DISTRIBUTED PROXIMITIES
PROCEEDINGS OF THE 40TH ANNUAL CONFERENCE OF THE ASSOCIATION FOR COMPUTER AIDED DESIGN IN ARCHITECTURE
VOLUME I: TECHNICAL PAPERS, KEYNOTE CONVERSATIONS

Editors
Brian Slocum, Viola Ago, Shelby Doyle, Adam Marcus, Maria Yablonina, Matias del Campo

Copy Editing
Rachel Fudge, Mary O'Malley, Paula Wooley

Graphic Identity
Adam Marcus, Viola Ago, Alejandro Sánchez Velasco

Graphic Design
Alejandro Sánchez Velasco

Layout
Carolyn Francis, Sebastian Lopez, Shelby Doyle, Adam Marcus

Printer
IngramSpark

ISBN 978-0-578-95213-0

PROCEEDINGS OF THE 40TH ANNUAL CONFERENCE OF THE ASSOCIATION FOR COMPUTER AIDED DESIGN IN ARCHITECTURE

VOLUME I: TECHNICAL PAPERS, KEYNOTE CONVERSATIONS

Editors
Brian Slocum, Viola Ago, Shelby Doyle, Adam Marcus, Maria Yablonina, Matias del Campo

acadia

DISTRIBUTED PROXIMITIES

CONTENTS

AUTOMATION AND AGENCY

CULTURE AND ACCESS

LABOR AND PRACTICE

SPECULATION AND CRITIQUE

ACADIA CREDITS

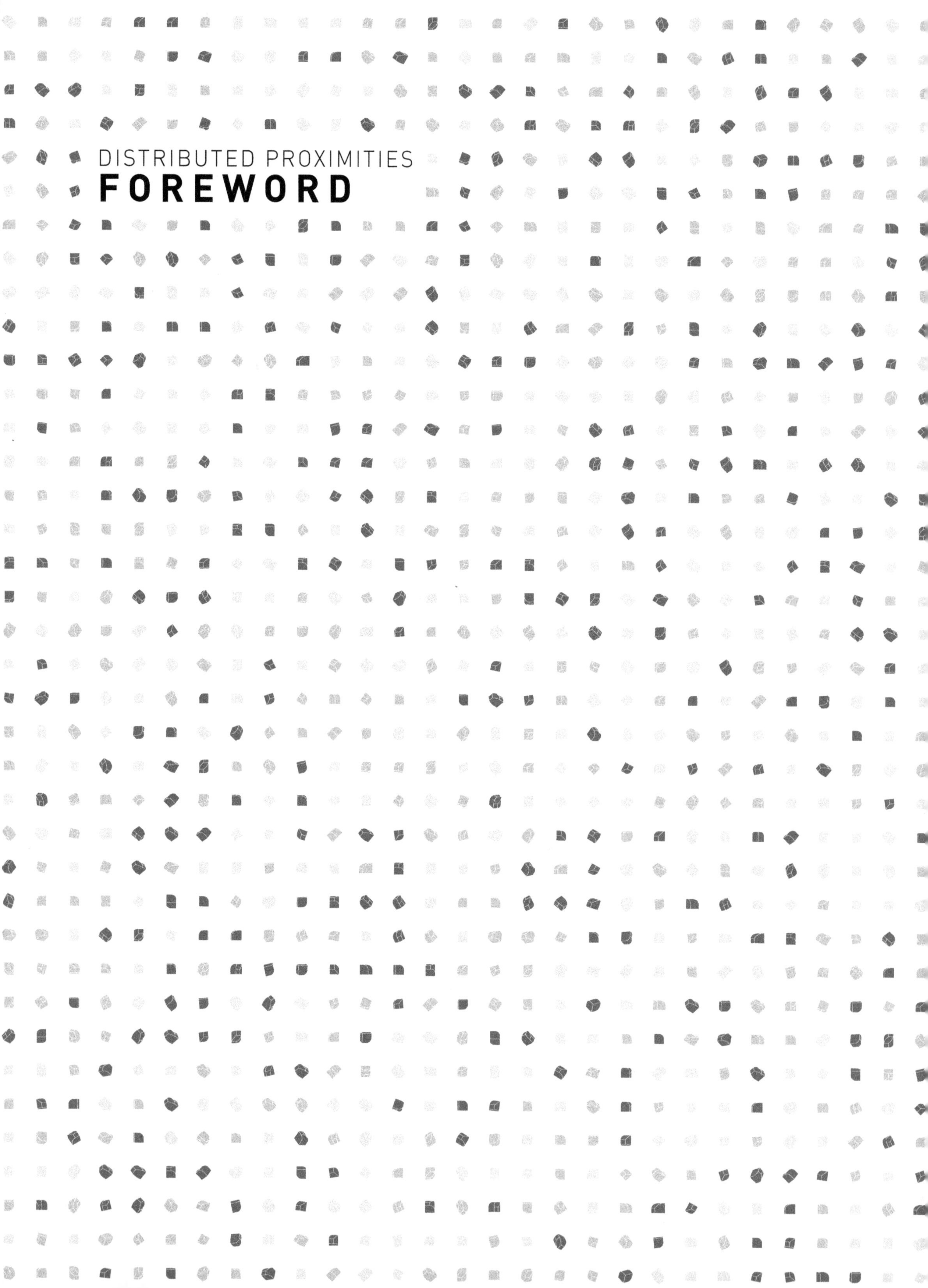

DISTRIBUTED PROXIMITIES

FOREWORD

Cultivating Transformative Practices

Kathy Velikov
ACADIA President 2018–2020
Associate Professor, University of Michigan Taubman College of Architecture and Urban Planning
Director, rvtr

It will be often repeated that 2020 has been an unprecedented year. We will all remember those few weeks in early March when the scale and implications of the coronavirus pandemic began to be apparent and when most activities that involved being around others were rapidly scaled down or cancelled and any activity that could do so moved to online space and digital screens. The transformations occurred breathlessly fast. Academic institutions, research labs, and offices were shuttered, and in-person conferences, including the 2020 conference that ACADIA had been planning with the University of Pennsylvania for October 2020, were cancelled. As ACADIA's primary activity is the exchange of knowledge through an annual conference (mandated in the organization's by-laws), the ACADIA Board of Directors moved to take over the rebranding, conceptualization, and organization of an online conference, workshops, and related events.

The tremendous energy and optimism of the six members of the Board who volunteered to lead this effort cannot be understated. On behalf of the ACADIA community, I would like to offer profound thanks to Viola Ago, Matias del Campo, Shelby Doyle, Adam Marcus, Brian Slocum, and Maria Yablonina for stepping up to the ambitious and time-consuming task of reinventing, organizing, and running ACADIA's 40th conference event, the 2020 *Distributed Proximities* conference. The team pushed the possibilities of an online conference to the limit, organizing a spectacular and smoothly run week-long event, hosted on a custom interactive website designed by Oliver Popadich. The amount of work that the chair team managed cannot be understated, and the incredible success of the 2020 conference is a testament to their efforts and inventiveness.

Working with the team, we recognized that this condition of temporary suspension of what we had grown accustomed to as usual activity could also be a period of metamorphosis. Not only was there a necessity to reinvent the playbook for ACADIA's annual conference, but this was also a moment to address the urgent need for making sense of the current situation. It was also an opportunity to actively put into practice the values of equity and inclusion that ACADIA had affirmed with the development of the Code of Conduct the previous year, and accelerate gender parity and increased racial diversity in the membership—two goals that the organization has been working to advance for the past several years. This mandate was not only taken on by the conference chair team, but also enthusiastically pursued by members of the Board through their committee work. In the spirit of the theme for the conference, we initiated a distributed, multipronged approach to these efforts, ensuring that they were coordinated and complementary.

This year's conference chair team rethought the keynote lecture format, which in the past had celebrated the accomplishments of a firm or an individual, to be staged instead as a series of critical conversations on the limits and possibilities of computation in contemporary design culture, with discussions on issues such as ecology, ethics, access, labor, and algorithmic biases. Over 85% of the speakers were female, and several represent BIPOC constituencies. The team also planned an unprecedented number of 15 workshops, taught online by leaders located in multiple countries, which greatly opened up the opportunities for different experiences with, access to, and levels of engagement with computational technologies. The conference chair team also inaugurated two new categories of juried submission to the annual conference: Videos and Field Notes. These new submission formats, along with the Projects, enabled more rapid, topical, and self-reflective ideas to be presented at the conference, expanding the range of possible conversations and access to a wider field of designers and thinkers, while maintaining the integrity of the selective peer review process for Technical Papers.

Matias del Campo, in addition to serving as a

conference chair, continued to also serve in his position as Development Officer, and this year secured one of the highest levels of sponsorship to supplement conference costs, including sponsorships from Autodesk, Zaha Hadid Architects, Epic Games, Grimshaw, and HKS Line. We developed a strengthened partnership with Autodesk, whose generous sponsorship this year enabled us to offer free registration for all students to the conference, and to also offer scholarships to attend the workshops to members of NOMA (National Organization of Minority Architects) as well as to students from Mexico and other international students. The response in registrations exceeded our expectations, with almost 2,000 free student attendees registering for the conference from all over the world, and with the number of female registrants for the first time exceeding the number of males. This pattern of near gender parity also held for the students who applied to the Autodesk-sponsored workshop grants. We thank Board members Jane Scott and Mara Marcu for their work in administering the increased number of student scholarships this year, as well as Chairs and Board members Shelby Doyle and Adam Marcus for coordinating and managing all of the workshops and attendees.

This year's conference saw a dramatic increase in international registrants. Participation was no longer limited to faculty and students who could afford not only the high fees associated with in-person events—where a significant proportion of the ticket costs go toward venue and equipment rentals, food, beverages, personnel, and physical paraphernalia—but also the travel and accommodation costs and time. The online conference also enabled relatively borderless access to anyone who had access to a computer, Wi-Fi, and an email account. It was therefore not limited to those who had the privilege to be able to obtain visas to travel to North America, and the registrants included many from countries that had not previously been represented at ACADIA. One question that the organization will need to grapple with when planning future conferences with in-person events is how to maintain this level of accessibility.

This year, the Board established a new Diversity Committee, which included Jason Kelly Johnson, Shelby Doyle, Behnaz Farahi, Tsz Yan Ng, and myself. Through the work of this committee, ACADIA has developed a partnership with NOMA and co-sponsored the inaugural ACADIA + Autodesk + NOMA Computational Design Award, a new category of award within NOMA's annual design competition. With June Grant now a member of the 2021 Board, we anticipate continuing to strengthen our relationship with NOMA and expanding ACADIA's mission as an organization that not only supports existing and established computational practitioners and researchers, but that also serves as a welcoming bridge and liaison into computational design for the next, more diverse generation of designers.

The sudden disruption caused by the pandemic has also enabled new relationships to be forged between ACADIA and our sibling organizations, eCAADe, CAADRIA, SiGRADi, and ASCAAD. As the presidents of the respective organizations reached out to each other to share information and strategies for transitioning to online conference formats, we also initiated efforts to take advantage of the online format to bring our organizations closer together. Together, we organized the first World CAAD PhD Workshop, held in early December 2020. The workshop introduced junior researchers at the PhD stage to the research cultures of different institutions and research cultures within the global computational design community. It offered doctoral students an opportunity to receive constructive feedback from prominent researchers and academics in the community, and provided an occasion to exchange ideas and position their research within a global research arena in computational design. Each sibling organization was represented at the workshop by three PhD student delegates as well as by experts from each community, and I thank Board member Jane Scott for working to organize the selection process and participating in the workshop. We hope to continue the PhD workshop both as part of future annual conferences and as a collaborative event across the sibling organizations.

This year also saw a milestone in the gender parity and diversity of the members of the ACADIA Board itself with, for the first time, more women being elected to the Board than men. The diversity of the elected Board has been steadily increasing, but it was not that long ago, in the 2015 election, when I recall being the only woman on the ballot; the following year, I was one of two female Board members, along with Dana Cupkova. I'd like to thank this year's elections committee—Andrew John Wit, Behnaz Farahi, and Tsz Yan Ng—along with the rest of the Board, for recruiting a strong pool of candidates for this year's elections and look forward to the leadership of the Board and new President Jenny Sabin in 2021.

Although in 2020 we experienced the loss of the pleasure of an in-person conference event—the casual conversations, debates, encounters, and engagement with new acquaintances that occur between paper presentations; in many ways, all of the things that make ACADIA feel like a family—it is also evident that a lot has been gained. We have benefitted from the expanded inclusivity and cultivation of greater equity and access, the ability to reach wider constituencies, and the decentering of dominant forms of practice and knowledge-making toward the emancipatory potentials of technology and socio-material reproduction. When we eventually reconvene in some form of in-person events, ACADIA may look and feel different than before. I hope so. I hope that it is a bigger, broader, and more inclusive family that welcomes alternative and unfamiliar conceptual and methodological practices, and will continue to be what it has always been: an open forum for sharing explorations in the use of computation in the making and remaking of our world.

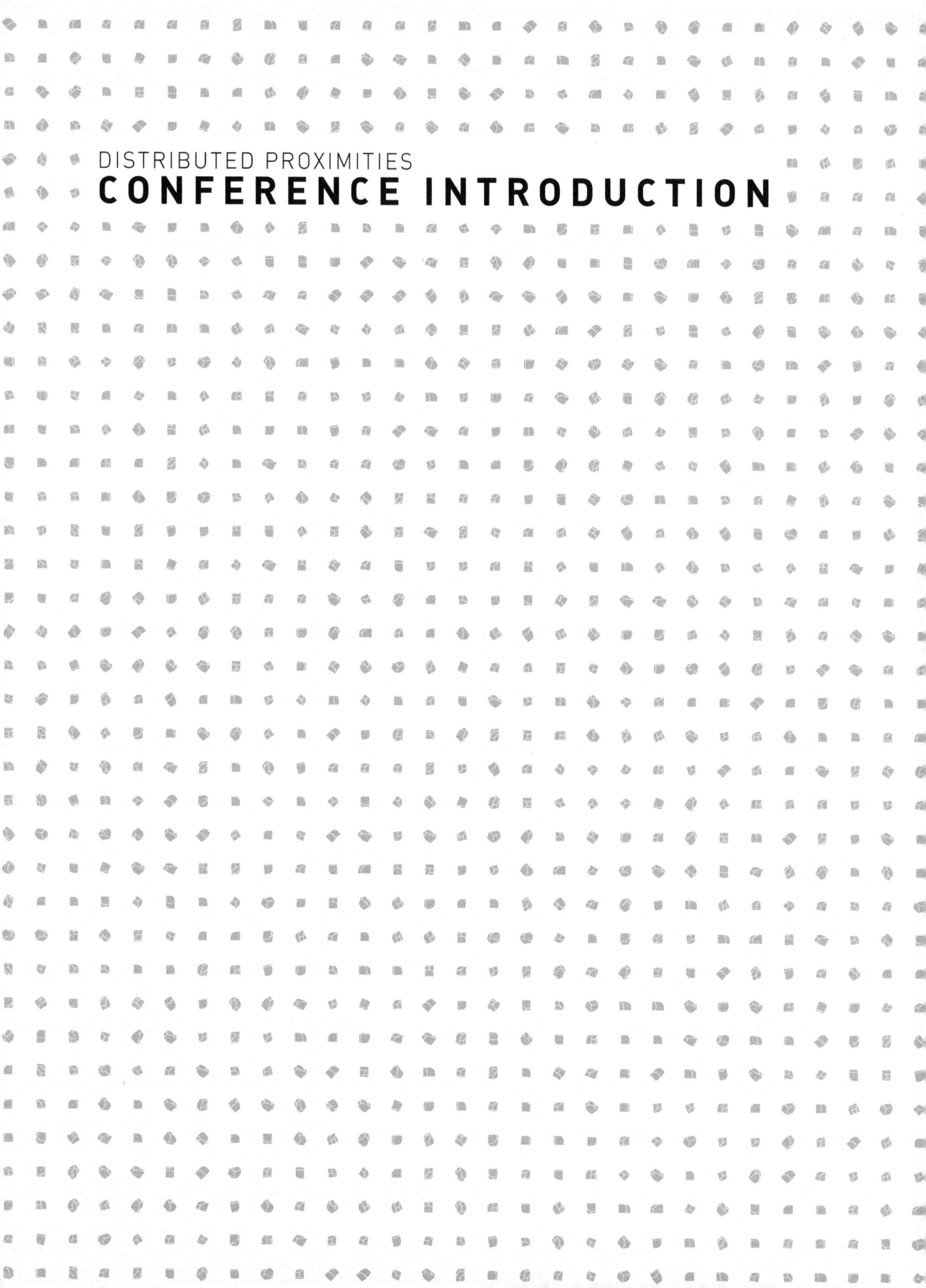

DISTRIBUTED PROXIMITIES

CONFERENCE INTRODUCTION

Postscript as Prologue

Introduction to the Proceedings of the 40th Annual ACADIA Conference

Viola Ago
Rice University
Matias del Campo
University of Michigan
Shelby Doyle
Iowa State University
Adam Marcus
California College of the Arts
Brian Slocum
Universidad Iberoamericana
Maria Yablonina
University of Toronto

While the ACADIA community has always been distributed, *ACADIA 2020 Distributed Proximities* was organized at a moment of truly unprecedented fragmentation in which many of us were working in isolation from collaborators, coworkers, and students. And yet, within this state of forced semi-autonomy, adaptations spontaneously emerged, and new proximities surfaced. Distributed models of collaboration, workflow, and production have catalyzed myriad experiments in remoteness, improvised virtual communities, and rapid retooling to address novel urgencies. A moment of crisis can be clarifying in that it provides an opportunity to reflect critically on both the motivations of a research agenda and its broader implications. This year was also an opportunity for ACADIA as an organization to reflect upon its own practices, habits, culture, and priorities; to recognize the interdependent coevolutionary nature of our planet, society, and built environment; and to collectively imagine alternate futures.

In March 2020, when ACADIA's Board of Directors, facing the onset of the global COVID-19 pandemic, began to consider alternatives to the organization's typical in-person conference, a survey was circulated among the membership inquiring about the pandemic's effects on research. More than 65% of respondents reported disruptions to their ongoing work, supporting a pivot to an alternative conference format that would address both the need for distancing and its impacts on academic research. Although a virtual conference by definition prohibits the kinds of direct interpersonal interaction that we have come to expect and enjoy each year, the Board of Directors saw this reformatting and reimagining of the ACADIA conference as an opportunity to critically reassess the discourse of computational design and consider how a more accessible format might encourage wider (and more inclusive) dialogue via a radical expansion in participation in the conversation.

In contrast to a typical ACADIA cycle, the 2020 conference was planned and executed by a set of individuals from various institutions spread throughout North America who are connected only by their commitment to the community rather than rooted in a single institution. The conference co-chair team brought together voices from across three countries: the United States, Canada, and Mexico, representing six institutions: California College of the Arts, University of Michigan, Iowa State University, Rice University, University of Toronto, and Universidad Iberoamericana. While the pandemic and all it entailed undoubtedly left its mark on the work presented and discussed at this year's online conference, removing the association with a single academic institution (with both implicit and explicit biases) gave the chairs the opportunity to foreground themes of importance to ACADIA and its mission. Among these are increasing the diversity of the computational design community, encouraging scholarship at the highest level, and providing a platform for respectful yet vigorous debate about this research and its positioning within multiple contexts, social as well as technical. From the outset, our shared intent was not only to shape this conference as an effective and compelling venue for advanced peer-reviewed research, but to embed it with an *aspirational* purpose: how might a conference embody values of inclusion, empathy, ethics, and criticality that can inform future trajectories of design computation?

In this spirit, we invited contributions that interrogate the current condition by prioritizing the processes and protocols by which work is produced, rather than only its artifacts. By framing the conference through the lenses of ethics, equity, and critique, we sought to foreground work that questions not just "how" we do what we do, but "why" we engage computation in our work, and the myriad consequences it may have both within and beyond the discipline.

To do so required reflecting upon nearly every aspect of the conference format and content, and deciding which aspects were ripe for reinvention. We brought together 21 speakers in multiple time zones to participate in six virtual keynote conversations about critical issues, to help situate the conference within an alternative collection of imaginaries in lieu of a series of loosely related monologues focusing on individual work. Leveraging the online format, we brought together 15 remote workshops with leaders and participants from six continents, creating a platform for a global group of participants to experiment with new modes of collaboration and remote fabrication. Emerging from the pandemic context was a special session showcasing work by members of the ACADIA community who participated in various initiatives for the fabrication of personal protective equipment. The Field Note and Video formats were added to the conference call for submissions to make space for other voices and other more immediate forms of engagement with and discussion about the community and its work. Additionally, in 2020, ACADIA inaugurated a collaboration with the National Organization of Minority Architects and the National Organization of Minority Architecture Students (NOMA/NOMAS), sponsoring attendance grants for both the conference and workshops, and exhibiting computational design work from the annual NOMA/NOMAS design competitions. In an attempt to foster the types of serendipitous interactions of an in-person conference, we collaborated with designer Oliver Popadich to develop a custom conference platform that deployed machine learning to visualize thematic affinities and proximities to the body of research presented at the conference; the resulting platform allowed the visualization of connections between people, work, and ideas that might otherwise have gone unnoticed. Additionally, Ultan Byrne's MMMURMUR, with its capacity to simulate the dynamics of physical gatherings, was an experiment in bringing the casual interactions of the coffee break or happy hour to an online atmosphere; to our great delight, this experiment exceeded expectations, providing a fun, gossipy gathering spot for welcome diversion after intense conference events and at the end of each day.

All of the above took place in conjunction with the ongoing rigorous research of the community; we began conference planning worried whether anyone would be able to submit, and we note with the benefit of hindsight the fierce determination and resilience of the community and its members in this regard. In terms of technical research submissions, ACADIA 2020 had the second highest number of submissions for peer review in the 40-year history of the conference and an unprecedented percentage (nearly 60%) of the group of accepted paper authors is female. Additionally, this year the Technical Chairs sought to achieve gender and geographic balance in the assignment of peer reviewers for each paper. We wish to thank all of our peer reviewers for their perseverance and professionalism; without them the publication and presentation of the research would simply not have been possible. Work was submitted from all over the world, and with political and financial barriers to conference attendance removed as a side effect of the pandemic, many who would otherwise have been unable to attend were able to present and have their research discussed at the conference, to the benefit of everyone in the ACADIA community. Finally, in what we take as an encouraging sign, students attended the conference in higher numbers than ever before,[1] achieving gender parity, representing six continents, and increasing the likelihood of future submission to and participation in ACADIA.

The six of us could never have imagined that, more than a year after beginning the process of organizing *Distributed Proximities*, the strange circumstances that gave rise to the conference theme not only persist but continue to define life and work in profound ways that we have really only begun to fathom. In keeping with this disjointedness, the nature of the online conference and this year's publication of these proceedings well after the closing of the conference proper have meant that what would normally carry an inaugural tone has simultaneously taken on a valedictory character—"what's past is prologue"[2]—conclusion as introduction. Seen in this manner, these two volumes serve to draw the curtain on *ACADIA 2020 Distributed Proximities*, recording within them the community's first attempts to comprehend and assimilate the formative events surrounding the conference's organization. However, at the same time we hope that they may be read as the opening remarks for a new kind of dialogue for ACADIA, a discourse that will be essential to the unfolding of the conversation about the long-term effects of distributed proximities as well as for the materialization of the future imaginaries so earnestly and provocatively discussed throughout the conference.

NOTES

1. Thanks in large part to the generous sponsorship of Autodesk.
2. William Shakespeare, *The Tempest*, ed. Ronald Herder (Mineola, NY: Dover Publications, 1999), 56.

Contribution Statement

Viola Ago
Rice University

Matias del Campo
University of Michigan

Shelby Doyle
Iowa State University

Adam Marcus
California College of the Arts

Brian Slocum
Universidad Iberoamericana

Maria Yablonina
University of Toronto

In support of transparency in authorial attribution, the conference chairs wish to briefly highlight the specific contributions of each member of the team to both the conference and this publication, in addition to their roles in the general overall planning for the ACADIA 2020 Conference. These categories are adapted from and expanded upon the CRediT (Contributor Roles Taxonomy) promoted and administered as an informal standard at CASRAI (https://casrai.org/credit/). Names are listed here in order of contribution to this volume.

Brian Slocum: Conceptualization (Conference Themes and Conference Platform), Writing - Original Draft, Writing - Review & Editing, Visualization, Supervision, Project Administration (Technical Papers Peer Review Process, Conference Budget, Conference Paper Sessions Organization).

Viola Ago: Conceptualization (Conference Themes and Conference Platform), Writing - Original Draft, Writing - Review & Editing, Visualization (Conference Graphics), Supervision, Project Administration (Technical Papers Peer Review Process, Conference Paper Sessions Organization).

Shelby Doyle: Conceptualization (Conference Themes and Conference Platform), Writing - Original Draft, Writing - Review & Editing, Visualization, Supervision, Project Administration (Keynotes Organization, Field Notes & Videos Review Process, PPE Panel Organization, Workshops Organization, AIA CEUs Administration).

Adam Marcus: Conceptualization (Conference Themes and Conference Platform), Writing - Original Draft, Writing - Review & Editing, Visualization (Conference Graphics), Supervision, Project Administration (Keynotes Organization, Field Notes & Videos Review Process, Awards Organization, Workshops Organization, Website Management, Conference Videoconferencing Management).

Maria Yablonina: Conceptualization (Conference Themes and Conference Platform), Writing - Original Draft, Writing - Review & Editing, Visualization, Supervision, Project Administration (Projects Peer Review Process, Curated Projects, Keynotes Organization).

Matias del Campo: Conceptualization (Conference Themes and Conference Platform), Writing - Original Draft, Writing - Review & Editing, Visualization, Supervision, Project Administration (Projects Peer Review Process, Curated Projects), Funding Acquisition.

General Statement Regarding Attribution

Attribution order for work submitted to ACADIA and published in this volume is determined by level of contribution, with the first author listed considered the principal author and subsequent authors listed in order of contribution to the work. If authors have contributed equally, those names are indicated with an asterisk. The only exception to this convention is that lab/studio leaders' names (if applicable) appear last on the list of authors.

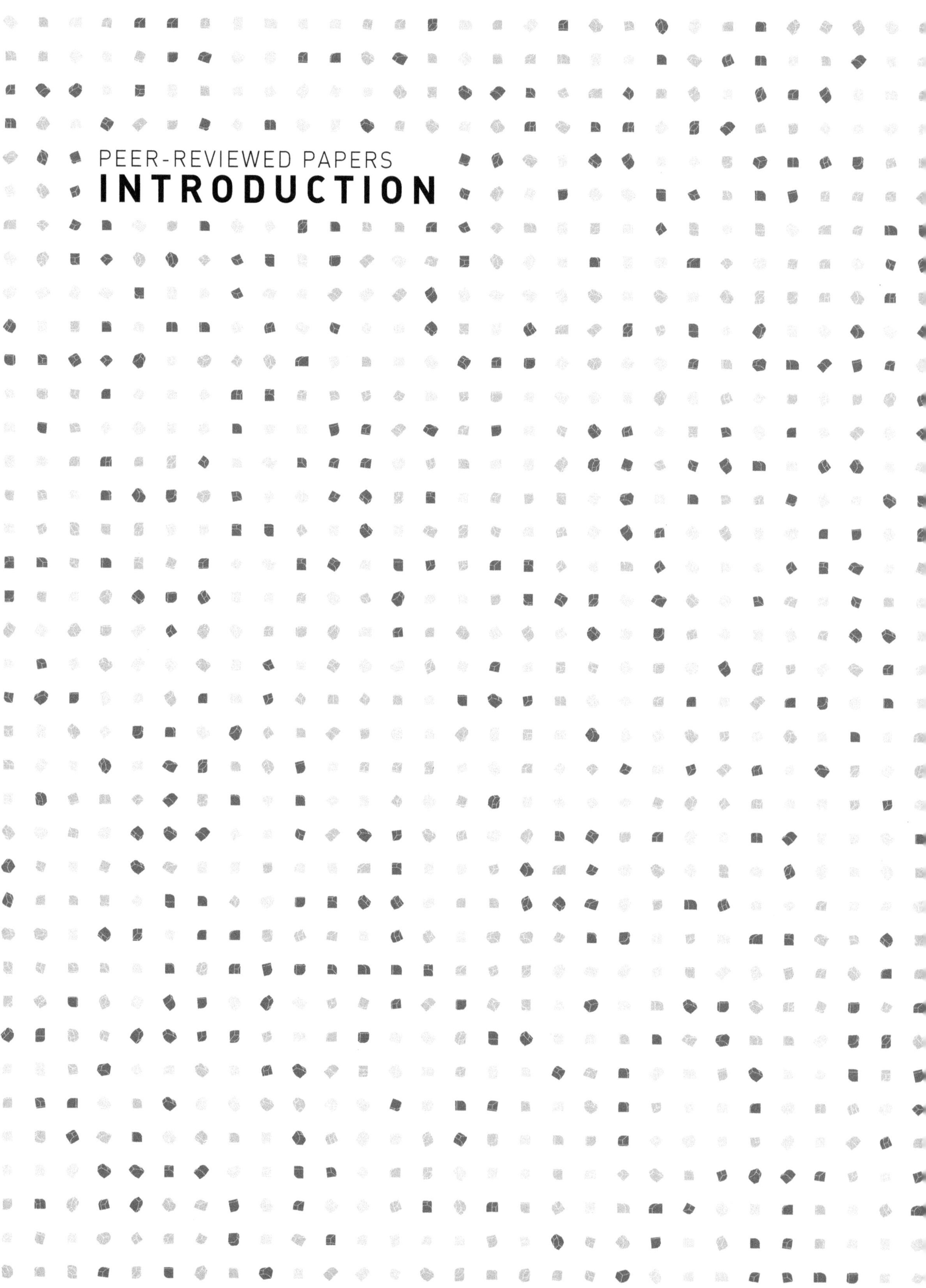

PEER-REVIEWED PAPERS

INTRODUCTION

Exquisite Corpus

Introduction to the Peer-Reviewed Papers of the 40th Annual ACADIA Conference

Brian Slocum
Universidad Iberoamericana

Viola Ago
Rice University

It took in the neighborhood of 0.26 seconds for the phrase "The New Normal" to become cliché. That's the time it took for the first person who spoke or typed the words to transmit them via radio waves to a communications satellite in geostationary orbit and for that device in turn to relay the data to the world (University of Waikato, 2021). Before anyone even processed the information, it was already overused, trite. The phrase ostensibly encapsulates how our respective and collective realities have been permanently altered by the pandemic. To begin, let us set aside the problematic word "normal." Because while purportedly focusing on the status quo, what the phrase "new normal" actually represents is "novelty" neatly packaged for consumption, a way to frame effects as new, and moreover the suggestion that this newer newness itself has an inherent value. But according to philosopher of science Thomas Kuhn, quoted by author Michael North in *Novelty: A History of the New*, "work within a well-defined and deeply-ingrained tradition seems more productive of tradition-shattering novelties than work in which no similarly convergent standards are involved" (Kuhn 1977, 234; cited in North 2013, 171). At present it may in fact be enough simply to recognize that the magnitude of the ongoing disturbance has opened cracks in accepted paradigms, and that rather than focus on novelty per se, we should instead attempt to understand why some characteristics of our collective version of "normal" have remained extraordinarily resilient despite recent shifts.

There is certainly merit in analyzing the transformations brought about by global events, for if ever there were a need to comprehend the disruptions to our shared existence, it would be now. A survey of our community showed that the research of nearly two-thirds of its members was being interrupted by the pandemic. In response, the collective of conference chairs sought to emphasize themes that would address this disruption by emphasizing works-in-process, adaptation, and retooling. While our immediate goal was to alleviate the effects of the interruptions and remove impediments to submission for those whose work was affected, we also (and perhaps more importantly) sought to convert what has been an unquestionably difficult situation into a moment for reflection and critical thought. We wanted to provide a moment for the community to pull back the veil, and to focus on giving multiple opportunities for a discussion of work—including technical research—that was unfinished, rough, and perhaps less polished, and in the process to promote a dialogue removed from the pressures of a "normal" conference, a dialogue that in its undistilled state might also incorporate themes that resonate beyond the ACADIA community, converging with the global zeitgeist more perhaps than at any time in recent memory.

A quick analysis of the final papers using a list of keywords, culled primarily from the conference call for submissions and paper session titles, yields some unexpected results (Fig. 1). Based on the abstract submissions, the effects of the pandemic seemed, anecdotally at least, to have been

	KEYWORD(S)		
769	ROBOT ROBOTS ROBOTIC ROBOTICS	46	ARTIFICIAL INTELLIGENCE
650	FABRICATE FABRICATION	46	CLIMATE
578	NEW NOVEL NOVELTY	46	COLLABORATE COLLABORATION
578	DATA	45	THE ENVIRONMENT
326	ENVIRONMENT	27	SPECULATE SPECULATION SPECULATIVE
200	AUTOMATE AUTONOMOUS AUTOMATION	26	RESILIENCE RESILIENT
186	AGENCY AGENT	17	BIAS
176	OPTIMIZE OPTIMIZATION	14	EQUITABLE INEQUITABLE EQUITY INEQUITY
173	PRACTICE PRACTICES	14	ECOLOGY ECOLOGIES
101	MACHINE LEARNING	11	DISRUPTION DISRUPTIVE
87	CRITICAL CRITIQUE	10	HEURISTIC HEURISTICS
87	ADAPT ADAPTATION ADAPTIVE	9	ETHICAL ETHICS
78	ACCESS ACCESIBILITY	7	UNEXPECTED
70	ERROR ERRORS	7	ACCIDENT ACCIDENTAL
59	LABOR	2	FAIL FAILURE FAILURES
57	CULTURAL CULTURE	1	GENDER
56	COVID COVID19 COVID-19 CORONAVIRUS PANDEMIC EPIDEMIC		

1 Technical Papers Keywords (listed in order of mentions).

borne out with an increased submission of software-based research on artificial intelligence, which we attributed to the phenomenon of lab closures. While there was indeed a high number of papers mentioning machine learning or artificial intelligence, of the keywords analyzed (Fig. 2), a pattern emerges showing that research involving "fabrication," "automation," and above all "robotics" continued apace during the pandemic, regardless of facility restrictions. Interestingly, words related to the conference themes and of significance to the immediate discussion, such as "bias," "climate," and "ethics," appear much less frequently than other, more familiar and technical terms like "optimization" and "automation." Of note especially is the lone appearance of the word "gender."

To the extent that the papers include discussion of pressing social issues, the pandemic, inequity, work in isolation, and investigations interrupted, what becomes strikingly apparent is the remarkable determination of the community to carry on undistracted in the face of uncertainty. As organizers, we were determined to produce a different kind of conference, and the work presented and published as part of *Distributed Proximities* is evidence of a great determination to continue all types of scholarship undeterred by a global pandemic. Returning to *Novelty: A History of the New*, North continues, this time summarizing Kuhn, "that it is the practical doggedness and not just the abstract dogmatism of normal science that makes it inevitably revolutionary" (North 2013, 172). And so while it may appear contradictory to focus on normality when keywords relating to novelty appear in all but one of the papers, the noteworthy resilience shown in the work published here contributes to the ongoing academic conversation (now in its forty-first year) in an unexpected and reassuringly "normal" way.

Summarizing and introducing the product of the conference has always been about striking a balance between distilling how the work has engaged the conference themes and a hindsight reading to look for patterns in what is currently being done. In looking back at the full content of the conference, we come to the realization that if the conference itself is a dynamic conversation on a yearly time-scale, then it follows that the body of shared knowledge being generated in the form of the research papers represents a more traditional discourse more on the order of decades or career-length time-scales. This past year more than ever, the former is exemplified by the keynote conversations introduced by our colleagues with corresponding transcriptions included in this volume alongside the peer-reviewed papers, while the latter represents a mature yet ever-evolving grand corpus. In keeping with the conference theme, the conference is a proximal forum more open to the influence of current events as well as tendencies in the focus and thinking of the computational design community, while the peer-reviewed research papers might be understood as a lengthier yet staccato conversation—a written *cadavre exquis*—distributed over time and location.

Of course, the conference dialogue may affect the broader discourse, if at all, only after many years. But while the *cadavre exquis* is meant to generate a shocking novelty through a purposefully random combination of disparate and intuitive contributions, novelty in the work of the computational design community has been more closely associated with the "normal science" of Kuhn, a steady, deliberate, and technical novelty achieved through this type of "tradition-shattering," productive normality. The circumstances are ripe for the evolution of a discourse that demonstrates both sociocultural and technical novelty by situating the technical work within the broader sociocultural contexts in which we operate, as well as discussing urgent issues that are inevitably impacted by that same work—a discourse that, in the words of conference keynote conversant Ruha Benjamin, "is defined not just by *what* we study but also *how* we analyze, questioning our own assumptions about what is deemed high theory versus pop culture, academic versus activist, evidence versus anecdote" (Benjamin 2019, 125). Even if this year's specific conference themes were perhaps only tangentially taken up by the community, the propitious emergence of a more critical discourse is an encouraging sign of the increasing interconnectedness between ACADIA's conference dialogue and its growing academic corpus.

The six paper sections that follow are meant to be a continuation of this exchange between the ephemeral discourse of the conference and the work presented under its auspices. Whereas previous years' proceedings have been organized either chronologically (by conference paper session) or according to technical subject matter, this year each of the keynote transcripts serves to "introduce" a curated collection of peer-reviewed technical papers. The conversations on "Ecology and Ethics," "Data and Bias," "Automation and Agency," "Culture and Access," "Labor and Practice," and "Speculation and Critique" provide an alternative framework through which to interrogate the technical content of the conference; it is hoped that these may provoke healthy debate and inspire further discussion.

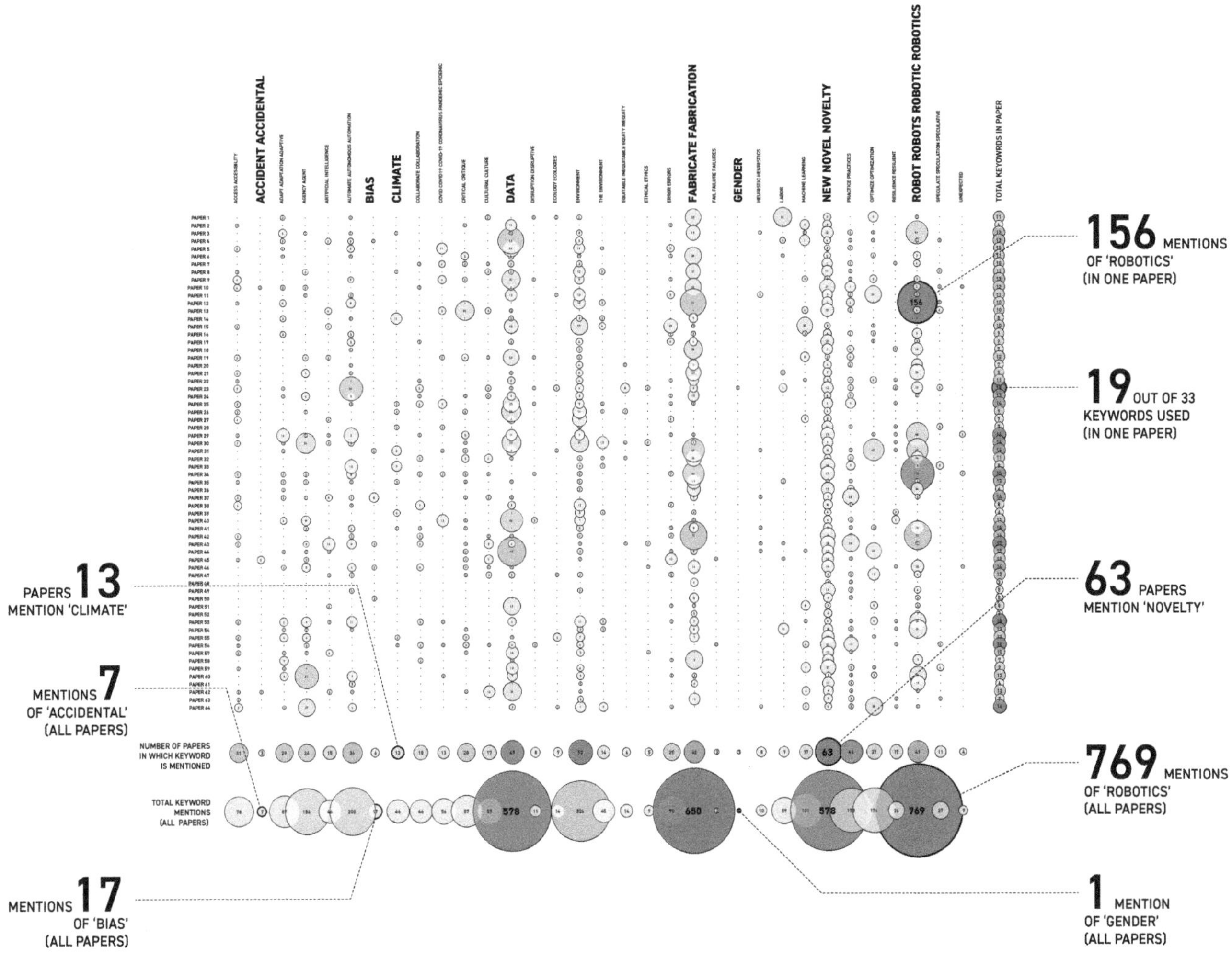

1 Technical Papers Keyword Analysis.

IMAGE CREDITS

Brian Slocum

REFERENCES

Benjamin, Ruha. 2019. *Race After Technology*. Cambridge, MA: Polity Press.

Kuhn, Thomas S. 1977. *The Essential Tension: Selected Studies in Scientific Tradition and Change*. Chicago, IL: University of Chicago Press.

North, Michael. 2013. *Novelty: A History of the New*. Chicago, IL: University of Chicago Press.

University of Waikato. 2021. "Satellite Communications," Science Learning Hub, accessed 22 May 2021, https://www.sciencelearn.org.nz/resources/270-satellite-communications

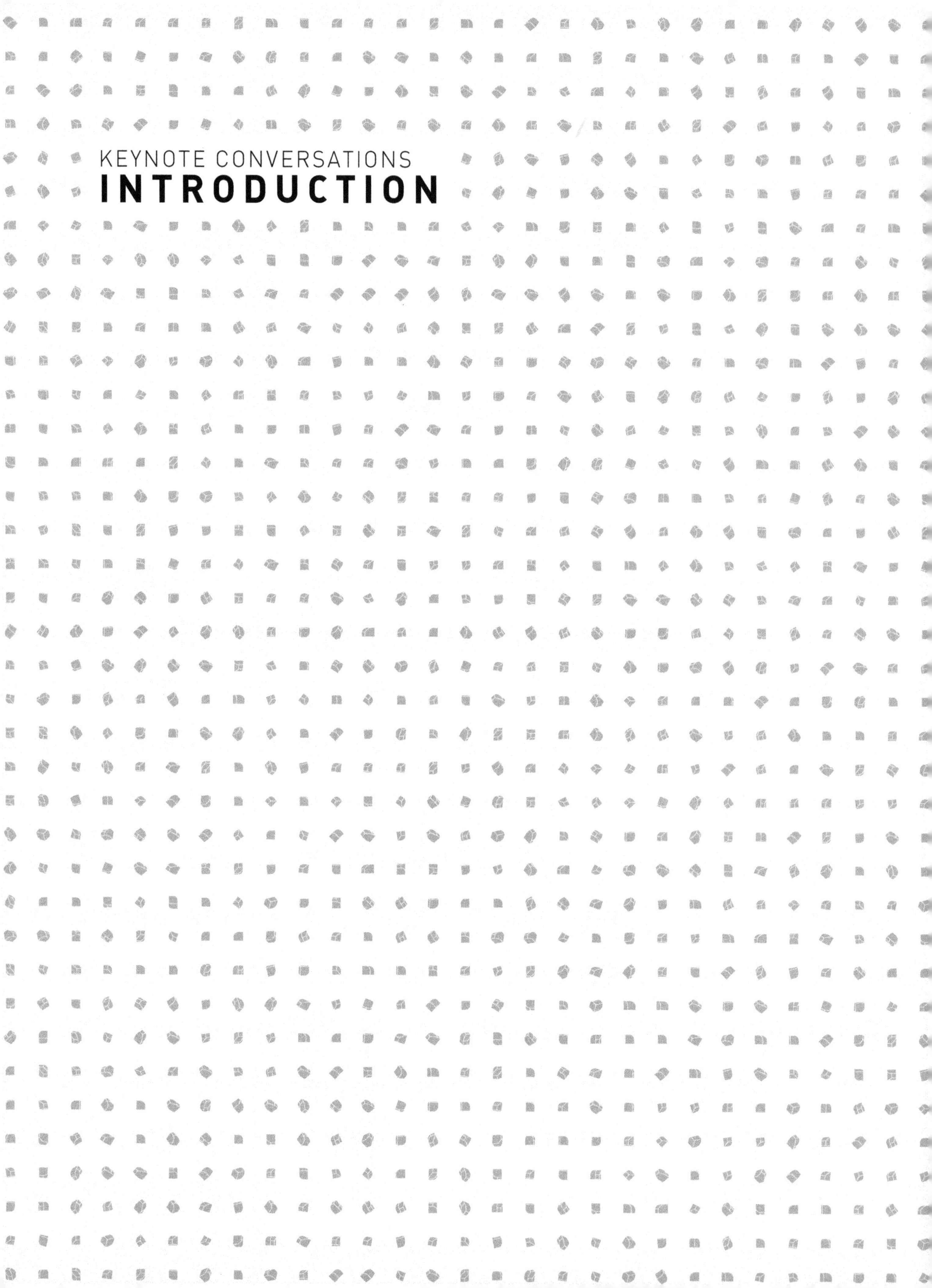

KEYNOTE CONVERSATIONS

INTRODUCTION

Distributed Dialogues

Introduction to the Keynote Conversations of the 40th Annual ACADIA Conference

Shelby Doyle
Iowa State University

Adam Marcus
California College of the Arts

Maria Yablonina
University of Toronto

The term "keynote" originated in musical theory and refers to the first note played to establish a key for a performance.[1] Extending this metaphor, a successful keynote speech opens a conference and sets the tone for the exchange of ideas that follows. In curating the keynote conversations for the *Distributed Proximities* conference, the co-chairs sought to establish a tone of criticality and reflection that would resonate throughout the event.

The 2020 *Distributed Proximities* conference was the first online gathering in the 40-year history of the ACADIA community. Necessitated by a global pandemic, the online format lowered the barriers of geography, travel, and time, thereby allowing for a convening of multiple voices around a series of urgent topics consequential to computational design. These topics became the basis for six prompts used to structure a series of keynote conversations: *Ecology and Ethics*, *Data and Bias*, *Automation and Agency*, *Culture and Access*, *Labor and Practice*, and *Speculation and Critique*. Scheduled adjacent to each keynote event were thematically related peer-reviewed paper sessions, thereby allowing the topics introduced through the keynotes to be further explored through the work of conference authors and attendees.

The 2020 keynotes presented an opportunity to reflect upon the habit and practice of the conventional keynote monologue format. A monologue is by definition delivered by a single person; in an academic context, this speaker is granted power to occupy a space and to amplify a specific view of knowledge and experience. The culture of a contemporary conference keynote is undoubtedly a sibling to the culture of "thought leadership" introduced by and broadly expanded through thousands of TED talks and similar speaking events. The aim of such an event is not to criticize or investigate, but rather to entertain and leave an impression, and sometimes even to educate and inspire the unsuspecting audience. As Daniel Drezner writes in his book *The Ideas Industry*, a thought leader "develops their own singular lens to explain the world, and then proselytizes that worldview to anyone within earshot."[2] The monologue format privileges the simplicity of a "big idea," a single voice, and a single solution to a problem over reflection and critique. However, the reality of any practice is inherently messy, complex, and resonant with many voices.

Keynote speakers—those selected to be "keynote worthy"—represent a value judgment about the priorities of a community or an organization. For the ACADIA community to effectively engage with contemporary urgencies—from racial justice to climate change—it must enlist the entirety of the community's collective intelligence. To do so entails making space for a diversity of both thought and people, as well as including voices from other disciplines whose work intersects with computational design in significant and critical ways. In this spirit, the intent in curating these six keynote conversations was to convene critical thinkers from fields as diverse as ecology, sociology, history of science, and labor activism to speculate on how the computational design community might expand its capacities to tackle the increasingly urgent challenges of our time.

Fostering a welcoming culture for ACADIA's computational design community requires active, intentional, and frequent reflection on our habits, expectations, and practices. The 2020 ACADIA keynote conversations are one such experiment, of hopefully many to come, that highlights the friction between our ability to describe the world through computational certainty and the fragile, messy, and powerful work of constructing culture.

Each keynote event consisted of short individual presentations by each of the speakers, followed by a conversation on the work. The edited transcripts included in this book contain the conversation components; recordings of all events can be accessed via ACADIA's Youtube page at: https://www.youtube.com/c/ACADIAorg.

NOTES

1. "keynote, n.". OED Online. March 2021. Oxford University Press. https://www.oed.com/view/Entry/103152?rskey=GM6R5s&result=1 (accessed April 26, 2021).
2. Daniel W. Drezner, *The Ideas Industry: How Pessimists, Partisans, and Plutocrats Are Transforming the Marketplace of Ideas* (Oxford: Oxford University Press, 2017), 9.

KEYNOTE CONVERSATION

ECOLOGY AND ETHICS

KEYNOTE EVENT

A Conversation on Ecology and Ethics

Jennifer Gabrys
University of Cambridge

Molly Wright Steenson
Carnegie Mellon University

Technologies of sensing, analysis, and simulation provide architects with new methods to understand, model, and interface with ecologies across scales, from the material to the planetary. In the context of the escalating climate crisis—and its exacerbation of social, political, and economic disparities worldwide—these technologies present opportunities for greater ecological awareness, citizenship, and democratic engagement. In this keynote conversation, Jennifer Gabrys and Molly Wright Steenson, two critical thinkers, practitioners, and scholars of computation, discuss how distributed and bottom-up approaches to sensing technologies might offer a counternarrative to the prevailing paradigms of Big Data.

Jennifer Gabrys, Chair in Media, Culture, and Environment in the Department of Sociology at the University of Cambridge, began the keynote event with a presentation of her research and engagement initiatives Citizen Sense and AirKit, which provide community access to DIY environmental sensing systems. Gabrys's work seeks to "generate ecological, ethical, and sociopolitical practices for sensing a planet in crisis," always transcending the merely technical by teasing out the latent social and political possibilities that exist within simple technologies like air quality sensors. Organized according to the chapters of her recent book *How to Do Things with Sensors*, the talk offered the DIY "how to" guide as a model for empowering citizens to deploy sensors and develop actionable environmental initiatives based on the collected data. The work, deeply grounded in practice and engagement, offers a critical yet ultimately optimistic vision for how technology might enable a more democratic and participatory ethos of ecological awareness.

Molly Wright Steenson, Senior Associate Dean for Research in the College of Fine Arts at Carnegie Mellon University, where she is also the K&L Gates Associate Professor of Ethics and Computational Technologies and Associate Professor in the School of Design, followed with a response that recast Gabrys's work within a broader discussion of ethics. Emphasizing that considering ethics within computational practices highlights the persistent role of the human, Steenson reiterated Gabrys's call for enlisting technology

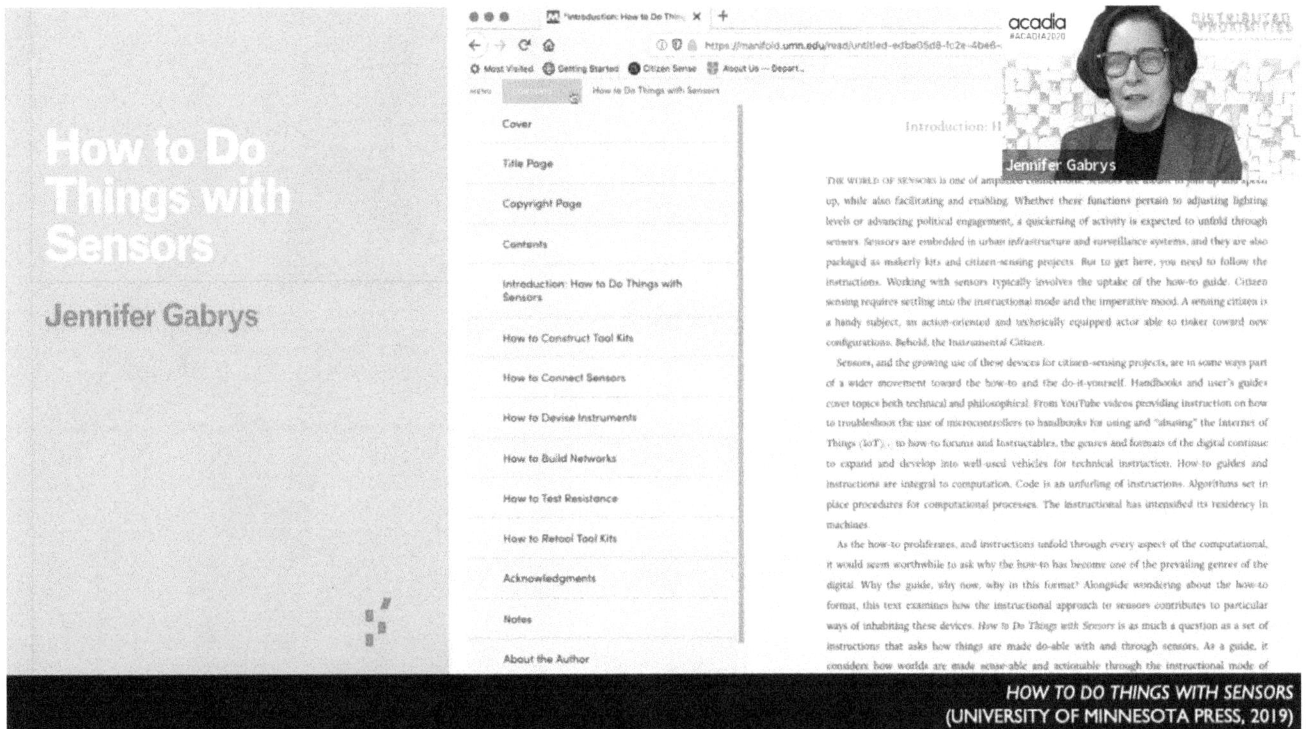

HOW TO DO THINGS WITH SENSORS (UNIVERSITY OF MINNESOTA PRESS, 2019)

1 "I want to ask how it's possible to generate ecological, ethical, and sociopolitical practices for sensing a planet in crisis. I look at this question from the perspective of citizen sensing. Rather than looking at this as a remote sensing problem, something undertaken by technocrats, I look at how practitioners as well as citizens engage in citizen sensing projects." —Jennifer Gabrys

in broader efforts to promote ecological citizenship and remake worlds. A wide-ranging conversation on these entangled questions of technology, ecology, and ethics followed, and is reproduced below in edited form.

For a recording of the entire event, please see this link: **https://www.youtube.com/watch?v=hxs2MrCGUCE**

Molly Wright Steenson (MWS): Given that the title of our session today is "Ecology and Ethics," I think it's important for us to consider the possibilities of ethics, and what exactly we mean by "ethics." We find that traditional definitions of ethics center on moral principles. Typically, if we look at morals, we see terms like "good," "bad," "right," "wrong," "evil"; these are about human characteristics and related to actions, desires, and human character.

These definitions of ethics and morals seem to be potentially limited, and there are opportunities for opening these up a bit more, both in the current moment in technology and through Jennifer Gabrys's work. Where does the moral fit into ethics frameworks for computation? And is ethics actually really what we're talking about?

I'm in the midst of a study with a group of faculty and students at Carnegie Mellon looking at how discussions about AI and ethics are taken up. We have found more than 210 different AI and ethics frameworks, toolkits, principles, codes of conduct, checklists, codes, and manifestos across the board. We've scraped Medium.com for discourse on artificial intelligence, ethics, design governance, regulation, machine learning, robotics, algorithms, design, and big data, among other topics. We're also doing this study across major publications like the *New York Times*, *Washington Post*, and *The Wall Street Journal*, and across academic journals.

What we're discovering is that when we start talking about ethics and technology, maybe not surprisingly, the figure of the human designer and technologist becomes part of the conversation. Which is to say that if you leave ethics completely out of a conversation about machine learning, you're going to find a lot of talk about algorithms. But if you start bringing in ethics, one of the first things that's going to come up is the word "technologists," as well as "human," "AI," and "bias."

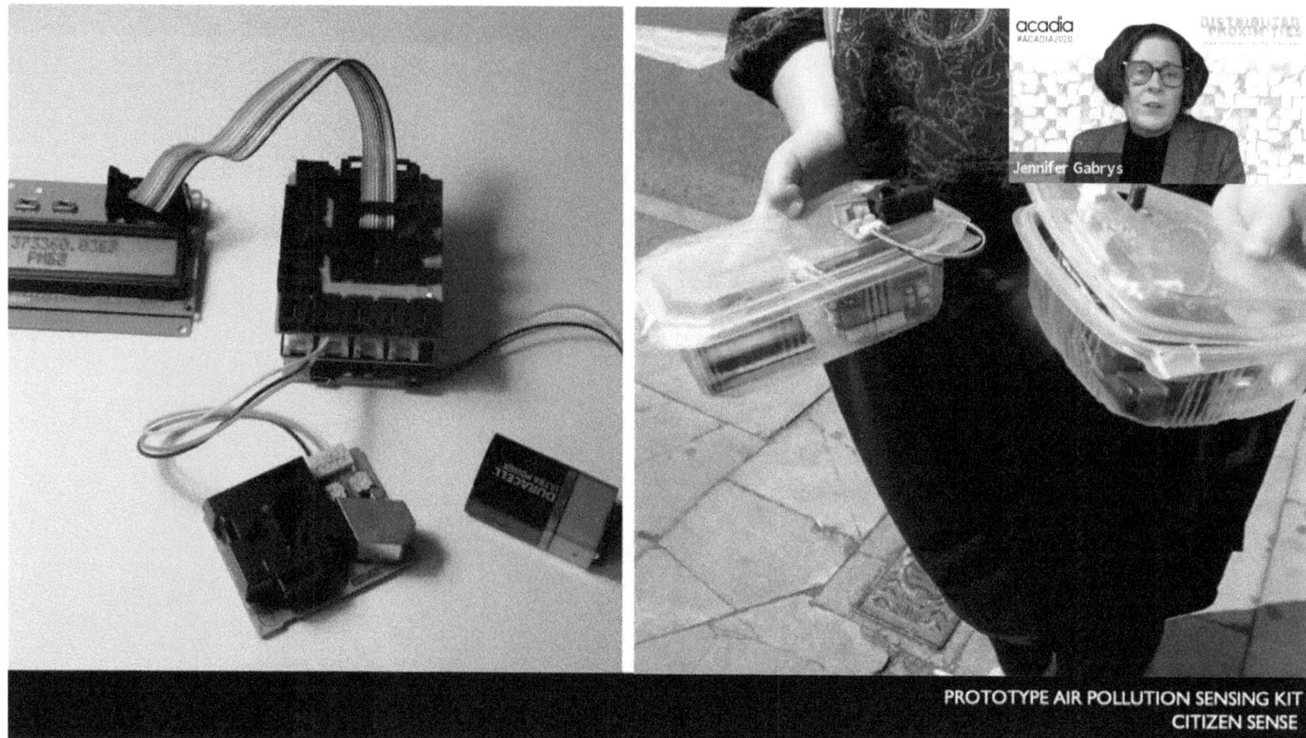

2 "In order to unravel the typically rigid contours of digital devices, many technology advocates have begun to assemble microcontrollers, sensors, and code to develop a more informed engagement with these machines. The toolkit actually becomes a way to fashion a more deliberate encounter with digital devices." —Jennifer Gabrys
[Image: Jennier Gabrys / Citzen Sense]

So if ethics in computation highlights the role of the human, then Jennifer Gabrys's work in *How to Do Things with Sensors* expands the territory of that conversation. This idea of "how to," she writes, "becomes an invitation to make, organize, orchestrate, conjure, and sustain people, technology, and worlds toward openings, rather than prescribed ends."[1]

In this amalgamation or assemblage of sensing the environment, sensors, and experience, "how to" relations, and informing, I'd like to know what kind of ethics we might find. And conversely, I'd like to know what ethics might find in this approach. Not just good/bad, right/wrong, good/evil, and the way we've been looking at morality tied to human character and morality tied to ethics, but rather a new view of the citizen who possesses rights, privileges, and responsibilities. Within sensing the environment, relations, and informing, perhaps we see "how to" as an ethics in the environment, both beyond the human and the more-than-human.

Jennifer Gabrys quoted Leanne Betasamosake Simpson's book *As We Have Always Done: Indigenous Freedom through Radical Resistance*, and I find myself continually coming back to this quote, in which Simpson says, "It became clear to me that *how* we live, *how* we organize, *how* we engage in the world—the process—not only frames the outcome, it is the transformation."[2]

So the question, then, is *how*? And: *how to*? And: *how to remake worlds*? So let's move to our conversation.

Jennifer Gabrys (JG): Thank you. This is a fantastic way to open up the conversation. And I think this point you raised about AI and ethics is really interesting in terms of the sorts of ethics that are mobilized in these 210 and counting examples of how ethics is captured and the way in which the ethical becomes the "how to."

I think it's really provocative to think of that as the how-to guide. Have you thought about it in that way?

MWS: Very much so. I just want to say that I appreciate your work being a new lens onto this because I think it greatly expands the way that we talk about AI. On one hand, I could quote Rumman Chowdhury, an AI strategist at

3 "To build something requires much more than making a digital device operational. A project to monitor and address air pollution involves building community networks as ongoing, contingent, and iterative practices that are ways of making and maintaining ecological, ethical, technical, and social infrastructures." —Jennifer Gabrys
[Image: Jennier Gabrys / Citzen Sense]

Twitter, who points out that "AI" is really just another word for "computation" or "computers" these days. But on the other hand, I think we have expectations that it's something greater. What I appreciate about an overlay of your work onto this question of ethics and computation is that we start to think about this in terms of ecology, environment, citizenship, and, as you concluded, in remaking worlds.

One of the things that I've been observing is the way that ethics frameworks are being developed by companies and by nonprofits. In companies such as Facebook or Microsoft, ethics is known as "responsible innovation," and no longer ethics. When it comes down to it, at the end of the day, technologists need to be implementing, operationalizing, and optimizing their code, as though they've left out a full area of design, observation, engagement, and making of the world where architects and designers find themselves. I wonder if you have some thoughts about the role of design within this broader process of sensing, engaging, and remaking?

JG: We very much work in a practice-based way, and I would say this is informed by my prior life working in landscape architecture and working also as a designer, and bringing these kinds of practice-based modes of inquiry to understand how technologies work in the world. It's not just designing an object so it looks and functions in a particular way. But it's also, from a more sociological perspective, seeing how people take up devices, put them to work, use them to generate data, make claims, and contact their regulators to file complaints, and then end up in different kinds of engagements—from productive meetings to altercations—when they have this pollution data.

I think that this is where design can really step into the breach. How do these technologies start to unfold in the world? How can we understand this through different processes of collaborative design and research? How can we see ethics not as something that is completed at the point that a technology is produced, but as something that is ongoing, will have to continually be revisited, and has to also include people as part of those processes so that these don't end up becoming, as we're seeing now, de-democratizing devices?

where does the moral fit into ethics frameworks for computation?

4 "When we start talking about ethics and technology, maybe not surprisingly, the figure of the human designer and technologist becomes part of the conversation." —Molly Wright Steenson

MWS: You're suggesting that ethics are not a destination, but an ongoing process—perhaps a journey. How would you describe ethics? How would you define it from your perspective and from your work?

JG: This is part of what the "how-to" guide really troubles. Rather than trying to define grand concepts like truth or ethics, can we instead begin to dismantle the subject along the way, and ask ourselves, how do we even know what we know? Is it possible to have provisional concepts that can then be put to work in the world and to continually remake those concepts by seeing what effects they have and by tuning them through these different experiments? This is a different way of approaching concepts, a concept like ethics, rather than saying that I have the definitive answer for what ethics is or ought to be. It's a kind of germination of a process for how to engage, how to approach situations, and how to continually remake them. If there's any definition of ethics, I would say it's being able to enter into these contingent engagements and to have the processes by which it's possible to form collectives, to address problems, and to realize more just worlds that are less destructive and less unequal.

This is where I think any approach (like we see in many arenas of political life these days) that would say, "Well, we have our foundational script; that's all we ever need," in fact is not good enough. It is the very life, interpretation, process, and engagement that makes that initial germ of a concept what it is in the world, whether we're talking about technology, environmental problems, or anything else that's currently troubling democracy.

MWS: You've laid out a process here for a broader set of cycles between approach, engaging, and remaking. I'm very much struck by this notion of the practical, the heuristic, the learning at hand, and the concept of tuning—something you write about in much of your work. What does it mean to get something in tune, so that it might sense, and so that the person, the entity, the relationships might better sense as well?

JG: This is a concept that I'm really interested in and have reworked from Isabelle Stengers's citation of Andrew Pickering's discussion of laboratory instruments.[3] I take this up and think about it as the way in which sensors are now working in the world, and how this is not just one human sensing subject saying, "I see or hear this thing," but rather it's about environments of sensation. It's about all sorts of different entities sensing together, and this tuning process, then, is a way to also think about environmental engagements and ethics. We could think about this in relation to climate change, for example, and how many different organisms are changing because of climate change. Plants are flowering out at different times. Birds are migrating at different times. So we can begin to see them as sensors who are tracking changes in environments, and begin to understand the changing environments that we're all involved in and also, in a way, responsible for.

This is a kind of tuning to collective conditions. It's a way to think about practice in an iterative sense, where there is not a single trajectory toward a certain outcome, but rather an ethos of how to engage and work with all of these different actors and conditions to have potentially less destructive environments.

MWS: In your talk, you spoke about the notions of "modest witness," "resistance," and data logging books: different ways of collecting knowledge that might on the surface seem to be passive, but are actually anything but. I'm reminded of the ways that sensors do in fact work. They collect. They channel. They are actively informing, in all of the ways that that means.

JG: Sensing is anything but a passive process. If we think about the work that sensors do, they tune our attention to some things and not others. They create a measurement of particulate matter, for instance, but they're not necessarily telling you about somebody's asthma or about the fact that one in nine people worldwide die from air pollution–related causes. They create certain kinds of measurements, certain kinds of experiences, and not others. This is also a point of tuning into what some sensing entities allow us to understand, but also what may not be included, so that we're aware of what our attention is oriented to and how it might be expanded.

This is why I like to use the term "expanded" as much as "tuning"—to think about how to really trouble these devices, and to make them work in ways that they're not necessarily designed to. When we work with citizens and participants to collect data, they have access to their data. People were really putting the data to work, for instance, by downloading and analyzing it in spreadsheets. In our Pennsylvania pollution-monitoring project, before we had created a tool for citizens to analyze their own data, they were calling state and federal regulators to ask that all sorts of different things that the sensors were not sensing be taken account of, because of the data that sensors were showing. So when there were pollution events, they were asking that certain industry operations be looked at, that follow-up monitoring be undertaken, and so on.

The other thing about sensing is that it can really spark all kinds of different and unexpected encounters. When we organized these community monitoring networks, and people started to work with our data, we found we really couldn't predict what they would do with it.

MWS: We have a question from Jose Sanchez in the audience: "How can we resist the appropriation of data that has been generated through citizen participation by private entities that aim to extract value from such initiatives?"

JG: This is a concern in terms of how citizen data can be used in many different ways. In our work, we were thinking quite carefully about our data collection as not being overly zealous. We collected very particular kinds of data about particulate matter levels. We did not collect location data through digital means. We actually had quite dumb location data that we made fuzzy on our digital platform. So with the northeastern Pennsylvania example, we had township-level data. We did that quite deliberately because Pennsylvania has had quite a lot of social tension in relation to fracking. This was in 2013-14 when we first started the project, and communities were really in conflict. Data became a way in which participants felt they could come to a collective agreement about whether and where pollution was occurring. Communities felt data was important for potentially addressing some of these rifts, but at the same time, people didn't want the data to be overly revealing. For this reason, we collected a very limited amount of data. I think this is very different from what private companies do when they often are amassing large data sets.

We also thought quite carefully about how the data could be used for different purposes. In fact, the data has not been appropriated by private entities. If anything, industry has been quite annoyed with the citizen data because we did show that we were able to attribute pollution to fracking infrastructure through bringing in wind and weather data, and through scraping some data online. This is not data they wanted to appropriate. But what did happen was that federal regulators at the Agency for Toxic Substances and Disease Registry (ATSDR of the EPA) conducted follow-up monitoring that corroborated the citizen data results.

They made a set of recommendations to the Department of Environmental Protection (PA DEP), who then expanded their air-quality monitoring network in response to the findings from the citizen air-quality data.

We haven't had encounters with private entities appropriating the data, I think in part because of the way we've designed our data collection to be as streamlined and specific as possible, and not to over-collect.

This is an important thing to consider if you're a designer working on data: How can you ensure that you're not going to be disclosing more than you need to disclose? How can you really work with participants to ensure that they have control of that data?

MWS: It's worth noting that the keynote event with Ruha Benjamin, Orit Halpern, and David Benjamin also engaged important questions of data and algorithmic bias, and some different concerns for data collection and its outcomes.

JG: Absolutely. I think Ruha Benjamin's work on the Citizen app is a really key example of how what people are being asked to contribute and collect is a much different kind of data.[4] It's a kind of citizen surveillance and reporting on your neighbor. I think this is also part of the ethos of these projects that generates a much different kind of citizen.

MWS: Indeed, as we frame this year's ACADIA conference, it is in part, at least, a conversation about data, how that data will play out, and the role of architecture more globally in that question.

We have a question from Rebecca Smith in the audience: "It sounds like you're suggesting that the reproduction of social/political inequalities might even arise quite explicitly from an emphasis on linear action, rather than open-ended making: that the action model projects knowledge, whereas the making approach allows for other forms of agency to enter into the production of knowledge itself. In your talk, you mentioned Donna Haraway and Isabelle Stengers. I'm also thinking of Daniela Rosner's *Critical Fabulations*.[5] Are there other frameworks you turn to in this area, or maybe could you speak more to this point?"

JG: The intention is not to create a binary to say that potentially more linear ways of working to be effective are less viable, but rather that often there will be a script for action. These scripts can be technological or sociopolitical, and I think here is where practice-based research really demonstrates how it's necessary to think about the ways in which those are much more porous practices and encounters.

This is where open-ended processes come in as practices of adjustment, again drawing from the pragmatists such as James and Dewey.[6] But there are also a number of Black Studies pragmatists, such as the work of early Cornel West and Eddie Glaude, who have written about the way in which social change unfolds through engagement and iteration and being open to certain kinds of change that might not have been anticipated in an initial program of action.[7] This really allows for ways to attempt to avoid dogma, to make sure that engagements are things that can allow a plurality of contributions.

You've also referred to the work of Daniela Rosner, Donna Haraway, and of course a much longer tradition of feminist technoscience. I'm also very informed by this broader area of inquiry, and I think this is a really great resource to bring to a venue like ACADIA, because feminist technoscience is always asking questions including: How are technologies made? Who gets to be recognized as the author of those devices? Who is the entity that is in charge of those scripts, and who holds power in relation to them? And who also recedes from view?

The "modest witness" that I am referring to here is Haraway's critique of Steven Shapin and Simon Schaffer's discussion of the modest witness, which acknowledges that many people are not able to operate as modest witnesses.[8] A certain type of scientist gets to be the modest witness, but women, people of color, and technicians—the very people who make devices run—are not allowed to be part of this arena of who works on technology. It's the white and privileged "gentleman" in his salon writing about the air pump who gets to be the modest witness, the one who is recognized as the authority, because he does not jam the signal of objectivity. I think this is where feminist technoscience has a lot to offer in terms of really opening up practice to an expanded range of actors and contributions that look at the kind of inequalities that have shaped who does and does not get to register in those spaces. It also acknowledges that these are not just human actors; there are all sorts of more-than-human actors who are part of this mix.

MWS: Another audience question, from Cassandra Frazier: "Working with sensors can present a red flag in terms of inequality, because not everyone has the same coding and technological knowledge. What do you think about this? Are

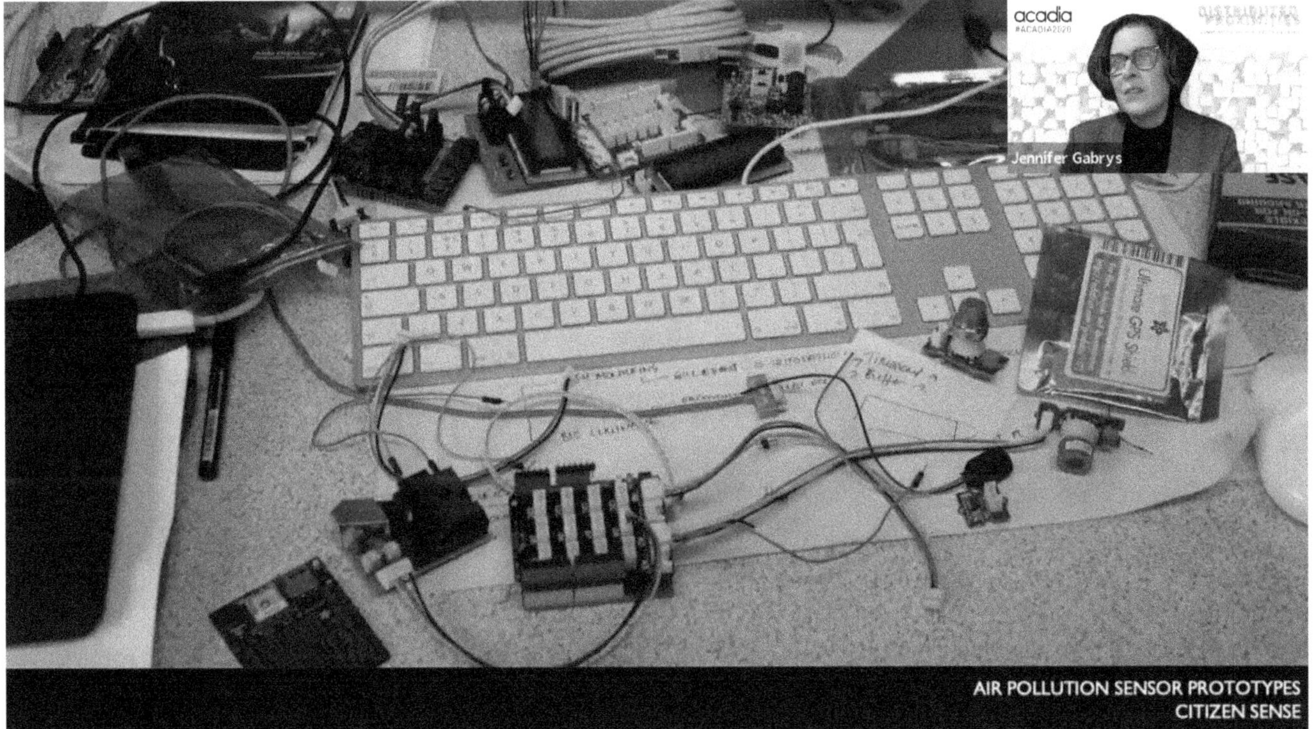

5 "We move away from making as a good in and of itself, where action is simply about getting practical in a hands on way.... This is the way in which I am proposing that we can rethink instruments and instrumentalities, not as linear trajectories towards certain outcomes, but rather as contingent operations that remake worlds." —Jennifer Gabrys
[Image: Jennier Gabrys / Citizen Sense]

there ways that these forms of knowledge can and should be made more accessible to all, in order for more citizens to be able to participate in collecting this data?"

JG: We've also written about this in a separate article in *New Media & Society* on recalibration, where we talk about the kind of dilemmas that arise when these kinds of maker communities are often composed of very particular kinds of actors.[9] Other scholars in science and technology studies have written about this in relation to hacker spaces. Often, people engaged in environmental justice and social organizing projects don't want to bother with assembling sensors from scratch, they would much rather work with devices that are plug-and-play.

The way in which politics and engagement is organized in a makerly space is often one particular kind of configuration that is about getting devices up and running. But communities have a different notion of what it means to get devices up and running. It's important to note that not everyone should have to or is interested in assembling sensors from scratch. To try to understand the claims that were being made for citizen sensing devices, we have tried to work in a critical way, and to think about what is being operationalized when people assemble their own sensors. Are they necessarily becoming enlightened citizens and addressing the problem of air pollution? What we found is that's far from the case. In fact, often those makerly discussions remain within a very particular milieu, and people who are more interested in addressing air pollution are working in different modalities all together.

We have tried to also incorporate a component of pedagogy as part of our public engagement. We've held data workshops, and we've composed data stories to present the citizen data in ways that attempt to work with narrative—not just measurement in the usual sense.[10] We've also held workshops to discuss the findings with participants and to compose action points. I think there are many different ways in which we could think about this troubleshooting as not just centering on a device, but as a kind of larger problem—in this case, air pollution—and how people can make contributions to that. It could be that they're contributing to the narratives for a data story, that they're proposing actions, that then they're even using the data (as with our southeast London example) to obtain funding to run transportation pilot experiments to remake the urban fabric. This very much became citizen data moving into citizen design. I think this doesn't have to just be people monkeying with wires and sensors; there are many ways in which people can contribute.

MWS: There are a couple of final questions from the audience. Jordan Nelson Long says, "I appreciate the framing of Black pragmatism as part of an ethical framework. It helps me situate your statement about ethics being iterative within the making/sensing/interpretive process. Nevertheless, we must also grapple with ethics in the first place in the moments before we embark on project work. This too is where damage is done. I'm curious about what frameworks might allow our projects, particularly those led by white folks and in partnership with industry, to engage in meaningful ethical reflection ahead of initial action."

There is a related question from Shane Burger: "How might we more broadly consider this in our opportunities as a professional or even a political body of architects and designers and computational people?"

JG: That's a really great and important question. Here's where I've always had a problem with frameworks to begin with. We really wrestled with this problem when we were doing our first case study in Pennsylvania. We had this research design, which was to look at how sensors are being used by citizens. But we didn't have a kind of objective in terms of how the data would be used. We began having conversations with these community groups who are already doing their own monitoring. They all had different agendas, and they were not in agreement about how best to address this. Some of them thought that fracking should be shut down entirely; others wanted to work with industry because they were receiving royalties. So we really entered this not from a fixed and settled initial condition of saying, "Here's our ethical framework. Let's now go out in the world." But rather, I would say it was something that rushed at us from all sides. And we then had to work within these conditions as a way of trying to create a collective project of monitoring air quality and trying to do something with that data.

I wonder if ethics doesn't necessarily start as a framework that is then disseminated in that way, but rather is something that requires engagement and encounter and collective deliberation to even begin to form and tune what those engagements might consist of. This really raises lots of different questions about what are the terms of those engagements, because it does almost seem to require certain forms of deliberation and engagement that could seem to be privileging some and not others. This is obviously a critique that's been raised in relation to various forms of democratic engagement. How can there be a plurality of engagements and ways of registering political encounters?

This is something I'm really wrestling with in a new book I'm writing called *Citizens of Worlds*. How can we think about citizenship, not in the singular, but as something that is really tied to ontological plurality and yet is inevitably going to be a site of struggle? This is, I think, something that really needs to be addressed in many different forms of design practice where there might be an initial script, but it will give rise to these plural ontologies. I think there isn't just one initial framework. There are all sorts of different approaches, citizens of worlds, that come to these practices. And that's where I think practice really becomes the way in which they meet and have to work through these different struggles. That's also where inequality really starts to become evident, and potentially can be addressed.

MWS: We've had a really wonderful and wide-ranging conversation that changes how we think of what a "how-to" is, what the environment is, what ecology is, where we interact with it, and what possibilities open up to us as citizens. As you write, "The more-than-knowledge that doing produces involves the very relations and networks that make worlds—and these are political inquiries and inhabitations."[11]

NOTES

1. Jennifer Gabrys, *How to Do Things with Sensors* (Minneapolis: University of Minnesota Press, 2019), 9.
2. Leanne Betasamosake Simpson, *As We Have Always Done: Indigenous Freedom through Radical Resistance* (Minneapolis: University of Minnesota Press, 2017), 19–20.
3. Isabelle Stengers, "A Constructivist Reading of Process and Reality," *Theory, Culture & Society* 25, no. 4 (2008): 91–110. See also Andrew Pickering, *The Mangle of Practice* (Chicago: Chicago University Press, 1995).
4. Ruha Benjamin, "The AntiBlack Box and Abolitionist Tools for the New Jim Code," presentation at 4S New Orleans, September 7, 2019, https://convention2.allacademic.com/one/ssss/4s19/index.php?cmd=Online+Program+View+Paper&selected_paper_id=1530800&PHPSESSID=odllsgekqppe8diu7sqjg1crb5.
5. Daniela Rosner, *Critical Fabulations: Reworking the Methods and Margins of Design* (Cambridge, MA: MIT Press, 2018).

6. For instance, see William James, *Pragmatism and Other Writings* (New York: Penguin Books, 2000); and John Dewey, "The Development of American Pragmatism," in *John Dewey: The Later Works, 1925–1953, Volume 2: 1925–1927*, ed. Jo Ann Boydston (Carbondale: SIU Press, 2008), 3–21.
7. Eddie S. Glaude, *In a Shade of Blue: Pragmatism and the Politics of Black America* (Chicago: University of Chicago Press, 2008); Cornel West, *The American Evasion of Philosophy: A Genealogy of Pragmatism* (Madison: University of Wisconsin Press, 1989).
8. See Donna Haraway, *Modest_Witness@Second_Millennium. FemaleMan©_Meets_OncoMouse™* (New York: Routledge, 1997); and Steven Shapin and Simon Schaffer, *Leviathan and the Air-Pump: Hobbes, Boyle, and the Experimental Life* (Princeton: Princeton University Press, 1985).
9. Helen Pritchard, Jennifer Gabrys, and Lara Houston, "Re-calibrating DIY: Testing Digital Participation across Dust Sensors, Fry Pans and Environmental Pollution," *New Media & Society* 20, no. 12 (2018): 4533–4552.
10. For a recent example of how Citizen Sense has created infrastructures for citizens to contribute to air-pollution sensing in multiple different registers, see the AirKit project, https://citizensense.net/projects/airkit/.
11. Gabrys, *How to Do Things with Sensors*, 84.

Jennifer Gabrys is Chair in Media, Culture, and Environment in the Department of Sociology at the University of Cambridge. She leads the Planetary Praxis research group, and is Principal Investigator on the European Research Council–funded project, Smart Forests: Transforming Environments into Social-Political Technologies. She also leads the Citizen Sense and AirKit projects, which have both received funding from the ERC. She is the author of *How to Do Things with Sensors* (University of Minnesota Press, 2019); *Program Earth: Environmental Sensing Technology and the Making of a Computational Planet* (University of Minnesota Press, 2016); and *Digital Rubbish: A Natural History of Electronics* (University of Michigan Press, 2011); and co-editor of *Accumulation: The Material Politics of Plastic* (Routledge, 2013). Her in-progress books include *Citizens of Worlds: Open-Air Toolkits for Environmental Struggle*. Her work can be found at citizensense.net and planetarypraxis.org.

Molly Wright Steenson is Senior Associate Dean for Research in the College of Fine Arts at Carnegie Mellon University, where she is also the K&L Gates Associate Professor of Ethics and Computational Technologies and Associate Professor in the School of Design. She is the author of *Architectural Intelligence: How Designers and Architects Created the Digital Landscape* (MIT Press, 2017), a history of AI's impact on design and architecture, and the co-editor of *Bauhaus Futures* (MIT Press, 2019). She was previously an assistant professor at the University of Wisconsin–Madison and an associate professor at the Interaction Design Institute Ivrea in Italy, home of the Arduino, and began her tech and design career at groundbreaking studios, consultancies, and Fortune 500 companies in 1995. Steenson holds a PhD in Architecture from Princeton and an MED from the Yale School of Architecture.

PEER-REVIEWED PAPERS

ECOLOGY AND ETHICS

"In this amalgamation or assemblage of sensing the environment, sensors, and experience, 'how to' relations, and informing, I'd like to know what kind of ethics we might find. And conversely, I'd like to know what ethics might find in this approach. Not just good/bad, right/wrong, good/evil, and the way we've been looking at morality tied to human character and morality tied to ethics, but rather a new view of the citizen who possesses rights, privileges, and responsibilities. Within sensing the environment, relations, and informing, perhaps we see 'how to' as an ethics in the environment, both beyond the human and the more-than-human."

—Molly Wright Steenson, "A Conversation on Ecology and Ethics"

In addition to work focusing on biological interactions and climate/environmental simulation for building envelope design, taking cues from the "Conversation on Ecology and Ethics," this section includes work involving the implementation of sensors and sensing, which in turn provides a segue to projects of "architectures of care," related to healthcare and the pandemic.

Irradiated Shade

Mapping, Modeling, and Measuring Urban UVB Exposure

Stephen Mueller
Texas Tech University

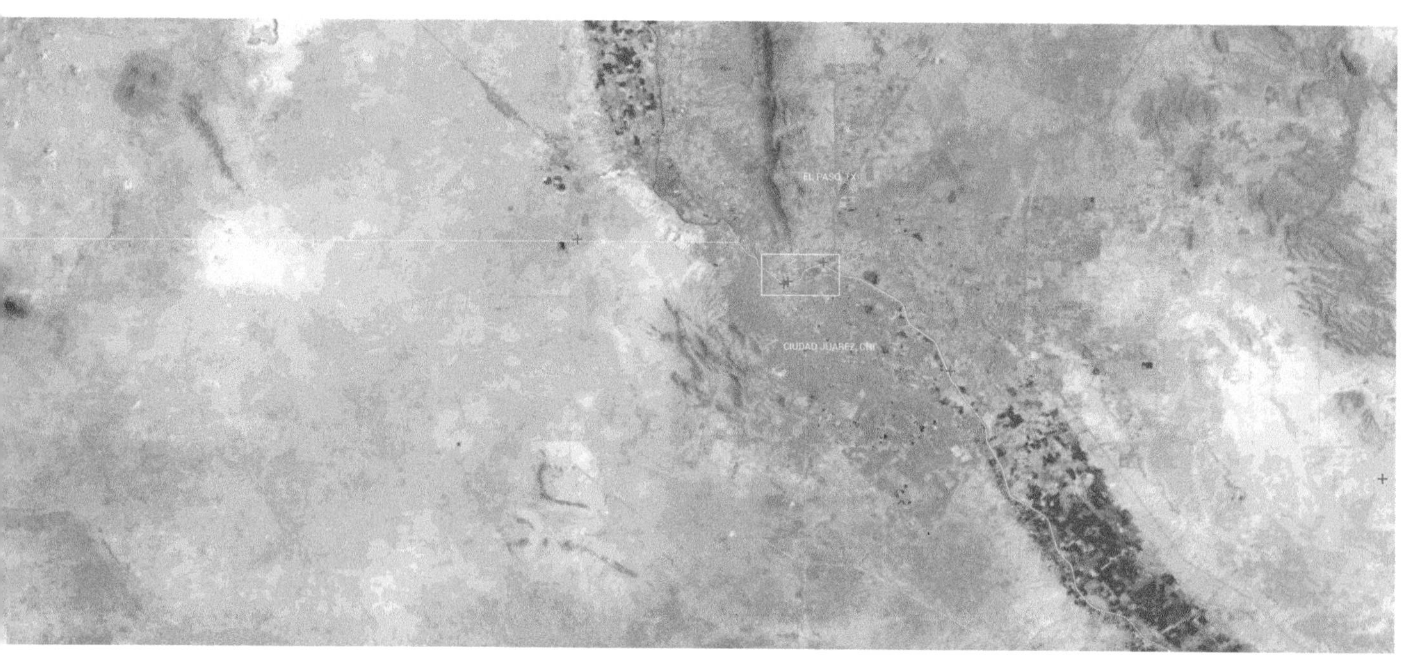

1 Land surface temperature map, El Paso/Ciudad Juárez Metroplex.

ABSTRACT

The paper details computational mapping and modeling techniques from an ongoing design research project titled Irradiated Shade, which endeavors to develop and calibrate a computational toolset to uncover, represent, and design for the unseen dangers of ultraviolet radiation, a growing yet underexplored threat to cities, buildings, and the bodies that inhabit them. While increased shade in public spaces has been advocated as a strategy for "mitigation [of] climate change" (Kapelos and Patterson 2014), it is not a panacea to the threat. Even in apparent shade, the body is still exposed to harmful, ambient, or "scattered" UVB radiation. The study region is a binational metroplex, a territory in which significant atmospheric pollution and the effects of climate change (reduced cloud cover and more "still days" of stagnant air) amplify the "scatter" of ultraviolet wavelengths and UV exposure within shade, which exacerbates urban conditions of shade as an "index of inequality" (Bloch 2019) and threatens public health. Exposure to indirect radiation correlates to the amount of sky visible from the position of an observer (Gies and Mackay 2004). The overall size of a shade structure, as well as the design of openings along its sides, can greatly impact the UV protection factor (UPF) (Turnbull and Parisi 2005). Shade, therefore, is more complex than ubiquitous urban and architectural "sun" and "shadow studies" are capable of representing, as such analyses flatten the three-dimensional nature of radiation exposure and are "blind" to the ultraviolet spectrum. "Safe shade" is contingent on the nuances of the surrounding built environment, and designers must be empowered to observe and respond to a wider context than current representational tools allow.

INTRODUCTION

The project seeks to expand the architect's toolkit in simulating and representing the impact of ultraviolet radiation on sites and bodies, through the production of custom representational tools, drawings, and shade structure designs. This paper will focus primarily on the challenges and efforts to conduct analyses at the urban scale within the study area to identify areas where solar radiation poses a high risk to populations despite apparent shade. This paper will describe the challenges of mapping solar radiation at an urban scale within a binational urban context; proposed approaches, computational tools, and workflows across geographic information system (GIS) and design software platforms to overcome these challenges, including a spherical projection algorithm developed specifically for this application; and the emerging representational outcomes.

CHALLENGES

The study focuses on applications within the El Paso/Ciudad Juárez metroplex, a binational territory defined by the inequitable distribution of public shade, where significant atmospheric pollution amplifies the "scatter" of ultraviolet wavelengths and UV exposure within public space. The metroplex spans the US-Mexico border and is characterized by a fragmented multijurisdictional datascape at the intersection of two nations and three states, a complex patchwork of disparate municipal, county, and regulatory domains (Kripa and Mueller 2021). These multiple regulatory boundaries divide the political administration of the territory while also imposing artificial divisions in the collection and distribution of geospatial data relevant to otherwise continuous, transboundary environmental phenomena, including urban UV exposure. As substantial portions of the metroplex population fluidly inhabit multiple jurisdictions on a daily or weekly basis, they cross territories with substantially changing capacities, standards, and protocols for urban environmental assessment. Shared, cross-border environmental and urban planning efforts capable of addressing environmental health risks and promoting environmental justice in the region are limited by both the technical challenges to overcome differences in data gathering and reporting methods across multiple jurisdictions, as well as changing attitudes toward international cooperation at the federal level.[1] Without complete, contiguous, and comparable data describing ultraviolet solar radiation exposure, the disparities and asymmetries in threats to public health across multiple and interrelated jurisdictions remain hidden and difficult to address.

An urban solar radiation analysis in the borderland capable of spanning multiple jurisdictional divisions currently relies on one of two distinct approaches. The first approach would entail a process of data assemblage. That is, researchers could gather discontinuous data from multiple domains and attempt to forge continuities and comparative analyses across the boundaries by addressing the discrepancies in the geographic or environmental data provided. Alternatively, investigators could seek out transboundary datasets that bypass the various data divides. In the study area, this approach would entail the collection of transboundary satellite data or open-source urban-level data. The data assemblage approach in the binational study area faces unique challenges, including the different languages, units of measurement, reporting frequencies, and methods of data collection between the US and Mexico. The alternative approach—to rely on already-contiguous transboundary datasets—faces its own challenges. Contiguous satellite data and imagery in the region is mostly available at a resolution unsuitable for urban-level analysis. High-resolution satellite data and imagery is available from national sources in the US and Mexico and faces a similar challenge to create comparable and contiguous analyses. Open-source urban-level data in the region, including physical and urban geographic features, is relatively incomplete.

In addition to these context-specific challenges, urban-scale solar radiation analysis in any context faces particular difficulties. First is the complexity of the phenomenon (Mueller 2021). Solar radiation levels in an urban environment are dependent on multiple physical and environmental conditions. Physical features (including both topographic elements and elements of the built environment that can impact shade, shadow, and reflectivity) and changing environmental factors (including solar angle, cloud cover, and amount of airborne particulate) can mitigate or amplify ultraviolet radiation exposure in an urban environment. Both direct and diffuse radiation can impact the relative risk of ultraviolet exposure, and each type impacts each site differently at different times of day. Second is the limited availability and application of tools, workflows, and representational methods for urban planners and designers to produce comparative analyses of urban sites incorporating these multiple factors to determine exposure risk and to evaluate proposed solutions to mitigate exposure.

METHODS

To address these challenges, the project takes a composite approach, leveraging readily available cross-border satellite data to begin with a continuous transboundary assessment, while selectively augmenting the relatively low resolution of the dataset with a series of higher-resolution overlays and computational mapping and modeling

2

3

4

5

2 Land surface temperature map. 3 Diffuse radiation map. 4 Direct radiation map. 5 Pedestrian intensity map.

techniques. Satellite imagery and sensor data serve as inputs for a series of initial mapping underlays that help to describe the major environmental conditions impacting urban ultraviolet exposure in the study region.

A digital elevation model (DEM) is a common input for solar radiation analysis in geographic information system (GIS) mapping platforms, as the slopes and shadows of topographic features impact the amount of radiation absorbed by a given exposure. The DEM available for the study area from the National Elevation Dataset provides topographic information in the metroplex at a relatively low 1 arcsecond resolution. Higher resolutions are available for US topography, but these datasets end abruptly at the international border. The available DEM can be used with built-in solar radiation analysis tools in ArcGIS Pro (ESRI 2021) to generate low-resolution, transboundary assessments of direct, diffuse, and total solar radiation in the borderland. But the model at this resolution approximates only topographic features, largely ignoring elements of urban geography (e.g., buildings and bridges). Additionally, this 2.5D height information fails to capture more complex, layered canopy conditions from street trees and other overhanging elements common to urban environments and likely to impact radiation exposure. Asymmetries in ultraviolet exposure with this method are most certainly below what Eyal Weizman has termed the "threshold of detectability" (Weizman 2017), and additional measures must be taken to increase the resolution of the investigation.

Three other readily available data sources can help to augment the analysis: optical, thermal, and height-field data. Satellite data from LANDSAT 8 includes both optical and thermal information at a resolution of 60 cm for the study area, and is contiguous across the international boundary, including portions of Ciudad Juárez. The LANDSAT program captures and publishes satellite imagery in different spectral bands, including optical and thermal bands. By processing the optical bands in GIS software, a false-color image of the urban environment can be produced, which in turn can help distinguish areas of vegetation, shown in red, within urbanized land, shown in light blue. Raster-based analysis comparing these aspects of the false-color image can identify likely areas of street trees impacting urban UVB exposure. By processing the information stored in the thermal bands, a land surface temperature map can be produced,[2] identifying areas in which populations may be exposed to the most heat stress, and therefore most likely to seek shade. To better analyze the impact of the three-dimensional urban environment on solar radiation exposure, a three-dimensional model of the buildings and other built structures is needed. The study area lacks comprehensive building footprint and building height data, and open-source data presents only a partial understanding. LiDAR (light detection and ranging) data sources[3] are published as point clouds of natural and man-made elements, which can also be used to conduct analyses of direct, diffuse, and total radiation. While this level of three-dimensional resolution is an essential and

6 Composite map.

expedient component of a study in this region, readily available datasets from the United States Geological Survey (USGS) capture only portions of the study region south of the international boundary.

Noting that no single available dataset—or single analysis from such dataset—can capture the full complexity of urban-scale solar radiation as outlined above, and that the resolution of any one dataset is inadequate to inform analyses below the scale of a city block, the project explored two parallel hypotheses and two parallel investigations.

First, by compositing available datasets and producing a series of graphic and computational overlays, we suggest that the compound effects of multiple urban and environmental factors contributing to urban shade and UV exposure may be better ascertained, and sites most at risk of "irradiated shade" may be identified.

Second, since the calculation of urban UV exposure depends primarily on "hidden" processes within GIS software platforms conditioned by three-dimensional constructs of the urban environment, we suggest that a higher-resolution analysis may be possible by translating the hidden logics of common solar analysis tools through computational algorithms, to produce detailed representations of the geometric and spatial relationships, and resulting conditions of solar radiation and shade on a specific site.

Composite and Computational Mapping

Our composite mapping efforts start with a focus on the area near the international boundary, where there is a high degree of pedestrian activity from travelers entering and leaving the US via pedestrian bridges. The channelized Rio Grande/Rio Bravo, tracking across the maps from left to right, serves as the international boundary. The midrise and high-rise urban core of downtown El Paso, Texas, is shown toward the top of the map, with lower-rise neighborhoods moving south into Ciudad Juárez. The maps are developed in ArcGIS Pro, using some built-in tools and raster-processing workflows to extend what is visible.

Processing the thermal band information from the LANDSAT data, we produced a *land surface temperature map* (Fig. 2) of the study region during the summer solstice, showing the cool mountain peaks and intense heat of the urban heat island within which populations seek shade. This base map begins to describe the character of the urban environment and some initial areas of likely risk, with increased heat island effects throughout the approach to the border and particular hot spots near the pedestrian bridges and transit connections near the port of entry.

We then produce a *direct solar radiation map* (Fig. 4), using the 1-arcsecond DEM and the Solar Radiation toolset in ArcGIS Pro. The resulting rather noisy map shows direct solar radiation averaged over the same period. The impact of the topography on solar exposure is evident, with the

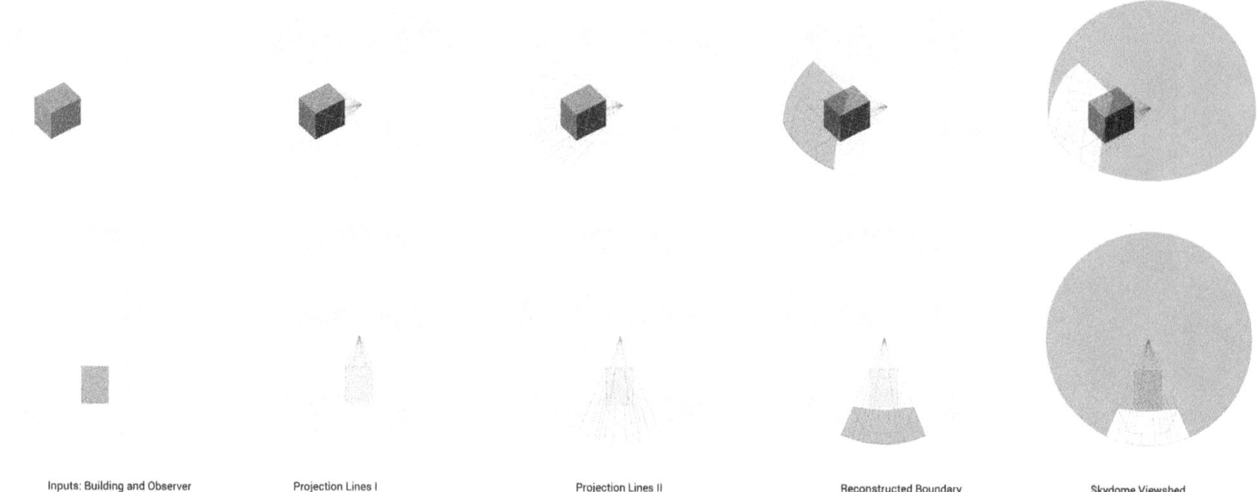

7 Spherical projection algorithm diagram.

low area of the river valley shown with a relatively even distribution of direct radiation. Higher topography and the building masses of the downtown core provide some protection from solar radiation away from the border. Building masses are registered in the checkerboard pixelization but clearly at a low resolution, given the source data.

Next we produce a *diffuse solar radiation map* (Fig. 3), also from the DEM and the built-in Solar Radiation toolset. The diffuse map begins to capture the effects of UV scatter in the border environment. Built into the calculation is a degree of cloud cover, which approximates the diffuse radiation bouncing off clouds and atmospheric particles. The UVB spectrum is more prominent in diffuse solar radiation, and its spread is conditional on the amount of sky visible to an observer at any given point. Diffuse radiation is thus impacted in this map by both the topography and the urban canyons. The map begins to capture a clearly unequal, asymmetrical distribution of UV protection in the study area. Relatively low amounts of diffuse radiation, shown in the yellow tones, are abundant in the urban core but few and far between in the approach to the bridges, a result of the low building heights, wide streets, reflective surfaces including transit zones and parking areas, and low number of street trees. These broad swathes of high exposure to diffuse radiation cover some of the lowest-income zip codes in the city, and in fact in all of the US, signaling access to urban UV protection as an underconsidered condition of environmental inequity.

To get even higher resolution on the distribution of radiation, we use LiDAR point cloud data to generate the urban terrain with better detail, making possible a more focused study at the block level, revealing areas of relatively high protection against diffuse radiation in the urban core, and conditions of general overexposure along the streets approaching the bridges.

The risk of harmful effects due to solar radiation are tied to the length of an individual's exposure, so we also find proxies for the likely locations of high intensities of pedestrian activity in the study area. We produce a *pedestrian intensity map* (Fig. 5), layering in municipal GIS data, like the location of bus and streetcar stations and population data, to calculate walking distance to transit stops. The distribution reveals some transit shadows along the approach to the Paso del Norte bridge and throughout the low-income neighborhoods, indicating increased exposure time for pedestrians seeking access to transit.

We next analyze the optical bands of the LANDSAT data and convert the raw data to a false-color image to reveal the distribution of vegetation, including likely areas for street trees. We note also that this protective amenity corresponds to areas already well-protected by taller buildings and topography, likely increasing the disparity of exposure conditions in the study area.

Using these maps as base layers, we then developed a *compound analysis workflow* that weights each input in order to identify areas of compound risk. The *composite map* (Fig. 6) reveals an abundance of ultraviolet exposure and a pronounced shade deficit near the international border. Major pedestrian areas near international bridges and ports of entry—where urban density, building heights,

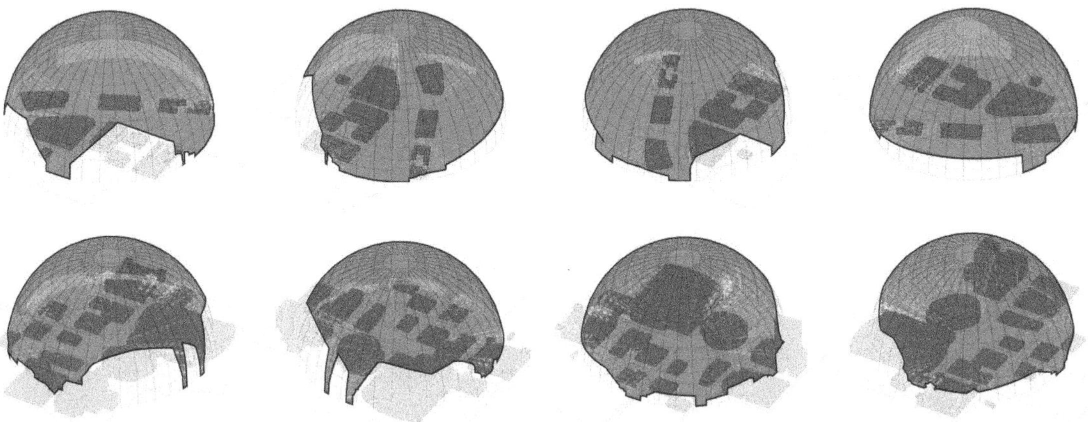

8 Urban sky exposure analysis using spherical projection algorithm.

and amount of street trees are low—are particularly overexposed. A number of hot spots emerge, demonstrating where ultraviolet exposure is most extreme. By running graphic and numeric overlays of the various base layers, we can begin to see some compound effects. By overlaying the land surface temperature and pedestrian intensity map, for instance, we can see and calculate the areas that are generally hotter, and in which pedestrians would have longer commutes. Overlaying the direct and diffuse radiation maps, we can better understand the need to design for changing concerns throughout a single urban corridor.

Spherical Projection Algorithm

To calculate solar radiation, ArcGIS Solar Analysis tools and other GIS platforms use a similar approach, first analyzing height data stored in a digital elevation model to compute a hemispheric viewshed, creating a kind of circular map of the areas of exposed sky. The resulting *viewshed map* is based on a sampling of the surrounding height field in a specified number of directions (Tovar-Pescador et al. 2006). Its accuracy is conditional on the resolution of the height data provided, and while a useful visualization, the map is left "behind the scenes" of the solar analysis tools, an intermediate step in the production of the more common visualizations: the *sunmap* and *skymap*.

The sunmap is a familiar architectural and urban solar analysis tool, describing the path of the sun at different times and days throughout the year. Calculations overlaying the sunmap with the viewshed diagram yield direct radiation values. The skymap calculates diffuse radiation values for different sectors of the sky dome. Calculations overlaying the skymap with the viewshed diagram yield diffuse radiation values (Tovar-Pescador et al. 2006). Both the sunmap and the skymap are shown in a similar hemispherical projection, similar to what would be captured by a fish-eye photograph. Researchers comparing this geometric computational approach in GIS software to the real-world analysis of urban environments have shown the computational to correlate accurately with empirical measurements. In one related example, researchers confirmed the relative accuracy of calculated Sky View Factors (SVF) using skymaps produced through fish-eye photography compared to the GIS simulation (Chen et al. 2012).

It has further been shown that exposure to indirect radiation under a shade structure correlates to the amount of sky visible from the position of an observer (Gies and Mackay 2004). To provide "safe shade," designers must be able to map and model the impact of the built environment on UVB exposure on urban sites with higher precision and evaluate the effectiveness of architectural designs in protecting populations from UVB scatter.

Borrowing from some of the hidden logics built into solar analysis in GIS software, we developed our own tools to visualize and assess conditions of urban UV exposure, translating the "behind the scenes" operations to a more immediate, interactive, and responsive design environment. To better understand the impact of building geometry on UV exposure in urban space, we developed a *spherical projection algorithm* (Fig. 7) in Rhino and Grasshopper (Robert McNeel & Associates 2020; Rutten 2020). The algorithm translates the hidden logic of the GIS calculations into an interface more familiar to architects and urban design professionals, and allows for real-time feedback for site studies and design evaluations, more immediate than waiting for GIS software or plug-ins to render results. This helps us to analyze the impact of existing building forms on diffuse UV exposure and assess the impact of any future intervention. By seeing the particular geometry of sky exposure from one or several public spaces, we can calibrate the extents of a new building mass or shade canopy to provide better protection

Drawing on the evidence that the amount of UV radiation entering a shaded condition is directly proportional to the amount of visible sky seen from the shade, we have developed a technique for spherical projection that takes any point in the city, scans the surrounding cityscape, and masks any obstructions on the sky dome (Fig. 8). This computational technique yields both a computable surface and a graphic representation of the areas of potential vulnerability, as well as metric information, including the percentage of sky cover and other orientation vectors. We can "unroll" this projection in a panorama-style drawing to better understand how the surrounding city offers protection against UV exposure, and work in this environment with design proposals in real time to see how interventions might additionally mask the sky dome. An additional algorithm unrolls the spherical projection in a panorama-style drawing, allowing designers to see the particular geometry of the skyline clearly in every direction so we can begin to assess and address these overexposed orientations.

The research team has begun deploying the algorithm at highly trafficked intersections in the borderland to reveal the varying degree of exposure to the sky, and therefore to diffuse radiation and damage from UVB. We then developed a custom technique to map and measure the sky exposure, and direction of exposure at each intersection, to find likely zones of exposure. We needed first to construct a comprehensive building model of the study region to more accurately physically compute three-dimensional conditions. By deploying the algorithm in the digital model, we further reveal trends in increased UVB exposure near the international boundary, in pedestrian areas approaching the crossing, where pedestrians are at the greatest risk of unhealthy exposure.

We have sampled every major pedestrian intersection in the study area near the border to compile a *sky exposure catalog* of the metroplex, color-coding each by their exposure area, graphically identifying areas at highest risk of exposure to diffuse radiation. The resulting masked sky dome represents an optimized form for maximum UVB protection for any given point in the city. From each masked sky dome we compute the ratio of exposure, rendering the most exposed forms in deepest orange, indicating the intersections with highest risks. The catalog reveals significant differences in urban ultraviolet exposure in the study region. From these assessments we can see at much higher resolution the differences in exposure along the pedestrian corridors and can locate areas most in need of additional protection. Each intersection yields a different and highly articulated sky exposure map, which we use as a computable surface (Fig. 9). Raw data from the surface area, for instance, allow us to make quick assessments about the extent to which each intersection is exposed to diffuse radiation. From the images, we can better see which orientations have clear channels of exposure from ground to sky.

RESULTS AND DISCUSSION

As we continue to develop the interface and the outputs from the computational toolset, we are integrating an ability to better visualize and assess the relationship of sky exposure to solar orientations, using the sky dome geometry as an input for other environmental analysis tools. Using the Ladybug plug-in for Grasshopper (Roudsari 2020), for instance, we can map monthly averages of high and low solar radiation on the sky exposure map of a single site to better understand where the geometry of the sky dome is exposed to the most dangerous orientations, and where the surrounding built environment is already providing adequate protection.

We plan to further develop the tools by integrating the science of UV exposure and scatter. We know that as the sun angle varies, it changes the angle of incidence for direct UVA radiation, and therefore the intensity of direct solar radiation. But we also know that UVB radiation typically enters the environment in a diffuse manner, with intensities that do not correlate to standard solar studies. Diffuse UVB radiation is at its highest just before and just after solar noon, so these are the hours of the design space for projects seeking to protect against UV radiation. We are planning to integrate the computational workflow with existing analytical tools in GIS software and environmental analysis plug-ins for Rhino/Grasshopper to incorporate these variables, and we plan to develop a shared tool or script for other designers to use.

CONCLUSION

The project suggests computational mapping and modeling techniques that urban and architectural designers may employ to more successfully investigate and address conditions of UV exposure within urban environments. The computational mapping workflow presented can assist designers in overcoming the challenges of attaining and assessing the necessary geographic and environmental information pertinent to a robust analysis of urban UV exposure while suggesting productive overlays to help in identifying areas of increased exposure risk. The mapping workflow leverages remote sensing and raster analysis techniques using transboundary data in GIS to increase the spatial resolution, continuity, and complexity of solar radiation analysis in an otherwise fragmented cross-border datascape. This workflow enables the identification of areas with limited protection from UV exposure, supporting investigations capable of supporting environmental and spatial justice initiatives in the US-Mexico borderland. The computational spherical projection algorithm further increases the spatial resolution of solar radiation analysis by translating the logics of radiation calculations into an interactive, three-dimensional design environment. This algorithm assists designers in understanding the built environment to better address diffuse solar radiation levels in apparent shade by producing clear representations of the exposed sky dome, a critical factor in preventing ultraviolet radiation from entering shaded conditions.

ACKNOWLEDGMENTS

Project team, POST (Project for Operative Spatial Technologies): Stephen Mueller, research director; Ersela Kripa, project director; Karla Padilla and Sofia Dominguez Rojo, research assistants. This project was supported in part by Columbia University GSAPP Incubator Prize.

NOTES

1. The US-Mexico Border Health Initiative, a major transboundary environmental health initiative, no longer publishes cross-boundary environmental data for the US-Mexico borderland. See https://www.usgs.gov/about/organization/science-support/international-programs/us-mexico-border-environmental-health
2. See, e.g., https://www.esri.com/arcgis-blog/products/product/analytics/deriving-temperature-from-landsat-8-thermal-bands-tirs/
3. See, e.g., USGS LiDAR Explorer: https://prd-tnm.s3.amazonaws.com/LidarExplorer/index.html#/

REFERENCES

Bloch, Sam. 2019. "Shade." *Places Journal*, April, 2017. https://doi.org/10.22269/190423.

Chen, Liang, Edward Ng, Xipo An, Chao Ren, Max Lee, Una Wang, and Zhengjun He. 2012. "Sky View Factor Analysis of Street Canyons and Its Implications for Daytime Intra-Urban Air Temperature Differentials in High-Rise, High-Density Urban Areas of Hong Kong: A GIS-based Simulation Approach." *International Journal of Climatology* 32, no. 1: 121–136.

ESRI. 2021. *ArcGIS Pro*. V.2.8. ESRI. PC.

Gies, Peter, and Christina Mackay. 2004. "Measurements of the Solar UVR Protection Provided by Shade Structures in New Zealand Primary Schools." *Photochemistry and Photobiology* 80, no. 2: 334–339.

Kapelos, George Thomas, and Mitchell Rolland Sutherland Patterson. 2014. "Health, Planning, Design, and Shade: A Critical Review." *Journal of Architectural and Planning Research* 31, no. 2: 91–111.

Kripa, Ersela, and Stephen Mueller. 2020. "An Ultraviole(n)t Border." *e-flux architecture*. https://www.e-flux.com/architecture/at-the-border/325756/an-ultraviole-n-tborder/.

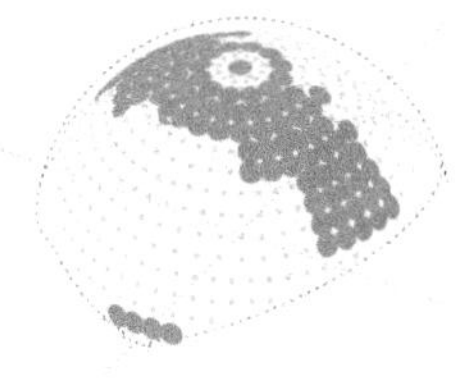

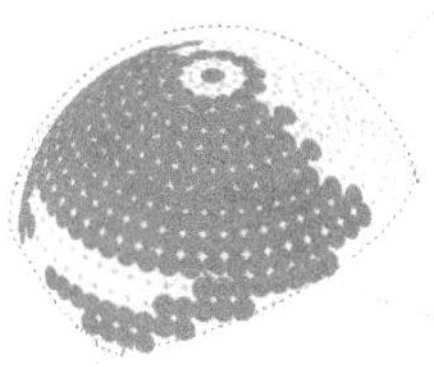
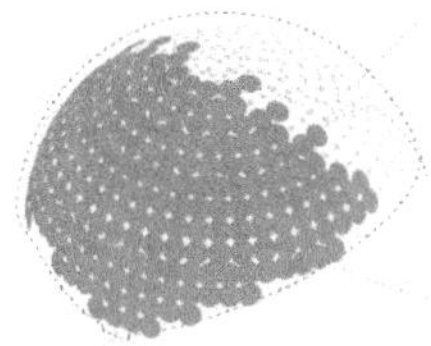
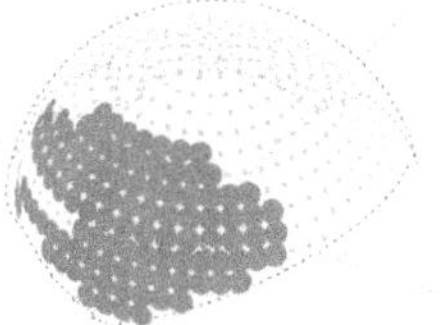
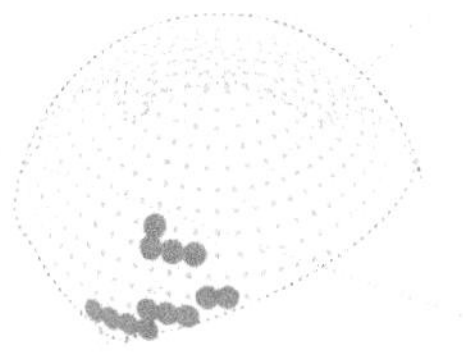
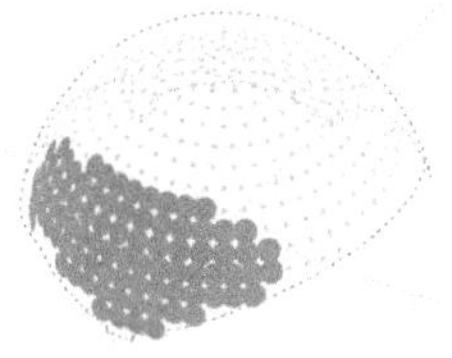

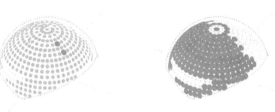

9 Solar radiation analysis of sky exposure computable surface.

Kripa, Ersela, and Stephen Mueller. 2021. "Inhabiting the Data Border." In *Less Talk More Action [Proceedings of the ACSA Fall 2019 Conference]*, Stanford, CA, 13–15 September 2019, edited by A. Larimer, D. Berke, D. Lin, D. Krafcik, J. Barton, and S. Bald, 86–90. ACSA Press.

Mueller, Stephen. 2021. "Designing for Irradiated Shade." In Carbon *[Proceedings of the 2020 AIA/ACSA Intersections Research Conference]*, Philadephia, PA, 30 September 2020. ACSA.

Robert McNeel & Associates. Rhinoceros. V.6.0. Robert McNeel & Associates. PC. 2020.

Roudsari, Mostapha Sadeghipour, and Chris Mackey. Ladybug Tools. V.1.1.0. Ladybug Tools LLC. PC. 2020.

Rutten, David. Grasshopper. V.1.0.0007. Robert McNeel & Associates. PC. 2020.

Tovar-Pescador, J., D. Pozo-Vázquez, J. A. Ruiz-Arias, J. Batlles, G. López, and J. L. Bosch. 2006. "On the Use of the Digital Elevation Model to Estimate the Solar Radiation in Areas of Complex Topography." *Meteorological Applications: A Journal of Forecasting, Practical Applications, Training Techniques and Modelling* 13, no. 3: 279–287.

Turnbull, David J., and A. V. Parisi. 2005. "Increasing the Ultraviolet Protection Provided by Shade Structures." *Journal of Photochemistry and Photobiology B: Biology* 78, no. 1: 61–7.

Weizman, Eyal. 2017. *Forensic Architecture: Violence at the Threshold of Detectability*. New York: Zone Books. doi:10.2307/j.ctv14gphth.

IMAGE CREDITS

All drawings and images by POST (Project for Operative Spatial Technologies).

Stephen Mueller is a Research Assistant Professor at Texas Tech College of Architecture (CoA) and founding director of research at POST (Project for Operative Spatial Technologies), a territorial think tank and CoA research center situated on the US-Mexico border. Mueller's research seeks novel applications for emerging spatial technologies to analyze, engage, and transform urban environments. POST engages transformations in the borderland through projects intersecting urban geography, border studies, and digital humanities. Mueller is a registered architect and founding partner of AGENCY, and the recipient of several awards, including the Rome Prize in Architecture from the American Academy in Rome and Emerging Voices award from the Architectural League of New York.

Coral Carbonate

Alex Schofield
California College of the Arts

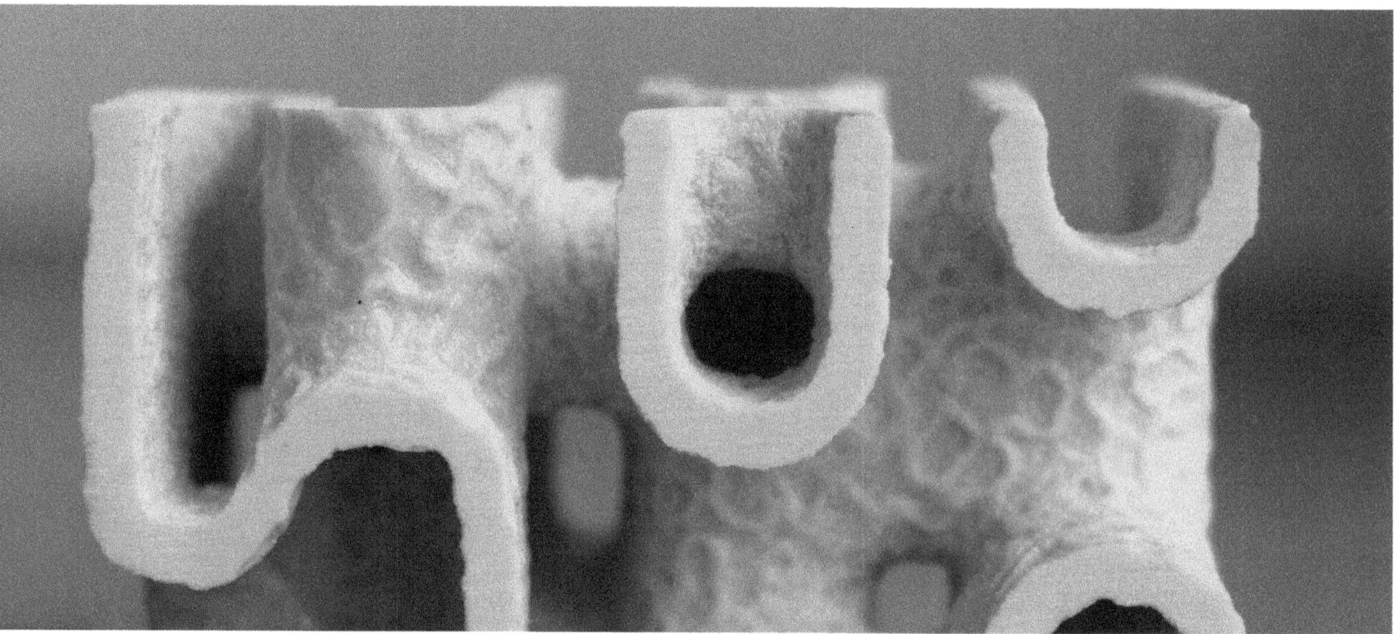

1

ABSTRACT

This work-in-progress paper describes a body of research that utilizes the invention and application of a novel method to 3D-print calcium carbonate ($CaCO_3$). The resultant 3D-printed objects can be computationally optimized and used as a scaffold for the growth of various aquatic life that exists at the interface of soft edges and the built, specifically (but not limited to) coral polyps. Rather than utilizing materials designed for anthropocentric terrestrial environments, we can harness materials and forms native to aquatic ecosystems in combination with advanced computation and fabrication techniques to help foster applied research in service to healthier ecosystems and cohabitation. This paper introduces the novel application of a 3D-printed calcium carbonate, mimicking a similar material composition to that of coral, and describes the additive manufactured medium with regard to 3D powder-printing methodologies. Hypothesis and proposal of morphogenesis in surface and volume are identified as key factors for interface with aquatic organisms. Current and future applications are additionally exhibited through a combination of material composition, surface, and form as targeted intervention and artificial restoration for aquatic ecosystems. While our planet requires anthropocentric mitigation strategies for reduction of greenhouse gases that contribute to aquatic life's greatest threats, we must simultaneously develop strategies for adaptation that immediately respond to the current realities of a changing climate.

1 Initial prototype of 3D-printed calcium carbonate exemplifying procedural surface and form.

2 "Reef Balls" being lowered into water as artificial reef.

3 Old New York City subway cars being lowered into water as artificial reef.

BACKGROUND

The footprint of our existence has had a catastrophic impact on ecosystems globally. In particular, coral reefs are being decimated by human-induced conditions quicker than they can recover and grow. This work-in-progress paper describes a novel application of a 3D-printed (3DP) coral, in the form of the material substrate calcium carbonate, as targeted intervention and artificial restoration for aquatic ecosystems. More specifically, calcium carbonate is 3D-printed to mimic the materiality that makes up the hard structural home of coral's living polyp inhabitants. This unique material development has led to the invention of a working prototype in support of a wide range of ocean life ecosystems by fabricating and reseeding a 3DP calcium carbonate scaffold. The 3DP calcium carbonate is currently being tested as structures, tiles, and frags used to further research and test live applications in support of artificial coral restoration, but also shows promise as biological substrate for the growth of other ocean life. The ultimate goal of such an intervention is the cultivation of a healthy and biodiverse aquatic ecosystem through adaptation and repair of physically damaged environments caused by anthropogenic sources. This project and application goes beyond a simple substrate to seed and supplement the growth of coral as it proposes a link between our anthropocentric built environment and surrounding natural ecosystems. Where there was once considered a hard edge between our built environment and aquatic ecosystems, a softer edge is being explored that considers our interface between the world beyond buildings.

Precedent

Scientists have begun to observe a rapid decline of underwater ecosystems due to anthropogenic carbon dioxide altering seawater chemistry (Fabry et al. 2008). Fifty percent of the world's coral reefs have died in the past 30 years, and it is anticipated that 90% will die in the next century (Burke et al. 2011). With rising oceanic temperatures and increase in ocean acidification, many aquatic organisms using calcification to create their homes are being rapidly destroyed. While we work on land to solve mitigation strategies to reduce greenhouse gases and pollution, we are simultaneously developing adaptation strategies that help respond to the immediate impacts of the climate change crisis. Alternative materials used in contemporary interventions for underwater ecosystems and coastline fabrication, such as concrete used for "Reef Balls" (*The Economist* 2014), Tetrapods (Chamberland et al. 2017), or even coral frags, often leach undesirable by-products and contribute a large carbon footprint in their production processes. Additionally, waste by-products from cities, such as old New York City subway cars

2

3

(Kennedy 2001), have been used as substrate for artificial reef restoration. These precedents exemplify solutions that utilize materials more common in the human built environment than those that make up the structures of aquatic life. Aquatic ecosystem restoration and intervention, most notably seen in artificial coral restoration, is a relatively new practice that requires further critical research in support of natural ecosystems as vital infrastructure for our planet.

METHOD

This paper establishes three primary subjects as methodology: material, surface, and form. Material ecologies (Oxman, Ortis, and Gramazio 2015) take the forefront in methodology and approach towards observation and biomimetic application (Knippers, Speck, and Nickel 2016). A viable additively manufactured calcium carbonate material is described in origin and composition with regard to mechanical means of binder jetting technology. Research and analysis of the resultant objects morphogenesis is described in the context of application in aquatic environments.

Material

For millennia, coral polyps (the soft, living organism of coral) have developed their own method of capturing carbon, as CO_2, from ocean water by converting it to calcium carbonate, $CaCO_3$, making up the hard skeleton

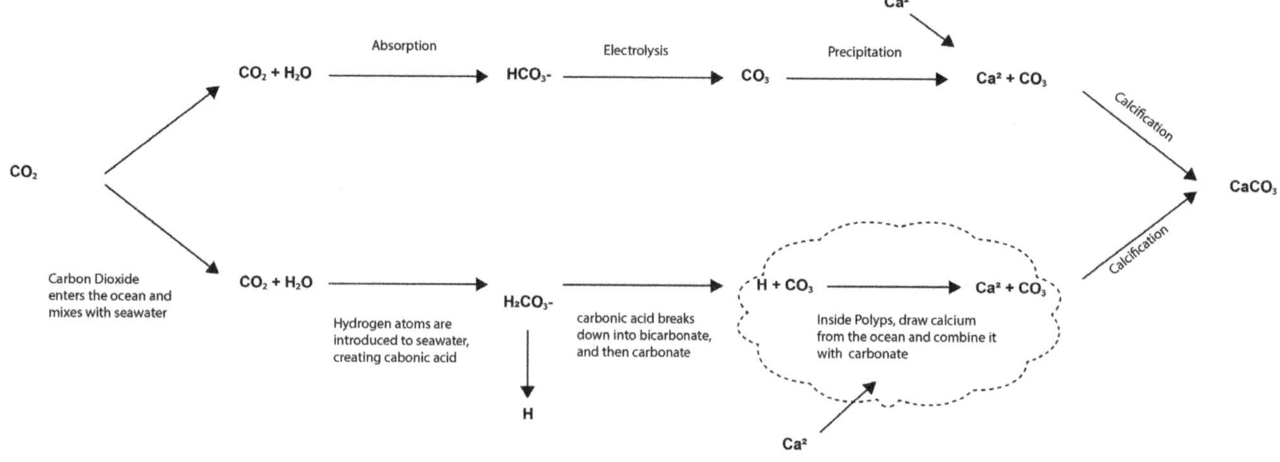

4 Diagram of carbon cycle from CO_2 to $CaCO_3$ both on land and in water.

scaffold in which the polyps inhabit. A material formulation of $CaCO_3$ was chosen to replicate a material most like that which is already produced and inhabited by coral polyps. Additionally, such a material is more domestic and familiar for a variety of other aquatic-based applications due to its composition and chemistry.

Material Sourcing

Natural $CaCO_3$ cycles and similar human-sourcing methodologies can be applied through sequestration of CO_2 from our atmosphere, resulting in a material more native in chemistry to aquatic life. Calcium can be found across our planet, making up more than 4% of the earth's crust as the fifth most abundant material, and thus $CaCO_3$ is widely accessible (IMA-NA n.d.). $CaCO_3$ can be found in geological sources (e.g., limestone, chalk, marble, and travertine) as well as biological sources (e.g., various shells and dark green vegetables). More recently, in the late 20th and 21st centuries, scientists have identified the transformation of CO_2 into a precipitated mineral carbonate through an ex situ mineral carbonation leading to carbonate crystallization in various polymorphs of $CaCO_3$ (Ribooga et al. 2017). Such discoveries and additional research identify promising options for carbon capture and storage in the production of viable material alternatives.

Material Application

The novel method in application of 3DP $CaCO_3$ is in recreating a similar material composition through contemporary fabrication methods of 3DP. Many contemporary 3DP techniques have championed the application of fused deposition modeling (FDM), using polymer-based substrates in distributed manufacturing techniques (Kreiger and Pearce 2013), though others have recognized potential in novel materials in additive manufacturing and their environmental impacts (Faludi et al. 2019). Binder jet applications, as an alternative, provide a method for fabrication (Utela et al. 2008) by utilizing the friable nature of $CaCO_3$ and its sedimentary properties as a viable solution in fabrication of solid substrate objects. The author has demonstrated novel invention and secured a proprietary patent for production and application of 3D-printed calcium carbonate material.

Material Formulation

With use of any additive manufacturing means, material composition is of utmost importance with regard to mechanical methods unique to each application. Not all materials will behave as desired for successful 3DP outcomes regarding chosen mechanical methodology. This paper focuses on material compositions with regard to binder jet 3D printing, which utilize one or more of the following: base material, adhesive agent, wicking agent, and hygroscopic agent. The base material comprises the majority of material composition in this application as calcium carbonate. An adhesive agent can be used to help stick or bind successive layers when activated by a binder solution to create either local or global strength in the object as it is fabricated. A wicking agent helps pull selectively applied liquid from the binder solution into the powder material, which maximizes hydration of the material composition and lowers surface tension in application of subsequent layers. A hygroscopic material can additionally be added to control transference of liquid and proper hydration of the material. The material agents work in combination, specifically for the use of calcium carbonate as material in 3D binder jetting applications, to produce the

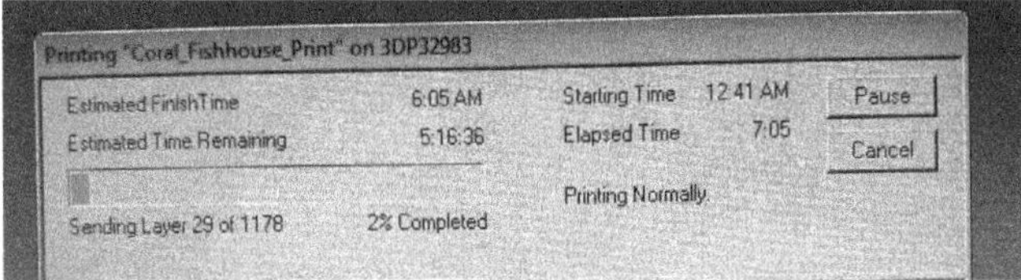

5

6

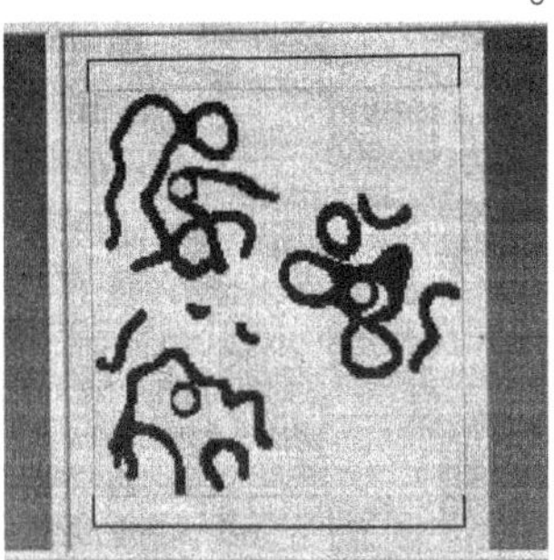

7

8

9

10

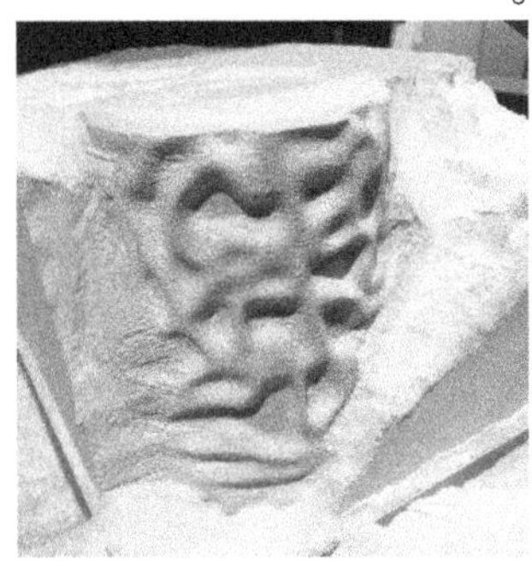

11

5 Printing progress of Zprint software used to communicate with Zcorp 310 3D printer.

6 Progress of 3D print from view of elevation, showing depth of 3D print bed.

7 Section layer showing area (in black) to deposit binder in the current layer of print progress.

8 Printing arm of Zcorp 310 printer scooping over a fresh layer of powder to be printed on.

9 Print cycle finished as printer is prepared by raising the print bed to reveal the 3D print.

10 Careful excavation of print bed to remove unused powder for reuse.

11 Final print fresh out of printer.

resultant coral carbonate body of work.

Material Binders

A unique characteristic of 3DP binder jetting technologies is its use of powder-based materials, or materials in their friable state. For this reason, a binding element must be chosen to keep the previously friable material composition from returning to its friable state postprinting. In an ideal solution for 3DP binder jetting, chemistry and material science play a large role in both the process and production of the resultant object. In the case of coral carbonate, a water-based binder was chosen with the aforementioned material formulation in order to act as a catalyst that activates the friable powder material, thus binding it. Key components to the water-based binder include: a water (H_2O) component as catalyst, an alcohol component to balance saturation and increase evaporation, and optional components of monosaccharides, which help in localized layer adherence as the binder is deposited. While traditional means of hydration to a binding element generally require prolonged agitation to introduce and activate the desired chemical reaction, 3DP binder jetting only introduces a liquid solution at a specified local coordinate, thus requiring a more complex consideration of binding material and techniques.

Material Longevity

The resultant 3DP object, freshly removed from a binder jet printer, might be thought of as being in its "green" state. It is strong enough to hold its shape and form, to exist in the world, but specific application in use of the object dictates a certain desired longevity. Further optional postprocessing may be chosen to increase the longevity of the object through a selection of techniques that include, but are not limited to, further hydration through an atmospheric application (e.g., steam bath), further application of heat (e.g., baking), or additional binder (e.g., resin). In the application of coral carbonate as an aquatic substrate, initial prototypes utilize the addition of bio-based resin to increase longevity of the object as its host organisms grow. While many different types of resins are currently used in aquatic applications, such as shipbuilding and even coral frag attachment, this paper advocates for a more critical thought to these resins, which are generally petroleum-based derivatives. Currently, there is an abundance of research into the production and application of a variety of bio-based resin alternatives to petroleum-based materials (Baroncini et al. 2016). In application of coral carbonate, a bio-based resin derived from bamboo was applied postprinting for use of increased longevity in order to ensure growth of the host substrate. Great consideration and a critical lens is taken to the addition of materials beyond the base calcium carbonate due to the sensitivity of aquatic organisms to leaching of their environmental materials. Further research and testing is required to identify a suitable length of object longevity in the inhabitance of aquatic organisms for further material optimization.

Surface

The methodology in design of a fabricated object is not just for one specific organism but for a diversity of intermingling agents that promote ecosystem health and increased calcium carbonate production (Herrán et al. 2017). Surface is an important characteristic of an object designed for aquatic applications in that it becomes real estate for many different organisms. In coral, an algae called Zooxanthellae utilizes coral polyp waste products to photosynthesize nutrients and food for the growing coral polyp in a symbiotic relationship. The Zooxanthellae live on the surface of the coral in order to maximize their exposure to sunlight. This observation leads to the conclusion that maximal surface area is an ideal and that increased rugosity, variation between surface highs and lows (i.e., roughness), provide an optimal surface for most algae and microorganisms that share similar symbiotic relationships (Marcus et al. 2018).

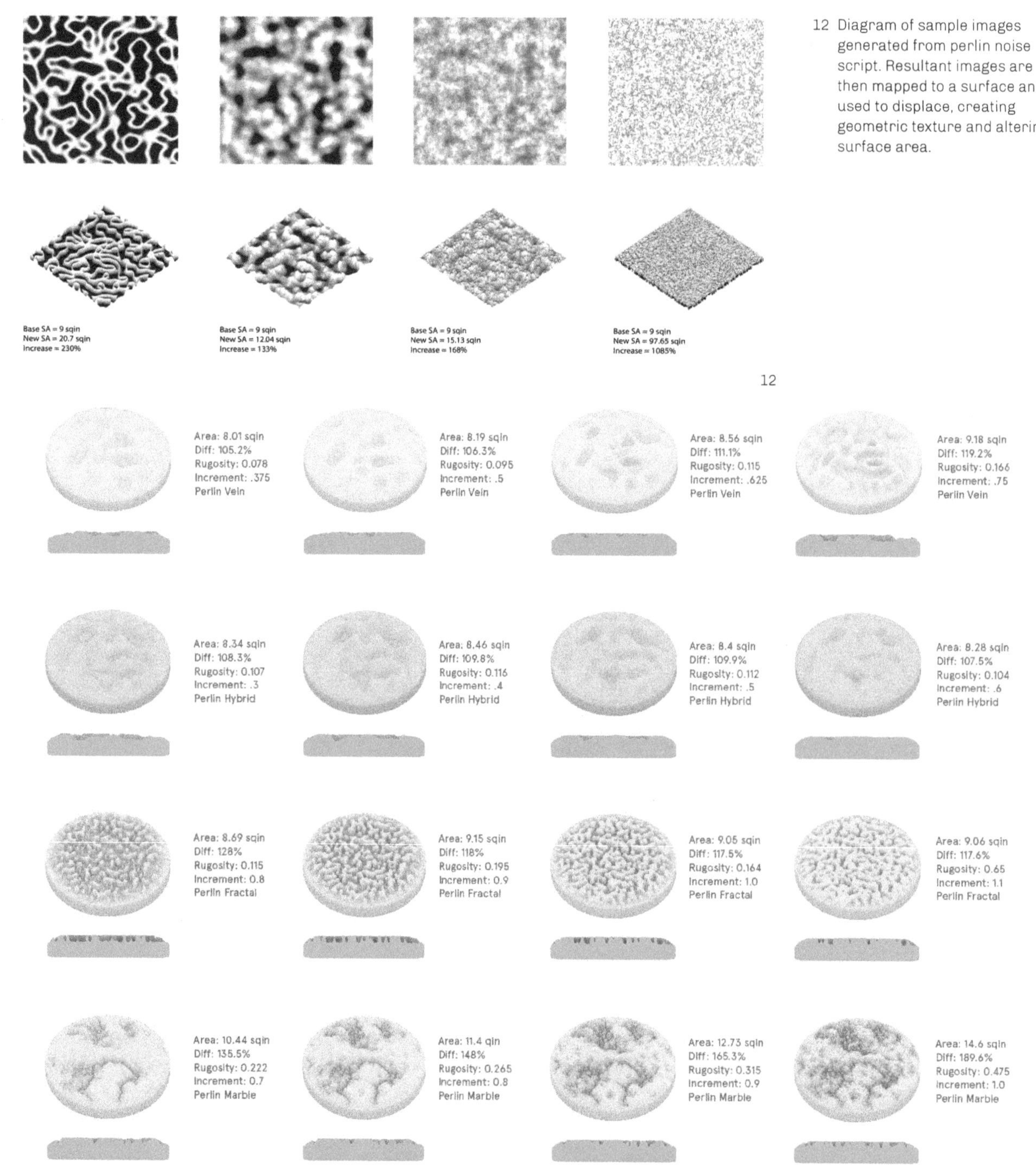

12 Diagram of sample images generated from perlin noise script. Resultant images are then mapped to a surface and used to displace, creating geometric texture and altering surface area.

13 Diagram of studies showing different perlin algorithms and resultant studies of surface manipulation.

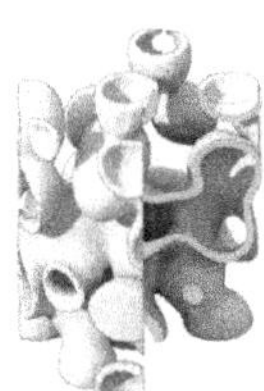

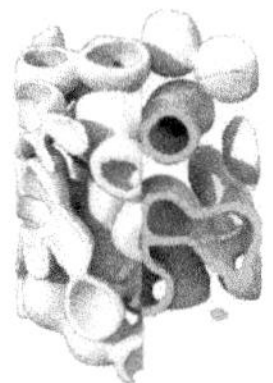

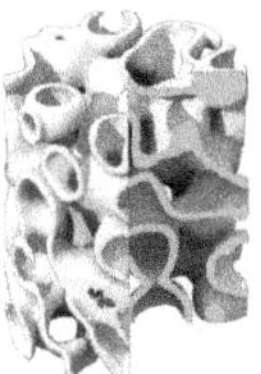

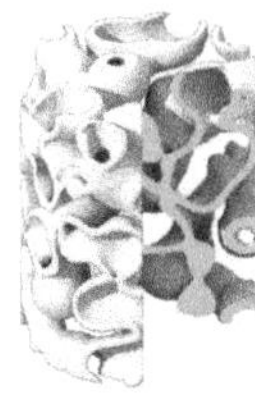

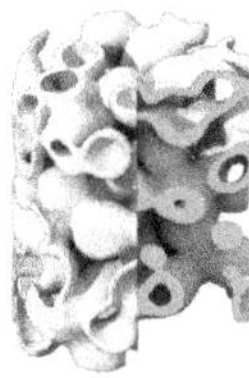

14 Studies showing volumetric production of form using isosurface algorithms.

15 Example of resultant model using isosurface algorithm.

The generation and creation of surface texture is very laborious when left to the hand and often imprecise or limiting with regard to mechanical or chemical means of surface manipulation. For this reason, and due to the precision and repeatability offered through fabrication of 3DP, computationally derived surfaces are employed through the creation of procedural materials in 3D modeling software. Procedural materials rely on algorithms that generate a 2D image in grayscale, which can deploy a seemingly infinite array of imagery. The algorithm generally utilizes a set of parameters that can be altered to change various desirable characteristics of the resultant image. The algorithm then maps itself globally to the selected surface and alters its surface topology with relation to color values coordinated by the image. If a geometric vertex falls within a specific value, it is moved at that specific amount with relation to the normal of its origin on the surface, easily creating vast amounts of variation in texture and surface for iteration and ultimate application. For this reason, computationally derived surfaces are employed through the creation of procedural algorithms as applied to UV space in order to maximize surface area through rugosity.

Form

Form, or the creation of volume, is another aquatic spatial consideration. Form can often take various subjective outcomes, but what might appear "beautiful" to terrestrial organisms might not necessarily be beneficial for aquatic ones. Form must also follow the symbiotic nature of the observed ecosystem by accommodating a multitude of aquatic organisms. An obvious solution would be to 3D scan existing aquatic structures and replicate the subsequent forms—however, most scanned models lack the complexity of interior spatial considerations that aquatic life desires at a multitude of scales. Additionally, such a methodology would limit itself to the characteristics or initial use of the 3D-scanned origin. This paper advocates for computational outcomes that sample selected environmental parameters to procedurally generate possible spatial outcomes.

A series of studies were performed in the generation of what were termed "fish houses" due to their intention to create refuge for smaller fish that seek protection from predators. While material and surface methodologies addressed aquatic organisms specifically at the scale of polyps and algae, formal methodologies address issues of growth and aggregation which begin to speak to a larger scale—in this case of fish. To create the fish houses, parameters of fish size were identified to be utilized as a driver for spatial delineation with regard to inhabitants and mobility. An initial point cloud with a varying distance domain of small fish sizes was produced within a stochastic framework to fit the inhabitants of different fish into a defined boundary. An isosurface algorithm (Lorensen and Cline 1987) was then deployed to produce the physical boundary and delineation between a series of points with relation to their values (as fish size). The application of computational isosurface algorithms not only accommodates variation in defined volumes but maintains structure through complex arches and maximizes surface area for subsequent application of procedural surface manipulation.

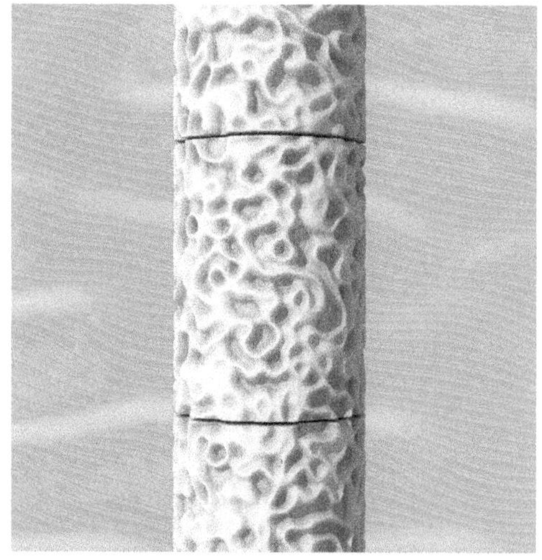

16

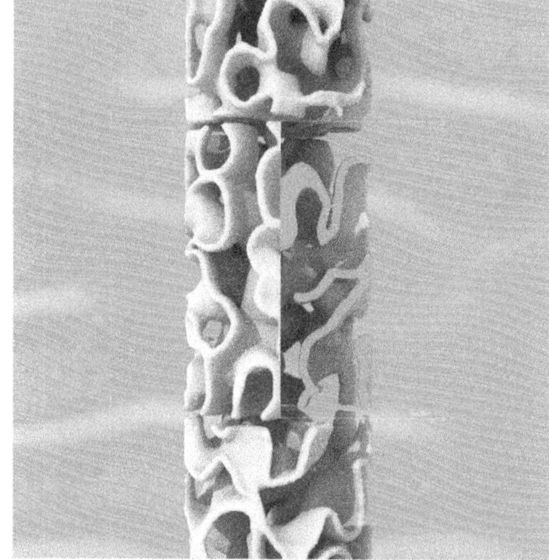

18

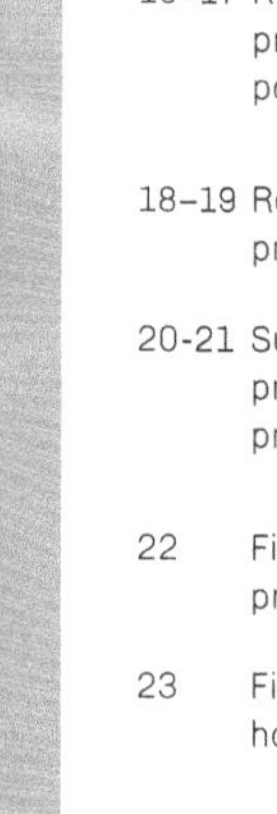

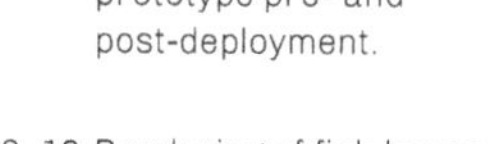

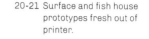

16–17 Rendering of surface prototype pre- and post-deployment.

18–19 Rendering of fish houses pre- and post-deployment.

20-21 Surface and fish house prototypes fresh out of printer.

22 Final fabricated surface prototypes.

23 Final fabricated fish houses.

17

19

Proof of Concept

The resultant product, as described through methods for design and fabrication, was successful in its novel invention of 3DP $CaCO_3$ substrate application. Initial prototypes have been fabricated and introduced in controlled environments to test coral polyps' acceptance of the substrate. Introduction of polyps appear to have established themselves, but future long-term observation of prototypes will be required to reach proper results and conclusions. In the short term, additional aquatic installations were established to study more immediate interaction with aquatic organisms in biodiverse ecosystems.

RESULTS

Initial live tests of the 3DP $CaCO_3$ were performed with coral polyps on frags within a controlled indoor tank before introduction to a live environment. Prolonged monitoring in live environments is needed to determine long-term aquatic growth, but all initial tests successfully observed the attachment of aquatic life. In 2019, to begin additional short-term studies while long-term coral prototypes were under way, 3DP $CaCO_3$ prototypes were deployed in the San Francisco Bay as hanging from the Architectural Ecologies Lab's study vessel "Float Lab." These prototypes were deployed to study the 3DP $CaCO_3$ substrate in its application of surface and volume servicing biologically diverse fouling environments and its many inhabitants. These are currently being monitored to study the ongoing impact of computationally derived surfaces and forms utilizing the 3DP $CaCO_3$. After only a couple months in the field, these prototypes were visited and observed an abundance of local aquatic species already having been established.

These prototypes will continue to be monitored, observing and measuring their growth and species. However, initial sampling yields some interesting observations. There appears to already be a great diversity of species embedded within the community of the prototypes; however, the identification of some invasive species raises questions as to how to assess what constitutes a "healthy" or "successful" ecological outcome given the opportunity provided by the 3DP $CaCO_3$ prototypes. Further

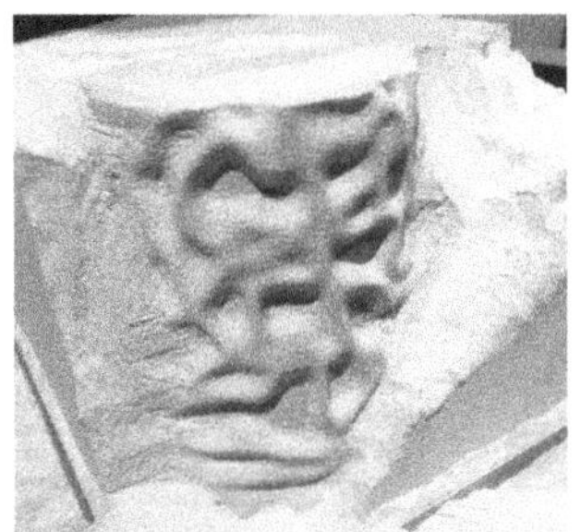

20

21

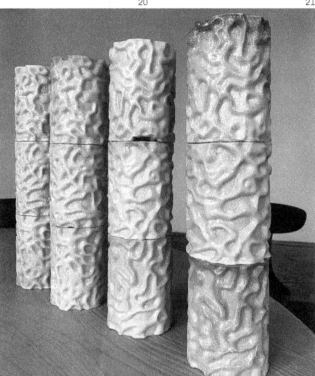

22

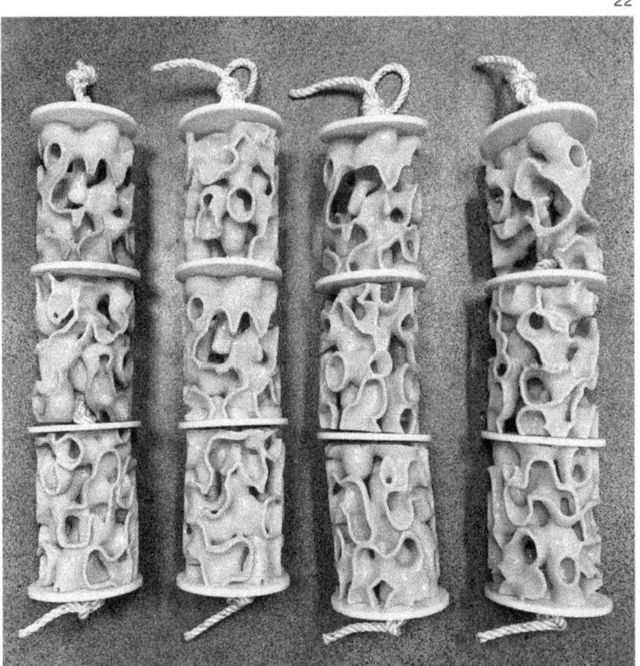

23

documentation and collection of data is required to assess long-term coral health and outcomes, diversity of species, local community health, as well as larger ecosystem fitness. However, it is important to note that by utilizing methods described by this paper, the computationally derived substrate was able to fulfill the accommodation of an ecosystem rather than any particular individual agent.

Parameters for Future Research

The observation of invasive species brings forward a new subject for consideration and future research: resource competition. As previously mentioned, surface becomes an important resource for aquatic organisms to establish themselves and spread in hopes to maximize access to sunlight. Such a resource is in high demand as there are many aquatic organisms vying for access to surface area with only a finite amount of real estate. Further research is required to identify surface parameters that favor and promote growth of desired inhabitants yet minimize and deter growth of undesirable invasive species. Additionally observed, specifically in contemporary coral propagation and artificial restoration, is also a conflict between the growth of coral polyps and other locally competing algae. How, then, might a surface be optimized, and what parameters might contribute to the selective success of desired agents while still contributing towards a larger ecological fitness?

Questions have also been brought forward with regard to calcium carbonate's longevity in an (oceanic) environment that is increasing in acidification. As our oceans increase in acidity, organisms that rely on their hard shells and skeletons made from calcium carbonate become susceptible to degradation and dissipation. In coral, the polyp has specifically evolved to produce calcium carbonate for its future growth and propagation—so regardless of the 3DP base prototype composition, the future growth and success of the coral would remain in question. For this reason, the author hypothesizes that the success of the coral lies not in an initial 3DP prototype but in the coral polyp's ability to establish itself and grow. Aquatic organisms do not require 3DP structures to exist and thrive; however, this initial established structure provides adaptive means to combat undesirable environmental factors in the early stages of propagation and establishment. This further raises the question of required longevity or long-term existence of the initial 3DP prototype. At what point does the initial 3DP prototype, as biological scaffold, become of diminished benefit to an established aquatic organism? How does longevity, as a parameter, affect the "success" of a 3DP prototype?

Additionally, future research requires more controlled tests with regard to identifying relationships in rates of colonization with regard to other standard materials currently used in aquatic restoration. A variety of specified aquatic environments must also be more critically selected and controlled to compare colonization and growth rates across applications and varied ecosystems.

CONCLUSION

Methodologies of computational design and fabrication utilizing $CaCO_3$ provide various benefits for a shift from an anthropocentric built environment to that of a symbiotic one. The results of this paper's research find application in oceanic artificial coral reef restoration as scaffold for polyps, coastal and intertidal ecosystem restoration in providing substrate as habitat, and waterfront interface as the softening of the terrestrial built environments' edge designed for aquatic organisms' benefit. As previously stated, many contemporary adaptive interventions fall short in poor consideration of material applications and little consideration of precedent aquatic populations. This paper's research and methodology finds success in the invention and methodological application in a 3DP $CaCO_3$ substrate for aquatic inhabitance.

24

25

26

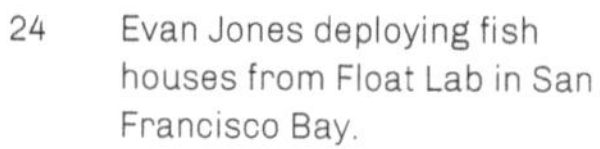

24 Evan Jones deploying fish houses from Float Lab in San Francisco Bay.

25–26 Removing the fish houses after several months in fouling environment.

ACKNOWLEDGMENTS

A special thank you to those who have engaged with this research in various capacity and contributed toward its larger collaborative endeavors: Jessica Gregory; Alex Davies; The Ocean Learning Center—Fabien Cousteau, Justin Muir; CCA Architectural Ecologies Lab—Adam Marcus, Margaret Ikeda, Evan Jones; and Benthic Lab, Moss Landing Marine Laboratories—John Oliver, Kamille Hammerstrom.

REFERENCES

Baroncini, E. A, S. Kumar Yadav, G. R. Palmese, and J. F. Stanzione. 2016. "Recent Advances in Bio-Based Epoxy Resins and Bio-Based Epoxy Curing Agents." *Journal of Applied Polymer Science* 133: 44103. https://www.doi.org/10.1002/app.44103.

Burke, Lauretta, Katie Reytar, Mark Spalding, and Allison Perry. 2011. *Reefs at Risk Revisited*. Washington, DC: World Resource Institute.

Chamberland, V.F., D. Petersen, J. R. Guest, et al. 2017. "New Seeding Approach Reduces Costs and Time to Outplant Sexually Propagated Corals for Reef Restoration." *Scientific Reports* 7, 18076. https://doi.org/10.1038/s41598-017-17555-z..

The Economist. 2014. "Artificial Reefs: Watery Dwellings." December 14. https://www.economist.com/technology-quarterly/2014/12/04/watery-dwellings.

Fabry, Victoria J., Brad A. Seibel, Richard A. Feely, and James C. Orr. 2008. "Impacts of Ocean Acidification on Marine Fauna and Ecosystem Processes." *ICES Journal of Marine Science 65, no. 3 (April)*: 414–432.

Faludi, Jeremy, Corrie M. Van Sice, Yuan Shi, Justin Bower, and Owen Brooks. 2019. "Novel Materials Can Radically Improve Whole-System Environmental Impacts of Additive Manufacturing." *Journal of Cleaner Production 245 (February)*: 1580–1590.

Herrán, Natalia, Gita R. Narayan, Claire E. Reymond, and Hildegard Westphal. 2017. "Calcium Carbonate Production, Coral Cover and Diversity along a Distance Gradient from Stone Town: A Case Study from Zanzibar, Tanzania." *Frontiers in Marine Science 4 (March)*: 412. https://doi.org/10.3389/fmars.2017.00412.

Industrial Minerals Association—North America (IMA-NA). n.d. "What Is Calcium Carbonate?" IMA-NA. Accessed December 7, 2020. https://www.ima-na.org/page/what_is_calcium_carb.

27 Sample of organisms observed growing on fish houses. Many native and invasive species observed.

Kennedy, Randy. 2001. "End of Line for Subway Cars: The Ocean Floor." *The New York Times*, August 22.

Knippers, Jan, Thomas Speck, and Klaus G. Nickel. 2016. "Biomimetic Research: A Dialogue Between the Disciplines." In *Biomimetic Research for Architecture and Building Construction; Biological Design and Integrative Structures*, 1–5. Cham: Springer.

Kreiger, Megan A., and Joshua M. Pearce. 2013. "Environmental Impacts of Distributed Manufacturing from 3-D Printing of Polymer Components and Products." *MRS Online Proceedings Library* 1492 (December): 107–112. https://doi.org/10.1557/opl.2013.319.

Lorensen, William E., and Harvey E. Cline. 1987. "Marching Cubes: A High Resolution 3d Surface Construction Algorithm." *SIGGRAPH Computer Graphics* 21 (4): 163–169. https://doi.org/10.1145/37402.37422.

Marcus, Adam, Margaret Ikeda, Evan Jones, Taylor Metcalf, John Oliver, Kamille Hammerstrom, and Daniel Gossard. 2018. "Buoyant Ecologies Float Lab. Optimized Upside-Down Benthos For Sea Level Rise Adaptation." In *ACADIA 2018: Recalibration: On Imprecision and Infidelity [Proceedings of the 38th Annual Conference of the Association for Computer Aided Design in Architecture (ACADIA)]*, Mexico City, Mexico, 18–20 October 2018, edited by P. Anzalone, M. del Signore, and A. J. Wit, 414–423. CUMINCAD.

Oxman, Neri, Christine Ortiz, Fabio Gramazio, and Matthias Kohler. 2015. Material Ecology: Design and Computational Issues [Special issue], *Computer-Aided Design* 60 (C).

Ribooga, Cheng, Kim Semin, Lee Seungin, Choi Soyoung, Kim Minhee, and Park Youngjune. 2017. "Calcium Carbonate Precipitation for CO2 Storage and Utilization: A Review of the Carbonate Crystallization and Polymorphism." *Frontiers in Energy Research* 5, 17. https://doi.org/10.3389/fenrg.2017.00017.

Utela, Ben, Duane Storti, Rhonda Anderson, and Mark Ganter. 2008. "A Review of Process Development Steps for New Material Systems in Three Dimensional Printing (3DP)." *Journal of Manufacturing Processes 10, no. 2 (July)*: 96–104.

IMAGE CREDITS

Figure 2: "Reef balls, lowering into Lake Pontchartrain" Louisiana Sea Grant College Program, Louisiana State University. https://www.flickr.com/photos/88158121@N00/3471140679/sizes/o/in/photostream/ licensed under CC BY 2.0.
Figure 3: "Art Reef," SDNRFigures, http://www.dnr.sc.gov/marine/pub/seascience/artreef.html, licensed under CC BY-SA 3.0.
Figures 24–27: © Evan Jones.

All other drawings and images by the author.

Alex Schofield is an Adjunct Professor of Architecture at California College of the Arts, San Francisco, and collaborator of the Architectural Ecologies Lab. He directs Objects and Ideograms, a design workshop based in Oakland, California. His award-winning work has been exhibited internationally and focuses on material innovations in fabrication and computation. Alex is a graduate of University of California, Berkeley, College of Environmental Design.

Knitted Bio-Material Assembly

Cultivating Building Materials for Sustainable Urban Development

Christine Yogiaman
Singapore University of Technology and Design, SUTD

Christyasto P. Pambudi
Singapore University of Technology and Design, SUTD

Dhileep Kumar Jayashankar
Singapore University of Technology and Design, SUTD

Peizhi Chia
Singapore University of Technology and Design, SUTD

Yuhan Quek
Singapore University of Technology and Design, SUTD

Kenneth Tracy
Singapore University of Technology and Design, SUTD

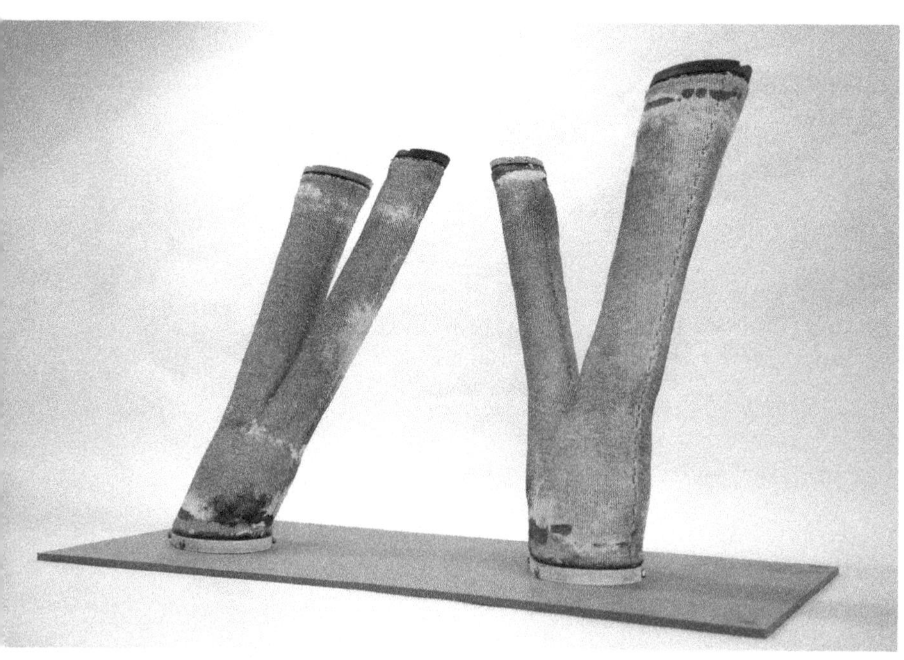

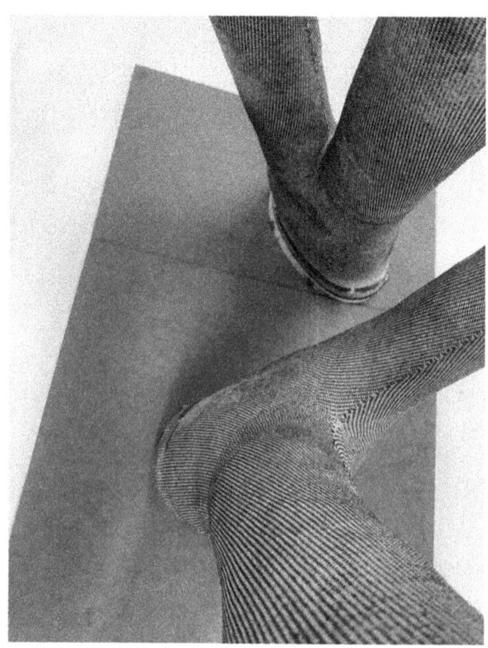

1 Two proof-of-concept prototypes for the design, fabrication, and cultivation of a new material type: knitted textile mycelium composite that has the capability to augment final material composite properties and provide formal freedom to designers.

ABSTRACT

Bio-fabrication of materials opens up novel opportunities for designers to innovate the functional possibilities of the designed output through variations in fabrication processes. Literature has seen an increased interest in this emerging material design practice that has recently been defined as "growing design" (Myers 2012). Our research work expands on the definition of this emerging material design practice to engage digital design and fabrication procedures in the intersection of biology, craft, and design. The aim is to cultivate a new material type—knitted textile mycelium composite that has the capability to augment final material composite properties and provide formal freedom to designers. 3D CNC knitting enables the fabrication of knitted textile that has control over the specificity of each knit loop, opening up design possibilities to grade functional differentiation when the knitted textile is used as a sacrificial mold for the cultivation of mycelium composite. The research presents various design-to-fabrication workflows that facilitate working with the indeterminate nature of 3D-knitted membrane and the dynamic nature of cultivating mycelium composite growth. Two architecture-scale prototype units were fabricated and cultivated, demonstrating the range of design freedom for this new material type.

INTRODUCTION AND BACKGROUND

Factors Contributing to Mycelium Composite Properties

Mycelium composites are being named a promising bio-fabricated material that is in line with a Cradle-to-Cradle approach (McDonough and Braungart 2010) and present environmental and sustainable possibilities that are in stark contrast to the exhaustive chain of extraction, processing, and subtractive shaping characteristic of current building materials (Karana et al. 2018). Mycelium refers to the network of interwoven filaments, hyphae, that compose the vegetative parts of fungus (Kavanagh 2005). The organic substrate, which is colonized and degraded by the mycelium fungus strain, provides the nutrients necessary for the hyphae growth (Pelkmans, Lugones, and Wösten 2016). Mycelium composite is a bulk material that results when the fungus is prevented from decomposing the substrate entirely, and the network of hyphae interlocks the particles of the substrate and form a thickened growth of air-exposed fungal skin (Haneef et al. 2017). The resultant mechanical properties of the mycelium composites depend on a wide range of factors, including type of fungal strain, composition of substrates, conditions of light, temperature and humidity during cultivation, and the postprocess treatment of the material. (Jones et al. 2017). Research on what factors contribute to the composite mechanical properties converged on the finding that the combination of factors that increase the thickness of fungal skin and the density of the hyphae network within the substrate correlate directly to the increased mechanical behavior of the mycelium composites (Appels et al. 2019)

This review allowed the research group to identify the design potential for knitted textile to serve as a sacrificial mold, permitting the augmentation and control of the resultant composite mechanical properties in two ways: first, as an external surface with independent structural properties that can be fused and bound to the layer of fungal skin and contributes to the resultant composite properties. Scanning electron microscopy (SEM) images for cross-sections of the cotton yarn knitted textile mold in a sample of mycelium textile composite were taken and studied. Figure 2 shows SEM images of hyphae growing through the porous knit loops. Second, the knitted textile is permeable, and the increased access to air will increase the resultant fungal skin and hyphae growth density (Fig. 3). The typical shaping method in the cultivation of the composite is the use of impermeable plastic molds that contain the substrate. In the middle of the cultivation process, the mycelium is de-molded and flipped in the mold in order to ensure even exposure of all sides to air and extend the growth of hyphae on the side that was previously in contact with the mold (Appels et al. 2019).

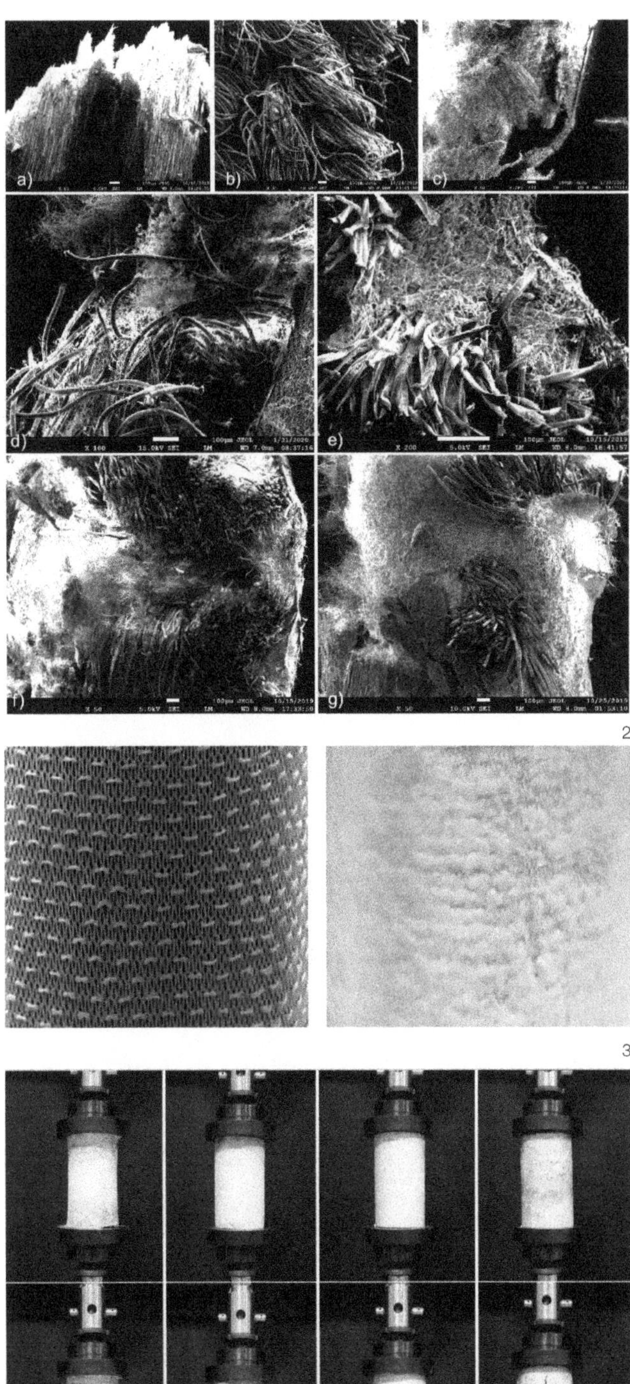

2 (a) Wood chip control; (b) fabric control; (c) mycelium control; (d, e) hyphae growing on yarn; (f, g) hyphae growing on and through the textile.

3 (left) Permeable textile mold at the start of cultivation; (right) hyphae growth through permeable textile mold surface.

4 Compression testing using ASTM C39 standard for textile mycelium composite lined with (a) ultra-high molecular weight polyethylene (UHMWPE); (b) acrylic; (c) cotton; and (d) control sample without textile lining..

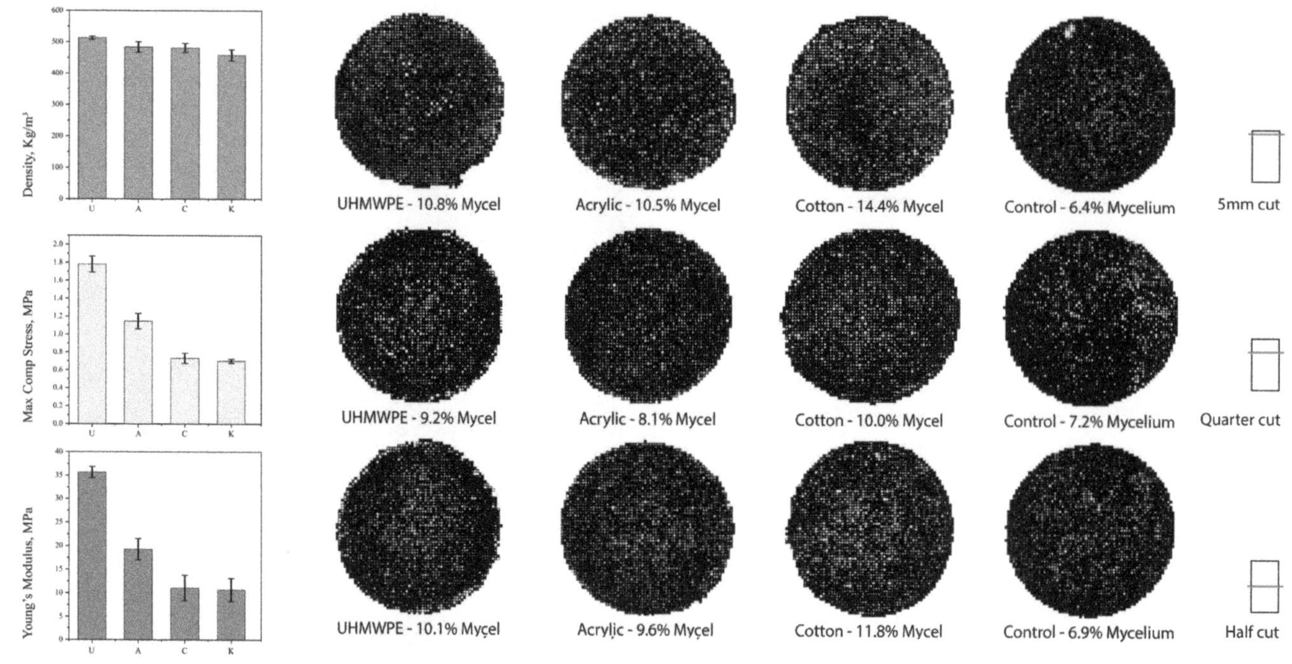

5

6

Knit Textile Mycelium Composite Testing

In the exploration of design parameters involved in using knitted textile as a sacrificial mold, the research group conducted a controlled experiment to determine if variations in yarns used contributes to increased mechanical properties and increased fungal growth density. The fungi species *Ganoderma lucidum* was used, with substrate composition of 42% woodchip, 40% tapioca, 15% wheat bran, and 3% lime.

Tubular single jersey textile was knitted with three yarn types: cotton, acrylic, and ultra-high molecular weight polyethylene (UHMWPE). These knitted textiles were used to line plastic pipe containers 72.5 mm in diameter and 120 mm in height to cultivate the knit textile mycelium composite samples. Substrates were loaded and compacted into the pipe containers. The containers were incubated in a sterile environment at 22°C. All the samples were left in the pipe containers for the first three days, and the pipe containers were removed for the next four days of incubation, leaving the textile lining and substrate directly exposed to air. This experiment procedure simulated the equivalent effect of having a porous knitted textile mold. After the seven-day cultivation period, the samples were put into four cycles of dehydration in the oven at 80°C for 12 hours and allowed to passively cool for 24 hours to incrementally complete the dehydration process. The experiment also included the cultivation of control samples, where the substrate was loaded and compacted into pipe containers without a knit textile lining. The substrates for control samples were left inside the pipe container for the seven-day period of the incubation as a simulation of a nonporous mold container.

Five samples of each textile mycelium composite type and control samples underwent compression testing using the ASTM C39 standard (ASTM 2020) (Fig. 4). Results show UHMWPE yarn textile mycelium composite has the highest Young's Modulus figure and is the stiffest of the different composites, followed by acrylic and cotton lined samples. Control samples performed the poorest compared to all samples lined with knit textiles (Fig. 5). This result supports the design opportunity that exists in using knitted textiles as an external surface with independent structural properties contribute to the resultant composite properties.

Cross-section cuts of each textile mycelium composite and control type samples were made at the top, quarter, and midway of the 120 mm tall samples. Images taken from three diameters along the height of the samples were analyzed for density of hyphae growth within the body of the substrate (Fig. 6). The results showed cotton-lined samples had the densest hyphae growth, followed by the UHMWPE samples and the acrylic, with the control having the least hyphae growth density. This result opened up the opportunity to control the density of hyphae growth through the inclusion of cotton or other nutrient-rich yarn types in the knit textile.

METHOD: KNIT TENSIONED TEXTILE MOLD TO AUGMENT PROPERTIES

Results from the testing introduced design possibilities to calibrate mechanical properties of cultivated mycelium composites with the ability to control textile graded properties using 3D CNC knitting. The designed knit textile mold

7

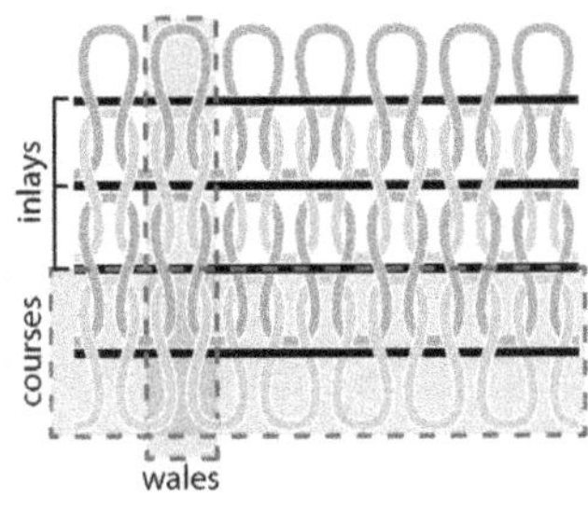

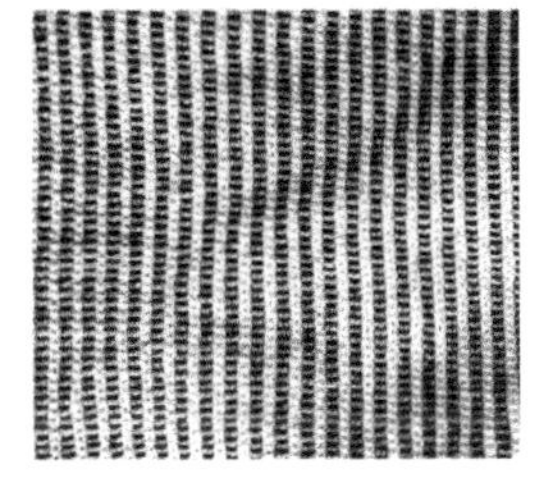

8

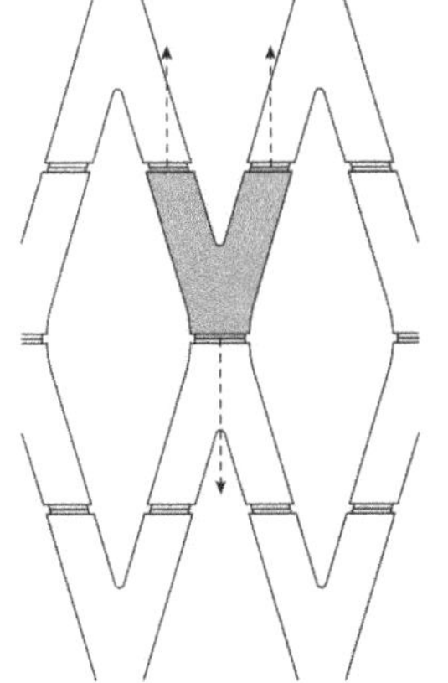

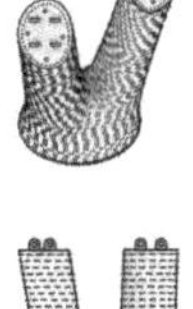

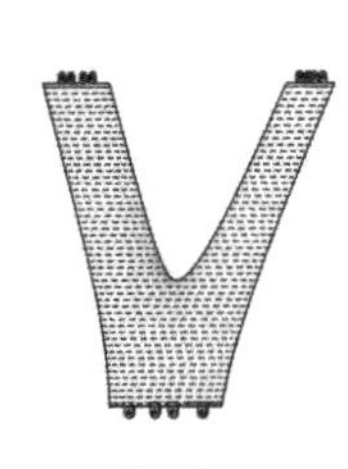

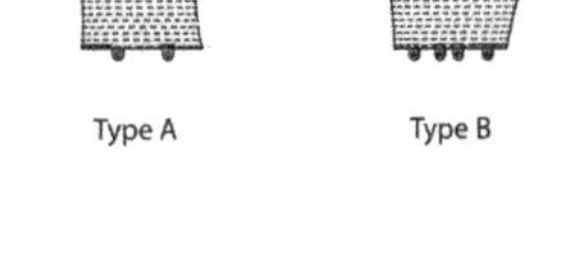

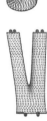

9

5 Test results for textile mycelium composite lined with (U) UHMWPE; (A) acrylic; (C) cotton; and (K) control sample.

6 Image analysis of hyphae growth density on cross-sections taken at top, quarter, and middle of the mycelium composite samples.

7 Two-part fixture with adjustable top shelf to increase the tension of the textile mold.

8 Tubular single jersey with inlay knit structure.

9 Form typology based on V-unit lattice formation; type A and B units.

consists of a knit structure made up of high-strength yarn base knit to maximize the resultant composite properties, and a simultaneous insertion of a nutrient-rich yarn on the same knit surface that encourages hyphae growth and increases the fusion of the high-strength textile skin with the composite body.

In developing the unit blocks for a prototypical knitted textile mycelium composite structure, the research team leveraged the increased stiffness properties of textile when tensioned. This stiffness allowed for the permeable knitted textile mold to be an effective mold container to resist the weight of the substrate when it is compacted into the mold during the cultivation setup. A two-part fixture was designed, with a fixed bottom shelf and an adjustable top shelf that could be adjusted to increase the tension of the textile mold (Fig. 7),

Geometries to be knitted were transformed into length measurements made up of a quantity of courses (a unit row of knit loop) and number of wales (a unit column of knit loop) (Fig. 8). Tubular single jersey is the stitch pattern selected for the mold, as it is a basic lightweight stitch pattern. This lightweight porous knit stretches freely in the direction of both its courses and its wales. Ultra-High molecular weight polyethylene (UHMWPE) blended with spandex and polyester yarn is used for this base body of the knit mold to allow the knit mold to stretch and tension. The design of the knit structure included another stitch pattern—inlays. Inlays were made by running a continuous yarn in between knit courses, moving in an alternating pattern in the front and behind a set of knit loops (Fig. 8). The inclusion of inlays that are independent of the base body of the knit mold allows for a freedom to designate yarn types that could be calibrated to specific needs. In this prototypical knitted textile mycelium composite structure, the inlay yarns were specified to be cotton or other nutrient-saturated yarns that will encourage hyphae growth and increase the bond between the UHMWPE high-performance textile skin with the composite body.

RESULT: PROTOTYPICAL KNITTED MYCELIUM COMPOSITE STRUCTURE

In developing a formal typology based on the attributes of a tubular tensioned textile mold and its fixture, a lattice of V-shaped branching units was proposed (Fig. 9). The allocation of horizontal joining plates aligned the stretch of the knitted textile mold between the joints and fixture. With this basic formal typology, a column structure made of two distinct V-shaped branching units was used to construct a column assembly. The prototypical 3 m tall column is composed of six units of type A and type B V-shaped branching units (Fig. 10).

Digital Design Adjustment Workflow

A digital design adjustment workflow was developed by the research team to calibrate distortions in the setup and cultivation of knit textile mycelium composites. The workflow aimed to achieve minimal geometrical discrepancy between digitally modeled geometry and final resultant geometry at the end of the setup and cultivation process.

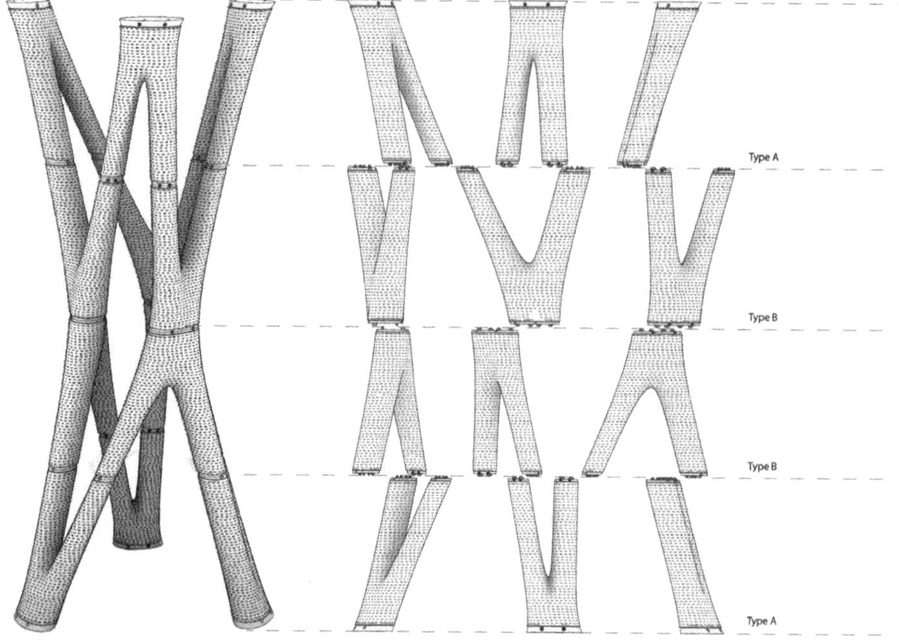

10 Prototypical 3 m tall column composed of six units of type A and type B V-shaped branching units.

These calibrated distortions were applied to a resultant geometry referred to as knit mold geometry.

The major contribution to distortion was the Poisson effect of the fabric when stretched along the vertical axis of the joining plates and fixture. To establish the vertical distortion resulting from the stretch, V-shape tubular knit textile was stretched along the direction to a maximum before evidence of breaking was observed. The Poisson effect caused the shrinking of the knit mold at the midlength of the tubular knit (Fig. 11a). To reverse this effect, the modeled geometry was run through a particle springs simulation with an outward force applied on its vertices to inflate it while fixing its end. The resultant geometry showed an inflated geometry towards the middle of its length. The rigidity and stiffness of the stretched mold withstands the undesirable geometric distortion that will result from compacting the substrate into the mold during the cultivation phase. The aim would be for the combined effect of this geometry reversal and the outward pressures exerted during the loading of the substrate to result in the intended final resultant geometry at the end of the cultivation phase (Fig. 11b). The knit mold geometry was determined through applying these combined calibrated distortions.

3D Knit Mold

The various angled branching V-shaped knit mold geometries need to be translated to quantities of courses and wales. To bypass the computationally complex translation of three-dimensional geometry to knit instructions, the research team experimented with a workflow that uses physics-based simulation to relax the knit mold geometry on a flat surface. Regions of creases that formed in excess of the flattened relaxed state were identified as the areas where decreased and increased surface needed to be removed or added to conform to the three dimensionalities of the angled V-shaped knit mold geometry. This was indicated by the height gradient mapping on the flattened knit geometry (Fig. 12). These regions of red and blue corresponded to locations where decreasing and increasing the number of wales through the courses were needed. This was done by splitting or merging the knit loops, respectively (Fig. 13).

Both type A and type B unit molds were knitted and installed in fixtures for cultivation. Two-part fixtures for each unit type were constructed with standard aluminum t-slot extrusions designed with a fixed base and a top frame that could be moved to increase the distance between the two parts of the fixture, allowing incremental tensioning of the textile mold (Fig. 14). 13.1 kg of substrate was packed into the type A mold, and 15.8 kg into the type B mold. Both prototypes were cultivated for 12 days and dehydrated in cycles over a period of three days.

CONCLUSION AND FUTURE WORK

The two prototypes served as proof of concept for the design, fabrication, and cultivation of a new material type—knitted textile mycelium composite that has the capability to augment final material composite properties and provide formal freedom to designers. Within this identified branching formal typology, various workflows have been established to facilitate working with the indeterminate nature of knit membrane and the dynamic nature of cultivating mycelium growth.

The research highlighted the design opportunities in using knit mold as an interface to grade and control the final composite properties. The functional division of using the base knit structure as the continuous structural layer that augments the mechanical properties of the mycelium composites frees up the ability for other knit types to be added intermittently and in areas local to where other additional functions are needed. In the case of this knit structure, the team had speculated on the potential to alter the density of cotton or nutrient-rich yarns to specific areas of the knitted textile mycelium composite. The current speculation is that the increased density of nutrient-rich yarns will increase the growth of hyphae in those areas, increasing the bond between the body of the composite to the knitted skin and increasing its structural performance locally (Fig. 12). With the current tubular single jersey base knit, the 3D knitting machine has the capacity to introduce a maximum of four strands of cotton yarn within each knit course. Figure 15 shows the possible gradient of inlays that could be knitted in the course-wise and wale-wise directions. Loading the prototypical 3 m tall column made up of type A and B branching units, the visualization of the range of load distribution could be mapped onto the base knit surface to differentiate areas of more and less inlay density (Fig. 16). The pursuit of developing 3D knitted textile mold as both a surface to augment structural properties and as an interface to encourage hyphae growth opened up novel opportunities for designers to innovate in the functional possibilities of the designed output.

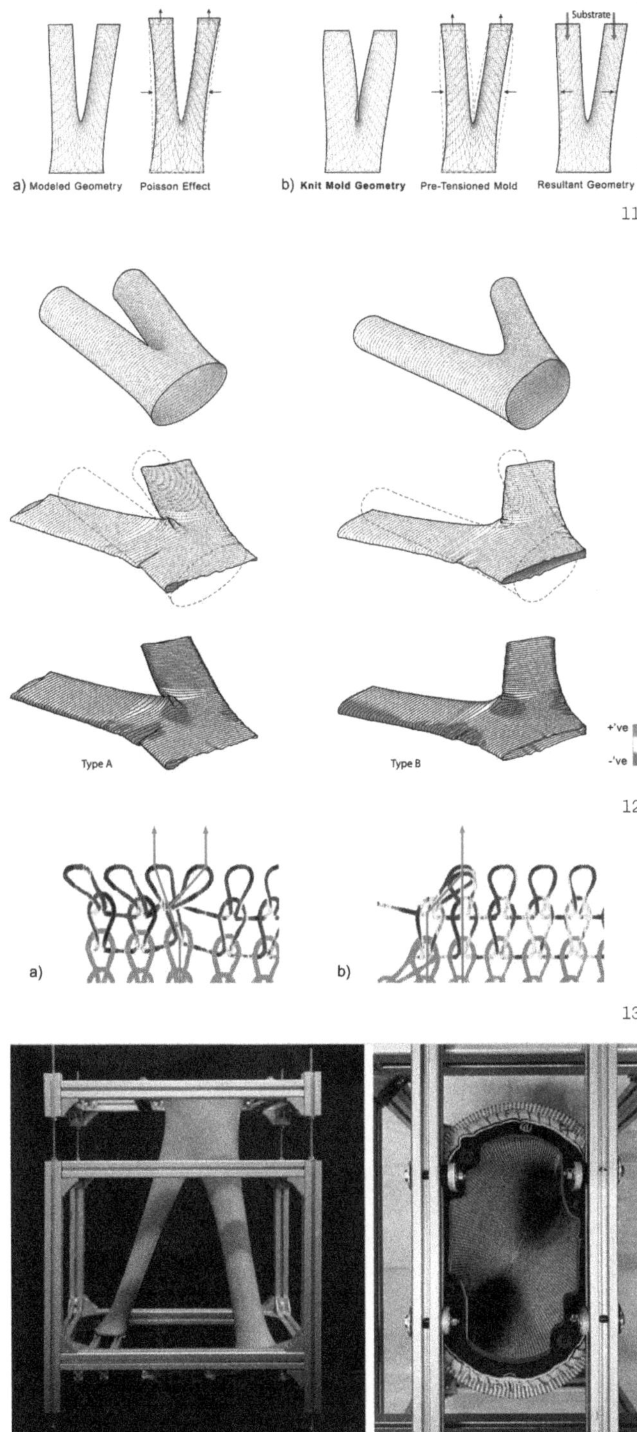

11 (a) Poisson effect caused the shrinking of the knit mold at the midlength of the tubular knit; (b) knit mold geometry was determined by applying combined calibrated distortions.

12 Height gradient mapping on the flattened knit mold geometry for type A and type B units.

13 (a) Splitting and (b) merging the knit loops.

14 Variable height-adjustable fixture constructed from standard aluminum t-slot extrusions.

ACKNOWLEDGMENTS

We would like to acknowledge SUTD's International Design Center (IDC) for funding that made this research possible. A special thank you to IDC's innovation lab, which supported our need of space; Dr. Franklin Anariba, who generously advised us on the field of material science; and our collaborator Mycotech Lab in Bandung, Indonesia.

REFERENCES

Appels, F. V. W., S. Camere, M. Montalti, E. Karana, K. M. B. Jansen, J. Dijksterhuis, and H. A. B. Wösten. 2019. "Fabrication Factors Influencing Mechanical, Moisture- and Water-Related Properties of Mycelium-Based Composites." *Materials and Design* 161: 64–71.

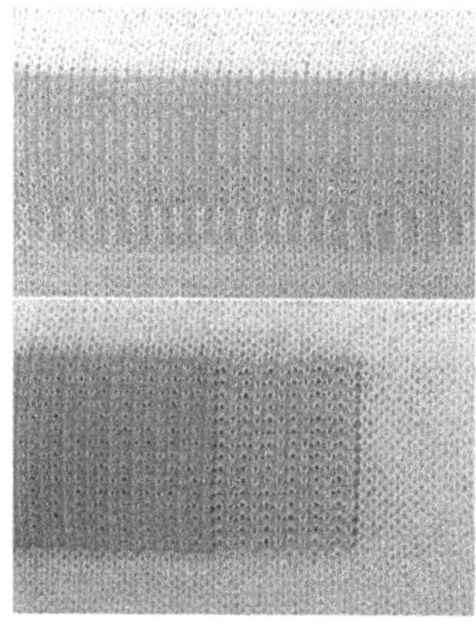

15 Increasing gradient of inlays knitted in the course-wise (top) and wale-wise directions (bottom).

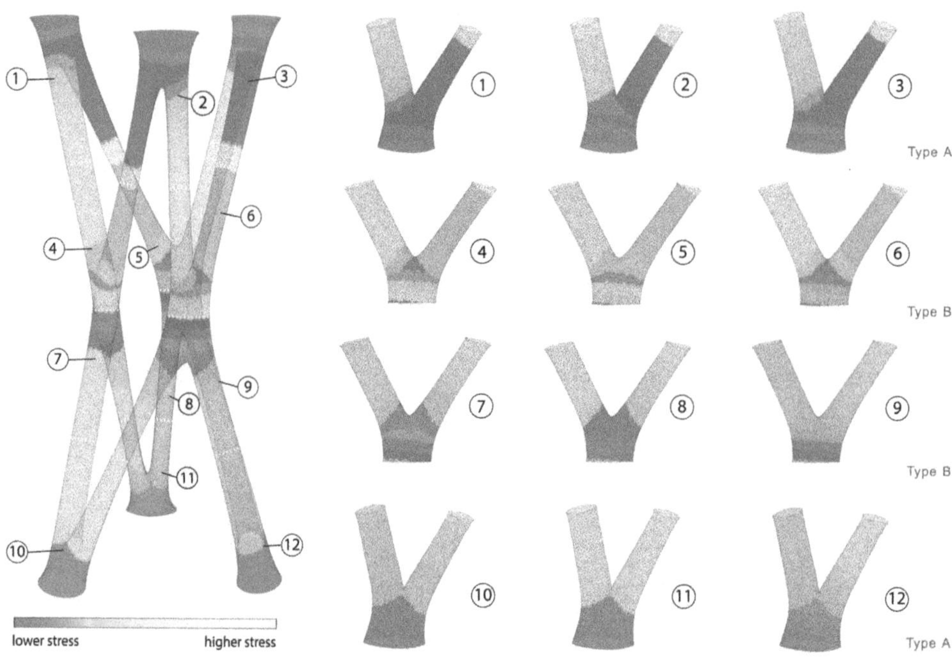

16 Load distribution on each type A and type B unit mapped onto the base knit surface to differentiate areas of more and less inlay density.

ASTM C39/C39M-20. 2020. *Standard Test Method for Compressive Strength of Cylindrical Concrete Specimens*. West Conshohocken, PA: ASTM International.

Haneef, M., L. Ceseracciu, C. Canale, I. S. Bayer, J. A. Heredia-Guerrero, and A. Athanassiou. 2017. "Advanced Materials from Fungal Mycelium: Fabrication and Tuning of Physical Properties." *Scientific Reports* 7 (41292).

Jones, M., T. Huynh, C. Dekiwadia, F. Daver, and S. John. 2017. "Mycelium Composites: A Review of Engineering Characteristics and Growth Kinetics." *Journal of Bionanoscience* 11 (4): 241–257.

Karana, E., D. Blauwhoff, E. J. Hultink, and S. Camere. 2018. "When the Material Grows: A Case Study on Designing (with) Mycelium-Based Materials." *International Journal of Design* 12 (2): 119–136.

Kavanagh, K. 2005. *Fungi: Biology and Applications*. Wiley.

McDonough, W., and M. Braungart. 2010. *Cradle to Cradle: Remaking the Way We Make Things*. New York: North Point Press.

Myers, W. 2012. *Bio Design: Nature, Science, Creativity*. High Holborn, UK: Thames & Hudson.

Pelkmans, J. F., L. G. Lugones, and H. A. B. Wösten. 2016. "15 Fruiting Body Formation in Basidiomycetes." In *Growth, Differentiation and Sexuality*. https://doi.org/10.1007/978-3-319-25844-7_15

IMAGE CREDITS

All drawings and images by the authors.

Christine Yogiaman is an Assistant Professor in Architecture and Sustainable Design Pillar at the Singapore University of Technology and Design. Christine directs Dynamic Assemblies Lab (DAL) in SUTD, a design research lab that explores emerging technologies through prototyping, simulation, and visualization. DAL's research focuses on several topics within building performance and digital fabrication, including responsive structures, 3D knitting, computational fluid dynamics, compliant mechanisms, fabric formwork, and tensegrity. By developing workflows that leverage these systems, DAL aims to broaden the palette of design possibilities for a more resilient and adaptable built environment.

Christyasto P. Pambudi is a research assistant in Dynamic Assembly Lab (DAL), actively involved in 3D knitting design research, including knit tensegrity shell, knit color relief, and knitted bio-material assembly. Having graduated from SUTD with a bachelor of science in architecture, Christyasto specializes in digital design and simulation

Dhileep Kumar Jayashankar is a research assistant in Dynamic Assembly Lab (DAL) and Digital Manufacturing & Design (DManD) Centre at the Singapore University of Technology and Design. He is a mechanical engineer by training and is currently working on digital fabrication, biomaterials, and 4D structures.

Peizhi Chia is a research assistant in SUTD who specializes in soft goods fabrication using CNC knitting and cut-and-sew techniques. Her research involvement spans across architecture, healthcare wearables, and geographic information systems. She graduated from the National University of Singapore with a BSocSci in geography.

Yuhan Quek is a research assistant in Digital Manufacturing & Design (DManD) Centre at the Singapore University of Technology and Design. He is trained as a engineering product designer, and is working on computation procedures related to CNC knitting.

Kenneth Tracy is an Assistant Professor of Architecture at Singapore University of Technology and Design, where he teaches design and directs the Dynamic Assemblies Lab (DAL). DAL's research combines expertise in material science, computation, engineering, and craftsmanship to investigate how performance-based design can inform the built environment. Expertise in making and design tools link Kenneth's teaching to his research and practice. In 2009 Kenneth founded Yogiaman Tracy Design (yo_cy), an experimental design firm with current projects in Indonesia and Singapore.

Surface Generation of Radiatively Cooled Building Skin for Desert Climate

Dorit Aviv
University of Pennsylvania

Zherui Wang
Princeton University;
SUNY Buffalo

Forrest Meggers
Princeton University

Aletheia Ida
University of Arizona

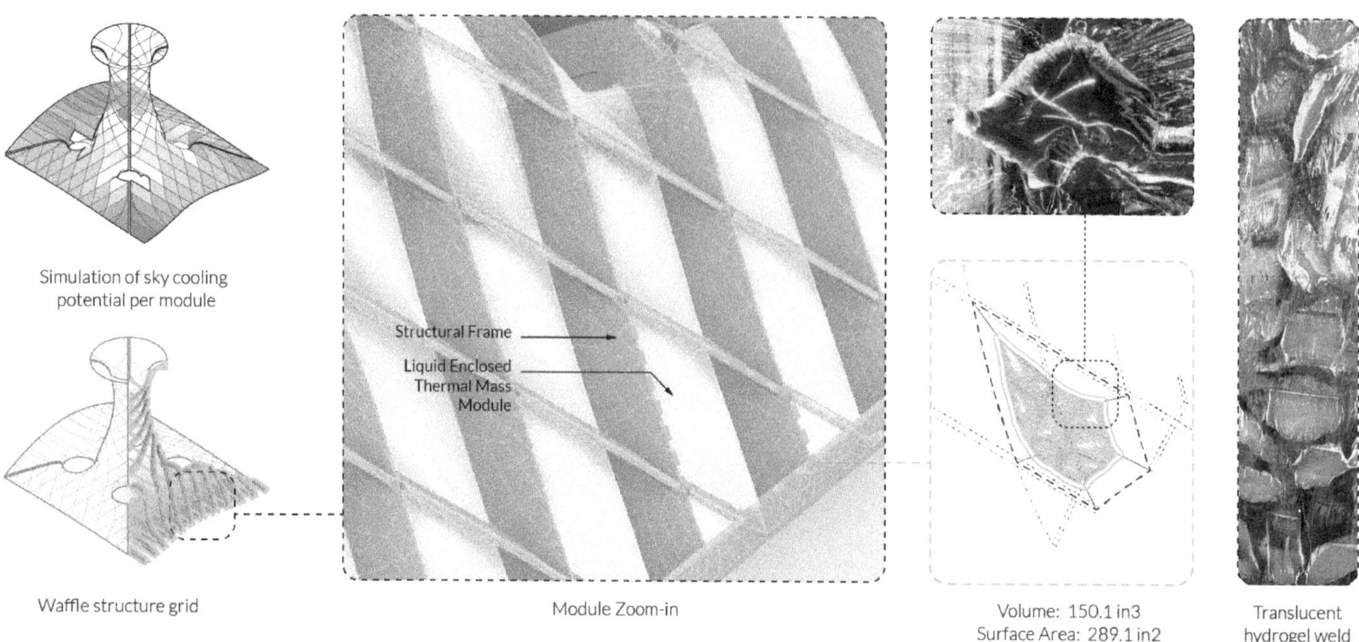

1 Diagram of skin development: digital surface generation, FEM simulation for liquid mass, and physical fabrication experiments with membranes and hydrogel.

ABSTRACT

A radiatively cooled translucent building skin is developed for desert climates, constructed out of pockets of high heat-capacity liquids. The liquids are contained by a wavelength-selective membrane enclosure, which is transmissive in the infrared range of electromagnetic radiation but reflective in the shortwave range, and therefore prevents overheating from solar radiation and at the same time allows for passive cooling through exposure of its thermal mass to the desert sky.

To assess the relationship between the form and performance of this envelope design, we develop a feedback loop between computational simulations, analytical models, and physical tests. We conduct a series of simulations and bench-scale experiments to determine the thermal behavior of the proposed skin and its cooling potential. Several materials are considered for their thermal storage capacity. Hydrogel cast into membrane enclosures is tested in real climate conditions. Slurry phase change materials (PCM) are also considered for their additional heat storage capacity. Challenges of membrane welding patterns and nonuniform expansion of the membrane due to the weight of the enclosed liquid are examined in both digital simulations and physical experiments. A workflow is proposed between the radiation analysis based on climate data, the form-finding simulations of the elastic membrane under the liquid weight, and the thermal storage capacity of the overall skin.

INTRODUCTION

Transparent Radiant Envelopes

Transparent and translucent building envelopes present a challenge for building energy management because of window assemblies' tendency to have higher solar transmittance and higher conductivity (U-Value) than opaque envelopes, leading to excessive heat loss or heat gain through those parts of the facade. A standard double-pane glass assembly, for instance, loses about 10 times more heat than a standard opaque wall. In this paper, we develop a translucent building skin for desert climates, which, instead of causing overheating under solar exposure, passively cools the building's interior using thermal storage by a translucent medium encapsulated within the transparent envelope. The liquid mass is cooled by the night sky, and thus maintains a low surface temperature, which in turn absorbs heat radiating from the building's occupants to keep them cool during the day.

As argued by Kiel Moe (2010), thermally active surfaces, which integrate liquids into architectural planes, have been part of architectural history for millennia: the Roman baths, for instance, take advantage of waste heat from water pools to warm up large thermal mass surfaces and allow for radiant heat transfer from these surfaces to human bodies in space. However, integrating liquid flow into transparent envelopes is challenging to both construct and to model. Faircloth et al. (2018) developed sensing and modeling techniques to analyze a facade prototype with paraffin wax phase change material encapsulated by PETG translucent plastic modules. Various architects have deployed skin systems containing liquids enclosed in elastic membrane: William Katavolos integrated water-enclosed plastic membranes in his design of the Autonomous House Unit to provide insulation and help plant growth (Gans 2006). Pasquero and Poletto (2020) demonstrated the use of ETFE membrane for enclosing water and algae in a 2-by-7-meter facade-scale installation.

We propose to use translucent high thermal-capacity materials encapsulated by a translucent membrane, which allows for passive cooling by transmission of radiative heat fluxes from the thermal mass to the sky. Heat capacitance is a factor in a material's thermal storage capacity,[1] calculated by the amount of energy input required to raise the temperature of a material by 1 degree. High thermal capacitance materials demonstrate heat retention over longer periods of time, serving as a radiant heat sink.

Radiative Cooling[2] of Thermal Mass by the Night Sky

The hot-dry climate of the desert offers unique passive cooling potential for building envelopes due to cold sky temperatures that are, for clear skies, about 20°C colder than the air temperature during the day, and often reach below-freezing temperatures during the nighttime (Berdahl and Fromberg 1982; Garg 1982). We develop a radiatively cooled building skin for the desert climate, constructed out of pockets of liquids with high thermal capacitance. However, despite the low sky temperature,[3] it is challenging to achieve net radiative cooling in desert climates because this climate is also characterized by extremely high direct solar radiation that would be absorbed by the thermal mass and cause it to heat during the day far beyond the cooling exchange with the sky. To avoid excessive heat gain by solar exposure, we use a wavelength selective membrane to encapsulate the thermal mass: the membrane is transmissive in the infrared range of electromagnetic radiation (Teitelbaum et al. 2019), but reflective in the shortwave range. It therefore prevents overheating from solar radiation and at the same time allows for passive cooling through exposure of the thermal mass to the desert sky. Raman et al. (2014) achieved radiative cooling to nearly 5°C below the ambient air temperature under direct sunlight using a wavelength-selective approach with a solar reflector, which reflects 97% of the incident sunlight while emitting strongly and selectively in the atmospheric transparency window.[4] During the night hours, the cooling potential of the thermal mass exposed to the night sky is much greater because of the lack of radiative heat gain from the sun and thus, during a 24-hour cycle, even in the midst of summer, it is possible to achieve substantial cooling of the building skin using this approach.

We use the cooling tower geometry we have predefined in our previous work (Aviv et al. 2020a) as a case study for this special skin deployment. To generate the skin, we subdivide an envelope surface and use a waffle structure as the framing device of the thermal mass modules (Fig. 1).

METHODS

Solar and Sky Exposure Simulations

To estimate the radiative cooling potential of the skin, each module is examined for its thermal potential based on exposure to the sky and the sun following steps 1–4:

1. A solar shortwave simulation is conducted with the aid of Ladybug environmental plugin for Grasshopper 3D (Roudsari 2013) for the overall envelope, providing kWh/m^2 (converted to kJ/m^2 for 24h) solar heat gain for each module, for one day on June 21.
2. A simulation for the radiative heat loss due to exposure to diffuse cold sky radiation is custom-built by the authors, using sky view factor calculation based on vector representation of heat flux (Aviv et al. 2020b). The

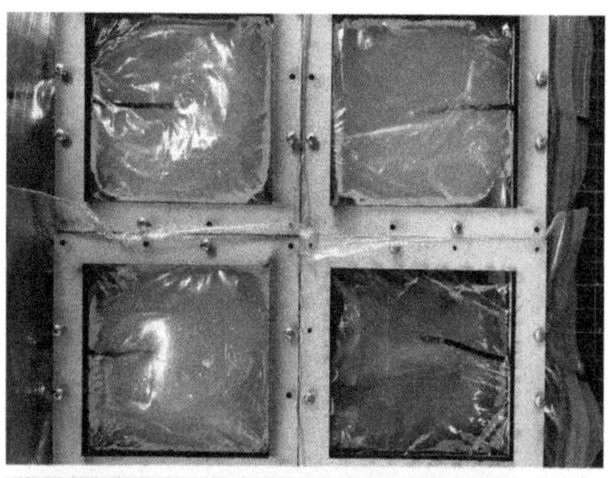
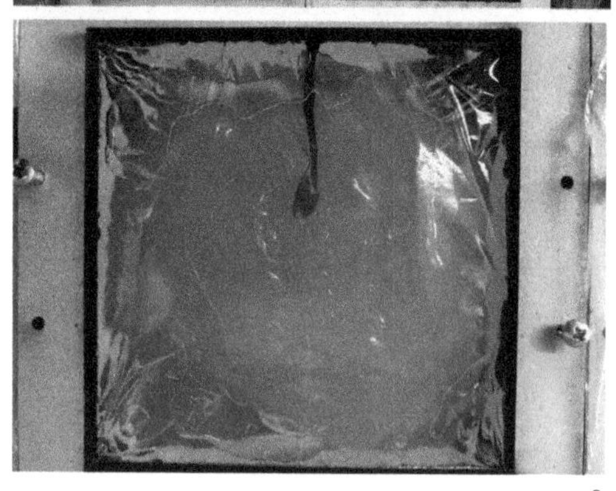
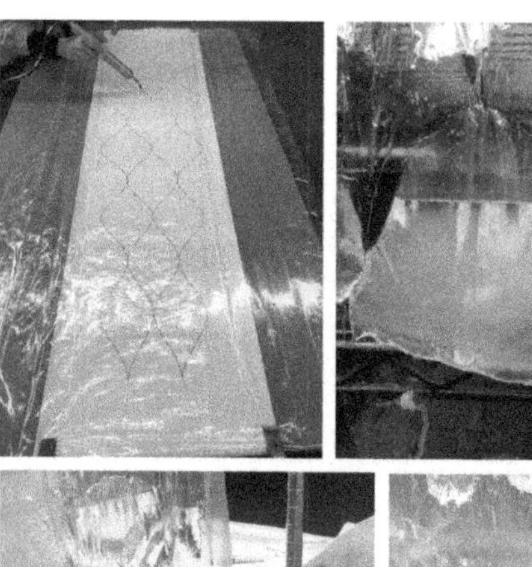

2 Hydrogel thermal testing modules. 3 LDPE welding and hydrogel membrane fabrication process with filled membrane cells.

mean radiant temperature[5] perceived at T_r (°K) at a point p (center point of each module) can be derived from Equation 1, where view factors $F_{p\text{-}i}$ between the point P and all the surroundings are used to weigh the surface temperatures T_i (°K):

$$T_r^4 = \sum_{i=1}^{n} T_i^4 F_{p \rightarrow i} \quad (1)$$

The surface temperature T_i is determined using hourly inputs of sky, air, and roof surface temperature variables on June 21, a peak scenario to bracket the maximum incoming daily solar value. The resultant T_r (°K) values for each hour of the day determined using Equation 1 are used as input in Equation 2 to calculate the total heat loss rate for each hour:

$$Q_r = \frac{1}{24} \sum_{i=1}^{24} A\sigma(T_s^4 - T_{ri}^4) \quad (2)$$

where Q_r is the mean of the radiant heat transfer rate (kW) throughout the day, A is the surface area in m^2, σ is the Stefan-Boltzman constant 5.670367 × 10^{-8} kg s^{-3} K^{-4}, T_s is the surface temperature (K), and T_{ri} is the mean radiant temperature (K) at each hour (i). To find the total energy loss from the surface in one day, the rate of heat transfer is multiplied by the duration in seconds.

3. To find the energy balance between the heat gain and heat loss, the results are weighted by the transmissivity (τ) vs. reflectivity (R) in the incoming solar shortwave versus in the longwave (thermal infrared transmission) of the membrane surface encompassing the thermal mass. We examine the radiative heat balance when changing the wavelength-specific balance of heat avoided by solar reflection (R) and heat rejected by thermal radiation (τ) to find the threshold that provides a negative heat balance (i.e. cooling).
4. The following equation is used to estimate the total thermal storage capacity of each module:

$$Q_{store} = \rho \times V \times C_p \times \Delta T \quad (3)$$

Q_{store} (J) is the total thermal energy loss when the module changes temperature by ΔT (°K), for a module of volume V (m^3) with a material density ρ (Kg/m^3) and specific heat capacity C_p (J/kg°K).

Membrane Form-Finding

As shown in Equations 2–3, the energy balance of each module depends on its volume and surface area. To find these variables, we conduct finite element analysis (FEM) simulations using Kangaroo Live Physics Engine plugin for Grasshopper (Piker 2013) and estimate the deformations caused by the weight of the enclosed liquid. The modules are anchored at each corner while movements are allowed for the edges. In order to control the amount of liquid enclosed within each module, we devise additional welding patterns to control the surface area and volume. Once these two variables are obtained, we can iteratively calculate the thermal storage potential of each module per Equations 2–4. The final objective of the simulation is to devise a welding pattern that on one hand provides enough structural stiffness to limit membrane subsidence caused by weight, while on the other optimizes both surface area and volume such that the cross-sectional thickness of the liquid based thermal storage material is evenly distributed across the membrane module.

Physical Tests

Physical tests for material thermal properties and fabrication methods demonstrate the empirical evidence to inform the digital simulations for radiant cooling module designs. Initial thermal testing experiments were conducted with polyelectrolyte hydrogels (PEG) encased in clear low-density polyethylene (LDPE) bags (Fig. 2). The testing modules were located on the rooftop of a cooling tower in Tucson, Arizona. Four volumes (50, 100, 150, and 200 mL) and thicknesses (6.3, 12.7, 19, and 25 mm) of hydrogel modules are studied with integrated thermistors for temperature difference over time from the dry-bulb temperature due to heat capacitance and radiant cooling properties. The material test modules are oriented in a horizontal full-sky exposure situation. An additional thermistor is placed on the roof, exposed to the air, subject to both convective and radiative heat transfer. The sensor measurements account for a 24-hour cycle for a typical September day. Initial fabrication studies were conducted with handheld plastic welding of LDPE and impregnation of liquid hydrogels with a syringe method (Fig. 3). These prototype membrane studies were oriented vertically during fabrication so that each pod could be filled with the liquid from a small hole punctured at the top of each cell. The general weight and pressure of the liquid upon the LDPE pocket results in a turgid condition toward the bottom of the pod(s), with a more restrained thickness at the upper zones.

Hydrogel (PEG) and Phase Change Material (PCM) Comparison

A PEG module is also compared to a PCM module under concurrent July solar and sky exposure conditions. Although PCM is lower density than water, its phase change enables greater capacity for thermal storage but also introduces kinetic deformation challenges for the plastic membrane enclosure, and its low viscosity may cause leaks. The PCM utilized is a 100% paraffin slurry with a 24°C melt-point obtained from Microtek Laboratories.

RESULTS

Solar and Sky Exposure Simulations

The results of the simulations shown in Figure 4 provide the basis for the radiant heat transfer potential of different areas of the surface. The membrane reflectivity in the shortwave is assumed to be 0.8 and transmissivity in the longwave is assumed to be 0.8 (Teitelbaum 2019, Tsilingiris 2003). Using those coefficients, the total diurnal net heat loss for one typical module with a surface area of 0.165m2, is ~300kJ, assuming clear sky and neglecting convective heat exchanges and transient heat transfer rate variations.

These results, however, are highly sensitive to the shortwave and longwave transmissivity (τ) vs. reflectivity (p) ratios of the enclosing membrane as seen in Figure 5. For instance, if the membrane shortwave reflectivity ratio decreases to 0.7, the net heat exchange would be positive rather than negative. In the conditions tested, the threshold for cooling is 0.76 reflectivity in the shortwave and 0.8 transmissivity in the longwave.

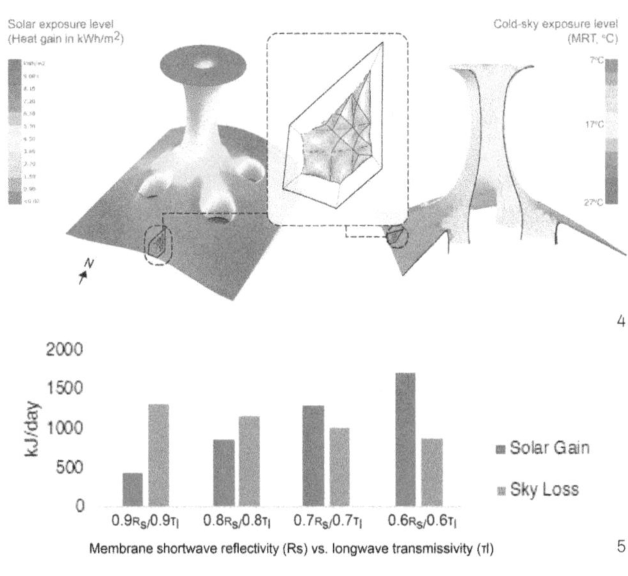

4 Results for solar exposure simulation total heat gain for the duration of one day, June 21 (left), and of cold-sky exposure expressed as the mean radiant temperature averaged over the day of points on the surface, with a sectional view showing 2-sided exposure (right).

5 Results for modeled solar gain vs. sky loss potential in kJ per day for one typical module.

Membrane-Mass Form-Finding

The results of the membrane form-finding simulations show that in comparison to the surface area/volume ratio of a module with no welding, welding from module centroid to corners and edges provides the greatest surface area ratio. While bracing from centroid to edges and from centroid to corners has similar surface area to volume ratio, bracing only at centroid has the least surface area to volume ratio. The original surface area of the module, before the simulated deformation, is 0.1649m². We can see in Figures 6b and 6c that each weighting distribution tested results in a different amount of membrane stretch, while the projected surface area shrinks. By subdividing modules into smaller pockets, we can maintain higher surface area to volume ratio with less overall module deformation.

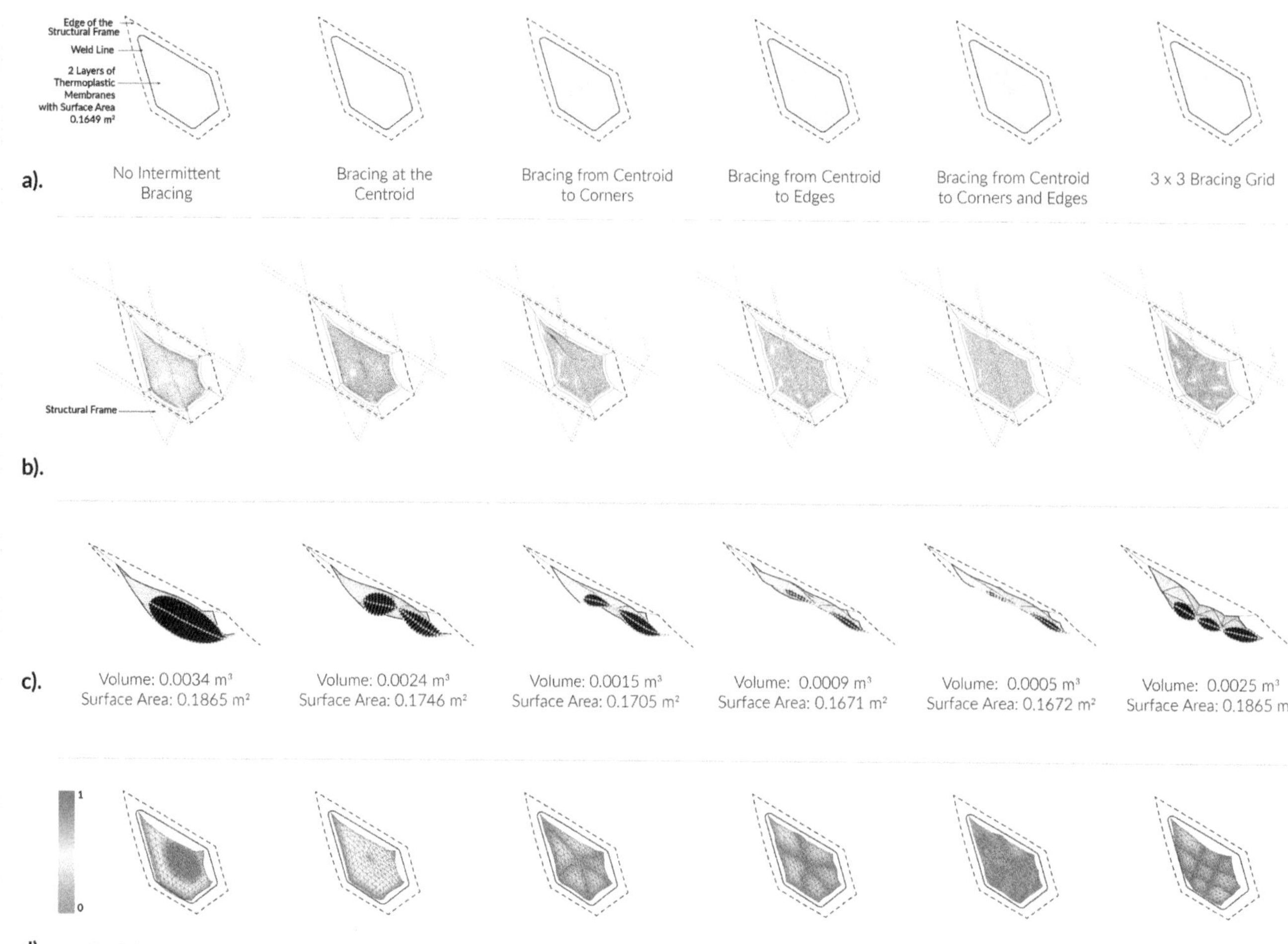

6 Sample results for the membrane expansion due to the liquid weight and welding patterns: (a) boundary condition and deployed welding patterns; (b) isometric view of the simulation results; (c) sectional view of the simulation results with respective surface area and volume; and (d) cross-sectional thermal mass thickness deviation compared to the global maximum found in each module with no intermittent bracing. 6

Further, because of conduction that will occur within each module volume, the thermal storage potential for a given module is dependent on the consistency of cross-sectional thicknesses of thermal mass material enclosed in membrane. In observing liquid subsidence produce uneven cross section distribution, we conduct thickness deviation tests in Figure 6d for all welding patterns, As a point of comparison, although bracing from centroid *to* edge and bracing from centroid *and* edge both have similar surface area and volume, the latter has a lower cross-sectional thickness deviation.

Based on the form-finding simulations results and Equations 2 and 3, we obtain that if ~300kJ of cooling is available per module per day, that would suffice to cool down the volume of water captured in the membrane by over 20°C. Conversely, for each of the volumetric configurations results, we can find the variation of the thermal storage potential of kJ/day, with a predefined goal temperature difference of 20°C, as shown in Table 1:

Table 1 Change in thermal storage capacity per volume per day.

Volume (m^3)	0.0034	0.0024	0.0015	0.0009	0.0005
Thermal Storage (kJ/day)	284.92	201.12	125.7	75.42	41.9

We are thus able to achieve a workflow between the FEM form-finding analysis and the radiative cooling and thermal storage calculations, combining geometric, structural, and thermal considerations for the design of the skin system. The membrane used is an elastic enclosure medium, and therefore the volume of the thermal mass filling is estimated by the form-finding method. The results in turn provide an estimate for the thermal storage capacity of the modules.

However, the thermal storage results include simplifications for a steady-state condition, while multidimensional transient heat transfer and convective losses are neglected. This simplification is acceptable when the air temperature and surface temperature are close, but when the radiant temperature diverges significantly from the air

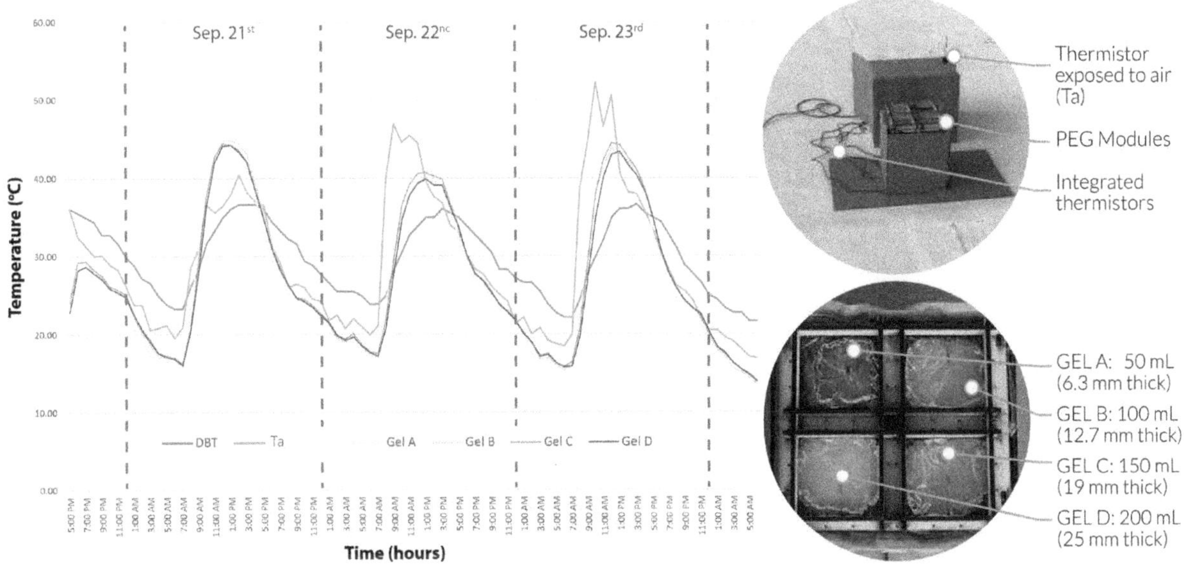

7 Hourly PEG material temperatures compared with outdoor dry-bulb and air-exposed thermistor during pilot test period September 21–23.

temperature, convective gains and losses will keep the mass closer to the air temperature and reduce the impact of the radiant heat transfer. Significantly, during the night, the convective impact will keep the thermal mass closer to the air temperature, and the full potential of sky cooling cannot be exploited unless a protective air gap is applied as done in Raman et al. (2014). To account for a more accurate transient heat transfer, a numerical model such as shown in Serale, Goia, and Perino (2016) for PCM or as provided in the "Conduction Finite Difference Solution Algorithm" developed by EnergyPlus (Department of Energy 2019) will be pursued in future work.

Hydrogel (PEG)

Results for the four PEG test modules of different volumes and thicknesses are presented for horizontal orientation over a three-day period in September (Fig.7). The material temperatures are compared with both the outdoor dry-bulb temperatures and to the readings from a thermistor exposed to both air and radiation exchanges, demonstrating the diurnal swing and solar and sky radiant influences on temperature fluctuations.

The PEG modules remain very close in temperature with each other throughout all periods of the testing. There is a slight variation in material temperatures at the peak of each day but a similar rate of heating and cooling occurs across all PEG modules. When compared with the outdoor dry-bulb temperature (DBT), the PEG modules experience both lower and higher peak temperatures and exhibit a rapid rate of cooling. In comparison with the temperature readings from the air-exposed thermistor, the PEG module temperatures remain lower during the morning heating periods while demonstrating a similar rate of cooling throughout the afternoon and evening. An anomaly appears on the first full testing date of September 21, when there are overcast sky conditions combined with slightly higher dry-bulb temperature, which suppresses the outdoor radiant temperature while the PEGs maintain sensible heat gain from the DBT. The PEG module material temperatures drop lower at night than both the outdoor air-exposed thermistor temperature and DBT. The comparison between the PEG modules themselves reveals that the module of the largest volume (Gel D) consistently displayed more thermal inertia during the daytime hours.

The next step will be to repeat the test but with a photonic membrane enclosure to avoid the heat gain peaks evident in Figure 7. Because of the convective losses, the temperature at night cannot be brought down much further than is already achieved in the tests we performed, but a reduction in solar heat gain thanks to the membrane will increase the cooling impact of the thermal mass.

Hydrogel (PEG) and Phase Change Material (PCM) Comparison

The initial physical material experiments, conducted for both thermal and fabrication behaviors, demonstrate specific constraints for the modules. The heat capacitance of the PEG is assumed close to that of liquid water (4.186 kJ/kgK), while the PCM heat capacitance ranges from solid (4.1 kJ/kgK) and liquid (3.1 kJ/kgK) states (Andrássy and Szánthó 2019). For a small module tested with a surface area of 0.09m^2, the total thermal energy loss potential is 163kJ for the PEG and 197.5kJ average for the PCM with the initial test modules of mass 1.18 kg each. Infrared (IR)

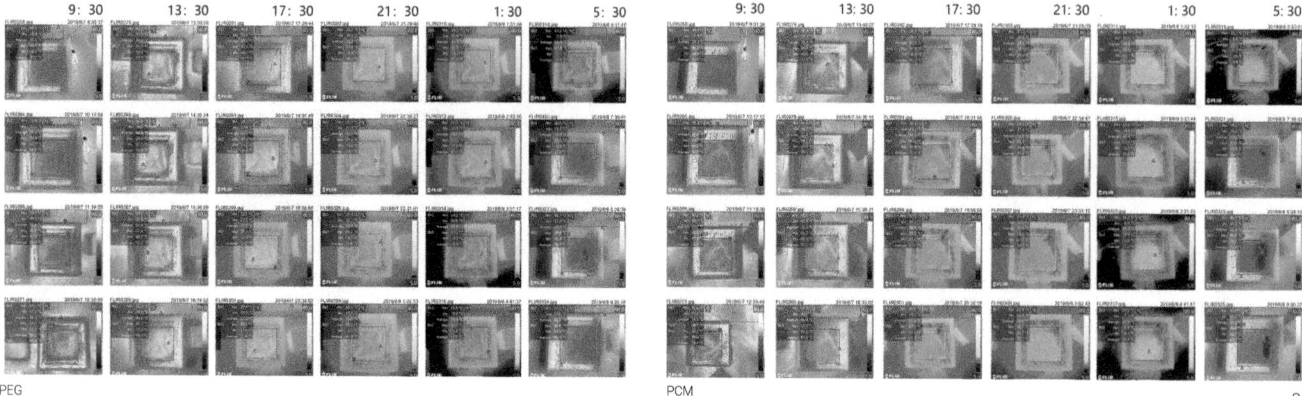

8 Infrared thermography images for PEG (left) and PCM (right) at hourly intervals during pilot-test period July 12–13.

thermography imaging (Fig. 8) demonstrates the material temperature comparisons of PEG and PCM modules at hourly intervals (top to bottom, left to right).

In the infrared thermography imaging, the PCM module maintains a more stable temperature throughout the day but heats up more quickly in the morning compared to the PEG module. The material module cooling rates occur in a similar fashion, with the low temperature occurring between 6:30 a.m. and 8:30 a.m. and with the PCM reaching slightly lower temperatures than the PEG. The results from this comparison, as previously published (Aviv et al. 2020a), also demonstrate these differentials with thermistor sensing measures.

CONCLUSION

This paper examines the morphology of a translucent radiatively cooled building skin in a desert climate, using high heat capacitance materials and a photonic membrane enclosure. To model the dependencies between surface geometry, volume, and material properties of the thermal mass and its enclosure, we created a workflow that integrates form-finding FEM simulations with heat transfer simulations and thermal storage analysis. This methodology relies on a feedback loop between form and performance, informed by computational simulations, analytical models, and physical tests.

On the site designated for full-scale construction of this special building skin in Tucson, Arizona, we devised a series of bench-scale tests to inform the model and test the individual module behavior. We were thus able to test the material response to solar and sky radiation exposure when encased with a transmissive membrane that allows for high absorbance of the thermal mass in all wavelengths. We also compared the behavior of hydrogel, which consists mostly of water—a material with very high specific heat—to that of a paraffin wax phase change material enclosed in the same membrane and exposed simultaneously to the elements.

The design and fabrication challenges of this building skin include the limited ability to predict the elastic membrane's shape changes when transient material processes such as thermal expansion and phase change occur, leading to leakage of the liquids through micro openings in the encapsulating membranes. We noted that the paraffin wax's low viscosity and high thermal expansion coefficient lead to leaks that are quite challenging to prevent with the membrane welding method currently deployed.

Future work will include a transient heat transfer model, informed by the physical tests, that will help to better characterize the thermal mass behavior. This model will also be informed by the completion of a full-scale prototype of the proposed building skin. Data collection from the prototype in the desert over a year will provide additional assessment of the simulations, and help evaluate the potential thermal and kinetic degradation factors of the hydrogel.

ACKNOWLEDGMENTS

We would like to thank Sean Rucewicz, Eric Teitelbaum, Maryam Moradnejad, Junren Tan, and Jiewei Li for their contributions to this project, and Princeton University Office of Sustainability, Princeton Council on Science and Technology, University of Arizona (UA) Accelerate for Success (AFS) grant, and Penn Praxis at the University of Pennsylvania for providing funding for this research.

NOTES

1. The ability of a body to store thermal energy, which depends on material heat capacity and/or its phase change properties.
2. Heat loss by thermal radiation heat transfer to colder surfaces.
3. The effective temperature for the radiative exchange of heat between terrestrial objects in the sky.
4. Allowing infrared wavelengths between 800 and 1400 nm to pass back out to the sky.
5. The weighted mean temperature of all the objects surrounding the body (Guo et al. 2019).

REFERENCES

Andrássy, Z., and Z. Szánthó. 2019. "Thermal Behaviour of Materials in Interrupted Phase Change." *Journal of Thermal Analysis and Calorimetry* 138: 3915–3924.

Aviv, Dorit, Maryam Moradnejad, Aletheia Ida, Zherui Wang, Eric Teitelbaum, and Forrest Meggers. 2020a. "Hydrogel-Based Evaporative and Radiative Cooling Prototype for Hot-Arid Climates." In *SimAUD 2020 [Proceedings of the Symposium on Simulation for Architecture & Urban Design]*, Vienna, Austria, 25–27 May 2020, edited by Angelos Chronis, Gabriel Wurzer, Wolfgang E. Lorenz, Christiane M. Herr, Ulrich Pont, Dana Cupkova, and Gabriel Wainer, 273–280. SCS.

Aviv, Dorit, Miaomiao Hou, Hongshan Guo, Eric Teitelbaum, and Forrest Meggers. 2020b. "Simulating Invisible Light: Adapting Lighting and Geometry Models for Radiant Heat Transfer." In *SimAUD 2020 [Proceedings of the Symposium on Simulation for Architecture & Urban Design]*, Vienna, Austria, 25–27 May 2020, edited by Angelos Chronis, Gabriel Wurzer, Wolfgang E. Lorenz, Christiane M. Herr, Ulrich Pont, Dana Cupkova, and Gabriel Wainer, 311–318. SCS.

Aviv, Dorit, and Axel Kilian. 2018. "Climate-Adaptive Volume: Solving the Motion Envelope of a Reconfigurable Cooling Aperture for Desert Climate." *Technology|Architecture+ Design* 2 (2): 186–195. https://doi.org/10.1080/24751448.2018.1497367.

Aviv, Dorit, and Forrest Meggers. 2017. "Cooling Oculus for Desert Climate—Dynamic Structure for Evaporative Downdraft and Night Sky Cooling." *Energy Procedia* 122: 1123–1128. https://doi.org/10.1016/j.egypro.2017.07.474.

Berdahl, Paul, and Richard Fromberg. 1982. "The Thermal Radiance of Clear Skies." *Solar Energy* 29 (4): 299–314.

Department of Energy. 2019. "Energy Plus Engineering Reference." Building Technologies Program, U.S. Department of Energy. https://energyplus.net/sites/all/modules/custom/nrel_custom/pdfs/pdfs_v9.2.0/EngineeringReference.pdf

Faircloth, B., R. Welch, M. Tamke, P. Nicholas, P. Ayres, Y. Sinke, and M. Ramsgaard Thomsen. 2018. "Multiscale Modeling Frameworks for Architecture: Designing the Unseen and Invisible with Phase Change Materials." *International Journal of Architectural Computing* 16 (2): 104–122.

Gans, Deborah. 2006. "William Katavolos." *Bomb Magazine* 97 (October).

Garg, H. P. 1982. *Treatise on Solar Energy: Fundamentals of Solar Energy Utilization*. England: John Wiley Sons.

Guo, Hongshan, Dorit Aviv, Mauricio Loyola, Eric Teitelbaum, Nicholas Houchois, and Forrest Meggers. 2020. "On the Understanding of the Mean Radiant Temperature within Both the Indoor and Outdoor Environment, a Critical Review." *Renewable and Sustainable Energy Reviews* 117: 109207.

Moe, Kiel. 2010. *Thermally Active Surfaces in Architecture*. New York: Princeton Architectural Press.

Pasquero, Claudia, and Marco Poletto. 2020. "Bio-Digital Aesthetics as Value System of Post-Anthropocene Architecture." *International Journal of Architectural Computing* 18 (2): 120–140.

Piker, Daniel. 2013. "Kangaroo: Form Finding with Computational Physics." *Architectural Design* 83 (2): 136–137.

Raman, A. P., M. A. Anoma, L. Zhu, E. Rephaeli, and S. Fan. 2014. "Passive Radiative Cooling below Ambient Air Temperature under Direct Sunlight." *Nature* 515 (7528): 540–544.

Roudsari, Mostapha Sadeghipour, Michelle Pak, and Adrian Smith. 2013. "Ladybug: A Parametric Environmental Plugin for Grasshopper to Help Designers Create an Environmentally-Conscious Design." In *Proceedings of the 13th Conference of International Building Performance Simulation Association (IBPSA)*, Chambery, France, 26–28 August 2013, edited by E. Wurtz, 3128–3135. IBPSA.

Serale, Gianluca, Francesco Goia, and Marco Perino. 2016. "Numerical Model and Simulation of a Solar Thermal Collector with Slurry Phase Change Material (PCM) as the Heat Transfer Fluid." *Solar Energy* 134: 429–444.

Smith, S. I. 2017. "Superporous Intelligent Hydrogels for Environmentally Adaptive Building Skins." *MRS Advances* 2 (46): 2481–2488.

Teitelbaum, Eric, Adam Rysanek, Jovan Pantelic, Dorit Aviv, Simon Obelz, Alexander Buff, Yongqiang Luo, Denon Sheppard, and Forrest Meggers. 2019. "Revisiting Radiant Cooling: Condensation-Free Heat Rejection Using Infrared-Transparent Enclosures of Chilled Panels." *Architectural Science Review* 62 (2): 152–159.

Tsilingiris, P. T. 2003. "Comparative Evaluation of the Infrared Transmission of Polymer Films." *Energy Conversion and Management* 44 (18): 2839–2856.

Dorit Aviv PhD is an architect and Assistant Professor at the University of Pennsylvania Weitzman School of Design, where she is the director of the Thermal Architecture Lab.

Zherui Wang is an academic professional researcher at Princeton University Andlinger Center for Energy and the Environment and a Peter Reyner Banham Fellow at SUNY Buffalo.

Forrest Meggers PhD is an Assistant Professor at Princeton University School of Architecture and the Andlinger Center for Energy and the Environment, and director of the C.H.A.O.S Lab,

---

Aletheia Ida PhD is an architect and Associate Professor at the University of Arizona, co-director of the Adaptive Environments Design Lab, and founding director of Ecollagency.

Embedded Sensing and Control

Concepts for an Adaptive, Responsive, Modular Architecture

Oliver Bucklin
University of Stuttgart: ICD

Larissa Born
University of Stuttgart: ITFT

Axel Körner
University of Stuttgart: ITKE

Seiichi Suzuki
University of Stuttgart: ITKE

Lauren Vasey
University of Stuttgart: ICD

Götz T. Gresser
University of Stuttgart: ITFT

Jan Knippers
University of Stuttgart: ITKE

Achim Menges
University of Stuttgart: ICD

1 ITECH Research Demonstrator 2018–19.

ABSTRACT

his paper investigates an interactive and adaptive control system for kinetic architectural applications with a distributed sensing and actuation network to control modular fiber-reinforced composite components. The aim of the project was to control the actuation of a foldable lightweight structure to generate programmatic changes. A server parses input commands and geometric feedback from embedded sensors and online data to drive physical actuation and generate a digital twin for real-time monitoring.

Physical components are origami-like folding plates of glass and carbon-fiber-reinforced plastic, developed in parallel research. Accelerometer data is analyzed to determine component geometry. A component controller drives actuators to maintain or move towards desired positions. Touch sensors embedded within the material allow direct control, and an online user interface provides high-level kinematic goals to the system. A hierarchical control system parses various inputs and determines actuation based on safety protocols and prioritization algorithms. Development includes hardware and software to enable modular expansion.

This research demonstrates strategies for embedded networks in interactive kinematic structures and opens the door for deeper investigations such as artificial intelligence in control algorithms, material computation, as well as real-time modeling and simulation of structural systems.

INTRODUCTION

The ITECH Research Demonstrator 2018–19 proposes a control system for kinematic architectural control system that reconfigures in response to multiple interface and sensor data input sources. To date, the majority of concepts for actively controlled adaptive architecture leverage mechanical actuation strategies, which require robust control systems with heavy emphasis on redundant safety and privacy (Barozzi et al. 2016; Bier et al. 2018; Urquhart, Schädelbach, and Jäger 2019). Ultralightweight material systems and customized fabrication processes open new technological opportunities for an architecture that can adapt to changing structural, climatic, and programmatic demands (Attia, Lioure, and Declaude 2020; Bier et al. 2018; Kilian and Sabourin 2017; Schnädelbach et al. 2016; Senatore et al. 2018; Sobek 2016). This project implements a hierarchical control system that draws input from physical sensors, graphic digital interfaces, and real-time data to drive the actuation of a modular carbon fiber-reinforced plastic (CFRP) architectural shading system.

AIM

The physical development of the Research Demonstrator, as described in Körner et al. (2020), proposes the use of compliant mechanisms with embedded pneumatic actuators to increase reliability and robustness of adaptive structures by minimizing mechanical complexity. The aim of the research described in this paper is to develop the complementary sensing, control, and interaction strategies that will enable the demonstrator to be reconfigured in real time in response to fluctuating programmatic and user demands.

The specific technical contributions of this system would include a modular control system to enable the flexible components to adapt to high-level geometric goal states (e.g., more closed for shading), with intelligent handling of kinetic constraints and material properties, in addition to a system of embedded sensors for reconstruction of the current geometric state of the demonstrator. Moreover, the aim was to enable real-time interaction and direct user control of the geometric reconfiguration of the structure through interactive tacit behaviors and user interfaces.

STATE OF THE ART

Robotically reconfigurable architecture has precedents in many contemporary research projects. Bier et al. (2018) describe the challenge of moving human-robot interaction out of the factory and into the built environment, where the building itself becomes robotic. They define a range of strategies that can be implemented to turn a building into an environment that responds to its occupants. The ITECH

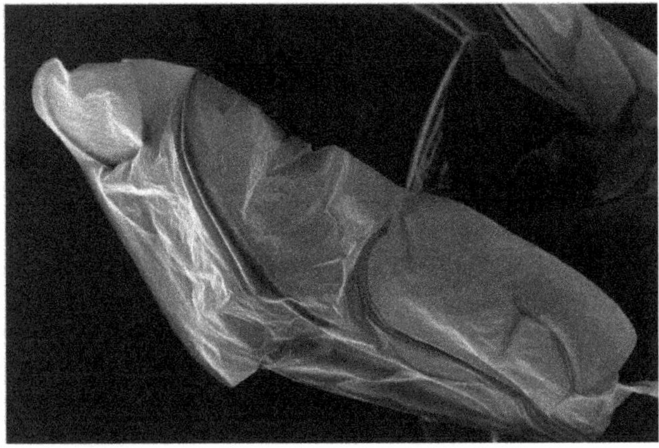

2

2 Hind wing of *Coleoptera coccinellidae* used as biological model for folding components of ITECH Research Demonstrator 2018–19.

Research Demonstrator 2018–19 seeks to implement the following state-of-the-art concepts and use them as criteria to evaluate the success of the system.

Material Interaction

Material interaction defines an interface where a physical material serves as both sensory input and reactive output interface. In his ongoing research, Sean Ahlquist (2015) investigates novel interactive interfaces that integrate sensing and interaction into a unified user experience. The research aims to increase the accessibility of interactions by removing barriers to comprehension. In this case, the architectural surfaces register direct touch input from users and react by changing form and appearance. Thus, abstract external interfaces are eliminated and direct interaction with the built environment can occur.

Feedback for Closed-Loop Control

Self-awareness is a system's ability to understand its own current state and capabilities and can give it the ability to respond to changing conditions. The Stuttgart Smart Shell, developed by University of Stuttgart's Institute for Lightweight Structures and Conceptual Design (ILEK) and Institute for System Dynamics (ISYS), in collaboration with Bosch Rexroth, demonstrates the potential for a self-aware structure to achieve higher structural performance than simple static structures (Neuhaeuser et al. 2013). The ultralight timber shell gathers information about changing load conditions, and then responds nearly instantaneously with a closed-loop control algorithm to optimize its shape to avoid requiring redundant material.

Digital Twins

The digital twin is a computational tool whereby a digital model is continuously updated in real time according to the physical state through the processing of sensor feedback.

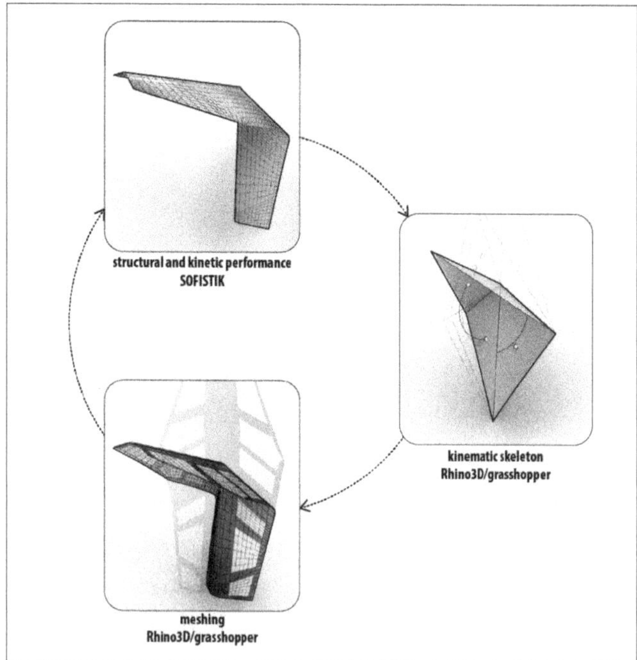

3

4

3 Computational design workflow for the physical component fabrication used as framework for this research. Adapted from Körner et al. (2020).

4 Actuation principle demonstrated by carbon fiber-reinforced plate bending via an integrated pneumatic cushion.

In "Self-Choreographing Network," Mathias Maierhofer and Valentina Soana implement a digital twin as both back-end control and front-end user interface for an adaptive, nondeterministic, bending-active structure (Maierhofer et al. 2019). The digital twin was able to bridge from the physical to digital realms through automated sensor-actuator feedback control, and from human to machine through a live graphical interface. The digital twin acts as a framework for integrating development concepts into a streamlined control platform.

METHODS

The overarching project ITECH Research Demonstrator 2018–19 consisted of multiple areas of development, resulting in two shading components produced on a six-axis industrial robot fitted with an industrial tape-laying end effector (Körner et al. 2020). Each origami-like folding component consists of four stiff plates joined by discrete elastic hinge zones with embedded pneumatic cushions for actuation. As a rigid origami mechanism, the folding elements would have one degree of freedom, with components folding to cantilever over a space. Elastic deformation of the used material and individual control of hinges could allow the components to extend the predefined motion path to generate additional adaptivity. To this end, each hinge is actuated individually via an electronically controlled proportional pressure regulator.

The actuation principle via pneumatic cushions is based on previous research by the University of Stuttgart's Institute for Building Structures and Structural Design and Institute for Textile and Fiber Technologies (Mader et al. 2020). A holistic overview of the project and the computational design, fabrication, and biomimetic aspects are covered in depth in separate publications (Körner et al. 2020). Adjacent components connect in sequence to supply pressurized air to further enhance modularity. Curled CFRP edges add stiffness to the panels and create a conduit to embed hoses and electrical signal wires inside the structure.

Control Hierarchy

The shading elements were used as a kinetic framework for developing the interactive control network detailed in this paper. Development focused on generating a flexible, modular control network that still responds to the specific challenges of the geometric, material, and mechanical systems. Custom hardware and software were developed into a control system that mirrors the physical component with a digital twin, enabling a hierarchy of inputs to enable both tacit and web-based interaction. The control system consists of three components: (1) feedback and closed-loop control; (2) direct occupant control; and (3) goal state generation.

Feedback and Closed-Loop Control

The most fundamental element of a control system is a feedback system, which in this case would require monitoring the components' geometry to ensure safe, accurate actuations. To establish closed-loop control in relationship to the pneumatic actuation, it was necessary to measure

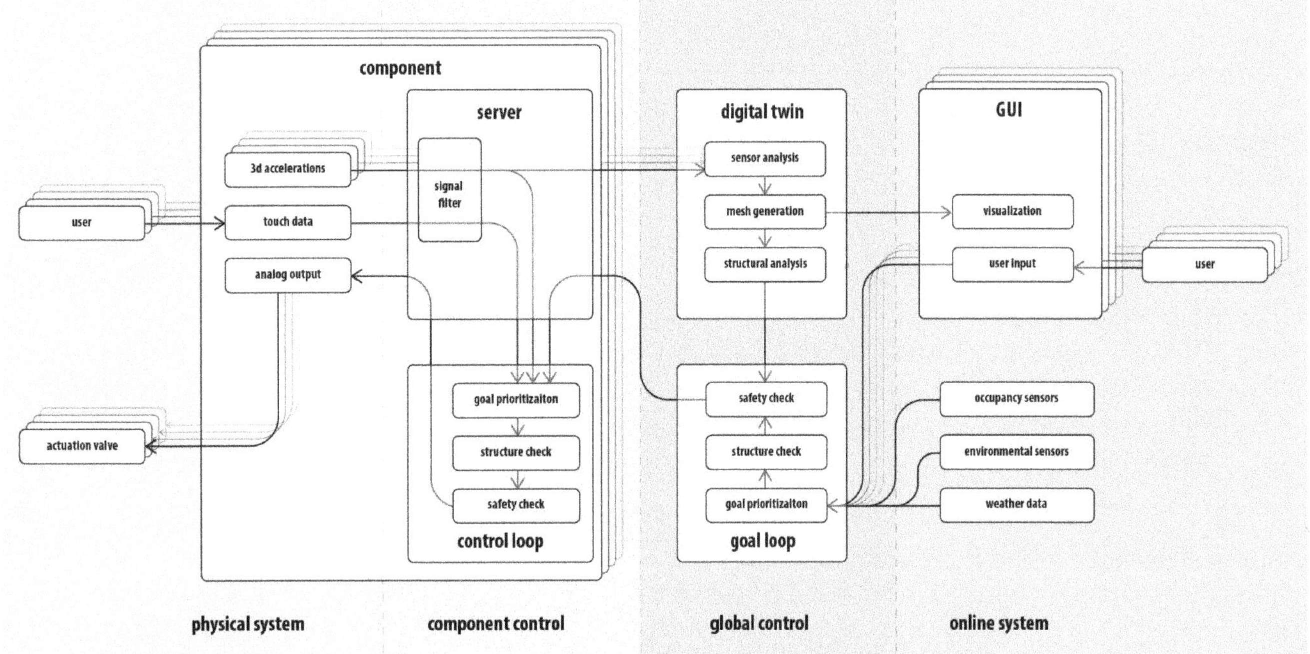

5 Proposed hierarchical control network structure with data flows.

each component's geometric configuration at a high frequency. To gather the relevant data, various sensor-based approaches were considered, with cost, robustness, accuracy, speed, and ease of integration being essential criteria for comparison.

The classical solution to embedded material sensing is a strain gauge, which measures local deformation along a single axis. When mounted on opposite sides of a structural member, two strain gauges can give the local bending state in a single coordinate direction. However, establishing a wireless strain gauge system was deemed to be overly complicated, and the cost of strain gauges increases exponentially with their accuracy and robustness. A second option is optical 3D scanning, which gives a very accurate point cloud image of a structure, allowing a high-resolution generation of a virtual model. However, this option would be computationally expensive and require a relatively large and expensive external sensor that could not be embedded in the component.

Ultimately, internal measurement units (IMUs) were chosen to monitor the component shape. These small, cheap sensors can give their orientation with respect to vertical by sensing the magnitude of gravitational acceleration along X, Y, and Z vectors. IMUs were placed at strategic points on the stiff component panels. By applying these incline values to the correlating points on a kinetic digital model, the relative angle between any two adjacent panels could be measured, and the current state of the physical component can be reconstructed digitally.

By integrating this into a closed-loop control loop, they can maintain or drive towards goal state positions. A proportional-integral-derivative (PID) control algorithm was proposed that calculates the amount of error between actual and desired hinge position states and executes proportional changes in the pneumatic regulator outputs.

Tacit Occupant Control

Several different methods were considered for enabling users to manipulate the components through direct, intuitive, material interaction. For example, by tapping on the structure, a user could elicit a specific type of geometric change such as opening or closing.

The IMUs used for geometric reconstruction could register user commands. The chosen sensors have a built-in double-tap recognition function, and there is precedent in many user interfaces where users double- or triple-click to manipulate graphical interfaces. This interaction was deemed to be too abstract, as users would have to be taught how to manipulate the component.

Ultimately, the electrical conductivity of the CFRP was leveraged to create a deeply embedded sensor. The electrical capacitance of the human body is used to generate signals in most touch-screen devices, and this same property can be used to create a touch sensor in a range of materials, including CFRP. By connecting panels of the components' base material to a simple circuit, human touch could be registered and utilized as a command input. This was coupled by direct behaviors that would elicit a new relative goal state. For example, tapping produces a new goal state that is relatively more closed than its current state.

Goal-State Generation

The components are indirectly controlled through a digital twin that generates goal states. These are geometric configurations generated by synthesizing data from various sources to coordinate multiple components simultaneously. An online graphical user interface allows users to manipulate the configuration of multiple components. These are considered as goal states because each component evaluates its own goal states based on safety and command priority and determines how to react.

Hardware

To measure the local orientation of each component's folding panels during operation, two IMUs are strategically placed on each panel. Various sensors were proposed, including six-axis and three-axis IMUs. The rotational measurements of six-axis IMUs would have simplified bending measurements but were found to have too much accumulated error over long periods of operation. The ADXL345 three-axis accelerometer was instead chosen for its robustness and simplicity. The I2C communication protocol allows multiple devices to communicate along a common set of wires, or bus, by calling each module with a unique identifier, or address. The ADXL345 has two built-in addresses, meaning four separate I2C buses would be required to communicate with the minimum eight IMUs required for monitoring. To allow communication to all sensors along a single bus, a custom-printed circuit board (PCB) was designed and fabricated that included an ATTiny44 microcontroller. This versatile chip can also be programmed to perform basic calculations and be used for various input and output functions, including reading and writing analog and digital signals and serial communication. These custom modules were given unique device identifiers so that potentially hundreds could be addressed on a single bus.

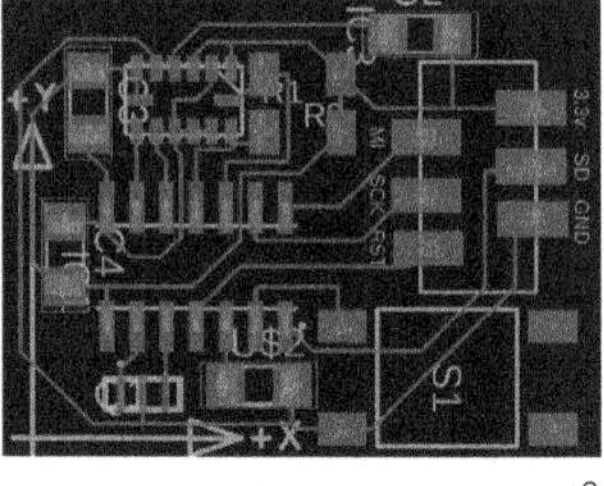

6

7

6 Printed circuit board layout as designed for custom IMU sensors used to analyze component geometry.

7 Completed IMU sensor ready for installation in component.

The I2C bus is also utilized for communication with two other custom PCB module types. The ATTiny44 controls the capacitance sensors that register human touch on four control pads found on each component. A digital-to-analog controller (DAC) uses a larger ATMega328 microcontroller, which features more outputs that are capable of pulse-width modulation. This feature simulates an analog voltage level that is amplified to achieve a 0-10-volt output to the proportional pressure regulators that drive the pneumatic actuation of the structure. All custom modules were programmed in the Arduino IDE with a combination of Arduino and C programming language.

Network Structure

The control network is structured with a three-layer hierarchy. At the lowest tier, the embedded sensors and actuators sense and manipulate the material directly. The central tier is the component controller, where inputs from sensors and the digital twin are interpreted and actuation commands are decided. The top tier, the digital twin, portrays sensor data and facilitates goal-state generation. The component controller is a Raspberry Pi 3, whose compact size and broad connectivity allow it to interface with physical devices and online networks. This controller prioritizes inputs, calculates movement commands, and outputs signals to the DACs using python scripts. DACs are installed on a separate I2C bus from sensors, isolating the actuators from potential interference during failsafe operations and to allow parallel sensing and actuation.

The controller also streams sensor data to the digital twin using TCP/IP protocols over Wi-Fi. Tests were conducted to attempt to reconstruct the component geometry in a physics-based model by applying IMU orientation values to a simulated component. This three-dimensional digital model is the central element of the digital twin, serving as a graphical feature to contextualize data and give users the current configuration of the demonstrator, allowing remote monitoring of the structure.

RESULTS

The hierarchical nature of the control system was able to respond to inputs at various levels. Data from embedded sensors allowed direct control of component geometry, and the online interface coordinated the movements of multiple components. The system achieves modularity at multiple levels; sensor and actuator modules could easily be added or replaced on the I2C bus, and additional components can easily be added to the digital twin.

The I2C bus proved to be unreliable over the 3 m component. The electrical capacitance of the communication wires

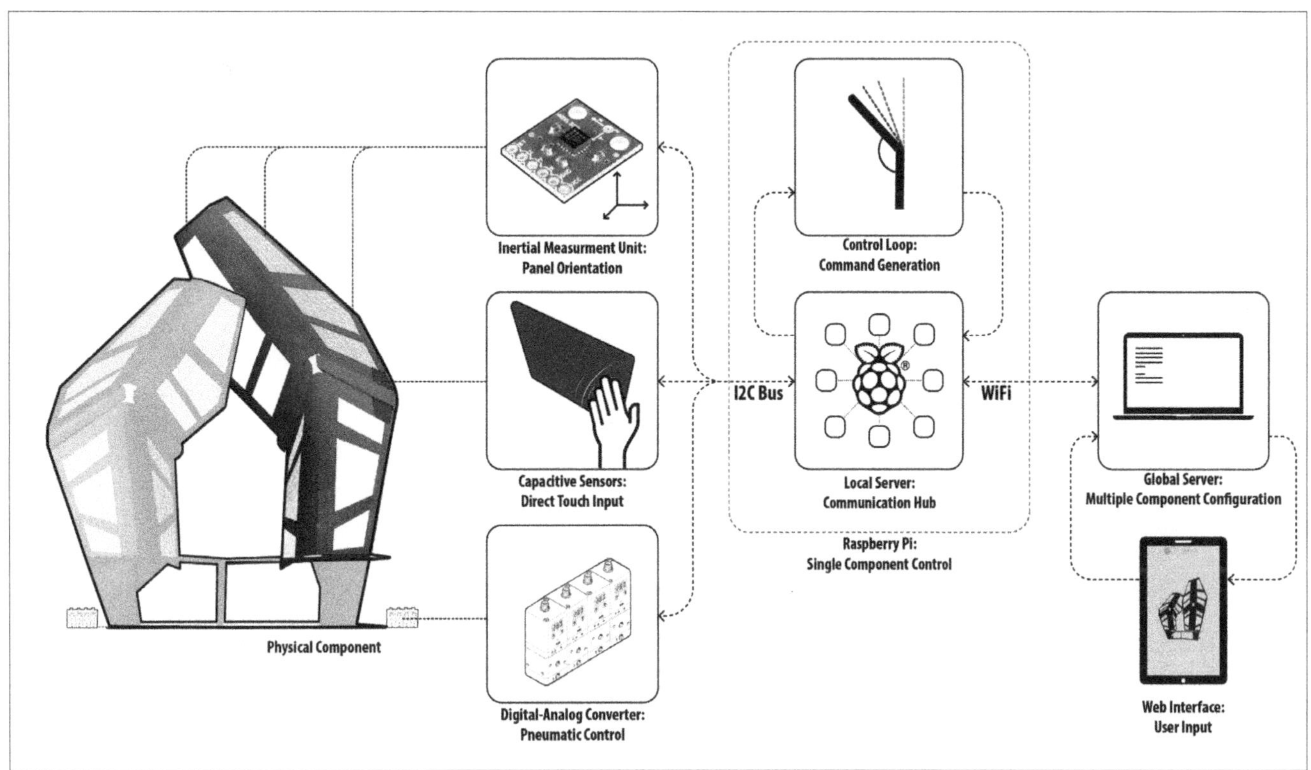

8

8 Hardware network centered around autonomous control of components adapted from Körner et al. (2020).

themselves caused signal losses of up to 25% from modules at the far end of the bus. This was remedied with changes to the physical circuit and software filtering. The included ATTiny44 microcontroller proved vital, as confirmation characters were used to verify the accuracy of data transfers. The IMU microcontrollers were programmed with additional functions to calibrate, offset, and filter electrical noise and physical vibrations. The touch sensors were very sensitive and would occasionally register false contacts. This was remedied by a self-calibration routine that would run at startup. Signals from the four physical touch pads are packed into a single byte to maximize transfer speed and would only transfer if the data had changed. These optimizations freed up processing power for the component controller to use for communication and decision-making.

In early tests, high angle bending caused signs of separation of the hinge plates; therefore, due to concerns about excessive stresses during disproportional actuation, lateral swinging movement was deemed infeasible. Thus, all hinges were operated in unison, with pressure values scaled proportionally based on maximum deflection pressure. The pneumatic cushions operate at very low pressures: 0.8 bar in the horizontal hinges and 0.4 bar in vertical hinges are sufficient to generate an 80° safe maximum deflection (Körner et al. 2020). This low value compared to the regulator's operational output range led to a reduced resolution in control. In addition, latency between input signal and regulator switching was 550 and 1300 milliseconds for turning on and off, respectively, which rendered a PID controller useless. Instead, for component operation, positional goals are sent directly as cushion air pressures, and predetermined maximum and minimum values set in the component controllers prevent overbending.

CFRP capacitive touch sensors enable material interaction. Components respond to inputs via the four CFRP touch-sensitive pads mounted above and below the horizontal hinges, which reliably reported touch inputs to the controller. Signals activate a time-based incrementor that raises or lowers cushion pressures. In this way, intuitively touching the material generated a direct physical reaction of the kinematic structure.

Multiple streams feed data about the components' geometry, physical interfaces, and online interactions to the component controller. This, coupled with the ability to react to the inputs, demonstrates self-awareness. The hierarchical nature of the control network, and that individual components have ultimate control over their own actuation output, demonstrates an effective implementation of decentralized control. The benefits are also demonstrated in input data streams, as measurement data is preprocessed at sensor modules.

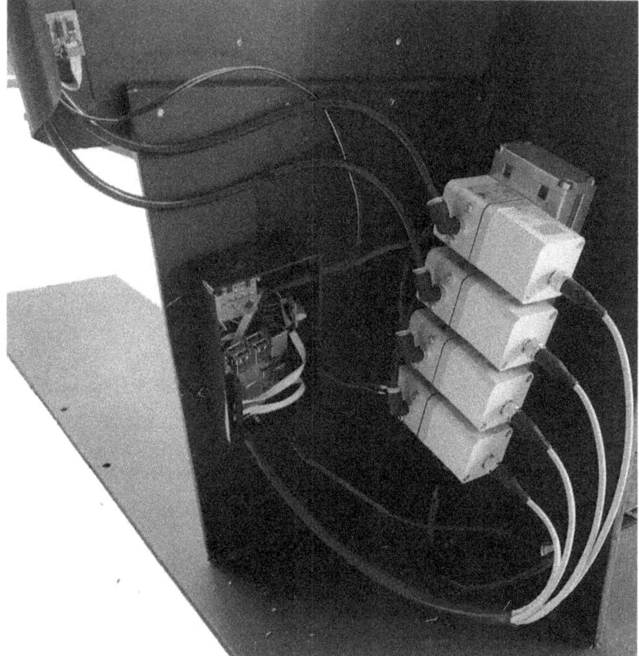

9

10

9 Control system installed on component.

10 CFRP touch panel used for direct command input.

The digital twin allows the synthesis of all input and output streams into one integrated model. This program generates the three-dimensional virtual model that makes the main graphical component of the digital twin. Because excessively heavy calculation would be required to analyze IMU data and simulate a physical model in real time, this data is instead compared to an array of precomputed meshes to select an approximated 3D model that best matches the current component state. Users access the digital twin via a mobile online interface and can view the demonstrator from any angle and access a real-time readout of sensor data. Users can also generate goal-state configurations for the entire demonstrator through simple up/down buttons. The digital twin thus enables the adaptation to transcend single component control and choreograph large-scale spatial changes.

DISCUSSION AND OUTLOOK

The developed control system could function as a framework to test new control concepts. These developments could come as improvements at every stage of control.

For position monitoring and control, a low computational intensity physical modeling system could simulate the components in real time, giving the system more self-awareness for decision-making. In addition to more accurate visual representation of the model, this could help understand the physical system; three-dimensional acceleration data could shed light on structural behavior by measuring displacement during high winds, find oscillation frequencies to help structural engineers verify their modeling techniques, and identify and warn operators of potentially dangerous situations. If fast-reacting proportional regulators were used, a PID controller would likely become a valid method for kinematic operation, and active damping could perhaps even be developed to stabilize components during dynamic conditions. Similarly, by monitoring the health of the electrical and mechanical systems required to operate the demonstrator, equipment failures could be proactively identified and remedied to ensure continuous operation.

The conductivity of the CFRP was useful in implementing the touch sensor pads. This could potentially be utilized to sense contact with components or inhabitants. Fabrication development could see power and communication wires embedded in layers of CFRP during robotic fabrication.

New functions could parse input from multiple users to generate subspaces within a larger aggregation of components. This could be done abstractly by requesting spatial types, or directly through a geometric model-based interface. Algorithms would need to be carefully considered to ensure equitable accessibility.

Weather data from online sources could inform demonstrator control, and a bank of on-site weather sensors like thermometers, rain sensors, and anemometers would give even more precise localized data. Occupancy sensors were considered that could evaluate how many users were using the structure and where they were located, adapting the structure to provide the maximum of shelter. Vision-based sensors that can discern human gestures or occupancy could be integrated. These could use three-dimensional mapping or be based on two-dimensional image recognition. The digital twin could be programmed to track occupant

11 Online user interface of the digital twin, used for user coordination of multiple components. Adapted from Körner et al. (2020).

patterns over days or seasons and to optimize reactions for certain end goals, such as maximum occupancy, maximum visit duration, or maximum unique visitors.

The complexity of such input parameters could be a strong candidate for machine learning to drive interaction. Simultaneous operation with potentially conflicting local commands and online coordination would present interesting challenges for parsing instructions during operation. From these inputs the demonstrator could develop unique and unexpected interactive behaviors.

CONCLUSION

The control system demonstrates a flexible, decentralized structure for organizing multiple data streams for interactive, adaptive architecture.

This project demonstrates how distributed computation can make physical control systems more robust. By implementing specialized modules with specific tasks, the entire system was made more flexible. Delegating computational tasks to satellite modules improved efficiency by locally calculating, filtering, and storing sensor values, which streamlined communication and reduced latency. Local control of each architectural component allows for failsafe operations in case of digital twin malfunction. High-level data is processed on a single powerful control computer.

Control functioned at local and global scales. Embedded sensors enable material interaction where the components react directly to human touch. An online digital twin allows coordinated control of multiple components. The digital twin functioned as an online interface for displaying relevant building data, and further development could allow the control system to link sensors and models to attain complex self-awareness. Linking data about the surrounding environment and inhabitants to the physical demonstrator would open the doors for broad exploration into behavioral adaptation of kinetic architecture.

ACKNOWLEDGMENTS

The research has been partially supported by the Deutsche Forschungsgemeinschaft (DFG, German Research Foundation) under Germany's Excellence Strategy—EXC 2120/1–390831618.
The presented research was partially developed within the master's program Integrative Technologies and Architectural Design Research (ITECH) at the University of Stuttgart. The following students were involved in the development of the presented demonstrator project: Miro Bannwart, Eliza Biala, Xiaoyu Chen, Rebeca Duque Estrada de Almeida Araujo, Farnaz Fattahi, Rob Faulkner, David Horvath, Niloofar Imani, You-Wen Ji, Fabian Kannenberg, Nate Kaylor, Denitsa Koleva, Jure Kozmos, I-Ching Lee, Ada Lezuchowska, Zhiqi Lin, Samantha Melnyk, Seyed Mobin Moussavi, Mona Mühlich, Seyed Ahmad Razavi, Tamara Rosales, Emi Shiraishi, Sanoop Siby, Piyanat Songkhroh, Hana Svatoš-Ražnjevic, Naomi Kris Tashiro, Babasola Thomas, Aditya Tiwari, Maria Wyller, Nima Zahiri, Ruqing Zhong. The project was made possible through collaborations with Compositence GmbH, the Department of Evolutionary Biology of Invertebrates and the Department of Palaeontology of Invertebrates at the University of Tuebingen, Autodesk, and Roy Hohlfeld.

REFERENCES

Ahlquist, Sean. 2015. "Social Sensory Architectures: Articulating Textile Hybrid Structures for Multi-Sensory Responsiveness and Collaborative Play." In *ACADIA 2015: Computational Ecologies: Design in the Anthropocene [Proceedings of the 35th Annual Conference of the Association for Computer Aided Design in Architecture (ACADIA)]*, Cincinnati, OH, 19–25 October 2015, edited by L. Combs and C. Perry, 263–273. CUMINCAD.

Attia, Shady, Romain Lioure, and Quentin Declaude. 2020. "Future Trends and Main Concepts of Adaptive Facade Systems." *Energy Science and Engineering* 8 (9): 1–18. https://doi.org/10.1002/ese3.725.

Barozzi, Marta, Julian Lienhard, Alessandra Zanelli, and Carol Monticelli. 2016. "The Sustainability of Adaptive Envelopes: Developments of Kinetic Architecture." *Procedia Engineering* 155: 275–284. https://doi.org/10.1016/j.proeng.2016.08.029.

Bier, Henriette, Alexander Liu Cheng, Sina Mostafavi, Ana Anton, and Serban Bodea. 2018. "Robotic Building as Integration of Design-to-Robotic-Production and -Operation." In *Robotic Building*, edited by H. Bier. Cham: Springer International Publishing. https://doi.org/10.1007/978-3-319-70866-9_5.

Körner, Axel, Larissa Born, Oliver Bucklin, Seiichi Suziki, Lauren Vasey, Götz T. Gresser, Achim Menges, and Jan Knippers. 2020. "Integrative Design and Fabrication Methodology for Bio-Inspired Folding Mechanisms for Architectural Applications." *Computer-Aided Design* 133: 102988. https://doi.org/10.1016/j.cad.2020.102988.

Mader, Anja; Larissa Born, Axel Körner, Gundula Schieber, Pierre-Alexandre Masset, Markus Milwich, et al. 2020. "Bio-Inspired Integrated Pneumatic Actuation for Compliant Fiber-Reinforced Plastics." *Composite Structures* 233: 111558. https://doi.org/10.1016/j.compstruct.2019.111558.

Maierhofer, M., V. Soana, M. Yablonina, S. Suzuki, A. Körner, J. Knippers, and A. Menges. 2019. "Self-Choreographing Network: Towards Cyber-Physical Design and Operation Processes of Adaptive and Interactive Bending-Active Systems." In *ACADIA 19: Ubiquity and Autonomy [Proceedings of the 39th Annual Conference of the Association for Computer Aided Design in Architecture (ACADIA)]*, Austin, TX, 21–26 October 2019, edited by K. Bieg, D. Briscoe, and C. Odom, 654–663. CUMINCAD.

Neuhaeuser, Stefan, M. Weickgenannt, C. Witte, Walter Haase, O. Sawodny, and W. Sobek. 2013. "Stuttgart Smartshell: A Full Scale Prototype of an Adaptive Shell Structure." *Journal of the International Association for Shell and Spatial Structures* 54: 259–270.

Schnädelbach, Holger, Petr Slovák, Geraldine Fitzpatrick, and Nils Jäger. 2016. "The Immersive Effect of Adaptive Architecture." *Pervasive and Mobile Computing* 25: 143–152. https://doi.org/10.1016/j.pmcj.2014.11.006.

Senatore, Gennaro, Philippe Duffour, Pete Winslow, and Chris Wise. 2018. "Shape Control and Whole-Life Energy Assessment of an 'Infinitely Stiff' Prototype Adaptive Structure." *Smart Materials and Structures* 27 (1). https://doi.org/10.1088/1361-665X/aa8cb8.

Sobek, Werner. 2016. "Ultra-Lightweight Construction." *International Journal of Space Structures* 31 (1): 74–80. https://doi.org/10.1177/0266351116643246.

Urquhart, Lachlan, Holger Schnädelbach, and Nils Jäger. 2019. "Adaptive Architecture: Regulating Human Building Interaction." *International Review of Law, Computers and Technology* 33 (1): 3–33. https://doi.org/10.1080/13600869.2019.1562605.

IMAGE CREDITS

All drawings and images by the authors.

Oliver Appling Bucklin is a research associate at the University of Stuttgart's Institute for Computational Design and Construction (ICD). Oliver holds a Master in Architecture from Harvard University and a Bachelor of Fine Arts from the University of Washington. Oliver's current research investigates sustainable building practices leveraging advanced modeling and fabrication in solid wood building envelopes. Further research covers embedded electronics and custom mechanics, including mobile robotics and integrating computational intelligence in industrial processes. Oliver is currently involved in the Performative Wood group at the ICD.

Larissa Born has been a research associate at the Institute for Textile and Fiber Technologies (ITFT) since 2014. In 2020, she received her doctorate in engineering (Dr.-Ing.) with distinction from the University of Stuttgart. Her scientific work is focused primarily on material development for compliant fiber-reinforced plastics with locally integrated hinges and actuators for adaptive, flexible systems. Her research within this field has received several awards, including for the bio-inspired facade shading systems flectofin, Flectofold, and Flexafold.

Axel Körner received his MSc in emergent technologies and design from the Architectural Association in London 2013 with distinction. Between 2008 and 2014, he worked for various architecture firms in Munich, Vienna, and London and taught at the AA School of Architecture in London. Since 2014 he has been a research associate at the Institute for Building Structures and Structural Design (ITKE) at the University of Stuttgart with focus on bio-inspired compliant mechanisms for architectural applications. In addition,

12 Completed ITECH Research Demonstrator 2018–19.

12

he has held several positions as visiting lecturer and organized international workshops on biomimetic, folding, and adaptive architectural applications.

Seiichi Suzuki is a postdoctoral researcher at the Bionic Lightweight Design and Functional Morphology Group at the Alfred Wegener Institute. He holds a Bachelor of Architecture from the Pontifical Catholic University of Ecuador, a Master's degree in Advanced Architecture from the Institute for Advanced Architecture of Catalonia, and a Master's degree in Advanced Design and Digital Architecture from the Pompeu Fabra University. Between 2013 and 2019, he held a research position at the Institute for Building Structures and Structural Design (ITKE). In 2020, Seiichi was awarded the title of Doctor in Engineering from the University of Stuttgart.

Lauren Vasey is a postdoctoral researcher at the ETH Zurich within the NCCR Digital Fabrication in the stream Construction Robotics, and is also a cluster leader of on-site robotics and digital fabrication within GKR. She received her PhD from the ICD, with great honor, where she conducted research in adaptive robotic fabrication methods and taught within the ITECH Master's Program for five years. From 2016 to 2020, she was an elected member of the Board of Directors of ACADIA serving roles on the scientific and steering committees, and was also an editor of *IJAC*.

Götz T. Gresser received his Diploma in Mechanical Engineering at the University of Stuttgart in 1991 and completed his PhD in 1998. Up to 2013 he held various leading positions at Rieter Maschinenfabrik AG in Winterthur, Switzerland. Since 2013 he has held the chair of Textile Technology, Fiber-Based Materials and Textile Machinery at the University Stuttgart. He is head of the Institute of Textile and Process Engineering (ITV) and the Institute for Textile and Fiber Technologies (ITFT). He is also chair of the German Institutes of Textile and Fiber Research Denkendorf (DITF) and managing director of ITV Denkendorf Produktservice GmbH.

Jan Knippers is a practicing consulting engineer and, since 2000, head of the Institute for Building Structures and Structural Design (ITKE) at the University of Stuttgart. His interest is in innovative and resource-efficient structures created at the intersection of research and development and practice. From 2014 to 2019, Jan was the coordinator of the DFG collaborative research center Biological Design and Integrative Structures. Since 2019 he has been deputy executive director of the Cluster of Excellence Integrative Computational Design and Construction for Architecture (IntCDC) and Vice-Rector for Research of the University of Stuttgart.

Achim Menges is a registered architect in Frankfurt and a full Professor at the University of Stuttgart, where he is the founding director of the Institute for Computational Design and Construction (ICD) and the director of the Cluster of Excellence Integrative Computational Design and Construction for Architecture (IntCDC). In addition, he has been a Visiting Professor in Architecture at Harvard University's Graduate School of Design and held multiple other visiting professorships. His research focuses on the development of integrative design at the intersection of computational design methods, robotic manufacturing, and construction, as well as advanced material and building systems.

Pedestrian Flow: Monitoring and Prediction

Nikol Kirova
IAAC

Areti Markopoulou
IAAC

Monitoring and prediction of pedestrian flows through smart material sensing surfaces towards informed dynamic mobility reconfiguration strategies

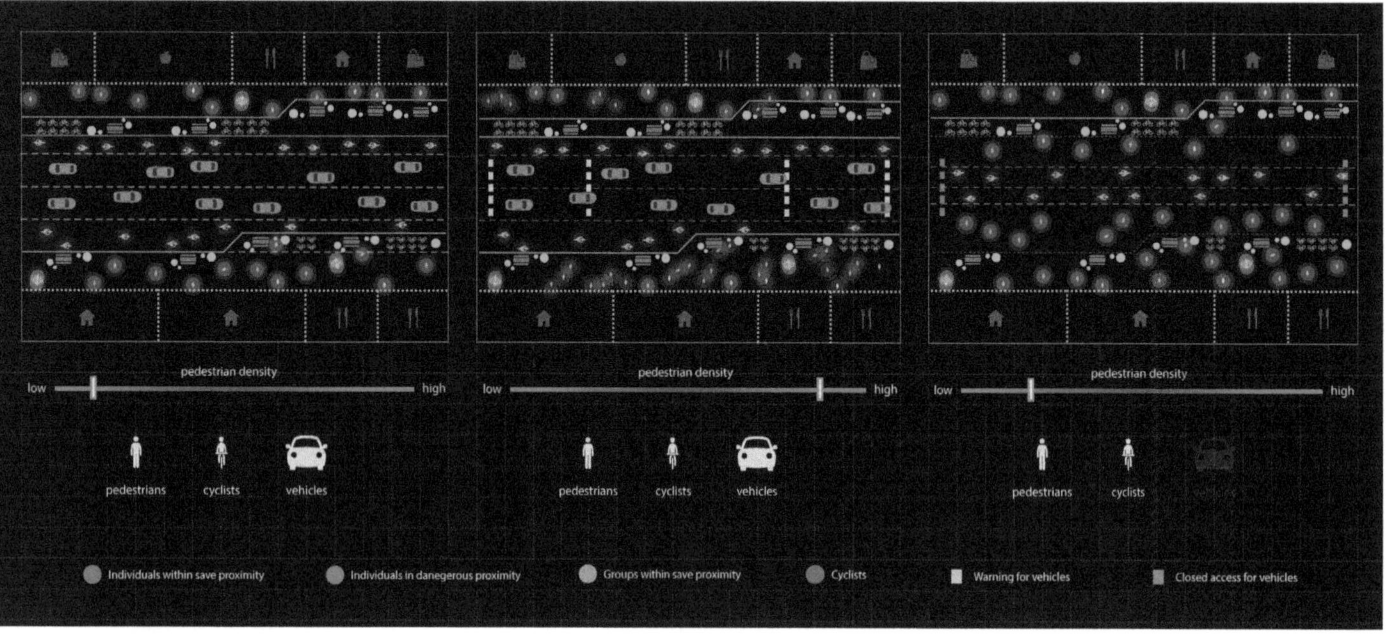

1

1 Proposal for a dynamic mobility plan reconfiguration based on a smart material-based sensing and actuating surface.

ABSTRACT

The worldwide lockdowns during the first wave of the COVID-19 pandemic had an immense effect on the public space. The events brought up an opportunity to redesign mobility plans, streets, and sidewalks, making cities more resilient and adaptable. This paper builds on previous research of the authors that focused on the development of a graphene-based sensing material system applied to a smart pavement and utilized to obtain pedestrian spatiotemporal data. The necessary steps for gradual integration of the material system within the urban fabric are introduced as milestones toward predictive modeling and dynamic mobility reconfiguration.

Based on the capacity of the smart pavement, the current research presents how data acquired through an agent-based pedestrian simulation is used to gain insight into mobility patterns. A range of maps representing pedestrian density, flow, and distancing are generated to visualize the simulated behavioral patterns. The methodology is used to identify areas with high density and, thus, high risk of transmitting airborne diseases.

The insights gained are used to identify streets where additional space for pedestrians is needed to allow safe use of the public space. It is proposed that this is done by creating a dynamic mobility plan where temporal pedestrianization takes place at certain times of the day with minimal disruption of road traffic. Although this paper focuses mainly on the agent-based pedestrian simulation, the method can be used with real-time data acquired by the sensing material system for informed decision-making following otherwise-unpredictable pedestrian behavior. Finally, the simulated data is used within a predictive modeling framework to identify further steps for each agent; this is used as a proof-of-concept through which more insights can be gained with additional exploration.

INTRODUCTION

With the emergence of the COVID-19 pandemic, many nations across the globe adopted similar protective measures that severely affected public space occupation. These events highlighted an opportunity to redesign mobility plans, streets, and sidewalks, allowing cities to become more resilient (Alter 2020; Bliss 2020; EFE 2020; Hawkins 2020; Topham 2020). Aside from the physical redesign of spaces for social distancing, the pandemic has also raised the need for continuous real-time monitoring of space and citizens' mobility. Different countries across the globe immediately began operating urban apps that monitor the geolocation of users in real time (Kim 2020; WHO 2020). Such practices were also present in some countries before the COVID-19 pandemic, and while they are helpful tools for enhancing security and health, the existing systems used for their application present critical aspects related to privacy (Council of the European Union and European Parliament 2016).

There are numerous "Smart City" oriented projects and visions investigating possibilities for the application of digital technologies such as ubiquitous computing and Internet of Things for urban flow monitoring. The latest events have suggested the importance of establishing new mobility infrastructures that respond to the dynamic flows in a rapidly adaptable manner. The "Imaging the Driverless City" by BIG (Bjarke Ingels Group) for the 2010 Audi Urban Future Initiative envisioned a city where self-driving cars move in harmony with their fellow pedestrian commuters. Such mobility plans require novel smart infrastructures where sensors are embedded in the pavement, "generating a ubiquitous network of smart streets that would control and direct the smart cars" (Hack 2016). The result of such vision is an elastic urban space that can expand and contract to accommodate peak traffic hours or allow a park or plaza to invade the car lanes to fit the demands and desires of its citizens in real time.

There is a series of available software and hardware that tracks either the geolocation of devices or requires the use of surveillance cameras with computer vision that directly track individuals based on face and/or body recognition (Martani et al. 2017). However, these systems require great computational power to achieve their goal and, as they target individuals, are considered invasive, infringing upon the privacy of parties during the tracking process. Additionally, according to studies, cameras in the public space can have a behavior-altering effect (Jansen et al. 2018). GPS-locating systems act as a background process within our smart devices and maybe unnoticed but provide personal information that can easily be exploited by companies and authorities for objectives that do not directly serve the quality of life or safety of citizens.

In contrast, research on "surface-based sensing," which measures the differences in capacitance or pressure of conductive surfaces, presents alternative models of urban and pedestrian flows monitoring (Akhmareh et al. 2016; Arshad et al. 2017; Goodman 2015). Surface-based sensing introduces the possibility of creating a "sensing ability" integrated into the materiality of a surface rather than using externally plugged-in systems of traditional monitoring hardware. Previous work has proven the accuracy of real-time sensing of people in motion, through the capacitance difference in conductive surfaces. Regardless, there is a lack of methodologies and applications of using the data acquired from materially integrated sensing surfaces to predict urban flows as well as to make informed decisions about the public space (Kirova et al. 2020).

The proposed system provides completely anonymous data that, by design, cannot be used to identify individuals. It also provides bidirectional communication between the inhabitants and space through its programmable response. This feature aims at creating an engaging environment rather than merely tracking and locating. It also contributes to redesigning the public space with a human-centric notion and through a dynamic privacy-respecting monitoring system for improving city resilience in response to unpredictable crises.

METHODOLOGY

This paper presents the application of a graphene-based material system for monitoring pedestrian traffic and density in the public space with a nonprivacy-invasive method, alongside the computational workflow, used to analyze the raw data gathered and interpret it to gain valuable insights for prediction. The paper uses an urban case study to demonstrate how the system would function if utilized in public space. It also provides an integration strategy foreseeing the possible impact the system might reach on various stages of its application. A computational workflow is established where an area is studied and optimized for allowing sufficient distancing between pedestrians without introducing additional physical monitoring infrastructure but rather by using the paving material as a data-gathering device. Proximity maps are generated by analyzing the distance between the agents in each frame. The aim of the proposed system is to inform temporary changes in the urban environment in an engaging and noninvasive manner.

2

3

5

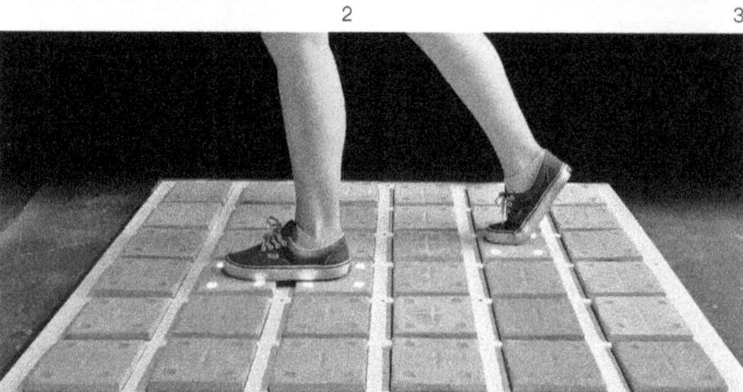

4

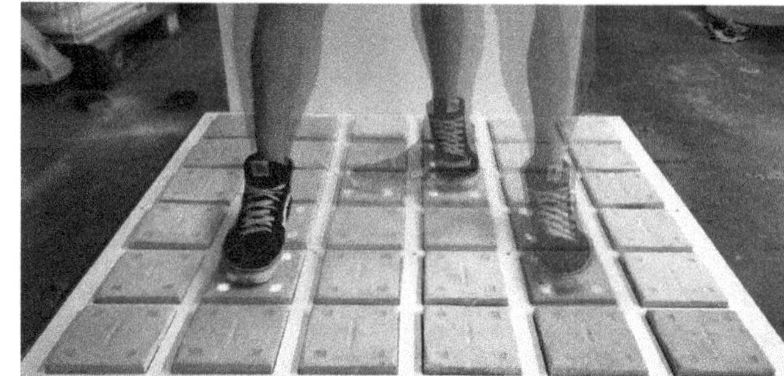

6

Material System

In our previous research, we prototyped graphene urban tiles with different base materials in the laboratory, demonstrating the graphene's extended surface-sensing potential and allowing accurate location of people on the pavement (Kirova et al. 2020). The core of the research lies in the integration of various performances within a material system. The sensing layer utilizes the principle of capacitive sensing and is composed of an XY graphene electrodes matrix, together acting as a sensor to locate a person coming in proximity to the material. The sensing system is coupled with active layers that can respond in real time or when needed (Figs. 4–6).

There are limitations to the length of each electrode that can be controlled. It was established that it is more efficient to have individual nodes or modules within a larger matrix (Figs. 2, 3). With the development of physical prototypes, a system acquiring high accuracy of signal and better control is created. Once the electrodes are embedded in concrete, which is a dielectric material and acts as an insulation, the sensing performance of the system increases. In terms of proximity, the tiles can sense up to 3 cm from the surface, but this range can be manually increased by placing additional electric resistance in the hardware. This system allows accurate determination of the position or proximity of an object on the floor at any given time. With this information, it is possible to determine the direction of motion of a user or conductive objects, their size, speed, and quantity (Kirova et al. 2020).

Adjusting the resolution of the matrix is linked with the traceability of pedestrians. When the resolution is increased, not only does the accuracy increase but so does the cost of production, maintenance, and energy consumption. Additionally, beyond a certain point, the precision of the system may contradict its main feature—gathering data noninvasively. When it starts providing high-resolution data, the possibilities to link patterns to individuals through computational processes become apparent.

As the system tracks users based on their interaction with the pavement surface, it is essential to space the electrodes such that all types of users can be sensed while also excluding unnecessary capacitive noise. To ensure both accuracy and privacy, the electrodes are spaced in 15 cm distances but deformed in order to decrease the distance between endpoints to 7 cm. This distance has been mainly determined based on the average human foot size. It is foreseen that the modules can become larger, and therefore with a lower resolution, in future iterations without compromising the value of the data.

Integration Strategy

The material system can be integrated within the built environment in several phases (Fig. 7). To capture enough pedestrian data and gain insights into urban fluxes, the system can be primarily installed in strategic locations. The strategy for integration in stages is meant to ease the adoption of the new technology and reduce initial costs.

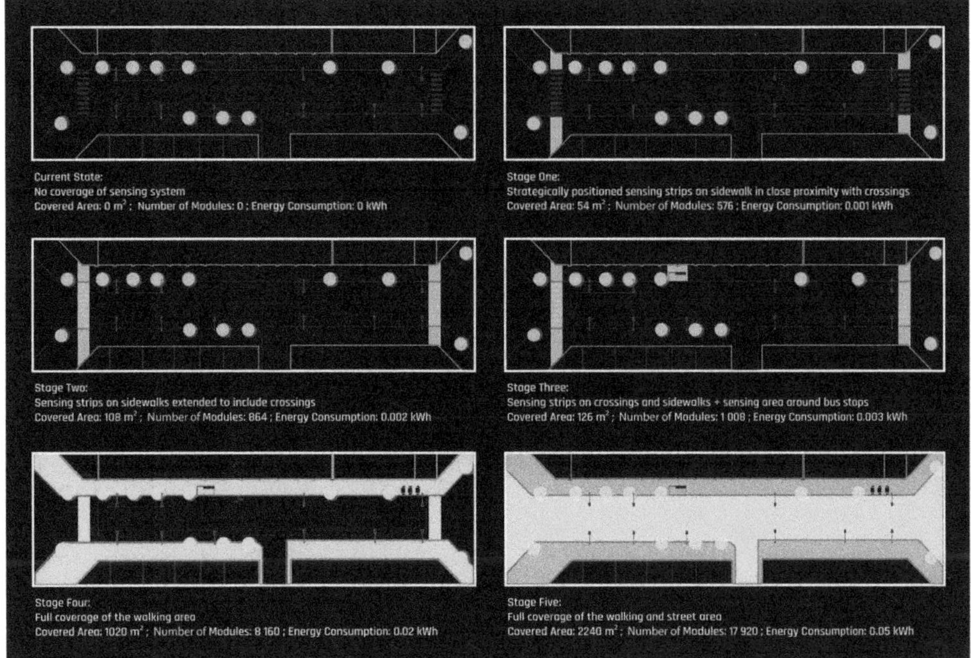

Current State:
No coverage of sensing system
Covered Area: 0 m² ; Number of Modules: 0 ; Energy Consumption: 0 kWh
Stage One:
Strategically positioned sensing strips on sidewalk in close proximity with crossings
Covered Area: 54 m² ; Number of Modules: 576 ; Energy Consumption: 0.001 kWh
Stage Two:
Sensing strips on sidewalks extended to include crossings
Covered Area: 108 m² ; Number of Modules: 864 ; Energy Consumption: 0.002 kWh
Stage Three:
Sensing strips on crossings and sidewalks + sensing area around bus stops
Covered Area: 126 m² ; Number of Modules: 1 008 ; Energy Consumption: 0.003 kWh
Stage Four:
Full coverage of the walking area
Covered Area: 1020 m² ; Number of Modules: 8 160 ; Energy Consumption: 0.02 kWh
Stage Five:
Full coverage of the walking and street area
Covered Area: 2240 m² ; Number of Modules: 17 920 ; Energy Consumption: 0.05 kWh

2 Concrete urban paving tile with embedded graphene capacitive sensor. Produced in the lab. Size: 150 × 150 mm.

3 Concrete urban paving tile with embedded graphene capacitive sensor and LED. Produced in the lab. Size: 150 × 150 mm.

4 Prototype of a matrix of sensing and actuation concrete urban paving tiles. Produced in the lab. Size: 1500 × 1500 mm.

5 Prototype of a matrix of sensing and actuation concrete urban paving tiles. Produced in the lab. Size: 1500 × 1500 mm.

6 Prototype of a matrix of sensing and actuation concrete urban paving tiles. Produced in the lab. Size: 1500 × 1500 mm.

7 Strategy for gradual integration of the smart material system into the urban fabric (in three stages).

To begin with, the process will require a minimum cost of installation while covering sufficient area to create dynamic light-emitting signage that implements changes in the mobility program. It is proposed that the crossings, which intersect the vehicular network to provide connections for pedestrians, can be used as indications for the first stage of integration. Replacing the static urban tiles with pedestrian traffic-capturing smart tiles that indicate changes in the mobility configuration aims to generate a more resilient and adaptive environment. At a later stage, the inclusion of other strategic locations, such as bus stops, building entrances, or areas of interest, would provide more data reliability.

At a mature stage of the technology adoption life cycle, it is envisioned that the entire sidewalk area will be covered with the material system. At this stage, it would be able to provide a high degree of both accuracy and engagement. Finally, proposing a liquid transition between walking and driving areas, the streets would evolve to host greater diversity of dynamically changing functions. When installed on the entire available paving surface, including sidewalks and streets, the system reaches the full extent of both monitoring and interaction with all agents in the public environment.

The material can be plugged into the electrical grid through a connection where street lamps are located. The energy consumption estimated for the system is not particularly high. As observed in strategy C, which proposes full integration in the city fabric for the urban area of 3,200 m^2 (of which 2240 m^2 have to be covered with the system), the energy consumption is estimated to be between 0.05 kWh and 170 kWh (Fig. 7). This wide range is mainly influenced by the proposed signage, which at this iteration of the research is achieved with LEDs.

The system has different impacts according to the scale on which it is applied. It is possible to integrate it over long periods by replacing existing modules (tiles) with smart tiles. Material costs would vary according to the scale of production, and a reliable estimate is not to be given at this stage of the research.

Predictive Modeling

The next step of the predictive modeling development consists of the integration of the system's collected data and the computational workflow to transform the potentially gathered data into knowledge about the public space (Fig. 8). The anonymously collected data from the graphene-based sensing floor allows extrapolation of insights about pedestrian mobility patterns, such as high density or absence of pedestrians within a specific zone and timing. To demonstrate those insights, an agent-based simulation is developed with the Unity engine (Unity Technologies 2019) to generate data similar to what the physical system would be able to provide.

The Unity environment works with 3D objects and is optimized for efficient and fast workflow in real time with complex geometries, materials, and animations. The simulation is developed based on an accurate 3D model of the study area modeled in Rhino and several scripts developed in Unity. The aim is to create an

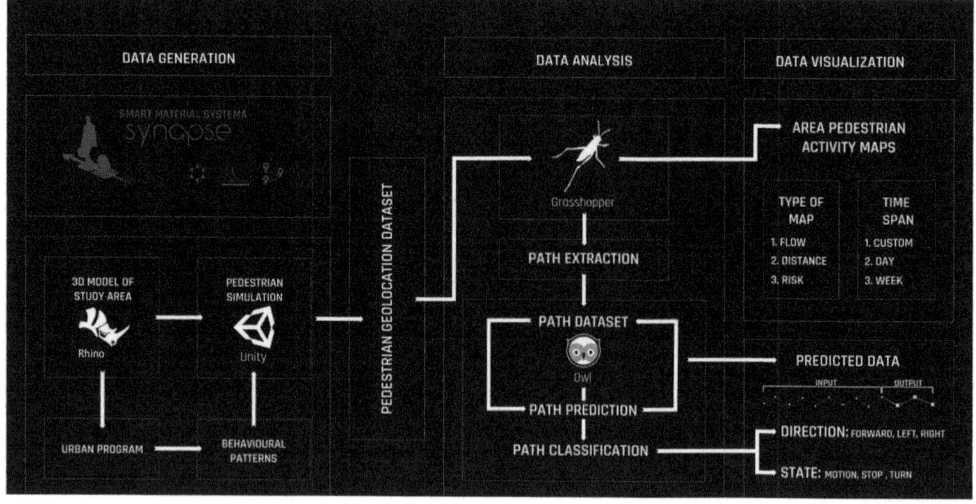

8

8 Computational workflow diagram.

9 Study area program and analysis visualization.

10 Weekly analysis and areas intervention proposal.

approximation of the pedestrian activity within the study area that requires minimal computational power and can be modified to further investigate a range of parameters. Individual agent profiles are not encoded. The programmed agent behavior is based on a logical approximation. In comparison to the simulation of motorized traffic, pedestrians are not bound to lanes or sidewalks. Pedestrian movement is influenced by both spatial configuration and the location of attractions (goals).

The pedestrian simulation is based on goal exploration, where the goals are organized and located according to the actual functions of the area. Agents move to/from and spend time on goals according to their functions. Within the simulation, agents do not have set interaction goals but follow sequential instructions. A simplified example during the workday would be going to work in the morning, followed by visiting a bar or restaurant during lunch break hours, leaving work in the afternoon, and going to a recreational or residential point in the evening. These simplified routines help achieve a certain realism to the simulated data but do not account for the unpredictability and complexity of actual pedestrian behavior. The benefits of the material system in comparison to the simulation are based on the accuracy of data, real-time monitoring of pedestrians, and guidance through light-emitting signage. Nonetheless, the simulation gives an idea of some patterns based on the spatial configuration of functions within the area that can be used to propose where a high density of pedestrian traffic is likely to occur.

To achieve a realistic walkway topology, the Navigation AI tool embedded in Unity is used. Most of the computation is internal, which makes it accessible for professionals with basic coding experience. Additionally, it allows for bidirectional and multidirectional flow to be generated. The navigation system in Unity allows us to provide powerful path-finding generating walkways for the agents with ease. The Navigation tool requires the generation of a simplified geometrical plane, referred to as navmesh. The navmesh enables characters to plot walkways around the various complex items in a scene. The navmesh agent is responsible for moving around a scene and finding paths based on the navmesh.

Through the developed simulation, the location of agents is recorded with an accuracy of one minute. The simulation ran for the period of one week and generated a data set of pedestrian activity for further analyses. The analyses are done with Rhino Grasshopper (Rutten 2020), where the data is managed, segmented, and organized into subsets. Primarily, based on individual frames, distance and density maps are combined to identify high-risk areas. Secondarily, interpolations between the frames of data are used to generate flow maps.

Individual paths are extracted based on the proximity between the recorded location points. A large data set of polylines, each made up of 10 segments or 11 points, is composed. Duplicated and similar paths are removed, creating a balanced training data set for a neural network that detects the type and relative direction of a path through classification programmed with the Owl2 plugin (Zwierzycki 2019). Furthermore, a prediction is achieved with Owl2, predicting the next three "steps" or points based on the same dataset. Predicting the angle and amplitude in order to show the possible next three points of the path is simply a proof-of-concept that path prediction with this method is attainable.

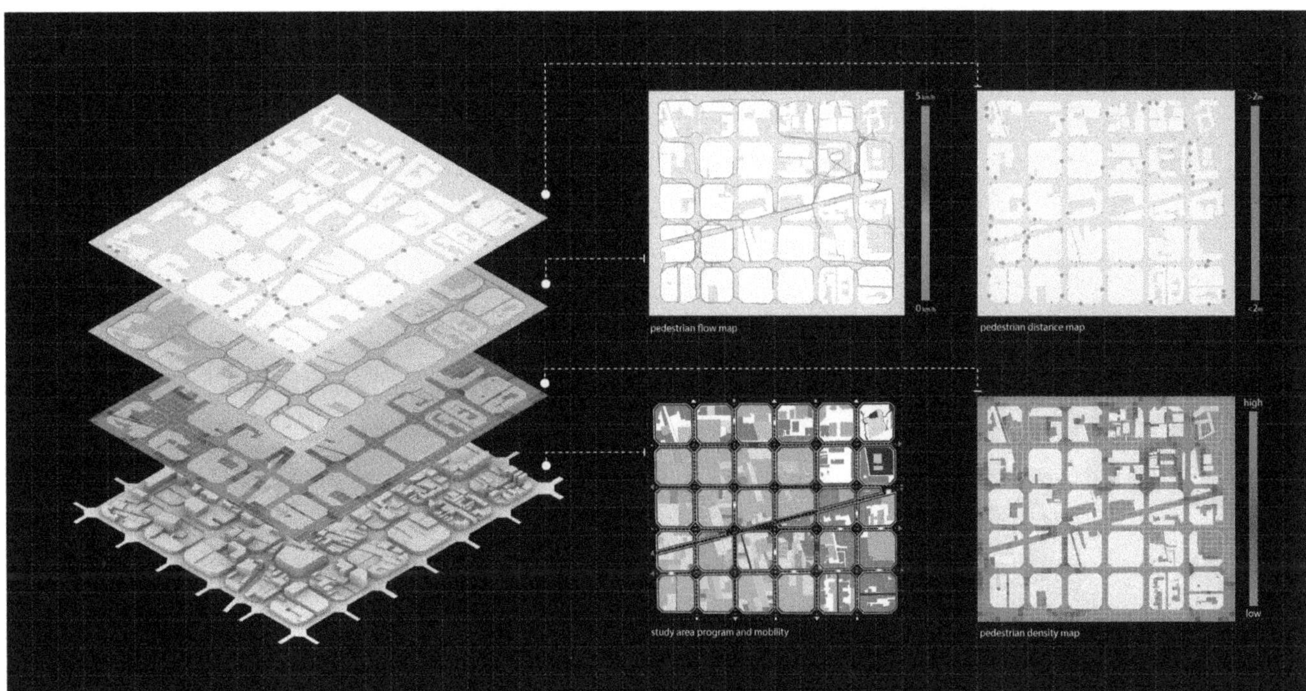

9

Monday x<2 distance

Tuesday x<2 distance

Wednesday x<2 distance

Thursday x<2 distance

Friday x<2 distance

Saturday x<2 distance

Sunday x<2 distance

Priority proposal

normally operational

pedestrian priority

Daily analysis on number of agents in less than 2m distance

One week data on risk points (x<2 distance)

Risk area map

Overlapping street directions to help identify possible interventions

10

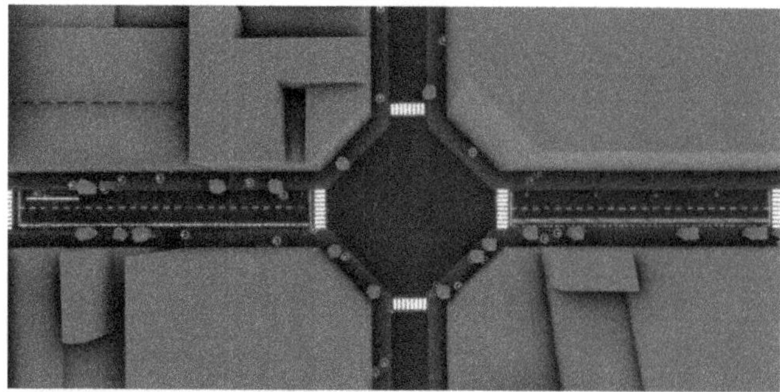

11

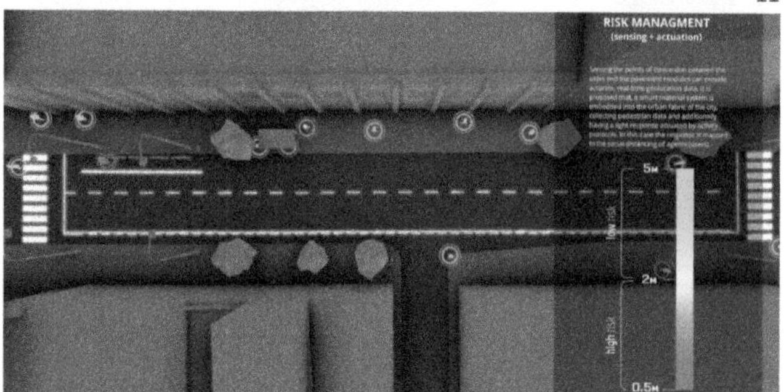

12

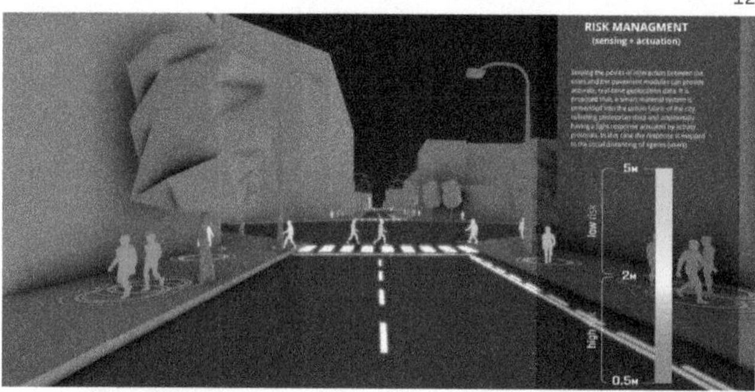

13

14

11 Top view from system demo video done in Unity showing agent dynamics and distancing.

12 Perspective view from system demo video done in Unity, showing risk management visualization.

13 Top view from system demo video done in Unity, showing risk management visualization.

14 Perspective view from system demo video done in Unity, showing potential external urban data visualization.

Case Study: Poblenou, Barcelona

The simulation is developed for a specific area familiar to the authors. The study area is 0.6 km^2, in the neighborhood of Poblenou, Barcelona (Spain). Poblenou is going through gentrification and has low but steadily increasing pedestrian activity sprawl by the emergence of office/co-working spaces, restaurants, bars, universities, and nightclubs. The area has a diverse ground-floor program with predominantly mixed-use. Based on the simulated pedestrian activity, various maps are generated to investigate how flow and density relate to the area. It is identified that there are zones with higher pedestrian traffic and density. By overlapping the simulated activity with other urban data such as land use, it becomes evident that there is a direct correlation between pedestrian density and the distribution of programs within the area. Furthermore, areas with steady and slow traffic that are linked to higher levels of transmission of airborne diseases are identified. The distance between agents at each frame is analyzed and mapped, demonstrating the range of risk zones.

Finally, in order to communicate the findings in a more visually engaging way, the Unity engine is used to create a series of animations where the diffuse color of the agents is mapped to their proximity to one another (Figs. 11–14). With the created animation it becomes clear which areas require higher risk management. Bus stops, crossings, and narrower sidewalks stood out as places where agents tend to pass within 2 m proximity. Additionally, by looking at hourly sets of data, it is observed that the zones of high pedestrian activity varies substantially. It is envisioned that if the sensing system is installed throughout the study area, the same visualization could be used for the acquired data rather than the simulated one.

Dynamic Mobility Reconfiguration

Based on the analysis of the simulated pedestrian patterns, it is evident that pedestrian behavior is dynamic and can differ depending on the time and day of the week. The unpredictability of actual pedestrian walking patterns cannot be obtained with the developed simulation. There are gaps in the data accuracy that can be filled only by actual data gained from the material system.

Nevertheless, based on the simulation, zones with high risk can be spotted and managed. The insights gained are used to identify streets where an additional pedestrian space is needed to allow safe use of the public space (Fig. 9). It is proposed that this is done by creating a dynamic mobility plan where temporal pedestrianization takes over at certain times of the day or during particular days as the density goes beyond certain limits and distancing is no longer possible. As the developed system also supports light indications and signals, it can further smooth the transition between states. Even when the system is integrated only in the crossing paths, it is possible to create sufficient indications to guide or stop traffic at certain times of the day (Fig. 10). Moving from conventional mode to pedestrian mode in an informed and flexible manner aims at the minimized disruption of road traffic without compromising public health and safety. Dynamically reconfiguring mobility plans can create a more resilient urban environment.

RESULTS AND DISCUSSION

The information acquired through the pedestrian simulation generates data similar to that which could be obtained with the material system. When the generated data set is analyzed, it conveys a correlation between spatial configuration and mobility. The in-depth data management sets the basis for predictive modeling and analytics on pedestrian spatial behavioral patterns. The absence of accurate, real-time information about an individual's spatial behavior leaves authorities and decision makers without a real space performance metric and consequently may lead to poor judgment and slow policy implementation in public space management and design. The research foresees that the creation of a system that combines hardware (sensing pavement system) with software (pedestrian flows predictive modeling) can be used both as a tool for real-time monitoring and as a planning tool enforcing spatial resilience.

Moving beyond monitoring, the research aims to challenge our understanding of how public space is occupied and how it could start adapting to a new set of spatial restrictions such as public health. The spatial distancing measures that have been implemented during the pandemic have shown the necessity of having a more connected and engaging urban environment.

The system can be used to inform temporary changes in public space. Through the identification of areas where distancing is not possible, risk zones where intervention is needed can be located. Such interventions are associated with but not limited to wider pavements for a more pedestrian-friendly environment that can lead to less noise and air pollution, greener space, and more adaptive street programs. Surface-based pedestrian monitoring can inform a dynamically adaptive public space typology where the balance between vehicle and pedestrian priority shifts according to the needs and the observed spatiotemporal patterns (Fig. 1). The analysis of the simulated data shows common patterns in density during morning and evening hours as well as higher pedestrian density on some streets than others. It is proposed that these streets are suitable for a transition between priority modes (Fig. 10).

CONCLUSION

The smart urban tile developed by the researchers is able to gather data on pedestrian activity when applied as a paving material in the public space. The developed system manages to monitor pedestrian behavior in real time with a nonprivacy-invasive method through surface-based capacitive sensing rather than GPS tracking or camera monitoring. As the material system is still under development, the capabilities of the technology are demonstrated through an urban pedestrian simulation. The Unity game engine and Rhino Grasshopper are used to generate and analyze pedestrian traffic. The demonstration is situated in the Poblenou neighborhood (Barcelona). Through the use of a case study, the research aims to communicate the value of using pedestrian flows in the design and decision-making process.

The changes in the use of the public space that occurred in the past year have opened a niche for alternative measures for health and safety alongside real-time monitoring and engagement. In states of emergency such as the COVID-19 pandemic, the developed system can be used to minimize risk within the public space without infringing on civil liberties or causing social segregation. The key benefits of using surface-based sensing, aside from the real-time data-acquiring capabilities, are its socially inclusive nature and seamless integration within the existing urban materiality. The system acts as a physical interface that can improve pedestrian engagement and information. In this way, the system contributes to the comfort, guidance, and personal privacy that inhabitants should be provided within the urban realm.

The visualized data representing simulated spatiotemporal pedestrian behavior exposes the benefits and value of an alternative real-time urban flow monitoring system. By recording traces of footsteps, the system can provide accurate, anonymous large-scale spatiotemporal information that becomes the base for dynamic density, flow and distance maps, trend prediction, and in-depth understanding of pedestrian behavior. The information could become particularly valuable when coupled with existing urban information such as land use, environmental, and mobility data. This paper covers the benefits of the sensing tool as well as setting up the basis for a computational workflow that could eventually support informed decision-making and a more adaptive urban environment. The computational workflow is effective in terms of data mapping and determining risk areas based on the simulated input data. The pedestrian activity simulation is to be further developed to include a wider range of agents in the urban traffic and an intervention-verification phase. Furthermore, the future steps of the research will focus on predictive modeling and trend extraction based on a more in-depth analysis of pedestrian paths.

ACKNOWLEDGMENTS

The research was initiated in the "Digital Matter" research studio of the master of advanced architecture at the Institute of Advanced Architecture of Catalonia. The initial student team included Hayder Mahdi and Shruti Jalodia. The research has received support at various stages of its development from Angelos Chronis, David Andres Leon, Raimund Krenmueller, Mateusz Zwierzycki, Ashkan Foroughi, Daniil Koshelyuk, and Rosen Rusinov.

REFERENCES

Akhmareh, A. Ramezani, M. Lazarescu, O. Bin Tariq, and L. Lavagno. 2016. "A Tagless Indoor Localization System Based on Capacitive Sensing Technology." *Sensors* 16 (9): 1448.

Alter, L. 2020. "Urban Design after the Coronavirus." *Treehugger*, April 8. https://www.treehugger.com/urban-design/urban-design-after-coronavirus.html.

Arshad, A., S. Khan, and R. Tasnim. 2017. "Simple Capacitive Floor Occupancy Sensor for Determining the Pattern of a Walking Person." *4th IEEE International Conference on Engineering Technologies and Applied Sciences (ICETAS), Salmabad*, 1–4. https://www.doi.org/10.1109/ICETAS.2017.8277879.

Bliss, L. 2020. "Mapping How Cities Are Reclaiming Street Space." *CityLab*, April 3. https://www.citylab.com/transportation/2020/04/coronavirus-city-street-public-transit-bike-lanes-covid-19/609190/.

Council of the European Union and European Parliament. 2016. "Regulation (EU) 2016/679 of the European Parliament and of the Council of 27 April 2016 on the protection of natural persons with regard to the processing of personal data and on the free movement of such data, and repealing Directive 95/46/EC (General Data Protection Regulation)." OJ L 119, April 27, 1–88. https://op.europa.eu/en/publication-detail/-/publication/3e485e15-11bd-11e6-ba9a-01aa75ed71a1/language-en/format-PDF/source-search.

EFE. 2020. "Milán le quitará al coche 35 km de carriles para dárselos a la bici y el peatón." *El Periódico*, April 21.

Goodman, D. H. 2015. "Aware Surfaces: Large-Scale, Surface-Based Sensing for New Modes of Data Collection, Analysis, and Human Interaction." Thesis, MIT School of Architecture and Planning, Program in Media Arts and Sciences. https://dspace.mit.edu/handle/1721.1/98643.

Hack, G. 2016. "Hearst Lecture: Gary Hack—Disruptive Changes and the Pattern of Cities." *Focus* 14 (1). https://digitalcommons.calpoly.edu/focus/vol14/iss1/9.

Hawkins, A.J. 2020. "There's No Better Time for Cities to Take Space Away from Cars." *The Verge*, March 23. https://www.theverge.com/2020/3/23/21191325/cities-car-free-coronavirus-protected-bike-lanes-air-quality-social-distancing.

Jansen, A. M., E. Giebels, T. van Rompay, and M. Junger. 2018. "The Influence of the Presentation of Camera Surveillance on Cheating and Pro-Social Behavior." *Frontiers in Psychology* 9: 1937. https://doi.org/10.3389/fpsyg.2018.01937.

Kim, M.S. 2020. "Seoul's Radical Experiment in Digital Contact Tracing." *New Yorker*, April 17. https://www.newyorker.com/news/news-desk/seouls-radical-experiment-in-digital-contact-tracing.

Kirova N., Markopoulou A., Mahdi H., Jalodia S. 2020. "A Smart Material System for Real-Time Urban Flow Data Collection Toward Responsive Environments and Informed Decision Making in Urban Spaces." *Impact: Design With All Senses*. DMSB 2019. Cham: Springer. https://doi.org/10.1007/978-3-030-29829-6_54.

Markopoulou, A., and C. Farinea. 2016. "Forward Urbanism in the Experience Age." In *Responsive Cities International Symposium Proceedings*, 7–8. Institute for Advanced Architecture of Catalonia.

Martani, C., S. Simon, A. Sinan, S. Kenichi, B. Dean, and J. Ying. 2017. "Pedestrian Monitoring Techniques For Crowd-Flow Prediction." *Proceedings of the Institution of Civil Engineers—Smart Infrastructure And Construction* 170 (2): 17–27. https://www.doi.org/10.1680/jsmic.17.00001.

Ramezani, A., M. Lazarescu, O. Bin Tariq, and L. Lavagno. 2016. "A Tagless Indoor Localization System Based on Capacitive Sensing Technology." *Sensors* 16: (9): 1448.

Rutten, David. 2020. *Grasshopper*. V.1.0.0007. Robert McNeel & Associates. PC.

Topham, Gwyn. 2020. "London Pedestrians and Cyclists May Get More Space on Roads." The Guardian, April 14, 2020. https://www.theguardian.com/uk-news/2020/apr/14/london-pedestrians-and-cyclist-may-get-more-space-on-roads-during-coronavirus-lockdown.

Unity Technologies. 2019. *Unity*. V.2019.0.1. https://unity.com/. PC.

WHO. 2020. "Global Surveillance for Human Infection with Coronavirus Disease (COVID-19): Interim Guidance." World Health Organization, January 31, 2020. https://apps.who.int/iris/handle/10665/330857.

Zwierzycki, Mateusz. 2019. *Owl*. V.2.1. https://www.food4rhino.com/en/app/owl. PC.

Nikol Kirova is an interdisciplinary Bulgarian architect with an educational background in interior design, urban planning, and advanced architecture. Currently, Nikol is a teaching assistant and a researcher at IAAC. She is developing a PhD focusing on design and construction with carbon-sequestering by-products. The common feature of her work is the search for alternative solutions for optimized construction, material-informed design, and spatial communication.

Areti Markopoulou is a Greek architect, researcher, and urban technologist working at the intersection between architecture and digital technologies. She is the Academic Director at IAAC in Barcelona, where she also leads the Advanced Architecture Group, a multidisciplinary research group exploring how design and science can positively impact and transform the present and future of our built spaces, the way we live and interact. Her research and practice focus on redefining the architecture of cities through an ecological and technological spectrum combining design with biotechnologies, new materials, digital fabrication, and big data.

BIM-Based Automatic Contact Tracing System Using Wi-Fi

Wonjae Yoo
Texas A&M University

Hyoungsub Kim
Ajou University

Minjae Shin
Hanyang University, ERICA

Mark J. Clayton
Texas A&M University

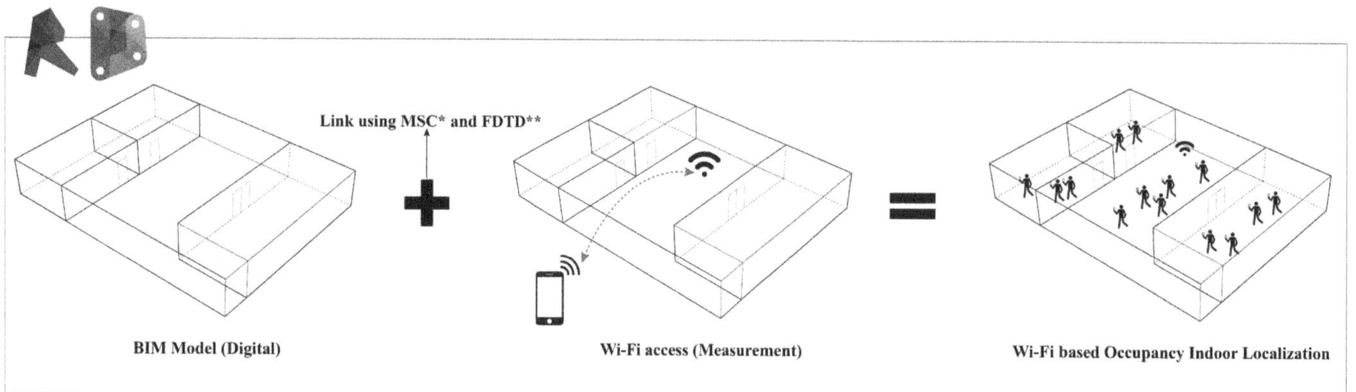

1 Graphical concept of the stations-oriented indoor localization (SOIL) system.

ABSTRACT

This study presents a BIM-based automatic contact tracing method using a stations-oriented indoor localization (SOIL) system. The SOIL system integrates BIM models and existing network infrastructure (i.e., Wi-Fi), using a clustering method to generate room-level occupancy schedules. In this study, we improve the accuracy of the SOIL system by including more detailed Wi-Fi signal travel sources, such as reflection, refraction, and diffraction. The results of field measurements in an educational building show that the SOIL system was able to produce room-level occupant location information with a 95.6% level of accuracy. This outcome is 2.6% more accurate than what was found in a previous study. We also describe an implementation of the SOIL system for conducting contact tracing in large buildings. When an individual is confirmed to have COVID-19, public health professionals can use this system to quickly generate information regarding possible contacts. The greatest strength of this SOIL implementation is that it has wide applicability in large-scale buildings, without the need for additional sensing devices. Additional tests using buildings with multiple floors are required to further explore the robustness of the system.

INTRODUCTION

The COVID-19 pandemic caused more than 2,000 deaths daily in the US, in early April 2020 alone (Danilchev 2020). The world crisis has highlighted the need to track COVID-19 cases, to prevent further transmission and death (Günther, Günther, and Günther 2020). In the early stages of the pandemic, there were fewer cases. At that point, it was possible to conduct manual contact tracing. However, with the exponentially increasing number of infected, an automatic contact tracing system has become necessary.

Several studies have suggested that sensing techniques (e.g., Bluetooth, Wi-Fi) could be applied to indoor contact tracing (Trivedi et al. 2020). Such research has assumed that occupants always carry smartphones that transmit signals to receivers. Received signals are then used to localize occupants and help determine who may have been in close proximity to the infected individual. However, these indoor localization techniques face challenges in terms of scalability. For example, a Bluetooth approach requires additional actions, such as installing a smartphone app and deploying beacons inside buildings (Basiri et al. 2017). Indoor localization based on Wi-Fi has been shown to be well-suited for large-scale buildings, relying solely on existing infrastructure (Yoo, Kim, and Shin 2020; Trivedi et al. 2020; Li et al. 2014). However, both approaches require further investigation on a sensing area for an offline survey, which can take months when applied to multiple large-scale buildings.

New interdisciplinary approaches to building information modeling (BIM) use have combined BIM and sensing techniques for facility management and construction monitoring purposes (Ghaffarianhoseini et al. 2017; Tang et al. 2019; Dave et al. 2018). Non-graphic data and 3D geometric objects encapsulated in BIM have been used to expand sensor-based localization studies. Li et al. (2014) and Yoo et al. (2020) utilized BIM to retrieve geospatial information of buildings and localized occupants based on time-series Wi-Fi data. Although these studies provided direction for using BIM for contact tracing in large buildings, the method's applicability in actual practice is still in question. For example, the approach used in Yoo et al. (2020) estimated Wi-Fi signal propagation using a signal path loss method, neglecting other signal propagation sources such as reflection. However, large-scale buildings are more complex in their signal propagation, due to the presence of multiple floors, furnishings, and ceiling materials, often resulting in inaccurate indoor localization results. Thus, more detailed signal propagation sources must be analyzed in multiple spaces during the indoor localization process in order to increase the accuracy of the results.

This research presents an automatic contact tracing system using the stations-oriented indoor localization (SOIL) system introduced in Yoo et al. (2020), along with detailed Wi-Fi signal propagation sources. Based on physical region information (e.g., the coordinates of a space) and building component data (e.g., material type and thickness) in a BIM model, the SOIL system can simulate Wi-Fi propagation using the electromagnetic field prediction method called the finite-difference time-domain (FDTD) algorithm. In the present research, simulation results were compared with actual Wi-Fi signals transmitted from occupants of an educational building. The robustness of the room-level indoor localization outcomes represented a successful combination of Wi-Fi-based localization and BIM, and offer increased scalability for contact tracing in large-scale buildings.

BACKGROUND

Indoor occupancy detection

Reliable and affordable indoor localization techniques are necessary for contact tracing applications. Achieving scalability to large-scale buildings is the most difficult aspect, and currently an obstacle to broad adoption for contact tracing purposes. In this section, we focus on two widely used indoor localization techniques, Bluetooth low energy (BLE) and Wi-Fi, to identify limitations inhibiting scalability.

BLE is an emerging technology driven by the need for continuous interfacing with low power sensors. Due to its minimal power requirements and extended period of operation (e.g., several months), BLE could be deployed throughout a building for indoor occupancy detection (Davidson and Piché 2017; Faragher and Harle 2015; Park, Dougherty, and Nagy 2018). Bluetooth devices within the range of deployed Bluetooth beacons connect to such beacons, establishing wireless communication between the two. However, BLE has a relatively low detection range compared to Wi-Fi, typically less than 20 m (Basiri et al. 2017). The short range of detection makes BLE a device-based occupancy detection approach. Thus, denser deployment would be required inside buildings for the purpose of indoor localization (Budina et al. 2015; Davidson and Piché 2017). A deployment plan determining the correct position of each beacon would be necessary for each building in order to adequately cover the sensing area of interest (Budina et al. 2015). In this context, BLE is difficult to apply in large buildings. Conversely, Wi-Fi uses existing infrastructure communication services. Due to its ubiquitous availability in commercial and residential

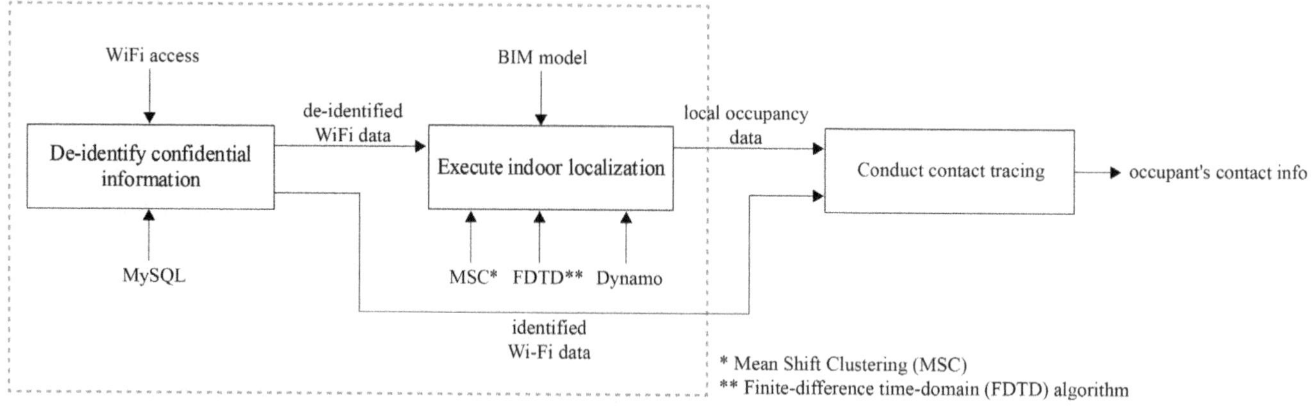

2 Conceptual framework for contact tracing system.

environments, Wi-Fi-based indoor localization could be used in a variety of circumstances and with greater accessibility.

Both BLE and Wi-Fi use the received signal strength indicator (RSSI) as a range measurement to estimate the locations of occupants. The RSSI is typically collected through a receiver, as a metric of signal link quality. In general, a higher RSSI indicates that a signal transmitter (i.e., a smartphone) is closer to a signal receiver, helping the practitioner estimate the locations of occupants carrying signal transmitters. However, the RSSI is significantly affected by the surrounding environment, resulting in signal attenuation and reflection and consequent location estimation errors. Thus, RSSI fingerprinting has become widely used among indoor localization approaches adopting BLE or Wi-Fi (Mendoza-Silva, Torres-Sospedra, and Huerta 2019).

The fingerprinting method has two phases: offline and online (He and Chan 2016). The offline phase, referred to as the training phase, records the RSSI based on a site survey. A practitioner visits each reference point for known locations and collects RSSI vectors for all signals detected from signal receivers. Then, the reference points and RSSI vectors are stored in a database for the online phase. During the online phase, Wi-Fi and BLE measurement data are collected to determine occupant locations. A localization system then compares similarities in measurement data with offline survey data and locates the transmitter at the nearest neighbor reference point. However, the fingerprinting approach requires a laborious offline survey of each site. This work could take months if used for multiple large-scale buildings. Therefore, a new approach that would reduce the burden of the offline survey portion and increase the scalability to broader scenarios is needed for the purposes of universal contact tracing.

Synergy of building information modeling and sensing technology

The use of BIM in the fields of architecture, engineering, and construction (AEC) has offered various benefits to adopters, including designers, contractors, and owners (Fountain and Langar 2018). BIM allows the user to characterize a building's geospatial information in an accurate 3D virtual environment (Ghaffarianhoseini et al. 2017). In the US, 72% of new buildings constructed in the last 10 years adopted BIM (Fountain and Langar 2018) and 96% of large firms were using BIM by 2016 (American Institute of Architects 2016). This trend in BIM adoption will continue in all AEC industries (Fountain and Langar 2018).

The combination of BIM with the Internet of Things (IoT) offers significant changes and benefits to construction monitoring, health and safety management, and facility management (Tang et al. 2019). For example, indoor localization systems can generate well-informed occupancy data that can be used in occupancy-based HVAC operation, enhancing energy management (Capozzoli et al. 2017). In emergency situations (e.g., building fires), room-level occupancy information is crucial to the quick navigation and rescue routing necessary to save human lives (Sergi et al. 2020; Li et al. 2014). In a construction environment, indoor localization and visualization techniques provide workers with warnings in hazardous situations and manage construction processes by tracking the locations of tagged materials (Fang et al. 2016). These approaches have great potential to extend BIM implementation to data-driven smart city management, facilitating a sustainable built environment through data sharing between BIM and the Geographic Information System (Wang, Pan, and Luo 2019).

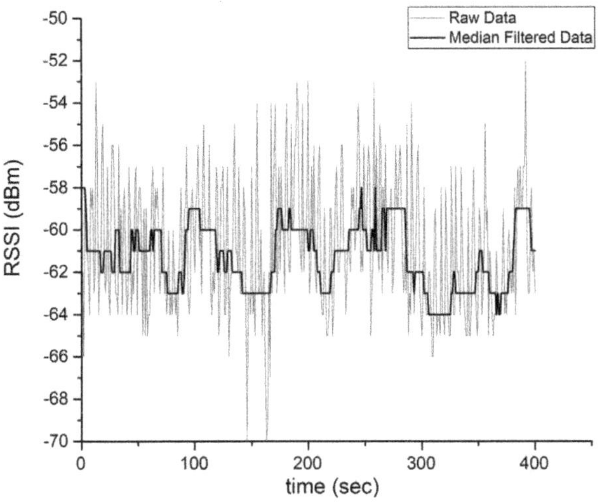

3 Results of the median filtering of raw RSSI data

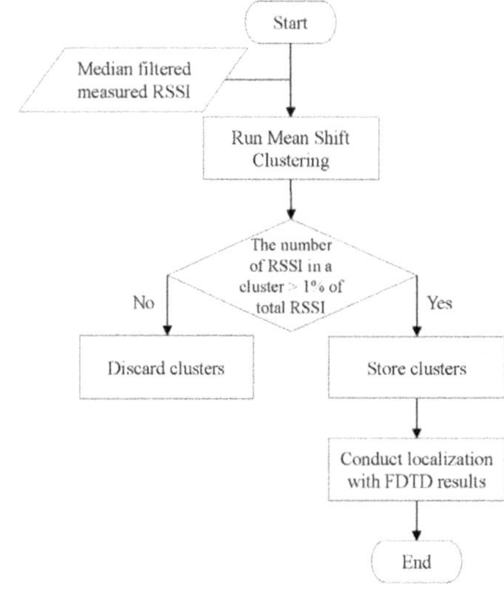

4 Data processing flow for signal sorting and indoor localization. 4

METHOD

The contact tracing system was developed using Dynamo, a visual programming tool in Autodesk Revit (Autodesk 2021). The present research employed the SOIL system introduced in Yoo et al. (2020), improving its accuracy to secure applicability in practice (i.e., in large-scale buildings) (Yoo et al. 2020). The SOIL system detects occupants' presence at the room level via Wi-Fi and a BIM model. The system employs the BIM model as a digital map to replace the offline survey used in the fingerprinting approach. In this process, stations (e.g., chair, sofa) in a BIM model are regarded as reference points to estimate the locations of sedentary occupants. We only adopted signals from sedentary occupants for indoor localization because they would have a relatively longer exposure time to an infected individual. Also, the signals offer less variation and noise, leading to a higher level of accuracy for localization.

Mainly, the SOIL system uses a signal path loss approach to estimate the RSSI for each reference point, and links it to measured Wi-Fi data to determine occupant locations. The current SOIL system does not consider signal travel sources such as reflection, refraction, and diffraction. Thus, the present study adopted the electromagnetic field prediction method called the FDTD algorithm to include the various signal travel sources that need to be considered in large and complex buildings. The improved SOIL system relies on Wi-Fi signals alone, so most commercial buildings can use this system to conduct contact tracing and analyze the locations of individuals who shared the same room at the same time with an infected individual. Figure 2 illustrates the overall data flow for this study, which included three major steps: 1) data preparation, 2) indoor localization, and 3) contact tracing.

Data preparation

The system collects Wi-Fi data, especially the RSSI and media access point (MAC) addresses, through the wireless infrastructure. A MAC address is a unique identifier assigned to smart devices by the manufacturer. In the present research, once a MAC address was collected, it was de-identified with random numbers and linked to falsified user identification to confirm the owner of the Wi-Fi-accessed device.

We pre-processed the collected Wi-Fi RSSI for use in the indoor localization algorithm. Median filtering (MF) was first conducted to remove the signal noise. MF is a method for minimizing the sum of the absolute values of the errors by replacing each sample with the median of neighboring samples (Boles, Kanefsky, and Simaan 1990). The outcome of the MF process is shown in Figure 3.

Mean shift clustering (MSC) was then performed to sort the signals into two groups: signals obtained while occupants were sedentary, and signals obtained while occupants were moving (Fig. 4). The system separated clusters into different groups based on the number of RSSIs. If the cluster had less than 1% of the total number of collected RSSIs, the system regarded it as a cluster composed of signals obtained while occupants were moving. Then, the system removed the clusters from the database and analyzed the remaining clusters for localization. MSC is a non-parametric clustering method introduced by Fukunaga and Hostetler (1975). It forms clusters iteratively for discrete samples underlying a feature space. This study utilized the characteristic of the MSC algorithm, which makes clusters without prior knowledge of the number of clusters. In this system, each cluster represented an RSSI

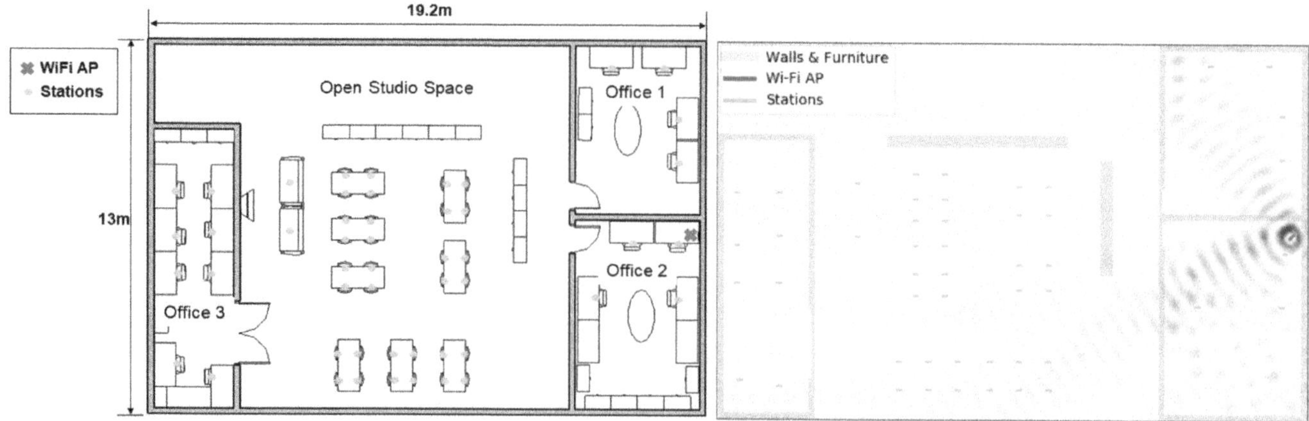

5 Test case BIM model (left) and FDTD simulation result for Wi-Fi propagation prediction (right).

group transmitted from Wi-Fi-accessed devices at the same station in the field. Since the number of signal groups varied depending on the number of occupants and occupied stations, the system adopted MSC to adapt to such an environment.

Indoor localization

In the localization system, the FDTD algorithm was used for electromagnetic field prediction. FDTD is a computational modeling approach used to solve Maxwell's equation while showing the Wi-Fi signal field distribution (Gorce, Jaffrès-Runser, and de la Roche 2007). Specifically, a 2D formulation was used in the present study because of the low computational cost; the area of interest was assumed to be infinite along the vertical direction.

The FDTD simulation required specific characteristics of the building elements for Wi-Fi coverage prediction. A BIM model provided a physical region and material type and thickness information for the experiment area to the FDTD simulation. The dielectric parameters associated with each material were stored in the system. Once the system retrieved a material type from the BIM model, it built a computational domain with the associated dielectric parameters. Thus, the simulation was able to predict Wi-Fi coverage by adapting to the environment, effectively increasing the scalability of indoor localization.

The FDTD was implemented on a uniform grid of the experiment area. Once the Wi-Fi access point (AP) was placed on a grid cell of the computational domain, the discretized electric and magnetic field distribution was calculated on the cell using time-dependent Maxwell's equations. Then, the information could travel to the neighboring grid cells. The electric field intensity was obtained for each grid through sufficient iterations (i.e., 1,000) and a Fourier transform was applied at an operating frequency of 5 GHz.

The 5GHz Wi-Fi frequency was selected (as opposed to 2.4 GHz) because the shorter wavelength allowed for greater discrimination from room to room through the observable differences in electric intensity. These observable differences led to a higher level of indoor localization accuracy (Yoo, Kim, and Shin 2020).

Once the electric field intensity was obtained, the local mean intensity (l) could be computed at each reference point (i.e., station) to remove the signal's small-scale fading effects, per the following equation:

$$l\,(\mathrm{m},\mathrm{n}) = \frac{1}{N^2}\sum_{m'=m-\frac{N-1}{2}}^{m'=m+\frac{N-1}{2}}\sum_{n'=n-\frac{N-1}{2}}^{n'=n+\frac{N-1}{2}}|E(m',n')|^2 \tag{1}$$

where N is the number of samples (in this study, three), m is the x-coordinate of a station, n is the y-coordinate of a station, and E is the electric field intensity.

Then, the local mean intensity (l) was stored in the database for the localization process. Similar to in other FDTD studies (Gorce, Jaffrès-Runser, and de la Roche 2007), the present research assumed that the RSSI was approximately proportional to the electric field intensity. Once the RSSI measurement data were obtained and processed for data preparation, a nearest neighbor linkage process was performed. The shortest distance from the pre-processed RSSI to the local mean intensity at a reference point determined the location of the device. The system assumed that the location of the Wi-Fi-accessed device was the location of the occupant. The localization results, including de-identified MAC addresses and measured times, were then stored in the system, ready to be reidentified for contact tracing.

Contact tracing implementation

Upon identifying that a COVID-19 positive individual occupied the building, a public health professional could run the proposed system to reidentify occupant data and

Indoor Localization Results

Date	Time (hh:mm:ss)	Randomized ID	Estimated Location
20190401	11:57:00	1	Open Studio Space
		3	Open Studio Space
		10	Open Studio Space
		2	Open Studio Space
		9	Office 3
		6	Office 2
		7	Office 2
	11:57:30	1	Open Studio Space
		3	Open Studio Space
		10	Open Studio Space
		2	Open Studio Space
		9	Office 3
		6	Office 2
		7	Office 2
...	...	...	...

Contact Tracing for ID #1

ID	Date	Time	Estimated Location	Possible Contacts
#1	20190401	11:00 – 12:32	Open Studio Space	#3, #10, #2
	20190402	...	...	...
	⋮			

Contact Tracing Final Form

ID	Contact Info	Likely Exposure Time	Date
#3	abc@de.com	92 min	20190401
#10	⋮	⋮	⋮
⋮			

6 Example of the localization results and contact tracing process.

Table 1 Material Properties and Parameters for FDTD Simulation

Material	Relative Dielectric Constant (ϵ_r)	Conductivity ($\sigma[S/m]$)
Wood Wall	2.5	0.08
Metal Furniture	1	10,000,000
Door	1.5	0
Air	1	0

FDTD Parameter	Value
Cell Size	0.1 m
Courant Number	0.7
Number of Iterations	7,000
Frequency	5 GHz

Table 2 Confusion Matrix for Indoor Localization Results

Total True Positive Accuracy: 95.6%	Estimated: Office 1	Estimated: Office 2	Estimated: Office 3	Estimated: Open Studio Space
Actual: Office 1	104	7	0	3
Actual: Office 2	0	102	0	0
Actual: Office 3	0	0	78	3
Actual: Open Studio Space	8	2	13	498

generate contact tracing forms. In this process, individuals' physical locations would be excluded and the infected patient's identity concealed to preserve privacy. The period of investigation would begin four days before the onset of symptoms and end at the date of COVID-19 confirmation. The system can determine the likely time of exposure to an infected individual based on the indoor localization results. In a default setting, the system would include people on the contact tracing form when the likely exposure time exceeded 15 minutes. The period of investigation and exposure time can also be manipulated by a public health professional to the extent of the available data (e.g., up to 10 seconds in the current setting).

RESULTS

We conducted the indoor localization test case in the Earnest Langford Architecture Center at Texas A&M University in College Station, Texas. Based on the localization results, the system generated a sample contact tracing form. The data were collected every 10 s from one part of the building for a week (Fig. 5). The dimensions of the area were 13 m x 19.2 m (length x width). We placed a Wi-Fi AP in Office 2 for the test. During the experiment period, 26 subjects connected one of their smart devices to the Wi-Fi AP. For the validation of the proposed method, the ground truth locations of occupants were assigned to Wi-Fi data based through an investigation on academic room schedules and Wi-Fi connection times.

The results of the FDTD simulation implemented in Dynamo Revit are shown in Figure 5. The dielectric properties of the materials and parameters used for the FDTD simulation are summarized in Table 1. The occupancy analysis for room-level has a less sensitivity to the FDTD results; therefore, human bodies and mechanical components such as an electrical wiring that may affect FDTD results are neglected in this study for the low computational cost. In Figure 5 (right), the color intensity of the wave represents the Wi-Fi signal strength. The simulation results show a Wi-Fi propagation that attenuates, reflects, refracts, and diffracts after meeting BIM elements (e.g., walls and furniture). After running the simulation, local mean intensities at stations were calculated and linked to the field-obtained RSSIs to determine the locations of occupants.

Table 2 shows the confusion matrix for the indoor localization results. The numbers in Table 2 represent the number of occupants counted every 15 minutes during the experiment. As described in Indoor localization Section, the estimated locations were determined by the linkage process of the measured signal strengths to the FDTD simulation results. The true positive accuracy indicates the proportion of correct room-level estimations across all estimations obtained through comparisons with ground truth occupants' locations (i.e., gray cells in Table 2); the system achieved a 95.6% total true positive accuracy across all spaces. The testing completed with FDTD illustrates the robustness of SOIL, as compared to the results of a previous study (Yoo, Kim, and Shin 2020) that achieved a 93% level of accuracy.

Figure 6 is an example of the localization outcome and contact tracing form generated by the system. Once ID #1 is confirmed to have COVID-19, a public health professional could run the SOIL system and reidentify the data to quickly trace possible contacts.

DISCUSSION

The SOIL system contributes to the field of public health, as well as building technology. The main benefit of the SOIL system is its applicability to large-scale buildings through the use of Wi-Fi and FDTD simulation. The FDTD simulation estimates a Wi-Fi signal at each station on a BIM model, replacing the conventional laborious RSSI fingerprinting process. Thus, the proposed approach allows the system to conduct indoor localization while adapting to a space layout in a building, allowing public health professionals to investigate contacts in multiple buildings.

It is worth noting that SOIL assumes that each person connects to Wi-Fi using only one smart device. This assumption may cause severe errors when it comes to occupancy counting, if occupants connect multiple devices to Wi-Fi APs in a natural field setting. In a future study, we will adopt a pattern recognition algorithm to consider similar RSSI patterns to be one device, reducing potential occupancy count errors caused by multiple smart devices.

The SOIL approach uses stations as reference points to estimate the locations of occupants. Hence, the system only considers sedentary occupants, sorting RSSIs using the MSC algorithm. Both sedentary and moving occupants have the potential to be exposed to viral transmission. However, based on the observations in Yoo et al. (2020), occupants' movement time spent traveling corridors is generally less than 1% of the total time spent in a building, especially in educational structures. Moreover, the Center for Disease Control and Prevention (CDC) defines close contact as "any individual within 6 feet of an infected person for a total of 15 minutes or more" (CDC 2020). Upon these findings, we concluded that the SOIL system could deliver a reasonable outcome for contact tracing by considering sedentary occupants.

Although this study adopted the 2D FDTD algorithm for its low computational cost, the system showed a robust result when estimating occupants' locations on a single floor, using one Wi-Fi AP. In a future study, we will collect Wi-Fi data from a multi-floor environment and multiple Wi-Fi APs. Wi-Fi signals may penetrate floors and ceilings and reach devices on other floors, causing localization errors. Hence, further investigation is required to evaluate the performance of 2D FDTD in future test cases. Comparisons between 2D and 3D FDTD approaches in terms of computational cost and localization accuracy are worthwhile because they are likely to increase the reliability of the system in large-scale buildings.

CONCLUSION

This study introduces an automatic contact tracing system using Wi-Fi and BIM. We adopted the SOIL system with the FDTD method to simulate Wi-Fi signal propagation, overcoming limitations in the conventional laborious fingerprinting approach. A BIM model provided material type and thickness information and the coordinates of the experimental area to the FDTD simulation, establishing a computational domain. The SOIL system was tested in an educational building for indoor localization and contact tracing form generation. The results show that the system can localize occupants with a 95.6% level of accuracy, allowing for reliable contact tracing .

Although the test was limited to a single floor, this approach shows the potential applicability to large-scale buildings by considering more signal propagation sources. In a future study, testing will be conducted in a multi-floor environment with more natural field settings, allowing occupants to use multiple smart devices. Further development of the SOIL system will increase its applicability to areas related to occupancy analysis, such as space programming and energy management.

REFERENCES

American Institute of Architects. 2016. "The Business of Architecture 2016: AIA Firm Report." Washington, DC.

Autodesk. *Dynamo*. V.2.10. Autodesk. PC. 2021.

Basiri, Anahid, Elena Simona Lohan, Terry Moore, Adam Winstanley, Pekka Peltola, Chris Hill, Pouria Amirian, and Pedro Figueiredo e Silva. 2017. "Indoor Location Based Services Challenges, Requirements and Usability of Current Solutions." *Computer Science Review* 24: 1–12.

Boles, W. W., M. Kanefsky, and M. Simaan. 1990. "A Reduced Edge Distortion Median Filtering Algorithm for Binary Images." *Signal Processing* 21 (1): 37–47.

Budina, Jan, Ondrej Klapka, Tomas Kozel, and Martin Zmitko. 2015. "Method of IBeacon Optimal Distribution for Indoor Localization In Modeling and Using Context." *Lecture Notes in Computer Science. Vol. 9405*, edited by Christiansen H., Stojanovic I., Papadopoulos G. Cham: Springer.

Capozzoli, Alfonso, Marco Savino Piscitelli, Alice Gorrino, Ilaria Ballarini, and Vincenzo Corrado. 2017. "Data Analytics for Occupancy Pattern Learning to Reduce the Energy Consumption of HVAC Systems in Office Buildings." *Sustainable Cities and Society* 35 (July): 191–208.

CDC. 2020. "Contact Tracing for COVID-19." Centers for Disease Control and Prevention. 2020. https://www.cdc.gov/coronavirus/2019-ncov/php/contact-tracing/contact-tracing-plan/contact-tracing.html.

Danilchev, Maria. 2020. "COVID-19 Daily Deaths vs. Top 15 Causes of Death (Average/Day) in the US. 2020." 2020. https://public.flourish.studio/visualisation/1727839/.

Dave, Bhargav, Andrea Buda, Antti Nurminen, and Kary Främling. 2018. "A Framework for Integrating BIM and IoT through Open Standards." *Automation in Construction* 95 (August): 35–45.

Davidson, Pavel, and Robert Piché. 2017. "A Survey of Selected Indoor Positioning Methods for Smartphones." *IEEE Communications Surveys and Tutorials* 19 (2): 1347–1370.

Fang, Yihai, Yong K. Cho, Sijie Zhang, and Esau Perez. 2016. "Case Study of BIM and Cloud–Enabled Real-Time RFID Indoor Localization for Construction Management Applications." *Journal of Construction Engineering and Management* 142 (7): 05016003.

Faragher, Ramsey, and Robert Harle. 2015. "Location Fingerprinting with Bluetooth Low Energy Beacons." *IEEE Journal on Selected Areas in Communications* 33 (11): 2418–2428.

Fountain, James, and Sandeep Langar. 2018. "Building Information Modeling (BIM) Outsourcing among General Contractors." *Automation in Construction* 95 (May): 107–117.

Fukunaga, K, and L Hostetler. 1975. "The Estimation of the Gradient of a Density Function." *IEEE Transactions on Information Theory* 21 (1): 32–40.

Ghaffarianhoseini, Ali, John Tookey, Amirhosein Ghaffarianhoseini, Nicola Naismith, Salman Azhar, Olia Efimova, and Kaamran Raahemifar. 2017. "Building Information Modelling (BIM) Uptake: Clear Benefits, Understanding Its Implementation, Risks and Challenges." *Renewable and Sustainable Energy Reviews* 75 (October 2015): 1046–1053.

Gorce, Jean Marie, Katia Jaffrès-Runser, and Guillaume de la Roche. 2007. "Deterministic Approach for Fast Simulations of Indoor Radio Wave Propagation." *IEEE Transactions on Antennas and Propagation* 55 (3 II): 938–948.

Günther, Christoph, Michael Günther, and Daniel Günther. 2020. "Tracing Contacts to Control the COVID-19 Pandemic." ArXiv. http://arxiv.org/abs/2004.00517.

He, Suining, and S. H. Gary Chan. 2016. "Wi-Fi Fingerprint-Based Indoor Positioning: Recent Advances and Comparisons." *IEEE Communications Surveys and Tutorials* 18 (1): 466–490.

Li, Nan, Burcin Becerik-Gerber, Bhaskar Krishnamachari, and Lucio Soibelman. 2014. "A BIM Centered Indoor Localization Algorithm to Support Building Fire Emergency Response Operations." *Automation in Construction* 42: 78–89.

Mendoza-Silva, Germán Martín, Joaquín Torres-Sospedra, and Joaquín Huerta. 2019. "A Meta-Review of Indoor Positioning Systems." *Sensors* 19 (20).

Park, June Young, Thomas Dougherty, and Thomas Nagy. 2018. "A Bluetooth Based Occupancy Detection for Buildings." *Proceedings of Building Performance Analysis Conference and SimBuild*, 807–814. IBPSA.

Sergi, Ilaria, Ada Malagnino, Roberto Conte Rosito, Vincenzo Lacasa, Angelo Corallo, and Luigi Patrono. 2020. "Integrating BIM and IoT Technologies in Innovative Fire Management Systems." *5th International Conference on Smart and Sustainable Technologies (SpliTech)*, 1–5. IEEE.

Tang, Shu, Dennis R. Shelden, Charles M. Eastman, Pardis Pishdad-Bozorgi, and Xinghua Gao. 2019. "A Review of Building Information Modeling (BIM) and the Internet of Things (IoT) Devices Integration: Present Status and Future Trends." *Automation in Construction* 101 (June 2018): 127–139.

Trivedi, Amee, Camellia Zakaria, Rajesh Balan, and Prashant Shenoy. 2020. "WiFiTrace: Network-Based Contact Tracing for Infectious Diseases Using Passive WiFi Sensing." ArXiv, 2005.12045.1-23.

Wang, Hao, Yisha Pan, and Xiaochun Luo. 2019. "Integration of BIM and GIS in Sustainable Built Environment: A Review and Bibliometric Analysis." *Automation in Construction* 103 (September 2018): 41–52.

Yoo, Wonjae, Hyoungsub Kim, and Minjae Shin. 2020. "Stations-Oriented Indoor Localization (SOIL): A BIM-Based Occupancy Schedule Modeling System." *Building and Environment* 168 (October 2019): 106520.

IMAGE CREDITS

All drawings and images by the authors.

Wonjae Yoo is a PhD student in the Department of Architecture at Texas A&M University. He has been working on BIM-centered model development for sustainable indoor and outdoor environment.

Dr. Hyoungsub Kim is an Assistant Professor in the Department of Architecture at Ajou University. His research focuses on building technology in the area of computational modeling and sustainable architecture.

Dr. Minjae Shin is an Assistant Professor in the Division of Architecture at Hanyang University ERICA in South Korea. His expertise is in the energy modeling and performance simulation for the design and development of sustainable buildings.

Dr. Mark J. Clayton is the William M Pena Professor of Information Management in the Department of Architecture at Texas A&M. He currently is focused on introducing BIM to students in undergraduate design and directing PhD students in developing advanced design software.

Indoor Positioning System for Occupation Density Control

Djordje Stojanovic
University of Melbourne

Milica Vujovic
Universitat Pompeu Fabra

Branko Miloradovic
Mälardalen University

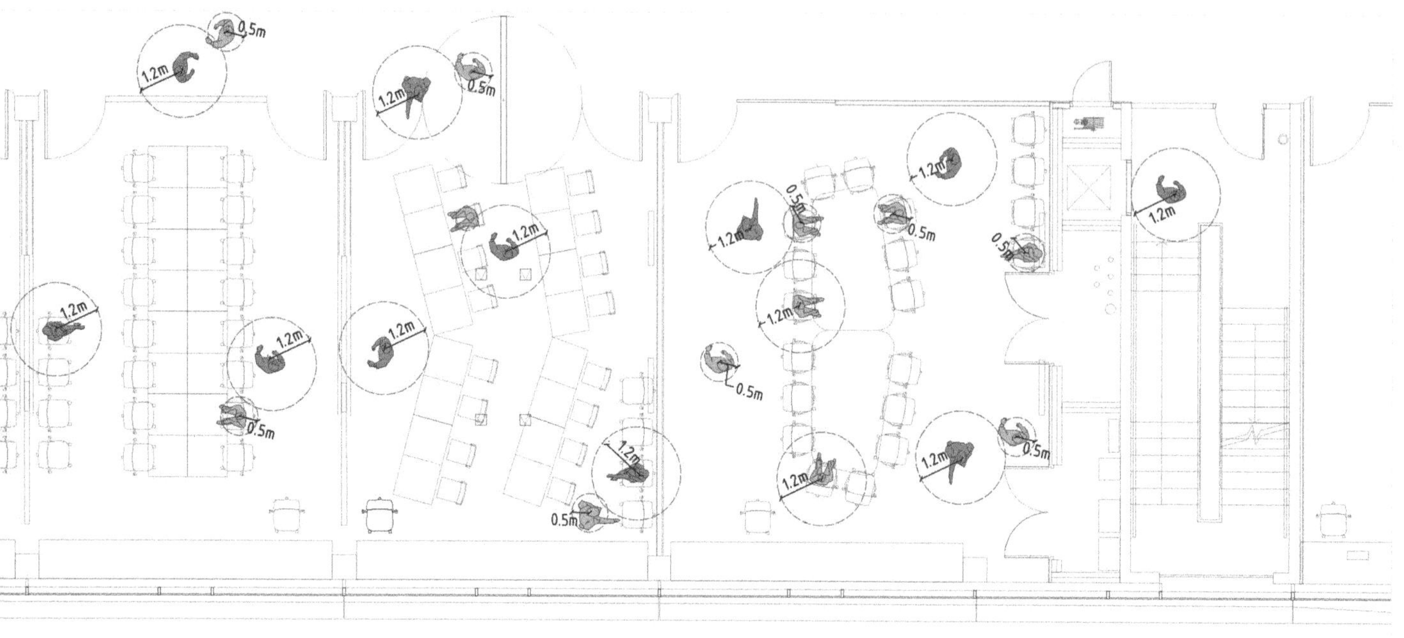

1 Indoor positioning system for occupation density control, concept drawing.

ABSTRACT

The reported research focuses on occupational density as an increasingly important architectural measure and uses occupancy simulation to optimize distancing criteria imposed by the COVID-19 pandemic. The paper addresses the following questions: How to engage computational techniques (CTs) to improve the accuracy of two existing types of indoor positioning systems? How to employ simulation methods in establishing critical occupation density to balance social distancing needs and the efficient use of resources? The larger objective and the aim of further research is to develop an autonomous system capable of establishing an accurate number of people present in a room and informing occupants if space is available according to prescribed sanitary standards. The paper presents occupancy simulation approximating input that would be provided by the outlined multisensor data fusion technique aiming to improve the accuracy of the existing indoor localization solutions. The projected capacity to capture information related to social distancing and occupants' positioning is used to ground a method for determining a room-specific occupational density threshold. Our early results indicate that the type of activities, equipment, and furniture in a room, addressed through occupants' positioning, may impact the frequency of distancing incidents. Our initial findings centered on simulation modeling indicate that data, composed of the two sets (occupant count and the number of recorded distancing incidents) can be overlapped to help establish room-specific standards rather than apply generic measures. In conclusion, we discuss the opportunities and challenges of the proposed system and its role after the pandemic.

INTRODUCTION

The reported research focuses on occupational density as an increasingly important architectural measure in the context of the COVID-19 pandemic. This paper examines the role of computational techniques (CTs) in making buildings less hospitable to viruses, and how autonomous and noninvasive occupancy detection systems can inform the way buildings are used and designed in the future. The ability to measure data from the built environment has rapidly increased, but occupancy analytics and indoor positioning systems' role in making buildings comply with infection control measures are not sufficiently explored nor fully discussed.

This paper outlines the research as follows. A brief literature review establishes state of the art on occupancy detection and indoor localization systems in the first section. The second section introduces the concept of real-time occupational density control applicable to school buildings and how simulation is employed. An examination of challenges follows, and the research method is described. The aim is to establish what instruments and techniques may be used, how to employ known indoor positioning systems, and what level of positioning precession is required to determine room-specific distancing criteria to help minimize the spread of infectious diseases and maintain efficient space usage. The data obtained would inform occupants and be used to train the system to determine dynamic occupancy limits in compliance with Workplace Directions (Public Health and Wellbeing Act) for Victoria, Australia. The next section presents the computational framework and simulation modeling for the Melbourne School of Design (MSD) building. Our research indicates that data—composed of (1) occupants or "available slots" count and (2) the number of recorded distancing incidents—can be overlapped to help optimize standards for individual rooms, rather than apply generic measures. In conclusion, we discuss results obtained by simulation and the benefits of the projected solution.

Related Work

Recent research involving occupancy data and indoor positioning can be categorized according to three questions: how to measure occupancy (Hobson et al. 2020; Sardar, Mishra, and Khan 2020; Sun, Zhao, and Zou 2020), how to clean and structure information once it is measured (Dai, Liu, and Zhang 2020; Datta and Chatterjee 2019; Liang, Hong, and Shun 2016; Saha et al. 2019), and finally how to use it to solve real-life problems (Hanse 2015; Hsu, Chen, and Perng 2020; Ouf, O'Brien, and Gunay 2019; Pallikere et al. 2019; Suzuki et al. 2015). Techniques most commonly applied for occupancy measuring include the use of passive infrared (PIR) sensors, carbon dioxide detectors, radio-frequency identification (RFID), Wi-Fi counters, optical and infrared cameras, and sensor fusion approaches involving a combination of devices to compensate for their individual insufficiencies (Hobson et al. 2019). Occupancy data is elusive and difficult to capture with high-level accuracy (Sun, Zhao, and Zou 2020). The proximity between occupants and dealing with a high number of people in the same room are particularly challenging (Berry and Park 2017). Inherent noise and occlusion in dynamic environments pose challenges for reliable occupancy measuring (Abbas et al. 2019; Großwindhager et al. 2017). The occupancy attribute indeed has two values only, occupied or not occupied (Kumar et al. 2018), but measuring and processing occupancy information may be complex when associated with time and space, and occupancy detection may be classified as tracking (Saha et al. 2019). Advanced computational techniques for data structuring and prediction are employed to improve accuracy and robustness and reduce operation costs of indoor positioning systems. There is an increasing number of studies (2,142 studies recorded in 2019 alone) into machine learning models such as logistic regression, artificial neural networks (ANN), the Markov chain model, decision trees, k-Nearest Neighbor (kNN), and support vector machines (SVM) related to buildings (Dai, Liu, and Zhang 2020). Finally, occupancy data is still primarily focused on the performance of building automation systems (BAS), resulting in energy savings. However, there are growing indications that occupancy data is valuable to architectural design (Gomez-Zamora et al. 2019), user experience (Hansen 2016), security, resource management (Suzuki et al. 2015), and public transportation (Hsu, Chen, and Perng 2020). This paper addresses challenges related to the accuracy and reliability of indoor positioning systems. It describes simulation methods to examine the potential of CTs to improve the usage and well-being of occupants. At the time the research was conducted and this paper submitted, workplace and activity directions issued by the Department of Health and Human Services, Victoria State government, restrict access to university buildings. Therefore, we relied on simulation modeling to develop the system and test its viability before real-life implementation is possible.

RESEARCH AIMS

This study aims to provide a crucial contribution to the development of a prudent solution for implementing social distancing measures in response to the COVID-19 pandemic. Our initial research recognizes challenges faced by current indoor localization systems, namely positioning accuracy and dealing with multiple occupants. In response, we propose the use of a multisensor data fusion approach to improve location precision and reliability of results. The principal aim is to ground the method for determining the room specific occupancy limits, using the rule of 1.5 m distance between users, or 4 m^2 per user as a departing point of the study. The paper addresses the following research questions: How to employ simulation methods in establishing a room-specific occupation density to balance between social distancing needs and the efficient use of resources? How to engage CTs to improve the accuracy of two existing types of indoor positioning systems?

This study aims to answer research questions by simulating an occupancy detection system operation at the micro level and in an indoor environment to benefit the use of educational buildings, where the introduction of social distancing rules imposes a new usage norm. The goal is to use findings obtained through simulation to enable further research leading to the development of an autonomous system capable of establishing the exact number of people present in each room or zone of the school and of informing occupants if space is available in that classroom, lab, or studio according to health and safety standards prescribed by Workplace Directions (Public Health and Wellbeing Act) for Victoria, Australia. To that end, we outline a computational technique to reduce measurement inaccuracies of the two existing occupancy detection systems. And we use simulation modeling to examine occupancy scenarios and set the foundations of a method for establishing a room-specific maximum of occupants while maintaining adequate distancing measures.

METHOD

An Approach to Improving the Positioning Precision

Our background research suggests that the existing indoor positioning solutions would require further development to facilitate studies related to social distancing requirements imposed by the COVID-19 pandemic. Therefore, we propose a technique that relies on an overlap between two existing types of occupancy detection systems, one employing RFID anchors and tags, and the other one based on the use of Wi-Fi counters and individual mobile devices (Fig. 2). System 1, such as Decawave DW1000, is a low-cost indoor positioning system based on the off-the-shelf ultra-wideband transceiver (Kulmer et al. 2017). It uses a single anchor and multipath wall reflections to establish an accurate position of a tag. The system operates up to a decimeter accuracy to update the position tags in real time while not requiring additional infrastructure. The frequent use of ID cards in school buildings eases implementing a solution based on personal tags. System 2, such as WiDeep, is a deep learning-based localization system with high accuracy (Abbas et al. 2019). It is designed to deal with inherent noise and device heterogeneity in counting mobile device signals to establish the number of people present in a specific room.

The two systems are based on related principles, employing different but well-known devices. The first uses an anchor or antenna and high bandwidth signals to locate tags or agents. The second utilizes a transmitter or a signature collector module, which scans for access points and analyzes signal strength to determine the distance and thus the location of individual mobile devices. However, both solutions employ advanced computational techniques to improve positioning accuracy. System 2 utilizes a two-phase fingerprinting-based approach of localization, composed of offline training and online localization. During the training phase, the signature collector module scans for access points, allowing the computational systems to learn their signal strengths and, in this specific solution, to building a deep neural network per each point of interest (Abbas et al. 2019). It is reported that the proposed CT improves traditional techniques' accuracy by 29.8%, with a consistent mean accuracy of 121 cm for the spatial configuration of interest to our study (Abbas et al. 2019). System 1 exploits signal reflections by incorporating floor-plan knowledge and using a positioning algorithm to improve accuracy (Kulmer et al. 2017). It is reported that the proposed technique demonstrates reliable results at an accuracy of 50 cm (Kulmer et al. 2017).

The initial plan to build the prototype and use data acquired by two systems for further research is replaced with simulation modeling due to the ongoing lockdown restrictions. The developmental framework for the multi-sensor data fusion technique involving the simultaneous and correlated operation of two systems, enhanced by CT to alleviate their limitations and increase the reliability of data needed for the next research phase, is outlined as follows.

The proposed input information consists of two categories, the number of people in the room and their location, established by each system separately. The output information is a verified number of occupants and a median position of each occupant measured by two systems. The number of occupants is verified when the count by two systems is the same, while occupants' position is determined at the intersections of two location areas established by two systems. Measurements from two systems are compared, and the average value is calculated to compensate for their individual insufficiencies and minimize a potential mistake. The two occupancy detection solutions' measurements are operating with acceptable tolerances of 0.5 and 1.2 m. However, neither one of the two systems on its own would be able to determine occupants' position with a needed

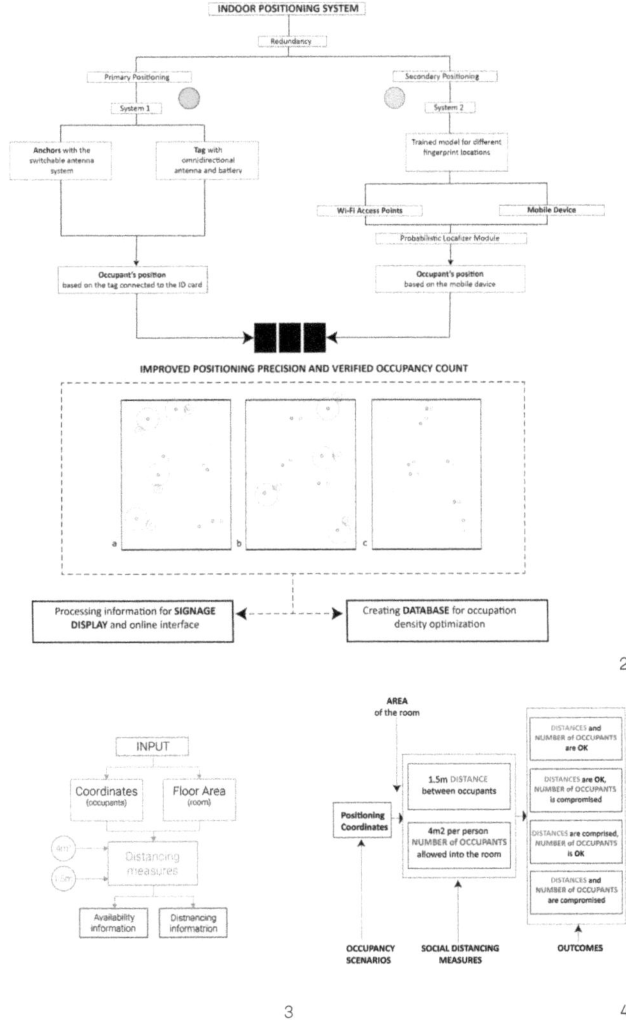

2 An approach to improving positioning precision.

3 Computational framework to examine current distancing measures.

4 Simulation framework for indoor positioning for MSD studio room.

level of accuracy to help implement social distancing rules. Their limitations are also related to dealing with multiple occupants. Previous studies involving these two systems (Abbas et al. 2019; Kulmer et al. 2017) and other research efforts related to indoor positioning (Berry and Park 2017) report challenges in establishing an occupant count when as little as three people are present in the same room.

The proposed CT is to reduce any potential error arising from the limited accuracy of sensing devices in establishing and confirming the location of Wi-Fi access points and RFID tags. Measurements from both systems are taken into account with their accuracy threshold. Each occupant's location is recorded as a circle area, R1.2 m for System 1, and R0.5 m for System 2, instead of a single point. It is anticipated that the two detection systems will provide marginally different locations, resulting in different centers and, therefore, misaligned areas of two circles. An intersection of these two areas is the increased precession zone. Initially, the count of people in the room as well as occupants' positioning may not coincide with the two systems. A signal passing through partitions may contribute to two systems giving different occupancy counts. A person standing close to the dividing wall may be accounted for as standing inside or outside a room. Both positioning and counting of occupants are essential to disease prevention measures, and this is how the proposed multisensor data fusion technique increases the positioning precision to help implement social distancing measures.

When information obtained by the two indoor positioning systems is compared and verified, it is processed as follows: the established number of occupants is checked against the maximum allowed in that room, calculated when the floor area is divided by an area designated for each occupant as an effective disease prevention measure. The result would be communicated as an instant message via a purpose-developed signage system, positioned at the room entrance and operating much like a street traffic light. Also, the number of occupants in each room would be displayed online in real time, allowing remote planning. At this research stage, occupancy data is randomly generated to enable the development of the intelligent and room-specific occupational density control presented in this paper. The following section presents the computational framework and introduces simulation modeling carried out to date.

Computational Framework

The computational framework shows how information that would be gathered by sensory devices, RFID anchors, and Wi-Fi counters is processed to create two valuable data sets. The input consists of the precise positioning for each occupant given with their coordinates and floor area. The maximum number of people allowed in that room is calculated when the floor area is divided by an area designated for each occupant as an effective COVID-19 prevention measure. There are two output categories, availability information, expressed as available slots, and distancing information, expressed as distancing incidents (Fig. 3).

More importantly, the overlap of these two categories is recognized for its potential to help optimize the number of people allowed in any room. While it is understood that fewer people in the room will result in easier distancing, we aim to establish an evidence-based technique for finding a critical threshold at which the distancing incidents rate

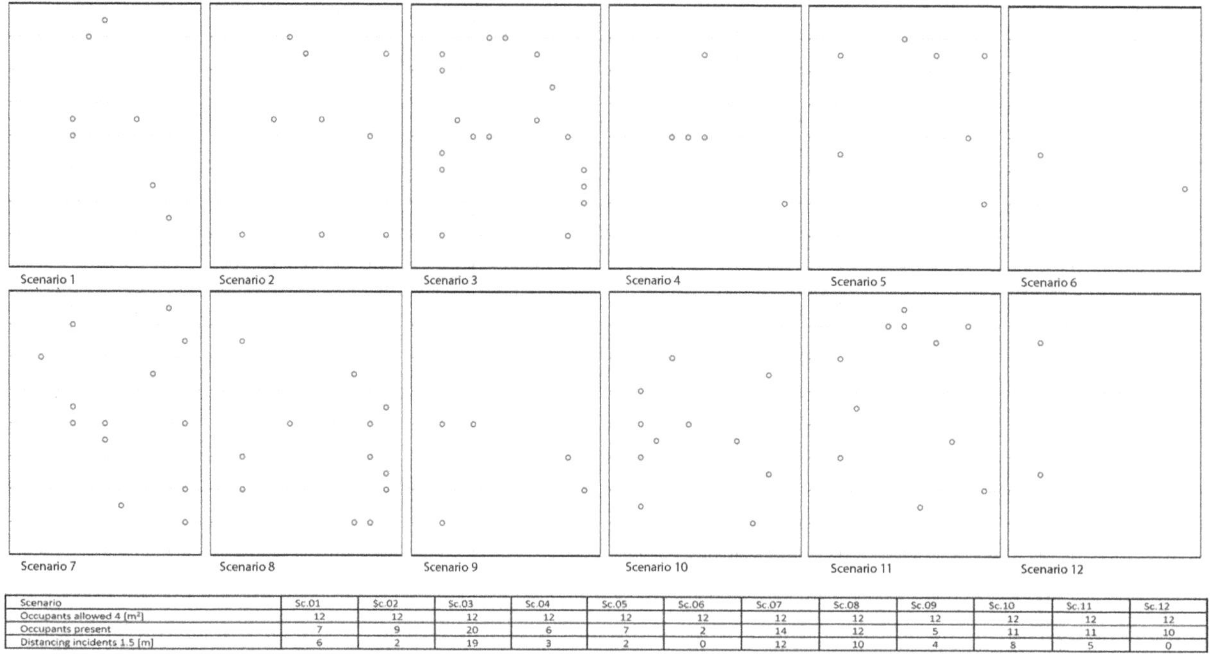

Scenario	Sc.01	Sc.02	Sc.03	Sc.04	Sc.05	Sc.06	Sc.07	Sc.08	Sc.09	Sc.10	Sc.11	Sc.12
Occupants allowed 4 (m²)	12	12	12	12	12	12	12	12	12	12	12	12
Occupants present	7	9	20	6	7	2	14	12	5	11	11	10
Distancing incidents 1.5 (m)	6	2	19	3	2	0	12	10	4	8	5	0

5 Visual output and data overview for 12 simulated scenarios for MSD studio room with a varied number of occupants. 5

starts to peak. The aim is to maximize the number of people and minimize the number of distancing incidents through the dynamic and responsive implementation of infection control measures. The study focuses on the micro environment of the MSD building. It examines one of many studio rooms measuring approximately 48 m² with a single doorway to the gallery-type access. Studios are designed with a capacity of 16 students. Under the new usage norms imposed by disease prevention measures, capacity is reduced by 25%.

Modeling Indoor Positioning at MSD Building

The simulation examines the correlation between distancing incidents and a generic density norm, converted to the number of people allowed in any room (Fig. 4). The objective is to simulate a number of occupancy scenarios to examine the efficiency of current distancing measures and establish a method for determining a room-specific maximum occupancy while maintaining adequate distancing measures. Social distancing measures of 1.5 m distance between users and 4 m² per user are employed as initial parameters, resulting in one of four possible outcomes because compliance with one measure does not necessarily mean compliance with the other. The two measures, distancing between occupants and area allocated per each occupant, do not impose the same occupancy limits. While the area of 4 m² can be notionally allocated to each user, human behavior is a lot less predictable and may often result in the 1.5 m distancing rule's breach. The type of activities, equipment, and furniture in a room may all impact the frequency of distancing incidents. In the end, people are not always able to judge the distance with sufficient accuracy or may not always be aware that another person is behind them. To that end, the record of distancing incidents and the number of people in the room at the time of the incident is important to establish an efficient occupancy limit. The simulation aims to establish the ratio of distancing breaches to the number of people present in a specific room. It is assumed that different occupational densities may be recommended for two rooms of the same size, in addition to generic prevention measures.

RESULTS

At the time of this paper's submission, university education in Victoria is delivered solely via online teaching mode, with a much expected return to the campus according to the new usage standards scheduled for early 2021. Therefore, we rely on simulation modeling to examine the correlation between availability and distancing data sets. The simulation model is developed to process data that would be provided by the proposed multisensor fusion technique, given as coordinates of occupants in the room and the room's occupational capacity derived from its size and social distancing parameters. For the purpose of presented research, the input data is generated randomly but in line with the plan acquisition to enable the objective to explore the overlap between distancing incidents and the number of people in the room (or the number of available slots). The simulation's visual output shows a schematic floor plan with occupants' locations recorded in three-minute

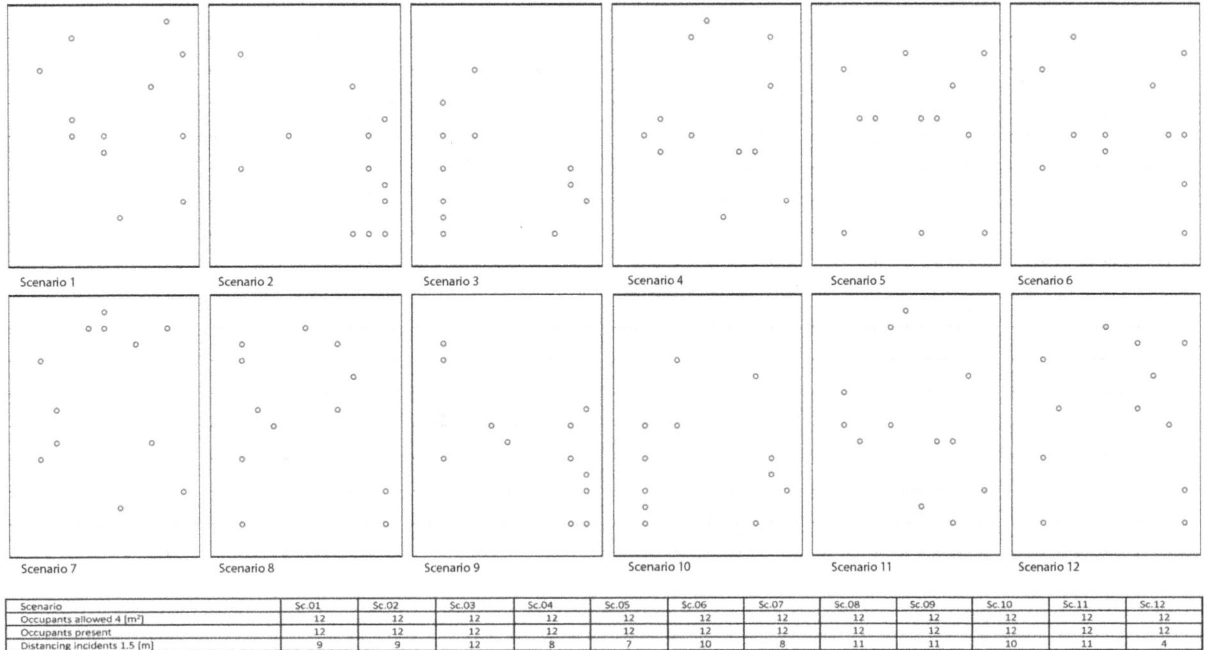

Scenario	Sc.01	Sc.02	Sc.03	Sc.04	Sc.05	Sc.06	Sc.07	Sc.08	Sc.09	Sc.10	Sc.11	Sc.12
Occupants allowed 4 [m²]	12	12	12	12	12	12	12	12	12	12	12	12
Occupants present	12	12	12	12	12	12	12	12	12	12	12	12
Distancing incidents 1.5 [m]	9	9	12	8	7	10	8	11	11	10	11	4

6 Visual output and data overview for 12 simulated scenarios for MSD Studio with the maximum number of occupants according to the current norm. 6

intervals. Color coding is used to mark compliance with distancing measures. Blue is for occupants complying with measures and red for those at a distance less than 1.5 m.

Initially, location modeling was conducted with a varied number of occupants in the room. As expected, a higher number of people in the room resulted in a higher rate of incidents. However, 12 scenarios (Fig. 5) show that distancing breaches may occur even with very few people in the room. Further location modeling was conducted to continue the probe into the correlation between the number of people in the room and distancing incidents. The next step in location modeling included the maximum allowed number of occupants, according to the prescribed occupancy density of 4 m² per person. Results show a high number of distancing incidents (Fig. 6). In the third step, location modeling was based on the revised norm and a lowered maximum of occupants, according to the corrected occupancy density norm of 7 m² per person. Results show a lower number of distancing incidents (Fig. 7).

CONCLUSION

The location modeling shows different occupancy scenarios for a studio room at the MSD building. Three groups of scenarios, differing by the number of occupants in the room and distancing norms, are presented to prove the validity and suitability of current prevention measures and develop a technique for establishing room-specific standards. The first group of scenarios shows the occurrence of distancing breaches under different occupancy counts. The second set shows distancing incidents when current occupational density norms are applied, and the third group shows the rate of incidents when corrected and more stringent occupancy norms are applied. It leads to the conclusion that maintaining social distancing will be challenging in practice, but also that current generic measures are inadequate for a studio room of the MSD building.
Our research reveals that neither generic density norms (1.5 m distance between users and 4 m² area per user), nor synchronized measures to maintain social distancing may be adequate. Those norms are not context-aware, as they do not account for the type of activity, furnishing, and many other factors. Our study is based on the context of an educational building, and the simulation is employed to examine the correlation between distancing incidents and occupancy count to determine a room-specific maximum of occupants while maintaining adequate social distancing measures. The presented findings address the first research question to balance social distancing needs and the efficient use of resources.

Our second research question, related to improving the precision levels of known occupancy detection systems (Berry and Park 2017; Sun, Zhao, and Zou 2020), is addressed with an outline of a technique employing two already developed but not sufficiently tested indoor poisoning solutions (Abbas et al. 2019; Kulmer et al. 2017) to help manage occupation density and implementation of social distancing measures. The paper outlines how CTs would be used to compensate for sensing devices'

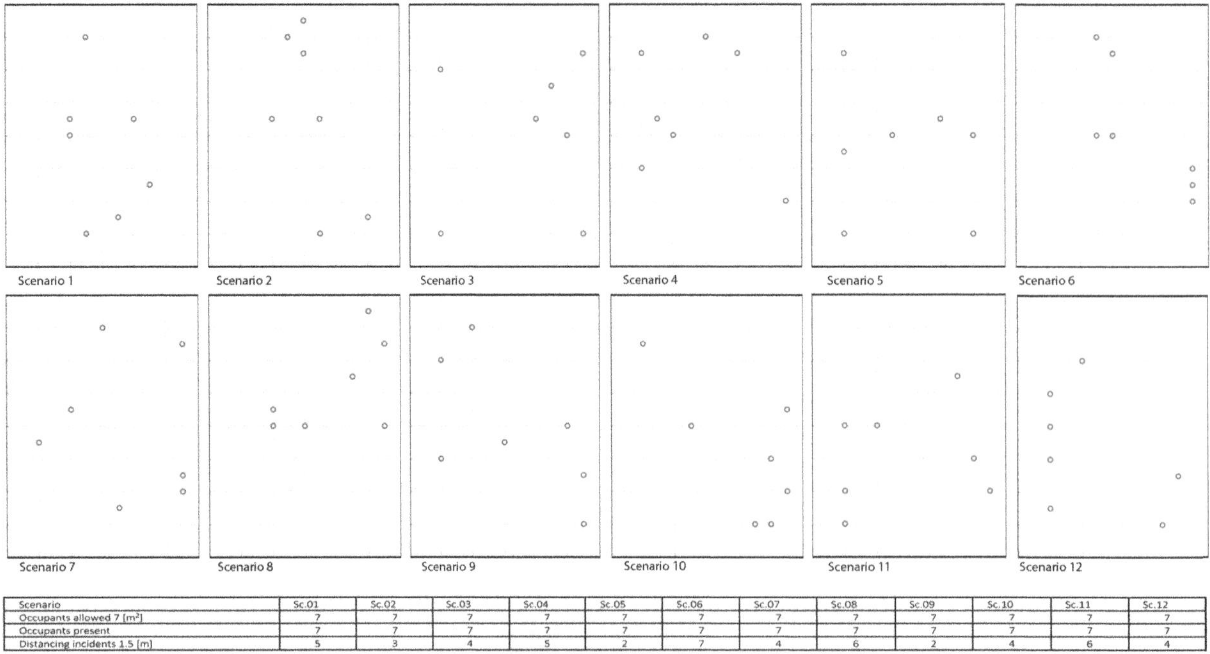

Scenario	Sc.01	Sc.02	Sc.03	Sc.04	Sc.05	Sc.06	Sc.07	Sc.08	Sc.09	Sc.10	Sc.11	Sc.12
Occupants allowed 7 [m²]	7	7	7	7	7	7	7	7	7	7	7	7
Occupants present	7	7	7	7	7	7	7	7	7	7	7	7
Distancing incidents 1.5 [m]	5	3	4	5	2	7	4	6	2	4	6	4

7 Visual output and data overview for 12 simulated scenarios for MSD studio with the maximum number of occupants according to the revised norm. 7

insufficiencies and improve indoor positioning accuracy while maintaining a noninvasive approach. It is indicated that further development of the proposal would lead toward a fully functional solution that would be used to inform occupants and thus help preemptively and noninvasively, rather than relying on location history, tracking, and tracing methods to minimize the spread of infection. In the latter study, we have employed simulation to compensate for the lack of real-life data imposed by the lockdown. Simulation has unlocked the possibility to probe further into the relation between distancing incidents and generic occupancy norms. The reliance on the simulation method imposes limitations, as many aspects of human behavior were not taken into account. Therefore, the presented method sets the ground for further research and establishes the optimal number of occupants specific for each room, which would indirectly consider the type of activity, occupants' awareness and preferences, and other more elusive aspects of human behavior. Further research would also focus on developing the proposed technique to address the needs of more complex spatial configurations such as open-plan space located in the central atrium of the MSD building.

This study's contribution is in developing a method for occupancy detection and employing occupancy information to help disease prevention in educational buildings while maintaining efficient use of resources. The findings presented in this paper demonstrate how computation is used to structure data and to enable evidence-based inquiry into occupation density as an increasingly important architectural measure. The research relies on the simulation method, replacing access to restricted spaces, providing hard-to-get data, and enabling timely development of the solution and its examination before real-life implementation. The resulting data sets could also be used for an accurate overview of usage to help facility management through more efficient occupancy scheduling and occupation density minimization. Occupancy data recorded over a more extended period would also enable designers to understand behavior patterns and what happens after building buildings. It provides a means to develop predictive analysis tools and evidence-based design methods centered on occupants' behavior. In the longer run, the database created through continual occupancy monitoring would help future research in several increasingly converging areas such as architectural design, facility management, learning environments, and health and disease prevention.

REFERENCES

Abbas, Moustafa, Moustafa Elhamshary, Hamada Rizk, Marwan Torki, and Moustaf Youssef. 2019. "WiDeep: WiFi-Based Accurate and Robust Indoor Localization System Using Deep Learning." In *Proceedings of IEEE International Conference on Pervasive Computing and Communications*, 1–10. Kyoto, Japan.

Berry, Jaclyn, and Kat Park. 2017. "A Passive System for Quantifying Indoor Space Utilization." In *ACADIA 2017: Disciplines and Disruption [Proceedings of the 37th Annual Conference of the Association for*

Computer Aided Design in Architecture (ACADIA)], Cambridge, MA, 2–4 November 2017, edited by T. Nagakura, S. Tibbits, M. Ibañez, and C. Mueller, 138–145. CUMINCAD.

Dai, Xilei, Junjie Liu, and Xin Zhang. 2020. "A Review of Studies Applying Machine Learning Models to Predict Occupancy and Window-Opening Behaviours in Smart Buildings." *Energy and Buildings* 223: 110159.

Datta, Suseta, and Sankhadeep Chatterjee. 2019. "An Efficient Indoor Occupancy Detection System Using Artificial Neural Network." *Advances in Intelligent Systems and Computing* 811: 317–329.

Gomez-Zamora, Paula, Sonit Bafna, Craig Zimring, Ellen Do, and Mario Vega Romero. 2019. "Spatiotemporal Occupancy for Building Analytics." In *Architecture in the Age of the 4th Industrial Revolution Proceedings of the 37th eCAADe and 23rd SIGraDi Conference*, edited by J.P. Sousa, J.P. Xavier, and G. Castro Henriques, 111–120. Porto, Portugal.

Großwindhager, Bernhard, Michael Rath, Josef Kulmer, Stefan Hinteregger, Stefan, Moustafa Bakr, Carlos Boano, Klaus Witrisal, and Kai Romer. 2017. "UWB-Based Single-Anchor Low-Cost Indoor Localization System." In *Proceedings of the 15th ACM Conference on Embedded Network Sensor Systems*, edited by M. Rasit Eskicioglu. Delft, Netherlands.

Hansen, Kai. 2016. "Designing Responsive Environments Through User Experience Research." *International Journal of Architectural Computing* 14 (4): 372–385.

Hobson, Brodie, Daniel Lowcay, Burak Gunay, Araz Ashouri, and Guy Newsham. 2019. "Opportunistic Occupancy-Count Estimation Using Sensor Fusion." *Building and Environment* 159: 106154.

Hsu, Ya-Wen, Yen-Wei Chen, and Jau-Woei Perng. 2020. "Estimation of the Number of Passengers in a Bus Using Deep Learning." *Sensors (Basel)* 20 (8): 2178.

Kulmer, Josef, Stefan Grebien, Bernhard Grosswindhager, Michael Rath, Mustafa Bakr, Erik Leitinger, and Klaus Witrisal. 2017. "Using DecaWave UWB Transceivers for High-Accuracy Multipath-Assisted Indoor Positioning." In the *Proceedings of 2017 IEEE International Conference on Communications Workshops (ICC Workshops)* edited by A. Jamalipour and C. Papadias, 1239-1245. Paris.

Kumar, Sachin, Shobha Rai, Rampal Singh, and Saibal K. Pal. 2018. "Machine Learning-Based Method and Its Performance Analysis for Occupancy Detection in Indoor Environment." In *Proceedings of Third International Symposium on Signal Processing and Intelligent Recognition Systems (SIRS-2017)*, 240–251. Manipal, India.

Liang, Xin, Tianzhen Hong, and Geoffrey Shen. 2016. "Occupancy Data Analytics and Prediction: A Case Study." *Building and Environment* 102: 179–192.

Ouf, Mohamed, William O'Brien, and Burak Gunay. 2019. "On Quantifying Building Performance Adaptability to Variable Occupancy." *Building and Environment* 155: 257–267.

Pallikere, Avinash, Robin Qiu, Parhum Delgoshaei, and Ashkan Negahban. 2019. "Incorporating Occupancy Data in Scheduling Building Equipment: A Simulation Optimization Framework." *Energy and Buildings* 209: 109655.

Saha, Homagni, Anthony Florita, Gregor Henze, and Soumik Sarkar. 2019. "Occupancy Sensing in Buildings: A Review of Data Analytics Approaches." *Energy and Buildings* 188–189: 278–285.

Sardar, Santu, Amit K. Mishra, and Mohammed Z. A. Khan 2020. "Indoor Occupancy Estimation Using the LTE-CommSense System." *International Journal of Remote Sensing* 41 (14): 5609–5619.

Sun, Kailai, Qianchuan Zhao, and Jianhong Zou. 2020. "A Review of Building Occupancy Measurement Systems." *Energy and Buildings* 216: 109965.

Suzuki, Larissa, Peter Cooper, Theo Tryfonas, and George Oikonomou. 2015. "Hidden Presence: Sensing Occupancy and Extracting Value from Occupancy Data." In the *Proceedings of the 4th International Conference Design, User Experience, and Usability: Interactive Experience Design, DUXU 2015*, edited by M. Aaron, 412–424. Los Angeles.

IMAGE CREDITS

All drawings and images by the authors.

Djordje Stojanovic is a Senior Lecturer at the University of Melbourne, Faculty of Architecture, Building and Planning. He is interested in how computational techniques and robotic systems enable more efficient space usage.

Milica Vujovic is an INPhINIT "la Caixa" Marie Curie PhD candidate at the ICT Department of Universitat Pompeu Fabra, Barcelona. She is an architectural and mechanical engineer with a history of working in academia, architecture, and mechanical and industrial engineering. Her research interests focus on mechatronics, human-computer interaction, and smart environments.

Branko Miloradovic is pursuing a PhD in Computer Science at Mälardalen University, Sweden. He is involved with the AFarCloud (ECSEL JU) project. His research interests include robotics, multirobot mission planning, combinatorial optimization, and evolutionary algorithms.

Dynamic Anthropometric Modeling Interface (DAMI)

A Kinect-Based Anthropometric Modeling Work Process for Patient Room Layout Optimization and Nurse Posture Evaluation

Mengni Zhang
Department of Design & Environmental Analysis, Cornell University

Clara Dewey
Department of Mechanical Engineering, Cornell University

Saleh Kalantari
Department of Design & Environmental Analysis, Cornell University

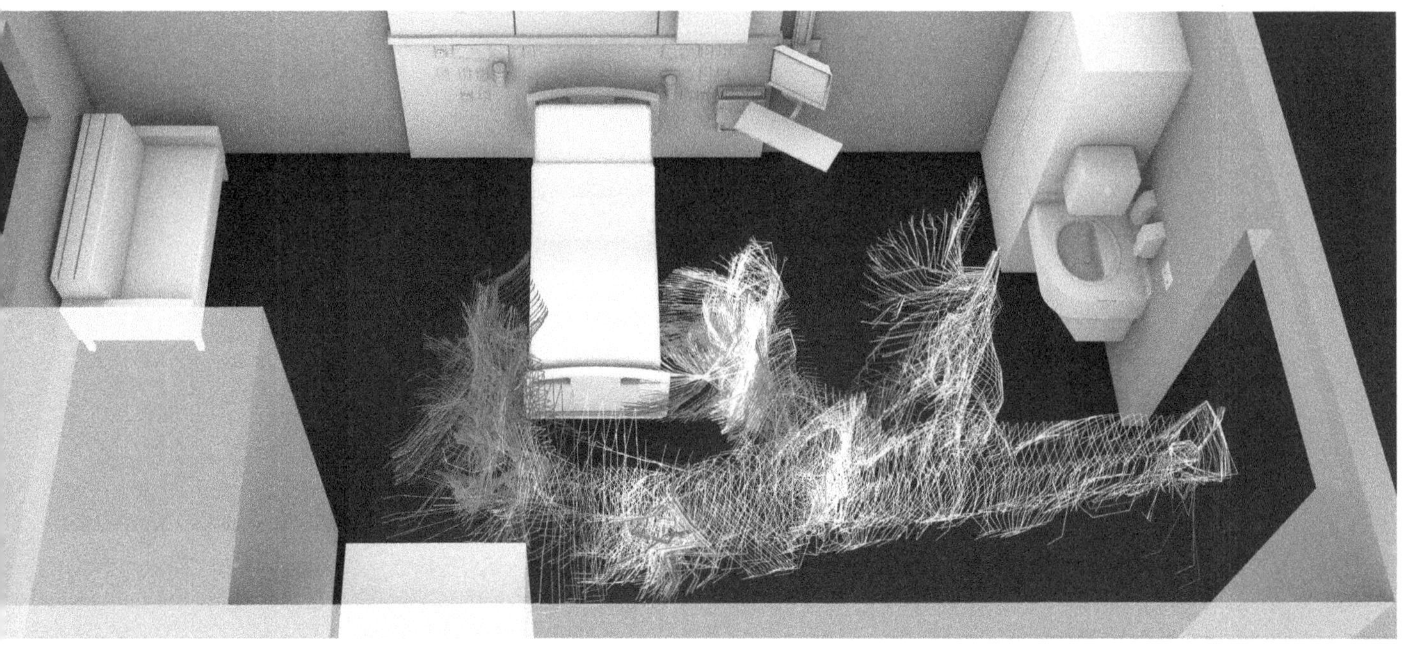

1

1 Sample continuous skeleton recordings placed in base patient room model with Rapid Entire Body Assessment (REBA) scores assigned in colors from white (good posture) to red (bad posture).

ABSTRACT

In this paper, we propose a Kinect-based Dynamic Anthropometric Modeling Interface (DAMI), built in Rhinoceros with Grasshopper for patient room layout optimization and nurse posture evaluations. Anthropometry is an important field that studies human body measurements to help designers improve product ergonomics and reduce negative health consequences such as musculoskeletal disorders (MSDs). Unlike existing anthropometric tools, which rely on generic human body datasets and static posture models, DAMI tracks and records user postures in real time, creating custom 3D body movement models that are typically absent in current space-planning practices. A generic hospital patient room, which contains complex and ergonomically demanding activities for nurses, was selected as an initial testing environment. We will explain the project background, the methods used to develop DAMI, and demonstrate its capabilities.

There are two main goals DAMI aims to achieve. First, as a generative tool, it will reconstruct dynamic body point cloud models, which will be used as input for optimizing room layout during a project's schematic design phase. Second, as an evaluation tool, by encoding and visualizing the Rapid Entire Body Assessment (REBA) scores, DAMI will illustrate the spatiotemporal relationship between nurse postures and the built environment during a project's construction phase or post occupancy evaluation. We envision a distributed system of Kinect sensors to be embedded in various hospital rooms to help architects, planners, and facility managers improve nurse work experiences through better space planning.

INTRODUCTION

Anthropometric charts have been widely used in human factors design across various industries since the 1960s. There are a few limitations associated with current anthropometric datasets and practices: 1) they are often based on outdated data from a limited number of individuals, and 2) the charts are 2D static representations of a limited number of postures, which hinder the integration of anthropometrics into the design process (Dianat, Molenbroek, and Castellucci 2018). In this paper, we propose a Dynamic Anthropometric Modeling Interface (DAMI) that allows designers to generate and evaluate patient room layouts based on task-specific dynamic nurse postures. This process bridges two existing fields: ergonomic assessments using Microsoft Kinect skeleton tracking (Microsoft n.d.), and room layout optimization using multi-objective programming. The goal is to create a work process that designers can use to consider ergonomic needs during space planning.

Traditionally, planning approaches involve consultations between ergonomists, designers, and stakeholders to understand existing problems and available resources (Brooks 1998). Within healthcare architecture, designers often use participatory strategies to study ergonomics, including methods such as dynamic simulation, site visits, process analysis, flow analysis, and field observation (Villeneuve et al. 2007). To solve issues associated with hospital room configurations, other researchers have gathered coalitions of experts to evaluate room layouts based on a defined set of issues such as patient safety, staff efficiency, and circulation (Pati et al. 2009). However, none of these methods consider the dynamic anthropometric data of users in relation to the built environment via continuous evaluations, especially for occupational safety purposes.

A generic patient room was used as the base to develop DAMI, due to the presence of ergonomically demanding tasks, and large financial and health implications related to healthcare designs. Studies have shown that nurses experience high rates of musculoskeletal disorders (MSDs), particularly low back pain (Sharafkhani et al. 2014). Environmental variables such as furniture ergonomics and room layouts are significant contributors to error rates in emergency care (Chaudhury, Mahmood, and Valente 2009). A survey of 23 occupational groups also noted that poor performance and ergonomics in the patient room may be caused by inadequate space around the patient bed, strenuous physical task demands, and lack of available horizontal surfaces (Lavender et al. 2015). By making more informed design decisions in medical planning, DAMI may help reduce nurse work-related pain and error rates.

RELATED WORK

Previously, researchers have used the Kinect sensor coupled with skeleton data correction to conduct a RULA (Rapid Upper Limb Assessment) in real workplace conditions (Plantard et al. 2016). The sensor has also been used to quantify repetitive motions, predict musculoskeletal disorders (Buisseret, Hamzaoui, and Jojcyzk 2018), and to serve as an ergonomic evaluation tool due to its low cost and almost immediate results (Horejsi et al. 2013). Kinect has even been used to train nurses on how to safely transfer a patient from the bed to a wheelchair (Huang et al. 2014). However, there is a lack of research that uses dynamic, continuous skeleton tracking for ergonomic assessments to inform layout designs. One close example is a tool that integrates the RULA/REBA (Rapid Upper Limb Assessment/ Rapid Entire Body Assessment) with a custom-made 3D body modeling system to design a workstation for modular construction workers (Li, Zhang, and Yu 2019). DAMI aims to push this investigation one step further beyond the furniture scale to provide means of designing ergonomically sound nurse workflow in an entire patient room.

The optimization plug-in used in this paper is Octopus for Grasshopper (Vierlinger 2018; Rutten 2020). This multi-objective solver has been used to create a "heuristic optimization workflow" for interactively exploring different building geometries (Ashour and Kolarevic 2015), and to implement a genetic algorithm to assist architects in exterior designs (Kocabay and Alaçam 2017). While these two examples focused on the building and urban scale, Octopus has also been used at the interior level, which is where DAMI will be implemented. One example is a project that optimized building layouts based on pedestrian flow information (Li, Zhang, and Yu 2019). Projects utilizing other tools for layout optimization include a novel multi-objective search method for configuring a hospital emergency department (Zuo et al. 2019) and a space-planning model using generative algorithms to subdivide planar structures (Nagy et al. 2017). However, one shared limitation among these projects is the absence of dynamic anthropometric data in the optimization process. DAMI aims to fill this gap by acquiring and using specific user body skeleton and point cloud data as input parameters for layout optimization and evaluation to assist designers in both schematic phases and postoccupancy evaluations of projects.

METHOD

DAMI was developed in five steps (Fig. 2) in Rhinoceros and Grasshopper with the following plug-ins: Firefly for generating Kinect skeleton (Payne and Johnson 2015), Project Owl for generating Kinect half point cloud (Chung 2017), and Octopus for optimization (Vierlinger 2018).

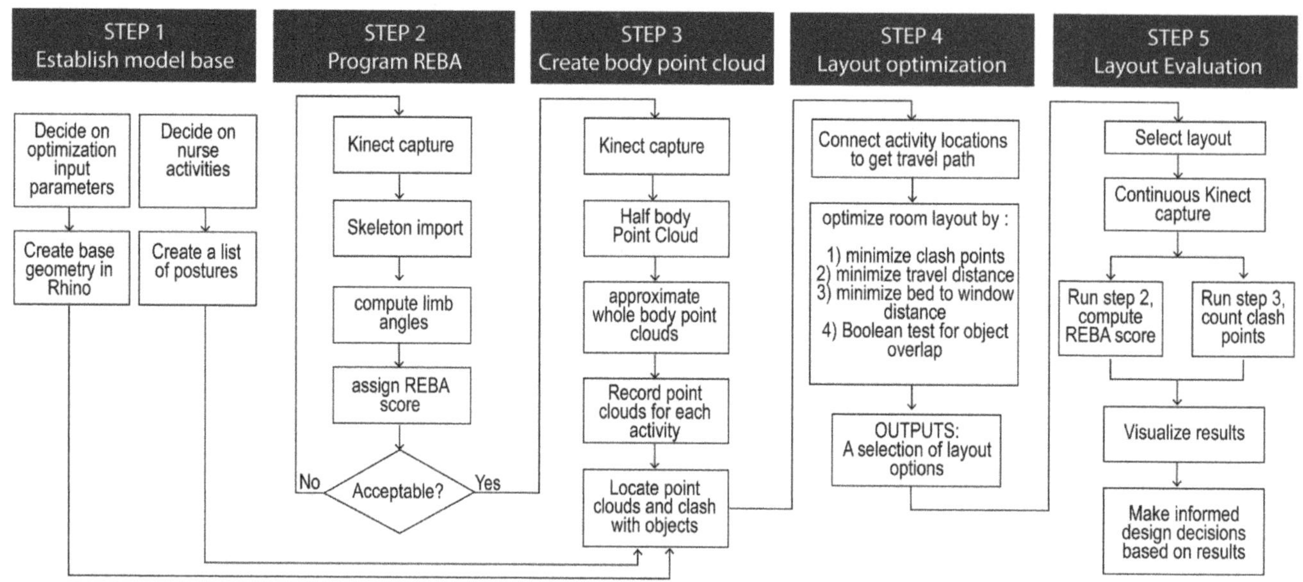

2

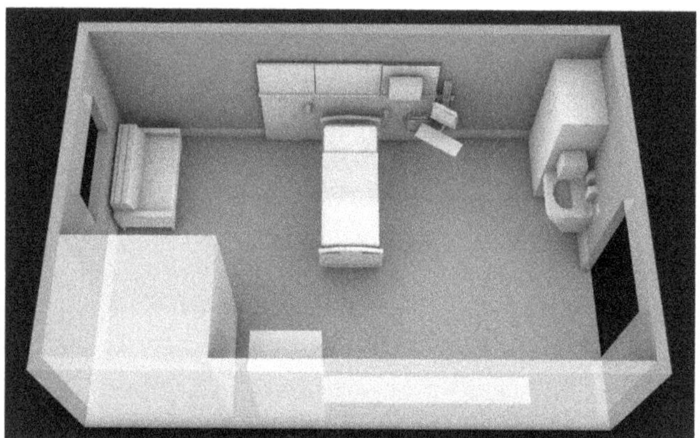

3

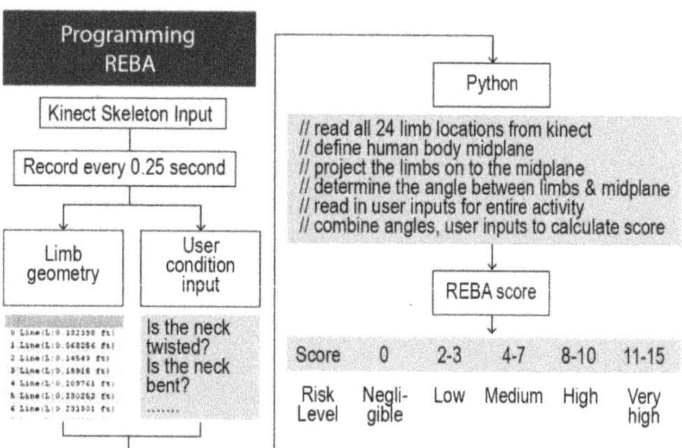

4

2 Overall framework for tool development.

3 Rhinoceros model of the base patient room with adjustable elements (door, window, furniture, and equipment).

4 Framework for generating the REBA scores.

Step 1: Establish Base Model

First, a 25 ft x 16 ft patient room model was built with typical architectural elements, including bathroom, patient bed, headwall, foot wall, charting computer, couch, wardrobe, and sink (Fig. 3). Each element is movable and will be used as an input parameter for layout optimization. Next, a list of potential nurse tasks was created based on existing studies (Freitag et al. 2007, 2013) to be used later for full body point cloud reconstruction. These tasks include: 1) helping patients sit up in bed; 2) standing up from a seated position; 3) squatting; 4) lifting from the floor; 5) making bed; 6) lifting patients' legs; 7) transferring materials; 8) walking; 9) charting; and 10) washing at the sink.

Step 2: Program REBA

In order to assess nurse postures, an industry tool—the Rapid Entire Body Assessment (REBA)—was selected (Hignett and McAtamney 2000). Current research that investigated eight different methods for determining ergonomic risk factors found that the REBA assessment was one of the most stringent in terms of predicting high risk situations (Chiasson et al. 2012). Normally, the REBA is a worksheet that is manually filled out by the investigator based on observations of the employee completing various tasks. For this project, the process was translated into a Grasshopper Python script that took in two types of input: 1) skeleton reading from Kinect, and 2) manual posture assessments including questions such as "What is the load carried?" or "How frequently is this task performed?" The overall development framework is presented in Figure 4.

The REBA assesses five different joint angles: Neck, Trunk, Upper Arm, Lower Arm, and Wrist. On the REBA worksheet, each angle was examined from the side view of the employee.

In order to digitally assess these angles in the same way and continually evaluate them as the employee moves around the room, a coordinate system that uses the body as the reference frame was needed. A plane was created between the employee's spine and right shoulder. A plane perpendicular to the shoulder-spine plane that intersected the employee's spine was designated as the "midplane." All limbs and joints were projected onto this midplane in order to emulate the REBA "side view" angle assessment. Each angle measurement then was used to assign a score for each joint.

The angle scores and user-input scores were combined to find the overall REBA score, using the same methods implemented on the worksheet. For this study, the authors made skeleton recordings of six selected nurse tasks. For each recording, a new REBA score was calculated every 0.25 seconds. Since the Kinect sensor often had unstable readings, the tool computed an average of every five REBA scores. The results can then be divided into five different risk levels (Hignett and McAtamney 2000) as summarized in Figure 4. This final skeleton posture data was used to help constructing point clouds in step 3.

Step 3: Reconstruct Full Body Point Cloud

One key factor that distinguishes our tool from others is its ability to create dynamic models with Kinect movements. The first difficulty to overcome was to reconstruct a full body point cloud based on Kinect's half body point cloud, as generated by Project Owl. Because our evaluation is at a room scale and therefore detail is not a key requirement in this process, our approach was to first assume that the human body is symmetrical.

As an example, the following sequence would allow us to generate the other half of the point cloud for a single limb (Fig. 5). Taking one example reading from Kinect, the skeleton information was imported into the model space as a line with a point cloud in front. By projecting the line onto the XY plane, the rotational angle θ_{xy} between the projected line and x axis can be found. Similarly, the rotational angle θ_R on the new plane R bounded by the original line and z axis can also be found. These two angles were then used to rotate the XZ plane to create a new plane for mirroring, denoted as plane M. After aligning the new plane with the original line, the point cloud was mirrored around plane M, the two point clouds were joined together to form one whole point cloud.

Taking this logic and applying it to the 24 limbs read from Kinect, 24 mirroring planes were created and stitched together to create one continuous surface. The half body point cloud was subsequently mirrored around this surface to create the full body point cloud as shown in Figure 6.

A second issue encountered relates to the fact that Kinect detects all objects in its field of view. Depending on the test environment, there can be noise and unwanted objects. To overcome this, the same continuous mirroring surface was extruded to create a volume, then a Boolean test was performed to separate the points that fall within the volume from those that were outside (Fig. 7).

A third problem inherent with the Kinect sensor was its reading instability. Joints can change locations even when the user is not moving, causing the skeleton lines to jolt.

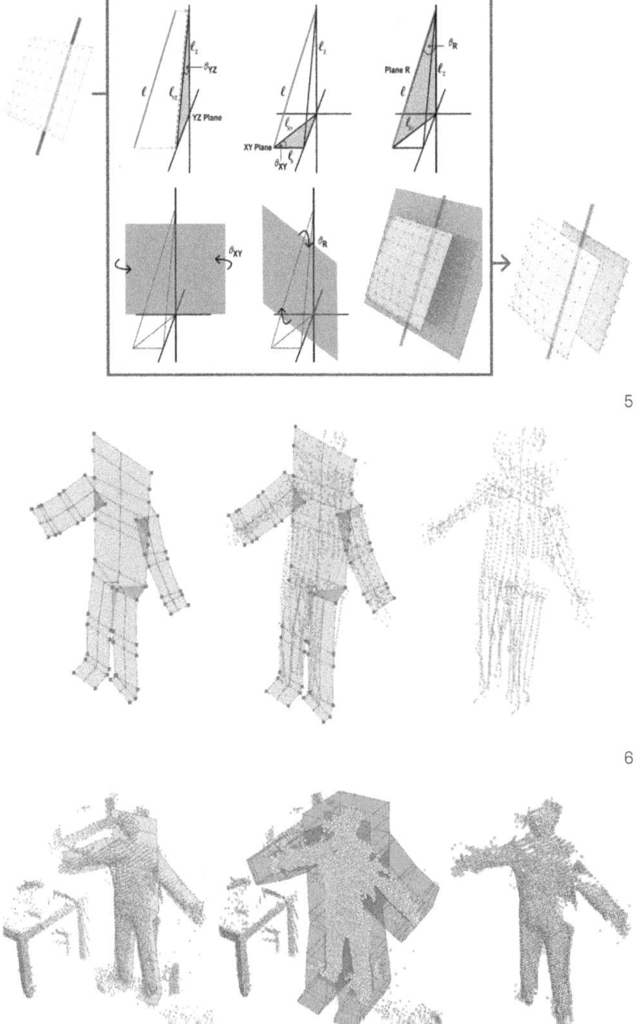

5

6

7

5 Logic sequence for approximating point cloud for one limb. From left: Kinect skeleton line reading, projecting line onto XY plane to get θ_{xy}, find new plane R bounded by original line and z axis to get θ_R, rotate XZ plane by θ_R and θ_{xy} to get mirroring plane M, mirror point clouds based on plane M.

6 Example showing the creation of one full body point cloud by mirroring Kinect half body point cloud over a continuous mirroring surface.

7 Example showing extruding the mirroring surface into a volume and performing a Boolean test to find which points fall within the volume (highlighted in green) and delete noise points that fall outside.

Instead of smoothing the data, which accepts some degrees of error, a better option was to delete the irregular positions entirely from the set. Examining the mirror planes created previously, if the reading was normal, the vertices interpolated from the skeleton joints will line up correctly to form one continuous surface. If the reading was abnormal, the joints will be shuffled to the incorrect place, causing the surface to become shattered or twisted. In Grasshopper, a continuous surface resulted in a list length of 1, while a discontinuous surface resulted in a list length of greater than 1. This was used to quickly detect and delete irregular readings from the data set (Fig. 8).

The next step was to make the full body point cloud dynamic by attaching each limb's associated points onto the Kinect skeleton. This was accomplished by taking the 24 planes created previously and extruding each into a volume. By intersecting and finding all the points that fall within each volume, the full body point cloud was subdivided into 24 groups of points, which were then moved onto the dynamic Kinect skeleton lines (Fig. 9).

Finally, the preselected nurse activities were simulated to record the corresponding point clouds. Six tasks were recreated: helping a patient sit up, making the bed, squatting, walking, charting, and washing at the sink. The chosen recording setting was in a relatively empty room, with minimum furniture present. The author stood approximately 1 meter away, directly facing the Kinect sensor while performing the tasks. Each recording lasted four to five seconds, with one position captured every second, resulting in a total of four to five point clouds per task, which were then merged into one whole point cloud. An example step-by-step recording of Task 1: lifting patient, is shown in Figure 10. The six recorded whole point clouds with task REBA scores are shown in Figure 11, and the corresponding REBA calculation parameters are shown in Figure 12.

Step 4: Layout Optimization

During a project's schematic design phase, DAMI could be used to rapidly generate an initial pool of optimized layouts for selection. This was achieved by minimizing four goals in Octopus: 1) total point cloud collision with objects; 2) total travel distance; 3) distance from bed to window; and 4) a Boolean test of object overlap. The input parameters were: entry door location, bathroom location, bathroom door location, bathroom size, patient bed location, bedside charting computer rotation angle, foot wall location, wardrobe

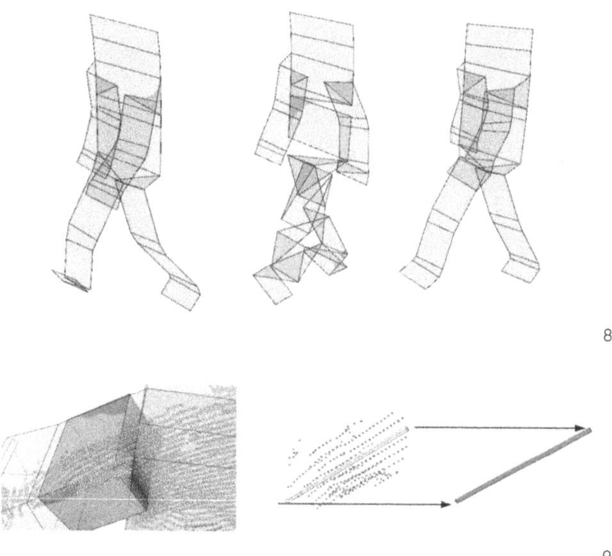

8

9

8 Example showing error reading detection. The middle figure indicates a discontinuous surface, which is a bad reading to be deleted from the set.

9 Example showing one segment of the body volume (upper right side arm) intersecting the body point cloud. The green highlighted points are then moved onto and associated with the dynamic Kinect skeleton (red line).

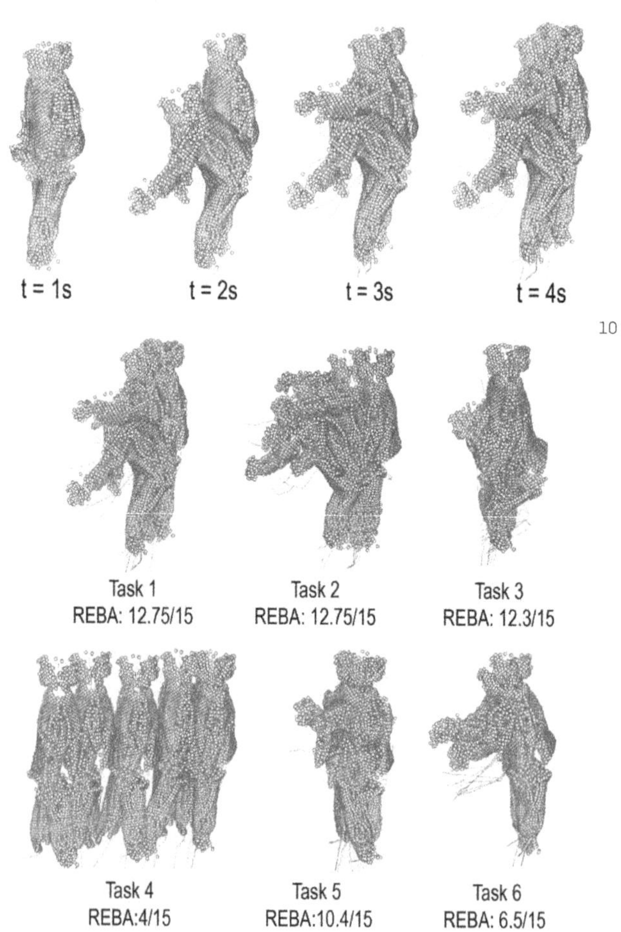

10

11

10 Example showing recording process for task 1: helping a patient sit up in bed. T=4s shows the final total point cloud for this task, to be used in later spatial layout optimization.

11 Total point clouds recordings with REBA scores calculated for the six selected tasks: 1) Helping a patient sit up; 2) making the bed; 3) squatting; 4) walking; 5) charting; and 6) washing at the sink.

location, window location, and window size. In order to set up the first optimization goal, three example tasks (Task 2: making bed, Task 5: charting, and Task 6: washing at the sink) were first located in the patient room and the recorded point clouds were moved to the corresponding locations, respectively. After connecting each task position with a straight line, the point cloud for walking was arrayed along the path. Next, 3D clearance zones around the patient bed, charting computer, and sink were created as simple cubes. A Boolean test was performed between the clearance boxes and the total point clouds to calculate how many points fall within the clearance volume. This completed the setup for the first goal of minimizing collision points (Fig. 13). For the second goal of minimizing total travel distance, a mass addition of the distances between each task point was performed. The third goal of minimizing bed to window distance was simply found by taking a measurement in model space between the geometric center of the patient bed to that of the window. The final goal of detecting object overlap was set as a Boolean test between 0 (no overlap) and 1 (overlap).

REBA parameter	Task 1	Task 2	Task 3	Task 4	Task 5	Task 6
Neck is twisted	True	True	False	False	True	False
Neck is bent	True	True	True	False	True	True
Trunk is twisted	True	True	True	False	True	True
Trunk side is bent	False	True	False	False	True	False
Leg raised	False	False	True	False	False	False
Leg adjustment	1	1	2	0	0	0
Load	2	2	1	0	1	1
Shock	False	False	False	False	False	False
Coupling score	2	2	0	0	1	1
Hold	True	True	True	False	True	True
Repeated	True	True	True	True	True	True
Large change	True	True	True	False	False	False
Shoulder raise	True	True	False	True	True	False
Upper arm abduct	True	True	False	False	True	False
Arm support	False	False	False	False	False	False
Wrist is bent	True	True	True	False	True	True

12

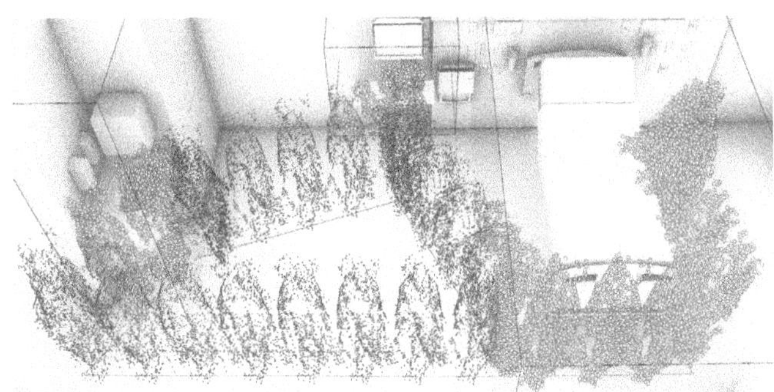

13

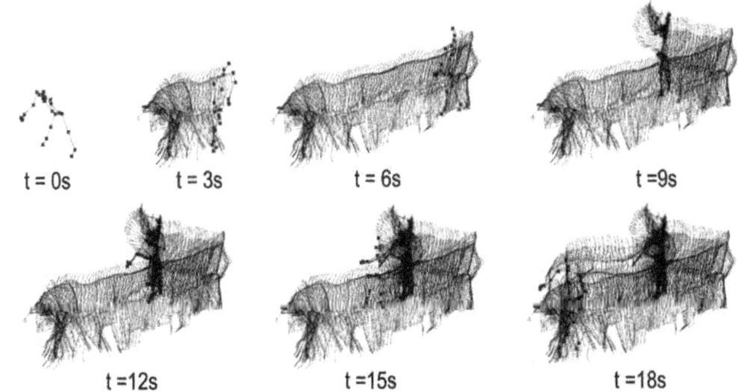

14

15

16

Step 5: Layout Evaluation

During the phase of construction mockup or postoccupancy evaluation, DAMI could provide valuable assistance in helping the facility management team and the architects to visualize and better understand the spatiotemporal relationship between nurse postures and the built environment. To demonstrate, a sample continuous skeleton recording was made in a room (roughly 25 ft x 16 ft) with furniture rearranged to imitate the location of a patient bed. The author simulated a walk-through around the space, and the skeletons were captured via Kinect in Rhinoceros (Fig. 14). These lines were then moved into the base patient room model (Fig. 15). The previously recorded point clouds were also attached to the task-associated skeleton lines (Fig. 16), including walking, charting, making bed, and helping a patient sit up in bed. This resulted in 608,100 generated points, which significantly affected computer performance. Therefore, for final visualization, the density of the point clouds was reduced by 90%, leaving around 60,000 points. Similar to point collision from step 4, green clearance zones around the patient bed, the foot wall wardrobe, and the bathroom were created to perform a Boolean test to understand point cloud encroachment (Fig. 16).

RESULTS

This section will be presented in two parts: 1) results for optimized layouts and 2) results for posture evaluations.

12 REBA input setting parameters for each of the tasks recorded.

13 Image showing point clouds located in base model with clearance zone boxes (green) and the collision points that fall within (red).

14 Continuous Kinect skeleton recording process.

15 Placement of recorded skeletons in the base patient room model.

16 Recorded point clouds are attached to the skeletons in model space. Clearance zones for point cloud collisions are shown as green boxes.

Part 1: Optimization Results

The optimization process was run for three hours, resulting in 50 generations with 1 second per iteration and 200 iterations per generation. This yielded approximately 10,000 room layout options. The results are compiled and shown in Figure 17 for Generation 1, 5, 10, 15, 20, 25, 30, 35, 40, and 45. Generation 50 is shown separately. On the graph, the x axis (green) shows total travel distance in inches, the y axis (red) shows total collision point count, and the z axis shows bed to window distance. Each cube on the graph represents one iteration. A red cube denotes an iteration with room objects overlap, a green cube denotes an iteration without objects overlap, and a semitransparent yellow cube denotes a past iteration included in this generation for optimization. For all generations, only green cubes are considered because objects must not overlap in the room.

One example layout is picked at every generation, circled in yellow and shown next to the graph. While it is impossible to pick a layout that fulfills all optimization goals, a hierarchy of importance can be set up to help compare the advantages and disadvantages of each selection, as summarized in Figure 18. This optimization process rapidly produces a catalog of options for designers to choose from. The result for Generation 50 is shown in Figure 19, with collision points ranging from 15505 to 19516, total travel distance ranges from 328 to 521 inches, and bed to window distance from 122 to 200 inches.

In order to improve the layout selection criteria, we can further rationalize each optimization goal such that the designer can make better judgments based on programmatic needs or user preferences. For example, shortening the total travel path can help reduce nurse fatigue. A lower bed to window distance implies increased daylight exposure. Construction cost is another important factor. The point cloud collision represents encroachment into equipment or furniture clearance zones, specified in regulations such as those published by the Facility Guidelines Institute (Facility Guidelines Institute 2018). Though movable objects and people are allowed within the clearance zone, minimizing the collision points can be interpreted as a way of improving the work environment efficiency for nurses. Example summaries of selection comparisons are shown in Figure 20.

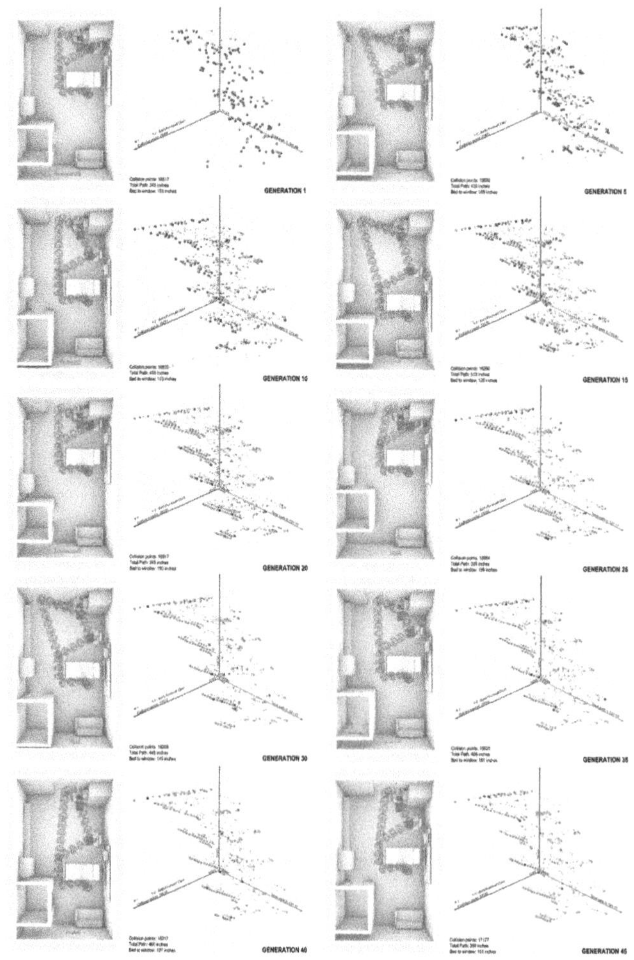

17

Generation Number	Travel Distance	Point Collision	Bed-Window Distance	Object Overlap
1	Low	Low	High	No Overlap
5	Medium	Low	Medium	No Overlap
10	Medium	Medium	Medium	No Overlap
15	High	Low	Low	No Overlap
20	Low	Low	High	No Overlap
25	Low	High	High	No Overlap
30	Medium	Low	Medium	No Overlap
35	Medium	Low	Medium	No Overlap
40	Medium	Medium	Low	No Overlap
45	Medium	Medium	Medium	No Overlap
50	Medium	Low	Medium	No Overlap

18

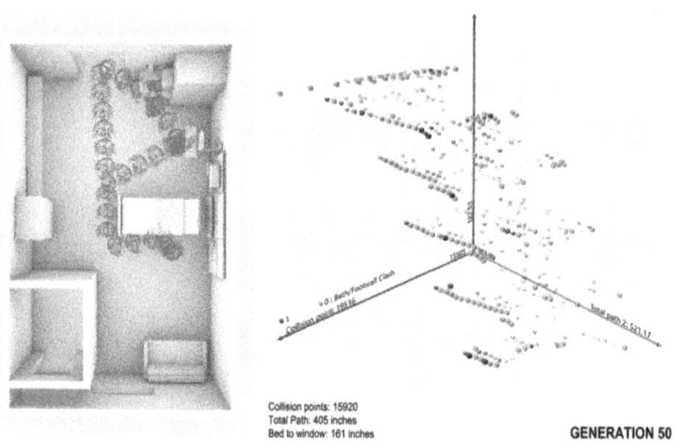

19

17 Optimization results, with selected room layout iteration noted as yellow circle in graph.

18 Table showing combination priorities for selecting layout options.

19 Generation 50 graph and selected iteration.

Part 2: Evaluation Results

The goal of the evaluation process is to help designers and facility managers visualize and better understand where in time and space poor postures would occur. To illustrate this, the example recording's REBA scores were used to construct a gradient color fill for the skeleton lines in model space, from white (with score 0 = negligible risk) to red (with score 15 = very high risk) (Fig. 21). By visualizing the REBA scores in space, one can see that the tasks performed at one side of the bed resulted in a much higher score than the other, implying a worse posture. Since the skeleton locations were recorded in a sequential manner with known intervals, the order of tasks can be easily tracked in Grasshopper. This allows the designer to visualize the location of users, the duration for each task, and the associated REBA scores to better understand the spatiotemporal relationship between the architectural environment and user posture.

Read together with the skeleton REBA graph, the point cloud collision illustration (Fig. 22) provides a more detailed view of potential clash regions between the nurse and the space.

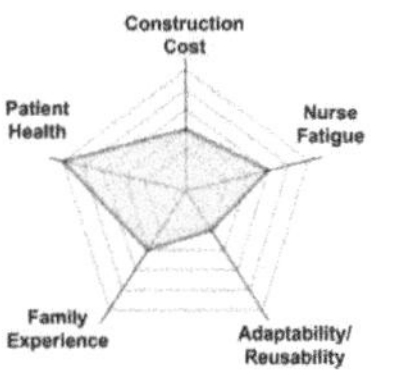

20

21

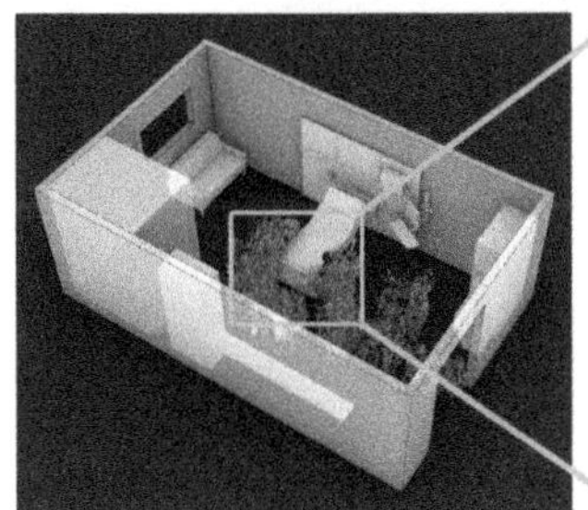

22

The body point clouds are represented here as spheres, the radius and color of which increase proportionally to the degree of clearance zone encroachment. This diagram reveals areas where there may be insufficient space to complete the task. In this example, collision points near the patient bed show the largest radius, indicating an increased chance of task conflict with the bed.

DISCUSSION

The results presented here serve as early validation of our concept, providing direct visualization that links together nurse tasks, posture REBA scores, and clearance encroachments, plus the factor of time in space. This can help architects, planners, and facility managers better understand when and where in the patient room poor ergonomics could occur and the associated tasks being performed. One potential issue is that the results generated during optimization were based on simplified input parameters. Not all selected options are actually suitable for construction, such as those that have inaccessible bathrooms. The aim of this paper is to explain the development of DAMI and demonstrate how to apply such a tool in a patient room. One interesting behavior from the optimization is the system's elimination of object overlaps even though this was not specified as a preference. At Generation 1, there were more red cubes than green ones, representing more iterations with object overlaps. From Generation 20, a distinct pattern started to emerge with increasing numbers of green cubes (Fig. 17).

However, there are also limitations. The first is a weakness with the Kinect sensor, which cannot detect blocked objects. If a nurse moves behind the patient bed, the point cloud generated would be inaccurate. The initial assumption of human body symmetry is another factor contributing to inaccuracies. The Kinect data is also uneven, which may impact the reliability of REBA scores. This can be resolved by choosing more advanced near-infrared light sensors. While the REBA scores can be calculated for task specific point cloud recordings, continuous task score estimations are not precise because the employee cannot pause during a task for the investigator to update REBA parameters. Therefore, the calculation settings also need to be dynamically built into the evaluation process.

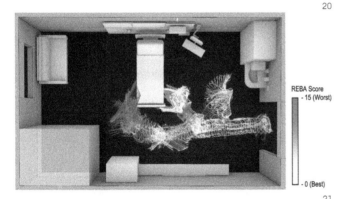

20 Example showing logic comparison and further reasoning to help designers finalize layout selection from the optimized pool of options.

21 Image showing continuous skeleton recording placed in base patient room model in Rhinoceros, with coloring according to their calculated REBA scores (range 0–15).

22 Image showing point cloud and collision points within object clearance zone, shown as spheres. The color and radius of the point sphere is proportional to how far it encroaches into the clearance area.

We envision a distributed system of sensors to be mounted in various spaces of a hospital, gathering skeleton and point cloud data. At the end of a nurse's shift, DAMI can provide summaries in easily understandable graphs and charts to assist various stakeholders in making evidence-based design decisions.

CONCLUSION

In this paper, we proposed DAMI, a Dynamic Anthropometric Modeling Interface aimed to optimize patient room layout and provide continuous evaluation of nurse postures with REBA scores. The results illustrate and reveal the important spatiotemporal relationship between task postures and the built environment. Architects, planners, and hospital facility managers can incorporate this work process to assess and improve the ergonomics of architectural spaces.

DAMI makes two contributions to the field of ergonomics and computational design. First, we are developing a novel real-time tracking work process based on the Kinect sensor that generates dynamic 3D human body point cloud models, which may accumulate into a new anthropometric database. The output can then be used directly by other designers to evaluate architectural spaces with respect to postures. Second, we are tailoring this tool specifically to the patient room environment and equipment layout, which is an under-studied area in anthropometry. Instead of focusing on how products can be fitted to accommodate varying body types, we want to investigate how architectural spaces can accommodate varying body dimensions and tasks.

For future studies, the base room model can be refined to incorporate more accurate input elements for the optimization process. In lieu of the mirroring method used in this paper, a neural network can be trained on existing data to generate the full body point clouds. A more controlled lab environment can also be used, such as a full-scale mockup room, similar to the actual construction process to create a more realistic testing environment. The processes can be applied to environments outside of the patient room as well, such as emergency rooms, waiting areas, or other high-traffic zones. Scenarios involving multiple users with overlapping pathways should be conducted to simulate complex situations. In addition, more user-based experiments must be performed to understand DAMI's reliability and validity.

REFERENCES

Ashour, Yassin, and Branko Kolarevic. 2015. "Heuristic Optimization in Design." In *ACADIA 2015: Computational Ecologies: Design in the Anthropocene [Proceedings of the 35th Annual Conference of the Association for Computer Aided Design in Architecture (ACADIA)]*, Cincinnati, OH, 19–25 October 2015, edited by L. Combs and C. Perry, 356–369. CUMINCAD.

Brooks, Ann. 1998. "Ergonomic approaches to office layout and space planning." *Facilities*. 16 (3/4): 73–78. DOI:10.1108/02632779810205602.

Buisseret, F., F. Dierick O. Hamzaoui, and L. Jojczyk. 2018. "Ergonomic Risk Assessment of Developing Musculoskeletal Disorders in Workers with the Microsoft Kinect: TRACK TMS." *Innovation and Research in BioMedical engineering* 39: 436–439. arXiv:1710.09682.

Chaudhury, Habib, Atiya Mahmood, and Maria Valente. 2009. "The Effect of Environmental Design on Reducing Nursing Errors and Increasing Efficiency in Acute Care Settings." *Environment and Behavior* 41 (6): 755–786. https://doi.org/10.1177/0013916508330392.

Chiasson, Marie-Ève, Daniel Imbeau, Karine Aubry, and Alain Delisle. 2012. "Comparing the Results of Eight methods Used to Evaluate Risk Factors Associated with Musculoskeletal Disorders." *International Journal of Industrial Ergonomics* 42: 478–488. https://doi.org/10.1016/j.ergon.2012.07.003.

Chung, H. 2017. "Project Owl." Accessed May 1, 2020. https://github.com/hodgoong/grasshopper-kinect2.

Dianat, Iman, Johan Molenbroek, and Héctor Ignacio Castellucci. 2018. "A Review of the Methodology and Applications of Anthropometry in Ergonomics and Product Design." *Ergonomics* 61 (12): 1696–1720. https://doi.org/10.1080/00140139.2018.1502817.

Facility Guidelines Institute. 2018. *Guidelines for Design and Construction of Hospitals*. New York: The Facility Guidelines Institute.

Freitag, Sonja, Rachida Seddouki, Madeleine Dulon, Jan Felix Kersten, Tore J. Larsson, and Albert Nienhaus. 2013. "The Effect of Working Position on Trunk Posture and Exertion for Routine Nursing Tasks: An Experimental Study." *Annals of Occupational Hygiene* 58 (3): 317–325. https://doi.org/10.1093/annhyg/met071.

Freitag, Sonja, Rolf Ellegast, Madeleine Dulon, and Albert Nienhaus. 2007. "Quantitative Measurement of Stressful Trunk Postures in Nursing Professions." *Annals of Occupational Hygiene* 51 (4): 385–395. https://doi.org/10.1093/annhyg/mem018.

Hignett, S., and L. McAtamney. 2000. "Rapid Entire Body Assessment: REBA." *Applied Ergonomics* 31: 201–205. DOI:10.1016/s0003-6870(99)00039-3.

Horejsi, Petr, Tomas Gorner, Ondrej Kurkin, Patrick Polasek, and Martin Januska. 2013. "Using Kinect Technology Equipment for

Ergonomics." *MM Science* (March): 388–389. DOI:10.17973/MMSJ.2013_03_201302.

Huang, Zhifeng, Ayanori Nagata, Masako Kanai-Pak, Jukai Maeda, Yasuko Kitajima, Mitsuhiro Nakamura, Kyoko Aida, Noriaki Kuwahara, Taiki Ogata, and Jun Ota. 2014. "Automatic Evaluation of Trainee Nurses' Patient Transfer Skills Using Multiple Kinect Sensors." *IEICE Transactions on Information and Systems* E97.D (1): 107–118. DOI:10.1587/transinf.E97.D.107.

Kocabay, Serkan, and Sema Alaçam. 2017. "A Multi-Objective Genetic Algorithm Framework for Earlier Phases of Architectural Design." In *Protocols, Flows and Glitches, Proceedings of the 22nd International Conference of the Association for Computer-Aided Architectural Design Research in Asia (CAADRIA)*, 293–303. Hong Kong: CAADRIA.

Lavender, Steven A., Carolyn M. Sommerich, Emily S. Patterson, Elizabeth B.-N. Sanders, Kevin D. Evans, Sanghyun Park, Radin Zaid Radin Umar, and Jing Li. 2015. "Hospital Patient Room Design: The Issues Facing 23 Occupational Groups Who Work in Medical/Surgical Patient Rooms." *HERD: Health Environments Research & Design* 8 (4): 98–114. https://doi.org/10.1177/1937586715586391.

Li, Xinming, Sanghyeok Han, Mustafa Gül, and Mohammed Al-Hussein. 2019. "Automated Post-3D Visualization Ergonomic Analysis System for Rapid Workplace Design in Modular Construction." *Automation in Construction* 98: 160–174. https://doi.org/10.1016/j.autcon.2018.11.012.

Li, Yunqin, Jiaxin Zhang, and Chuanfei Yu. 2019. "Intelligent Multi-Objective Optimization Method for Complex Building Layout Based on Pedestrian Flow Organization: A Case Study of People's Court Building in Anhui, China" *Proceedings of the 24th CAADRIA Conference* 1, 271–280. Hong Kong: CAADRIA.

Microsoft. n.d. "Kinect for Windows." Accessed May 2020. https://developer.microsoft.com/en-us/windows/kinect/.

Nagy, Danil, Lorenzo Villaggi, Dale Zhao, and David Benjamin. 2017. "Beyond Heuristics: A Novel Design Space Model for Generative Space Planning in Architecture." In *ACADIA 2017: Disciplines and Disruption [Proceedings of the 37th Annual Conference of the Association for Computer Aided Design in Architecture (ACADIA)]*, Cambridge, MA, 2–4 November 2017, edited by T. Nagakura, S. Tibbits, M. Ibañez, and C. Mueller, 436–445. CUMINCAD.

Pati, Debajyoti, Thomas E. Harvey Jr., Evelyn Reyers, Jennie Evans, Laurie Waggener, Marjorie Serrano, Rachel Saucier, and Tina Nagle. 2009. "A Multidimensional Framework for Assessing Patient Room Configurations." *HERD: Health Environments Research & Design Journal* 2 (2): 88–111.

Payne, A., and J. K. Johnson. 2015. "Firefly." Accessed May 1, 2020. http://www.fireflyexperiments.com/.

Plantard, Pierre, Hubert P.H. Shum, Anne-Sophie Le Pierres, and Franck Multon. 2016. "Validation of an Ergonomic Assessment Method Using Kinect Data in Real Workplace Conditions." *Applied Ergonomics* 65: 562–569. Published online ahead of print. DOI:10.1016/j.apergo.2016.10.015.

Rutten, David. *Grasshopper*. V.1.0.0007. Robert McNeel & Associates. PC. 2020.

Sharafkhani, Naser, Mahboobeh Khorsandi, Mohsen Shamsi, and Mehdi Ranjbaran. 2014. "Low Back Pain Preventative Behaviors Among Nurses Based on the Health Belief Model Constructs." *Sage Open* 4 (4): 1–7. https://doi.org/10.1177/2158244014556726.

Vierlinger, R. 2018. "Octopus." Accessed May 1, 2020. https://www.food4rhino.com/app/octopus.

Villeneuve, J., S.L.M. Remijn, J. Lu, S. Hignett, and A.E. Duffy. 2007. "Ergonomic Intervention in Hospital Architecture." In *Meeting Diversity in Ergonomics*, edited by R.N. Pikaar, E.A.P. Koningsveld, and P.J.M. Settels, 243–270. DOI:10.1016/B978-008045373-6/50016-7.

Zuo, Xingquan, Bin Li, Xuewen Huang, Mengchu Zhou, Chunyang Cheng, Chunyang Cheng, Xinchao Zhao, and Zhishuo Liu. 2019. "Optimizing Hospital Emergency Department Layout via Multiobjective Tabu Search." *IEEE Transactions on Automation Science and Engineering* 16 (3): 1137–1147. DOI:10.1109/TASE.2018.2873098.

Mengni Zhang is a PhD student at Cornell University's Architectural Robotics Lab. He is majoring in Human Behavior & Design with minor focuses in Information Science and Electrical & Computer Engineering. His research centers on the design and implementation of multi-agent assistive robots in healthcare environment.

Clara Dewey is a recent graduate of Cornell University with a B.S. in Mechanical Engineering and minor in Design & Environmental Analysis. She has researched a variety of human-product interactions, and now explores the intersection of product development, user-centered design, and sustainability.

Saleh Kalantari is an Assistant Professor at Cornell University's Department of Design and Environmental Analysis. He is the director of the Design and Augmented Intelligence Lab (DAIL) at Cornell, where his research group investigates human–technology partnerships in the design process, and the resulting opportunities for innovation and creativity. He has previously taught at the University of Houston and Washington State University.

Affective Computing for Generating Virtual Procedural Environments Using Game Technologies

Claudiu Barsan-Pipu
CAUP-Tongji University
Neomorph Studio

Nathalie Sleiman
Arden University
NS Interiors

Theodor Moldovan
Transylvania University
Neomorph Studio

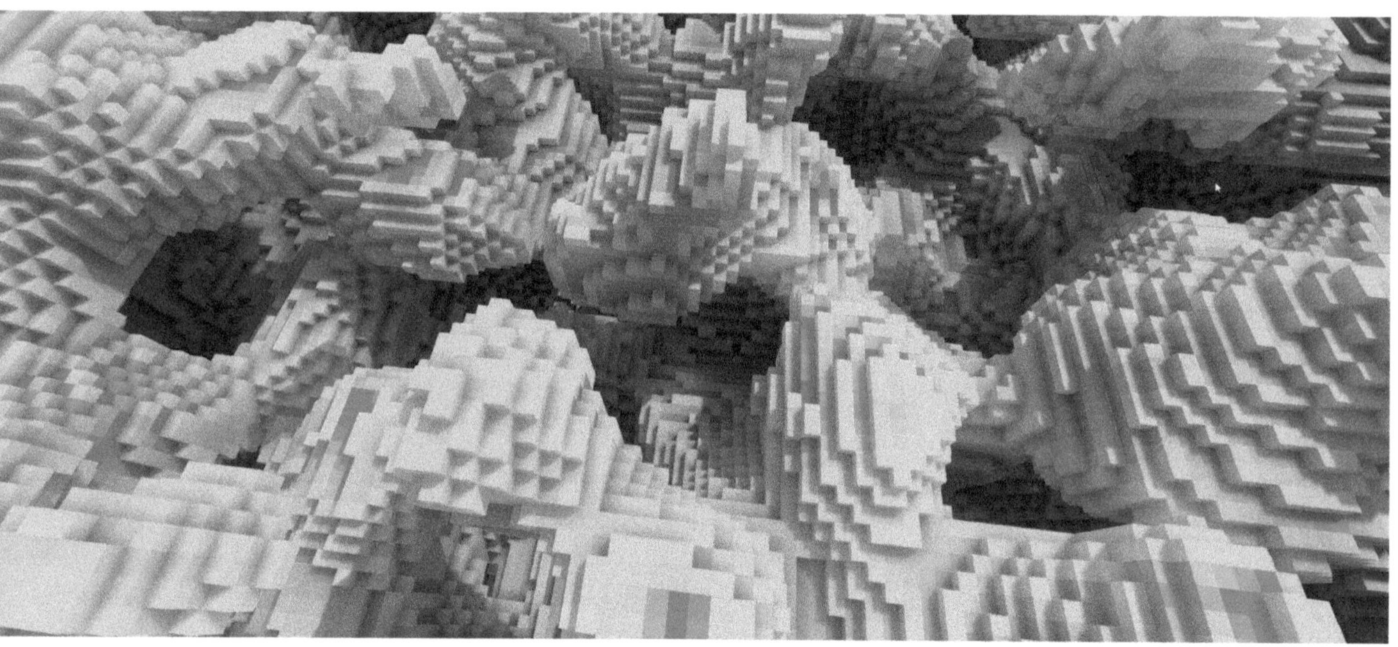

1 Game engine virtual reality environment view of a procedural volumetric 3D complex noise morphology rendered in real-time using VGI (voxel global illumination) based on the affective response measured via brain-computing interfacing and generated using eye-tracking within the proposed experimental system.

ABSTRACT

Architects have long sought to create spaces that can relate to or even induce specific emotional conditions in their users, such as states of relaxation or engagement. Dynamic or calming qualities were given to these spaces by controlling form, perspective, lighting, color, and materiality. The actual impact of these complex design decisions has been challenging to assess, from both quantitative and qualitative standpoints, because neural empathic responses, defined in this paper by feature indexes (FIs) and mind indexes (MIs), are highly subjective experiences. Recent advances in the fields of virtual procedural environments (VPEs) and virtual reality (VR), supported by powerful game engine (GE) technologies, provide computational designers with a new set of design instruments that, when combined with brain-computing interfacing (BCI) and eye-tracking (E-T) hardware, can be used to assess complex empathic reactions. As the COVID-19 health crisis showed, virtual social interaction becomes increasingly relevant, and the social catalytic potential of VPEs can open new design possibilities. The research presented in this paper introduces the cyber-physical design of such an affective computing system. It focuses on how relevant empathic data can be acquired in real time by exposing subjects within a dynamic VR-based VPE and assessing their emotional responses while controlling the actual generative parameters via a live feedback loop. A combination of VR, BCI, and E-T solutions integrated within a GE is proposed and discussed. By using a VPE inside a BCI system that can be accurately correlated with E-T, this paper proposes to identify potential morphological and lighting factors that either alone or combined can have an empathic effect expressed by the relevant responses of the MIs.

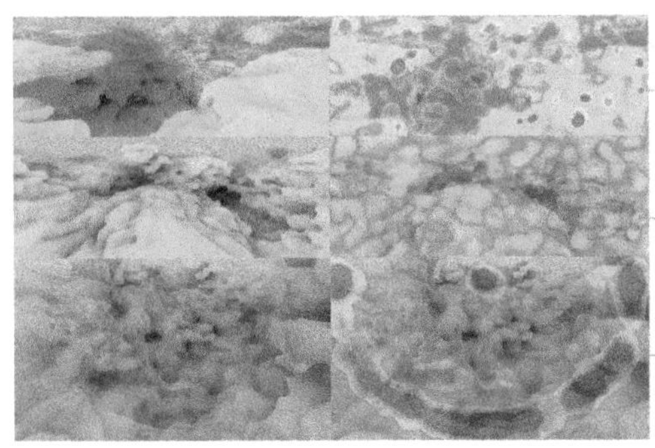

2 Feature-to-affect correspondences between the smoothed VPE and the guiding E-T interest heat map.

INTRODUCTION

Background Research

Architects have long sought to create spaces that can relate to or even induce specific emotional conditions in their users, such as states of relaxation or engagement (Balakrishnan, Sundar and Shyam 2006). Different approaches have been used to structure and guide the perceived spatial-empathic experience of humans (Franz and Bülthoff 2003). Dynamic or calming qualities were given to these spaces by controlling form, perspective, lighting, color, and materiality (Haeusler 2009; Strohmeier et al. 2016). The actual impact of these complex design decisions has been challenging to assess (Farahi 2018; Shemesh et al. 2016) from both quantitative and qualitative standpoints, as neural empathic responses, defined in this paper by feature indexes (FIs) and mind indexes (MIs), are highly subjective experiences (Barrett 2018). With the recent advances in the fields of virtual procedural environments (VPEs) and virtual reality (VR), supported by increasingly powerful game engine (GE) technologies, computational designers are provided with a new set of design instruments that, when combined with newly integrated brain-computing interfacing (BCI) and eye-tracking (E-T) hardware (Zhang, Jeng, and Zhang 2018), can be used to assess complex empathic reactions (Davidson 2004).

In Barsan-Pipu (2020), an immersive virtual cyber-physical system is proposed that uses a deep learning model, namely reinforcement learning, to analyze and learn the emotional response of a designer in relation to the psychological arousal factor (without being able to determine the valence) with a powerful procedural back-end integrated within a GE. An experimental and VR compatible dry-electrode electroencephalogram (EEG) system was used to record real-time EEG information from the parietal and occipital areas of the brain, while E-T was used to spatially control the focus and spatial deformation areas over a 3D surface powered by the procedural back-end. The end goal of the artificial intelligence (AI) system was to produce designs via complex geometric variations of the input surfaces that would excite the designer in terms of psychological arousal, without knowing if the user would find the resulting spatial design exciting in a positive or negative way. It basically learned how to provoke a "love-hate" type of emotional spatial design response based on a continuous feedback loop. In Shemesh et al. (2016), researchers investigated the human perception of different geometries of spaces in a cave-type VRE and assessed the emotional response of two categories of users with regards to their architectural background: expert and nonexpert users. Results seemed to indicate that the nonexperts preferred the smoother shapes, and the experts—with architectural background—had a preference for sharper-featured spaces. The curvature of the geometry was found to be highly relevant for both test groups. In Haeusler (2009), a subtle connection between human emotion and forms of urban representation was achieved via empathic feedback loops expressed over three-dimensional voxel surfaces. The emotions here are derived using facial analysis using feature-based recognition. In Grandchamp and Arnaud (2016), an inflatable dome with internal video projections of procedural real-time fractal images was used to engage a dynamic feedback loop, where the BCI based on an Emotiv Epoch 14 channel EEG was used to alter in real time the images being projected on the virtual dome based on the empathic response of the user, in search of a state of relaxation proper for meditation. Finally, Banaei et al. (2017), using inside a VRE a complex EEG cap with 128 electrodes covering the entire scalp, analyzed the empathic response that combines the psychological arousal and resulting pleasure (valence) of different typologies of interior spaces, illustrating again a preference for rounder, smoother spaces vs. sharper, more rigid spaces within a sample population with no architectural training.

The above references, while approaching in various ways the problematic of assessing a basic emotional response to different types of spaces, predefined or dynamically (procedurally) generated, suffer from limited immersiveness and often simplistic or flattened out—when projected on surfaces—spatial characteristics. More immersive and complex spatial models for VREs are needed that are able to combine multisensorial data in compact and affordable devices—for example, by joining precise E-T and dry-electrode BCI systems within a unified VR head-mounted display (HMD) solution, as proposed by the current research. While more simplistic than their medical-grade, expensive laboratory equipment counterparts, these new

3

4

5

approaches can still provide relevant results that, while less accurate, can enable new methodologies of assessing and generating spaces that consider the affective response of their users.

Research Objectives

As the COVID-19 global health crisis showed, virtual social interaction is increasingly relevant. As physical social distancing may become the norm, the social catalytic potential of VPEs can open new design possibilities. The research presented here attempts to introduce the cyber-physical design of such an affective computing system (Picard 1995). It focuses on how empathic data can be acquired in real time by exposing subjects within a dynamic, procedurally generated VR-based VPE and assessing their emotional responses while controlling the actual generative parameters via a live feedback loop. It is worth noting that the scope of this paper is limited to presenting the setup and procedures required, and only touches slightly on the data analysis and result interpretation, as those aspects are envisioned to be the subject of a follow-up work with a larger and more representative user sample. The notion of emotional or affective response is seen in its simplified form as a series of brain-pattern changes interpreted by the analysis of the EEG data, relying on the features and capabilities of the software and hardware BCI solution. The goal of this research was not to provide a medical-grade validation of the EEG technology but rather to focus on a simpler yet relevant solution design, much more seamlessly integrated with the VR HMD, which would provide more comfort for development and user usage, employing affordable EEG and VR HMD devices as a valid future direction for enabling wider access to this kind of technology. A combination of such affordable VR, BCI, and E-T solutions integrated within a GE is proposed and discussed.

Figure 6 illustrates the main schematic components of the proposed system.

METHODOLOGY

Procedural Volumetric Density-Based (VDB) Voxel Environments

At the core of the proposed cyber-physical method is a VDB voxel-based procedural system combining various generative elements. In its current form, the procedural system is based on three-dimensional noise fractal algorithms. It can produce evolving VPEs with either raw/coarse (voxel) (Fig. 3) or smoothed results, via the Marching-Cubes method (Fig. 4). This algorithmic selection could be easily expanded, for example, by incorporating L-Systems or Cellular Automata implementations, or other generative techniques such as spatial combinatorics or recursion. Still, for the scope of this investigation, the variety and complexity of spatial outcomes produced by the chosen techniques were deemed sufficient. Each generative algorithm exposes a set of control parameters and, due to the voxel system approach, enables smooth or discrete transitions between these parameters as well as between the different algorithms. This results in an ample range of morphological complexity occurring at various scales (Fig. 7). Because proper lighting represents a crucial feature for spatial human perception, a voxel-based real-time global

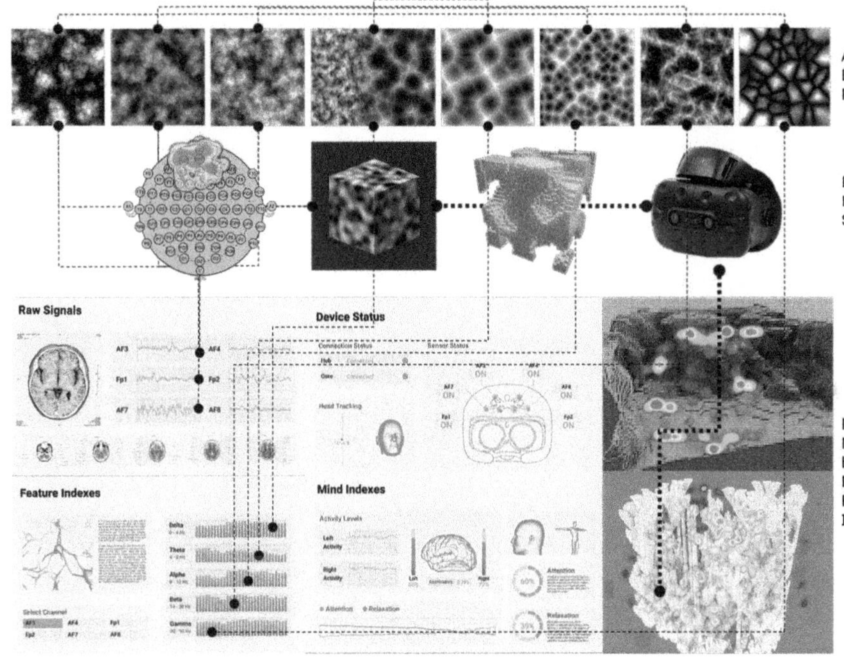

6

3 Aerial (flight mode) view of the coarse VDB voxel-based VPE showing the dynamic heat map overlay.

4 Ground-level (teleportation mode with gravity active) representation of the VPE showing transition from coarse to smooth voxel surfaces based on the focus areas illustrated by heat map.

5 Illustration of the user interface showing the raw values defining the feature indexes (EEG electrodes and channels/electrode activations) in world view.

6 Schematic conceptual overview of the method proposed in the current paper highlighting the main relations between its core components.

illumination (VRGI) solution was implemented, enabling dynamic shifts in direct and indirect lighting conditions. Finally, color abstraction was used to represent materiality, since the goal of the experiment focuses on assessing the primordial empathic response to different dynamic spatial morphologies and lighting conditions. Thus, the detailing was abstracted and intentionally kept to a minimal level. These components come together and create the dynamic VPEs used for this experiment.

Feature and Mind Indexes with Eye-Tracking

Another critical component of the experiment is the high-resolution VR HMD system integrating BCI and E-T functionalities. Supporting the BCI interface, a six-channel prefrontal dry-electrode EEG system enables filtered and raw signal acquisition at 500 Hz, as well as extraction of FIs (alpha, beta, gamma, theta, delta) and MIs (attention, relaxation, hemisphere balance) at 10 Hz using its internal software signal-processing module accessed by exposing the provided SDK functionality inside the GE.

The prefrontal cortex is responsible for the brain's executive functions and complex cognitive-behavioral processes as well as controlling emotions. Aggregation of the FIs based on the brainwaves recorded by each electrode results in the MIs, expressed by the attention, relaxation, and brain hemispheres activation balance. These MIs represent the performance metrics for the evaluation of the affective responses triggered by the different VPEs. E-T is used to associate the empathic response to a specific area of the VPE, thus enabling feature-to-affect relations (Fig. 2) to be observed via a dynamic heat map system accounting for eye gazes and fixations (Fig. 8).

Experimental Hardware and Software System

The experiment was developed on a VR-ready desktop computer running Windows using a GE (Unity[1] in this case), benefiting from the rapid iteration speed, photorealistic rendering capabilities, and readily available hardware integration for HTC Vive Pro Eye,[2] via SteamVR[3] and LooxidLabs LooxidLink SDK.[4] An overview of the experimental hardware setup is given in Figure 9.

A procedural 3D complex noise generator was implemented on the CPU, using SIMD[5] instructions, providing a wide range of volumetric noises, such as Perlin, Simplex, Cellular (Worely), or Alligator. The parametric properties of these generative 3D complex noises were exposed to the system and linked to the various FIs and MIs acquired by the LooxidLink BCI interface. Local changes of these parameters occurred based on the current focus areas, determined by gazes and fixations, defined here as sequences of gazes with a small spatial variation evaluated over 200 ms intervals that were recorded for each session and made invisible to the users. For analysis, while hidden to the user wearing the VR HMD and only visible on the monitors of the VR desktop system used for the experiments, a real-time E-T heat map was generated based on the acquired eye data. For visualization purposes, the real-time heat map was implemented as a postprocessing effect in deferred rendering mode using the G-buffer[6] and depth buffer, and the custom solution was implemented so

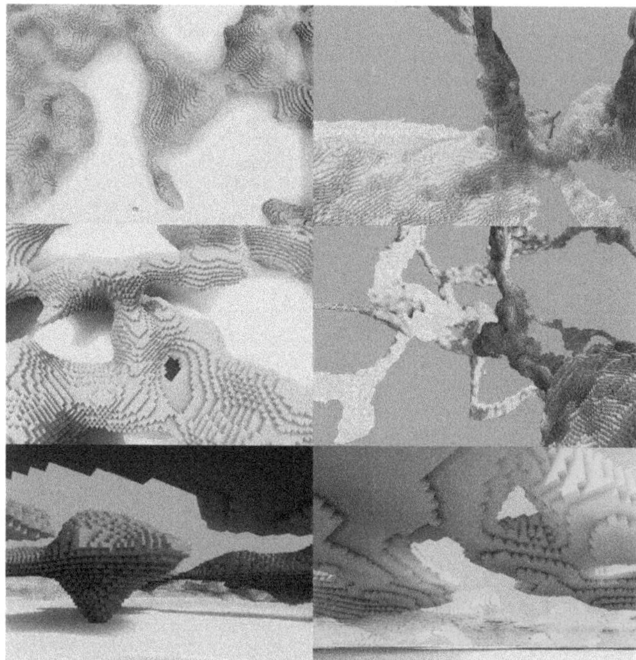

7

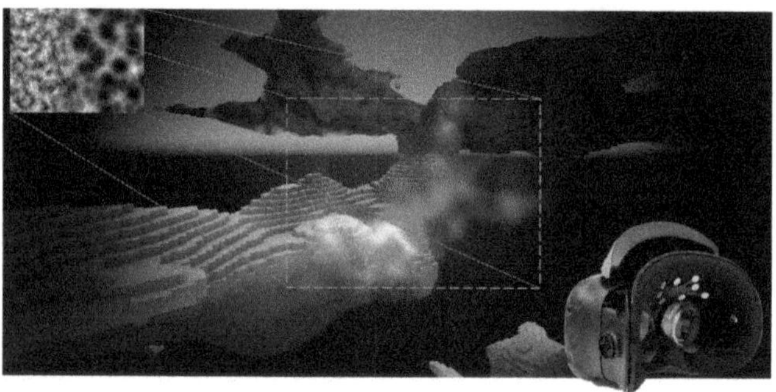

8

7 Volumetric density-based (VDB) voxel procedural system combining various generative elements. In its current form, the procedural system is based on three-dimensional complex noise models controlled by different parameters resulting in a high variation of the resulting morphologies.

8 Eye-tracking is used to associate the empathic response to a specific area of the VPE, thus enabling feature-to-affect relations to be observed via a dynamic heat map system accounting for eye gazes and fixations.

that there is no need to generate UV texturing coordinates and that the solution would be independent of geometric complexity, solely relying on ray-cast intersection with the procedurally created mesh colliders. The experiment allowed the generation of the heat map based on the E-T data, employing both a head-tracking approach and a gaze-based approached, using HTC Vive Pro Eye's integrated high-fidelity E-T system. Mounted on the HTC Vive Pro Eye HMD was the six-channel LooxidLabs BCI adapter, with its prefrontal dry-electrode EEG system enabling filtered and raw signal acquisition and extraction of the FIs (alpha, beta, gamma, theta, delta) and the MIs (attention, relaxation, hemisphere balance) (Fig. 10). A dedicated spatial user interface (UI) was adapted and extended from LooxidLink's SDK to visualize in real time the connection quality, the FIs and MIs, and the current 3D noise pattern being used (Fig. 5). This spatial UI was not directly visible to the users during the experiments but was implemented as a system that could be enabled to check for proper electrode connectivity and visualize real-time EEG data, as well as the active noise pattern. From the user's perspective, no UI system was required to interact with the VPE.

Experiment Description

A concept-validation experiment involving eight volunteer architecture master students (five men, three women) aged 23 to 26 was run, where each participant spent 10 minutes inside the VPE. While the initial conditions for all participants were identical, the individual empathic responses, namely the FIs and MIs that were controlling the procedural parameters, led to different spatial evolution for each participant. The goal of this experiment was not a full validation of the proposed setup, which would have required a much more thorough testing environment and procedural rigor but rather served as the base to observe the behavior of the cyber-physical system when used by different users and identify relevant spatial quality aspects, such as comfort, focus, orientation, smoothness, colorfulness, and complexity.

For each participant, after ensuring proper BCI connectivity for the six dry electrodes and accurate VR E-T calibration, the formal evolution generated by the real-time empathic response was tracked for 10 minutes. The cyber-physical system was designed in such a manner as to connect the various FIs and MIs received in real time via the BCI interface to different parameters of the procedural 3D noises. Note that both the types of volumetric noises used at every moment, as well as the parameters and properties of these noises, were automatically and dynamically altered based on the BCI feedback loops and the focus areas, recorded and later visualized via the real-time heat map. For example, the color and smoothness aspects of the resulting morphologies were controlled by different thresholds of the attention and relaxation parameters, as well as their ratio, whereas brain hemisphere activations and their balance were used to smoothly switch between the various 3D noise types implemented. Each user could freely move within the VRE either by using the HTC Vive Pro Eye's VR controllers to fly freely or by enabling gravity and using a more conventional VR teleportation system, while also given the option to dynamically switch between the two means of locomotion. In order to avoid motion sickness, a potential risk for users not accustomed to free flight mode inside VR, gravity-enabled teleportation was used as the implicit motion system. Two flight speed options were provided for the free locomotion mode, while collision detection was

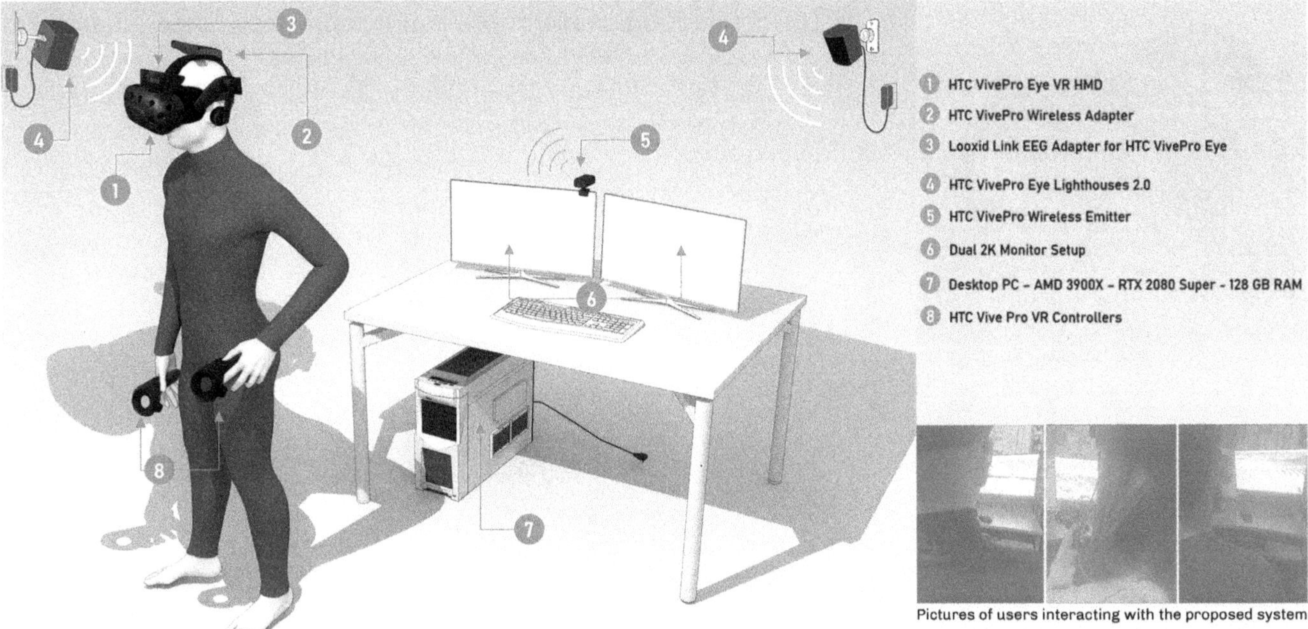

9 Experimental setup and the hardware components were used by eight volunteers (master's-level architecture students) who interacted with the procedural virtual environment.

used to prevent users from moving through the visible surfaces, thus avoiding potential confusing spatial perception and keeping the experience consistent and smooth (Fig. 12). Furthermore, in order to sustain a frame-rate suitable for an enjoyable VR experience while also performing voxel-based global illumination (VRGI) computations in real time, a somewhat simplified model of VRGI was used with only two indirect light bounces, and the simulations were run on a robust system powered by an AMD Zen 2 Ryzen 9 3900X CPU, nVidia RTX2080 Super GPU with 8GB of DDR6 VRAM, 128 GB DDR4 RAM @ 3200 MHz, 1TB PCIE Gen. 4 SSD running Windows 10 Pro, built using Unity 2019.4 LTE.

RESULTS AND DISCUSSION

By using a VPE inside a BCI system that can be accurately correlated with E-T, this paper proposes to identify potential morphological and lighting factors that either alone or in combination can have an empathic effect expressed by a relevant response of the MIs. The interactive aspect of the resulting VPEs is given by the real-time feedback loop, where the averaged values of the FIs and MIs over 3,500 ms were fed as parametric control input for a new iteration in the focus area, identified via the E-T heat map controlling the generative algorithms, lighting, and color parameters (Fig. 11). Given the inherent affective response variations in relation to the resulting space morphologies, including curvature, smoothness, coloring, and lighting, the results also exhibited a significant variation between the experiment's participants. More relaxing states of mind, defined here by the value of the relaxation MI, were observed and expressed via the smoothing of the voxel volume and a preference for warmer colors, whereas focus states, connected to the attention MI, were often expressed by intense multicolor scenes, and by more and lengthier fixations, leading to areas with increased complexity and spatial detailing. Figure 13 illustrates the eight resulting VPEs after the 10-minute session, showcasing a wide range of outcomes but also revealing some spatial structures and lighting conditions that led to calming or highly engaging results.

The curvature and formal richness played an important role for all users. However, the male participants seemed to find geometrical spaces with more flat surfaces more relaxing, while female participants found highly featured complex spaces more intimidating, which corresponded to heightened attention but much lower calming values (Fig. 14). The aforementioned conclusions were based on the measured MIs and validated by the informal description of the experience after it was completed, described in terms of the spatial qualities perception relevance for comfort, focus, smoothness, colorfulness, complexity, and orientation for all participants (male and female), female-only participants, and male-only participants as illustrated in Figure 15. Finally, Figure 16 presents the average mind indexes (relaxation, attention, left and right hemisphere activation) for four perceived complexities of spatial features, ranging from flat-dominant, low-complexity, medium-complexity, to high complexity attributes, showing a direct correlation between attention and complexity and an inverse relation of relaxation to complexity.

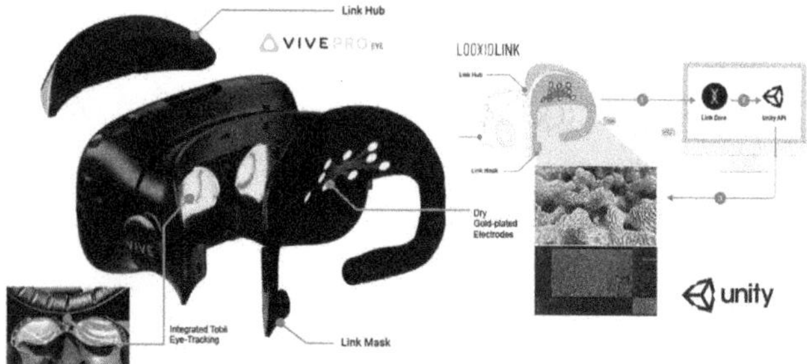

10 BCI interface: a six-channel prefrontal dry-electrode EEG system enabling filtered and raw signal acquisition at 500 Hz and extraction of feature indexes (alpha, beta, gamma, theta, delta) and mind indexes (attention, relaxation, balance) at 10 Hz interfacing with the Unity game engine. 10

Limitations

While visually complex, the CPU-based procedural noise models used in this research are still limited in terms of morphological output and variation. Computation speed could also be improved by using GPU Compute Shaders. Being abstract by design, the VPEs limit the users' perception of these spaces as being proper architecture; however, architectural and urban like-qualities have been acknowledged, especially due to the VRGI lighting system used. Constant voxel size might also influence the scale perception, though this is less observable in the case of the smoothed resulting morphologies. Feature-to-affect mapping was developed intuitively, based on the eye-tracking focus areas and direct empirical affective assignments of index and mind features values to parameters of the procedural noise models. More complex nonlinear models of assignment should be developed and tested. While using totally-dry electrodes embedded in the VR HMD hardware proved to be more user-friendly than the alternative saline-wet/gel or semi-dry variants, the limited amount of data coming from the specific area of the prefrontal cortex being scanned limits the nuances of interpreting the affective results in terms of psychological arousal and especially relating to measuring valence, providing only a simplified concept of emotion. An EEG system with more channels and a more complete electrode distribution covering all cerebral areas would provide a much clearer picture of the brain activation patterns. However, no such dry-electrode VR HMD-compatible system currently exists. Another important limitation is the small sample size of the user group used for data acquisition, and by the fact that all participants were in a way biased in the way they relate to space by their prior architectural background, all having studied architecture.

Future Research

One direction of further investigation entails the exploration of more complex and computationally efficient procedural generative systems that can enable designers to actively create a plethora of computational algorithms, broadly extending the morphological repertoire that users can empathetically access and use. Converting the resulting morphologies into more recognizable, natural, architectural or urban-like spaces by increasing detail and using easily relatable formal and scale-specific vocabularies should also become the subject of additional work. Further development should allow for scale variation of the patch and voxel components, as well as much smoother transitioning and interpolation between them. By making use of AI and specifically via deep learning models, more complex and relevant feature-to-affect mappings for affective assignments of index and mind features values to parameters of the procedural generative models could be identified and developed. By extending the area of the brain where EEG acquisition is possible beyond the prefrontal cortex, more nuanced evaluations of affective results in terms of psychological arousal and valence will be possible. Significantly increasing the user sample size for data acquisition and including nonarchitecture subjects while using a thorough statistical comparison of the results, both within each specific group of experts and nonexperts as well as between the two, could help obtain more pertinent and widely generalizable information. Finally, by exploring multiuser interactions and finding ways to procedurally generate virtual environments that successfully combine the relevant affective features of each participant with their interaction peers is proposed as a potential further investigative direction.

CONCLUSION

The information obtained via this approach is designed to be extrapolated beyond the scope of this paper to a much larger sample group and, with the future addition of artificial intelligence, and particularly that of deep learning methods, the minimization of the inter- and intra-subject variability of observed empathic responses is sought. VPEs can provide innovative opportunities for nontectonic design approaches, where empathy-driven participatory architectures will entail a significant shift in the role of designers and architects. Their new responsibilities as open-ended system designers require a firm reliance on complex computational and procedural systems that can operate at both the depth and the sensibility these new virtual social interaction spaces demand. Potential applications stemming from this research are the creation of complex relaxing or focus spaces within homes, offices, schools, maternity wards, and hospitals, as well as purely experiential (nonmaterialized, nontectonic) empathetically adaptive virtual environment scenarios for social interaction as an extension of the current social networks into VR. In order

11 Interactive view of the VPE showing the dynamic update of the morphology based on the user's gaze. The 3D environment is updated based on E-T fixations, while the smoothness of the space is controlled by the empathic response. 11

for the results of this investigation to be transformed into the aforementioned VPE spaces, additional polishing steps would be required, as the current experiment only provides a morphological base that needs to be properly adapted to each of the specific spatial destinations. Also, adequate integrated hardware and software VR solutions must be deployed alongside these VPEs, thus enabling the system to be potentially transformed and adapted for true real-life applications.

NOTES

1. Unity game engine: https://www.unity.com
2. HTC Vive Pro Eye HMD from HTC: .https://www.vive.com/eu/product/#pro%20eye%20series
3. SteamVR platform: https://www.steamvr.com/en/
4. LooxidLabs LooxidLink Software Development Kit (SDK): https://looxidlabs.com/looxidlink/
5. Single instruction–multiple data (SIMD): Parallel computation feature of modern CPUs .
6. G-buffer is collective term designating all textures used to store lighting-relevant data for the final lighting pass in deferred rendering mode.

ACKNOWLEDGMENTS

The authors would like to thank the reviewers for their valuable comments and revision on an earlier version of the manuscript, which helped improved the present manuscript.

ETHICAL CONSIDERATIONS

Informed Consent Statement: Informed consent was obtained from all individual participants included in the study and the recorded data was completely anonymized. The purpose and research procedures were presented in detail, and all questions raised by the participants before and after the experiment were answered. All potential risks and hazards of using the VR environment were explained and an accommodation session was run for each participant. Participants were informed that they could opt-out of the experiment at any moment, should any aspect of the procedure become problematic from a psychological or physiological perspective. One of the female participants experienced mild motion sickness, but she decided to continue and finalize the experiment when offered to quit.

Conflicts of Interest: The authors declare no conflict of interest.

REFERENCES

Balakrishnan, Bimal, Loukas N. Kalisperis Sundar, and S. Shyam. 2006. "Capturing Affect in Architectural Visualization—A Case for integrating 3-dimensional visualization and psychophysiology." In *Communicating Space(s) [24th eCAADe Conference Proceedings]*, 664–669. Volos.

Banaei, Maryam, Hatami Javad, Yazdanfar Abbas, and Gramann Klaus. 2017. "Walking through Architectural Spaces: The Impact of Interior Forms on Human Brain Dynamics." *Frontiers in Human Neuroscience* 11: 1–14.

Barrett, Lisa Feldman. 2018. *How Emotions Are Made: The Secret*. Boston: Mariner Books.

Barsan-Pipu, Claudiu. 2020. "Artificial Intelligence Applied to Brain-Computer Interfacing with Eye-Tracking for Computer-Aided Conceptual Architectural Design in Virtual Reality Using Neurofeedback." In *Proceedings of the 2019 Digital FUTURES. CDRF 2019*, 124–135. Singapore: Springer.

Davidson, RJ. 2004. "What Does the Prefrontal Cortex 'Do' in Affect: Perspectives on Frontal EEG Asymmetry Research." *Biological Psychology* 67: 219–233.

Farahi, Behnaz. 2018. "HEART OF THE MATTER: Affective Computing in Fashion and Architecture." In *ACADIA 2018: Recalibration: On Imprecision and Infidelity [Proceedings of the 38th Annual Conference of the Association for Computer Aided Design in Architecture (ACADIA)]*, Mexico City, Mexico, 18–20 October 2018, edited by P. Anzalone, M. del Signore, and A. J. Wit, 206–215. CUMINCAD.

Franz, G., M. Von der Heyde, and H. H. Bülthoff. 2003. "An Empirical Approach to the Experience of Architectural Space in VR—Exploring Relations Between Features and Affective Appraisals of Rectangular Interiors." In *Digital Design [21th eCAADe Conference Proceedings]*, 17–24. Graz.

Grandchamp, Romain, and Arnaud Delorme. 2016. "The Brainarium: An Interactive Immersive Tool for Brain Education, Art, and Neurotherapy." *Computational Intelligence and Neuroscience* 2016. Article ID 4204385.

Haeusler, Matthias Hank. 2009. "Modulations of Voxel Surfaces Through Emotional Expressions to Generate A Feedback Loop Between Private Mood and Public Image." In *Proceedings of the 14th International Conference on Computer Aided Architectural Design Research in Asia*, 173–182. Yunlin.

Picard, R. W. 1995. *Affective Computing*. M.I.T Media Laboratory Perceptual Computing Section Technical Report No. 321, 1–16. Cambridge, MA.

12

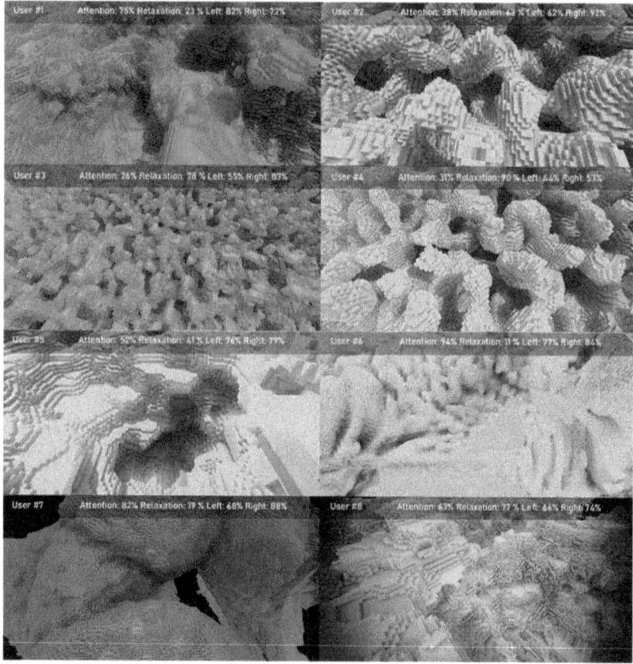

13

12 Two screenshots of the prototype VPE showing the electrode activation (lower left corner) and the current noise pattern (lower right corner).

13 Eight resulting VPEs after the 10-minute sessions, showcasing a wide range of outcomes and revealing some spatial structures and lighting conditions that led to calming or to highly engaging results.

Shemesh, A., R. Talmon, O. Karp, I. Amir, M. Bar, and Y. J. Grobman. 2016. "Affective Response to Architecture—Investigating Human Reaction to Spaces with Different Geometry." *Architectural Science Review*: 116–1125.

Strohmeier, Paul, Juan Pablo Carrascal, Bernard Cheng, Margaret Meban, and Roel Vertegaal. 2016. "An Evaluation of Shape Changes for Conveying Emotions." In *Proceedings of the 2016 CHI Conference on Human Factors in Computing Systems (CHI '16)*, 3781–3792. New York.

Zhang, L.M., T. S. Jeng, and R. X. Zhang. 2018. "Integration of Virtual Reality, 3-D Eye-Tracking, and Protocol Analysis for Re-Designing Street Space." *CAADRIA(23)*, 431–440. Beijing.

IMAGE CREDITS

All drawings and images by the authors.

Claudiu Barsan-Pipu is a cross-disciplinary computational designer with a background in architecture, fine arts, engineering, and game technologies. Working at the intersection between science and art, and passionate about the complexity theory paradigm, he contributed to developing new artificial intelligence and evolutionary computational models for urban and architectural investigations and recently incorporated powerful game technologies into virtual reality environments for conceptual design. He launched his own computational design agency, neomorph studio (www.neomorph.io) in 2017, where together with an interdisciplinary team, he explores state-of-the-art ideas and technologies, with a strong focus on AR/VR, brain-computing interfacing, and AI. He is also a guest lecturer at the Ion Mincu University of Architecture and Urbanism in Bucharest, Romania, and a PhD candidate of the International DigitalFUTURES program at Tongji University in Shanghai, China, under the supervision of Prof. Neil Leach.

Nathalie Sleiman has a widespread background covering interior design, psychology of design, and neuroscience. She is currently studying psychology at the University of Arden, in the UK. She runs her own creative practice, ns interiors, where she investigates how psychology can be applied to architecture and interior design, supporting mental health and well-being.

Theodor Moldovan is an enthusiastic game developer and computer science student in the Applied Informatics Department of Transylvania University in Brasov, Romania, and is passionate about the latest advancements revolving around AR/VR and artificial intelligence. He also works at neomorph studio, where he is responsible for experimenting and exploring the potential applications and implications of state-of-the-art technologies in design and other complementary fields.

14

14 Additional morphologies as well as interior spaces generated by users during the experiment (morphology and coloring were developed via the proposed cyber-physical system).

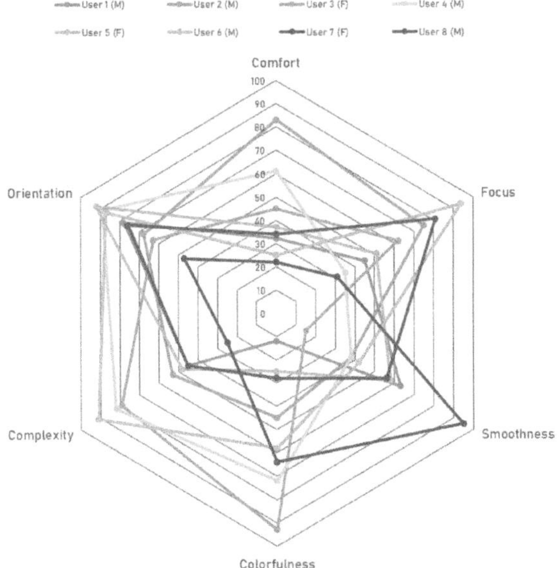

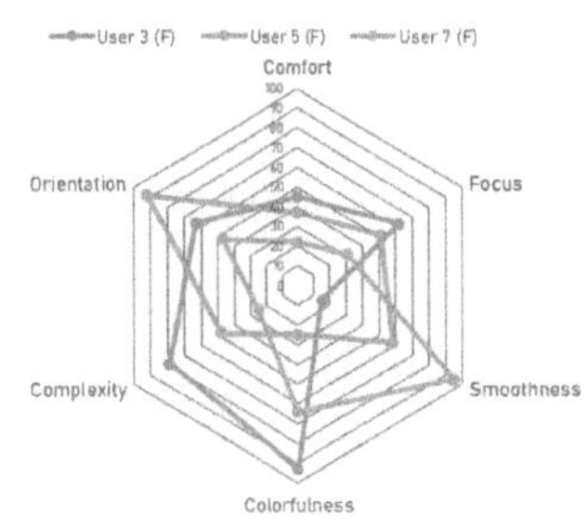

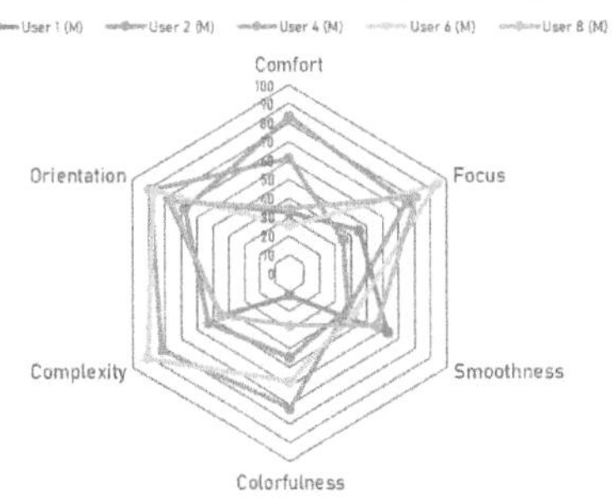

15

Average Mind Indexes based on Spatial Complexity

100
90
80
70
60
50
40
30
20
10
0

Flat-dominant Spatial Features
Low Complexity Spatial Features
Medium Complexity Spatial Features
High Complexity Spatial Features

■ Average Attention MI
■ Average Relaxation MI
■ Average Left Hemisphere Activation MI
■ Average Right Hemisphere Activation MI

16

15 Spider chart representations of the spatial qualities perception relevance (comfort, focus, smoothness, colorfulness, complexity, orientation) for all participants (left), female-only participants (top right) and male-only participants (bottom right).

16 Average mind indexes (relaxation, attention, left and right brain hemispheres activations) values based on estimated spatial complexity, expressed via flat-dominant, low-complexity, medium-complexity, and high-complexity spatial features.

Anxious Landscapes

Correlating the Built Environment with Mental Health through Deep Learning

David Newton
University of Nebraska-Lincoln

1 Aerial images of census tracts generated by a generative adversarial network that was trained on satellite images of tracts with high incidence of anxiety.

ABSTRACT

Advances in the field of machine learning over the last decade have revolutionized artificial intelligence by providing a flexible means to build analytic, predictive, and generative models from large datasets, but the allied design disciplines have yet to apply these tools at the urban level to draw analytic insights on how the built environment might impact human health. Previous research has found numerous correlations between the built environment and both physical and mental health outcomes—suggesting that the design of our cities may have significant impacts on human health. Developing methods of analysis that can provide insight on the correlations between the built environment and human health could help the allied design disciplines shape our cities in ways that promote human health. This research addresses these issues and contributes knowledge on the use of deep learning (DL) methods for urban analysis and mental health, specifically anxiety. Mental health disorders, such as anxiety, have been estimated to account for the largest proportion of global disease burden. The methods presented allow architects, planners, and urban designers to make use of large remote-sensing datasets (e.g., satellite and aerial images) for design workflows involving analysis and generative design tasks. The research also contributes insight on correlations between anxiety prevalence and specific urban design features—providing actionable intelligence for the planning and design of the urban fabric.

INTRODUCTION

Mental health is a pressing global health problem. It is estimated that mental health disorders such as depression and anxiety account for the largest proportion of disability-adjusted life years, which is a measure of global disease burden (Whiteford et al. 2015). Previous research in urban planning has found numerous correlations between the built environment and physical health measures, such as rates of obesity, high blood pressure, asthma, and diabetes (Marshall, Piatkowski, and Garrick 2014; McConnell et al. 2006; Müller et al. 2018; Simons et al. 2018). This research suggests that the design of our neighborhoods and cities may have significant impact on human health, but there has been less research on how mental health may be impacted by urban design features (Moore et al. 2018). Developing methods of analysis that can reveal correlations between the built environment and mental health is, therefore, a significant and underaddressed problem that is the focus of this research.

Previous research has largely relied on inferential statistical methods to find correlations between design features and health measures (Hoisington et al. 2019). More recent work has explored data-driven methods from the field of machine learning (ML), such as deep learning (DL), which offers an unparalleled ability to use large image databases (e.g., satellite, aerial, point-of-view images) to train models to estimate health outcomes (Maharana and Nsoesie 2018; Suel et al. 2019; Xie et al. 2016). Further, deep learning methods offer new ways to analyze images and find visual features that might correlate to specific health measures. Previous work has largely focused on physical health measures, however, and has paid little attention to the development of deep learning methods that can identify specific visual features in the built environment that might correlate with mental health measures.

This research, therefore, addresses these gaps in previous work and contributes knowledge on the use of generative and discriminative deep learning methods in combination for urban analysis involving mental health. The research specifically targets the prevalence of anxiety because it is responsible for a significant share of the global disease burden discussed previously. These methods can be used and adapted by architects, planners, and urban designers for design workflows involving analysis and generative design tasks. In addition to the methodological contribution, the research also contributes insight on potential correlations between urban design features and anxiety.

BACKGROUND

Deep learning is a branch of machine learning that has demonstrated the ability to outperform competing approaches, including human experts, in a variety of image processing, recognition, prediction, and generation tasks (Liu et al. 2017). Deep learning can be divided into two main categories: discriminative and generative deep learning. Discriminative deep learning can take advantage of large labeled datasets to build a model capable of classification and regression tasks. Generative deep learning processes can learn the probability distribution that underlies a selected dataset. This distribution can then be sampled from to create new data instances. Both these processes can work with many forms of data (e.g., images, drawings, text, 3D models, sounds, etc.), making it extremely useful to disciplines like design—whose data tends to be image-based.

There is a limited but growing body of research exploring the use of deep learning in conjunction with satellite images to find correlations between urban morphology and health/quality of life measures. Previous research in this area has explored the use of satellite images to predict poverty levels in Africa (Jean et al. 2016). Researchers have also used satellite images of census tracts in U.S. cities to estimate levels of obesity (Maharana and Nsoesie 2018). There has also been research that uses point-of-view images of the city to estimate a variety of social, environmental, and health measures (Suel et al. 2019). This precedent work all uses discriminative deep learning methods and does not address the problem of finding correlation between specific image features and outcomes. Further, this work has not yet dealt with anxiety and has not come from the design disciplines. This research attempts to address these gaps by contributing knowledge for the allied design fields on the comparative application of both discriminative and generative deep learning processes to identify correlations between urban morphology and anxiety.

METHODOLOGY

There are two primary input datasets used in this research. The first dataset is comprised of 7,949 color census tract satellite images of California from 2017 obtained through the U.S. Census Bureau (2018). The images are cropped to the census tract shape. Pixels outside the tract shape are set to white. Each image is scaled to fit within a square pixel area of 299 x 299 pixels. This dimension was determined through experiments to provide the best ratio of training speed to accuracy.

These census tract images were then matched with a second dataset comprised of survey data on anxiety rates for adults per census tract from the 2017 California Health Interview Survey (CHIS). The CHIS is the largest state health survey in the United States, covering 58 counties and providing health information on a spectrum of physical and mental health measures for adults, teenagers, and children through

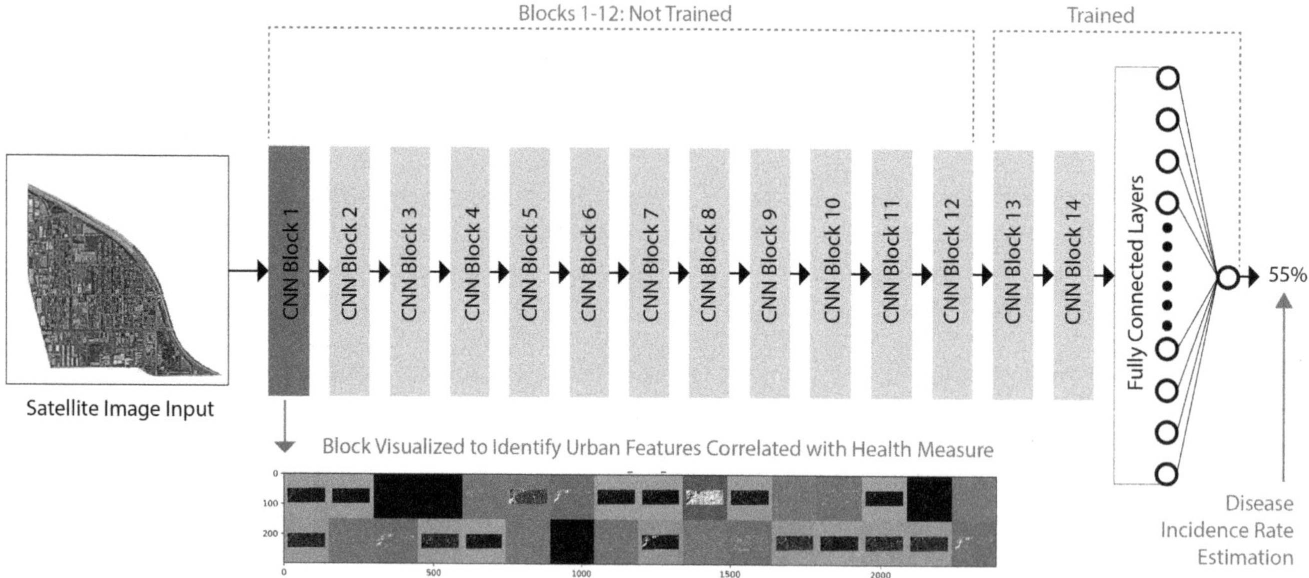

2 The Xception architecture is shown along with modifications made for the estimation and visualization tasks of this research. 2

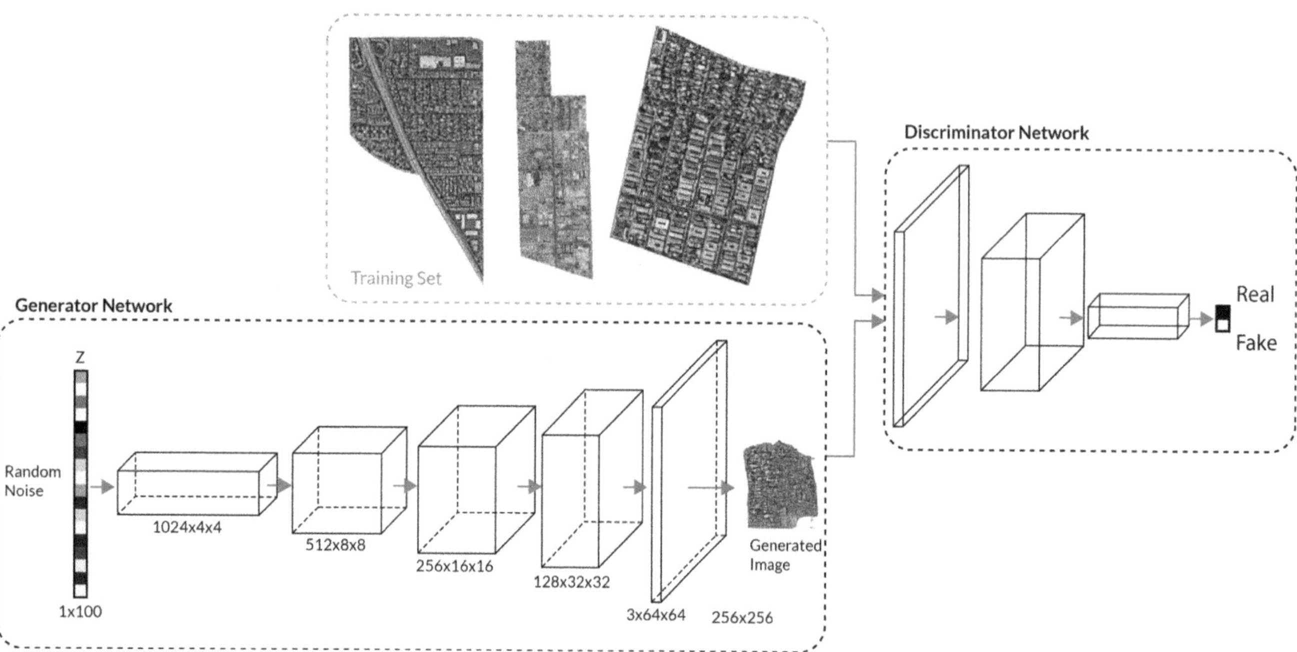

3 The WGAN architecture is comprised of generator and discriminator networks. 3

a self-reporting survey (California Health Interview Survey. 2017).

This dataset is used to train two different deep learning models. One is a discriminative deep learning model and the other is a generative deep learning model. The results from each are then analyzed and compared with one another through a mixed-methods approach to identify possible correlations between urban design features and anxiety.

The first model uses the Xception Convolutional Neural Network (CNN) architecture. Xception is a state-of-the-art discriminative deep learning architecture (Chollet 2017). The architecture is modified to provide a regression value that estimates the rate of anxiety given a census tract image (Fig. 2). Transfer learning is used to train only the 13th, 14th, and final fully connected layers in order to take advantage of the abilities of available pretrained models. This CNN architecture is trained and tested on the previously described datasets for 100 epochs with the following training and testing split: 6,359 samples for training; 1,590 samples for testing. The model is tested for its accuracy in estimating rates of anxiety from satellite images of census tracts using the mean absolute error (MAE) cost function. The MAE is used to ascertain

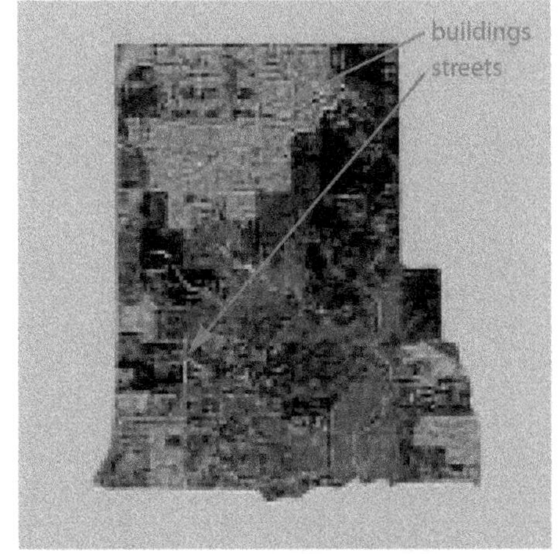

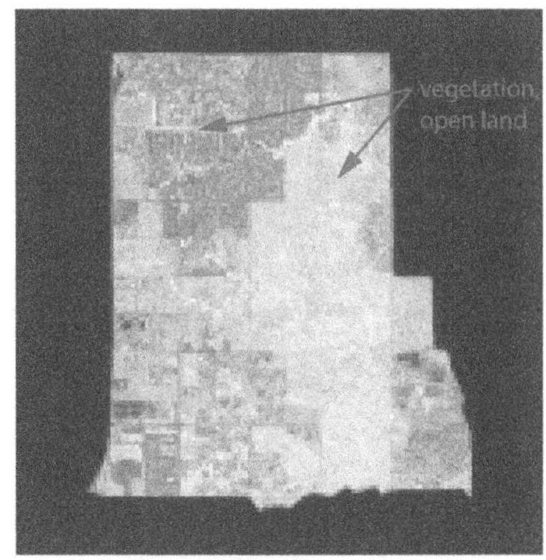

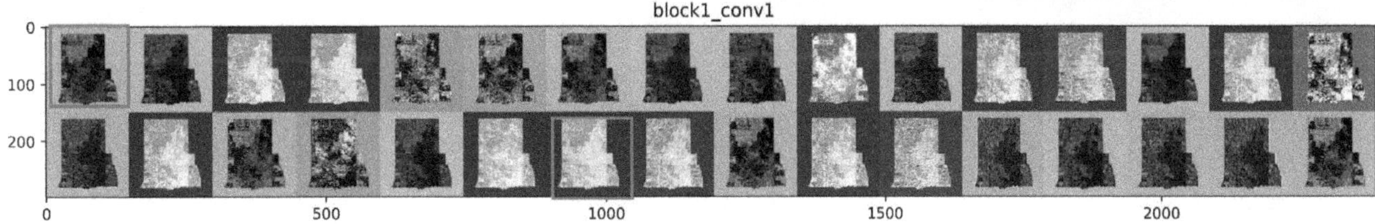

4 (Bottom) The visualization of the first convolutional block of the Xception architecture. (Top) The most active feature maps of the convolutional block for all high incidence rates of anxiety along with overlaid analysis. 4

whether the satellite images have significant correlation with the chosen health measure.

To identify visual features in satellite images that might correlate with anxiety, the neural layers of the Xception architecture are analyzed using a mixed-methods approach. Specifically, the feature maps from the first convolutional block that are most active for high incidence of anxiety are numerically identified (Fig. 2). Feature maps represent the visual features learned by the model in order to distinguish images of high anxiety incidence from low incidence. Once the most active feature maps are identified, they can be visually assessed and interpreted qualitatively to identify visual features that are most active in relation to high rates of anxiety.

The second model uses a generative adversarial network deep learning architecture called the Wasserstein Generative Adversarial Network (WGAN) (Arjovsky, Chintala, and Bottou 2017). The WGAN architecture (Fig. 3) is trained over 1,000 epochs to learn the probability distribution that underlies the dataset of satellite images for both high and low incidences of anxiety. Once learned, the WGAN samples from these distribution models to create new satellite images of census tracts with both high and low incidences of anxiety. These images are then qualitatively assessed to identify urban design features that may be correlated with high and low incidence of anxiety. Correlations identified by both methods are then compared and contrasted with existing research on anxiety to gauge the performance of each process to identify correlations.

RESULTS AND DISCUSSION

The discriminative deep learning model using the Xception CNN architecture is first trained and tested on the given datasets to validate whether the visual features in satellite images correlate in any meaningful way to rates of anxiety. The results demonstrate that the model is able to achieve a mean absolute error of 21.4% for its estimates of anxiety rates per census tract as compared to the data from the CHIS. This error rate means the model can predict the percentage of people with anxiety in a census tract given just a satellite image within a range of 21.4% higher or lower than the real measured percentage rate. This accuracy suggests that visual features in satellite images of census tracts have significant correlation with anxiety and that, in principle, it should be possible to identify these features.

In order to identify these visual features, the neural layers of the Xception architecture are analyzed to identify the most active feature maps for high rates of anxiety. The most active feature maps are numerically identified and shown in Figure 4. After identifying these maps, they are qualitatively assessed by visually identifying the image features with the brightest pixels in these maps. These bright pixels indicate visual features that are most active in the model's determination of high anxiety

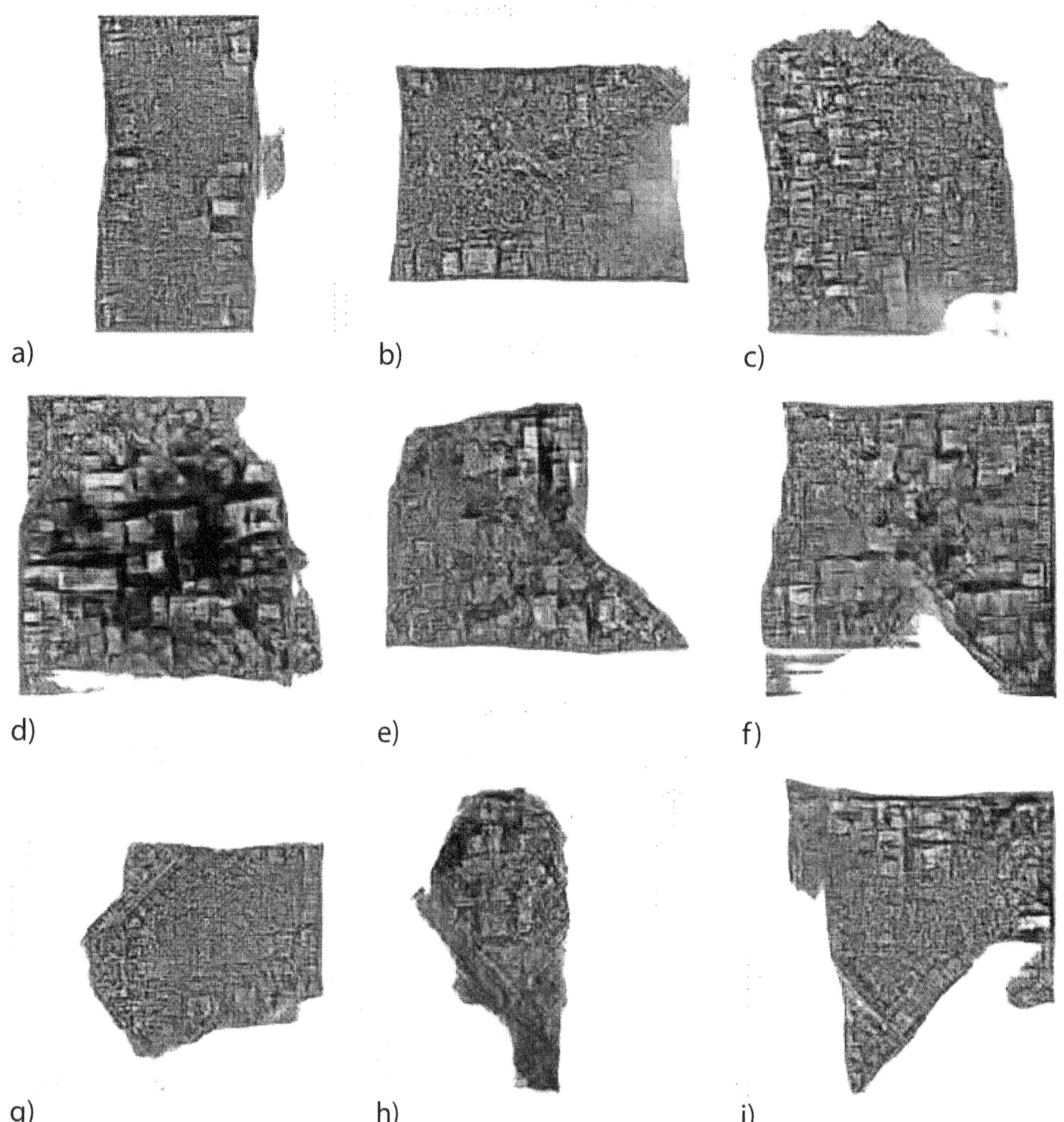

5 Generated samples from a WGAN model trained on high incidence of anxiety: (a–c) Dense urban fabric with no natural spaces and an air pollution-like haze; (d–f) Large buildings and high density create large areas with low lighting levels; (g–i) Samples that seem to have an airport next to them, another possible pollution source. 5

incidence. Feature map #0 shows high activation (i.e., brighter pixels) in relation to proxies for density such as buildings and streets. Feature map #22, in contrast, shows high activation in relation to proxies for natural spaces, such as vegetation and open land. These maps, therefore, imply that building density and access to natural spaces may have a correlation with high rates of anxiety. It is unclear, however, how high or low measures in either category correlate to anxiety rates. This illustrates some of the limitations of the visual interpretation of feature maps.

Next, the results from the WGAN generative DL architecture are presented and discussed. Figure 5 shows generated census tract images from the WGAN architecture after being trained on images from census tracts with high levels of anxiety. A qualitative visual analysis reveals a number of similarities shared by these images that may have significant correlation with high rates of anxiety. All the generated images show a high degree of urbanization and density. Figures 5a–c show high levels of density with no green spaces. There is also an orange haze on the images, which appears similar visually

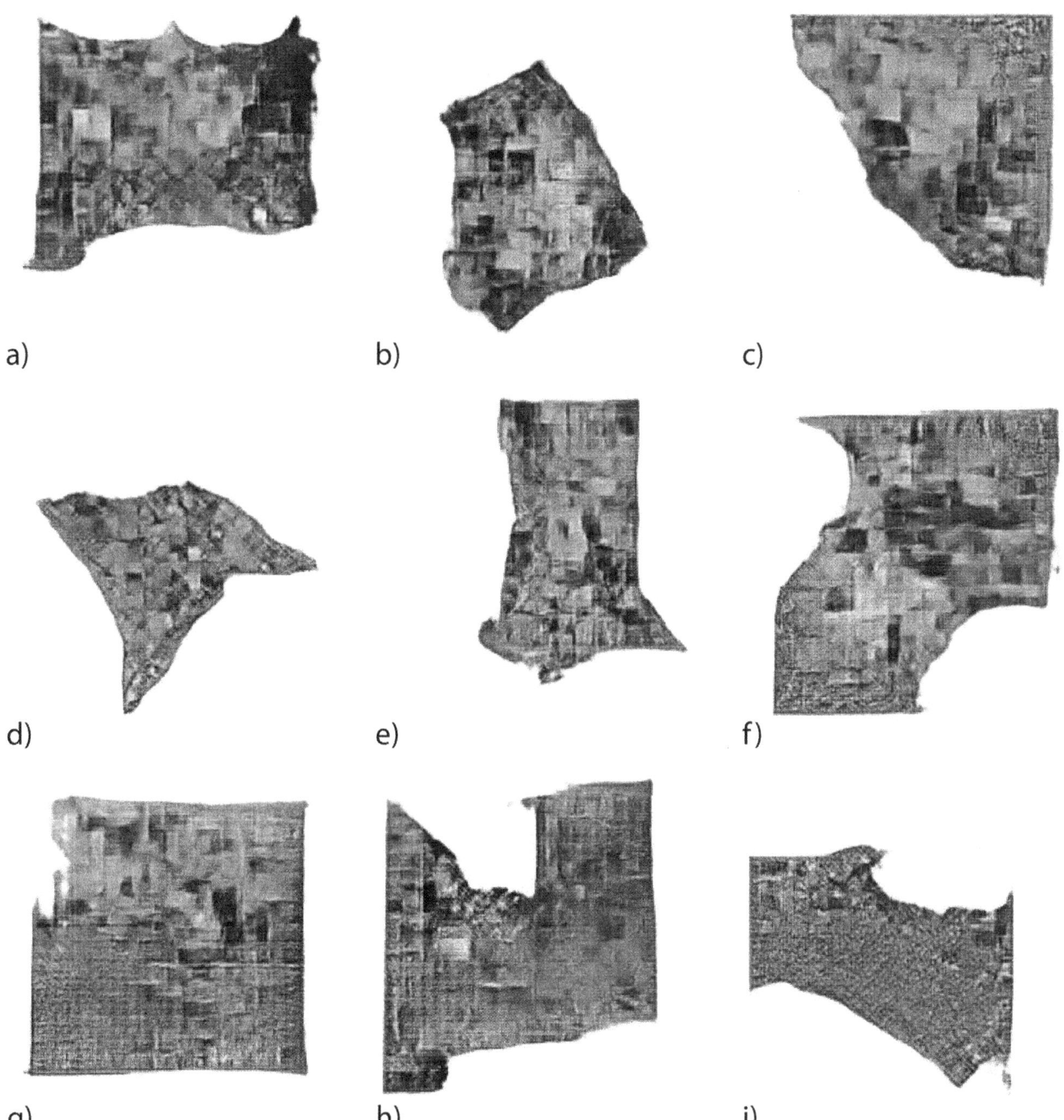

6 Generated samples from a WGAN model trained on low incidence of anxiety: (a–f) Census tracts dominated by natural landscapes; (g–i) Green spaces and natural environments integrating into urban fabric. 6

to images of air pollution. Figures 5d–f show high density urban grids that limit access to light and produce high levels of dark spaces. These images share visual similarities to images of downtown urban areas with high-rise buildings. Figures 5g–i show generated images that seem to have airport and/or highway infrastructure next to a dense urban grid. These infrastructural features infer a possible correlation with pollution sources involving air and sound.

In contrast to these results, Figure 6 shows generated samples from the WGAN architecture after being trained on images with low levels of anxiety. Green spaces, access to light, and medium to low density all seem to be dominant urban design features in these images. Specifically, Figures 6a–f show images of landscapes dominated by green spaces and open land. These spaces are often gridded in a similar fashion as agricultural fields. In contrast, pixels resembling the hardscapes of cities and neighborhoods are relegated to small concentrations on the boundaries of the images. This pattern changes in Figures 6g–i, where green spaces are more directly integrated within a medium-density urban fabric. In these images, an increase in the prevalence of hardscapes is joined by the appearance of blue pixels resembling water features (e.g., small lakes, ponds, coastal spaces). In summary, the WGAN results indicate that natural landscape features (e.g., green spaces, open land, mountains, water features), access to light, and medium to low density may have a meaningful correlation with low anxiety rates.

The results from both experiments are compared and contrasted with precedent research involving anxiety and the built environment to ascertain their efficacy. Existing research has found significant correlations between mental health and exposure to natural light and natural views (Braubach 2007; Codinhoto et al. 2009). Increased levels of urbanization have also been correlated with higher rates of mental illness (Peen et al. 2010). Existing research, therefore, supports the findings of both the Xception and WGAN findings. The WGAN process, however, provided additional insight and indicated a correlation to air pollution that has been found by existing research (Bolton et al. 2013; Chen et al. 2018). Further, the WGAN results implied a correlation of low anxiety with proximity to water features. This association has also been found by existing research (Garrett et al. 2019).

These results imply that generative deep learning methods may have a significant advantage over discriminative methods in identifying correlations between visual features in the built environment and anxiety. Further, generative methods are able to provide information as to how the amount of a particular visual feature might correlate to rates of anxiety. The discriminative method, in contrast, does not provide insight into this relation.

CONCLUSIONS

The results of the research demonstrate the efficacy of using discriminative and generative deep learning methods in combination for urban analysis in relation to anxiety. They demonstrate a useful workflow that architects and urban designers can use to make use of satellite and aerial images of the city to help identify correlations between the morphology of the built environment and anxiety. This insight can then be used to inform more healthy urban policy, planning, and design.

The research found that generative deep learning methods provided the most correlational insight and were able to identify significant visual features that were not found in the discriminative deep learning method tested in this research. This implies that GANs could be useful as analytical tools for design and not just as generative tools. The research, therefore, opens the door to a new way of using GANs within the design and planning disciplines.

Future work will investigate other health measures, as well as the efficacy of these processes at scales both below and above the scale of the census tract. Further, exploring the accuracy of deep learning models with other remote-sensing datasets singularly and in combination could help to better understand the correlation of urban morphology and mental health. These are just a few areas of development in a terrain that is largely new and full of opportunities for the design disciplines to engage creatively.

ACKNOWLEDGMENTS

This research was supported by funding from the College of Architecture at the University of Nebraska-Lincoln. This work was completed utilizing the Holland Computing Center of the University of Nebraska, which receives support from the Nebraska Research Initiative.

REFERENCES

Arjovsky, Martin, Soumith Chintala, and Léon Bottou. 2017. "Wasserstein Generative Adversarial Networks." In *Proceedings of the 34th International Conference on Machine Learning (PMLR)*, Sydney, Australia, 7–9 August 2017, 214–223. PMLR.

Bolton, Jessica L., Nicole C. Huff, Susan H. Smith, S. Nicholas Mason, W. Michael Foster, Richard L. Auten, and Staci D. Bilbo. 2013. "Maternal Stress and Effects of Prenatal Air Pollution on Offspring Mental Health Outcomes in Mice." *Environmental Health Perspectives* 121 (9): 1075–1082. https://doi.org/10.1289/ehp.1306560/

Braubach, Matthias. 2007. "Residential Conditions and Their Impact on Residential Environment Satisfaction and Health: Results of the WHO Large Analysis and Review of European Housing and Health Status (LARES) Study." *International Journal of Environment and Pollution* 30 (3–4): 384–403. https://doi.org/10.1504/IJEP.2007.014817.

California Health Interview Survey. 2017. "Adult Public Use Files." UCLA Center for Health Policy Research. CHIS. Accessed January 2019.

Chen, Chen, Cong Liu, Renjie Chen, Weibing Wang, Weihua Li, Haidong Kan, and Chaowei Fu. 2018. "Ambient Air Pollution and Daily Hospital Admissions for Mental Disorders in Shanghai, China." *Science of the Total Environment* 613: 324–330. https://doi.org/10.1016/j.scitotenv.2017.09.098.

Chollet, François. 2017. "Xception: Deep Learning with Depthwise Separable Convolutions." In *Proceedings of the 2017 IEEE Conference on Computer Vision and Pattern Recognition (CVPR)*, Honolulu, HI, 21–26 July 2017, 1800–1807. IEEE. https://doi: 10.1109/CVPR.2017.195.

Codinhoto, Ricardo, Patricia Tzortzopoulos, Mike Kagioglou, Ghassan Aouad, and Rachel Cooper. 2009. "The Impacts of the Built Environment on Health Outcomes." *Facilities* 27 (3–4): 138–151. https://doi.org/10.1108/02632770910933152.

Garrett, Joanne K., Theodore J. Clitherow, Mathew P. White, Benedict W. Wheeler, and Lora E. Fleming. 2019. "Coastal Proximity and Mental Health Among Urban Adults in England: The Moderating Effect of Household Income." *Health & Place* 59: 102200. https://doi.org/10.1016/j.healthplace.2019.102200.

Hoisington, Andrew J., Kelly A. Stearns-Yoder, Steven J. Schuldt, Cody J. Beemer, Juan P. Maestre, Kerry A. Kinney, Teodor T. Postolache, Christopher A. Lowry, and Lisa A. Brenner. 2019. "Ten Questions Concerning the Built Environment and Mental Health." *Building and Environment* 155: 58–69. https://doi.org/10.1016/j.buildenv.2019.03.036.

Jean, Neal, Marshall Burke, Michael Xie, W. Matthew Davis, David B. Lobell, and Stefano Ermon. 2016. "Combining Satellite Imagery and Machine Learning to Predict Poverty." *Science* 353 (6301):790–794. https://doi.org/10.1126/science.aaf7894.

Liu, W., Z. Wang, X. Liu, N. Zheng, Y. Liu, and F. E. Alsaadi. 2017. "A Survey of Deep Neural Network Architectures and Their Applications." *Neurocomputing* 234: 11–26. https://doi.org/10.1016/j.neucom.2016.12.038.

Maharana, Adyasha, and Elaine Okanyene Nsoesie. 2018. "Use of Deep Learning to Examine the Association of the Built Environment with Prevalence of Neighborhood Adult Obesity." *JAMA Network Open* 1 (4): e181535–e181535. https://doi.org/10.1001/jamanetworkopen.2018.1535.

Marshall, Wesley E., Daniel P. Piatkowski, and Norman W. Garrick. 2014. "Community Design, Street Networks, and Public Health." *Journal of Transport & Health* 1 (4): 326–340.

McConnell, Rob, Kiros Berhane, Ling Yao, Michael Jerrett, Fred Lurmann, Frank Gilliland, Nino Künzli, Jim Gauderman, ED Avol, and Duncan Thomas. 2006. "Traffic, Susceptibility, and Childhood Asthma." *Environmental Health Perspectives* 114 (5): 766–772. https://doi.org/10.1289/ehp.8594.

Moore, T.H.M., J.M. Kesten, J.A. López-López, S. Ijaz, A. McAleenan, A. Richards, Selena Gray, J. Savović, and S. Audrey. 2018. "The Effects of Changes to the Built Environment on the Mental Health and Well-being of Adults: Systematic Review." *Health & Place* 53: 237–257. https://doi.org/10.1016/j.healthplace.2018.07.012.

Müller, Grit, Roland Harhoff, Corinna Rahe, and Klaus Berger. 2018. "Inner-City Green Space and Its Association with Body Mass Index and Prevalent Type 2 Diabetes: A Cross-Sectional Study in an Urban German City." *BMJ Open* 8 (1): e019062. https://doi.org/10.1136/bmjopen-2017-019062.

Peen, Jaap, Robert A. Schoevers, Aartjan T. Beekman, and Jack Dekker. 2010. "The Current Status of Urban-Rural Differences in Psychiatric Disorders." *Acta Psychiatrica Scandinavica* 121 (2): 84–93. https://doi.org/10.1111/j.1600-0447.2009.01438.x.

Simons, Elinor, Sharon D Dell, Rahim Moineddin, and Teresa To. 2018. "Associations Between Neighborhood Walkability and Incident and Ongoing Asthma in Children." *Annals of the American Thoracic Society* 15 (6):728-734. https://doi.org/10.1513/AnnalsATS.201708-693OC

Suel, Esra, John W Polak, James E Bennett, and Majid Ezzati. 2019. "Measuring Social, Environmental and Health Inequalities Using Deep Learning and Street Imagery." *Scientific Reports* 9 (1): 6229. https://doi.org/10.1038/s41598-019-42036-w.

U.S. Census Bureau. 2018. "TIGER/Line Shapefiles." Accessed December 27, 2018. https://www.census.gov/cgi-bin/geo/shapefiles/index.php.

Whiteford, Harvey A., Alize J. Ferrari, Louisa Degenhardt, Valery Feigin, and Theo Vos. 2015. "The Global Burden of Mental, Neurological and Substance Use Disorders: An Analysis from the Global Burden of Disease Study 2010." *PloS One* 10 (2): e0116820. https://doi.org/10.1371/journal.pone.0116820.

Xie, Michael, Neal Jean, Marshall Burke, David Lobell, and Stefano Ermon. 2016. "Transfer Learning from Deep Features for Remote Sensing and poverty Mapping." In *Proceedings of the 30th AAAI Conference on Artificial Intelligence*, Phoenix, AZ, 12–17 February 2016, 3929–3935. AAAI.

IMAGE CREDITS

All drawings and images by the author.

David Newton is an Assistant Professor at the University of Nebraska-Lincoln where he leads the Computational Architecture Research Lab (CARL). CARL is dedicated to the research and development of next-generation computational design technologies that make for a more environmentally and socially sustainable built environment. Professor Newton holds degrees in both architecture and computer science. This background informs a research and teaching agenda that is cross-disciplinary in nature and enables research of issues that straddle both disciplines and might otherwise be inaccessible to the field of architecture.

KEYNOTE CONVERSATION

DATA AND BIAS

KEYNOTE EVENT

A Conversation on Data and Bias

Ruha Benjamin
Princeton University

Orit Halpern
Concordia University

David Benjamin
Columbia University / The Living

As computational design practices become increasingly dependent on data collection and processing, a critical reflection on the ethical, cultural, and political implications of data-driven design practices is necessary. Abundant commercial "smart home" appliances promise the comforts of a fully automated living environment populated by ambient sensing devices at the "negligible" price of the user's personal data. Machine learning and cloud-based computing strategies marketed as inherently intelligent with a hint of mystery and magic are in fact entirely black-boxed solutions based on multitudes of harvested data. Data-driven processes create the false promise of objectivity, fairness, and neutrality. In this context, designers must critically engage with the questions of inherited bias and investigate responsible design approaches to working with (and/or against) data collection, data processing, and algorithmic automation. In this keynote conversation, three scholars and design practitioners who engage critically with the questions of machine learning, data collection, and data bias convened to discuss the implications of these technologies for both design and a broader sociopolitical context.

Ruha Benjamin, Professor of African American Studies at Princeton University, began with a sociological and historical perspective on how technology is and always has been entangled with issues of race and bias. In her talk, Benjamin walked through a number of case studies from her book *Race After Technology: Abolitionist Tools for the New Jim Code*,[1] explaining how "technology is mirroring back at us—and also deepening and naturalizing—these distinctions that permeate everyday life." Benjamin concluded with a call to designers to use their expertise in recognizing and making patterns to subvert the logics of inequality and oppression that often underpin the rise of new technologies.

Orit Halpern, Associate Professor in Sociology and Anthropology at Concordia University, followed with a presentation of her research into how algorithmic logics of optimization and financialization have enabled extractive industries to achieve new levels of efficiency and ecological destruction. Situating these practices within a broader history of settler-colonial economics, Halpern called for a break with languages of efficiency and optimization,

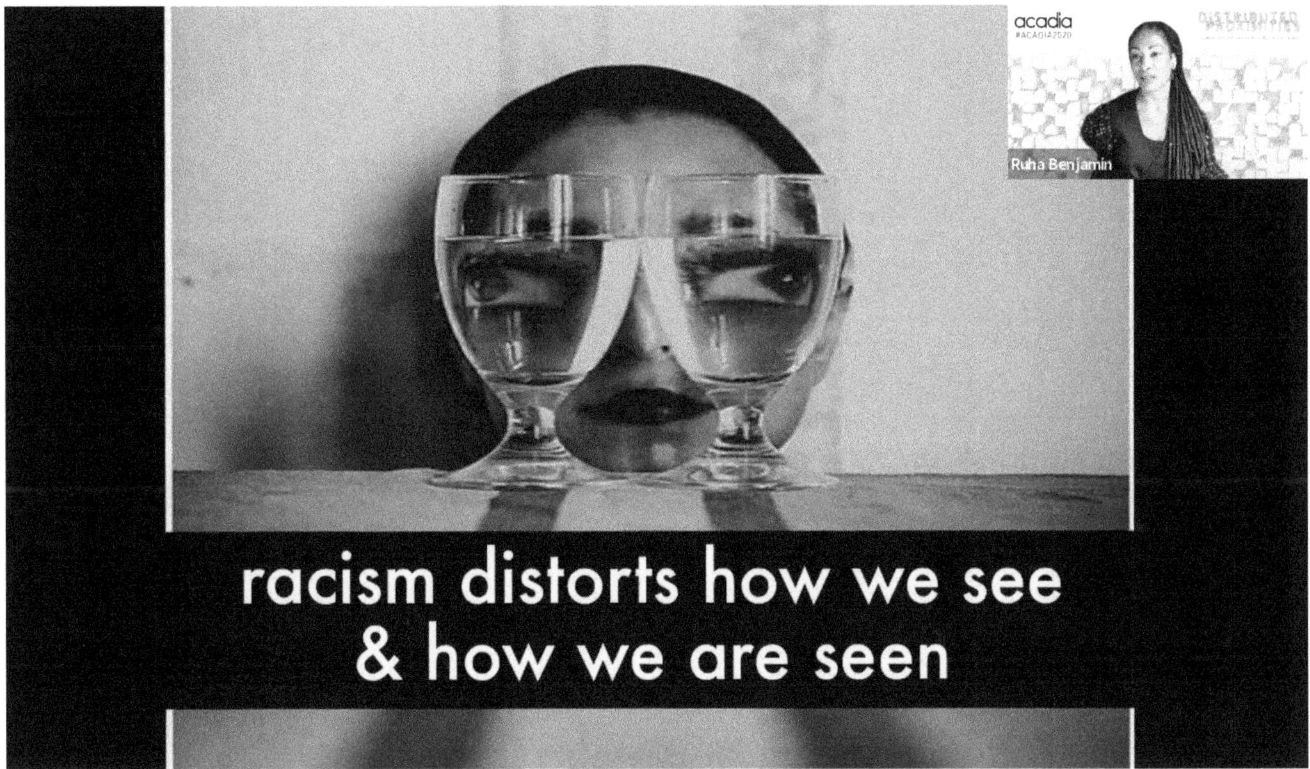

1 "Racism, among other axes of domination and difference, distorts our vision. It distorts not only what we see *out there*—our external view, our ability or inability to understand the social patterns around us, to understand the multiple crises we face—but it also distorts our interpersonal vision—how we see one another at an individual level. It even distorts how we understand ourselves: our internal vision." —Ruha Benjamin

and encouraged designers to embrace the power of imagination to rethink how these existing systems might be reinvented in a more just way.

David Benjamin, Founding Principal of The Living and Associate Professor at Columbia University Graduate School of Architecture, Planning, and Preservation, concluded with a brief response speculating how designers might engage directly with questions of data neutrality and bias. Benjamin presented his *Twin Mirror* project, an installation commissioned for the 2017 Seoul Biennale of Architecture and Urbanism which deployed machine-learning technology and facial-recognition algorithms to reveal their very lack of neutrality and objectivity. A lively conversation among all three participants followed, and is reproduced below in edited form.

For a recording of the entire event, please see this link: **https://www.youtube.com/watch?v=9t0u8CwdC9s**

David Benjamin (DB): Both of your presentations raise important issues that are sometimes missing from conversations in schools of architecture, but which I think are so important and relevant. As someone who both teaches in an architecture school and practices as a designer and architect, I'm thinking about how some of these ideas might play out in architecture and the built environment. And I'm also thinking about how to make some of these complex issues legible to a public audience.

First I'd like to talk a little more specifically about the tools we're using—tools like machine learning and optimization. We've explored some of the effects of the tools, but I also want to talk about the tools themselves, including how they work and who made them. A colleague of mine who is a computer scientist recently commented, "Architects have been hijacked by computer scientists," the implication being that we're using tools that we didn't necessarily write, invent, or perhaps even ask for. But I want to transition that into something maybe more active and ask both of you to reflect on how important you think it is for architects and designers, or for sociologists or historians of science, for that matter, to be able to get under the hood, to understand all the technical details of how things like machine learning work, and to maybe even be able to tinker with them or write alternatives or suggest feature changes. Is this

2 "While ecology and infrastructure may not appear to be intuitive places to be thinking about big data, I think that rethinking figurative ground, landscapes, and the boundaries of systems says a lot for how we model problems, and ultimately how structural injustices are built into big data and machine learning systems." —Orit Halpern

something that you think about as a way to become more active in this context? How important is it for all architects to really be fluent in the language of algorithms?

Ruha Benjamin (RB): My own thinking around this is that it's great if an individual can have multiple fluencies—the architectural, the sociological, the historical—but at the same time, realistically, we can't all do and know everything. One of the workarounds is to think about what kind of teams we want to have. What forms of expertise—disciplinary and otherwise—do we want around the table as we're both building and adopting tools? To have that expertise around the table is vital. At the same time, in conversations about data and bias, I think the technological literacy or know-how is too often over-emphasized. Too often, the social and historical literacy and know-how are discounted because of the hierarchies of knowledge that map our own universities.

When we talk about understanding the tools that we use, I also think about the *social* tools: how we often are using various conceptual and social tools without really understanding them. I write about how race itself is a technology that we often employ in our work by relying on common-sense notions without understanding what's under the hood of race. But there's an imperative to understand what's in the black box of the algorithm. And so I would really encourage us to include in our repertoire, or in our toolkit, respect for and a honing of the social and conceptual tools as much as we want to have expertise around the hardware and the software and the algorithms.

In the same way that you described computer science kind of taking over architecture, I write a little bit in chapter five of *Race After Technology* of how design thinking has taken over almost everything.[2] That's an example of a conceptual tool that in some ways we could say has colonized or infected or created a hegemony in which we talk about so many things in the language of and through the lens of design thinking, without enough reflexivity, and enough thinking about: Where did that come from? Who does it serve? I love the question, and I would just expand it to include things in addition to algorithms and automated systems.

3 "The project reflects back to the viewer these two versions of reality through a kind of twin mirror. Neither version of reality is neutral or objective; both are biased. We think that by seeing them together, we may be able to get under the hood and apply some judgment to these kinds technologies. Maybe to become a little suspicious and to recognize their flaws." —David Benjamin

DB: This idea of bringing together teams, that no one individual can have all of the literacy—I think that's really critical and actionable for designers and architects. I also think collaboration comes much more naturally to this current generation, which seems much more skeptical of the solitary genius model.

Orit Halpern (OH): I would also urge a sense of humility or humbleness, and acknowledge that no team will have all the knowledge. Partial perspective and reflexivity are key, because there is a constant valorization of certain types of knowledge over others that can serve a deeply political function. Interdisciplinary teams are crucial in this regard. When I speak of "interdisciplinary," or perhaps "intersectional," what I mean is people who come from genuinely different backgrounds and forms of knowledge and practice.

DB: I wonder if there exist what we might call antidotes to the insidious effects of bias and data and algorithms? Maybe humility would be one? But I was also thinking—just picking up some of the terms from your presentations—of others: imagination, activism, pattern-making, visualization. These can be tools, antidotes, or ways to counterbalance some of what we encounter. I wonder if you have other thoughts about what we should be looking for or striving for?

RB: In thinking about ways forward, it is really important to incorporate a power analysis as an essential component of whatever we do. I mean this both in terms of thinking about the relationship between knowledge and power, and also "old-school" power in terms of social and political power: how pre-existing hierarchies and pre-existing power dynamics shape every step of the process. This includes the questions that we start with, in terms of what we want architecture or design or technology to solve or to intervene in. I would urge us to recognize that these questions are already weighted with certain forms of power that are over-determined by history and by our current social order—before we pick up any tool or develop any team to address it. How, at the point of posing questions, can we begin to subvert power, and subvert the typical ways of thinking and doing things? Rather than waiting until downstream—further along in the process where there's already momentum, it's harder to turn left or right—how can we think about this at the starting point? What does that look like to begin to have a rigorous power analysis at the point of posing questions? Because that leads us down certain rabbit holes and away from others, depending on how we're framing whatever the thing is we want to build, and who it's going to serve.

Even the word "client"—if we think about what it means to privilege the client versus other publics, or other users, already sends us down certain trajectories. I think that there's a lot we can do very early in the process.

OH: I'm not sure about solutions, but one thing I've found helpful is to create *situations* as a pedagogical tool. For example, in the context of my research on extraction, it's a particular problem to have to envision the future of a mine, or to incorporate different opinions from indigenous groups or from people who are in the communities that are relying on these extraction industries.

I think at a fundamental level, there's also a question about vocabulary, because it's hard to envision a reclamation or smartness project or any design problem without avoiding questions about optimization and efficiency. Once you fundamentally have those locked in, you're going to be developing a racist, inequitable system. Already from the start, you have built in a series of premises and biases.

I don't have any one-step solutions to offer, but I think that there are ways to put people in knowledge situations where they actually have to contend with these questions as designers.

DB: Could you connect back to the notion of a so-called good version of circularity that you mentioned in your talk? How might we start to imagine a better version of a circular economy?

OH: In the particular case of mining, you're starting with a premise that the economy will allow more mining to commence. So you have kind of an impossible scenario there, from certain environmental or ecological or human rights concerns. When thinking about economies, it is important to consider who and what the economy is for, and where value is actually being assigned.

I'm actually very interested in environmental movements that use financial strategies and re-direct them towards fights such as stopping oil pipelines. I may critique those kinds of instruments, but as Ruha has suggested in acknowledging our abilities for pattern-making, every assemblage that we face presents more opportunities for action.

The most generic mode of thinking about this is betting on solar energy. But there are more complicated affiliations between environmental movements and finance.

DB: In a sense, you're talking about identifying levers of change. If we think about the current moment and its multiple crises—the pandemic, climate change, economic inequality, racial justice—what levers might we identify to amplify our efforts and create beneficial change? Education comes to mind, as well as regulation, activism, and imagination, which Ruha brought up in such a compelling way.

RB: I often say that my ground zero is really thinking about pedagogy and education. For me, that's the groundwork where we seed alternatives, where we begin to plant seeds in the minds and hearts of students, encouraging ways of thinking outside the box, thinking beyond certain kinds of boundaries. I do acknowledge that both regulation and policy (such as the algorithmic accountability bill that I mentioned in my talk) are crucial when considering the entire pathway of protections that have to be fostered in order to transform the ecosystem in which we develop technology. Also, organizing is critical—both among professionals who work in a particular sector, such as technology, and within grassroots communities. In my talk, I mentioned Data for Black Lives and the Detroit Community Technology Project, two organizations that are emblematic of this kind of work.[3]

We also need to think about the arts in the most expansive sense possible, consisting of not just people who consider themselves professional artists, but also those who we might call cultural workers, who challenge us to question and create different kinds of norms and values.

In regard to imagination and speculation more broadly, I'm teaching a class now called Black Mirror: Race, Technology, and Justice. For their practicum, students are working on a speculative design project around COVID and race, in which they're taking a lot of the conceptual tools that we've been reading about and actually applying them in a project that requires them to build that muscle of imagination. Today, when they were in their breakout groups, I posed the question, "Can you have a conversation among your group about whether you're still bounding yourself within our current reality? Or are you pushing the boundaries? Are you really

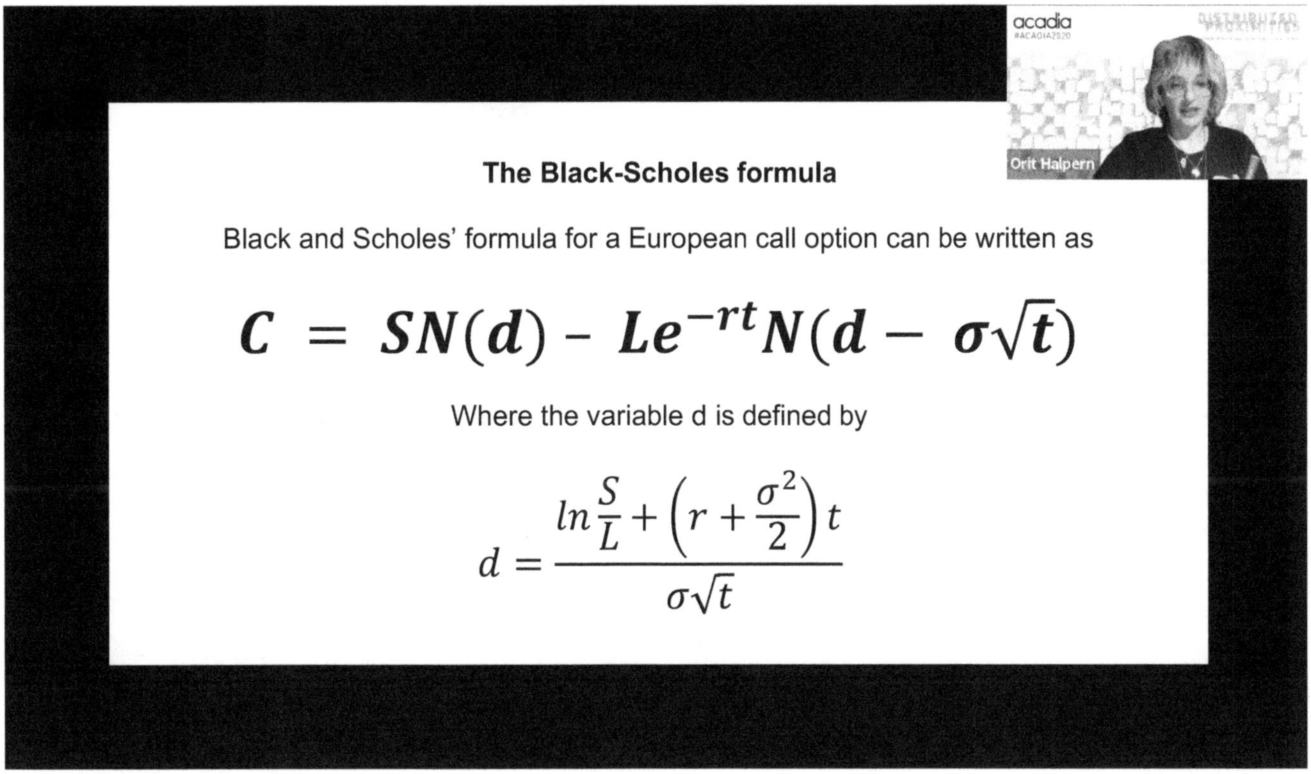

acadia
#ACADIA2020
Orit Halpern

The Black-Scholes formula

Black and Scholes' formula for a European call option can be written as

$$C = SN(d) - Le^{-rt}N(d - \sigma\sqrt{t})$$

Where the variable d is defined by

$$d = \frac{ln\frac{S}{L} + \left(r + \frac{\sigma^2}{2}\right)t}{\sigma\sqrt{t}}$$

4 "These mining sites demonstrate how computational and algorithmic technologies that are used to get resources out of the increasingly fatigued Earth, such as the Black-Scholes equation used to price derivatives, reformulate older extractive and settler-colonial economies." —Orit Halpern

trying to have at least one dimension that is in a near future that you can imagine?" It's so hard, I think, especially for people who are successful in our academic structure; the imaginative muscle has atrophied in some ways. We have to think about what that future looks like. Otherwise, we'll continue to build new versions of the same old thing: the same systems, the same apps that have a different gloss, but that have the same underlying power and social dimensions. As a teacher, I believe it's vital to build imagination and speculation into my pedagogy. The ability to imagine a different future is science-fictional.

OH: Pedagogy is certainly the first start, and particularly public education. I think there's a real question about producing the infrastructures of possibility for all human beings, and that continues to be a primary and central concern, particularly right now. It's important to recognize what Kathryn Yusoff has noted in her book *A Billion Black Anthropocenes or None*, that these crises are not new and have been endured by a lot of people for a very long time.[4] The discourse of crisis often facilitates a survivalist mentality that makes certain things and certain lives and certain types of knowledge sacrificable, and I find that intolerable.

I'm actually quite positive and confident that research creation can bring people together from across the arts, humanities, social sciences, sciences, engineering, and design to think collectively and differently. I'm seeing a lot of this happen already around climate and around race. I see the incredible potency of pedagogy, but I also understand that pedagogy links to politics in its fundamental commitment to plural democracy, which is difficult to continue to envision but essential to fight for, both within the university and outside of it.

Ultimately, I believe that re-narrativization and the production of fiction are the potent tools we have really at this juncture to envision a world other than the one we have right now.

DB: One question from the audience: "Do you think the social dynamics, digital literacy, and societal needs will be more open to change post-COVID?"

RB: I think we're at a crossroads. I think they can be more open. I can see a way forward in which they're more open. But I also see a way that this has created an opening for the people who want to re-entrench power and monopolize

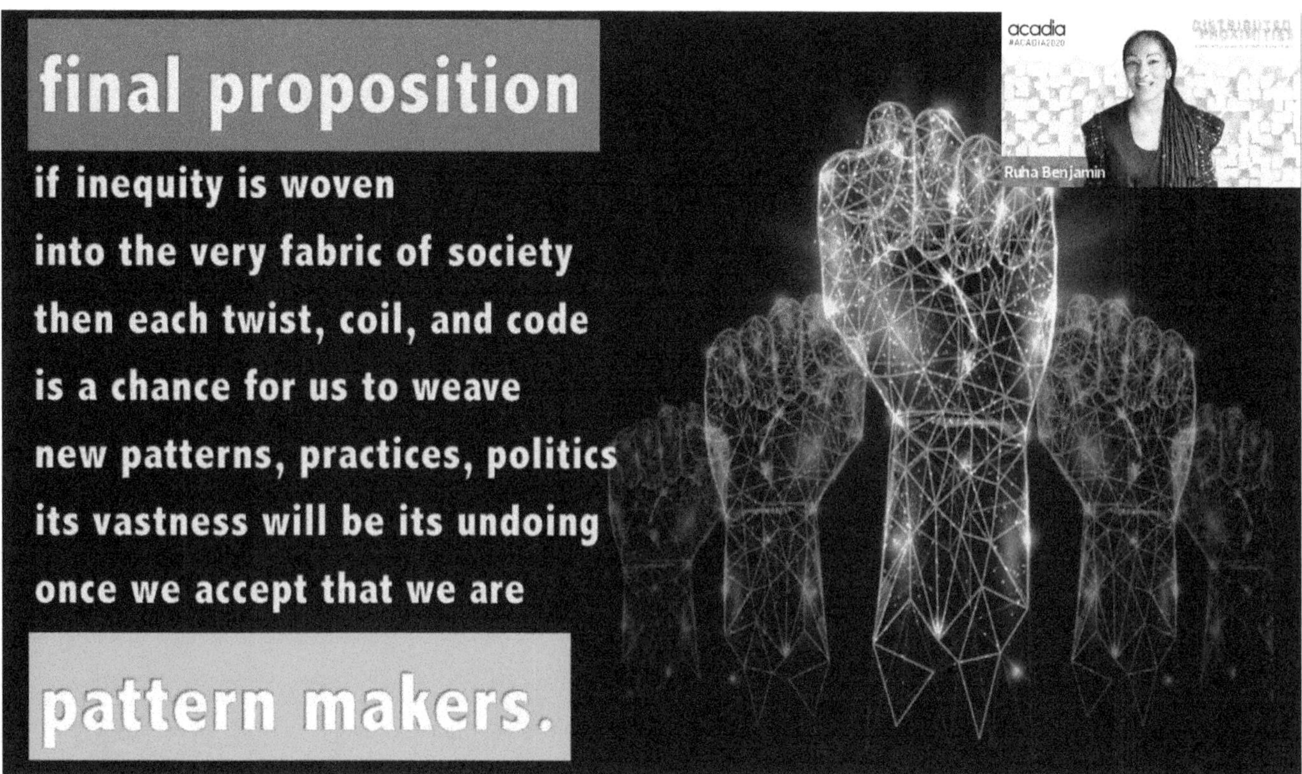
final proposition
if inequity is woven
into the very fabric of society
then each twist, coil, and code
is a chance for us to weave
new patterns, practices, politics
its vastness will be its undoing
once we accept that we are
pattern makers.
acadia
Ruha Benjamin

5 "If inequity is woven into the very fabric of society, then each twist, coil, and code is a chance for us to weave new patterns, practices, and politics. The vastness of the problem we are up against will be its undoing once we accept that we are pattern makers." —Ruha Benjamin

resources. So it's an opening from below but also from above, to fill a vacuum and to use the crisis as a way to fill it with tech fixes and other short-term solutions that will just maintain the status quo and perhaps even deepen inequality and social domination, which I think we're seeing already. If we just look at the rising unemployment rate next to the increasing net worth of the richest handful of people, you see a widening of the gap that all of the mutual aid in the world can't can't fill, as heartening as that work is. And so I think we have to stay both sober and also hopeful in terms of what's possible at this crossroads.

OH: I'm always a pessimistic optimist. I wouldn't be doing what I'm doing if I didn't think things will get better. Finance actually hasn't experienced too much of a crisis as a result of the pandemic, but there has been a massive reallocation of capital, which presents an opportunity to act and to reflexively question the infrastructures of society. The pandemic as an infrastructural problem has really highlighted structural violence, inequity, and environmental destruction.

I've been thinking a lot about how in this moment we might create a politics of uncertainty. How can we prepare people to be ready to deal with diverse possible futures, and with diversity in general? It is in this sense that I remain pessimistically optimistic.

DB: It does seem to be a moment of reset, and maybe it is a moment to be pessimistically optimistic, but it's going to take work to take advantage of this moment of reset. One final observation that comes out of both of your presentations and this conversation: we are, of course, workers and professionals and academics, but we're also *citizens*. I think that's important for architects to remember. We often tell ourselves we're not controlling the situation here, we're at the mercy of our clients, we're just doing the job, we need to get paid, and so on. But today we've discussed the importance for one to declare what one will do and what one won't do—to acknowledge one's role as a citizen making decisions based on values.

NOTES

1. Ruha Benjamin, *Race After Technology: Abolitionist Tools for the New Jim Code* (Cambridge, UK: Polity, 2019).
2. Ibid., chap. 5.
3. Data for Black Lives, https://d4bl.org/; Detroit Community Technology Project, https://detroitcommunitytech.org/.
4. Kathryn Yusoff, *A Billion Black Anthropocenes or None* (Minneapolis: University of Minnesota Press, 2018).

Ruha Benjamin is Professor of African American Studies at Princeton University, founder of the Just Data Lab, and author of *People's Science: Bodies and Rights on the Stem Cell Frontier* (Stanford University Press, 2013) and *Race After Technology: Abolitionist Tools for the New Jim Code* (Polity, 2019), among other publications. Her work investigates the social dimensions of science, medicine, and technology with a focus on the relationship between innovation and inequity, health and justice, knowledge and power. Professor Benjamin is the recipient of numerous awards and fellowships including from the American Council of Learned Societies, the National Science Foundation, the Institute for Advanced Study, and the President's Award for Distinguished Teaching at Princeton.

Orit Halpern is an Associate Professor in Sociology and Anthropology at Concordia University. Her work bridges the histories of science, computing, and cybernetics with design. She completed her PhD at Harvard. She has published widely and has held numerous visiting scholar positions including at the Max Planck Institute for History of Science in Berlin and at Duke University. She is currently finishing a book that is a history and theory of "smartness," examining the changing relationship between ecology, finance, and artificial intelligence. Her future research investigates how we are designing planetary futures and managing uncertainty through an array of techniques ranging from biomimetic design to artificial intelligence. She is also the director of the Speculative Life Research Cluster, a laboratory bridging the arts, environmental and biosciences, and the social sciences.

David Benjamin is Founding Principal of The Living, Director at Autodesk Research, and Associate Professor at Columbia University Graduate School of Architecture, Planning, and Preservation. His work engages technology and the environment, with a focus on real-world applications that explore topics such as generative design, low-carbon materials, and reusable design intelligence. Recent projects include the Airbus NIS Engine Factory (a low-carbon lighthouse project for the future of manufacturing), the Princeton University Embodied Computation Lab (a new building for research on robotics and IoT), Pier 35 EcoPark (a 200-foot-long floating pier in the East River that changes color according to water quality), and Hy-Fi (a branching tower for MoMA PS1 made of a new type of biodegradable brick).

PEER-REVIEWED PAPERS

DATA AND BIAS

"[I]n conversations about data and bias, I think the technological literacy or know-how is too often over-emphasized. Too often, the social and historical literacy and know-how are discounted because of the hierarchies of knowledge that map our own universities."

—Ruha Benjamin, "A Conversation on Data and Bias"

"Today 'big data' is regularly touted as the solution to economic, social, political, and ecological problems; a new resource to extract in a world increasingly understood as resource constrained."

—Orit Halpern, *Beautiful Data*

The term "data mining" carries with it connotations of the extractive practices Halpern highlights in the conversation (and in her work in general). Considering the proliferation of large data sets used in the training of machine learning models, this section is composed almost entirely of research incorporating various forms of artificial intelligence. Here these tools are employed in a wide array of research from a meta-analysis of architecture writing to urban design and various forms of optimization.

AD Magazine

Mirroring the Development of the Computational Field in Architecture 1965–2020

Nadja Gaudillière-Jami
Technische Universität Darmstadt, DDU (Digital Design Unit), Department of Architecture;
GSA Laboratory, ENSA Paris-Malaquais

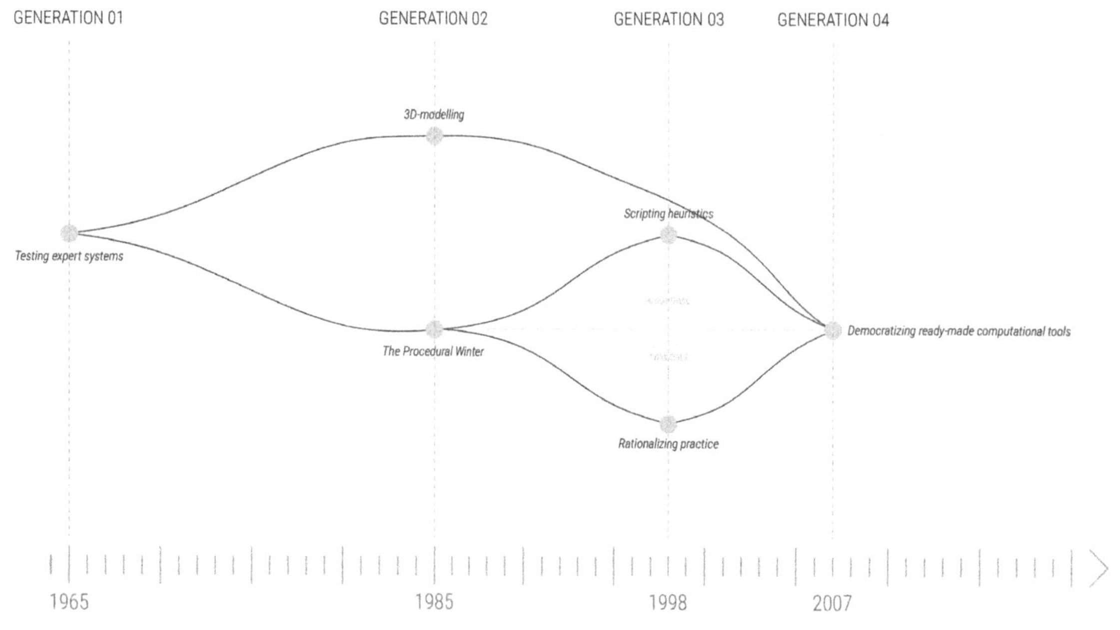

1

1 Chronology of the computational field in architecture 1965–2020.

ABSTRACT

This paper aims to contribute to a history of computational design and to a historiography of the field by proposing a study of the development of sociotechnical networks of computation in architecture between 1965 and 2020 as shown in *AD* magazine. The research focuses on two aspects: (1) a methodological approach for the constitution of a comprehensive history of the field and the application of that methodology to a corpus of items published in *AD*, and (2) questions the relevance of the outlook into computational design as given by the magazine in comparison to a more comprehensive history taking into account other sources. First, the paper presents the history and the editorial line of *AD*, as well as its pertinence as a primary source. Second, a brief account of the history emerging from this research is given, with a focus on four different periods: pioneering research of the 1960s–1970s, emergence of 3D modeling tools and the *procedural winter* in the 1980s–1990s, constitution of a large-scale academic and professional network in the 2000s, and democratization of algorithmic design tools in the 2010s. Third, observations are made on editorial choices of the magazine and the biases of its account of computational research, with a special focus on the period 2000–2020, during which many issues have been dedicated to computational design themes, therefore making potential biases more visible. Despite the preponderance of specific topics, editors, and contributors, *AD* magazine provides an outlook into key concerns of the community at given times. The main biases identified, including a strong focus on the themes of biodesign and rationalization of practices, mirror the biases of the computational field itself, demonstrating the value of *AD* as an archive for the history of the field.

INTRODUCTION

The computational movements in architecture are characterized not only by the common resort to specific design tools—programming tools—but also by the conditions that enabled research on this topic to blossom: a specific sociohistorical context of emergence. The computational movements organize around a series of practitioners, of research units and classes hosted by specific architecture schools and institutions, as well as around events such as exhibitions and conferences. Furthermore, computational movements in architecture are characterized as much by the technical aspects of the practice as by the structuration of the community of its practitioners, identifying it as a sociotechnical network (Latour 1987) still to be described.

In existing literature, several aspects of this sociotechnical network have been studied. In particular, the work of Mario Carpo (2011, 2017) must be mentioned as a recent historical and global overview of the computational movements in architecture. If numerous archaeologies of the digital in architecture already exist as well, including the book of that name by Greg Lynn (2013), they consist in the majority of an assembly of emblematic projects, presentations, and texts by the architects and designers of the computational field. Only a few studies of the development of specific digital tools exist (Serraino 2002; Smith 2017), focusing mainly on the 1990s and early 2000s and on the development of 3D modeling. While these works all contribute to an understanding of past and present use of computational design tools in architecture, none provide a global study of the associated sociotechnical network as such.

In the sociological study of science and technology, a sociotechnical network is a system of social, cultural, and economical links tying a given series of stakeholders together. In order to highlight the topology of a given network, one can follow specific technical objects, as is done in the present research with algorithmic design tools. Sociotechnical networks exist at different scales, from large state or societal-wide sociotechnical landscapes to smaller niche systems, such as the computational field, also a microcosm of larger contemporary architecture-related sociotechnical systems. The effect of sociotechnical networks on the trajectory of innovations in contemporary societies[1] and on our relationship to technical objects has been studied by several major thinkers of our time (Edgerton 2006; Latour 1987; Simondon 1958). The study of such networks in the computational field can be of interest for two reasons. First, the ability of such study to unveil the articulations between communities of practices and algorithmic design tools as well as the reasons why given tools are favored rather than others, be it for technical, economical, or cultural reasons. Second, while the amount and diversity of experimentations in the computational field makes it difficult to build an all-encompassing coherent historical account, focusing on practices themselves by following algorithms through their sociotechnical networks enables the emergence of common threads out of this diversity, making a comprehensive history of computational movements in architecture possible. The first has been documented in Gaudillière (2020a, 2020b), and the current research focuses on the second.

This paper aims to contribute to a practical and epistemological history of computational design and to a historiography of the field by proposing a study of the development of sociotechnical networks of computation in architecture between 1965 and 2020 as shown in *AD* magazine. The research focuses on two aspects: (1) a methodological approach for the constitution of a comprehensive history of the field and the application of that methodology to a corpus of items published in *AD* in the past 55 years, and (2) questions the relevance of the outlook into computational design as given by the magazine in comparison to a more comprehensive history taking into account other sources. First, the paper presents the history and the editorial line of *AD* magazine, as well as its pertinence as a primary source. Second, a brief account of the history emerging from this research is made, with a focus on four periods: pioneering research of the 1960s–1970s, emergence of 3D modeling tools and the *procedural winter* in the 1980s–1990s, constitution of a large-scale academic and professional network in the 2000s, and democratization of algorithmic design tools in the 2010s. Third, observations are made on editorial choices of the magazine and the biases of its account of computational research, with a special focus on the period 2000–2020, during which many issues have been dedicated to computational design themes, therefore making potential biases more visible. Despite the preponderance of specific topics, editors and contributors, *AD* magazine provides an outlook into key concerns of the community at given times. The main biases identified, including a strong focus on the themes of biodesign[2] and rationalization of practices, mirror the biases of the computational field itself, demonstrating the value of *AD* as an archive for the history of the field.

AD MAGAZINE, A COMPANION TO THE COMPUTATIONAL FIELD SINCE THE 1960S

AD Magazine

In order to contribute to the mapping of sociotechnical networks of computation, the choice of sources for the constitution of the corpus of practitioners, institutions, firms, and projects; typologies and tools; conceptual approaches; and references constituting the network is instrumental. *AD* magazine, given its history and editorial line, appears to be a particularly suitable source for the constitution of a primary corpus. *Architectural Design (AD)* magazine was founded in 1930 and has since continuously been published, first by Academy and later by Wiley. Twelve issues a year were released until the magazine switched to six per year in 1987, with each issue being the occasion for *AD* to invite a guest editor to focus on a specific concern of architectural design. For decades, *AD* magazine has represented a key reference for many practitioners of the field, in particular for technological developments of the discipline, and since the dawn of the computational turn in architecture, it has been recognized at large as a reference for this specific area.

Compared to other print titles in architectural press, *AD* has the advantage of having more in-depth content than *Architectural Digest*, *Dezeen*, or *Archdaily*, with a more rigorous editorial selection process for the contents than the latter two. It is an intermediary between titles focused on written theoretical essays such as *Log* and those focused on practical issues of construction such as *Detail*. Furthermore, *AD*'s editorial line presents an especially open mindset towards innovation and in particular towards computational design than many magazines, and has done so since early on in the digital age. As an example, reviews of the Seroussi Pavilion Competition and the exhibition that followed in the French press have been studied and show that as late into the computational turn as 2007, generalist architectural press in France was still very critical of anything that might involve experimenting with algorithmic design (Gaudillière 2019).

Furthermore, to the author's knowledge, no study of *AD* magazine as a resource on the history of computational design exists, despite the very complete archive of the development of the field it represents and the valuable inputs it could provide in several domains.

Methodology

The methodology outlined here is the complete approach proposed for the constitution of a database to be used as the basis for a comprehensive history of the field. As explained above, this methodology has been used for a global survey of the computational field. As part of this survey, *AD* magazine archives have been studied. This paper describes the observations made based on the *AD* archives, and balances them with a comparison to the observations using the entire database and methodology. First, information has been gathered from various sources. *AD* magazine issues were the first consulted, thus creating a database listing every project mentioned in it that referred to computational design. This database was then completed using exhibition catalogs[3] and conference proceedings.[4] Interviews were conducted with a series of practitioners, some of them also having given access to their private archives. Three types of objects were considered for the research: practitioners' trajectories, design projects, and design tools, all followed through the sociotechnical network and for each of which a series of information was gathered in the sources.

The corpus studied in order to establish the database consists of 456 *AD* issues, from issue no. 1 of 1965 to issue no. 6 of 2020, and eight issues from the *AD Reader* series, accessed in the KADK (Copenhagen), ENSAPB (Paris), and ENSAMV (Paris) libraries. Of these 464 issues, 134 contained items relevant to the proposed study of the computational field in architecture. 1,398 projects cited in the articles and 139 written essays were identified and integrated to the database for further analysis. Four categories of items have been established, with specific sets of information gathered on each: First, the editorial team of *AD* magazine in place at the time of the release as well as the guest editors have been extracted for each issue. Second, for projects, the practitioners and firms participating, the computational framework, the type of algorithm, and the area of focus have been listed. Third, for studio classes featured, students, teachers, institutions, computational framework, type of algorithm, and area of focus have been listed. Fourth, for written essays, author, institution, references, area of focus, and theoretical position have been listed. Finally, the network is mapped out by establishing ties between practitioners and firms, practitioners and institutions—where each one studied and taught—as well as by documenting which project was created by whom using which type of algorithm, thus mapping generations and clusters of development throughout time.

A BRIEF HISTORY OF THE COMPUTATIONAL FIELD IN ARCHITECTURE

Clusters of development forming the network throughout four successive generations have been observed, with each generation marked by the transmission of theoretical and practical knowledge from the previous to the next, and by the extension of the network to further clusters. The starting point of this history is the constitution of the first clusters of research in computational architecture in the 1960s, and unfolds following the chronology depicted in Figure 1, with four periods and six major approaches to the role played by algorithmic tools. While the history of the computational field in architecture as uncovered in this research deserves a much longer and detailed text, the brief description that follows is intended as a reference point regarding a few key issues—programming knowledge of practitioners, level of development of technical setups and algorithms, and network constitution—in order to further comment on the outlook into this history provided by *AD* magazine.

Pioneers of Computation

The first generation encompasses the work of pioneers such as Nicholas Negroponte, Cedric Price, and the Frazers, with limited technical setups such as the one used at MIT by the Architecture Machine Group (ARCH MAC) for the URBAN 5 project in 1973, resorting to room-size processors, tiny cathodic screens, and light pens (Steenson 2014). Those inquiries took place in only a few academic institutions (MIT, Bartlett School of Architecture, AA, UCLA, UTS), bringing together a handful of practitioners who relied on collaborations with computer scientists to develop not only programs in early languages such as FORTRAN but also pioneering research in the fields of computer science and artificial intelligence (AI). In particular, alongside other research groups that would soon become the MIT Medialab, the ARCH MAC contributed significantly to the development of verbal communication between a computer and a human in natural languages (Brand 1987). The primitive technical setups also entailed the traditional limits of computerized logic systems of the time, in particular the combinatorial explosion and the problem of commonsense knowledge (McCorduck 2004), on which architectural design heavily relies. At the time, practitioners of the computational field pursued their work in close proximity to the field of artificial intelligence, then in early development. As a consequence, this period is also characterized by many enquiries on the nature of the design process—while Nigel Cross's texts are especially known to our field, he is not the only one to have drawn from attempts at coding scripts enabling the automation of design decision-making to a long-term reflection on the nature of the discipline—a characteristic of pioneering experimentations that would then fade with time.

The Procedural Winter

The second period is marked by a split in two parallel fields of development. On one hand, 3D-modeling tools appeared, first in the animation industry and then in architectural practices, which started resorting to them to handle complex geometries—developing into the well-known curvy shapes that would in part characterize the digital turn in architecture in later years. This is the most documented period and setup, with both historical pieces on 3D-modeling software developed in specific firms and analysis of the impact of such tools on the practice (Serraino 2002; Smith 2017). Following the appropriation of existing 3D-modeling tools such as Maya, it is the moment where architects' making of their own tools has been established as a key marker of the digital field in architecture—with architects embracing 3D modeling and creating their own software, such as form*Z in Chris Yessios's company auto.des.sys or Digital Project in what would become Gehry Technologies. It is also the moment of appearance of a representation bias: as 3D modeling went on to develop in everyday architectural practice, digital tools would for many be reduced to representation tools with affordances equivalent to pen and paper. The algorithms on which modeling is based were concealed behind the complex geometrical explorations the software enabled, and the procedural processes at large those algorithms enable were also hidden away.

While 3D modeling boomed, the research on algorithmic design processes entered a *procedural winter*, a term coined to describe what computer scientists and historians of artificial intelligence call the *Winter of AI* (McCorduck 2004). Research in computational design slowed down, with the network of practitioners hardly expanding and little experimentation with scripting programs being conducted. This stagnation echoes the situation of the AI field, where research also slowed and funding considerably diminished, as researchers struggled to make significant progress in tackling major issues like limited computer power, intractability, and Moravec's paradox. A few of the new practitioners working in computational architecture kept trying to solve the main issues of decision-making automation and made a few unsuccessful attempts at producing industrialized expert system solutions for standard architectural practice. Most practitioners new to the field at the time, such as Bernard Cache and Patrik Beaucé, rather than looking into these unloved and unfunded problems, focused on experimentations with digital fabrication and the associated theory of nonstandard fabrication, producing major texts of the theoretical framework of the following years (Cache 1995).

The Golden Years

While research in computational architecture withered during the procedural winter, it did not disappear. Later years were marked by an exponential development of the network in two different directions again. On one hand, the computational field developed into a more generalist and construction-oriented practice. Engineering offices such as Arup and Bollinger + Grohmann, in association with classic architectural practices such as Dominique Perrault Architecture and SANAA, started mobilizing algorithms for postrationalization of designs in order to build them, but they also looked into developing design tools enabling prerationalization in order to save time and money. Large architecture offices such as Foster & Partners, Skidmore Owings & Merrill, and Zaha Hadid Architects created small in-house research groups to look into the potential of computational design tools. The software industry also began to take growing interest in the field, first with Bentley Systems conducting research and proposing software packages such as Generative Components, followed by McNeel and Autodesk, whose interest would ultimately lead to the integration of Grasshopper into Rhinoceros and of Dynamo into Revit.

At the time, the network was becoming denser not only through the appearance of these various private firms as new stakeholders but also through the multiplication of university groups and master's programs dedicated to computational practices in architecture (such as CITA, Mediated Matter group, and EmTech). Within these groups, researchers also maintained professional practices, giving rise to a multitude of small experimental offices such as biothing, EZCT, Xefirotarch, supermanoeuvre, kokkugia, R&Sie(n), OCEAN, and theverymany. The activity of these practitioners is characterized by a fine-tuned mastery of programming, acquired by some in the course of complementary training to their architecture studies and honed by regular practice. While these practitioners tended to use the same software and programming languages—in particular Maya/MEL and Rhinoceros/Python, very popular before and after 2007, respectively—they created a custom algorithm for each new project. These algorithms were assembled from a patchwork of many specialized computer tools (sometimes up to 10 or 15) and were the marker of a genuine craft of programming. Moreover, these algorithms were often inspired by algorithmic structures developed in other fields (biology, animation), which were hijacked to be used for the production of architectural objects.

Much more than the first split, this one happened by separating academy and industry in their goals and practices. At this point, nevertheless, a lot of links remained between the two branches, constituting a dense network of exploration of the potential of computational tools, both in a heuristic and in a rational approach.

Democratizing Computational Tools

The different groups of practitioners that have emerged over the generations all share an interest in computational tools and their potential for architectural design. While they have different visions, they are all involved in transmitting the knowledge they have helped to develop and are committed to ensuring that their knowledge and vision is shared. Thus, in the most recent period of development, the democratization of algorithmic design tools to a great number of practitioners has become a key issue. However, the combination of the hijacking of algorithmic structures originating from other disciplines, the search for a certain efficiency in professional computational practices, and the need for practitioners to be able to rapidly transmit their knowledge leads to the promotion of algorithmic typologies and the constitution of associated software, rather than to the transmission of an in-depth knowledge of a scripting craft for architectural design. These ready-made tools have in the latest period of development taken over from custom algorithms in the field (Gaudillière 2020a).

If some software enables the development of custom libraries and extensions, ready-made software solutions enabling easy use of algorithmic typologies popularized by previous generations are spreading rapidly, and they allow computational practices to exit the initial network, with the appearance of many new users all over the world. The interfaces of these pieces of software are decisive components—they make democratization possible by allowing amateurs to access and manipulate complex algorithmic models. As these models are increasingly based on algorithmic typologies, they make use of predefined rules that users can access to set up their model. Over the decades, from tailor-made algorithms to ready-made software solutions, the thickness of interfaces is increasing more and more, and the parameters on which an algorithmic model is based are not always easily accessible. Algorithmic design tools then become black-box software. Users who are less familiar with programming techniques are therefore constrained in their use of the tools and guided by the tool developer and the structure they put in place. In the case of computational architecture, this also means being pushed to adopt the programmer's vision of the discipline and the role to be played by algorithms (Gaudillière 2020a). Neophyte users therefore tend to build a biased practice, influenced by the structure of ready-made software solutions and with little or no opportunity to question or modify these structures. Some typologies and the tools associated with them also predominate due to their ease of adaptation for amateur interfaces. Others, on the contrary, are more difficult to adapt and thus see their use diminish (Gaudillière 2020b). Some approaches to computational design are promoted through these black-box tools, in particular a rationalization bias through which attempts are made to systematically anchor architectural decision-making in scientific knowledge and scientific methodologies.

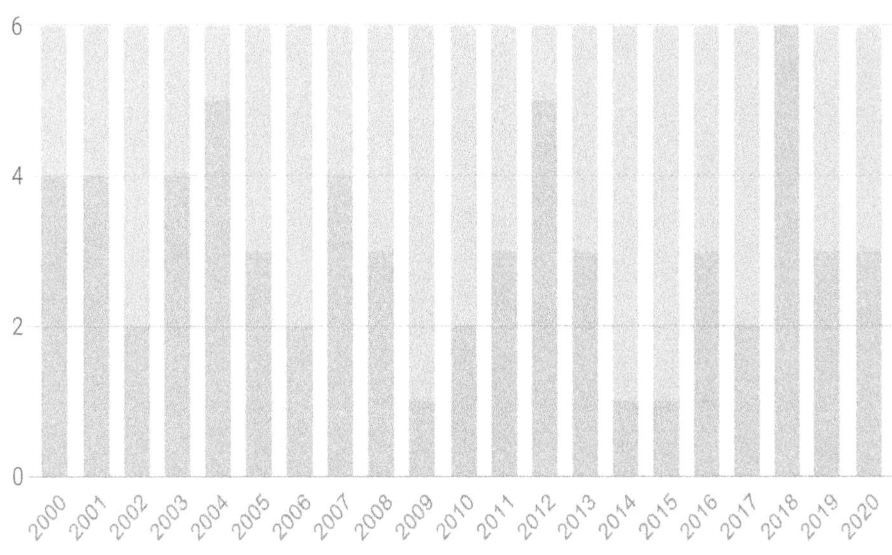

2 Number of *AD* issues dedicated to computational design issues, 2000–2020.

Several factors influence this rationalization bias: first, the inheritance of a mechanistic bias, with a recent resurgence; second, the split between industry and academy and the related structure of sociotechnical networks in the field, leading to the promotion mainly of computational tools spreading a capitalist approach; third, the current democratization dynamic is at work, with little questioning of those black-box tools and with little epistemological reflection on the nature of the discipline. This contributes to strengthening the rationalization bias in the field, to the detriment of the diversity of practices that has characterized not only the computational field since its early developments but architecture as a discipline itself.

AD MAGAZINE: A BIASED HISTORY?

Using *AD* magazine as a source has enabled us an overview of the history of the computational field in architecture, by contributing to the identification of key practitioners and projects over 55 years. But as a magazine with a given editorial line, *AD* has made curation choices over the years, and in order to assess the accountability of the development of the field as based on *AD* issues as sources, the biases that might have been triggered by such choices must be evaluated. To assess this potential bias and to highlight nuances of *AD* magazine's editorial line, the *AD* corpus has been cross-referenced with the general study. And while the contents displayed in *AD* over time generally fit the cross-referenced account made in this paper of the development of the computational field, editorial choices tend to highlight some practitioners and themes much more often than others. Examples of editorial choices and potential biases in the account of the experimentations in the computational field have therefore been studied for the 2000–2020 period. As this is the period in which a greater number of *AD* issues were dedicated to topics relevant to the computational field, editorial choices and potential biases thus become more apparent.

During that period, *AD*'s structure has slightly evolved but continues to consist of articles and project presentations by the guest editor related to the issue's theme, as well as a series of short fixed sections with regular writers, such as Craig Kellogg, Will McLean, Valentina Croci, and Neil Spiller. The editorial team, lead by Helen Castle since 1999, has evolved over the years, and now includes several key figures of the computational field.[5] Between 2000 and 2020, 126 issues of *AD* magazine were published, as well as 8 issues from the *AD Reader* collection. Of those, 62 issues of the magazine and four readers were dedicated to themes relating to the computational turn (Fig. 2)—almost half, with a slight increase over the years. This points to the importance granted by the magazine to the stakes of computational practice in architecture.

Figure 3 shows themes of the computational-related issues throughout the years. Eight categories have been identified:

- Biodesign-themed issues look at morphogenetic design processes, biomimicry, evolutionary algorithms, and biomaterials. Twelve have been published in the past 20 years, for example, the 2004 "Emergence: Morphogenetic Design Strategies" issue and the 2015 "Material Synthesis: Fusing the Physical and the Computational" issue.

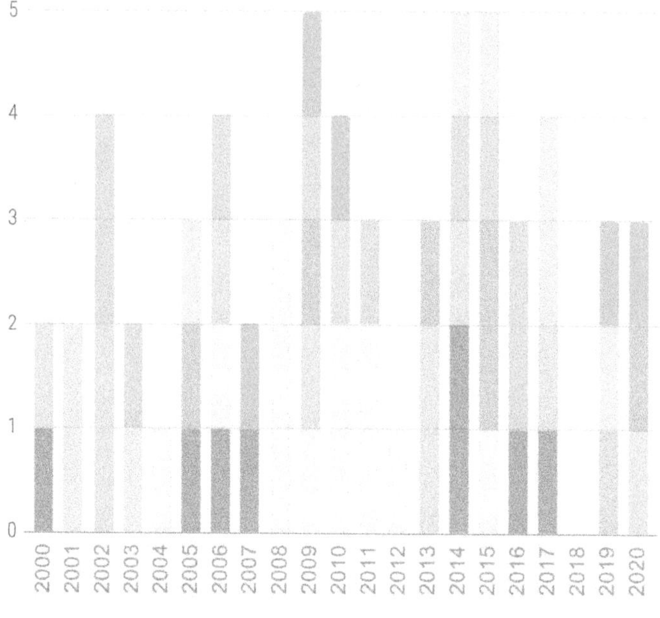

3 Themes of *AD* issues dedicated to computational design issues, 2000–2020.

- Rationalization-themed issues look at construction-oriented practices. Eleven have been published, for example, the 2002 "Versioning: Evolutionary Techniques in Architecture" issue and the 2013 "The Innovation Imperative: Architectures of Vitality" issue.

- Theory-themed issues look at possible global keys for the understanding of the computational paradigm in architecture. Two readers and 11 issues have been released, for example, the 2011 "Mathematics of Space' issue and the 2019 "Discrete: Reappraising the Digital in Architecture" issue.

- Fabrication-themed issues look into novel fabrication methods such as robotic processes and into nonstandard fabrication workflows and frameworks. One reader and six issues have been released, for example, the 2014 "Made by Robots" issue.

- Urbanism-themed issues look into questions regarding smart cities and analysis and design tools for the city. Six issues have been released, for example, the 2020 "Urban Futures: Designing the Digitalised City" issue.

- Aesthetics-themed issues look into the potential of computational design techniques for a renewal of the formal complexity of architecture. Five issues have been released, for example, the 2010 "Exuberance" issue.

- Global issues (three and a reader) offer an overview of the computational field as a whole at the time of publication, and other themed issues (eight and a reader) regroup topics that are unrelated to the major themes identified.

As can be seen in Figure 3, some themes are represented twice as often as others. While it is understandable that theoretical issues would often be edited, as the computational field is in constant evolution and still in need of a global understanding of the diversity of experiments of the past decades, the large number of issues dedicated to biodesign and to rationalization indicates an editorial choice. The biodesign theme has had a particularly prolific period (2008–2013), and although the history laid out by *AD* does not fundamentally differ from the history documented with cross-referenced sources, the importance given to the subject as an all-encapsulating narrative far outweighs the other narratives that played a role in the field. This can be explained by the fact that the morphogenetic narrative, as an inheritance of cybernetics and of the Paskian architecture paradigm (Pickering 2009) is one of the historically most ancient and therefore well-accepted understanding prisms for the computational in architecture. The presence of numerous rationalization-themed issues, on the other hand, accompanies the rise of the bias of the same name in the field that we described earlier.

Figure 4 shows the most-cited institutions and firms in computational design-themed issues of that period—from three mentions for the smallest circles to 111 for the most

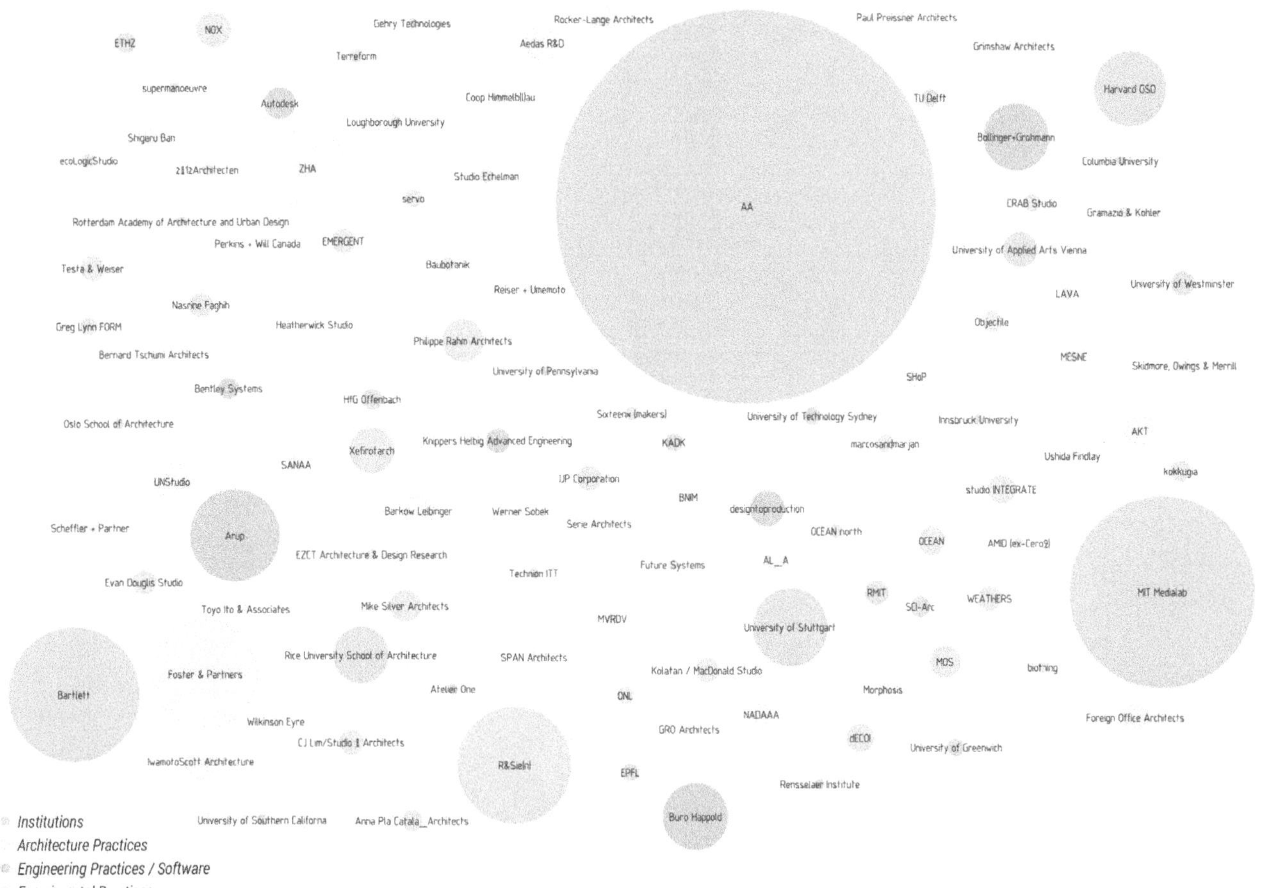

4 Most frequently mentioned firms and institutions in *AD* issues dedicated to computational design issues, 2000–2020.

cited (the AA School). In Figure 5, the first tab shows the most frequently invited contributors, the number of papers they have authored in issues they have not edited, and their background; the second tab shows the repartition of all the contributors in computational-themed issues. The third tab shows the most frequently invited guest editors, as well as the number of mentions of projects they have led in all of the computational issues—including the ones they have edited themselves. It shows that some guest editors have been invited for several issues, while other practitioners instrumental to the constitution of the field have never been invited. Taking into account both the issues edited and the contributions, out of 905 contributors and editors, 15 have been invited for a major feature in 1 issue out of 10, and 3 have been invited for a major feature in one issue out of 5. Furthermore, some guest editors tend to feature much of their own work or works by close collaborators in issues they edit, also distorting the overview given by *AD* magazine, as can be seen in the number of mentions column. This highlights the existence of an "*AD* network" of practitioners and curators, hinting to the fact that being featured in *AD* magazine or invited as a guest editor is guided by a system of cooptation—a phenomenon not rare in the world of editing and curating but that still weighs on the accuracy of the narrative of the computational field as offered by *AD*.

Overall, despite a tendency to always put the same people forward, *AD* nevertheless remains a mirror of key concerns of the time in the computational field. At some periods, it has taken the pulse of the field very accurately—in particular, two issues looking into open-source match very closely the concerns expressed by practitioners interviewed about the period of release of these issues—while at other periods it has been a more loose account. On the topic of computational design tools and their control as well, *AD* mirrors the vision of the field, encouraging black-box tools by providing little technical detail about the projects featured and accompanying a wave of democratization sustaining a rationalist approach.

CONCLUSION

The study has allowed for the creation of a database listing all the items referenced in *AD* as well as the information gathered on them. General observations on the genesis of

Contributor	Number of contributions***	Background
Mark Burry	9	Architect
Patrik Schumacher	9	Architect
Michael Weinstock	8	Architect / Academic
Greg Lynn	7	Architect / Academic
Neri Oxman	7	Academic
Ben van Berkel	6	Architect
Mario Carpo	6	Academic
Peter Cook	6	Architect
Francois Roche	6	Architect
Dennis Shelden	6	Architect / Academic
Benjamin H. Bratton	5	Academic
Manuel DeLanda	5	Academic
Hernan Diaz Alonso	5	Architect / Academic
Mark Garcia	5	Academic
Achim Menges	5	Architect / Academic
Antoine Picon	5	Academic
Philippe Morel	5	Architect / Academic
Leon van Schaik	5	Academic
Philip F Yuan	5	Architect / Academic

Number of contributions	Number of contributors
1	735
2	97
3	31
4	11
5	10
6	7
7	3
8	1
9	2
10	3*
11	1*
16	2*
19	1*
Total contributors**	905

* Contributors for a fixed section
** Including contributors co-authoring papers
*** In issues other than the ones edited by the contributor

Editor	Computational issues edited	Total number of issues edited	Number of mentions	Background	Part of the editorial board
Achim Menges	7	7	51	Architect / Academic	No
Michael Hensel	5	7	36	Architect / Academic	Yes
Neil Leach	4	4	7	Curator	No
Bob Sheil	4	4	7	Academic	No
Ali Rahim	4	4	17	Architect	No
Lucy Bullivant	3	4	0	Curator	No
Mark Garcia	3	4	0	Academic	No
Neil Spiller	3	5	4	Academic	No
Michael Weinstock	3	3	28	Architect / Academic	No
Mark Burry	2	2	13	Architect	Yes
Richard Garber	2	2	3	Architect	No
Christopher Hight	2	2	6	Designer / Academic	No
Hina Jamelle	2	2	4	Architect	No
Leon van Schaik	2	2	3	Academic	Yes

5 Most frequently invited contributors and guest editors of *AD* issues dedicated to computational design issues, 2000–2020.

the field have been extracted, as has information on instrumental contributions by practitioners and institutions, on the first appearance of the various algorithmic typologies, and on their frequency of use throughout time, showing their historical development. An account of the development of the computational field is provided based on this information, showing the four stages of development of the network and the impact of the modalities of transmission of knowledge throughout time and throughout the network. Furthermore, the *AD* history is compared to the global, cross-referenced network history, enabling a study of the curation bias entailed by *AD*'s editorial line and choices. Finally, this database could be used in various research projects either as an overview of the existing contributions to specific issues of the field or by further exploiting the referenced data. As an example, the present research has focused on mapping the development of the network through its projects and tools, but much remains to be said on the areas of focus, the writings, and sets of references used by the practitioners in their essays and the epistemological ramifications of the computational field they render visible, thus contributing to a theoretical history of the computational turn.

ACKNOWLEDGMENTS

The author would like to thank the Architecture of Order Research Cluster and the Hessian State Ministry of Higher Education, Research and the Arts: State Offensive for the Development of Scientific and Economic Excellence (LOEWE) for supporting this research.

NOTES

1. In particular, the stakeholders involved in a given sociotechnical network influence, depending on their interests, the adoption and promotion of given technical artifacts and the disregarding of others.
2. This field has been given various names across the period, from "morphogenetic design" to "biodesign" but always reflects a common interest in natural phenomenon and materials.
3. *The Gen(h)ome Project, Naturaliser l'architecture, Architectures Non-Standard, Archilab, scriptedbypurpose, L'architecture au-delà des formes*, as well as archives of the

Canadian Center for Architecture and of the FRAC Centre.

4. RobArch, Design Modeling Symposium, ACADIA, eCAADe, CAADRIA.
5. Members of the editorial board currently include: Will Aslop, Denise Bratton, Paul Brislin, Mark Burry, André Chaszar, Nigel Coates, Peter Cook, Teddy Cruz, Max Fordham, Massimiliano Fuksas, Edwin Heathcote, Michael Hensel, Anthony Hunt, Charles Jencks, Helen Castle, Jayne Merkel, Mark Robbins, Deborah Saunt, Leon van Schaik, Patrik Schumacher, Ken Yeang, and Alejandro Zaera-Polo.

REFERENCES

Brand, Stewart. 1989. *The Medialab: Inventing the Future at M.I.T.* New York: Penguin Books.

Cache, Bernard. 1997. *Terre Meuble*. HYX.

Carpo, Mario. 2011. *The Alphabet and the Algorithm*. Cambridge, MA: MIT Press.

Carpo, Mario. 2017. *The Second Digital Turn: Design Beyond Intelligence*. Cambridge, MA: MIT Press.

Cross, Nigel. 1977. *The Automated Architect*. London: Pion.

Cross, Nigel. 2006. *Designerly Ways of Knowing*. Springer.

Edgerton, David. 2006. *The Shock of the Old: Technology and Global History Since 1900*. Oxford: Oxford University Press.

Eisenman, Peter. 1984. "The End of the Classical: The End of the Beginning, the End of the End." *Perspecta* 21: 154–713.

Gaudillière, Nadja. 2019. "Towards an History of Computational Tools in Automated Architectural Design—The Seroussi Pavilion Competition as a Case Study." In *Intelligent & Informed: Proceedings of the 24th CAADRIA Conference—Volume 2*, edited by M.Haeusler, M. A. Schnabel, and T. Fukuda, 581–590. Victoria University of Wellington, Wellington, New Zealand.

Gaudillière, Nadja. 2020a. "Evolutionary Tools and the Practice of Architecture: from Appropriated Typology to Becoming the Black Boxes of CAAD." In *Proceedings of the 4th International Conference of Biodigital Architecture & Genetics*, edited by A. Estevez. iBAG-UIC Barcelona.

Gaudillière, Nadja. 2020b. "Computational Tools in Architecture and their Genesis: The Development of Agent-based Models in Spatial Design." In *RE: Anthropocene, Design in the Age of Humans—Proceedings of the 25th CAADRIA Conference—Volume 2*, edited by D. Holzer, W. Nakapan, A. Globa, and I. Koh, 497–506. Chulalongkorn University, Bangkok, Thailand, 5–6 August 2020.

Latour, Bruno. 1987. *Science in Action*. Cambridge, MA: Harvard University Press.

Lynn, Greg, ed. 2013. *Archaeology of the Digital*. London: Sternberg Press.

Masure, Anthony. 2014. "Le design des programmes : des façons de faire du numérique." PhD thesis, Université Paris-1 Panthéon Sorbonne.

McCorduck, Patricia. 2004. *Machines Who Think: A Personal Inquiry Into the History and Prospects of Artificial Intelligence*, Taylor & Francis.

Pickering, A. 2009. "Gordon Pask: From Chemical Computers to Adaptive Architecture." In *The Cybernetic Brain: Sketches of Another Future*. Chicago: University of Chicago Press.

Serraino, Pierluigi. 2002. *History of Form*Z*. Basel: Birkhauser.

Simondon, Gilbert. 1958. *Du mode d'existence des objets techniques*. Paris: Editions Aubier-Montaigne.

Smith, Robert. 2017. *Fabricating the Frank Gehry Legacy: The Story of the Evolution of Digital Practice in Frank Gehry's Office*. CreateSpace.

Steenson, Molly W. 2014. *Architectural Intelligence: How Designers and Architects Created the Digital Landscape*. Cambridge, MA: MIT Press.

IMAGE CREDITS

All drawings and images by the author.

Nadja Gaudillière-Jami is a PhD researcher at the GSA Laboratory (ENSAPM), a researcher at the Digital Design Unit (TU Darmstadt), co-founder of XtreeE and vice president of the NGO thr34d5.

A Machine Learning Method of Predicting Behavior Vitality Using Open Source Data

Yunjuan Sun
School of Architecture
Harbin Institute of Technology

Lei Jiang
Bartlett School of Architecture
University College London

Hao Zheng
School of Design
University of Pennsylvania

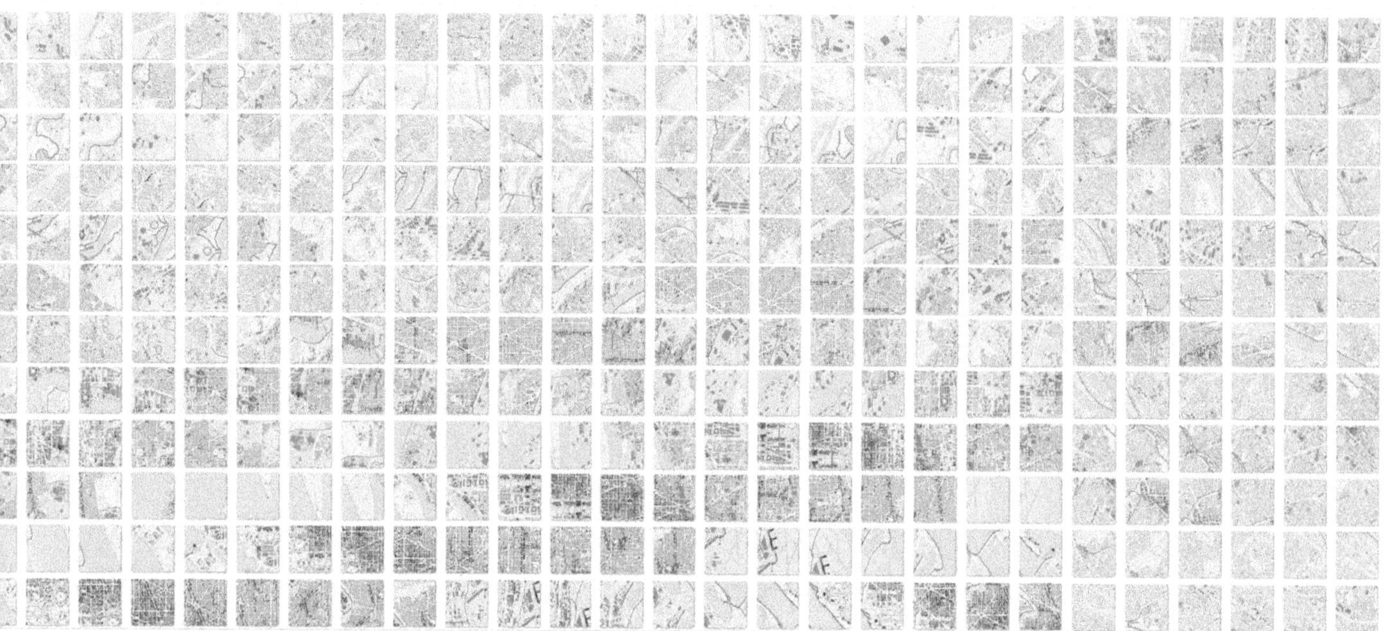

1 The datasets for GAN training representing urban form and function.

ABSTRACT

The growing popularity of machine learning has provided new opportunities to predict certain behaviors precisely by utilizing big data. In this research, we use an image-based neural network to explore the relationship between the built environment and the activity of bicyclists in that environment. The generative model can produce heat maps that can be used to predict quantitatively the cycling and running activity in a given area, and then use urban design to enhance urban vitality in that area. In the machine learning model, the input image is a plan view of the built environment, and the output image is a heat map showing certain activities in the corresponding area. After it is trained, the model yields output (the predicted heat map) at an acceptable level of accuracy. The heat map shows the levels and conditions of the subject activity in different sections of the built environment. Thus, the predicted results can help identify where regional vitality can be improved. Using this method, designers can not only predict the behavioral heat distribution but also examine the different interactions between behaviors and aspects of the environment. The extent to which factors might influence behaviors is also studied by generating a heat map of the modified plan. In addition to the potential applications of this approach, its limitations and areas for improvement are also proposed.

INTRODUCTION

Problem Statement

Previous studies about cycling behaviors have mainly used the subjective evaluation method, the behavior research methods, and statistical methods like regression analysis. The subjective evaluation method often uses questionnaires to analyze the impact of environmental factors on cyclists through statistical analysis (Antonakos 1993). The behavior research method analyzes the selection of riding routes to infer the environment preferences of the travelers (Howard and Burns 2001). The first evaluation method has a larger subjective factor and lacks analysis of spatial factors affecting its use. The second method is more convincing, but the data required is more expensive and difficult to obtain. Statistical methods are widely used to reveal those factors that have great impact on cycling use. However, those data types are mostly quantitative or qualitative indicators, such as numerical indicators used to measure traffic accessibility, land use diversity, and street attributes. There is almost no use of the city plan, which contains the information of the urban form and natural environment. Moreover, it is difficult to avoid the collinearity between multiple variables and quantify the influence of each factor. Therefore, it is difficult to make accurate quantitative predictions based on the built environment. However, by experimenting with various inputs and model types using open source data and generative adversarial networks (GANs), we can easily compare the influence of different factors in behaviors and reveal different interactions between built environment and various activities. The method of using generative adversarial neural networks has innovations in data types and learning methods.

Background

The advancement of technologies like artificial intelligence, wearable sensors, and positioning techniques have created the potential to study the relationship between human behaviors and the built environment. Revealing the human–environment relationship can provide strategies like optimizing spatial layouts, designing the visual environment in the planning stages, and evaluating them later. These techniques can play a crucial role in constructing the physical space to meet people's requirements. The popularity of shared bicycles and the influence of riding behavior in the built urban environment has become a hot spot in academia (Fraser and Lock 2011). The design and optimization of the cycling environment has become an important issue in urban planning, and it can benefit from an increased understanding of how the built environment affects cycling.

Research on Bicycling Behavior

Research on bicycling behavior mainly includes four aspects: first, willingness and satisfaction of bicycling, which mainly analyze the residents' evaluation factors through questionnaire surveys. Second, spatiotemporal patterns of biking behavior (for example, Zhou 2015 analyzed massive bike-sharing data from July to December in 2013 and 2014). Third, examining factors affecting bicycling flows and usage. Many scholars have found that the diversity of land use, accessibility to destinations, street design, and urban form are highly related to bicycling behavior (Faghih-Imani et al. 2014). Fourth, using machine learning to predict the cycling demand of the site to effectively allocate public resources. Wang and Kim (2018) adopted long short-term memory neural networks (LSTM) and gated recurrent unit (GRU) models to predict the short-term number of available bikes in docking stations with one-month historical data.

Machine Learning Methods in Urban Planning

The application of machine learning at the micro level of urban planning mainly focuses on analysis of the spatial environment. These applications include measuring physical settings, predicting human perceptions of a place (Zhang et al. 2018), generating street images (Steinfeld 2019), and developing intelligent tools for designers. (Naderi and Raman 2005). Especially in the usage of GANs, image generation and prediction techniques have been widely applied in the image-based tasks. Previous research about using GANs in the urban field includes image classification, geographic knowledge discovery (Mao et al. 2017), and scene generation,

Project Goal

In this research, through machine learning that uses an image-based neural network, we explore the relationship between the built environment and heat maps of riding activity. The generative model can produce heat maps, and the meaning of the generated image is a visualization of the number of bicycle trips. The closer it is to red, the more active it is. By assessing the value of the RGB channel of each pixel in the generated heat map, the method allows designers to quantitatively explore the influence of modifications.

Using machine learning to quantitatively analyze and predict urban behaviors, this research challenges the traditional subjective analysis and generative methods in urban design and planning, and proposes a workflow of evaluating urban metrics by building predictive machine learning models. The data collection method, as well as the model training process, provides urban designers

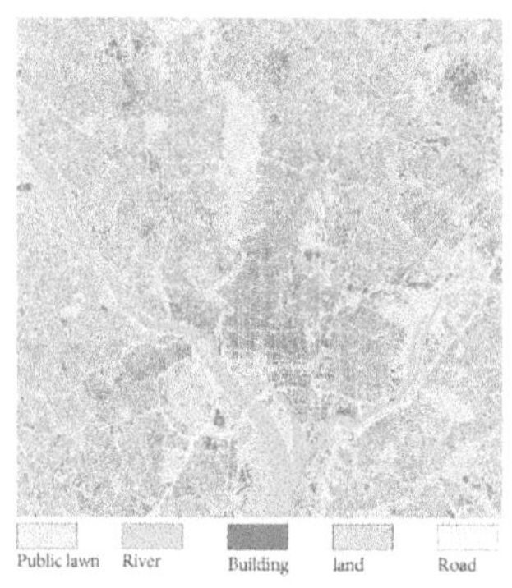

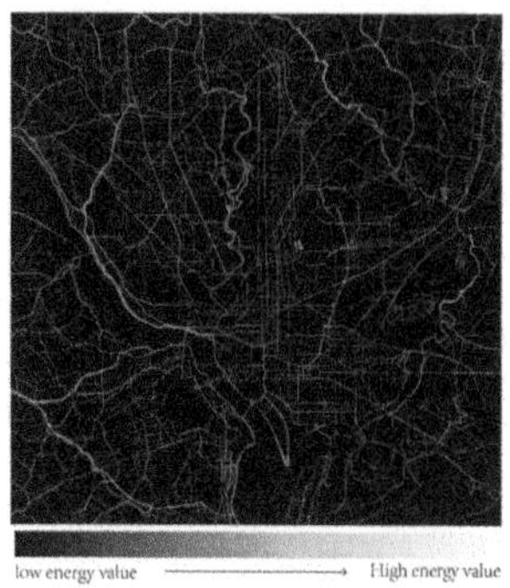

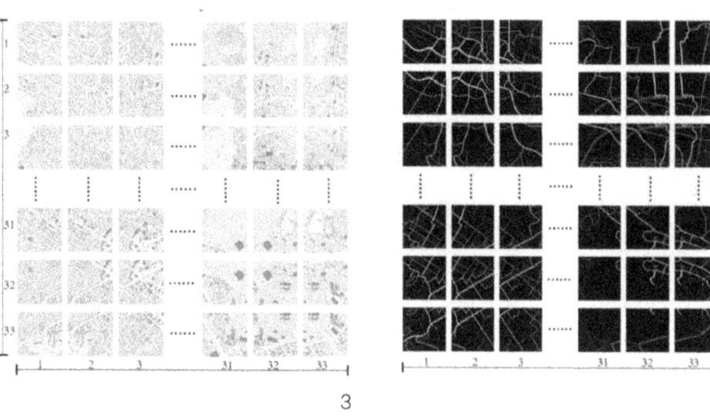

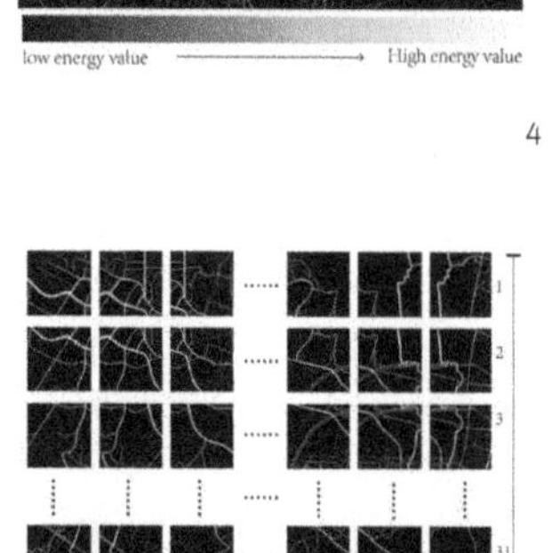

6 Comparison of the inputs for two models.

7 Visualization of points of interest and cycleways.

2 Map of the built environment.

3 Cut images of the map.

4 The ride heat map.

5 Cut images of the heat map.

with further inspirations and tools for explorations, thus revealing a novel machine learning approach in urban planning.

METHOD

Collection of Built Environment Plans

We use Mapbox to customize the map style in the studio and use different colors to distinguish such things as buildings, roads, green spaces, and natural elements in the built environment. Then, local maps of Washington and its suburbs are automatically intercepted (Fig. 2). Through image processing, the whole map is cut into small images (Fig. 3) with a resolution of 700×700 using the PIL library in Python. This operation makes the size of each picture uniform and suitable for the data format of machine learning.

Collection of Regional Cycling Heat Map

Using Strava (Strava Inc. 2021), and by selecting the type of activity, we can get a heat map based on the movements of all public users in a given area. First, the heat distribution map of partial areas in the window is intercepted multiple times. Then all the intercepted areas are stitched into a large thermal map that is aligned with the image of the built environment. Finally, the zoom level and picture size are fine-tuned to ensure that the thermal map and the image of the built environment are aligned in latitude and longitude. Then the heat map (Fig. 4) is cut into small images (Fig. 5) with 700×700 resolution.

Collection of Points of Interest and Road Classification Associated with Ride Behavior

To test whether adding information like points of interest (POI) and road classification improves the accuracy of the images, we build two input models (Fig. 6) to compare the predicted result. The input for the first model contains only the basic urban form information, while the input for the second model uses two sizes of circles to represent two types of POI related to cycling. The first type includes art centers, attractions, malls, monuments, museums, playgrounds, public buildings, supermarkets, viewing areas, and the zoo. These have a great correlation with recreational cycling (Liu and Lin 2019). The second type includes functional places like schools, restaurants, and hotels. In addition to POI, cycleways are represented by purple on the city map. The classification and geographic locations of POI and roads are all downloaded from OpenStreetMap in Shapefile (.shp) format. Then the related POI and roads are selected by attributes and visualized in ArcGIS (ESRI 2019) (Fig. 7). By intercepting the window in ArcGIS, overlapping it with the map, and cutting it into small images with 700×700 resolution, the inputs for the second model are obtained.

Neural Network Structure and Training

The task for the machine learning model is to learn the relationship between the input built environment plan and the output rider heat map. An image-based GAN with convolution and deconvolution kernels is used as the

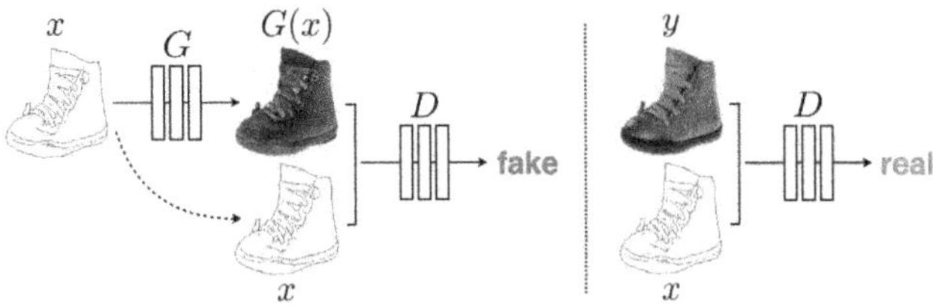

8 Training a conditional GAN (Isola et al. 2017).

framework. The conditional GAN from Goodfellow et al. (2014) and pix2pixHD from Isola et al. (2017), an open-source project, are used to develop the algorithm for this research. pix2pixHD means pixel-to-pixel translation, and the size of the input and output images remains the same.

The model pix2pixHD contains two neural networks, Generator (G) and Discriminator (D), which are trained simultaneously (Fig. 8). The Generator transforms an input image to an output image with the same size, using convolutional layers, residual layers, and deconvolutional layers. The Discriminator distinguishes the image generated by the Generator from the ground truth image. The Generator feeds forward the generated result to the Discriminator, while the Discriminator feeds back the loss and gradient to the Generator. Thus, the Generator is trained to generate the fake images closer to the ground truth, while the Discriminator is trained to better tell the fake image apart. The two networks "compete" with each other, so this system is called "adversarial."

Practically speaking, to apply pix2pixHD in addition to providing the program with image pairs described previously, some important hyper-parameters also need to be defined. First, there are no instance maps, thus the function to read and use instance maps should be turned off. Second, we want the program to directly use RGB colors as input, so we set the label_nc as 0. Third, during experiments we found the early training epochs with a constant learning rate would not improve the network after 70 epochs; thus, we set the learning rate for the first 70 epochs of the training process as a constant value but the learning rate for the following 30 epochs as decaying values. All other settings are the same as the default settings.

In this model, the input image is a plan view of the built environment, and the output image is a cycling heat map of the corresponding area. Of all the samples, 83% are put into the training set, and the other 17% are the testing set. The training set is used to train the model, and the testing set is used to verify the accuracy of the model. After training, the model can predict the area with an unknown cycling heat map. This can then guide the transformation of urban design. Figure 9 shows the image pairs in each training epoch, indicating that the training is complete with high accuracy in epoch 100.

RESULTS AND DISCUSSION

Predicted Results of Testing Set

When identifying images for the test set to represent different regions of the city, we select three vertical columns and three horizontal columns from the middle of the entire data area. The training set includes a variety of urban and suburban areas (Fig. 10 left). In order for all features to be tested, we divided the test area and training area manually. Because the distribution of urban features is not uniform, it is better to select the test set manually than randomly from the overall map. The selected examples of the synthesized results in the first model have different levels of accuracy compared with the corresponding parts of the real riding heat map (Fig. 10 right). The overall accuracy of the predicted heat map is ideal, since it can roughly distinguish the heating conditions of different sections.

Definition of Error

To measure the prediction error, we define the basis for calculating the error between the synthesized image and the real image. The overall accuracy is based on the accuracy of small fractions in an image, which combine to show the comprehensive accuracy of the whole image. First, we divide the 700×700 resolution synthesized heat map of the testing set and the corresponding real image into many 10×10 resolution fractions. For each RGB channel, we sum the value for each pixel in the fraction (Fig. 11). We then accumulate the absolute difference in each channel's sum of corresponding fractions between the real images and the synthesized images. We calculate the errors by dividing the first result by the number of pixels (Fig. 12). The error is the average difference of one pixel in each channel.

To establish the perception of the error value and show the improvement of accuracy in the prediction, the error values of two artificial cases are calculated as a reference (Fig. 13). In the first case, all the synthesized images are black, and in the second case, the synthesized images are rotated versions of the real heat map. The error values of these two cases are shown in Table 1.

Comparing the Accuracy of the Two Models

By using different information as inputs to predict the heat map and then analyzing the accuracy of results, we can reveal the core elements that influence specific behavior. The difference between the inputs of the two models is that the inputs for the second model contain information

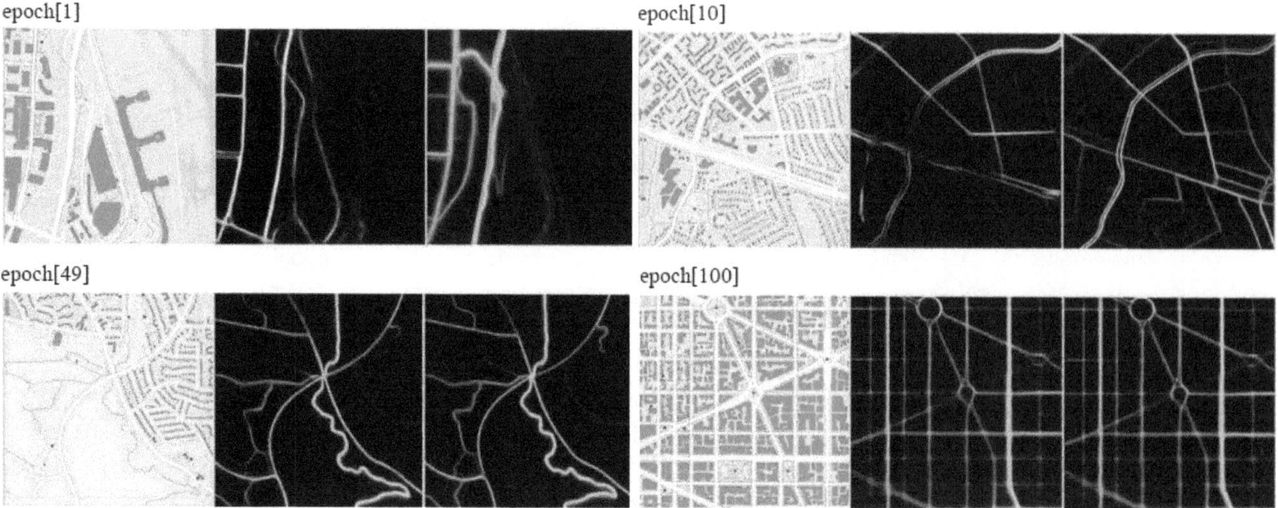

9 Training images and re-generated images in four training epochs. For each group of images, the left image is the urban plan, the middle is the generated heat map, and the right is the real heat map.

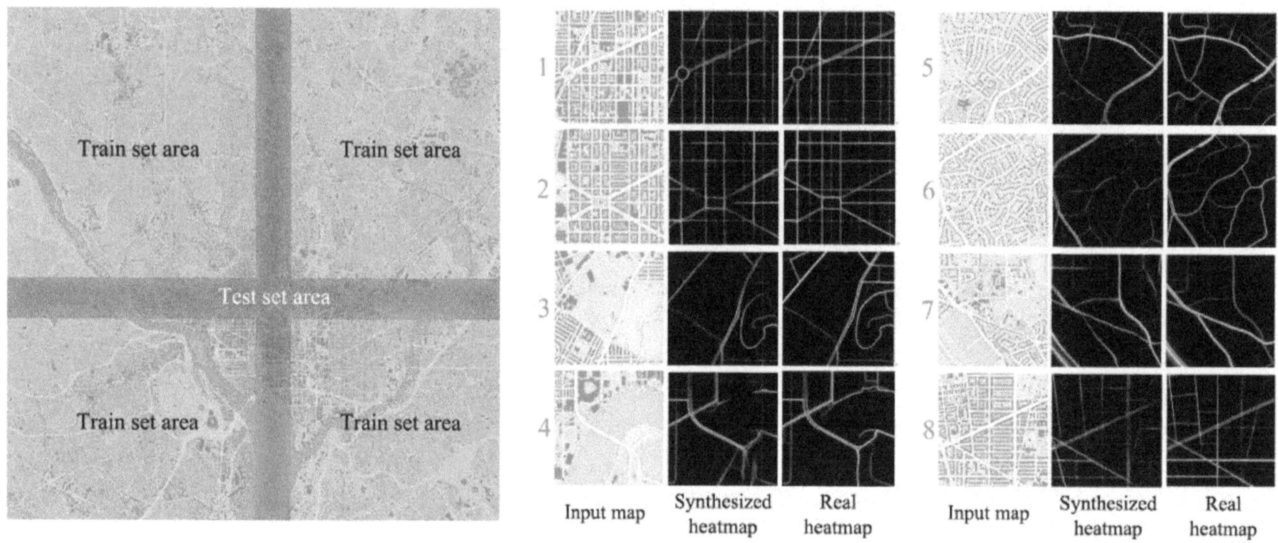

10 Left: the training set area and the testing set area; right: examples of predicted results.

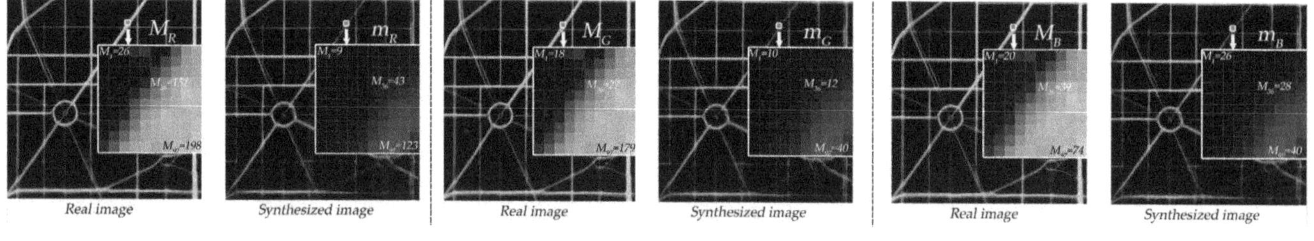

11 Illustration of error calculation formulation.

Error R=$\sum |sum(M_R) - sum(m_R)|/N$ M_R、$m_R \in Z^{10\times10}$ and where N is the number of pixels

Error G=$\sum |sum(M_G) - sum(m_G)|/N$ M_G、$m_G \in Z^{10\times10}$ and where N is the number of pixels

Error B=$\sum |sum(M_B) - sum(m_B)|/N$ M_B、$m_B \in Z^{10\times10}$ and where N is the number of pixels

12 Error calculation formulation for each channel.

on POI and road attributes. By analyzing the difference in the synthesized results of the two models, and the reasons behind them, the important factors affecting riding behavior can be identified. Moreover, by analyzing the characteristics of the areas where the prediction results of the two models are both poor, it is possible to make conjectures about factors related to riding that can be included in a subsequent prediction model.

The absolute difference between the average errors of models 1 and 2 (Table 2) is 0.8, which is nearly 6% of the absolute difference (30.5 – 16.7 = 13.8) between the average error of reference case 1 (Fig. 13 left) and model 1 (Fig. 14 left). Because the absolute difference between reference case 1 and model 1 can show a very significant improvement, it therefore can be concluded that the predictive ability of model 2 is better than model 1. However, it is possible to extract the characteristics that model 1 has learned during the GAN training process. It has learned the mapping between road width, road form, surrounding natural elements, and the vitality of the road. Comparing the two images with the largest differences in error value from the two models shows that model 2 better reflects the attributes of the cycling track. So that model has a strong overall ability to predict the cycling activity of the area, including the cycling track. This also shows that the vitality of cycling is highly related to the cycleway (Fig. 14). Moreover, analyzing the situations where the predictive ability of both models is poor shows that both models are worth improving in the complex city context, where intricate roads exist (Fig. 15). Some reasons for this might be the lack of integration of 3D environmental factors like landscape elements, inappropriate representation of urban functions by using only POI, and not including the impact of population distribution on vitality. In subsequent efforts, more experimental models and comparisons of results can be used to explore the factors that affect the vitality of cycling.

APPLICATIONS

Comparison of Cycling and Running Models

With trained machine learning models, urban designers can predict the vitality distribution of a given plot. In addition to the cycling heat map, a machine learning model for running heat maps is trained. By using these two motion models to predict the same plot and comparing the synthesized heat maps of different activities, the differences in the interaction between the two kinds of movement and the environment can be summarized (Fig. 16). For example, running behavior is more likely to follow green roads and streets with smaller scales than cycling. Cycling is less dependent on public grassland and greening than running, but it is more dependent on the pathways that connect the city. Besides, riding is more dependent on straight roads, and running paths are often curved landscape greenways. Using this method to compare the behavioral preferences

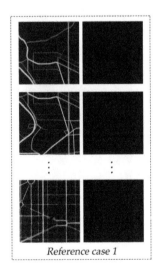

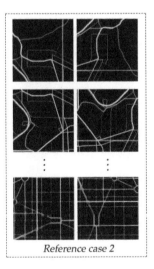

Reference case 1 | Reference case 2

13 Two reference cases.

Reference cases	Error R	Error G	Error B	Average Error
1	43.4	23.1	25.0	30.5
2	33.9	19.0	9.2	20.7

Table 1. Error value of two reference cases.

Model number	Error R	Error G	Error B	Average Error
1	28.5	14.9	6.8	16.7
2	27.1	13.9	6.7	15.9

Table 2. Error value of two models.

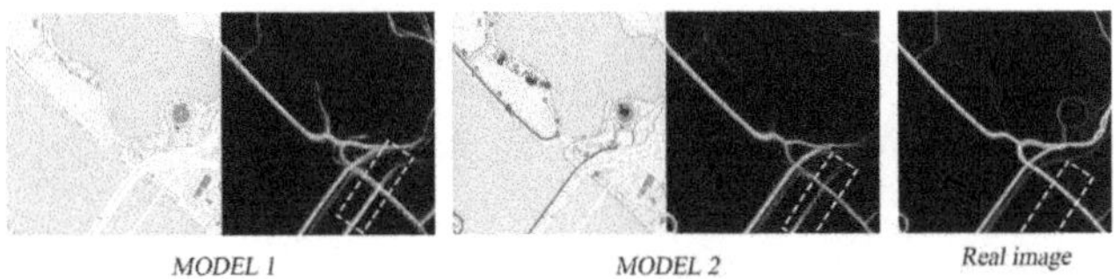

14 Comparing the two images with the largest differences in error value.

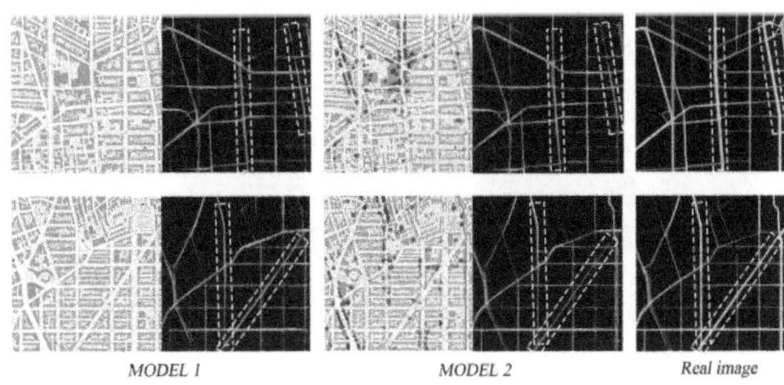

15 Analyzing cases where the predictive ability of both models are all poor.

of the two activities can avoid errors caused by a small number of samples, because the generated results are predicted results based on the learning of a wide range of samples.

Evaluate the Impact of the Modified Factors

Furthermore, by generating a heat map of the revised plan, designers can see the effect of the modified factors on the vitality distribution, thus obtaining real-time feedback and evaluation of the revised design. For example, by modifying the road width, the green area, and the floor area ratio, the predicted activity heat map before and after the changes can be compared, and thus the effect of the corresponding design strategy can be visually presented (Fig. 17). For example, after widening the road, the vitality value of the road has been significantly improved. Cycling activities are strongly related to the main roads of the city, which inspires us to pay attention to the construction of special

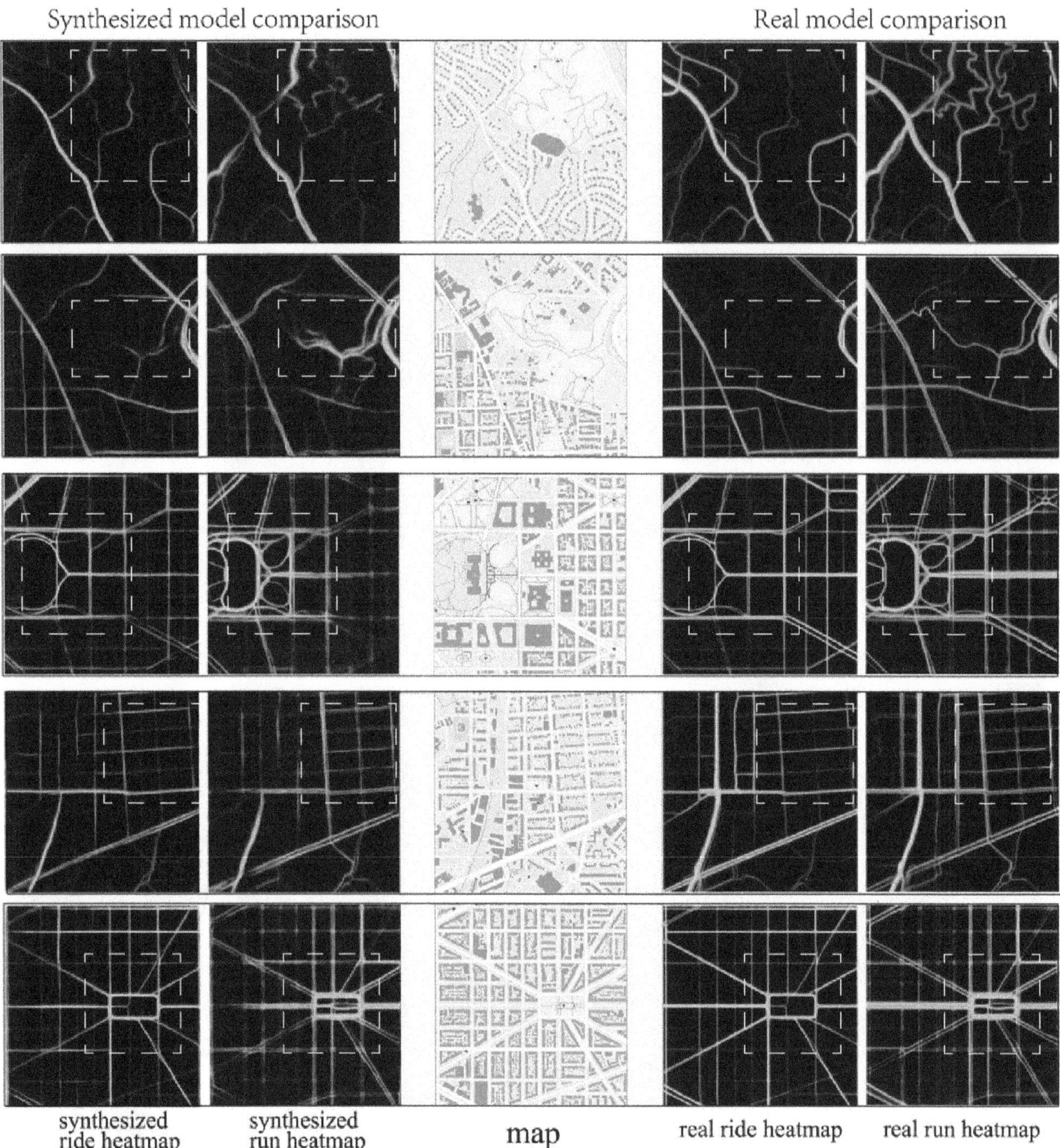

16 Comparison of cycling and running models. Left: synthesized image; middle: input image; right: real image.

cycling lanes on those roads. For another example, when the floor area ratio of the building is increased, riding vitality decreases. We can infer that people prefer to ride in areas with clear views. By iteratively updating the urban plan design according to the predicted heat map, the machine learning model can serve as a critic and supervisor, guiding the designers to find a better design with more active behavior vitality.

CONCLUSION

This method of using generative machine learning models with big data provides new capabilities for studying environmental behavior. Not only is it possible to derive the principles of interaction and the factors that determine behavior by analyzing different models, but it also can support urban designers in their efforts to improve their designs through real-time feedback of the evaluation results. Compared with previous methods, this approach solves the shortcomings of subjective evaluation and the difficulty of obtaining data. Taking the cycling and running heat maps as an example, this method shows the capability of predicting the behavioral vitality of an urban area, thus providing guidance for revising an urban design plan. By comparing the accuracy of two models with different input, it has been shown that it is possible to improve predictive ability by continuously optimizing the attributes of the information being used for input.

Subsequent research will seek to improve the accuracy and analytical results with more features. By enriching the features of the urban environment—for example, by adding information on the height and other attributes of buildings or the distribution of residents—the machine learning model can take a variety of scientific and social factors into account. This should yield a more accurate generative model with further guidance for design strategies. In addition to optimizing the input, we will continue to construct more advanced machine learning models that are more in line with the predictive characteristics. For example, modeling a place with graphs to predict its characteristics and using GCNs model to calculate vitality indices can help integrate elements such as environmental factors, street-view imagery, and socioeconomic data from POI. The last point is that because the GAN is not aware of destinations that are off the edge of each image segment, the GAN's ability to consider context that is not in a given image but may be in a neighboring image is limited. In order to address this problem, we need to develop a more advanced model.

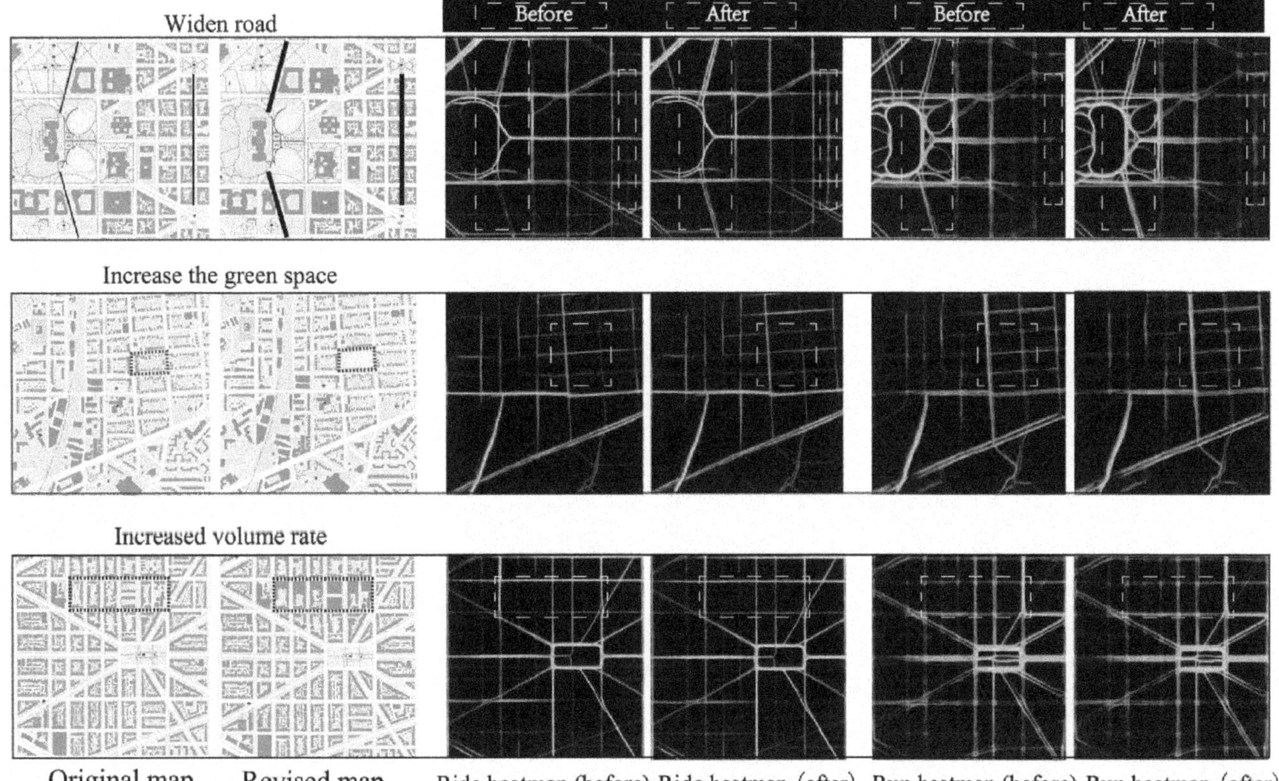

17 Using generative models to predict the influence of revised factors.

REFERENCES

Antonakos, C. L. 1993. "Environmental and Travel Preferences of Cyclists." PhD dissertation, University of Michigan.

ESRI. 2019. *ArcGIS*. V.10.8. Environmental Systems Research Institute. PC.

Faghih-Imani, A., N. Eluru, A. M. El-Geneidy, M. Rabbat, and U. Haq. 2014. "How Land-Use and Urban Form Impact Bicycle Flows: Evidence from the Bicycle-Sharing System (BIXI) in Montreal." *Journal of Transport Geography* 41 (August): 306–314. https://doi.org/10.1016/j.jtrangeo.2014.01.013.

Fraser, S.D.S., and K. Lock. 2011. "Cycling for Transport and Public Health: A Systematic Review of the Effect of the Environment on Cycling." *The European Journal of Public Health* 21 (6): 738–743.

Goodfellow, I., J. Pouget-Abadie, M. Mirza, B. Xu, D. Warde-Farley, S. Ozair, A. Courville, and Y. Bengio. 2014. "Generative Adversarial Nets." *Advances in Neural Information Processing Systems*: 2672–2680. Cambridge, MA: MIT Press.

Howard, C., and E. K. Burns. 2001. "Cycling to Work in Phoenix: Route Choice, Travel Behavior and Commuter Characteristics." *Transportation Research Record: Journal of the Transportation Research Board* 1773: 39–46.

Isola, P., J. Zhu, T. Zhou, and A. A. Efros. 2017. "Image-to-Image Translation with Conditional Adversarial Networks." arXiv preprint. https://arxiv.org/abs/1611.07004.

Liu, H. C., and J. J. Lin. 2019. "Associations of Built Environments with Spatiotemporal Patterns of Public Bicycle Use." *Journal of Transport Geography* 74 (1): 299–312. https://doi.org/10.1016/j.jtrangeo.2018.12.010.

Mao, H., Y. Hu, B. Kar, S. Gao, and G. McKenzie. 2017. "GeoAI 2017 Workshop Report: The 1st ACM Sigspatial International Workshop on GeoAI: AI and Deep Learning for Geographic Knowledge Discovery: Redondo Beach, CA, USA—November 7, 2016." *SIGSPATIAL Special* 9 (3): 25.

Naderi, J. R., and B. Raman. 2005. "Capturing Impressions of Pedestrian Landscapes Used for Healing Purposes with Decision Tree Learning." *Landscape and Urban Planning* 73 (2–3): 155–166. https://doi.org/10.1016/j.landurbplan.2004.11.012.

Steinfeld, Kyle. 2019. "GAN Loci: Imaging Place using Generative Adversarial Networks."In *ACADIA 19: Ubiquity and Autonomy [Proceedings of the 39th Annual Conference of the Association for Computer Aided Design in Architecture (ACADIA)]*, Austin, TX, 21–26 October 2019, edited by K. Bieg, D. Briscoe, and C. Odom, 392–403. CUMINCAD.

Strava Inc. 2021. *Strava*. V.209.0.0. Strava Inc. Android and iOS.

Wang, B., and I. Kim. 2018. "Short-term Prediction for Bike-Sharing Service Using Machine Learning." *Transportation Research Procedia* 34: 171–178. https://doi.org/10.1016/j.trpro.2018.11.029.

Zhang, Fan, Bolei Zhou, Liu Liu, Yu Liu, Helene H. Fung, Hui Lin,and CarloRatti. 2018. "Measuring Human Perceptions of a Large-Scale Urban Region Using Machine Learning." *Landscape and Urban Planning* 180 (September): 148–160.

Zhou, X. 2015. "Understanding Temporal Patterns of Biking Behavior By Analyzing Massive Bike Sharing Data in Chicago." *PLoS ONE* 10 (10): 1–20. https://doi.org/10.1371/journal.pone.0137922.

IMAGE CREDITS

Figure 8: "Training a conditional GAN to map edges to photo." From Isola et al. (2017).

All other drawings and images by the authors.

Yunjuan Sun holds a Master of Architecture degree from the Harbin Institute of Technology. Her research interests include geospatial modeling, applied artificial intelligence in 3D spatial analytics and crowd behavior, perception, and behaviors in urban environments through the application of innovative geographic information system (GIS) methods.

Lei Jiang holds a Master of Architecture degree from the University College London and a Bachelor of Architecture degree from the University of Portsmouth. Based on the study of artificial intelligence techniques and the environmental perception application at UCL, he focuses his research on machine learning, urban studies, and architectural design.

Hao Zheng is a PhD researcher at the University of Pennsylvania, Stuart Weitzman School of Design, specializing in machine learning, digital fabrication, mixed reality, and generative design. He holds a Master of Architecture degree from the University of California, Berkeley, and Bachelor of Architecture and Arts degrees from Shanghai Jiao Tong University.

Clustering and Morphological Analysis of Campus Context

Based on a Convolutional Autoencoder Model

Peiwen Li*
Department of Architecture, Southeast University, China

Wenbo Zhu*
Department IEOR, University of California, Berkeley

*Authors contributed equally to the research.

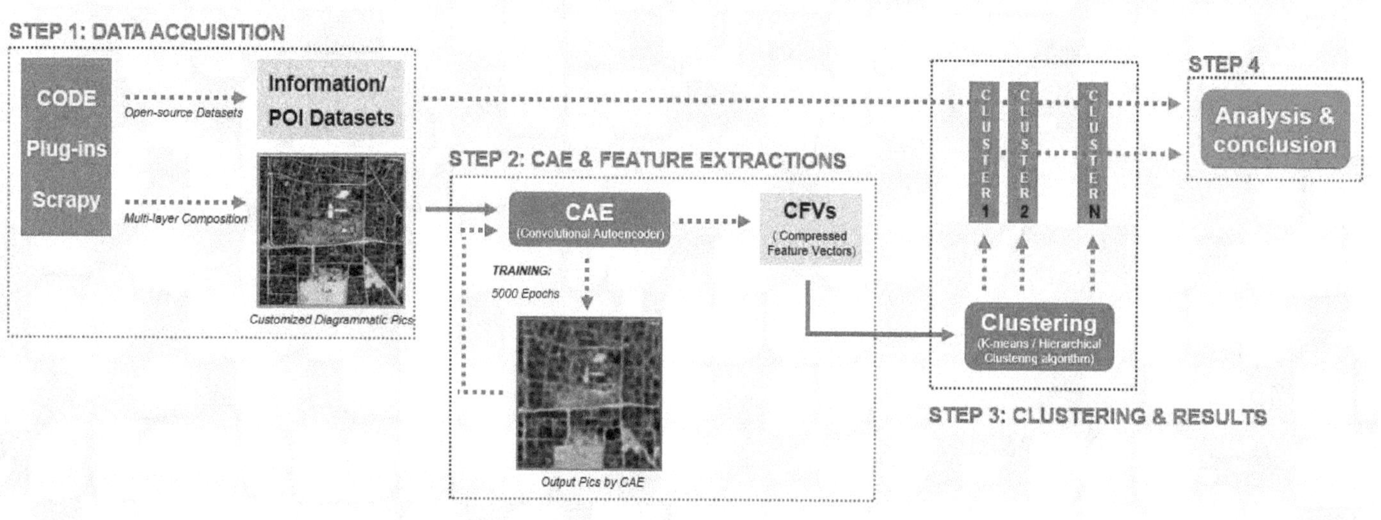

1 The framework and the strategy of this research.

ABSTRACT

"Figure-ground" is an indispensable and significant part of urban design and urban morphological research, especially for the study of the university, which exists as a unique product of the city development and also develops with the city.

In the past few decades, methods adapted by scholars of analyzing the figure-ground relationship of university campuses have gradually turned from qualitative to quantitative. And with the widespread application of AI technology in various disciplines, emerging research tools such as machine learning/deep learning have also been used in the study of urban morphology.

On this basis, this paper reports on a potential application of deep clustering and big-data methods for campus morphological analysis. It documents a new framework for compressing the customized diagrammatic images containing a campus and its surrounding city context into integrated feature vectors via a convolutional autoencoder model, and using the compressed feature vectors for clustering and quantitative analysis of campus morphology.

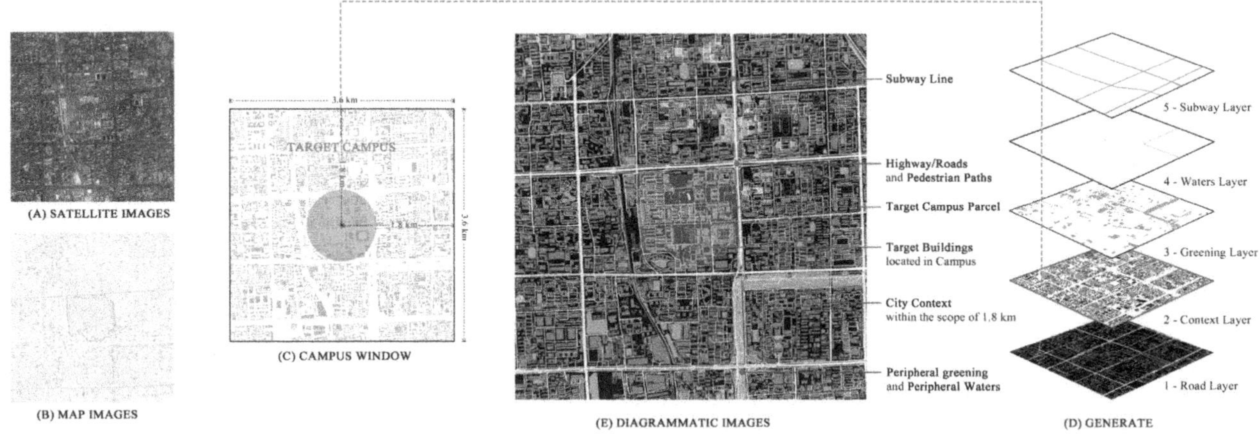

2 Satellite image, map, and one customized image for a single sample campus generated from five layers of tile maps.

INTRODUCTION

The relationship between "figure" and "ground" is critical to urban design, which results in the frequent application of figure-ground diagrams in the process of analyzing urban morphology. The university, as a unique product of the city's evolution, has gradually developed from the "university street" intertwined with the city in the early days to the "college quadrangle" composed of atriums, and finally evolved into the comprehensive "university campus" with various styles and forms.

Traditional classifications and analysis methods are difficult to apply to the increasingly complicated and diverse campus morphology. With the continuous usage of emerging technologies, scholars have begun to use computational methods such as simulation software, machine learning algorithms, and deep learning tools to quantitatively analyze the urban morphology and characteristics (which differ from qualitative research thinking in the traditional research theoretical framework), for instance, using spatial syntax to compute the connectivity value/depth value/integration degree of the external spatial morphology of Nanjing primary schools (Meng 2018); using machine learning algorithms to quantify and visualize the influence of different impact factors inside the figure-ground images (Xin et al. 2017); and using neural network models to perform feature extraction and morphological clustering of residential plans (Dong et al. 2018). These strategies of urban morphological research provide a new analysis pattern of campus studies.

On this basis, this paper proposes a new research framework based on deep learning and clustering on partial Chinese university campuses with their surrounding context: First the research constructed the database by using Scrapy (Zyte 2021) and other plug-ins to synthesize 500 customized diagrammatic images containing campus/context/traffic network/green areas/water information and other basic datasets, then the image data was input to the convolutional autoencoder (CAE) model to get the compressed feature vectors (CFVs), which are used to quantify the differences between morphological differences by using hierarchical clustering algorithms.

METHODS

Data Acquisition

Maps and satellite images are frequently used in urban morpho-typology studies, which contain city context information (buildings/infrastructure/public space along with its morphology/topology), traffic information (roads with different levels/overpasses/railways), site information (water/landscape features), and other information (traffic flow/stream of pedestrians/light and shadow). However, while integrating rich city scenes, both methods contain more noise than relevant information, especially for the large-scale range of urban context in campus studies. Confronted with such a dilemma, for reference, Rhee tried to use the small-scale customized diagrammatic images of Pittsburgh including height obtained in geographic information systems (GIS) as the input of machine learning (Rhee

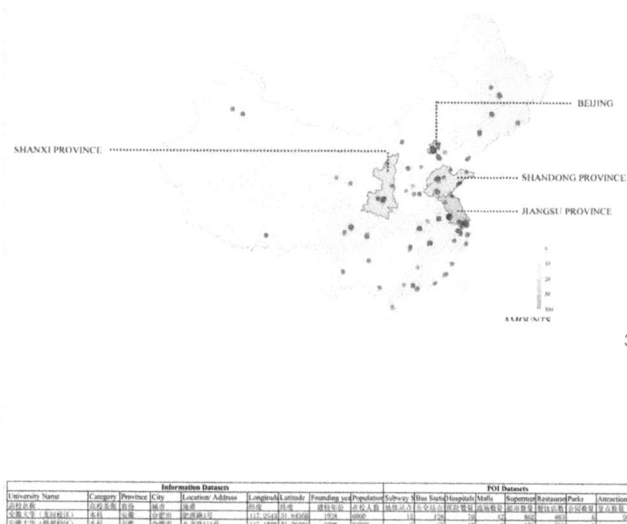

3

Information Datasets									POI Datasets							
University Name	Category	Province	City	Location/ Address	Longitude	Latitude	Founding year	Population	Subway S	Bus Statio	Hospitals	Malls	Supermar	Restauran	Parks	Attractions
高校名称	高校类别	省份	城市	地址	经度	纬度	建校年份	在校人数	地铁站点	公交站点	医院数量	商场数量	超市数量	餐饮店数	公园数量	景点数量
安徽大学（龙河校区）	本科	安徽	合肥市	[illegible]	[illegible]	[illegible]	1928	[illegible]	12	128	79	42	862	863	6	[illegible]
安徽大学（磬苑校区）	本科	安徽	合肥市	[illegible]	[illegible]	[illegible]	1928	[illegible]	3	67	10	8	[illegible]	[illegible]	2	18
安徽建筑大学（北校区）	本科	安徽	合肥市	[illegible]	[illegible]	[illegible]	1958	[illegible]	11	98	27	23	[illegible]	[illegible]	4	22
安徽建筑大学（南校区）	本科	安徽	合肥市	[illegible]	[illegible]	[illegible]	1958	[illegible]	1	55	7	8	[illegible]	[illegible]	0	9
北京大学	本科	北京	北京市	[illegible]	[illegible]	[illegible]	1898	29617	11	101	23	19	[illegible]	[illegible]	16	[illegible]
北京师范大学	本科	北京	北京市	[illegible]	[illegible]	[illegible]	1902	[illegible]	14	[illegible]	77	20	[illegible]	[illegible]	19	[illegible]
清华大学	本科	北京	北京市	[illegible]	[illegible]	[illegible]	1911	47762	9	[illegible]	[illegible]	17	[illegible]	[illegible]	11	341
北京科技职业学院	专科	北京	北京市	[illegible]	[illegible]	[illegible]	1997	/	0	[illegible]	11	2	[illegible]	[illegible]	4	14
北京体育职业学院	专科	北京	北京市	[illegible]	[illegible]	[illegible]	2008	/	13	142	67	31	[illegible]	[illegible]	13	61
集美大学	本科	福建	厦门市	[illegible]	[illegible]	[illegible]	1918	[illegible]	4	58	6	14	511	[illegible]	5	[illegible]
厦门大学	本科	福建	厦门市	[illegible]	[illegible]	[illegible]	1921	[illegible]	3	78	14	12	[illegible]	872	9	[illegible]
华南理工大学（大学城校区）	本科	广州	广州市	[illegible]	[illegible]	[illegible]	1952	[illegible]	4	93	8	6	173	878	11	72
华南理工大学（五山校区）	本科	广州	广州市	[illegible]	[illegible]	[illegible]	1952	55377	13	145	38	43	[illegible]	[illegible]	6	117
深圳大学（粤海校区）	本科	广州	深圳市	[illegible]	[illegible]	[illegible]	1983	[illegible]	19	199	10	61	[illegible]	[illegible]	22	[illegible]
贵州大学	本科	贵州	贵阳市	[illegible]	[illegible]	[illegible]	1902	[illegible]	4	158	12	12	251	[illegible]	6	34
海南大学	本科	海南	海口市	[illegible]	[illegible]	[illegible]	1958	[illegible]	0	128	27	21	[illegible]	[illegible]	7	[illegible]

4

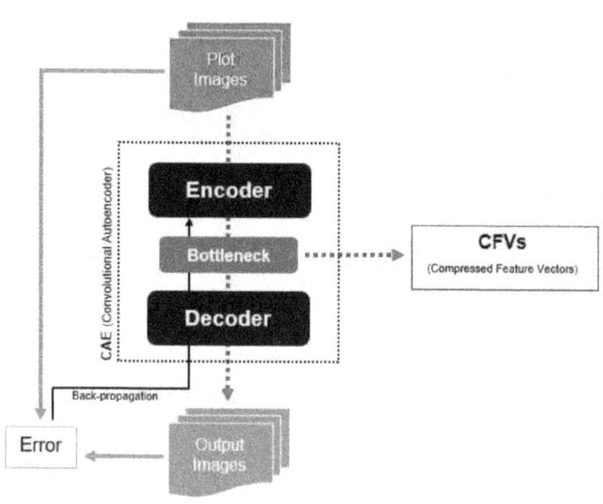

5

et al. 2019), which proved to increase the focus degree of feature extraction.

In the case of the university campus, which is the object of this research, using customized diagrammatic images can greatly reduce the interference of noise disturbance in the images while enabling the extraction of campus features from the large-scale urban features with which these campuses are often intertwined. Therefore, this paper adopted customized diagrammatic images retaining highly relevant and synthetic information such as the campus structures, campus boundary, urban context, traffic network, subway lines, green areas, and water features in the research area composed of clear color blocks, which is convenient for human understanding and machine learning and training (Fig. 2).

This paper selects 500 campuses of 286 representative universities in China as the research samples (distribution information is shown in Fig. 3). Five layers of tile maps were downloaded from the map platform through Scrapy and have been automatically synthesized into one image (the size of each sample image is 1024 x 1024 pixels). To get the proper range for the campus window, we set the campus in the center at the same scale and half of the window range to be 1.8 km. At the same time, basic information about each campus (latitude and longitude, year of establishment, number of students, population data, etc.), and different types of point of interest (POI) data around campus are obtained and summarized as the feature values for further research and analysis (Fig. 4).

Neural Network and CAE Model

Neural networks, an emerging structural model in the field of deep learning research in recent years, are widely used in various classification, prediction and clustering tasks. Particularly in the image field, traditional image classification methods, such as the scale-invariant feature transform (SIFT) algorithm, mainly focus on local features of the image, and find extreme points and their related descriptor information at the spatial scale. Deep learning methods, however, such as convolutional neural networks (CNNs), can learn image features of different dimensions by setting different receptive fields to simulate human vision, providing new methods for image classification and clustering tasks. The emergence of deep CNN frameworks, such as AlexNet, further enables neural network methods to better understand images and has achieved significant improvements in the classification task of the imageNet dataset.

Feature vectors are required when performing clustering or comparison tasks. When dealing with high-dimensional datasets containing noise, to some extent the autoencoder (AE), a nonlinear model, proves to be a good choice for learning features. However, faced with complicated images, which are obviously high-dimensional and retain much more noise, the CAE network will be a relatively suitable feature extractor for this type of dataset. Compared with the traditional AE, CAE adds several convolutional layers before the fully connected layer, which can better perform downsampling and upsampling for image data. At the same time, because of combining convolutional layers,

	Test Autoencoder model			Final Autoencoder model (using the architecture 2)
	Architecture 1	Architecture 2	Architecture 3	
The size of the input image	[1000, 1000, 3]	[1024, 1024, 3]	[2048, 2048, 3]	**[1024, 1024, 3]**
The number of kernels in each convolutional layer	16, 16, 8, 8	16, 16, 8, 8, 4	16, 16, 8, 8, 4	**16, 16, 8, 8, 4**
Kernel sizes	11*11, 9*9, 5*5, 3*3	11*11, 9*9, 7*7, 5*5, 3*3	3*3, 3*3, 2*2, 2*2, 2*2	**11*11, 9*9, 7*7, 5*5, 3*3**
The size of max pooling layers	2*2, 4*4, 5*5, 5*5	2*2, 2*2, 2*2, 2*2, 2*2	2*2, 2*2, 2*2, 2*2, 2*2	**2*2, 2*2, 2*2, 2*2, 2*2**
The size of output CFVs in bottlenec	[5, 5, 8]	[32, 32, 4]	[64, 64, 4]	**[32, 32, 4]**
The size of the output image	[1000, 1000, 3]	[1024, 1024, 3]	[2048, 2048, 3]	**[1024, 1024, 3]**
Training samples	226	226	226	**1000** (500 * 2 - by data augmentation)
Training epochs	1000	1000	1000	**5000**
Time consuming of each epoch	23s	30s	45s	**143s**
Training loss	0.5942	0.5084	0.5548	**0.4833**
Input image / Output image of the autoencoder				

6

3 Distribution heat map of selected 500 university campuses.

4 Partial university campus datasets obtained through Scrapy.

5 The structure of the convolutional autoencoder model to extract the features.

6 The architectures and output image of 3 CAE testing models and the final model.

CAE enables the model to extract feature of images from various dimensions and sizes better and more descriptively when compared with the 2D features obtained by AE.

The structure of the CAE consists of encoder layers, a bottleneck layer, and decoder layers. The core function of the encoder layers is extracting the features of input diagrammatic images through each convolutional layer and reducing the dimension of feature vectors through each max pooling layer, as the decoder layers perform an inverse operation to the encoder. By training, the model continuously optimizes the extracted features and minimizes the difference (error) between the plot images as input and the reconstructed images as output (Fig. 5).

Training Process

The customized diagrammatic images obtained in the previous step will be used as the input of the CAE, and the high-dimensional feature vector obtained in the middle layer of the CAE network will be taken as the output of the neural network for clustering and morphological quantification in the next step.

In the experiment, before the final training process, three different structures of CAE model with different parameter settings are employed for pre-training (Fig. 6). By comparing the losses and generated results of the three models, the Architecture-2 adopts a combination of decreasing pooling windows from a large range to a small range (kernel size to be 11 x 11, 9 x 9, 7 x 7, 5 x 5, 3 x 3), which performs better in image identification and feature extraction. Therefore, the Architecture-2 is selected as the final training framework with better performance in learning the global characteristics of the campus area, road networks, and context structures in the input image. At the same time, the customized diagrammatic images are subjected to the process of data augmentation to double the sample size (in order to preserve the north-south direction of the image, only a mirror operation is performed), and then input to the training model.

Figure 7 illustrates the workflow of CAE and visualizes the partial middle output of different network layers. Although the neural network is similar to a "black box," it is still observable that morphological features such as context density, water/green areas, and campus boundaries are continuously extracted as the network goes deeper, and finally compressed into the 4096 (32 x 32 x 4) dimensional feature vectors by the middle layer. And in the decoder, the compressed high-dimensional feature vector is reversely restored to a 1024 x 1024 size image as output. Part of the input sample images and the output images of the experiment are shown in Figure 8. The neural network nearly completely restores the morphological characteristics of the input image such as the campus boundary and surrounding site features. The next step of the experiment will use the output of the middle layer, the 4096-dimensional feature vectors, for further analysis.

CLUSTERING AND RESULTS

Clustering Process

Clustering is mainly taken through classification methods

or based on a certain predefined distance, by which similar objects are divided into different groups or classified into more subsets. The members belonging to the same clustered category are similar in the defined spatial distance, and they tend to have similar attributes. The task of image clustering often involves the feature extraction of a certain image and the definition of corresponding distance.

In order to quantitatively describe the morphological features of the samples, unsupervised machine learning is performed for a similarity analysis of the whole set in this study to cluster the 4096-dimensional compressed feature vectors (CFVs) from the middle layer of the neural network in the previous step. Specifically, this research uses machine learning algorithms, including K-means clustering and hierarchical clustering. Due to the small size of experimental samples at this stage of the experiment, the results taken by the K-means clustering algorithm and visualized through the t-Distributed Stochastic Neighbor Embedding (t-SNE) algorithm (van der Maaten 2008) after dimensionality reduction are not considerable because K-means clustering requires specification of the classification labels or the number of clusters beforehand and relies on manual adjustment of parameters with greater randomness (Fig. 9).

In contrast, the hierarchical clustering algorithm can avoid the corresponding disadvantages of a K-means algorithm, and can illustrate the entire clustering process more intuitively via a dendrogram (the result using a hierarchical clustering algorithm is shown in Fig. 10). It can be seen that the result is a hierarchical tree with multiple levels. By determining the location to cut the dendrogram into clusters (in this study, we chose the feature vectors within a distance of less than 40 to be regarded as a cluster), 9 clusters are observed, including 95 campus samples.

Analysis of clusters

As stated above, 9 clusters are observed that exhibit some degree of morphological similarity. In this section, we discuss the basic campus data obtained combined with POI data information in the database to analyze the clustering results of different types of customized diagrammatic images.

Among these, cluster 1 recognizes the curvilinear characteristics of the campus boundaries, and the road networks surrounding the campus also tend to be irregular. Using OpenCV (OpenCV 2021) to identify the proportion of the red area (the campus boundary) in each picture, we calculate the average campus area ratio of each image in one cluster to be 22.5, ranking second among the 9 clusters. This cluster can be summarized as a "large-area irregular

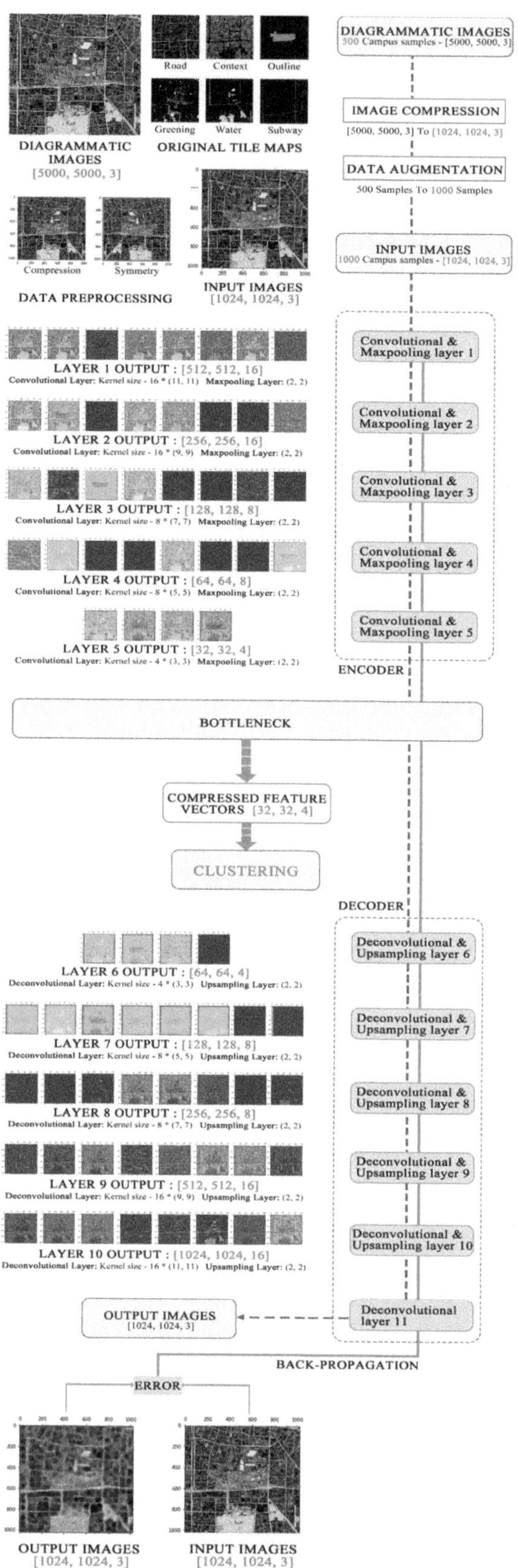

7 Workflow and visualization of middle-output from each layer of the final CAE model.

7

campus". At the same time, this type of campus is mostly located on the northwest side of the main road, while the southeast side of the main road features mostly areas of water or blocks with insufficient development.

When it comes to clusters 2 and 3, the context density of the surrounding city is relatively low, and most of these campuses appear to be located in suburban areas. By comparing the average value of POIs of these two clusters with other clusters, they both share the minimal functional facilities surrounding, and the average establishment year of these campuses tends to be relatively recent. Moreover, the average POI quantity in cluster 3 is greater than that of cluster 2, and the campuses in cluster 2 appear to have been established within the past 20 years. These two types of clusters can be summarized as "low-density suburban campus". Cluster 4 has the same characteristics as the previous type; in addition to having the highest percentage of average campus area ratio/average number of students in campus, it also shows a high degree of regularity and completeness. This category can be summarized as "giant-new regular campus".

Clusters 5, 6, and 7 share obvious landscape characteristics: large areas of water and green space. These types of campuses also have the most scenic spots/parks POI, which can be summarized as a "campus around landscape," but each cluster still has some slight differences. For example, the average green area ratio in cluster 7 is much higher than that in clusters 5 and 6, indicating that cluster 7 is led by the morphology of green areas; while in cluster 5, the proportion of each campus in the area is relatively similar, with the average campus area ratio to be 15.8; and the campuses in cluster 6 share a continuous landscape belt (green space/water area) that divides the images in half, with the campus tending to be located adjacent to the landscape belt.

Clusters 8 and 9 are both campuses in high-density urban areas, so their average establishment year is the earliest, and the average number of surrounding POIs is also ranked in the top two; cluster 8 identifies the characteristics of multiple campuses and can be defined as an "urban multi-campus campus"; the campus area of cluster 9 is generally smaller and more regular and can be defined as an "urban integral campus."

CONCLUSION

This paper introduces a new quantitative framework in the field of urban morphology into the research of university campus morphology by constructing a database containing highly relevant information on customized diagrammatic

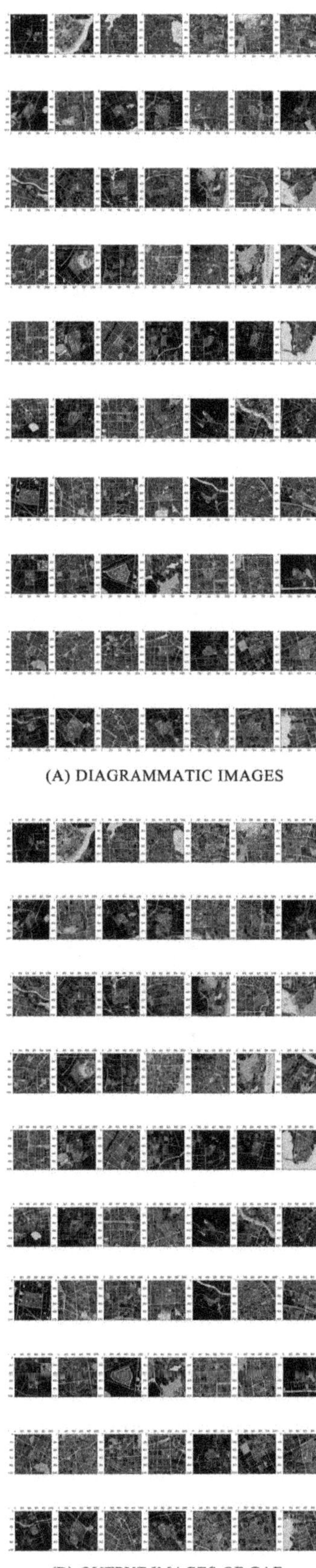

8 A selection of input sample images and output images from the experiment.

images of each campus and including other identifying auxiliary data. Employing a CAE model framework to extract compressed feature vectors facilitates the classification of different clusters (via a hierarchical clustering algorithm), thus enabling quantitative exploration of underlying morphological differences between campuses. Through comparison and analysis, each cluster is shown to share certain similarities and differences in morphology, such as surrounding urban context features, landscape features, traffic features, and campus boundary features. Additionally, some clusters appear to show that a campus is often located on the north side of a main road; this inertial campus planning is also worthy of further discussion. At this time, it remains difficult to reflect on the internal characteristics or structures of each individual campus in the clustering results. This may be related to sample size and customized styles used within the investigation. Based on this, further research will expand the data sample size, increase the color contrast in the customized images, and add the generation experiment to further explore the different types of campus morphology in the understanding of the machine. This research framework is also applicable to research on the morphology of other architectural typologies such as hospitals, residential areas, public spaces, etc.

REFERENCES

Dong, J., L. Li and D. Han. 2019. "New Quantitative Approach for the Morphological Similarity Analysis of Urban Fabrics Based on a Convolutional Autoencoder." *IEEE Access* 7: 138162–74.

Li, X., S. Cheng, K. Li, and C. Chen. 2017, "Data Analysis of Urban Fabric—A Case Study of Hankou Yanjiang Area." *Architectural Journal* (S1): 7–13.

Meng, Zhang. 2018. "Research on Outer Space Morphology of Primary and Secondary Schools Based on Space Syntax." Master's thesis, Southeast University.

OpenCV. 2021. *OpenCV*. V.4.5.2. https://github.com/opencv/opencv/tree/4.5.2.

Rhee, Jinmo. 2019. "Context-rich Urban Analysis Using Machine Learning—A Case Study in Pittsburgh, PA." In *Architecture in the Age of the 4th Industrial Revolution—Proceedings of the 37th eCAADe and 23rd SIGraDi Conference*, edited by J.P. Sousa, J. P. Xavier, and G. Castro Henriques, 343–52. Portugal. CUMINCAD.

van der Maaten, L. J. P. and G.E. Hinton. 2008. "Visualizing High-Dimensional Data Using t-SNE." *Journal of Machine Learning Research* 9 (Nov): 2579-2605.

Zyte. 2021. *Scrapy*. V.2.5.0. https://scrapy.org.

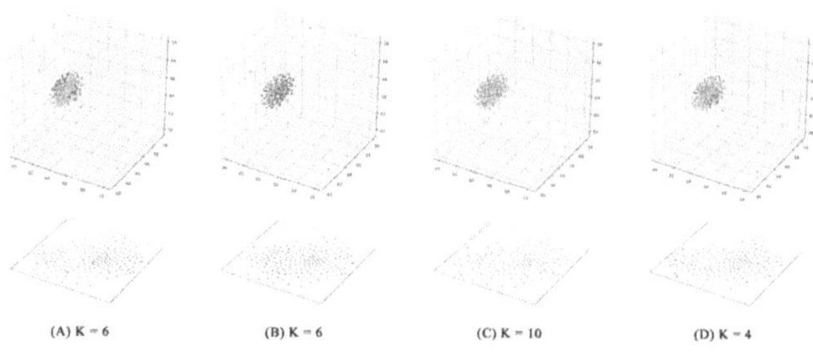

9

9 Different results produced by different settings of the k value in the K-means clustering algorithm.

10 Dendrogram and partial results produced by the hierarchical clustering algorithm.

IMAGE CREDITS

All drawings and images by the authors.

Peiwen Li Graduate student, Southeast University, Nanjing, China. 2014–2018 Bachelor of Engineering, Information Engineering, Southeast University.
2018–2021, Architecture Design and Theory Major, School of Architecture, Southeast University, Master of Engineering.

Wenbo Zhu Machine learning engineer, ByteDance, China. 2014–2018 Bachelor of Administration (Industrial Engineering) and Bachelor of Science (Mathematics), Beihang University. 2018–2019 Master of Engineering, Industrial Engineering and Operations Research, University of California, Berkeley.

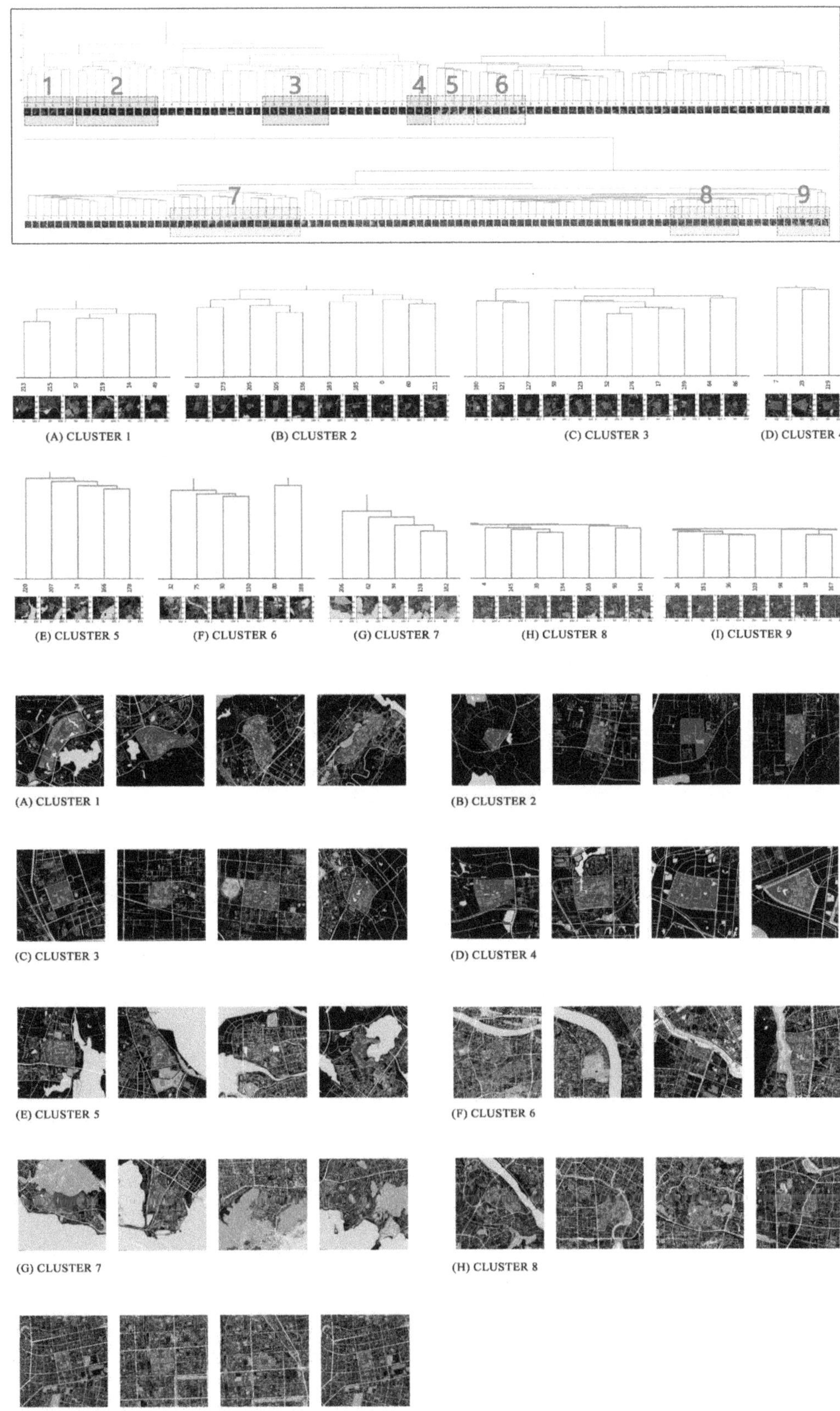
1
2
3
4
5
6
7
8
9
(A) CLUSTER 1
(B) CLUSTER 2
(C) CLUSTER 3
(D) CLUSTER 4
(E) CLUSTER 5
(F) CLUSTER 6
(G) CLUSTER 7
(H) CLUSTER 8
(I) CLUSTER 9
(A) CLUSTER 1
(B) CLUSTER 2
(C) CLUSTER 3
(D) CLUSTER 4
(E) CLUSTER 5
(F) CLUSTER 6
(G) CLUSTER 7
(H) CLUSTER 8
(I) CLUSTER 9

10

Machine Learning for Comparative Urban Planning at Scale: An Aviation Case Study

Ahmed Meeran
Singapore University of Technology and Design

Sam Conrad Joyce
Meta Design Lab,
Singapore University of Technology and Design

1

1 San Fransisco Airport before and after U-Net segmentation showing class labels.

ABSTRACT

Aviation is in flux, experiencing 5.4% yearly growth over the last two decades. However, with COVID-19 aviation was hard hit. This, along with its contribution to global warming, has led to louder calls to limit its use. This situation emphasizes how urban planners and technologists could contribute to understanding and responding to this change.

This paper explores a novel workflow of performing image-based machine learning (ML) on satellite images of over 1,000 world airports that were algorithmically collated using European Space Agency Sentinel2 API. From these, the top 350 United States airports were analyzed with land use parameters extracted around the airport using computer vision, which were mapped against their passenger footfall numbers.

The results demonstrate a scalable approach to identify how easy and beneficial it would be for certain airports to expand or contract and how this would impact the surrounding urban environment in terms of pollution and congestion. The generic nature of this work-flow makes it possible to potentially extend this method to any large infrastructure and compare and analyze specific features across a large number of images while being able to understand the same feature through time. This is critical in answering key typology-based urban design challenges at a higher level and without needing to perform on-ground studies, which could be expensive and time-consuming.

INTRODUCTION

Aviation has been one of the most consistently growing industries over the last two decades, representing a 15-year doubling period of passenger numbers (ICAO 2018) resulting in many airports being built. However, in 2020, aviation was one of the worst-hit industries by the global pandemic (IATA 2020). Even before that, there were increasing calls to limit its use due to its contribution to global warming, urban congestion, and noise pollution. This calls for a potential urban reform targeting the larger pieces of infrastructure constituting the urban ecosystem.

Airport planning and infrastructure construction should be a critical element of this rethink: the construction of airports uses large amounts of land, often near cities, and can be disruptive, expensive, and time-consuming. When in operation, airports result in exposure to noise and environmental degradation. But at the same time, the connections can enrich cities, society, culture, and economies. The lack of readily available data for airport planning and design can be a problem for governments and decision makers, especially when comparing airports in different countries.

Geographic information system (GIS) and satellite imagery have been some of the key tools aiding planners and designers in their workflows. Satellite images are not just pleasing to look at; they also hold large amounts of structured data that are often overlooked (Demir et al. 2018). From explaining variation in geographies to visualizing change of seasons and understanding the changing urban density, satellite images contain useful data for urban designers and architects. Currently, the lack of a consistent and scalable method to extract useful data from raw satellite images is at the point where complex analysis is being performed manually or, in some cases, compromised altogether. This is where the potential of artificial intelligence (AI) and machine learning (ML) could be leveraged to build a system that can help understand changing land-use patterns in real time and, in turn, be able to make higher-level planning decisions at the early stages of design conceptualization.

BACKGROUND

Data-driven urban planning has been important and successful in recent sustainable planning and policy decision-making practices (Sadik-Khan 2017). With recent developments demonstrating sophisticated learning of large-scale urban data using convolutional neural networks (CNNs) and deep neural networks (DNNs), global organizations are now turning towards the practical implementation of using AI for the betterment of humanity for causes like peacekeeping and disaster mapping (Microsoft Corporation 2020; United Nations 2019). DeepSat (Basu et al. 2015) aims to address the issue of classifying high-dimensional satellite imagery data to detect and segment common land-use categories like the presence of water, forest, agricultural, and dense urban land using a deep belief network (DBN). A technique composed of supervised ML over a sequence of unsupervised learning was used to detect large-scale damage in postdisaster contexts using a United Nations Institute for Training and Research (UNITAR) dataset (Gueguen and Hamid 2015). With rapid urbanization, especially in developing economies, geospatial analytics leading to accurate information on current land-use practices will be a useful tool for urban planners and policymakers (Malarvizhi, Vasantha Kumar, and Porchelvan 2015).

This work attempts to build on the existing approach for generating meaningful planning insights from raw satellite imagery using AI and machine vision. Although existing work in this domain relies primarily on satellite imagery from specifically curated datasets from Google Maps API (Basu et al. 2015), UNITAR (Gueguen and Hamid 2015), and Urban Atlas (Albert, Kaur, and Gonzalez 2017), we aim to develop an AI-supported approach to collect, model, process, and synthesize meaningful planning data, leveraging trained image recognition on publicly available satellite image sources. This will enable designers and stakeholders to look at the variables from a higher level of abstraction, and in this case to better understand the impact of aviation on urban land use—specifically by leveraging an approach that analyzes many of the same typologies so that holistic policy decisions, as well as specific but relativistic entity decisions, might be supported.

METHODOLOGY

Image Collection

We used open-access satellite imagery data sourced from the Sentinel2 satellite, which was launched by the European Space Agency's (ESA) Copernicus mission in 2015 for earth observation. This satellite and ones like it might change the way we work with earth observation, since accessibility is very problematic when it comes to satellite data, which are often gatekept for national security reasons. Also, since the revisit time is just five days, it is possible to closely monitor the natural earth phenomenon, adding great value to areas such as geology and meteorology.

The images are rendered in three resolutions (60 m, 20 m, 10 m), with 10 m representing the side length of 1 pixel (100 m2 ground area). A tile in sentinel terminology is a single capture, which is usually 100 km^2 of a region. Sentinel2 is on a sun-synchronous orbit, moving pole to pole and capturing the whole of the earth's surface under similar daylighting.

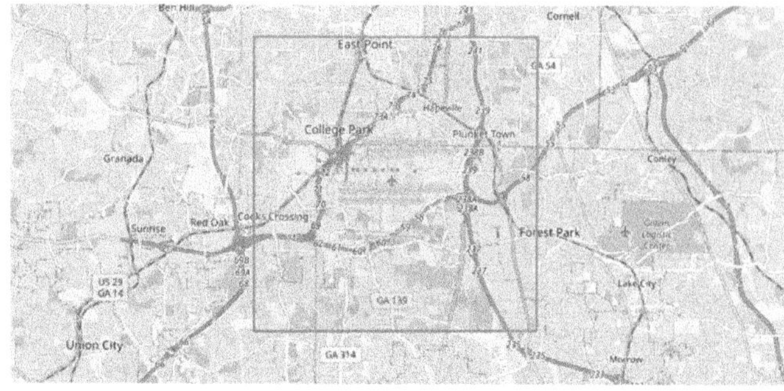

2 Spatial boundary showing the 10 km² area of interest over Atlanta International Airport (ATL), Georgia, USA.

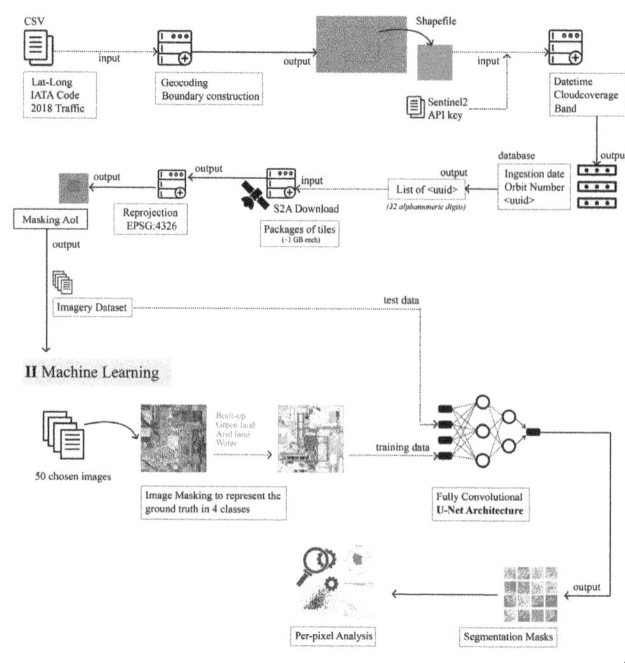

3

The satellite also captures other bands, such as vegetation index, near infrared, ultra-blue aerosol, and shortwave infrared, although these bands are available only in lower resolutions (20 m and 60 m). Another key aspect of this mission is that the images can be accessed not just through their web interface (European Space Agency 2014) but also be extracted from the Sentinel2's Python API, which gives high control in defining the parameters for returned images.

The API also supports other keyword arguments such as:

Datetime – A range of dates can be passed as a string to query the database for available sentinel tiles. A short correction was made to get the best possible image during spring–summer due to season inversion across hemispheres.

Cloudcoverpercentage – A number indicating the preferred cloud coverage for the tile.

Limit – The number of tiles in a single search.

Contains – Ensures a strict intersection of the shapefile with the tile (100% inclusion).

The focus here is on extracting the world's top 1,000 airports (based on passenger footfall in 2018) and explore key typology-based questions, specifically: airport expandability, land encroachment, and interaction between urban zones and airport activity. The approach is a scalable methodology that can be applied to many airport sites to explore, through comparative data, the current impact of airports on existing land usage, if airports could expand or contract, and how beneficial or challenging it would be to do so. The approach and ML training is generally for large-scale land-use analysis but here applied to understand the relationship between airports and cities. For the sake of demonstration, we chose to analyze the top airports in the United States, mainly because American airports are leaning towards the saturation phase in terms of passenger footfall numbers, and it would be the right time for the authorities to take action to answer the

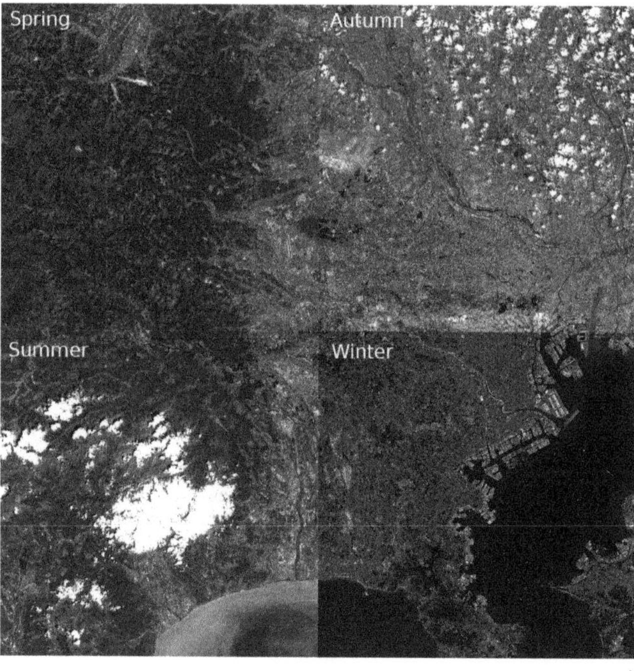

4

3 The general automated process workflow to collect, compile, and analyze aerial imagery from ESA Sentinel2 satellite.

4 Sentinel image of Tokyo, Japan, visualized across all four seasons.

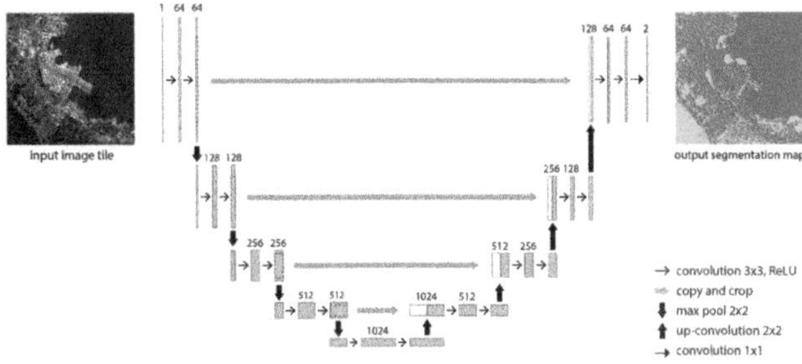

5

5 Schematic visual of the U-Net Architecture.

million-dollar question, Is it viable for airports to expand or contract?

One of the primary motives of this study is to understand the US airports as data points and take general macro-level planning to rethink whether they should contract or be removed based on a few key parameters like land use, size of the airport, and passenger traffic.

To collect aerial imagery, we need the geo-coordinates such as latitude and longitude of the desired location. We sourced this data from Aviation Fanatic (Tóth 2011) and compiled it into a CSV file. This was then combined with the IATA's open-access dataset of world airports, which we used to validate the authenticity of Aviation Fanatic. A spatial boundary around the airport was constructed (Fig. 2) using Python's Pygc (Python Software Foundation 2017), a spatial projection library. A square boundary of side 10 km was chosen, keeping the terminal building at the center, and the shapefile produced was parsed to Sentinelsat, the Python API, to query for matches of the spatial boundary in the satellite's database.

The API returned a list of "Products" (a 100 km² tile), each of which has a string-based identifier and contains other metadata, including its date of capture and orbit number. The list of Products was then sorted to get the least clouded tile and the best one downloaded using its unique identifiers and the corresponding 10 m true color tiles were extracted computationally from the file structure. This was performed in series and in batches to preserve the repeatability of the process, since the volume of data involved was in the order of hundreds of gigabytes. This also works as a failsafe mechanism: in event of a program crash, it can then be tracked to its nearest batch number, thus saving time. The tiles were then converted to world projection EPSG:4326 using the library GDAL (Frank et al. 1998). This was a critical step, as Sentinel collects imagery across the globe, and each country uses a different EPSG code that best represents its aerial map. For scalability reasons, all the satellite images collected were transformed to the web Mercator standard for visualization later.

The Pygc spatial boundary constructed earlier was used to clip out the area of interest from the projected larger tile, which is the 10 × 10 km square around the terminal and runways. These were then stored to file as RGB images, and their metadata (date, time, cloud cover, and satellite order) retained for further analysis.

Image Recognition

The next step was to devise a methodology to understand the land-use features in the airport images. For this we devised four unique classes of land use (agricultural land, arid land, built-up land, and water), which our ML model was trained to predict across our entire dataset.

We used the U-Net Architecture (Ronneberger, Fischer, and Brox 2015) for feature extraction from our images for several reasons. First, it is fully convolutional and symmetric in nature, which ensures the resolution of both the images and the features are preserved. Second, U-Net is known for its high convergence rate with low sizes of training database, reducing human labeling time. Traditionally, in ML practices dataset sizes are in the order of 104, but in our case, it is much lower and U-Net was able to work with lower numbers of data. Third, its supervised nature of learning enabled us to manually provide area labels in the training dataset that we want the model to predict over the full set. U-Net has already been used effectively in geology (Karchevskiy, Ashrapov, and Kozinkin 2018) and diagnostic radiology (Dong et al. 2017).

Initially, 25 airport images were human selected to approximate the entire dataset in terms of diversity in the level of urbanization, cloudiness, proximity to the sea, and other natural features. These images were then manually segmented using the four classes as a key, using Photoshop for the ground truth labels. The black pixels on the leftmost of Figure 6 were features that did not fall into the four basic classes. However, for future versions of this work we recommend fine-tuning the manual labeling process for better accuracy of prediction.

The images were stored, along with their original RGB variants, which together were fed into the U-Net. Initially, we found that the U-Net was not able to predict images that had higher cloud coverage, sometimes classifying clouds as desert (arid). Hence a second round of sampling was carried out with 25 more images (50 in total) to include some wider cases such as cloud-ridden and semi-arid. The masks were converted into a one-hot encoding to preserve the land-use classes for a more accurate prediction. The model was then trained on an Nvidia GTX 1060 GPU and converged in four hours with an accuracy of about 70% at 300 epochs. U-Net provided reasonably accurate predictions with just

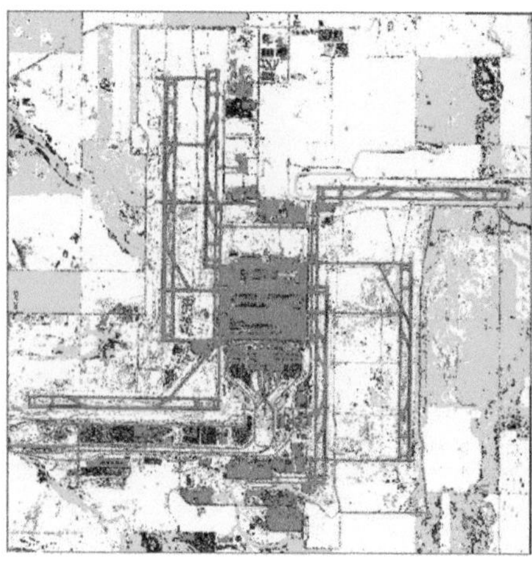

6 From left: Ground truth mask showing multiple urban land use; the RGB Sentinel2 image of O'Hare Airport (ORD) Chicago used for identification; and land use predictions from trained U-Net.

50 sample training points, which further strengthened our confidence in using this architecture.

The prediction masks were then stored to file using a similar naming convention as that of the RGB airport images. At this point, it is interesting to note the versatility of this method in being able to be scaled up as well as manipulated due to its open-source nature. The flexibility of this workflow could easily allow us to perform longitudinal analyses on a single image over time to monitor phenomenon such as land-use change, area lost to forest fire, and land reclamation or construction progress monitoring. At the same time, cross-sectional or comparative analyses can be performed across the entire dataset based on one or more parameters to generate meaningful insights pertaining to urban planning and design.

ANALYSIS

Once the predictions from the U-Net model of the four land-use classes were extracted, we then proceeded with per-pixel analytics based on the ground truth parameters to extract analytical metrics from the images. A visual representation (Fig. 8) shows the geographic context as well as the number of airports per state. This helped us understand which states are vulnerable in terms of the impact their airports cause to the surrounding urban fabric in the form of passenger traffic congestion and pollution.

To understand the level of urbanization around airports, it is crucial to first understand the land-use distribution derived from the U-Net. A pie chart showing the land-use composition was plotted at the respective airport locations (Fig. 10) in a map showing the share of each land-use metric against the total available land area. The data shows airports located towards the coastal region had a fair share of water being represented in the plot, whereas the composition of arid (yellow) land began to rise in the dry Midwestern region. This in turn proved that the model provided reasonably accurate results, especially the level of detail, considering the size of the dataset involved in training our model and the resolution of the images supplied.

For this relatively simplistic study, we defined two key variables which will enable us to compare the ground reality with the results predicted by the ML system. The ground reality is given by the passenger footfall numbers (2018 data), and the urbanization ratio is given by taking the total of the red pixels from the image predictions, which correspond to the built-up pixels from the true-color RGB images. Both variables were normalized by dividing each data point against the maximum value found across the entire dataset.

The two variables were then plotted against each other (Fig. 11) to understand if there is a correlation between passenger footfall and urbanization in general, but primarily to explore which airports are near saturation in terms of urbanization or passenger traffic, or both.

RESULTS AND DISCUSSION

One of the main motives of this research was to find out if airports have been impacting the surrounding urban fabric and how can it be quantified to an extent where higher-level urban planning decisions can be taken based on analytics. Based on the scatter plot (Fig. 11), the initial and more general trend identified was that more congested airports tend to cause a greater negative impact on the surrounding urban context. This was further confirmed by the leading diagonal of the scatter plot. There were also cases of airports that are less crowded but comparatively more urbanized, as well as airports that are semi-urban/arid but highly crowded. To account for these cases, we devised an action strategy with four unique categories based on their

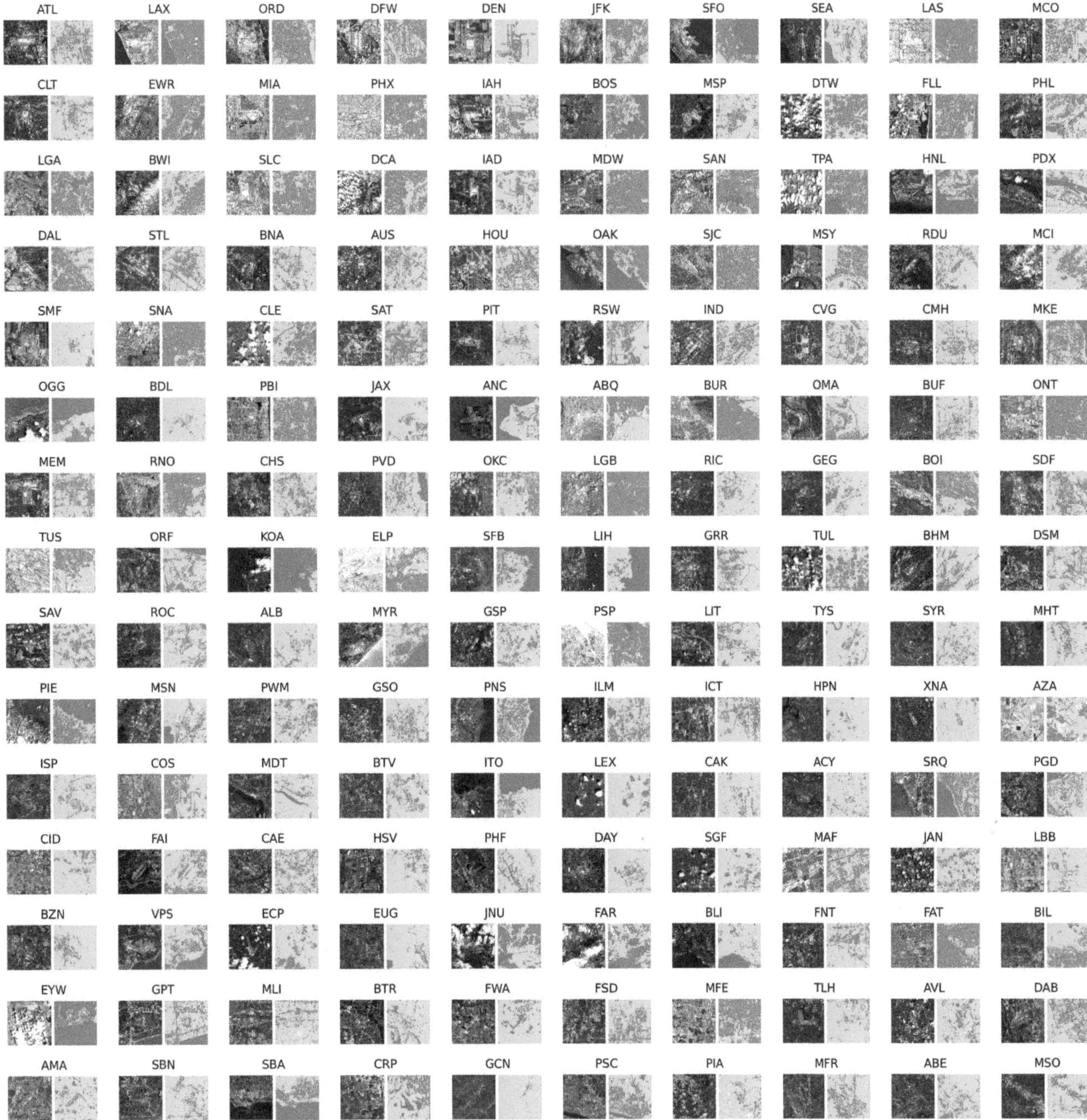

7 RGB images visualized along with their U-Net multiclass predictions of 150 of the top 350 airports in the United States. 7

current congestion-to-urbanization ratio. These categories were:

Safe to Expand – Congested but semi-urban airports.

Remove – Less congested but highly urbanized airports.

Monitor – Both more congested and more urbanized airports, requiring attention in the future.

Leave – Low impact airports that do not require any intervention now.

These categories were determined using the scatter plot (Fig. 12) as an index, by assigning cut-off values for each axis. Although this is a basic measure using only two factors, and in both cases the cut-off value is chosen arbitrarily, they could be reinforced through the addition of more variables, consumer travel patterns, and domestic-international share of flights to be able to offer a more precise output. The variables could also be linked to observe which airports are borderline over/under acceptable limits as defined by the government or local population. However, we reserve this for a future version of this work.

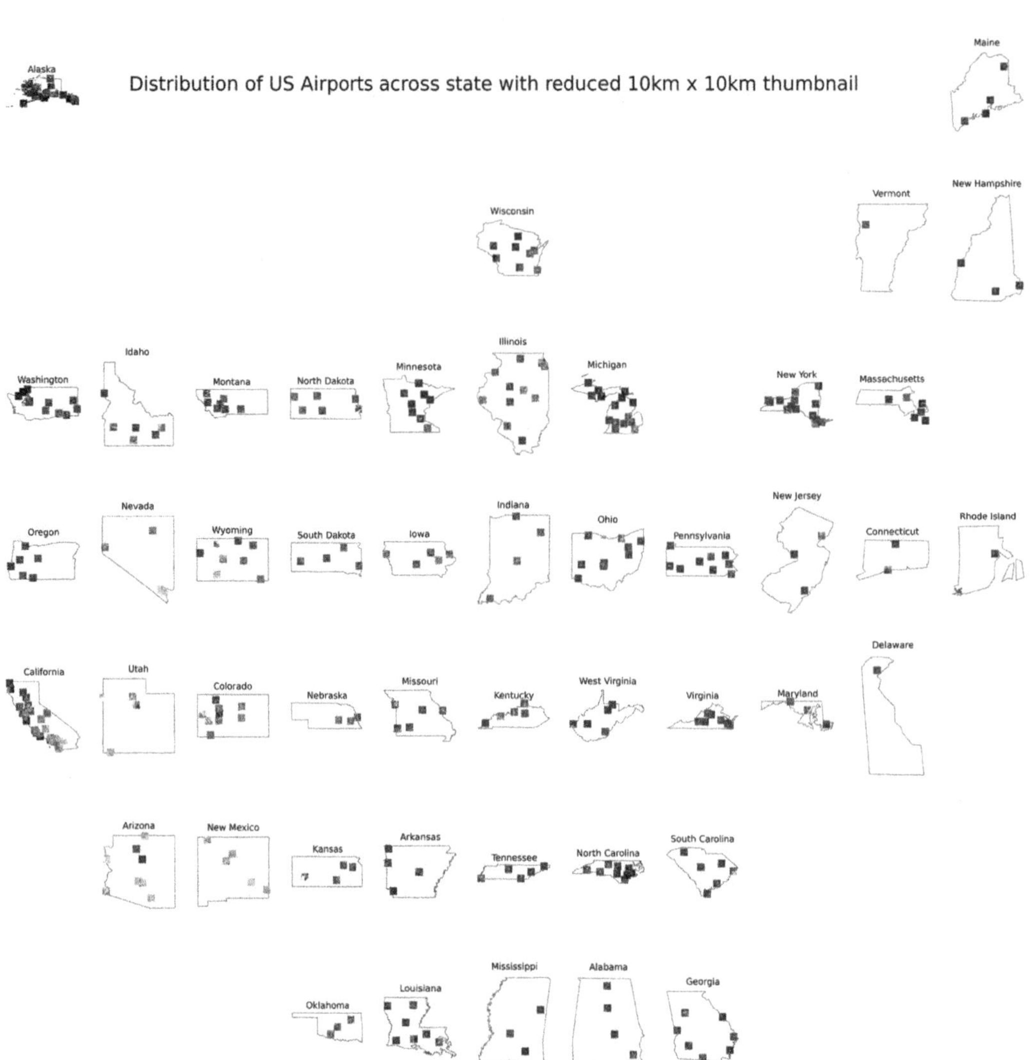

8

The results obtained from the scatter plot are interesting in of themselves, although the findings are more indicative and not to be applied from this study alone. As expected, we found at least 10 airports that had been causing serious impact to their surroundings, as highlighted in red. The majority of the airports fell under the "Monitor" category, which could be justified considering the general rising trend of increasing air passenger traffic numbers in the US combined with the optimism revolving around building and expanding cities. These airports need to be closely monitored, and we feel that governments and planning authorities should consider this band of airports more seriously and plan for them with greater emphasis on their sustainability. It is suggested that the green band should be treated carefully to avoid misinterpretation. Though they might be safe to expand, their feasibility and sustainability

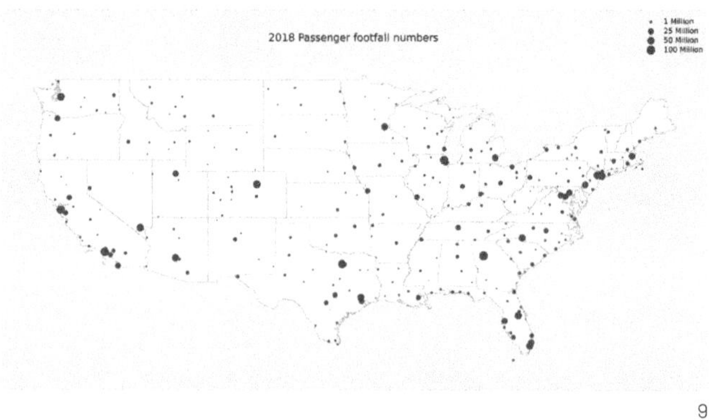

9

8 Distribution density of US airports by state, visualized at their approximate respective locations.

9 Airport passenger traffic in the US in 2018.

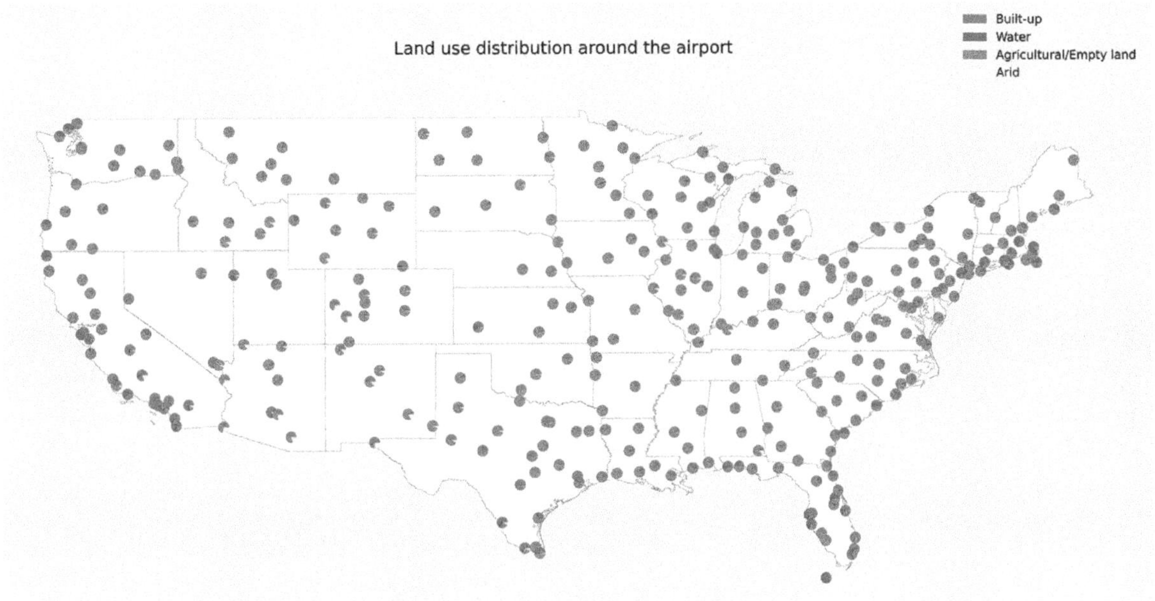

10

must be put at top priority. The rest of the airports currently have no pressure on them in terms of passenger numbers or urban congestion. Nonetheless, the results obtained here must be treated cautiously in general, since few parameters are used and hence the study is simplistic in nature.

CONCLUSION

Technology-driven urban planning could be the key to the greater goal of rethinking individual and network planning in the aviation industry. In this study, we explored the current situation of US airports in terms of two key variables: one of which was the ground truth (passenger traffic data) and the other was predicted by a ML system trained to identify different types of land use from raw satellite imagery. This approach shows that it is computationally possible to longitudinally analyze airports for key high-level parameters based on ML summaries of complex raw aerial data. The open-source nature of the methodology makes it both scalable and repeatable, and thus suitable for varied requirements, with major benefiters being country and state governments, especially those rapidly developing without up-to-date mapping. The ability to extract complex and critical information related to land-use patterns and perform per-pixel analytics from a simple aerial image is interesting, and we feel that this could potentially change the way the aviation industry foresees its challenging adaption path ahead. We believe this workflow could aid urban planners, policymakers, and environmentalists, especially with the growing concern around the ever-expanding nature of aviation and urban infrastructure with direct impacts to people through noise pollution and urban congestion and to nature through shifting land-use patterns.

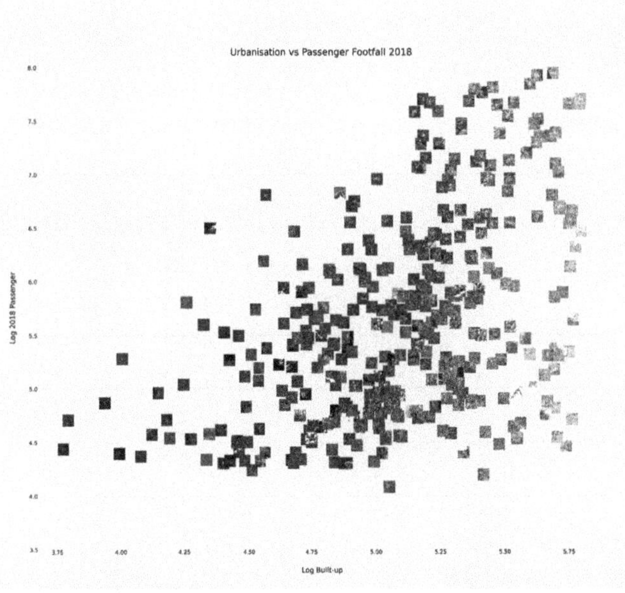

11

10 Land-use distribution around the airport based on the four different class labels.

11 Level of urbanization plotted against passenger footfall numbers, with each airport represented by its corresponding aerial image.

We strongly feel that this methodology provides an interface to compare the different contributing parameters in analyzing such impacts at a higher level very much at the early stages of design conceptualization. The generality of this approach makes it more intriguing and applicable to similar large infrastructure of concern, such as transport hubs and seaports etc., to name a few.

Investigations into this typology-driven exploration are ongoing, including generating design solutions for airport

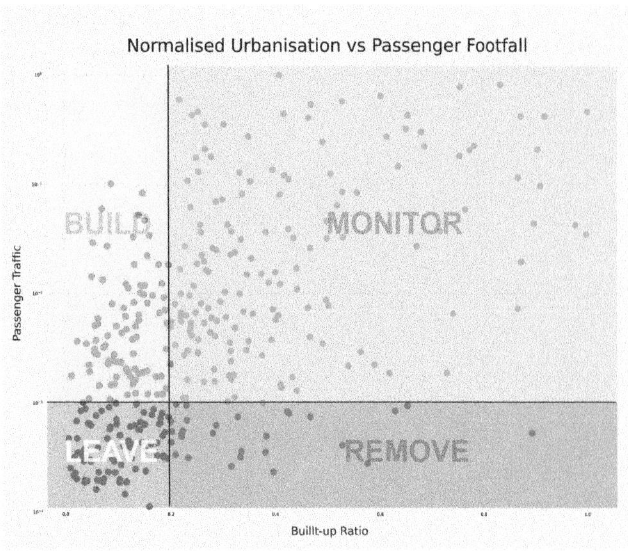

12 Urban congestion vs. airport passenger traffic with axis cut-off values for action strategy.

terminals. Combined with this study, generative adversarial networks and design space exploration by Meta Parametric design (Ibrahim and Joyce 2019) could be leveraged to explore alternative design options at the early stage of architectural design through analytics at the building, site, and urban levels.

LIMITATIONS AND FURTHER WORK

Given that this study focused on airport expansion purely in terms of land availability around the terminal building, we are aware that variables such as planning regulation, zoning, noise pollution, land cost, and traveler preferences were not explicitly taken into consideration. We leave this more sophisticated analysis for future work. As researchers, we see ML helping to streamline many time-intensive planning processes such as those shown. AI in planning has the immense potential to amplify human efforts, vastly increasing the number of examples or the breadth of area examined, crucial in the field of comparative analysis for design. This study demonstrates steps towards using ML to understand land-use patterns, using satellite imagery over a whole continent, which is specifically useful in an aviation planning context in which each airport relates to a larger global network.

REFERENCES

Albert, Adrian, Jasleen Kaur, and Marta Gonzalez. 2017. "Using Convolutional Networks and Satellite Imagery to Identify Patterns in Urban Environments at a Large Scale." In Proceedings of the 23rd ACM SIGKDD International Conference on Knowledge Discovery and Data Mining, 1357-1366. New York, NY: ACM.

Basu, Saikat, Sangram Ganguly, Supratik Mukhopadhyay, Robert Dibiano, Manohar Karki, and Ramakrishna Nemani. 2015. "DeepSat – A Learning framework for Satellite Imagery." In *Proceedings of the 23rd SIGSPATIAL International Conference on Advances in Geographic Information Systems*, 37:1-37:10. New York, NY: ACM.

Demir, Ilke, Krzysztof Koperski, David Lindenbaum, Guan Pang, Jing Huang, Saikat Basu, Forest Hughes, Devis Tuia, and Ramesh Raskar. "DeepGlobe 2018: A Challenge to Parse the Earth through Satellite

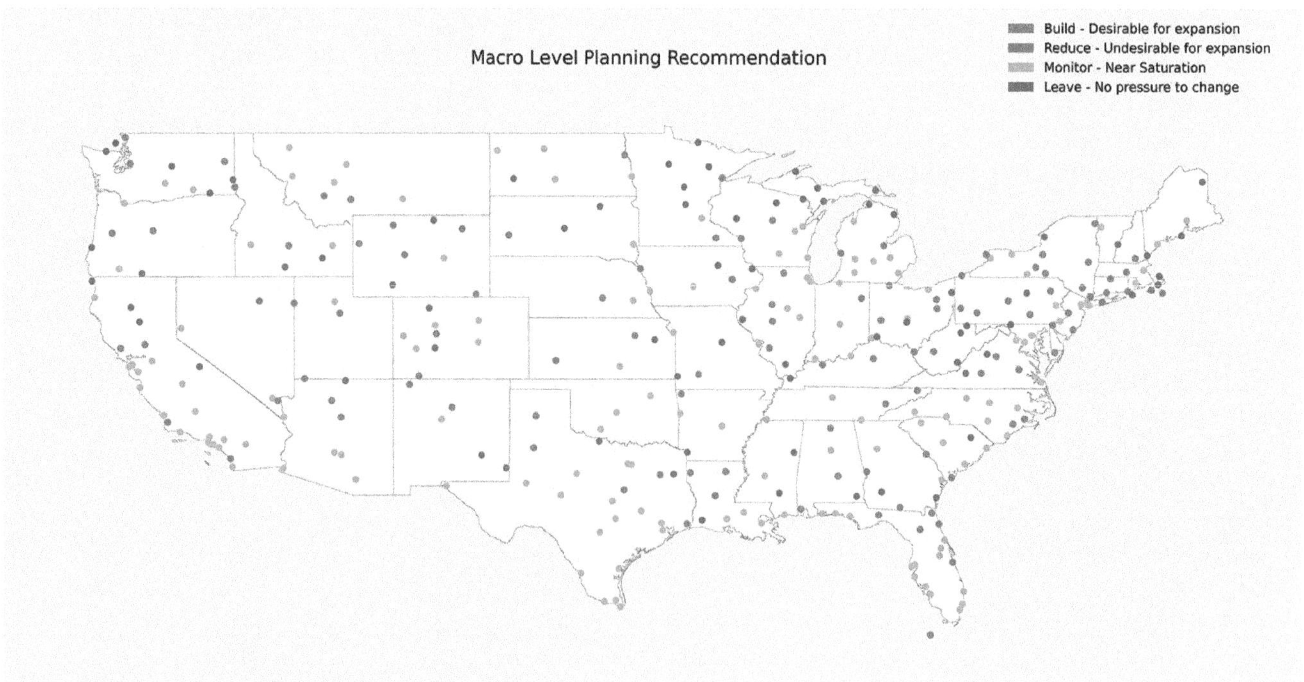

13 Macro-level planning recommendation for US airports.

Images." *2018 IEEE/CVF Conference on Computer Vision and Pattern Recognition Workshops (CVPRW)*. https://doi.org/10.1109/CVPRW.2018.00031.

Dong, Hao, Guang Yang, Fangde Liu, Yuanhan Mo, and Yike Guo. 2017. "Automatic Brain Tumor Detection and Segmentation Using U-Net Based Fully Convolutional Networks." *Annual Conference on Medical Image Understanding and Analysis,* 506–517. Edinburgh, UK.

European Space Agency. 2014. API Hub. https://scihub.copernicus.eu/twiki/do/view/SciHubWebPortal/APIHubDescription.

Frank, Warmerdam, Rouault Even, et al. 1998. *GDAL*. https://gdal.org/index.html.

Gueguen, Lionel, and Raffay Hamid. 2015. "Large-Scale Damage Detection Using Satellite Imagery." *CVPR 2015*. Boston: Computer Vision and Pattern Recognition.

IATA. 2020. "COVID-19 Impact on Asia-Pacific Aviation Worsens." Pressroom, April 24. https://www.iata.org/en/pressroom/pr/2020-04-24-01/.

Ibrahim, Nazim, and Sam Joyce. 2019. "User Directed Meta Parametric Design for Option Exploration." In *ACADIA 19: Ubiquity and Autonomy [Proceedings of the 39th Annual Conference of the Association for Computer Aided Design in Architecture (ACADIA)]*, Austin, TX, 21–26 October 2019, edited by K. Bieg, D. Briscoe, and C. Odom, 50–59. CUMINCAD.

ICAO. 2018. "Long-Term Traffic Forecasts Passenger and Cargo." International Civil Aviation Organization.

Karchevskiy, Mikhail, Insaf Ashrapov, and Leonid Kozinkin. 2018. "Automatic Salt Deposits Segmentation: A Deep Learning Approach." ArXiv. https://arxiv.org/abs/1812.01429.

Malarvizhi, K., S. Vasantha Kumar, and P. Porchelvan. 2015. "Use of High Resolution Google Earth Satellite Imagery in Landuse Map Preparation for Urban Related Applications." *International Conference on Emerging Trends in Engineering, Science and Technology*. Thrissur.

Microsoft Corporation. 2020. "AI for Humanitarian Action." https://www.microsoft.com/en-us/ai/ai-for-humanitarian-action.

OECD. 2008. *The Impacts of Globalisation on International Air Transport Activity*. Guadalajara: OECD.

Python Software Foundation. 2017. *Pygc*. V.1.1.0. https://pypi.org/project/pygc/. PC.

Ronneberger, Olaf, Philipp Fischer, and Thomas Brox. 2015. "U-Net: Convolutional Networks for Biomedical Image Segmentation." *LNCS* 9351: 234–241.

Sadik-Khan, Janette. 2017. *Streetfight: Handbook for an Urban Revolution*. Penguin Books.

Tóth, Bálint. 2011. Aviation Fanatic. https://www.aviationfanatic.com.

United Nations. 2019. "Unite Maps Initiative." August. https://geoportal.dfs.un.org/arcgis/apps/sites/#/unitvemaps.

World Bank. 2020. "Urban Development Overview." April 20. https://www.worldbank.org/en/topic/urbandevelopment/overview.

IMAGE CREDITS

Figures 4 and 6 (middle): © Sentinel-2 ESA Copernicus.

All other images and graphics are produced by the authors.

Ahmed Meeran is a master's student at the Singapore University of Technology and Design, pursuing his degree in Engineering Innovation by Design. He earned his Bachelor's in Architectural Technology (first-class honors) from the Indian Institute of Technology Kharagpur with a minor specialization in MS Economics. Ahmed aims to use emerging technologies to streamline mundane processes in design workflows and is currently exploring the use of artificial intelligence systems and generative frameworks for early-stage design option exploration. He aims to broaden his knowledge in leveraging large-scale systems to collect and analyze Big Data to take meaningful policy decisions that impact people in their everyday lives. Ahmed also works on data visualization with a special emphasis on urban morphology to understand cities and the built environment in a useful way.

Sam Conrad Joyce is an Assistant Professor at the Singapore University of Technology and Design, in the Architecture and Sustainable Design pillar. He explores possibilities at the intersection of technology-driven research and design practice, having worked at Foster + Partners on projects such as the Mexico City Airport. He heads up The Meta Design Lab, an interdisciplinary group seeking out, conceiving, developing, and testing future architectural capabilities, specifically, how AI and Big Data can find design insight and generate novel solutions, with the ultimate goal that humans and computers might work together as collectively superior cocreators.

Data-Driven Midsole

Performance-Oriented Midsole Design Using Computational Multi-Objective Optimization

Runjia Tian*
Graduate School of Design, Harvard University

Yujie Wang*
Department of Architecture, Massachusetts Institute of Technology

Onur Yüce Gün
R&D Innovation Studio, New Balance Athletics Inc.

*Authors contributed equally to the research.

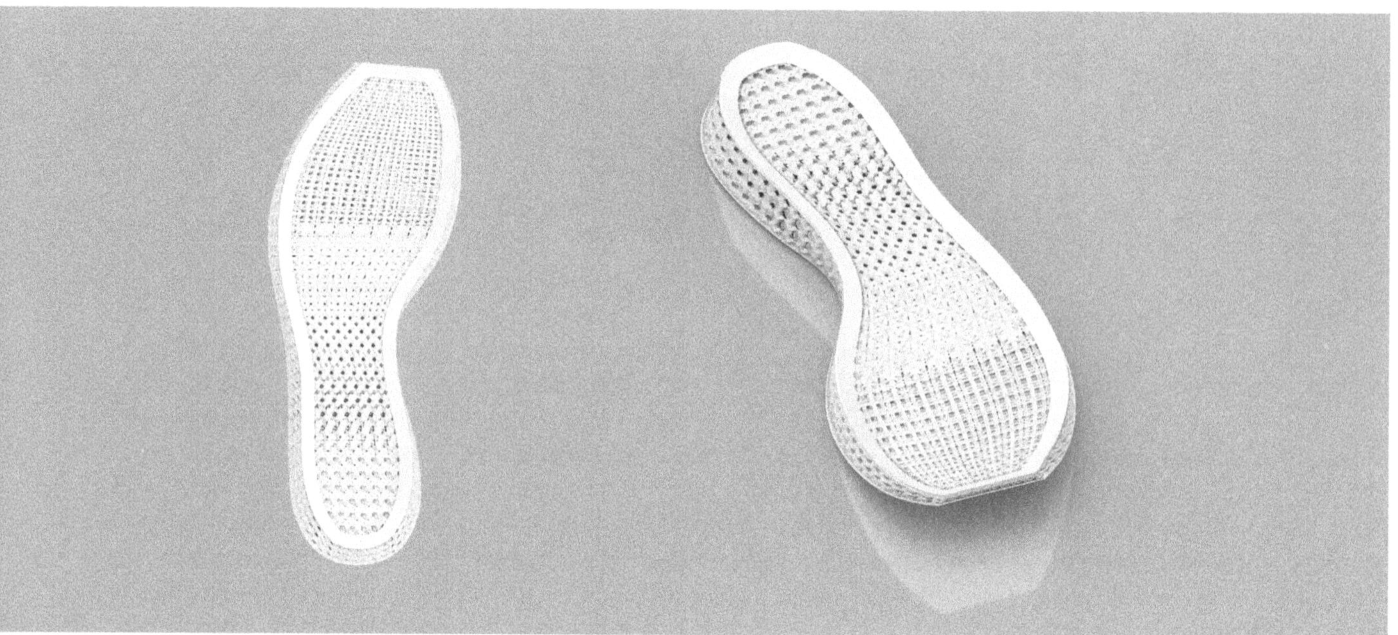

1 Midsole design using deep temporal clustering and computational multi-objective optimization.

ABSTRACT

With the advancement of additive manufacturing, computational approaches are gaining popularity in midsole design. We develop an experimental understanding of the midsole as a field and develop designs that are informed by running data.

We streamline two data types, namely underfoot pressure and surface deformation, to generate designs. Unlike typical approaches in which certain types of lattices get distributed across the midsole according to average pressure data, we use ARAMIS data, reflecting the distinct surface deformation characteristics, as our primary design driver. We analyze both pressure and deformation data temporally, and temporal data patterns help us generate and explore a design space to search for optimal designs. First, we define multiple zones across the midsole space using ARAMIS data clustering.

Then we develop ways to blend and distribute auxetic and isosurface lattices across the midsole. We hybridize these two structures and blend data-determined zones to enhance visual continuity while applying FEA simulations to ensure structural integrity. This multi-objective optimization approach helps enhance the midsole's structural performance and visual coherence while introducing a novel approach to 3D-printed footwear design.

INTRODUCTION

3D printing has been broadly applied to product prototyping and fabrication. With the advancement of data science and volumetric modeling toolkits, there are opportunities in the footwear industry to employ computationally generated lattice systems in place of conventional components and materials to enhance performance with new design possibilities.

As a layer between the upper and the outsole, the midsole of a shoe performs as the main cushioning, stability and pronation control component. Midsole materials, subcomponents, and overall composition determine the quality of the running experience, and thus numerous running shoes end up featuring a broad range of midsole components and materials.

With the advancement of data science and volumetric modeling toolkits, we see an opportunity in the footwear industry to replace these components and materials through employing computationally generated lattice systems (Nazir et al. 2019) . We develop a data-driven design approach, utilizing multi-objective optimization and performance simulations.

In recent years, New Balance partnered with Nervous System to develop 3D-printed midsoles for performance running shoes in which 3D pressure data determined the 3D-printed lattice geometry.

The authors also experimented with traditional measures to design a midsole using a pressure-data-driven approach. In this case, we designed a midsole composed of lattice units whose structural unit angle and member diameter are proportionate to the underfoot pressure data in the midsole (Fig. 1).

Such approaches only take into consideration the instant or averaged sum of underfoot data. Nonetheless, typical midsole deformations are temporal processes such as running and jogging. The rich temporal information embedded in the change of external force across time is flattened and untapped. The ARAMIS data[1] is a set of midsole deformation data captured by stereo cameras during a unit duration of the running process on both sides of the midsole. During each frame, the strain and deformation for each lattice on the midsole were calculated (Fig. 5).

We see an opportunity to add to this data-driven approach by taking the temporal implications of running and ARAMIS dataset into consideration: various parts of the midsole come into effect during various human movement stages.

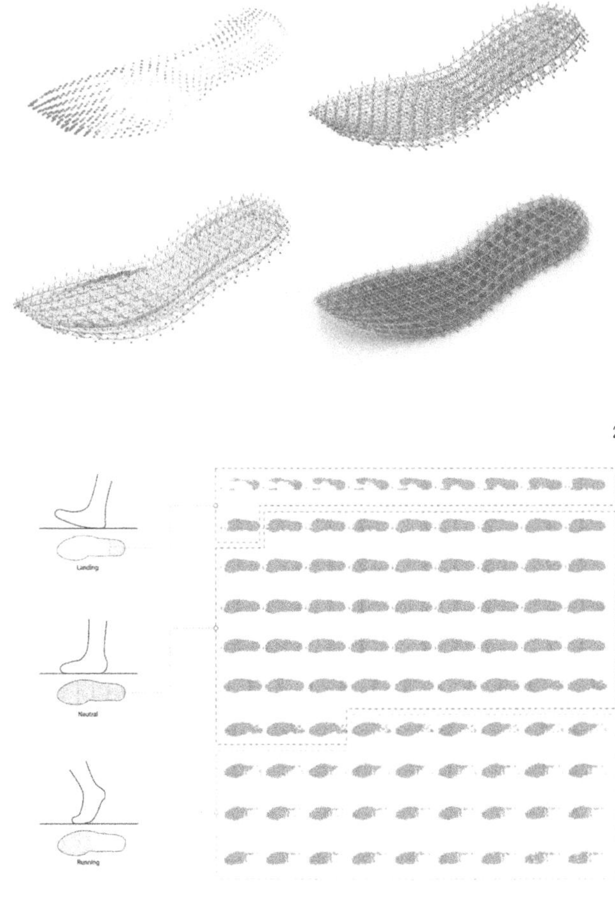

2 Pressure data-driven material distribution.

3 Visualization of sequential pressure data demonstrating running experience in three stages.

This can be used to inform lattice distribution and design (Fig. 2). This approach will augment the static pressure-data-driven approach and bring new opportunities and insights into computational midsole design.

METHODOLOGY: COMPUTATIONAL MULTI-OBJECTIVE OPTIMIZATION DESIGN

We develop a computational multi-objective optimization approach that takes both ARAMIS data and underfoot pressure data into design and evaluation processes. We apply a lattice system as a parametric design framework for the midsole design and determine the optimal lattice structure for each group of lattice units using deep-temporal clustering as a segmentation algorithm. We then evaluate the generated designs through performance-based computational simulations and determine each segment's optimal structure combination. We use underfoot pressure data to

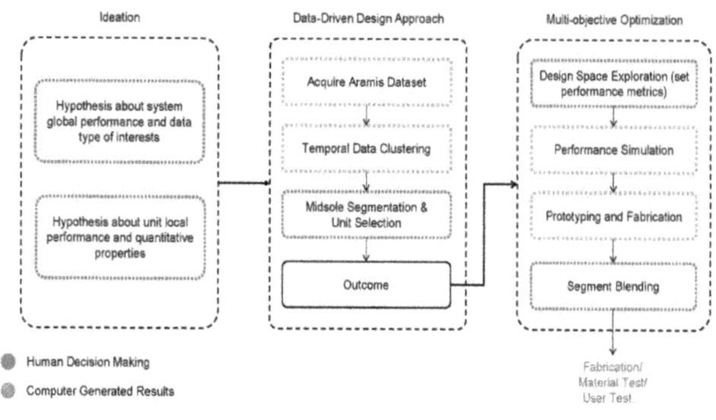

4

ARAMIS Data: Surface Strains + Camera Sensing

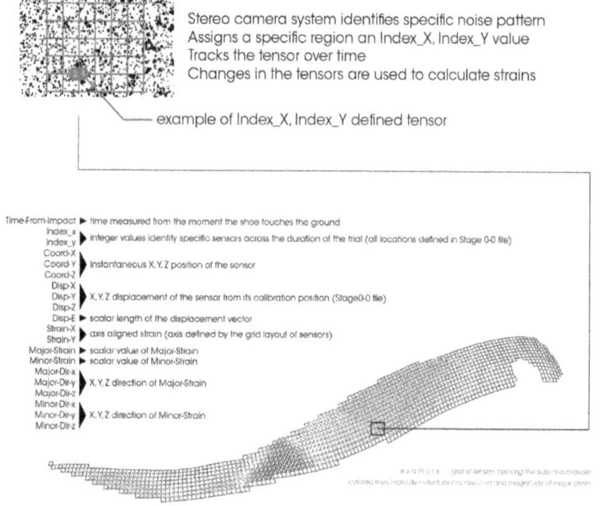

5

4 Holistic computational multi-objective optimization workflow.

5 ARAMIS data overview.

determine the optimal form factor and material distribution for each lattice unit. Meanwhile, we research ways to implement aesthetic decisions into the design.

A holistic approach is critical in this method as we intend to unify and synthesize the performance and aesthetic goals and computation and human agency in the design process. The approach is composed of three steps: ideation, data-driven approach, and multi-objective optimization.

Ideation

The synthetic workflow starts with an ideation phase driven by human designers. In this phase, the designers define high-level shape grammars and hypotheses for performance space (Fig. 4).

The first hypothesis is the global-local hypothesis. It assumes that the global system performance corresponds to the case where each local segment's performance is optimal. Therefore, the midsole's optimal global performance of impact absorption is achieved where each segment deformation is at its local minima. Similarly, each segmentation archives its best performance metrics when each lattice unit resists its local temporal strain effect to its best.

The second hypothesis proposes a blending hypothesis. In this case, the designer assumes that the strain is interpolated along the major axis of midsole and that the aesthetics metric is optimal when the lattice units between the center of two segments are smooth volumetric interpolation of lattice units on the two poles.

Data-Driven Approach

The performance-based midsole design starts with ideating how available data types affect the running experience.

There are two types of footwear data available in this project: the under-foot pressure data[2] and ARAMIS data. Both are sequential, making it possible to track the midsole's behavior over a specific period.

The under-foot pressure data reflects the load distribution of midsole upper surface in the running process, but it cannot be used for temporal analysis due to its limited frame counts.

There have been many explorations of using under-foot pressure data as a primary form factor for additive manufacturing (Brennan-Craddock, Wildman, and Hague 2012) and midsole designs (Dong, Tessier, and Zhao 2019). The approach we present challenged this conventional footwear data usage by proposing a new design agenda that treats ARAMIS data as the primary factor and pressure data as the secondary factor.

The ARAMIS data set (Fig. 5) includes measurements of the surface deformation of the inner and outer side-surface for midsole, and is created by New Balance Inc. using digital-image-correlation (DIC) systems (Chu et al. 1985). The data set includes more than 200 instantaneous frames of optically measured position data and surface strains for midsole deformations. We used the midsole side surface data, which is composed of a grid of 152 × 18 data points. Each data point in the data set contains the unique x and y index for the point, the coordinate of the point on that frame, the displacement of the point in x and y direction compared to the calibration status, the strain in x, y, and z direction,

	TIME-FROM-IMPACT	INDEX_X	INDE-Z	DISP-X	DISP-Y	DISP-Z	RAIN-Y	MINOR-STRAIN	MAJOR-DIR-X	MAJOR-DIR-Y	MAJOR-DIR-Z	MINOR-DIR-X	MINOR-DI Y
0	0.2	17	1·4	39.77452	121.0083	-21.8903	1.33741	0.51291	-0.93437	0.307481	-0.18748	-0.37157	-0.81124
1	0.2	18	1·4	39.75324	120.1739	-21.9601	1.31835	0.45842	-0.30454	0.841156	-0.45419	-0.9579	-0.26649
2	0.2	19	1·2	39.37608	118.9675	-22.0656	1.31615	0.51291	-0.26445	0.869291	-0.42283	-0.96716	-0.2336
3	0.2	20	1·8	38.97893	117.7658	-22.1595	1.31918	0.51797	-0.71256	0.655539	-0.25018	-0.70497	-0.64315
4	0.2	21	1·8	38.57319	116.5678	-22.2199	1.44937	0.51814	-0.82937	0.535644	-0.16114	-0.56125	-0.75946
5	0.2	22	1·6	38.18861	115.3623	-22.3428	1.47966	0.52383	-0.8369	0.528042	-0.14506	-0.54848	-0.77002

130 frames of inside of midsole ARAMIS data

features = ['Disp-X','Disp-Y','Disp-Z','Disp-E','Major-Strain','Minor-Strain','Major-Dir-x',
'Major-Dir-y','Major-Dir-z','Minor-Dir-x','Minor-Dir-y','Minor-Dir-z']

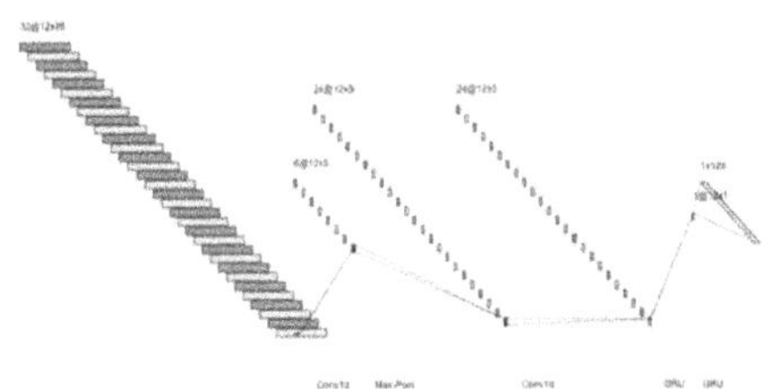

Deep Temporal Clustering with Recurrent Neural Network Autoencoder

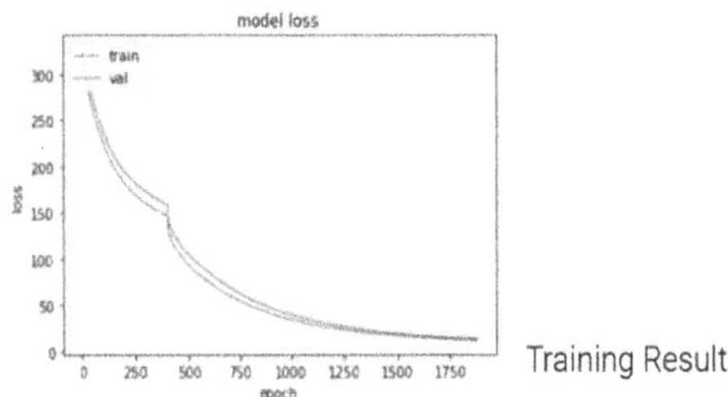

Training Result

6 ARAMIS data sample and deep temporal clustering algorithm.

6

and the x, y, and z directions of minor and major strain. Here we use the primary strain vector and the displacement vector as major features for temporal clustering.

Data clustering allows us to understand different zones of the midsole's behavior and come up with different data interpretations to inform various types of designs. Applying the deep temporal clustering (Madiraju et al. 2018) and K-Shape clustering (Paparrizos and Gravano 2015) algorithms to the ARAMIS data, we can discover a reasonable range of segments with the available frames of displacement and strains.

- Deep temporal autoencoder: We first extract time series data for each data point in the ARAMIS data set based on the deformation pattern for the strain and displacement. Then we use a long-short term memory (LSTM) (Hochreiter and Jürgen 1997) autoencoder composed of multiple LSTM layers to learn a latent representation of the temporal data for all data points in the data set. The strain data and displacement data are concatenated as input vectors to the neural network. We minimize the mean-squared error (MSE) and Kullback–Leibler (KL) divergence as the loss function of the autoencoder. With the LSTM autoencoder, we reduce the dimensionality of input data from a high-dimensional signal to a one-dimensional signal, which allows us to further use the K-shape algorithm for further clustering the temporal pattern (Fig. 6).
- K-shape clustering: Then we use the K-shape algorithm for clustering the latent time series for each data point in the ARAMIS data set. K-shape uses a normalized version of the cross-correlation measure algorithm that compares the time series's shape (Paparrizos and Gravano 2015).
- Obtain optimal segmentation: In the deep temporal clustering approach above, we have a hyperparameter—cluster number—that we need to determine using validation. We first select a reasonable range of cluster numbers (between 4 and 8) that do not convey too overwhelming visual variation while maintaining the design's shape diversity (Paparrizos and Gravano 2015). We select the optimal clustering number with validation where the number of clusters is maximum while all segments maintain a reasonable number of data points. We maximize the number of segments in the midsole to obtain a diversity of unit structures to reflect the midsole deformation process's temporal pattern.

Then we segment the whole midsole into optimal zones with optimal lattice units to be distributed in each segment. The pressure data is then utilized to affect material distribution in terms of the lattice units' member diameter.

Computational Optimization Approach

Predefined and tested metrics help evaluate design iterations across design spaces in computational optimizations (Ma, Wu, and Matusik 2020). In this project, we set up two optimization goals for lattice units. The primary goal is to create a rigid and protective structure to resist the load (Alderson et al. 2019). We achieve this by selecting lattice units with a smaller vertical displacement under

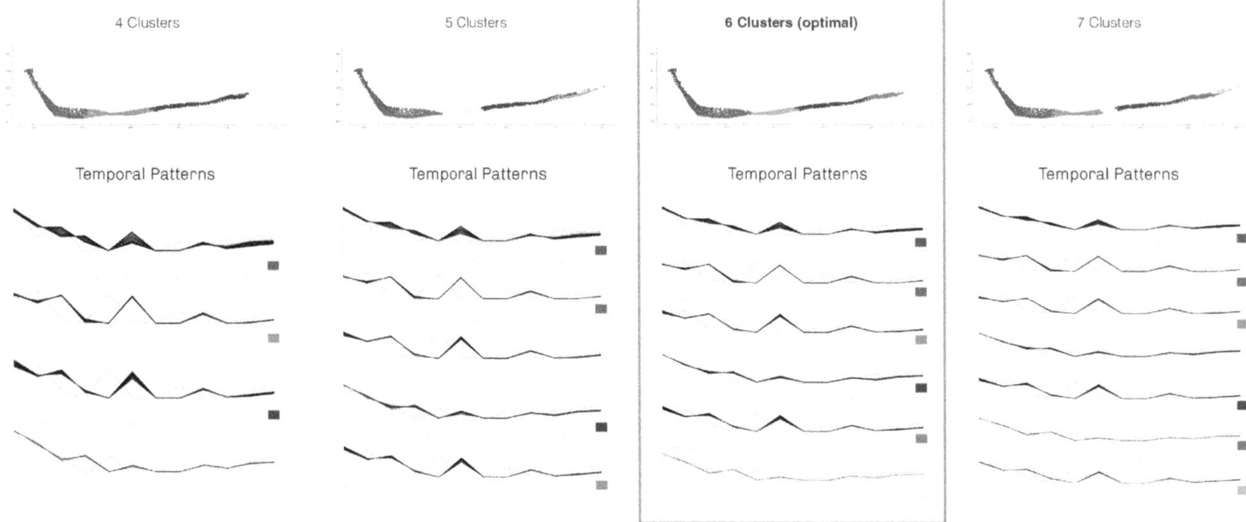

7

pressure in proportion to the overall unit height (shifting ratio). The secondary goal is to achieve a smaller overall material-to-volume ratio, which yields lighter solutions for similarly performing designs.

- Design space exploration: We make iterations with selected design variables for design space exploration (Gün 2010). We control the lattice system's form factors and focus on the performance of the lattice unit with two variables as the internal form factor: the scale ratio for compactness and the member diameter for manufacturing feasibility.
- Performance simulation: We set up multiple optimization objectives and search for optimal unit cell design. The simulation results are then evaluated according to two metrics: the shifting ratio (reflecting rigidity to deformation) and the volume ratio (reflecting material efficiency). Finite element analysis (FEA), which subdivides a large complex system into smaller, simpler solvable parts through discretization in the space dimensions, is implemented here to quantify the displacement of members of the lattice units when being applied to the same load by treating auxetic units as beam-like structures (Wang 2018) and gyroid units as shell-like structures (Yang et al. 2019).
- Prototyping and fabrication: We made a 1:1 partial prototype with resin 3D printing thanks to New Balance Sports Research Lab. This experiment helped understand the actual material performance and behavior through physical impressions and simple material tests to understand how the segments respond to pressure and deformation.
- Segment blending: Segment blending creates a smooth transition between segments by tuning material density and blending the unit cell structure. The blending factors are associated with the characteristics of adjacent segments. Parameters of lattice unit structure in adjacent segments are tuned to achieve coherent aesthetics through gradient transition.

RESULTS AND DISCUSSION

A Performance-Based Midsole Design Using Computational Multi-Objective Optimization

The authors designed and prototyped a midsole that functioned as part of the sneaker with a lattice system as a experiment for the proposed workflow.[3]

A multi-objective optimization system was designed to evaluate the performance of designs. First, a family of unit structures was selected based on heuristic speculations. Within this family, each unit was tested with simulation in accordance with each temporal cluster. The unit with optimal performance was matched to the respective cluster.

Lattice System Design

The midsole design used a lattice system as a flexible structure, as this system could be easily deformed and remapped. We tested various lattice units, starting from an auxetic structure that provides cushioning and bouncing to a solid minimal surface structure that provides resistance in the pronation process (Wang 2018).

We apply a uniformly distributed lattice system of 18 × 20 × 6 in x, y, and z dimensions. The lattice system's size is

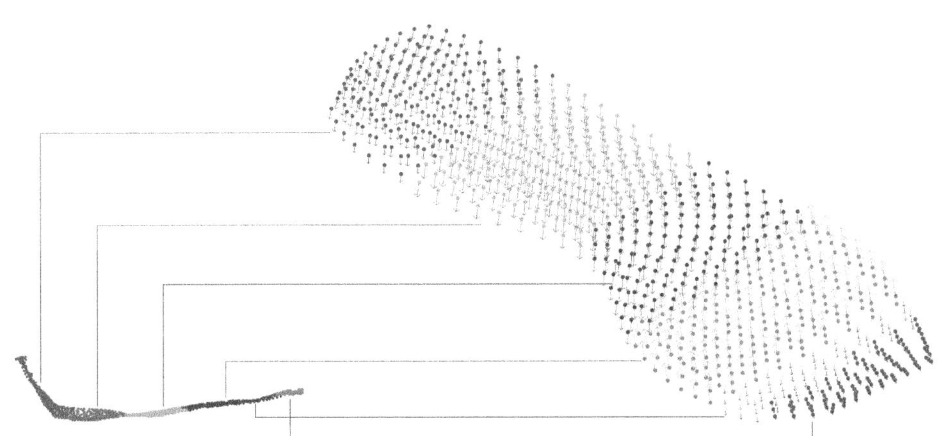

7 Principle component analysis visualization of the latent space of temporal data clustering and K-shape analysis.

8 Lattice unit segmentation based on deep temporal clustering.

8

constrained by the fabrication precision and the consistency with the data grid size in the ARAMIS data.

Temporal Clustering and Midsole Segmentation

Our deep temporal clustering network comprises a mixture of one-dimensional convolutional layers, max-pooling layers, and multiple gated recurring unit (GRU) layers. The decoder is composed of a similar structure of deconvolutional layers, unspooling layers, and GRU layers.

Then we train the deep temporal autoencoder on the feature-engineered ARAMIS data set with MSE and KL divergence. The training process converged after 2,000 epochs on both the training set and validation set to prevent overfitting.

We obtain a low-dimensional latent representation that captures each data point's essential temporal pattern with the deep temporal clustering. Then we use the K-shape clustering to further visualize the temporal pattern for the latent signal representation for each data point across all time stamps (Fig. 7).

We experiment with cluster numbers 4–8 to observe the result for temporal clustering. Then we visualize the clustering result for various cluster numbers in the latent space with principal component analysis. All cluster numbers seemed reasonable.

From this visualization, we observe that cluster number 5 does not differentiate temporal patterns between clusters, underfitting the clustering task, and in the case of cluster number 7, two clusters have temporal patterns that are too similar, therefore overfitting the clustering task. Therefore, we determined that cluster number 6 would be used as the optimal hyperparameter (Fig. 8).

Design Space Exploration of Unit Structure

A multi-objective optimization system was designed to evaluate the performance of the designs. First, a family of unit structures was selected to test metamaterial properties. Within this family, each unit was tested via simulation in accordance with each temporal cluster. The unit with optimal performance was matched to the respective cluster.

With controlled form factors of the lattice system, we generated lattice unit iterations for performance simulations focusing on two internal unit form factors as input variables: the scale ratio for compactness and member diameter for material manufacturability.

The form factor was further determined with a pressure data set about the material grading. The structure performance was then validated with simulation for testing.

After six iterations of design and performance simulation, we concluded that Schoen Gyroid surfaces, shell-based Schoen Gyroid surfaces, Schwarz P surfaces, and Schoen I-WP surfaces would produce reasonable shape blending effects as well as balanced deformation characteristics of minimal surface structures (Fig. 9).

Multi-Objective Optimization of Cluster Performance

Various lattice units were tested, starting from an auxetic structure that provides cushioning (Wang 2018)

Unit Cell Type	Auxetic			Hybrid Isosurfaces			Struct-based Gyroid		
Form Factor	scale factor			Octo + IWP			density factor		
	0.3	0.6	0.9	20%+80%	50%+50%	80%+20%	0.3	0.6	0.9
Visualization									
Shifting Ratio (%) [Rigidity]	7	13	17	9	9	7	9	6	4
Volume Ratio [Material Efficiency]	0.09	0.25	0.38	0.24	0.27	0.34	0.13	0.22	0.3

9 Finite element analysis (FEA) performance simulation of lattice units. 9

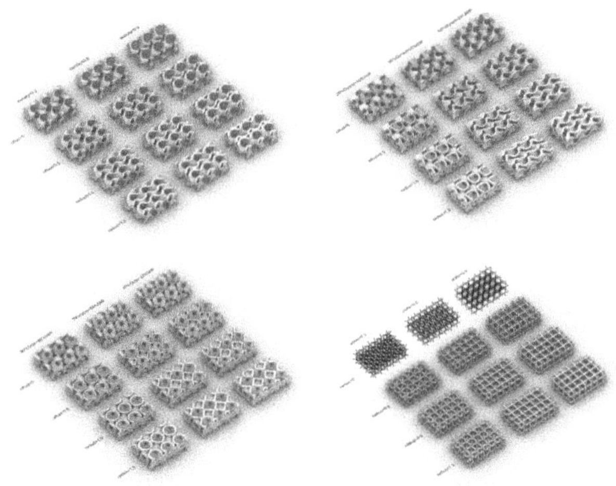

10

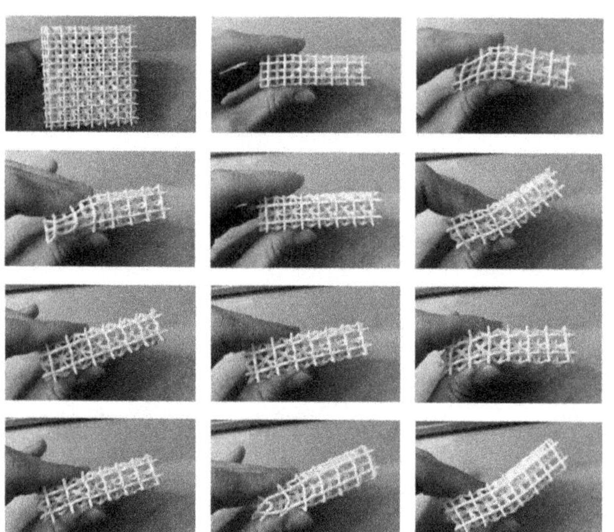

11

10 Design space exploration with lattice unit clusters.

11 Partial prototype and deformation experiments with thermoplastic powders via SLS printing.

and bouncing, to a solid minimal surface structure that provides resistance in the pronation process (Yang et al. 2019).

According to two metrics, the simulation results are evaluated: the shifting ratio (reflecting rigidity to deformation) and the volume ratio (reflecting material efficiency). The shifting ratio is the vertical displacement in proportion to the overall unit height responding to the same vertical load applied to the unit surface area. It reflects the rigidity of the unit to deformation by measuring how geometry responds to the same load. The volume ratio is the lattice unit's material volume in proportion to the uniform unit cell volume. It reflects the material efficiency of the lattice unit in the additive manufacturing process. We aim to select unit cells with a lower shifting ratio (higher rigidity) and lower volume ratio (higher material efficiency) and hybridize them into segments responding to optimal ARAMIS data segmentation through iterative performance simulations (Fig. 10).

Finite element analysis (FEA) conducted with Kiwi!3D (str. ucture 2020), a plugin for Rhino and Grasshopper enabling the integration of isogeometric analysis (IGA) into the CAD environment, is implemented to quantify the displacement of members of the lattice units when applied to the same load on the unit surface area. Auxetic units are treated as beam-like structures (Wang 2018), and gyroid units are treated as shell-like structures (Yang et al. 2019) in the simulations. Material properties of additive manufacturing are also applied in the simulation.

Prototyping and Fabrication

Partial prototypes of the segment samples were 3D printed with photopolymer/rebound resin powder by a selective laser sintering (SLS) printer to test physical properties and material performance (Fig. 11). Further material testing in a rigorous lab environment would be an ideal next step.[4]

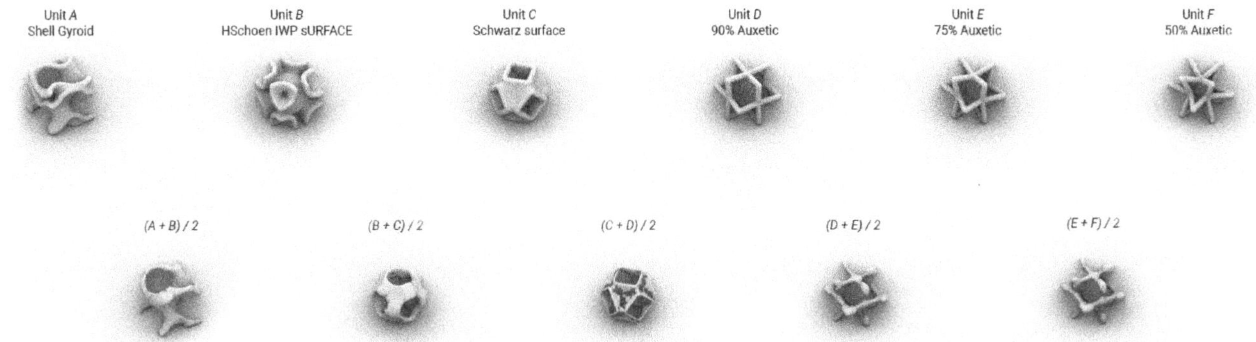

12 Volumetric blending of lattice units and resulting lattice structure.

Volumetric Blending and Optimal Selection

With the blending hypothesis, we decided to interpolate the lattice units volumetrically in adjacent segments to create a midsole design that could reflect a delicate balance of local and global temporal strain patterns. We tested with various lattice unit structure set choices and discovered the optimal unit set that allows reasonable material density after the blending process.

We implemented the blending algorithm using the Dendro for Rhinoceros 3D Library. Dendro is a volumetric modeling library for Rhino/Grasshopper built on top of the OpenVDB library (ecrlabs 2020). We perform a trilinear volumetric interpolation between the optimal structural units to populate the lattice units between structure segment centers. This blending process serves both aesthetic and functional purposes (Fig. 12).

Various lattice units were tested both individually and hybrid to search for the optimal midsole design. We tested with six combinations of the same primitive lattice units and selected the optimal design based on both the evaluation metrics derived by computational optimization and the form density evaluation metrics that influence aesthetic quality (Fig. 13).

CONCLUSION

Unlike the standard approach in which certain types of lattices get distributed across the midsole according to an averaged pressure data, in this project we use ARAMIS data reflecting the distinct surface deformation characteristics as our primary design driver (instead of averaged pressure data). We proposed a data-driven workflow for midsole design.

Our approach demonstrated how to use deep temporal clustering to analyze the sequential pattern of running experience and segmentation of midsole areas. We developed a multi-objective computational system for midsole design optimization. Furthermore, we employed computational simulations to make informed decisions to iterate our designs. We developed a method for blending lattice units with different topological configurations.

As computational optimization tools become central in decision-making processes, human interventions become even more crucial for setting and running such systems efficiently and intuitively.

Our holistic approach could be applied to a scenario in which the design resides in a context with an explicit temporal pattern. The shape-blending approach reveals the material response to external force and strain and will serve as a generic aesthetic quality that could be used in various scenarios in performance optimization.

Computational optimization requires quantitative metrics to run, and thus, subjective decision-making, such as visual choices, cannot easily be quantified (Gün 2017). However, such decisions remain significant for design space exploration. While computational optimization tools remain central in decision-making processes, human interaction becomes even more crucial for setting and running such systems in efficient and intuitive ways. Revisiting the challenges of blending visual and performative design goals in this project, we aim to develop systems to enhance human input into our optimization system through more holistic computational design approaches in the future.

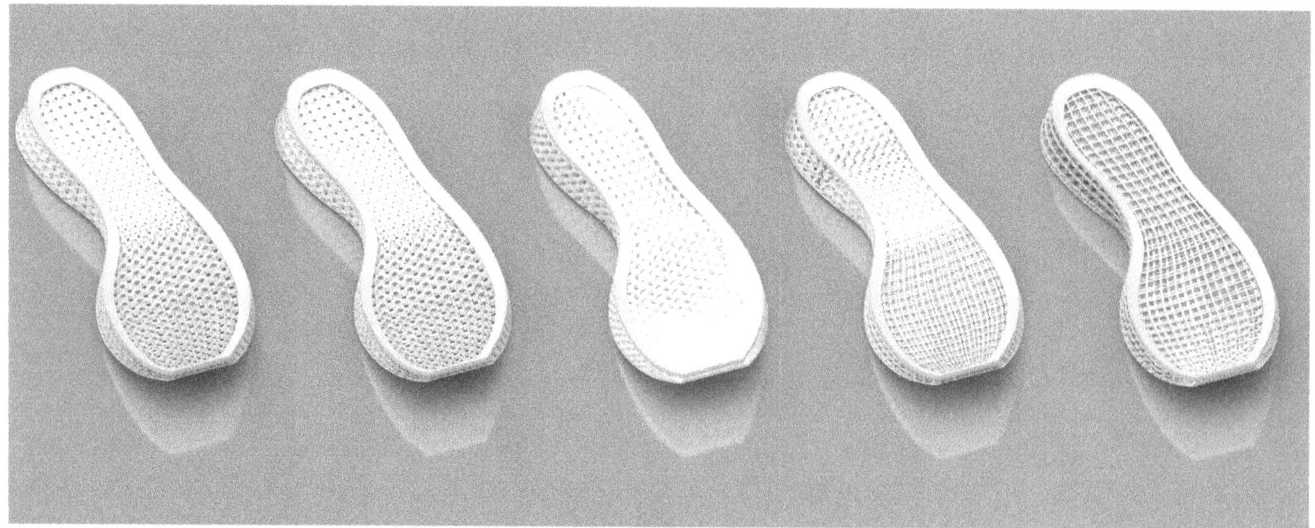

13 Various iterations of midsole designs.

ACKNOWLEDGMENTS

We want to express our gratitude to Onur Yüce Gün, the MIT Department of Architecture, and NEW Balance R&D Innovation Studio for their generous support.

NOTES

1. The ARAMIS data set is proprietary information created by New Balance Inc.
2. Data source available through New Balance Sports Research Lab.
3. We developed the proposed workflow in a computational design class 4.s56 Special Subject: Shape Grammars — Superseding Parts, Computing Wholes, taught by Onur Yüce Gün PhD at Massachusetts Institute of Technology in 2020. The course's objective was to "employ computational design with a critical inquiry of conventional part-to-whole relationships."
4. This experiment has been postponed due to COVID-19. Future research will incorporate more physical prototype testing.

REFERENCES

Alderson, A., K. L. Alderson, K. E. Evans, J. N. Grima, M. R. Williams, and P. J. Davies. 2005. "Modelling the Deformation Mechanisms, Structure–Property Relationships and Applications of Auxetic Nanomaterials." *Physica Status Solidi* 242 (3): 499–508.

Brennan-Craddock, J., D. Brackett, R. Wildman, and R. Hague. 2012. "The Design of impact Absorbing Structures for Additive Manufacture." *Journal of Physics: Conference Series* 382 (1): 012042.

Chu, T. C., W. F. Ranson, and Michael A. Sutton. 1985. "Applications of Digital-Image-Correlation Techniques to Experimental Mechanics." *Experimental Mechanics* 25 (3): 232–244.

Dong, Guoying, Daniel Tessier, and Yaoyao Fiona Zhao. 2019. "Design of Shoe Soles Using Lattice Structures Fabricated by Additive Manufacturing." In *Proceedings of the Design Society: International Conference on Engineering Design*, 719–728. Cambridge University Press.

ecrlabs. 2020. *Dendro for Grasshopper*. V. 0.9.0. PC.

Gün, Onur Yüce. 2010. "Geometric Gestures" In *Elements of Parametric Design*, edited by Robert Woodbury, 171–184. USA & Canada: Routledge.

Gün, Onur Yüce. 2017. "Computing with Watercolor Shapes." In *Computer-Aided Architectural Design: Future Trajectories [Proceedings of the 17th International Conference, CAAD Futures 2017]*, Istanbul, Turkey, 12–14 July 2017, edited by Gülen Çağdaş, Mine Özkar, Leman Figen Gül, and Ethem Gürer, 252–269. Springer.

Hochreiter, Sepp, and Jürgen Schmidhuber. 1997. "Long Short-Term Memory." *Neural Computation* 9 (8): 1735–1780.

Ma, Pingchuan, Tao Du, and Wojciech Matusik. 2020. "Efficient Continuous Pareto Exploration in Multi-Task Learning." In *International Conference on Machine Learning*, 6522–6531. PMLR.

Madiraju, Naveen Sai, Sadat, Seid M, Fisher, Dimitry, and Karimabadi, Homa. 2018. "Deep Temporal Clustering: Fully Unsupervised Learning of Time-Domain Features." arXiv:1802.01059 [cs.LG], February 4. https://arxiv.org/abs/1802.01059v1.

Nazir, Aamer, Abate, Kalayu Mekonen, Kumar, Ajeet, and Jeng, Jeng-Ywan. 2019. "A State-of-the-art Review on Types, Design, Optimization, and Additive Manufacturing of Cellular Structures."

International Journal of Advanced Manufacturing Technology 104 (9): 3489–3510.

Paparrizos, John, and Luis Gravano. 2015. "K-Shape: Efficient and Accurate Clustering of Time Series" In *SIGMOD '15 [Proceedings of the 2015 ACM SIGMOD International Conference on Management of Data]*, Melbourne, Australia, 31 May–4 June 2015, edited by Timos Sellis, 1855–1870. Association for Computing Machinery.

str.ucture. 2020. *KIWI!3D*. V. BETA 0.5.0. PC.

Wang, Fengwen. 2018. "Systematic Design of 3D Auxetic Lattice Materials with Programmable Poisson's Ratio for Finite Strains." *Journal of the Mechanics and Physics of Solids* 114: 303.

Yang, Lei, Raya Mertens, Massimiliano Ferrucci, Chunze Yan, Yusheng Shi, and Shoufeng Yang. 2019. "Continuous Graded Gyroid Cellular Structures Fabricated by Selective Laser Melting: Design, Manufacturing and Mechanical Properties." *Materials & Design* 162: 394–404.

IMAGE CREDITS

Figure 5: © New Balance Sports Research Lab (SRL) and Chris Wawrousek.

All other drawings and images by the authors.

Runjia Tian is a master in design studies technology track student at Harvard Graduate School of Design. Trained as an architect, Runjia is a multidisciplinary advocate of architecture, computation, and engineering. He investigates the future of design through the synergetic engagement of creative computation, extended reality, multimodal media, and machine perceptions. His more recent research focuses on the enactive cocreation between human designers and artificial intelligence. Runjia has authored/coauthored several peer-reviewed publications on architecture, urban design, and technology. He is the cofounder of AiRCAD, with research and working experience at MIT CSAIL and at Autodesk.

Yujie Wang is a master of architecture student at Massachusetts Institute of Technology. As an interaction design architect and creative technologist working across intelligent systems, sensory experiences, tangible products, and intangible services, Yujie investigates the future of social and technological systems by mediating human and machine perception and transforming how people interact with media such as mixed reality, brain-computer interface, self-driving vehicles, and adaptive built environment. He is the cofounder of Muser and AiRCAD, with research experience at Media Lab and Harvard Medical School and professional experience at Philips Healthcare.

Onur Yüce Gün is a seasoned computational designer and instructor. Trained as an architect, Onur holds a PhD and a Masters in Design and Computation, both earned at MIT. Onur instituted the Computational Geometry Group at KPF NY in 2006. His computational architecture work has been published in *Elements of Parametric Design* (Gün 2010). In 2009, he developed the curriculum and directed İstanbul Bilgi University's undergraduate program in architecture. He has taught at MIT, RISD and Adolfo Ibáñez University in Chile. He is currently the Creative Manager of Computational Design at New Balance and develops computational design workflows and futuristic concepts with a specific concentration on dfAM (design for additive manufacturing).

Simulation and Calibration of Graded Knitted Membranes

Yuliya Sinke Baranovskaya
CITA/KADK
The Royal Danish Academy

Martin Tamke
CITA/KADK
The Royal Danish Academy

Mette Ramsgaard Thomsen
CITA/KADK
The Royal Danish Academy

1 Fragment from the simulation digital environment, where the point cloud data is overlapped with the mesh-based geometry of a knitted membrane.

ABSTRACT

The grading of knit changes its geometrical performance and steers membrane expansion. However, knit possesses challenges of material predictability and digital simulation, due to its multiscalar complexity and anisotropic properties. Taking as a challenge the lack of digital solutions incorporating CNC-knit performance into the design model, this paper presents a novel approach for the design-integrated simulation of graded knit, informed by an empirical dataset analysis in combination with genetic optimization algorithms.

Here the simulation design tool reflects the differences of industrially knitted textile panel behavior through digital mesh grading. Diversified fabric stiffness is achieved by inter-twining the yarn into variegated stitch types that steer the textile expansion under load. These are represented digitally as zoned quad meshes with each segment assigned a stiffness value.

Mesh stiffness values are optimized by minimizing the distance between the point clouds and the digital mesh, which are documented through deviation colored maps.

This work concludes that design properties—pattern topology, stitch ratio, pattern density—play an important role in textile panel performance under load. Stiffness values derived from the optimization are higher for shallower designs and lower for the deeper cones.

INTRODUCTION

In recent years numerous projects (Gupta et al. 2020; Popescu et al. 2020; Ramsgaard Thomsen et al. 2015, 2019) have displayed the potential of CNC knits as a next-generation material for textile architecture in its integrated detailing, material differentiation, and sustainable production. Knit grading changes the geometrical performance of the textile, allowing it to steer the membrane expansion in the predefined areas under load. However, knits possess challenges of material understanding, predictability, and digital simulation, due to their multi-scalar complexity and anisotropic properties.

Currently, there are no digital solutions that would integrate the simulation of CNC-knit performance into a design model to specify fabrication data. Instead, the workflow is solved through a laborious sample-based prototyping, which inhibits scaling up and accessibility of knit application in architecture.

This paper presents a novel approach for the design-integrated simulation of CNC knits, informed by an empirical dataset analysis with the help of genetic optimization algorithms.

Existing simulation methods from fashion and computer graphics focus on human body templates, without taking into account the material stretch; rather, they represent fabric being draped over the mannequin (Kaldor, James, and Marschner 2008; ShimaSeiki 2007; STOLL 2007; Yuksel et al. 2012). Often these models are not connected to the fabrication machinery logic, although the behavior of the fabric is very realistic.

The application of knit in architecture aims to use fabrics under tension, where the geometrical performance and precision are highly crucial (Tamke et al. 2016). However, precise textile engineering methods of modeling through colliding stitches become computationally infeasible when scaling up (Kyosev and Renkens 2010). Architectural domain tools for woven membrane form-finding, although scalable, miss graded properties integration across the surface. Thus, the digital models for knitted membranes should reflect the differentiated surface properties of knit as these affect the geometry and material performance. Therefore, it is necessary to find ways to integrate graded properties of knit into design models (Ramsgaard Thomsen et al. 2016) in order to gain material understanding, inform its composition for fabrication, and promote the use of knit in architecture.

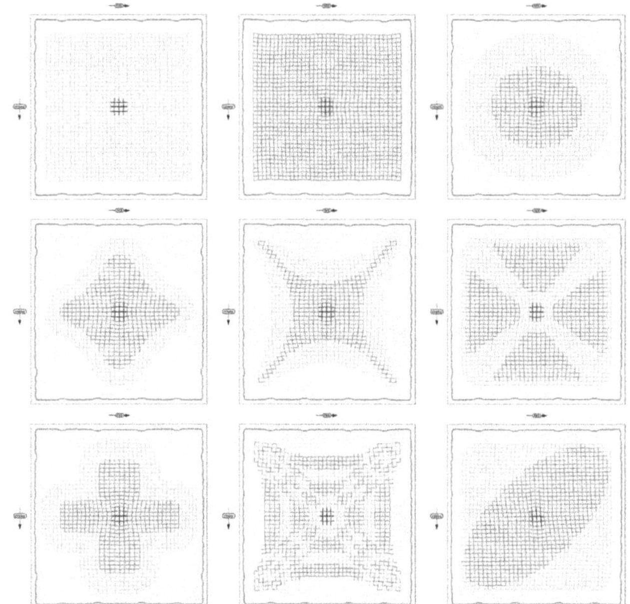

2 Nine selected designs for the experiment.

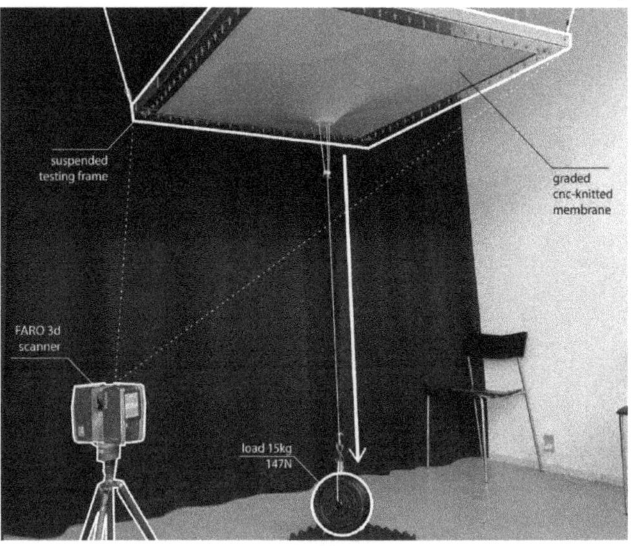

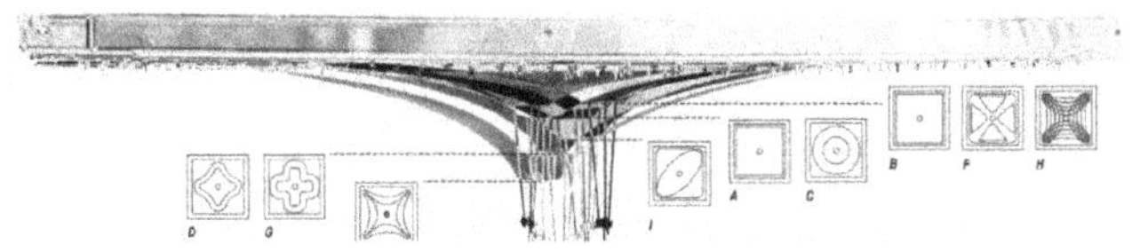

3 Testing setup: graded CNC-knitted membrane tensioned to a suspended frame, loaded with 15 kg and scanned with FARO laser scanner.

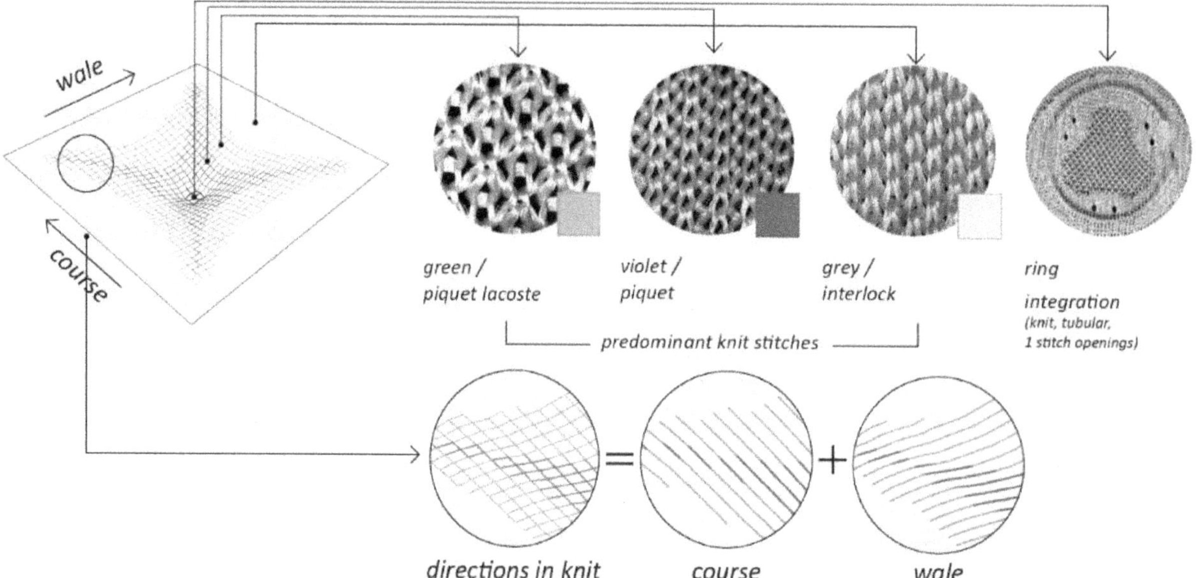

4 Digital setup for graded knitted membranes: mesh bars are sorted by color and divided into groups by the direction of wales and courses. 4

METHOD FOR SIMULATION AND TESTING OF GRADED KNITTED TEXTILES

Digital and Physical Correlation

In this paper, we present the development of a simulation method for graded knitted membranes through the KnitVault experiment that is designed to validate the method by testing the correlation between the digital and the physical aspects of the exercise.

The digital tool aims to follow the differences of physical textile panel behavior by incorporating variegated knit properties through the digital mesh grading. Despite the same yarn being used for the entire membrane surface fabrication, intertwining it into the different stitches results in a diversified fabric stiffness. As a direct yarn-to-yarn stitch modeling is computationally heavy, the abstraction of the knitted surface into a quad-based mesh is a compromise (Fig. 4).

The physical side of the experiment is supported by the industrially knitted textile panels with varied topology patterns (Fig. 1), where three predominant stitch types (piquet, piquet lacoste, and interlock) are used to steer the surface degree of expandability under load (Fig. 4). Nine pattern configurations (Fig. 2), selected for the experiment, were designed manually to create different stitch-ratio proportions and pattern-drawing geometries. Although looking back to these decisions, the designs could be more irregular in order to challenge the experiment setup.

As the textiles are knitted on the industrial CNC-knitting machine using digitally generated bitmaps and equivalent machine settings throughout the production, the pattern difference is the only varied parameter between the panels. Once fabricated and attached to the frame, the dissimilarity in planar pretension is noticeable across the designs, which indicates the effect of patterns on the textile behavior.

Next, the panels are loaded with a 15 kg weight from the center, which results in different stretch depths, related to the pattern differences (Fig. 3). Each geometry is scanned with a FARO laser scanner in order to transfer the data into the digital environment. The processed point clouds of the loaded panels are compared to the corresponding simulations (K2 Engineering plug-in for Kangaroo [Brandt 2016]) for further digital tool calibration.

The directionality of the quad-mesh (UV arrangement) associates with the wale-course nature of knitted structures, where heterogeneous properties are defined through the mesh segments' stiffness assignment across the surface, defined by the pattern boundaries and the direction. The direction of knit is important to take into account, as it contributes to an anisotropic behavior of the fabric. Therefore, separate stiffness values are assigned to the course and wale directions of the mesh.

While the stiffness of the yarn is normally a known value, provided by the producer, *the stiffness of the knitted fabric made of this yarn remains unknown*, as various stitches can be used to form the textile. For that reason, it poses an interesting challenge to understand these relations in order to build a reliable, yet computationally viable, simulation tool of graded knitted fabrics.

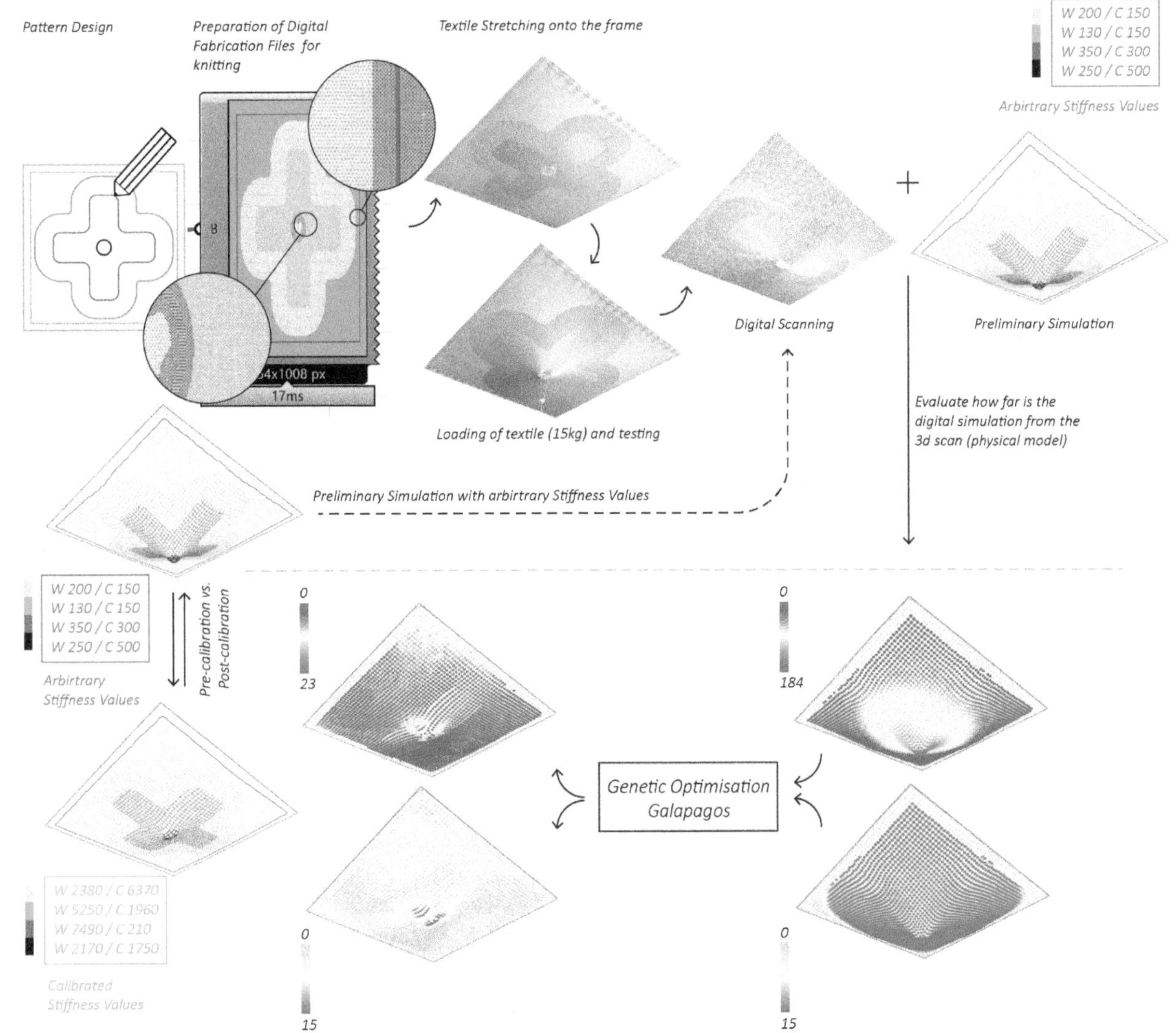

5 Diagram of the workflow for graded knitted membrane design, digital setup, simulation, testing, and digital tool calibration. 5

Digital Deviation Optimization

At first, when the real stiffness values are yet undiscovered, arbitrary numbers are assigned to the pattern zones in order to complete the simulation. This gives an arbitrary mesh geometry to work with.

The simulation follows the same steps as in the physical installation of the fabric onto the test rig. In the beginning, the textile sample is stretched in plane with the testing frame and only then loaded with the weight. In the same way the pretension is introduced in the digital environment. These pretension values are then used in the second step of the simulation, when the pretensioned mesh is loaded with the 147 N in the z (down) direction (Fig. 6a, b, c). This allows us to build a more correct simulation of the three-dimensional geometry, corresponding more closely to the real behavior.

The point clouds are translated to the mesh geometry by projecting an arbitrary mesh (in red) to it and rebuilding the same topology mesh (in blue, Fig. 6e). This way there are two meshes with identical topologies that can be overlapped and compared. The comparison lies in calculating the distances between the mesh nodes (Fig. 6f), where it is visualized through the red-yellow-blue color mapping projected onto the simulation mesh (Fig. 6g). In the magenta mapping, the nodes are colored pink if the distance exceeds 15 mm (Fig. 6h).

At first, the mesh with the arbitrary values deviates a lot from the point cloud geometry (Fig. 6d). The prevalence of the magenta nodes (Fig. 6h) means a high degree of discrepancy between the simulation and the equivalent physical geometry. The aim of the task is to lower the distance between the red and the blue mesh by achieving

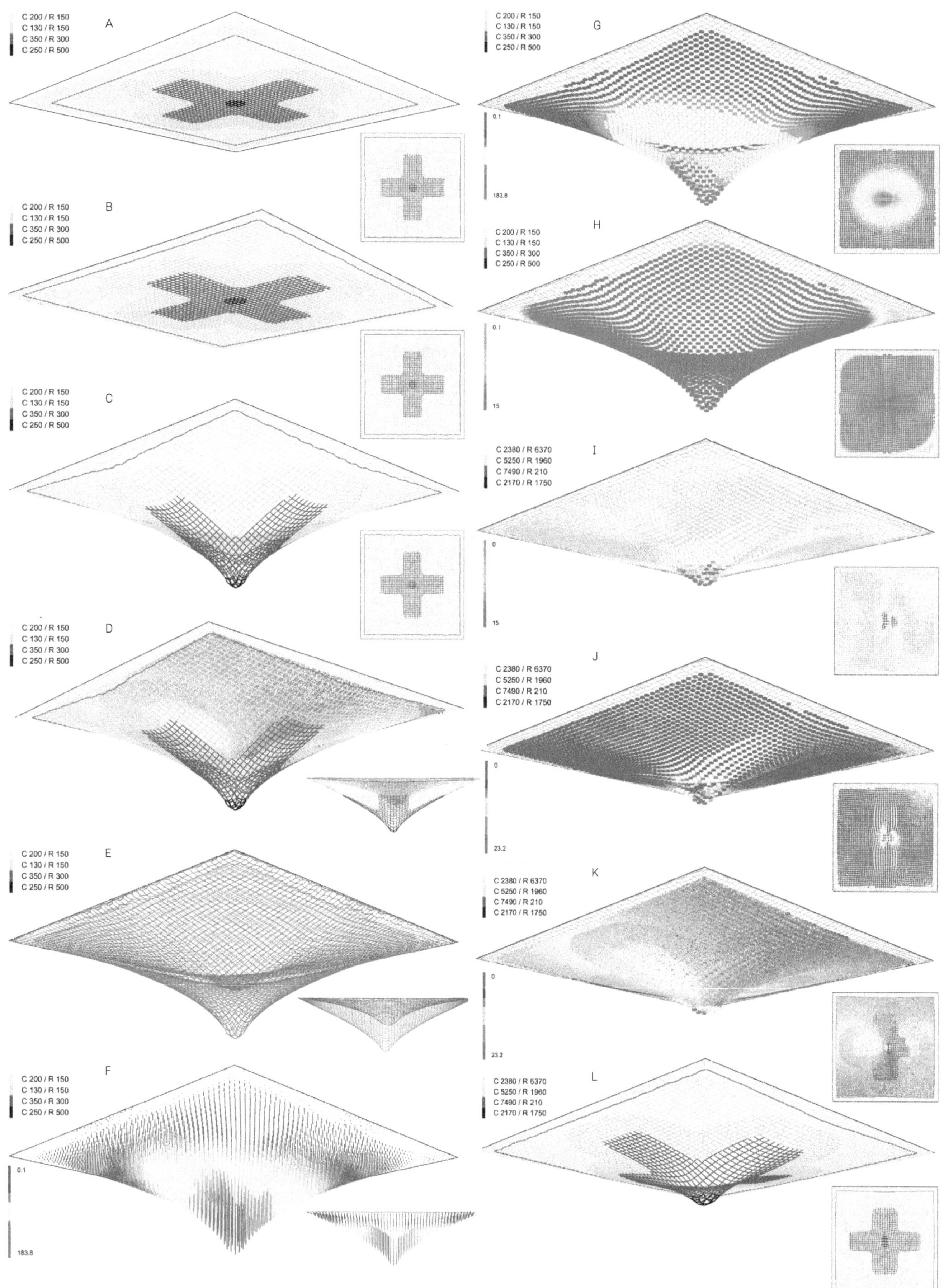

6 Step-by-step actions of graded membrane stiffness value optimization membrane design, digital setup, simulation, testing, and digital tool calibration

7 Incremental improvement of the stiffness value set by reduction of deviation value between the simulated mesh and the point cloud. 7

the smallest maximum distance and reducing the number of magenta nodes in the simulated mesh.

To derive the set of unknown stiffness values, a genetic optimization algorithm is used to minimize the distance between the digital mesh and the point cloud of the corresponding textiles (Fig. 5). The optimization loop is established with the Galapagos plug-in for Grasshopper Rutten 2020), integrated in a double solver simulation with Kangaroo (Piker 2017) and K2 Engineering workflows. Here the engine is going over the stiffness value combinatorics within the given boundaries (150–8500 MPa) and applying them to the mesh zones. With each stiffness value application, the algorithm is measuring the distance from the resulting simulated mesh to the point cloud. If it exceeds the maximum desired value, the search for the optimal stiffness values continues until the deviation is acceptably low. On average, the search for each design solution took 10–15 hours and an average of 20,000–25,000 iterations. Figure 7 shows the incremental reduction of both magenta nodes and the maximum distance, while the mesh is getting closer to the point cloud geometry.

RESULTS AND DISCUSSION

This paper describes the method of stiffness value determination for graded knitted membrane material. Initially, unknown mesh stiffness values are optimized, using corresponding point clouds as target geometries for minimizing the distance to the mesh. As a result of the exercise, the stiffness values that would bring the digital mesh very close to the corresponding physical model geometry have been found (Fig. 8). The tolerance between the point cloud and the simulated mesh is between 16 mm and 36 mm, which is acceptable for the expandable fabrics. Although the results for each geometry were very promising, the stiffness values for the same fabric type differ from design to design, and the cross-application of discovered values would give deviating results. This means, for example, that the stiffness values that work perfectly for design D would not work for F. This challenge provoked the authors to rethink the method and to find a potential system in the results to improve the method for the future development of the work.

For that reason all the discovered stiffness value sets are cross-applied to all the other designs. This exercise is explained in Figure 9 through D-, C-, and E-based optimized results. The results for each cross-application are sorted based on the deviation from the corresponding point cloud: from the smallest in the target design to the most deviating in the rest of them. When looking at the selection of design pairs based on their stitch ratio proportion similarity (D/G, C/E, I/H, E/H), interesting findings emerged. In the analysis of the results, the following aspects are taken into account:

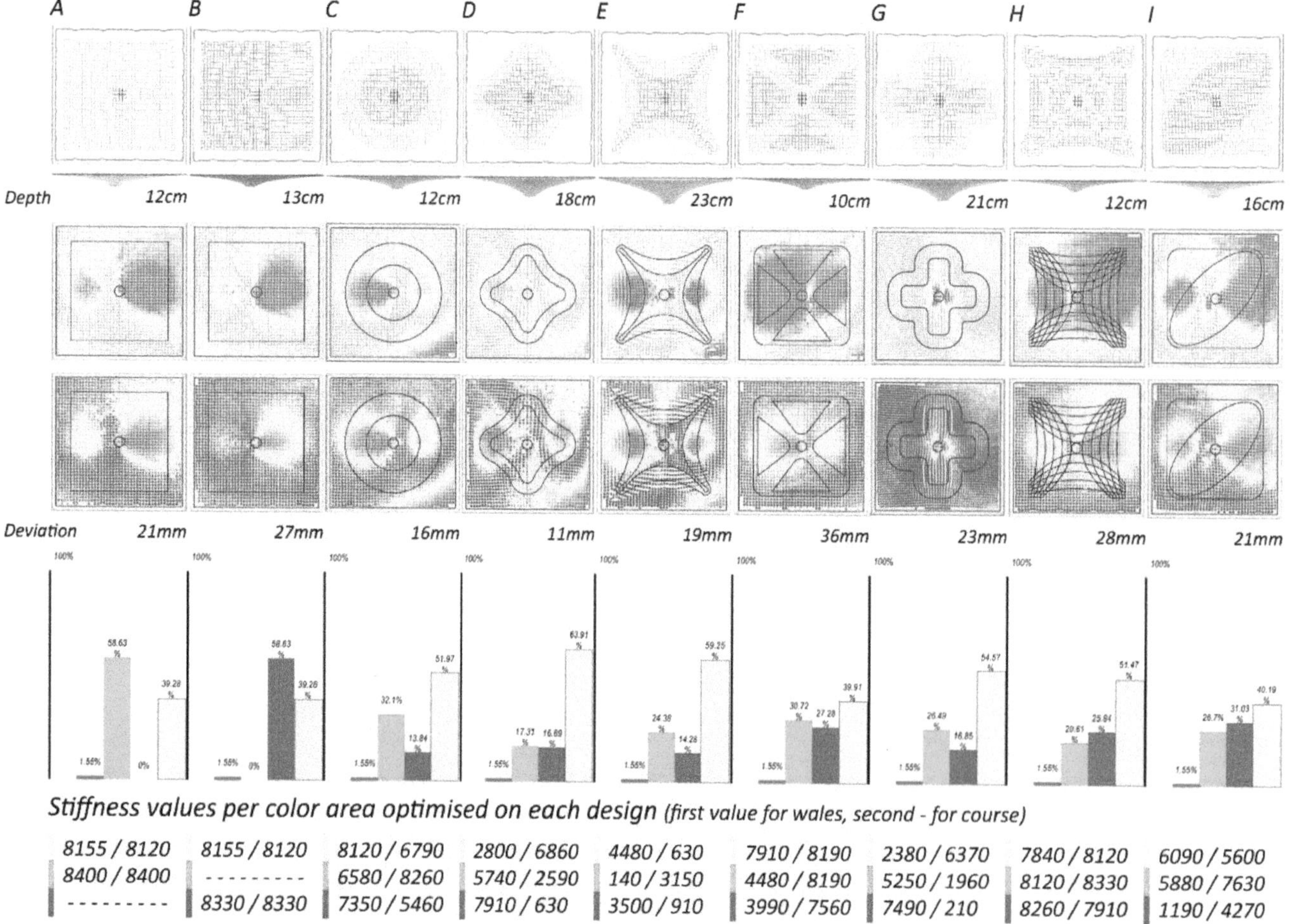

8 Diagram showing (top to bottom) the tested design range, optimization results mapped onto the mesh, stitch ratio proportions, and stiffness values. 8

stitch ratio, geometry of the pattern, and the depth of the cones under the stretch.

Cross-application of stiffness values between topologically similar patterns ("cross-like" in D/G) shows less deviation from the equivalent point clouds (Fig. 9 top), while topologically different patterns, although with similar stitch ratio (C/E), resulted in a larger error to the point clouds (Fig. 9 middle). Topologically similar designs with a close stitch ratio (E/H) but variation in pattern density (dispersed checkerboard vs. large shapes) performed a noncompatibility of stiffness values. The numbers resulting from optimization on the shallower designs (A, B, C, F, H) are higher, while the values trained on deeper geometries (D, E, G) are lower (Fig. 10). This is logical, as the stiffer mesh has more resilience against the load and therefore results in a shallower cone.

Overall, the value of discovered stiffness values remains doubtful, as it is unreliable to reuse them for pattern geometry other than the one that was used to train the optimization. The discrepancies among the stiffness values can be explained by the lack of pattern boundary tracing. As the pattern linework was not traced in the point clouds, it is challenging to evaluate whether the simulated mesh has taken the exact right shape. Possibly, while the overall mesh boundaries were quite close after optimization, the inner boundaries of the pattern might remain off.

Additionally, in the described optimization setup, the relations between the stitch type areas were not defined but rather left too open. The same stiffness value range condition (150–8500 MPa), introduced to all the zones, created a situation where the same stitch type zone is obtaining both the low and the high stiffness values in the different designs.

REFLECTION AND CONCLUSION

Despite the challenges encountered in the universality of the method, the presented workflow is an important step toward an understanding of the graded knit behavior. The optimization of stiffness values per design showed a high degree of precision, interlinking the pattern design, fabrication data, physical testing data, and the corresponding digital simulation.

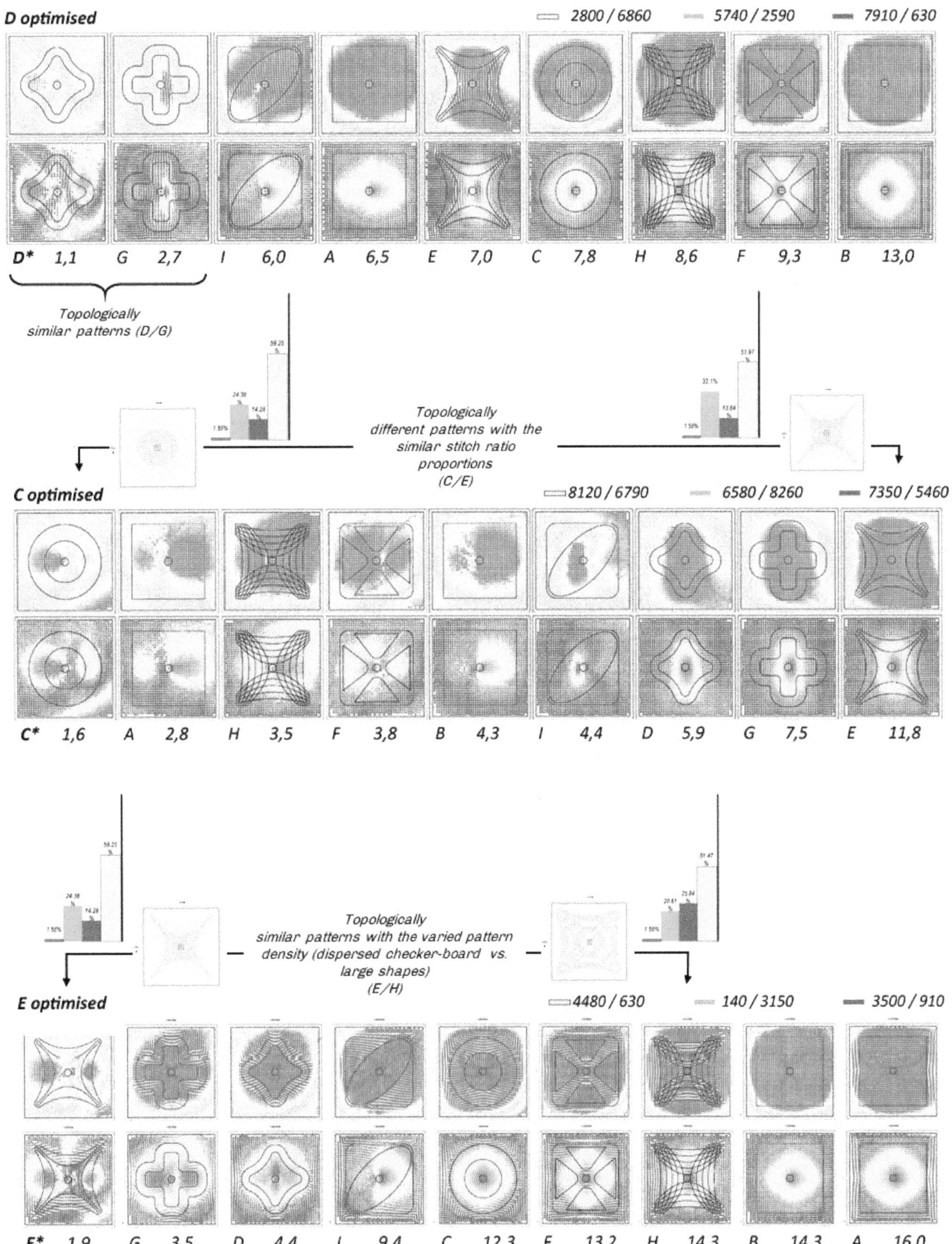

9 Results of the cross-application of the stiffness values trained on a particular design.

9

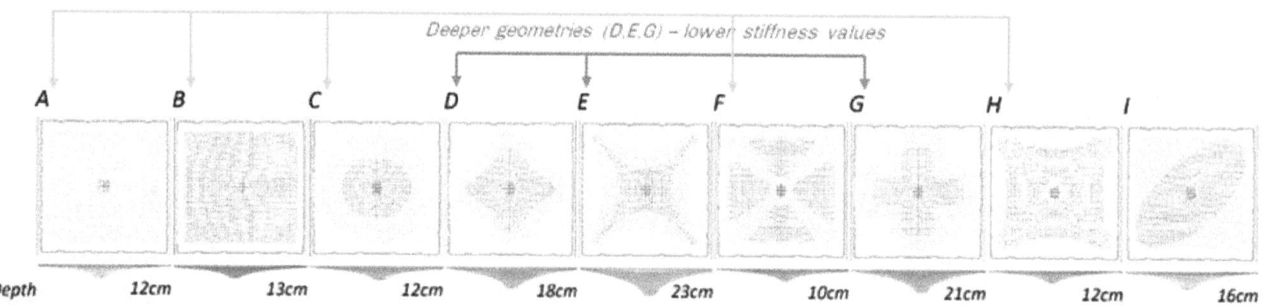

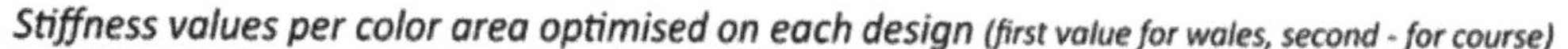

Stiffness values per color area optimised on each design (first value for wales, second - for course)

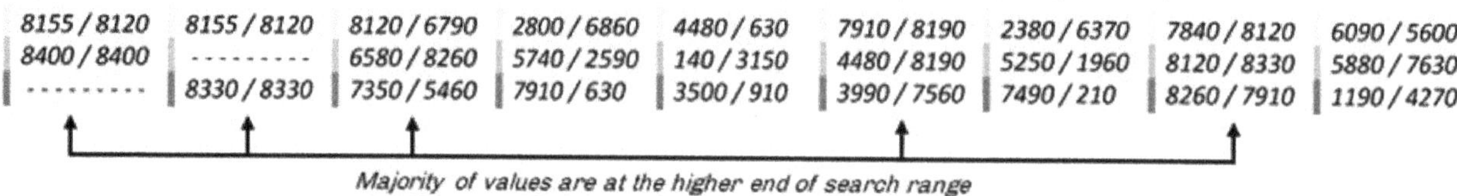

8155/8120 | 8155/8120 | 8120/6790 | 2800/6860 | 4480/630 | 7910/8190 | 2380/6370 | 7840/8120 | 6090/5600
8400/8400 | --------- | 6580/8260 | 5740/2590 | 140/3150 | 4480/8190 | 5250/1960 | 8120/8330 | 5880/7630
--------- | 8330/8330 | 7350/5460 | 7910/630 | 3500/910 | 3990/7560 | 7490/210 | 8260/7910 | 1190/4270
Majority of values are at the higher end of search range

10 The resulting stiffness value sets for each panel design.

10

A future research work would imply a further increase of digital complexity, introducing a wider search range of stiffness values, finding a way to quantify the pattern density (dispersed vs. large zones), establishing the relations between the stitch types (stiff vs. expandable), and introducing additional springs for reflecting the stitch type differences. These implementations might potentially increase the method's precision, transforming it to the tool for generating stiffness values for heterogeneous knitted membranes.

A more reliable digital tool for graded knitted membranes would allow for a greater confidence in design with this challenging but high potential material for architectural applications. Predictability of graded knit material behavior would build trust in using it for large-scale architectural elements, where heterogeneous material density and elasticity can contribute to functionality and structural performance while being highly sustainable and waste-free in manufacturing.

ACKNOWLEDGMENTS

Many thanks to SIA ViolaStils for a productive collaboration on textile panels production, especially to Vladimirs Dementjevs and Jelena Bruzuka.

REFERENCES

Brandt, Cecilie. 2016. "Calibrated Modelling of Form—Active Structures." MSc thesis. Copenhagen, Denmark: DTU Danish Technical University.

Gupta, Sachin, Ying Tan, Pei Chia, Christyasto Pambudi, Yu Quek, Christine Yogiaman, and Kenneth Tracy. 2020. "Prototyping Knit Tensegrity Shells: A Design-to-Fabrication Workflow." *Springer Nature Applied Sciences Switzerland* 2 (7). https://doi.org/10.1007/s42452-020-2693-4.

Kaldor, Jonathan M., Doug L. James, and Steve Marschner. 2008. "Simulating Knitted Cloth at the Yarn Level." In *ACM Transactions on Graphics* 27 (3): 1-9. https://doi.org/10.1145/1360612.1360664.

Kyosev, Yordan, and Wilfried Renkens. 2010. "Modelling and Visualization of Knitted Fabrics." In *Modelling and Predicting Textile Behaviour*, edited by X. Chen, 255–262. Woodhead Publishing. https://doi.org/10.1533/9781845697211.1.225.

Piker, Daniel. 2017. *Kangaroo Physics*. V.2.42. https://www.food4rhino.com/en/app/kangaroo-physics. PC.

Popescu, Mariana, Matthias Rippmann, Andrew Liew, Robert Flatt, Tom Van Mele, and Philippe Block. 2020. "Structural Design, Digital Fabrication and Construction of the Cable-Net and Knitted Formwork of the KnitCandela Concrete Shell." *Structures*, no. 31 (June): 1287–1299. https://doi.org/10.1016/j.istruc.2020.02.013.

Ramsgaard Thomsen, Mette, Martin Tamke, Anders Holden Deleuran, Ida Katrine Friis Tinning, Henrik Leander Evers, Christoph Gengnagel, and Michel Schmeck. 2015. "Hybrid Tower, Designing Soft Structures." In *Modelling Behaviour*, edited by M. R. Thomsen et al., 87–99. Springer International Publishing.

Ramsgaard Thomsen, Mette, Martin Tamke, Ayelet Karmon, Jenny Underwood, Christoph Gengnagel, Natalie Stranghöner, and Jörg Uhlemann. 2016. "Knit as Bespoke Material Practice for Architecture." In *ACADIA 2016: Posthuman Frontiers: Data, Designers, and Cognitive Machines [Proceedings of the 36th Annual Conference of the Association for Computer Aided Design in Architecture (ACADIA)]*, Ann Arbor, MI, 27–29 October 2016, edited by K. Velikov, S. Ahlquist, M. del Campo, and G. Thün, 280–289. CUMINCAD.

Ramsgaard Thomsen, Mette, Yuliya Sinke Baranovskaya, Filipa Monteiro, Julian Lienhard, Riccardo La Magna, and Martin Tamke. 2019. "Systems for Transformative Textile Structures in CNC Knitted Fabrics – Isoropia." In *Softening the Habitats [Proceedings of the TensiNet Symposium 2019]*, Milan, Italy, 3–5 June 2019, 95–110. TensiNet Association.

Rutten, David. 2020. *Grasshopper*. V.1.0.0007. Robert McNeel & Associates. PC.

ShimaSeiki. 2007. *SDS-One APEX*. https://www.shimaseiki.com/virtual_sampling/.

STOLL. 2007. *M1 Plus*. https://www.stoll.com/en/software/m1plusr/.

Tamke, Martin, Yuliya Baranovskaya, Anders Deleuran, Filipa Monteiro, Raul Manuel Esteves Sousa Fangueiro, Natalie Stranghöhner, Jörg Uhlemann, Michel Schmeck, Christoph Gengnagel, and Mette Ramsgaard Thomsen. 2016. "Bespoke Materials for Bespoke Textile Architecture." In *Spatial Structures in the 21st Century*, edited by K. Kawaguchi, M. Ohsaki, and T. Takeuchi. Tokyo, Japan.

Yuksel, Cem, Jonathan M. Kaldor, Doug L. James, and Steve Marschner. 2012. "Stitch Meshes for Modeling Knitted Clothing with Yarn-Level Detail." *ACM Transactions on Graphics* 31 (4): Article 37. https://doi.org/10.1145/2185520.2185533.

IMAGE CREDITS

All images and drawings are by the authors.

Yuliya Sinke Baranovskaya is a PhD Fellow at CITA—Centre for IT and Architecture. She is conducting her research within the UN Sustainable Goal 12 Responsible Consumption and Production framework, where she is investigating the application of CNC-knitted membranes in architecture and in particular the aspects of digital simulation and design models for graded textile properties.

Martin Tamke is pursuing design-led research on the interface and implications of computational design and its materialization. He joined the newly founded research center CITA in 2006 and shaped its design-based research practice. His focus is on new design and fabrication models and workflows with an emphasis on feedback from environment and process. The latest research focuses on biobased material and is characterized by strong interdisciplinary links to computer science, with a focus on machine learning and 3D sensing; structural engineering, with a focus on simulation and ultralight hybrid structures; and material science, with a focus on bespoke CNC knit, engineered timber, and additive fabrication with recycled and biobased materials.

Mette Ramsgaard Thomsen examines the intersections between architecture and new computational design processes. During the last 15 years her focus has been on the profound changes that digital technologies instigate in the way architecture is thought, designed, and built. In 2005 she founded the Centre for IT and Architecture research group (CITA) at the Royal Academy of Fine Arts, School of Architecture, Design and Conservation, where she has piloted a special research focus on the new digital-material relations that digital technologies bring forth. Investigating advanced computer modeling, digital fabrication, and material specification, CITA has been central in forming an international research field examining the changes to material practice in architecture.

Generating and Optimizing a Funicular Arch Floor Structure

Hao Zheng
Xinyu Wang
Zehua Qi
Shixuan Sun
Masoud Akbarzadeh

Polyhedral Structures Laboratory, Stuart Weitzman School of Design, University of Pennsylvania

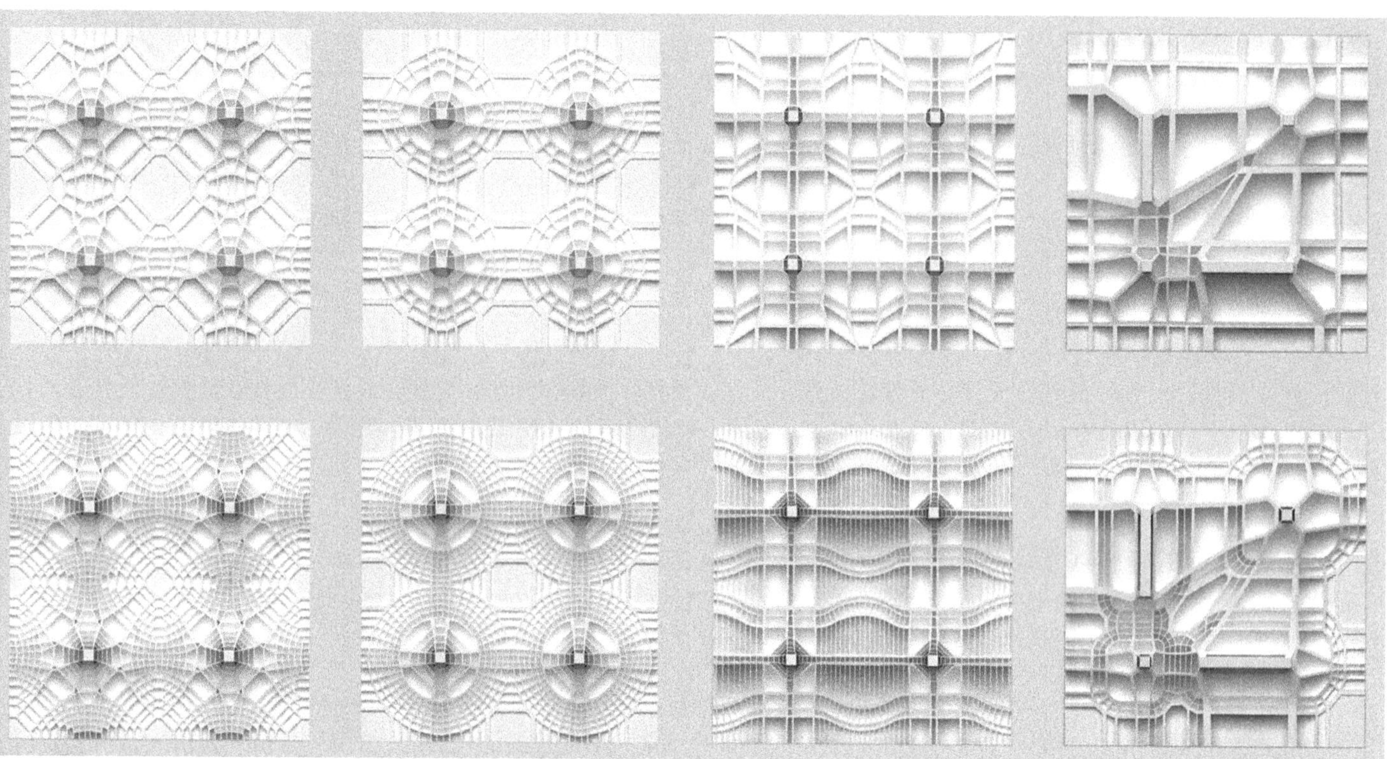

1 Different structural forms generated by graphic statics.

ABSTRACT

In this paper, we propose a geometry-based generative design method to generate and optimize a floor structure with funicular building members. This method challenges the antiquated column system, which has been used for more than a century. By inputting the floor plan with the positions of columns, designers can generate a variety of funicular supporting structures, expanding the choice of floor structure designs beyond simply columns and beams and encouraging the creation of architectural spaces with more diverse design elements. We further apply machine learning techniques (artificial neural networks) to evaluate and optimize the structural performance and constructability of the funicular structure, thus finding the optimal solutions within the almost infinite solution space. To achieve this, a machine learning model is trained and used as a fast evaluator to help the evolutionary algorithm find the optimal designs. This interdisciplinary method combines computer science and structural design, providing flexible design choices for generating floor structures.

2 History of concrete roof structures. From top left to bottom right: (a) Riverside Church; (b) Lanificio Gatti; (c) Palazzo del Lavoro; (d) floor design from Block Research Group; (e) Zoology Lecture Hall at the University of Freiburg; (f) Dfab House. Image credits: (a) Henry C. Pelton; (b) Pier Luigi Nervi; (c) Pier Luigi Nervi; (d) Philippe Block; (e) Bruno Krupp; (f) NCCR Digital Fabrication.

INTRODUCTION

Background

The Maison Dom-Ino was invented more than 100 years ago by Le Corbusier (Anderson 1984) and is still widely used in open floor-plan designs. The column supports the beam while the beam supports the ceiling, which covers the main space.

However, with the development of computational design techniques, a new possibility is emerging: a funicular arch structure that can replace columns and beams. Recent developments and explorations in funicular arch structures by Rafael Guastavino, floor designs by Philippe Block (Adriaenssens et al. 2014), and reinforced concrete by Luigi Nervi have brought out new aesthetics and the possibilities of more economical structure systems (Fig. 2).

Graphic Statics

In the design of the funicular arch structures, the graphic statics method is widely used to evaluate and generate the force and form. Graphic statics (2D/3D) is a geometry-based structural design and analysis method. The history of graphic statics can be traced back to the Hellenistic Age, when Archimedes used algebraic formulas and illustrations to explain in his book *On the Equilibrium of Planes* that the weight of an object is inversely proportional to the distance under equilibrium conditions in the law of levers.

The Renaissance was the beginning of modern mechanics. Galileo Galilei, Robert Hooke, and Isaac Newton made great contributions to the scientific development of mechanics. Specific to graphic statics, mechanics contains three important factors: forces are represented as vectors, forces can be composed and decomposed, and a balance of forces can be achieved under equilibrium conditions. In 1586, Simon Stevin (1586) proved the parallelogram rule of the decomposition and synthesis of forces with the load test on an inclined plane, pioneering the use of geometry to find the equilibrium of forces. In 1864, after systematically reviewing and expanding the field's knowledge, Karl Culmann named this subject "*graphische Statik*" (graphic statics) in his book *Die Graphische Statik* (Culmann 1864), which was widely accepted by the academic community. Graphic statics was then formally established with the successful follow-up research in 2D graphic statics (Bow 1873; Cremona 1890; Maxwell 1864, 1870).

However, 2D graphic statics has its own limitations (Akbarzadeh 2016); only 2D abstractions of 3D structures can be designed, although Culmann (1864) also proposed a 3D solution of graphic statics, which was never explained or proven in detail in his book. Maxwell (1864) applied this 3D method to a specific case of geometric operation, but the complex calculations stopped him from further research in 3D graphic statics, and this theory has been left intact since 1864.

But with the recent development of computing power, the complex geometric calculations of 3D graphic statics can be now performed through digital computation. Thus, 3D graphic statics has attracted the attention of researchers again. Aided by computers, architects developed digital algorithms to generate 3D forms from 3D force diagrams (Akbarzadeh, Van Mele, and Block 2015; Block and Ochsendorf 2007; Fivet and Zastavni 2013; Schrems and Kotnik 2013; Theodoropoulos 2000; Van Mele and Block 2014; Van Mele et al. 2012). The computational solution of 3D graphic statics helps designers generate 3D polyhedral forms by manipulating force diagrams with given boundary conditions.

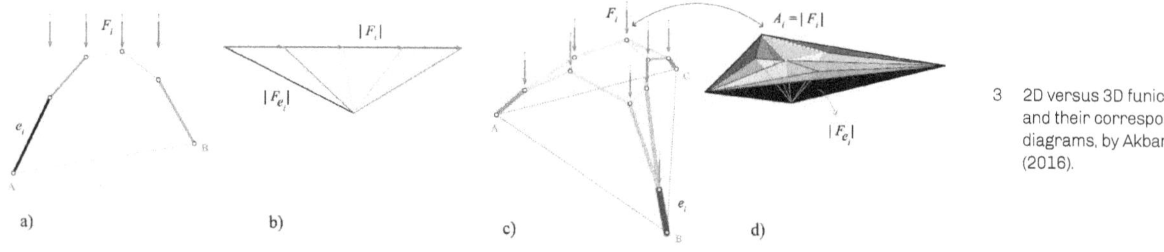

3 2D versus 3D funicular solutions and their corresponding force diagrams, by Akbarzadeh et al. (2016).

In the form-finding of 3D graphic statics, the transformation rules from force diagrams to form diagrams work much as they do in 2D. Figure 3 shows the comparison of 2D and 3D graphic statics, where (b) and (d) are the force diagrams and (a) and (c) are the form diagrams. Each applied load F_i in the force diagram represents a corresponding load force F_i in the form diagram, with the two perpendicular to each other. Each exterior supporting force F_{ei} in the force diagram results in a structural member *ei* in the form diagram, which shows the corresponding form of a force diagram. But the difference is that, in 2D graphic statics, the forces are drawn as lines, while in 3D graphic statics the forces are represented as planar surfaces, so the forces and the corresponding forms in 3D graphic statics have one more dimension than the forces and forms in 2D graphic statics.

By generating or adjusting the polyhedral force geometries, different funicular forms can be provided using 3D graphic statics. The advantage of this form-finding algorithm is that the generated structures are always in equilibrium under a given boundary condition. As long as the force diagram is a set of closed polyhedrons, the corresponding form can stay balanced under the action of applied forces. Therefore, when designing a form with given applied loads, architects can divide the force polyhedrons with additional interior faces to achieve complexity while maintaining the form equilibrium.

Machine Learning

Besides the focus on 3D graphic statics, the interest in the application of machine learning to design and optimization has increased considerably (Showkatbakhsh, Erdine, and Rodriguez 2020; Zheng 2020), in which researchers regard machine learning models as evaluation tools to help find the optimized options in design solutions.

For example, a machine learning model can be trained to classify images of geometries based on the architect's aesthetic tendency (Turlock and Steinfeld 2019). Examples of the funicular structures are translated into black-and-white spatially distinguished images, then used to train a convolutional neural network (CNN) model. The authors randomly generate a large number of structural models, flatten them into images, and then ask volunteers if they think the images are beautiful. By this method, the trained CNN can learn the aesthetic indicators in the sense of architecture based on the answers of the volunteers. Combined with the traditional structural evaluation indicators, the program can find a solution that is evaluated to be both beautiful and structurally stable.

Furthermore, neural networks can be used to solve the computational problem in the field of structural optimization (Aksöz and Preisinger 2019). The authors use an artificial neural network (ANN) to learn the stress conditions and coping methods in finite element analysis, then use the generated sample data to train the neural network, and finally apply the trained neural network to generate structure solutions based on the stress conditions given by the user. In order to simplify the problem, the authors divide the complex structure system into small units, and the overall structure is composed of each small unit optimized by the ANN. Similarly, the structural computation process is optimized by training ANN models (Yetkin and Sorguç 2019), but the optimization is applied to small truss structures.

Problem Statement and Objectives

In this paper, we aim to answer the following questions: (1) how to integrate the novel strategies in structure and computation and develop a digital process that could translate and optimize routine structural systems into funicular structures as another design option for architects; and (2) how to redefine and optimize the construction module using machine learning techniques.

Therefore, in this research, we propose a geometry-based generative design method to generate and optimize a floor structure with funicular building members. This method challenges the antiquated column system, which has been used for more than a century. By inputting the floor plan with the positions of columns, designers can generate a variety of funicular supporting structures, resulting in more choices for designing a floor structure, rather than only columns and beams. This ability to generate floor

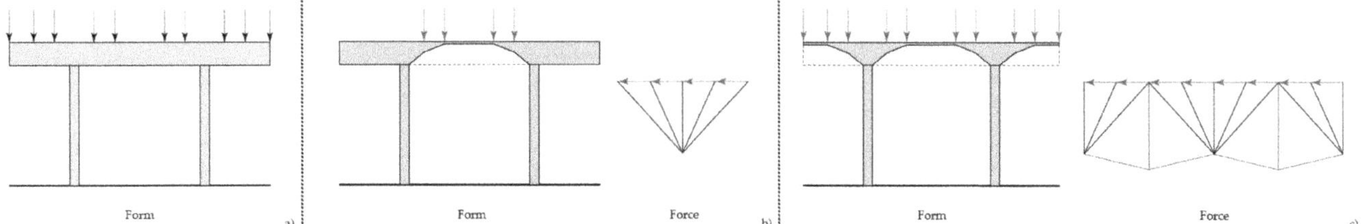

4 Funicular solution for 2D domino structure: (a) flat structure; (b) arch structure and its force diagram; (c) extendable arch structure and its force diagram. 4

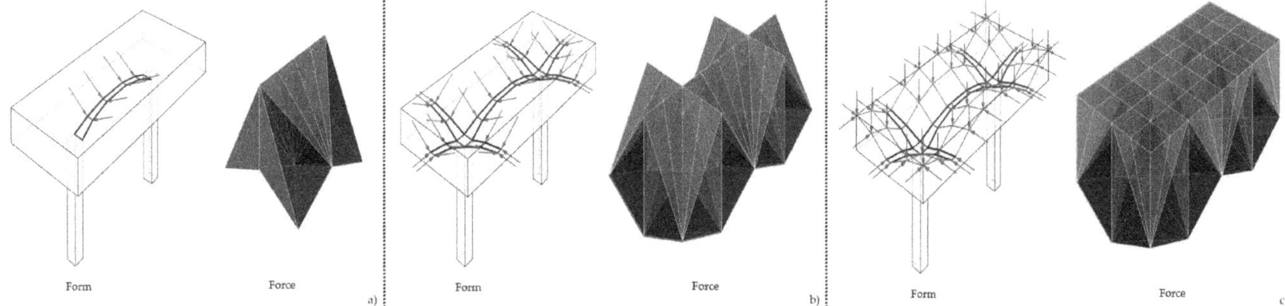

5 Funicular solution for 3D domino structure: (a) flat structure; (b) arch structure and its force diagram; (c) extendable arch structure and its force diagram. 5

structures with funicular forms can foster the development of architectural spaces with more diverse design elements. We further apply machine learning techniques (ANNs) to evaluate and optimize the funicular structure's structural performance and constructability, thus finding the optimal solutions within the almost infinite solution space. To that end, a machine learning model is trained and used as a fast evaluator to help the evolutionary algorithm find the optimal designs. This interdisciplinary method bridges computer science and structural design, providing flexible design choices for generating floor structures.

METHODOLOGY

The Topology and the Subdivision

To redesign a space with the Maison Dom-Ino system into funicular forms, the topology should be defined, including the graph relationship (connectivity) between each column. For any floor plan with columns in any position, straight lines can be drawn between pairs of columns, representing the main structural members. Once there is at least one line connecting to each column and no lines are overlapping, the topology is legal, and the complete graph shows the initial structural members.

Figures 4 and 5 explain the logic for constructing forces that generate a more efficient and ecological funicular solution from a regular domino module as force and form dual diagrams. Shown in Figure 5, in the funicular alternative, the connection between two columns is reestablished with a funicular arch by designing an aggregable 3D force diagram. Aggregating the forces causes the connections in the form to further expand to boundaries or other supports, which ultimately become the main structural network among the columns. The total applied load, on the other hand, is represented by a horizontal polygon face at the top of the force diagram. Subdividing the total applied load and converging the subdivided faces to different points in the force diagram allows additional load paths to be generated in the form, and through them the applied loads are transferred to the main structures.

Additionally, Figures 6 and 7 show the steps for generating funicular-arch floor structures from 2D layouts. The first step is to identify connections between vertical structural elements and establish the connectivity map. From the connectivity map, one can determine the force boundary that demonstrates how the applied load is distributed to each structural member. The 3D force diagram is then created for each force boundary. The force diagrams can be aggregated to generate the resulting form. Further, as shown in the different topologies for layouts with columns and walls, the geometries of the constraints can also affect the connectivity map and the force distribution.

Regarding the graph as an initial form diagram, the force diagram can be generated using the graphic statics method as a dual geometry (Akbarzadeh, Van Mele, and Block 2015). The force diagram represents the internal and external force distribution. Subdividing the force diagram divides the internal forces into several subforces, thus resulting in internal structural members. With the final subdivided force diagram, the graphic statics method is used again to generate the form diagram as a dual diagram under the boundary constraints of the initial site. Therefore, a

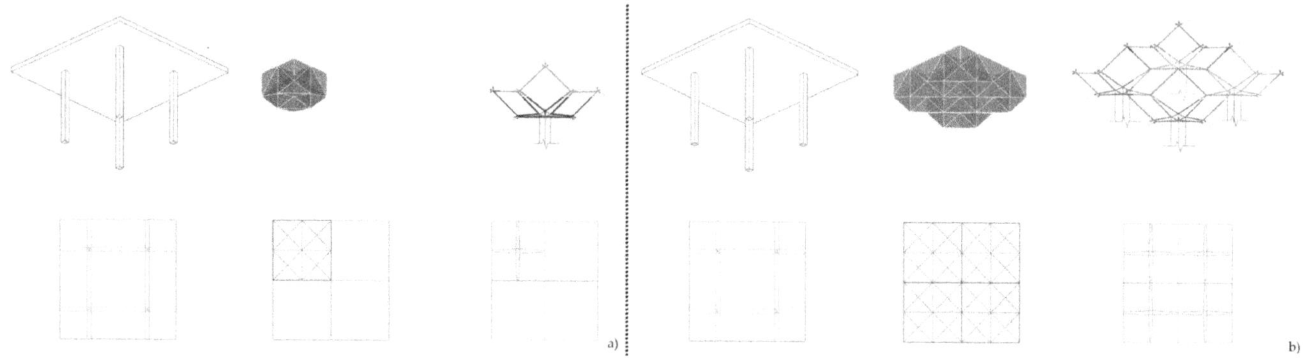

a) b)

6 Funicular solution derived from simple layout (with 4 columns). 6

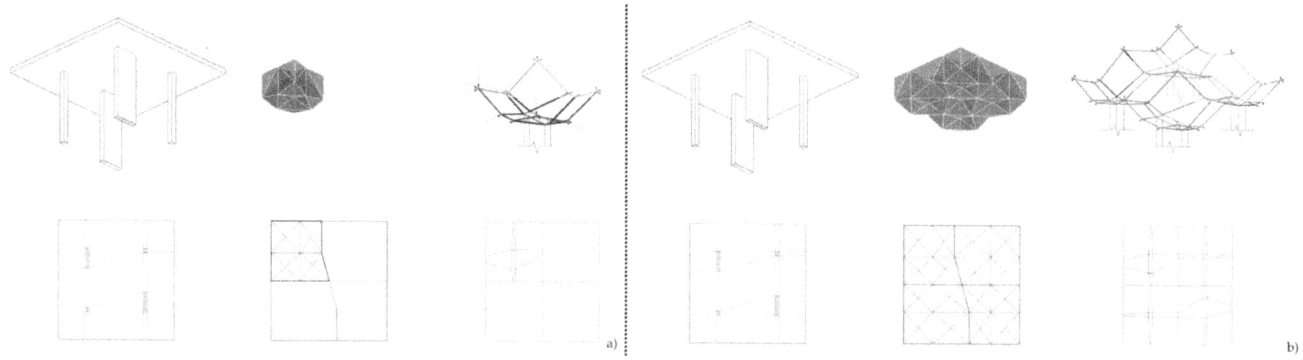

a) b)

7 Funicular solution derived from simple layout (with 2 columns and 2 walls). 7

8 Subdivision exploration. 8

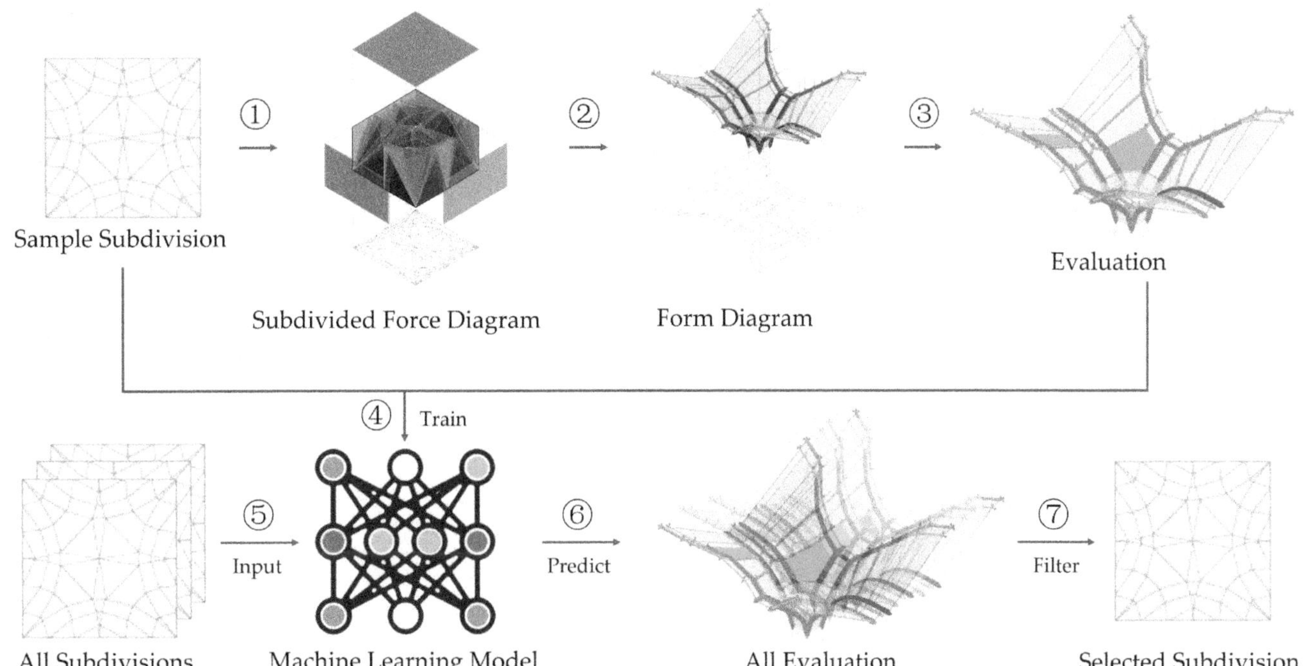

9 Workflow of machine learning assisted form-finding. 9

funicular arch structure can be designed through this method. With different subdivision strategies, the method can provide designers with highly complex and diverse design options (Fig. 8).

Machine Learning Form-Finding

There is an almost infinite number of structural forms with different topology and subdivision rules. Optimization is achieved by evaluating each form in terms of its structural performance and material usage. However, traditional optimization methods—for example, enumeration and genetic algorithms (GAs)—usually incur an unacceptable time cost during the process. Therefore, we propose a feed-forward neural network that learns the mapping between the topology using the subdivision rules and the evaluation criteria (Fig. 9). By training with a small amount of pregenerated data, the trained neural network gains the ability to predict the structural performance and the material use with high accuracy within milliseconds. Using this neural network model, the form-finding process requires less time, finding the best solutions (Zheng, Moosavi, and Akbarzadeh 2020).

In detail, the sample subdivision patterns are generated as the training set, in which the parameters to control the subdivision become the input neurons of the neural network. The subdivided form diagrams can be generated according to the subdivided force diagrams and then be evaluated based on their structural properties, which become the output neurons of the neural network. With the sigmoid as the activation function and the mean square error as the loss function, an ANN can be constructed and trained, containing several hidden layers according to the training accuracy.

After training, the neural network becomes an agent with the knowledge to quickly evaluate structural properties. With the trained neural network model, all possible combinations of the subdivision parameters can be input for evaluation, and, according to the outputted values, the solutions with the best performance can be filtered, thus finding the best forms.

RESULTS

The Redesign of Space with Random Columns

To test the feasibility of this method, we randomly generate a space with a rectangular floor plan and 11 columns. We choose this example as the case study of using the funicular structure to redesign the architectural space (Fig. 10.1). The center points of those 11 columns can be regarded as the connecting points for the topology. The topology of those connecting points contains 10 fixed lines to the boundary and 30 optional internal lines, which further results in 88 different types of topology. The subdivided force diagrams can be generated by subdividing the 88 force diagrams derived from the topology with a controlling parameter from 0 to 1; the funicular forms can then be created.

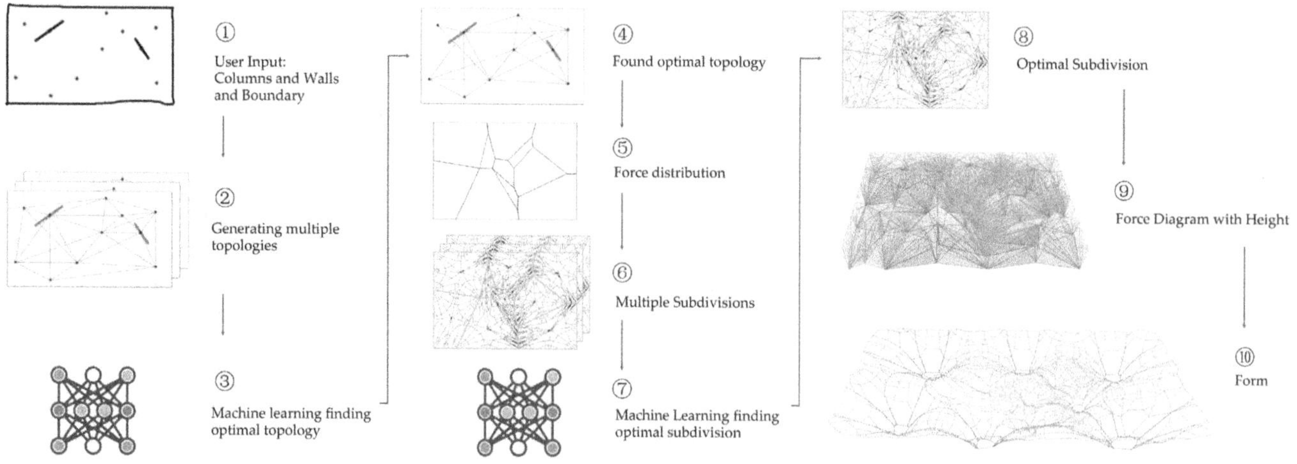

10 Workflow for generating and optimizing a funicular arch floor structure.

10

Machine Learning Models

In the process of generating the funicular forms, there are 88 types of topology and one parameter with continuous values, which control the generation. Therefore, each form can be represented by an 89-dimension input vector (1 value for the subdivision parameter, and 88 values to represent the typologies using a "one-hot encoding" method appropriate for nonordered categorical data), and the evaluation is a two-dimension output vector showing the values of the two criteria. After the experiment, we found an optimal setting for the hidden layers and the activation and loss functions that result in a high level of accuracy in predicting the structural performance and material use from the topology and the subdivision rules.

In detail, Figure 10 shows the workflow of the machine learning process. After receiving the input settings of the columns and walls from the users, different topological graphs can be generated as sets of parameters representing the initial boundary of each force cell (Fig. 10.2). By training a neural network (Fig. 10.3) with the method described above, one can find the best topological graph with the smallest average edge length, indicating the most equal distribution of the main forces (Fig. 10.4).

With the selected topological graph as the initial boundaries (Fig. 10.5), different subdivision rules are applied, resulting in multiple force diagrams (Fig. 10.6) and the corresponding form diagrams. Another neural network (Fig. 10.7) can be trained and used to find the best force and form diagrams, with the input as the subdivision parameters and the output as the structural properties.

For the output evaluative value, we choose to use the material usage as the criterion. In Figures 11 and 12, we apply some of our most successful subdivision strategies to the simplest layouts and compare the volume of the generated arch floor structure with that of a typical slab. As shown in the statistics, our generated results save from 30% to 50% in materials compared to those obtained through the regular method of parallel grids, but the best material-saving solution is found by the neural network.

Finally, the trained neural network finds the optimal results as the subdivision parameters (Fig. 10.8). By transforming the subdivision parameters into the 3D force diagram (Fig. 10.9) and its corresponding form solution, the network can generate the best form with the largest material savings (Fig. 10.10).

Form- Finding Results

After training with the generated samples, the neural network has the ability to act as an evaluation agent to give real-time feedback on the two criteria values. Under the guidance of the neural network model, forms with better structural performance and lower material use are found (Fig. 12).

CONCLUSION AND DISCUSSION

Architectural space structured with the Maison Dom-Ino system can be redesigned using a funicular structure generated by the graphic statics method. The topology and subdivision rules control the generation of the force diagrams; therefore, the funicular forms are also generated as a dual geometry.

A trained neural network model can find the forms with the user-defined evaluative metrics. The machine learning model is trained and used as a fast evaluator to help the evolutionary algorithm to find the optimal designs. This method spans the interdisciplinary border of computer science and structural design, providing flexible design choices for generating floor structures.

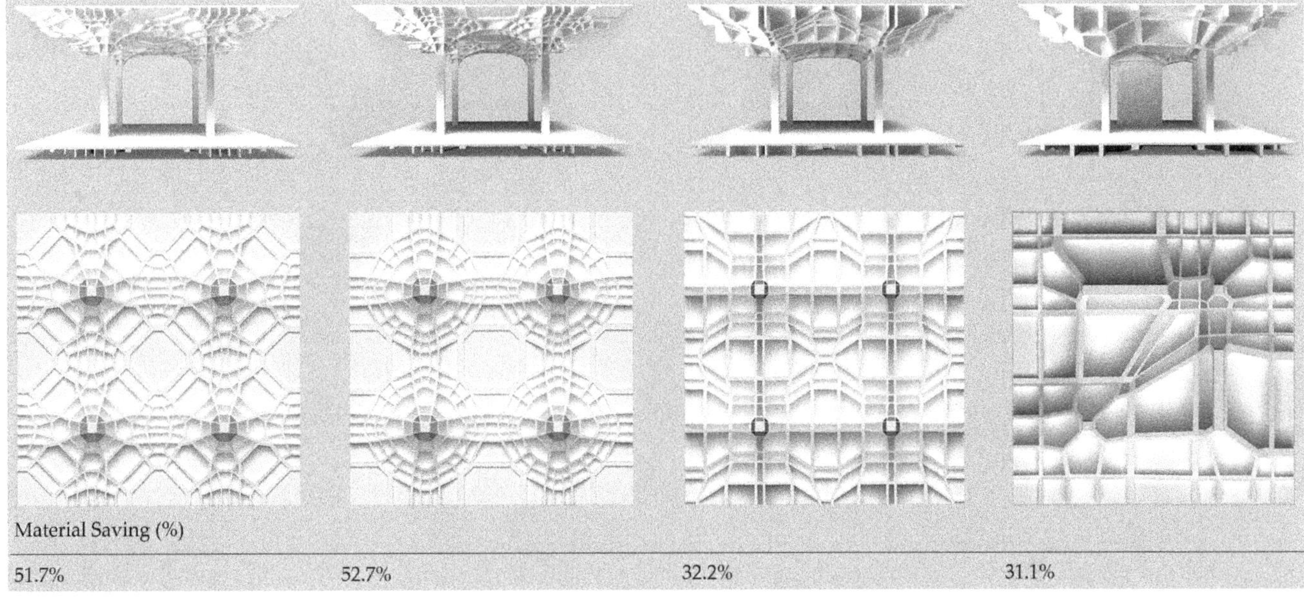

11 Material saving comparison I.

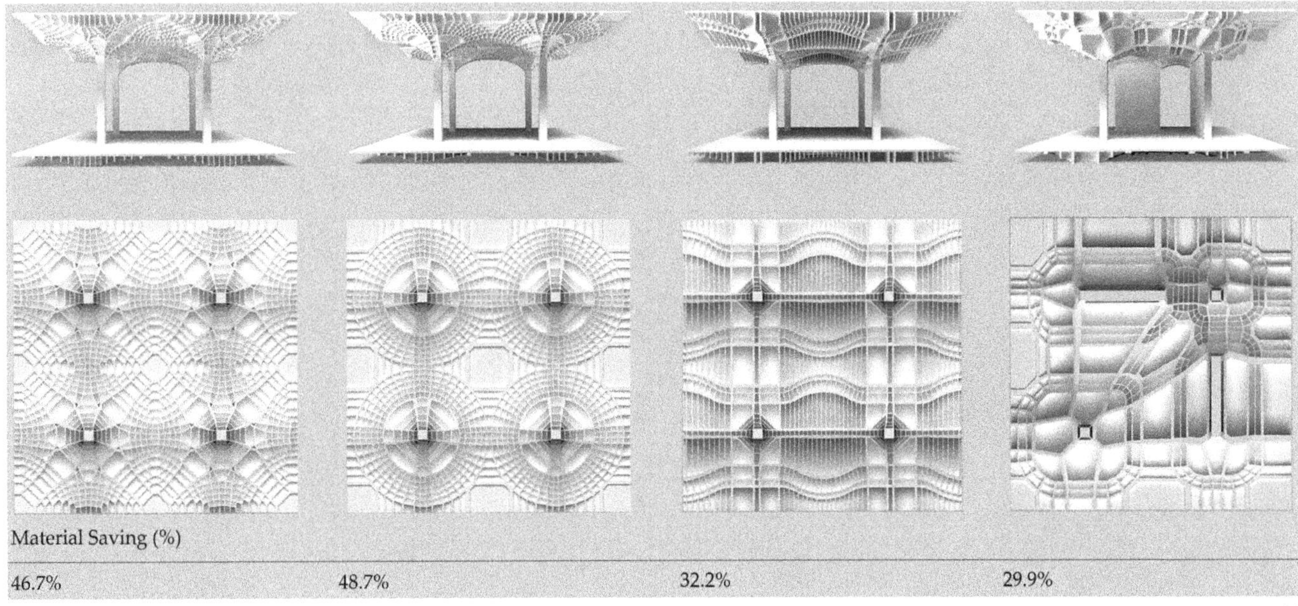

12 Material saving comparison II.

The future research of this project includes improving the topology and subdivision rules, as well as increasing the accuracy and processing speed of the machine learning model.

REFERENCES

Adriaenssens, S., P. Block, D. Veenendaal, and C. Williams. 2014. *Shell Structures for Architecture: Form Finding and Optimization*. Routledge.

Akbarzadeh, M. 2016. "3D Graphical Statics Using Reciprocal Polyhedral Diagrams." PhD dissertation, ETH Zurich.

Akbarzadeh, M., T. Van Mele, and P. Block. 2015. "On the Equilibrium of Funicular Polyhedral Frames and Convex Polyhedral Force Diagrams." *Computer-Aided Design* 63: 118–128.

Aksöz, Z., and C. Preisinger. 2019. "An Interactive Structural Optimization of Space Frame Structures Using Machine Learning." In *Impact: Design With All Senses [Proceedings of the Design Modelling Symposium]*, Berlin, Germany, edited by Christoph Gengnagel, Olivier Baverel, Jane Burry, Mette Ramsgaard-Thomsen, and Stefan Weinzierl, 18–31. Springer.

Anderson, S. 1984. "Architectural Research Programmes in the Work of Le Corbusier." *Design Studies* 5 (3): 151–158.

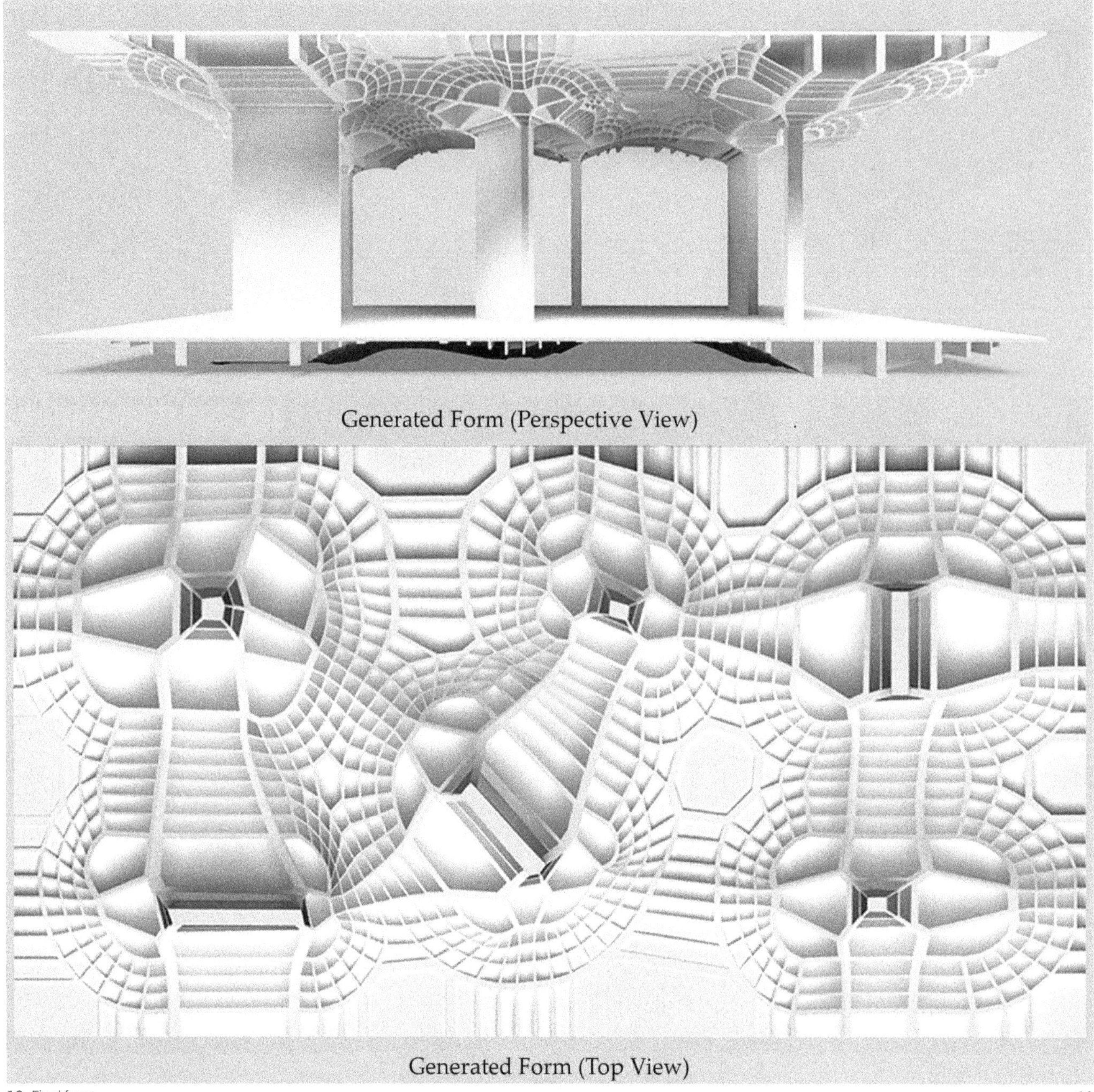

12 Final form.

12

Block, P.,and J. Ochsendorf. 2007. "Thrust Network Analysis: A New Methodology for Three-Dimensional Equilibrium." *Journal of the International Association for Shell and Spatial Structures* 48 (3): 167–173.

Bolhassani, M., M. Akbarzadeh, M. Mahnia, and R. Taherian. 2018. "On Structural Behavior of a Funicular Concrete Polyhedral Frame Designed by 3D Graphic Statics." *Structures* 14: 56–58.

Bow, R. H. 1873. *Economics of Construction in Relation to Framed Structures*. Cambridge: Cambridge University Press.

Cremona, L. 1890. *Graphical Statics: Two Treatises on the Graphical Calculus and Reciprocal Figures in Graphical Statics*. Oxford: Clarendon Press.

Culmann, K. 1864. *Die Graphische Statik*. Zurich: Verlag Meyer & Zeller.

Fivet, C., and D. Zastavni. 2013. "Constraint-Based Graphic Statics: New Paradigms of Computer-Aided Structural Equilibrium Design." In *Beyond the Limits of Man [Proceedings of IASS Annual Symposia]*, Wroclaw, Poland, 23–27 September 2013, edited by J.B. Obrębski and R. Tarczewski, 1–6(6). International Association for Shell and Spatial Structures (IASS).

Maxwell, J. C. 1864. "XLV. On Reciprocal Figures and Diagrams of Forces." *The London, Edinburgh, and Dublin Philosophical Magazine and Journal of Science* 27 (182): 250–261.

Maxwell, J. C. 1870. "I.—on Reciprocal Figures, Frames, and Diagrams of Forces." *Earth and Environmental Science Transactions of the Royal Society of Edinburgh* 26 (1): 1–40.

Schrems, Maximilian J., and Toni Kotnik. 2013. "Statically Motivated Formfinding Based on Extended Graphical Statics (EGS)." In *Open Systems [Proceedings of the 18th International Conference on Computer-Aided Architectural Design Research in Asia (CAADRIA 2013)]*, Singapore, 15–18 May 2012, edited by R. Stouffs, P. Janssen, S. Roudavski, and B. Tunçer, 843–852. CAADRIA.

Showkatbakhsh, M., E. Erdine, and A. L. Rodriguez. 2020. "Multi-Objective Optimization of Robotically Bent In-Situ Reinforcement System." *The 11th Annual Symposium on Simulation for Architecture and Urban Design (SimAUD)*, 177–184. Vienna, Austria.

Stevin, S. 1586. *Der Beghinselen der Weeghconst van Christoffel Platijn*. Amsterdam: Françoys van Raphelinghen.

Theodoropoulos, C. 2000. *Shaping Structures: Statics*. Cambridge, MA: MIT Press.

Turlock, M., and K. Steinfeld. 2019. "Necessary Tension: A Dual-Evaluation Generative Design Method for Tension Net Structures." In *Impact: Design With All Senses [Proceedings of the Design Modelling Symposium]*, Berlin, Germany, edited by Christoph Gengnagel, Olivier Baverel, Jane Burry, Mette Ramsgaard-Thomsen, and Stefan Weinzierl, 250–262. Springer.

Van Mele, T., and P. Block. 2014. "Algebraic Graph Statics." *Computer-Aided Design* 53: 104–116.

Van Mele, T., L. Lachauer, M. Rippmann, and P. Block. 2012. "Geometry-Based Understanding of Structures." *Journal of the International Association for Shell and Spatial Structures* 53 (4): 285–295.

Yetkin, O., and A. G. Sorguç. 2019. "Design Space Exploration of Initial Structural Design Alternatives via Artificial Neural Networks." In *Architecture in the Age of the 4th Industrial Revolution [Proceedings of the 37th eCAADe and 23rd SIGraDi Conference]*, Porto, Portugal, 11–13 September 2019, edited by J.P. Sousa, J.P. Xavier, and G. Henriques, 55–60. CUMINCAD.

Zheng, H. 2020. "Form Finding and Evaluating Through Machine Learning: The Prediction of Personal Design Preference in Polyhedral Structures," In *Proceedings of the 2019 DigitalFUTURES*, Shanghai, China, 7–8 July 2019, edited by Yuan P., Xie Y., Yao J., Yan C. 169–178. Singapore: Springer. https://doi.org/10.1007/978-981-13-8153-9_15.

Zheng, H., V. Moosavi and M. Akbarzadeh. 2020. "Machine Learning Assisted Evaluations in Structural Design and Construction." *Automation in Construction* 119: 103346.

IMAGE CREDITS

Figure 2: image credits listed in the caption.
Figure 3: © Masoud Akbarzadeh. 2016.

All other drawings and images by the authors.

Hao Zheng is a PhD researcher at the University of Pennsylvania, Stuart Weitzman School of Design, specializing in machine learning, digital fabrication, mixed reality, and generative design. He holds a Master of Architecture degree from the University of California, Berkeley, and Bachelor of Architecture and Arts degrees from Shanghai Jiao Tong University. Previously, Hao worked as a research assistant at Tsinghua University and UC Berkeley with a concentration on robotic assembly, machine learning, and bioinspired 3D printing. His teaching experience includes workshop tutor at Tongji University; lecturer at Macau University of Science and Technology; lecturer at the University of Pennsylvania; and teaching fellow at Shanghai Jiao Tong University.

Xinyu Wang, **Zehua Qi**, and **Shixuan Sun** are research assistants at Polyhedral Structures Laboratory, Stuart Weitzman School of Design, University of Pennsylvania.

Masoud Akbarzadeh is a designer with a unique academic background and experience in architectural design, computation, and structural engineering. He is an Assistant Professor of Architecture in Structures and Advanced Technologies and the Director of the Polyhedral Structures Laboratory (PSL). He holds a DSc from the Institute of Technology in Architecture, ETH Zurich, where he was a Research Assistant in the Block Research Group. He holds two degrees from MIT: a Master of Science in Architecture Studies (Computation) and an MArch, the thesis for which earned him the renowned SOM award. He also has a degree in Earthquake Engineering and Dynamics of Structures from the Iran University of Science and Technology and a BS in Civil and Environmental Engineering. His main research topic is three-dimensional graphical statics, which is a novel geometric method of structural design in three dimensions. In 2020, he received the National Science Foundation CAREER Award to extend the methods of 3D/polyhedral graphic statics for education, design, and optimization of high-performance structures.

Encoded Images

Representational Protocols for Integrating cGANs in Iterative Computational Design Processes

Gabriella Rossi
CITA/Royal Danish Academy

Paul Nicholas
CITA/Royal Danish Academy

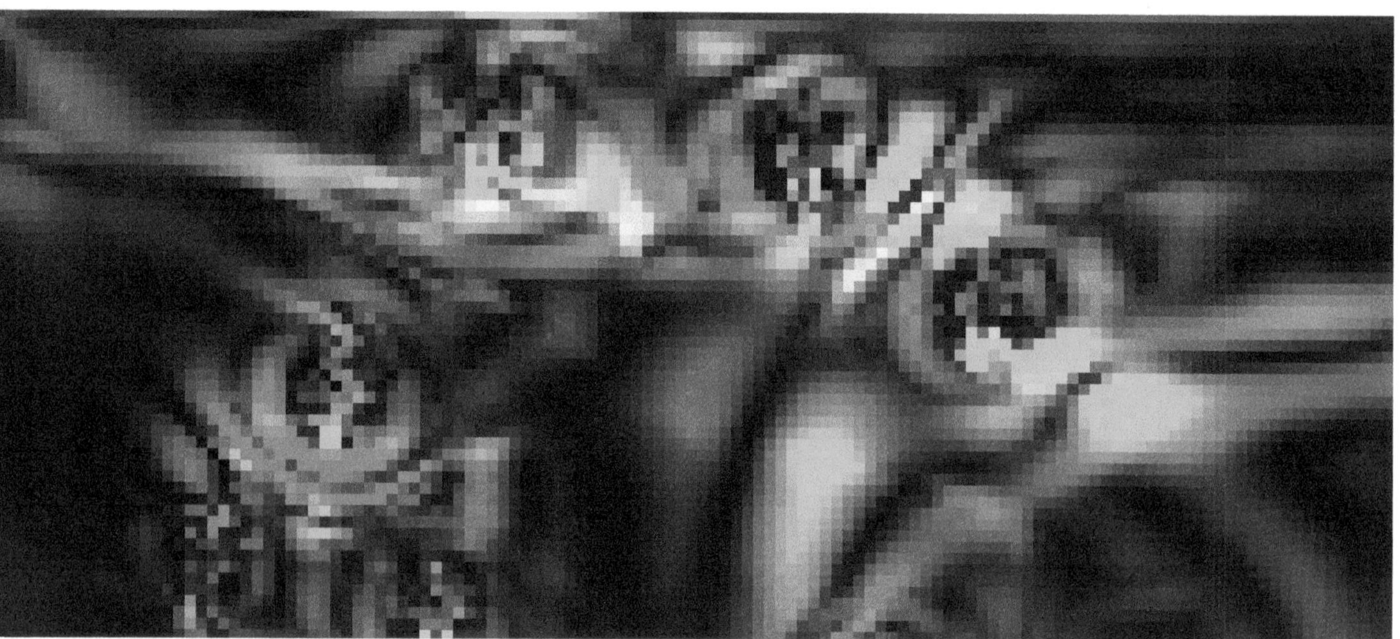

1

1 Encoding bending energy of a thin metal shell as a 128 × 128 false-color RGB image. This image is part of a larger training set used to train a cGAN to replace finite element analysis structural simulation.

ABSTRACT

In this paper, we explore conditional generative adversarial networks (cGANs) as a new way of bridging the gap between design and analysis in contemporary architectural practice. By substituting analytical finite element analysis (FEA) modeling with cGAN predictions during the iterative design phase, we develop novel workflows that support iterative computational design and digital fabrication processes in new ways. This paper reports two case studies of increasing complexity that utilize cGANs for structural analysis.

Central to both experiments is the representation of information within the data set the cGAN is trained on. We contribute a prototypical representational technique to encode multiple layers of geometric and performative description into false color images, which we then use to train a Pix2Pix neural network architecture on entirely digital generated data sets as a proxy for the performance of physically fabricated elements. The paper describes the representational workflow and reports the process and results of training and their integration into the design experiments. Last, we identify potentials and limits of this approach within the design processes.

INTRODUCTION

The field of machine learning (ML) includes a vast ecology of algorithms (Goodfellow, Bengio, and Courville 2016) that, while not designed with architecture in mind, possess potent architectural application. Their exploration and application in architecture is now growing (Darko et al. 2020). In particular, image-based neural networks, which have become the state of the art across diverse disciplines, possess architectural potential along two trajectories. The first is their potential as design generators. By interpolating through design space parameters, they can offer new design solutions (Chaillou 2017; Del Campo 2020). Their second, and larger, potential is to break the boundaries that serialize design, analysis, and fabrication. In establishing a new mode of connecting design and analysis, neural networks (NNs) offer the potential for iterative and interactive analysis-driven design. Examples of this approach are the Lace Wall project by CITA (Tamke et al. 2016), where NNs are used to develop a quick intuition-based structural analysis, or the use of NNs to shortcut computationally heavy wind analysis (Galanos et al 2019; Mokhtar et al 2020). In establishing a new mode for connecting design and fabrication, NNs unlock the possibilities for adaptive and interactive complex fabrication processes. Good examples of this are the use of NNs to learn springback behavior and adapt toolpath generation in the Bridge Too Far (Zwierzycki, Nicholas, and Thomsen 2017) and English Wheel projects (Rossi and Nicholas 2018), as well as to learn fabrication parameters (Brugnaro 2017).

These are complex problems requiring substantial specificity and an awareness of spatial and temporal correlations, which therefore challenge the traditional schism between design and analysis in contemporary practice. Solving them in a standard manner via computationally heavy analysis processes is incompatible with iterative design processes that emphasize quick feedback to support the flow of design exploration. There are two limiting aspects: first, they require specialist knowledge to establish input parameters and boundary conditions, and second, any change—large or small—in a design iteration triggers a lengthy computational wait time.

In this paper, we describe how a state-of-the-art image-based neural network model, the conditional generative adversarial network (cGAN) (Isola et al. 2017), can be used to address these complexities. By using finite element analysis (FEA) in the training process, we are able to replace analytical modeling with cGAN predictions in the design exploration process. This enables us to encode a cGAN model with specific material, geometric, and structural parameters and boundary conditions through a one-time training process, and to exploit the faster predictive response possible with that model during iterative design exploration. The relative imprecision of the cGAN in relation to the FEA used in training is made up for by the speed of the prediction and lack of expert knowledge needed. This approach allows us to develop novel workflows that support iterative computational design and digital fabrication processes in new ways.

We report two case studies of increasing complexity that utilize cGANs for structural analysis. The first case predicts structural performance of an undulating building facade panel directly from point-cloud scanning. The prediction is used to drive the geometry generation for a conformally 3D-printed reinforcement pattern. The second case predicts the structural performance of a double shell from a generative surface input, and is used to inform incrementally formed structural corrugation on metal sheets. Central to both experiments is the representation of information within the data set the cGAN is trained on. By introducing an experimental representational technique to encode multiple layers of geometric and performative description into false-color images, we are able to train a Pix2Pix neural network architecture on entirely digital generated data sets as a proxy for the performance of physically fabricated elements.

METHOD

Representation

The most important parameter of neural network training is the data itself. Neural networks are able to discern features in data, from local orders to higher abstract orders of latent space and random noise, an ability critical to making correct predictions. Since architectural ML applications use nonstandard data sets, methods to gather information and develop appropriate representational protocols are essential to get a computer to know and use information, as recognized in Gero's seminal paper (Gero 1991). A key question becomes, How does one reconcile the complexity of architectural description with the limits associated with neural networks—specifically their input shapes? How can geometry, performances, and boundaries be translated into a simpler representational space of 0s and 1s, and how can networks engage beyond single dimensions and single data types, so as to describe a spatial condition?

A superficial attraction of cGANs for architectural application is that they are trained on images, architecture's traditional mode of representation. cGANs have been trained on low-resolution scans of hand-drafted plan drawings to generate new plan drawings (Challiou 2017; Kvochick 2018). Other contemporary research has

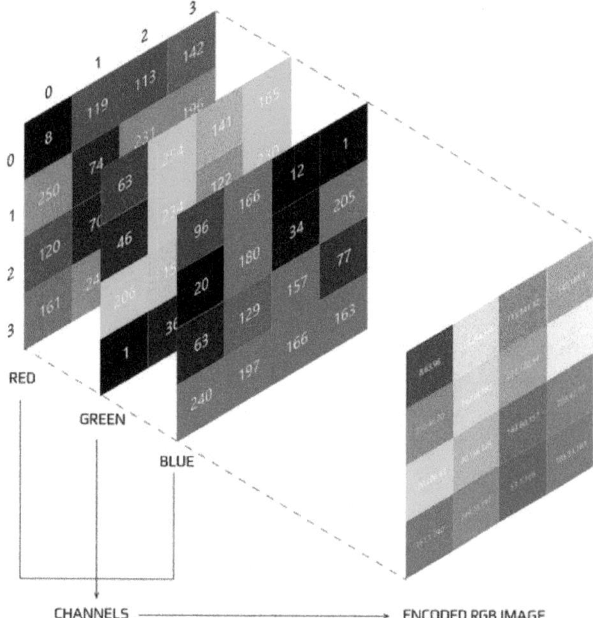

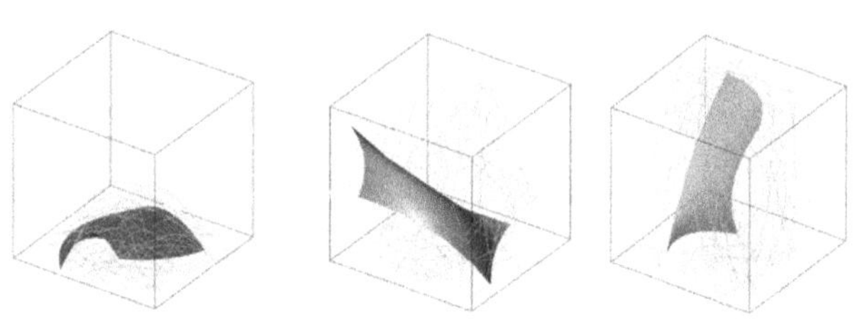

2 Image composition methodology: Each pixel of the three image channels becomes an information carrier for multisourced multidimensional data, compiled into one RGB-encoded image that is fed to the neural network for training and predicting.

3 Heuristic generation of surface data set populating the design space.

explored the image-to-image translation to shortcut CFD simulation (Galanos et al. 2019; Mokhtar et al. 2020; Musil et al. 2019), using a 2D ground-floor plan input to represent building boundaries. However, in cases such as these, the limits of 2D representation enforce a radically simplified representation of architectural form, so that it can be encoded into a one-dimensional representational space.

Our research goes beyond using the image as an illustration towards encoded images that express both geometries and performances. In this way, we shift the underlying representational understanding from an illustrative image to a multidimensional abstract compilation of information. This allows us to better capture subtleties of architectural form and performance, and thereby enable richer predictions. We propose an approach to encode multidimensional and multisourced data into false-color images. We use the image's three channels as information carriers, RGB. These encoded images are used to train networks that are able to produce fast predictions based on the correlation of the different datasets encoded into the image (Fig. 2).

This understanding develops from our prior research into similar representational approaches (Rossi and Nicholas 2018), where false-color images are generated to train a convolutional autoencoder. We go further by developing a custom representation approach that translates both geometric features, and performances into images that can be analyzed by a neural network.

Synthetic Data Set Generation

Image-based neural networks require a large amount of data to be able to correctly correlate features between input and output. This is often a bottleneck in architectural applications. In fact, while other disciplines either use standard data sets for competing in benchmarking
2 (computer science) or make their data sets available under open source licenses for collaboration (medicine), data sets for architectural applications simply do not exist. In fact, the few applications we reference in the first section all rely on the production of their own data sets. Data sets can be generated either by digitizing physical prototypes (Brugnaro and Hanna 2017; Nicholas et al. 2017; Rossi and Nicholas 2018), where data augmentation becomes necessary due to the usually limited amount of samples.
3 Other data sets are produced digitally through screenshotting of orthogonal views, simulation results, or perspective renderings.

In both case studies we present in this paper, we use a digital synthetic data set generated on Grasshopper for Rhino (Rutten 2020) to train the network. The two case studies use the same approach with different complexities of the design space and different resolution. We set up a parametric model that defines the design space. Fully aware of the dangers of data set misrepresentation and bias, we carefully compose our design space with respect to the problem against which the network will subsequently be deployed, and we use pseudorandom distributions in order to avoid introducing bias and artificial limits to the dataset. Heuristically, we iterate through the parametric model and create thousands of samples (Fig. 3). Here we encode the geometries as input text file. The geometries are subsequently passed to finite element analysis engine Millipede (Michalatos 2014), where material and load case properties are applied, and the results are subsequently encoded into a text file. Using a custom Python script, the text files are then translated into input image–output image couples that are fed to the neural network.

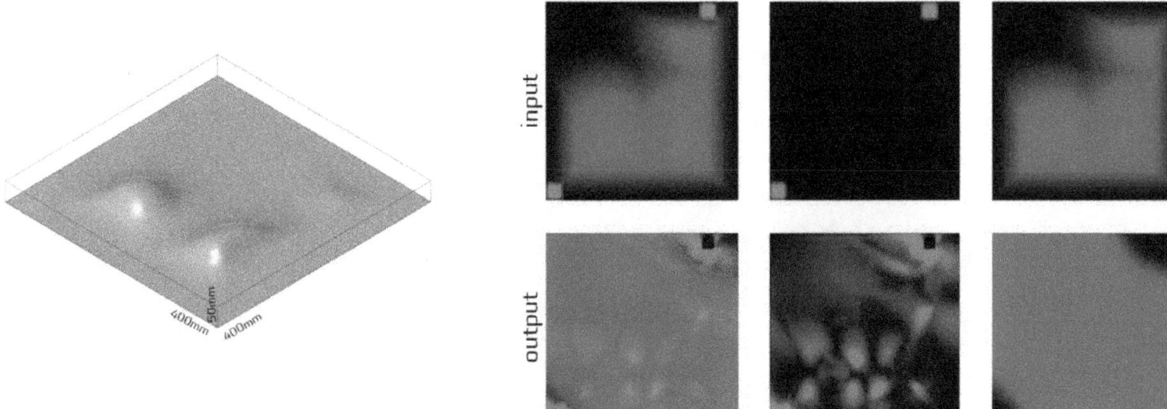

4 Data set encoding for case study 1 and its design space. Inputs are a height map capturing the panels' undulating geometry and support conditions, and outputs are Von Mises stress and deflection.

Network Architecture

In both case studies, we use a standard Pix2Pix architecture to translate a set of input images into output images. The choice of this particular network architecture is due its ability to correlate patterns present in the input image to features in the output image. This robust architecture has been demonstrated across different application cases and employs two networks that are training in tandem: a convolutional autoencoder named "generator," which compresses the input image to latent space and then decompresses it back to an image, and a classifier named "discriminator," which acts as a filter for how plausible the output image is. The first case we describe utilizes 64 × 64 RGB images, whereas the second case uses 128 × 128 RGB images. We use standard hyperparameters as provided in the original architecture.

Integrated Deployment of the Network in Rhino/Grasshopper

After training, we save the weight configuration as an h5 file. We then deploy the network in Grasshopper in order to integrate it within the ongoing computational design workflow. This is achieved via a Grasshopper-based interface. The designer shapes the surface for which they wish to evaluate the performance. It is encoded into a text file and sent to the network to query. The network produces a prediction in under 5 seconds (compared to 45 seconds for a 64 × 64 resolution, and 2.5 minutes for a 128 × 128 using the plugin Millipede FEA simulation tool). The prediction results are automatically parsed within Grasshopper, where they can be first visualized, and afterwards used to inform the fabrication process in the rest of the Grasshopper definition, as a field of values.

TRAINING EXPERIMENTS

Case 1: Facade Panels under Wind Load

We tested the workflow in a workshop collaboration with University of Technology Sydney. It demonstrates a cGAN trained to predict structural behavior of a building facade panel under wind load on the basis of its 3D scan in the form of a point cloud. The prediction is used to drive the generation of a reinforcement pattern that is conformally 3D-printed onto the panel itself.

Design Space Definition

The design space in this case is a simple rectangular panel with the dimensions 40 × 40 cm. The panel is populated by a random amount of out-of-plane peaks between 1 and 5. These peaks have random heights with an upper limit of 50 mm. This design space definition mirrors the physical limitations of panel manufacturing. The panels are assumed to be held by a random amount of support points ranging from 2 to 4 and positioned within a 50 mm offset region from the panel edges itself. Using the generative workflow outlined in the Synthetic Data Set Generation section, we generate a data set with 2,500 samples for training and 250 samples for testing.

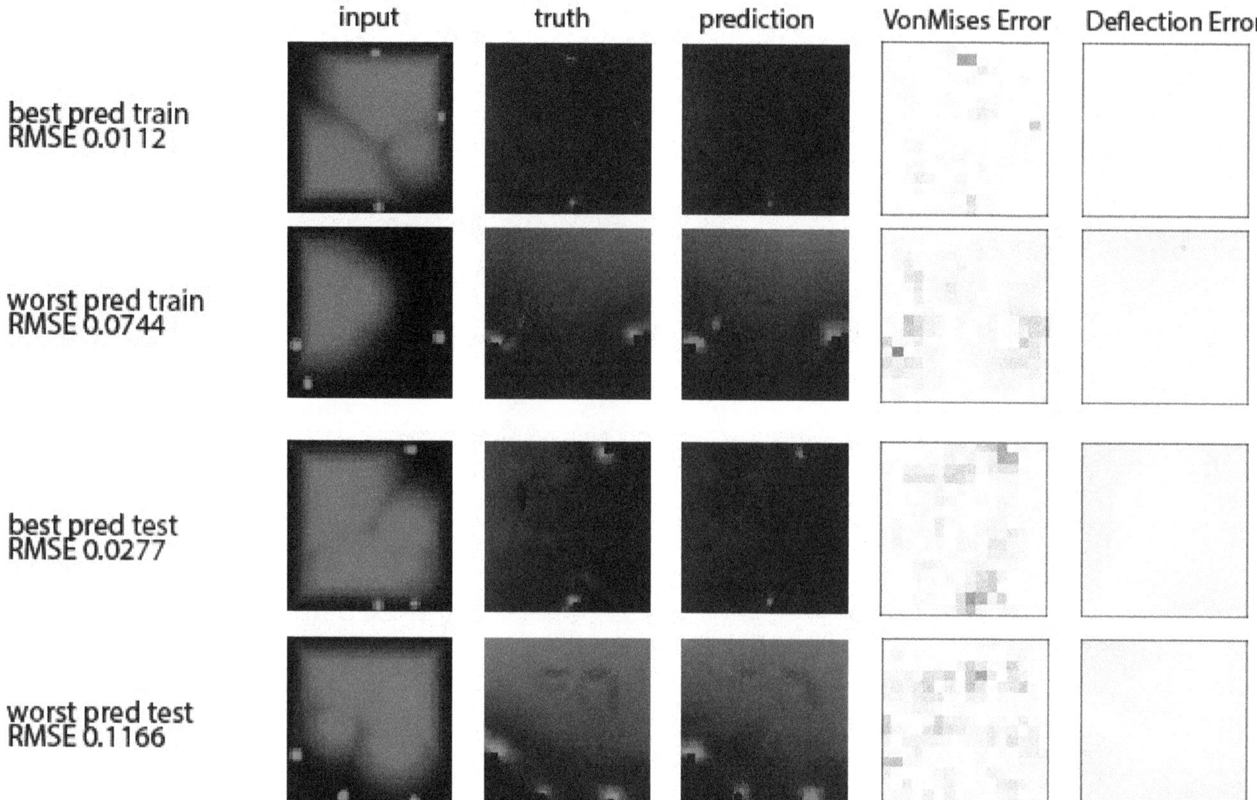

5

5 Best and worse predictions on both training set (top) and test set (bottom) of the trained cGAN for case study 1. We also plot the inverted pixel error upsampled to 16 × 16 for both red "Von Mises" and blue "deflection" channels.

6 Conformal robotic 3D printing of differentiated PETG reinforcement pattern on panel, predicted from the 3D scan of the panel itself (top) and close-up details of 3D-printed geometry (bottom).

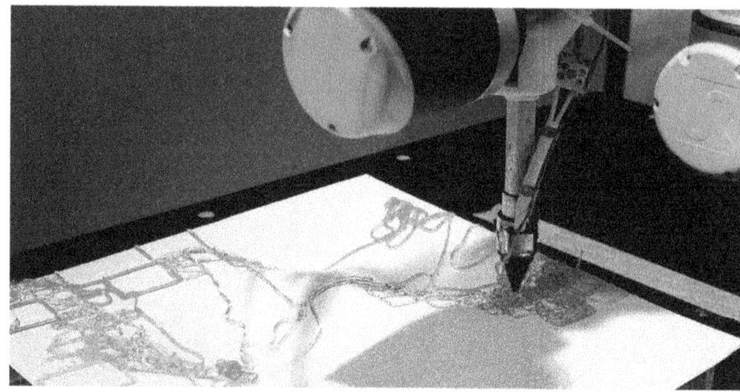

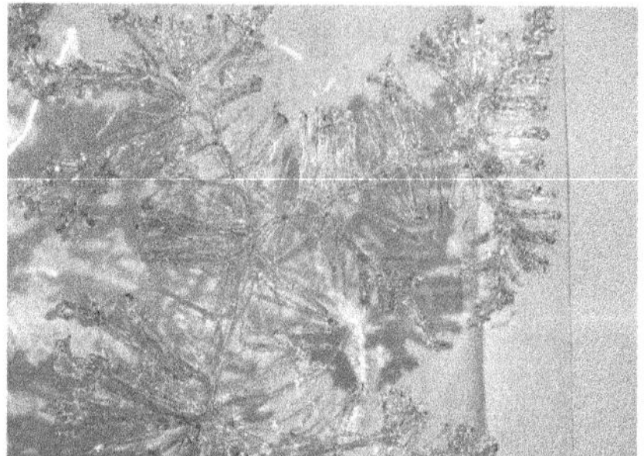

6

Image Encoding

The designed surface, as well as its support condition, is encoded into the input image. The blue channel represents the geometry topography in the form of a gradient height-field where black is flat and saturated blue signifies a z height of 50 mm. The red channel represents the two, three, or four points at which the panel would be held on the facade. The panel is assumed to be subjected to a normal load of 1000 Pa. The FEA results are encoded in the output image: the blue channel represents the deflection of the panel in mm. The red channel represents the Von Mises stress. The ranges of these forces are determined to remap the whole data set from its real extents to 0 to 255 (Fig. 4).

Training Results

When used for generative purposes, the performance of GANs and cGANS is usually evaluated through the Inception Score metric, meaning how realistic to the human eye is the generated image (Salimans et al. 2016). However in order to evaluate the cGAN as a simulation engine, we look at the root mean squared error (RMSE) between the ground truth and the predicted image. The best predicted sample from the 2,500-sample training set scored 0.0112,

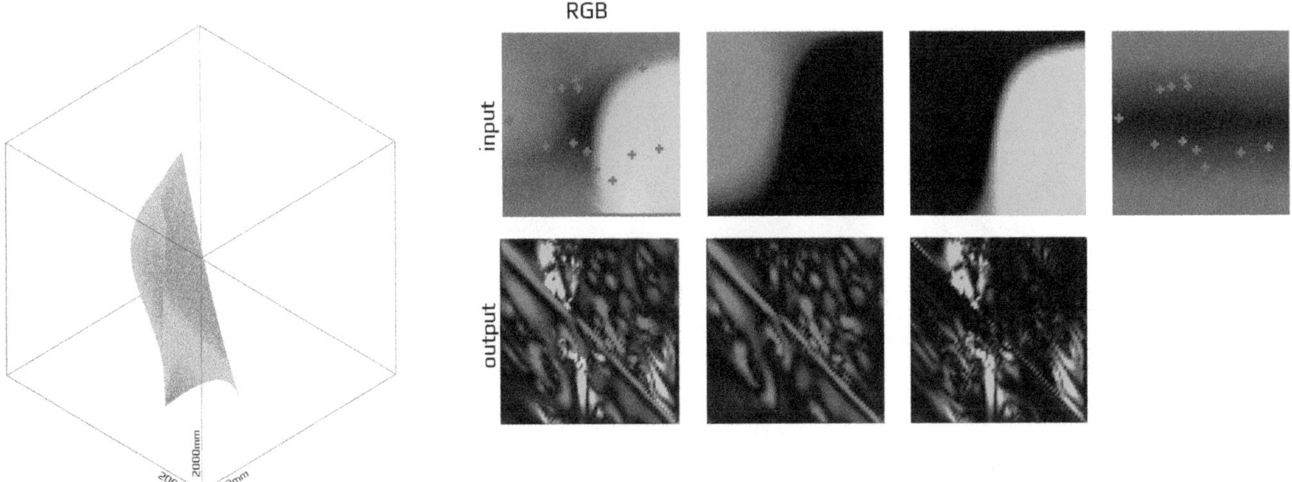

7 Data set encoding for case study 2 and its design space: inputs are a dot product map capturing the panels, undulating curvature, and support conditions, and outputs are bending energy for shell 1 and 2.

whereas the worst 95th percentile scored 0.0744. As for the 250-sample test set, the best predicted result scored 0.0277, and the worst 95th percentile scored 0.1166. To get better insight into the individual metric predictions, we split the channels and compare separately red, the Von Mises Stress, and blue, the deflection. We do so on an upsampled 16 × 16 version of the prediction rather than the original 64 × 64 image size, which yields a 60 mm/pixel resolution, in order to better capture the general behavior prediction, rather than the specific outliers. With pixel value being 1/255 numerical value assigned to each picture of the image, we have found that the average tolerance for the Von Mises stress was 12 pixel values, and that for the deflection it was 8 pixel values (Fig. 5).

Conformal 3D Printing

The predictions of the network are used as a value field to drive the generation of structural reinforcement toolpaths, which are printed on the back of the panels and act to rigidize them. We have developed multiple families of reinforcement, some with recursive subdivision to drive material deposition at different densities, more sparse where there is less stress and more concentrated where the material is more stressed, and some that deposited along the stress lines. We report on the printing setup, pattern generation algorithms, and results in Nicholas et al. (2020).

Case 2: Freeform Thin Metal Shells

The second iteration of the workflow was tested during the workshop "Material Hyper-specificities for Digital Futures 2020" in August 2020 and for "Augmented Assemblies" for Computation in Architecture master students at the Royal Danish Academy in October 2020. It demonstrates a cGAN trained to predict bending behavior of a freestanding thin metal double-shell 70 mm deep under self and wind load on the basis of its simplified NURB representation. The prediction is used to drive the generation of an incrementally formed rigidization pattern applied to a thin metal sheet using a dual robotic setup.

Design Space Definition

The design space in this case is more complex given that it is not panel-based but rather considers three-dimensional structural shells. We define a 2 × 2 × 2 cube in which a NURB surface is generated based on two random second-degree profile curves and two random second-degree edge curves. Three sets of rules guarantee the creation of a UV surface, which we categorize as follows: (1) "wall type" when the first curve belongs to the bottom side of the cube and the second is on the top side; (2) "arch type" when both curves are on the bottom side of the cube; and (3) "cantilever type" when the first curve belongs to the bottom side and the second curve belongs to one of the four lateral sides of the cube. The surfaces are tested for self-intersection at an intra-shell offset of 70 mm. The two shells are assumed to be connected by a random number of connection points ranging from 15 to 30 for structural stability. Using heuristics, we generate a data set of 6,000 different surfaces and connections. The data set is larger than the previous case study to be better representative of the design space.

Image Encoding

The designed surface, as well as its support condition, is encoded into the input image. While all surfaces are UV-remappable, in this case the geometry variation needs to be described in more than one direction, since that is

input | truth | prediction | Bending Shell1 | Bending Shell2

best pred train
RMSE 0.0291

worst pred train
RMSE 0.1811

best pred test
RMSE 0.0398

worst pred test
RMSE 0.2178

8 Best and worse predictions on both training set (top) and test set (bottom) of the trained cGAN for case study 2. We also plot the inverted pixel error upsampled to 32 × 32 for both red "shell 1" and green "shell 2" channels of the assembly

9 Dual-robotic incremental sheet-forming station. Here 0.3 mm aluminum sheets are rigidized using patterns generated based on the design surface structural prediction. Different exploration of tessellation and pattern expression were explored.

an important parameter to how it will react to the load. We use all three channels of the image for that. We sample the surface to 128 × 128 mesh, and we calculate the dot product between the face normal and the load vector. If the dot product is negative, it is mapped onto the red channel; if the dot product is positive, it is mapped onto the green channel. This means that darker areas of the image are points where the surface is parallel, and thus unaffected by the load. The blue channel represents both the connection points between the two shells but also a gradient representing the distance in height between the supported edge and the point on the surface, since all surfaces are not equal in height. The FEA results are encoded in the output image. In this case, we are interested only in one metric: the bending energy, defined as the Euclidean distance between the two principal bending moments at one point. We map the bending energy of shell 1 on the red channel and that of shell 2 on the green channel. The ranges of these forces are determined to remap the whole data set from its real extent to 0 to 255 (Fig. 7).

8

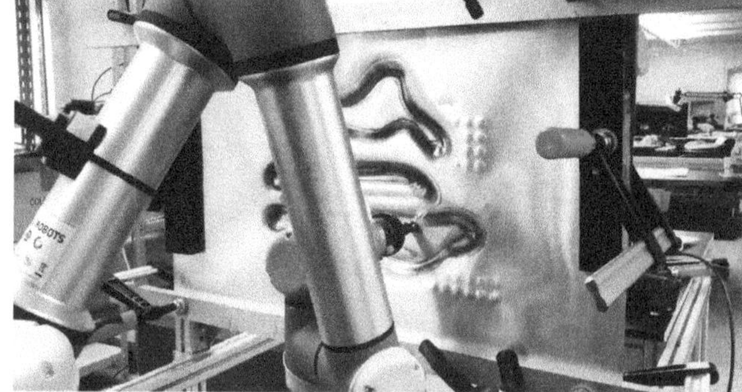

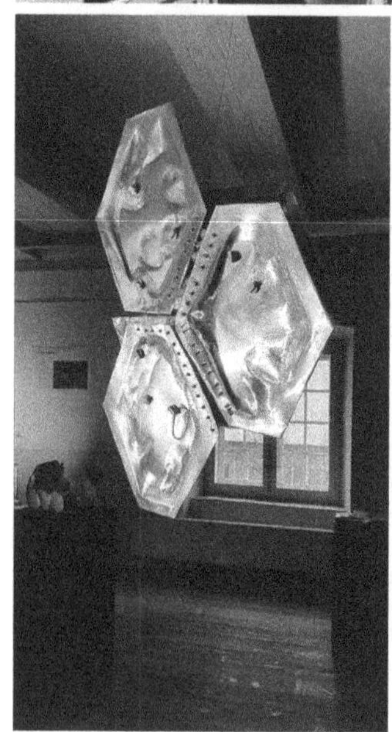

9

Training Results

We evaluate the network performance using the same method explained in case study 1. Here, the best predicted sample from the training set scored 0.0291, whereas the worst 95th percentile scored 0.1811 . As for the test set, the best predicted result scored 0.0398, and the worst 95th percentile scored 0.2178. We analyze the channels separately at a 32 × 32 pixel resolution. The average error on the red channel encoding the bending behavior of shell 1 is 33 pixel value and 30 pixel values for shell 2, represented on the green channel (Fig. 8).

Incremental Sheet Forming

The designer creates a macro surface, which is offset. Each shell is then tessellated according to parameters of curvature and panel scale using k-means clustering. Next, the connection points are generated as the intersection of the panels of the two shells to guarantee structural stability. This information is encoded using the method described in "Image Encoding" as an input image and sent to the network for prediction. Predicted bending energy is used as field values to drive the generation of corrugations for incremental sheet forming.

The fabrication workflow to generate these thin shells is multiscalar and is based on CITA's previous research in incremental sheet forming (Nicholas et al. 2016). The macro surface is split into its constituent panels, and a custom Grasshopper workflow generates the robotic toolpath for each panel, combining both corrugation geometry from one side and connecting cones on the other. Working within the restraints of the workshop time frame, only parts of the student designs could be fabricated. The sheets are formed using a dual UR5e setup, with the two robots each performing single-sided forming. The setup is calibrated using OptiTrack sensors, and the mesh forming is recorded using an Intel Real-Sense camera for monitoring and assessment of forming tolerances.

DISCUSSION

This paper has described a prototypical representational technique and successfully tested this technique through two design workshops. At the workflow level, we have found our approach to be very efficient. Querying the network for prediction takes under 5 seconds, no matter the resolution, whereas running a FEA using Millipede for Grasshopper takes 45 seconds at a 64 × 64 resolution, and 2.5 minutes at a 128 × 128 resolution. From the perspective of the designer, the relative speed of our approach and its lack of delay allows for iterative design and immediate visualization of the results without having to leave the design environment, or wait for disruptive and lengthy feedback from simulation engines. This supports an integration between design, analysis, and fabrication.

The workshops have demonstrated scalability to a certain point. In the two cases, the resolution of the images used to train the predictive model was chosen to match the size and detail of the architectural elements: in the first case study, the 64 × 64 resolution onto a 400 × 400 mm panel yields a precision of 6 mm in the prediction for 3D printing, whereas in the second case study we used 128 × 128 on a 2 × 2m surface, yielding a mesh resolution of 15 mm suitable for smooth incremental sheet forming. For larger structures, an increase of resolution could be chosen—resolutions of 512 or 1024 are becoming commonplace for image prediction.

At the specific level of neural networks, we have explored feeding the same model architecture with different data sets encoded in a similar way. We have understood the sensitivity of the network with respect to the variability of the parameter space from which the data set was generated. The network developed in case study 1, which has a simpler design space, was capable of high-precision predictions without substantial error. It was also able to predict stress distribution for load cases that were not present in the dataset; for instance, 1 support point or 5 support point cases. The network developed in case study 2, however, was less precise. While it was able to correctly correlate the connection points with the vortex accumulation of bending energy, it was less precise in correctly grasping the range of amplitude of the bending energy. We believe this is a by-product of the variability of the design space, where we have allowed for possible but nonsensible surfaces to be generated, which increases the range of bending response to contain a significant amount of outliers. Due to our normalization workflow, it is possible that the feature information is thus compressed, which results in the network being presented with multiple inputs for very similar outputs in the training set. This could be addressed in future work through dimensionality reduction or careful filtering of the training set.

CONCLUSIONS AND REFLECTIONS

In this paper, we introduced a prototypical representational technique to encode multiple layers of geometric and performative information into false-color images and exemplified this through two novel use case scenarios for neural networks within architecture. We demonstrated how the use of ML to short-circuit normative modeling practices can enable new associations of information, such as point clouds and structural performance. We showed how networks can be trained exclusively on entirely synthetic, digitally generated data sets, as opposed to images taken from real life or the captured performance of physically fabricated elements. Although we are limited to the number of channels an image has (3 or 4), with careful selection of the descriptive parameters from the design space this proves to be enough to describe a high level of architectural complexity. By separating the channels for validation, we are able to evaluate the metric-specific predictive capacity of the network. Furthermore, we showed how cGANs can offer an alternative to computationally heavy and laborious simulations. The speed and ease of input encoding and result parsing within Grasshopper make our cGAN workflow an immediate design tool for the end user. This allows for quick iterative design explorations while being able to get immediate analytical and predictive feedback on the design performance for real-time computational and fabrication processes.

At a higher level, this research seeks to contribute thinking towards the architectural use of machine learning, specifically in recognizing that descriptions of architectural objects typically bring together multiple sets of data that include form, material, performance, and environment. In showing how an image representation can be encoded to move beyond the illustrative, we propose that cGANs and similar image-based models are powerful tools for the further integration of design analysis and fabrication, and that more effort should be put into deploying and calibrating them for this usage. For instance, alongside the efforts being put into generating new architecture-specific data sets, we should also investigate architecture-specific evaluation measures that are appropriate to problems, metrics, and the tolerances that are being predicted. Just as we value tools that have different levels of predictive accuracy within the contemporary design workflows—for example, tools like Millipede or Karamba that are directly deployed in Grasshopper versus having to export to a standalone FEA even if it meant a compromise of accuracy—we should also develop machine learning models that occupy a similar spectrum of speed-accuracy tradeoffs relevant to specific architectural tasks.

ACKNOWLEDGMENTS

We would like to thank the student participants of the following workshops: "Making Sense of Sensing" at the University of Technology Sydney, "Material HyperSpecification" at Digital Futures 2020, and "Augmented Assemblies" at Computation in Architecture at the Royal Danish Academy.

REFERENCES

Brugnaro, Guilio, and Sean Hanna. 2017. "Adaptive Robotic Training Methods for Subtractive Manufacturing." In *ACADIA 2017: Disciplines and Disruption [Proceedings of the 37th Annual Conference of the Association for Computer Aided Design in Architecture (ACADIA)]*, Cambridge, MA, 2–4 November 2017, edited by T. Nagakura, S. Tibbits, M. Ibañez, and C. Mueller, 164–169. CUMINCAD.

Chaillou, Stanislas. 2019. "IA & Architecture." Thesis, Harvard Graduate School of Design. https://issuu.com/stanislaschaillou/docs/stanislas_chaillou_thesis_.

Darko, Amos, Albert PC Chan, Michael A. Adabre, David J. Edwards, M. Reza Hosseini, and Ernest E. Ameyaw. 2020. "Artificial Intelligence in the AEC Industry: Scientometric Analysis and Visualization of Research Activities." *Automation in Construction 112*: 103081.

del Campo, Matias, Sandra Manninger, and Alexandra Carlson. 2020. "Hallucinating Cities: A Posthuman Design Method based on Neural Networks." In *Proceedings of SimAUD2020*, 255-262. Newbury Park, CA: SAGE Publications.

Galanos, Theodore, Angelos Chronis, O. Vesely, A. Aichinger, and R. Koenig. 2019. "Best of Both Worlds: Using Computational Design and Deep Learning for Real-Time Urban Performance Evaluation." In *1st International Conference on Optimization Driven Architectural Design*. Amsterdam, Netherlands: Elsevier Ltd.

Gero, John. 1991. "Ten Problems for AI In Design." In *Proceedings of Artificial Intelligence In Design '91*. Oxford, England: Butterworth-Heinemann. http://papers.cumincad.org/data/works/att/46ce.content.04041.pdf.

Goodfellow, Ian, Yoshua Bengio and Aaron Courville. 2016. *Deep Learning*. Cambridge, MA: MIT Press.

Isola, Phillip, Jun-Yan Zhu, Tinghui Zhou, and Alexei A. Efros. 2017. "Image-to-image Translation with Conditional Adversarial Networks." In *Proceedings of the IEEE Conference on Computer Vision and Pattern Recognition*, 5967–5976. New York, NY: IEEE.

Kvochick, Tyler. 2018. "Sneaky Spatial Segmentation. Reading Architectural Drawings with Deep Neural Networks and Without Labeling Data." In *ACADIA 2018: Recalibration: On Imprecision and Infidelity [Proceedings of the 38th Annual Conference of the Association for Computer Aided Design in Architecture (ACADIA)]*, Mexico City, Mexico, 18–20 October 2018, edited by P. Anzalone, M. del Signore, and A. J. Wit, 166–175. CUMINCAD.

Michalatos, Panagiotis. 2014. *Millipede*. V.1. Grasshopper Component. PC.

Mokhtar, Sarah, Aleksandra Sojka, and Carlos Cerezo Davila. "Conditional generative adversarial networks for pedestrian wind flow approximation." *Proceedings of SimAUD2020*. May 25-27. Online. 2020

Musil, Josef, Jakub Knir, Athanasios Vitsas, and Irene Gallou. 2019. "Towards Sustainable Architecture: 3D Convolutional Neural Networks for Computational Fluid Dynamics Simulation and Reverse DesignWorkflow." arXiv preprint. arXiv:1912.02125.

Nicholas, Paul, David Stasiuk, Esben Nørgaard, Christopher Hutchinson, and Mette Ramsgaard Thomsen. 2016. "An Integrated Modelling and Toolpathing Approach for a Frameless Stressed Skin Structure, Fabricated Using Robotic Incremental Sheet Forming." In *Robotic Fabrication in Architecture, Art and Design 2016*, 62–77. Cham: Springer.

Nicholas, Paul, Mateusz Zwierzycki, Esben Clausen Nørgaard, Scott Leinweber, David Stasiuk, Mette Ramsgaard Thomsen, and Christopher Hutchinson. 2017. "Adaptive Robotic Fabrication for Conditions of Material Inconsistency: Increasing the Geometric Accuracy of Incrementally Formed Metal Panels." In *Fabricate 2017*, 114–121. London: UCL Press.

Nicholas, Paul, Gabriella Rossi, Ella Williams, Michael Bennett, and Tim Schork. 2020. "Integrating Real-Time Multi-Resolution Scanning and Machine Learning for Conformal Robotic 3D Printing in Architecture." *International Journal of Architectural Computing* (August). https://doi.org/10.1177/1478077120948203.

Rossi, Gabriella, Paul Nicholas. 2018. "Re/Learning the Wheel: Methods to Utilize Neural Networks as Design Tools for Doubly Curved Metal Surfaces." In *ACADIA 2018: Recalibration: On Imprecision and Infidelity [Proceedings of the 38th Annual Conference of the Association for Computer Aided Design in Architecture (ACADIA)]*, Mexico City, Mexico, 18–20 October 2018, edited by P. Anzalone, M. del Signore, and A. J. Wit, 146–155. CUMINCAD.

Rutten, David. 2020. *Grasshopper*. V.1.0.0007. Robert McNeel & Associates. PC.

Salimans, Tim, Ian Goodfellow, Wojciech Zaremba, Vicki Cheung, Alec Radford, and Xi Chen. 2016. "Improved Techniques for Training GANS." *Advances in Neural Information Processing Systems* 29: 2234–2242.

Tamke, Martin, Mateusz Zwierzycki, Anders Holden Deleuran, Y. Sinke Baranovskaya, I. Tinning Friis, and M. Ramsgaard Thomsen. 2017. "Lace Wall-Extending Design Intuition through Machine Learning." In *Fabricate: Rethinking Design and Construction*, edited by Achim Menges, Bob Sheil, Ruairi Glynn and Marilena Skavara, 98-105. London, England: UCL Press.

Zwierzycki, Mateusz, Paul Nicholas, and Mette Ramsgaard Thomsen. 2018. "Localised and learnt Applications of Machine Learning for Robotic Incremental Sheet Forming." In *Humanizing Digital Reality*, 373–382. Singapore: Springer.

IMAGE CREDITS

Figures 1–9: © Gabriella Rossi and Paul Nicholas, CITA, Royal Danish Academy

---

Gabriella Rossi is a PhD Fellow at CITA, Royal Danish Academy. Her work focuses on the intersection between machine learning and robotics, exploring novel materialities and manufacturing workflows applied to architecture. She teaches in the master's program Computation in Architecture at the Royal Danish Academy, and has guest taught at the University of Technology Sydney and Southeast University in Nanjing. Previously, she worked as a computational design specialist at Odico Construction Robotics and researcher at Politecnico di Milano. She is member of the Danish Association of Architects.

Paul Nicholas is an Associate Professor at the Royal Danish Academy and leads the international master's program Computation in Architecture. Paul holds a PhD in Architecture from RMIT University, has practiced with Arup consulting engineers, and taught in Australia, China, and Europe. Paul's research explores the idea that new material practices necessitate new relationships across the traditional boundaries separating design, fabrication, and materiality. Current research projects explore machine learning, biomaterials, adaptive robotic fabrication, and multiscalar modeling.

BIM Hyperreality

Data Synthesis Using BIM and Hyperrealistic Rendering for Deep Learning

Mohammad Alawadhi
Texas A&M University
Wei Yan
Texas A&M University

1

1 3D model generated using photos and a render-trained GAN.

ABSTRACT

Deep learning is expected to offer new opportunities and a new paradigm for the field of architecture. One such opportunity is teaching neural networks to visually understand architectural elements from the built environment. However, the availability of large training datasets is one of the biggest limitations of neural networks. Also, the vast majority of training data for visual recognition tasks is annotated by humans. In order to resolve this bottleneck, we present a concept of a hybrid system—using both building information modeling (BIM) and hyperrealistic (photorealistic) rendering—to synthesize datasets for training a neural network for building object recognition in photos. For generating our training dataset, *BIMrAI*, we used an existing BIM model and a corresponding photorealistically rendered model of the same building. We created methods for using renderings to train a deep learning model, trained a generative adversarial network (GAN) model using these methods, and tested the output model on real-world photos. For the specific case study presented in this paper, our results show that a neural network trained with synthetic data (i.e., photorealistic renderings and BIM-based semantic labels) can be used to identify building objects from photos without using photos in the training data. Future work can enhance the presented methods using available BIM models and renderings for more generalized mapping and description of photographed built environments.

INTRODUCTION

The inability of a cognitive intelligence—either human or artificial—to distinguish between reality and simulated reality has been coined as *hyperreality* in philosophical discourse, first by Baudrillard (1995). Humans as much as computer machines can struggle to differentiate between a photo and an imitation of a photo—either as art or a 3D rendering. This argument is evident in hyperrealistic building visualizations (digitized architecture) and counterpart actualized buildings (built architecture) that are common practice in the architecture, engineering, and construction (AEC) industry, which are being augmented by a growing interest in virtual reality and augmented reality. By considering hyperrealism with the proliferation and advancement of artificial intelligence technology for solving machine cognition tasks, the authors' work was an attempt to exploit hyperreality between synthetic photorealistic renderings and photos of buildings for teaching machines to detect building objects—as defined through BIM. This attempt constituted: (1) exploring methods to create machine learning datasets that rely on BIM and photorealistic rendering instead of manual annotation, and (2) testing said methods using current neural network technology.

The introduction of artificial neural networks into architectural discourse is a recent phenomenon owing itself to the recent breakthroughs of *deep* neural networks at solving complex machine learning tasks, paving the way to a new paradigm of *deep learning*. Neural networks are inspired by biological neurons; in a sense, they are an abstract model of the brain. Their typical structure is composed of an input layer of nodes, hidden layers of nodes, and an output layer with a single node, with connections between them that have weights, which are multiplied and adjusted. They require training by showing them many examples. An area where deep neural networks have excelled is in image processing tasks, which include image classification, object detection, semantic segmentation, image-to-image translation, and image generation, among other tasks. Since architecture is a visually oriented field, a significant portion of previous work was interested in using these image-based deep learning models within the field. However, few have explored using the knowledge contained in digital BIM models to train deep learning models.

In their work, Krijnen and Tamke (2015) followed by Kim et al. (2019) used BIM-based data to train neural networks for BIM model quality assurance and data integrity. As et al. (2018) developed a methodology to train neural networks using BIM-based graph models and subjective scores. The previously mentioned literature did not explore the applications of BIM-trained neural networks in the real built environment, an area in which this paper is interested. Braun and Borrmann (2019) proposed using camera-aligned BIM models and photos of construction sites to train neural networks, though no training was conducted. This paper is particularly interested in the use of synthetic data to train a neural network that can be used on real-world data (i.e., photos). When given an example photo of a building, a trained network would segment the image into predicted building objects. This application would be useful for building surveys and building energy modeling (BEM).

The potential of neural networks is limited by the availability of large, high-quality training data. Also, web data and manual annotation are the dominant data acquisition methods in visual recognition (Mayer et al. 2018). A solution idea for this data acquisition problem is using both BIM and photorealistic rendering for generating training data. By considering the ubiquity of BIM and 3D rendering in the architecture field, BIM can generate building object data that can be used with photorealistic renderings to train a neural network.

3D renderings can be impossible to differentiate from photos, and even computer programs can struggle to differentiate between them (Lyu and Farid 2005). Synthetic data—in the form of 3D renderings—were used for training machine learning models to understand indoor architectural scenes (Georgakis et al. 2017; Handa et al. 2015; Peng et al. 2017; Zhang et al. 2017). Machine learning models trained using a dataset supplemented by photorealistic renderings can outperform programs trained with only hand-labeled photos (Richter et al. 2016). Photorealistic renderings also reduced the number of manually annotated photos required for training (Georgakis et al. 2017; Richter et al. 2016). Neural networks trained on photorealistic renderings can accurately estimate depth and part segmentation in photos (Varol et al. 2017) and can produce results near or beyond state-of-the-art performance (Handa et al. 2015; Zhang et al. 2017).

While previous research in other fields has explored the use of synthetic data in the form of annotated photorealistic renderings for training neural networks that can predict objects from photos, there is no example that utilized this in conjunction with BIM—an object-oriented process. Therefore, it can be hypothesized that a neural network trained with BIM and photorealistic renderings of buildings would work well when tested on photos of buildings. Proving this hypothesis true would mean that available BIM models and visualization renderings that are already being used in the AEC industry can be leveraged instead of manually labeling building photos.

For testing the previously discussed hypothesis, Conditional GANs (CGANs)—a variation of GANs—can be trained with RGB image pairs of BIM renderings and photorealistic renderings for semantic segmentation of building objects. GANs are an emerging type of neural network introduced by Goodfellow et al. (2014) that is based on implementing two neural networks competing in a zero-sum game (Goodfellow 2017). These neural networks are set up where one network is a generator that creates samples with the same distribution as the training data, while another network is a discriminator that determines whether the samples are real or fake (Goodfellow 2017). The generator network is trained to deceive the discriminator (Goodfellow 2017). GANs have a large potential in the future of machine learning technology. CGANs are successful solutions for image processing problems that involve translating an input image into a corresponding output image (Isola et al. 2018); for example, a building façade image and a corresponding labeled façade image. GANs, as opposed to state-of-the-art semantic segmentation neural networks, can be used for semantic segmentation problems in addition to other image-to-image translation tasks, which demonstrate their applicability and flexibility for architectural problems, including generative design (Chaillou 2019), urban image generation (Steinfeld 2019), depth estimation, and detecting architectural elements from photos.

Utilizing GANs for achieving machine understanding of basic objects of the built environment can be useful for a multitude of tasks in real-world conditions. For example, a neural network that is trained to predict basic building objects from photos can be used on building photos that are acquired from photogrammetry surveys, as one of the challenges of automated BEM from photogrammetry is the annotation of basic building-element objects such as windows. Automating the annotation process using machine learning can be used instead of manual annotations; therefore, a photogrammetry-based building model annotated using a neural network can be useful for producing object-oriented building models including BEM and BIM models.

In the scope of our work, we tackle the issue of manual annotation in deep learning by developing methods for data synthesis derived from BIM data and photorealistic rendering. We experimented with a single-sample test case of a building that includes on-site photos, a corresponding BIM model, and a photorealistic 3D model of that building. Then, we used *BIMrAI*—the rendering output of our data synthesis system—to train a neural network. We evaluated the testing results on photos in terms of how well the network performed and analyzed the methods in terms of potential usefulness for mapping the built environment and automatic BIM creation. The following section describes the methods that were developed.

METHODS

The authors developed a system using BIM and 3D software tools to generate synthetic training data for a neural network model that conducts semantic segmentation on photos. The network model that was chosen for testing the efficacy of the system is *pix2pix*—a state-of-the-art CGAN developed by Isola et al. (2018) for image-to-image translation: meaning it translates an input RGB image to a corresponding output RGB image. In this case, the network was trained to translate photorealistic renderings to color-ID renderings—i.e., the network was adapted for the task of semantic segmentation, which is segmenting an input image into color-labeled objects. This approach was used to conduct semantic segmentation based on building objects, where each color label corresponds to a building object (Fig. 4).

The system was tested with a real building sample: a single-story farmhouse with an L-shaped floor plan including five surrounding buildings. The synthetic training data was generated using two 3D models: a BIM model and a corresponding photorealistic model—based on photogrammetry—of the same building that was acquired from previous work (Alawadhi and Yan 2018). It is possible to generate the data using a single BIM model with photorealistic materials; however, this approach was not taken in the scope of this experiment.

Setting up the system for data synthesis is a four-step process: (1) assigning BIM object colors, (2) running scripts for model alignment and (3) the orbiting camera, and (4) rendering. The workflow process of this system is as follows: Using 3ds Max (a 3D software tool), an imported Revit model of the sample was aligned to the photorealistic model. The alignment was conducted using a three-point-click method. The imported BIM objects—namely, the walls, windows, doors, columns, and roofs—were assigned specific user-defined RGB colors, which are blue, cyan, purple, red, and green, respectively. An animated camera that orbits around the models was automatically created using parameters (3D positions and focal length) derived from drone camera data in the photogrammetry file.

Figure 2 shows two instances of the user interface (UI) illustrating camera positions and matching views to the aligned models where (a) is the photorealistic model and (b) is the imported BIM model (with the photorealistic model hidden).

2a

2b

3

2 UI instances showing (a) the photorealistic model and (b) the BIM model.

3 Batch-rendered views with simulated lighting for each scene state.

The camera has a keyframe on each second of the animation timeline, where each keyframe represents a different camera view of the models for a total of 110 views. Thirty-eight different scene states were set up for the photorealistic model to simulate lighting conditions based on location and time of day in order to simulate realism in the training data. Figure 3 shows render samples of the photorealistic model under different conditions, where each image represents a time of day with different illumination and shadows. Given the large variations that can be produced with different views and lighting, the system inherently applies data augmentation that is often applied to training data. Another scene state was set up for the imported and color-labeled BIM model. As outputs, photorealistic renderings and corresponding color-labeled renderings were produced automatically via a batch rendering process for all 39 scene states using 3ds Max. In total, 4,180 image pairs of matching photorealistic views and color-labeled model views were rendered in three days using a single PC. For future work, this duration can be drastically reduced using a render farm.

The output renderings of this system were processed for use as training data for the neural network. Each rendered pair was resized to two squares and stitched together—as 256-pixel square input and output—using Python scripting for training the GAN for translating the photorealistic renderings into the BIM-based object color renderings.

Figure 4 shows the basic structure of the GAN. Given a latent vector *z*, input photorealistic rendering *c*, and output color-labeled rendering *x*, the generator network *G(c,z)* is trained to generate the RGB color labels from the photorealistic renderings *c* to fool the discriminator network *D(c,x)*. The discriminator network *D(c,x)* is trained to detect the correct labels *x* from the false labels. There is also the L1 loss, which is a regression problem between the generator's labels and the original labels *x*. The L1 loss can be disregarded in other GAN applications but is considered useful for image segmentation tasks (Isola et al. 2018); therefore, it was included in this experiment. The full loss equation in Figure 4 shows the relationship between the three loss functions: the generator loss, the discriminator loss, and the L1 loss.

Table 1 shows the main hyperparameters for training the GAN model. Total training time on the *BIMrAI* dataset was approximately 15 hours using a single GPU. After training, the network was tested on real-world photos of the sample building. Unlike conventional GANs in which photo images are used as training data in the GAN, in this work, only the photorealistic renderings and BIM-based color labels were used as training data. The purpose is twofold: (1) to explore if generated synthetic imagery can be used as training data for deep learning, and (2) whether the results are adequate or not.

Table 1 GAN Training Parameters

Dataset Size (render pairs)	Model Resolution (pixels)	Hyperparameters (pix2pix)		
		Batch Size	Learning Rate	Training Epochs
4,180	256 x 256	1	0.0002	200

As for evaluating the results of the trained GAN on the photos, besides evaluating the results subjectively, it is difficult to evaluate GANs objectively (Borji 2018; Salimans et al. 2016) as opposed to conventional segmentation networks. However, since the GAN was used for the same task, an evaluation method was developed to plot the accuracy based on standard metrics that are used to evaluate conventional segmentation networks, such as per-object pixel accuracy and intersection-over-union (IoU). The first step of this evaluation method is to apply a color quantization algorithm on the predicted outputs of the network for reducing the RGB colors to match the original RGB integer values that were defined in the training data synthesis system. Afterward, an evaluation tool was developed using Python. The ground truth renderings and the color-quantized GAN outputs were encoded as numerical labels corresponding to pixels and their object class (e.g., wall, window, etc.). The evaluation method might be detrimental to the evaluation scores in cases where GAN-predicted RGB pixels do not correspond to the user-defined object class's RGB integers, possibly resulting in mislabeled pixels after

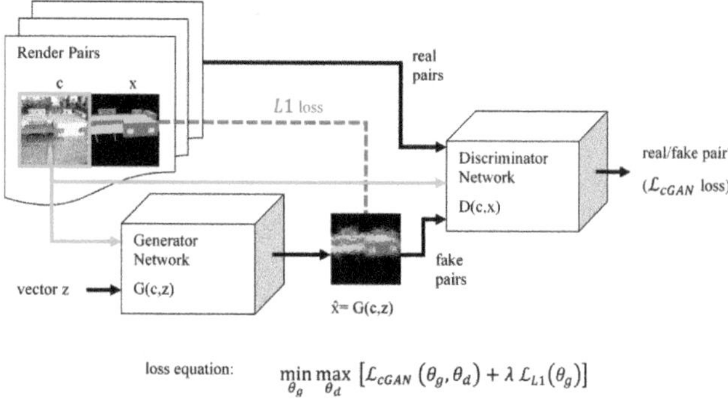

4 CGAN model. Source: Figure adapted from Herranz (2018).

color quantization and label encoding. However, this is not a concern if the network has been trained well, as the pixels with observable RGB color inconsistencies introduced by the GAN would be nonexistent or very small. Also, this did not appear to be a problem in this experiment. Therefore, the presented method can be used for evaluating semantic segmentation results of the GAN objectively while identifying that a technical bias might arise in future work.

The evaluation tool uses the binary classification of object classes per-pixel. The classes are *wall*, *window*, *door*, *column*, *roof*, and *background* objects. The evaluation metrics in the tool are the accuracy, precision, recall, F1 score, and the mean IoU. The accuracy is calculated by dividing the sum of true positives *tp* and true negatives *tn*—which are predicted pixels that have the same positive and negative classifications as the ground truth—by the total number of pixel classifications. Accuracy was calculated globally (for all pixels) and for pixels per-object. The precision, recall, and F1 score take the false positives *fp* and false negatives *fn* into consideration for more in-depth analysis and are given by the following:

$$precision = \frac{tp}{tp + fp}, \quad recall = \frac{tp}{tp + fn}, \quad F1 = 2 \cdot \frac{precision \times recall}{precision + recall}$$

The mean IoU is another important metric for gauging the overlap between ground truth *a* and predicted *b* segmentations. IoU is scored from 0 to 1, where 1 indicates matching prediction and ground truth segments. The IoU is calculated for each class, then averaged between all classes, and is given by the following:

$$IoU(a, b) = \frac{a \cap b}{a \cup b} = \frac{tp}{tp + fp + fn}$$

The intersection between *a* and *b* is synonymous with *tp*, and the union between *a* and *b* is the sum of *a* and *b* segmentations. The mean IoU is considered a more rigorous metric than accuracy for segmentation tasks because it is sensitive to class imbalance in the data, whereas using accuracy only could give misleadingly high scores if class imbalance is an issue. Therefore, both accuracy and mean IoU were considered when evaluating the GAN results.

RESULTS AND REFLECTION

The trained GAN was tested with real-world photos of the sample. Based on qualitative observation and comparing GAN predictions with the ground truth, the trained network was able to predict objects from the photos with acceptable accuracy—with minor misidentifications (Fig. 5). Overfitting can be an issue if the training data (renderings in the test) is too similar to the testing data (photos). In the case of this test, there are noticeable differences between the renderings and the photos when compared side-by-side. Specifically, there are differences between simulated and real geometry, lighting, colors, and details when compared by human eyes. However, more future work will be needed to test if this network would work well on photos of another building sample. Most likely, the network would need to be trained on more buildings.

Therefore, what can be concluded from this test is that rendering can be generalized as a data synthesis method for deep learning, although more future work will be needed for data synthesis using BIM and rendering methods to achieve improved generalization, which is the ability to perform object recognition on other buildings for which we do not possess BIM models using the trained network. Neural networks that are trained using a large amount of data with a good amount of variance within a specific data distribution have shown to have good generalization when deployed on unseen data. For example, a neural network for predicting building objects that is trained with a large number of building images will most likely perform accurately on other unseen building images that are similar in typology. However, there is a bottleneck in data acquisition, as curating training data for deep learning is a labor-intensive task. The results show promise in tackling this issue through data synthesis using BIM and photorealistic rendering, both of which are ubiquitous in the field of architecture.

As for analyzing the results quantitatively, the GAN outputs were evaluated empirically using the evaluation tool, and the resulting metrics are shown in Table 2. The average accuracy is 93% (rounded) and the mean IoU is 0.64, which are good compared to the results from state-of-the-art benchmarks on street scene datasets used for autonomous driving applications (Table 3). For this specific building case study, the results demonstrate that a GAN can be trained using only photorealistic renderings and BIM-based labels to identify building elements from photos.

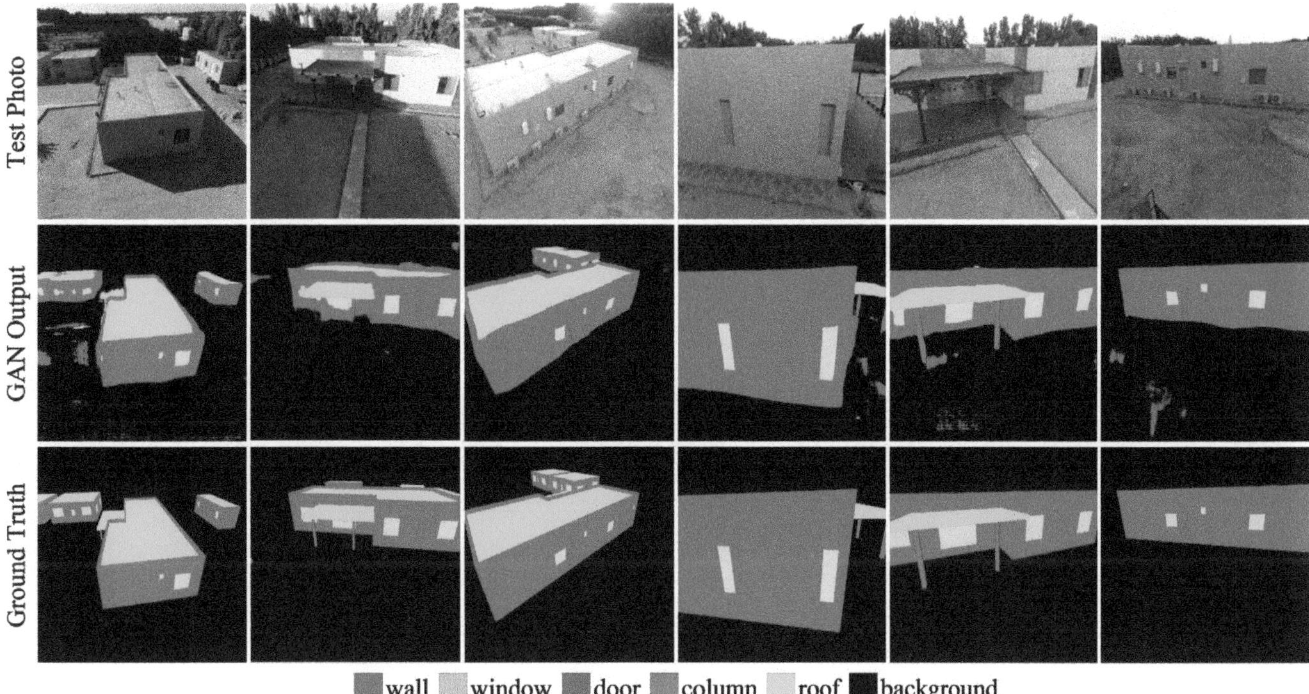

5 Predicted GAN outputs from photo inputs.

5

Table 2 GAN Semantic-Segmentation Evaluation

Accuracy (%)	**92.82**
Per-Object Accuracies (%)	
Wall	93.69
Window	85.81
Door	55.83
Column	88.89
Roof	76.36
Background	94.49
Precision	0.934
F1	0.926
mIoU	**0.641**

Table 3 Results Comparison with Street Scene Benchmarks

Dataset	Model	Accuracy (%)	mIoU	Source
CamVid	FC-DenseNet103	91.5	0.669	Jégou et al. 2017
	BiSeNet	-	0.687	Yu et al. 2018
Cityscapes	PSPNet	-	0.802	Zhao et al. 2017
	BiSeNet	-	0.789	Yu et al. 2018
	pix2pix	86	0.35	Isola et al. 2018
	CycleGAN	58	0.16	Zhu et al. 2020
GTAV-to-Cityscapes	CBST	-	0.47	Zou et al. 2018
	ADVENT	-	0.455	Vu et al. 2019
BIMrAI (Ours)	pix2pix	**92.82**	**0.641**	This Paper

Further, to study and speculate on potential applications of the trained network, the predicted outputs from the GAN were automatically remapped onto a photogrammetry-based model. A photogrammetry software was used for the remapping process. The software normally uses photos for both the geometry and texture creation; however, for the texture, the photos were replaced with the GAN predictions obtained from the previous phase. The resulting *semantic mesh model*—i.e., the model with predicted outputs of the network projected in 3D—can be seen in Figures 1 and 6. This semantic mesh model can be used in the future as a basis to construct a BIM model from a photogrammetry model, which is in great demand for applications such as BEM, building operation, renovations, etc.

An observation from this experiment is that remapping the predicted images on the 3D model seemed to increase the fidelity of the predicted colors, as incorrect predictions were blended away with correct predictions from different image angles. The blended predictions benefited from the high average accuracy of the GAN to rectify single-image prediction colors in photo angles where the network underperformed. Figure 7 shows the increased prediction accuracy from the photogrammetry texture creation process when compared to single-image prediction. Photogrammetry tools implement texture mapping algorithms using Bayesian inference methods, such as Markov random field for high-quality texture blending (Lempitsky and Ivanov 2007). The blended prediction method (Fig. 6)

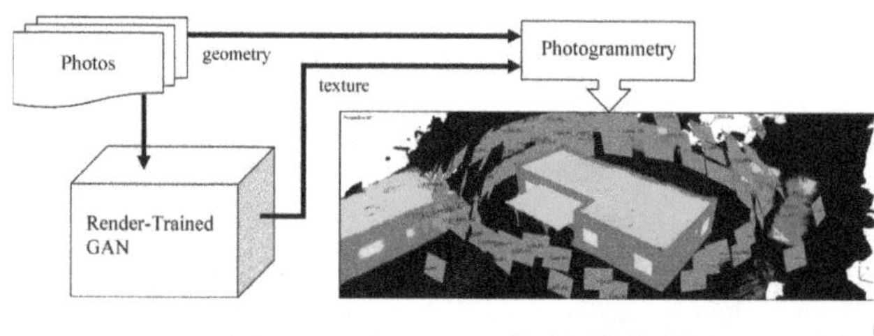

6

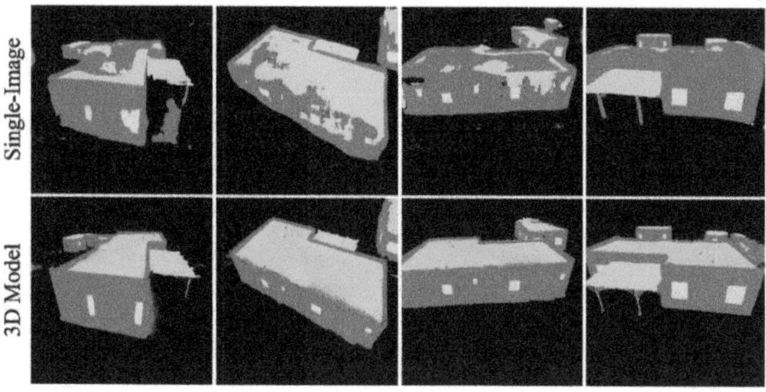

7

6 Process for generating semantic mesh model toward BIM creation.

7 Single-image vs. 3D-projected and blended predictions.

has the potential to be integrated with probabilistic inference to improve real-time machine learning prediction with accumulated prior predictions.

CONCLUSIONS AND FUTURE WORK

Teaching neural networks to detect building objects from photos requires training, i.e., showing them many examples (up to thousands or even millions). Training datasets are often acquired by manually labeling data, which is labor-intensive and time-consuming. Ideas from the architectural field can be introduced to improve this process, specifically BIM and 3D rendering. BIM can generate synthetic data—as building object data—that can be used in conjunction with photorealistic renderings as training data in a deep learning neural network for understanding architectural elements in photos (or video images) about the built environment.

We presented valid methods for training-data synthesis using BIM and photorealistic rendering. Based on our results, we identify the following limitations and avenues for improvement: Generalization should be improved in the future by using more samples and training with more data. We assume that with enough data, we would be able to generalize trained networks on building photos for which we do not have corresponding training data (BIM models and renderings). Also, future work can explore using hyperreal parametric BIM to automatically create large and fully synthetic datasets of photorealistic building models. As for the described semantic mesh model that was generated using photogrammetry-based texture creation, geometry processing methods would need to be developed to construct a valid BIM model in an appropriate file format.

The intended applications and significance of the methods described in this paper can be summarized in the following: Synthetic data generation methods provide virtually unlimited training data for deep learning. BIM and photorealistic rendering can generate high-quality training data for the applications of deep learning in architecture and will help overcome the bottleneck of labor-intensive data acquisition, especially in architecture, where complex 3D and BIM data needed for training are already provided in the AEC industry. The same method can be applied to other industries where semantic models are available. As future work, the system presented in this paper can be augmented using hyperreal parametric BIM and generative design methods to generate synthetic big data for training deep learning models to improve the generalization of the presented methods.

REFERENCES

Alawadhi, Mohammad, and Wei Yan. 2018. "Geometry from 3D Photogrammetry for Building Energy Modeling." In *Proceedings of the 22th Conference of the Iberoamerican Society of Digital Graphics (SIGraDi)*, São Carlos, Brazil, November 7–9. São Paulo: Blucher, 5: 631–637. https://doi.org/10.5151/sigradi2018-1867.

As, Imdat, Siddharth Pal, and Prithwish Basu. 2018. "Artificial Intelligence in Architecture: Generating Conceptual Design via Deep Learning." *International Journal of Architectural Computing* 16 (4): 306–327. https://doi.org/10.1177/1478077118800982.

Baudrillard, Jean. 1995. *Simulacra and Simulation*. Translated by Sheila Faria Glaser. Ann Arbor: University of Michigan Press.

Borji, Ali. 2018. "Pros and Cons of GAN Evaluation Measures." ArXiv:1802.03446 [Cs], October. http://arxiv.org/abs/1802.03446.

Braun, Alex, and André Borrmann. 2019. "Combining Inverse Photogrammetry and BIM for Automated Labeling of Construction Site Images for Machine Learning." *Automation in Construction* 106 (October): 102879. https://doi.org/10.1016/j.autcon.2019.102879.

Chaillou, Stanislas. 2019. "AI + Architecture: Towards a New Approach." Thesis, Harvard University Graduate School of Design. https://view.publitas.com/harvard-university/ai-architecture-thesis-harvard-gsd-stanislas-chaillou/.

Georgakis, Georgios, Arsalan Mousavian, Alexander C. Berg, and Jana Kosecka. 2017. "Synthesizing Training Data for Object Detection in Indoor Scenes." ArXiv:1702.07836 [Cs], September. http://arxiv.org/abs/1702.07836.

Goodfellow, Ian. 2017. "NIPS 2016 Tutorial: Generative Adversarial Networks." ArXiv:1701.00160 [Cs], April. http://arxiv.org/abs/1701.00160.

Goodfellow, Ian J., Jean Pouget-Abadie, Mehdi Mirza, Bing Xu, David Warde-Farley, Sherjil Ozair, Aaron Courville, and Yoshua Bengio. 2014. "Generative Adversarial Networks." ArXiv:1406.2661 [Cs, Stat], June. http://arxiv.org/abs/1406.2661.

Handa, Ankur, Viorica Patraucean, Vijay Badrinarayanan, Simon Stent, and Roberto Cipolla. 2015. "SceneNet: Understanding Real World Indoor Scenes With Synthetic Data." ArXiv:1511.07041 [Cs], November. http://arxiv.org/abs/1511.07041.

Herranz, Luis. 2018. "Generative Adversarial Networks and Image-to-Image Translation." Luis Herranz, August 7. http://www.lherranz.org/2018/08/07/imagetranslation/.

Isola, Phillip, Jun-Yan Zhu, Tinghui Zhou, and Alexei A. Efros. 2018. "Image-to-Image Translation with Conditional Adversarial Networks." ArXiv:1611.07004 [Cs], November. http://arxiv.org/abs/1611.07004.

Jégou, Simon, Michal Drozdzal, David Vazquez, Adriana Romero, and Yoshua Bengio. 2017. "The One Hundred Layers Tiramisu: Fully Convolutional DenseNets for Semantic Segmentation." ArXiv:1611.09326 [Cs], October. http://arxiv.org/abs/1611.09326.

Kim, Jinsung, Jaeyeol Song, and Jin-Kook Lee. 2019. "Inference of Relevant BIM Objects Using CNN for Visual-Input Based Auto-Modeling." In *Proceedings of the 36th International Association for Automation and Robotics in Construction (ISARC)*, May, 393–398. https://doi.org/10.22260/ISARC2019/0053.

Krijnen, Thomas, and Martin Tamke. 2015. "Assessing Implicit Knowledge in BIM Models with Machine Learning." In *Modelling Behaviour: Design Modelling Symposium 2015*, edited by Mette Ramsgaard Thomsen, Martin Tamke, Christoph Gengnagel, Billie Faircloth, and Fabian Scheurer, 397–406. Cham: Springer. https://doi.org/10.1007/978-3-319-24208-8_33.

Lempitsky, V., and D. Ivanov. 2007. "Seamless Mosaicing of Image-Based Texture Maps." In *Proceedings of 2007 IEEE Conference on Computer Vision and Pattern Recognition (CVPR)*, Minneapolis, MN, June 17–22, 1–6. https://doi.org/10.1109/CVPR.2007.383078.

Lyu, S., and H. Farid. 2005. "How Realistic Is Photorealistic?" *IEEE Transactions on Signal Processing* 53 (2): 845–850. https://doi.org/10.1109/TSP.2004.839896.

Mayer, Nikolaus, Eddy Ilg, Philipp Fischer, Caner Hazirbas, Daniel Cremers, Alexey Dosovitskiy, and Thomas Brox. 2018. "What Makes Good Synthetic Training Data for Learning Disparity and Optical Flow Estimation?" *International Journal of Computer Vision* (April). https://doi.org/10.1007/s11263-018-1082-6.

Peng, Wenzhe, Fan Zhang, and Takehiko Nagakura. 2017. "Machines' Perception of Space: Employing 3D Isovist Methods and a Convolutional Neural Network in Architectural Space Classification." In *ACADIA 2017: Disciplines and Disruption [Proceedings of the 37th Annual Conference of the Association for Computer Aided Design in Architecture (ACADIA)]*, Cambridge, MA, 2–4 November 2017, edited by T. Nagakura, S. Tibbits, M. Ibañez, and C. Mueller, 474–481. CUMINCAD.

Richter, Stephan R., Vibhav Vineet, Stefan Roth, and Vladlen Koltun. 2016. "Playing for Data: Ground Truth from Computer Games." ArXiv:1608.02192 [Cs], August. http://arxiv.org/abs/1608.02192.

Salimans, Tim, Ian Goodfellow, Wojciech Zaremba, Vicki Cheung, Alec Radford, and Xi Chen. 2016. "Improved Techniques for Training GANs." ArXiv:1606.03498 [Cs], June. http://arxiv.org/abs/1606.03498.

Steinfeld, Kyle. 2019. "GAN Loci." In *ACADIA 19: Ubiquity and Autonomy [Proceedings of the 39th Annual Conference of the Association for Computer Aided Design in Architecture (ACADIA)]*, Austin, TX, 21–26 October 2019, edited by K. Bieg, D. Briscoe, and C. Odom, 392–403. CUMINCAD.

Varol, Gül, Javier Romero, Xavier Martin, Naureen Mahmood, Michael J. Black, Ivan Laptev, and Cordelia Schmid. 2017. "Learning from Synthetic Humans." In *Proceedings of 2017 IEEE Conference on Computer Vision and Pattern Recognition (CVPR)*, Honolulu, HI, July 21–26, 4627–4635. https://doi.org/10.1109/CVPR.2017.492.

Vu, Tuan-Hung, Himalaya Jain, Maxime Bucher, Matthieu Cord, and Patrick Pérez. 2019. "ADVENT: Adversarial Entropy Minimization for Domain Adaptation in Semantic Segmentation." ArXiv:1811.12833 [Cs], April. http://arxiv.org/abs/1811.12833.

Yu, Changqian, Jingbo Wang, Chao Peng, Changxin Gao, Gang Yu, and Nong Sang. 2018. "BiSeNet: Bilateral Segmentation Network for Real-Time Semantic Segmentation." ArXiv:1808.00897 [Cs], August. http://arxiv.org/abs/1808.00897.

Zhang, Yinda, Shuran Song, Ersin Yumer, Manolis Savva, Joon-Young Lee, Hailin Jin, and Thomas Funkhouser. 2017. "Physically-Based Rendering for Indoor Scene Understanding Using Convolutional Neural Networks." ArXiv:1612.07429 [Cs], July. http://arxiv.org/abs/1612.07429

Zhao, Hengshuang, Jianping Shi, Xiaojuan Qi, Xiaogang Wang, and Jiaya Jia. 2017. "Pyramid Scene Parsing Network." ArXiv:1612.01105 [Cs], April. http://arxiv.org/abs/1612.01105.

Zhu, Jun-Yan, Taesung Park, Phillip Isola, and Alexei A. Efros. 2020. "Unpaired Image-to-Image Translation Using Cycle-Consistent Adversarial Networks." ArXiv:1703.10593 [Cs], August. http://arxiv.org/abs/1703.10593.

Zou, Yang, Zhiding Yu, B. V. K. Vijaya Kumar, and Jinsong Wang. 2018. "Domain Adaptation for Semantic Segmentation via Class-Balanced Self-Training." ArXiv:1810.07911 [Cs], October. http://arxiv.org/abs/1810.07911.

IMAGE CREDITS

All drawings and images by the authors.

Mohammad Alawadhi is a doctoral student currently researching the intersection between artificial intelligence and architecture. He has an MSc in Architecture from Texas A&M. His interests include machine learning applications in architecture, computational design, and building energy modeling.

Wei Yan PhD is the Mattia Flabiano/Page Southerland Design Professor at Texas A&M University. He teaches computational methods in design and conducts research in BIM, simulation, optimization, AR, and AI, with projects funded by the NSF, NEH, DOE, Autodesk, etc.

Text-to-Form

3D Prediction by Linguistic Descriptions

Hang Zhang
University of Pennsylvania

The house has two floors. It has three bedrooms, two washrooms, two studys, two livingrooms, two storage and two balconys. Bedroom1, bedroom2, washroom1, storage1, study1, livingroom1, storage2 and balcony1 are all located on the first floor, while the others are on the second floor. Livingroom1 is in the center, it has 60 square meters. Balcony1 is on the south with 12 square meters. Bedroom1 is located in southwest and has 20 square meters. Bedroom2 is on the west with 24 square meters. Washroom1 is on the northwest which has 14 square meters. Study1 has 22 square meters and on the north. Storage1 has 8 square meters and lays between washroom1 and study1. Storage2 has 18 square meters and is located on the southeast. There is a livingroom2 on the center with 32 square meters. Balcony2 is the same as balcony1. Bedroom3 is on the southwest with 15 square meters. Washroom is on the northwest with 16 square meters. Study2 has 19 square meters and is located on the north. All of the rooms have one 900mm door and one 2000mm window. The height of the railings of the balcony is 1500mm. The house has 240mm wall and 200mm floor. The roof is inclined, the middle height of the roof is 1500mm.

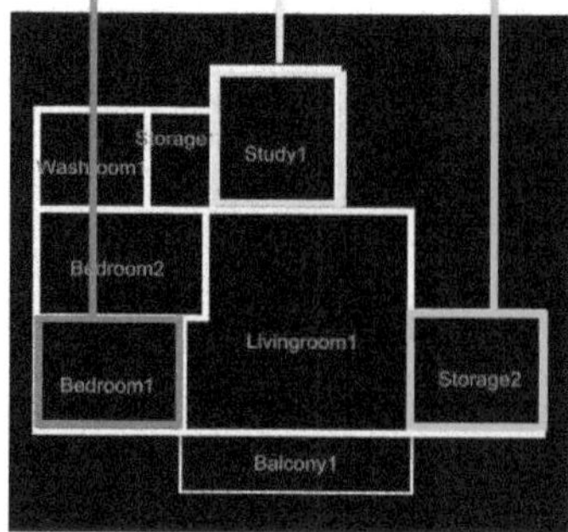

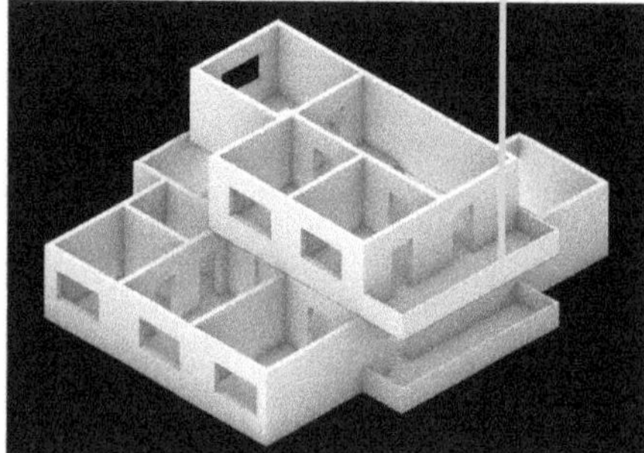

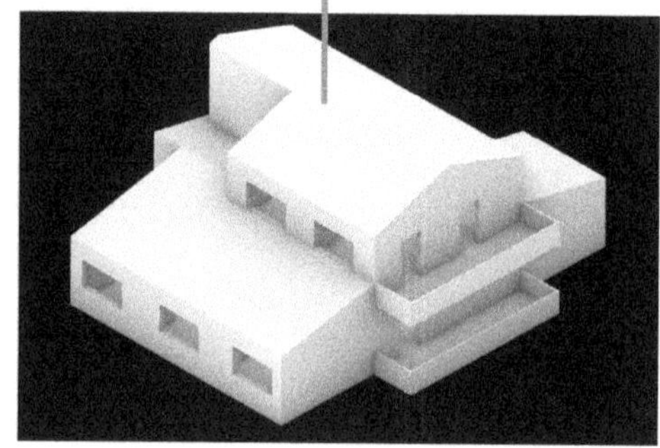

1 Selected results of the Linguistics-based Architectural Form Generative Model (LAFGM) that makes 3D form predictions based on the corresponding descriptions.

ABSTRACT

Traditionally, architects express their thoughts on the design of 3D architectural forms via perspective renderings and standardized 2D drawings. However, as architectural design is always multidimensional and intricate, it is difficult to make others understand the design intention, concrete form, and even spatial layout through simple language descriptions. Benefiting from the fast development of machine learning, especially natural language processing and convolutional neural networks, this paper proposes a Linguistics-based Architectural Form Generative Model (LAFGM) that could be trained to make 3D architectural form predictions based simply on language input.

Several related works exist that focus on learning text-to-image generation, while others have taken a further step by generating simple shapes from the descriptions. However, the text parsing and output of these works still remain either at the 2D stage or confined to a single geometry. On the basis of these works, this paper used both Stanford Scene Graph Parser (Sebastian et al. 2015) and graph convolutional networks (Kipf and Welling 2016) to compile the analytic semantic structure for the input texts, then generated the 3D architectural form expressed by the language descriptions, which is also aided by several optimization algorithms. To a certain extent, the training results approached the 3D form intended in the textual description, not only indicating the tremendous potential of LAFGM from linguistic input to 3D architectural form, but also innovating design expression and communication regarding 3D spatial information.

2

3

Input Text	GAN-INT-CLS [10]	Ours CGAN	Ours CWGAN
Dark brown wooden dining chair with red padded seat and round red pad back.			
Circular table, I would expect to see couches surrounding this type of table.			
Waiting room chair leather legs and armrests are curved wood.			
A multi-layered end table made of cherry wood. There is a rectangular surface with curved ends, and a square storage surface underneath that is slightly smaller.			
Brown colored dining table. It has four legs made of wood.			

4

2 Text2Scene: Generate various forms of compositional scene representations from natural language descriptions.

3 Text-to-image: Make the text-to-image translation while guaranteeing semantic consistency via novel global-local attentive and semantic-preserving framework.

4 Text2Shape: The first attempt at learning joint embeddings of freeform text descriptions and colored 3D shapes.

INTRODUCTION

In the semiotic sense, the appearance, materiality, and function of a building can be abstracted into a language symbol system, while these architectural elements themselves contain the experience and history of both design and construction. Architects are transmitters of information, and the design process is manifested as the gradual transformation of ideas and concepts into iconic signs, along with two-way communication between the architect and the user or viewer. The former conveys the "intention" to the latter through the "sign," and the latter's understanding of the sign (social convention) limits and affects the former's application of the sign.

During the progress of architectural design that starts with initial conception, through repeated elaboration, and ends up with the final production, architects are accustomed to expressing their design intention with 2D drawings (plans, sections, etc.) or 3D models (digital renderings, physical models, etc.). While encountering communications for sharing architectural theories or thoughts, specifying design requirements, and even getting feedback from reviewers, it is unavoidable to transfer information via both linguistic texts and verbal descriptions in these scenarios.

However, the content conveyed by words is always abstract or even obscure, leading to a high-level threshold of verbal and reading skills. Especially for architectural projects and studies, designers must ensure their own text description accurately conveys design intention and conception, while at the same time, they must do their best to absorb design thoughts and connotations from other literature.

For the past few decades, the artificial intelligence (AI) field of study has been exploring the imitation of logic from the human mind. One of its fundamental branches, natural language processing (NPL), is gradually emerging as having great potential to forge links between natural language and physical spatial information. Benefiting from the development of convolutional neural networks (CNNs) (Krizhevsky et al. 2012) and generative adversarial networks (GANs) (Goodfellow et al. 2014), state-of-the-art progress has been made regarding text-to-visual element translation. A Text2Scene model (Fig. 2) was designed to generate various forms of compositional scene representations from natural language descriptions (Tan and Ordonez 2019). Guaranteeing semantic consistency during text-to-image generation was addressed by MirrorGAN (Fig. 3), which proposed a novel global-local attentive and semantic-preserving framework (Tingting et al. 2019). Text2Shape (Fig. 4) was the first attempt at learning joint embeddings of freeform text descriptions and colored 3D shapes (Chen et al. 2018).

Nevertheless, regarding architectural form-finding, the current relevant research cannot satisfy the mapping and transformation demands from language expression to complex 3D spatial form. Generally, from word vectors to visual perception, the input-output data association in

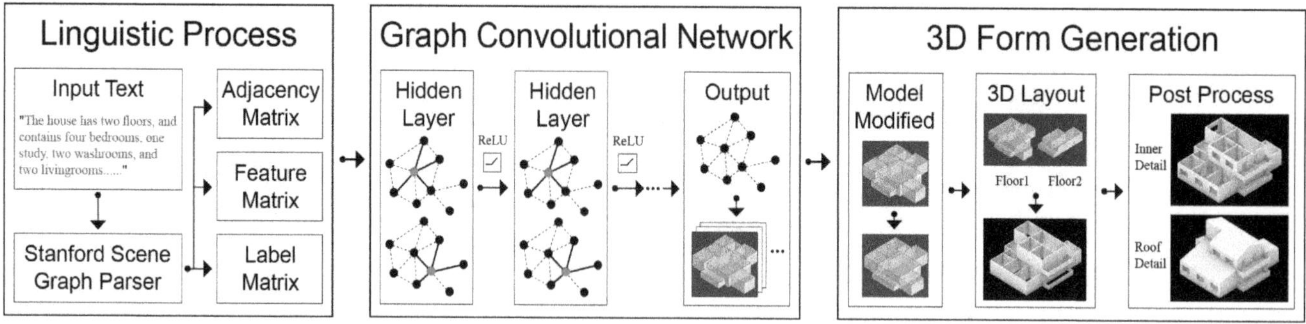

5

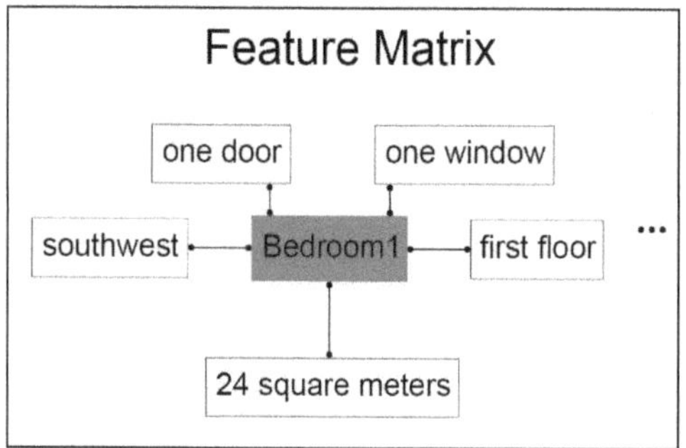

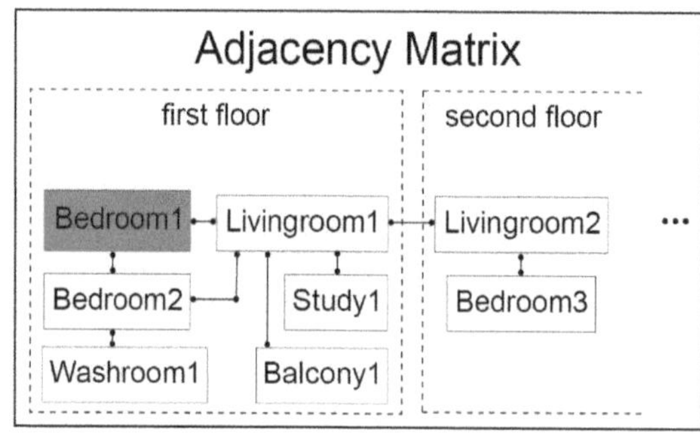

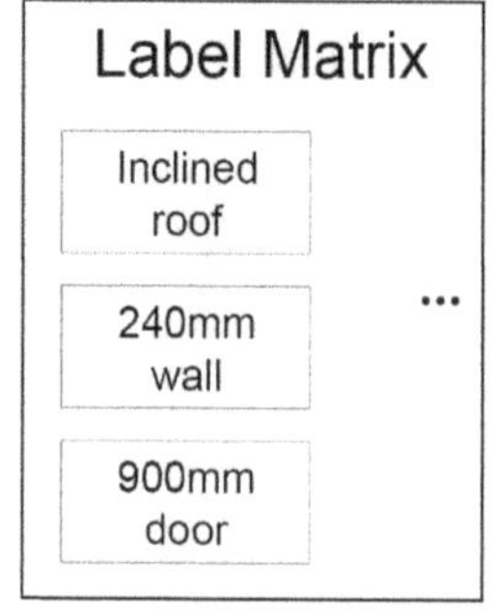

6

deep learning has mainly focused on 2D pixels or 3D voxels. Compared with the regression optimization for geometric features of a single object, the architectural structure lays more emphasis on the spatial geometric arrangement and multidimensional layout relations, leading to the particular requirement of CNN design and general work flow optimization for this task.

METHODOLOGY

General Workflow

On the basis of these previous works, this paper proposes a workflow for 3D form prediction from the corresponding descriptions, named the LAFGM (Linguistics-based Architectural Form Generative Model). As Figure 5 shows, the LAFGM contains three basic parts: linguistic process, training on a graph convolutional network (GCN), and 3D form generation via postprocessing. The linguistic process transfers the description information into the training matrix, then the GCN makes the 3D boundary prediction. With the postprocessing, the auto-modeled 3D form is generated based on both the label matrix and rule set of 3D layout modification.

Linguistic Process

To begin with, the author applied the Stanford Scene Graph Parser (Sebastian et al. 2015) to transfer the language information input into three types of graph structures (Fig. 6). The feature matrix records the attributes of each entry unit, specifically room location, size, floor, etc. In addition, the adjacent relation between the horizontal plane and vertical floors is stored by the adjacency matrix. Finally, the label matrix will pickle the overall feature information of the building (thickness of the wall, height of the floors, etc.) and flow directly into the Grasshopper components (Rutten 2020), providing specific optimization during final model generation.

5 The main process of the LAFGM contains 3 basic parts: linguistic process, training on graph convolutional networks, and 3D form generation via postprocessing.

6 Detail of the parsed matrix structure, which includes 3 basic matrices: feature, adjacency, and label.

Figure 7 shows the samples of the training input. The data set of this research was manually collected from open sources of villa floor plans on the internet; each drawing has corresponding linguistic data that was manually populated and modified based on language templates. This process was inspired by state-of-the-art natural language generation (NLG) research (Gatt and Krahmer 2018). When the matches of the drawings and descriptions is finished, 938 of the paired data were put in the training set and 124 in the evaluating set.

To illustrate the more detailed structure of the graph parsed results, Figure 8 shows one sample of the processed framework and index for each linguistic element. The parser will iterate through all the training data, assigning an index to each different type of word based on its pretrained vocabulary system. Within every single sentence, all phrases will be transformed into a tree

......one washroom, one balcony, one livingroom, and one kitchen. bedroom1 covers 12 square meters located in east. storage1 has 11 squares in east. In addition, washroom1 is in center with 3 square meters. balcony1 is in east with 4 square meters. livingroom1 covers 38 square meters located in center. study1 covers 7 square meters located in west......

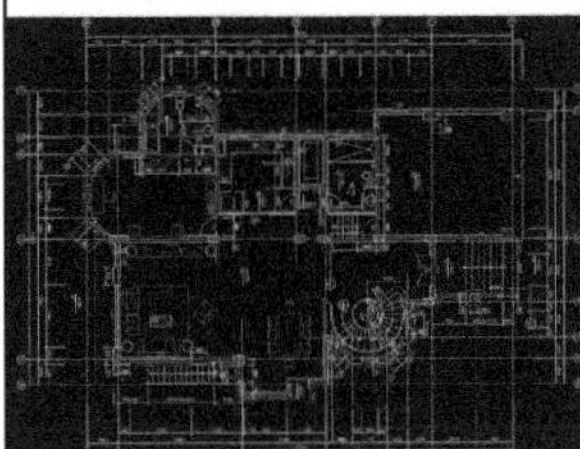

......two storages. Specifically, bedroom2 has 14 squares in southeast. Additionally, bedroom2 has 13 squares in southwest. bedroom3 has 6 squares in northeast. Additionally, washroom2 is in east with 6 square meters. livingroom1 covers 37 square meters located in center. study2 is in north with 4 square meters, storage2 is in southeast with 10 square meters......

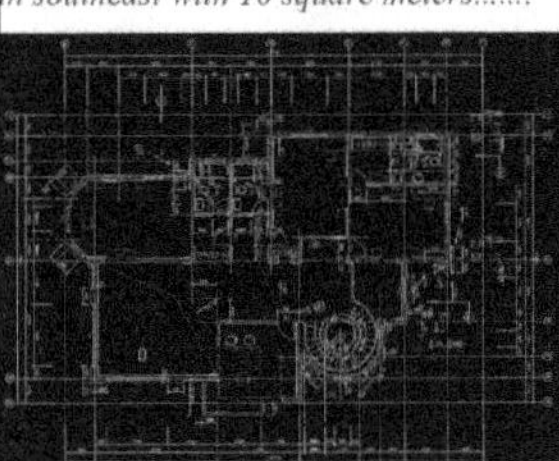

......and three balconys. washroom1 is in east with 7 square meters. washroom2 has 5 squares in east. In addition, washroom3 covers 4 square meters located in west. livingroom2 is in south with 30 square meters. study1 has 8 squares in the center. Besides, livingroom1 covers 7 square meters located in southwest. storage2 holds 12 square meters and located in......

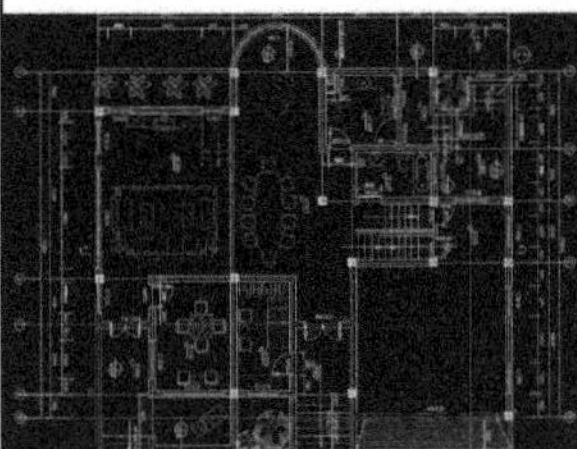

......bedroom2 is in northeast with 15 square meters. bedroom3 covers 15 square meters located in southwest. kitchen1 is in northwest with 7 square meters.balcony1 is in south with 10 square meters. In addition, balcony2 covers 10 square meters located in north. bedroom4 covers 9 square meters while in the northeast, and livingroom2......

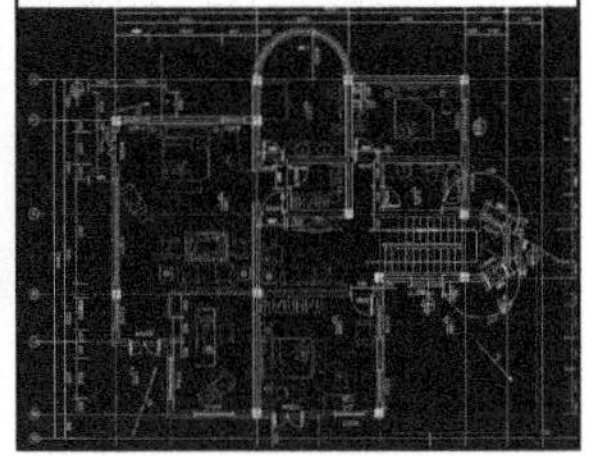

......

7

The house has two floors. It has three bedrooms, two washrooms, two studys, two livingrooms, two storages and two balconys. Bedroom1, bedroom2, washroom1, storage1, study1, livingroom1, storage2 and balcony1 are all located on the first floor, while the others are on the second floor. Livingroom1 is in the center, it has 60 square meters. Balcony1 is on the south with 12 square meters. Bedroom1 is located in southwest and has 20 square meters. Bedroom2 is on the west with 24 square meters. Washroom1 is on the northwest which has 14 square meters. Study1 has 22 square meters and on the north. Storage1 has 8 square meters and lays between washroom1 and study1. Storage2 has 18 square meters and is located on the southeast. There is a livingroom2 on the center with 32 square meters. Balcony2 is the same as balcony1. Bedroom3 is on the southwest with 15 square meters. Washroom is on the northwest with 16 square meters. Study2 has 19 square meters and is located on the north. All of the rooms have one 900mm door and one 2000mm window. The height of the railings of the balcony is 1500mm. The house has 240mm wall and 200mm floor. The roof is inclined, the middle height of the roof is 1500mm.

(a)

```
(ROOT
  (S
    (NP (DT The) (NN house))
    (VP (VBZ has)
      (NP (CD two) (NNS floors)))
    (. .)))
```

(b)

```
(ROOT
  (S
    (NP (PRP It))
    (VP (VBZ has)
      (NP
        (NP (CD three) (NNS bedrooms))
        (, ,)
        (NP (CD two) (NNS washrooms))
        (, ,)
        (NP (CD two) (NNS studys))
        (, ,)
        (NP (CD two) (NNS livingrooms))
        (, ,)
        (NP (CD two) (NNS storages))
        (CC and)
        (NP (CD two) (NNS balconys))))
    (. .)))
```

(c)

```
(ROOT
  (S
    (NP
      (NP (NNP Bedroom1))
      (, ,)
      (NP (NNPS bedroom2) (, ,) (NNPS washroom1) (, ,) (NNPS storage1) (, ,) (NNPS study1) (, ,) ......
        (CC and)
        (NNPS balcony1)))
    (VP (VBP are) (RB all)
      (VP (VBN located)
        (PP (IN on)
          (NP (DT the) (JJ first) (NN floor)))
        (, ,)
        (SBAR (IN while)
          (S
            (NP (DT the) (NNS others))
            (VP (VBP are)
              (PP (IN on)
                (NP (DT the) (JJ second) (NN floor)))))))
    (. .)))
```

(d)

```
(ROOT
  (S
    (NP (NNP Balcony1))
    (VP (VBZ is)
      (PP (IN on)
        (NP
          (NP (DT the) (NN south))
          (PP (IN with)
            (NP (CD 12) (JJ square) (NNS meters)))
    (. .)))
```

```
(ROOT
  (S
    (NP (NNP Bedroom1))
    (VP
      (VP (VBZ is)
        (VP (VBN located)
          (PP (IN in)
            (NP (NN southwest)))))
      (CC and)
      (VP (VBZ has)
        (NP (CD 20) (JJ square) (NNS meters))
```

(e)

```
(ROOT
  (S
    (NP
      (NP (DT The) (NN height))
      (PP (IN of)
        (NP
          (NP (DT the) (NNS railings))
          (PP (IN of)
            (NP (DT the) (NN balcony)))
    (VP (VBZ is)
      (NP (CD 1500) (NNS mm)))
```

```
(ROOT
  (S
    (S
      (NP (DT The) (NN roof))
      (VP (VBZ is)
        (ADJP (JJ inclined))))
    (, ,)
    (S
      (NP
        (NP (DT the) (JJ middle) (NN height))
        (PP (IN of)
          (NP (DT the) (NN roof))))
      (VP (VBZ is)
        (NP (CD 1500) (NNS mm))))
```

8

structure so as to carry off key information from the same branches.

Once the parsing is finished, the output can be formatted as NumPy data for further matrix generation (Harris 2020). The sample information of Figure 8 will be extracted as follows:

(a) feature_input = {'floor1','floor2'} (b) valid_output.shape = [13,6] (c) 'floors1' = {'bedroom1','bedroom2','washroom1','storage1','study1','livingroom1','storage2','balcony1'}; num_floors2 = 5; 'floors2' = {'bedroom3','washroom2','livingroom2','study2','balcony2'} (d) 'balcony1' = {'south',12}; 'bedroom1' = {'southwest',20} (e) 'height' = (1500); 'inclined' = (True); 'inclined_height' = (1500).

Floor1		
1	2	3
4	5	6
7	8	9
Floor2		
10	11	12
13	14	15
16	17	18
Not Exist		0

Northwest	North	Northeast
West	Center	East
Southwest	South	Southeast

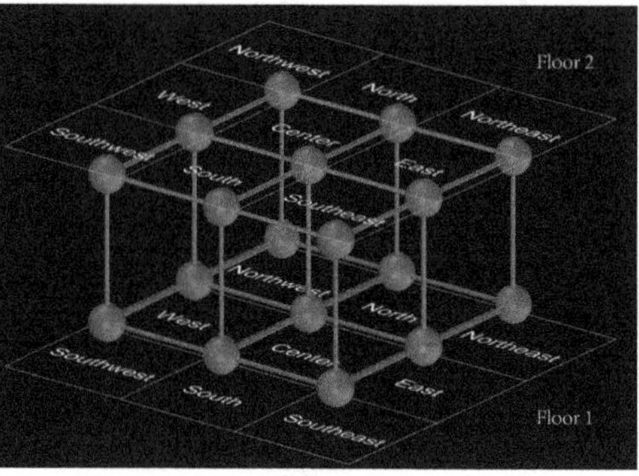

9

Name	bedroom1	bedroom2	bedroom3	bedroom4	washroom1	washroom2	......
bedroom1	0	1	1	0	0	0	
bedroom2	1	0	0	0	1	1	
bedroom3	1	0	0	0	0	1	
bedroom4	0	0	0	0	0	0	
washroom1	0	1	0	0	0	0	
washroom2	0	1	1	0	0	1	
washroom3	0	0	0	0	0	0	
study1	0	0	0	0	1	0	
study2	0	0	0	0	0	0	
study3	0	0	0	0	0	0	
livingroom1	1	1	0	0	0	0	
livingroom2	0	0	1	0	0	0	
livingroom3	0	0	0	0	0	0	
livingroom4	0	0	0	0	0	0	
balcony1	0	0	0	0	0	0	
......	......	......	......	......	......	......	

10

7 Samples of training input that contain the 2D plan drawings and corresponding linguistic descriptions.

8 One sample of the processed framework and index for each linguistic element: (a) floor conditions; (b) room conditions; (c) floor distributions; (d) detail of the single room information; (e) details for the label data.

9 The corresponding positions of room distributions could be marked as the sequential index.

10 The final adjacency matrix of this sample.

Machine Learning

Several previous attempts have been made regarding 3D architectural form-finding via machine learning. A method for making the data-driven 3D form generation of design alternatives has been made by combining an autoencoder architecture for point clouds (Bidgoli and Veloso 2018) or vectors (de Miguel et al. 2019). A GAN was used to make the anonymous composition of 3D form (Liu, Lia, and Srivastava 2019). 3D form style transfer on two levels of scale (overall and detailed) through multiple GANs has also been trained on both serial stack and multiview datasets (Zhang and Blasetti 2020).

This paper aims to make 3D architectural form predictions expressed by the linguistic descriptions while specifically using a GCN to compile the analytic semantic structure. As shown in Figure 5, the GCN described in this paper uses two layers in total, with a rectified linear unit (ReLu) as the inner activation function and Softmax (Goodfellow et al. 2016) as the final activation function. The optimizer during each training loop will be the Adam optimization algorithm (Kingma 2014). As a result, the overall function is:

$$Z = f(X, A) = \mathrm{softmax}\left(\hat{A}\ \mathrm{ReLU}\left(\hat{A}XW^{(0)}\right)W^{(1)}\right)$$

Here, the $W^{(0)}$ and $W^{(1)}$ are the weights of the two GCN layers, while *X* is the feature matrix and *A* is the adjacency matrix. The GCN is a semisupervised learning method for graph-structured data. It is based on a variant of an efficient CNN that operates directly on the graph. The selection of the convolution architecture is stimulated by the local first-order approximation of the spectral graph convolution. The model is scaled linearly according to the number of edges and learns to encode the hidden layer representation of local graph structure and node characteristics. This graph-based training logic makes the GCN perfectly matched for the parsed data structure from the previous language processing steps.

Matrix Data Set Generation

To prepare the training matrix for the GCN, several translation rules were made to map the parsed NumPy data into the feature matrix and adjacency matrix.

The training input of adjacency is a sparse matrix composed of 0 and 1, where 1 represents the adjacency relationship between two elements. In the source information describing the location of each room, the data type will be the spatial orientation of the relative position (center, north, southeast, etc.). Based on the multilayer structure of the 3D spatial relationship (this paper mainly focuses on two floors), the corresponding positions of room distributions could be marked as the sequential index (Fig. 9). The final

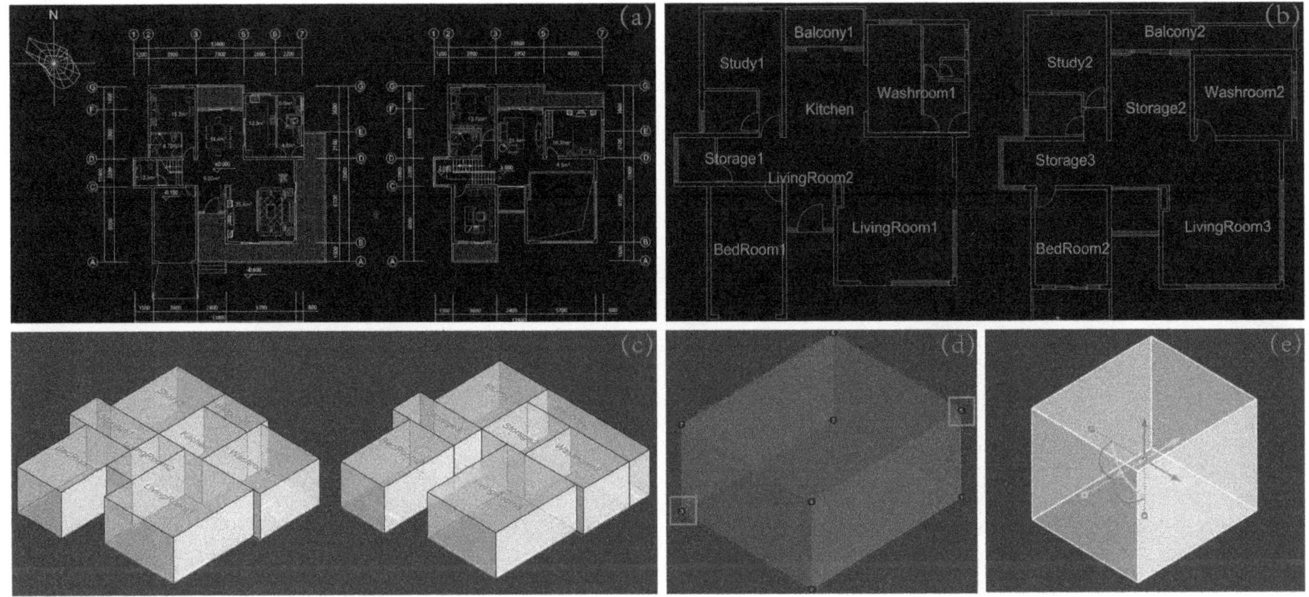

11

	Input		Output					if not exist : 0
Name	Location	Area	Xminus	Yminus	Zminus	Xplus	Yplus	Zplus
bedroom1	7	20	0	2	0	5	6	3.3
bedroom2	4	24	0	6	0	6	10	3.3
bedroom3	16	16	0	2	3.3	4	6	6.6
bedroom4	0	0	0	0	0	0	0	0
washroom1	1	14	0	10	0	4	13.5	3.3
washroom2	10	16	0	10	3.3	4	14	6.6
washroom3	0	0	0	0	0	0	0	0
study1	2	22	5	10	0	9.5	15	3.3
study2	11	18	5	10	3.3	9.5	14.5	6.6
study3	0	0	0	0	0	0	0	0
livingroom1	0	64	5	2	0	13	10	3.3
livingroom2	14	32	4	2	3.3	8	10	6.6
livingroom3	0	0	0	0	0	0	0	0
livingroom4	0	0	0	0	0	0	0	0
balcony1	7	12	5	0	0	13	2	1.1
......	......	......	......	......	......	......	......	......

12

adjacency matrix (Fig. 10) is generated through the welting condition on the same layer and the similar condition between upper and lower layers.

The feature matrix mainly records the value description of the spatial size and its location index, in which the input data is obtained by the linguistic text, and the ideal output data is extracted from the corresponding CAD model. Figure 11 illustrates one sample of a general process from collecting architectural plan drawings to their theoretical 3D layout coordinates: (a) original plan data with all model layers; (b) filter the layers which include the essential boundary information; (c) build the bounding box based on the 2D layout and "height" value from parsed NumPy data; (d) extract the minus and plus nodes values based on the WorldXY plane in Grasshopper; (e) basic XYZ coordinate relationship.

When dealing with the raw data from architectural and engineering drawings, the redundant information is

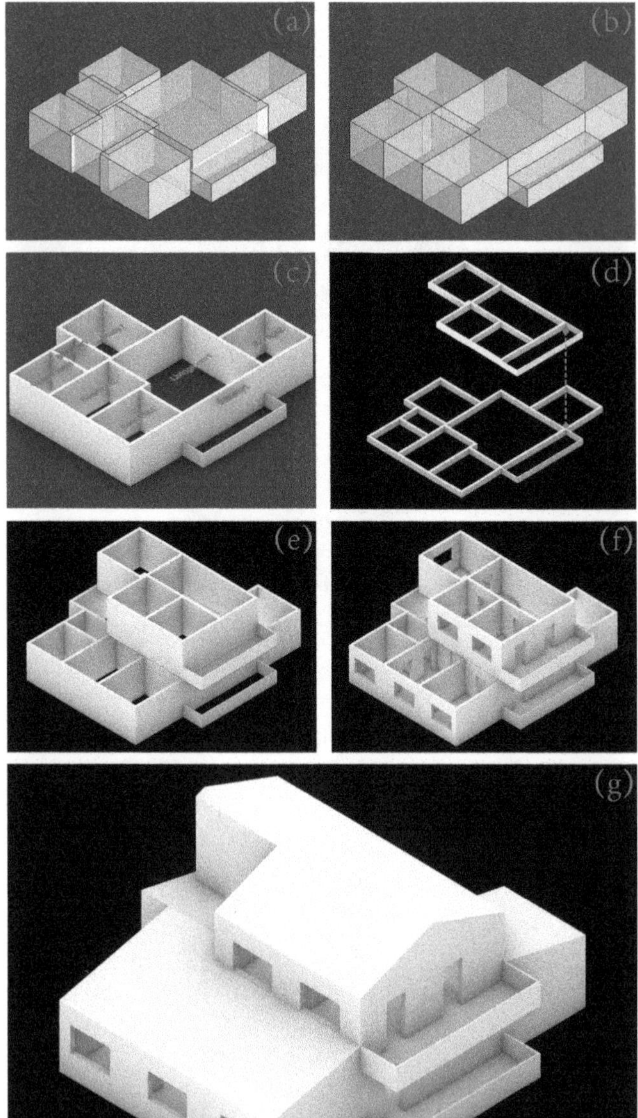

13

11 One sample of the general process from collecting architectural plan drawings to their theoretical 3D layout coordinates: (a) original plan data; (b) filter the essential information; (c) build the bounding box; (d) extract the minus and plus nodes; (e) basic xyz coordinate relationship.

12 Training input and output of feature matrix.

13 General workflow of postprocess: (a) basic reconstruction of the bounding box; (b) modification method for aligning the room boundary; (c) wall generation from label matrix; (d) multilayer modification; (e) fixed two-layer model; (f) postprocessing for generating windows and doors; (g) final step of covering the roof of 2 types.

removed by the filtering step. Due to the limitations of 2D layouts, the generation of a bounding box approximates the spatial domain that the building is supposed to have, whose z-axis value is offered by the language description. However, it is not necessary to store the whole coordinate data from every single corner of the bounding box. While on the basis of the formatted WorldXY plane in Grasshopper, the corner points that have the highest or lowest value of x, y, and z can be navigated.

Thus, as shown in Figure 12, the training input is given by both the layout locations and their area numbers, while the ground truth output will be the x, y, and z values of the minus and plus corner points. Note that if the room does not exist in this training batch, all of its values in both adjacency matrix and feature matrix will be 0, so as to help maintain the same data structure.

Finally, the customized loss function can be obtained based on the mean square error of minus and plus corner values:

$$\text{Loss} = \text{MSE}(\text{y\_true} - \text{y\_pred}) = (\text{y\_true(minus)} - \text{y\_pred(minus)})^2 + (\text{y\_true(plus)} - \text{y\_pred(plus)})^2$$

while specifically:

$$(\text{y\_true(minus)} - \text{y\_pred(minus)})^2 = (\text{y\_true(Xminus)} - \text{y\_pred(Xminus)})^2 + (\text{y\_true(Yminus)} - \text{y\_pred(Yminus)})^2 + (\text{y\_true(Zminus)} - \text{y\_pred(Zminus)})^2$$

the plus corner loss function will share the same structure as the minus corner. The y_true and y_pred correspondingly refer to the ground truth value of the corner coordinate and the predicted value from the trained model.

Postprocessing

Since the GCN training is generally processed on bounding box layout, postprocessing is required to satisfy the detailed final architectural model generation. As the language input has also been parsed to contribute the label matrix ("900 mm door" and "2000 mm window," etc.), the postimprovement steps can be performed via Grasshopper components, where the key values are extracted as input data for label recognition and parameter setting.

As Figure 13 shows, the general workflow of postprocessing modifies the spatial information obtained through GCN training, predicting the architectural form that conforms to the language description to a certain extent: (a) basic reconstruction of the bounding box from the trained prediction of the GCN; (b) the modification method for aligning the room boundary; (c) wall generation via "thickness" value from the label matrix; (d) the multilayer modification that fixes the deviation between the upper and lower layers; (e) fixed two-layer model; (f) postprocessing for generating windows and doors; (g) the final step of covering the roof of 2 types.

The training of deep learning is always accompanied by a deviation that cannot be ignored. Even if this paper has adjusted the GCN parameters and trained to 200 epochs,

The building has 2 floors. It contains three bedrooms, two washrooms, two studys, two balconys, two livingrooms, three storages, and one kitchen, while the livingroom1, livingroom2, bedroom1, storage1, study1, balcony1,kitchen, and washroom1 are on the first floor. Bedroom1 covers 18 square meters located in southwest. Livingroom1 has 33 squares in southwest, and livingroom2 in south with 9 square meters. Kitchen is located in the center and has 11 squares. the Washroom1 has 25 square meters and is on the east. The study1 is located on the northwest with 25 square meters, and balcony1 in the north with 5 squares. Storage1 covers 11 square meters and in the west. Moreover, the bedroom2 has 19 square meters and is on the southwest. The livingroom3 is located on the southeast with 35 squares. Storage2 is in the middle and has 10 squares, while the study2 is in the northwest with 23 square meters. The washroom2 covers 19 square meters in the east and the balcony2 is located on the north with 12 squares. All of the rooms have one 900mm door and one 2100mm window. The height of the railings of the balcony is 1500mm. The house has 240mm wall and 200mm floor. The roof is Flattened.

The building contains 2 floors, with two bedrooms, two washrooms, one study, one balcony, two livingrooms, two storages, and one kitchen, while the livingroom1, bedroom1, storage1, study1, balcony1, kitchen, and washroom1 are on the first floor. Bedroom1 will have 22 square meters in notrhwest. Kitchen is in the center and with 13 squares. The Washroom1 has 18 square meters and is located on the west. Livingroom1 has 35 squares while in south. The study1 is located on the east with 27 square meters, and balcony1 lays in the north with 8 squares meters. In addition, the Bedroom2 has 19 square meters and is on the southwest. The study2 is on the west with 19 square meters. Storage1 covers 11 square meters and in the North. Moreover, The Storage2 is located on the northeast with 29 squares. The washroom2 covers 19 square meters in the east. At last, Livingroom2 has 39 squares while in east. All of the rooms have one 1000mm door and one 2000mm window. The height of the railings of the balcony is 1500mm. The house has 240mm wall and 210mm floor. The roof is Flattened.

The building has 2 floors. It has two bedrooms, two washrooms, two studys, two livingrooms, one storage, and the livingroom1, bedroom1, storage1, study1, and washroom1 are all located on the first floor. Livingroom1 covers 18 square meters located in southwest. Livingroom2 has 33 squares in the center, and Bedroom1 in east with 37 square meters. Washrooms1 is located in the west and has 11 squares meters. The Study1 has 25 square meters and is on the south. Moreover, the study2 is located on the south with 17 square meters, and balcony1 in the north with 5 squares. Storage1 covers 19 square meters and in the northwest. In addition, the Bedroom2 has 22 square meters and is on the south. The Washroom2 is located on the northeast with 9 squares. Storage2 is in the middle and has 10 squares. All of the rooms have one 900mm door and one 2000mm window. The house has 260mm wall and 220mm floor. The roof is Flattened.

14

14 Three samples of generated 3D model through the LAFGM.

each individual room will still overlap each other during the output reconstruction, which obviously does not meet the expectations of building generation. Based on the principle that the center position will not change, all adjacent bounding boxes should calculate the overlapping domains within the central geometry, leading to coordinate data corrections guided by the nearest adjacent corner, so as to align the rooms of the generated model.

Moreover, spatial alignment correction is also required between the upper and lower models. As both the top and bottom centers were fixed during the previous step, this paper set up a chosen point (southeast corner) to match the coordinates, while also modifying the z-axis value for each corner point to maintain the coherence of these spatial geometries. Finally, as the detailed data are extracted to guide the creation of the windows, doors, and roofs, the final 3D model form is defined.

RESULTS AND DISCUSSION

Figure 14 shows three samples of the generated 3D models through the LAFGM. This text-to-form workflow was able to make the approximate 3D model prediction of the building based on certain language descriptions. However, due to the limitation of the number of training sets that are confined to the 1,062 pairs, as well as the shortage of keyword definitions that are limited to several variable parameters, there is no obvious diversity of the results produced.

In addition, it is obvious that, among the written descriptions of the architectural design intention, the layout relationship and dimensions of each room need to be further specified. The keyword units of both feature matrix and adjacency matrix rely highly on these explanations in order to obtain detailed information and participate in computation, which, however, result in the rigid requirement for literal narration. It does not accord with the situation of daily use of language. An ideal natural language translation workflow needs to conform to the language usage habits of most people, which requires the improvement of this serious defect through the training of a large quantity of data with high diversity and clear geometric modeling descriptions.

At the same time, LAFGM's data types still lack diversity. At present, the part involved in GCN training is mainly focused on the layout and area values of spatial rooms, while the doors, windows, beam-column structures, and other architectural elements are not involved in the learning process. This forced LAFGM to use additional postoptimization algorithms to predict and generate the above building elements. The graph structure-based neural network is able to make convergence and prediction of the spatial location relationship with relatively high efficiency, while on the other hand, this structure also limits the configurational demands of freeform design, along with the restriction of training data selection or production. As a result, the final predicted output through the LAFGM was limited to the degree of simple block stacking.

CONCLUSION

At present, LAFGM is almost the first attempt in deep learning to predict three-dimensional spatial morphology through natural language processing. Based on the learning process trained by more than 1,000 sets of 2D architectural plan drawings and their corresponding linguistic descriptions, this workflow could be able to make an architectural form prediction that generally conforms to the description expectation, enabling abstract descriptive language to be associated with the concrete and straightforward layout form.

Even though there are still many limitations and shortcomings, the general framework has great potential to make further progress. Future work could focus on optimizing and improving the data set and effectively integrating the labels of corresponding architectural elements, so as to make text-to-form more flexible and diversified. Or it could try more natural language processing algorithms, such as the CovLSTM-based model (Shi et al. 2015) that makes the sequence-to-sequence transition while releasing the staid language structure restrictions in GCN training.

Moreover, there is no doubt that architectural design and communication will embrace a new stage when machine learning enables mature and accurate transformation between language and forms. When communicating with party A through text-to-form, partners and even students, will help remove the misunderstanding between communication, as the abstract language will be concretized into graphical models or images. While obtaining the predicted feedback during linguistic communication, designers will be able to explore innovative design or form-finding through the "mind" of AI, which will be similar to the real-time design and optimized suggestions via machine learning (Zhang et al. 2018). More significantly, profound architectural ideas will be able to be extracted into more understandable visual forms through professional architectural terms.

REFERENCES

Bidgoli, Ardavan, and Pedro Veloso. 2018. "DeepCloud. The Application of a Data-driven, Generative Model in Design." In *ACADIA 2018: Recalibration: On Imprecision and Infidelity [Proceedings of the 38th Annual Conference of the Association for Computer Aided Design in Architecture (ACADIA)]*, Mexico City, Mexico, 18–20 October 2018, edited by P. Anzalone, M. del Signore, and A. J. Wit, 176–185. CUMINCAD.

Chen, K., C. B. Choy, M. Savva et al. 2018. "Text2shape: Generating Shapes from Natural Language by Learning Joint Embeddings." In *Asian Conference on Computer Vision*, 100–116. Cham: Springer.

de Miguel, Jaime, Maria Eugènia Villafane, Luka Piškorec, and Fernando Sancho-Caparrini. 2019. "Deep Form Finding—Using Variational Autoencoders for Deep Form Finding of Structural Typologies." In *Architecture in the Age of the 4th Industrial Revolution [Proceedings of the 37th eCAADe and 23rd SIGraDi Conference, Volume 1]*, Porto, Portugal, 11–13 September 2019, edited by J. P. Sousa, J. P. Xavier, and G. Castro Henriques, 71–80. eCAADe.

Gatt, Albert, and Emiel Krahmer. 2018. "Survey of the State of the Art in Natural Language Generation: Core Tasks, Applications and Evaluation." *Journal of Artificial Intelligence Research* 61: 65–170.

Goodfellow, I., J. Pouget-Abadie, M. Mirza, B. Xu, D. Warde-Farley, S. Ozair, A. Courville, and Y. Bengio. 2014. "Generative Adversarial Nets." *Advances in Neural Information Processing Systems*: 2672–2680.

Goodfellow, I., Y. Bengio, A. Courville. 2016. "6.2.2.3 Softmax Units for Multinoulli Output Distributions." In *Deep Learning*, edited by I. Goodfellow, Y. Bengio, and A. Courville, 180–184. Cambridge: MIT Press.

Harris, C.R., K. J. Millman, S. J. van der Walt, et al. 2020. "Array programming with NumPy." *Nature* 585, 357–362. DOI: 0.1038/s41586-020-2649-2.

Kingma, Diederik P., and Jimmy Ba. 2014. "Adam: A method for stochastic optimization." arXiv preprint arXiv:1412.6980.

Kipf, T. N., and M. Welling. 2016. "Semi-Supervised Classification with Graph Convolutional Networks." arXiv preprint. arXiv:1609.02907.

Krizhevsky, A., I. Sutskever, and G. Hinton. 2012. "Imagenet Classification with Deep Convolutional Neural Networks." *Advances in Neural Information Processing Systems*: 1097–1105.

Liu, Henan, Longai Liao, and Akshay Srivastava. "An Anonymous Composition." 2019. In *ACADIA 19: Ubiquity and Autonomy [Proceedings of the 39th Annual Conference of the Association for Computer Aided Design in Architecture (ACADIA)]*, Austin, TX, 21–26 October 2019, edited by K. Bieg, D. Briscoe, and C. Odom, 404–411. CUMINCAD.

Rutten, David. 2020. *Grasshopper*. V.1.0.0007. Robert McNeel & Associates. PC.

Sebastian, Schuster, Ranjay Krishna, Angel Chang, Li Fei-Fei, and Christopher D. Manning. 2015. "Generating Semantically Precise Scene Graphs from Textual Descriptions for Improved Image Retrieval." In *Proceedings of the Fourth Workshop on Vision and Language*, Lisbon, Portugal, 18 September 2015, 70–80. Association for Computational Linguistics.

Shi, X, Z. Chen, H. Wang et al. 2015. "Convolutional LSTM Network: A Machine Learning Approach for Precipitation Nowcasting." *Advances in Neural Information Processing Systems* 28: 802–810.

Tan, F., S. Feng, and V. Ordonez. 2019. "Text2Scene: Generating Compositional Scenes from Textual Descriptions." In *Proceedings of the 2019 IEEE/CVF Conference on Computer Vision and Pattern Recognition (CVPR)*, Long Beach, CA, 15–20 June 2019, 6703–6712. IEEE.

Tingting, Qiao. Jing Zhang, Duanqing Xu, and Dacheng Tao. 2019. "Mirrorgan: Learning Text-to-Image Generation by Redescription." In *Proceedings of the 2019 IEEE/CVF Conference on Computer Vision and Pattern Recognition (CVPR)*, Long Beach, CA, 15–20 June 2019, 1505–1514. IEEE.

Zhang, Hang, and Ezio Blasetti. 2020. "3D Architectural Form Style Transfer through Machine Learning." In *Anthropocene, Design in the Age of Humans [Proceedings of the 25th CAADRIA Conference, Volume 2]*, Bangkok, Thailand, 5–6 August 2020, edited by D. Holzer, W. Nakapan, A. Globa, and I. Koh, 659–668. CUMINCAD.

Zhang, Yan, Arnod Grignard, Alexander Aubuchon, Kevin Lyons, and Kent Larson. 2018. "Machine Learning for Real-time Urban Metrics and Design Recommendations." In *ACADIA 2018: Recalibration: On Imprecision and Infidelity [Proceedings of the 38th Annual Conference of the Association for Computer Aided Design in Architecture (ACADIA)]*, Mexico City, Mexico, 18–20 October 2018, edited by P. Anzalone, M. del Signore, and A. J. Wit, 196–205. CUMINCAD.

IMAGE CREDITS

Figure 2: Tan et al. 2019.
Figure 3: Tingting et al. 2019.
Figure 4: Chen et al. 2018.

All other drawings and images by the author.

Hang Zhang is a postgraduate student from University of Pennsylvania. In the past two years, he has published several investigations regarding the application of machine learning-aided architectural form finding and structural optimization. More recently, he has been interested in NLP (natural language processing), DRL (deep reinforcement learning), and intelligent robotic fabrication, trying to contribute to the interdisciplinary cooperation fields related to design, bio-inspired material, AI, and robotics.

Space Allocation Techniques (SAT)

Computable Design Problems and Integrated Framework of Solvers

Nirvik Saha
Georgia Institute of Technology

John Haymaker
Perkins & Will

Dennis Shelden
Rensselaer Polytechnic Institute

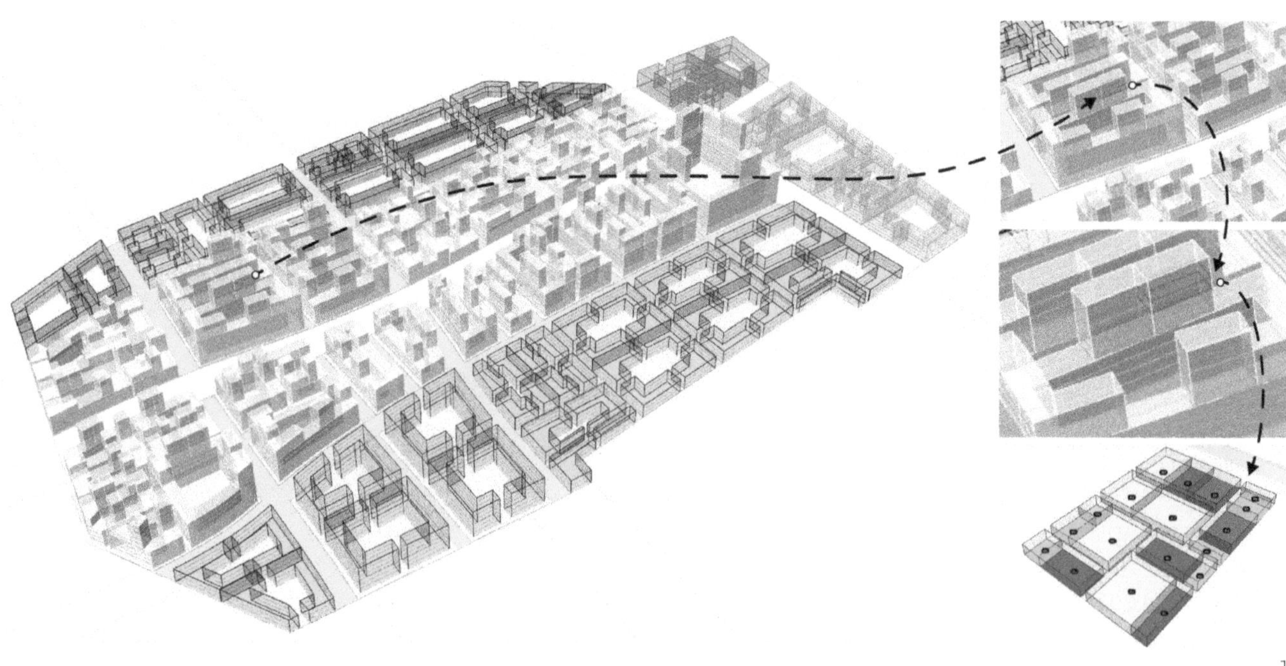

1 DOTs provides an integrated framework of solvers to address a top-down design process from urban planning to site parcellation and massing to floor plans. This is illustrated by the study where the proposed solution is used for urban planning. The site is parcellated and a schematic massing is generated. For each mass, the floor plates are extracted and the floor plan is generated.

ABSTRACT

Architects and urban designers use space allocation to develop layouts constrained by project-specific attributes of spaces and relations between them. The space allocation problem (SAP) is a general class of computable problems that eluded automation due to combinatorial complexity and diversity of architectural forms. In this paper, we propose a solution to the space allocation problem using reinforcement learning (RL). In RL, an artificial agent interacts with a simulation of the design problem to learn the optimal spatial organization of a layout using a feedback mechanism based on project-specific constraints. Compared to supervised learning, where the scope of the design problem is restricted by the availability of prior samples, we developed a general approach using RL to address novel design problems, represented as SAP.

We integrated the proposed solution to SAP with numerous geometry modules, collectively defined as the space allocation techniques (SAT). In this implementation, the optimization and generative modules are decoupled such that designers can connect the modules in various ways to generate layouts with desired geometric and topological attributes. The outcome of this research is a user-friendly, freely accessible Rhino Grasshopper (C#) plugin, namely, the Design Optimization Toolset or DOTs, a compilation of the proposed SAT. DOTs allows designers to interactively develop design alternatives that reconcile project-specific constraints with the geometric complexity of architectural forms. We describe how professional designers have applied DOTs in space planning, site parcellation, massing, and urban design problems that integrate with performance analysis to enable a holistic, semi-automated design exploration.

SPACE ALLOCATION PROBLEM (SAP)

In the domain of architecture and urban design, space allocation is well-known with numerous applications in the design of building layouts and urban planning schemes (Keller 2006). From prior descriptions of space allocation, (Lopes et. al. 2010; Martin 2006; Shekhawat 2018), we define the space allocation problem (SAP) as a project-specific organization of spaces, constrained by geometry of spaces and relations between activities, hosted by the spaces. Since each design problem is unique, SAP-related geometric and topological constraints vary significantly between design projects. Determining an optimal solution is nontrivial because the number of permutations exhibits exponential growth, limiting the exploration (Galle 1986). Researchers and practitioners address SAP as a combinatorial problem, which is optimized by generating alternatives of a layout and evaluating each alternative based on predefined constraints to find an appropriate spatial organization (Jagielski and Gero 1997). The combinatorial complexity of the SAP combined with the expected geometric diversity of architectural formations provides scope for computation to aid design processes.

This paper presents a novel solution to SAP using reinforcement learning for combinatorial optimization, which drives geometric modules to assist designers in developing architecture or urban design schemes. Collectively, we refer to these modules as space allocation techniques (SAT). We developed a minimal set of SAT, which can be connected in various ways to provide a modular approach to SAP-related design problems. The contribution of this research is the formulation, implementation, and validation of the proposed SAT.

To allow intuitive access to designers and support community-led analysis tools, we wrapped the modules into a plugin for the Rhino-Grasshopper environment, namely, the Design Optimization Toolset (DOTs), available at https://github.com/nirvik00/DOTS/. The components operate in a top-down manner to generate spatial output from generic inputs with minimum human intervention to iterate and manage the process of exploration of architectural and urban design schemes (Fig. 1). Together, the DOTs-components (Fig. 2) address the diversity of geometric forms in architecture and urban design, using SAT for distribution of spaces from a point, along a curve, and partitions of a closed curve, and include numerous massing typologies. The geometry modules operate procedurally to develop spaces that meet geometric constraints such as area, setbacks, floor area ratio (FAR) distribution, etc. Simultaneously, a customized reinforcement learning algorithm optimizes user-defined topological attributes of the

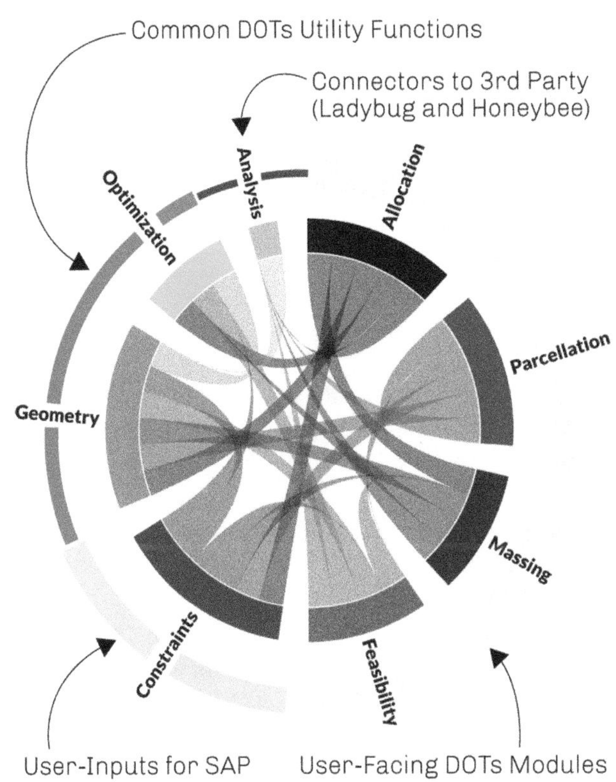

2

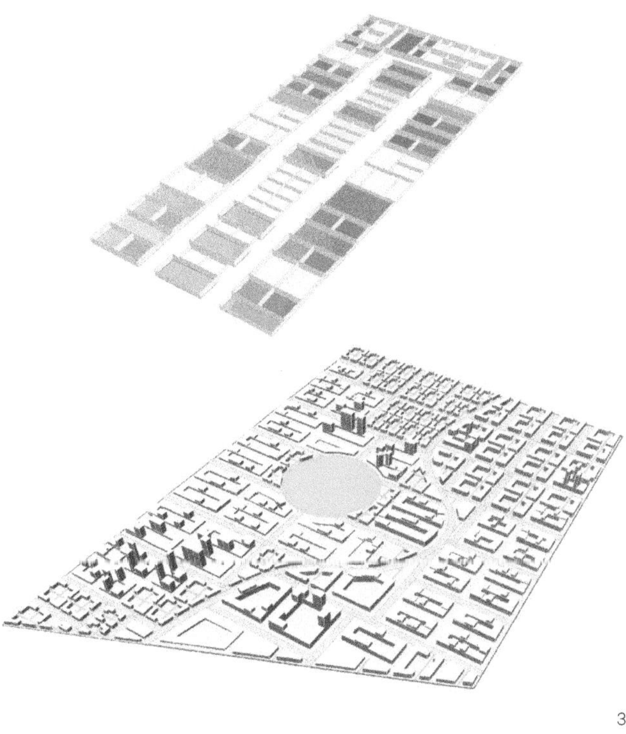

3

2 Overall classification of components in DOTs.

3 Sample of floor plans and urban planning schemes generated by DOTs.

layout such as adjacencies, the proximity between spaces, access to views, and orientation.

The efficiency of the SAT algorithms and the generic formalism of SAP allows the proposed solution to serve as an assistant in a rapid, iterative design process. The output of this process provides a foundation for subsequent performance analysis and design development. Apart from the generation of design, we illustrate the application of DOTs in conjunction with analytical tools such as Ladybug and Honeybee to provide recommendations to designers. In this paper, we describe the proposed techniques and demonstrate applications to industry case studies concerning space planning and urban design (Fig. 3).

SAP and Recent Developments in Design Automation

Prior research on the SAP has been extensively discussed by Liggett (2000), where the origin of the problem is traced to the quadratic assignment problem (Armour and Buffa 1963) in facility planning and plant layouts. Since then, architectural researchers have classified constraints based on geometric and topological criteria that serve as cost functions to reward or penalize certain arrangements (Rodrigues et al. 2013). The numerical score of a layout is used to guide an iterative optimization process such as genetic algorithms (Calixto and Celani 2015). The introduction of new technologies provides a scope to enhance the user interaction, rapidly develop design prototypes in a flexible manner, scale the solution, and extend the solution to design problems with additional geometric or topological constraints.

As deep learning techniques evolve, data-driven approaches are increasingly being applied to generate tentative layouts using prior samples of layouts. Huang and Zhang (2018) demonstrate the application of generative adversarial networks (GANs) for "drawing review, digitization, and drawing assistance," which assists designers in performing repetitive tasks. Researchers use GANs to demonstrate solutions at the scale of family dwellings (Wu et al. 2019) and extended a GANs-based approach to develop layouts from a "bubble-diagram," or a graph of desired spatial relations (Nauata et al. 2020). The discriminator and generator networks in GANs are trained using data sets of existing architectural plans where the generator develops variations acceptable to the discriminator, and together they provide variations based on a scheme provided by the training data. The supervised-learning solutions to a design problem, such as GANs, are useful when large data sets of similar design problems exist. But usually, designers are engaged in unique design problems, studied as SAP in prior research, where the problems are entirely customized by project-specific constraints that include types of spaces, area requirements, relations between the spaces, or access to views and orientation.

We propose a general solution to design problems by formulating a SAP, and ensure the scalability of the algorithm as well as the geometric diversity using advances in another branch of machine learning, namely, reinforcement learning. RL is a class of machine learning, which is known to be effective in combinatorial optimization (Mazyavkina et al. 2020) with applications in various domains such as game AI (Shao et al. 2019), operations research (Hubbs et. al. 2020), or healthcare (Yu, Liu, and Nemati 2020). We adapted the RL to control geometric operations and apply the solution to SAP in architecture and urban design.

SPACE ALLOCATION TECHNIQUES

Our approach to SAP consists of an interaction between optimization and geometry modules where the optimization algorithm allocates spaces in a layout and the geometry module generates an architectural pattern such as double-loaded corridors or partitions of a floor plate. Geometry modules conduct procedural operations to discretize the layout, generate a topological model of the layout for optimization, and convert an optimized topological model back to geometric forms. The optimization module operates on the topological model of the layout, which is a graph with spaces as attributes of the vertices, and reconfigures the vertices to address desired proximities, access to orientation, views, etc. (Fig. 4). The geometry and optimization modules are decoupled such that various pattern generators access the optimization functions by an intermediate topological representation. Using this formulation, we developed an extensible SAT framework to simultaneously provide a solution to the design problems, represented as SAP, and address the diversity of architectural or urban design formations. In the following sections, we describe the optimization process along with a sample of the geometry modules.

Combinatorial Optimization with Reinforcement Learning

The proposed solution to SAP is based on the theory of reinforcement learning (Sutton and Barto 1998). In our adaptation of RL, an agent operates on the topological representation of the layout and learns to associate spaces to locations by evaluating the effect of constraints or rewards on a sample layout and predicting future rewards, provided by an alternative spatial organization. Key elements of RL are adapted to SAP and described as follows:

- The *environment* is generated dynamically when the optimization module is invoked. The environment parses user-input interfaces such as spreadsheets to extract numerical values of topological and geometric constraints. The inputs received from the geometry module include a set of discrete locations inside or along the bounding curve of the layout where spaces can be placed (vertices of the graph or topological model) and SAP constraints. During the optimization process, the environment computes the numerical values of a sample layout using the design constraints, which act as a feedback signal to determine the desirability of the samples.
- *States* are the set of all locations (vertices of the graph) to which spaces are allocated. The states are generated by a geometry module and used by the optimization module to assign spaces, represented as an attribute of the vertex of the graph or topological model of the layout (Figs. 4b–c).
- An *agent* is an algorithmic construct that traverses the states while associating a space to that location and receives rewards from the environment. This process is referred to as an interaction with the environment. The agent tries to maximize the rewards by iteratively choosing an alternative action at a state and updating the attribute of the topological model.
- The *action* taken by an agent is the mechanism of interaction between the agent and environment where the agent chooses a space to assign to a state, receives rewards for the assignment, and moves to the next state.
- A *reward* is a numerical value (scalar) provided by the environment to the agent as feedback for actions. The reward is calculated by evaluating the effect of the action on the user-defined constraints. A positive reward signifies desired action whereas a negative reward implies an undesired action. The SAP is extended by introducing additional constraint types and their effect on the layout, described by numerical feedback signals.
- The *value function* is used to estimate the cumulative rewards that an agent can accrue from the current state to the terminal state. The sole purpose of the agent is to maximize the value function.
- *Q-learning* in space allocation is implemented by a simulation where the agent traverses the states (locations), assigning spaces to each location, and computes the discounted rewards, given by the adjacency and orientation calculations in this implementation.
- The *policy* is a map of an agent's action at all states. Initially, the agent starts with an arbitrary policy and improves it over several iterations. An optimal policy has the maximum value function leading to a space

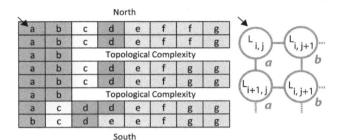

Spaces	Number	Orientation	Adjacency	
a	7	east=100	a=20	c=20
b	7	south=100	g=20	
c	6		a=20	d=20
d	7	east=100	c=5	
e	7	south=10	f=15	
f	8	north=20	e=15	
g	10	north=10	b=20	

4a

4b

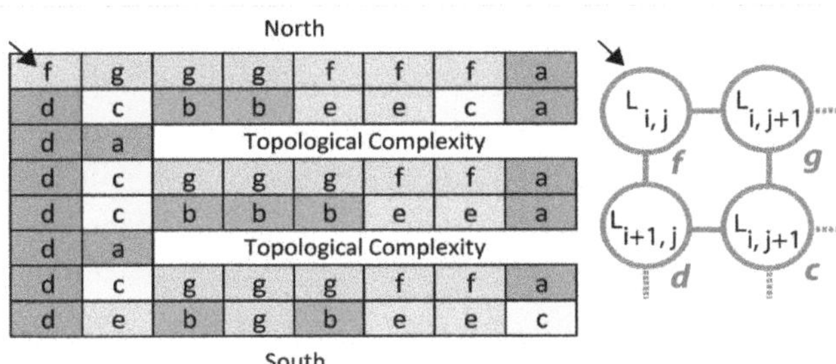

4c

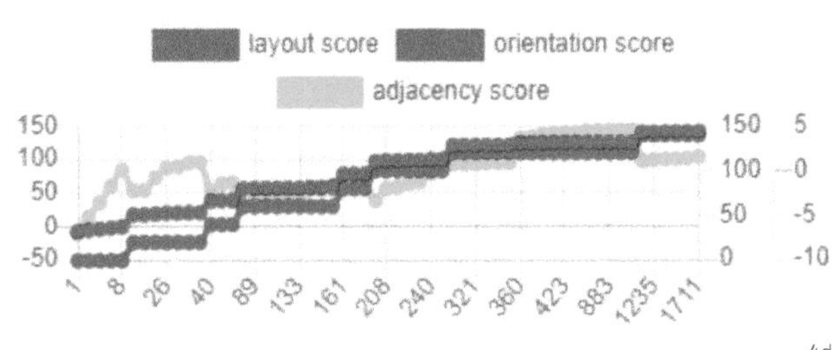

4d

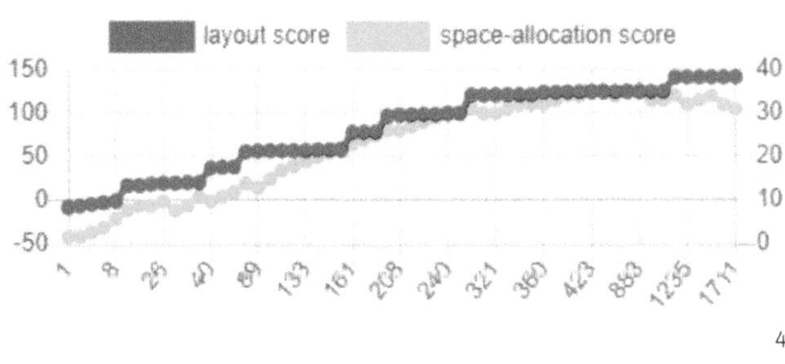

4e

4a Constraints for number of each type of spaces, their adjacency, and access to orientation are illustrated and analyzed in a topological SAP problem.

4b,c Initial and optimized layouts, indicating the topological structure used for running the RL algorithms.

4d Graph showing the improvement of scores over a number of iterations.

4e Graph showing the increase increment of layout score with respect to cumulative change in the layout.

allocation that satisfies the constraints.

- A *Q-table* is a cache of action values at each state. The agent updates the Q-table during the process of exploration. The agent uses this cache to estimate the value at a state and reduce the combinatorial complexity of the SAP by eliminating exploratory traversals. During the process of optimization, a designer may partially develop the Q-table, reevaluate the constraints, and resume the optimization process with altered constraints without losing information. Or, the Q-tables provide a way to save optimal substructures of the layout such that until better relations are discovered by the agent, the substructure is retained. Even if the constraints are altered, the agent targets spaces that exhibit suboptimal relations without disturbing optimal relations. Q-tables can be saved and reused in other projects with similar constraints to drastically reduce the time required to develop a solution.
- The agent maximizes rewards by balancing the processes of *exploration and exploitation*. Exploration is the process where the rewards for various state action sequences are computed as the agent stochastically chooses actions to maximize rewards during state traversal. While exploration allows the agent to find actions that yield greater rewards, after several iterations, the agent may follow an exploitation-based space allocation where the agent assigns the highest known values to a state without testing alternatives or calculating rewards as a consequence of that action. An epsilon-greedy policy is used during the process of policy improvement to ensure that the agent scans alternatives with minimum moves.
- *Deep Q-networks* (DQN) utilize neural networks (deep learning) to predict the value of action during the exploration phase. The neural network is trained using the Markov chain Monte Carlo (McMC) algorithm by computing the rewards, updating the error, and adjusting the network. Once trained, the neural network acts as a regression model to predict the values at a state during the feed-forward phase, greatly reducing the combinatorial complexity of the problem.

In our implementation of reinforcement learning for SAP, the agent starts with an arbitrarily generated policy and improves the policy over several episodes (traversal from initial to terminal state) by interacting with the environment. During the interaction, the agent takes an action (chooses a space) at a state (location), and moves to the next state. This process is continued until the terminal state is reached and all spaces have been allocated. Iteratively, the agent improves the initial policy by choosing alternative actions to increase the cumulative rewards. A Q-table is maintained

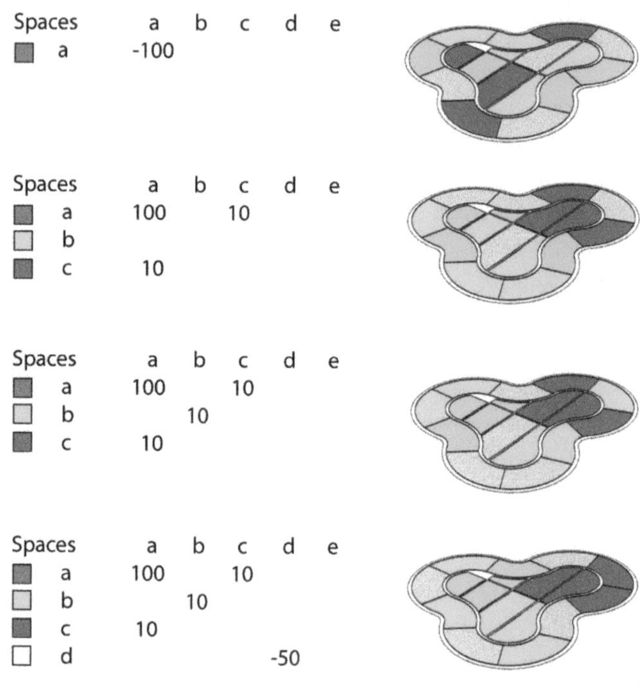

5 Designer interaction with DOTs components for developing rapid prototypes in a flexible manner. In this image, two different types of geometry modules are used. The designers can change constraints in an external spreadsheet and update the spatial organization.

to record the action value or value functions of explored states. A Monte Carlo evaluation controls the trajectories taken by the agent during exploration such that the agent returns the space allocation that yields maximum value. The epsilon-greedy policy ensures a comprehensive exploration and value estimates of a state, and eliminates traversals with low rewards. To demonstrate the scalability of the proposed solution, the algorithm is tested on a sample topological representation of a layout with 52 spaces with adjacency and orientation constraints, where the overall learning strategy is illustrated by Figs. 4a–e. The Q-table addresses the flexibility of design processes where designers continuously alter the constraints and try variations on some parts of the layout while retaining the parts of the layout that exhibit optimality (Fig. 5). In the following sections, we describe two geometric modules that develop spatial organization and generate architecturally appropriate layouts.

Sample of SAT Modules to Address Geometric Diversity

To address the diversity of forms used by designers, we developed geometric modules as sequential sets of operations that generate typical patterns of architectural and urban layouts from a building program with constraints. For instance, the same set of geometric operations leads to spaces along the periphery of a floor plate and parcels along a site curve, or double-loaded corridors correspond to parcels on opposite sides of a street. Formal massing typologies, such as a courtyard or podium, are generated procedurally using constraints such as floor space ratio (FSR), setbacks, or stepbacks. By combining the geometry modules, complex patterns are generated across scales of buildings and urban planning. A sample of geometry modules, the layout of spaces along a curve, and the subdivision of the curve are illustrated in the following sections.

Binary Partition

The internal region of a closed curve is split into the area and adjacency requirements using an equivalence relation between requirements and geometric operations on the closed geometric shape of the boundary (Fig. 6). The relation is such that the boundary of the curve is split in correspondence with cumulative areas of the two subsets of requirements. Recursively, the entire region can be split with a guarantee that it will meet the area requirements. These operations form a binary tree which is manipulated by the optimization module to determine appropriate relations between spaces based on constraints.

Spaces Along a Curve

The region along a curve is discretized into locations for spaces using the algebraic formulation of the curve such that a peripheral band of cells is generated at regular intervals of the curve to match the number of spaces required. An array of point locations is extracted from the cells to form the topological model of the layout. The optimization module operates on the topological representation of the layout and returns the location array with appropriate spaces allotted to each element. To generate the geometry of spaces, the region along the curve is discretized into cells with thin sections, which are procedurally joined to generate the area of spaces. In conjunction with binary partition, a variety of architectural patterns can be generated using this formulation (Figs. 6, 7).

DESIGN OPTIMIZATION TOOLSET (DOTS)

When the SAT modules are used in conjunction as workflows, each module addresses the substructures of an architectural scheme, and the workflows provide an avenue to expand the scope of SAT in addressing design problems. Simultaneously, the sequential application of SAT modules to a design problem represents the blueprint of a solution, which can be transferred to similar problems by updating the constraints of the problem. A designer may explore alternative geometric formations using the SAT workflows or study the effect of constraints on an architectural scheme. To facilitate the flow of information between the SAT modules, we developed a framework, namely, Design Optimization Toolset (DOTs), where the modules of SAT are embedded in the Grasshopper components of DOTs

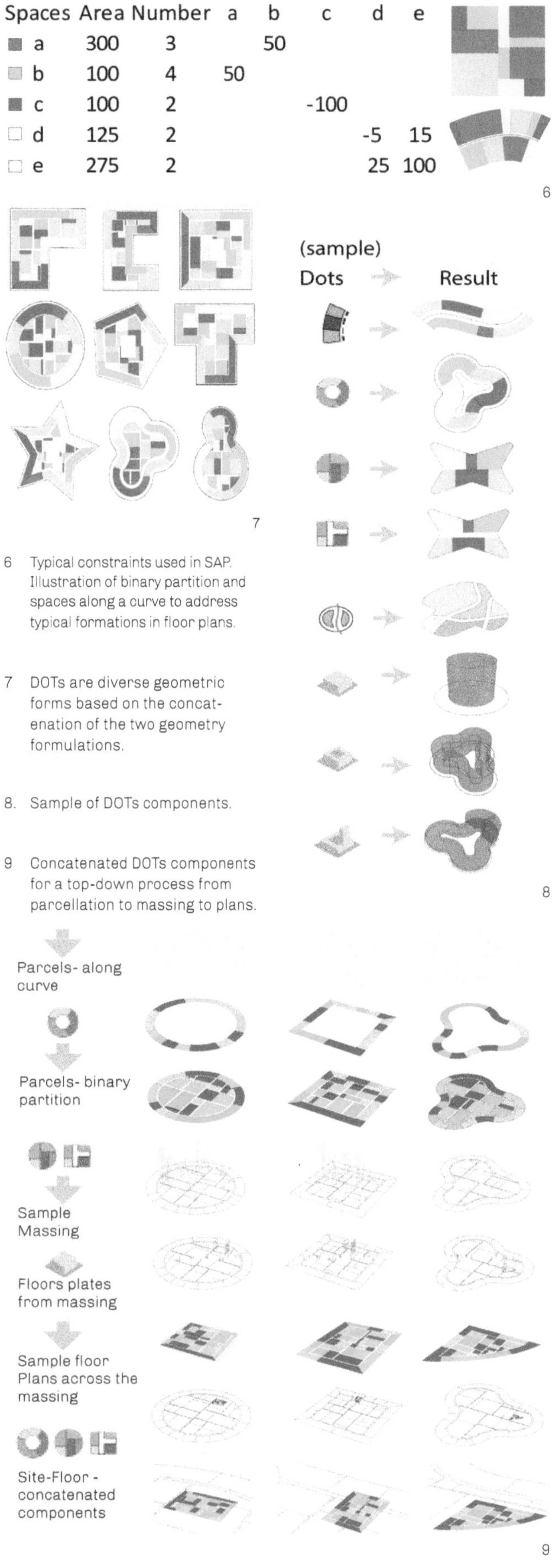

Spaces	Area	Number	a	b	c	d	e
a	300	3		50			
b	100	4	50				
c	100	2			-100		
d	125	2				-5	15
e	275	2				25	100

6 Typical constraints used in SAP. Illustration of binary partition and spaces along a curve to address typical formations in floor plans.

7 DOTs are diverse geometric forms based on the concatenation of the two geometry formulations.

8. Sample of DOTs components.

9 Concatenated DOTs components for a top-down process from parcellation to massing to plans.

using the C# Rhinocommon API (Fig. 8). DOTs is an extensible framework that allows designers to address complex SAP by concatenating components to create workflows. For instance, Figure 9 illustrates a potential workflow to emulate a top-down process from large-scale planning to the floor plans of a building. Once a workflow is developed, it can be reused in similar problems because the SAT are generalized to topological and geometric variations.

Case Studies to Demonstrate Generality across Scales

We developed and tested the SAT, as implemented in DOTs, on space planning and urban planning case studies to generate corresponding spaces and parcels. Each case study demonstrates the scope for exploring variations of geometry and constraints.

Space Planning case study: This case study illustrates the application of the proposed SAT in architectural space planning processes. The original plan was created using a conventional design process (Fig. 10) and exhibits unusual geometric shapes with varying organization of spaces at periphery, quadrants, and center. Using the same geometric and adjacency constraints used by the original designer (Fig. 11), we were able to generate alternatives for convex, non-convex curves and orthogonal shapes, using the same DOTs workflow (Fig. 12).

Urban Design case study: We worked with designers to develop a DOTs workflow for planning a mixed-use science park (Figs. 13, 14). The campus integrates high-tech facilities within a parkland with recreational facilities, and the program requires robotic manufacturing, labs, offices, amenities, etc. Our solution modifies the planar space planning allocation described above to include a three-dimensional allocation of activities, constrained horizontally by the building type, and vertically by the elevation of the floor plate. The urban layout is served by a circulation system that is hierarchical and includes primary streets, pedestrian/cycle streets, secondary streets, service streets, and pedestrian paths.

Case Studies: DOTs and Performance Analysis

Space allocation is generally an early-stage design process where a variety of numerous design alternatives are required to develop project-specific recommendations before the design stage. Since DOTs generates spatial output from project requirements, analysis can be conducted on probable alternatives to explore the effect of constraints. In the following sections, two instances of collaborative research are presented at the scale of multi-level buildings and urban scale (campus planning) to illustrate the utilization of the proposed SAT to assist

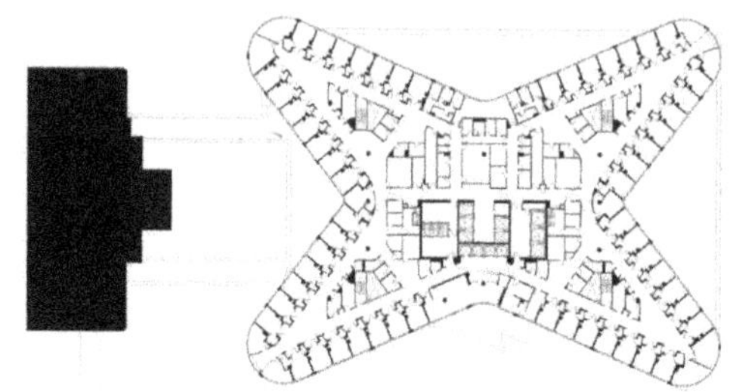

10

Spaces (sample)	Id	Area	Number	z1.a	z1.b	z1.c	z1.d	z1.e	z1.f	z1.g
Workstation	z1.a	1	2	-90	100	50				
Meds	z1.b	1	1			50				
clean_supplies	z1.c	1	1			50	100	50	50	50
Staircase	z1.d	2	1				0	100	100	100
Nour	z1.e	0.75	1				100		100	
Evs	z1.f	0.75	1					100		100
Linen	z1.g	0.75	1						100	

Spaces (sample)	Id	Area	Number	z3.a	z3.b	z3.c	z3.d	z3.e	z3.f
Trmt	z3.a	1	1		100				-90
Respite	z3.b	1	2	100	100				-90
share office	z3.c	0.75	1			200			
food_gallery	z3.d	1	1					100	100
ptot_therapy	z3.e	0.5	1				100		200
Evs	z3.f	0.5	1				100		200

11

Using DOTs

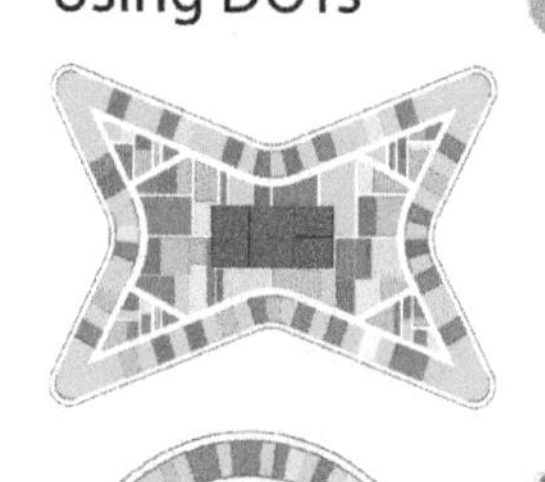

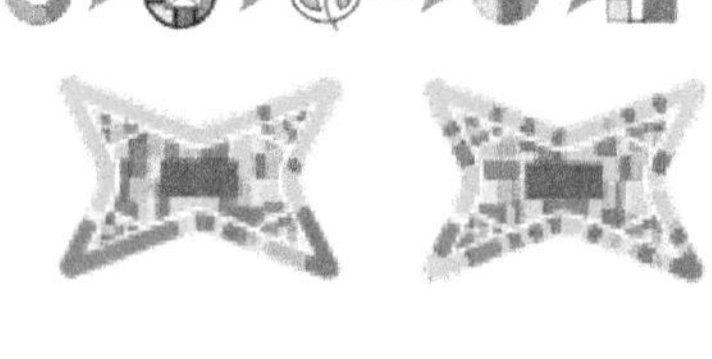

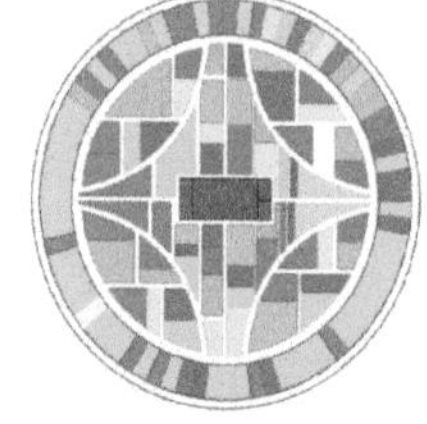

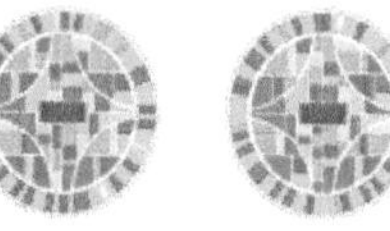

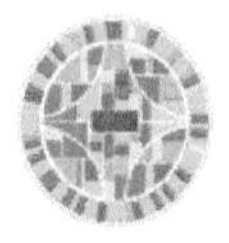

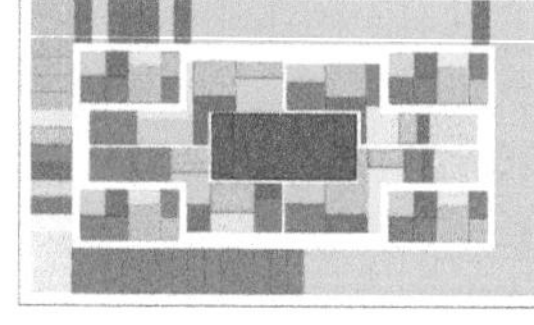

12

10 Sample layout generated by designers.

11 Sample constraints to formulate a SAP.

12. Concatenated DOTs components to replicate the solution and explore diverse geometric forms and constraints.

in performance analysis and provide guidelines for the subsequent design process.

K-12 massing study for energy and daylight: Rezzae et al. (2019) demonstrate the application of a multiobjective workflow in K–12 school design to increase energy and daylight performances. A DOTs workflow was developed based on program requirements. Constraints of window-wall ratio and orientation were included for analysis. The project-specific constraints included a range of dimensions for each space and their tentative adjacency requirements. Since the adjacencies did not fully constrain the spaces, the solution generated equivalent exhaustive configurations (1,080 in number) of a three-dimensional layout of the school. The objective of the study is to provide recommendations to the design team at the early stage of the design process that achieve spatial constraints while maximizing daylighting and minimizing energy consumption (Fig. 15).

Campus massing study for energy and human comfort: Chang et. al. (2019) describe an application of the proposed SAT in site planning and subsequent multiobjective optimization. The collaborative research explored generative campus planning where site parcellation, massing, and feasibility studies were analyzed for proximity, building dimensions, and topography. The alternatives (Fig. 16) were used to study multivariate relationships in campus planning. The design options were analyzed to determine the optimal conditions for solar radiation, energy performance, and sky-view factor (Fig. 17). The multivariate analysis demonstrated relationships between urban forms and performance criteria. The findings provided recommendations for optimal solar potential and the building coverage ratio, and the optimal energy balance and the threshold for sky-view factor. These relationships contributed to the development of design strategies and guidelines for designing a sustainable campus.

SPACES
- a Manufacturing-I
- b Manufacturing-II
- c HUB

SPACES
- d Lab/office
- e Amenity

Sample of Grid-Based SAP (initial experiment)

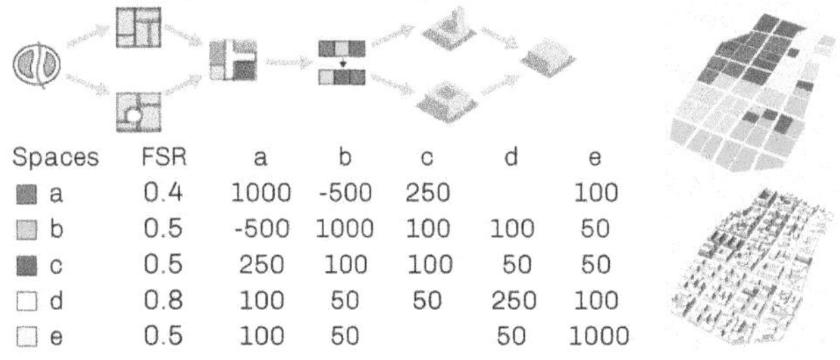

Spaces	FSR	a	b	c	d	e
a	0.4	100	50	-25	-85	-100
b	0.5	50	100	50	-25	-50
c	0.5			100		
d	0.8				100	100
e	0.5				100	100

Sample response to typologies, access & SAP

Spaces	FSR	a	b	c	d	e
a	0.4	1000	-500	250		100
b	0.5	-500	1000	100	100	50
c	0.5	250	100	100	50	50
d	0.8	100	50	50	250	100
e	0.5	100	50		50	1000

13

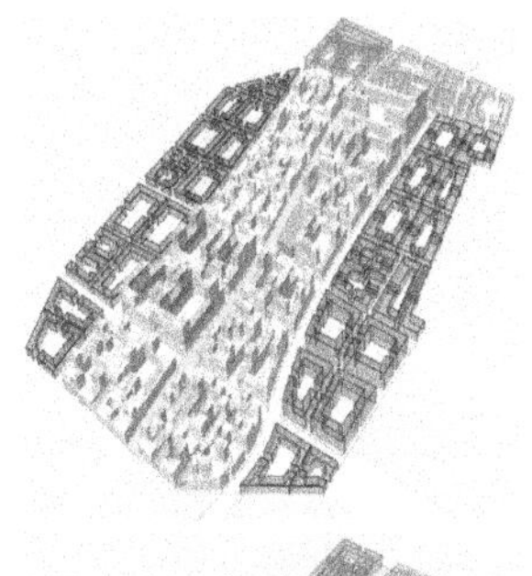

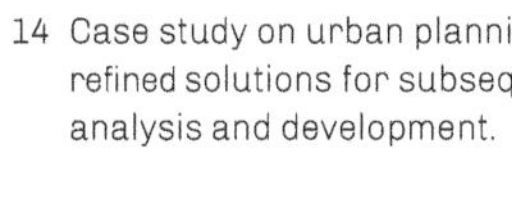

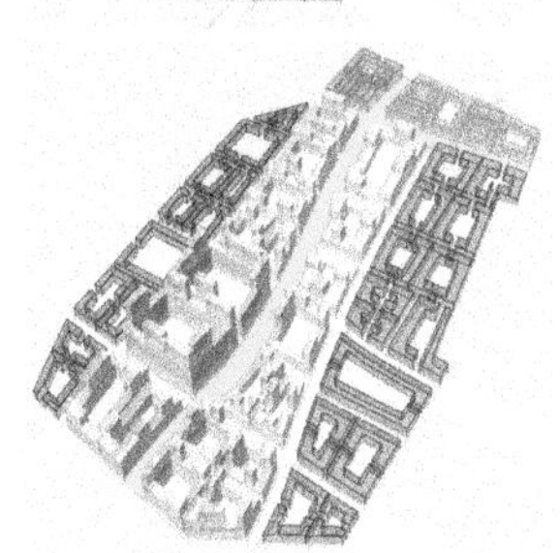

14

13 Case study on urban planning: initial steps in determining the SAP constraints and develop the DOTs workflow. Designers considered various options by altering FSR, typologies, and spatial relations.

14 Case study on urban planning: refined solutions for subsequent analysis and development.

15 K-12 study: Parallel coordinates plot showing various analytical parameters and the sample of architectural scheme.

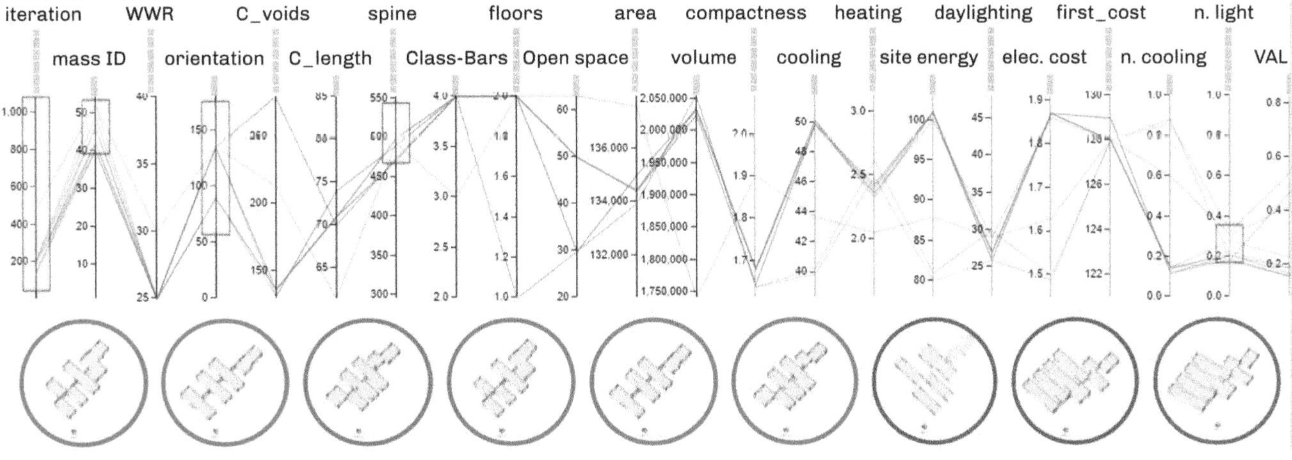

15

SUMMARY AND FUTURE DEVELOPMENT

This research proposes a general solution to SAP using reinforcement learning to drive various geometric operations, collectively defined as space allocation techniques (SAT). The SAT modules utilize basic project requirements and generate architecturally appropriate building layouts, site parcellation, and massing. SAT is combined into an integrated framework, DOTs, a Rhino-Grasshopper plugin that generates layouts for subsequent analysis, decision-making tools, and design development. DOTs hides the complexity of internal functions and allows a designer to further develop or analyze the spatial output of DOTs using external plugins such as Ladybug or Honeybee.

In our interaction with designers, we find that the process of designing with a computational aid such as DOTs needs further examination. Additionally, research is necessary to address the formulation of design problems to better understand spatial requirements that respond to allied processes regarding energy, structural design, and mechanical systems. To address these limitations, we developed the DOTs framework as an extensible library that anticipates new geometry, optimization, and analytical methods.

16

1000
800
600
400
200
0

0 5 10 15 20

LEGEND

floor space ratio
sky view factor (%)
average solar radiation (kWh/sqm)
potential solar power (kWh/sqm)
annual energy demand (kWh/sqm)
number of thermal zones
ground coverage ratio (%)
external wall area x 1000 sqm

17

16 Campus planning study: Sample layouts or schemes generated by the SAT.

17 Campus planning study: Graph showing all the analytical fields studied based on the samples generated.

ACKNOWLEDGMENTS

We would like to thank Professor Perry Yang, Dr. Soowon Chang at Eco Urban Lab (Georgia Institute of Technology), and the designers and Process Lab researchers at Perkins & Will for applying the proposed generative techniques in their analytical methodology for urban (campus) design.

REFERENCES

Armour, G. C., and E. S. Buffa. 1963. "A Heuristic Algorithm and Simulation Approach to Relative Location of Facilities." *Management Science* 9 (2): 294–309.

Calixto, V., and G. Celani. 2015. "A Literature Review for Space Planning Optimization Using an Evolutionary Algorithm Approach: 1992–2014." In *SIGraDi 2015 [Proceedings of the 19th Conference of the Iberoamerican Society of Digital Graphics]*, Florianopolis, Brazil, 23–27 November 2015, 662–671. CUMINCAD.

Chang, S., N. Saha, D. Castro-Lacouture, and P. P. J. Yang. 2019. "Multivariate Relationships between Campus Design Parameters and Energy Performance Using Reinforcement Learning and Parametric Modeling." *Applied Energy* 249: 253–264.

Galle, P. 1986. "Abstraction as a Tool of Automated Floor-Plan Design." *Environment and Planning B: Planning and Design* 13 (1): 21–46.

Huang, W., and H. Zheng. 2018. "Architectural Drawings Recognition and Generation through Machine Learning." In *ACADIA 2018: Recalibration: On Imprecision and Infidelity [Proceedings of the 38th Annual Conference of the Association for Computer Aided Design in Architecture (ACADIA)]*, Mexico City, Mexico, 18–20 October 2018, edited by P. Anzalone, M. del Signore, and A. J. Wit, 156–165. CUMINCAD.

Hubbs, D., P. Hector, S. Owais, N. Sahinidis, I. Grossmann, and J. Wassick. 2020. "OR-Gym: A Reinforcement Learning Library for Operations Research Problem." arXiv preprint. ArXiv abs/2008.06319 .

Jagielski, J., and J. S. Gero. 1997. "A Genetic Programming Approach to the Space Layout Planning Problem." In *CAAD Futures 1997 [Proceedings of the 7th International Conference on Computer Aided Architectural Design Futures]*, Munich, Germany, 4–6 August 1997, edited by R. Junge, 875–884. Springer.

Keller, Sean. 2006. "Fenland Tech: Architectural Science in Postwar Cambridge." *Grey Room 2006* (23): 40–65. doi: https://doi.org/10.1162/grey.2006.1.23.40.

Liggett, R. S. 2000. "Automated Facilities Layout: Past, Present and Future." *Automation in Construction* 9 (2): 197–215.

Lopes, R., T. Tutenel, R. M. Smelik, K. J. de Kraker, and R. Bidarra. 2010. "A Constrained Growth Method for Procedural Floor Plan Generation." In *Proceedings of the 11th International Conference of Intelligence Games Simulation*, Leicester, UK, 17–19 November 2010, 13–20. GAME-ON.

Martin, J. 2006. "Procedural House Generation: A Method for Dynamically Generating Floor Plans." Paper presented at the *Symposium on Interactive 3D Graphics and Games*, Redwood City, CA, 14–17 March.

Mazyavkina, N., S. Sviridov, S. Ivanov, and E. Burnaev. 2020. "Reinforcement Learning for Combinatorial Optimization: A Survey." arXiv preprint. arXiv:2003.03600.

Nauata, N, K. Chang, C. Chin-Yi, G. Mori, and Y. Furukawa. 2020. "House-GAN: Relational Generative Adversarial Networks for Graph-constrained House Layout Generation." *European Conference on Computer Vision*. arXiv preprint. arXiv:2003.06988.

Rezaee, R., T. Marshall, S. Bernal, N. Saha, and J. Haymaker. 2019. "Constructing and Exploring Building Configurations Based on Design and Multi-Performance Criteria." In *16th Conference of IBPSA [Proceedings of Building Simulation 2019]*, Rome, Italy, 2–4 September 2019, edited by V. Corrado, E. Fabrizio, A. Gasparella, and F. Patuzzi, 2990–2997. International Building Performance Simulation Association.

Rodrigues, E., A. Gaspar, and A. Gomes. 2013. "An Approach to the Multi-Level Space Allocation Problem in Architecture Using a Hybrid Evolutionary Technique." *Automation in Construction* 35: 482–498.

Shao, Kun, Zhentao Tang, Yuanheng Zhu, Nannan Li, and Dongbin Zhao. 2019. "A Survey of Deep Reinforcement Learning in Video Games." arXiv preprint. arXiv:1912.10944.

Shekhawat, K. 2018. "Enumerating Generic Rectangular Floor Plans." *Automation in Construction* 92: 151–165.

Sutton, R.S., and A. G. Barto. 1998. *Reinforcement Learning: An Introduction*. Cambridge, MA: MIT Press.

Wu, W., X. M. Fu, R. Tang, Y. Wang, Y. H. Qi, and L. Liu. 2019. "Data-Driven Interior Plan Generation for Residential Buildings." *ACM Transactions on Graphics (TOG)* 38 (6): 1–12.

Yu, C., J. Liu, and Shamim Nemati. 2020. "Reinforcement Learning in Healthcare: A Survey." arXiv preprint. arXiv:1908.08796.

Nirvik Saha PhD is a Postdoctoral Fellow at the CASE, RPI. Nirvik investigates design processes as geometric systems developed by artificial agents. The research advances automation in architecture and urban design using web technologies, computer graphics, and machine learning. The research is being used by globally renowned design firms and startups.

John Haymaker PhD, AIA, is Perkins & Will's Director of Research, overseeing the firm's investigations into materials, design process, building technology, resilience, regeneration, human health, and wellness. John works with researchers, designers, and academics to expand the firm's knowledge base in pursuit of state-of-the-art design solutions. He also oversees the firm's Research Labs, Innovation Incubator program and nonprofit research arm, AREA Research. Previously a professor of civil engineering at Stanford University, and of architecture and building construction at Georgia Institute of Technology, John has contributed more than 100 professional and academic articles on design process communication, optimization, and decision-making.

Dennis Shelden is an Associate Professor and director of the Center for Architecture, Science and Ecology (CASE) at the Rensselaer Polytechnic Institute. He is an expert in applications of digital technology to building design, construction, and operations, with experience spanning across research, technology development, and professional practice, including multiple architecture, building engineering, and computing disciplines. Prior to joining CASE, he led the development of architect Frank Gehry's digital practice as director of R&D and director of computing of Gehry Partners, and as cofounder and CTO of Gehry Technologies. He has taught at MIT, Georgia Tech, UCLA, and SCIARC and is a licensed architect in California.

KEYNOTE CONVERSATION

AUTOMATION AND AGENCY

KEYNOTE EVENT

A Conversation on Automation and Agency

Erin Bradner
Autodesk

Sougwen 愫君 Chung
SCILICET

Stefana Parascho
Princeton University

Elly R. Truitt
University of Pennsylvania

Georgina Voss
London College of Communication,
University of the Arts London

Industrial robotics and the hardware and software of automation have been at the center of the discourse on computational design and digital fabrication for more than a decade. Initially developed for the execution of repetitive tasks in the context of serialized production and manufacturing, robots and industrial machines have been repurposed, reprogrammed, and rethought for an array of new tasks, as well as new approaches to what they can do and what they can represent. However, the meaning, histories, and array of metaphors surrounding robots inform design and creative practice. This keynote conversation brought together five designers, scholars, artists, and practitioners whose work engages with robotics and automation, specifically focusing on their implications in design and creative practice, and their complex cultural and political histories.

Stefana Parascho, Assistant Professor at Princeton University and Director of the CREATE lab, began with a presentation of her work with geometrically complex construction systems, discussing the role of robotic technology and low-level tool development in architectural research, teaching, and practice. Erin Bradner, Director of Autodesk's Robotics Lab in San Francisco, followed with a talk titled "Robot Reality Check," in which

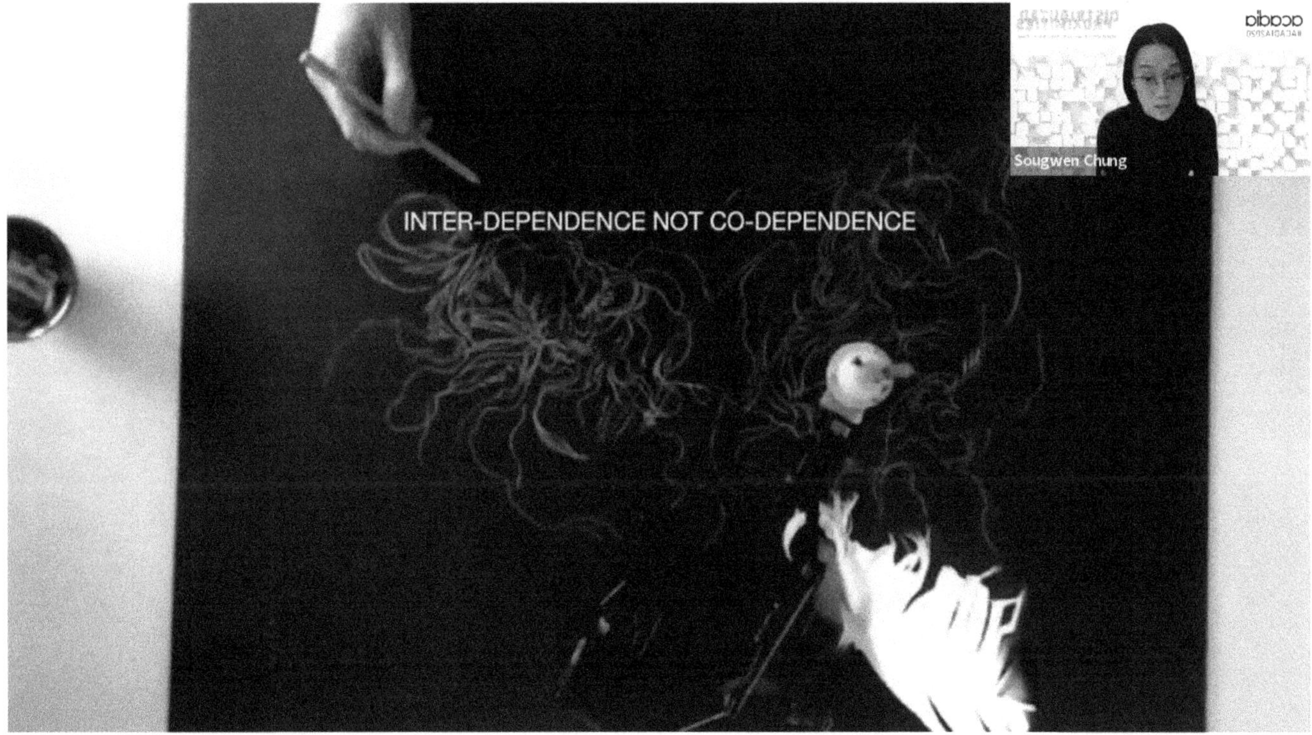

1 "I have wondered, and I've speculated, that maybe the future of human creativity may not be in what it makes, but in how it comes together to explore new ways of making, human and nonhuman alike." —Sougwen Chung
(Image: Sougwen Chung)

she identified the signal through the noise of robotics and automation, and discussed the current and future technology drivers underpinning the new ways robots are being appropriated in industry.

Artist and researcher Sougwen Chung then presented her speculative critical practice that spans performance, installation, and drawing, exploring the dynamics between humans and technical systems. Elly R. Truitt, an Associate Professor of the History of Science at the University of Pennsylvania, followed with a talk titled "Automation, Presence, and Agency," which discussed the historical and cultural contexts of automata and technical mechanical systems.

Georgina Voss, Reader in Systems and Deviance in the Design School at London College of Communication, University of the Arts London, and co-founder and lead of Supra Systems Studio, concluded the talks with a response and led a lively conversation, which is reproduced below in edited form.

For a recording of the entire event, please see this link: **https://www.youtube.com/watch?v=xMB-A5pKAcE**

Georgina Voss (GV): Anytime there is a panel on the ideas around automation, agency, and robotics, it always has a particular heft and weight in the public imaginaries. But it also feels, particularly in this past year, that the conversation has grown not only in the sense of technical advances that we've seen over the past decade, but also in thinking about what futures are coming, what is on the horizon.

We have been questioning our roles in building automation technologies, and investigating what they look like, and how they behave. Who constructs and who uses these systems? Words like "robotics" and "automation" have a certain buzz to them, representing really solid expectations of what they might bring into being. The idea of sociotechnical imaginaries—imagination and images of social life that might center around the development of certain technologies—is particularly potent for automation. By realizing that the senses of how these systems behave and what they do are imaginary, one can begin to tease them apart, to ask what is expected, what should we have on the horizon, what should be coming to us.

I was genuinely delighted to see in the four talks we just heard, that across history, time, and different forms of

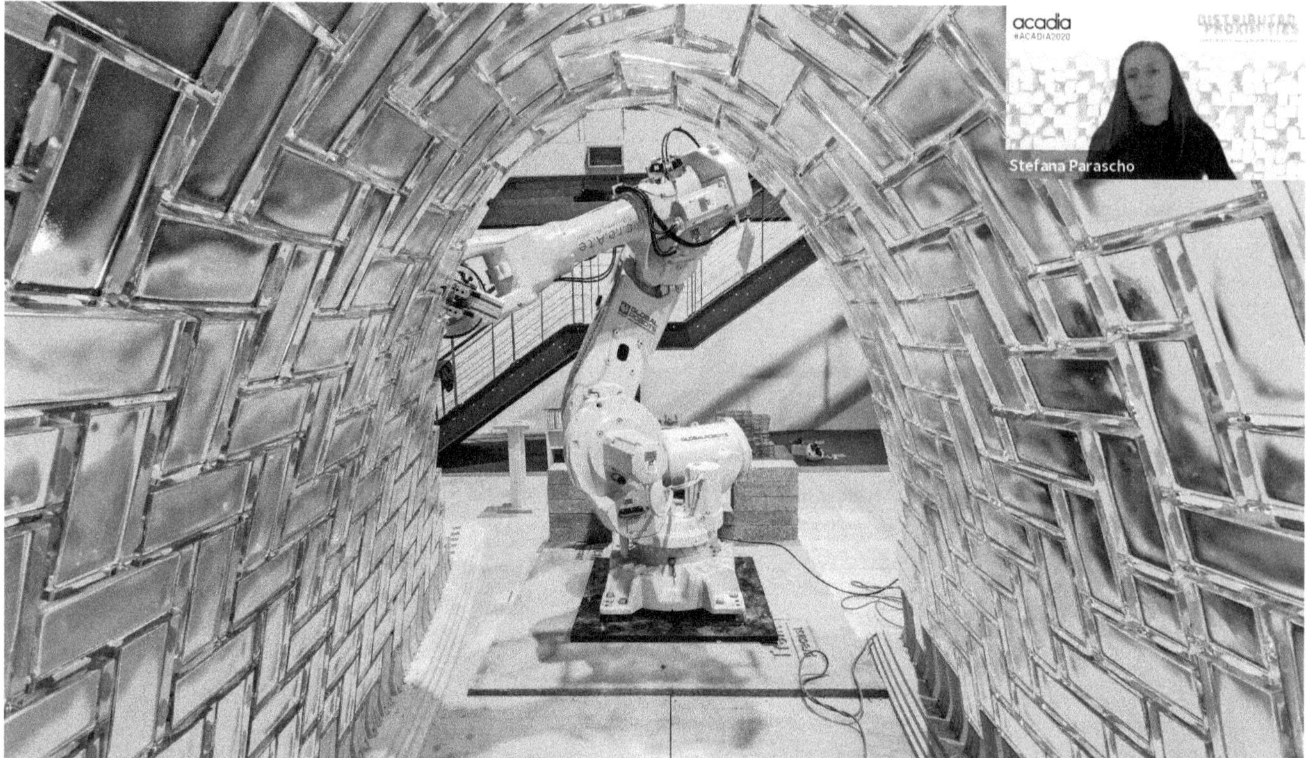

2 "There are tensions within our own discipline over the value of technological developments when compared to the value of creativity and critical thinking. While the technical architectural field might often feel closer to engineering than to the humanities, I think we, as architects, are in a unique position to reflect on the broader implications of technical tools and design. I am convinced that we cannot do this without a very deep and thorough understanding of the underlying technical details." —Stefana Parascho
(Image: CREATE Laboratory Princeton / SOM – photo by: Maciej Grzeskowiak)

practice and engagement, there is a sense of teasing apart, tugging, questioning the ideas of how these technologies are going to work, uncovering a layer of complexity and richness that is beneath the surface and the buzz.

To start with Elly's wonderful talk on the very long history of automation, I can imagine coming to this topic for the first time, thinking that automata or robots are always in a certain shape and size. As Elly says, we can go centuries back to look at the alternative forms and behaviors that they can exist in. They might be very different than what one might expect, but they still inhabit and carry with them a lot of the power dynamics that we see working through technical systems today.

There is a similar shift in assumptions in Stefana's teaching and practice that sits in the context of certain expectations around robots and off-the-shelf computational tools in architecture. In fact, what she is proposing is that we need to overhaul these expectations and rethink the tools, often from scratch, to allow more control, more agency, more knowledge, and a deep understanding of what it is we are doing, rather than defaulting to what existing tools allow us to do. Stefana challenges us to create a holistic image of the richness and the complexity of connections between technologies beyond the fixed form of what the automatons in these spaces might be.

Sougwen also challenges the idea of cultural expectations and norms, both about drawing practices and about technical forms. With her own very specific form of practice, she clearly demonstrates that this is not a dry conversation, but rather people who are doing this, people having fun, and people butting against the systems we are building. As she beautifully puts it, this practice is about actively shaping a cultural imagination. Her work is also tapping back into and sitting within a very rich history of automation and robotics, acknowledging that none of these technologies are really new; they have been around for a long time, have taken, and might yet take many forms.

And finally, coming to Erin and her work in looking towards the future—or rather, multiple possible futures, instead of just one that is specifically robot-driven. Again, there is a set of societal expectations about what roles we are going to have, what jobs, and what technological areas will exist. However, Erin is suggesting a broader space that is much more open to being shaped and discussed, rather than something that is coming down the train tracks at us.

What I loved about these talks was that everyone here explored and challenged assumptions baked into a lot of discussions and representation around automation, robotics, and technical systems. Moreover, you all have said, "Well, this is what we can do about it." The conversation goes beyond discourses and moves into making, into practice, into teaching, and ultimately into new forms of engaging with technical systems. As we return to the initial principles of automation, querying what robotics might be, we are also cracking that space open. Unfortunately, given the times we find ourselves in, we are not in Elly's courtly pageant space having water spat on us by irate automatons, but we are in a space that, as many of the panelists talked about, is rich with emergent new technologies of machine learning and sensor-rich environments, which transform machines we work with and ourselves into parts of a much wider network with expanded modes of practice.

I would like to revisit the idea of sociotechnical imaginaries, the idea that there is often a public imagination of what automation is, what AI is, what a robot is. I want to emphasize that these imaginaries have power for a reason. They can be seductive, as Elly talked about. They can be impressive, amazing, they can discomfort us, they can terrify us, they have affect, they do things to us, we buy into them. I speak for myself here, but we have 146 people in the audience, and I imagine that you all are here for a reason as well, because you are excited and want to know about all these facets of automation and computational systems. We think they are really fascinating and great, but it is also necessary to reflect on ourselves and the choices we are making in why we choose to engage with them. We can choose to both think, "Wow these things are really fascinating," and simultaneously reflect on the power dynamics that run through them.

I will wrap up my introduction there, and move on to a round of questions, one for each panelist, just like Christmas.

Stefana, I am really fascinated about the work you showed around building your own tools. I was wondering, what challenges have you encountered in doing that, and at what point did you realize that the tools available to you just weren't going to work off-the-shelf? How does that work in teaching, for students who are given this wide-open space to play with, rather than something that is more constrained by the design environment of something more rigid?

Stefana Parascho (SP): The challenges that I've encountered are pretty much everything you can imagine, from just not knowing where to start, to learning to dive into technical areas that every time are completely new. There is no such thing as doing the same thing twice in research, particularly when engaging with new technologies and new fields of inquiry every single time. In every project, it feels like I'm a beginner and I have to figure out where to start, what to aim towards. It takes some time to build the confidence to just dive into new concepts and new methods, but it also gets more fun and fruitful with every new project.

In terms of building my own tools, I wouldn't say that I have tried all of the existing tools and figured that they weren't enough. The necessity of custom-built tools for custom processes was almost implied when I began working with these machines, maybe partially because there weren't many software tools available at the time. So, I dove into making my own tools and developing solutions early on—partially because I was curious, and it was fun, and partially because I wanted to do new non-trivial things with the machines, so the solutions weren't really there.

With teaching, I will admit that it is often challenging. Many times students come with expectations of quickly implementing a robotic process, but then they realize: Wait a second, why aren't you giving us a magic plugin where we can click a button and things just happen? I put a lot of emphasis on exactly not falling for that one-click solution and having them engage with the low-level knowledge that is behind the systems, which often is not the easiest way. But this knowledge is necessary to meaningfully work with new technologies. I hope what they get out of it is the confidence that these tools and technologies aren't something that we as designers and architects don't have control over, but they are something we can engage with at every level, which in turn opens up more possibilities than working with black-box tools. I don't think they would have ended up developing or even imagining the processes and projects they've made if they hadn't engaged with all of the underlying challenges and troubleshooting at the early stage.

GV: It's something I think about a lot with my teaching work, and it's really nice to hear that a lot of the same issues come up. I also appreciate that particular idea of doing it through practice, where a bounded space only gives you so much to play with. But when you crack it open, you're suddenly dealing with much wider expectations, and that's so lovely.

Elly, thank you for a brilliant talk on the history of technology. You locate, particularly in this talk, the historical figure of the automaton put to use by power in different ways, whether through the court or a type of showmanship. Given that to create an automaton, one requires a lot of resources—time, money, wood, metal, etc.—I was wondering, are there examples you can think of, or interesting stories where people with maybe fewer resources than those you've talked about were able to either push back, make something, or create a counternarrative in some way?

I am curious if there are some fascinating alternative imaginaries that come through history?

Elly Truitt (ET): There are a few examples where individuals push back against automata. For example, a common trope across cultures is the story of the learned man (philosopher, sorcerer, or scholar) and his automaton-child. In the Latin West, these stories have been attached to Albert the Great, a medieval bishop and natural philosopher; to René Descartes; and to Thomas Edison. In some of these examples, like in the stories of Albert the Great and Descartes, the automaton is destroyed. But it's destroyed by people who are presented as being ignorant. They don't understand the true technology, and so they are afraid and let their fear speak for them.

Your question makes me think also about these moments in the historical record where you can get a sense of the other people involved, a sense of where these objects are appearing and the larger ecologies they appear as a part of. Even though, for example, the duke or the count may have been the one who says, "This is what I want, this is what I want it to do, this is what I want it to look like," we see in the historical record other people who were involved. For instance, the mechanical monkeys had to be sent to the refurbisher or the repelter every year or two. And you begin to imagine this person in that job thinking every year, "Oh, here it comes. Again, it's the monkeys." I think it's important to remember that even though those artisans may not speak to us as directly, in some ways, they're there in the records. We have to remember the ways in which they are contributing to the process or changing it in some way. I unfortunately haven't come across many examples of the truly liberatory automata or servants that I might hope for. But I continue to hope that people like Erin and Sougwen and Stefana will help get us there.

GV: That brings to mind the idea of a wider network of production that exists around technical systems. I've been thinking a lot about how the current critical discourse around technical systems is often heavily weighted towards people who work in senior management or technical roles. There is an entire range of other people who are involved historically, working in those processes, and who may be more marginalized and have less power, as you say, comparable to the pelt manager, but also have a valuable part to play in the network. I would love to read whichever fiction writer picks up that guy's story and turns it into great historical science fiction.

Sougwen, it is always lovely to hear you talk about your practice and see it as well. In the beginning, you talk about how over the past decade in your work you have been challenging and questioning your own expectations of what your drawing practice is in relationship to the idea of computational systems and engagement. At the end of your talk, you mentioned how you are reframing and rethinking this idea in relationship to what is happening now, and how that gets embedded into your practice and life. What are the challenges you're facing, and are the questions you are asking now comparable to the ones that belong to the longer thread of ideas that began 10 years ago around your drawing practice? How have those ideas evolved, where are you now, and how do you feel about it?

Sougwen Chung (SC): That's a big series of questions. And of course, they're ones that I've been thinking about a lot, given that I'm spending a lot of time in my studio recently, and acknowledging how much the world has changed.

Prior to this year, I was thinking a lot about automation as not just a technical challenge but one that has considerable social implications and emotional responses. The role of machines in society, and their role in displacing large swaths of the workforce—that creates a very real anxiety, and a fear of being replaced. So, I see it as part of my practice to address, reframe, and rethink the dynamic between the human and the machine and what it can mean. To address the role of imagination in human agency alongside machines. Simply put, not as *either/or*, but *and*.

This has developed into broader investigations into the

3 "In considering agency, I am going to examine the links between automation and enslavement over about 900 years, from 950 until the middle of the 19th century. Both artificial servants and enslaved persons appear as liminal objects that glorify the individual at the center of the court, comment on a spectrum of humanity, and embody the use of technology to articulate power over nature." —Elly Truitt
[Image: A ceremonial "Kammermoor," early 18th century.]

intertwining of human and machine: How can we expand beyond interactions towards relation, towards a co-creation with machines, AI systems, and even VR technology, to really expand our model of singular authorship, in regards to the notion of a Copernican awareness, and the decentering of the human subject as that sole node of authorship, the center around which the world revolves?

I think we've come to this expanded awareness in part due to the prevalence of synthetic sensory technologies, cobbled together as a kind of sensory apparatus that allows us to observe beyond ourselves. We are able to actually connect in new ways and see through machine learning algorithms as they provide feedback to our process. Observing the mass amounts of information we have at our disposal and thinking about what that does to the human subject is really interesting.

In my practice, I explicitly bring in machine feedback systems because it helps with my own anxiety about potential futures. The practice of co-creation with machines also helps us imagine new futures through embodied making, which I not only narrativize, but also design, think about, and write about.

For me, part of the practice results in the creation of visual artifacts with two functions. The first function is that the artifacts exist as visual representations of a developing recurrent neural network model. The second, a painting, is an artistic artifact that grounds modes of speculation and contemplation. The dual interpretation of the results of this human-machine process excites me in that it engages fields of science and art in tandem. As a painting, it exists within a cultural practice that can engage the larger narrative of art history. This is important to me because I feel that a lot of the time, I've seen conversations about art and technology ignore and de-historicize what came before, that erase cultural histories in the name of progress and innovation.

I'm interested in works and approaches to art, AI systems, and robotics that facilitate larger conversations about our collective potential, and the continued evolution of cultural

4 "If there is anything that these advances in synthetic sensing technologies have shown us, it is that we are undergoing a certain Copernican trauma. What I mean by that is a recognition that the self is not at the center of the process, and that we are all interconnected. This realization becomes a profound decentering of the human subject." —Sougwen Chung
(Image: Sougwen Chung)

practices like mark-making. That's what excites me about imagining potential futures with machines or AI.

GV: Your last statement beautifully articulates something I know a lot of us have been thinking about: we see whenever there is a narrative around computational technologies, it can be very ahistorical, like a giant shiny wall moving forward with nothing behind it. It is just always there, always new, and always shiny. And that is particularly surprising in the art space, given that the history of art, as much as the history of technology, is so fascinating and so rich. I think it is a very useful articulation of how by gluing onto the computational technologies, or even by breaking them apart, suddenly the richness of a historical practice becomes a thing that exists now, in this moment.

And since we are talking about futures, it brings me to my question for Erin. What I found fascinating about your talk is that you explicitly stated in the very beginning that you are not a futurist. You presented a very rich and intriguing range of ideas in a very pragmatic way, basically saying that the future is not this blinding thing that is going to terrify us, but something we can and should take a look at, and maybe discover that it is not what one expects.

I am curious to know how this version of the future, not as jetpacks on the moon, but rather something that is more complex and layered, is received—whether you present it internally at Autodesk or externally to larger audiences? Is there a sense of pushback against the preliminary expectation? And to add to that question, what has surprised you in your own work as you have been researching and developing this area of technological futurity?

Erin Bradner (EB): I intentionally explain that I am not a futurist primarily because that word often throws folks off. It creates this image of someone gazing into a crystal ball, and more importantly implies that there is only one future to be seen, and a certain continuum that can be extrapolated along a linear trajectory. Within our organization, we have come to a point where we acknowledge that there are many parallel possible futures, depending on what lens we are looking through: a social lens, a technical lens, or an economic lens. In that sense, this notion of multiple futures

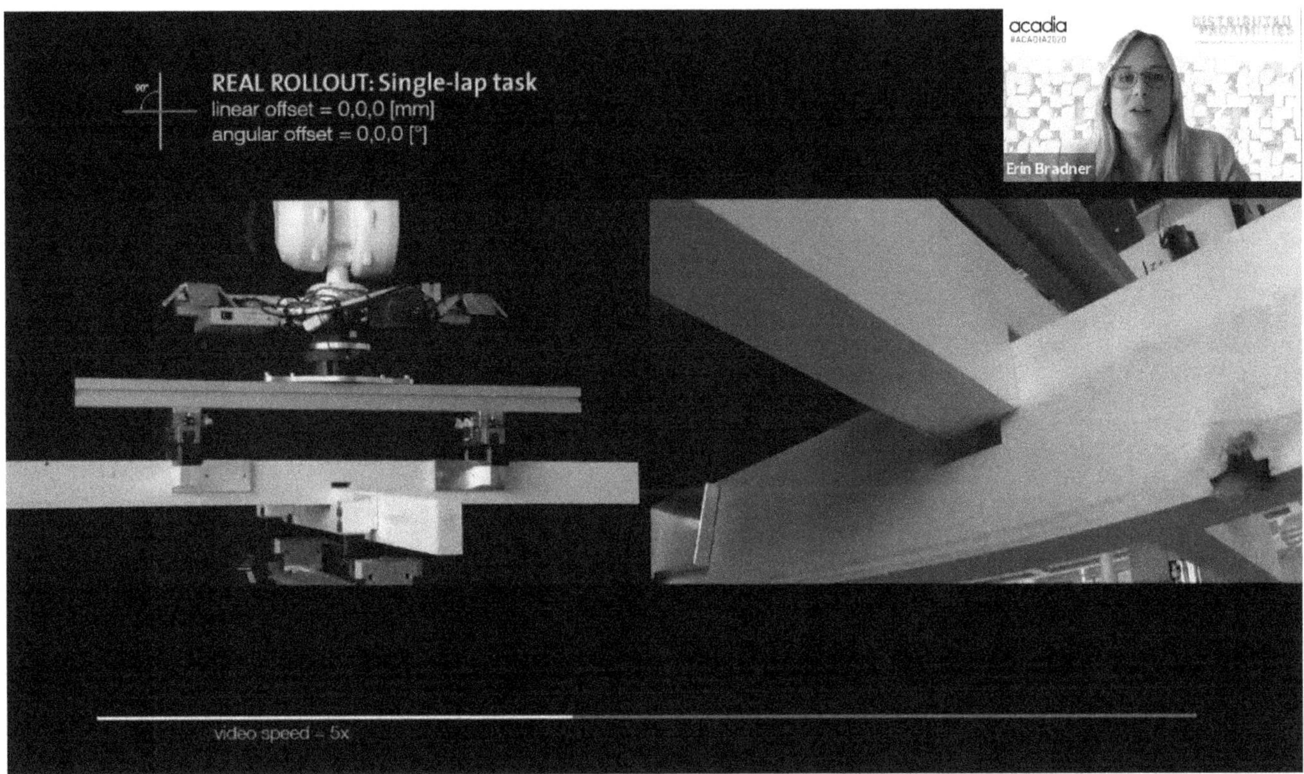

5 "Rather than stand in the dark and stare into the unknown, let's extrapolate what we know and look at the technologies underpinning advances in robotics and see where they are headed. My team and I have identified five drivers: Inherently Adaptive, Sensor Rich, Automatically Programmed, Highly Connected, and Easy to Use." —Erin Bradner
(Image: Research into machine learning for timber assembly, by ETH Zurich and Autodesk)

is well received and incorporated within the organization. And it is important to outline that this multiplicity of futures is not a dichotomy between either a dystopian or a utopian future. There are desirable futures and there are undesirable ones, and it behooves all of us to analyze all of the possible scenarios, as many as we can imagine. We need to imagine first and then identify what it is we need to do to navigate towards the desirable futures: desirable for the environment, desirable for society, desirable for the economy, and so forth.

To answer your question about what surprises me in my work, I am fascinated by how profoundly interdisciplinary the act of looking into the future around technology is. This is especially true in robotics. Stefana's work, with her embrace of custom toolmaking, is a great example of this. Everyone who is pushing the boundaries of robotics is operating this way, soldering and wiring new systems, literally and metaphorically, from the ground up. At the same time, they need to understand the implications of how it is applied, for instance in Stefana's case, in architecture, investigating the interplay between design and fabrication, developing new ways of crafting not just a pragmatic design but also an aesthetically pleasing one. This interdisciplinary nature of robotics is what surprised me most when I first joined this team.

GV: I think we are all on team interdisciplinarity here. We may not be able to necessarily pronounce it, but we certainly believe in it.

For me, as someone who has looked at imaginaries and socioeconomic futures, the plurality of futures feels so important. It sometimes feels like there's one steering force, and you can strap yourself to the engine in order to get that future somehow. But what we are talking about here is the future being a broader, messier array, where there are active choices. It is not about being sucked into a vortex of a 30-year time horizon, but rather about the choices that are made along the way and who gets to make them.

We have a question from the audience. Shelby Doyle asks: "As architectural robots have evolved into many species of design collaborators rather than human proxies or perfect slaves, does this shift in thinking change us? Does rejecting frameworks of enslaving technology shift our thinking about ourselves as designers and how we locate and value human labor or how we engage with computational labor practices?"

EB: I can answer as a computer scientist rather than as an architect. What we look to do with our technology development is not to automate the process of designing and making, but to produce tools that allow this interplay between the technology and the designer. Sougwen described this well as interdependence. We are striving towards a design characteristic, and a relationship between our robots and our designers, that is interdependent and collaborative, rather than dependent on automation.

SC: Even though terms like "enslaving technology" are very loaded, I do think that certain human skills become atrophied through a linear approach of engaging with robots, where the machine is a task-execution device. By framing my work as a collaboration, I create a space where not only are both human and machine processes evolving, but where the self-limiting engagement of the two deepens the connection between human and machine collaborators. That is the future I would like to be heading towards, one where it is not about control or execution, but about catalyzing new types of knowledge through interaction and entanglement.

SP: This understanding of the machine as a collaborator rather than task executor can be seen as an alternative route for the architectural profession, away from the image of an architect as a lonely creative genius who generates something that is later executed by someone else. Our relationship to the labor of making and executing processes, be it machine labor or human labor, must inform and shape our design process at its earliest stage.

ET: Speaking more broadly, but to take up the points that Erin, Stefana, and Sougwen have made, I wonder if taking the view of a spectrum from augmented human abilities and autonomous intelligent machines, rather than a binary of human/robot, might allow us to humanize our machines, and lead to new areas for growth and creativity.

Erin Bradner is the Director of Autodesk Inc.'s Robotics Lab in San Francisco. She and her research team are developing tools to enable industrial robots to intelligently make things by sensing, responding, and adapting to new information in real time. Under Erin's leadership, Autodesk's Robotics Lab is using artificial intelligence and closed-loop controls to teach robots new workflows in manufacturing and AEC. Prior to leading the Robotics Lab, Erin co-founded the Generative Design practice at Autodesk; through research and thought leadership, she helped incubate the technology from concept to commercialization. Erin is driven to discover how to leverage intelligent software tools for smarter building, manufacturing, and design. In her past lives, Erin consulted on the first commercial intelligent agents and cloud storage systems; and contracted at IBM, Boeing, and AT&T. Erin is a co-author on patents in advanced design and publishes in academia. She holds a PhD in Information and Computer Science.

Sougwen 笄君 Chung is an artist and researcher whose work explores the dynamics between humans and systems. Her speculative critical practice spans performance, installation, and drawings which have been featured in numerous exhibitions at museums and galleries around the world. Chung is a former research fellow at MIT's Media Lab and a pioneer in the field of human-machine collaboration. In 2019, she was selected as the Woman of the Year in Monaco for achievement in the arts and sciences and was a featured speaker at TED in Mumbai, India. In 2018 she was an inaugural E.A.T. Artist in Residence in partnership with New Museum and Bell Labs, and was awarded a commission for her project *Omnia per Omnia*. In 2016, Chung received Japan Media Art's Excellence Award for her project *Drawing Operations*.

Stefana Parascho is Assistant Professor at Princeton University and director of the CREATE Laboratory Princeton, where her research focuses on computational design and robotic fabrication. Before joining Princeton University in 2019, she obtained her PhD from ETH Zurich, Gramazio Kohler Research. She received her Diploma in Architectural Engineering in 2012 from the University of Stuttgart and has worked with DesignToProduction Stuttgart and Knippers Helbig Advanced Engineering. Throughout her research, she has explored existing computational design methods and their potential role for architectural fabrication, ranging from agent-based design tools to multi-robotic assembly techniques. Her goal is to strengthen the connection between design, structure, and fabrication and the interdisciplinary nature of architecture through the development of accessible computational tools and robotic fabrication methods. Current projects include research on cooperative robotic assembly techniques for self-supporting structures, including spatial structures, bending-active systems, and masonry construction. In addition, she is currently exploring methods of further integrating different fabrication systems into the design decision-making process.

Elly R. Truitt is Associate Professor of the History of Science at the University of Pennsylvania and the author of *Medieval Robots: Mechanism, Magic, Nature, and Art* (University of Pennsylvania, 2015), as well as scholarly articles on medieval astronomy, pharmacobotany, the history of automata, early mechanical clocks, and premodern concepts of artificial intelligence. Her work has also appeared in *Aeon*, *The TLS*, and *History Today*, and she has contributed to several programs on BBC Radio Four. She is currently at work on several projects, on the topics of Roger Bacon, speculative technology, and temporality; the co-creation of the categories of "modern science" and "medieval history" in the nineteenth century; and how medieval technologies produced narratives of Christian temporality and universality. Her research has received support from the National Science Foundation, the Andrew J. Mellon Foundation, the Huntington Library, and the Max Planck Institute for the History of Science.

Georgina Voss is an artist, writer, and educator. Originally trained in technology anthropology and industrial economics, her work explores the politics, presence, and deviance of large-scale machines and technical systems through performance, multimedia installation, writing, and investigative research projects. Georgina's work has been exhibited and performed in spaces including Tate Modern, Auto Italia South East, STUK (Leuven), London Design Festival, and TAC Eindhoven. Her writing has been published in places including *The Atlantic*, *The Guardian*, *Science as Culture*, *Economic Science Fictions* (MIT Press, 2018), *Journal of Economic Geography*, and *Journal of Homosexuality*. She is currently working on her second book, on experiencing systems, with Verso. Georgina is Reader in Systems and Deviance in the Design School at London College of Communication, University of the Arts London, and co-founder and lead of Supra Systems Studio. She is also founder and co-director of the consultancy Strange Telemetry, and currently a resident of Somerset House Studios.

PEER-REVIEWED PAPERS

AUTOMATION AND AGENCY

"As we return to the initial principles of automation, querying what robotics might be, we are also cracking that space open. [We] are in a space that [...] is rich with emergent new technologies of machine learning and sensor-rich environments, which transform machines we work with and ourselves into parts of a much wider network with expanded modes of practice."

—Georgina Voss, "A Conversation on Automation and Agency"

Providing a more nuanced take on automation, this talk provides a framework for redefining it as a form of distributed, shared authorship between a variety of human and non-human agents. Included are papers that incorporate material, morphological, bacterial, artificial, and robotic agents that emerge as components of the "wider network" and "expanded modes of practice" described in the conversation.

How Machines Learn to Plan

A Critical Interrogation of Machine Vision Techniques in Architecture

Matias del Campo
University of Michigan, Taubman College of Architecture and Urban Planning

Alexandra Carlson
University of Michigan, Michigan Robotics

Sandra Manninger
SPAN/IAAC

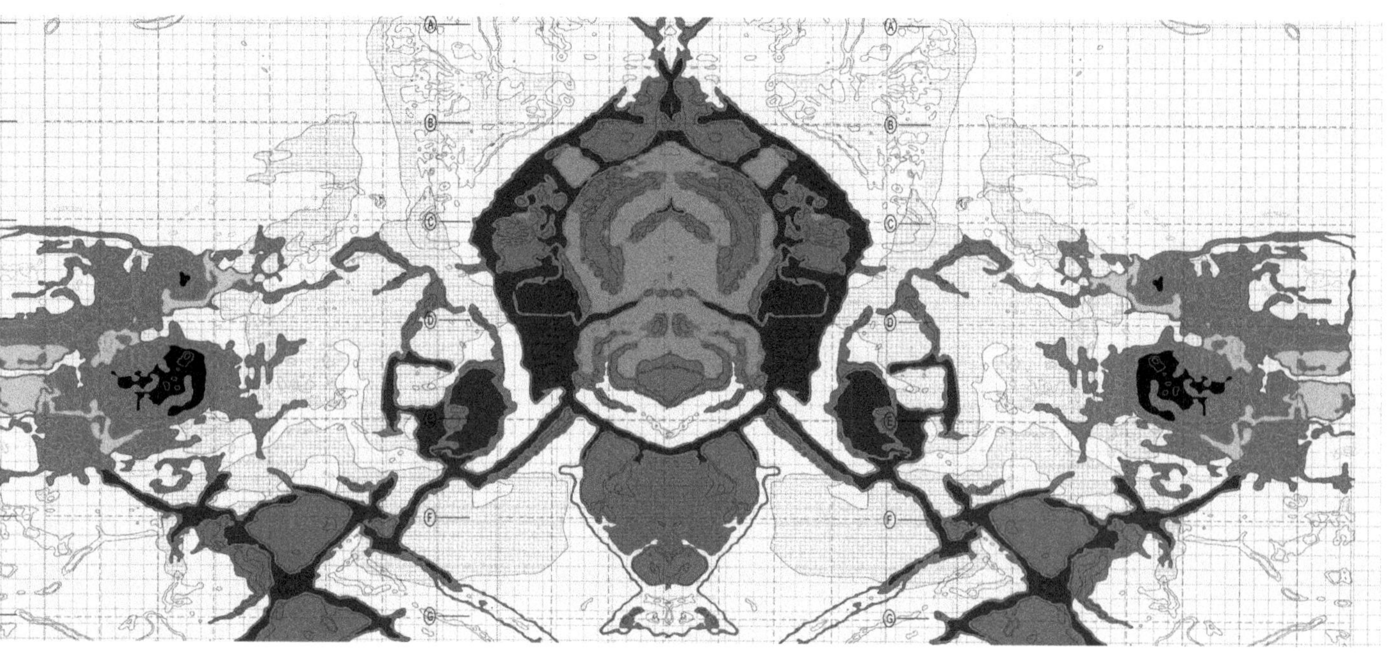

1

1 Close-up of one of the resulting plans based on the StyleGAN2 process between Baroque and Modern plans.

ABSTRACT

This paper strives to interrogate the abilities of machine vision techniques based on a family of deep neural networks, called generative adversarial neural networks (GANs), to devise alternative planning solutions. The basis for these processes is a large database of existing planning solutions. For the experimental setup of this paper, these plans were divided into two separate learning classes: Modern and Baroque. The proposed algorithmic technique leverages the large amount of structural and symbolic information that is inherent to the design of planning solutions throughout history to generate novel unseen plans. In this area of inquiry, aspects of culture such as creativity, agency, and authorship are discussed, as neural networks can conceive solutions currently alien to designers. These can range from alien morphologies to advanced programmatic solutions. This paper is primarily interested in interrogating the second existing but uncharted territory.

INTRODUCTION

Paraphrasing Alan Turing (1950), the renowned computer science and artificial intelligence (AI) pioneer, the authors ask, "Can machines learn to form plans?" This inquiry spawns questions that delve deeply into the interrogation of creativity, sensibility, and agency. This paper includes a set of definitions in order to facilitate the conversation. To motivate the use of AI applications, specifically deep neural networks, to create well-informed planning solutions, we define the following: we say "well-informed" in the sense of being able to resolve uncertainty or to convert raw data into valuable information in a creative fashion. Creativity, in the framework of the present conversation, is the ability to find novel, surprising, or valuable solutions based on existing information and knowledge. These creations can be intangible (theories, political ideas, philosophical concepts, jokes) as well as tangible (sculptures, buildings, paintings, instruments, doodles). Sometimes even in combination, considering that a computer is a tangible object that can produce intangible products through the input of an agent. Agency is defined by both unconscious, involuntary behavior as well as goal-driven, deliberate action with specific intentions. For this to come to fruition, agents are required to demonstrate evidence of immediate awareness of their own physical activities as well as perception of the environment in order to realize the objective of the planned activity. Sensibility is probably the most difficult category to describe in an abbreviated fashion. In the case of the conversation presented in this paper, sensibility is framed as the ability of creative minds to conceive unique aesthetic expressions that are unique to them and inherently difficult to replicate. (Please refer to the "Background and Definitions" section for more details.) Given these definitions, the goal of this paper is to address the question: How can the abstract, aesthetic, symbolic concept of "the plan" (Fig. 1) be realized through an algorithm?

We propose that the best candidate for algorithmic planning is deep neural networks (Zhang et al. 2018), specifically GANs (Goodfellow, Bengio, and Courville 2016). This is a family of powerful, high-performance algorithms that comprise a branch of the research on artificial intelligence and machine learning that has unparalleled success in performing visual tasks. They are designed to learn from visual input in a fashion similar to humans. When applied to collections of images, neural networks learn to extract salient visual features/patterns from the input image pixel values, and optimize these features to perform visual tasks. Neural networks (Sarvepalli and Kumar 2015) are purely mathematical functions that are structured and trained to extract features from their input that will maximize task performance; while they are tools that have no self-awareness nor can they make conscious design and aesthetic choices, we as designers can utilize them as tools to see the world in a different way and leverage this new sight to inform the design process.

At its most basic level, a plan is represented as pixel values in an image, which means the myriad aforementioned meanings captured in a plan are also built into these pixel values. We demonstrate that neural networks applied to images of plans can learn visual features that extend beyond merely modeling simple textures/pixel patterns in images to capture the structure and thus symbols that are captured in plans, and use these to propose new ones. Thus, the goal of this paper is to demonstrate and explore a plan design technique based on the style and spatial features learned by neural networks, influenced by aesthetic processes of humans.

BACKGROUND AND DEFINITIONS

In order to create a clear framework for the conversation laid out in this paper, specific boundaries in terms of the definitions have to be made. In the following we attempt to specify the definitions used in this paper as they pertain to artificial intelligence and architecture.

Agency

In the Western philosophical tradition (Hume 1898), causal chains do not produce our choices, as would be the case with objects responding to natural forces, thus giving us—humans—agency. Free will and agency are closely related but not identical. They share traits, in that agency is undetermined but significantly free. In contrast to inanimate objects, humans can make decisions and enforce them on the world (for the moment we will leave out the metaphysical question as to how humans make decisions). In any case, it entails moments of moral agency, as particular acts of human agency need thought and consideration about the outcomes. For this paper, we rely on agency as part of the debate on action theory (Davidson 2001). This can be exemplified for example with the philosophical traditions established by Hegel (Speight 2001) and Marx (Pratten 1993) that consider human agency in a collective fashion Thus, for our frame of thinking we consider the relation between human and neural network as such a collective with a particular agency. In this framework, idealist (Hegel 1975) and materialist (Brosio 2000) considerations collide with aspects of determinism (Millican 2010) and indeterminacy (Hertzmann 2020).

Authorship

Relevant for the frame of conversation in this paper are the positions of Roland Barthes and Michel Foucault regarding

2 The database of Baroque plans collected for a data set consisting of 1,918 plans. The data set includes plans that are distorted in order to increase the number of plans. The distortion allows us to maintain the main Baroque features such as symmetry, concave/convex surfaces, and the figure/ground articulation.

the nature of authorship and author at large. These critics interrogated the role and relevance of authorship pertaining to the interpretation or meaning of text—this can be expanded to all areas of artistic production, as for example to architecture in the present text of this paper. Barthes, for example, attributed meaning to the language and not the author of the text. Instead of relying on the legal authority to exude authorship, Barthes (1982) assigns authority to the words and language itself. Foucault's critical position vs. the author can be found in the argument he presents in his essay "What Is an Author?" (Foucault 1998). Foucault argues that all authors are writers, but not all writers are authors—echoing a broadly shared sentiment in architecture: not all architecture is building and not every building is architecture.

Creativity

We will rely on the help of Margaret A. Boden (2009, 83) with regard to the definition of creativity: "First things first. Human creativity is something of a mystery, not to say a paradox. One new idea may be creative, while another is merely new...Creativity is the ability to come up with ideas or artefacts that are new, surprising, and valuable. 'Ideas,' here, includes concepts, poems, musical compositions, scientific theories, cooking recipes, choreography, jokes ... and so on, and on. 'Artefacts' include paintings, sculpture, steam-engines, vacuum cleaners, pottery, origami, penny-whistles...and you can name many more."

Culture

Culture, in the frame of conversation presented in this paper, relies on a definition borrowed from anthropology: a set of implicit and explicit values, ideas, concepts, and rules of behavior that permit a socially connected group to perform and perpetuate itself. Culture is a dynamic and evolving social construct based in reality and shared by the members of a specific social population (Hudelson 2004). It is expressed in twofold fashion in that it produces a material culture, which serves as a vessel for a shared symbolic culture.

Sensibility

When the authors utilize the term *sensibility*, it is specifically geared towards aspects of artistic sensibility. To unfold the term, the authors rely on Alexander Gottlieb Baumgarten's (1750) and Immanuel Kant's (1781) definitions of aesthetics

3 Part of a representation of a town in a Neolithic wall painting from Çatal Hüyük, Turkey, dated to the early seventh millennium BCE. Approximately 3 m in length. Image reproduced from J. Mellaart, "Excavations at Çatal Hüyük, 1963, Third Preliminary Report," *Anatolian Studies* 14 (1964): 55 and pl. V. Photograph by James Mellaart.

as a basis to explain our use of sensibility in this paper, which concludes with the insight that aesthetics is, at its very core, a theory of sensibility—evoking a response in the observer. This assertion discusses the arts of the past as much as the arts of the present, recognizing the aesthetic value as a specific feature of all experience. Or as Arnold Berleant (2015, 4) put it: "Such a generalized aesthetic enables us to recognize the presence of a pervasive aesthetic aspect in every experience, whether uplifting or demeaning, exalting or brutal. It makes the constant expansion of the range of architectural and of aesthetic experience both plausible and comprehensible."

What we mean by sensibility is the perceptual awareness developed and guided through training and exercise. To this extent, it is certainly more than simple sensual perception, and closer to something like a guided or educated sensation. An education that has to be continuously fostered, polished, and extended, through encounters and activities, in order to maintain the ability to execute tasks with an aesthetic sensibility. This ability is attributed in the Western traditions primarily to the arts—to painting, sculpture, music, literature, and so on—with architecture being this strange animal living somewhere between engineering and the arts.

Plans and Other Architectural Machinations

The set of computational methods discussed in this paper are based primarily on generative adversarial networks (GANs), which are a subset of deep neural networks. One of the primary qualities of these networks is their ability to learn specific features based on large image databases. To this extent, they are inherently fit in performing learning processes from architectural databases. For the task presented in this paper, the authors put together databases of plan images of specific styles—Baroque (Fig. 2) and Modern (Fig. 4).

So how do machines learn to plan? In a similar fashion as humans: by analyzing data that we have absorbed throughout our careers that relates to the problem at hand. In many cases, architects have to sit down and analyze precedent cases that can be applied to a specific architectural program, whether this be housing, infrastructure, hotels, or factories. Artificial neural networks are capable of processing this information much faster than any human ever could—however, is this a creative process?

Let's start with the plan itself. The oldest known architectural representation has been identified as possibly

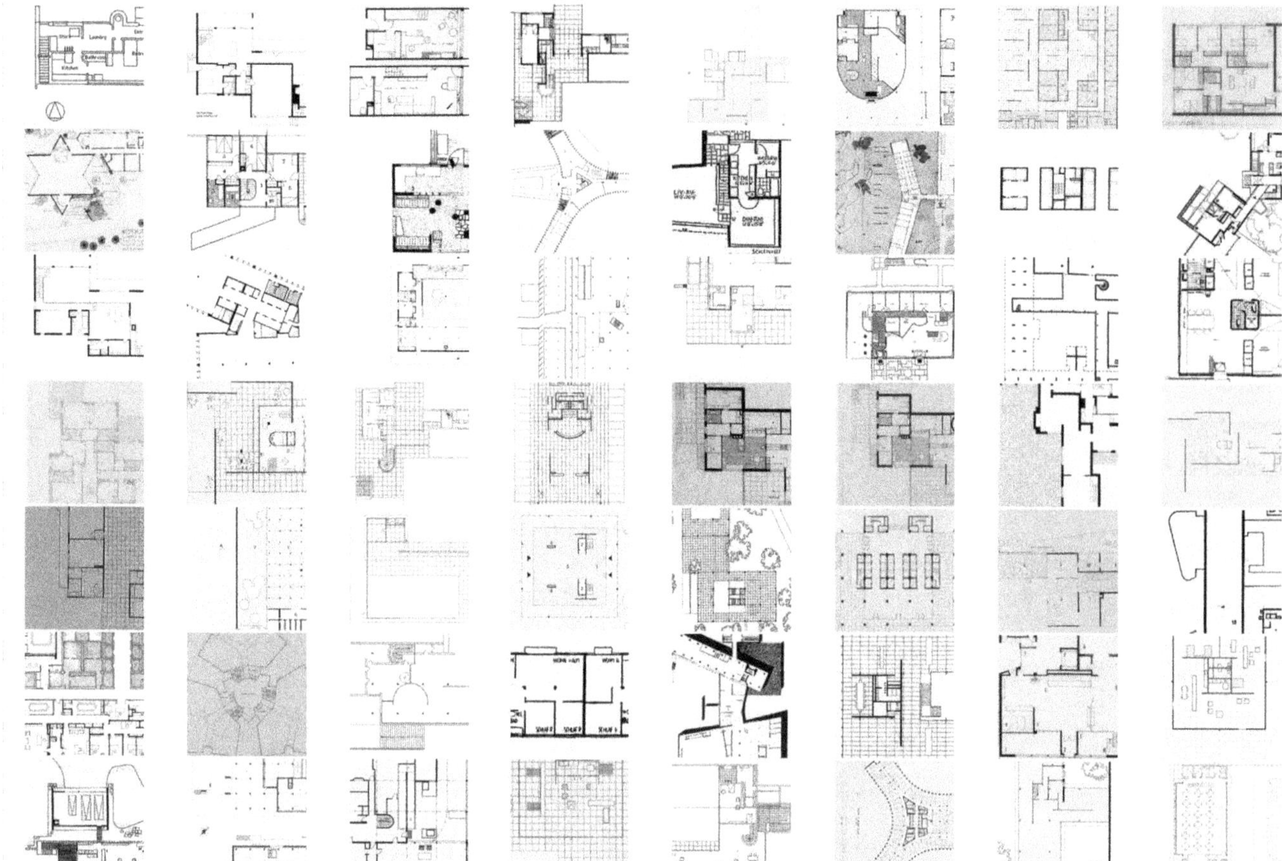

4 A set of Modern plans used as target images.

representing a city in plan view (Rochberg 2012) (Fig. 3). From this starting point, around 9,000 years ago, the discipline has continuously produced plans—whether in the form of planning drawings on clay tablets, papyri, hide, paper, or digital media—or in the form of the documentation of existing buildings. The rise of the Albertian paradigm (Carpo 2011) manifested plans, sections, and elevations as the standard abstraction of architectural thinking—a unique machination of the discipline. It seems only evident that this vast archive of the discipline represents an extraordinary collection of possible solutions for design problems. An archive of architectural imagination that so far has been untapped by methodologies facilitating the interrogation of big data. A quick search on Google results in more than eight billion hits tagged plan—filtering through this information shows the enormous bandwidth of contributions of the discipline. (This is proof also for the popularity of architectural terms as metaphors in the general language.) This vast deposit of architectural knowledge is there, waiting to be quarried—not to replicate existing architectures but to transform into well-informed solutions for current and future problems. Talking about the future, it seems only prudent to interrogate aspects of utopia (Eisenman 1996) and ideology (Agrest and Gandelsonas 1996) embedded in the black lines of an abstract device such as a plan. It might not be surprising that a plan itself constitutes a vessel that holds abstract concepts describing ideologies beyond its morphology, aesthetics, and program. The plan also encompasses political, social, and economic conditions. The authors are aware of this problem, but addressing all of the sociopolitical and economic implications of planning would by far exceed the limits of this paper. The focus in the interrogation presented in this paper is the inherently human ability to not only perform pattern and symbol recognition (Lladós et al. 2001) but also pattern and symbol generation (Cunha et al. 2015).

METHODS: MODELING THE STYLE OF FLOOR PLANS

Neural networks can be trained to perform generative tasks like image rendering. To accomplish this task, neural networks learn the distribution of visual information and salient visual features/pixel patterns over all possible images in the input data set. Conceptually, this means that the network learns to interpolate between the images in

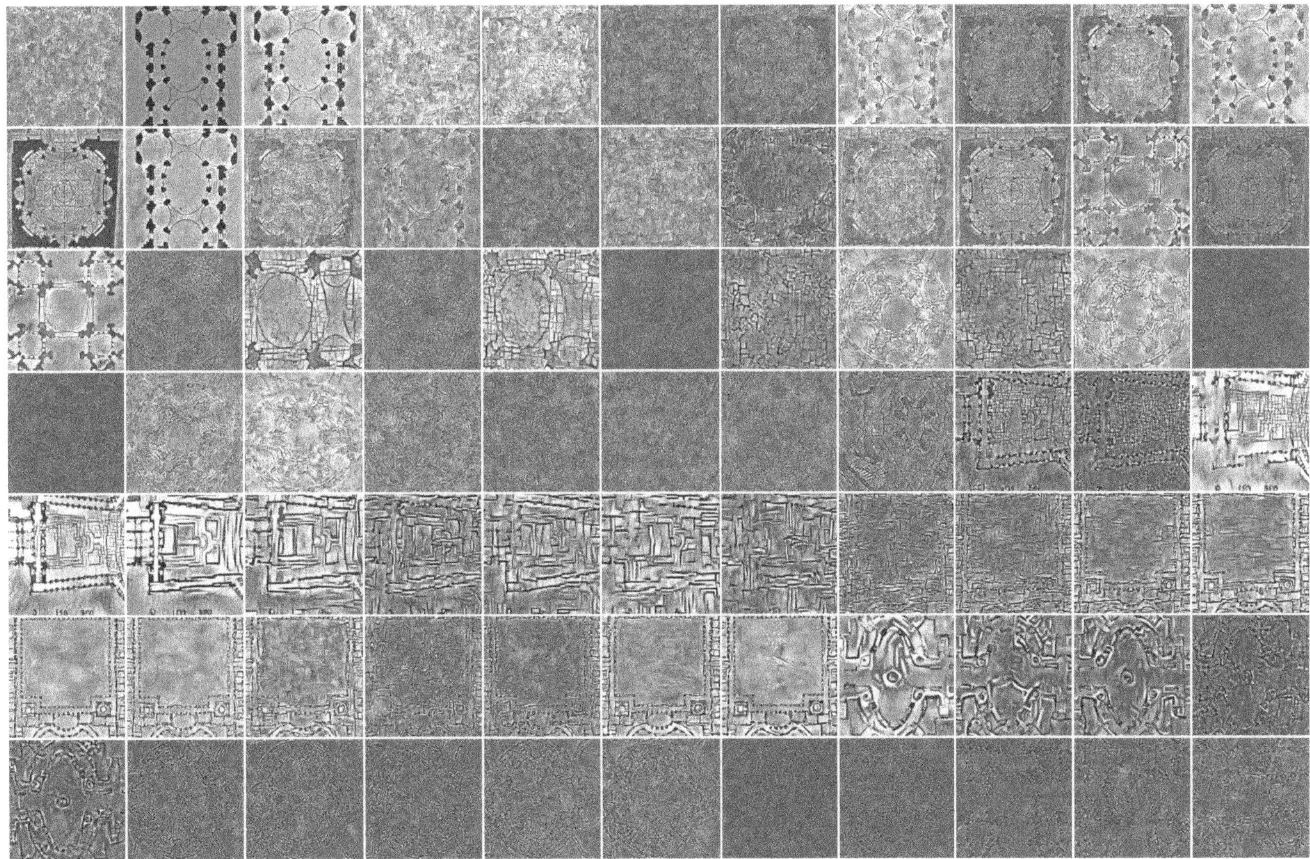

5 Neural networks learn the distribution of visual information and salient visual features/pixel patterns over all possible images in the input data set.

their training set to "imagine" previously unrealized images (Fig. 5) (Goodfellow, Bengio, and Courville 2016). GANs are state-of-the-art generative networks. In a GAN framework, the generative neural network, called the generator, is trained by a second neural network, called the discriminator. The generator network renders candidate images, and the discriminator evaluates them by comparing the rendered images to real images. Both networks are trained simultaneously, and they are adversaries to one another. The generative network's training objective is to "fool" the discriminator network by producing novel synthesized images that appear to have come from the set of real images. The discriminator, conversely, tries to detect patterns within the synthetic data that do not occur in real images. With this adversarial training strategy, the generator learns the distribution over real-world visual information, which results in the production of novel photorealistic images that trick the discriminator. By learning to interpolate between images, we can build data sets that force the GAN to learn the space between images that capture different architectural semantic content, like topographic maps and city plans, to generate innovative plans and layouts. Note that GANs learn features of the real world (from the training data set) in an entirely bottom-up fashion; we as the trainers of these algorithms exert our influence insofar as the design of the training set, but we cannot determine what features the GAN learns from pixels. To generate a mash-up of architectural styles, we take advantage of how GANs learn to model the distribution of visual information in the real world, i.e., by learning to interpolate between the images within the training data set. We collected a data set of images whose content spanned a wide range of Modern-style floor plans and Baroque-style floor plans. When a GAN is trained on this specially curated data set, it learns the pixel patterns that connect and define the visual space between the images in the data set. The trained GAN can be used to produce novel images that incorporate elements/visual features across all the styles in the training data set. Because of this, we hypothesize that a GAN can be used to generate unseen and unique floor plans that incorporate symbolic elements (e.g., room voids, windows, walls) and stylistic elements (e.g., width of walls, symmetry, curves) from both Baroque and Modern plans. To examine if GANs are able to capture these stylistic and symbolic elements from pixels, we train a state-of-the-art GAN, called StyleGAN2 (Karras et al. 2020), on our Modern

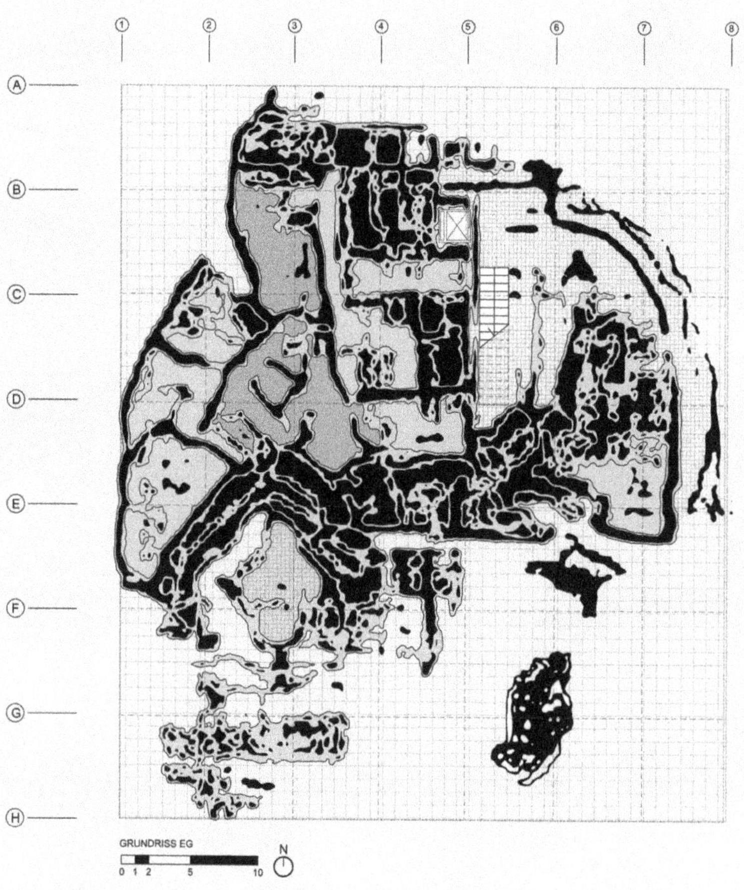

6 Resulting plan.

and Baroque floor plan data set. We use this trained StyleGAN2 to then generate images, and to evaluate the presence (or absence) of our desired features.

DISCUSSION

The analysis of the results revealed some interesting insights as to what the GAN processes (Fig. 6). It is interesting to observe that the Baroque influence on modern plans consists of a thickening of walls, and an increased subdivision of space. The GAN learns to transform from the inherent symmetry of Baroque plans into asymmetric conditions inherited from the Modern floor plan database. The struggle between these two conditions is expressed in strange, massive pochés populating parts of Modern plans. It is a stretch, though, to describe these plans as Modern as they are operating outside Modern criteria of planning such as continuous floor space, striving for a dissolution of material assemblies. These plans combine the voluptuousness and thickness of Baroque materiality with the asymmetry, openness, and rationality of a Modern floor plan, resulting in hybrid conditions. To the surprise of the authors, when using databases of Baroque or Modern architecture plans to design new projects, the results don't look Baroque or Modern. They result in something new, different, alien, strange, and wonderfully beautiful—maybe the first genuine 21st-century architecture.

CONCLUSION

In conclusion, we reiterate the main question of this paper: Can machines learn to plan? If so, how? To unpack this problem, let's first attempt to describe how we as humans plan. Every form of planning requires the knowledge of abstract high-level concepts performed in a hierarchical sequence—the epistemological question, however, as to how humans acquire the skill to learn such abstractions remains a mystery. What we do know is the sequence of decision-making steps (targets) along this hierarchy that allows a plan to manifest itself. Though this concept is uniformly applicable, the authors will rely on examples from architecture. Let's take the example of an architecture competition—say, an airport. It starts with a raw mental sketch ("design an airport and deliver the result at the competition deadline"). This first mental sketch is then subdivided into a detailed sequence of subtargets necessary for the planning process (read the competition brief, calculate hour estimates, assemble a team, etc.). Then a set of sub-subtargets follows that allows us to refine the process further, breaking up the planning process into a series of events necessary to move successfully through it, down to the bodily action of moving the muscles of your fingers to make a first sketch for the competition—producing the first physical outcome of the planning process. Though in most daily routines ("cook a meal, go shopping"), the planning process can be quite linear, the architecture planning process is at times defined by multiple parallel processes (plans are being drawn, the model is getting built while the structural engineers are working on their structures report—this would be a typical competition scenario), which provides an additional layer of subtarget planning to achieve the goal of delivering the competition entry on time. The implementation of subtargets allows humans to plan efficiently along a timeline in order to achieve the goals of the plan, which includes tasks, rewards, and the respective environmental structure. As these behavioral patterns can be read as a consistent formal model, they can be implemented as computational principles, capable of performing hierarchical planning (West 2018). Now, this would be an example of a human planning process, but what about artificial intelligence? How can AIs learn to plan? For an AI to replicate the human planning process in any way, shape, or form, it needs three things: intentionality, intelligence, and adaptability (Kumar 2020). All of these are crucial in a planning process—any planning process—whether it is planning an airport or your walk to the kitchen to make a sandwich. With this in mind, it can be stated that the application of generative adversarial networks, as presented in this paper, forms one of the milestones in the research on synthetic planning processes. It provides insight as to how neural networks can interrogate the pixel space of an image and recognize specific features. This being said, there is still a critical component missing, which is the integration of semantic information in the process that allows the neural network to perform more specific tasks than the identification of a style. Despite the fact that the resulting images are highly inspirational, there is a need to critically interrogate the resulting plans for their performative aspects. How do they subdivide space? How does the circulation perform? Does it make sense structurally and programmatically? These are necessary questions that will push the research on neural architecture further. To achieve this, there is work necessary in regards to building up databases that include many more examples, as well as detailed semantic information so that neural networks start to learn what is a wall, what is a door, what is a window, what is a room, which rooms are they. Based on this information, neural networks can start acquiring the knowledge to apply abstract high-level concepts in a hierarchical sequence, thereby allowing machines to plan.

However, this task cannot be done by one architect alone, or by one institution alone. Taking cues from computer science, the architecture discipline has an opportunity here to contribute to this emerging field of architectural production by being part of a concerted effort in the creation of databases to facilitate planning processes. Furthermore, these databases can serve not only as repositories of architectural ideas but also as tools for architectural research in history and theory. Circling back to the beginning of the paper, the architecture discipline is in a unique position in that solutions found millennia ago are continuously transformed to serve current architectural applications.

ACKNOWLEDGMENTS

The authors would like to thank Dean Jonathan Massey (UoM) and Associate Dean of Research Geoffrey Thün (UoM) for their continuous support and the robotics department of the University of Michigan for providing knowhow, time, and effort to make this research possible. In particular Jessy W. Grizzle, the Elmer G. Gilbert Distinguished University Professor Jerry W. and Carol L. Levin Professor of Engineering and Director of Robotics. We additionally wish to thank Justin Johnson, assistant professor in the computer science department of the University of Michigan.

REFERENCES

Agrest, D., and M. Gandelsonas. 1996. "Semiotics and Architecture—Ideological Consumption or Theoretical Work." In *Theorizing a New Agenda for Architecture: An Anthology of Architectural Theory 1965–1995*, edited by K. Nesbitt, 112–121. New York: Princeton Architectural Press.

Barthes, R. 1982. "The Death of the Author, Essay 1967." In *A Barthes Reader*, edited by S. Sontag. New York: Hill and Wang.

Baumgarten, A. G. 1750. *Aesthetica*. Frankfurt: J.C. Kleyb.

Berleant A. 2015. "Aesthetic Sensibility." *Ambiances* 1. https://doi.org/10.4000/ambiances.526.

Boden, M. 2009. "Creativity in a Nutshell." *Think* 5: 83–96.

Brosio, R. A., 2000. "Various Reds: Marx, Historical Materialism, Critical Theory, and the Openness of History." *Counterpoints* 75: 79–120. http://www.jstor.org/stable/42976139.

Carpo, M. 2011. *The Alphabet and the Algorithm*, Cambridge, MA: The MIT Press.

Cunha, João, Pedro Martins, Amílcar Cardoso, and Penousal Machado. 2015. "Generation of Concept-Representative Symbols." In *Workshop Proceedings from the Twenty-Third International Conference on Case-Based Reasoning (ICCBR 2015)*, Frankfurt, Germany, 28–30 September 2015, edited by Joseph Kendall-Morwick, 156–160. ICCBR.

Davidson, D. 2001. *Essays on Actions and Events: Philosophical Essays, Volume I.* Oxford: Clarendon Press.

Eisenman, P. 1996. "The End of the Classical—The End of the Beginning, The End of the End." In *Theorizing a New Agenda for Architecture: An Anthology of Architectural Theory 1965—1995*, edited by K. Nesbitt, 212–227. New York: Princeton Architectural Press.

Foucault, M. 1998. "What Is an Author?" In *Aesthetics, Method and Epistemology*, edited by J. D. Faubion, 205–222. New York: The New Press.

Goodfellow, Ian, Yoshua Bengio, Aaron Courville, and Yoshua Bengio. 2016. *Deep Learning*. Cambridge, MA: MIT Press.

Hegel, G. W. F. 1975. *Aesthetics. Lectures on Fine Art.* 2 vols. Trans. T. M. Knox. Oxford: Clarendon Press.

Hertzmann, A. 2020. "Visual Indeterminacy in GAN Art." *Leonardo: SIGGRAPH 2020 Art Papers* 53 (4).

Hudelson, P. M. 2004. "Culture and Quality: An Anthropological Perspective." *International Journal for Quality in Health Care* 16 (5): 345–346. https://doi.org/10.1093/intqhc/mzh076.

Hume, D. 1898. *A Treatise of Human Nature, Part III, section XV (Rules by which to judge of causes and effects)*, 173–176. Oxford: Clarendon Press.

Kant, I. 1781. *Kritik der Reinen Vernunft*. Riga: Verlag Johann Friedrich Hartknoch.

Karras, Tero, Samuli Laine, Miika Aittala, Janne Hellsten, Jaakko Lehtinen, and Timo Aila. 2020. "Analyzing and Improving the Image Quality of stylegan." In *Proceedings of the IEEE/CVF Conference on Computer Vision and Pattern Recognition (CVPR)*, Seattle, WA, 13–19 June 2020, 8107–8116. IEEE. http://doi.org/10.1109/CVPR42600.2020.00813

Kumar, A. 2020. "Teaching AI to Learn How Humans Plan Efficiently." Towards Data Science, August 24. https://towardsdatascience.com/teaching-ai-to-learn-how-humans-plan-efficiently-1d031c8727b.

Lladós, Josep, Ernest Valveny, Gemma Sánchez, and Enric Martí. 2001. "Symbol Recognition: Current Advances and Perspectives." In *Graphics Recognition Algorithms and Applications. GREC 2001. Lecture Notes in Computer Science*, edited by D. Blostein and Y. B. Kwon, 104–127. Berlin, Heidelberg: Springer. https://www.doi.org/10.1007/3-540-45868-9_9.

Millican, P. 2010. "Hume's Determinism." *Canadian Journal of Philosophy* 40 (4): 611–642. muse.jhu.edu/article/411607.

Pratten, S. 1993. "Structure Agency and Marx's analysis of the labor process." *Review of Political Economy* 5 (4): 403–426. https://www.doi.org/10.1080/09538259300000029.

Rochberg, F. 2012. "The Expression of Terrestrial and Celestial Order in Ancient Mesopotamia." In *Ancient Perspectives: Maps and Their Place in Mesopotamia, Egypt, Greece, and Rome*, edited by Richard Talbert, 9–46. Chicago: University of Chicago Press.

Sarvepalli, Sarat Kumar. 2015. "Deep Learning in Neural Networks: The Science behind an Artificial Brain." https://www.doi.org/10.13140/RG.2.2.22512.71682.

Speight, A. 2001. *Hegel, Literature and the Problem of Agency*. Cambridge: Cambridge University Press.

Turing, A. M. 1950. "Computing Machinery and Intelligence." *Mind* 59 (236): 433–460.

West, Darrel M. 2018. "What Is Artificial Intelligence?" A Blueprint for the Future of AI, 2018–2019. Brookings Institution, October 4. https://www.brookings.edu/series/a-blueprint-for-the-future-of-ai/

Zhang, W. J., G. Yang, Y. Lin, C. Ji, and M. M. Gupta. 2018. "On Definition of Deep Learning." *2018 World Automation Congress (WAC)*, 1–5. https://www.doi.org/10.23919/WAC.2018.8430387. Goodfellow, Ian, Yoshua Bengio, and Aaron Courville. 2016. *Deep Learning*. Cambridge, MA: MIT Press.

IMAGE CREDITS

Figure 3: Photograph by James Mellaart.

All other drawings and images by the authors.

Matias del Campo is a registered architect, designer, and educator. SPAN, which he founded with Sandra Manninger in Vienna/Austria, is a globally acting practice best known for their application of contemporary technologies in architectural production. Their award-winning architectural designs are informed by advanced geometry, computational methodologies, and philosophical inquiry. Matias del Campo is a recipient of the Accelerate@ CERN fellowship and the AIA Studio Prize. He is Associate Professor of Architecture at Taubman College for Architecture and Urban Planning, University of Michigan.

Alexandra Carlson attended the University of Chicago for her undergraduate degree, where she studied psychology and physics. She is currently a robotics PhD candidate with the Ford Center for Autonomous Vehicles at the University of Michigan. Her graduate studies focus on robust computer vision for autonomous vehicles. Her research develops an experimental framework that identifies visual features within images that contribute to the failure of deep neural networks (e.g., noise from the camera, as well as noise from the surrounding environment), and then uses these insights to develop neural network architectures that can more effectively distinguish between objects.

Sandra Manninger is a registered architect, teacher, and researcher. She is coprincipal of SPAN. The focus of the practice lies in the integration of advanced design and building techniques that fold nature, culture, and technology into one design ecology. Her work is part of the permanent collection of the FRAC Collection, the Luciano Benetton Collection, the MAK & the Albertina in Vienna. She currently serves at Tsinghua SIGS and at IAAC.

Drawn, Together

Kyle Steinfeld
University of California, Berkeley

Machine-Augmented Sketching in the Design Studio

1

1 Sketches produced by students of an upper-division undergraduate research studio offered at UC Berkeley in spring 2020 using the Sketch2Pix augmented drawing tool.

ABSTRACT

Changes in the media through which design proceeds are often associated with the emergence of novel design practices and new subjectivities. While the dynamic between design tools and design practices is complex and nondeterministic, there are moments when rapid development in one of these areas catalyzes changes in the other. The nascent integration of machine learning (ML) processes into computer-aided design suggests that we are in just such a moment.

It is in this context that an undergraduate research studio was conducted at UC Berkeley in the spring of 2020. By introducing novice students to a set of experimental tools (Steinfeld 2020) and processes based on ML techniques, this studio seeks to uncover those original practices or new subjectivities that might thereby arise. We describe here a series of small design projects that examine the applicability of such tools to early-stage architectural design. Specifically, we document the integration of several conditional text-generation models and conditional image-generation models into undergraduate architectural design pedagogy, and evaluate their use as "creative provocateurs" at the start of a design. After surveying the resulting student work and documenting the studio experience, we conclude that the approach taken here suggests promising new modalities of design authorship, and we offer reflections that may serve as a useful guide for the more widespread adoption of machine-augmented design tools in architectural practice.

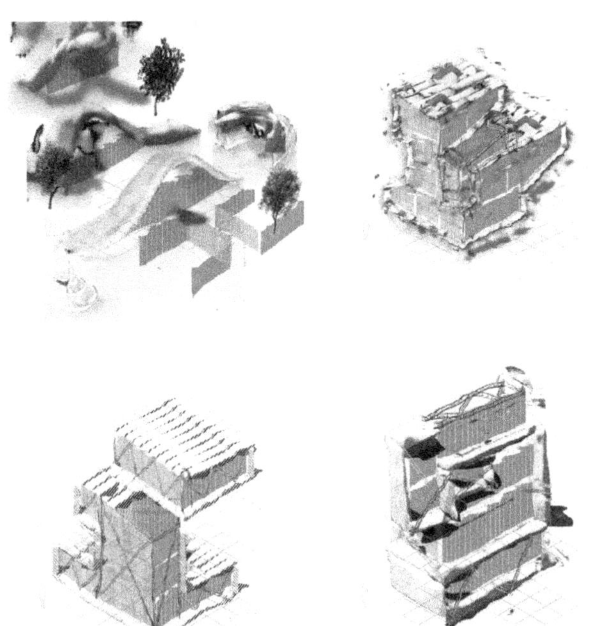

INTRODUCTION

It has been observed (Carpo 2017) that changes in the media through which design proceeds—that is, the means and methods of design—are often associated with the emergence of novel design practices and new subjectivities—the manner in which a designer may act, make decisions, and assert their agency. While there is not a direct deterministic link between design tools and the culture of design practice—between, for example, design software and design subjectivities—there have been moments at which rapid development in one of these areas catalyzes changes in the other (Loukissas 2012).

Just as the adoption of scripting in the early 2000s facilitated new practices such as rule-based design (Hensel, Menges, and Weinstock 2013), and as the later broad acceptance of parametric modeling tools facilitated new practices such as generative design (Leach 2009), we may expect to see that a more widespread availability of design tools based on statistical inference will similarly engender novel design practices. As such, the nascent integration of ML processes into computer-aided design suggests that we may be in the midst of one such moment.

2 Four axonometric projection drawings produced using the Sketch2Pix augmented drawing tool. Robert Carrasco, 2020.

3 Landscape drawing produced using the Sketch2Pix augmented drawing tool. Nicholas Doerschlag, 2020.

Such a paradigm shift from computer-aided design to machine-augmented design would be most welcome. Existing models for computer-aided design fail to directly support what is arguably the important moment in early-stage design: that point before an idea is fully manifest, when we first recognize the pattern of a compelling solution that lies latent in our problem. Insofar as machine learning is inherently relational, imagistic, historical, and concerned with the recognition of pattern, we posit that this technology may be better suited than the currently dominant modes of computational design in supporting the abductive nature of early-stage design (Steinfeld 2017).

Of particular interest here is one mechanism that has been shown to be important to supporting creative thinking: the "provocation." Speaking of the role that provocations can play in the creative process, Edward de Bono (2015) coined the term "po" to describe an intentionally disruptive stimulus that is used to facilitate creative thinking. While de Bono clearly articulated the concept, he was far from the first to notice the utility of disruptive points of origin in creative fields. Preceding concepts and works include Pierre Boulez's aleatorism (Riley 1966), which describe compositions resulting from actions made by chance, and Brian Eno and Peter Schmidt's "Oblique Strategies" (1975), a series of prompts for overcoming creative blocks printed on cards.

The work of the studio seeks to understand how ML tools might function as tools of creative provocation in particular, and of tools of early-stage design more broadly. This question comes at an opportune time. Triggered by new advances in machine learning, and the development of methods for making these advances visible and accessible to a wider audience, the past five years has seen a burst of renewed interest in generative practices across the domains of fine art, music, and graphic design. In this context, this work seeks to further our understanding of ML tools in architectural design.

METHODS

Here we present a set of technical tools and pedagogical methods introduced in an undergraduate research studio conducted at UC Berkeley in the spring of 2020 with the aim of examining the applicability of ML processes to early-stage architectural design, and of uncovering any original practices or new subjectivities that might thereby arise.

We first enumerate the specific tools used by the students in this course, which include several "off-the-shelf" conditional text-generation models and conditional image-generation models, as well as an augmented architectural drawing tool developed by the authors (Steinfeld 2020). We then describe a series of small design projects that structure students' engagement with these tools, and present a selection of student work and a survey of student experience of the studio.

THE TOOLS OF THE STUDIO

The ML tools employed by the studio fall into two broad categories: conditional generative models, including conditional text-generation models and conditional image-generation models, and general-use "platforms" that facilitate access to these generative models. We enumerate each of these tools here in ascending order of their importance to the work of the studio.

Assorted Text Generation Models

A text generation model (Li et al. 2017) generates synthetic text that completes a given passage based on the corpus on which the model was trained. Among the most successful text generation models at the time of writing is the GPT-2 model (Radford et al., 2019), which serves as the basis of two online tools used by the studio: Talk to Transformer (Kin, 2019) and AI Dungeon (Walton 2019).

The Artbreeder Platform

Artbreeder (Simon 2019) is a web-based creative tool, created and maintained by Joel Simon while at Stochastic Labs in Berkeley, CA, that allows people to collaborate and explore high-complexity spaces of synthetic images generated by various generative adversarial networks (GANs). The studio employs two models hosted on Artbreeder: the "general" model that appears to be an implementation of BigGAN (Brock et al. 2019) and the "landscapes" model that is a custom-trained implementation of the same.

The Runway Platform

The RunwayML platform (Valenzuela 2018) is an ML model training, hosting, and distribution service. This platform is used in a variety of ways in the studio, and represents a critical link in a central workflow of the class: the connection between ML models generally, and the sketching environment of Adobe Photoshop. This workflow is discussed in a section below. The studio also made use of a particular web-based implementation of Runway, the Runway Generative Engine, which creates synthetic images from textual captions.

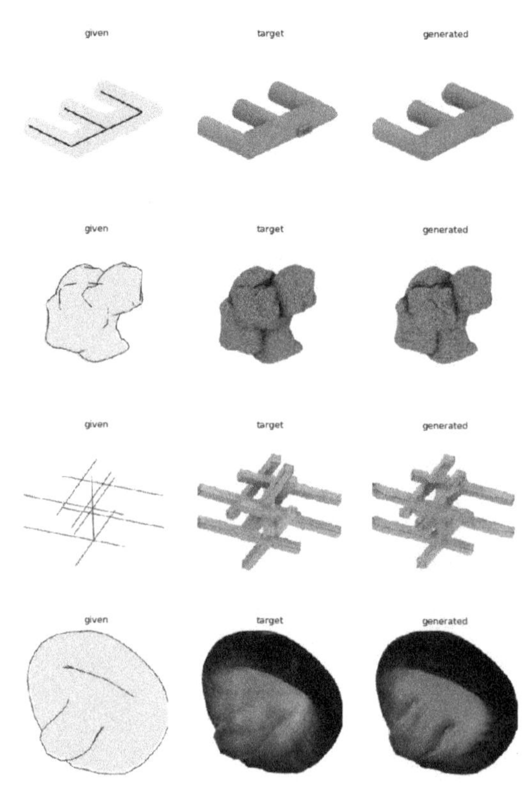

4

The Sketch2Pix Generative Model

Sketch2Pix is an augmented architectural drawing tool developed by the authors (Steinfeld 2020) that supports architectural sketching augmented by automated image-to-image translation processes (Isola et al. 2016). This tool enables novice undergraduate designers to conceptualize, train, and apply their own personal AI "drawing partners." The RunwayML platform forms a link between student-trained image-to-image translation models and the sketching environment of Photoshop. Because students hold agency both over the training and the application of these "bots," and as such are able to configure these tools to meet the perceived demands of a given design problem as well as the subjective dictates of their trainer's tastes, we observe that the approach taken here suggests promising new modalities of design authorship.

THE WORK OF THE STUDIO

Here we discuss the pedagogical approach taken by the studio in integrating ML tools as "creative provocateurs" in early-stage design.

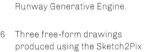

5

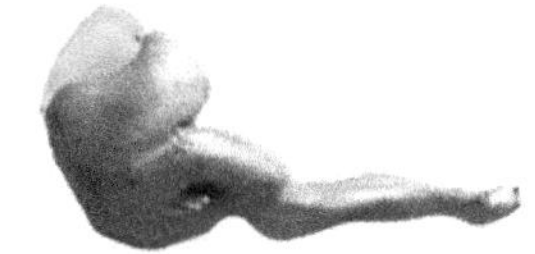
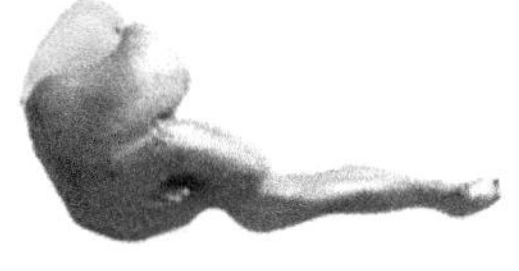
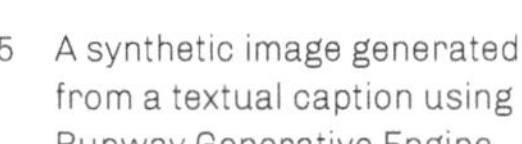
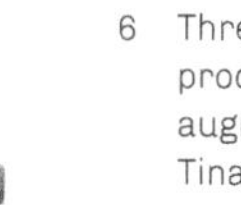
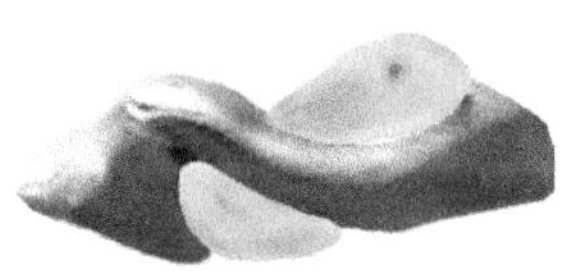

6

4 Depictions of the operation of four separate Sketch2Pix "brushes" authored by students.

5 A synthetic image generated from a textual caption using Runway Generative Engine.

6 Three free-form drawings produced using the Sketch2Pix augmented drawing tool. Tina Nguyen, 2020.

Given the speculative nature of the course, rather than privilege the development of a singular design project, the studio proceeds through a series of three lightly connected "propositions" that explore the potential role of ML tools in design. By proceeding in short bursts, the studio values patience in allowing the discovery of small questions to aggregate into larger and more elaborate proposals. The role of each ML tool differs, and each proposition offers a chance to better know the underlying technology and how it might figure in a larger process of design.

While the studio is primarily driven by method, such an investigation benefits from the comprehensive details of an architectural design problem. This raises the question: What is an appropriate test bed for ML tools as technologies of the artificial? The studio responds with a focus on the Northern California landscape, and on the interface between the built environment and the natural environment.

In the following sections, we detail each of the three propositions completed by the studio, illustrated by a small sample of student work. But first, we briefly discuss an ongoing practice of conceptual sketching that permeated the semester.

Augmented Sketching as a Daily Practice

Given the novelty of the augmented sketching tools adopted by the studio, students are asked to engage in a practice of daily sketching, and to post these sketches for public display. This practice served to encourage increased competency with these tools. The primary conduit for the public display of this work is an Instagram hashtag related to the course: #ARCH100D. The graphic material found at this hashtag relates to each of the propositions listed here.

Proposition One: Strange Fruit

This two-week proposition introduces students to the nature of the ML tools employed in the course, and provides a platform for understanding the utility of these tools as design prompts.

Here, students are instructed to select a fruit or vegetable grown in Northern California and to conduct basic research on its life cycle, including the climate in which it was grown and who may have participated in its production. Next, based on this research, students collaborate with a text generation bot to author a narrative about a person involved in the production of the produce, including an explicit description of the various settings involved. Then, based on this story, students use the Runway Generative Engine to create a storyboard of scenographic images generated from textual captions.

In parallel with this exercise, students utilize the Sketch2Pix tool to train an augmented drawing assistant—in the parlance of the studio, a "brush"—based on their chosen produce. As is detailed in another scope of work, the technical process of training these brushes combines 3D scanning, calibrated rendering, and a custom implementation of a Pix2Pix model (Isola et al. 2016). Once trained, this brush allows students to sketch imagined three-dimensional forms and spaces in collaboration with

7

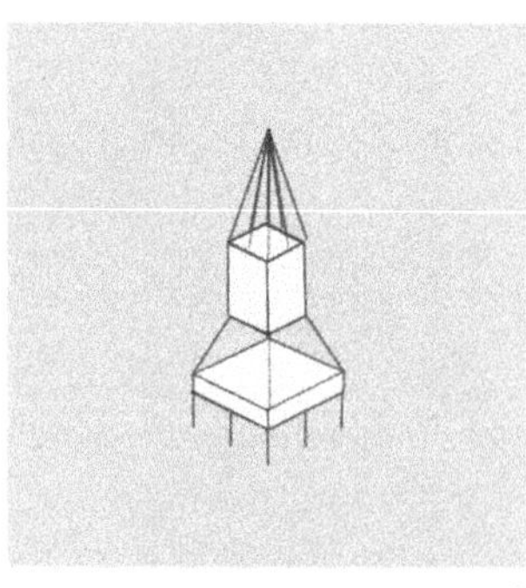

8

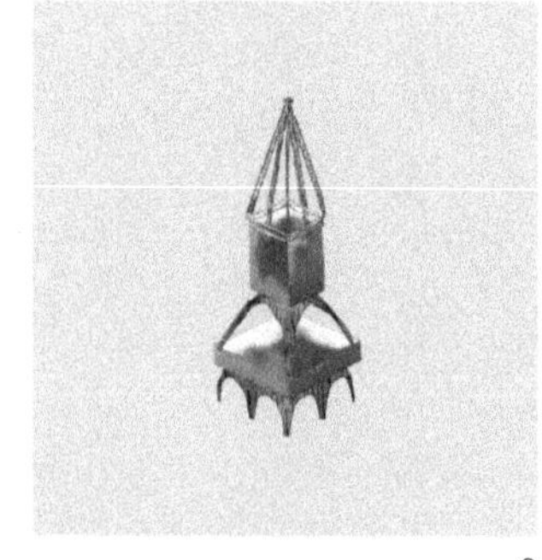

9

7 Physical interpretive models produced in response to the nearby augmented sketches. Any media available while under pandemic lockdown. Tina Nguyen, 2020.

8 Human-authored input in an augmented drawing process. Tina Nguyen, 2020 .

9 Computer-generated result in an augmented drawing process. Tina Nguyen, 2020.

a conditional image generation model that generates the colors, textures, and forms that are related to the produce on which the brush is trained. At the end of this two-week period, students present a graphic interpretation of the images generated from captions, applying their brushes in the service of embedding a set of three-dimensional forms and spaces.

While this first proposition serves primarily to build familiarity with the requisite tools, we can clearly see the positioning of the ML generative model as an early-design provocateur, as it serves to provoke a creative response in the tradition of Eno, Schmidt, and Boulez.

Proposition Two: Landscapes of Change

This two-week proposition expands on some of the tools introduced in the previous proposition, Artbreeder and Sketch2Pix in particular, and seeks to extend these further into the realm of architectural production.

To begin, students again train an augmented drawing assistant, or brush, using more familiar subject matter: the architectural model. Here, students construct a series of nonscaled physical models that employ an intentional formal language common to academic design studios. Examples include a series of foam-core massing models; a collection of plaster "blob" models; and a third series of linear basswood matrix models. These models are then 3D scanned such that, employing the process mentioned above, they may serve as the basis of a training set for a brush. The result is an augmented drawing assistant that transforms hand-drawn sketches into "deepfake" photographs of architectural models. These tools were then deployed in the service of the design of a dwelling for a specific site.

To conceptualize an appropriate site for these dwellings expressed as deepfake architectural models, students are asked to return again to Artbreeder. First, selecting from a number of sites at the border between urban and rural spaces in the San Francisco Bay Area, students speculate on the changes likely to occur at this site over a span of 100 years. Then, students work with the gene-splicing feature of the Artbreeder landscape model to produce images that evoke their chosen site and animations of this imagined transformation. This approach to the generation of images—via a manipulation of "genes," or archetypal features discovered during training—is a mode of authorship unique to the latent space of generative adversarial networks (GANs), and is distinct from other modes of large-space exploration currently practiced in architectural design (Woodbury and Burrow 2006).

At the end of this two-week period, students again present a graphic interpretation that functions as an early-stage design proposal. Here, following the steps described above, the proposal is expressed as a photomontage that shows a deepfake architectural model situated in a synthetic landscape.

Proposition Three: Four Elements of a Synthetic Architecture

The final proposition of the studio extends over nearly four weeks. Continuing the movement of the studio toward the language of architecture, here we focus on developing a more formal language of building systems, expressed through a single drawing type: the axonometric.

Following Gottfried Semper (2010), and using Artbreeder as a provocateur once again, students each make a coordinated proposal for four elemental building systems. Each of these forms the basis of the training of a separate Sketch2Pix brush, which is then employed to produce a number of sketch proposals of dwellings. As above, these dwellings are proposed for a synthetic landscape but are developed simultaneously through two types of projected drawings: exploded axonometric and perspective.

To develop this collection of four related brushes, students first make use of the Artbreeder general model to create four synthetic images that are suggestive of forms related to each of Semper's four elements.[1] In crafting these images, students again make use of Artbreeder's ability to specify and edit the genes of an image, which allows for adjustments to be made in terms of the intensity of influence of imagistic archetypes.

Next, following the four archetypal images generated by Artbreeder, students compose collections of textured 3D models in Rhinoceros (Robert McNeel & Associates 2020) and Blender (Blender Online Community 2021) to serve as the basis of corresponding Sketch2Pix brushes. Similar to the deepfake architectural models, these digital models must be authored in a manner distinct from traditional modes of architectural production. Due to the nature of the data extraction and training processes, the specific geometries and overall forms found in these models holds less impact on the behavior of the resulting brush than imagistic features, such as textures, colors, and small-scale formal relationships.

As in previous propositions, at the end of this four-week period, students present an early-stage design proposal. Here, the proposal is expressed in exploded axonometric.

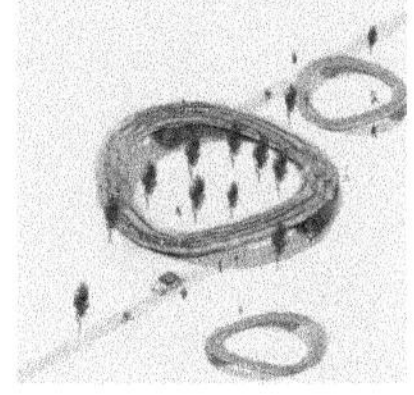

10

10 Four free-form drawings produced using the Sketch2Pix augmented drawing tool. Can Li, 2020.

RESULTS AND REFLECTION

In this paper, we describe a series of small design projects conducted in the spring of 2020 that examine the applicability of machine-augmented tools to early-stage design, with the aim of uncovering any original practices or new subjectivities that may arise. Upon reflection, it is possible to extract a number of observations that hold ramifications for the further adoption of machine-augmented tools in architectural practice.

First, as demonstrated by those projects that rely on the gene-mixing and gene-editing capabilities of Artbreeder, we suggest that the epistemic action of latent space exploration may be different from that of known forms of design space exploration (Woodbury and Burrow 2006). We suggest this difference in that imagistic archetypes that serve as the "genes" of latent space do not result from a user-defined set of parameters but, in the case of unsupervised learning models, are "discovered" during training. Further research is needed to distinguish the ways in which latent space exploration may differently support design cognition.

Next, we observe that an ML generative model functions as a novel and effective form of early-design provocateur, in the tradition of Eno, Schmidt, and Boulez. While similarly functioning to serve as a quasi-random "po" deliberately used to facilitate creative thinking, it is notable that the forms and images conjured by ML processes are not random but rather are associations drawn from a specific body of experience (the training data set) that may or may not be apparent to a user. This feature suggests a novel form of "guided" provocation, in which an author consciously selects the predilections of their drawing assistant to be provoked in an intentional way in relation to the particularities of a design problem.

Finally, we highlight a new form of subjectivity offered by machine-augmented design. In the training of Pix2Pix brushes, including the critical step of crafting data sets for training, we find a new authorial position that should not be overlooked by designers engaging with this media. In stark contrast to other modes of computational authorship, such as parametric modeling, design action expressed through the defining of a training data set is curatorial more than logistic or compositional. It is an action that may be regarded as uncomfortably indirect by designers new to the media: suggestive of imagistic traits more than deterministic of formal or geometric ones. This new locus of subjectivity holds broad ramifications for the future of computational design education, and suggests that connections must be strengthened with allied knowledge domains, such as data science and critical data studies.

11

12

11 An axonometric drawing produced as a collage of results of the Sketch2Pix augmented drawing tool and 3D scans of Santa Monica, CA. Nicholas Doerschlag, 2020.

12 An axonometric drawing produced as a collage of results of the Sketch2Pix augmented drawing tool and 3D scans of Berkeley, CA. Nicholas Doerschlag, 2020.

ACKNOWLEDGMENTS

The project also owes a debt to a number of technologists and creative practitioners who inspired our approach. These include but are not limited to:

- Scott Eaton (2020), a mechanical engineer and anatomical artist who uses custom-trained transfer models as a "creative collaborator" in his figurative drawings.
- Nono Martinez Alonso's thesis "Suggestive Drawing Among Human and Artificial Intelligences" (2017) is an important precedent as it similarly deploys the Pix2Pix model in the service of a creative design tool, and serves as an early demonstration of the potential of computer-assisted drawing interfaces.
- Stanislas Chaillou's thesis "AI + Architecture, Towards a New Approach" (2019) also uses Pix2Pix as a part of a larger stack of processes that lead to an architectural result.

We would also acknowledge that this research is closely related to an upper-division undergraduate research studio offered at UC Berkeley in the spring of 2020. This studio was instructed by the author and attended by an inspiring group of 16 students. We would like to thank the students of this course for the generous willingness to participate in the case study described here. This resilient group of young designers faced difficult circumstances with grace, and adopted unfamiliar methods with enthusiasm: Daniel Barrio, Robert Carrasco, Sarah Dey, Nicholas Doerschlag, Siri Dove, Payam Golestani, Garrick Home, Uade Imoukhuede, Nehal Jain, Can Li, Gabi Nehorayan, Tina Nguyen, Andre Phan, TJ Tang, Rose Wang, Leo Zhao.

NOTES

1. These are understood as the: Mound, or massive elements (often stone, earthwork, or concrete) that relate a building to its ground. Roof, or linear elements (such as timber or steel) that offer protection from the elements. Enclosure, or planar elements (such as sheet materials or textiles) that produce spatial division and social separation. Hearth, or objects (such as mechanical systems or furniture) that provide thermal comfort, ventilation, and cooking, and offer a focus of social life (Semper 2010).

REFERENCES

Blender Online Community. 2021. *Blender*. V.2.93. Stichting Blender Foundation, Amsterdam. http://www.blender.org.

Brock, Andrew, Jeff Donahue, and Karen Simonyan. 2018. "Large Scale GAN Training for High Fidelity Natural Image Synthesis." In *Proceedings of the 7th International Conference on Learning Representations*. New Orleans, LA: openreview.net https://openreview.net/forum?id=B1x-sqj09Fm.

Burry, M. 2011. *Scripting Cultures: Architectural Design and Programming. Architectural Design Primer*. John Wiley & Sons.

Carpo, Mario. 2017. *The Second Digital Turn: Design Beyond Intelligence*. MIT Press.

de Bono, Edward. 2015. *The Mechanism of Mind: Understand How Your Mind Works to Maximise Memory and Creative Potential*. Random House.

Eno, Brian, and Peter Schmidt. 1975. "Oblique Strategies." Opal.Limited Edition, Boxed Set of Cards. RMAB.

Hensel, Michael, Achim Menges, and Michael Weinstock. 2013. *Emergent Technologies and Design: Towards a Biological Paradigm for Architecture*. Routledge.

Isola, Phillip, Jun-Yan Zhu, Tinghui Zhou, and Alexei A. Efros. 2016. "Image-to-Image Translation with Conditional Adversarial Networks." *CoRR*. abs/1611.07004.

King, Adam. 2019. "Talk to Transformer." https://app.inferkit.com/demo

Leach, Neil. 2009. "Digital Morphogenesis." *Architectural Design* 79 (1): 32–37.

Li, Jiwei, Will Monroe, Tianlin Shi, Sébastien Jean, Alan Ritter, and Dan Jurafsky. 2017. "Adversarial Learning for Neural Dialogue Generation." In *Proceedings of the 2017 Conference on Empirical Methods in Natural Language Processing*, 2157–2169. Copenhagen, Denmark: Association for Computational Linguistics. https://doi.org/10.18653/v1/D17-1230.

Loukissas, Yanni Alexander. 2012. *Co-Designers: Cultures of Computer Simulation in Architecture*. Routledge.

Radford, Alec, Jeffrey Wu, Rewon Child, David Luan, Dario Amodei, and Ilya Sutskever. 2019. "Language Models Are Unsupervised Multitask Learners." *OpenAI Blog* 1 (8): 9.

Riley, Howard. 1966. "Aleatoric Procedures in Contemporary Piano Music." *The Musical Times* 107 (1478): 311–312.

Robert McNeel & Associates. 2020. *Rhinoceros*. V.6.0. Robert McNeel & Associates. PC.

Semper, Gottfried. 2010. *The Four Elements of Architecture and Other Writings*. Trans. Harry F. Mallgrave and Wolfgang Herrmann. Cambridge University Press.

Simon, Joel. 2019. *Artbreeder*. https://artbreeder.com.

Steinfeld, Kyle. 2017. "Dreams May Come." In *ACADIA 2017: Disciplines and Disruption [Proceedings of the 37th Annual Conference of the Association for Computer Aided Design in Architecture (ACADIA)]*, Cambridge, MA, 2–4 November 2017, edited by T. Nagakura, S. Tibbits, M. Ibañez, and C. Mueller, 590–599. CUMINCAD.

Valenzuela, Cristóbal. 2018. *RunwayML—Machine Learning for Creators*. RunwayML. https://runwayml.com.

Walton, Nick. 2019. *AI Dungeon*. AI Dungeon. https://aidungeon.io/.

Woodbury, Robert F., and Andrew L. Burrow. 2006. "Whither Design Space?" *Artificial Intelligence for Engineering Design, Analysis and Manufacturing* 20 (2): 63–82. https://doi.org/10.1017/S0890060406060057.

IMAGE CREDITS

All drawings and images by the author or the students listed above.

Kyle Steinfeld is an Associate Professor of Architecture at UC Berkeley. In his academic and scholarly work, he seeks to illuminate the dynamic relationship between the creative practice of design and computational design methods, thereby enabling a more inventive, informed, responsive, and responsible practice of architecture.

Topological and Material Formation

A Generative Design Framework for Additive Manufacturing Integrating Material-Physics Simulation and Structural Analysis

Robert Stuart-Smith
University of Pennsylvania
University College London

Patrick Danahy
University of Pennsylvania

Natalia Revelo La Rotta
University of Pennsylvania

1 Close-up rendered perspective view of a column-like element created using the three-part research method that involves the generative design of a topological and material formation, and the material-physics simulation of the continuous AM extrusion process.

ABSTRACT

Extrusion-based additive manufacturing (AM) is gaining traction in the construction industry, offering lower environmental and economic costs through reductions in material and production time. AM designs achieve these reductions by increasing topological and geometric complexity, and through variable material distribution via custom-programmed robot tool paths. Limited approaches are available to develop AM building designs within a topologically free design search or to leverage material affects relative to structural performance. Established methods such as topological structural optimization (TSO) operate primarily within design rationalization, demonstrating less formal or aesthetic diversity than agent-based methods that exhibit behavioral character. While material-extrusion gravitational affects have been explored in AM research using viscous materials such as concrete and ceramics, established methods are not sufficiently integrated into simulation and structural analysis workflows. A novel three-part method is proposed for the design and simulation of extrusion-based AM that includes *topoForm*, an evolutionary multi-agent software capable of generating diverse topological designs; *matForm*, an agent-based AM robot tool-path generator that is geometrically agnostic and adapts material effects to local structural and geometric data; and *matSim*, a material-physics simulation environment that enables high-resolution AM material effects to be simulated and structurally and aesthetically analyzed. The research enables designers to incorporate and simulate material behavior prior to fabrication and produce instructions suitable for industrial robot AM. The approach is demonstrated in the generative design of four AM column-like elements.

INTRODUCTION

Extrusion-based additive manufacturing (AM) is gaining traction in the construction industry, offering lower environmental and economic costs through reductions in material and production time (Buswell et al. 2007; Essop 2020; Khoshnevis, Kwan, and Bukkapatnam 2001). AM designs achieve these reductions by increasing topological and geometrical complexity, and through variable material distribution via custom-programmed robot tool paths. Limited approaches are available to engage AM building-design within a topologically free design search or to leverage material affects relative to structural performance. Established formal methods such as topological structural optimization (TSO) operate primarily within design rationalization (Jipa et al. 2016), overconstraining aesthetics and demonstrating less formal diversity than agent-based methods that exhibit behavioral character (Snooks and Stuart-Smith 2011). While material-extrusion gravitational affects have been explored in AM research using viscous materials such as concrete and ceramics (Rael and San Fratello 2017), established methods are not sufficiently integrated into simulation and structural analysis workflows compared to alternative AM approaches (Ansys n.d.). Limited investigations have been undertaken into how material effects might feed back into design and engineering approaches, to date, operating primarily through sensor-in-the-loop methods (Im, AlOthman, and del Castillo 2018), necessitating extensive physical prototyping.

A generative method is proposed that builds on the authors' multi-agent research (Stuart-Smith 2011, 2018) to provide a novel approach to the design and simulation of extrusion-based AM (Fig. 2) that includes:

- *topoForm*—an evolutionary multi-agent software capable of generating diverse topological designs with integrated structural and geometric performance (Figs. 3–7).
- *matForm*—an agent-based AM tool-path generator that is geometrically agnostic and able to produce gravitational material affects while adapting to local structural and geometric data (Figs. 8–11).
- *matSim*—a material-physics simulation environment that enables high-resolution AM material effects to be simulated, structurally and aesthetically analyzed (Figs. 1, 12–14, 16).

The method enables designers to incorporate and simulate material behavior prior to fabrication and produce instructions suitable for industrial robot AM. The approach is demonstrated through the design and simulation of four AM column-like elements (Fig. 15).

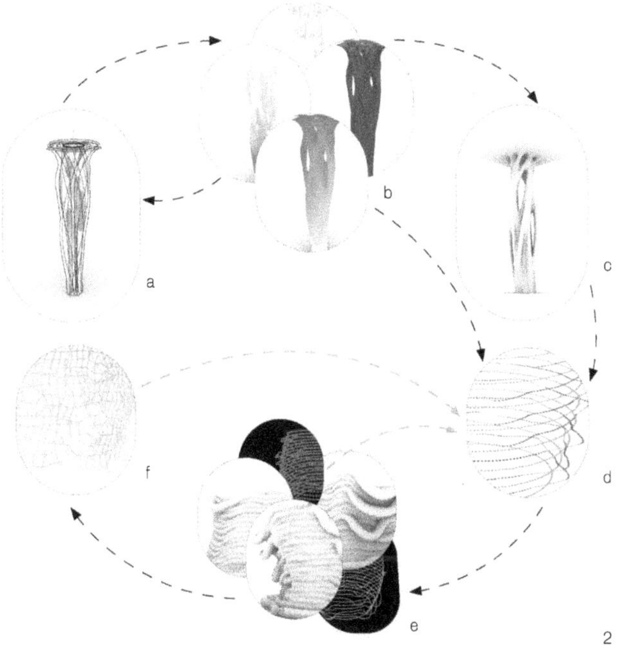

2 Research methodology. Step 1, topoForm: (a) multi-agent topology generation; (b) geometric and structural analysis as part of an evolutionary fitness evaluation; (c) evolved column-like geometric result. Step 2, matForm: (d) agent-generated robot tool path. Step 3, matSim: (e) manufacturing simulation; (f) postsimulation structural analysis.

METHODS

The research provides a novel approach to the design computation of continuous AM geometries that allows for a flexible exploration of topological and material considerations within design while incorporating structural and geometric performance prior to and following an AM simulation. Three custom software packages were developed— *topoForm*, *matForm*, and *matSim*—and utilized in the development of four design solutions for a 3.5 m high column-like geometric element to demonstrate the utility, adaptability, and aesthetic capabilities of the method.

topoForm Generative Design Software for Column-like Topological Design

topoForm is an evolutionary multi-agent design software tasked with developing multimanifold topological designs that integrate multiobjective design criteria for column-like geometries. *topoForm* is an extension of multi-agent software developed by the authors (Stuart-Smith 2018) that encodes design decisions within a group of autonomous particles that interact with each other and their environment through vector-based steering behaviors inspired by Craig Reynolds' (1989) OpenSteer algorithm. Kokkugia's software has been utilized for the design of multiple building projects (Stuart-Smith 2011), with *topoForm* extending this framework by integrating multiobjective evolutionary optimization. Several agent behavioral parameters are assigned to operate as genes, capable

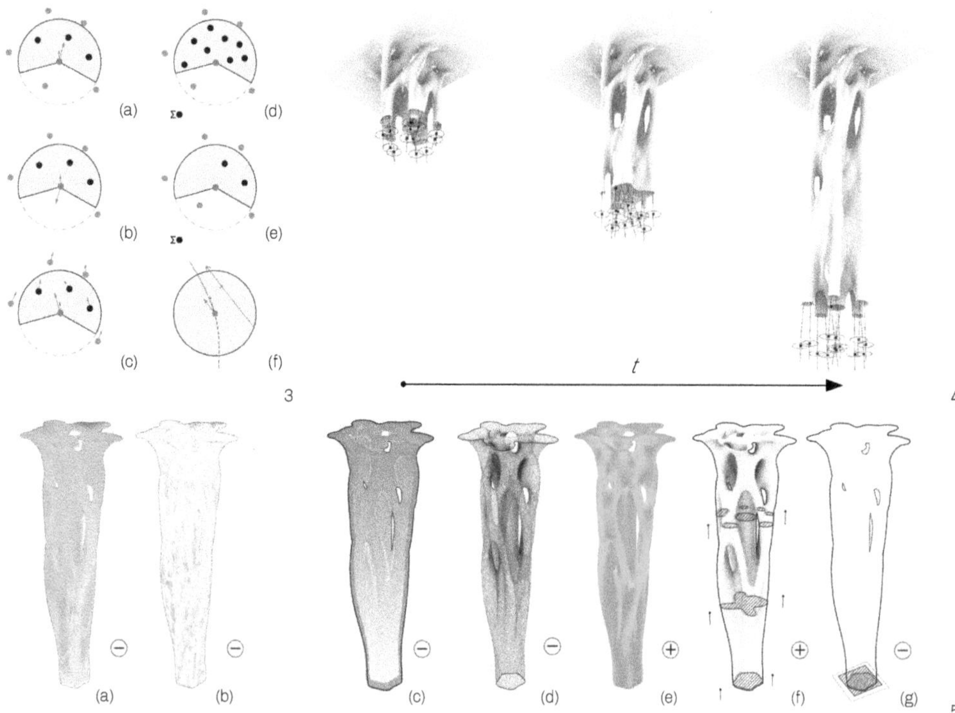

3 *topoForm* agent rules: (a) cohesion; (b) separation; (c) alignment; (d) state change: crowding; (e) state change: isolation; (f) vector guide alignment.

4 Evolutionary multi-agent topological formation of a column-like geometry. Motion trajectory curves interpolated as an isosurface mesh.

5 Multiobjective fitness criteria. Structural analysis: (a) deflection; (b) principle stress. Geometric: (c) volume; (d) surface area; (e) mean curvature; (f) plan-sectional area; (g) base bounding area.

6 Abbreviated results of an evolutionary solver run: population of 20-40 genomes for 35 generations.

7 *topoForm* evolutionary results demonstrating diverse topological order and formal character. (a) midevolution phenotypes; (b) final generation results showing variations of surface area, volume, and curvature.

of impacting the behavior of a multi-agent simulation and resulting mesh interpolation for each genome outcome within an evolutionary search. These settings are varied over an evolutionary sequence comprising of a population of 30 geometrical outcomes evolved over 36 generations (evolutionary cycles) in relation to diverse structural and geometric fitness criteria. The process is repeated multiple times with varied ratios of a multiobjective fitness criteria to demonstrate the topological, geometric, and aesthetic variability of the method.

Each population of design variants is generated through an object-orientated Python code, where instances of an agent class are tasked with descending from 3.5 m in altitude to zero over a time-based simulation of 300 time frames, generating motion trajectory curves that are interpolated by an isosurfacing method into a multimanifold surface. Agent motion is updated each frame (iteration), ceasing motion if they arrive at zero altitude. Variables influencing agent motion and spatial set-out parameters are exposed to evolutionary variance. An evolutionary search adjusts values for genes, including agent seeding conditions, vector-behavior values, and mesh interpolation settings (Fig. 3). The Python agent code employed Grasshopper's Galapagos as an evolutionary solver due to its availability and easy integration within a Rhino3D 3D modeling environment workflow (Rutten 2013).

Genome: Agent Behavior and Mesh Interpolation

Each agent operates as a particle whose motion is governed by programmed autonomous decisions. Agents are characterized by an (x,y,z) position, a radius (range of perception), field-of-view (cone of vision), a state (1 or 2), and vectors governing their velocity, maximum velocity, maximum force (a variable limiting the influence of any one behavior). Each agent updates its position over time by calculating a series of vector influences that are weighted to provide a combined influence over the agent's acceleration, which is added to its velocity each time-frame. Initial agent seeding conditions enabled variations in the number, distribution, and orientation of agents. Three horizontally oriented concentric circles were located on the origin at 3.5 m in the z-axis world space. Evolutionary variance informed the number of agents equally distributed along these circles, their relative positions along each circle, and initial orientation vectors (Fig. 3).

Agent rules exposed to evolutionary variance included steering behaviors, agent motion variables, and rules that governed each agent's ability to change state. Steering behaviors included separation, cohesion, alignment, agent-trail seeking, agent-trail alignment, vector alignment (Figs. 3a–f). Agent motion variables included agent radius, maximum velocity, and maximum force. Agents changed between one of two states at any point during the simulation. State changes would occur when an agent was either isolated or crowded in by other agents. This evaluation was based on a variable exposed to evolutionary variance that specified the number of other agents within an agent's radius. Each agent state impacted the value of agent motion variables and steering behaviors. Changes of state therefore resulted in changes to an agent's behavior.

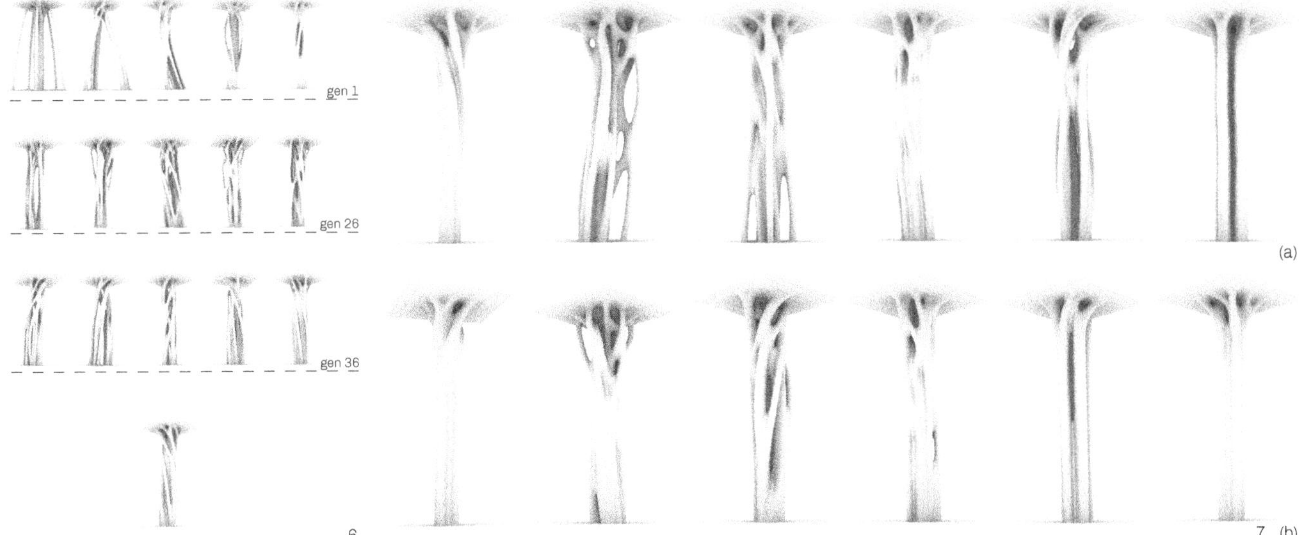

Each agent's behavior over time resulted in a motion trajectory curve. All agents' curves were interpolated as a polygon mesh isosurface using Grasshopper's Cocoon plugin (Stasiuk 2015). Cocoon variables, including a radius threshold around each curve and a charge-strength (degree of influence) of curve groups, were also exposed to evolutionary variance. Each of the above agent and mesh interpolation rules operated as a gene with variances ranging between 0.0 to 1.0 in increments of 0.01 within each genome. Each genome resulted in a column-like mesh geometry that was then analyzed to provide a fitness evaluation within the evolutionary sequence.

Fitness Evaluation and Breeding

Mesh outcomes were structurally analyzed for stress and deflection, and geometrically analyzed for surface area, volume, mean curvature, base bounding area, and plan-sectional area at three intermediate heights (penalized for containing small profiles below 80 mm diameter)(Fig. 5). Analysis metrics were remapped and weighted to reward topological complexity while minimizing deflection and volume within the following multiobjective fitness criteria:

$$fitness = \sum \left(\frac{w_1 Deflection}{D_1} + \frac{w_2 Stress}{D_2} + \frac{w_3 Vol}{D_3} + \frac{w_4 SrfArea}{D_4} + \frac{w_5 Crv}{D_5} + \frac{w_6 planAreas}{D_6} + \frac{w_7 baseArea}{D_7} \right)$$

Whereby D_n represents the domain of each item in order to return a 0–1 value prior to weighting with a scale-factor of w_n for each parameter. The evolutionary solver was run multiple times to develop a series of column-like geometries from different ratios of w_{1-7} related to design criteria that varied surface area to volume and curvature ratios.

Structural analysis was undertaken in Karamba3D (Preisinger 2013) as a shell analysis, with an assumed 10 mm thickness. The bottom of each geometry was marked as a support structure, while the geometry was loaded with self-weight and a live load of 300 KN along its top profile (determined by assuming each geometry represented a column in a grid array spacing of 10 × 10 m where the floor was loaded with 3 KN/m^2 live loading). Stress and deflection values informing fitness evaluations were based on the average/range of values exhibited within the result. Evolutionary outcomes were ranked, with 0.05 selected for breeding to generate the subsequent generation of genomes. In order to avoid incestuous and zoophilic breeding, an in-breeding factor of 0.625 and out-breeding factor of 0.375 were specified in Galapagos, to allow variation in genomes to be evident early in the evolutionary process and reasonable levels of convergence in later generations of the evolution sequence (Figs. 6, 7).

matForm Material Formation

While a building element's structural performance is primarily characterized by its material properties, geometry, and scale, its material distribution can also impact structural integrity and aesthetics. Extrusion-based AM manufactures a geometry by depositing layers of material in a sequence of vertically stacked horizontal contours. Material gravitational effects can be generated when an extrusion contour deviates locally to produce overhangs relative to contour layers below, or through variations in extrusion velocity, both of which result in material settlement effects that modify layer bonding, visual continuity, and intricacy. Enabling material-distribution scale design decisions to be undertaken is tedious, while it is difficult for such rules to be successfully adaptive to topologically diverse designs.

A geometrically agnostic Python program called *matForm* was developed, capable of generating custom AM toolpaths suitable for manufacture or digital simulation, and adaptive to a polygonal mesh input. Hybridizing deterministic and

8 *matForm* method: (a) deposition sequence developed locally on inverted *topoForm* result; (b) variable AM print contour curves generated by a variable sequence of agent states; (c) unwrapped "DNA" of a column's agent states laid out as a graph.

9 *matForm* adapts to (a) *topoForm* mesh result, including structural (b) deflection and (c) stress; (d) mean curvature; and (e) inclination.

10 The AM print trajectory is created as an agent executes a series of deterministic substitution rules and nondeterministic adaption rules relative to local mesh data.

11 Agent queries a region of the mesh to obtain local data.

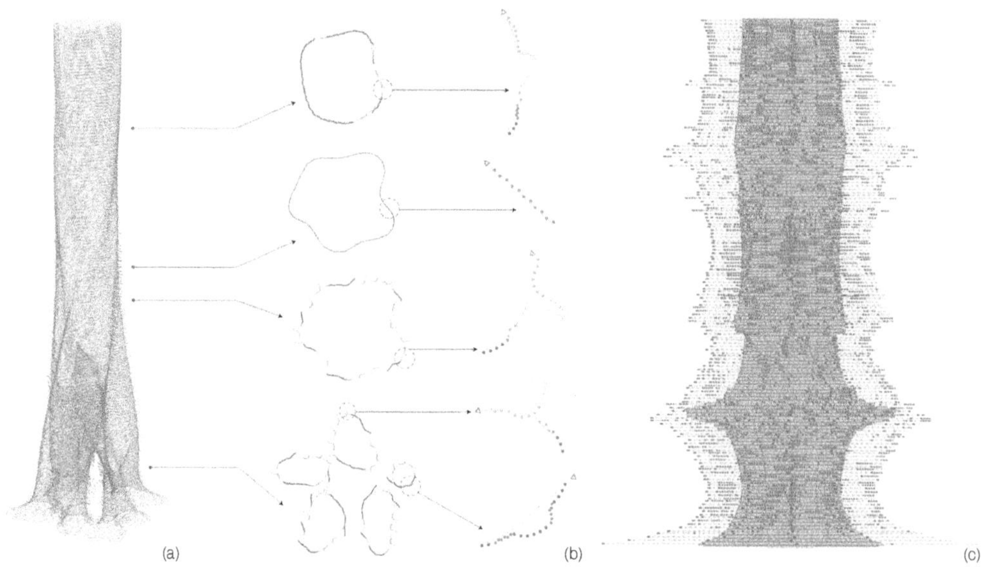

(a) (b) (c)
8

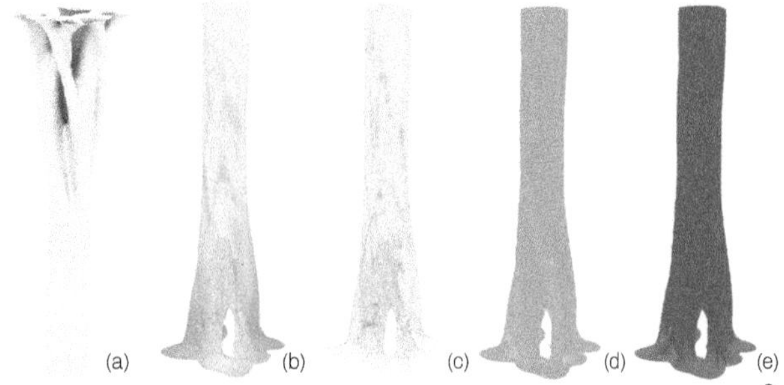

(a) (b) (c) (d) (e)
9

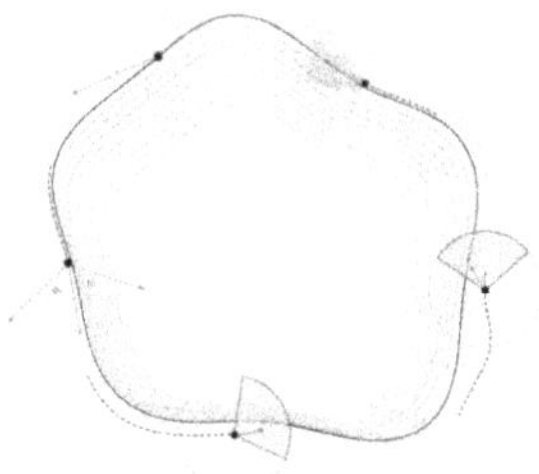

10

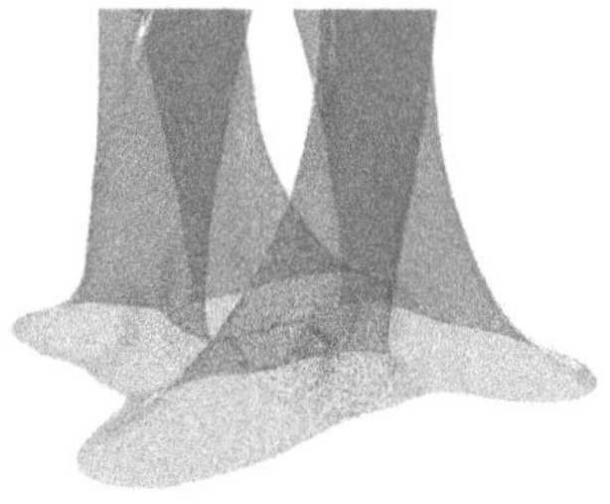

11

nondeterministic computation methods, a library of designed material deposition-scale behavior-based sequences was able to be developed in isolation while a series of nondeterministic rules ensured that such sequences also adapt to local variations in a mesh input's structural and geometric conditions such as curvature, inclination, or structural loading. An agent-based method employs both deterministic and nondeterministic rules to produce an AM robot toolpath and velocity sequence (Fig. 8). The method creates a list of waypoints through a time-based simulation where an agent representing the robot tool's center-point (TCP) updates its position along a contour by calculating and summing a series of steering vectors to determine the TCP's next position and velocity as a controlled deviation relative to the original mesh geometry contour.

Vectors influencing the agent's velocity include a vector steering towards the closest position on a mesh contour, aligning to a contour's closest tangent, rotating in the plane of a contour by a specified angle, and moving a specified distance within a single time frame (velocity). A series of agent-states were developed that each defined different values and weightings of the above rules (Fig. 10). The agent's motion is varied using substitution rules that determine the agent's state in relation to its previous state (deterministic rule) along with local variations relative to the input geometry's structural and geometric properties and the agent's previous motion (nondeterministic rules) (Figs. 9, 11). Commencing at the base of a geometry, the *matForm* TCP agent follows each ascending contour layer, deviating locally to produce overhangs and velocity changes in the contour that determine material-extrusion gravitational effects, storing each waypoint and velocity decision in a Python list. The resulting sequence of waypoints and velocities may be directly input into an ABB RAPID program to be used for industrial robot AM (as tested in Penn's 636 Material Formations course) or input into *matSim* to digitally simulate robot AM and resulting material settlement effects.

matSim AM Material-Physics Simulation Software

matSim simulates material settlement during continuous extrusion AM by depositing material relative to a robot's motion in simulated time. Extruded material is abstracted to a particle-spring chain, with functions that approximate bonding, slippage, and collapse in relation to a virtual robot's toolpath, velocity, and gravitational force. The app simulates the deposition sequence and exports a 3D mesh, polyline for the center of the deposition, and lines denoting physical bonding connections between layers of material. The mesh provides visual design feedback and representation while the

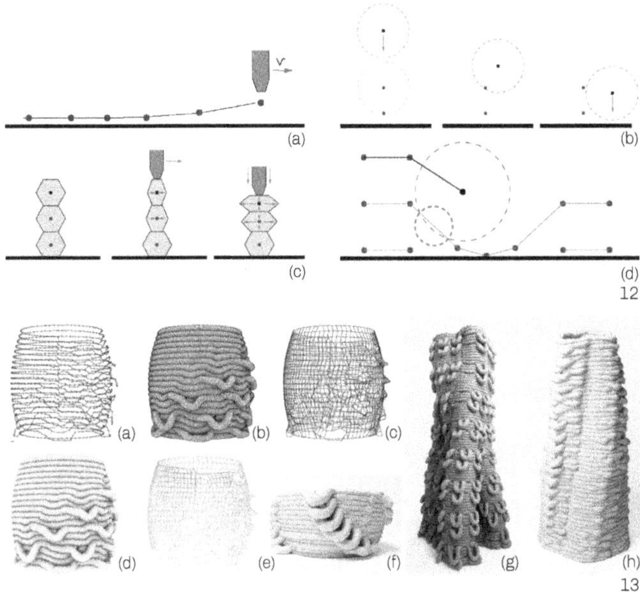

12 Particle-springs physics rules: (a) deposition, bonding; (b) particle-to-particle; (d) particle-to-spring; (c) variable extrusion profile relative to velocity and deposition height.

13 Results from *matSim*: (a) polyline center line; (b) mesh; (c) bonding links. Post-*matSim* analysis: (d) rendered visualization; (e) structural analysis; (f–h) ceramic 3D prints undertaken in University of Pennsylvania course 636: Material Formations utilizing *matForm*, demonstrating similar gravitational effects to *matSim*.

polyline and bonding connections can be utilized to perform a high-resolution structural analysis of the proposed 3D print (Fig. 13).

matSim is a custom-developed Java app that imports and exports data to and from a Rhino3D model. Imported information is comparable to data that directly informs a robot manufacturing process; a series of waypoints for the robot toolpath, the velocity the robot should move through each waypoint, and a Boolean value governing whether material should be extruded. The app animates a virtual robot TCP by moving the end-effector point at a velocity specified by the previous waypoint towards the next specified in the robot toolpath waypoint list. Particles are created at the TCP location at a constant rate (at every nth time frame). The spacing between particles is thus related to the velocity the robot is traveling within the simulation. Each particle has a mass and is influenced by gravity and springs that connect the particle to particles deposited directly before or after (providing the robot was extruding at both points in time). Springs were coded using Hooke's Law (Lengyel 2012), with a spring's force

$$f(x) = \frac{d_1}{t_1} + \frac{d_2}{t_2} + \frac{((p_1 - p_2) - r)}{S(p_1 - p_2)(\frac{1}{m_1 G} + \frac{1}{m_2 G})}$$

14 Function to determine spring length between two particles: *d*, particle's distance traveled; *t*, time; *p*, particle position in x,y,z; *r* rest length; *S*, spring strength; *m*, mass; *G* gravity.

being calculated at each time frame in relation to velocity, time, and each particle's mass and gravity (Fig. 14).

Particles descend under gravity until coming to rest either by touching previously deposited material or at zero altitude. Material bonding is determined by a particle's proximity and inclination to both settled particles and springs, relative to each particle and spring's radius (based on a material extrusion diameter variable). A series of functions evaluate whether a particle is within range of either another particle or the closest point on a neighboring spring, and if in range, whether the angle of inclination to an existing particle/spring would cause a particle to adhere relative to the particle's velocity and a friction coefficient. Where a particle comes to rest due to contact with a neighboring particle or spring, a bonding connection is established, and the bonding link line is stored in a list. Together with the particle-spring chain simulation result, all bonding connections are exported for use in postsimulation structural analysis. A 3D mesh is also generated around the springs, with n-sided polygonal cross sections oriented on the bisecting angle between connected springs, scaled and proportioned relative to robot velocity and extrusion height. Mesh faces are built by connecting across segments of two adjacent cross sections to create a ring of quad-mesh faces. Physical AM prints have demonstrated that when a layer is deposited in layer heights smaller than the material extrusion diameter, a greater proportion of material is pushed out sideways from the contour to compensate for the loss of space in the vertical axis. To approximate this, when a particle spring is deposited at a height above a previous layer less than the material extrusion diameter, the vertical height of

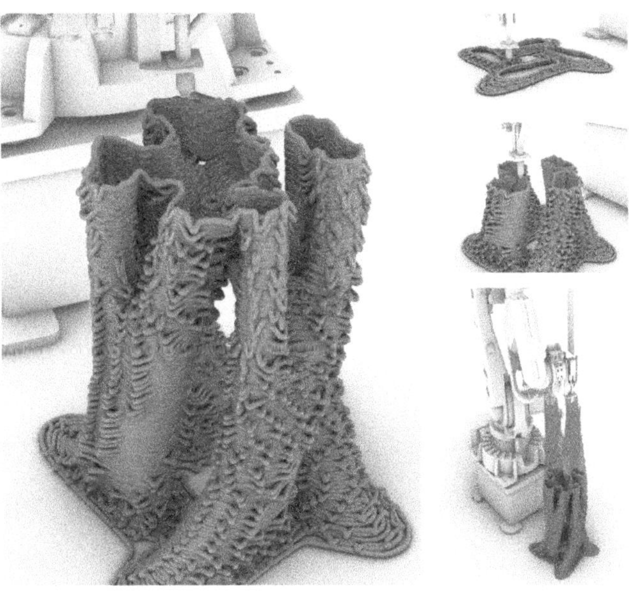

15 *matSim*: Simulation of industrial robot continuous extrusion AM material deposition of column-like geometry generated by *matForm*.

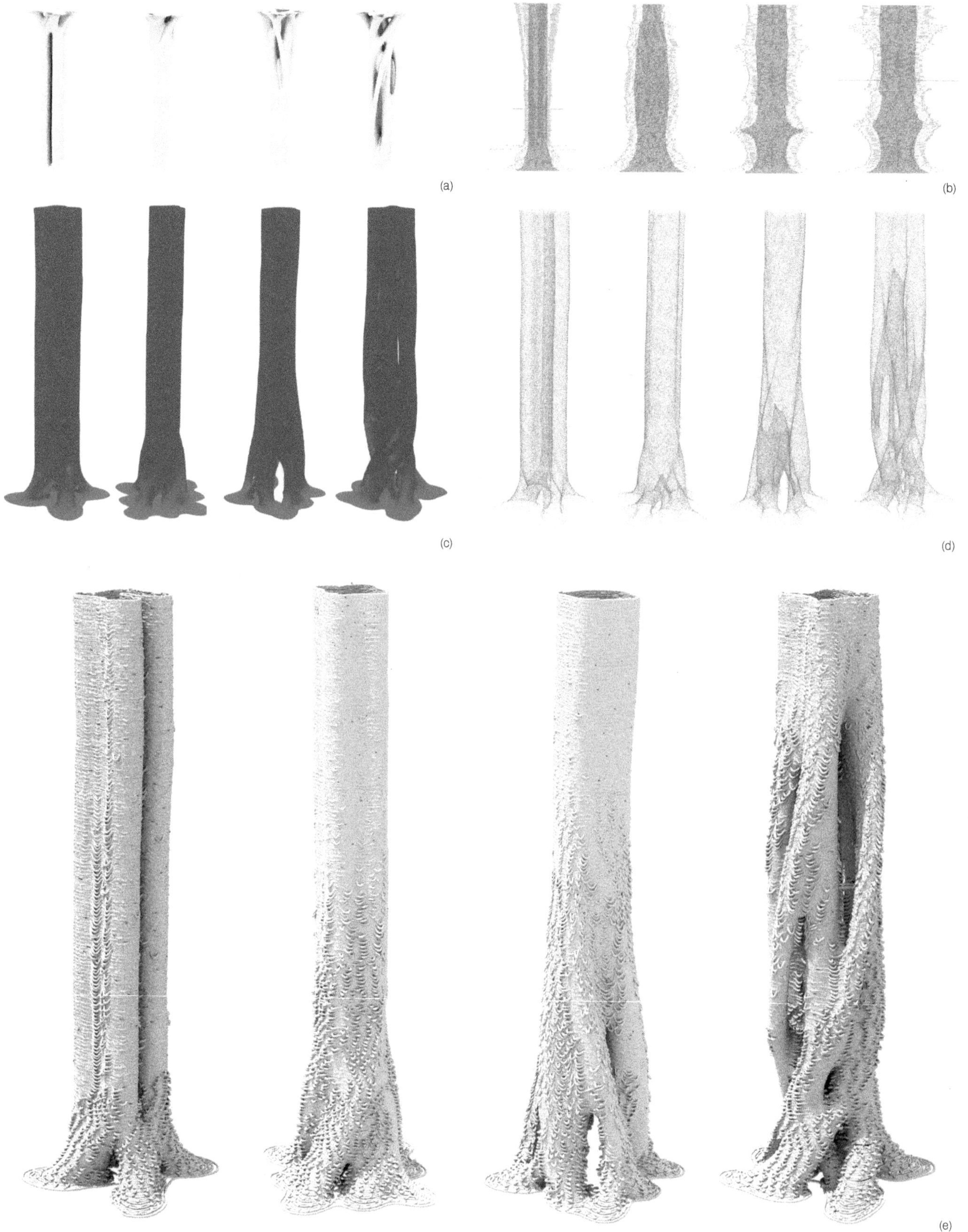

16 Four column-like geometries developed using the three-part proposed method: (a) column-like topological formations produced by *topoForm*; (b) unwrapped "DNA" of agent states for *matForm* results. Different distributions generated from identical *matForm* rules demonstrate local adaptation to topoForm geometries; (c) comparison of local inclination data on four *topoForm* geometries; (d) *matForm* generated AM print trajectories with differentiated agent states produced by identical *matForm* rules; (e) rendered perspective views of *matSim* results from the four *topoForm+matForm* design outcomes demonstrating integrated topological, formal, and material variation from the three-part method.

its cross section is reduced accordingly and the width of the cross section proportionally widened to maintain the same cross-sectional area. Similarly, due to the constant flow rate of the material extrusion process, increases in robot velocity result in a reduced extrusion cross-sectional area as the material volume is distributed over a greater distance. This is approximated in the simulation by scaling a particle's mesh cross section based on the length of the last deposited spring relative to a prior observed extrusion diameter at a velocity of 10 mm/s on University of Pennsylvania's IRB4600-60 robots.

Demonstration of the Approach in the Design of Four Column-like Elements

In order to test the utility, adaptability, and aesthetic capabilities of the three-part method, multiple design solutions for a 3.5 m high column-like geometric element were developed. Four column-like geometric outcomes were produced by running the *topoForm* evolutionary algorithm four times with different ratios of the fitness criteria and selecting a fit genome from each run's final generation. A custom AM toolpath for each of the selected outcomes was generated using *matForm* (Fig. 16d). The four geometries utilized an identical *matForm* rule set so that each result could be compared in order to evaluate the degree of adaptation demonstrated by variability in the four outcomes. The four outcomes were then input into *matSim* to simulate the extrusion sequence and resulting material settlement effects (Fig. 16e). *matSim* results were structurally analyzed in Karamba3D, and visually assessed in 3D perspective renderings, enabling feedback and error-checking prior to potential future manufacture (Fig. 17b).

RESULTS AND DISCUSSION

topoForm

Results from four evolutionary sequences using different multiobjective fitness criteria produced diverse topological and formal outcomes. Each sequence's initial generation of column contained a population average fitness value of 3.57, while final generations averaged 1.55, demonstrating a significant performance improvement. Early-generation outcomes contained several results with dispersed thin elements that were weak in structural performance. Later generations produced more convergent geometries with increased plan cross-sectional area, suggesting the combination of the geometrical fitness criteria with structural criteria was mutually beneficial. Design outcomes were notably more voluminous than industry-standard concrete columns. While concrete columns are typically solid, *topoForm*'s structural analysis was shell-based, and therefore likely encouraged surface-based rather than volumetric solutions. Fitness criteria such as surface area, volume, and curvature also encourage multimanifold topological surface solutions to provide increased structural performance. Future developments could incorporate a variable density lattice infill, which would likely reduce the volume of results.

matForm

A generative design method for producing AM toolpaths with material gravitational effects must be geometrically agnostic to be useful for widespread adoption. Such design flexibility requires adaption to local geometrical and structural data. The research demonstrated such capabilities, with discoveries informing rule sequencing and scale as follows:

- Areas of high mean curvature were found to require rules that avoided large trajectory deviations, otherwise excessive material collapse would result.
- Regions with significant inclination (+/-) required shorter agent-trajectory lengths to limit excess material buildup, otherwise substantial material settlement caused collapse. This was achieved by agent-state sequences with fewer steps or by scaling down the motion rules related to each agent step.
- Areas of high structural stress or deflection required substantial material continuity. In addition to continuous layering with minimal deviation, porous layers caused by material settlement could gain sufficient strength due to their increased depth and interconnectivity.

Based on the above aesthetic and structural feasibility required AM trajectories to be varied relative to geometric properties, validating the hybrid deterministic/nondeterministic approach of the agent-based method. An identical *matForm* rule set was utilized on four *topoForm* geometric outcomes (Fig. 16a). Each resulted in a unique distribution of agent-state rules without substantial serial repetition, demonstrating significant local adaptation (Figs. 16b, 16e). While *matForm* results may be directly utilized in industrial robot AM, the outcomes could not be manufactured due to lab closures caused by the COVID-19 pandemic. Fortunately, *matForm* results could be simulated and aesthetically and structurally assessed using the *matSim* method.

matSim

matSim outcomes for the four *matForm* results illustrate the capabilities of the method in simulating high-resolution material-physics for continuous extrusion AM at the scale of column-like building elements. The method simulated robot deposition trajectories of 396,671 waypoints with ease, although these took up to 188 minutes to complete on a desktop computer with a 16 Core processor with Boost Clock of 4.0Hz and 64 Gb RAM. Future work parallelizing the app for GPU computing would substantially reduce run time. The simulation successfully enabled visual and structural

(a)

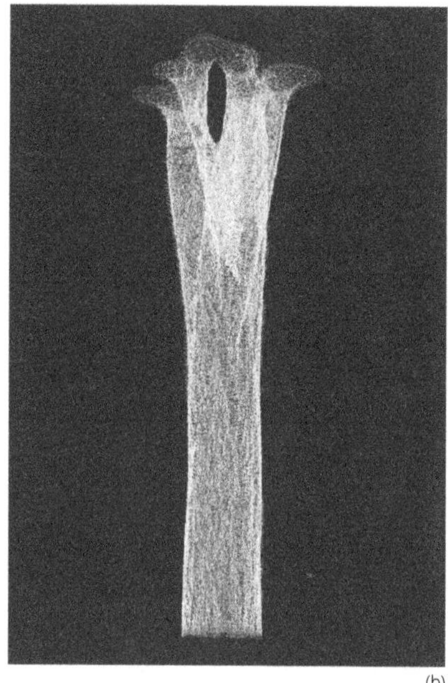

(b)

(c)

17 Selected images from one of the four column-like geometrical outcomes demonstrating the research method's ability to provide results suitable for visual and structural feedback of high-resolution continuous extrusion AM designs prior to manufacture: (a) closeup rendering of *matSim* mesh result; (b) post-*matSim* high-resolution structural analysis of simulated AM result; (c) rendering from *matSim* mesh result.

feedback by providing a closed manifold mesh geometry output and a network of lines that were utilized for structural analysis of simulation results.

Evaluation of the Combined Use of the Three Methods

As *topoForm* was tasked with producing hollow multimanifold geometries, surface area is a reasonable means to evaluate material efficiency relative to geometry. However, *matForm* toolpath length (material quantity) and material settlement estimated in *matSim* would determine whether material was distributed efficiently relative to the *topoForm* geometry, illustrating the merits of the three-stage approach. An identical *matForm* rule set was utilized on all four column-like *TopoForm* outcomes. *matSim* simulation results of these demonstrated:

- Different geometrical conditions resulted in different feature distributions, as depicted in the distribution of different agent states (Fig. 16b) and scaling of these features (Fig. 16e).
- Comparing the four *matForm* results to geometric and structural analysis of their *topoForm* surfaces, confirms a close adaptation to variable surface properties, including mean curvature, inclination (depicted), structural stress, and deflection (Fig. 16e).
- Distribution and character of material-gravitational effects is noticeably adapted to each geometry and does not exhibit substantial serial repetition.

topoForm extends architectural research in evolutionary design, multi-agent design, and AM TSO methods by introducing a topologically free generative design method that enables a wide range of multimanifold column-like designs to be developed in relation to structural, geometric, and aesthetic criteria. *matForm* created extrusion toolpath designs that adapted to local geometrical and structural data, demonstrating *matForm* can operate on multimanifold geometries of greater complexity than prior research using agent-based programming of a robot's tool-center point motion to direct the settlement of extruded material under gravitational force for variable qualitative design effects. The *matSim* simulation enabled visual feedback and structural analysis to be performed on the high-resolution *matForm* design outcome. The polygon mesh output provided extensive variation in character of material features and propagation affects with sufficient degrees of subtlety and geometric quality to be useful as a design and visualization aid (Figs. 1, 17).

CONCLUSION

Continuous AM building construction is already an internationally established practice despite limited design-engineering workflows available that leverage topological and material formation. The proposed method enables these to be incorporated within design and premanufacture workflows through material-physics simulation and a generative design approach that integrates structural, geometric, and robot motion parameters. The research provides additional design control and feedback on topology and material-scale organization and effects, enabling improvements to material and structural efficiency, and their relation to aesthetic design criteria. Continuation of the research would benefit from further validation studies in relation to the production and scanning of material prototypes, and in extending the design method to address full building-scale tectonics. Future application of the research could provide reductions to material quantities used in AM building construction, thereby also reducing the economic and environmental impact of AM buildings, supporting a more affordable built environment while enhancing design aesthetic development prior to manufacture. The software framework could also be extended and made publicly available to encourage an expansion of generative design and material simulation approaches within the broader design community.

ACKNOWLEDGMENTS

This research was undertaken with the support of the University of Pennsylvania's Weitzman School of Design's ARI Robotics Facility, chair of architecture Winka Dubbeldam, ARI Robotics Lab technician David Forero, and computer scientist Sanjana Rao contributing to *matSim* software development. Author contributions: Robert Stuart-Smith developed the three software apps, design workflow, and paper text. Patrick Danahy contributed to *matSim* mesh methods and *matForm* rule sets, ran evolutionary sequences, and produced the rendered visualizations. Natalia Revelo La Rotta developed *matForm* rule sets, diagrams, and IRB4600 physical print tests to validate *matSim*.

REFERENCES

Ansys. n.d. "Additive Manufacturing Simulation." Accessed June 23, 2020. https://www.ansys.com/products/structures/additive-manufacturing.

Buswell, R. A., R. C. Soar, A. G.F. Gibb, and A. Thorpe. 2007. "Freeform Construction: Mega-Scale Rapid Manufacturing for Construction." *Automation in Construction* 16 (2).

Essop, Anas. 2020. "SQ4D 3D Prints 1,900 Sq Ft Home in 48 Hours." 3d Printing Industry, January 13. https://3dprintingindustry.com/news/sq4d-3d-prints-1900-sq-ft-home-in-48-hours-167141/.

Frazer, John. 1995. *An Evolutionary Architecture*. London: Architectural Association.

Im, Hyeonji Claire, Sulaiman AlOthman, and Jose Luis García del Castillo. 2018. "Responsive Spatial Print: Clay 3D Printing of Spatial Lattices Using Real-Time Model Recalibration." In *ACADIA 2018: Recalibration: On Imprecision and Infidelity [Proceedings of the 38th Annual Conference of the Association for Computer Aided Design in Architecture (ACADIA)]*, Mexico City, Mexico, 18–20 October 2018, edited by P. Anzalone, M. del Signore, and A. J. Wit, 286–293. CUMINCAD.

Jipa, Andrei, Mathias Bernhard, Benjamin Dillenburger, Mania Meibodi, and Mania Aghaei-Meibodi. 2016. "3D-Printed Stay-in-Place Formwork for Topologically Optimized Concrete Slabs." In *Proceedings of the 2016 TxA Emerging Design + Technology Conference*, San Antonio, TX, 3–4 November 2016, edited by Kory Bieg, 96–107. Texas Society of Architects.

Khoshnevis, B., R. Russell, H. Kwon, and S. Bukkapatnam. 2001. "Crafting Large Prototypes." *IEEE Robotics and Automation Magazine*. https://www.doi.org/10.1109/100.956812.

Lengyel, E. 2012. *Mathematics for 3D Game Programming and Computer Graphics*. 3rd ed. ITPro Collection. Delmar Cengage Learning.

Preisinger, C. 2013. "Linking Structure and Parametric Geometry," *Architectural Design 83*: 110-113. doi: 10.1002/ad.1564.

Rael, Ronald, and Virginia San Fratello. 2017. "Clay Bodies: Crafting the Future with 3D Printing." *Architectural Design 87* (6): 92–97. https://www.doi.org/10.1002/ad.2243.

Reynolds, C. W. 1999. "Steering Behaviors for Autonomous Characters." *Game Developers Conference*, 763–782. https://www.doi.org/10.1016/S0140-6736(07)61755-3.

Rutten, David. 2013. "Galapagos: On the Logic and Limitations of Generic Solvers." *Architectural Design* 83 (2): 132–135. https://www.doi.org/10.1002/ad.1568.

Snooks, Roland, and Robert Stuart-Smith. 2011. "Nonlinear Formation: Or How to Resist the Parametric Subversion of Computational Design." In *Apomechanes: Nonlinear Computational Design Strategies*, edited by Pavlos Xanthopoulos, Ioulietta Zindrou, and Ezio Blasetti, 192. Asprimera Publications.

Stasiuk, David. 2015. "Cocoon." July 22. http://www.bespokegeometry.com/2015/07/22/cocoon/.

Stuart-Smith, Robert. 2011. "Formation and Polyvalence: The Self-Organisation of Architectural Matter." In *Ambience'11 Proceedings*, edited by Annika Hellström, Hanna Landin, and Lars Hallnäs, 20–29. Boras: University of Borås.

Stuart-Smith, Robert. 2018. "Approaching Natural Complexity—The Algorithmic Embodiment of Production." In *Meeting Nature Halfway*, edited by Marjan Colletti and Peter Massin, 260–269. Innsbruck University Press.

Robert Stuart Smith is an Assistant Professor of Architecture in University of Pennsylvania's Weitzman School of Design and director of the Masters of Science in Design: Robotics & Autonomous Systems (MSD-RAS) program. He also directs the Autonomous Manufacturing Lab (AML): University of Pennsylvania (Architecture) & University College London (Computer Science).

Patrick Danahy is a part-time lecturer in the University of Pennsylvania Weitzman School of Design and a research assistant in the Autonomous Manufacturing Lab.

Natalia Revelo La Rotta is a research assistant in the Autonomous Manufacturing Lab and MArch candidate in the University of Pennsylvania Weitzman School of Design.

Turbulent Casting

Bacterial Expression in Mineralized Structures

Thora H Arnardottir
Martyn Dade-Robertson
School of Architecture, Planning and Landscape, Newcastle University

Helen Mitrani
School of Engineering, Newcastle University

Meng Zhang
Department of Applied Sciences, Northumbria University

Beate Christgen
School of Natural and Environmental Sciences, Newcastle University

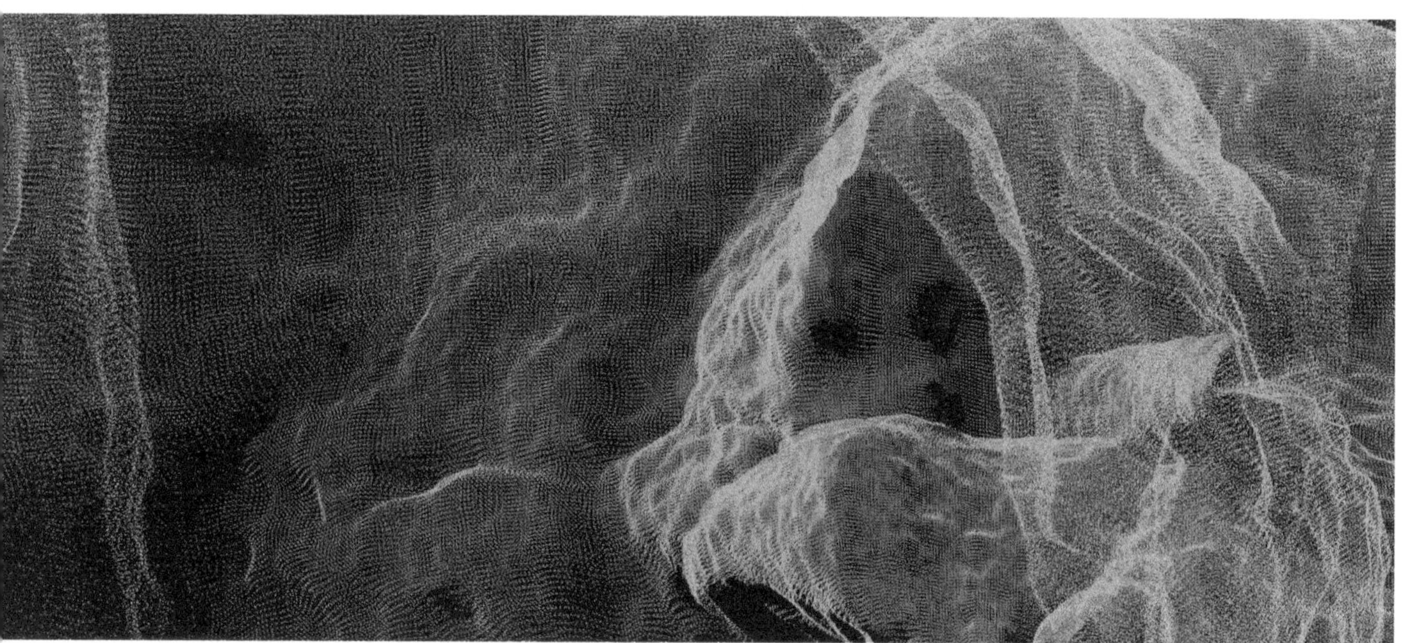

1 Tectonic landscape in the point cloud construction resulting from the 3D scanning process of a biomineralized form.

ABSTRACT

There has been a growing interest in living materials and fabrication processes including the use of bacteria, algae, fungi, and yeast to offer sustainable alternatives to industrial materials synthesis. Microbially induced calcium carbonate precipitation (MICP) is a biomineralization process that has been widely researched to solve engineering problems such as concrete cracking and to strengthen soils. MICP can also be used as an alternative to cement in the fabrication of building materials and, because of the unique process of living fabrication, if we see bacteria as our design collaborators, new types of fabrication and processes may be possible. The process of biomineralization is inherently different from traditional fabrication processes that use casting or molding. Its properties are influenced by the active bacterial processes that are connected to the casting environment. Understanding and working with interrelated factors enables a novel casting approach and the exploration of a range of form types and materials of variable consistencies and structure.

We report on an experiment with partial control of mineralization through the design of different experimental vessels to direct and influence the cementation process of sand. In order to capture the form of the calcification in these experiments, we have analyzed the results using three-dimensional imaging and a technique that excavates the most friable material from the cast in stages. The resulting scans are used to reconstruct the cementation timeline. This reveals a hidden fabrication/growth process. These experiments offer a different perspective on form finding in material fabrication.

INTRODUCTION

Industrial-scale materials manufacture often creates an enormous strain on our environment. In construction, concrete is the most widely used material in the world and a significant contributor to the world's carbon dioxide emissions, producing more than four billion tons every year (Lehne and Preston 2018).

Nature, however, is the producer of hard calcareous materials in various forms through biological processes that have evolved over millions of years with relatively little energy expenditure. While biologically produced materials, such as limestone, are common in the built environment, we tend to make use of biological materials after the organisms that created them are dead. The possibility of using living cells through biological processes offers the opportunity of replacing traditional types of fabrication and assembly with guided growth (Zolotovsky, Gazit, and Ortiz 2017) and new collaborations between nonhuman/biological processes in fabrication (Camere and Karana 2018). These processes entail the biological processing of elements from the environment such as carbon, water, and sources of energy to form mineralized structures (Mann 2001). Microbial calcium carbonate precipitation (MICP) is efficient in constructing hard calcareous materials at room temperatures and pressures. The process of MICP requires active bacteria, a passive aggregate, and a catalyst for inducing the mineralization process to create a binder for the aggregate material.

MICP has already been demonstrated in building construction, including, for example, the inclusion of microbial spores in concrete to enable self-healing of concrete cracks (Jonkers et al. 2010) and for the creation of an MICP-based cement to create bricks or other natural stone-like building elements (Dosier 2016; BioMason 2020). While having the potential to transform traditional construction, the use of MICP as a novel fabrication method has not been substantially explored. There has also been extensive design speculation on the use of MICP in architecture, including, for example, the injection of bacterial solutions into sand dunes to stabilize them and creation structures for human habitation (Larsson 2010) and as a method for constructing furniture using similar approaches (Hussey 2014). Projects such as these rarely go beyond design concepts, as the process of MICP-based material casting is not straightforward to perform.

While MICP-based materials can be produced in similar ways to more traditional cementitious materials, using microbes as active agents in MICP offers opportunities for form-making and material construction that are unique to

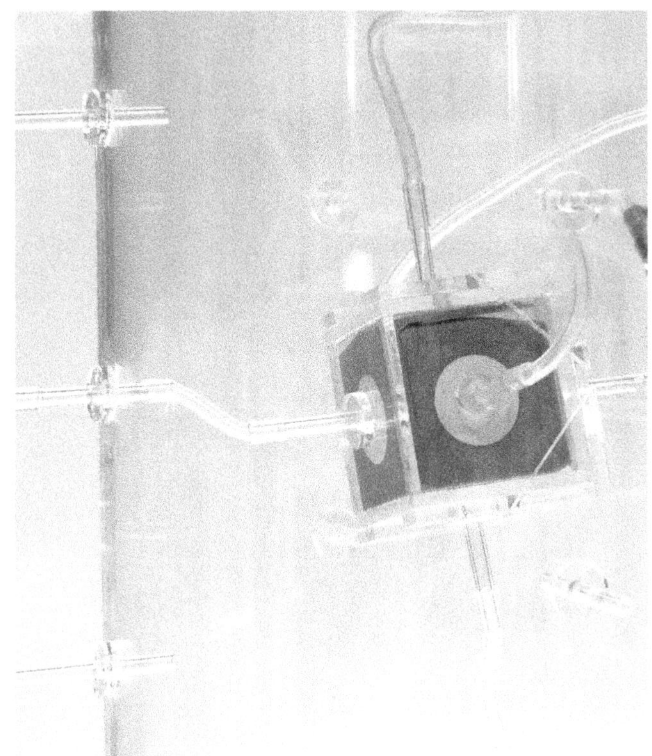

2

3

2 Prototype 2, casting vessel showing connection between the suspended mold and the bioreactor.

3 Prototype 3, casting volumes showing the series of molds set up.

4

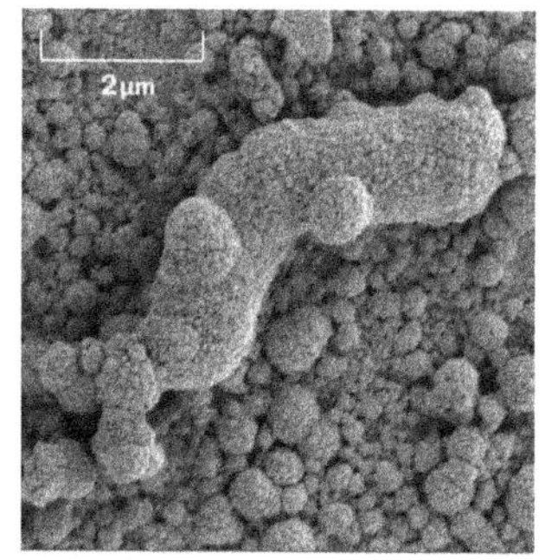

5

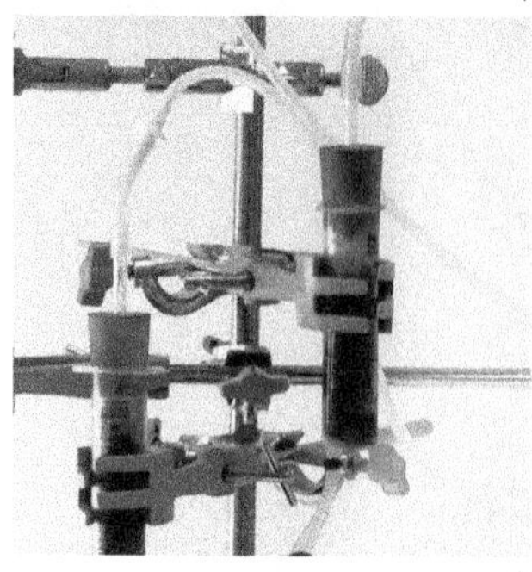

6

7

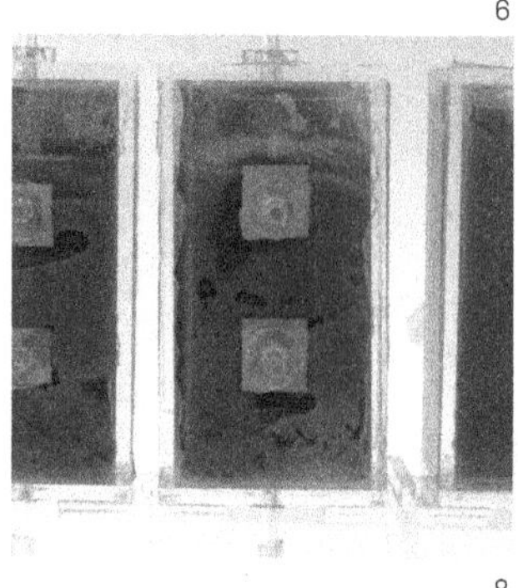

8

9

4 SEM of a calcified *Sporosarcina pasteurii* in agarose hydrogel.

5 SEM of a calcified *Sporosarcina pasteurii* in agarose hydrogel.

6 Prototype 1, casting volume.

7 Prototype 2, casting volume.

8 Prototype 3 casting volumes.

9 Prototype 4, casting volume.

the medium. However, to move beyond the state of the art requires repeatable hands-on experiments based on the production of meaningful material samples with the potential to scale up. In this paper, we present ongoing research into MICP in order to inform design engagement with a living organism in the creation of a mineralized material.

This paper focuses on the correlation between the fluid-solid interface that influences the flow of liquid through porous media (Wood, He, and Apte 2020). It explores how this phenomenon affects the fabrication process of bacterial-induced biomineralization and frames the living bacteria as co-designers in a construction system. It reveals a process of biological computation where the fabrication shows sensitivities to inputs that lead to different material outputs. Through this exploration, it will be shown that the MICP process is inherently different from traditional fabrication processes using, for example, casting and molding. We present initial studies of a casting process involving MICP in the sand that show the complex network of interactions essential in the control of biomineralization. The experiments focus first on the biological function of the bacteria in the precipitation of calcium carbonate and the optimal environment needed to support them. The project experiments with the design of experimental vessels to influence the cementation process. Finally, in order to capture the calcification in these experiments, the cementation pattern formation was analyzed using a three-dimensional scanning (Fig. 1) and a novel excavation technique that allows the dynamic build-up of the cementation process to be visualized.

METHODS

MICP is a biomineralization process where the precipitation of calcium carbonate occurs in response to microbial activity in specific environmental conditions. In our experiments, we incubated bacterium *Sporosarcina pasteurii* in various physical and chemical conditions for growth and mineral precipitation.

The bacterial cells use biological and chemical processes to form inorganic carbonate crystals by creating a microenvironment where hydrolysis of urea and the increase in pH around the cell induce the production of calcium carbonate ($CaCO_3$) crystals. The bacteria act as a nucleation site for $CaCO_3$ precipitation (Figs. 4–5). Mineral crystals are not produced by the bacteria but rather induced in response to an enzyme-initiated change in environmental pH. Many factors can affect this process, including the growth rate of the bacteria, availability of oxygen and nutrients, as well as the chemical components. These are interdependent parameters that can affect the construction of a biomineralized material at different scales.

For this casting process, we looked at these variables as tuning parameters to experiment with form-finding in the fabrication of cemented material. The parameters that we explore in this paper are:

- **The microbial factor:** as the biological and chemical activity of the bacteria in the mineral production of calcium carbonate crystals.
- **The granular factor:** through sand shape and size that dictates the structural control and binding possibilities.
- **The casting factor:** how the mold influences spatial control of the elements contained inside and how fluid matter is applied.

- **The fluid factor:** the chemical control of a mixture of nutrients, urea and calcium chloride, to apply to the system (the cementation media).

Although the tuning of each of these factors will affect the formation of a biomineralized structure, the biological elements of the bacterium are not being altered in a direct way, that is, the bacterium was not genetically modified. The bacterium is, however, affected by the environment, and changes in those factors can speed up or slow down their reaction time, spatial distribution, reproduction, and survival.

Apparatus

In this study, prototype casting vessels were developed as part formwork and part bioreactors in order to explore the different influences, such as casting and fluid factors, and direct the cementation process. These prototypes facilitate the biocementation process by containing sand fine enough to allow the bacteria to move between the grains, and by pumping the nutrient-rich liquid media with the substrate chemicals, urea and calcium chloride, to facilitate the essential bacterial activity to induce mineral crystal formation.

The casting vessels are constructed, using digital fabrication, from clear acrylic that allows visual observation and silicon tubing. The tubing allows injection of cementation liquid into the mold using peristaltic pumps at certain intervals per day as well as letting effluent waste liquid out. The acrylic mold is lined with acetate film to allow for easy release from the mold and filter paper in order to contain the sand and keep it from flowing back into the inlet tubes. The vessel is first filled with sand that is injected with a bacterial culture that has been incubated overnight in a shaking incubator at 30°C, to allow the bacterial cells to grow and attach to the sand grains. After this stage, the volume is connected to the pumps via tubing and the cementation solution is injected to initiate the mineralization process. The fresh solution is pumped through the vessel at 3–4 hour intervals over 7–10 days. In this process, pH levels are monitored from the effluent each day. It is important to maintain a pH of close to 9 in order to enable the bacterial cells to induce crystal formation. If the pH starts dropping below 9, it is a good indicator that the cell density has dropped or the bacteria are not receiving the nutrients they need. The rate of precipitation induced by the bacterial cells can also be increased by increasing the amount of calcium chloride in the liquid medium.

Each type of vessel (Figs. 6–9) is designed to deliver the liquid media into the sand volume through a different flow strategy in order to see the different effects they have on the cement formation. Initial experimentation followed known cementation procedures using plastic syringes (Whiffin 2004) to inject media upwards through a cylindrical volume (Fig. 6). This first prototype was used to experiment with:

- different sand sizes;
- the way the bacteria culture was mixed in the sand;

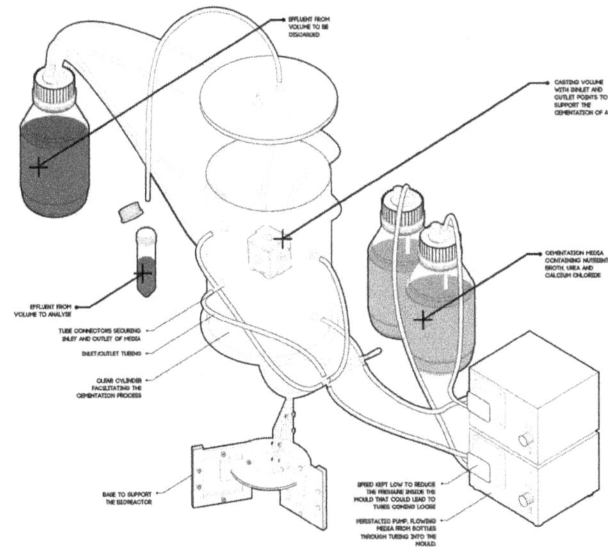

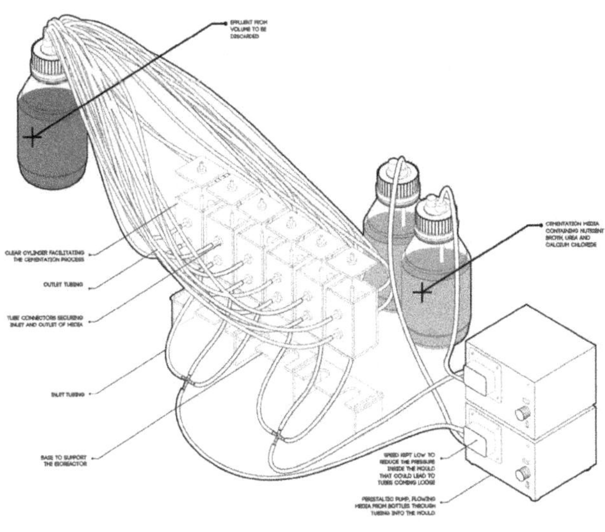

10 Exploded view of prototype 2 showing running setup and the connections with inlet media and effluent through peristaltic pumps.

11 Exploded view of prototype 3 showing running setup and the connections with inlet media and effluent through peristaltic pumps.

12

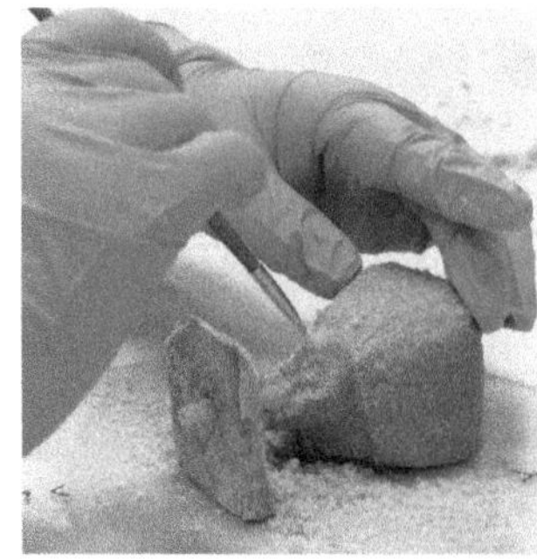

13

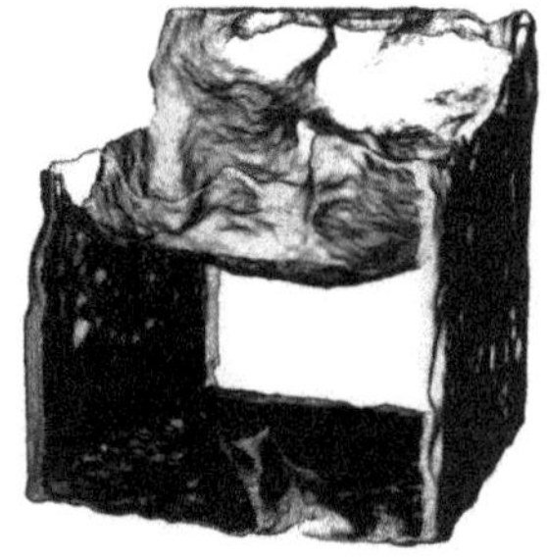
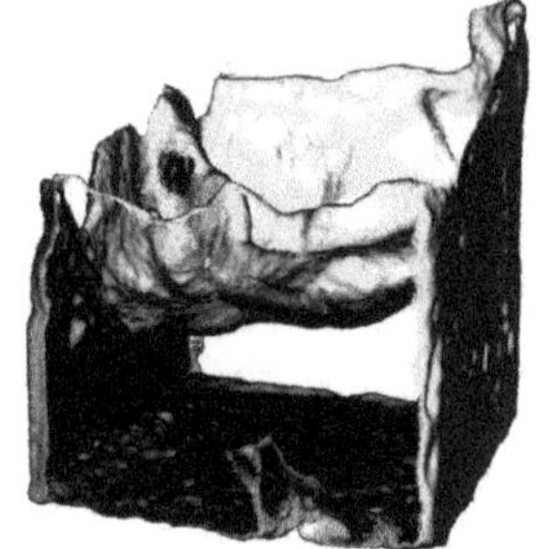

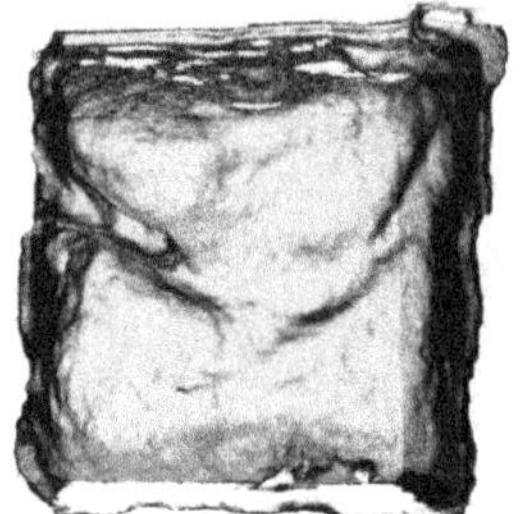

14

12 Loose sand removed from internal parts of the sand cast from prototype 2.

13 Sand cast being brushed with gentle strokes as the looser sand is removed from a volume in prototype 3.

14 Point cloud construction resulting from 3D scanning a sample. Visible flow patterns emerge from sand cast from prototype 2, showing two stages of the erosion.

- if applying heat or extra oxygen in the nutrient media would make a significant difference in the cementation procedure; and
- how long the cementation reaction would take.

Once optimal conditions were established, we used sand of 150–300 µm, the bacterial culture was either poured or injected into the volume in a liquid medium and when the cementation treatments started, we kept the volume at room temperature (21–23°C). In these experimental vessels, due to their small size, at least six days of cementation treatments were needed to form a solid sample piece.

The second prototype vessel (Figs. 2, 7, 10) has the shape of a 5 x 5 cm cube with tube inserts on all sides. This setup allowed media to flow not only from below, as in the first vessel, but through multiple injection points on all sides. This method eliminated the preferential flow that occurred when only pumped in one direction. Only three sides were selected for inflow of cementation media while the other three openings allowed effluent out, and this arrangement was changed every two days. This setup ran for 10 days before the sample cube was removed and dried. Eliminating preferential flow by changing flow paths created a relatively homogeneously cemented cube shell.

The third prototype (Figs. 3, 8, 11) was made of 5 x 10 cm cuboids in which the cementation media was injected through the center of a volume through a perforated tube connected in the middle of the cast with effluent media pushed out through the outlets positioned at the sides. This was to ensure that the internal parts of the sand volume were supplied with sufficient amounts of nutrients and reactant chemicals for the bacteria where previous prototypes prevented this access by cementing and blocking off where the inflow reached the volume. This prototype was set up as six identical volumes stacked together. Each cast was connected to a pump that supplied cementation media to all volumes at the same time. This setup ran for 12 days. Every other day during this treatment, one volume was disconnected from the stack, opened, and dried. This was to create a series of mineral formations where we are able to track the stages of cementation.

The fourth prototype (Fig. 9) was made of acrylic tubes 10 cm in diameter and 2.5 cm in height; as with the previous version, the vessel was designed to be injected from the inside. Openings were cut into a central plastic piece that was connected with tubing to the pumps and effluent points positioned on the exterior of the acrylic tube. This prototype was set up as three identical volumes stacked side by side, which ran for six days. What distinguished it from the previous setup was the ability to rotate the whole vessel in order to eliminate preferential flow or static air pockets in specific parts of the volume. The volumes were then opened and dried and analyzed alongside the other prototypes.

3D Scanning

For each of these different fluid injection methods, 3D scanning was used to explore the biomineral formation that occurs within the volume (Figs. 1, 17), something that is not visible during the process. Scanning at different times in the process can give us a glimpse into the patterns that form at different stages in the cementation process. The 3D scans were processed using EinScan-SE, a digital scanning program that uses programmed light patterns (Salvi et al. 2010). Between 30 and 100 scans were used to reconstruct the samples, producing a digital representation of the cemented objects in a 3D point cloud. Similar scanning techniques have been used in detecting and analyzing biological growth (Sollazzo, Baseta, and Chronis 2016). The resulting casts from the prototypes were 3D scanned in a sequence from the moment they were removed from the casts and in steps, as the sand grains were gradually brushed using a small spatula and brush where the material was more friable (Figs. 12–13). This excavation process allows us to trace back the cementing formation and reveal the different densities the material is able to form through time. These produced between 3–4 stages in the point cloud model depending on how friable the material was. Once these point models were generated, they were exported to Rhinoceros 3D (Robert McNeel & Associates 2020) (Fig. 14) and sliced to create topological sections (Fig. 15) that highlighted the transformation of the cast. These resulting scans can be seen as a timeline of the stages of cementation and allow us to visualize material changes over time.

RESULTS & DISCUSSION

The 3D scans from the excavation process reveal patterns of flow in both space and time. This was especially apparent in the case of the third prototype, where excavation revealed that the initial solidification occurred at the top of the volume (Fig. 16). As days passed, the cementation spread to the rest of the volume from close to the central injection tube outwards, eventually cementing the bottom of the volume.

The material samples explored in this study reveal that the way in which the flow is channeled in the sand constitutes a key factor in how the cemented form develops in the volume. The clear visualization resulting from the 3D scans highlights paths of the preferential flow of reactant media and its concentration in specific parts of the vessel. This preferential flow results in areas of a higher density of calcium carbonate precipitation. As bacteria mineralize, the flow of liquid changes its path, always finding the path of least resistance around solid formations and triggering crystallization in the remaining areas of the cast. As the liquid flows within the volume, it meets a shifting environment, whose topology is determined by the activity of the bacteria and resulting cemented formations. The natural patterning of the precipitate mostly depends on the distribution of bacteria cells and on the concentration of the reactants that trigger biomineralization activity. The various degrees of friability in the cemented material indicate that the flow meets the sand at different speeds through the volume. The speed of the flow decreases due to blocking caused by

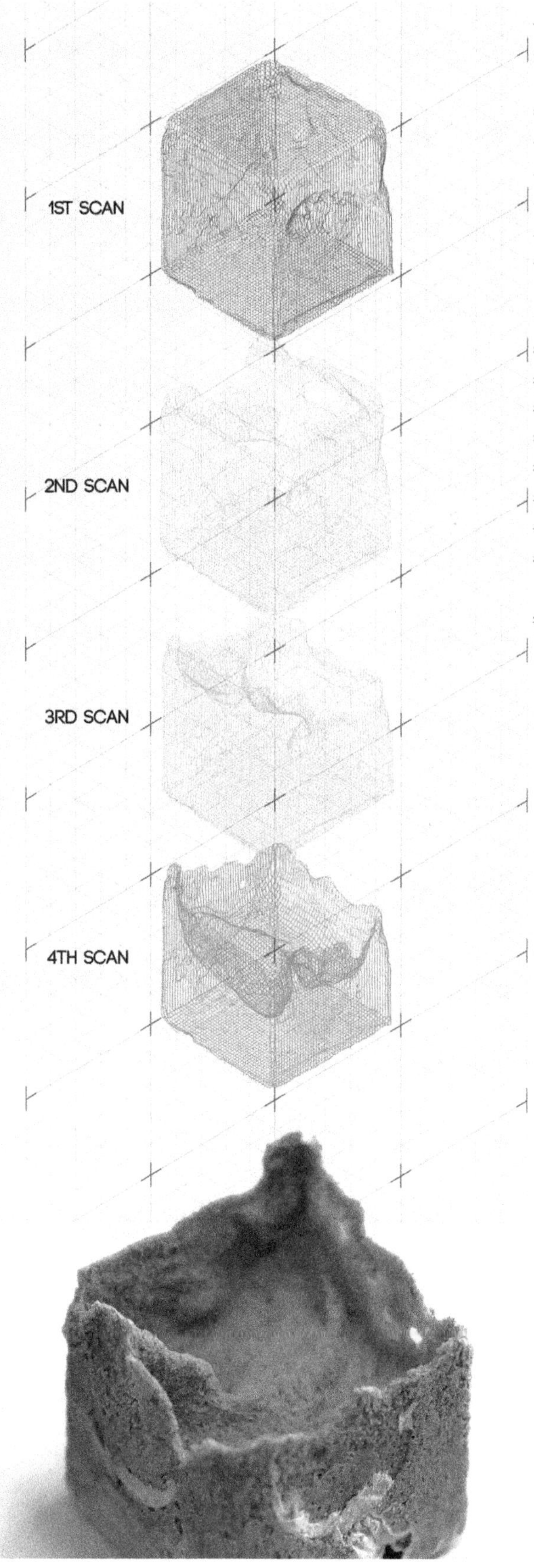

15 Topological sections of the timeline stages of a sample from prototype 2.

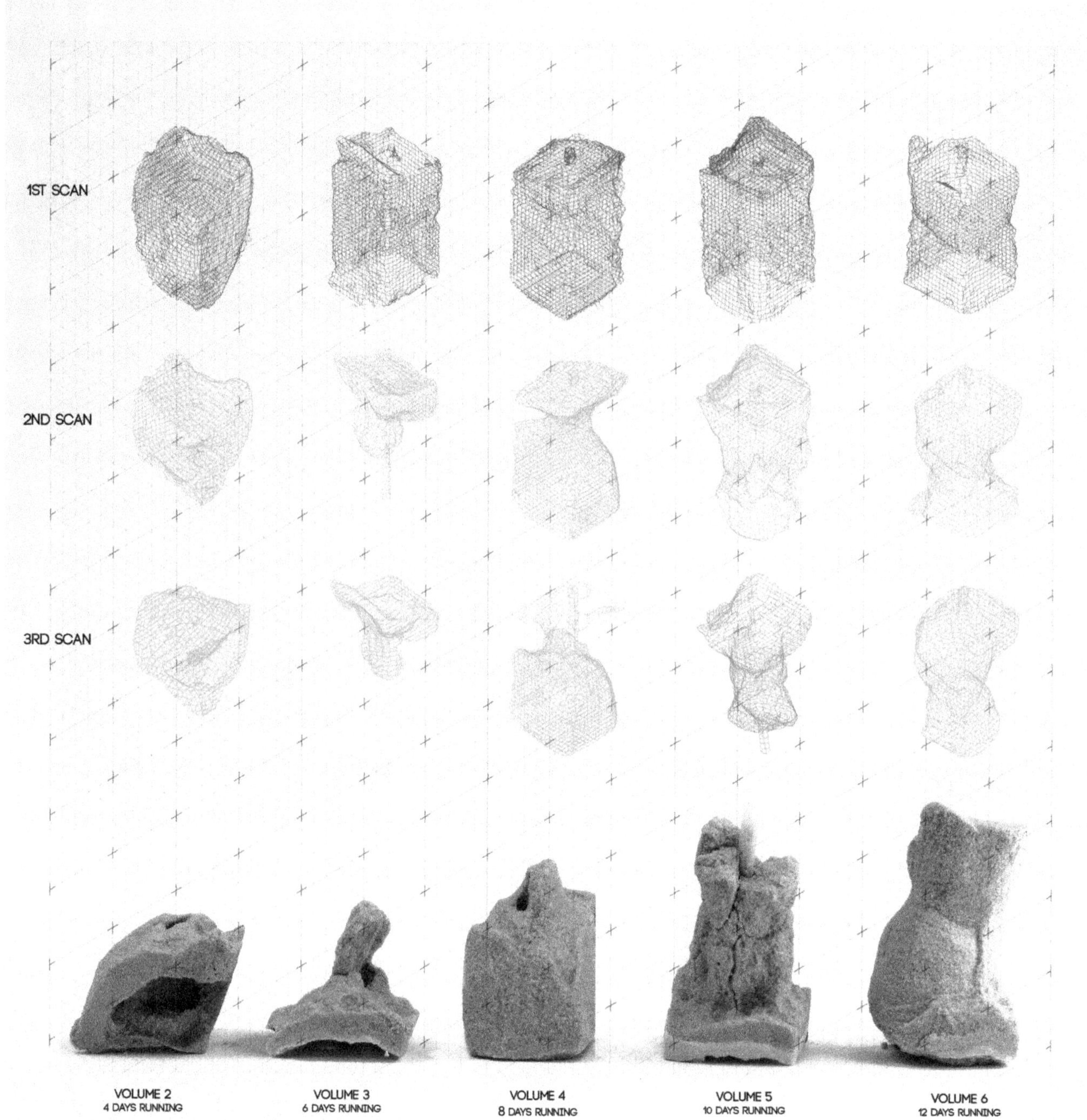

16 Topological sections of the timeline stages of the different samples from prototype 3, showing the different formation from a 4-day treatment to 12 days of cementation treatment with the resulting casts standing (in reverse) on the top cementation.

precipitation (Saad et al. 2019). In other circumstances, a decreasing dimension of the flow channel would correspond to an increase in pressure, and therefore in speed, but in this case, the internal circulation channels are still filled with sand, so the pressure is transmitted to the pump where it is forced to slow down. Where cement begins to block areas of flow, the reactant will have to circle in order to reach the non-cemented areas. As the speed of the flow diminishes, the bacteria left in these areas are starved of nutrients and start to die off. When, and if, the flow reaches these areas, the crystal formation will consequently be minor, causing the sand to be bound less tightly and to be more friable.

CONCLUSION

These results demonstrate the unique complexity of a casting process that involves living systems. The bespoke vessels allow the exploration of biomineral fabrication, and our experiments show that, while containing consistent features, each cast is unique and represents a story

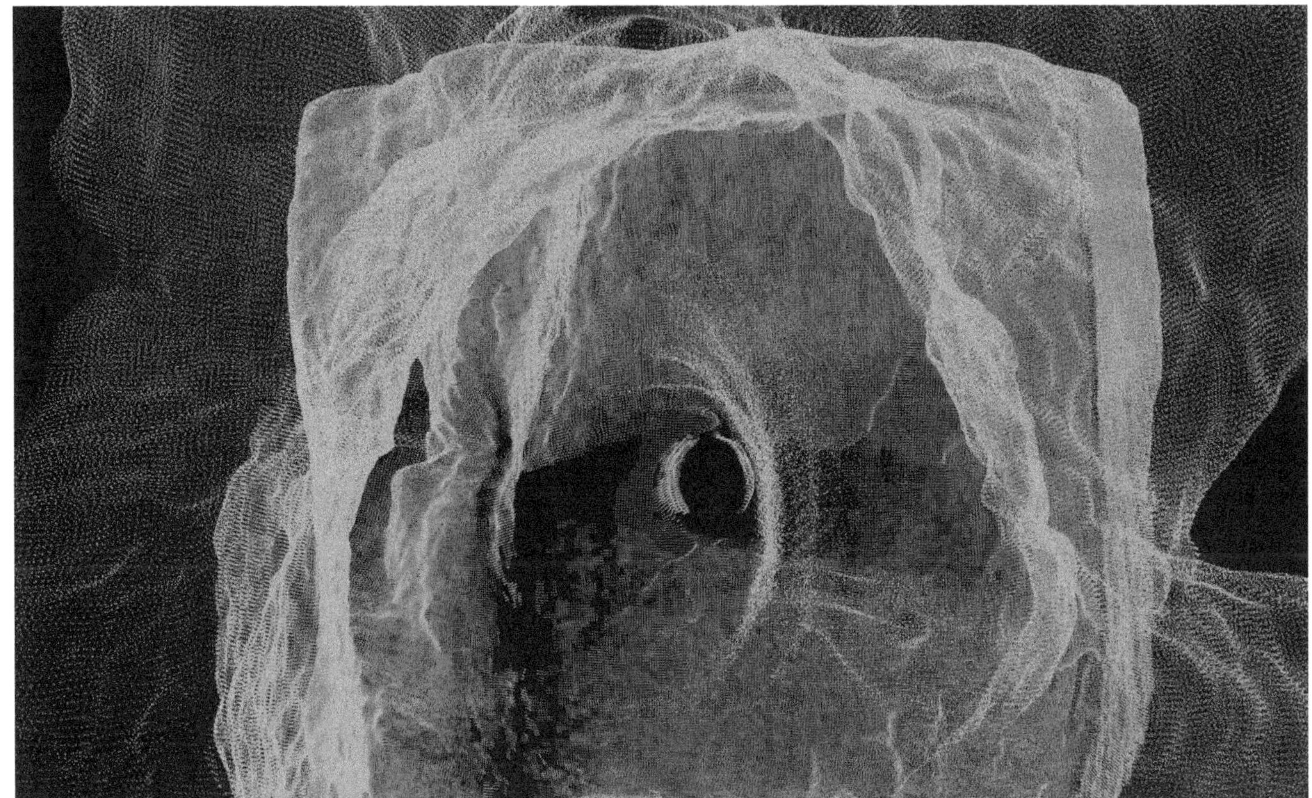

17 Tectonic form in the point cloud construction resulting from the 3D scanning process from prototype 3 in volume 5. Seen from the bottom of the shape looking up though the gap left by the injection tube.

of the living dynamic processes of the casting process. The results are not a homogeneous material but graded and sculpted volumes. Through these experiments and 3D imaging, we recognize that the control of the designer, through the casting process, is only partial. By controlling environmental factors through the vessel, we generate optimal conditions for the bacteria to live and for cementation to occur, but we cannot fully control the outcomes. The biomineralization process, as applied in architecture, is a particularly complex and radically different medium with which to fabricate compared to traditional nonliving materials. The mineralization process is not produced by the organism itself but is an induced chemical reaction in the environment caused by the bacteria. Therefore, these experiments encourage speculation regarding how this bacterial process is expressed and formed within aggregates such as sand through the fluid delivery of a catalyzing agent.

Although only preliminary work is presented in this paper, this technique of capturing the formation in reverse time, by removing material from the sample layer by layer and scanning each step, offers an exploration into form-finding and challenges the idea that, in casting, the material takes the form of the cast. The process reveals heterogeneity that is hidden in the casting process but may offer new architectural aesthetic possibilities and materials that reveal their fabrication process and the imprints of life. Further avenues of exploration would be to build up additional data from these experiments that could be used to simulate the process and to scale up the casts for architectural applications in the built environment.

ACKNOWLEDGMENTS

The authors would like to thank the other members of the Thinking Soils project for their advice and suggestions. Thinking Soils is funded by the ESPRC (EP/R003629/1). Thanks to Ed Robinson, technical support officer, at the Hub for Biotechnology in the Built Environment (HBBE) for his fabrication assistance. The HBBE is funded by Research England.

REFERENCES

BioMason. 2020. BioLITH® Tiles. 2020. https://www.biomason.com/product/biolith/.

Camere, Serena, and Elvin Karana. 2018. "Fabricating Materials from Living Organisms: An Emerging Design Practice." *Journal of Cleaner Production* 186: 570–584. https://doi.org/10.1016/j.jclepro.2018.03.081.

Dosier, Ginger. 2016. Methods for Making Construction Material Using Enzyme Producing Bacteria. US 20110262640 A1, issued 2016.

Hussey, Matt. 2014. "Stools Made of Sand and Urine by Peter Trimble." *Dezeen*, February 8, 2014. https://www.dezeen.com/2014/02/08/stools-made-of-sand-and-urine-by-peter-trimble/.

Jonkers, Henk M., Arjan Thijssen, Gerard Muyzer, Oguzhan Copuroglu, and Erik Schlangen. 2010. "Application of Bacteria as Self-Healing Agent for the Development of Sustainable Concrete." *Ecological Engineering* 36 (2): 230–235. https://doi.org/10.1016/j.ecoleng.2008.12.036.

Larsson, Magnus. 2010. "Dune: Arenaceous Anti-Desertification Architecture." In *Macro-Engineering Seawater in Unique Environments*, edited by Viorel Badescu and Richard Cathcart, 431–63. Berlin, Heidelberg: Springer-Verlag. https://doi.org/10.1007/978-3-642-14779-1_20.

Lehne, Johanna, and Felix Preston. 2018. *Making Concrete Change: Innovation in Low-Carbon Cement and Concrete* (Chatham House Report). https://www.chathamhouse.org/2018/06/making-concrete-change-innovation-low-carbon-cement-and-concrete.

Mann, Stephen. 2001. *Biomineralization. Principles and Concepts in Bioinorganic Materials Chemistry*. New York: Oxford University Press.

Robert McNeel & Associates. 2020. *Rhinoceros*. V.6.0. Robert McNeel & Associates. PC.

Saad, Ahmed Hassan, Haslinda Nahazanan, Zainuddin Md Yusoff, Bujang Kim Huat, and Muskhazli Mustafa. 2019. "Properties of Biomineralization Process in Various Types of Soil and Their Limitations." *International Journal of Engineering and Advanced Technology* 9 (1): 4261–4268. https://doi.org/10.35940/ijeat.A1756.109119.

Salvi, Joaquim, Sergio Fernandez, Tomislav Pribanic, and Xavier Llado. 2010. "A State of the Art in Structured Light Patterns for Surface Profilometry." *Pattern Recognition* 43 (8): 2666–2680. https://doi.org/10.1016/j.patcog.2010.03.004.

Sollazzo, Aldo, Efilena Baseta, and Angelos Chronis. 2016. "Symbiotic Associations." In *ACADIA 2016: Posthuman Frontiers: Data, Designers, and Cognitive Machines [Proceedings of the 36th Annual Conference of the Association for Computer Aided Design in Architecture (ACADIA)]*, Ann Arbor, MI, 27–29 October 2016, edited by K. Velikov, S. Ahlquist, M. del Campo, and G. Thün, 470–476. CUMINCAD.

Whiffin, Victoria S. 2004. "Microbial CaCO3 Precipitation for the Production of Biocement." PhD thesis, School of Biological Sciences & Biotechnology, Murdoch University, Western Australia. http://researchrepository.murdoch.edu.au/399/2/02Whole.pdf.

Wood, Brian D., Xiaoliang He, and Sourabh V. Apte. 2020. "Modeling Turbulent Flows in Porous Media." *Annual Review of Fluid Mechanics* 52: 171–203. https://doi.org/10.1146/annurev-fluid-010719-060317.

Zolotovsky, Katia, Merav Gazit, and Christine Ortiz. 2017. "Guided Growth: The Interplay among Life, Material and Scaffolding." In *Active Matter*, edited by S. Tibbits, 83–88. Cambridge, MA: MIT Press.

IMAGE CREDITS

Figures 1–3, 6–17: © Arnardottir, 2020.
Figures 4–5: © Christgen, 2019.

Thora H. Arnardottir is a PhD researcher and an experimental designer with a background in architecture. Her work addresses the possibilities of integrating biological systems in the built environment. Her research aims at understanding how to implement—instead of exploit—living materials in construction processes. Sitting at the intersection of design and biological fabrication, her work fosters the production of relationships of care for the living, centered on the production of hybrid assemblages. Her work combines biotic agency with design concepts and innovative crafting techniques.

Martyn Dade-Robertson is a Professor of Emerging Technology at Newcastle University where he specializes in design computation with a particular interest in emerging technologies, particularly synthetic biology. He is the co-director of the HBBE and has degrees in Architectural Design, Architectural Computation, and Synthetic Biology. He is the author of over 40 peer-reviewed publications, including the book *Living Construction* (2020).

Dr. Helen Mitrani is a Lecturer in Civil Engineering at Newcastle University and a chartered engineer. She obtained her PhD in Seismic Geotechnics from the University of Cambridge for work on novel liquefaction remediation methods for existing buildings. She then moved to industry to work as a structural engineer for Arup, in their London and Newcastle offices. During this time she was involved in the design and construction of diverse and challenging structures, including a new facility for testing 100-meter-long wind turbine blades. Her current research includes the development of responsive materials for civil engineering and novel ground improvement techniques.

Dr. Meng Zhang is an Associate Professor in Microbial Biotechnology at Northumbria University. Her PhD was in Proteomics studies of streptococcal pathogens, and she has worked on biocatalysis as a postdoctoral researcher for eight years. More recently, Meng has established new interdisciplinary research interest, applying microbial biotechnology in the built environment, particularly in the fabrication of functionally graded biomaterials. She has worked on several UK research council funded projects, and is co-leader for Living Construction theme in HBBE. Collaborating with architects, synthetic biologists, and civil engineers, she has published more than 20 peer-reviewed articles on the related topics.

Dr. Beate Christgen is a Senior Research Associate in the School of Natural and Environmental Sciences at Newcastle University. With a background in applied chemistry, advanced wastewater treatment, and environmental molecular microbiology, she studies changes in natural and engineered microbial systems and how to exploit these systems for a sustainable future. Her research includes investigations of bioelectrochemical systems for energy and product generation from wastewater, the impact and mitigation of the biological methane cycle in the Arctic on climate change, antibiotic resistance gene abundance and dissemination through wastewater and in terrestrial ecosystems, and microbial-induced calcium carbonate precipitation in hydrogels.

Formica Forma

Explorations in Insect-Robot Collaboration for Emergent Design and Manufacturing

Andrea Ling
ETH Zurich

Mahshid Moghadasi
Cornell University

Kowin Shi
Cornell University

Junghsien Wei
Cornell University

Dr. Kirstin Peterson
Cornell University

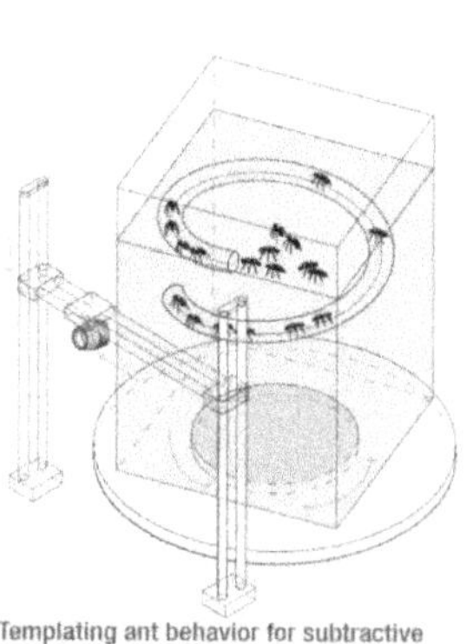

Templating ant behavior for subtractive fabrication with digitally controlled UV light

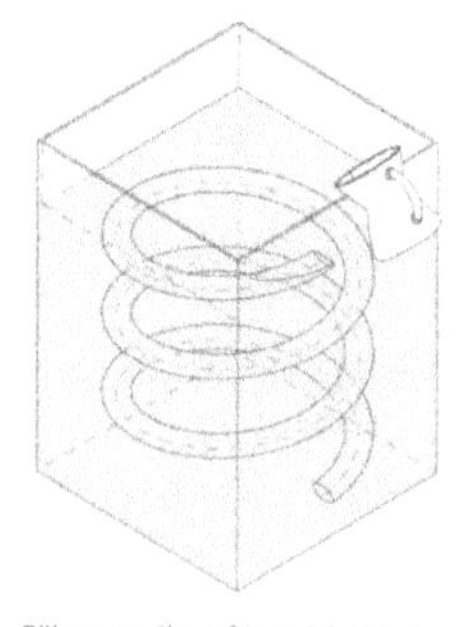

Silicon casting of templated ant tunnel

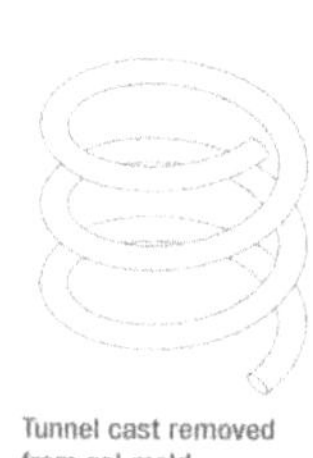

Tunnel cast removed from gel mold

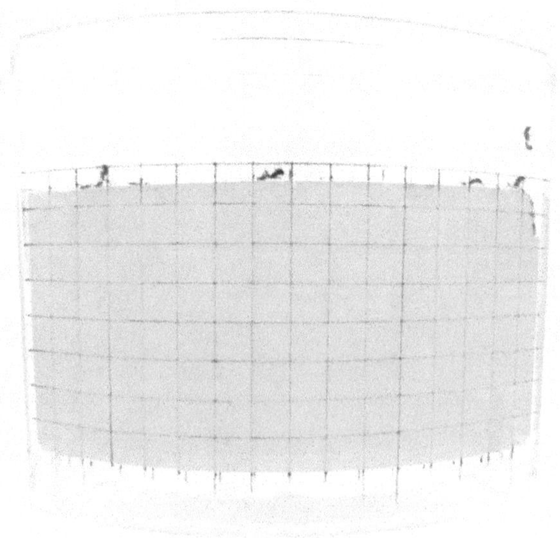

1, 2

1 Possible experimental structure where ants can dig out tunnels in nutrient ant gel with appropriate UV stimulus. Tunnel in gel can then be cast.

2 Control arena (16 × 14 × 3 cm), marked with 1 × 1 cm grid, with no UV light stimulus, 10 ants digging over 7 days.

ABSTRACT

Hybrid robot systems that cooperate with live organisms is an active area of research, in part to leverage biological advantages such as adaptivity, resilience, and sustainability. *Formica Forma* explores new possibilities of codesigning and cofabricating in partnership with Western Harvester ants to build forms that would be challenging with industrial techniques.

Using a robotically controlled UV light (350–405 nm) as an environmental stimulus to bias digging behavior, we guide 600 ants to dig ~141 cm of tunnels in transparent ant gel over 646 hours. Predictability, fidelity to the UV source, repeatability, dig efficiency, amount of ant activity, and tunnel preference were studied. The resulting branching tunnels were cast in silicone to demonstrate the ability to harness this in subtractive fabrication with inexpensive, self-maintaining biological fabricators.

Results showed that ants can follow the UV light as a path guide (when the light is moving) or target it as a goal (when the light is both moving and static), with longer digging effect from the moving UV stimulus. Ants showed high fidelity to the light path, aligning their tunnel direction exactly with changes in the UV position, tuning the fabrication in real-time with environmental alterations. Population size did not seem to affect digging speed or efficiency, and the ants' preexisting preferences factored into which tunnels were dug out.

The research develops a hybrid biodigital way of working with biological swarms where the individual agency and the intrinsic stochasticity of the system offer possibilities in real-time adaptability and programmability through environmental templating.

INTRODUCTION: INSECT AS PARTNER

In this paper, we focus on merging digital and biological fabrication to leverage biological advantages, particularly those associated with swarm systems, such as adaptability, sustainability, and robustness, with the design intentionality afforded by digital technologies. Projects such as Ren Ri's *Yuansu* beehive sculptures (Cascone 2014), Mediated Matter's *Silk Pavilion* (Oxman et al. 2014), and Agnieszka Kurant's *AAI* termite mounds (Walsh 2015) show cultural and engineering potential when human intent partners with biological agency, where design effort is placed not on developing artifact form but, rather, templating environmental conditions and designing processes for novel fabrication technologies.

Designing with biological systems, however, often means one is incorporating a degree of inherent agency and loss of control into the system, and requires an adjustment in design thinking for successful collaboration. We use Western harvester ants (*Pogonomyrmex occidentalis*), which are attracted to close-range UV light (Kayser 2018), and a robot-actuated UV light source to modify ant behavior as they construct tunnels in transparent nutrient gel. Six hundred ants were monitored over a period of 646 hours, digging ~141 cm of UV-templated tunnels, using the light as both a guide and target. The hypothesis was that the ant response is significant and accurate enough to direct the overall structural direction, despite individual level variance in tunnel direction. We were able to show preliminary success based on this idea with data collected from eight different experiments. More importantly, this project proves the feasibility of design with hybrid authorship instead of a strictly deterministic and human-generated model, a unique feature offered by this biodigital cooperative system.

The work develops methodologies towards adaptable sustainable fabrication through interaction with a swarm of ants and shows that their constructed tunnels are consistently biased by the presence of UV light but are also dependent on low-level stochastic interactions. We found that the ant-robot collaboration could form features that would be difficult with digital manufacturing and that the system was adaptable and robust in response to variability among individuals. The bio-hybrid approach, however, requires a shift in expectations due to the inherent agency and stochasticity of the system. The work offers insight on how to adjust design protocols in response to an inherently noisy aggregate system, with potential application to other hybrid biological-digital systems as well as in robotic swarm systems where individual agents have a high degree of autonomy and stochastic behavior.

3

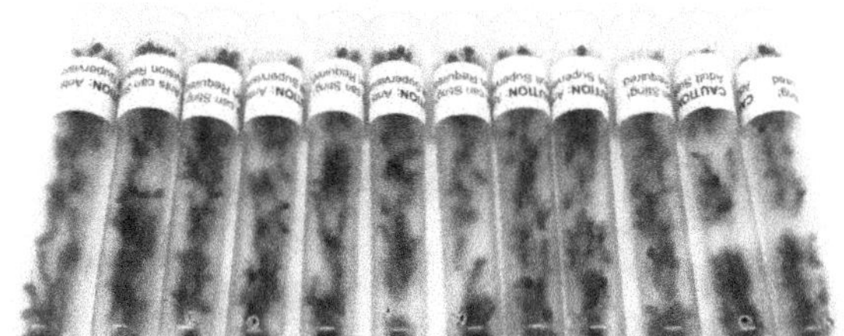

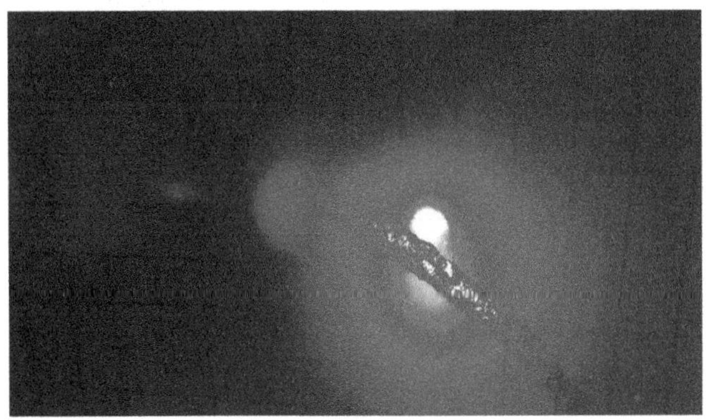

4, 5

3 *Silk Pavilion II*, 2020, The Museum of Modern Art, Neri Oxman & the Mediated Matter Group. This second iteration of the pavilion employed 17,532 silk worms on a robotically controlled scaffold to spin the silk skin of the structure.

4 *Pogonomyrmex occidentalis*, 600 specimens ordered from commercial supplier.

5 *Pogonomyrmex occidentalis* is attracted to close-range UV light ~ 350–405 nm wavelength.

BACKGROUND

Employing biological organisms as viable manufacturing platforms has gained traction in the field of synthetic biology and living material synthesis, where microbial organisms are used for their ability to procreate, synthesize new material, sense environmental conditions, and respond to disturbances in such conditions (Gilbert, Tang et al. 2019; Nguyen et al. 2018). Parallel efforts have only just begun in partnering biological organisms with robotic systems and larger-scale fabrication platforms. The term "partner" is used specifically, as one of the long-term goals is to develop bio-hybrid systems that favor mutualism between organism and machine over exploitation. The logic is that a symbiotic system, beneficial to both parties, can be ethical and will persist far longer than a system that exploits or kills the biological partner. The challenge, then, is to learn about the behavior of these autonomous partners such that the designed system can indeed be beneficial and will have a reliable degree of predictability.

In the *Silk Pavilion I*, the Mediated Matter group worked with 6,500 live silkworms to construct an architectural-scale pavilion. The group harnessed the silkworms' ability to adapt to different scaffold conditions, including variations in local temperature, aperture size, and z-height, to create a variable-density cladding on top of a parametrically designed and robotically fabricated scaffold that is configured by humans into a geodesic dome. Rather than boiling silk cocoons (thus sacrificing the silkworms) in order to harvest silk—as is done industrially—the silk remains on the pavilion and the worms are free to pupate and turn into moths. With his *Yuansu* series of honeycomb sculptures, the artist Ren Ri influences how the bees construct their hives by manually changing the orientation of their enclosure every seven days; the human artist dictates overall directionality in the shape of the hive but relinquishes fine-scale geometric authorship to the bees. In *Project coelicolor*, designer Natsai Audrey-Chiesza employs *Streptomyces coelicolor*, a common soil bacteria that produces vibrant magenta to indigo pigments, as painters of patterns on silk, setting color by precisely controlling nutrient type, level, pH, and temperature, as well as fixing shape by creating jigs within which the bacteria can work.

In all these projects, programmability and predictability of the outcome depend on setting the appropriate environmental conditions and stimuli to induce corresponding bottom-up behavior from the organisms to meet top-down expectations. We use similar stigmergic principles of coordination to guide our proposed collaboration with *Pogonomyrmex occidentalis*. Harvester ants demonstrate complex behaviors such as construction and foraging, which are the result of interactions that arise from individual stochastic occurrences (Gordon 2002). Coherent collective behavior emerges as the sum of these simple, distinct response-stimuli occurrences. Stimuli can be a variety of environmental cues; for instance, many species of ants use the angle of light polarization in the UV spectrum to navigate between foraging sites and their nests (Freas and Schultheiss 2018), while others use changes in relative humidity as a trigger to change the layout of their nest. Significantly for this work, *P. occidentalis* are highly influenced by ultraviolet light (350–405 nm) (Capinera 2008; Freas and Schultheiss 2018; Ho et al. 2017), burrowing or moving toward the location of highest light intensity.

This species of ant has female workers up to 10 mm in length, with colonies that can survive up to 20 years with a viable queen (Wikipedia n.d.). They are excellent tunnel diggers and create nests that are up to 5 m deep and 1 m in diameter. This time scale and nest size are usable for building systems, and invite the possibility of having ants live in the final structure for several years with the ability to alter the structure in response to changing conditions. *P. occidentalis* was also chosen because it is a commercially available, inexpensive, and simple organism to monitor, with a limited range of simple individual behaviors that aggregate into collective construction. On a colony level, the worker ants are most likely sisters of approximately the same age (Mayer 2016) and are genetically similar (Cole and Wiernasz 1997), reinforcing the hypothesis that much of their collective development is based on responses to environmental cues rather than inherited variation.

METHODS

We conducted experiments in a clear acrylic ant arena (30 × 30 × 2.5 cm, marked with a 1 × 1 cm grid) filled with nutrient gel that ants can dig tunnels in and that provides nutrients and water. A Gearlight S100 UV LED flashlight (UV) was fixed onto a six-axis, 40 cm reach, custom robotic arm (Shi 2019) that moves the light along preprogrammed paths in the arena to test the ant's response to a moving light guide (tests 1, 2, 3a, 3b; Fig. 6). For tests 4, 5, and 6, the same arena is partitioned into two equal halves and an adjustable stationary mount was used to carry a UV flashlight in each partition (15 cm apart; Fig. 7) to test the ant's response to a stationary stimulus. A smaller control arena (16 × 14 × 3 cm), without UV, was used to test baseline ant behavior, vitality, and dig rate. All tests were run indoors, at 21°C, with normal indoor humidity. All the tests were recorded via time-lapse photography, with active ants per hour counted.

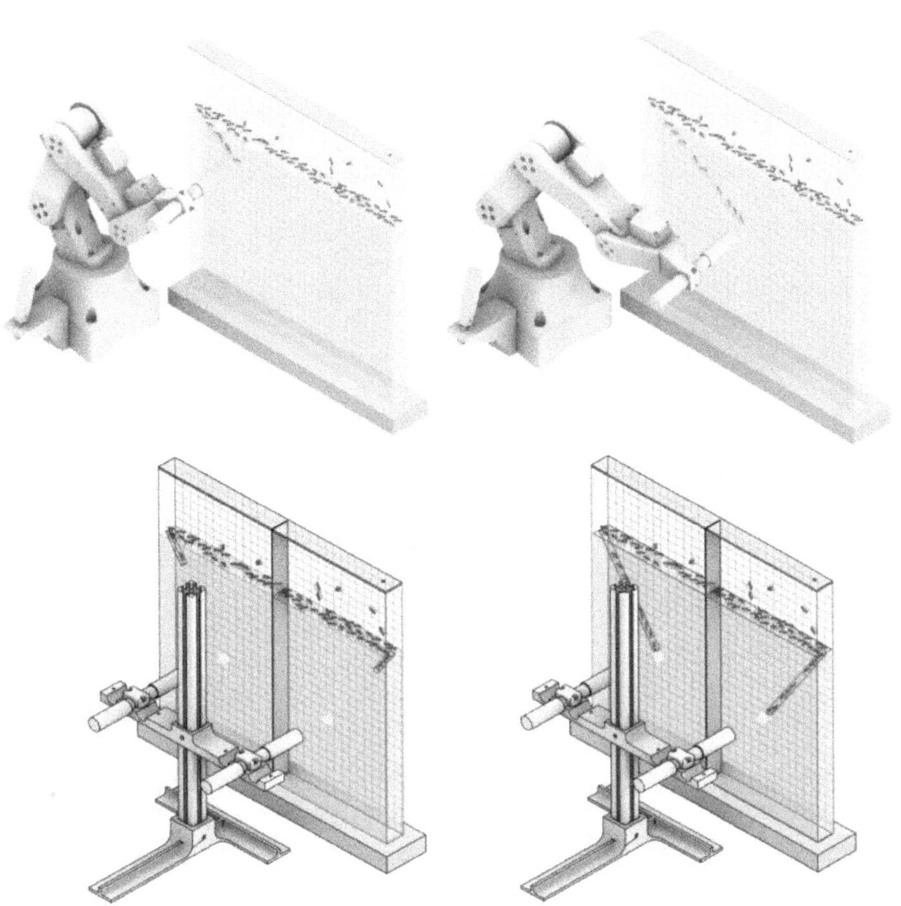

6,7 8

6 Experiment setup for tests 1, 2, 3: UV LED fixed to 6-axis custom robot arm, moving in manually programmed path across gel-filled arena.

7 Experiment setup for tests 4, 5, 6: two UV LEDs fixed to stationary stand, 15 cm apart (1 LED per partition). Arena is partitioned into 2 equal halves.

8 Tunnels are cast in 2-part silicone, and the ant gel is reheated and reused for next test.

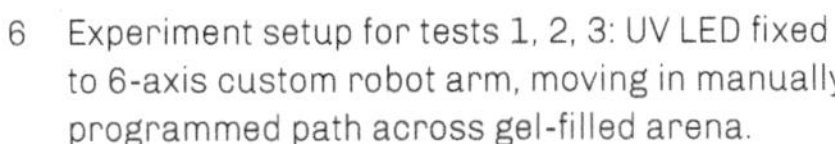

We ran eight experiments of three to seven days each, with different ant populations. With the hypothesis that the ants would always be biased to dig towards the UV, we explored the following:

- Predictability: How likely are the ants to follow the UV as a guide or target it as a goal?
- Fidelity: How precise is the digging to the UV path (guide) or target (goal)?
- Repeatability across different ant populations and numbers with identical stimulus.
- Efficiency: How much material is removed with time?
- Activity: Is dig rate affected by population size?
- Tunnel preference: Given the multiple ways that ants can dig towards the UV goal, how likely will the ants dig in the prescribed path towards the UV instead of alternative routes?

After the ants dug a significant area, we cast the complex tunnel shapes in silicone and reused the gel after casting (Fig. 8). This is of interest because fine branch structures found in nature, like ant tunnels, are often onerous or resource-intensive to fabricate, especially with subtractive technologies, so using inexpensive, self-maintaining biological fabricators offers an alternative possibility.

RESULTS

Test 0, the control, had 10 ants digging under 24-hour fluorescent light, but no UV light, for seven days. Once acclimated to the arena, the ants dug tunnels at an average rate of 2 mm per hour, although the digging was highly episodic, with periods of no digging interspersed with periods of rapid digging. The ants show a strong preference for hard edges and would dig straight down from the four corners of the enclosure before digging any branches or diagonal tunnels up. Out of 10 initial ants, only up to 4–5 ants dug at one time, and most of the digging was done by only 1–2 ants for the duration of the test. These preferences and patterns—starting tunnels at hard intersections, with most digging by a small fraction of available ants, at episodic intervals—were consistent throughout all the tests.

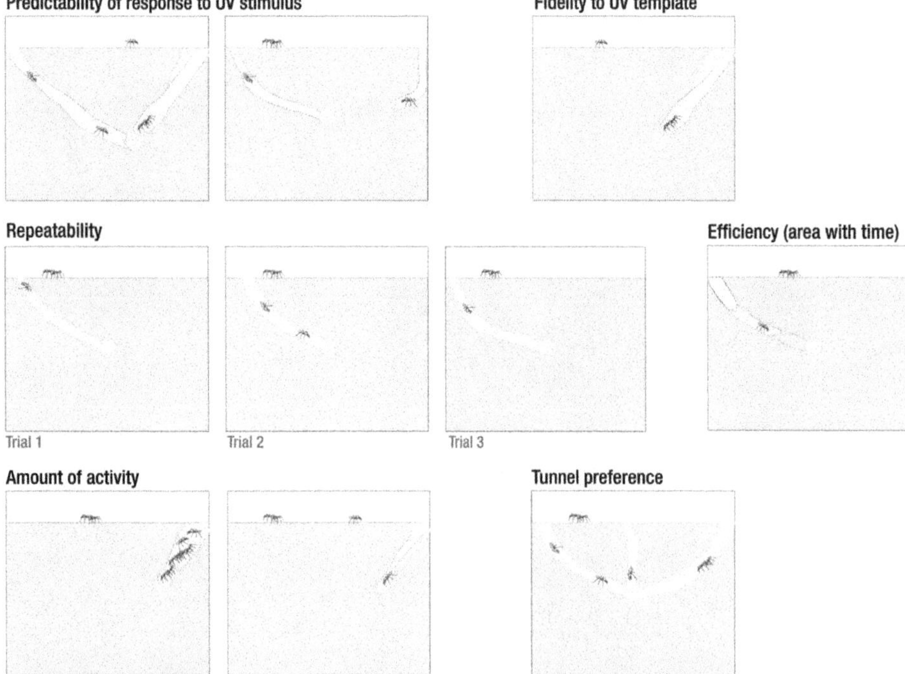

9 600 ants were observed to test the following:

(a) Predictability of response to the UV stimulus: How likely will the ants follow or target the UV?

(b) Fidelity: How precisely do the ants follow or target the UV?

(c) How repeatable are the results among different ant populations and sample sizes given identical stimulus?

(d) Efficiency: How much material is removed with time?

(e) Amount of activity: Is dig rate affected by population size or time in the arena?

(f) Tunnel preference: Given the multiple ways that ants can dig towards the UV goal, how likely will the ants dig in the prescribed path towards the UV instead of alternative routes?

9

Test 1 (Fig. 10) had 30 ants and a moving UV light along a preprogrammed path on the robotic arm. The ants moved initially to the right and left front corners of the arena. When presented with moving UV light, the active ants on the right side dug the templated path with remarkable fidelity, following the path of the robot arm, including the areas of UV light dispersion (tunnel A). Some ants on the left side started a second tunnel (B), digging towards the UV light instead of alongside with it. When an additional 30 new ants were introduced (test 2), the active ants chose to develop tunnel B (UV goal), instead of tunnel A (UV guide). Again, the ants did this with high fidelity, matching vector changes in the robotic arm with their own directional change to always directly target the UV light (Fig. 11). For both tests 1 and 2, the majority of the digging was done in the first 48 hours, with rapid decrease in dig rate afterwards.

Tests 3a and 3b show how branching tunnels can be templated with a moving UV light that traces a path off of tunnel B (the entrance to tunnel A is blocked with fresh ant gel). Sixty new ants chose between following the UV light as a guide or targeting it as a goal. Test 3a had the UV light moving downward and left, off a midpoint of tunnel B. Some ants followed the UV light, creating branch tunnel D, while the majority of the diggers chose to start a new tunnel C, from the left corner towards the UV light target. The majority of the digging was done in the first three days, after which dig rate dropped dramatically. Test 3b directed another 60 ants to dig a second branch tunnel E with the UV moving from another midpoint along tunnel B; the majority of the diggers followed the UV path and dug tunnel E, instead of developing tunnel D further, with most of the digging in the first 48 hours.

Tests 4, 5, 6 (Fig. 12) show different populations of ants (15, 30, 45, 60, 75, and 90) that were presented with identical static UV light in the middle of the ant gel partition. New ants and refreshed ant gel were used for each test. Five out of the six test populations dug from the same starting point in near-identical paths towards the UV goal, regardless of total population size, number of diggers, or whether the ants were on the left or right side of the partition. In test 6, the 15 ants on the left partition dug from the opposite corner compared to the other sets, and the 75 ants in the right partition dug an additional vertical tunnel after they had completed the first expected tunnel. While this consistency is not comparable to the repeatability and precision of industrial systems, it is significant for a system based on insects with biological agency.

Two exceptions were noted, both caused by slight gel inconsistencies:

- In test 6, in the right partition (15 ants), there was a gap between the plastic divider and the ant gel, which we believe made starting a tunnel on the left easier than at the right side which was the norm for the ants before.
- In test 6, in the left partition (75 ants), the vertical tunnel was started at the discontinuous interface between the old undisturbed gel and the new gel that was poured in to replace the gel disturbed by the previous tunnel.

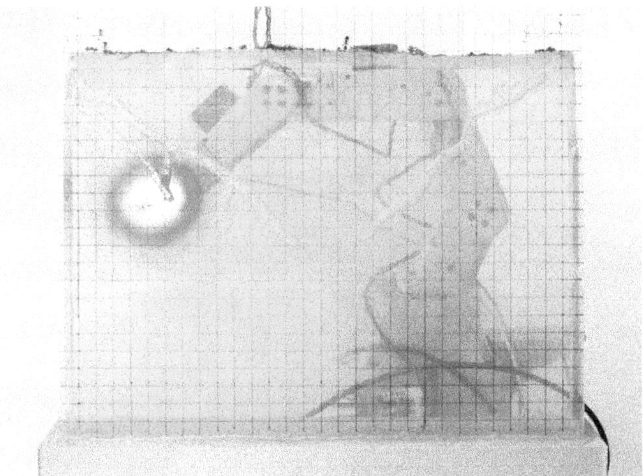

10 Tests 1, 2, 3a, 3b; Tunnels A–E dug over time, in response to moving UV guide. Color block units signify the amount of tunnel dug in 24 hours. UV guide starts in different positions (dashed circle) for tests 1, 2, 3a, 3b. End point of robot path indicated by small circle.

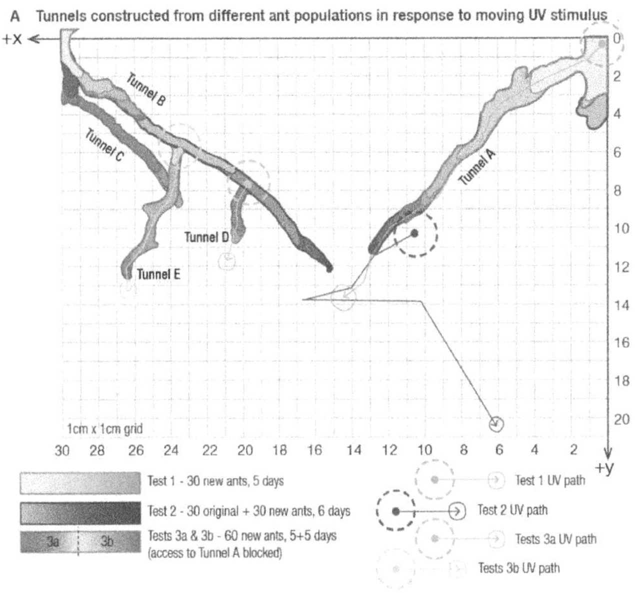

10

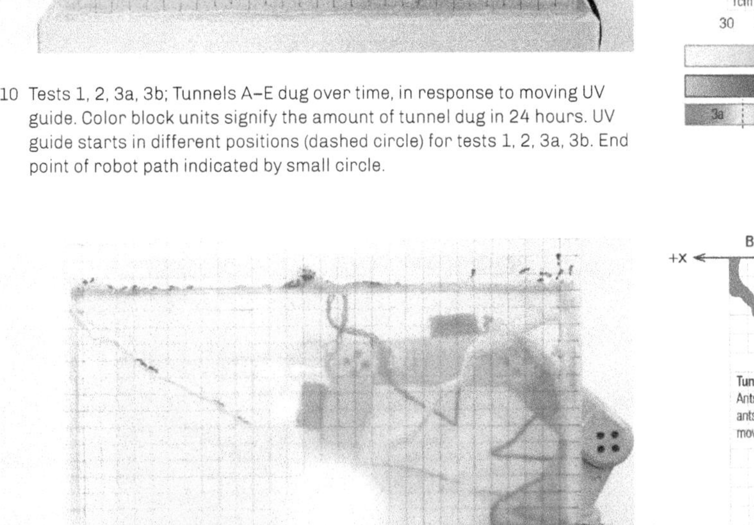

11 Development of Tunnel B during Test 2; ants change tunneling direction (as indicated by colored arrows) to match changing position of UV light path (dashed line). Color blocks indicates tunnel dug in 24 hours.

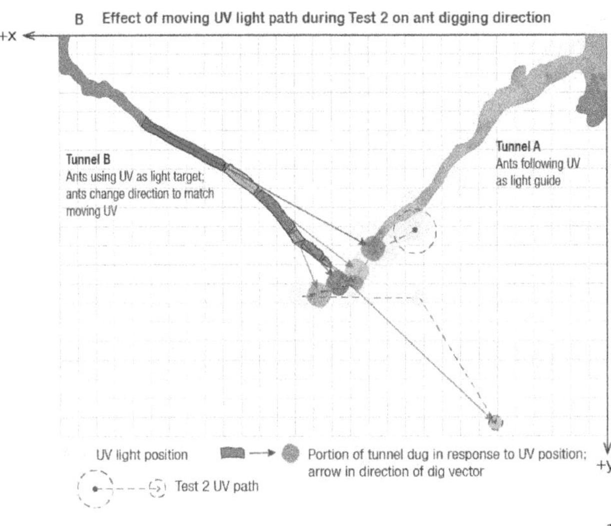

11

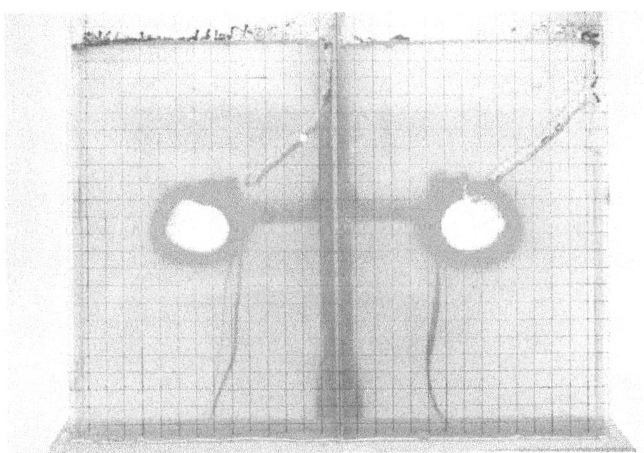

12 Tests 4, 5, 6: Tunnels F–L dug by different ant populations in response to stationary UV goal. Color blocks signify the amount of tunnel dug in 10 hours. Tunnels are dug by different numbers of ants using the same stimulus to test repeatability and effect of population size on dig rate.

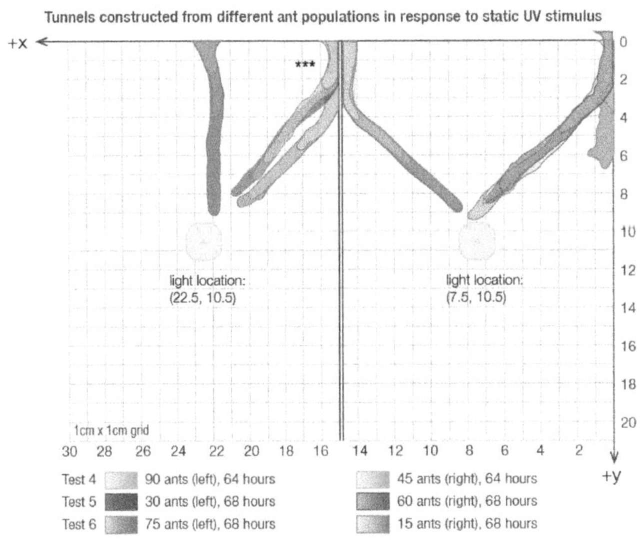

12

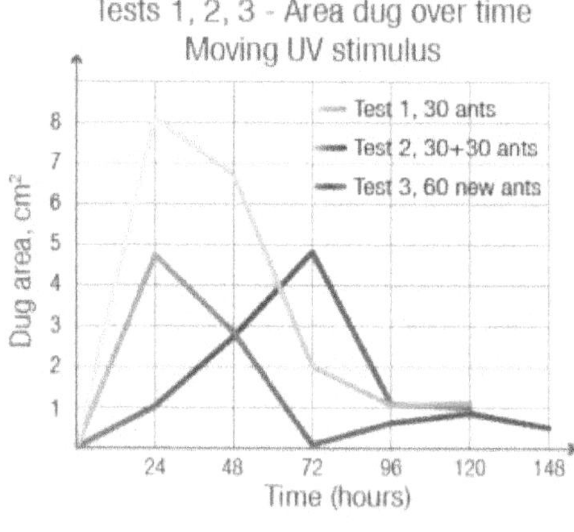

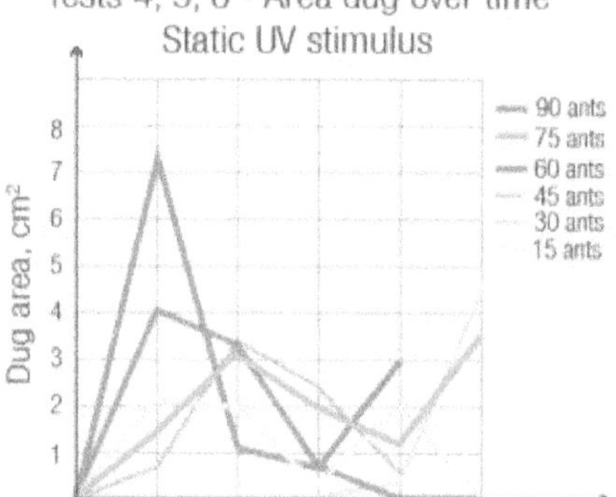

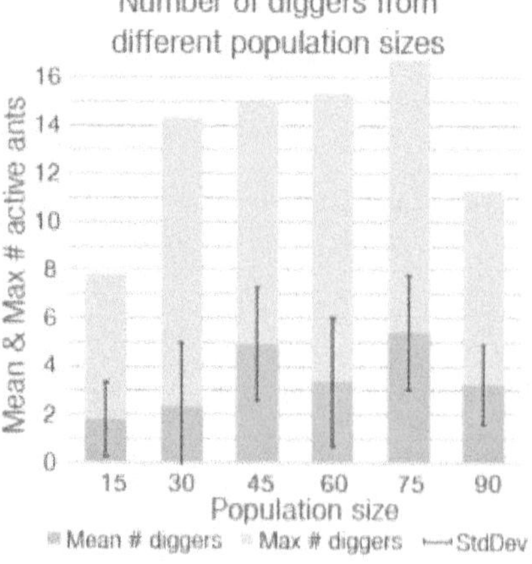

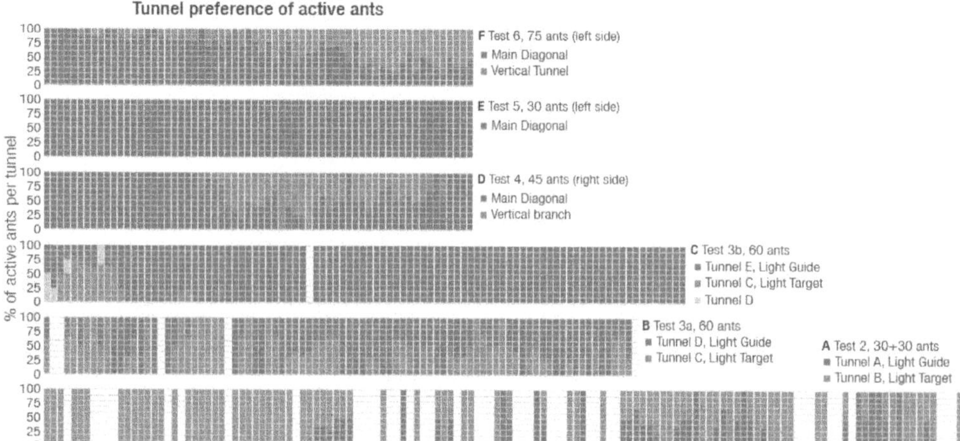

13, 14, 15

13 Area of gel dug by ants over time in response to the moving UV guide. Peak digging activity is noted to be in the first 24–72 hours of the test, after which activity rapidly drops off.

14 Area of gel dug by ants over time in response to the static UV goal. Peak digging activity is noted to be in the first 10–20 hours of the test, after which activity drops off; this is less than half the time they are active with a moving UV light. Some sample populations exhibit an increase in digging activity after 30–40 hours again to develop secondary tunnels. Intensity of digging activity is not correlated to population size.

15 Mean and maximum number of active digging ants in different population sizes of ants for tests 4, 5, 6. Increasing the population size of ants is correlated with a slight increase in maximum number of digging ants but without a significant increase in the mean number of digging ants, or an increase in dig rate.

16

16 Tunnel preference of active digging ants in each test when ants dig multiple tunnels in response to same UV stimulus. Blue indicates the proportion of active ants that dug the expected tunnel in response to UV; orange indicates the proportion of active ants that dug alternative tunnels in response to UV. Test 2 shows majority of active ants dug tunnel B, using the moving UV as a target instead of as the predicted UV guide (tunnel A). Test 3a shows half the ants chose the expected branch tunnel D, while half chose to develop alternative tunnel C. Test 3b shows a majority of ants digging branch tunnel E. Test 4 shows a majority of the ants in the 45 ant partition digging the main diagonal path and some starting a small vertical branch. Test 5 shows all the ants in the 30 ant partition digging the expected diagonal. Test 6 shows majority of ants in 75 ant partition digging the main diagonal, but after it is completed, they shift towards digging a second vertical tunnel.

Population size did not seem to affect digging speed or efficiency (Figs. 13, 14), nor did it significantly alter the number of active ants digging at any time (Fig. 15). That is, smaller population sizes could dig their tunnels as fast or faster, and had proportionally more active ants, than the larger population sizes. Figure 15 shows the average and maximum number of digging ants as a function of ant population. While larger populations generally had more actively digging ants and the mean number of diggers increased with population size, doubling the number of ants did not double the number of diggers, and at 90 ants, both the maximum and mean number of diggers decreased. This indicates that arena size and environmental conditions play a large role in digging activity rather than population size.

The amount of ant activity was correlated with static or moving UV light, with ants responding more vigorously and for a longer duration to a moving UV light source than a static one. With the moving source, ants would search until they found the changing UV light direction, either matching its direction or changing course to target it. Also significant was that in addition to the UV bias, ants have other preferences when digging, like starting tunnels at the hard corners of the arena or where there were discontinuities in the gel. This was especially notable in tests 4, 5, and 6, where the UV stimulus was in the middle of the arena; instead of starting from a point with the shortest path to the UV light, the ants preferred to start at the corners downwards and then switch directions to diagonally reach the UV light. These preexisting preferences, combined

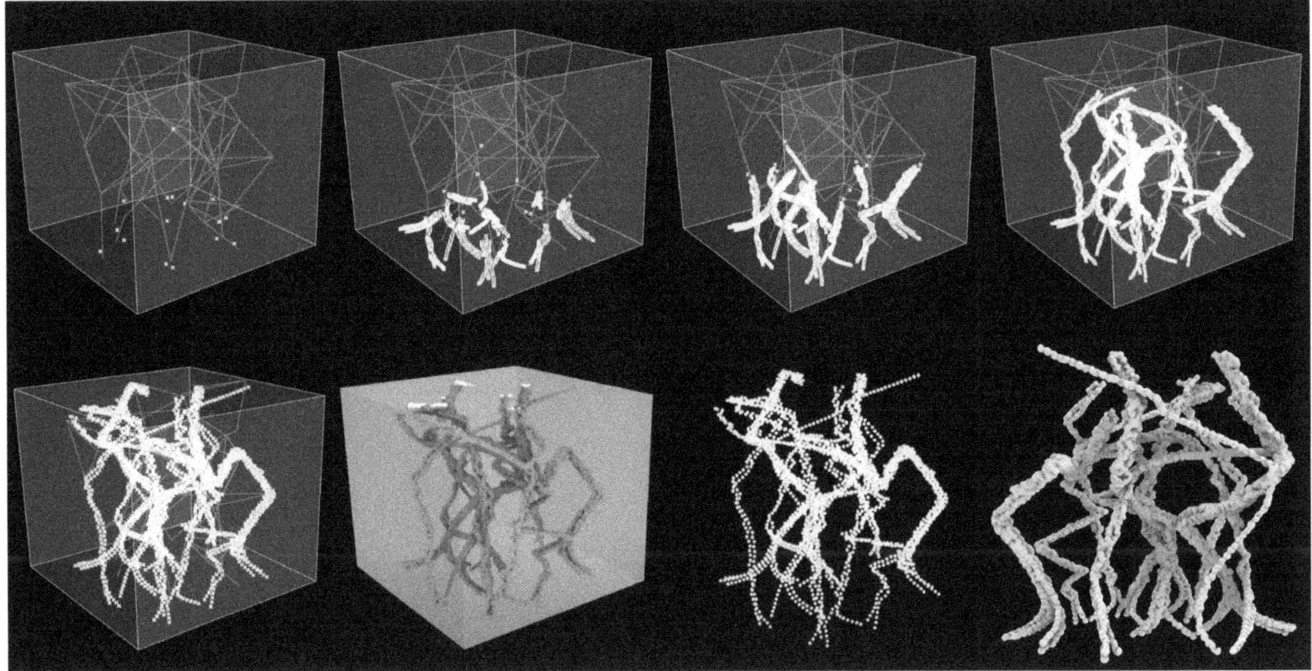

17

17 Future work using 3 dimensional gel arena with multiple moving UV light guides and multiple starting points. UV light (yellow points) follow toolpaths (purple lines) to attract ants along the tool path.

with the random local interaction of ants before collective trends can emerge, resulted in the multiple tunnels dug in response to the same UV light in numerous tests (Fig. 16).

Notable in this work is the large population of lazy ants in all the tests—up to 96% of the ants would rely on usually fewer than five hard working ants to dig the majority of the tunnels at any given time. Prior work (Aksoy and Camlitepe 2018) shows that generally at least 50% and up to 75% of a colony's ants in situ are inactive, potentially as nature's backup in case the working ants are hurt. Another potential reason for the high proportion of lazy ants in our sample sets may be that, given that we purchased these ants commercially, our sample set likely has a high proportion of older foraging ants that normally favor duties outside of the nest (and can thus be captured.) This indicates that the age range of the workers used in the experiments is important to clarify, or that a whole colony be used, in future work.

After the tests, the ant gel tunnels were successfully cast with a two-part silicone and easily removed. The gel can then be reheated and reused to create new tunnels. This suggests that casting in ant-dug tunnels would be a feasible way to subtractively form molds that would be difficult to mill. Given some of the inherent unpredictability of the tunnel paths, this would likely be a feasible manufacturing method for forms where granular detail is not critical as long as it meets higher-level goals, such as having more material cast at any point where the UV light might have been stationary or having multiple cast lines to every point the UV light was.

CONCLUSION: WHAT DO ANTS GET YOU?

Our study is a preliminary proof-of-concept that shows that ant tunneling can be consistently biased by UV light, and that this guided tunneling could be harnessed with design intent. UV biasing can be implemented with the UV light as a goal as well as a guide, with initial results showing that targeting it as a goal is more successful. Preexisting geometric features in the gel (cracks or discontinuities) or by the arena boundaries (hard interfaces) have a strong effect on where tunnels start, but eventually the ants will always be biased by the UV light, as shown by the consistent targeting of the UV stimulus in our stationary tests and the ability to prompt new branches off of old tunnels with our moving tests. Peak tunneling rates ranged from 3.3 to 8.1 cm^2 of material removed per day and was uncorrelated to the number of worker ants available but was strongly correlated to the amount of time that the workers were in the arena. The tunnels created in the ant gel can be easily cast and the gel can be melted and reused for new tunnels.

The project demonstrates that by manipulating the UV stimulus, we can provoke high-level predictable patterns of ant response, albeit with substantial low level noise. The ant gel we use provides nutrition and water and can potentially sustain the colony, while the ants inexpensively dig tunnel forms that are hard to create with existing technologies. They point towards a design approach where instead of prescriptively planning and detailing the *only* desirable outcome, the designer tunes a system towards probabilistically guaranteed outcomes that result from emergent processes with hybrid authorship. And while the system we designed cannot currently compare with the precision and consistency of an industrial fabrication system, it offers new fabrication possibilities with real-time adaptability to unexpected impedances, programmability through environmental templating, self-perpetuating sustainability, and the ability to fabricate challenging structures. This can help establish methodology for codesigning with distributed natural agents that allows for decentralized adaptive tunability during fabrication, with principles that can be applied to artificial systems of autonomous agent collectives.

This is a starting point; improvements include additional replicates of the original toolpaths and testing with larger populations, such as a whole colony or with ants of a known age. Future work also includes prototyping in 3D (to move beyond planar tunnels) and with multiple dynamic UV light sources and starting points, as in Figure 17. Finally, there is the desire to increase the precision of the UV templating as well as the scale of the structures that the ants can form to increase the feasibility of use in novel fabrication workflows.

ACKNOWLEDGMENTS

Thank you to Dr. Markus Kayser for discussing his initial tests from 2016 and to the Collective Embodied Intelligence Lab for their time.

REFERENCES

Aksoy, V., and Y. Camlitepe. 2018. "Spectral Sensitivities of Ants—A Review." *Animal Biology* 68 (1): 55–73. https://www.doi.org/10.1163/15707563-17000119.

Capinera, J. L., ed. 2008. *Encyclopedia of Entomology*. Dordrecht: Springer Science+Business Media B.V.

Cascone, Sarah. 2014. "Artist's Honeycomb Sculptures Made by Bees Spark Buzz." *Artnet News*, July 7. https://news.artnet.com/exhibitions/artists-honeycomb-sculptures-made-by-bees-spark-buzz-56554.

Cole, B. J., and D. C. Wiernasz. 1997 "Inbreeding in a Lek-Mating Ant Species, *Pogonomyrmex occidentalis*." *Behavioral Ecology and Sociobiology* 40 (2): 79–86. https://www.doi.org/10.1007/s002650050318.

Freas, C., and P. Schultheiss. 2018. "How to Navigate in Different Environments and Situations: Lessons From Ants." *Frontiers in Psychology* 9: 841.

Gilbert, Charlie, T.-C Tang, W. Ott, B. A. Dorr, W. M. Shaw, G. L. Sun, T. K. Lu, T. Ellis. 2021. "Living Materials with Programmable Functionalities Grown from Engineered Microbial Co-Cultures." *Nature Materials* 20 (January): 691-700. https://doi.org/10.1038/s41563-020-00857-5.

Gordon, D. M. 2002. "The Regulation of Foraging Activity in Red Harvester Ant Colonies." *American Naturalist* 159 (5): 509–518. https://www.doi.org/10.1086/339461.

Ho, P. H. C., C. Smuts, M. A. R. Kayser, and J. Hernandez. 2017. "Ant-Based Modeling: Agent-Based City Simulation with Ants." In *CHI EA '17 [Proceedings of the 2017 CHI Conference Extended Abstracts on Human Factors in Computing Systems]*, Denver, CO, 6–11 May 2017, edited by Gloria Mark and Susan Fussell, 475–475. Association for Computing Machinery.

Kayser, Markus. 2018. "Towards Swarm-Based Design: Distributed and Materially-Tunable Digital Fabrication Across Scales." PhD thesis, Massachusetts Institute of Technology.

Mayer, J. 2016. "Ants." *General Entomology*. North Carolina State University. March 25. https://projects.ncsu.edu/cals/course/ent425/library/tutorials/behavior/ants.html.

Nguyen, P. Q., N.-M. Dorval Courchesne, A. Duraj-Thatte, P. Praveschotinunt, N. S. Joshi. 2018. "Engineered Living Materials: Prospects and Challenges for Using Biological Systems to Direct the Assembly of Smart Materials." *Advanced Matter* 30 (19): Article 1704847. https://doi.org/10.1002/adma.201704847.

Oxman, Neri, Jared Laucks, Markus Kayser, Jorge Duro-Royo, and Carlos Uribe. 2014. "Silk Pavilion: A Case Study in Fibre-Based Digital Fabrication." In *Fabricate: Negotiating Design & Making*, edited by Fabio Gramazio, Matthias Kohler, and Silke Langenberg, 248–255. Zurich: gta Publishers.

Shi, Kowin. 2019. *SkookumAsFrig/Mini_6DOF_Arm*. Python. https://github.com/SkookumAsFrig/Mini_6DOF_Arm.

Walsh, Nicole. 2015. "Meet the Woman Making Art with Termites." *Vice*, August 7. https://www.vice.com/en/article/8qvmwz/meet-the-woman-making-art-with-termites.

Wikipedia. n.d. "Pogonomyrmex Occidentalis." Article. Last modified January 3, 2021. https://en.wikipedia.org/wiki/Pogonomyrmex_occidentalis.

IMAGE CREDITS

Figure 3: © *Silk Pavilion II*, Neri Oxman & the Mediated Matter Group, 2020. The Museum of Modern Art, New York, photographed by Denis Doorly.

All other drawings and images by the authors.

Andrea Ling is an architect, artist, and biodesigner at ETH Zurich. She holds an MS from the MIT Media Lab and an MArch from the University of Waterloo. Her research is on how the critical application of biologically mediated design processes can move society away from exploitative systems of production to regenerative ones.

Mahshid Moghadasi is a MS student in Matter, Design, Computation at Cornell and research associate at JSLab. She holds a BArch and MS in architectural technology from University of Tehran. Her research is focused on robotic assemblies in architecture.

Kowin Shi is an automation hardware engineer at Uber ATG. He has an MEng in ECE and BS in mechanical engineering from Cornell. His current work focuses on autonomous car delivery.

Junghsien Wei is an MEng student in electrical and computer engineering at Cornell. His research is on autonomous control in robotics, focusing on drones, autonomous cars, and blimp delivery.

Kirstin Petersen PhD explores the design of bio-inspired robot collectives and their natural counterparts. She leads the Collective Embodied Intelligence Lab at Cornell University in electrical and computer engineering. She did her PhD at Harvard University and the Wyss Institute for Biologically Inspired Engineering and a postdoc at the Max Planck Institute for Intelligent Systems,

Towards a Distributed, Robotically Assisted Construction Framework

Using Reinforcement Learning to Support Scalable Multi-Drone Construction in Dynamic Environments

Zhihao Fang
Carnegie Mellon University

Yuning Wu
Carnegie Mellon University

Ammar Hassonjee
Carnegie Mellon University

Ardavan Bidgoli
Carnegie Mellon University

Daniel Cardoso-Llach PhD
Carnegie Mellon University

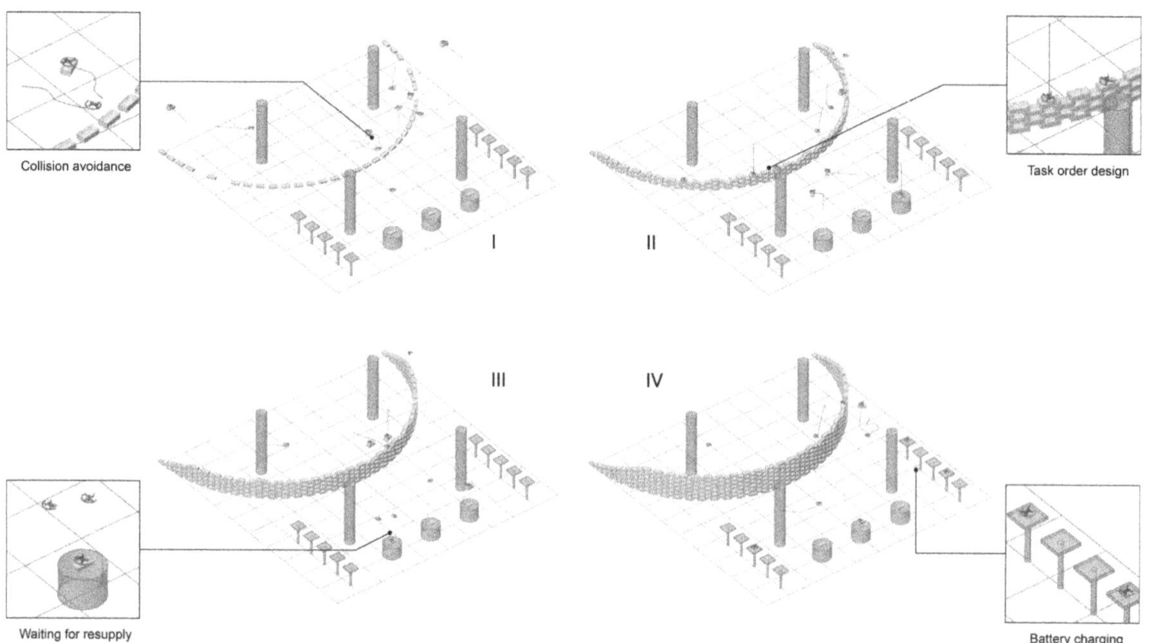

1

1 Four snapshots from the brick-laying simulation. A video of the entire simulation can be seen in Computational Design Lab (2020).

ABSTRACT

In this paper we document progress towards an architectural framework for adaptive and distributed robotically assisted construction. Drawing from state-of-the-art reinforcement learning techniques, our framework allows for a variable number of robots to adaptively execute simple construction tasks. The paper describes the framework, demonstrates its potential through simulations of pick-and-place and spray-coating construction tasks conducted by a fleet of drones, and outlines a proof-of-concept experiment. With these elements the paper contributes to current research in architectural and construction robotics, particularly to efforts towards more adaptive and hybrid human-machine construction ecosystems.

The code is available at: https://github.com/c0deLab/RAiC

INTRODUCTION

Our research investigates how recent advances in deep learning and reinforcement learning (RL) techniques might help improve the performance and adaptivity of robotically assisted construction systems, opening up new possibilities for semiautonomous technologies to support construction teams on- and off-site. Our vision is that networks of smaller, more adaptive robots might more flexibly and effectively assist building construction. We document progress towards a computational framework based on state-of-the-art reinforcement learning techniques that enables users to define simple construction tasks to be executed by a variable number of robots. The framework follows a centralized learning, decentralized execution approach. On the one hand, a server supervises task distribution and monitors the overall progress. On the other, each drone independently runs an RL algorithm for collision-free navigation and follows a series of rule-based macro actions to execute certain tasks. Our experimental scenario comprises a group of drones performing simple construction tasks—pick-and-place, and spray-coating—dynamically. We approach this as both a dynamic task-assigning problem and as a spatial one. We use problem modeling techniques to conceptualize a scenario of coordination involving multiple robots, supply and deployment sites, and a dynamic task list. We further discuss opportunities and limitations for this scenario of coordination in the context of the architecture-engineering-construction industries.

In the first section of this paper we discuss the state-of-the-art in multi-drone construction, identifying some shortcomings. In particular, we note the lack of a usable general framework for the introduction of these technologies in support of building processes. We then discuss our approach through an experimental scenario comprising both a software prototype, simulations, and progress towards a hardware prototype. Through simulations we test our software's capacity to coordinate a small group of drones in two kinds of construction-related activities: pick-and-place tasks and spray-coating. This section is followed by a discussion on the limitations of our approach, next steps, and notes on our broader vision on human-robot ecosystems of construction.

Background

Despite their original and ongoing applications in warfare, unmanned aerial vehicles (UAV), or drones, have recently been utilized in a variety of fields, including scientific research (Marris 2013), agriculture (Maes and Steppe 2019; Zhang and Kovacs 2012), and environmental monitoring (Lucieer et al. 2014; Nishar et al. 2016), and have gained popularity among flight and aerial photography/cinematography enthusiasts and specialists (Mademlis et al. 2018; Nägeli et al. 2017). A limitation of drones compared with industrial robots and rovers is their lower payload capacity, larger margins of error (Goessens, Mueller, and Latteur 2018), and shorter battery life.

On the positive side, drones are more agile, can cover larger distances, and can reach greater heights (Chaltiel, Maite, and Abdullah 2018). In addition, when equipped with sensors (Dackiw et al. 2019) and robust path-planning algorithms, they can operate in a wider range of conditions. Moreover, as recent works have shown, groups of drones can be programmed to execute tasks synchronously and "collaborate" in scenarios such as large-scale public displays (Intel n.d.). Drones' agility and flexibility can thus offer important advantages in architectural and construction-related tasks and, over the last decade or so, have attracted the attention of architectural and construction researchers.

Recent research in the field of autonomous construction has explored drones' potential to support construction tasks including, but not limited to, frame structure assembly (Lindsey, Mellinger, and Kumar 2011), bricklaying (Augugliaro et al. 2014), 3D printing (Hunt et al. 2014), tensile structure weaving (Ammar 2016), modular canopy structures (Wood et al. 2018), real-scale masonry construction (Goessens, Mueller, and Latteur 2018), roofing (Romano et al. 2019), and spraying mortar (Chaltiel et al. 2018). The majority of these efforts have employed a single drone, rather than a fleet of multiple drones. Among the exceptions is a 2011 project developed at the University of Pennsylvania comprising an array of quadcopters assembling truss-like structures consisting of "beams" and "columns" with magnets embedded at joints with a gripper (Lindsey, Mellinger, and Kumar 2011). The drones are controlled by a turn-taking algorithm that coordinates a pick-and-place process wherein drones take materials from a supply station to the construction, and assemble the structure following predetermined routes.

Another example of multirobot construction, exhibited live at the Fonds Régional d'Art Contemporain du Centre in Orléans, France, is the flight-assembled architecture, an installation comprising a 6 m tall tower composed of 1,500 foam modules deployed by four quadcopters (Augugliaro et al. 2014). Here, the researchers designed a state machine for additive drone-based construction: four drones worked collaboratively, each picking up a foam brick, transporting it to the building area, placing the brick at the designated target, and charging when needed. For planning the drones' trajectories, this project relies on a space reservation system preventing collisions. To avoid creating deadlocks when two drones try to swap positions, the team created separate "freeways" at different altitudes for the drones. Some researchers go beyond the homogeneous array of robots and combine multiple types of robots to address the limitations of drones. Felbrich et al. (2017) combined the accuracy of the industrial robotic arms with the reachability of drones to fabricate long-span structures.

These projects usefully demonstrate some potential applications of multiple drones in construction tasks. However, these approaches lack generalizability and scalability. For example, while working with predefined trajectories may suit certain construction types in strictly controlled environments, it would not be useful in dynamic and less structured ones—such as those characteristic of construction sites where multiple builders and tradespeople participate. Thus, it is important to consider how automated systems may interface with human teams at the design, operation, and maintenance stages. The literature in architectural and construction robotics is also sparse in examples of dynamic human-robot interactions. An exception is (Wood et al. 2018), who propose a model of interaction between the users and their UAV configurable architectural system where users could directly manipulate the system behavior by defining the growth patterns. They also propose an indirect interface between the users and the system through a learning mode, where the system could potentially collect data to study the patterns of interactions between users, environment, and their system. However, these researchers do not take concrete steps towards implementation.

HYPOTHESIS

We hypothesize that reinforcement learning techniques under a "centralized learning, decentralized execution" paradigm can enable a more flexible and generalizable software framework for robotically assisted construction that is more resilient to the dynamic nature of actual construction environments. Our technical approach relies on a server for task scheduling, progress monitoring, and drone management where each drone is equipped with reinforcement learning-based navigation algorithms for collision avoidance, and a library of rule-based macro actions, which are sequences of steps for accomplishing discrete subtasks such as building, resupplying, charging, and deviation handling. In addition, we use proximal policy optimization (PPO), a policy-based reinforcement learning algorithm (Schulman et al. 2017), to train a variable number of drones to navigate without collision. Coordination can thus be achieved in task execution time through specific task order and waiting mechanisms. Combining these technical strategies, a software framework can open up opportunities for more adaptive and efficient systems for robotically assisted construction and to interface dynamically with construction teams on site.

METHODS

Technical Framework

Our framework has a server for task distribution, progress monitoring, and drone management, allowing each drone to operate in a decentralized fashion. Each drone runs an RL-based navigation and collision avoidance algorithm and relies on rule-based macro actions to accomplish specific subtasks such as charging, resupplying, and placing objects (Fang 2020). Following the state machine proposed by Augugliaro et al. (2014), each drone follows the following states: (1) moving to the supply station for resupply; (2) navigating to the designated target position to install the blocks; and then, depending on its remaining battery, (3) issuing another task request; or (4) moving to the charging station to charge or change its battery.

Traditionally, centralized methods may suffer from combinatorial complexity when the number of robots grows, whereas decentralized methods may suffer from an incomplete solution with limited quality guarantees. Despite methods such as MAPP (Wang and Botea 2011), FAR (Wang and Botea 2008), and WHCA* (Silver 2005), the aforementioned limitations are inherent in the problem context. Given these limitations, reinforcement learning (RL) has emerged as an alternative approach in recent years. Through experiments, we are able to observe some key caveats that may improve generalizability and scalability concurrently, combining the advantages of both sides.

Our proposed system is more scalable, since introducing new drones to the system will not add significant load to the central server (Fig. 2). Given enough resources, the framework supports a virtually unlimited number of drones as well as various scales of construction tasks. RL navigation and collision avoidance makes the framework adaptable to a variety of environments, and is thus generalizable as long as tasks are structured as macro actions, following the state machine. Although this research is focused on scenarios with multiple drones, the problem itself only includes the simplest setting of multi-agent system (MAS), i.e., homogeneous agents without inter-agent communication or collaboration. Therefore at this stage, this research does not consider other topics featured in common MAS research, i.e., communication,

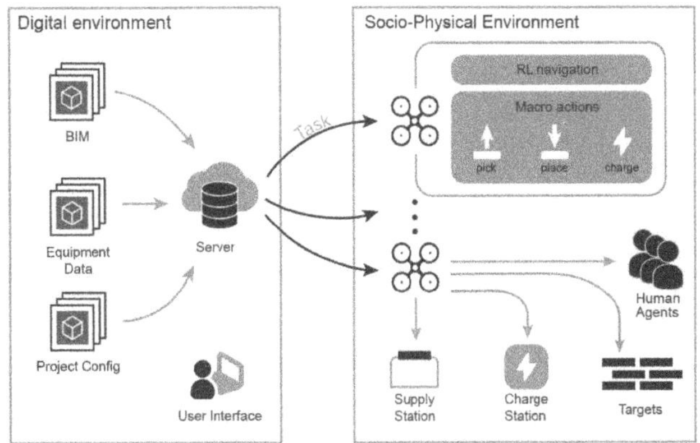

2

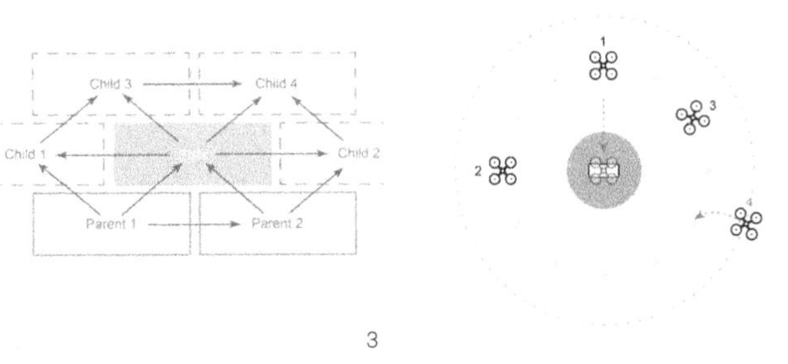

3

4

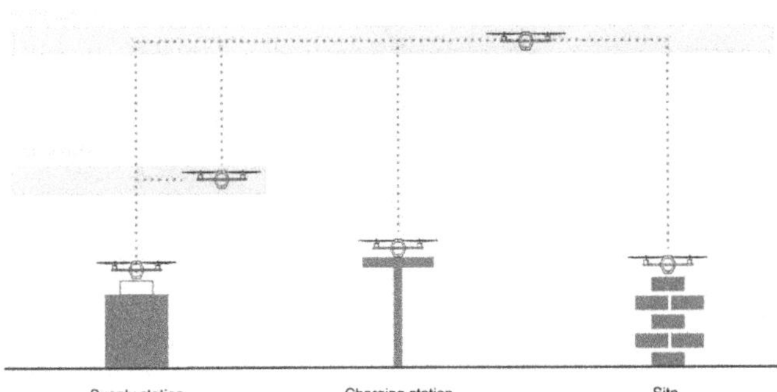

5

2 The proposed framework and its components.

3 Brick dependency concept.

4 Waiting mechanism.

5 Drone altitude allocation.

interaction, fault tolerance, adaptivity, cooperative and competitive environment.

Multi-Drone Coordination

In our framework, three auxiliary procedures support the coordination of multiple drones: (1) task order, (2) waiting mechanisms, and (3) altitude allocation.

A *task order algorithm* determines the execution order of tasks. For instance, in a bricklaying process, the task order algorithm determines which bricks should be installed first and which ones should be followed. We use a directed acyclic graph (Fig. 3) to encode bricklaying order as a series of dependencies. Bricks at the bottom are considered as "parent" items that should be laid before the "children" at the top. In addition, the drone's dimensions play a key role in defining such dependencies, as the system needs to constantly determine whether there is enough space for the drone to place the next brick. During construction, the server will only schedule the placement of bricks whose "parent" bricks are successfully installed. This approach eliminates the possibility of collision between the drone and other bricks during the construction process.

This task is presented to illustrate how simple construction tasks can be defined within the framework and is not meant to advocate drone bricklaying in particular as a construction methodology.

A *waiting mechanism* is designed to let drones take turns to resupply (Fig. 4). We define each supply station surrounded by a circular waiting zone. If a drone needs to resupply at an already occupied station, it can hover at the nearest available waiting position until the system summons it in a first in, first out (FIFO) order. Every time a drone finishes resupplying at the station, the server will signal the first drone waiting in the queue to initiate the resupplying process.

To simplify the path-planning process and to reduce it to a 2D problem, we assign a specific *altitude* to each drone. This assignment minimizes the down-wash effect among the drones. Additionally, a waiting altitude is defined below the flight altitude for drones to wait at the supply station, reducing the risk of waiting drones being approached by other active drones (Fig. 5).

Reinforcement Learning for Navigation

An RL model controls drones' navigation. Its objective is to learn an optimal policy such that drones are able to navigate from a starting to a target position without collision, including other drones, humans, walls, obstacles, etc., which are detected by the sensors at runtime. We use a proximal policy optimization (PPO) reinforcement learning model adapted from (Long et al. 2018), to learn the optimal policy. Compared with other uses of multi-agent reinforcement learning models such as Multi-Agent Deep Deterministic Policy Gradient (MADDPG), for example (Qie et al. 2019), we focus on the scalability of drone numbers, where communication among peer drones is not a major concern. Therefore, all the drones share the same RL model.

We modeled the problem in a software simulation environment based on the implementation of Multi-Agent Particle Environment (Lowe et al. 2017), an OpenAi Gym environment featuring a multi-agent particle world with a continuous observation and action space along with some basic simulated physics. The environment is defined as a 2.5D world, where the drone is allowed to fly only on either a horizontal plane during navigation or along a vertical axis to take off or land.

During the training phase, observations from different drones are collected into a common buffer in a decentralized manner before feeding into the neural network. The network input contains three types of observations: (1) simulated lidar ray data; (2) drone velocity; and (3) relative position of the target. Lidar data is specifically encoded with two CNN layers before concatenating with velocity and position. The network is updated using a composite loss that takes into account generalized advantage estimation (GAE) in a clipped manner (Schulman et al. 2017). The network outputs an acceleration vector for the drone's next movement. For better generalization, we also added Gaussian sampling.

The drone is rewarded if it reaches its target or makes an approaching step towards it, and it is penalized for getting away from the target or collision. For the criteria of reaching the target, the distance between the drone and its target should be within a tolerance distance and the velocity of the drone should be lower than a threshold. This ensures drones do not overpass the target because of inertia.

RL Training

We use a two-stage training method to learn the policy. The first stage comprises five agents in a randomly generated scenario. In every episode, five random targets, each associated with an independent drone, are generated on a 2D square arena. Each drone is expected to reach its target within a maximum limit of time steps. Later, 10 agents were trained in a scenario with a number of sparsely distributed threats. We trained the model for a total of 50 thousand episodes. We tested the model on 20 agents on a 20 × 20 m square arena with six randomly generated obstacles (Fig. 6). The results show that the model is robust to scale up to let more agents reach targets without collision. Compared with other methods (i.e., MADDPG, DDPG), the increase in the number of agents will not have a drastic effect on the training time.

EXPERIMENTS

We tested our framework in simulations of two hypothetical construction activities: bricklaying and spray-coating. The simulations were designed to test the RL algorithm's capacity to control each drone autonomously and independently from the server after being assigned to a task.

Bricklaying Simulation

A curved brick wall modeled in Rhinoceros and Grasshopper holds metadata (i.e., position, orientation, type, and dependency) for each brick, which are entered as inputs into the control framework. The test site comprises charging and supply stations, each with designated waiting areas. In the simulation, drones are deployed into charging stations prior to assembly. Four "threats" are defined in the working area to account for common obstacles in a construction site such as columns, stacks of materials, walls, and humans. Based on multiple tests, the optimal number of drones in this scenario was set to 10. We observed that despite the robustness of the RL algorithm to control the drones, crowded environments will result in resource competition between the drones and eventually lead to a significant waste of time in the resupply or charging queues.

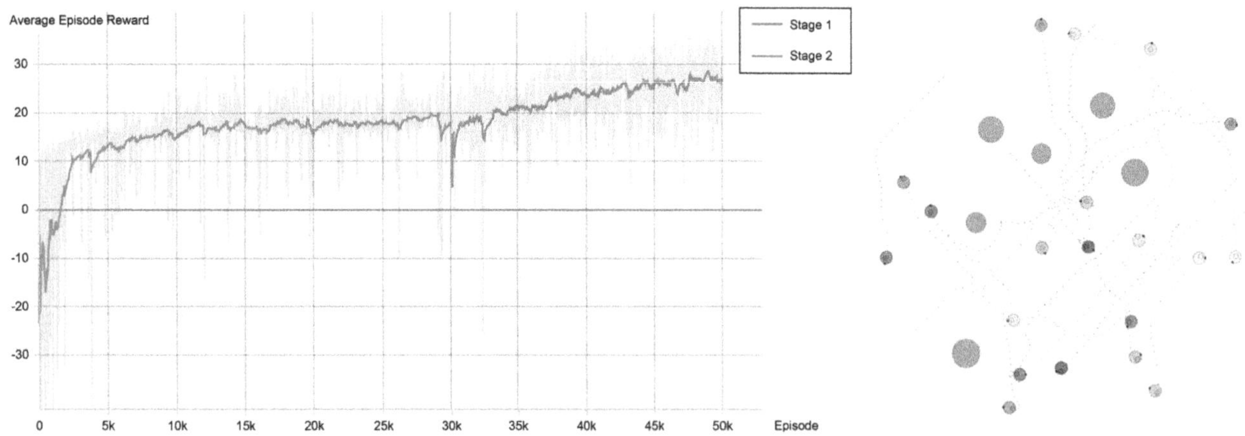

6 Average episode reward during the training model (left); evaluation of 20 agents reaching their targets (right).

6

In this experiment (Fig. 1), the framework was able to successfully decompose the task of building the curved wall into subtasks based on the units, distribute these tasks among multiple drones, and execute them without collisions in an environment that the drones had not "seen" before. Notably, the experiment showed an improvement in scalability over Augugliaro et al. (2014), which incorporates only four drones, and only allows two to fly at the same time. Our framework allows all 10 drones to operate efficiently and without collision at the same time. The experiment thus demonstrates the scalability and extensibility of the system.

Facade Coating Simulation

We also tested the system in a facade coating simulation. Following the outline of the pick-and-place state machine, drones are supposed to refill spray material and spray at designated locations. We use six drones to coat a dome-like object with another color (Fig. 7). Though different from bricklaying, the simulation is smooth and it shows how the system can be utilized in different scenarios.

The simulation demonstrates that the proposed navigation algorithm can be efficiently scaled up to control a flock of drones until they face a logistics bottleneck, e.g., charging and resupply limitations. Accordingly, we expect the algorithm to be efficiently scalable until the drones exhaust the logistical resources or hit the physical limitations of the work environment. Regarding the generalizability of the algorithm, we are actively working to adapt the algorithm to control unmanned ground vehicles (UGV) in a construction manufacturing scenario, which will be reported in a separate publication.

Progress Towards a Proof-of-Concept Implementation

We are currently developing the hardware setup to test the framework in a physical proof-of-concept implementation. The proposed hardware setup is designed solely to test the path-planning algorithm. However, deploying drones in indoor and unknown environments in close proximity to human users requires the use of adequate safety features for indoor and unpredictable environments (Shahmoradi et al. 2020), such as safety boxes and collision avoidance algorithms.

We developed a quadcopter drone that meets the specific functional and performance requirements that cannot be achieved by off-the-shelf products. Such requirements include a 500-gram payload capacity, integration with RL high-level flight commands, customizable flight control, telemetry hardware integration, and expansion points for attaching a gripper arm.

The drone is built on a lightweight F450-family frame with various attachment points for custom hardware integration. Motors are chosen to provide sufficient power to lift the 1,500 grams of drone empty weight as well as an additional 500 grams of payload. The selected battery pack can provide approximately 15 minutes of fly time at this

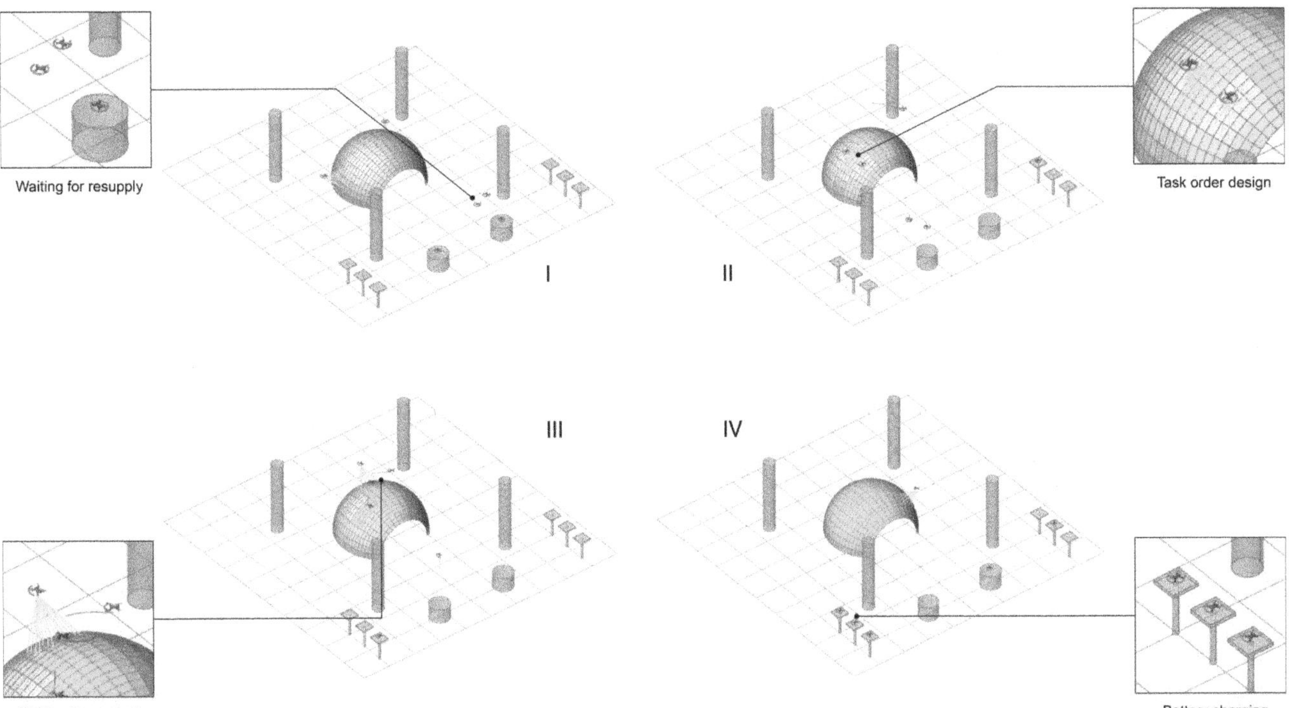

7 Four snapshots of the facade coating simulation, representing another use case scenario of the multi-drone framework.

7

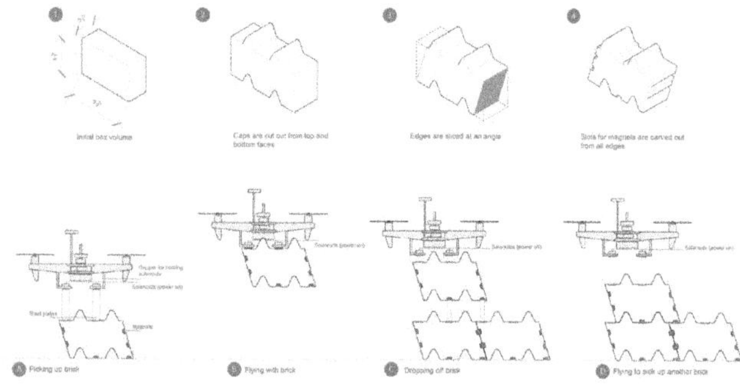

8

9

8 Design development of drone-compatible building components and illustration of magnetic-based drone gripping mechanism.

9 An illustration of the long-term vision for a distributed robotically assisted construction framework.

payload. A GPS/compass module is used to maintain real-time positioning in open spaces. To improve accuracy in real-time localization, this positioning system is combined with motion capture markers. A Pixhawk flight controller connected to an onboard radio transmitter for the flight control enables manual override through a handheld radio remote controller unit. In addition to the flight controller, a Raspberry Pi 4 board is used to relay high-level flight control commands between the RL algorithm running on a remote computer and the Pixhawk board controller via the Wi-Fi network. To monitor real-time flight data, a radio telemetry device connected to the Pixhawk controller collects and relays flight data to a ground-based computer. In addition, the drone is equipped with an underside custom arm to accurately pick up, transport, and release blocks. The arm is designed for holding solenoid electromagnet modules for picking blocks. Two electromagnets are attached to the two ends of the custom arm.

Custom-designed bricks have been designed and fabricated for use in this experiment. Each brick is equipped with a 1 × 1 in steel plate on its pickup point. A solenoid actuator controls the behavior of electromagnets on the arm to attract and release the steel plate on the designated pick and place points, respectively. In order to account for discrepancies between the drones' simulated location and their real location during the operation, these customized bricks have slanted faces, pointed caps, and embedded magnets on all faces so that the blocks can self-align into position when placed (Fig. 8).

DISCUSSION

Overview of Contributions

This paper presented a framework based on reinforcement learning techniques under a "centralized learning, decentralized execution" paradigm that enables a more flexible and generalizable approach to robotically assisted construction. We developed and trained a reinforcement algorithm for semiautonomous path planning for UAVs in dynamic environments, showing through simulations the successful, collision-free execution of two construction activities: bricklaying and spray-coating. Improving on previous literature, the RL model serving as the framework's back-end proved to be successful with a variable number of drones, and without prior knowledge of the obstacles in the environment. In addition to these simulations, we discussed progress towards a hardware prototype for testing the framework in practice.

Limitations and Next Steps

While the real-world testing of the framework has been delayed by the pandemic, we expect to deploy it and document results in the spring of 2021. While the RL algorithm proved to be successful in the simulations, we are not expecting to find one universal trained model to address all construction scenarios and environments. Instead, our framework entails the need to develop a growing library of RL models accounting for the specific characteristics of different construction environments and tasks. This will require close studies of such environments. At a technical level, we intend to optimize the framework for on-the-edge computing using the Raspberry Pi board in order to generate high-level flight commands onboard. In addition, we intend to replace the temporary motion capture-based localization method with lidar scanners to accurately scan the environment and detect peer drones, obstacles, and human agents in real time.

While our interest is in creating systems that support "real" activities on site, the tasks we accomplished in this paper are quite simple compared to those taking place on actual construction sites. However, we believe that our RL framework provides the flexibility to incorporate a greater

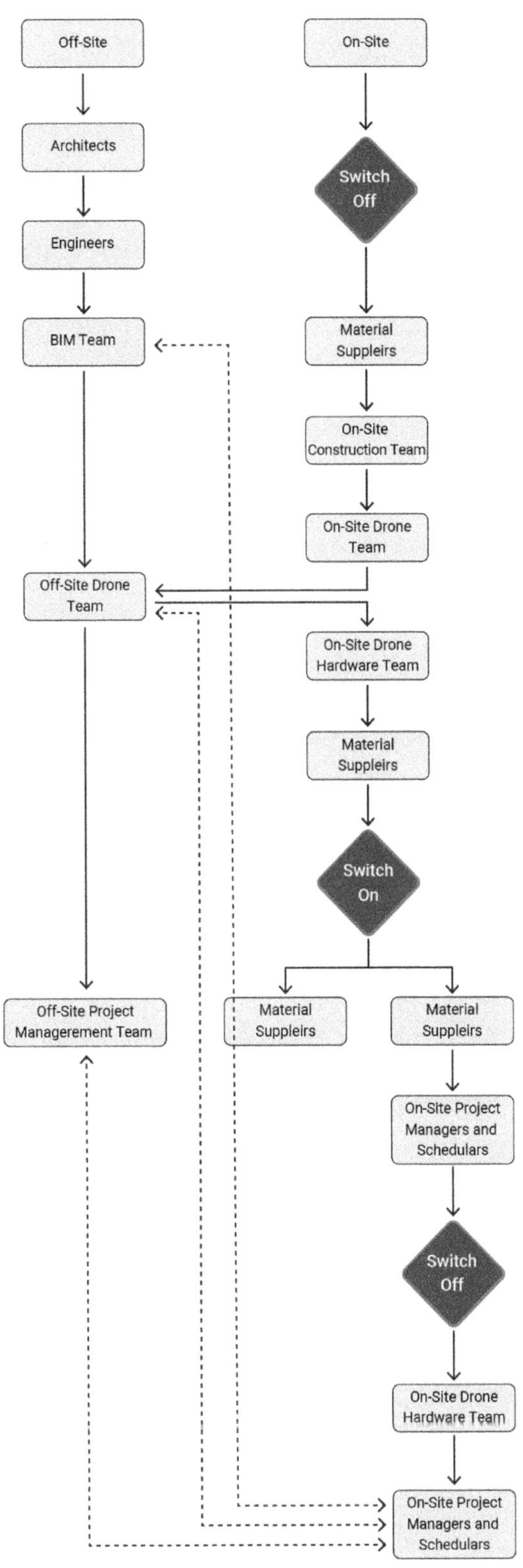

10

10 Long-term construction workflow pipeline showing different human roles involved and the process for implementing an advanced future framework in an unstructured environment.

degree of complexity, including changing environmental conditions, human workers, machinery, and scaffolding. Further work needs to be done to be able to test for these contingencies.

As discussed before, the limited payload capacity of drones limits their applicability to actual construction scenarios. This could be addressed by including new macro actions that entail the collaboration of multiple drones in carrying a single component. While this scenario is interesting, our framework is flexible, and we are currently in the process of adapting it to other types of robots and autonomous vehicles with greater carrying capacity.

Human-Robot Ecosystems of Construction: A Broader Vision for the Future

The framework described in this paper contributes to current efforts towards robotically assisted construction, and towards a longer-term vision of human-machine construction ecosystems where human builders are supported by semiautonomous technologies. The pipeline diagram in Figure 10 conceptualizes such a vision by speculating on how roles might be redistributed across human experts and nonhuman actors in a design and construction context. Off-site teams consisting of component manufacturers, architects, engineers, and the BIM team—all of whom collectively design and model the structure to be built—might be joined by simulation and robotics experts analyzing the building model and using it to identify and define tasks apt for robotic execution. On-site teams including conventional construction roles such as construction laborers, project supervisors, and managers, material suppliers, as well as a dedicated team of drone hardware experts, might be joined by robotically assisted construction experts in charge of programming, supervising, and maintaining robotic systems on site. Shaping these emergent roles and contributing to hybrid and humane construction ecosystems is an important task for researchers at the intersection of architecture and computing today.

ACKNOWLEDGMENTS

The authors would like to thank Yanwen Dong, Michael Hasey, and Willa Yang from the MS Computational Design program at CMU School of Architecture who contributed to this project. We would also like to express our gratitude towards the Design Fabrication Lab (DFab) at the School of Architecture at Carnegie Mellon University for their assistance with fabrication.

REFERENCES

Ammar, Mirjan. 2016. "Aerial Construction: Robotic Fabrication of Tensile Structures with Flying Machines." PhD dissertation, ETH Zurich.

Augugliaro, Federico, Sergei Lupashin, Michael Hamer, Cason Male, Markus Hehn, Mark W. Mueller, Jan Sebastian Willmann, et al. 2014. "The Flight Assembled Architecture Installation: Cooperative Construction with Flying Machines." *IEEE Control Systems Magazine* 34 (4): 46–64.

Chaltiel, Stephanie, Maite Bravo, Sebastien Goessens, Pierre Latteur, Masoumeh Mansouri, and Ismail Ahmad. 2018. "Dry and Liquid Clay Mix Drone Spraying for Bioshotcrete." In *Creativity in Structural Design [Proceedings of the IASS Symposium 2018]*, Boston, MA, 16–20 July 2018, edited by Caitlin Mueller and Sigrid Adriaenssens, 1–8. International Association for Shell and Spatial Structures (IASS).

Chaltiel, Stephanie, Maite Bravo, and Ibrahim Abdullah. 2018. "Adaptive Strategies for Mud Shell Robotic Fabrication." *International Journal of Environmental Science & Sustainable Development* 3 (2): 64–74.

Computational Design Lab. 2020. "Reinforcement Learning to Support Scalable Multi-Drone Construction in Dynamic Env. Simulation." https://youtu.be/oe1T1j5nVqM.

Dackiw, Jean-Nicolas, Andrzej Foltman, Soroush Garivani, Keith Kaseman, and Aldo Sollazzo. 2019. "Cyber-Physical UAV Navigation and Operation 1 Waypoint Navigation Interface for Drones through Augmented Reality." In *ACADIA 19: Ubiquity and Autonomy [Proceedings of the 39th Annual Conference of the Association for Computer Aided Design in Architecture (ACADIA)]*, Austin, TX, 21–26 October 2019, edited by K. Bieg, D. Briscoe, and C. Odom, 360–367. CUMINCAD.

Fang, Zhihao. 2020. "Towards Multi-Drone Autonomous Construction via Deep Reinforcement Learning." Master's thesis. Carnegie Mellon University.

Felbrich, Benjamin, Nikolas Frueh, Marshall Prado, Saman Saffarian, James Solly, Lauren Vasey, Jan Knippers, and Achim Menges. 2017. "Multi-Machine Fabrication: An Integrative Design Process Utilising an Autonomous UAV and Industrial Robots for the Fabrication of Long Span Composite Structures." In *ACADIA 2017: Disciplines and Disruption [Proceedings of the 37th Annual Conference of the Association for Computer Aided Design in Architecture (ACADIA)]*, Cambridge, MA, 2–4 November 2017, edited by T. Nagakura, S. Tibbits, M. Ibañez, and C. Mueller, 248–259. CUMINCAD.

Goessens, Sébastien, Caitlin Mueller, and Pierre Latteur. 2018. "Feasibility Study for Drone-Based Masonry Construction of Real-Scale Structures." *Automation in Construction* 94: 458–480.

Hunt, Graham, Faidon Mitzalis, Talib Alhinai, Paul A. Hooper, and Mirko Kovac. 2014. "3D Printing with Flying Robots." In *2014 IEEE International Conference on Robotics and Automation (ICRA)*, Hong Kong, China, 31 May–7 June 2014, 4493–4499. IEEE.

Intel. n.d. "Intel Drone Light Show Fact Sheet." Accessed November 10, 2020. https://www.intel.com/content/www/us/en/technology-innovation/drone-light-show-fact-sheet.html.

Lindsey, Quentin, Daniel Mellinger, and Vijay Kumar. 2011. "Construction of Cubic Structures with Quadrotor Teams." In *Proceedings of Robotics: Science and Systems (RSS). Vol. VII.* Cambridge, MA: MIT Press.

Long, Pinxin, Tingxiang Fan, Xinyi Liao, Wenxi Liu, Hao Zhang, and Jia Pan. 2018. "Towards Optimally Decentralized Multi-Robot Collision Avoidance via Deep Reinforcement Learning." ArXiv:1709.10082 [Cs], May. http://arxiv.org/abs/1709.10082.

Lowe, Ryan, Yi I. Wu, Aviv Tamar, Jean Harb, Pieter Abbeel, and Igor Mordatch. 2017. "Multi-Agent Actor-Critic for Mixed Cooperative-Competitive Environments." *Advances in Neural Information Processing Systems* 30: 6379–6390.

Lucieer, Arko, Darren Turner, Diana H. King, and Sharon A. Robinson. 2014. "Using an Unmanned Aerial Vehicle (UAV) to Capture Micro-Topography of Antarctic Moss Beds." *International Journal of Applied Earth Observation and Geoinformation, Special Issue on Polar Remote Sensing* 27 (part A): 53–62. https://doi.org/10.1016/j.jag.2013.05.011.

Mademlis, Ioannis, Nikos Nikolaidis, Anastasios Tefas, Ioannis Pitas, Tilman Wagner, and Alberto Messina. 2018. "Autonomous Unmanned Aerial Vehicles Filming in Dynamic Unstructured Outdoor Environments." *IEEE Signal Processing Magazine* 36 (December): 147–153. https://doi.org/10.1109/MSP.2018.2875190.

Maes, Wouter H., and Kathy Steppe. 2019. "Perspectives for Remote Sensing with Unmanned Aerial Vehicles in Precision Agriculture." *Trends in Plant Science* 24 (2): 152–164. https://doi.org/10.1016/j.tplants.2018.11.007.

Marris, Emma. 2013. "Fly, and Bring Me Data: Unmanned Aerial Vehicles Are Poised to Take Off as Popular Tools for Scientific Research." *Nature* 498 (7453): 156–159.

Nägeli, Tobias, Lukas Meier, Alexander Domahidi, Javier Alonso-Mora, and Otmar Hilliges. 2017. "Real-Time Planning for Automated Multi-View Drone Cinematography." *ACM Transactions on Graphics* 36 (4): 132:1–132:10. https://doi.org/10.1145/3072959.3073712.

Nishar, Abdul, Steve Richards, Dan Breen, John Robertson, and Barbara Breen. 2016. "Thermal Infrared Imaging of Geothermal Environments and by an Unmanned Aerial Vehicle (UAV): A Case Study of the Wairakei – Tauhara Geothermal Field, Taupo, New Zealand." *Renewable Energy* 86 (February): 1256–1264. https://doi.org/10.1016/j.renene.2015.09.042.

Qie, H., D. Shi, T. Shen, X. Xu, Y. Li, and L. Wang. 2019. "Joint Optimization of Multi-UAV Target Assignment and Path Planning Based on Multi-Agent Reinforcement Learning." *IEEE Access* 7: 146264–146272. https://doi.org/10.1109/ACCESS.2019.2943253.

Romano, Matthew, Yuxin Chen, Owen Marshall, and Ella Atkins. 2019. "Nailed It: Autonomous Roofing with a Nailgun-Equipped Octocopter." ArXiv:1909.08162 [Cs], September. http://arxiv.org/abs/1909.08162.

Schulman, John, Filip Wolski, Prafulla Dhariwal, Alec Radford, and Oleg Klimov. 2017. "Proximal Policy Optimization Algorithms." ArXiv:1707.06347 [Cs], August. http://arxiv.org/abs/1707.06347.

Shahmoradi, Javad, Elahe Talebi, Pedram Roghanchi, Mostafa Hassanalian. 2020 "A Comprehensive Review of Applications of Drone Technology in the Mining Industry." *Drones* 4 (3): 34.

Silver, David. 2005. "Cooperative Pathfinding." *Aiide* 1: 117–122.

Wang, Ko-Hsin Cindy, and Adi Boeta. 2008. "Fast and Memory-Efficient Multi-Agent Pathfinding." In *ICAPS'08 [Proceedings of the Eighteenth International Conference on International Conference on Automated Planning and Scheduling]*, Sydney, Australia, 14–18 September 2008, edited by Jussi Rintanen, Bernhard Nebel, J. Christopher Beck, and Eric Hansen, 380–387. AAAI Press.

Wang, Ko-Hsin Cindy, and Adi Boeta. 2011. "MAPP: a Scalable Multi-Agent Path Planning Algorithm with Tractability and Completeness Guarantees." *Journal of Artificial Intelligence Research* 24 (1): 55–90. https://dl.acm.org/doi/10.5555/2208436.2208439

Wood, Dylan, Maria Yablonina, Miguel Aflalo, Jingcheng Chen, Behrooz Tahanzadeh, and Achim Menges. 2018. "Cyber Physical Macro Material as a UAV [Re]Configurable Architectural System." In *Robotic Fabrication in Architecture, Art and Design 2018. ROBARCH 2018*, edited by J. Willmann, P. Block, M. Hutter, K. Byrne, and T. Schork. Springer: Cham. https://doi.org/10.1007/978-3-319-92294-2_25.

Zhang, Chunhua, and John M. Kovacs. 2012. "The Application of Small Unmanned Aerial Systems for Precision Agriculture: A Review." *Precision Agriculture* 13 (6): 693–712. https://doi.org/10.1007/s11119-012-9274-5.

IMAGE CREDITS

Zhihao Fang is a recent graduate of Carnegie Mellon's Master's in Computational Design program.

Yuning Wu is a current PhD student in the Computational Design program, CoDe LAB, and a Master's candidate in Machine Learning at Carnegie Mellon University.

Ammar Hassonjee is a current fourth-year student at Carnegie Mellon University in the Bachelor of Architecture program also minoring in Human-Computer Interaction.

Ardavan Bidgoli is a current PhD candidate and Robotics Fellow in Carnegie Mellon's Computational Design Program, CoDe LAB.

Daniel Cardoso-Llach PhD is an Associate Professor of Computational Design at Carnegie Mellon and the track chair of the Computational Design program as well as a codirector of CoDe LAB.

Designing [with] Machines

Task- and Site-Specific Robotic Teams for in-Situ Architectural Making

Maria Yablonina
Institute for Computational Design and Construction, University of Stuttgart; Daniels Faculty of Architecture, Landscape and Design, University of Toronto

Nicolas Kubail Kalousdian
Institute for Computational Design and Construction, University of Stuttgart

Achim Menges
Institute for Computational Design and Construction, University of Stuttgart

1 Robotically fabricated filament-wound object produced by a team of task- and site-specific robots. The robotic system was developed according to the Designing [with] Machines methodology, following the design criteria defined by the site.

ABSTRACT

The aim of this research is to investigate the potential of a design and fabrication workflow that is centered around the development of task- and site-specific robotic systems for in-situ architectural making: Designing [with] Machines (D[w]M). The project proposes an alternative strategy to the established logic of design for production, in which design decisions are a function of affordances and limitations of available fabrication equipment.
D[w]M engages the designer to define their own parameter ranges for the fabrication process through simultaneous development of fabrication machines and complimentary material, and architectural systems. In addition to affording more flexibility, D[w]M offers an opportunity to develop robotic fabrication systems uniquely tailored for deployment on sites that are not suited for conventional robotic equipment.

In this paper, D[w]M workflow is outlined in the description of a task- and site-specific robotic system for additive fabrication of a tensile filament-wound object in an in-situ environment. Specifically, the presented project investigates design opportunities afforded by cooperative operation of multiple mobile single-axis robots deployed along linear structural elements of the given site. In utilizing column and beam elements as machine locomotion substrates, the system contributes them to the robotic assembly as parts of the in-situ digital fabrication machine.

INTRODUCTION

The community of researchers and practitioners in the field of computational design and digital fabrication over the past two decades has grown around two significant technological tendencies: an increasing availability of industrial robotic hardware (Gramazio, Kohler, and Willmann 2014) and rapid development of open-framework CAD software (Burry 2015; Davis and Peters 2013). The combination of the two has enabled a rich body of work focusing on investigation and discovery of novel materials, fabrication methods, methodologies, and ultimately entirely new design possibilities and design spaces (Menges 2015).

Since the early 2000s, when multiple research institutions began experimenting with industrial manufacturing equipment for architectural fabrication (Bonwetsch, Gramazio, and Kohler 2006), industrial robot arms have become an almost iconic symbol of robotics in architecture and relevant areas of research. Initially developed for performing complex repetitive motions in a manufacturing environment, the robot arm has enabled free-form movement, liberating architectural practice from traditional modes of production. In inheriting industrial machine bodies, designers have been freed to focus on more architecturally relevant questions of geometry, material, scale, and program within the design spaces afforded by the machine. However, along with its benefits, any machine brings with it constraints and limitations inherited from the manufacturing line environment for which it was initially designed.

What happens if the technologies of production are approached in the same way as custom-designed software? Can architecture-specific hardware design be included in the global design undertaking, shifting the approach of digital architecture beyond design-for-production toward the design of and with fabrication hardware? Bock and Linner (2015) outline the concept of coadaptation of construction product and robotic technology to enable efficient construction automation. Building on the notion of robot-oriented design, a coevolution of object and machine beyond the automation of conventional construction tasks, and toward alternative architectural approaches, can be considered.

While acknowledging the opportunities accessed by co-opting industrial infrastructure, this research aims to question whether the architectural research community would be better served by developing the tools and expertise to design, craft, and deploy architecture-specific robots. Designing [with] Machines proposes an expansion of the collection of available tools with task- and site-specific machines that enable venturing into new design opportunities and contexts for digital fabrication. Moreover, it outlines a design practice wherein the designer's role is shifted from a consumer of fabrication technology to an active participant in its development.

STATE OF THE ART

Task-Specificity

The history of construction robotics and automation is rich with examples of on-site task-specific machines and devices. Single-task construction robots (STCR), which originated from research initiatives of construction companies in Japan in the 1980s, today occupy a sizable niche in the conventional construction industry (Bock and Linner 2016). In contrast to the specificity of STCRs in industry, the field of research in computational design and digital fabrication has only recently begun to explore single-task robots. Research projects that deploy nongeneric robots demonstrate that the development of architecture-specific machines can introduce entirely new digital fabrication design spaces far beyond automation of conventional construction tasks. A growing number of computational design researchers have endeavored to explore custom robotic solutions, including climbing (Jokic et al. 2014; Kayser et al. 2019; Yablonina and Menges 2019b), driving (Werfel, Petersen, and Nagpal 2014), aerial (Augugliaro et al. 2014; Wood et al. 2019), and cable robots (Dierichs et al. 2019), all developed and tailored for the fabrication task. Moreover, the field of architecture-specific robots spans beyond fabrication tasks toward architectural robotics (Gross and Green 2012) wherein the machine itself is the architectural object (Kilian 2018) or part of it (Maierhofer et al. 2019), designed to respond and adapt to human input through actuation.

Site-Specificity

Moving away from typical fabrication contexts and toward robotic in-situ fabrication requires examination of the relationships between the machine and the space it occupies. Specifically, in the case of smaller mobile robots, the relationship between the environment and the machine is expressed in the locomotion strategy. Current developments in in-situ mobile construction robotics are mostly limited to generic wheeled mobile platforms operating on the floor or on the ground, carrying a manipulator for transportation, placement, and deposition of construction material (Dörfler 2018; Dritsas and Soh 2019). This locomotion method is well-suited for conventional construction scenarios where a structure is erected from the ground up. It complies with the sequence of project delivery where phases of design, bid, and construction occur once in a linear sequence. However, introducing robotic fabrication in existing built spaces offers an opportunity to leverage the features of the built environment as locomotion surfaces for the fabrication robots.

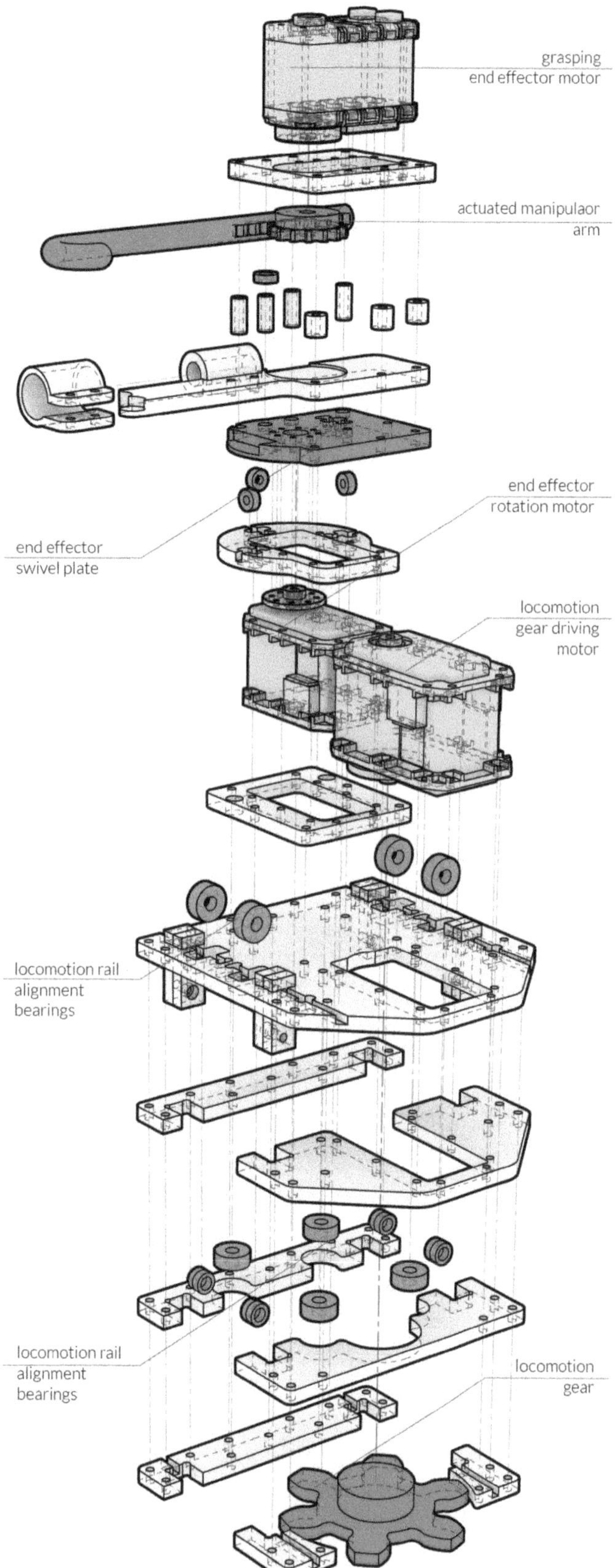

2

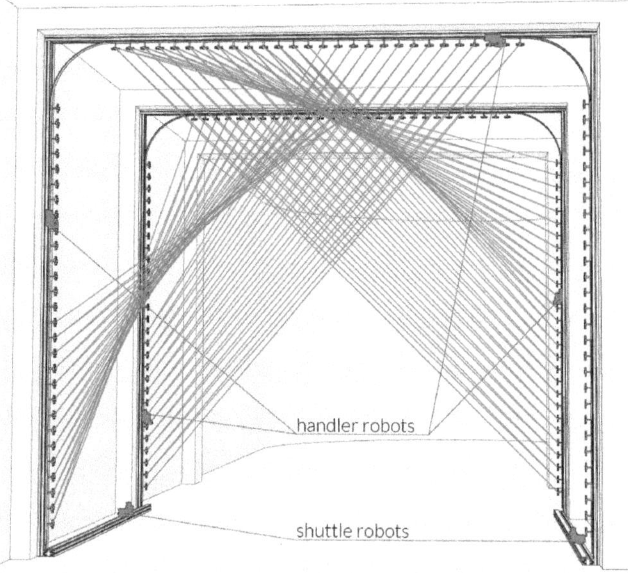

3

In the fields of building maintenance and surveying, the variety of locomotion methods is as rich as the variety of structures and elements surveyed, including examples of facade-and window-climbing machines (Elkmann et al. 2002), aerial vehicles (Daftry, Hoppe, and Bischof 2015), and pipe-climbing robots (Chattopadhyay et al. 2018). Investigation of site-specific robotic locomotion systems beyond maintenance applications toward fabrication of in-situ architectural objects allows us to explore the opportunities that existing building stock can offer as a site for new layers of digitally fabricated architectures. Locomotion along the features of an existing architectural space implies robotic workspaces that match the geometric constraints of a given site. Consequently, this provides an opportunity to actualize parts of the architectural environment as machine components, and to consider machines as extensions of the environment.

Designing [with] Machines

The presented research calls for a further investigation into architectural specificity of robotic hardware, proposing to deploy task- and site-specific robots in existing architectural environments, leveraging site features as substrates for both the fabrication machines and the resulting artefacts. The D[w]M approach in this paper is demonstrated in the description of a project that exists within the context of a larger body of work focusing on task- and site-specific robots for production of filament wound architectures in-situ in interior spaces (Yablonina and Menges 2019a). Previous work by the authors has investigated typical interior elements as substrate for the robotic fabrication process: walls and sheet materials. This project develops an in-situ system that relies on the vertical and horizontal

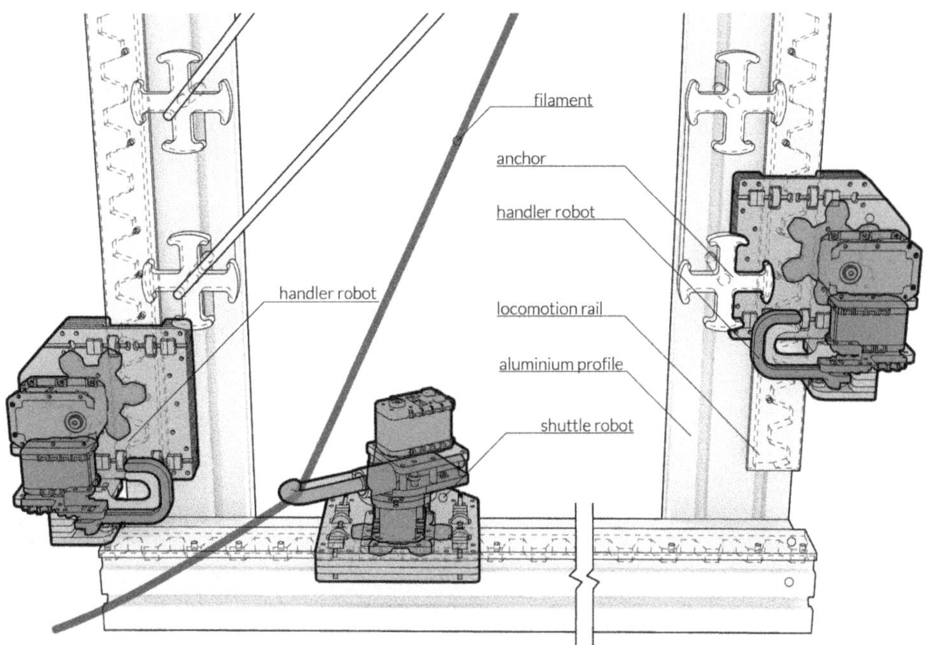

4

2 Shuttle robot assembly diagram. Shuttle and handler robot parts were custom designed and fabricated using CNC milling and 3D printing techniques. Robotic actuation was implemented using off-the-shelf motors and hardware parts.

3 In-situ robotic fabrication system: overview diagram. Custom robotic locomotion rails were prefabricated and installed in situ. Each rail connected a pair of columns and a beam spanning between them, forming a continuous robot locomotion track.

4 Overview of the robotic fabrication team. Shuttle robot deployed on one of the two floor rails connected a pair of vertical rail frames, enabling a hand-off routine and consequently a volumetric work envelope.

structural elements of the environment, forming a robotic work envelope between columns and beams (Figs. 1, 3).

METHODS

As introduced in this research, the D[w]M approach can be described as a series of interdependent relationships between the machine, the site, and the produced artefact. Throughout system development, these relationships must be considered in parallel, changes in one variable inherently impacting others. In the interest of clarity, this entanglement of variables can be classified into pairs of relationships centering on the machine as a linking parameter: machine-site, machine-material, machine-machine, and machine-designer relationships. Summary of these relationships results in the overall robotic architectural system: the global machine-object relationship.

The machine-site relationship describes hardware methods for anchoring the robotic equipment to the architectural elements on-site and actuation along them. The machine-material relationship describes hardware and software methods for material manipulation and anchoring, including the calibration of the robotic payload and work envelope to the properties of the fabrication material. The machine-machine relationship describes methods of linking multiple machine work envelopes into a global envelope of the robotic team, including hardware methods of machine-machine cooperation and software methods for multimachine system control. Finally, the machine-designer relationship describes the additive fabrication sequence and the computational design workflow for the artifact design within the machine affordances and limitations.

The following sections are structured according to the sequence of outlined relationships, serving as a narrative structure for describing various stages of technical and design development conducted throughout the project. However, this linear narrative does not reflect the integrative design process wherein the interdependent robotic, material, architectural, and computational parameters are co-designed. Insight into the workflow and the sequence of design decision loops within the D[w]M process is presented in the results section.

Overall System Description

The robotic system developed in this project comprised four machines: two material handlers, a material shuttle, and a filament tensioning device (Fig. 4). The material handlers and the material shuttle moved along rails installed on the columns, beams, and floor of the interior space. Material handlers were equipped with an end effector that enabled them to wrap a loop of filament around the anchors installed along the column and beam rails. The material shuttle robot, moving on the floor between a pair of material handlers, handed off the filament supplied by the feeder device from one side of the fabrication space to the other, allowing arrays of filament to span between the rails. The four machines received routine execution commands from a centralized server computer, based on a predefined filament winding syntax. The syntax was computed based on designer input processed by the computational design tool.

Machine-Site Relationship

The on-site structural elements served as the starting point and the design criteria for the development of the robotic

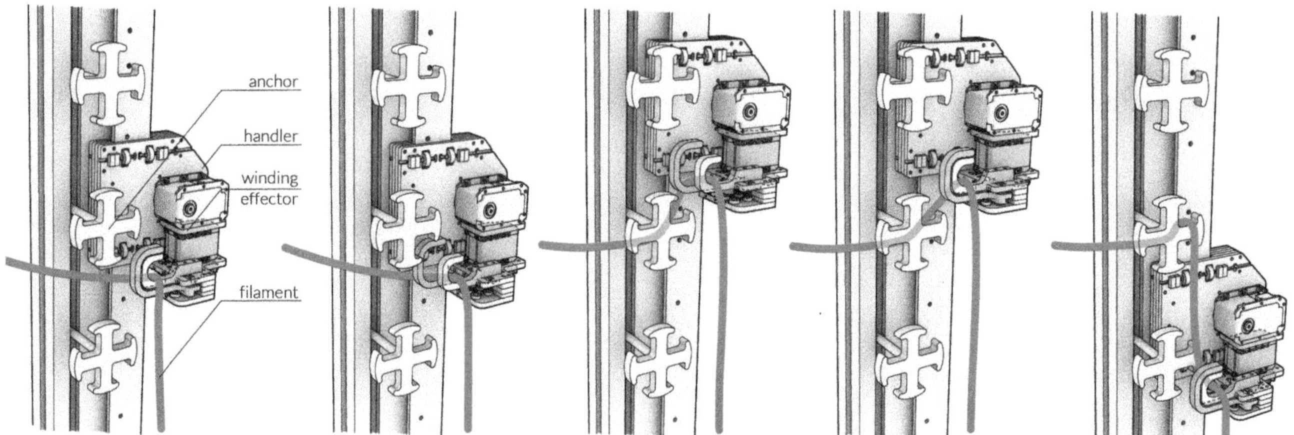

5 Handler robot anchoring routine sequence diagram. An actuated filament gripping claw allowed to entangle a loop of filament around the cap of an anchor.

actuation system. A mechanical rail-based locomotion strategy was identified as the most promising approach for the required design parameters. The system consisted of two parts: single-axis fabrication robots and guide rails installed on the columns and beams of the architectural environment. The rails served as interfaces between the on-site elements that acted as the structural frame for the system and the robots that relied on the rack-and-pinion gear for locomotion and positioning. The rails were fabricated out of compliant plastic material (HDPE) that ensured the prefabricated rail system could be fit to site, adapting to the tolerances of the built environment. A continuous rail was mounted to each pair of column and beam profiles, bridging the gaps between the vertical and horizontal sections with a circular bent element, thus creating a continuous track for the robots.

The robot body assembly was fabricated out of CNC-milled (ABS plastic sheets) and 3D printed parts (co-polyester plastic filament) (Fig. 2). The locomotion was enabled by a high torque servo motor (Dynamixel MX64) that drove the locomotion gear wheel. The assembly was completed with a set of passive wheels that clamped to the rail geometry, ensuring smooth motion and reliable attachment of the robot to the rail in both vertical and horizontal locomotion scenarios. Accuracy of robot positioning along the rail relied on the ability to control the locomotion wheel motor position. Thus, the selection of the locomotion motor was driven by the requirement for motor torque and resolution. The combination of a mechanical rack-and-pinion system and an internal closed-loop control system built into the motor control interface ensured accurate positioning of the robot along the rail. Tolerance resulted from on-site installation imprecisions, which were a constant parameter and thus did not accumulate over time. Once the robotic system was installed and calibrated to the rail, the tolerances remained within the acceptable range of 4mm.

Machine-Material Relationship

The machine-material relationship was expressed in the handling mechanisms and routines, developed in accordance with the following fabrication criteria: the robot's ability to grasp and move a loop of filament, its ability to attach filament to anchors, and the ability of the system to control the filament tension throughout the fabrication process. The two end effector mechanisms on the handler and the shuttle robots were designed to grasp, manipulate, anchor, and hand off the material. The material feeder device was developed to hold the material supply spool and control the filament tension throughout the fabrication process.

The grasping mechanisms on both the handler and the shuttle robots consisted of actuated hook arm elements that could carry the filament loop. The shuttle robot end effector assembly contained two actuators: one that afforded rotation of the effector to interact with both material handlers on either side of the shuttle robot's track, and one linear actuator that extended the hook arm to grasp, release, and hand off the filament loop (Fig. 6). The end effector assembly on the handler robot contained a single actuator that enabled the anchoring routine (Fig. 5).

Machine-Machine Relationship

The fabrication process relied on the machines' ability to perform tasks cooperatively. Overlapping work envelopes of the handler and the shuttle robots formed the fabrication system's work envelope, enabled by local cooperative mechanisms and global routine sequencing. Local cooperative routines described interactions between the handler and the shuttle robots at their work envelope boundaries. The cooperative hand-off routine between the handler and the shuttle robots relied on a sequence of subroutines performed by both robots' filament manipulation effectors wherein a loop of filament was transferred from one robot to the other. The global routine sequencing described the order of operations performed by all the machines within the robotic team to achieve a successful fabrication process.

Enabled by the locomotion, anchoring, hand-off, and active tensioning routines, the cooperative robotic fabrication sequence was established. One instance of the sequence, described by a cycle of robotic operations necessary to span a single strand of filament between two anchors, consisted of six steps. First, the handler robot carrying a loop of material navigated to an anchor and performed the anchoring routine. Next, it navigated back down to the hand-off location and passed the loop to the shuttle robot, which traversed to the other side of the fabrication space and handed the material loop to the second handler robot. The same six operations were then repeated, starting with the second handler robot. During the six steps, the feeder device controlled the filament tension accordingly.

Each of the fabrication robots developed for this case study was inherently constrained to a narrow work envelope defined by the single-axis locomotion system. However, when combined into a cooperative multimachine team, the work envelopes were linked to form a three-dimensional work envelope of the overall robotic fabrication system and the resulting design space. A single material handler robot traversing along a bent column-beam rail offered a triangle of possible material placement solutions defined by the rail geometry. Two handlers working cooperatively with the shuttle robot, as enabled by the hand-off routine, form a solution space described by a triangular prism defined by the two rails. Once two robotic teams are working in parallel within the fabrication space, the solution space of the overall system is described by two combined prisms, covering approximately 75% of the overall fabrication space volume afforded by the site (Fig. 7).

Machine-Designer

The robotic mechanisms, routines, and task sequences described above enable an additive fabrication process where strands of filament are sequentially deposited to form a tensile object spanning the six linear elements in the architectural space (four columns and two beams). Design of the fabricated object was developed to match the robotic system's affordances and limitations, as well as the site parameters. The fabricated object's geometry, density, and pattern were informed by designer-defined parameters of anchor placement and winding sequence. The anchor placement along the rails defined the boundary condition and the resolution of the fabricated object, while the winding syntax defined the geometry and pattern. Design workflow and a computational design tool were developed to enable design exploration following the parameter ranges defined

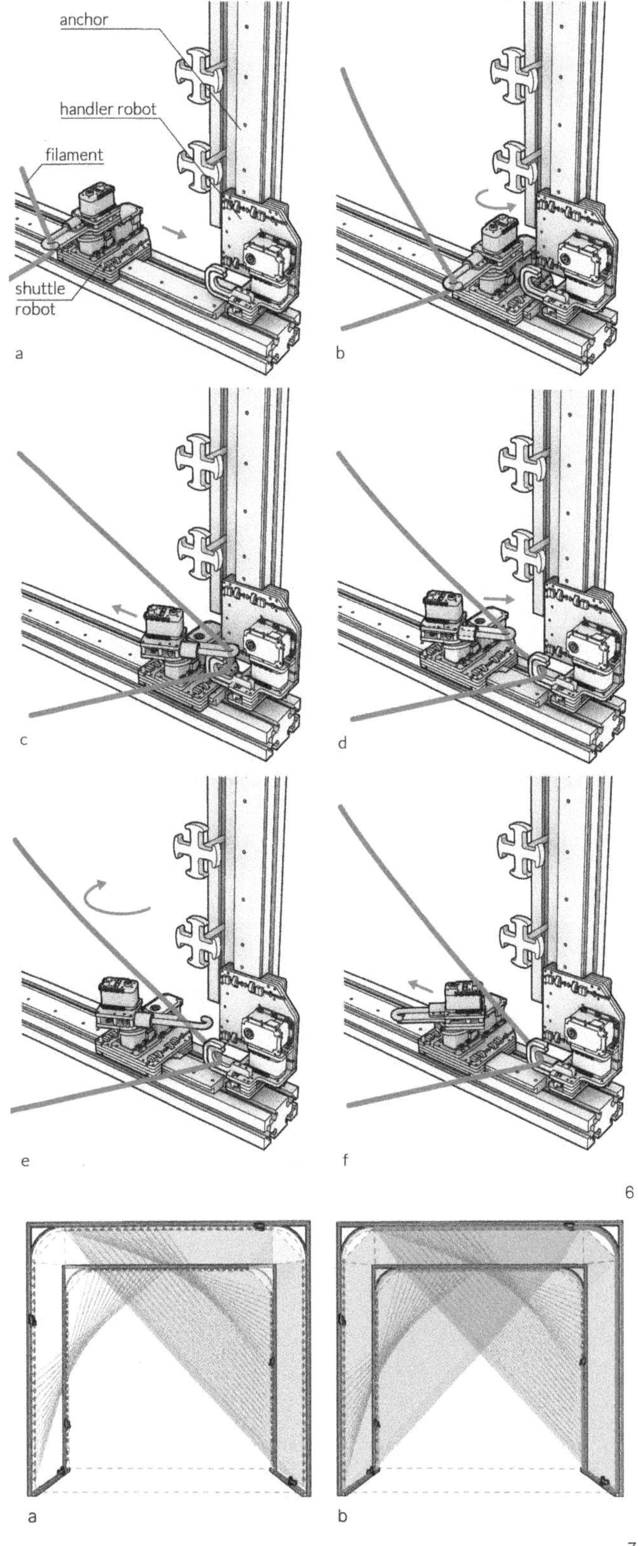

6 Shuttle to handler robot hand-off routine sequence diagram: a) shuttle robot approaches the handler robot; b) shuttle manipulation arm rotates; c) the filament wraps around the handler robot hook; d) the shuttle robot moves back on the rail, opens the grasping hook; e) the shuttle manipulation arm is rotated back, releasing the filament; f) the shuttle robot moves out of the way, and the handler robot proceeds to the anchoring routine.

7 Overlapping robotic work envelopes and the global design space: a) work envelope of a 3-robot system; b) work envelope of a 6-robot system.

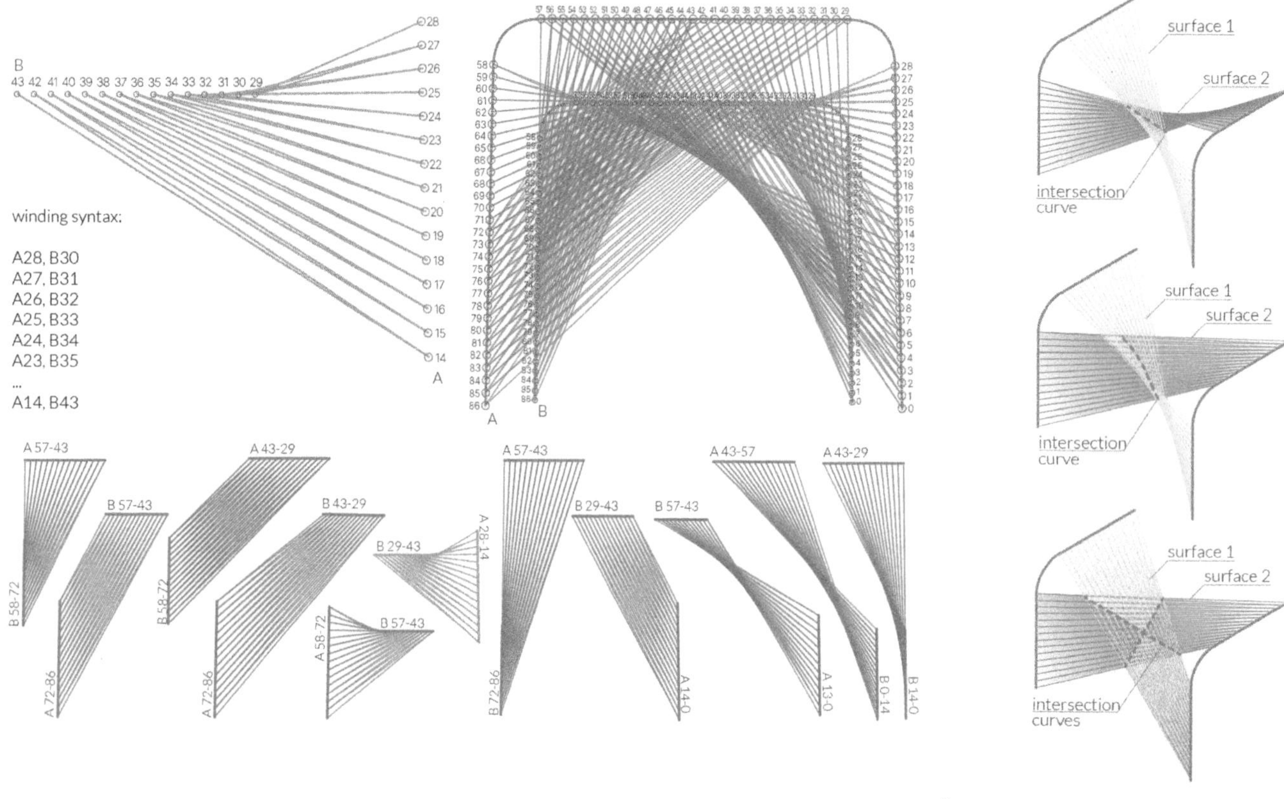

8

9

by the robotic process and the site. The development of the design workflow required identification of the global filament winding logic: how filament strands were arranged to form the geometry of the fabricated object. The global geometry consisted of arrays of nonintersecting filament strands forming layered surface-like elements (Fig. 8).

The computational design tool was developed in Rhino+ Grasshopper CAD environment (Robert McNeel & Associates 2020; Rutten 2020). It provided the designer with a workflow that produced variations of the filament winding pattern, benchmarked it against the robotic limitations, and generated the winding syntax document used for the robot control commands. The designer interacted with the tool by sequentially defining wound surface layers to be added to the design. The tool verified each input against the constraints of the robotic system and added it to the design preview if successful (Fig. 9). Once the design was finalized, the system proceeded to generate the global winding syntax in two steps: individual syntaxes for each surface element were computed, followed by a sorting process that ensured that all filament-filament intersections were accounted for (Fig. 10). The resulting syntax was manually evaluated in a model scale to ensure fabricability and to visually evaluate the design results in the physical space. The filament winding syntax could be used in reverse for the unwinding process, in the reconfiguration scenario.

RESULTS AND VALIDATION

The project concluded with the implementation of the robotic system on-site and subsequent fabrication of a tensile filament object under the authors' supervision. The object was fabricated within a robotic work envelope of 4.2 x 3.4 x 4 meters, defined by four columns and two beams on site. The object consisted of approximately 350 strands of 8 mm thick polyamide rope, spanning the anchor points installed along the rails. The overall length of the material used was approximately 1800 m. The fabricated object consisted of a series of overlapping and intersecting ruled surfaces, each described by an array of nonintersecting rope strands wound by the robots. The resulting arrangement created a range of optical effects when observed from various vantage points in the exhibition space.

Prior to the final fabrication sequence, a series of object reconfiguration tests were performed. A set of two intersecting filament surfaces were produced, unwound, and rewound in a new configuration, demonstrating that the robotic system is well-suited for applications beyond fabrication, wherein parts of the object can be iteratively removed, making space for new designs to be fabricated in their place. The ability of the fabrication system to construct and deconstruct the object opens new design spaces where the design goal is a dynamic time-based shift between multiple geometric expressions rather than a static finalized shape. However, further development of the computational

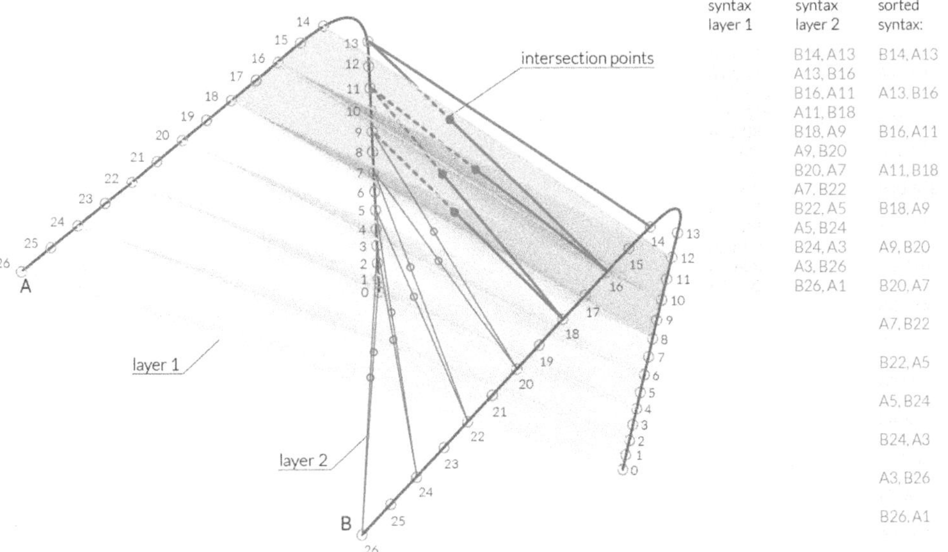

10

8 Global winding syntax diagram. The design consisted of iteratively adding layers of filament to the overall configuration. Each layer was benchmarked against robotic system constraints prior to being added to the global syntax file.

9 Surface-surface intersection constraints. The robotic system was not able to fabricate pairs of surfaces that produced multiple intersection curves. The computational design tool evaluated each surface in the design stage to ensure that only fabricable features made it to the final design and winding syntax.

10 Winding syntax sorting principle. In order to define the sequence of anchoring command executions, arrays of filament surfaces were sorted based on the intersection point sequence.

design tool and robotic control system is necessary to implement the scenario at a full scale. In its current state, the reconfigured parts of the object and the necessary robotic routines were generated manually, by reversing the winding syntax and redesigning the areas where the parts were removed.

Technical Validation

Regarding the technical development of the robotic and the architectural aspects of the presented system, the following features were successfully implemented and evaluated: site-specific robotic system, robotic localization and control system, task-specific material manipulation and anchoring, cooperative multi-robot routines, and object design methodology completed with a computational design tool.

Further development of the following technical aspects of the system are necessary for successful implementation in a nonsupervised fully autonomous operation mode: power supply, filament management and tensioning, proximity sensing, and design tool. The fabrication robots were powered via a cable suspended from the robot to the power source on the ground. During robotic locomotion along the horizontal beams, the power cable spanned the fabrication space, significantly impacting aesthetics and visitor safety. Potentially, a rail-integrated power line would be a cleaner solution. The filament tensioning device developed for this project lacked necessary tension-sensing resolution, requiring the filament to be supplied manually during the demonstrator object fabrication process. Further development of the tensioner device and the routines for switching between multiple filament bobbins are essential for a fully autonomous system operation. To implement the system in a reconfiguration scenario, an additional network of sensors needs to be implemented to inform reconfiguration choreography and ensure visitor safety. Moreover, a reconfiguration scenario would require significant rethinking of the computational design tool. In its current state the design tool is tailored for the design of objects rather than sequences of multiple configurations. Thus, further development of time-based interaction and geometry manipulation is necessary at the artifact design stage.

Designing [with] Machines Methodology Validation

The robotic system and the fabricated demonstrator object outline the affordances of the D[w]M methodology. Co-design and co-development of a robotic system and the material manipulation fabrication strategy allowed leveraging of the site properties and fabrication of a large-scale object directly in situ. Moreover, it offered an opportunity to consider this system beyond fabrication toward possible reconfigurable architecture applications.

The D[w]M methodology entails approaching a design task in an integrative manner, wherein affordances and limitations of robotic systems are considered in parallel with the design decisions. In this project, a choice of locomotion motor torque impacts the footprint and the geometry of the robot's body; in turn, the robot footprint defines the minimal distance between two filament anchors; this spacing limits filament density of the fabricated object and, as a result, defines the thickness and weight of the material, thus looping back to establishing the minimum requirements for the motor torque (Fig. 11). The D[w]M method consolidates multiples of closed and linked design decision loops like the one described. To be clear, some of the technical design parameters are more rigid than others (a motor can only be so strong). However, a workflow wherein technical and design decisions propagate

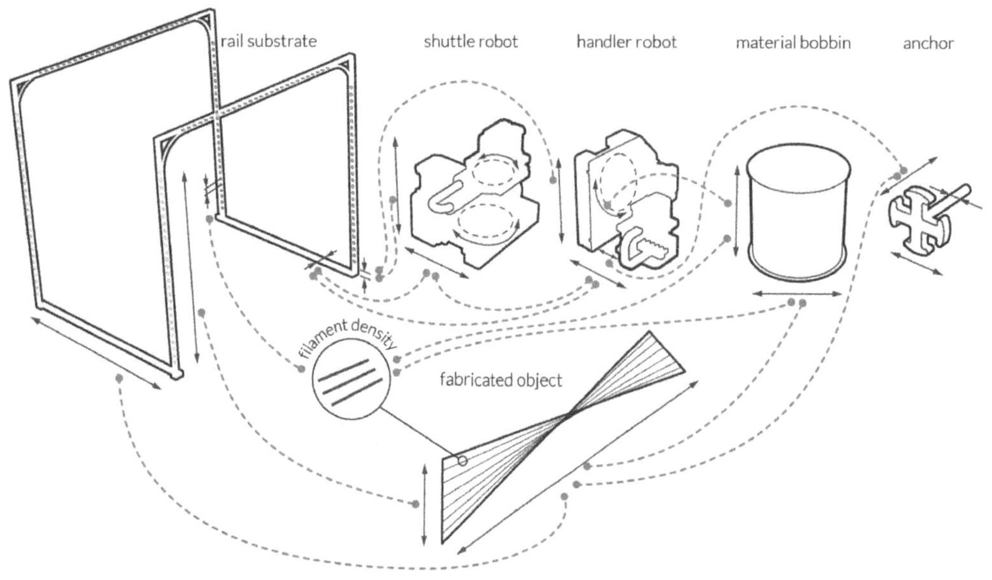

11 Design decision propagation diagram. Throughout the project development, hardware and software design and prototyping were conducted in relationship to the initial design criteria and the site parameters. As the robotic system development progressed and hard limitations were discovered, the design criteria and the fabrication logic were adjusted accordingly. Thus, the robotic system, the material system, and the design space of the fabricated object co-evolved throughout the development.

across the traditional disciplinary domain boundaries of the design process offers the flexibility of soft parameter ranges that can be adjusted at any point within the loop. At its current stage of development, Designing [with] Machines requires manual tracing of the parameters and design decision propagation. Future development of robust computational workflows for interdependent parameter linking and adjustment throughout the process is necessary to achieve the efficient implementation of the methodology.

CONCLUSION

Designing [with] Machines lays the foundation for further development of design practices, wherein novel design spaces can begin to emerge from the deliberate entanglement of robotic, structural, programmatic, and aesthetic variables. Moreover, it frames a conversation on the role of the designer in the development of robotic fabrication technologies. Designing [with] Machines is not implying that every designer become a robot builder, or that every design school get rid of their robot arm in favor of custom robotic systems. It suggests making space for task- and site-specificity in the arsenal of digital fabrication tools and in design practices.

This work proposes that we reconsider our roles as consumers of technologies and challenge our acceptance of having to work around and adapt to robotic hardware, software, and control and integration protocols made available by the robot manufacturing and distributing companies. Designing [with] Machines allows us to speculate on future interdisciplinary practices in which the designer is an active participant in the advancement of robotic technologies relevant to the design practice. Accepting such revised roles would allow for building new machine-artefact, machine-environment, and machine-designer relationships, beyond exclusively focusing on the objects a given machine can produce.

REFERENCES

Augugliaro, Frederico, Sergei Lupashin, Michael Hamer, Cason Male, Markus Hehn, Mark W. Mueller, Jan Willmann, Fabio Gramazio, Matthias Kohler, and Raffaello D'Andrea. 2014. "The Flight Assembled Architecture Installation: Cooperative Construction with Flying Machines." *IEEE Control Systems* 34 (4): 46–64.

Bock, Thomas, and Thomas Linner. 2015. *Robot-Oriented Design: Design and Management Tools for the Deployment of Automation and Robotics in Construction*. Cambridge: Cambridge University Press.

Bock, Thomas, and Thomas Linner. 2016. *Construction Robots: Elementary Technologies and Single-Task Construction Robots*. Cambridge: Cambridge University Press.

Bonwetsch, Tobias, Fabio Gramazio, and Matthias Kohler. 2006. "The Informed Wall: Applying Additive Digital Fabrication Techniques on Architecture." In *ACADIA 06: Synthetic Landscapes, [Proceedings of the 25th Annual Conference of the Association for Computer Aided Design in Architecture (ACADIA)]*, Louisville, KY, 12–15 October 2006, edited by G. Luhan, P. Anzalone, M. Cabrinha, and C. Clarke, 489–495. CUMINCAD.

Burry, Mark, ed. 2015. "Scripting Cultures." In *Scripting Cultures*, 8–12. Hoboken, NJ: John Wiley & Sons, Inc.

Chattopadhyay, Parimal, Shivani Ghoshal, Abhijit Majumder, Harihar Dikshit, and A. Majumder. 2018. "Locomotion Methods of Pipe Climbing Robots: A Review." *Journal of Engineering Science and Technology Review* 11 (4): 154–165.

Daftry, Shreyansh, Christof Hoppe, and Horst Bischof. 2015. "Building with Drones: Accurate 3D Facade Reconstruction Using MAVs." In *2015 IEEE International Conference on Robotics and Automation (ICRA)*, 3487–3494. Seattle, WA: IEEE.

Davis, Daniel, and Brady Peters. 2013. "Design Ecosystems: Customising the Architectural Design Environment with Software Plug-Ins." *Architectural Design* 83 (2): 124–131.

Dierichs, Karola, Ondřej Kyjánek, Martin Loučka, and Achim Menges. 2019. "Construction Robotics for Designed Granular Materials: In Situ Construction with Designed Granular Materials at Full Architectural Scale Using a Cable-Driven Parallel Robot." *Construction Robotics* 3 (1): 41–52.

Dörfler, Kathrin. 2018. "Strategies for Robotic in Situ Fabrication." PhD dissertation, Zurich, Switzerland: ETH.

Dritsas, Stylianos, and Gim Song Soh. 2019. "Building Robotics Design for Construction: Design Considerations and Principles for Mobile Systems." *Construction Robotics* 3 (1–4): 1–10.

Elkmann, N., T. Felsch, M. Sack, J. Saenz, and J. Hortig. 2002. "Innovative Service Robot Systems for Facade Cleaning of Difficult-to-Access Areas." In *IEEE/RSJ International Conference on Intelligent Robots and System* 1:756–762. Lausanne, Switzerland: IEEE.

Gramazio, Fabio, Matthias Kohler, and Jan Willmann, eds. 2014. *The Robotic Touch: How Robots Change Architecture*. Zurich: Park Books.

Gross, Mark D., and Keith Evan Green. 2012. "Architectural Robotics, Inevitably." In *Interactions* 19: 28.

Jokic, Sasa, Petr Novikov, Shihui Jin, Stuart Maggs, Cristina Nan, and Dori Sadan. 2014. "Small Robots Printing Big Structures. http://robots.iaac.net/.

Kayser, Markus, Levi Cai, Christoph Bader, Sara Falcone, Nassia Inglessis, Barrak Darweesh, João Costa, and Neri Oxman. 2019. "Fiberbots: Design and Digital Fabrication of Tubular Structures Using Robot Swarms." In *Robotic Fabrication in Architecture, Art and Design 2018*, edited by J. Willmann, P. Block, M. Hutter, K. Byrne, and T. Schork, 285–296. Cham: Springer.

Kilian, Axel. 2018. "The Flexing Room Architectural Robot: An Actuated Active Bending Robotic Structure Using Human Feedback." In *ACADIA 2018: Recalibration: On Imprecision and Infidelity [Proceedings of the 38th Annual Conference of the Association for Computer Aided Design in Architecture (ACADIA)]*, Mexico City, Mexico, 18–20 October 2018, edited by P. Anzalone, M. del Signore, and A. J. Wit, 232–241. CUMINCAD.

Maierhofer, Mathias, Valentina Soana, Maria Yablonina, Seichi Suzuki, Axel Koerner, Jan Knippers, and Achim Menges. 2019. "Self-Choreographing Network: Towards Cyber-Physical Design and Operation Processes of Adaptive and Interactive Bending-Active Systems." In *ACADIA 19: Ubiquity and Autonomy [Proceedings of the 39th Annual Conference of the Association for Computer Aided Design in Architecture (ACADIA)]*, Austin, TX, 21–26 October 2019, edited by K. Bieg, D. Briscoe, and C. Odom, 654–663. CUMINCAD.

Menges, Achim. 2015. *Material Synthesis: Fusing the Physical and the Computational: Architectural Design Profile 237*. London: Wiley.

Robert McNeel & Associates. 2020. *Rhinoceros*. V.6.0. Robert McNeel & Associates. PC.

Rutten, David. 2020. *Grasshopper*. V.1.0.0007. Robert McNeel & Associates. PC.

Werfel, J., K. Petersen, and R. Nagpal. 2014. "Designing Collective Behavior in a Termite-Inspired Robot Construction Team." *Science* 343 (6172): 754–758.

Wood, Dylan, Maria Yablonina, Miguel Aflalo, Jingcheng Chen, Behrooz Tahanzadeh, and Achim Menges. 2019. "Cyber Physical Macro Material as a UAV [Re]Configurable Architectural System." In *Robotic Fabrication in Architecture, Art and Design 2018*, edited by J. Willmann, P. Block, M. Hutter, K. Byrne, and T. Schork, 320–335. Cham: Springer.

Yablonina, Maria, and Achim Menges. 2019a. "Towards the Development of Fabrication Machine Species for Filament Materials." In *Robotic Fabrication in Architecture, Art and Design 2018*, edited by J. Willmann, P. Block, M. Hutter, K. Byrne, and T. Schork, 152–166. Cham: Springer.

Yablonina, Maria, and Achim Menges. 2019b. "Distributed Fabrication: Cooperative Making with Larger Groups of Smaller Machines." *Architectural Design* 89 (2): 62–69.

IMAGE CREDITS

All drawings and images by the authors.

Maria Yablonina is an Assistant Professor at the Daniels Faculty of Architecture, Landscape, and Design, and the Robotics Institute at the University of Toronto. Her research focuses on the development of custom robotic solutions in architecture and art.

Nicolas Kubail Kalousdian is a PhD candidate and a Research Associate at the Institute for Computational Design and Construction at the University of Stuttgart.

Achim Menges is a full Professor at the University of Stuttgart, where he is the founding director of the Institute for Computational Design and Construction (ICD) and the director of the Cluster of Excellence Integrative Computational Design and Construction for Architecture (IntCDC).

ELAbot

Cyber-Physical Design and Elastic Behavior of a Bending Active Textile Hybrid Robotic Structure

Valentina Soana
Autonomous Manufacturing Lab, University College London

Harvey Stedman
Autonomous Manufacturing Lab, University College London

Durgesh Darekar
Autonomous Manufacturing Lab, University College London

Vijay M. Pawar
Autonomous Manufacturing Lab, University College London

Robert Stuart-Smith
Autonomous Manufacturing Lab, University College London
University of Pennsylvania

1 ELAbot self-forming and achieving multiple states of equilibrium.

ABSTRACT

This paper presents the design, control system, and elastic behavior of ELAbot: a robotic bending active textile hybrid (BATH) structure that can self-form and transform. In BATH structures, equilibrium emerges from interaction between tensile (form active) and elastically bent (bending active) elements (Ahlquist and Menges 2013; Lienhard et al. 2012). The integration of a BATH structure with a robotic actuation system that controls global deformations enables the structure to self-deploy and achieve multiple three-dimensional states. Continuous elastic material actuation is embedded within an adaptive cyber-physical network, creating a novel robotic architectural system capable of behaving autonomously.

State-of-the-art BATH research demonstrates their structural efficiency, aesthetic qualities, and potential for use in innovative architectural structures (Suzuki and Knippers 2018). Due to the lack of appropriate motor-control strategies that exert dynamic loading deformations safely over time, research in this field has focused predominantly on static structures. Given the complexity of controlling the material behavior of nonlinear kinetic elastic systems at an architectural scale, this research focuses on the development of a cyber-physical design framework where physical elastic behavior is integrated into a computational design process, allowing the control of large deformations. This enables the system to respond to conditions that could be difficult to predict in advance and to adapt to multiple circumstances. Within this framework, control values are computed through continuous negotiation between exteroceptive and interoceptive information, and user/designer interaction.

INTRODUCTION

This paper presents the development of ELAbot: a robotic bending active textile hybrid (BATH) structure that can self-form and transform through continuous elastic material actuation. ELAbot achieves multiple states of equilibrium through the integration of a robotic actuation system that controls the global deformation of the BATH structure, causing large elastic changes of state (Fig. 1). Continuous elastic material actuation is embedded within an adaptive cyber-physical network, creating a novel robotic architectural system capable of behaving autonomously through a material machine-human negotiation (Fig. 2). This research focuses on the design and operation methods used to develop an elastic robotic system at architectural scale. It explores the role of robotics in architecture beyond the use of robots as construction tools.

Over the last 20 years, advancements in computational design processes and in the implementation of robotic solutions in architecture have facilitated not only process optimization but also the design, fabrication, and assembly of novel systems. The traditional separation between design and physical space, however, remains deeply rooted. Design usually takes place in the digital space and construction in the physical space. This separation privileges process simplicity and prevents the exploration of material dynamic behaviors as design drivers. Form is generally imposed on materials, which need to adapt to design intentions. As Buckminster Fuller and Frei Otto anticipated, engineers and architects are increasingly looking at formation processes through material and force—for structures that could be created with the minimum amount of material (Meissner and Möller 2017, 15).

Today, this is facilitated by technological advancements in simulation, where the integration of material behaviors into computational design processes enables physical material and structural parameters to act as active design generators (Menges 2015, 32). New opportunities are emerging from cyber-physical systems in which sensor feedback and robotic control can be embedded in real time into computational processes. This new paradigm of computational construction extends the design phase to the physical domain (Menges 2015, 29). Cyber-physical systems can continuously generate, evaluate, and update control values, enabling the system to plan for conditions that could be difficult to predict in advance—and to respond to any unexpected changes in circumstances: This approach allows actual material behaviors to be used as design parameters in physical space and in real time, which is particularly beneficial for the use of nonlinear elastic systems.

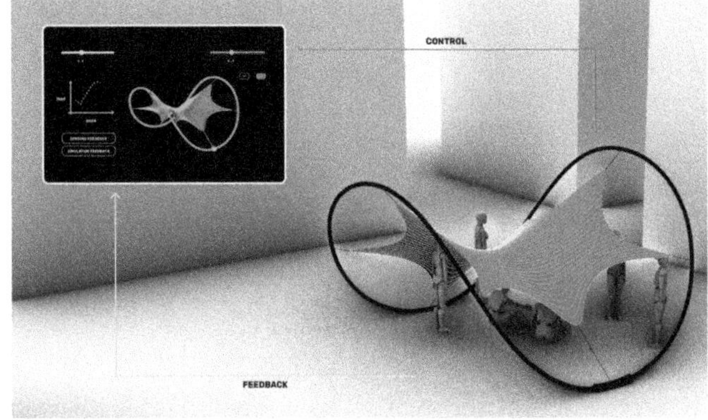

2 ELAbot cyber-physical feedback system. 2

The distinction between simulated material behavior and actual material behavior is relevant here, because simulations only approximate reality and mechanical accuracy is computationally expensive. In addition, simulation environments cannot consider all the physical conditions acting on the system at a specific moment in time, which can be subject to unexpected internal and external dynamics. Cyber-physical robotic research in architecture is, however, predominantly focused on design-to-construction workflows, reinforcing the dominant paradigm of digital-physical separation. This might be explained by the assumption that architectural structures are designed for one final state and that, once built, the design cannot be changed. However architectural systems exist within dynamic environments. Embedding robotic operations in the built environment enables novel architectural models, whereby multiple configurations can be achieved through cyber-physical negotiation between human and nonhuman agents (Bier 2018, 98).

When developing systems that can respond to different conditions, material adaptivity is a central concern. Due to their capacity to perform reversible elastic deformation, compliant materials are intrinsically adaptive (Lienhard 2014). They can respond to changes in conditions through large deformations, giving them significant kinetic potential. Lightweight adaptive structures are made of compliant systems integrated with actuators that trigger multiple states (Sobek et al. 2006).

Motivation

The creation of adaptive environments that could change state in response to different criteria has been a design ambition for over 50 years. Visions from the 1960s can now be revisited given recent advancements in autonomous systems. Beyond this opportunity, this research is driven by the need to address current challenges facing the built environment that require systems to respond to environmental changes, minimize material waste, and consider public participation, responding to multiple human conditions.

Intelligent adaptive structures can be designed through the development of lightweight elastic robotic systems. In these structures, material resources can be minimized as large global changes of state can be achieved through the strategic placement of robotic actuators that leverage material behavior, without the need for complex mechanical systems. Performative potential is enhanced by these materials' ability to achieve multiple double curvature geometries, starting from simple, lightweight planar elements.

ELAbot is part of an ongoing research agenda that seeks to establish a design approach for the assembly and control of robotic elastic structures that operate at architectural scale. The research extends the previous project "Self-Choreographing Network" developed at the University of Stuttgart (Maierhofer et al. 2018). "Self-Choreographing Network" was a room-scale spatial architectural robot comprising a network of linear elastic rods connected by robotic joints capable of implicitly changing the topology to trigger significant deformations, while being monitored by a digital twin that could make the system aware of its own state. ELAbot expands the design potential of this approach by leveraging BATH properties to develop a novel material machine kinetic system. The integration of textiles into bending active systems augments structural performances, accentuating senses of three-dimensionality and enclosure. At the same time, this adds a new level of structural complexity, requiring the development of new design and control methods. In order to respond to these challenges, a novel adaptive cyber-physical network was developed. Within this framework, control values are computed through continuous negotiation between exteroceptive and interoceptive information, and user/designer interaction.

Given the complexity of controlling the material behavior of nonlinear kinetic elastic systems at an architectural scale, ELAbot's development requires a highly interdisciplinary approach.

BACKGROUND

Architectural Vision: From Adaptive to Robotic Architecture

ELAbot's design ambitions recall discussions about adaptive, mobile, cybernetics, and intelligent architecture from the 1960s. Archigram's visions fostered new ideas of what architecture could be: mobile; acting spontaneously, in nonstandard ways; temporarily transforming spaces (Chang 2018). Yona Friedman's mobile architecture explored how simple lightweight elements could create complex, flexible, transformable, and deployable structures. Friedman's People's Architecture was based on participatory experiences where the public could contribute to the design, challenging established top-down models, seeking alternative design procedures through participation, trial and error, and open-ended and evolving processes (Hanru 2017). Cedric Price sought to overcome the idea that architecture needs to be steady, stable, and predetermined, instead leaving space for pleasure, surprise, playfulness, and provocation (Steenson 2017)—notions he envisioned in the Fun Palace. His collaboration with John Frazer and the cybernetician Gordon Pask attempted to merge information science and design to define a new concept of interactive architecture (Chang 2018). New multidisciplinary models emerged around that time, notably from Nicholas Negroponte's Architecture Machine Group (AMG). The AMG's work was situated at the intersection of architecture, artificial intelligence (AI), engineering, and art, proposing a new vision that investigated how AI interfaced with the physical environment (Steenson 2017). Research developed in these years did not translate into built projects, though it greatly influenced architectural design thinking. In early 2000 Kas Oosterhuis, through the work of the HyperBody group, conceived architectural systems as living creatures; embedded sensing and actuation systems enabled their structures to adapt to internal and external conditions (Chang 2018).

ELAbot shares these design visions but takes a very specific approach to adaptivity, pursuing them through the actuation of a BATH system.

Elastic Structures: Bending Active Textile Hybrids

In BATH structures, material behavior drives geometrical shape (Suzuki 2018) and equilibrium emerges from interaction between tensile (form active) and elastically bent (bending active) elements (Ahlquist and Menges 2013; Lienhard et al. 2012). Their ability to respond to force manipulation through geometrical variation produces an elastic response to deformation that achieves different physical states through actuation.

State-of-the-art BATH research demonstrates their structural efficiency, aesthetic qualities, and potential for use in innovative architectural structures (Suzuki and Knippers 2018). However, the relationship between elastic potential and changes in continuous motion remains underexplored. Due to the lack of appropriate motor-control strategies that exert dynamic loading deformations safely over time, state-of-the-art work in lightweight elastic structures predominantly focuses on static structures. A prerequisite for exploring the dynamic design space is the development of an appropriate motor control system that can safely enable large deformations.

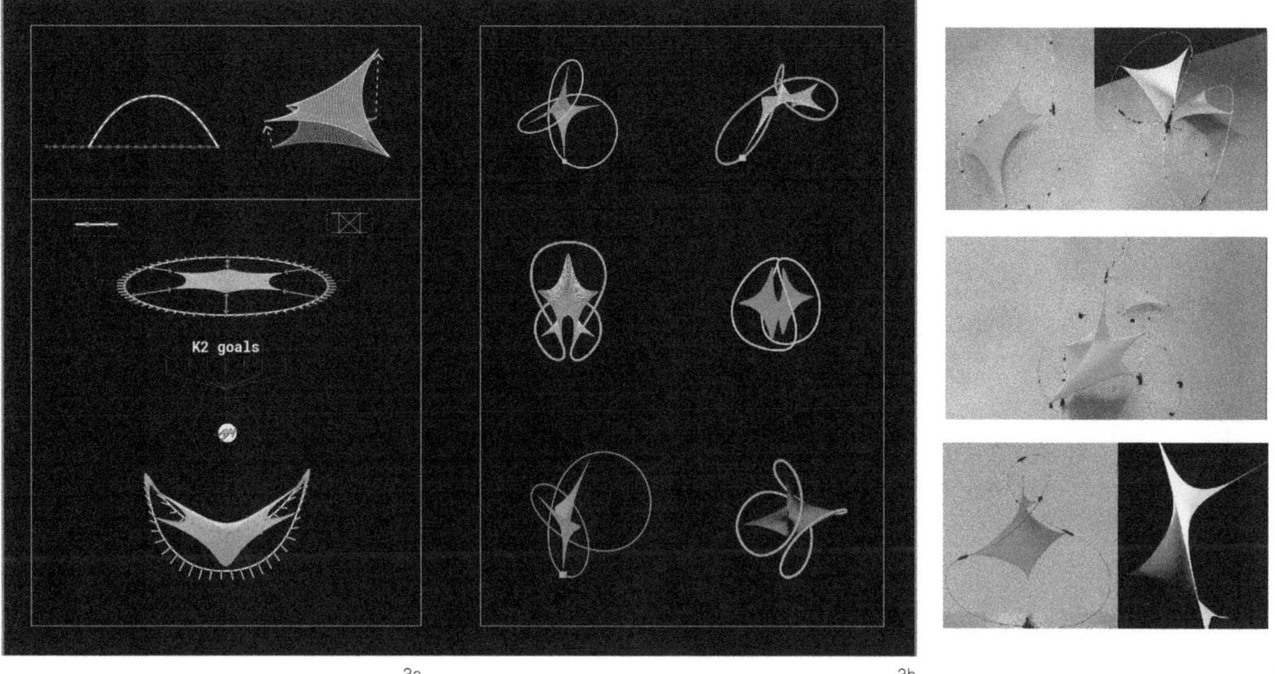

3 ELAbot design process: (a) simulation in Kangaroo 2.0 (K2) physics plug-in for Grasshopper; (b) simulation design studies; (c) physical design studies.

Robotic Systems

ELAbot's design process follows the structure of a robotic design workflow. A robotic system and a robotic controller require an understanding of system dynamic behavior and definition of the tasks to be performed. This involves the determination of a model to represent target system behavior. Based on this, the design of control laws sets the relationship between inputs (feedback) and outputs (actuation). In closed control loops, sensors and actuators are interconnected in a cycle. Control theory integrates strategies where the mechanical states of a dynamic system are related to the input/output values (Astrom and Murray 2008). Given the complexity of controlling nonlinear elastic behavior in uncontrolled environments, a cyber-physical control system that integrates physical feedback (such as current shape and load) into the digital model (simulation) enables computational processes that define control values, taking current state into consideration.

The nature of task determination and target actions differ in standard and architectural robotic design processes. In the design of architectural robots, quantitative objectives are combined with qualitative aims. The system strives both to maintain stability and to achieve a specific shape that reflects design intentions. Since ELAbot is approached as a robotic system, its development also addresses questions relating to operability and decisions about the relationship between human supervision and material-machine agency.

METHODS

ELAbot's development comprises four main research areas: (1) multi-state design: implementation of physical and computational form-finding methods to define and evaluate the assembly geometry and its dynamic performance; (2) design, assembly, and operation of the robotic system; (3) system calibration and characterization; and (4) decision-making strategies and methods to enable informed behavior (Fig. 3).

Multi-State Design

The design phase consisted of multi-state form-finding to define the assembly geometry and its dynamic performance. BATH systems cannot be designed using conventional geometrical approaches, as their form is dependent on the equilibrium of forces between bending active and form active tensile elements. Simulation studies were conducted with the Kangaroo 2.0 (K2) physics plugin for Grasshopper (Piker 2015), which simulates physical behavior using dynamic relaxation techniques. The process involves discretization of the linear elements (bending rods) and mesh surfaces (textile) in a particle-spring system, and the definition of parameters (goals) such as bending or tensile strength and topological rules. Based on these values, the K2 physics solver computes the form-found geometry (Fig. 3a).

Several design studies were conducted in the simulation by changing the solver input variables (Fig. 3b). In parallel, physical prototypes were built to validate simulation outputs and calibrate material behavior (Fig. 3c). The studies were based

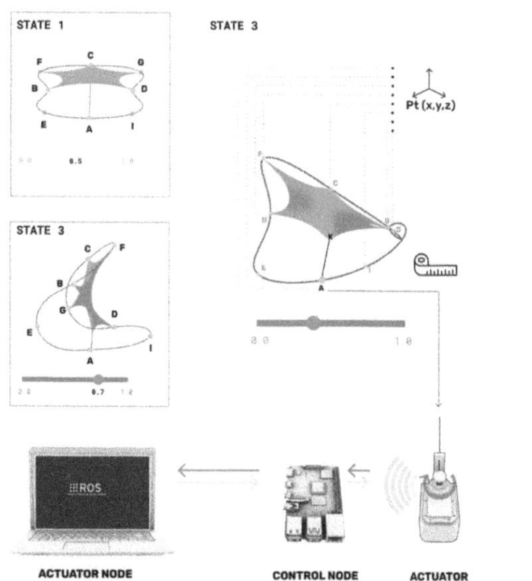

4a

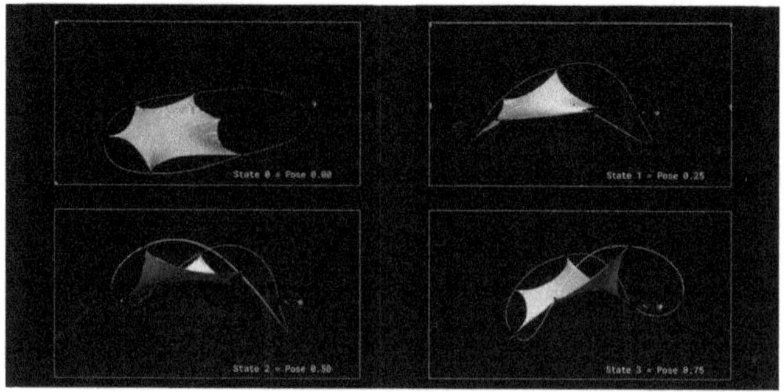

4b

4 Robotic system design, assembly, and operation: (a) assembly geometry and robotic system design; (b) operation and calibration phase.

on a configuration comprising a bending loop connected to a tensile surface. Dynamic studies were produced by changes in connection conditions between the loop and the textile (length and position). The main design goal was to enable the system to self-form (moving from a two-dimensional to a three-dimensional state) and to achieve multiple three-dimensional states, with the minimum number of elements and actuators. In the selected system, all connections between the bending loop and the tensile surface were fixed except for one, which allowed variable length. The change of length could drive implicit topological changes and variation of the global geometry. The selected topology was chosen because of the simplicity of the system, which relied on one actuation point to achieve the target behavior.

Robotic System Development

Robotic development was divided into two complementary parts: design and assembly of the physical system—including the mechanical incremental tensioning mechanism (ITM)—and development of a custom feedback-control logic for the actuator, developed in the ROS environment (Robot Operating System) (Quigley et al. 2009) (Fig. 4a). The feedback-control system operated through ROS in order to define a modular message-based communication structure between computational environment and physical system.

Simulation study results informed the physical structure, including the number of linear elements made of glass fiber rods (GFR) and/or carbon fiber rods (CFR), the cutting pattern for the elastic tensile surface (four-way nylon and/or Lycra fabric) and the topological conditions. Custom 3D-printed parts were fabricated to connect the rods in a circular loop, to connect the tensile surface to the rod loop, and to create the custom actuation system. The ITM is comprised of a Dynamixel smart actuator capable of sensing together with a custom-mounted spooling mechanism. The ITM was connected to the rod with a 3D-printed case. Changing the length of the cable that connected the rod to the textile caused a change of distribution of tensile forces acting on the textile surface, inducing bending stresses into the rod loop and causing tensile and bending deformation as a result.

According to prototype scale, either a Dynamixel AX-12A or a Dynamixel MX-64 was used. A custom motor-control feedback system was created based on the Dynamixel SDK software development kit for ROS. This enabled the operator to write control motor values (such as goal velocity and position) and read feedback data (such as present load and present position). Using this framework, goal positions and velocities were sent to the motor with the latest issued command, overwriting previous goal modes and ensuring safe and rapid control. A control system-specific variable defined as goal "pose" was developed by combining goal velocity control with position feedback. This allowed the operator to calibrate the system and declare a minimum and maximum position for the motor to reach (in relation to full motor rotations). The custom control function enabled the mapping of minimum and maximum values to 0.00 and 1.00. The operator could then input any number in this range to describe a position along the actuation axis. Once a goal pose was defined, goal rotations and velocities were computed to achieve the target pose position. This was particularly helpful to determine the actuation state of the system in different prototypes (geometry and scale). In this way the actuation value (pose) was computed in relation to the length of the cable. The actuation value (pose) was mapped in relation to the global geometry (Fig. 4b). Geometry was described by measuring the distance between selected points of the BATH loop. Initial planning included the implementation of the OptiTrack system. Preliminary tests were conducted using the OptiTrack Unity 3D plugin (OptiTrack 2018) which allows real-time streaming of data from the Motive OptiTrack software platform into Unity. Optical markers were placed into the bending rod, and their position displacement was streamed as changes of X, Y, Z coordinates.

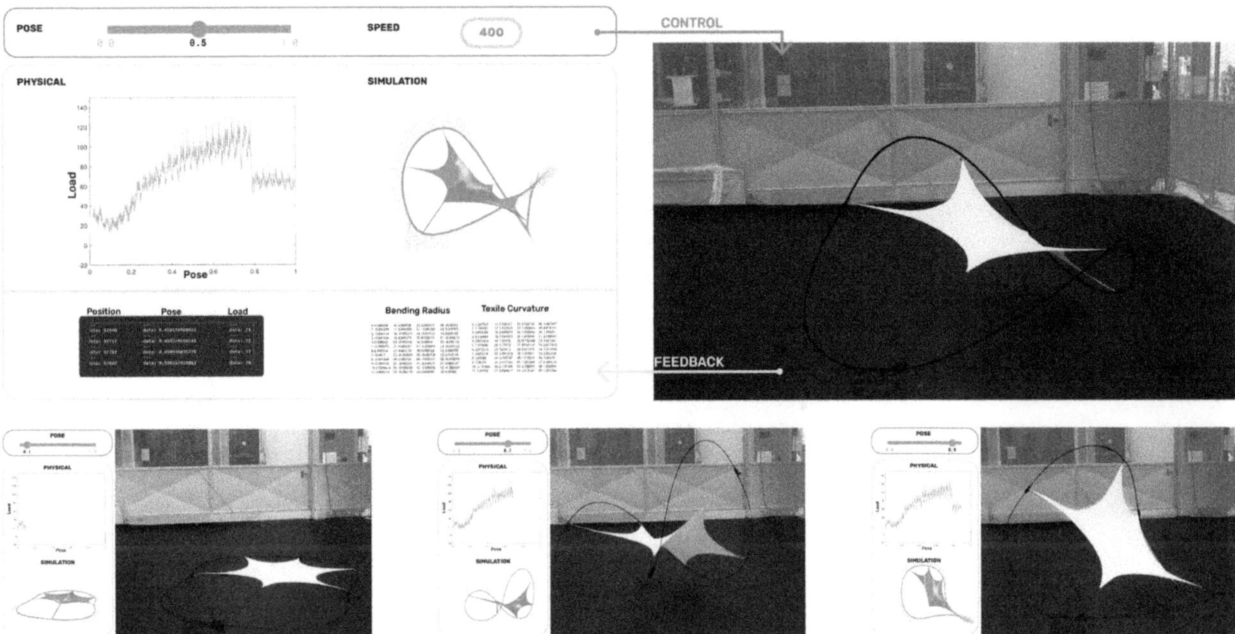

5 ELAbot during calibration and characterization phase at different states.

5

Feedback motor control was operated through ROS. This enabled a modular message-based communication structure, and the processing and exchange of data between different devices (laptop and Raspberry Pi controller, for example) through a subscribing and publishing logic. All executables/nodes were registered to the ROS network, allowing different devices to access (subscribing or publishing) all available control and feedback data/topics (speed, position, rotation, pose, load, etc.). Actuator and sensor information were therefore readily available throughout the network, facilitating communication for system control and analysis.

System Calibration and Characterization

Several physical prototypes were tested at multiple scales. Once the system was assembled, it was calibrated and characterized in order to enable subsequent informed behavior. Key control data (such as velocity and pose) were calibrated in relation to global outputs (geometrical changes) and analyzed through physical (load sensor feedback) and numerical analysis (bending radius and tensile curvature). This enabled calibration of control values to achieve specific goals (shapes) and identification of critical values to be corrected, stored, and monitored (Fig. 5).

Development of the Cyber-Physical Network

The design of the cyber-physical control network required real-time data exchange to be established between robotic (ROS) and digital (Grasshopper/Kangaroo) environments (Fig. 6). Central to the communication was the custom developed graphical user interface (GUI), developed in Unity (Unity Technologies 2019) and designed to foster interaction. The GUI was divided into three main parts: feedback visualization, simulated geometry, and control buttons.

The GUI was connected to the ROS network using the RosSharp libraries (Bischoff 2018) via WebSocket, through the RosBridge protocol (Mace and Lee 2013). It was also connected to the simulation environment in Grasshopper/Kangaroo via UDP and TCP protocols. Through this pipeline, robotic operations could be updated based on simulation and user feedback in addition to sensor feedback (load). All feedback values could be visualized and processed in the GUI, enabling the user/designer to directly overwrite current values. In addition, accumulated load values against structure poses were represented in a graph and rendered as a texture in the interface to facilitate intuitive physical analysis.

In the simulation, geometry was continuously updated based on robotic feedback. Geometrical data of the simulation particle-spring system were formatted and transferred to Unity, where the rod and mesh were rebuilt and rendered using built-in geometry renderers. Unity GUI methods were used to visualize feedback values and create a number slider for pose control and input fields for goal positions and velocities. These were then mapped to RosSharp publishers and subscribers and connected to the relevant ROS topics, extending the control of the Dynamixel actuators to the GUI.

In order to enable human interaction beyond the GUI, a color detection function was developed based on OpenCV library (Bradski 2000) and integrated into the ROS network. The

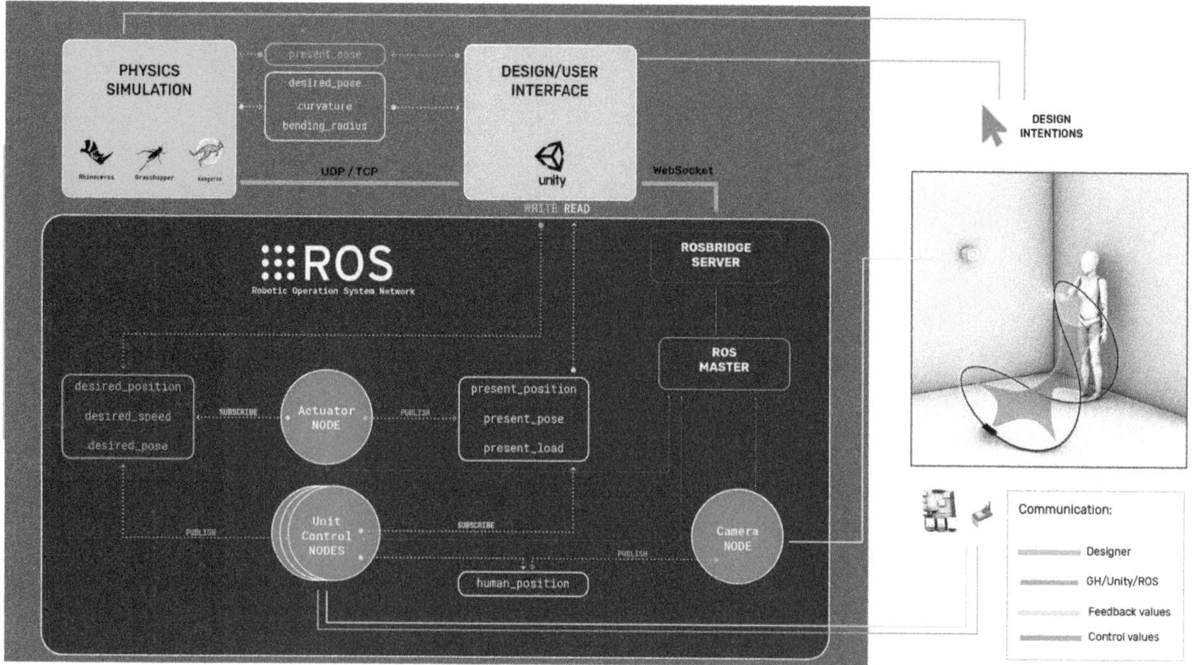

6 Cyber-physical network overview showing overall communication pipeline between the simulation, GUI, and ROS environment. 6

setup included a webcam and a high-contrast colored object. Calibration of the selected color was performed through RGB pixel analysis of several images, enabling the identification of a range of RGB values. The NumPy library (Harris 2020) was used to define RGB limits in the form of arrays. The Imutils library (Rosebrock 2021) was used to detect the contours of the colored object, ignoring any object that was outside its edge. A bounding rectangle and center point were identified. Real-time video processing enabled identification of the location of the colored object relative to the pixel of the laptop screen; based on this, relevant position values were computed. These values were stored as a topic on the ROS network. Control functions could therefore subscribe to the topic, which was used to affect current goal velocity and pose of the actuator system.

Decision-Making and Behavior

Based on data available through the cyber-physical network (Fig. 7), different operation modes were tested to explore the spectrum of possible behaviors (autonomous, human controlled, hybrid). The robotic system actuation state was controlled by goal pose and goal velocity values. These values were computed taking the following parameters into account: (1) design intentions; (2) user input; (3) human movement (colored object detection); (4) simulation feedback (bending radius); (5) motor-sensor feedback (present load and present velocity). Each parameter was described as one or multiple variables. Design intentions corresponded to a sequence of poses. User input was a goal pose value coming from the GUI. Human movement corresponded to the colored object screen pixel position, from the camera. Simulation feedback was a variable with the highest bending radius value. Motor-sensor feedback variables were identified as present load and present velocity. A series of control packages were developed in ROS to process and integrate these variables in the determination of the goal pose. A standard operation workflow included some basic steps: initial determination of a series of poses by the designer/operator, definition of critical values to be monitored (load, velocity) and control packages where conditional functions could generate and update the goal pose based on feedback. Based on different operation modes, each variable had a different weight/influence in the computation or update of the goal pose. If the mode of operation was purely autonomous, simulation feedback had a stronger impact in the determination of the next goal pose, and human-related variables had a limited influence in sequence correction. If the mode of operation was design-oriented, the initial pose sequence correction would only take place if a critical value was reached, signaling that structural stability was in jeopardy. User-oriented mode would privilege GUI inputs and motion. Development of the different logics aimed to explore how to build a control logic based on the negotiation of multiple variables.

RESULTS

Based on these methods several tests were made, including with different materials. The final prototype was comprised of a loop of four bending active protruded CFRs, measuring 4 mm in diameter and 2,000 mm in length (bending loop circumference: 8,000 mm). The selected dimension was chosen to enable the loop to bend at multiple states

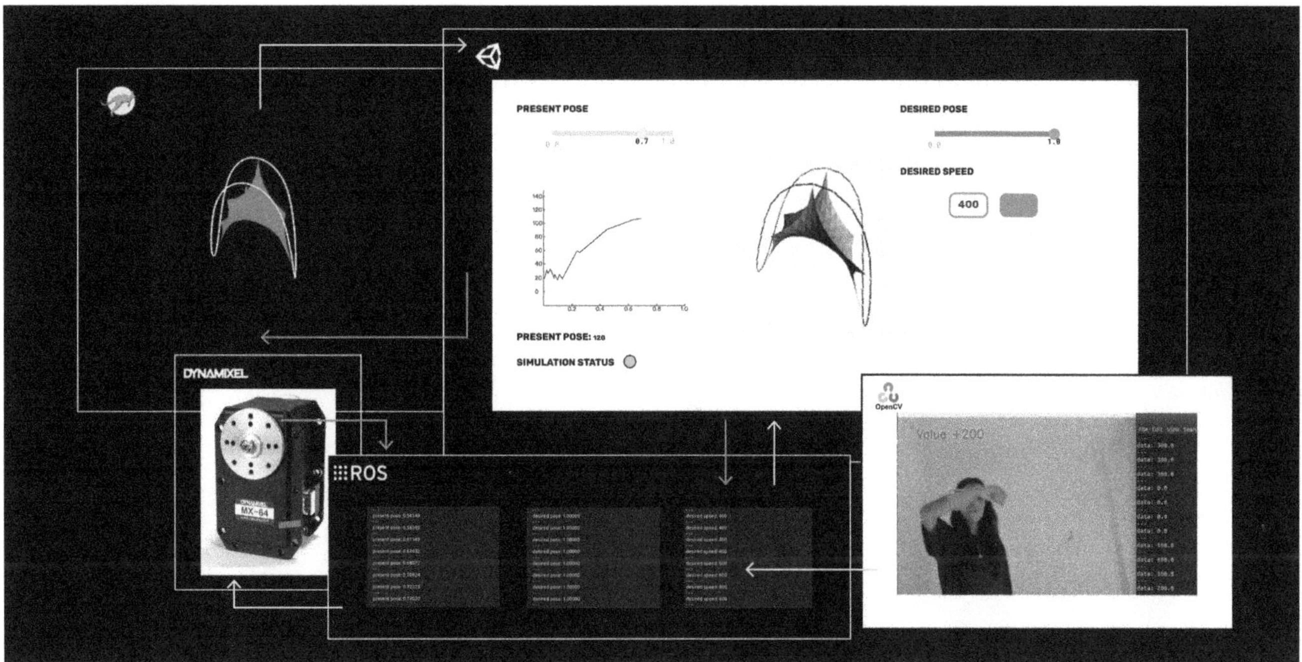

7 Demo showing cyber-physical network operations: processing and exchange of feedback control data between simulation, user interface, and ROS. 7

while maintaining stability. The loop was connected to a custom-cut four-way stretch fabric made of nylon (80%) and Lycra (20%). The cutting pattern was generated in the simulation. The same configuration was tested with GFRs, the main difference being the capacity of the CFR loop to start from a two-dimensional state and achieve a three-dimensional shape without the need of additional external force, demonstrating higher stiffness than the GFR loop. Custom connections were 3D printed. For the final ITM, the Dynamixel X-64 was used due to its torque value and high sensor feedback precision. The system was designed, assembled, calibrated, and characterized as described in the "Methods" section. The pose/load analysis gave a clear overview of system behavior at multiple states. From the characterization phase expected pose/load and bending radius values were input into the control functions. This enabled monitoring for any unexpected behavior. In the final test, the designer started the system by defining a series of pose values (target sequence). The system loaded these input values, which were translated into motor operations, while the GUI would display the feedback status and digital twin (from the simulation). The designer could directly overwrite the current pose and velocity through the slider in the GUI. Critical values were monitored. The previously described camera vision functionality—based on color detection—was used to influence the pose sequence, based on human body movement. A high-contrast pink-colored band was put on a human wrist. Its position relative to screen pixels was translated into a pose correction variable that would affect goal pose, alternating the preloaded sequence (Fig. 8a). While ELAbot demonstrated consistent behavior over time (based on analysis data), unpredictable external conditions could be detected by sensor feedback (load values). This caused the system to stop and compute the previous safe pose, then goal pose, until the load value was below the critical threshold (Fig. 8b). The final prototype was tested in indoor and outdoor environments (Fig. 9). It was interesting to observe in outdoor testing how environmental conditions such as wind could have radical effects, contributing to system actuation.

This prototype was the first attempt to explore and validate the methods developed. With the intention to extend and refine the behavior, this research opens new design possibilities in which adaptivity can be achieved through embodied intelligence.

CONCLUSION

Ongoing development work focuses on scale increments, in order to emphasize the architectural potential of the system as an inhabitable robotic structure. This will require multihierarchical topological solutions, combined with extra multimodal sensors and new learning processes, in order to augment autonomy and awareness. Extra sensors will also be integrated to gain ground truth datasets for future bending and tensile behavior characterization (in addition to refinement of external tracking). More fundamentally, the research will continue to interrogate deeper questions about autonomy and the role of robots in architecture, shifting the focus from tools to intelligent agents that can sense surroundings and act accordingly (Murphy 2019). This opens exciting scenarios in which the architectural system

8a

8b

8 ELAbot behavior: (a) human interaction; (b) load feedback affecting current pose.

is conceived not as a passive receiver of individual design visions but rather as a spatial interface that can process and display information—and that can compute decisions that would be very difficult for a human to manually process. At the same time, human desires and collective preferences are integrated data that contribute to the autonomous behavior. The work will continue to evolve through a multidisciplinary approach—translating creative tension between robotics and engineering approaches into design processes in order to develop resilient, self-aware systems that are structurally autonomous, intelligent, and playful.

ACKNOWLEDGMENTS

The presented work was developed at the Autonomous Manufacturing Lab (AML), Department of Computer Science at the University College of London. The research is supported by the Engineering and Physical Sciences Research Council (EP/N018494/1, EP/S031464/1 and EP/R513143/1). The authors would like to thank Mathias Maierhofer for his valuable feedback and support.

REFERENCES

Ahlquist, Sean, and Achim Menges. 2013. "Frameworks for Computational Design of Textile Micro-Architectures and Material Behavior in Forming Complex Force-Active Structures." In *ACADIA 13: Adaptive Architecture [Proceedings of the 33rd Annual Conference of the Association for Computer Aided Design in Architecture (ACADIA)]*, Cambridge, ON, Canada, 24–26 October 2013, edited by P. Beesley, O. Khan, and M. Stacey, 281–292. CUMINCAD.

Astrom, Karl J., and Richard M. Murray. 2008. *Feedback Systems: An Introduction for Scientists and Engineers*. Princeton, N.J: Princeton University Press.

Bier, Henriette. 2018. "Robotic Building as Integration of Design-to-Robotic-Production and -Operation." In *Robotic Building*, edited by Henriette Bier, 98. Cham: Springer Nature Switzerland AG.

Bischoff, Martin. 2018. *Ros Sharp*. V.1.3. https://github.com/siemens/ros-sharp.

Bradski, G. 2000. "The OpenCV Library." *Dr. Dobb's Journal of Software Tools* 25, no. 11 (November): 122-125.

Chang, J. 2018. "From Interactive to Intra-active Body." In *A+BE | Architecture and the Built Environment, HyperCell*, edited by Jia-Rei Chang. 47–80. https://doi.org/10.7480/abe.2018.1.3749.

Hanru, Hou. 2017. "Yona Friedman, an Ideal World That We Can Build Together." In *About Yona Friedman. People's Architecture*, edited by Elena Motisi. Rome: Fondazione MAXXI.

Harris, C.R., K. J. Millman, S. J. van der Walt, et al. 2020. "Array programming with NumPy." Nature 585, 357–362. DOI: 0.1038/s41586-020-2649-2.

Lienhard, Julian. 2014. "Bending-active Structures: Form-Finding Strategies Using Elastic Deformation in Static and Kinetic Systems and the Structural Potentials Therein." PhD diss., Univ. of Stuttgart.

Lienhard, Julian, Holger Alpermann, Christoph Gengnagel, and Jan Knippers. 2012. "Active Bending; A Review on Structures Where Bending Is Used as a Self-Formation Process." In *From Spatial Structures to Space Structures [Proceedings of the International IASS–APCS Symposium 2012], Seoul*, South Korea, 21–24 May 2012, 650–657. SAGE Journals. https://doi.org/10.1260/0266-3511.28.3-4.187.

Mace, Jonathan, and J. Lee. 2013. *Rosbridge suite*. V.0.4. https://github.com/RobotWebTools/rosbridge_suite.

Maierhofer, Mathias, Valentina Soana, Maria Yablonina, Seiichi Suzuki Erazo, Axel Körner, Jan Knippers, and Achim Menges. 2018. "Self-Choreographing Network." In *ACADIA 19: Ubiquity and Autonomy [Proceedings of the 39th Annual Conference of the Association for Computer Aided Design in Architecture (ACADIA)]*, Austin, TX, 21–26 October 2019, edited by K. Bieg, D. Briscoe, and C. Odom, 654–663. CUMINCAD.

Meissner, Irene, and Eberhard Möller. 2017. *Frei Otto: A Life of Research Construction and Inspiration*. Munich: DETAIL Gmbh & Co.

Menges, Achim. 2015. "The New Cyber-Physical Making in Architecture: Computational Construction." *Architectural Design* 85 (5): 14–21. https://doi.org/10.1002/ad.1950.

Murphy, Robin R., and Arkin, Ronald C. 2019. *Introduction to AI Robotics*. Cambridge, MA: MIT Press.

OptiTrack. 2018. *Motive*. V.2.1. https://optitrack.com/software/motive/.

9 ELAbot performing in an outdoor environment. ELAbot autonomous behavior affected by wind. 9

Piker, Daniel. 2015. *Kangaroo*. V.2.0. https://www.food4rhino.com/en/app/kangaroo-physics.

Quigley, Morgan, Ken Conley, Brian Gerkey, Josh Faust, Tully Foote, Jeremy Leibs, Rob Wheeler, and Andrew Y. Ng. 2009. "ROS: An Open-Source Robot Operating System." *ICRA Workshop on Open Source Software* 3 (3.2): 5.

Rosebrock, A. 2021. *Imutils*. V.0.5.4. https://github.com/jrosebr1/imutils.

Sobek, Werner, Patrick Teuffel, Agnes Weilandt, and Christine Lemaitre. 2006. "Adaptive and Lightweight." In *Adaptables 2006, TU/e [Proceedings of the International Conference on Adaptable Building Structures]*, Eindhoven, Netherlands, 3–5 July 2005, 38–42. Technische Universiteit Eindhoven.

Steenson, Molly Wright. 2017. *Architectural Intelligence: How Designers and Architects Created the Digital Landscape*. Cambridge, MA: MIT Press.

Suzuki, Seiichi, and Jan Knippers. 2018. "Digital Vernacular Design: Form-Finding at the Edge of Realities." In *ACADIA 2018: Recalibration: On Imprecision and Infidelity [Proceedings of the 38th Annual Conference of the Association for Computer Aided Design in Architecture (ACADIA)]*, Mexico City, Mexico, 18–20 October 2018, edited by P. Anzalone, M. del Signore, and A. J. Wit, 232–241. CUMINCAD.

Unity Technologies. 2019. *Unity*. V 2019.0.1. https://unity.com/.

IMAGE CREDITS

All drawings and images by the authors.

Valentina Soana is a PhD researcher at the Autonomous Manufacturing Lab (AML), Department of Computer Science, and lecturer at the Bartlett School of Architecture at University College London. Her research focuses on the design of robotic material systems for autonomous architectural structures.

Harvey Stedman is a research assistant at the Autonomous Manufacturing Lab (AML), Department of Computer Science at the University College of London. His research focuses on the development of scalable teleoperation interfaces for robots.

Durgesh Darekar is a research assistant at the Autonomous Manufacturing Lab (AML), Department of Computer Science at the University College of London. His research focuses on aerial robotics.

Vijay M. Pawar PhD is the director of the Autonomous Manufacturing Lab (AML) and TouchLab, Department of Computer Science at the University College of London. He leads a multidisciplinary team of computer scientists, optical metrology, robotics, and manufacturing experts developing autonomous and semiautonomous tools to help humans and machines work together across multiple scales.

Robert Stuart-Smith is the director of the Autonomous Manufacturing Lab (AML), Department of Computer Science at the University College of London, the director of AML/PENN, and Assistant Professor of Architecture at Weitzman School/University of Pennsylvania. He specializes in robotic manufacturing and generative design.

Prototype as Artefact

Design Tool for Open-ended Collaborative Assembly Processes

Lidia Atanasova
TU Munich

Daniela Mitterberger
ETH Zurich

Timothy Sandy
ETH Zurich

Fabio Gramazio
ETH Zurich

Matthias Kohler
ETH Zurich

Kathrin Dörfler
TU Munich

1

1 Prototype-as-Artefact fabrication workflow: Thanks to novel augmented reality technologies, two users and a robot collaborate in the assembly of a complex wooden structure in alternating physical actions. The spatial timber assembly being constructed follows a predefined assembly grammar but is not planned at the beginning of the process, its configuration is instead designed during fabrication.

ABSTRACT

In digital design-to-fabrication workflows in architecture, in which digitally controlled machines perform complex fabrication tasks, all design decisions are typically made before production. In such processes, the formal definition of the final shape is explicitly inscribed into the design model by means of corresponding step-by-step machine instructions. The increasing use of augmented reality (AR) technologies for digital fabrication workflows, in which people are instructed to carry out complex fabrication tasks via AR interfaces, creates an opportunity to question and adjust the level of detail and the nature of such explicit formal definitions. People's cognitive abilities could be leveraged to integrate explicit machine intelligence with implicit human knowledge and creativity, and thus to open up digital fabrication to intuitive and spontaneous design decisions during the building process. To address this question, this paper introduces open-ended Prototype-as-Artefact fabrication workflows that examine the possibilities of designing and creative choices while building in a human-robot collaborative setting. It describes the collaborative assembly of a complex timber structure with alternating building actions by two people and a collaborative robot, interfacing via a mobile device with object tracking and AR visualization functions. The spatial timber assembly being constructed follows a predefined grammar but is not planned at the beginning of the process; it is instead designed during fabrication. Prototype-as-Artefact thus serves as a case study to probe the potential of both intuitive and rational aspects of building and to create new collaborative work processes between humans and machines.

INTRODUCTION

In contemporary digital workflows from design to fabrication in architecture, the formal definition of the final shape is explicitly inscribed into the design model, and all design decisions are made prior to production. This applies in particular to digital fabrication processes, in which digitally controlled machines require such formal definitions for the execution of fabrication tasks by means of detailed and step-by-step machine instructions (Gramazio, Kohler, and Willmann 2014). While useful for fully automated applications in typical industrial settings, with the recent surge in novel augmented reality (AR) technology for digital fabrication workflows, in which users carry out complex fabrication tasks instead of a machine (Jahn et al. 2020; Larsson, Yoshida, and Igarashi 2019; Mitterberger et al. 2020), this approach does not allow users to contribute creatively to the fabrication process in any meaningful way. User involvement in digital fabrication raises questions about the level of detail and the nature of such explicit formal definitions. One such question is to what extent digital fabrication processes could be opened up to intuitive and spontaneous decisions by humans during fabrication, in order to integrate explicit machine intelligence with implicit human knowledge and creativity, and thus to create novel human-robot collaborative workflows.

To address this question, this paper proposes Prototype-as-Artefact fabrication workflows (Risatti 2007), which challenge the notion of a top-down linearity of design-to-fabrication workflows and explore the possibilities of making bottom-up design decisions while building in a human-robot collaborative setting. This paper describes the development of an assembly grammar that defines a set of rules on how to assemble elements into local configurations but leaves the overall design open to branch out in various directions and shapes during construction. This grammar sets the basis for the collaborative assembly of a complex spatial timber structure constructed with alternating building actions by two users and a collaborative robot, featuring both intuitive and rational aspects. Recent technological advancements in AR technology and sensor-enabled context-awareness (Sandy and Buchli 2018) establish a shared workspace between users and a collaborative robot via the visual interface of a mobile device. This context-aware AR technology makes it possible to iteratively register intuitive and spontaneous human building actions with a high geometric precision, to evaluate them in the computational design engine, and to supplement these actions with robot-controlled building tasks. The robotic tasks are computed in response to the user's intuitive building choices by using the explicit rules and geometric boundary conditions of the assembly grammar. This interactive process ultimately leads to the emergence of a final shape.

We present the results of a spatial timber assembly constructed by humans and a robot, and their complementary roles in creating and building. We outline the contextual background of prototype-as-artefact fabrication workflows and the current state of the art in this area of research. Then we present the method of the design tool and the fabrication workflow between humans and robots in a shared geometric workspace. We elaborate on the developed assembly grammar, and the collaborative building process it enables, including task distribution strategies between the two users and the robot. Next, we describe the results of the case study of the complex timber structure enabled by the developed workflows and interaction concepts. Finally we present the conclusion and offer a future outlook of this research. In closing, we discuss whether such a balanced integration of robotic fabrication processes in coordination with humans could open up new avenues for design and digital fabrication in architecture.

CONTEXT

Nonlinear Digital Design-to-Fabrication Workflows

The computational theory of making grammars, presented by Knight and Stiny (2015), extends the theory of shape grammars for the study and the digital representation of the temporal performance of craft in contrast to representing solely the product (Knight and Stiny 2015), ultimately aiming at replacing top-down hylomorphic thinking with bottom-up material processes of formation (Ingold 2010). By understanding the act of making in craft "as doing and sensing with stuff to make things," they described its underlying creative processes by segmenting the spatial and temporal properties of applying rules for both actions of making and sensory perception. Such processes are open and do not fully determine the outcome in advance. They allow practitioners and users to change plans on the fly, for example, to pursue new design ideas that are triggered by the pattern in progress, or to accommodate for mistakes (Knight 2017). Also, in Sennett's observations on Ruskin's worldview (Sennett 2008), he advocates for craft processes as "lost spaces of freedom," in which craftspeople experiment with ideas and techniques, risk mistakes and delays, and "can at least temporarily lose control." In the context of contemporary industrialized production, the early Enlightenment thinking summarized by Sennett offers clues as to how such spaces could be regained: "The enlightened way to use a machine is to judge its powers, fashion its uses, in light of our own limits rather than the machine's potential. A machine ought to propose rather than command, and humankind should certainly walk away from the command to imitate perfection" (Sennett 2008, 105). Rather than competing against the machine, exploring the relationship between rationalized industrial production techniques and traditional craft could show us entirely new ways in which we make and build architecture.

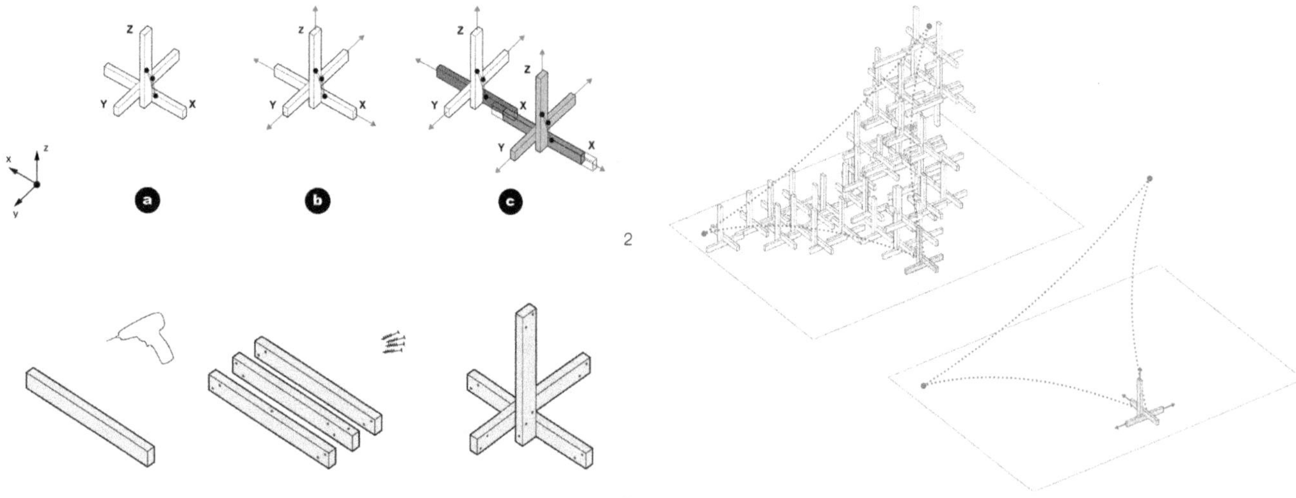

2

5

3

Our proposed geometric aggregation strategy therefore aims to combine the bottom-up principle of making in craft with computational methods in design and fabrication. While the final configuration of the spatial timber assembly is unplanned, the process of assembly is governed by a simple rule-based geometric process (described in "Method") in combination with human decision-making and physical constraints. As such, this strategy aims to integrate physical boundary conditions of material processes in architecture (robotic reach) into the open-ended design process, which often cannot be anticipated directly by human intuition. In this scenario, in which the final geometric result is not explicitly determined before fabrication, computation strategies are used to inform the user about possible design spaces and the feasibility of their design intent by making physical and material constraints explicit during the fabrication process. The novelty of this project lies in the creation of a collaborative fabrication framework between humans and robots for unplanned structures, in which both creativity (since users have a certain influence on the final result of the physical structure) and rationalization (since the machine computes and performs fabrication steps in response to the actions by the user) are fostered. This type of open-ended construction has advantages over a conventional top-down digital fabrication process: for example, it combines global target definitions with local connections between parts and ensures the constructability of each part during construction.

State of the Art

Various concepts and methods for nonlinear and open-ended digital fabrication workflows in architecture via direct and indirect user-input technologies have been demonstrated in recent years. Interactive Fabrication shows how users can direct the fabrication of a physical form with real-time user input (Willis et al. 2011). In Interlacing, camera tracking allows the 2D observation of a robot workspace, enabling a robot to process material inputs and make design decisions within a constrained design space during fabrication (Dörfler, Rist, and Rust 2012). In RoMA, an interactive fabrication system provides an in-situ modeling experience (Peng et al. 2018). As a designer creates and adapts a model using the RoMA CAD editor in AR, a 3D-printing robotic arm sharing the same design volume concurrently constructs the designed features. In FormFab: Continuous Interactive Fabrication, the interactive manipulation of a thermoplastic sheet allows for shape explorations directly in the physical space (Mueller et al. 2019).

While novel technology and approaches allow a major leap forward, these processes still show various trade-offs. For example, few investigations have been performed on how to utilize user input as a feedback to the computational design engine directly via the built structure. While the input of sensors defines the robot actions for manipulating an object in Interactive Fabrication, RoMA, and FormFab, the physical result is not registered and is therefore not directly part of an interactive loop. While Interlacing aimed to provide such feedback directly via the built structure, it was highly constrained by lacking adequate sensor and 3D registration technology and intuitive human-machine interfaces. Most importantly, all described processes have been performed at object scale and have not tested or evaluated the principles at the architectural scale and in the context of architectural production.

In Prototype-as-Artefact, user input is processed directly via the built structure by tracking elements that are placed spontaneously by users and by feeding this information back to the digital model. This approach allows for an interactive and collaborative workflow between humans and robots at architectural scale.

METHOD

The aim of the research was to develop a set of workflows and technologies to facilitate an interactive human-robot collaborative workflow for assembly tasks, with a particular

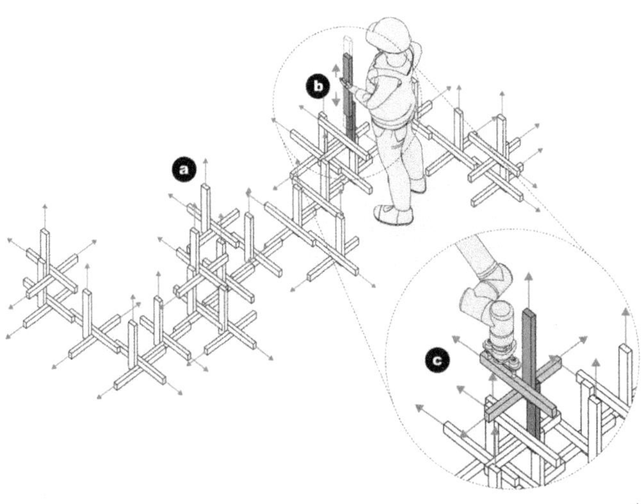

4

2 Assembly grammar: (a) module of three discrete elements represented by three nodes of a graph; (b) arrows displaying all possible directions in which the assembly can be continued; (c) placing new module within a range.

3 At the start of the process, users define an origin, described by one module, and global growth directions of the structure, specified by target points in space. The inscribed design space and resulting building options are based on these initial constrains and are continuously calculated throughout the process according to user input.

4 Assembly steps distributed between users and a collaborative robot according to a set of design rules and options: (a) arrows displaying the design options; (b) keystone element is placed freely at a chosen location within a possible domain; (c) complementing elements 2 and 3 are computed based on location of the keystone element and placed by the robot.

5 Material system: one module consists of equally sized predrilled timber elements mechanically connected with wood screws.

consideration for the unique needs and circumstances of architecture and construction. The following sections describe the various building blocks and implemented methods necessary for realizing this research project.

Assembly Grammar

In reference to Terry Knight's "making grammar," this research proposes an assembly grammar that describes rules for temporal processes next to geometrical ones. The design rules of the proposed assembly grammar allow for building spatial structures by mechanically connecting discrete elements in subsequent fashion. In the digital model, referred to as the Assembly Information Model, each element is represented by a node of a graph; the edges of the graph correspond to the connections between the elements. Each element features two connectors on both ends on the long side, representing two options where a new element can be mechanically attached, defining an open design space of discrete and variable structures (Rossi and Tessmann 2017).

The Assembly Information Model was implemented by using the data structures available through the open-source Python-based COMPAS framework (Mele et. al 2017).

The initial design rule that directly affects the geometrical outcome is described by the configuration of three perpendicular elements into a module with a predefined range of connection possibilities. Due to the module's perpendicular spatial arrangement, each element has a different type assigned to it—each module consists of one element of type X, one of type Y, and one of type Z. These also refer to the orientation of the elements along a respective axis in the digital design model (Fig. 2). The connection between two modules (but not the connection between elements within a single module) is represented as a parent-child connection, in which the module that is already mounted is referred to as the parent and the newly mounted one as its child. The first element of the child module inherits its parent's type: parent type X -> child type X, Y -> Y and Z -> Z. The type of the parent module's first element and correspondingly of its child determines the type and sequence of the placement and mounting of the subsequent two elements. Depending on the parent type, the sequence can have the following order: If the parent is type X, the mounting sequence is [X, Y, Z]. If the parent is type Y, its sequence is [Y, X, Z]. If the parent is type Z, its sequence is [Z, X, Y]. There are a few exceptions to these rules, for example, the mounting sequence for type Y changes to [X, Y, Z] when building on the ground, due to reduced accessibility of the space underneath previously mounted elements and the base of the structure.

To introduce differentiation in the design space where a structure can be built with higher or lower density, parent-child connections are fixed in angle but leave some variability in the range of the mounting distance along the element's axis. For this, two conditions must be satisfied: (1) Sufficient contact surface must be provided between the child and the parent where the mechanical connectors are installed but also allowing for the remaining two elements to be placed. With elements 40 cm long and a minimum overlapping length of 4 cm of the connected pieces, this results in a range of 15 cm within which an element can be freely placed along the respective axis. (2) The child must always be mounted on the same side of the parent element (on either the left or the right), otherwise the initial design rule cannot be fulfilled. If the mounting position within the structure differed, the spatial arrangement of the module would alter and prevent the modules from connecting, which would affect its structural performance and stability.

User Input

The assembly grammar stipulates that the placement of the first element of a new module, referred to as the keystone element, is carried out via a spontaneous user input within the

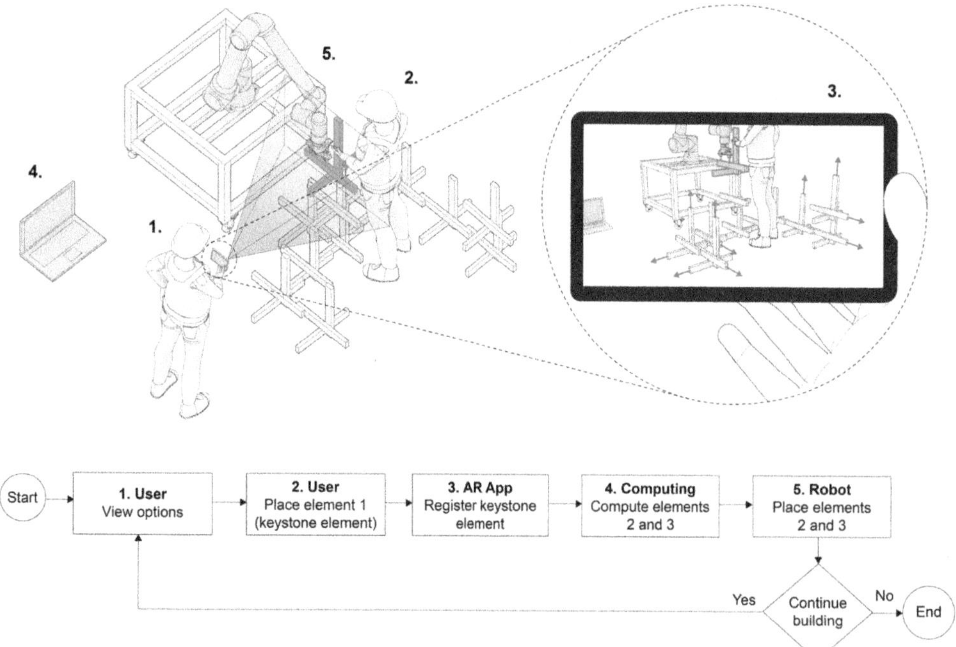

6 Setup and flow chart of the open-ended collaborative human-robot assembly workflow, enabled by novel assistive AR technology and sensor feedback.

7 The visual display of the AR device can superimpose cues on the real-world video stream designed to assist the builders with information, in this particular case with visual cues on the design space in which they can make their design choices.

given design space, that is, the free range and direction of an element's placement at open connector locations (Fig. 4). The boundary conditions constraining the design space can be subject to performance criteria such as stability criteria of the overall structure, target conditions of growth directions, workspace limitations of a robot, or collision avoidance between elements. After a user determines the orientation and location of the keystone element, the design algorithm computes the subsequent two elements of the module as a response to the user's choice. If the computed elements were to collide with the existing structure, any colliding objects are detected and omitted by the algorithm and thus not added to the assembly. With each added module, the potential design space, represented by the amount of open connectors, can grow.

Material System

To realize the prototype, same-sized timber elements with dimensions of 24 × 48 × 400 mm were used, which were predrilled and could later be mechanically connected into an overlapping shear connection with wood screws (Fig. 5). The spatial arrangement of the elements within a module results in three drilling patterns for each element type. These patterns enable a separate mechanical connection of each element to the other two elements, whereas the whole pattern necessary for the connection between modules remains the same for each element. The choice for the single shear screw connection type was influenced entirely by the requirement of enabling variable placement of the mechanical connectors along the longitudinal side of the elements. For fastening the elements, torx stainless steel countersunk wood screws with lengths of 40 and 60 mm were used. The screws are inserted through the holes of the predrilled element that is to be attached to the structure and screwed in the desired member of the structure with a portable electric screwdriver. By inserting two rather than only one screw at the lap joint, sufficient stiffness of the connection has been reached. The screw connection also enables an easy disassembly of the structure and reuse of both timber and screws.

Collaborative Human-Robot Assembly Setup

The setup of the proposed collaborative workflow for assembling the timber structure in alternating physical actions consists of two users equipped with a mobile AR device and complemented by a semi-mobile collaborative robot (Fig. 6). The mobile AR device enables both the users and the robot to build on the same workpiece, which is enabled by two key features: (1) The AR device's visual display can superimpose cues on the real-world video stream designed to assist the builders with information, in this particular case with visual cues on the design space in which they can make their design choices. (2) The simultaneous visual-inertial tracking capabilities of the AR device (Sandy 2018) allow the users to continually digitize their building actions (i.e., design choices); this is achieved by tracking and registering the precise position of newly placed keystone elements of the timber structure and by feeding this information back to the design engine (Fig. 7).

Open-Ended Assembly Workflow

The collaborative workflow consists of alternating user and machine actions of assembling timber elements into the spatial structure, in which each spontaneous user action is followed by a robot action. The combination of the timber elements into

7

modules of three thereby represents the alternating assembly sequence between the user (keystone element, freely placed by hand) and the robot (second and third element, computed and placed by the robot).

One iteration starts with the user tracking the built structure and observing the design space visualized via the AR interface (Fig. 7). The design space is visualized in the representation of arrows superimposed onto the built timber structure, in which the arrows indicate the open connectors and possible directions where the structure can be built and branched out. The location of the arrows are subject to various boundary conditions, in this case, the definition of initial target locations to where the structure should grow, as well as the current robot workspace. The user can then choose any location within the given design space to place the keystone element (Fig. 8a); while the chosen connection is then fixed in angle, the distance along the parent element's axis is subject to the user's decision. After the element is placed and mechanically fixed, its precise location (position and orientation) is then registered by the user via the AR device (Fig. 8b) and fed back to the design engine (Fig. 8c). In response to the user's freely placed element, the design engine then computes the location of the two subsequent elements to complement the module (Fig. 8d). For robotically placing the two computed elements, their corresponding robotic pick-and-place routines need to be calculated. The planning scene creation and the motion planning are done through COMPAS FAB, the robotic fabrication package for the COMPAS Framework (Rust et al. 2018), by using the MoveIt! Package from the Robot Operating System (ROS) backend (Coleman et al. 2014). In the closing of one iteration, the two elements are placed according to the computed robot motions (Fig. 8e).

Interoperability and Cross-Platform Communication

To ensure interoperability between the multiple devices and back-end computational processes, a necessary component is a scalable middleware technology as the communication infrastructure for the distributed system. In this case, this was achieved by using ROS, which is currently the state-of-the-art in robot middleware, providing a simple socket-based programmatic access to robot interfaces and algorithms, which external processes can access through the rosbridge package and roslibpy of COMPAS FAB. Here, the ROS system architecture is used to connect the multiple instances of (a) the design computation process embedded within the computer-aided design environment Rhino/Grasshopper (Robert McNeel & Associates 2020; Rutten 2020), (b) the mobile AR app for visualization and tracking, (c) the ROS MoveIt! Planner, and (d) the collaborative robot. The associated hardware consists of (a) a Windows PC (running the design computation process and a rosbridge client), (b) a Linux PC (running the ROS master, MoveIt!, and a rosbridge server), (c) an Android phone (running a rosbridge client within the AR app), and (d) the UR robot controller. For a viable communication, all devices have to be connected within the same Wi-Fi network.

RESULTS

To test the developed workflow and toolsets, a case study was conducted whereby two users and one collaborative Universal Robot (UR10e) interactively constructed a medium-scale architectural prototype. The prototype was realized on a building floor area of 2 × 3 m consisting of 6 MDF boards with dimensions of 1 × 1 m each and 6 mm thickness. This MDF flooring served both as a base for mounting the prototype with the elements placed on the ground to it and as a neutral background for the tracking. Additionally, dark lightproof, nonreflective fabric was suspended around the building area to exclude unnecessary surface edges from the tracking scene. To provide constant lighting conditions and thus uniform tracking results, only artificial light was used over the entire building process. A free space described by a 120 cm rail between the base of the prototype and the black coverings was used for the robot to be moved around within, as well as to allow for enough space for the robot motions.

Over three days, 102 timber elements were installed (Fig. 9), of which 16 were freely placed and tracked by a user, 56 were placed by the robot from three different locations, and 30 were placed by a user which could have been placed by the robot but were placed manually instead. This manual placement was made possible via the app, as the elements calculated by the design algorithm were visualized and the user could

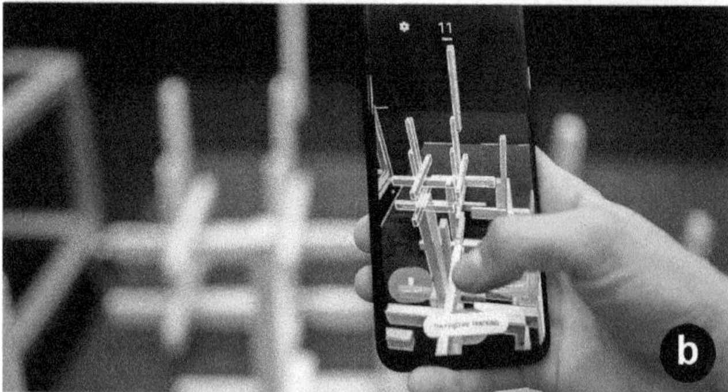

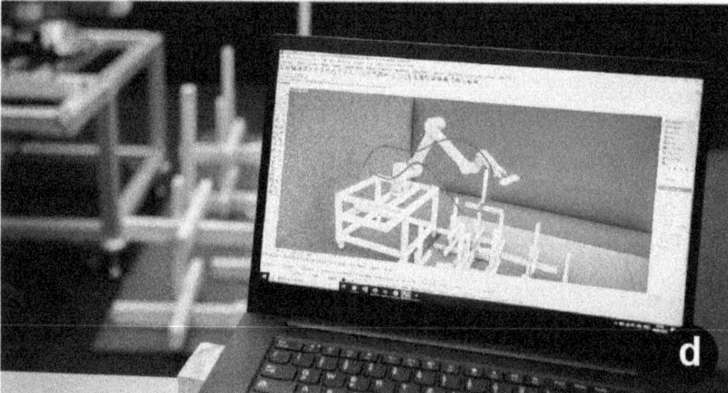

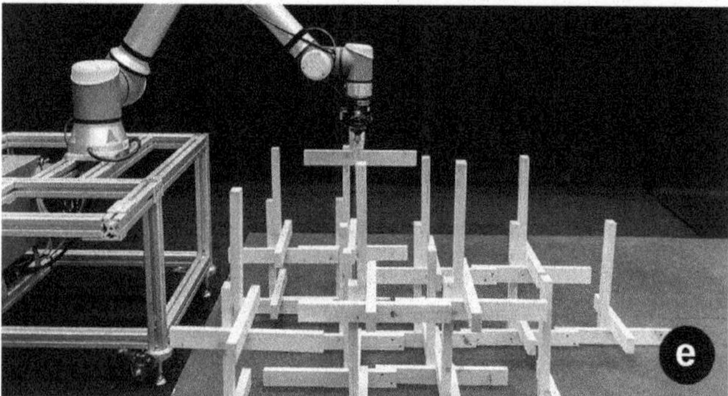

8

follow the superimposed outlines of the digital model over the video stream when placing them. At each of the robot's three locations, its origin was determined by manually matching recorded corner points of the built structure with the robot's measurement tip with their point location in the digital model. The tracking accuracy was observed to be well within 3 mm as indicated by ground truth measurements with the robot's measurement tip. The color gradients in the error plot (Fig. 10) indicate the deviation in distance (red) and rotation (blue) from the estimated object poses to the poses of the planned elements, which follow a rectilinear grid as defined by the design algorithm.

CONCLUSION AND OUTLOOK

Conclusion

The research presented in this paper has explored a novel open-ended digital fabrication workflow by introducing nonlinear principles of craft into a usually linear design-to-fabrication process. On the basis of an implemented design tool for the sensible distribution of tasks between humans and robots, this novel workflow could be carried out by two users and a collaborative robot. They all worked together in designing and assembling an unplanned spatial structure, combining explicit machine intelligence and implicit human knowledge and creativity. The realization of this concept was facilitated by state-of-the-art object tracking technology of an AR app, which provided the ability to register single objects precisely in 3D space and in relation to the built structure. The concepts and methods have been successfully evaluated and validated in one case study, the collaborative assembly of a branching spatial timber structure.

In this study, the global growth directions and local branching rules of the structure to be constructed were defined by the users at the start of the process. During the process, the users could follow the suggested directions that were visualized for them via the AR app, but make individual and spontaneous decisions within these suggested options. As such, the process facilitated the creative participation of humans in a digital building process by integrating creative decisions during the ongoing process. Design computation in this case was utilized not only to calculate a finished structure ready to be fabricated but to continually calculate a potential design space and resulting building options based on the users' decisions/input, as well as its corresponding robotic fabrication procedures. The result of this project was a timber structure—a complex 3D branching structure with varying densities—sequentially designed and built collaboratively on the basis of the user's design input and physical boundary conditions. In summary, the project has made it possible to question the typical roles of designers, builders, and robots. Transferred to practical applications for the architecture, construction, and engineering

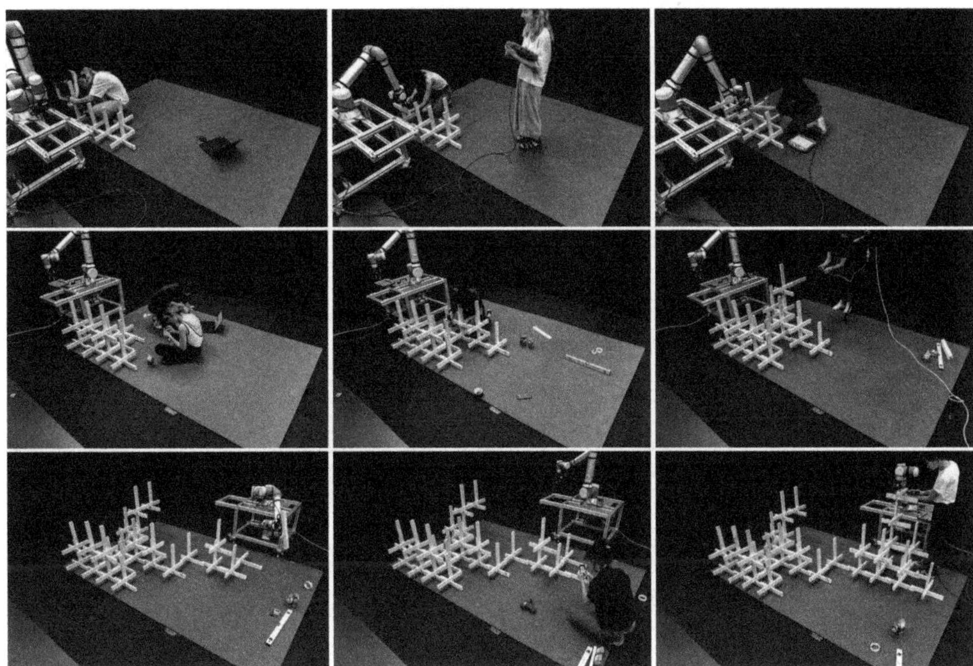

8 (a) The user can place an element freely within the boundaries of the AR-visualized design space. (b) After placing, the user must register the pose of the element via the tracking feature of the mobile AR app. (c) The registered pose is then transmitted to the CAD environment of the mobile AR app. (d) The two subsequent elements of one module and their respective robotic pick-and-place routines are then computed in response to the registered pose. (e) Finally, the robot places the two computed elements. At their target location, the user can fix the elements with screws.

9 Snapshots from the time lapse of the open-ended collaborative fabrication process.

9

industry, the proposed workflow also lays the foundation for future scenarios, implementing advanced technologies on the construction site, in which builders could actively intervene, physically or cognitively, supporting or steering automated processes towards higher levels of robustness and efficiency in complex or unforeseen scenarios.

Outlook

While this research allowed us to demonstrate the core concept of nonlinear and open-ended digital design-to-fabrication workflows, many directions for future work have been identified:

Structural evaluation: While structural evaluation is usually important for the final shape, in this research, maintaining structural stability during production is of great importance to ensure its equilibrium without further support. Due to the number of built elements compared to the scale, the built prototype's structural behavior could be intuitively anticipated by the users and thus affect their design decisions during building. This reduced the necessity for structural feedback through the design engine. Instead, locations were selected for new elements to be placed on the existing structure that were intuitively viewed as stable to continue building, such as by being mounted close to the structure's center of mass. However, the user's intuitive decision-making will require additional methods for evaluating the structure's stability, such as real-time structural analysis as an integrative part of design generation and computation of the design possibilities once the structure's complexity, such as by introducing cantilevering modules.

Mobile robot: Future applications of a robotic manipulator for collaborative fabrication should explore more elaborate robotic tasks to fully unfold its potential. Instead of a semi-mobile robot manipulator on a wheeled base and manually performed localization of the robot's origin, a mobile robot on an automatically movable base, and automating the robot localization by using the object registration capabilities of the mobile AR app, could be used.

Variability: The implemented bottom-up design strategies could be applied to building elements that vary in size and shape, as in the case of found material.

Scale: The process could be scaled up to enable the fabrication of larger structures to validate the stated concepts for fabrication at full architectural scale.

Gamification of construction: Future research will also look more closely at gamification in construction and its impact on the professions of architects and builders.

ACKNOWLEDGMENTS

This paper and the research were supported by incon.ai, which provided the AR tracking technology. We thank Begüm Saral for help with the fabrication of the prototype.

REFERENCES

Coleman, D., I. A. Şucan, S. Chitta, and N. Correll. 2014. "Reducing the Barrier to Entry of Complex Robotic Software: a MoveIt! Case Study," *Journal of Software Engineering for Robotics* 5(1): 3–16. doi: 10.6092/JOSER_2014_05_01_p3.

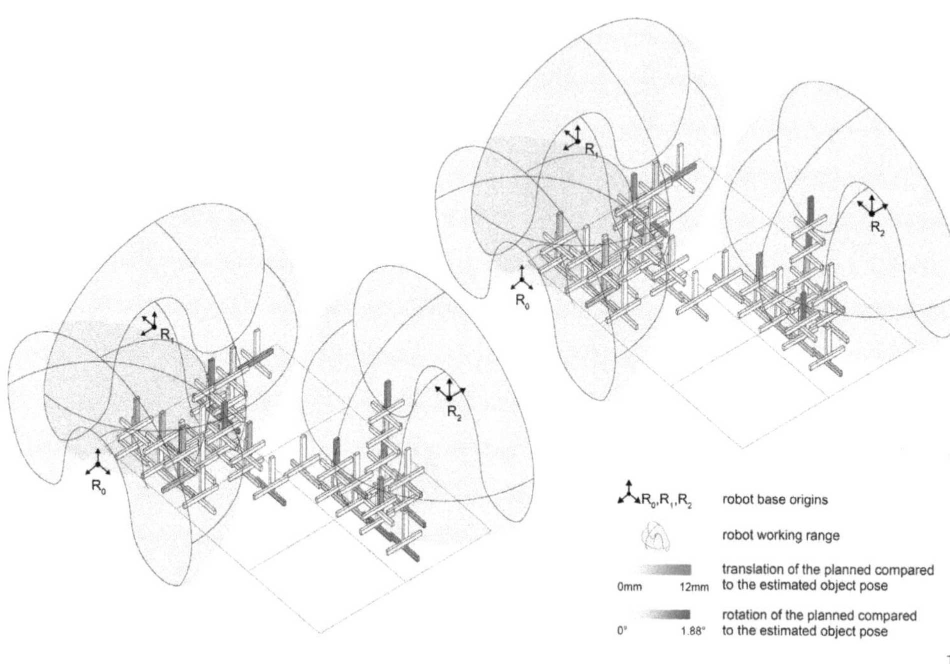

10

10 The color gradient indicates the divergence in translation (red) and rotation (blue), between the planned and estimated object poses, assuming they were to follow the rectilinear grid.

11 Potential design outcome: An overlaid structure, consisting of 290 timber elements generated following the rules of assembly grammar, within the design space defined by the realized prototype and following the branching directions specified by the users during building.

Dörfler, Kathrin, Florian Rist, and Romana Rust. 2012. "Interlacing: An Experimental Approach of Integrating Digital and Physical Design Methods." In *Rob|Arch 2012: Robotic Fabrication in Architecture, Art and Design*, edited by S. Brell-Çokcan and J. Braumann, 82–91. Vienna: Springer-Verlag Wien.

Gramazio, Fabio, Matthias Kohler, and Jan Willmann. 2014. *The Robotic Touch: How Robots Change Architecture*. Zurich: Park Books.

Ingold, Tim. 2010. "The Textility of Making." *Cambridge Journal of Economics* 34 (March): 91–102.

Jahn, Gwyllim, Cameron Newnham, Nick van den Berg, Melissa Iraheta, and Jackson Wells. 2020. "Holographic Construction." In *Impact: Design With All Senses*, 314–324. Cham: Springer.

Knight, Terry. 2017. "Craft, Performance, and Grammars." In Proceedings of the *2nd International Workshop on Cultural DNA*, Daejoen, South Korea, 13 January 2017.

Knight, Terry, and George Stiny. 2015. "Making Grammars: From Computing with Shapes to Computing with Things." *Design Studies* 41: 8–28.

Larsson, Maria, Hironori Yoshida, and Takeo Igarashi. 2019. "Human-in-the-Loop Fabrication of 3D Surfaces with Natural Tree Branches." In SCF '19 *[Proceedings of the ACM Symposium on Computational Fabrication]*, Pittsburgh, PA, 16–18 June 2019, edited by Stephen N. Spencer, 1–12. Association for Computing Machinery.

Mele, Tom Van, Andrew Liew, Tomás Méndez Echenagucia, and Matthias Rippmann. 2017. "COMPAS: A Framework for Computational Research in Architecture and Structures." http://compas-dev.github.io/compas/.

Mitterberger, Daniela, Kathrin Dörfler, Timothy Sandy, Foteini Salveridou, Marco Hutter, Fabio Gramazio, and Matthias Kohler. 2020. "Augmented Bricklaying." *Construction Robotics* 4 (3–4): 151–161. https://doi.org/10.3929/ethz-b-000466341.

Mueller, Stefanie, Anna Seufert, Huaishu Peng, Robert Kovacs, Kevin Reuss, François Guimbretière, and Patrick Baudisch. 2019. "FormFab: Continuous Interactive Fabrication." In *TEI '19 [Proceedings of the Thirteenth International Conference on Tangible, Embedded, and Embodied Interaction]*, Tempe, AZ, 17–20 March 2019, 315–323. Association for Computing Machinery.

Peng, Huaishu, Jimmy Briggs, Cheng-Yao Wang, Kevin Guo, Joseph Kider, Stefanie Mueller, Patrick Baudisch, and François Guimbretière. 2018. "RoMA: Interactive Fabrication with Augmented Reality and a Robotic 3D Printer." In *CHI '18 [Proceedings of the 2018 CHI Conference on Human Factors in Computing Systems]*, Montreal, Canada, 21–26 April 2018, 1–12. Association for Computing Machinery.

Risatti, Howard. 2007. *A Theory of Craft: Function and Aesthetic Expression*. The University of North Carolina Press.

Robert McNeel & Associates. *Rhinoceros*. V.6.0. Robert McNeel & Associates. PC. 2020.

Rossi, Andrea, and Oliver Tessmann. 2017. "Geometry as Assembly Integrating Design and Fabrication with Discrete Modular Units." *Proceedings of eCAADe 2017* 2: 201–210. eCAADe.

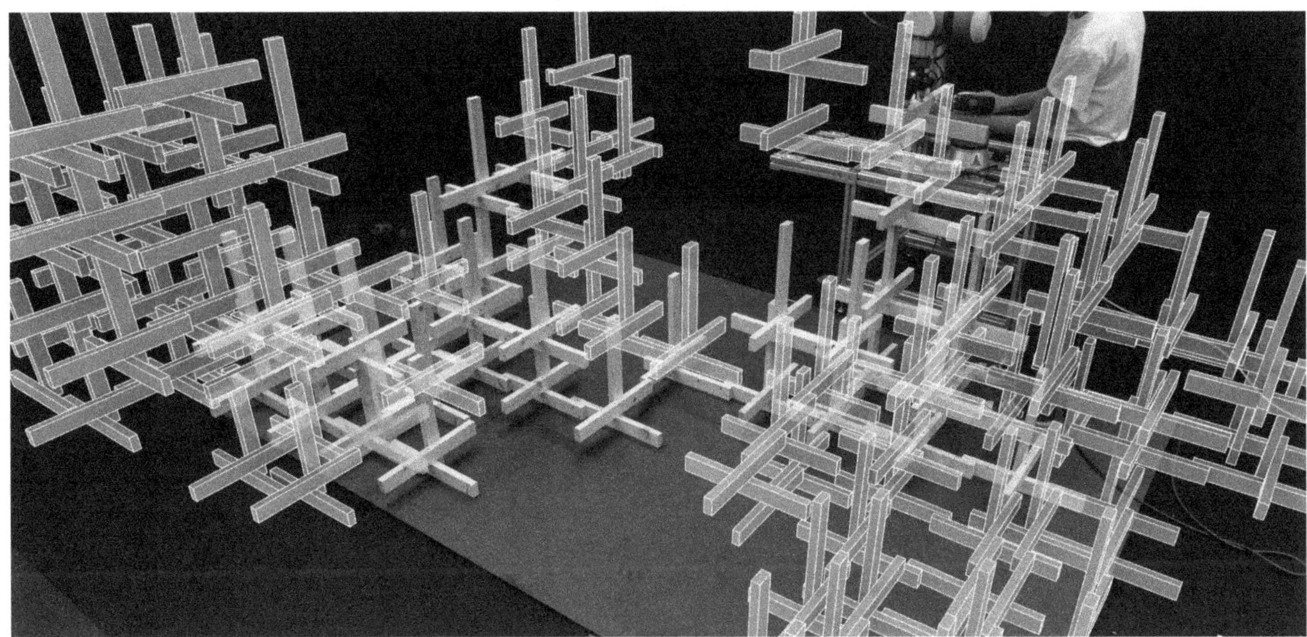

11

Rust, R., G. Casas, S. Parascho, D. Jenny, K. Dörfler, M. Helmreich, A. Gandia, I. Ariza, M. Pacher, B. Lytle, Y. Huang. 2018. *{COMPAS~FAB}: Robotic Fabrication Package for the COMPAS Framework*. Gramazio Kohler Research, ETH Zürich. https://github.com/compas-dev/compas_fab/. DOI:10.5281/zenodo.3469478.

Rutten, David. 2020. *Grasshopper*. V.1.0.0007. Robert McNeel & Associates. PC.

Sandy, Timothy, and Jonas Buchli. 2018. "Object-Based Visual-Inertial Tracking for Additive Fabrication." *IEEE Robotics and Automation Letters* 3 (3).

Sennett, Richard. 2008. *The Craftsman*. New Haven, CT: Yale University Press.

Temeltaş, Handan. 2017. "Collaboration and Exchange between 'Craftsman' and 'Designer': Symbiosis towards Product Innovation." *The Design Journal* 20 (1): S3713–S3723.

Willis, K D D, C Xu, K.-J. Wu, G. Levin, and M. D. Gross. 2011. "Interactive Fabrication New Interfaces for Digital Fabrication." In *TEI '11 [Proceedings of the Fifth International Conference on Tangible, Embedded, and Embodied Interaction]*, Funchal, Portugal, 22–26 January 2011, 69–72. Association for Computing Machinery.

Lidia Atanasova is an architect and PhD researcher at the TT Professorship Digital Fabrication (Augmented Fabrication Lab), a research group based at the Faculty of Architecture and associated with the Faculty of Civil, Geo and Environmental Engineering at TU Munich.

Daniela Mitterberger is an architect and a PhD researcher and A&T PhD Fellow at the Chair of Architecture and Digital Fabrication (Gramazio Kohler Research) at ETH Zurich. She is also the cofounder and director of MAEID—FutureRetrospectiveNarrative, a multidisciplinary architecture practice based in Vienna.

Timothy Sandy received his PhD in robotics, as a part of the NCCR Digital Fabrication at ETH Zurich, in 2018. In 2020, he was awarded an ETH Pioneer Fellowship and is building the spinoff incon.ai to provide augmented reality guidance tools to fabricators and construction workers.

Fabio Gramazio is an architect and cofounder of Gramazio Kohler Research, an architectural robotics laboratory at ETH Zurich. Gramazio Kohler Research has been formative in the field of digital architecture, creating a new research field merging advanced architectural design and additive fabrication processes through the customized use of industrial robots.

Matthias Kohler is an architect and cofounder of Gramazio Kohler Research, an architectural robotics laboratory at ETH Zurich. Gramazio Kohler Research has been formative in the field of digital architecture, creating a new research field merging advanced architectural design and additive fabrication processes through the customized use of industrial robots.

Kathrin Dörfler is leading the TT Professorship Digital Fabrication (Augmented Fabrication Lab) at the Faculty of Architecture and the Faculty of Civil, Geo and Environmental Engineering at TU Munich. Research in the Augmented Fabrication Lab is dedicated to fabrication-aware design and robotic fabrication processes.

Adaptive Textile Facades Through the Integration of Shape Memory Alloy

Maxie Schneider*
Ebba Fransén Waldhör*
Weißensee School of Art and Design

Paul-Rouven Denz*
Puttakhun Vongsingha
Natchai Suwannapruk
Priedemann Facade-Lab

Christiane Sauer
Weißensee School of Art and Design

*Authors contributed equally to the research.

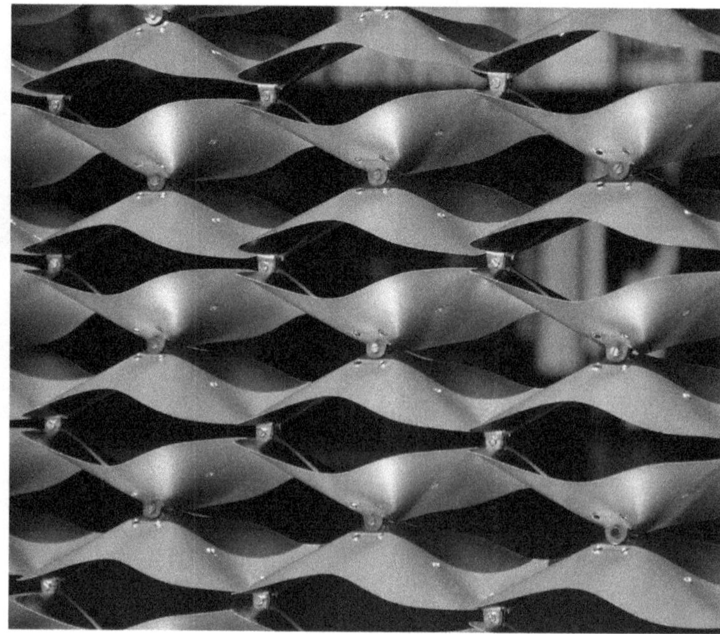

1 Two concepts for adaptive textile facade screens: ADAPTEX Mesh (left) and ADAPTEX Wave (right).

ABSTRACT

The R&D project ADAPTEX showcases a material-driven and computationally informed design approach to adaptive textile facades through the integration of shape memory alloy (SMA) as an actuator. The results exhibit thermally responsive and self-sufficient sun-shading solutions with innovative design potential that enhance the energy performance of the built environment. With regard to climate targets, an environmentally viable concept is proposed that reduces the energy required for climatization, is lightweight, and can function as a refurbishment system. Two concepts—ADAPTEX Wave and ADAPTEX Mesh—are being developed to be tested as full-scale demonstrators for facade deployment by an interdisciplinary team from architecture, textile design, facade engineering, and material research. The two concepts follow a material-driven, low-complexity design strategy and differ in type of kinetic movement, textile construction, integration of the SMA, reset force, and scale of permeability. In this paper, we describe the computational design process and tools to develop and design current and future prototypes and demonstrators, providing insights on the challenges and potentials of developing textiles with integrated shape memory alloys for architectural applications.

INTRODUCTION

The European Green Deal calls for a resilient climate adaptation of future building systems in order to combat the effects of climate change. Furthermore, the decarbonization of heating and cooling technologies of buildings can save up to 18% of currently consumed energy (European Commission 2020).

The facade, as an interface between the building and its environment, plays a key role in regulating the building's energy performance and efficiently preventing the overheating of interior spaces. Shading strategies are commonly considered the best method to prevent direct solar radiation from penetrating the interior space and overheating. New generations of facades are shifting towards multifunctionality and adaptive systems, allowing them to alter their behavior in response to the environment, as well as the integration of additional functional components and layers (Loonen et al. 2015). This polyvalent approach potentially results in a more complex system that can lead to maintenance issues—especially for mechanical actuators of kinetic facades (Loonen et al. 2011). The implementation of "smart materials" that display an intrinsic control or self-adjustment capacity can help reduce over-complexity, maintenance, and recycling issues, as shown in the literature review by Fiorito et al. (2016).

ADAPTEX explores the potential of implementing shape memory alloy (SMA) as an actuator for an adaptive, lightweight textile facade (Fig. 1). As a small size actuator with inherent sensing capabilities, SMA has the potential to supersede complex motors, driving mechanisms, and control systems. If thermally activated by solar energy, it eliminates the need for energy consumption in operation.

As the SMA responds to temperature changes in its immediate environment, it can be utilized to activate a surface and control the permeability of the textile surface: adjusting parameters like light transmission and reflection. The aim is to create a responsive textile system that regulates solar gain by maximizing daylight autonomy and view and minimizing overheating and glare, as well as meeting all relevant sun-shading criteria as defined by Kuhn (2017).

Textiles offer several advantages as architectural facades: their light weight, unique configurability, and flexibility in application (Sauer 2019). Furthermore, the assumption in ADAPTEX is that the structure of textiles—the interlocking of filaments—and the near-endless possibilities for material configuration make them especially suitable for the integration of filament-shaped, functional components such as SMA, and enable their transfer to an architectural scale (Denz 2017). The textile, the SMA and the environment are understood as a coherent system, in which the elements work together to create a cyclical movement between a closing and opening of the surface.

METHODOLOGY

The research is a collaboration of an interdisciplinary team from the fields of architecture, engineering, textile design, textile fabrication and smart materials research, bringing together all relevant expertise on the topic. Through a research-by-design approach, various application scenarios were developed on the basis of an initial requirement matrix that combined criteria defined by the different disciplines, as well as multi-scalar influences ranging from hard constraints to more flexible parameters (Denz et al., 2021). After a thorough evaluation, the two most promising concepts, Mesh and Wave (Fig. 1), were further developed through physical prototyping and computational design processes.

To facilitate the design and planning process a series of parametric design tools were developed. The tools were created with Grasshopper—a graphical algorithm editor which is integrated in the NURBS based 3D computer-aided design software Rhinoceros (Grasshopper 2009). The design criteria such as textile thickness, angle and transition behavior were translated into algorithmic parameters which were used in investigating and optimizing the openness factor, the permeability, as well as material interaction of ADAPTEX. Furthermore, the environmental context was explored by a comprehensive analysis of weather data in various climatic settings. Relevant data from the EnergyPlus Weather Data (.epw) such as dry-bulb temperature, day/night temperature differences, solar radiation, sunshine hours, and solar hours were mapped against the SMA activation temperature. The evaluation enhances the selection

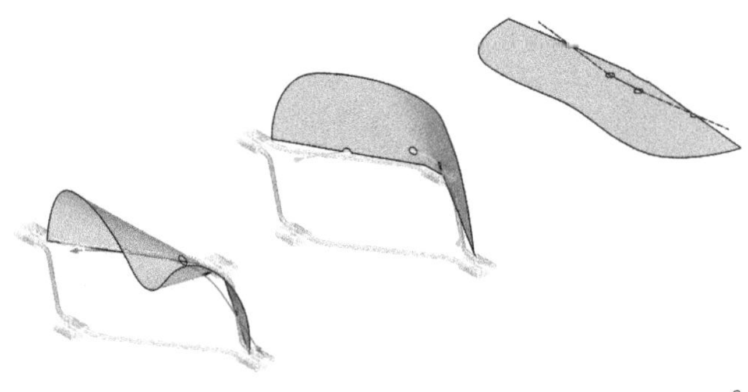

2

2 ADAPTEX Wave: Design principle of kinetic actuation.

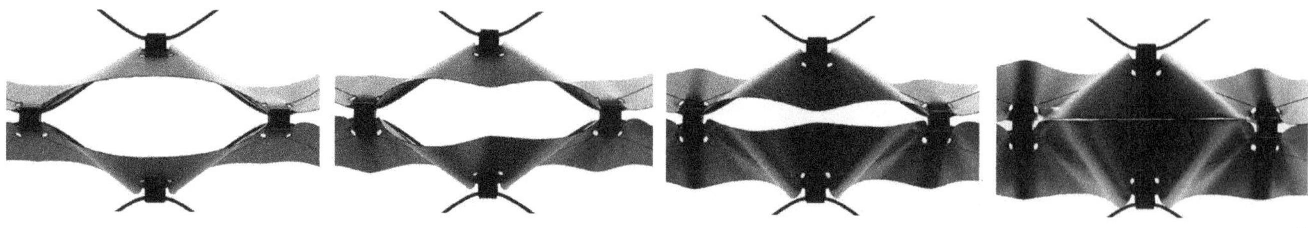

3 ADAPTEX Wave: Sequence of kinetic movement.

process of the optimal SMA for the context of a specific project site (Fig. 15).

STATE OF THE ART

In recent years, researchers have increasingly investigated the use of SMA within an architectural context, especially in attempts to replace mechanical control systems of shading devices (Addington and Schodek 2005). The review by Fiorito et al. (2016) shows that SMA is one of the most favorable actuators in research for shape-morphing solar shading systems. It has been used in various scales of applications, both as a subcomponent and integrated into the shading surface itself. An example where the SMA is a subcomponent can be seen in the project Harvest Shade Screens, where one SMA wire and a tension spring is used to control multiple louvers (Grinham et al. 2014). Decker and Zarzycki (2014) also employ one SMA actuator that reacts to ambient temperature to control a vertically moving screen system. The single actuator consists of a spring set and is designed as an independent component separated from the shading membrane itself. A more modular and integrated approach can be seen in the project Air-flow(er), where multiple individual, rigid panels are opened and closed by two sets of counteracting SMAs (Payne and Johnson 2013).

While the integration of SMA in architectural textile is relatively limited, a number of experimental approaches have shown promising results. The project Blind strives for a media facade by anchoring SMA springs within an elastic membrane with eye-like openings (Khoo, Salim, and Burry 2001). Coelho and Maes (2009) have been successfully embroidering SMA on a felt textile to activate louvers. A concept with modular textile umbrella-shaped elements has been developed into a full-scale mock-up by Finnsdottir and Sauer (2014). Adaptive textile shading devices have been investigated in terms of energetic (Chamilothori, Kampitaki, and Oungrinis 2013), material performance in glass fiber-reinforced polymers (GFRP) and occupants perception (Baehr-Bruyère et al. 2019).

ADAPTEX aims at feasible, scalable sun-shading systems for building envelope application. A core part is therefore the development of a full-size facade system for testing in a real environment (Denz, Vongsingha et al. 2021) through an iterative process of designing, modeling, and testing of smaller-scale demonstrators (Denz, Sauer et al. 2021).

COMPUTER-AIDED PHYSICAL PROTOTYPING

ADAPTEX Wave

In ADAPTEX Wave, a cyclic actuation is achieved by designing the interplay between the material strain of a textile band and an SMA wire. By fixing wave-shaped, semi-rigid textile bands at specific points to a cable net, a strain is created in the material (Fig. 2). Each band is interwoven across its entire length with a linear SMA wire, which contracts by 5% when activated, thereby forcing the band to buckle. This leads to a closure of the overall surface (Fig. 3). Due to the material strain, the textile band is able to move back to its original position after the elastic deformation. In the first full-scale prototype, the textile bands are made of an opaque, durable, flexural-resistant, glass-fiber-reinforced fabric. In an iterative form-finding process, variations of opening angles and actuator positions were derived.

ADAPTEX Wave: Parametric 3D-Model

Starting from simple paper-based geometric prototypes, the system layout was digitally modeled to obtain an optimal geometry in correspondence with the various shape changes. The textile geometry was continually optimized both on the physical model and within the CAD environment, in a continual exchange between design and analytical processing. Properties and bending behavior of different

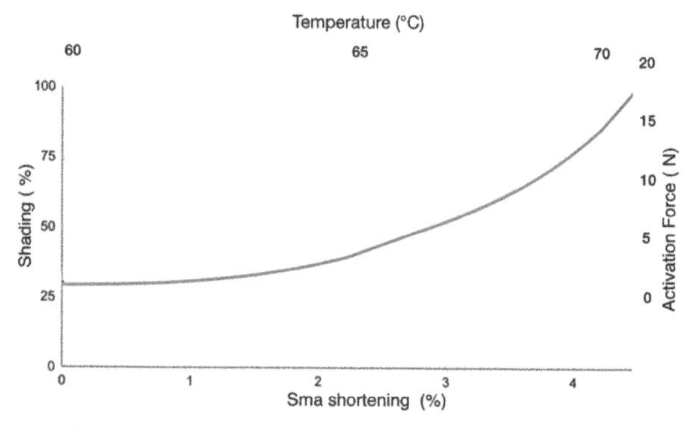

4 ADAPTEX Wave: shading and activation force in relation to SMA shortening.

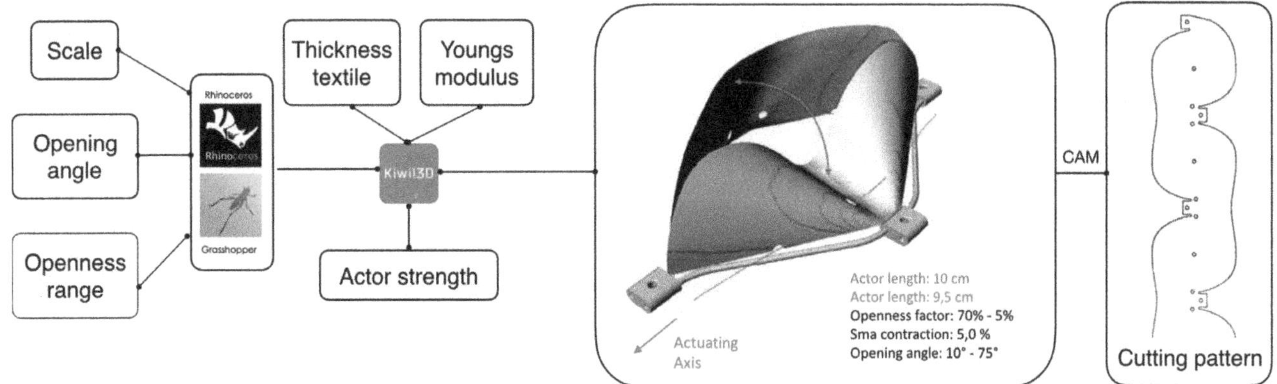

5 Loads and boundary conditions as well as material parameters can be assigned to the structure inside Rhino.

5

textiles, the position of the SMA, as well as joining techniques and manufacturing possibilities, are explored and fed back into the digital 3D model. The digital representation of the material parameters enables a functional optimization of the material system. This makes it possible to integrate the complex multiscalar interdependencies of the textile hybrid system and to predict the behavior of the physical prototype (Fig. 4).

The plugin Kiwi!3D for Rhino/Grasshopper (Bauer et al. 2018) is especially helpful as it performs an isogeometric analysis of the system (after nonlinear Kirchhoff-Love theory for thin plates) and allows for incorporating material values such as Young's modulus, element thickness, as well as the specific pull-force of the SMA. The finite element analysis (FEA) can be directly integrated into conventional NURBS-based CAD designs. This feature is extremely beneficial since a direct structural feedback can be provided to the designer. The kinetic movement and possible resulting stresses in the dynamic computer simulations form an integral part of the design process. Based on the geometric simulation of the optimal relaxed and deformed shape of the textile, two-dimensional cutting patterns for manufacturing the textile bands can be generated (Fig.5).

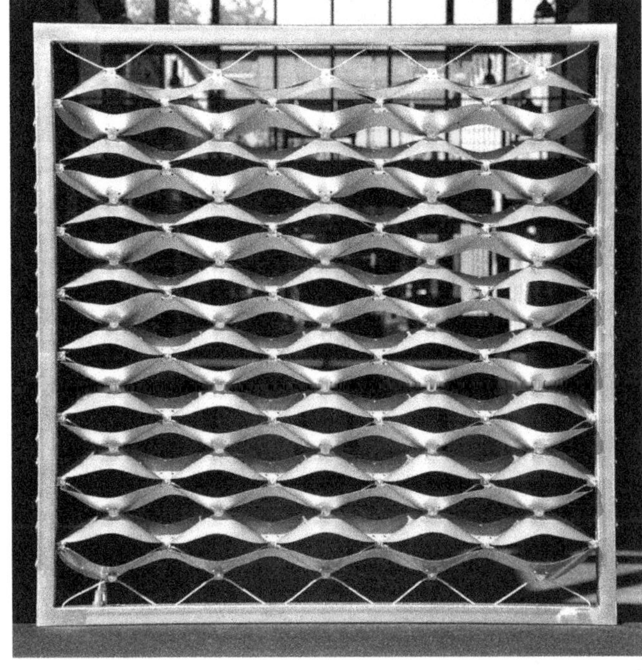

6

6 ADAPTEX Wave: Front view of closed 1 × 1 m prototype.

7

7 ADAPTEX Wave: Detail of prototype, open and closed state.

8 ADAPTEX Mesh in basalt and glass fiber.

9 Close-up of a 0.1 mm SMA wire embedded into the textile.

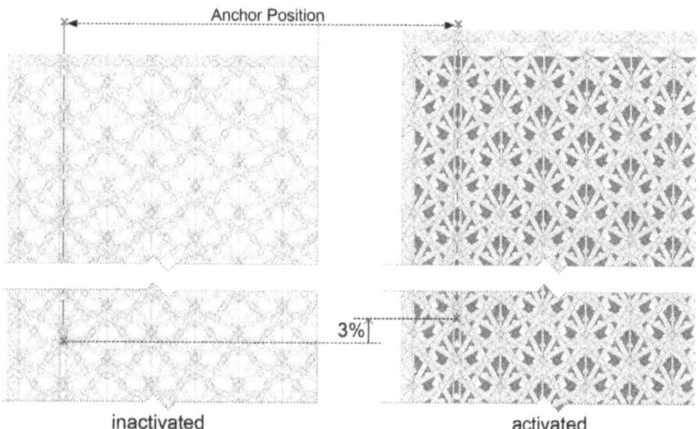

10 The length of the SMA (red) depends on the scale of the textile pattern, as it is set to contract 3% in activation. The lower the contraction, the more cycles are possible. However, a too-small shape change (< 1%) is challenging to control.

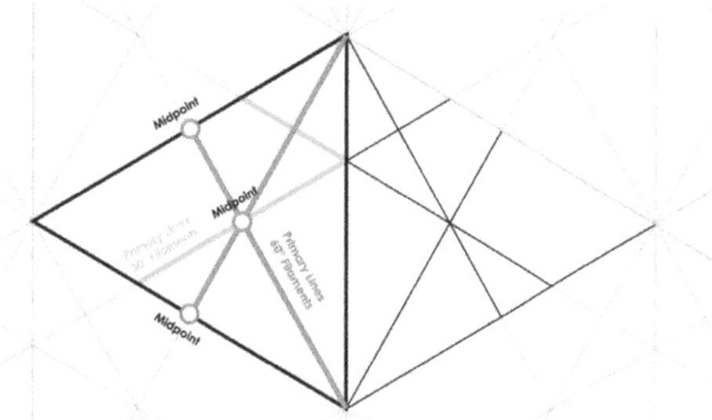

11 Pattern design.

ADAPTEX Wave: Result

The soft kinetic of ADAPTEX Wave (Fig. 6) displays a muscle-like behavior that is smooth and silent. As the textile band is interwoven with the SMA wire following a precisely calculated path, the relatively small actuation of 5% in contraction results in a transition of an openness factor switching between 70% and 0–5% (Fig. 7). As the bands are separate elements, a partial activation in the surface is possible.

ADAPTEX Mesh

In ADAPTEX Mesh, the aim is to develop a resource-efficient, simple system with a high Technology Readiness Level (TRL). The basic principle is that of two or more membranes with identical perforations aligned in front of each other to provide maximum permeability. As one of the membranes slides upwards, the overall permeability of the total surface decreases. The advantage of this principle is the small vertical movement generating a considerable impact in terms of shading efficiency. Different variations of this principle have been explored as a theoretical concept, for example, by Karamata and Andersen (2014) and by Hoberman as metal screen systems (2015). In ADAPTEX Mesh, the design of the textile membranes evolved through an iterative process between physical prototyping and digital modeling—from woven, orthogonally structured fabrics towards the realization as a structurally and optically optimized multiaxial noncrimp fabric with fully integrated SMA wires (Fig. 8). In the first full-scale prototype, the textile is fabricated from durable glass fiber facing the exterior (as it reflects incoming sunlight and lowers the energetic impact), and in a darker basalt fiber facing the interior (as it enhances the visibility from inside to outside, due to higher contrast).

ADAPTEX Mesh: Textile Construction and SMA Integration

Multiaxial, noncrimp textiles made up of layers of nonundulating filaments are commonly used as reinforcement fabrics in construction, as the load-absorbing filaments can be placed along the principal stress lines (Carvelli, Lomov et al. 2015). This method of constructing fabric lends itself well to creating a perforated structure that can be designed and adapted to the specific requirements of an adaptive sun shading system controlled by SMA. The filaments can be laid specifically to counterbalance the pull-force of the SMA so as to prevent deformation of the fabric. The required rigidity can be calibrated through the filament angle and thickness so that the textile remains flexible enough to be rolled for transportation.

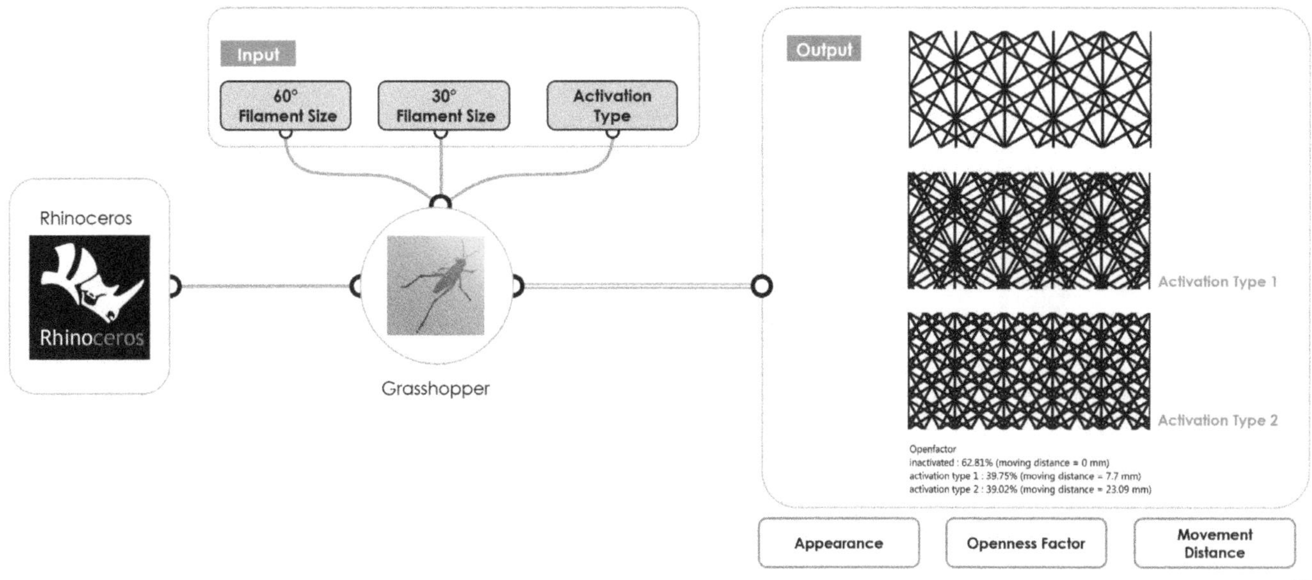

12 ADAPTEX Mesh: Rhino-based tool for openness factor analysis.

12

Furthermore, the layering of nonundulating fibers makes it possible to create a linear geometry guiding the integrated SMA within the textile structure (Fig. 9). This enables a flexible distribution of SMA wires over various kinds of geometries. The SMA runs within this linear geometry (Fig. 9), and is fixed at one end within the textile. The other end is attached to the supporting frame (Fig. 10). As the SMA is activated, it contracts by 3% and thereby slides the entire membrane a few centimeters upwards. As the temperature drops and the SMA cools down, the weight of the fabric ensures that it moves back to its original position driven by gravity only.

ADAPTEX Mesh: Computational Pattern Design

The size and the geometry of the overlapping areas determine the openness factor and can easily be adapted to specific building requirements. The textile pattern (Figs. 9, 11) was transferred into a parametric 3D model that serves

13 ADAPTEX Mesh: Front view of closed 1 × 1 m prototype.

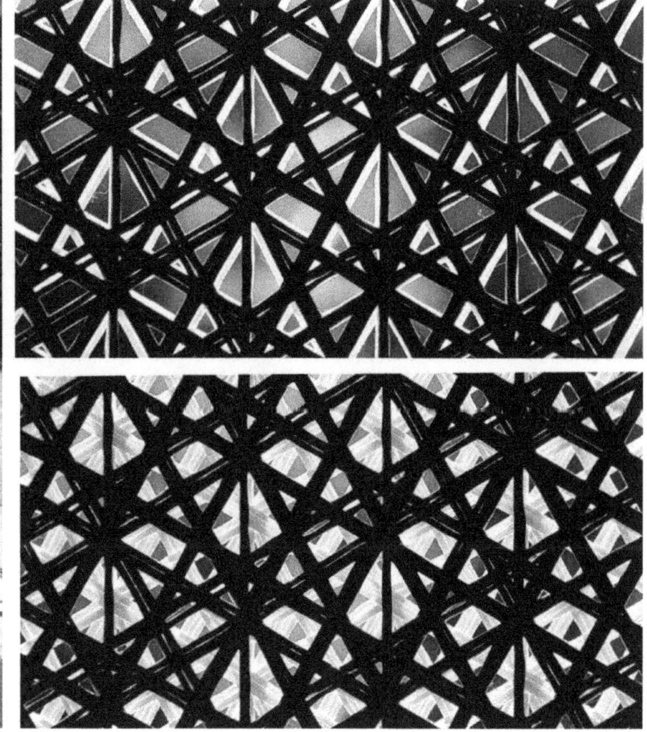

14 Detail of prototype, open and closed state.

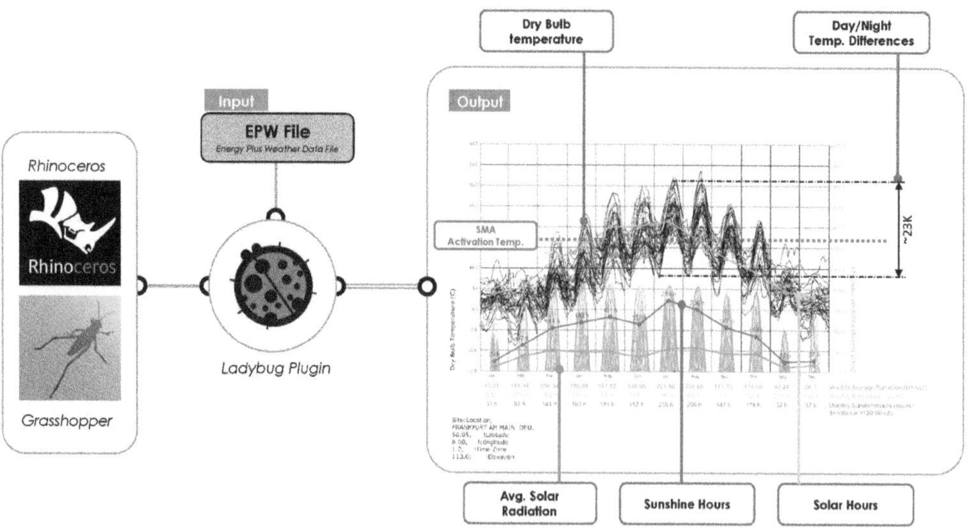

15 Integrated information flow chart of weather data analysis.

as a basis for subsequent fabrication and allows for easy adjustment of filament width and orientation. A Rhino-based tool for analyzing and evaluating openness factors was developed (Figs. 11, 12).

The program generates combinations of various widths of the filaments, according to a predefined range, and analyzes the openness factor of the system in three different states: inactivated, activation type 1, and activation type 2 (Fig. 12). Activation types 1 and 2 differ in length of movement, where the latter renders a more light-diffusing pattern than the former. The required openness factor is generally defined by the building requirements, and the most suitable corresponding pattern and movement type can be selected according to the result of the analysis. Commonly, the selection will be based on the suitable openness factor and the biggest difference between the activated and inactivated positions, ensuring an optimal daylight scenario. The parametric tool also enables scaling of the pattern, adjusting for application demands such as requirements of illuminance level, glare protection, shading effect, facade size and position, etc., and further iterations in the development process.

ADAPTEX Mesh: Result

ADAPTEX Mesh works as a cyclic sensor-actuator-reset system and follows a resource-efficient strategy for deployment of SMA. The pattern can be adapted to many different scenarios. As the one screen slides on top of the other, dynamic variations of the original pattern appear, intensified by the materiality of the glass fiber filaments and the parallax effect of the double layers (Figs. 13, 14). As a sun-shading screen, its intricate aesthetics link to a long tradition of the Islamic mashrabiya and Indian jali.

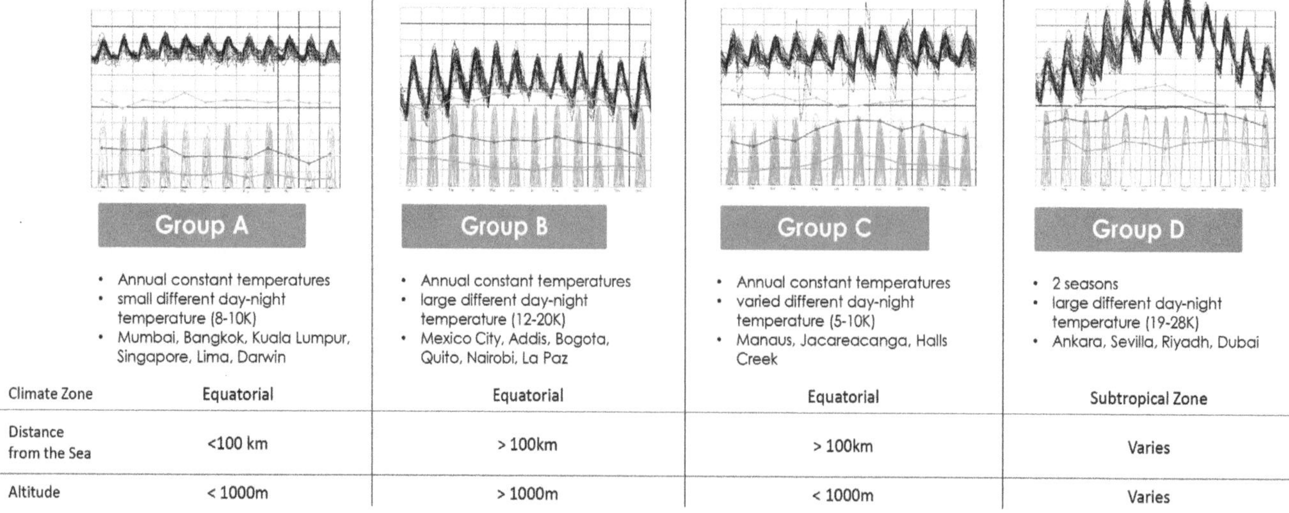

Group A
Annual constant temperatures
small different day-night temperature (8-10K)
Mumbai, Bangkok, Kuala Lumpur, Singapore, Lima, Darwin
Group B
Annual constant temperatures
large different day-night temperature (12-20K)
Mexico City, Addis, Bogota, Quito, Nairobi, La Paz
Group C
Annual constant temperatures
varied different day-night temperature (5-10K)
Manaus, Jacareacanga, Halls Creek
Group D
2 seasons
large different day-night temperature (19-28K)
Ankara, Sevilla, Riyadh, Dubai
Climate Zone
Equatorial
Equatorial
Equatorial
Subtropical Zone
Distance from the Sea
<100 km
> 100km
> 100km
Varies
Altitude
< 1000m
> 1000m
< 1000m
Varies

16

16 Location groups for weather data analysis. Locations categorized in groups based on the weather data extracted from EPW. The characteristics of each city result in unique weather conditions.

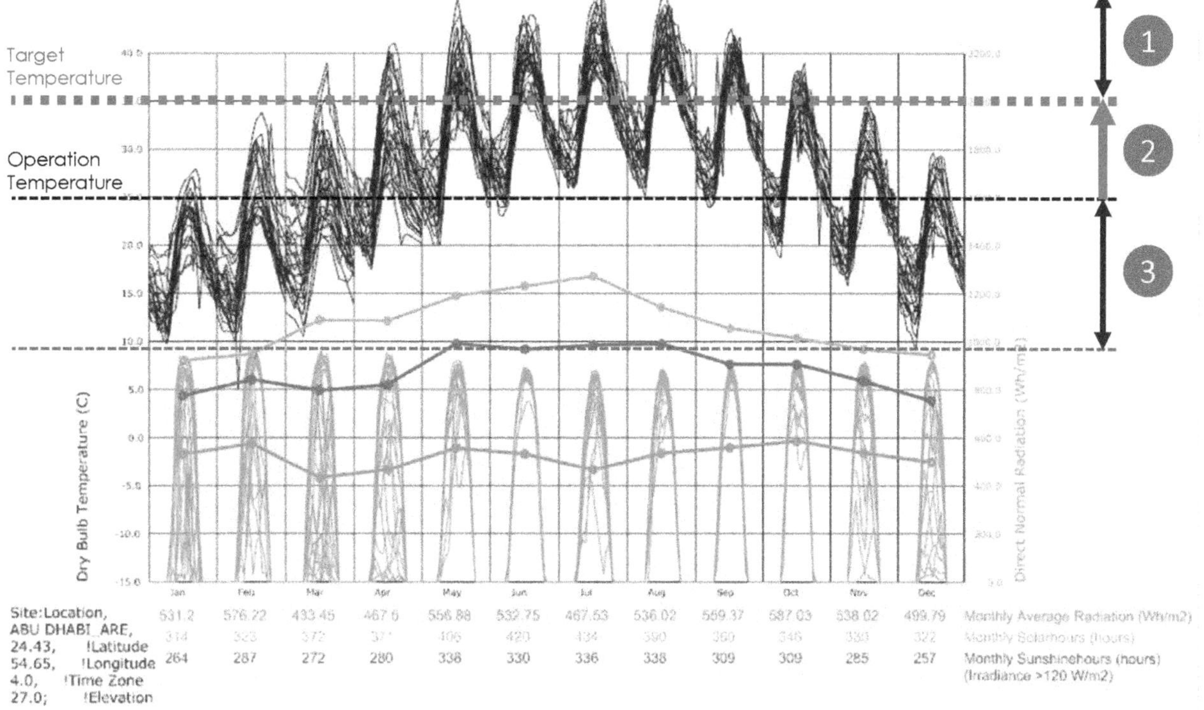

17 Example of weather data integrated information in Abu Dhabi, with a suggested activation temperature of 35° Celsius.

COMPUTATIONAL SIMULATIONS

Weather Data Analysis

As the SMA is activated by changes in the surrounding temperature, the relationship between solar radiation, temperature, and time must be investigated and analyzed. With the help of a systematic compilation of relevant weather data information, ideal locations and suitable SMA activation temperatures for different scenarios can be identified. The aim is to design both Wave and Mesh for a self-sufficient operation, activated only during essential time periods such as temporary exposure to high direct solar radiation and/or high ambient air temperature.

Assumption of ideal locations for an autarkic implementation of the system include areas with high solar radiation, high air temperature differences between day and night, and stable temperature ranges throughout the year. Following this criteria, 19 cities near the equatorial zone were selected and investigated with the following data: dry bulb temperature (exterior temperature without influence from solar radiation), daily direct solar radiation, and daily solar hours and daily sunshine hours (solar irradiance > 120 W/m²). The data was retrieved from the EnergyPlus Weather (EPW) database and compiled in visual charts for easy comparison (Fig. 15).

By cross-referencing the data, suitable locations and a range of SMA activation temperatures could be determined. According to the results, the locations were classified into four groups as shown in Figure 16.

The most suitable group is B with a high day-night temperature difference and a constant annual temperature, followed by groups A and C. For group D, a successful implementation depends on the chosen activation temperature—the sun shading could be activated during day in summer, deactivated at night, and inactivated in most parts of winter.

The example in Figure 17 shows the result of Abu Dhabi (group D). The activation temperature (target temperature) is set at 35°C. It was predicted that there could be three different situations. The first situation starts from May–September, in which during the day the dry bulb temperatures are higher than the activation temperature. In this situation, the sun shading will be activated during the day and deactivated during the night, solely through the drop in air temperature. The second situation starts from February–May and October–December, where low temperature might not activate the system at all, unless there is solar radiation directly on the actuation area. And in the third situation, in January, the system might remain inactivated at all times.

To facilitate the evaluation process, the data is extracted and illustrated in an integrated set of graphs. This obtained data along with other relevant information such as geographical location, facade orientation, building function, and user preferences enable the SMA activation temperature to be defined.

As the SMA reacts to the ambient temperature, the results of the Weather Data Analysis have a crucial role in determining the position of the ADAPTEX screen within the facade. For example, the cavity of a double-skin facade possesses higher ambient temperature and at the same time prevents direct influence from short-term weather changes like wind or clouds. For implementations in locations with high solar radiation but low dry bulb temperature, the placement of the system within the cavity of a double-glazed unit can enable the solar radiation to be transformed into thermal energy and increase the local temperature of the textile surface. Moreover, various stages of closure and ventilation of the cavity could also further influence the operation of the system.

The sun-shading system can also be positioned at the facade exterior, with an SMA that reacts at lower temperature and is activated only by direct radiation. Since the system is fully exposed to weather and highly ventilated, the activation and deactivation process is presumably faster in comparison to the sun shading located inside the cavity of a double-skin facade or similar.

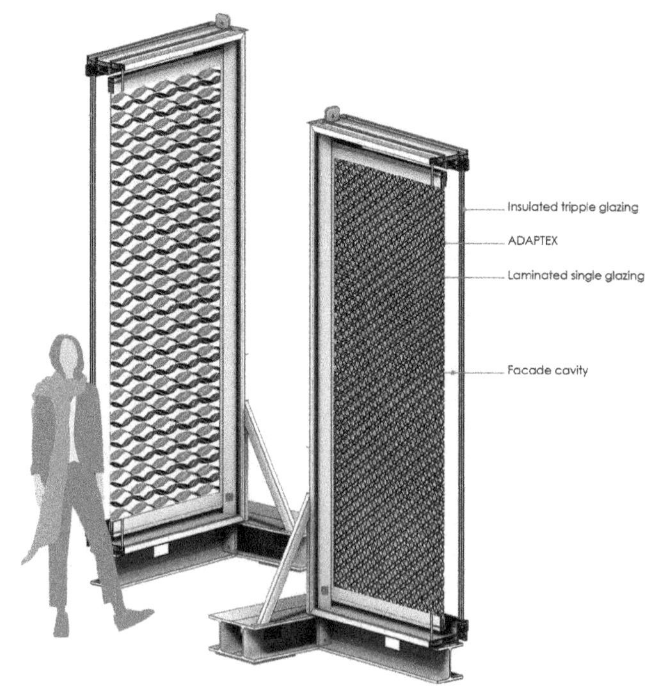

18 3D model for production planning of the double-skin facade with ADAPTEX prototype located inside the facade cavity.

The performance of the sun shading in relation to the position in the facade is currently being tested at the Fraunhofer Institute for Solar Energy Systems with 1 × 1 m prototypes. As a next step, the concepts will be scaled up and tested within real-size facade units (Fig. 18) and implemented on an existing facade in Oman, as part of the follow-up project ADAPTEX Klima+. Within these further development stages, challenges that arose in the making of the first small-scale prototypes (Figs. 6, 13) will be dealt with, and the project will evolve from a prototyping stage to more industrial construction processes (Denz, Vongsingha et al. 2021).

DISCUSSION AND OUTLOOK

The development of textile facade actuators based on shape memory alloys requires highly interdisciplinary expertise (Denz, Sauer et al. 2021). Due to the large number of influencing factors, such as location-specific air temperature, position within the facade, and the technical constraints of the SMA, the design of such systems is not automatically transferable or scalable. This requires an approach where several interconnected parametric design tools become inevitable.

ADAPTEX Wave and ADAPTEX Mesh, with their distinct properties arising from their materials and manufacturing processes, both illustrate a material system where the parameters of the SMA, the textile, and the surrounding environment work together to constitute a resilient cyclic actuation. By avoiding mechanical construction and relying on a soft textile operation logic with few components, the aim is to achieve a durable, simple, and flexible design solution, made possible by computer-aided design processes.

The two concepts propose a dynamic and demand-oriented sun-shading solution for buildings, as the autarkic textile facade controls solar transmission and thereby regulates the energy efficiency as well as user comfort of the building. Furthermore, lightweight textile structures reduce the amount of deployed materials and mechanical devices in comparison to conventional shutters and louvers, and thereby minimize the energy and material consumption required for construction, transportation, and operation. The next step of our research is to develop and realize a full-scale facade unit, with the help of the parametric digital tools presented in this paper.

ACKNOWLEDGMENTS

The authors would like to thank the further project partners of ADAPTEX: Fraunhofer IWU, VERSEIDAG-INDUTEX, Carl Stahl ARC, ITP, and SGS Ingenieurdienstleistungen, as well as the additional support by i-Mesh. The authors gratefully acknowledge the support within the ADAPTEX research project by the smart[3] e.V. and its funding by the German Federal Ministry of Education and Research (BMBF).

REFERENCES

Addington, M., and D.L. Schodek. 2005. *Smart Materials and New Technologies: For the Architecture and Design Professions.* Oxford: Architectural Press.

Baehr-Bruyère, J., K. Chamilothori, A.P. Vassilopoulos, J. Wienold, and M. Andersen. 2019. "Shaping Light to Influence Occupants' Experience of Space: A Kinetic Shading System with Composite Materials." *Journal of Physics: Conference Series* 1343 (1): 012162.

Bauer, A.M., P. Längst, R. La Magna, J. Lienhard, D. Piker, G.C. Quinn, C. Gengnagel, and K. Bletzinger. 2018. "Exploring Software Approaches for the Design and Simulation of Bending Active Systems." In *Creativity in Structural Design, Annual Symposium of the IASS—International Association for Shell and Spatial Structures*, 1–8. Boston.

Carvelli, V., S. V. Lomov et al. 2015. " Fatigue of Textile Composites" In *Woodhead Publishing Series in Composites Science and Engineering.* https://doi.org/10.1016/B978-1-78242-281-5.09002-7.

Chamilothori, K., A.M. Kampitaki, and K.A. Oungrinis. 2013. "Climate-Responsive Shading Systems with Integrated Shape Memory Alloys." In *Conference Proceedings of the 8th ENERGY FORUM 2013 on Advanced Building Skins.* Bressanone Italy.

Coelho, M., and P. Maes. 2009. "Shutters: A Permeable Surface for Environmental Control and Communication." In *Proceedings of the 3rd International Conference on Tangible and Embedded Interaction 2009*, 13–18. Cambridge.

Decker, M., and A. Zarzycki. 2014. "Designing Resilient Buildings with Emergent Materials." In *ECAADe* 32: 179–184.

Denz, P.-R. 2017. "Textile Building Skin. New Functionality Due to Smart Textiles." In *EfnMOBILE 2.0—Efficient Envelopes.* TU Delft.

Denz, P.-R., C. Sauer, E. Fransen Waldhör, M. Schneider, and P. Vongsingha. 2020. "Smart Textile Sun-Shading Current Results from R&D Project ADAPTEX." In *Proceedings of the 15th Advanced Building Skins Conference,* Bern, Switzerland, 26–27 October *2020*: ABS.

Denz, P.-R, C. Sauer, E. Fransen Waldhör, M. Schneider, and P. Vongsingha. 2021. "Smart Textile Sun-Shading—Development of Functional ADAPTEX Prototypes." In *Journal of Facade Design and Engineering / PowerSKIN Conference Proceedings.* Forthcoming.

Denz, P.-R., P. Vongsingha, M. Schneider, E. Fransen Waldhör, and C. Sauer. 2021. "Integration of SMA-driven Smart Textile Sun Shading into real-size façade units." In *Engineered Transparency 2021.* Berlin: Ernst & Sohn. Forthcoming.

European Commission. 2020. "COMMUNICATION FROM THE COMMISSION TO THE EUROPEAN PARLIAMENT, THE COUNCIL, THE EUROPEAN ECONOMIC AND SOCIAL COMMITTEE AND THE COMMITTEE OF THE REGIONS: A Renovation Wave for Europe - greening our buildings, creating jobs, improving lives," Doc. 52020DC0662. October 14. Brussels: European Union. https://eur-lex.europa.eu/legal-content/EN/TXT/?uri=CELEX%3A52020DC0662.

Finnsdóttir, B., and C. Sauer. 2014. "Change/Solar Curtain. Design Project Department of Textile and Surface Design." *Weißensee Kunsthochschule Berlin.* http://www.kh-berlin.de/projektuebersicht/Project/overview/changesmart31780.html.

Fiorito, F., M. Sauchelli, D. Arroyo, M. Pesenti, M. Imperadori, G. Masera, and F. Ranzi. 2016. "Shape Morphing Solar Shadings: A Review." In *Renewable and Sustainable Energy Reviews* 55: 863–884.

Grinham, J., R. Blabolil, and J. Haak. 2014. "Harvest Shade Screens Programming Material for Optimal Energy Building Skins." In *ACADIA 14: Design Agency [Proceedings of the 34th Annual Conference of the Association for Computer Aided Design in Architecture (ACADIA)]*, Los Angeles, CA, 23–25 October 2014, edited by D. Gerber, A. Huang, and J. Sanchez, 281–290. CUMINCAD.

Habu, T. 2011. "Applications of Shape Memory Alloys (SMAs) in Electrical Appliances." In *Shape Memory and Superelastic Alloys*, 87–99. Woodhead Publishing.

Hoberman C., 2015. "Transformable: Building Structures That Change Themselves." In *Building Dynamics: Exploring Architecture of Change,* edited by Branko Kolarevic and Vera Parlac. Abingdon: Routledge.

Karamata, B., and M. Andersen. 2014. "Concept, Design and Performance of a Shape Variable Mashrabiya as a Shading and Daylighting System for Arid Climates." In *30th PLEA Conference-Sustainable Habitat for Developing Societies* 2, 344–351. CEPT, University Ahmedabad.

Khoo, C.K., F. Salim, and J. Burry. 2011. "Designing Architectural Morphing Skins with Elastic Modular Systems." *International Journal of Architectural Computing* 9 (4): 397–419.

Kuhn, T.E. 2017. "State of the Art of Advanced Solar Control Devices for Buildings." *Solar Energy* 154: 112–133.

Loonen, R. C. G. M., J. M. Rico-Martinez, F. Favoino, M. Brzezicki, C. Menezo, G. La Ferla, and L. Aelenei. 2015. "Design for Façade Adaptability: Towards a Unified and Systematic Characterization." In *Proc. 10th Energy Forum-Advanced Building Skins*, 1274–1284. Bern, Switzerland.

Loonen, R. C.G.M., Marija Trcka, Jan Hensen, and Wim Kornaat. 2011. "Climate Adaptive Building Shells for the Future? Optimization with an Inverse Modelling Approach." In *ECEEE Summer Study*, 1413–1422. European Council for an Energy Efficient Economy.

Payne, A.O. and J.K. Johnson. 2013. "Firefly: Interactive Prototypes for Architectural Design." *Architectural Design* 83 (2): 144–147.

Rutten, D. 2007. *Grasshopper*. V.6.0. PC and MacOS. Robert McNeel and Associates.

Sauer, C. 2019. "Entwerfen. Upscaling Textiles. Experimenteller Materialentwurf im räumlichen Kontext." In *Experimentieren. Einblicke in Praktiken und Versuchsaufbauten zwischen Wissenschaft und Gestaltung*, edited by Marguin, S., Rabe, H., Schäffner, W., Schmidgall, F. Bielefeld: transcript Verlag, 51-66. https://doi.org/https://doi.org/10.14361/9783839446386.

Maxie Schneider is an architect and researcher. She studied Architecture and urban planning in Dresden (Technical University) and Berlin (Berlin University of the Arts). At the Weißensee School of Art and Design she teaches in the Department of Textile and Surface Design. In the affiliated research facility Design and Experimental Materials Research (DXM), she investigates adaptive facades through the integration of smart materials. In addition to technical textiles, her particular focus is on the crossover of textile prototyping and computational tools. With a strong interest in unconventional material systems and hybrid tectonics, she develops solutions for a sustainable material, design, and building culture. In 2020 she joined the practice based PhD program at TU Berlin.

Ebba Fransén Waldhör is an artist, designer and lecturer working in spatial installation and design research with a primary focus on textiles. As a design researcher at the department of Design and Experimental Materials Research at the Weißensee School of Art she investigates shape memory alloys in textiles and how these can be used in an architectural context. Alongside her research and teaching work, she develops experimental spatial concepts and scenographies for artists, writers, and institutions.

Paul-Rouven Denz studied architecture and urban planning at the University of Stuttgart and the E.T.S.A. Madrid with a focus on "resource-efficient construction" and "building construction". Mr. Denz has gained a wide range of experience during showcase building and research projects on sustainability in Germany and abroad. He also successfully participated in architectural and innovation competitions. Paul-Rouven Denz worked among others at Foster & Partners (London), Werner Sobek (Stuttgart), Fraunhofer IAO (Stuttgart), IBK2 (University of Stuttgart, Stuttgart), Gutierrez-delaFuente Arquitectos (Madrid) and ATOL architects (Shanghai). At Facade-Lab, the competence center of Priedemann Facade Experts group, Mr. Denz focuses as Head of R&D on research on new façade technologies, materials, systems and planning processes. Since 2017 Paul-Rouven Denz is also a PhD guest researcher at TU Delft, Faculty of Architecture and the Built Environment, investigating Smart Textile Skin solutions for material and energy efficient building envelopes.

Puttakhun Vongsingha is an architect/façade engineer. He studied Architecture at KMITL in Thailand. After a couple of years working as an architect, he took his Master's degree in building technology in TU Delft, the Netherlands. Afterward, for the last 5 years he was supporting the R&D department of Priedemann Facade-Lab GmbH, Germany. During those periods, he worked in multiple R&D projects, which involved energy producing/harvesting façade, environmentally responsive façade, new and innovative building components, and materials. Finding a solution for new and challenging problems is always something he enjoys doing. Thus, his main interest is to bring construction technologies to a higher level of sustainability.

Natchai Suwannapruk is a designer with experiences in both architecture and façade design disciplines. He began his career as an architect after graduating from the International Program in Design and Architecture at Chulalongkorn University in Thailand. With a passion in sustainability he holds the certifications of LEED Green Associate (2013-15) and TREES-A. After four years as an architect in Thailand, he decided to pursue his master's studies in Building Technology at TU Delft in the Netherlands. Currently he works as a Designer/Researcher at Priedemann Facade-Lab GmbH in Berlin to support design and research in innovative and sustainable solutions for engineering challenges.

Christiane Sauer is an architect and since 2013 Professor for Material and Design at Weißensee School of Art and Design Berlin. Her focus lies on developing and designing material systems for the architectural context based on textile structures, active materials and functional surfaces. She heads the research facility DXM - Design Experiment Material and conducts research within the interdisciplinary Research Cluster of Excellence Matters of Activity, Image Space Material. She has lectured internationally on new material developments, e.g. SCI-Arc, Los Angeles or Cornell University, NY. As a practicing architect she worked for international firms such as OMA Rotterdam and founded formade - studio for architecture and materials in Berlin. She has been active as author, contributor and moderator in the field of new materials and is member of the German Architects Association BDA and the Berlin Chamber of Architects.

Shape-Programmed Self-Assembly of Bead Structures

Cameron Nelson
Cornell University, College of Architecture, Art and Planning

Jenny Sabin
Cornell University, College of Architecture, Art and Planning

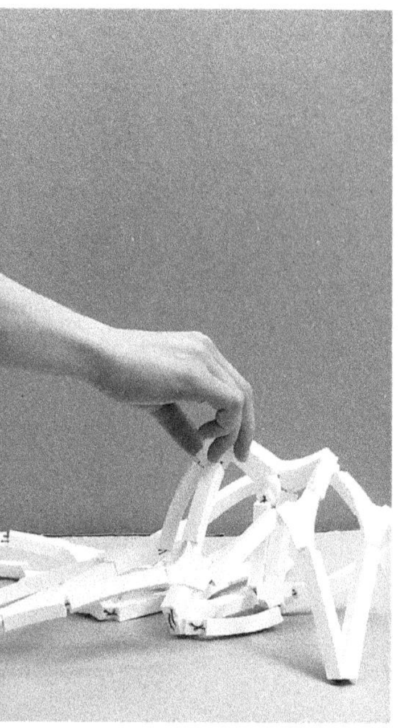
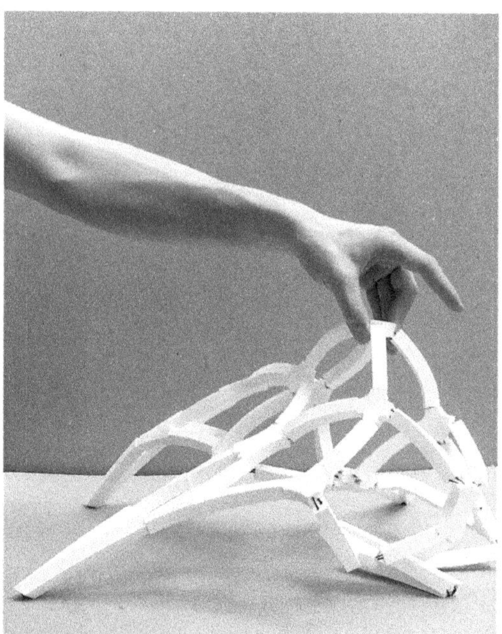
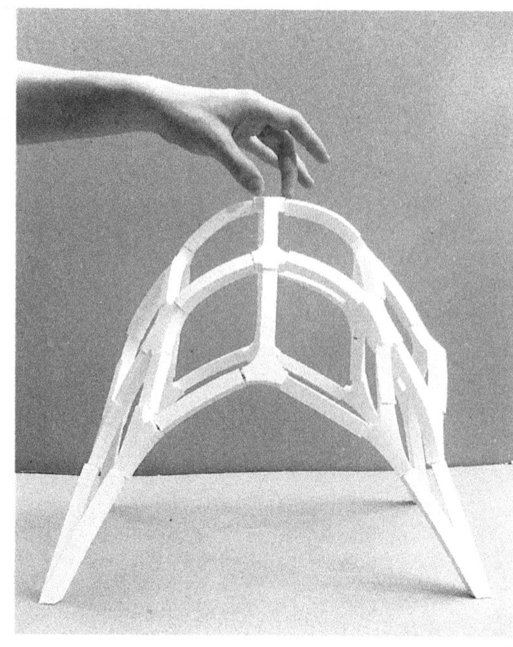

1

ABSTRACT

This paper demonstrates the potential of a robust, low-cost approach to programmable matter using beads and string to achieve complex shapes with novel self-organizing and deformational properties.

The method is inspired by the observation that beads forced together along a string will become constrained until they spontaneously rigidify. This behavior is easily observed using any household string and flat-faced beads and recalls the mechanism behind classic crafts such as push puppets. However, specific examples of architectural applications are lacking.

We analyze how this phenomenon occurs through static force analyses, physical tests, and simulation, using a rigid body physics engine to validate digital prototypes. We develop a method of designing custom bead geometries able to be produced via generic 3D-printing technology, as well as a computational path-planning toolkit for designing ways of threading beads together. We demonstrate how these custom bead geometries and threading paths influence the acquired structure and its assembly. Finally, we propose a means of scaling up this phenomenon, suggesting potential applications in deployable architecture, mortarless assembly of nonfunicular masonry, and responsive architectural systems.

1 A beadwork assembly can order itself into a self-standing structure with little to no aid.

2 Graph augmentation process. Left to right: framework, interfaces, and full solid geometry.

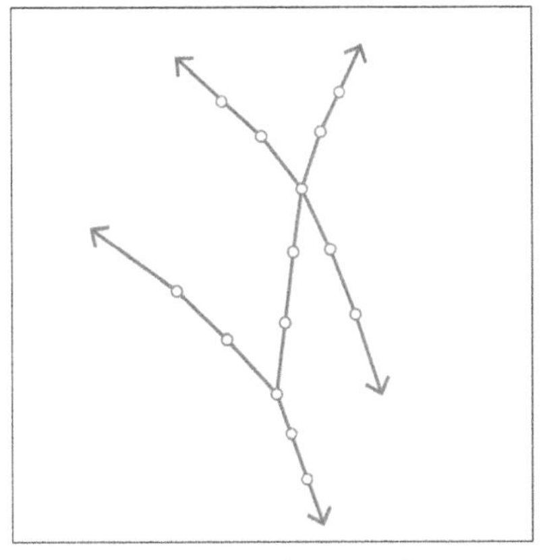
connectivity graph

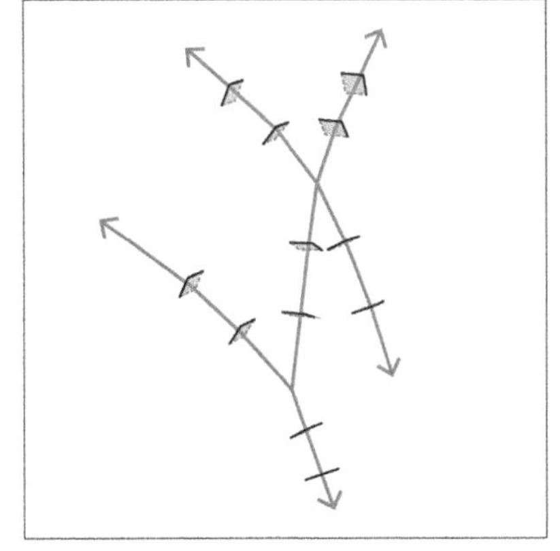
perpendicular faces

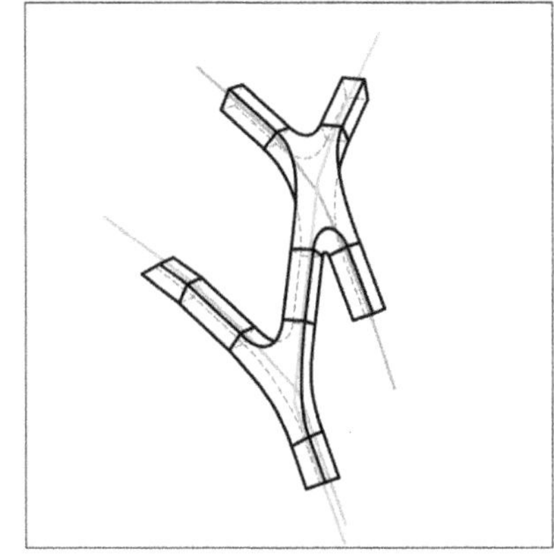
lofted beads, with string

2

INTRODUCTION

Self-assembly at the microscale has been the subject of extensive biochemical research. This phenomenon has recently been shown to extend to the macroscale, as demonstrated by projects like Fluid Crystallization by MIT Self-Assembly Lab (Tibbits 2014). In such experiments, mimicking the biochemical example, components move freely in a fluid like air or water and are dependent on specialized "handshake mechanisms" like magnetic links. Related projects such as the Macrobot (Tibbits 2011) perhaps bear closer comparison with the present work, in that they encode a global geometry into a series of part-to-part rules. We consider the present work to be a continuation of this line of inquiry, deviating in its novel use of only tensile cord and solid geometry to achieve similar results without specialized components.

Research in lightweight, mortarless, tensegrity structures, such as the Periscope Tower by Matter Design Studio (Clifford and McGee 2011), offers further parallels. We seek to extend such examples, though, by applying tension dynamically, taking full advantage of the shape-changing qualities of flexural materials in addition to the structural qualities of rigid ones. Furthermore, beads as a tensegrity have the novel property of distributing compressive forces externally and tension internally, which contrasts with tensegrities commonly seen in deployable architecture such as inflatables and the iconic bar-and-cable systems of Kenneth Snelson and Buckminster Fuller.

Our work is also tangent to research in low-energy adaptive architectural systems, like TU Delft's Hyperbody "Muscle Tower II" (Bier 2011) and other large-scale prototype structures such as those built at University College, London (Senatore et al. 2017) and the University of Stuttgart (Sobek and Teuffel 2001). However, the focus of these projects is on control protocols for large batteries of actuators, rather than on the building components or structural units themselves, which tend to be traditional materials such as steel and standard mechanisms such as hydraulic pistons. Indeed, if the tensioning of the string in a beadwork structure is handled by pistons or other digitally controlled actuators, many of the same principles could be applied. On the other hand, bead structures are also versatile enough to be implemented as passive or human-powered systems, and can be designed, assembled, and upkept cheaply while still exhibiting qualities of adaptability and self-repair.

METHODS

Bead Shape

We considered beads to be solids with one or more hollow channels that may or may not intersect. This allows Y- and X-shaped beads (Fig. 2), as well as more complicated topologies. The most important aspect is the geometry of the contact surfaces, which determines orientation constraints and interlocking behavior as well as the torque between adjacent beads. For example, generic flat interfaces constrain position but not relative rotation, whereas interlocking interfaces can potentially fully constrain adjacent beads.

For complex geometries our design process begins from a skeletonized "framework": a connectivity graph with nodes embedded in 3D space. The edges of the graph are a placeholder for the network of string(s), which are added later. This is to be as generic as possible. In contrast with other workflows such as graphic statics, our choice of framework is essentially arbitrary, and need not necessarily reflect any kind of preoptimization or force analysis. For example, the geometry in Figure 6 is not a true

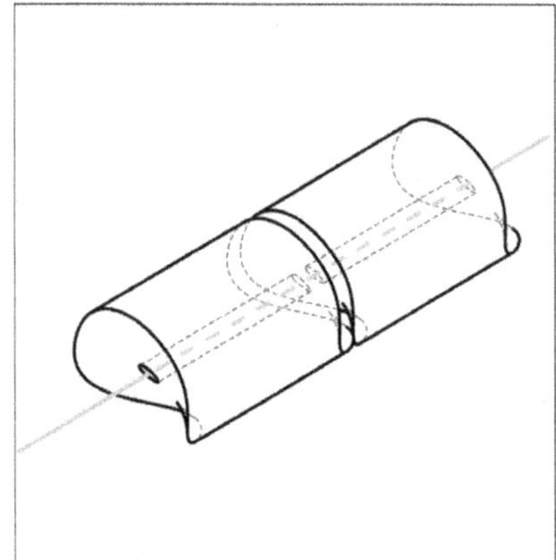

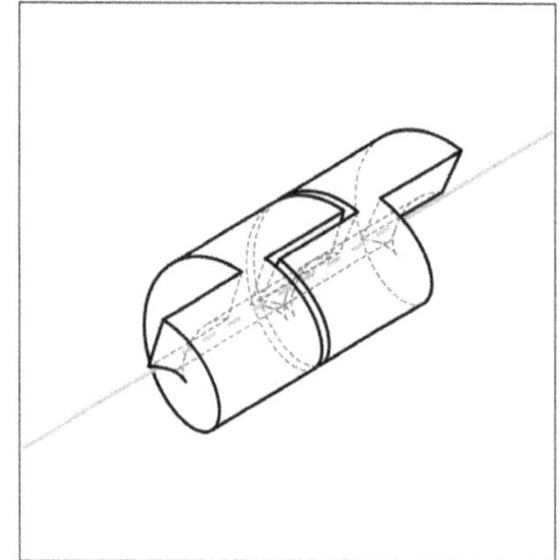

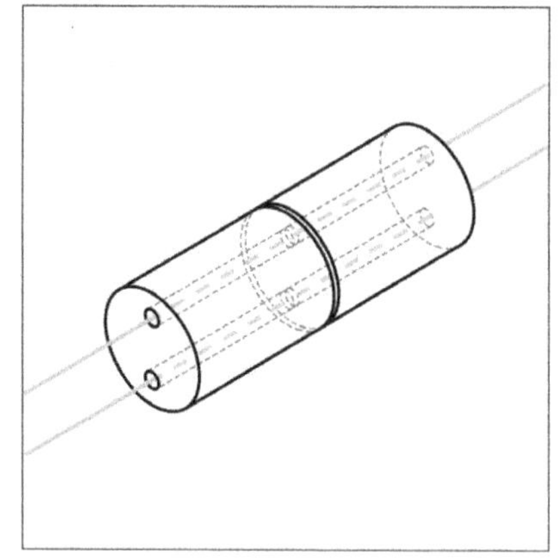

3

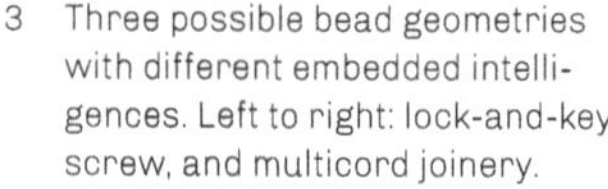

3 Three possible bead geometries with different embedded intelligences. Left to right: lock-and-key, screw, and multicord joinery.

4 Still from rigid body simulation.

5 Simulation of bead shape that spontaneously arranges in an alternating pattern, (a) before, (b) after, and (c) physically.

4

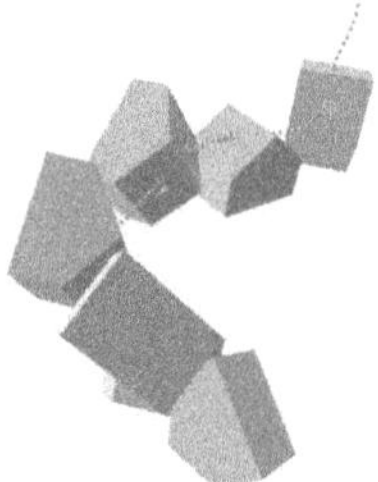

5a

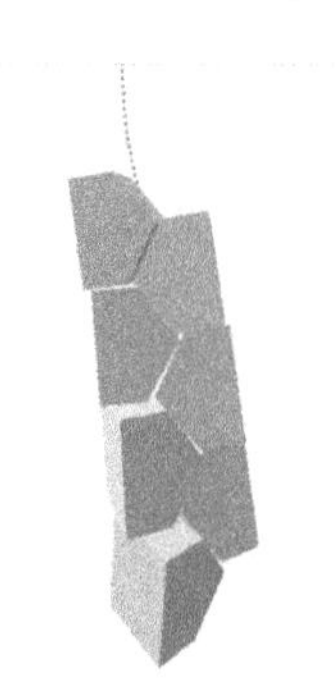

5b

5c

funicular dome, and hence cannot stand without a tensile string holding the beads in compression. It would immediately collapse as a pure, mortarless masonry gridshell. Conceptually, the emphasis is not upon static form-finding to produce an ideal geometry at time of manufacturing but rather to produce a robust assembly that will weather unpredictable loading conditions and still return to its original state.

To generate printable bead geometries, we apply a method we term "graph augmentation": given a framework, we build volumetric beads about the edges such that the interface between two adjacent beads is aligned to the perpendicular plane of the edge between them in the framework (Fig. 2).

Relative orientation of beads can be shape-programmed by a variety of approaches, such as lock-and-key-type, screw-type, and multicord interfaces (Fig. 3). Bead orientations need not be maximally constrained to exhibit self-organization, however. For example, self-assembly of a regular 180° alternating pattern was observed in a simple 1D sequence of beads subject to agitation and gravity, in both physical tests and simulation (Fig. 5). We hypothesized we could use the same principle to create any angle of alternation, and with our simulation pipeline we were able to validate this intuition instantly.

Simulation

Dynamic architectural systems place unique demands on the designer to understand their behavior in time as

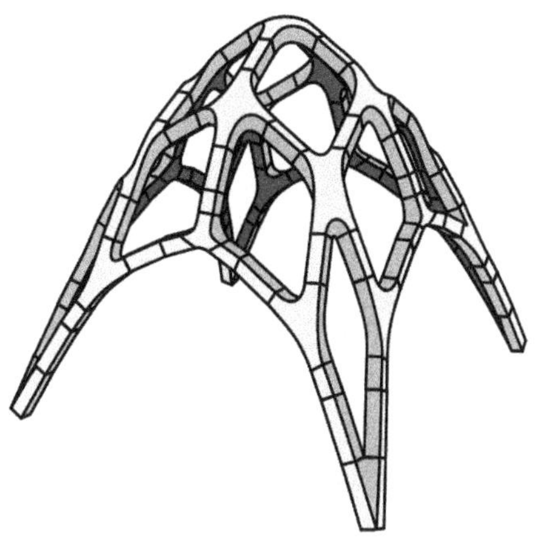

6 A complete generic dome framework (left) and the 3D printable bead geometries generated via graph augmentation.

a continuum and subject to a complex array of forces. Whereas physical scale models traditionally served this purpose, to mitigate rapid-prototyping turnaround times and quickly validate hypotheses we developed a pipeline from Rhino3d Grasshopper (Rutten 2020) to the physics engine Bullet (Fig. 4) (Coumans and Bai 2017). While this engine is primarily used for game physics and machine learning for robotics, its robust rigid-body collision physics makes it a natural choice for simulating string-bead interactions. String physics simulation methodologies generally fall into two categories: soft-body and rigid-body approximations. The latter approach treats a string as a chain of many small rigid bodies, each affixed to the next by a virtual joint. While soft-body approximations are specialized for deformable matter and may better simulate a string in isolation, simulations of beadwork are more reliable when strings and beads are approximated by the same type of object.

Thus, we treated a string as a chain of many small rigid bodies, each affixed to the next by a point-to-point constraint, since this approach has been validated for speed and accuracy (de Jong, Wormnes, and Tiso 2014; Gołębiowski et al. 2016). One difficulty in simulating beads and strings, especially when real-time interactivity is desired, is the computational burden produced by simulating collisions between concave mesh objects such as hollow beads. A standard workaround is to decompose each concave mesh into a series of convex parts whose collisions can be calculated much more quickly and accurately. Our simulation workflow employed both manual and automatic convex decomposition functionalities. General algorithms such as volumetric hierarchical approximate convex decomposition (VHACD) are widely used when geometry is not known beforehand (Mamou 2014). However, since our beads had predictable topology, we wrote custom convex decomposition scripts to yield more consistent and accurate results. Real-time interactivity in the simulations enabled invaluable feedback between *in silica* experiment, human understanding, and physical prototypes.

Threading Path

For any network topology more complex than a single row of beads in series, there may be many ways to thread them such that a cord passes through each bead at least once. For instance, we might use several threads each following a different path, and some beads might be threaded with multiple cords. There are many properties of a given threading path one might wish to optimize; here we consider (1) material economy, (2) ease of assembly, (3) shape control, and (4) mechanical effort.

Material economy: When the objective is to minimize the length of a single string, this reduces to the well-known Route Inspection problem (Edmonds and Johnson 1973). We implemented an algorithm using linear programming in the Python module PuLP (Mitchell and Dunning 2011), which solves this problem exactly. However, the threading paths can be highly asymmetric.

Ease of assembly: Often, when assembling a system by hand, a symmetrical threading path can be more intuitive to follow. The symmetries of a network are encoded in its automorphism group, a collection of ways of rearranging nodes of the graph such that path continuity is always preserved. By performing any such rearrangement on the vertices of a path, we obtain a topologically symmetric copy. The challenge then is to determine a set of one or more paths whose symmetric copies will cover the edges of the graph with the fewest overlaps. For example, in the threading diagram in Figure 15, there are only two unique paths that have been transformed into eight copies by a

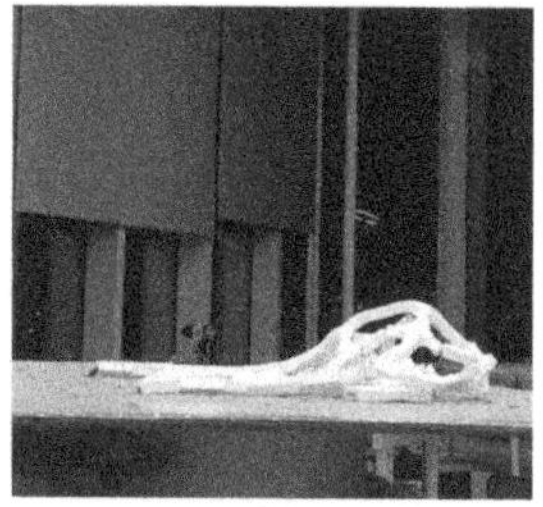

7a

7b

8a

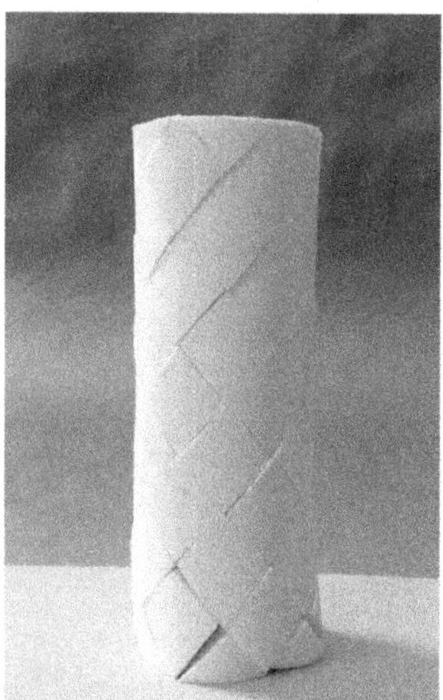

8b

7 Initial dome prototype: (a) before, and (b) after tensioning cord.

8 Tubular prototype exhibiting all X-type beads for greater geometric constraint. Self-repairing qualities are seen (a) before, and (b) after tensioning.

9 A simple indeterminate arch exhibiting multiple stable states (a–c) that appear more or less frequently in accordance with how they minimize a function of the kink angles; (d) shows a closeup of a kink.

9a

9b

9c

9d

subgroup of the graph's symmetries—in this case, the mirror symmetries. Unlike true mirror symmetry, though, graph automorphisms are topological in nature, making them robust to warping. This more generalizable approach to path planning can identify redundancy even in geometries that do not bear obvious symmetry.

Shape control: Geometric constraints upon one bead with respect to its neighbors can come not only from the bead's shape but also potentially from the threading pattern. As mentioned above and shown in Figure 3, multi-thread systems offer the benefit of constraining rotations. Two strings will fully constrain adjacent beads with planar interfaces, and three strings will fully constrain arbitrarily shaped beads, in the same sense that three points of contact are required to stabilize a chair. The dome model shown in Figure 1 exhibits a two-cord system with planar interfaces. A different approach to multicord threading patterns can be seen in the tubular prototypes in Figure 8. Here each bead represents a node of degree 4 in the model's graph representation. Thus, with a minimum of four points of contact per bead, the structure is fully constrained in position and orientation.

Mechanical effort: Minimizing the cumulative change in angle of a thread's path presents another possible criterion, since static analyses reveal that sharp angles can hinder force transmission by more than 70% (see "Static Force Analysis" below). Hence, less sharp angles will also minimize the force required to tension the bead system. In any network wherein all nodes are of even degree, we can break this problem into numerous smaller problems: for each node, we need to construct a matching among the incident edges such that the sum of the angles between matched pairs is minimized. This subproblem can be solved as a linear program, and if solved for each node independently, the resulting global threading path is guaranteed to minimize sharp turns in the threading path. In the special

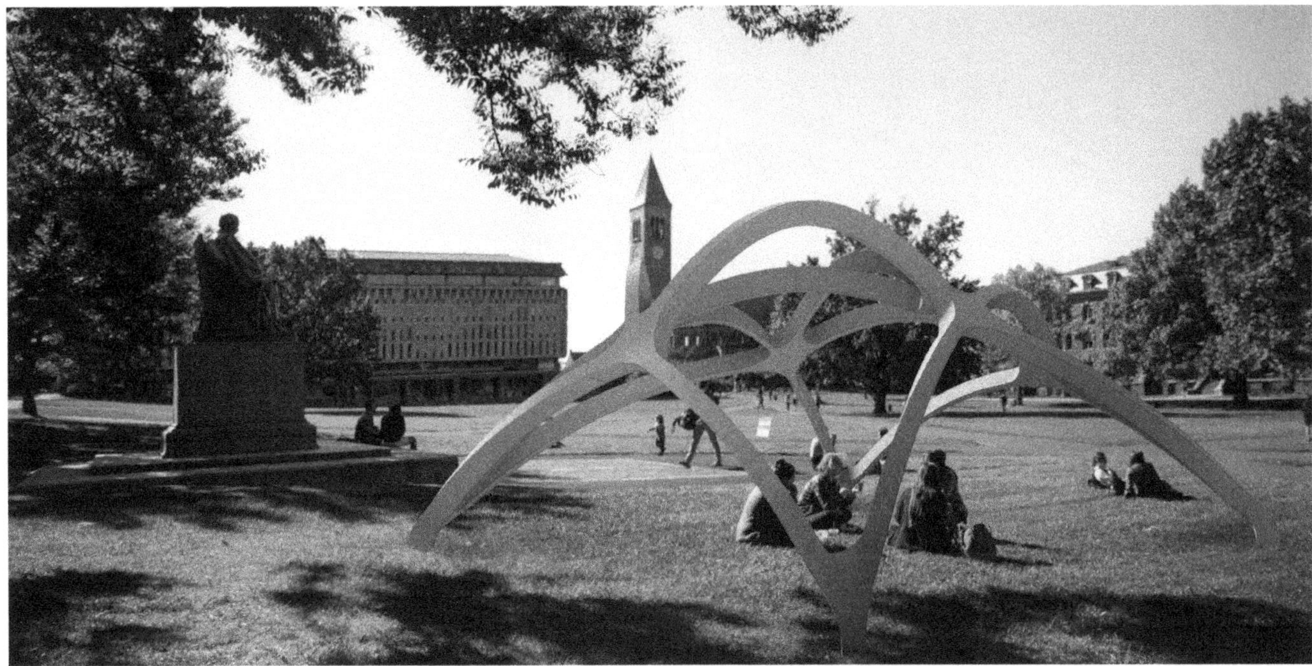

11 Foam stereotomy could produce beadwork structures at larger scales, preserving volumetric shape programming while maintaining light weight. 11

case of a two-cord bead system, like those discussed above, all nodes have even degree by default. Even-degree frameworks also permit the use of the much simpler Fleury's Algorithm for generating an Euler Tour, which is a single path that crosses each edge in a graph exactly once, necessarily in the shortest possible way. Fleury's Algorithm, therefore, perfectly solves the Route Inspection problem for this special subcategory of frameworks.

These methods assume the existence of a static framework; however, one could also begin with a surface and place nodes and edges upon this surface in a manner conducive to more optimal threading paths. For example, a geodesic naturally minimizes the cumulative change in angle of a path between two points on a surface; hence a geodesic gridshell, though it may require many independent cords, compensates with a comparatively low activation energy. The tubular models in Figure 8 offer one example of this approach, as helices are geodesics on a cylinder.

RESULTS & DISCUSSION

Prototypes

We applied our techniques to a simple dome-shaped gridshell structure. The beads were 3D printed in generic polylactic acid (PLA) thermoplastic, and the threading was performed by hand with cotton cord. The first prototype had a footprint of approximately 5 in × 5 in. When the cords at each of the four feet were pulled, the beads spontaneously formed a rigid dome structure (Fig. 7). This success motivated a second prototype at approximately three times scale, with a 15 in × 15 in footprint, this time threaded such that two strings passed through each bead. This gave more control at the expense of increased friction. To compensate, the dome's assembly was minimally aided (Fig. 1). When tension was removed from the upright dome, the slightest touch would collapse the structure, demonstrating that this is not a true funicular dome but a tensegrity reliant on tension and compression in balance. Conversely, starting from a slack state, as the dome's apex was lifted into place simultaneously with a gradual reintroduction of tension, the remainder of the structure assembled of its own accord. This "one-handed" assembly behavior not only demonstrates the influence of threading path and friction on global behavior but also promises further use cases. For example, as a counterweighted window similarly retains its position after it is adjusted, a heavy structure could form and unform only with gentle assistance. This could potentially lead to a novel kind of masonry construction with improved safety, user-friendliness, and sustainability.

Analysis

Self-organization is a suggestive term used with varying definitions in the discipline of architecture. Inevitably there is some input energy, and even physical or biological definitions allow that this force may come from without the system itself, subtly augmenting the meaning of "self"-organizing. For example, Brownian motion is caused by particle bombardment, and in the Self-Assembly Lab's Fluid Crystallization project, a wave chamber is agitated to ensure intermixing of the floating magnetic modules (Tibbits

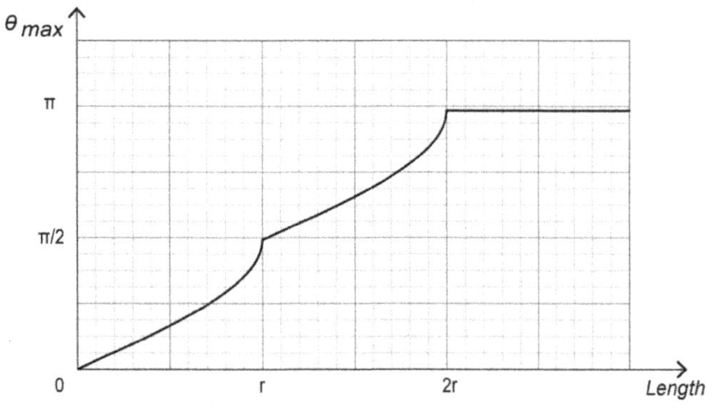

12

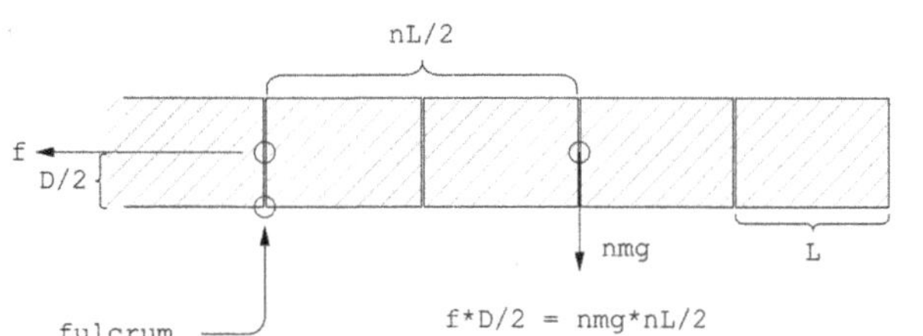

13

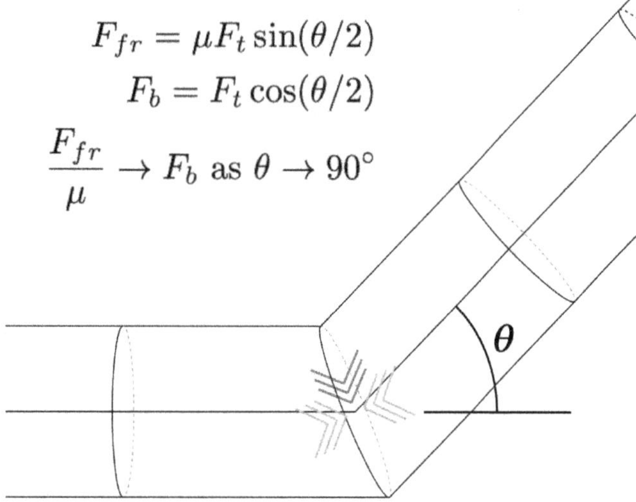

14

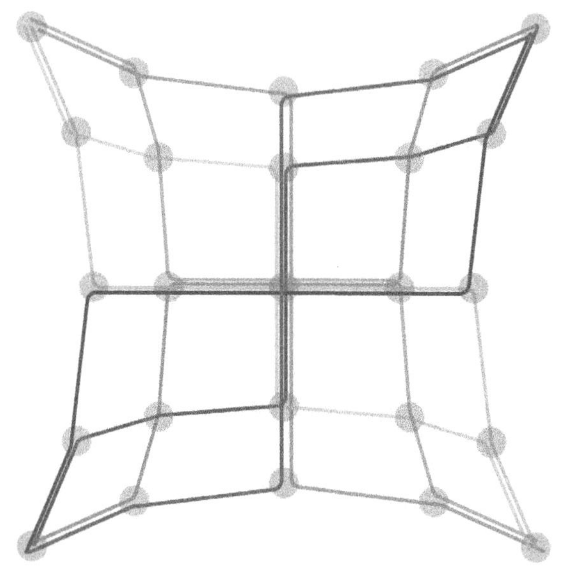

15

12 Maximum angle attainable between cylindrical beads as a function of the length of cord separating them. Note that $\theta_{max} \rightarrow 0$ as $l \rightarrow 0$, continuously but with discontinuous first derivative at $l = 2r$ and $l = r$. This graph illustrates the shrinking of the configuration space with the tensioning of the system.

13 The figure assumes a cantilever subjected to gravity. Bead diameter $D = 2r$ is inversely related to required tension f. L represents the bead length, m the mass per bead, and n the number of beads being supported. Because n is inversely proportional to both m and L, f is constant for changing n.

14 Two beads being compressed along a cord, demonstrating the effect of miter angle on friction between bead and cord. If θ is the supplement of the miter angle, $F_b = F_t \cos(\theta/2)$ and $F_{fr} = F_t \sin(\theta/2)$. For example, if $\theta = \pi/2$, we would expect $F_{fr} \approx 71\%F$.

15 A diagram of the threading path applied to the initial dome prototype (Fig. 7), as viewed from above. Here, symmetry is emphasized.

2014). Therefore, we adopt the interpretation that self-organization indicates an unordered form of agitation that nevertheless yields an ordered result. Inherent indeterminacy is, therefore, a hallmark of self-organization, by our definition.

A small "arch" model helps illustrate this principle (Fig. 9). Rather than a smooth arc, it forms a limited number of "kinks" in the sequence of beads. Repeatedly slackening and tensioning this arch, we observed that while the arch shape was different each time, certain arrangements of kinks were more likely to form in proportion with how much they minimized tension, or equivalently how much they maximized the angles at the joints. This probabilistic model strikes a balance between indeterminacy and order. Conversely, for a set of n kinks at specified positions in the sequence of beads, the angles formed at the respective kinks are consistently the same. We hypothesized that these angles are such that, if one views the arch as an $n+1$ bar linkage in the plane, then the sum of the squares of the angles between adjacent members is maximized.

In this example, "organization" can be quantified as the size of the system's configuration space, that is, the volume spanned by the valid domains in its parameter space. For example, we could measure the maximum angle between consecutive beads with respect to the distance separating their facing ends. If we define the length of cord between the centers of two cylindrical beads' flat faces as l, the radius of the beads as r, and the maximum angle between the two beads' axes as θ_{max}, we obtain the set of equations below whose plot is shown in Figure 12, revealing a continuous monotonic decrease in θ_{max} as l decreases:

$$\theta_{max} = \begin{cases} \pi & \text{if } 2r \leq l \\ \pi - \arccos((l-r)/r) & \text{if } r \leq l \leq 2r \\ \arcsin(l/r) & \text{if } 0 \leq l \leq r \end{cases}$$

In practice, this means that any shortening of the cord, such as by tension, will reduce the size of the configuration space until the system is forced into a constrained shape.

Static Force Analysis

In theory, using infinitely strong and frictionless materials, one can create a self-organizing bead structure approximating any given framework. In practice, however, friction, strength, and geometry play a role that can be limiting or fruitful. Consider the radius as the maximum distance from a point of contact between two beads to the string where it passes through them. A greater radius reduces the required tension force by supplying more torque. However, assuming constant density and cross-section, the aspect ratio of radius to length is unimportant. Figure 13 illustrates that n beads each l/n in length will require the same force to rigidify as m beads each l/m in length, for any n, m > 0.

Friction can significantly affect the transfer of tension. We observed this behavior even in relatively low-friction systems like the PLA and cotton-cord dome prototypes. In mitered beads like these, unlike in a straight chain of beads, the tension force applied to the cord is differently distributed, as seen in Figure 14. As the miter angle decreases, the normal force F_b between beads decreases, and the friction force F_{fr} between the string and the beads increases, requiring considerably greater force to pull.

Scale and Manufacturing

These considerations take on increasing importance as one begins to consider bead structures at larger scales. 3D printing has provided a natural means of producing these custom bead geometries, whose internal voids would present a challenge to most traditional subtractive manufacturing methods. In the interest of scaling bead structures to the human or building scale, novel materials and manufacturing methods ought to be considered. Using 3D-printed beads, but simply more of them, is one possibility. This offers the challenge of much more highly segmented frameworks, which become correspondingly more indeterminate as each vertex in the framework presents a potential for error, and this error may quickly accumulate into large displacements. Hierarchical approaches wherein substructures are rigidified incrementally could offer one solution.

A second approach is to use a large-scale volumetric material, such as foam, which offers high stiffness-to-density ratios. Precedents for large-scale foam tensegrities include the Periscope Tower by Matter Design Studio (Clifford and McGee 2011). This wind-prone structure was also stabilized by tension members, but differs from bead structures in that the cables were static and external to the foam blocks. Assuming traditional manufacturing methods of hot wire cutting and milling, which are less easily applied to complex concave surfaces, the challenge lies in how to run cords internally through a foam bead. One approach is to slice the bead along a plane through the desired thread path, then carve out half of the channel in each half of the bead before reassembling. To avoid the need for adhesives, the two halves of the bead can then be joined by wrapping with a secondary cord around the outer surface. This process of slicing and recombining recalls the "convex decomposition" process used to preprocess digital bead geometries for rigid body simulation, in a natural extension of the simulation-to-physical prototyping workflow. A visualization of what a large format bead test structure might look like is shown in Figure 11. Such a structure could provide rigid shelter while using no mortar and still be safe and robust to unusual loads such as high winds or children climbing upon it.

CONCLUSION

This preliminary study examined the potential of beads as a medium for controlled self-assembly and deployable structures. The potential applications of this technique are diverse, including but not limited to:

- rapidly deployable structures for disaster relief, temporary installations, and leisure.
- low-energy shape actuation for soft robotics and medical prosthetics, such as the CardioARM medical snake robot that uses a similar mechanism to control the joints of a many-segmented probe (Ota et al. 2009).
- assembly from a distance for autonomous structures in extreme environments as suggested by projects like MIT Self-Assembly Lab's Aerial Assembly project (Staback et al. 2017).

Rigid body simulation has also proven a valuable tool for rapid prototyping and experiment. The two prototypes presented in this paper demonstrate some potential challenges of threading and scale that must be further investigated to validate these concepts for human-scale applications. Whereas graph augmentation offers a generic and versatile framework for design, further research should leverage our current understanding of forces and complexity to produce more robust specimens. Our approach to self-assembly is also virtually agnostic to the materials used. Even off-the-shelf materials are sufficient to demonstrate the behaviors discussed, but scaling up the combination of stiffness and lightness will place more constraints on the variety of suitable materials. In the context of existing research on self-assembly for architecture, though, this is a departure from the specialized handshake mechanisms heretofore seen, such as magnets, bimetals, shape-memory polymers, and thermo- or hygro-active materials. The self-assembly of beads offers a novel approach with potentially greater control of shape formation, tunable and reversible rigidity, and structural robustness.

ACKNOWLEDGMENTS

The authors would like to acknowledge the M.S. Matter Design Computation program of the Department of Architecture, Cornell College of Architecture, Art, and Planning, and the Sabin Lab at Cornell University.

REFERENCES

Bier, Henriette. 2011. "Robotic Environments." In *Proceedings of the 28th International Symposium for Automation and Robotics in Construction (ISARC)*, Seoul, South Korea, 29 June – 2 July 2011, 863–868. IAARC.

Clifford, Brandon, and Wes McGee. 2011. "Periscope Foam Tower." In *Fabricate 2011*, edited by Ruairi Glynn and Bob Sheil, 77–80. London: UCL Press.

Coumans, Erwin, and Yunfei Bai. 2018. *Pybullet*. https://pybullet.org/wordpress. V.2.88. PC.

Dear, Tony, Blake Buchanan, Rodrigo Abrajan-Guerrero, Scott David Kelly, Matthew Travers, and Howie Choset. 2020. "Locomotion of a Multi-Link Non-Holonomic Snake Robot with Passive Joints." *The International Journal of Robotics Research* 39 (5): 598–616.

de Jong, J., K. Wormnes, and P. Tiso. 2014. "Simulating Rigid-Bodies, Strings and Nets for Engineering Applications Using Gaming Industry Physics Simulators." Paper presented at *i-SAIRAS: International Symposium on Artificial Intelligence, Robotics and Automation in Space*, Montreal, June 17-19. European Space Agency.

Edmonds, Jack, and Ellis L. Johnson. 1973. "Matching, Euler Tours And the Chinese Postman." *Mathematical Programming* 5 (1): 88–124. https://doi.org/10.1007/bf01580113.

Gołębiowski, W., R. Michalczyk, M. Dyrek, U. Battista, and K. Wormnes. 2016. "Validated Simulator for Space Debris Removal with Nets and Other Flexible Tethers Applications." *Acta Astronautica* 129: 229–240. https://doi.org/10.1016/j.actaastro.2016.08.037.

Mamou, Khaled. 2014. *V-HACD: Volumetric-Hierarchical Approximate Convex Decomposition*. V.2.0. PC.
Mitchell, Stuart, and Iain Dunning. 2020. *PuLP: A Linear Programming Toolkit for Python*. V.2.0. PC.

Ota, Takeyoshi, Amir Degani, David Schwartzman, Brett Zubiate, Jeremy McGarvey, Howie Choset, and Marco A. Zenati. 2009. "A Highly Articulated Robotic Surgical System For Minimally Invasive Surgery." *The Annals of Thoracic Surgery* 87 (4): 1253–1256. https://doi.org/10.1016/j.athoracsur.2008.10.026.

Rutten, David. *Grasshopper*. V.1.0.0007. Robert McNeel & Associates. PC. 2020.

Senatore, Gennaro, Philippe Duffour, Pete Winslow, and Chris Wise. 2017. "Shape Control and Whole-Life Energy Assessment of an 'Infinitely Stiff' Prototype Adaptive Structure." *Smart Materials and Structures* 27 (1): 015022. https://doi.org/10.1088/1361-665x/aa8cb8.

Sobek, Werner, and Patrick Teuffel. 2001. "Adaptive systems in architecture and structural engineering." In *Smart Structures and Materials 2001: Smart Systems for Bridges, Structures, and Highways*, vol. 4330, pp. 36-45. International Society for Optics and Photonics, 2001.

Staback, Danniely, MyDung Nguyen, James Addison, Zachary Angles, Zain Karsan, and Skylar Tibbits. 2017. "Aerial Pop-Up Structures." In *ACADIA 2017: Disciplines & Disruption [Proceedings of the 37th Annual Conference of the Association for Computer Aided Design in Architecture (ACADIA) ISBN 978-0-692-96506-1]*, Cambridge, MA 2-4 November, 2017, 582–589. CUMINCAD.

Tibbits, Skylar. 2011. "A Model for Intelligence of Large-Scale Self-Assembly." In *ACADIA 11: Integration through Computation [Proceedings of the 31st Annual Conference of the Association for Computer Aided Design in Architecture (ACADIA) ISBN 978-1-6136-4595-6]*, Banff (Alberta) 13-16 October, 2011, 342-349. CUMINCAD.

Tibbits, Skylar. 2014. "Fluid Crystallization: Hierarchical Self-Organization." In *Fabricate 2014*, edited by F. Gramazio, M. Kohler, and S. Langenberg, 297–303. Zurich: UCL Press.

IMAGE CREDITS

All drawings and images by the authors.

Cameron Nelson received their BA in architecture and mathematics from Yale University. They are currently an MS candidate in the Matter Design Computation program at Cornell University College of Architecture, Art and Planning.

Jenny E. Sabin is the Arthur L. and Isabel B. Wiesenberger Professor in Architecture and Associate Dean for Design Initiatives at Cornell College of Architecture, Art, and Planning. She is the principal of Jenny Sabin Studio and director of the Sabin Lab at Cornell. Sabin holds degrees in ceramics and interdisciplinary visual art from the University of Washington and a Master of Architecture from the University of Pennsylvania. Her work has been exhibited at the FRAC Centre, Cooper Hewitt Design Triennial, MoMA, and the Pompidou. Sabin won MoMA & MoMA PS1's Young Architects Program with her submission, Lumen, 2017.

Spatial Assembly with Self-Play Reinforcement Learning

Tyson Hosmer
Bartlett School of Architecture, University College London

Panagiotis Tigas
Machine Learning Computer Science, Oxford University

David Reeves
Bartlett School of Architecture, University College London

Ziming He
Bartlett School of Architecture, University College London

1 Rendered spatial assembly of spatial parts (*NoMAS* 2019).

ABSTRACT

We present a framework to generate intelligent spatial assemblies from sets of digitally encoded spatial parts designed by the architect with embedded principles of prefabrication, assembly awareness, and reconfigurability. The methodology includes a bespoke constraint-solving algorithm for autonomously assembling 3D geometries into larger spatial compositions for the built environment. A series of graph-based analysis methods are applied to each assembly to extract performance metrics related to architectural space-making goals, including structural stability, material density, spatial segmentation, connectivity, and spatial distribution. Together with the constraint-based assembly algorithm and analysis methods, we have integrated a novel application of deep reinforcement (RL) learning for training the models to improve at matching the multiperformance goals established by the user through self-play. RL is applied to improve the selection and sequencing of parts while considering local and global objectives. The user's design intent is embedded through the design of partial units of 3D space with embedded fabrication principles and their relational constraints over how they connect to each other and the quantifiable goals to drive the distribution of effective features. The methodology has been developed over three years through three case study projects called *ArchiGo* (2017–2018), *NoMAS* (2018–2019), and *IRSILA* (2019-2020). Each demonstrates the potential for buildings with reconfigurable and adaptive life cycles.

INTRODUCTION

The rise of artificial intelligence (AI) in the domain of architecture has enormous potential for enhancing our creative processes while raising a series of new problems and questions. In training an AI to "design," where does the design agency lie, what is the role of the AI and the role of the architect in the process, and how is an architect's design intent in the context of an architectural problem communicated to the machine?

In parallel, rapid advancement of computation, digital manufacturing, and robotic automation of construction and assembly processes offers us the opportunity to develop buildings as systems of prefabricated and reconfigurable building elements rather than continuing to focus on design processes that result in continuous, layered, and inflexible forms with unsustainable life cycles (Brand 1995; GlobalData 2018; Ngwepe and Aigbavboa 2015). With the aid of computation and opportunities of automated robotic systems, we can reappraise linear building life cycles holistically by creating design platforms for developing buildings as adaptive assembly systems.

We present a semiautonomous and generalizable method enabling architects to define their space-planning objectives and develop an alphabet of design elements as inputs for an AI agent to generate building compositions that are valid, constructable, and match the architect's design objectives. Spatial assembly with self-play reinforcement learning is a constraint-solving framework for generating spatial assemblies from sets of digitally encoded spatial parts designed by architects and assembled using policies learned through self-play reinforcement learning. An architect's design intent is embedded through the detailed design and classification of a library of specific spatial parts and their predefined relational syntax to form an assembly-aware design language while defining a series of weighted objectives negotiated by the AI to semiautonomously generate assemblies. Graph analysis methods are applied in the loop to score each spatial assembly by extracting performance metrics related to space-making goals and constraints. Policies for local selection and sequencing of spatial parts are developed through self-play reinforcement learning to negotiate local and global objectives. This method enables a productive and symbiotic relationship between architect and machine, empowering the architect to develop their own constructable language and communicate their intent while working with an AI to rapidly explore the complex design space of assembly configurations within their requirements.

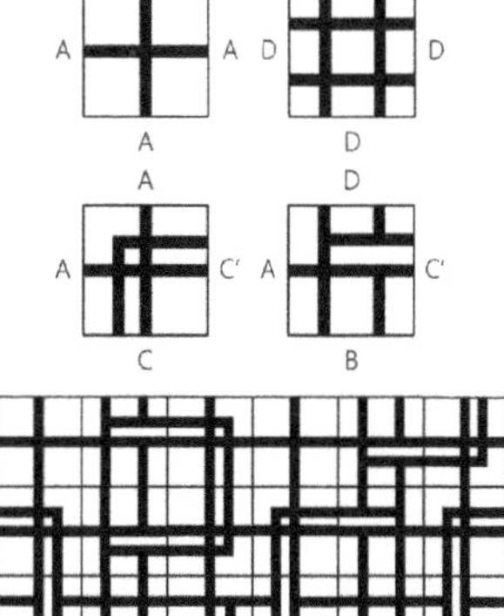

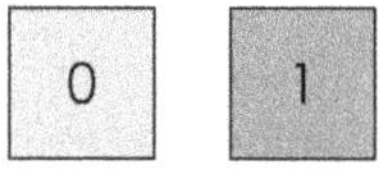

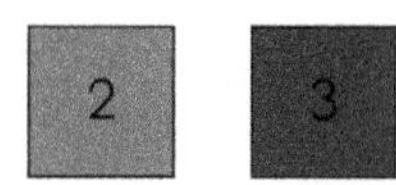

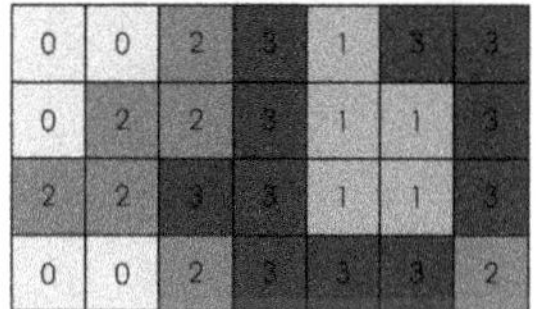

2 Spatial assembly constraint solver diagrams of geometric and class constraints.

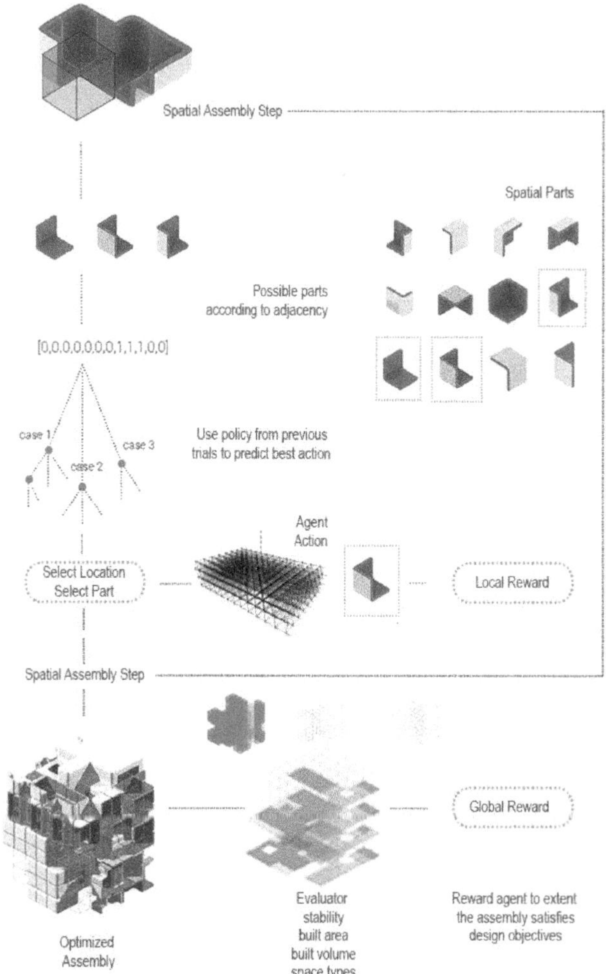

3 Spatial assembly with self-play reinforcement learning algorithm sequence diagram.

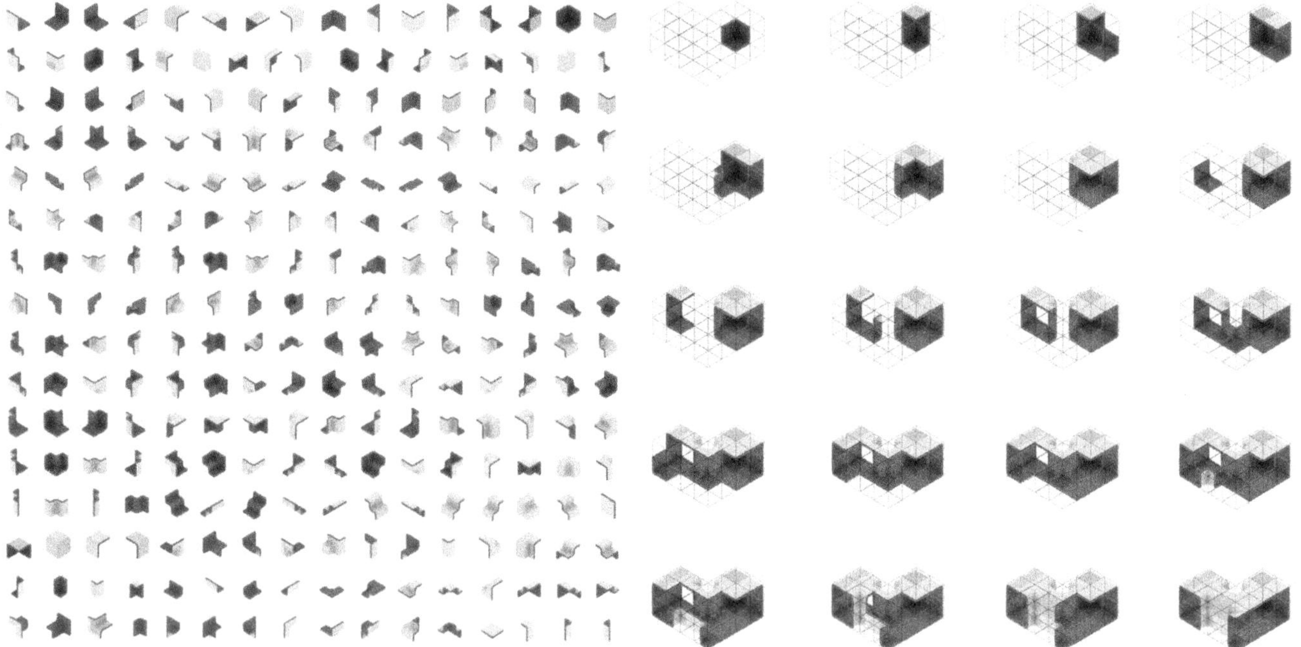

4 Spatial parts library (*NoMAS* 2019).

5 Spatial assembly sequence (*NoMAS* 2019).

BACKGROUND

The work is motivated by two key objectives: (1) to enable a creative and productive relationship between the architect and an artificially intelligent agent; and (2) to develop architecture as a system of constructable and reconfigurable parts. The notion of developing a complementary relationship in the design process between an architect and an intelligent agent was core to much of the early work of Nicholas Negroponte and the Architecture Machine Group. He described design as the "step-by-step process of sharpening both comprehension and representation of one's image of the problem" (Negroponte 1970, 19). Although the recent accelerated advancement of computer processors and neural network architectures has given us the potential to realize Negroponte's concept of an "AI assistant," the core problem remains the same: How do architects effectively communicate their design intent to the machine? Chaillou states two main challenges this presents to architects developing an AI assistant: "(1) they have to pick up an adequate taxonomy i.e., the right set of adjectives that can translate into quantifiable metrics for the machine, and (2) they must select, in the vast field of AI, the proper tools and train them" (Chaillou 2019c, 14).

We first considered generative adversarial networks (GANs) as a mechanism in our generative design strategy (Goodfellow et al. 2014). Image-based GANs have shown promising results in learning significant features and their relationships across large image-based data sets (Isola et al, 2018) and have been used to learn planning strategies for buildings (Chaillou 2019a; Chaillou 2019b; Zheng and Huang 2018), but have key limitations. Output images are composed through the "blending" of latent features and are therefore decoupled from precise geometric constraints. To construct a building from the outputs would require additional steps of interpretation and translation to constructable geometries and building elements. 3D-GANs have been developed for 3D shape generation from labeled data sets of 3D shapes (Wu et al. 2016), but output geometries are also "blended" from latent features, making them unsuitable for building construction without additional rationalization.

GAN solution spaces are dependent on the quantity and quality of input data sets, and learning is developed through interpolation within them. Alternatively, we focused on extrapolation to explore potential new solutions through constrained self-play. This strategy is similar to that of AlphaGo, the expert AI player at the game of Go (Silver 2017). Go's quantity of potential moves first required a decision tree guided by a Monte Carlo tree search. After training with a large data set of known games, the AI struggled to beat expert players. The training process was moved to the symbolic level by using the rules as constraints and utilizing self-play reinforcement learning to generate and explore new unrealized games, resulting in an AI that consistently surpasses expert human players. We extend this approach by considering the design of buildings as a complex game of assembling parts.

The automated assembly of serial elements for reconfigurable structures through predefined connectivity

6 Multiscalar spatial assemblies (*NoMAS* 2019).

7 Graph analysis methods (*NoMAS* 2019).

logics relates to the research concept of "digital materials" developed at MIT Center for Bits and Atoms (Gershenfeld 2015; Popescu 2006). The research utilizes computational models considering the combinatorics of discrete digital components with predefined connectivity logics, offering the potential for robotic reconfiguration and reversibility. This principle has been extended with the work of "discrete architecture," which develops design strategies to negotiate issues of construction efficiency with design flexibility and aesthetics through the assembly of a small number of distinct generic building elements (Retsin 2019).

To develop an efficient and generalizable implementation, we model the architectural assembly process as a constraint solving problem (CSP). CSPs consist of a finite set of rules and objects, whose composition/combination must satisfy constraints (Krzysztof 2003). CSP solvers have been effective in computation logic problems across many domains, including-decision making, game development, and logic puzzles (Miguel 2001; Modi 2001; Simonis 2005). Design innovation through constraint solving has been explored by Axel Killian (2006a, 2006b), focusing on constraints in design exploration and bidirectional constraint solving methods. Our solution extends principals from texture synthesis (Efros and Leung 1999), model synthesis (Merrell 2009), and wave function collapse (WFC) (Gumin 2016a; Karth and Smith 2016), which have been applied in procedural content creation and in game development. They are used to generate larger textures (texture synthesis), 3D geometries (model synthesis), or any content (WFC) by extracting features and their relations from user inputs used as constraints in the generative process.

Building parts cannot be "blended" like textures, and the assembly of building parts relies on discrete geometric relations. We develop spatial parts as generic digital objects with constraints defining valid and invalid connectivity and additional flexible classification constraints. They act as content-agnostic containers, enabling the architect to store several concurrent representations of architectural elements, processes, and metadata attached to them. Our approach is developed with self-play reinforcement learning to evaluate each local decision considering the current state of the assembly and guide the choices of assembly to negotiate the goals set by the architect.

METHODOLOGY

Spatial Assembly Constraint Algorithm

The base constraint algorithm builds assemblies from parts by sequentially evaluating the state of the work-in-progress assembly, selecting a location, and placing parts that fulfill adjacency constraints (Fig. 5). First, a graph topology is selected as an organizational grid (cubic, octahedral, etc.), which is used to place spatial parts. Spatial parts are generic containers of geometric representations and metadata, such as abstract and more detailed 3D meshes, and properties, such as material and area as well as adjacency constraints defining their compatibility with neighboring parts. We define a set of spatial parts as a spatial parts library (Fig. 4). The designer defines how parts can be connected as geometric constraints

8 Translation spatial parts to coconut fiber monocoque prototypes (*NoMAS* 2019).

9 Prototype of spatial part (*NoMAS* 2019).

and class constraints. Geometric constraints define the allowed connectivity relationships with respect to labels attached to parts. That is, a part with adjacency labeled A can connect with parts with adjacencies labeled A or C, and this connection is only allowed for the corresponding geometrically aligned adjacencies of the parts (Fig. 2). Class constraints are connectivity constraints referring to the entire part, which act as an additional filter. For example, a part with class 0 can be connected with part of class 0 or 2, but not class 1 or 3 (Fig. 2). Class constraints can be applied as a grouping of related parts, such as parts used for public spaces versus parts used for private spaces.

Evaluator

To inform the decision of where and what part to place next, the algorithm evaluates the work-in-progress structure *S* at each step and upon completion. We have devised several evaluation metrics related to the space planning and structure of the assembly that are used to score the assembly in relation to the objectives set by the designer. For example, we capture each part's physical properties and measure average and maximum displacement of the assembly using a simulation with the Unity physics engine (Unity Technologies 2019). Another example is the spatial connectivity evaluation, which analyzes the graph relations of the parts and assemblies to measure the connective qualities of rooms (Figs. 7, 12, 20). The evaluate function returns a vector that aggregates all the evaluations conducted from this step, for example, connectivity, stability score, spatial segmentation, etc. Specific evaluation functions are explored in more detail in the various projects in the "Results" section (Figs. 7, 12, 20).

Node and Part Selector

The constraint solver depends on two main functions, nodeSelector and partSelector. nodeSelector is responsible for identifying the location to place a part next. It takes as input the graph *G*, the work-in-progress structure *S* with the current occupancy of parts, plus the evaluations evals, which are used to identify the best place to add a part. partSelector takes the graph *G*, the structure *S*, and the selected position *n*, plus the evaluations evals, to make an informed decision of what part to add at this location within the potentially valid parts.

As parts are placed, constraints are propagated through the graph and nodes become increasingly constrained, making this an NP-hard CSP to solve without contradictions (nodes with no possible valid parts to place). WFC attempted to solve this by using the "minimum entropy heuristic" (Gumin 2016a; Karth and Smith 2016). Entropy was defined as a measure of how many different elements the algorithm can potentially connect at a node without invalidating the constraints. Only considering partially constrained nodes and selecting locations with the lowest entropy (least possible elements) efficiently reduces the probability of contradiction; however, it is agnostic to the objectives input by the user beyond those inherently captured in the part constraints and is incapable of learning from past experiences.

10 3.5 m reconfigurable spatial assembly prototype (*NoMAS* 2019).

11 Spatial parts translated to 3.5m spatial assembly prototype (*NoMAS* 2019).

Self-Play Reinforcement Learning

To solve these limitations, we utilize reinforcement learning with self-play (Sutton and Barto 2018) to train a neural network to learn a policy for the nodeSelector and part-Selector through experiences (data) to negotiate multiple objectives of the designer while limiting the probability of contradictions. Reinforcement learning is well-suited as it does not require an existing data set and generates the data in the simulator. The critical aspect of AlphaGo's success was that the machine could play billions of games in a Go simulator that had never existed and learn from them through self-play (Silver 2017). We have built an architectural "simulator" with the spatial assembly constraint solver that autonomously builds and evaluates potential assemblies while incorporating the designer's intentions as reward functions. The problem of reinforcement learning is learning an effective policy that, given a state, returns the best action which maximizes the expected reward. We define its key variables and how they are set up in our framework:

State: The state captures the information required to specify a situation, such as the current state of a chess board. In our case, the state describes the work-in-progress assembly as a graph with occupied nodes, the parts placed in them, unoccupied nodes with the propagated degree of constraint on them (array of parts that can be placed in them), and an array of evals updated at each step.

Action: An action is what is applied on the state to mutate it to a different state. For example, moving a piece in a chessboard (action) changes the board to a different situation (state). An action in our case involves (1) selecting an available location in the graph to place a part, and (2) selecting and placing a valid part at that location.

State transition matrix: A state transition matrix describes how each action influences the states. In our case, when a part is placed, it increases the level of constraint (lowers number of valid parts) on its neighbors and this is propagated through the graph after each action.

Reward: A reward specifies to what extent the goal of the task was satisfied by taking an action (i.e., did this move of the piece contribute to the player winning?). Rewards are given at each step and at the completion of a whole assembly or when a contradiction occurs. The evaluator is used to analyze the assembly and evaluate the results in relation to the designer's input goals. For example, to maximize daylight, a positive reward is given as more area is added in high-exposure areas while a negative reward is added when they are placed in more shadow.

```
Training Spatial Assembly:
Initialize policy π randomly
while not converged do
    Initialize the structure as S = 0
    while valid(S) do
        e = evaluate(S)                          ▷ evaluate structure S
        n = nodeSelector(G, S, e, π)             ▷ Select node from the graph G
        p = partSelector(G, S, e, n, T, π)       ▷ Select part from Parts library T
        R = getReward(G, S, n, p)
        Add (S, p, n, e, r) in the replay buffer D
        S' = updateStructure(G, S, n, p)
        S = S'
    end while
    update policy π with replay buffer D using PPO (Schulman 2017).
```

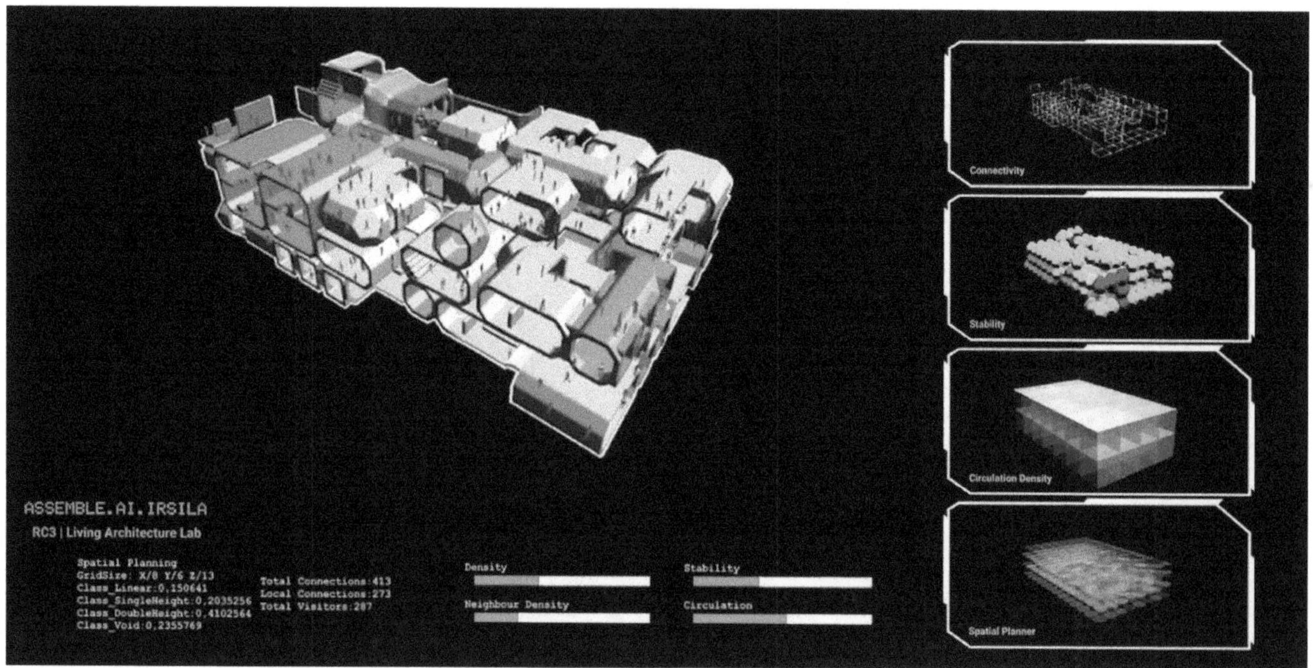

12 Spatial assembly interface + spatial assembly graph analysis methods (*IRSILA* 2020).

Training (Fig. 3): To train our algorithm we make use of proximal policy optimization (Schulman 2017), but other options are possible as well, such as soft actor critic (Haarnoja 2018). At each step during training, the agent evaluates the state and applies the action (selects nodes and parts) to get a reward that is being used by proximal policy optimization to update the policy. At the completion of a valid assembly, it is evaluated, and additional reward is given. When a contradiction arises before completion, a negative reward is given.

RESULTS AND DISCUSSION

This methodology was developed over three years in a research through teaching context in The Bartlett Architectural Design, Living Architecture Lab, Research Cluster 3 led by Tyson Hosmer, Octavian Gheorghiu, Panagiotis Tigas, David Reeves (2017–2019), and Valentina Soana (2019–2020). The methodology was tested with our students in three design projects, *ArchiGo* (2018) (Fig. 20), *NoMAS* (2019), and *IRSILA* (2020), with the last two described here as case studies.

NoMAS (Nomadic Modular Adaptive System) extended this method as a proposed platform for distributed digital ownership of shared housing in which users purchase digital parts that can be deployed physically in a series of different locations owned by the *NoMAS* company. A digital nomad would select a site partially shared by others, insert their spatial preferences and parts ownership quantities, and the platform would propose potential housing assembly options by negotiating multi-user, company, and context-based goals and constraints. The objectives and constraints for the assembles included: (1) site context constraints (irregular boundaries, limits on buildable footprints and height, limits on public, private, and green space); (2) preferences and objectives of multiple neighboring users (floor area and volume, percentages of types of space, degrees of spatial density or openness, degrees of privacy, height level); and (3) incentives of the company (minimized material cost, maximized shared spaces).

The architects designed a bespoke multiscalar library of spatial parts (Fig. 4) and input them into our framework to generate assemblies within different contexts for shared housing. The spatial parts contained both generic geometric representations as well as detailed representations embodying their fabrication and assembly strategy (Fig. 8). Building components were designed in detail as lightweight coconut fiber monocoque structures with hidden bolted interfaces enabling reversible assembly (Figs. 8, 9). The smallest scale digital part had a 1:1 relationship with prefabricated monocoque elements approximately 1–1.5 m and light enough to be manually assembled and disassembled. This was proven in the assembly of a 3.5 m high reconfigurable prototype for the Bartlett BPro Show in 2019 (Figs. 10, 11).

The project successfully integrates multiple scales of spatial parts and geometric and detailed representations for spatial planning, prefabrication, and assembly (Fig. 6). Although built from parts, the specific geometric and monocoque structural principles developed by the architects enabled a continuous multiscalar spatial

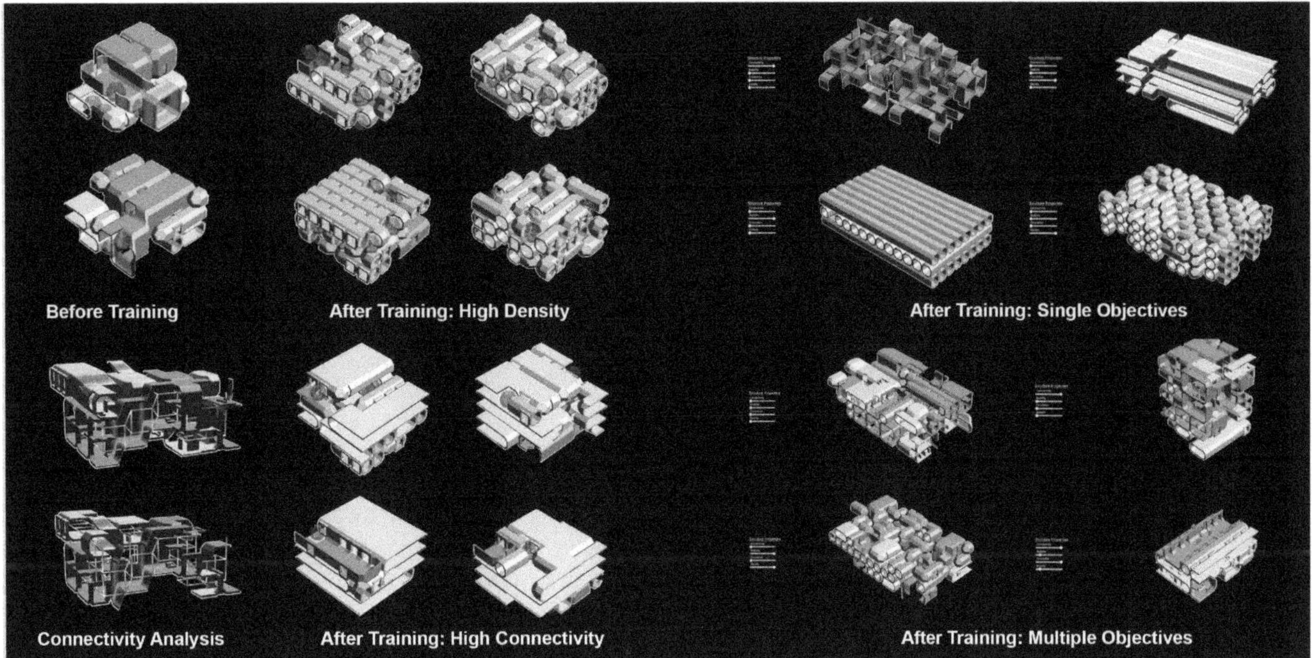

13 Reinforcement learning single objective outcomes (*IRSILA* 2020).

14 Reinforcement learning single objective outcomes (*IRSILA* 2020).

language. Self-play RL was used to develop policies for generating housing assemblies that fulfill input objectives and constraints. Metadata from spatial parts and graph analysis methods were used to evaluate and score each assembly according to stability, build area, build volume, and percentages of classes of spatial parts (Fig. 7).

IRSILA (Integrated Reconfiguration System in Living Architecture) was proposed as a reconfigurable cultural center for art (Fig. 18). It is a building system developed symbiotically with a distributed robotic assembly and reconfiguration system (Fig. 17). The architects designed spatial parts as voxelized clusters of smaller prefabricated building components that interface directly with the robotic assembly system (Figs. 15, 16). The project successfully demonstrates the integration of multiple scales and levels of detail bridging spatial planning with construction and assembly. Spatial parts contained abstract geometric representations as well as detailed representations of the prefabricated subparts with metadata related to the material distribution and assembly strategy

By defining spatial parts with both geometric constraints of connectivity and class constraints and metadata related to a spatial program, output assemblies could be defined and assessed for programmatic distribution, including percentages of interior and exterior space, galleries, cafes, and larger open spaces. Additionally, they were evaluated using physics-based analysis in Unity for stability (Unity Technologies 2019) and graph analysis for volume, spatial connectivity, and density of spatial segmentation (Fig. 12).

The algorithm was trained to develop a series of policies for both single objectives and multiobjectives (Figs. 13, 14). Single objective policies included: (1) maximizing density; (2) maximizing connectivity; (3) maximizing stability; and (4) alignment of proportional distributions of space types with inputs. Multiobjective policies were developed for weighted combinations of the objectives, yielding assemblies that negotiate between multiple goals. An additional interface was developed to enable a user to select areas of a built assembly to be reconfigured while maintaining "frozen" portions of the structure. This enabled the architect to intervene and select areas that they were happy with while generating new options for portions of the assembly.

The two projects effectively demonstrate the flexibility of the framework to support architects developing two unique design languages, in different design contexts, at different scales, and with different logics of prefabrication and assembly. *NoMAS* exhibits an opportunity to use this in a platform that negotiates the requirements and desires of multiple neighboring people that is applicable to developing new socioeconomic models of shared living. The virtually one-to-one translation of digital parts into prefabricated and assembled monocoque elements illustrates an opportunity to develop integrated modular building products much like IKEA furniture for more adaptive buildings. Alternatively, *IRSILA* demonstrates how spatial parts can be used to organize subsystems of smaller building components with constraints related to robotic assembly, opening opportunities to develop distributed robotic building systems that reorganize a building autonomously.

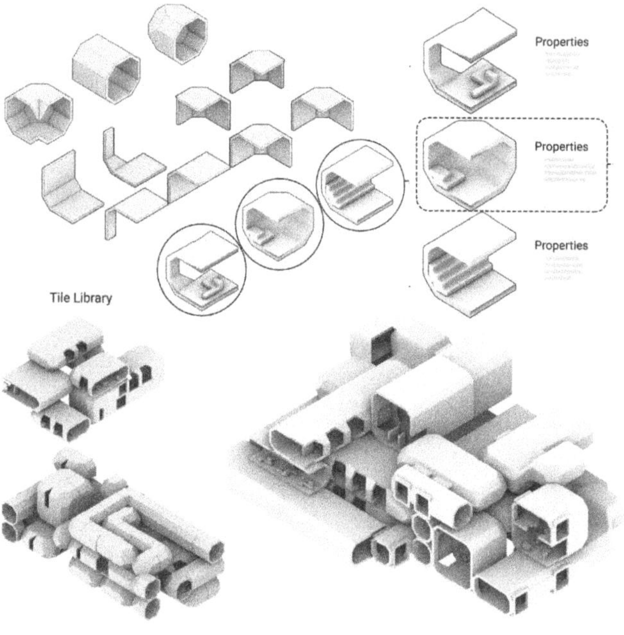

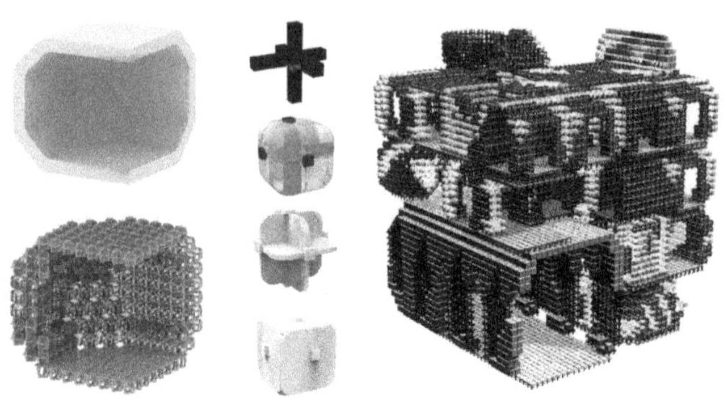

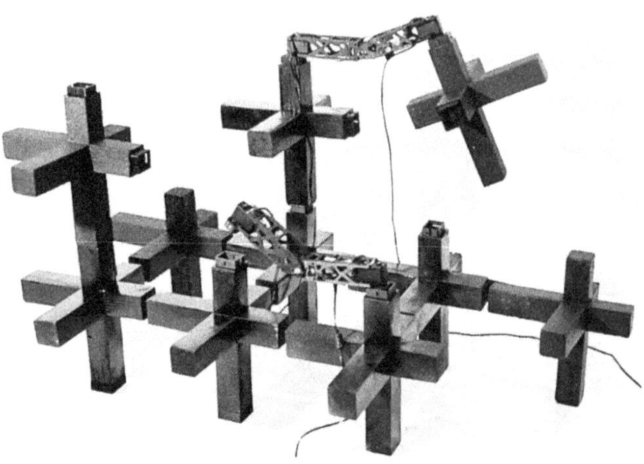

15 Spatial parts + assemblies (*IRSILA* 2020).

16 Spatial parts translation to robotic material system (*IRSILA* 2020).

17 Distributed robotic assembly system prototype, multirobot collaboration (*IRSILA* 2020).

Self-play RL offers the opportunity for the machine to explore complex options as an intelligent tree search within the design context and rules of assembly. It was found to be successful in generating valid outcomes based on the input objectives; that is, machine-learned policies generated assemblies with improved scores closely aligned to user input objectives. The primary challenge returns to questions of symbiosis between the human designer and machine assistant. That is, how well can an architect define and communicate the complexity of the design problem along with their design intention to the machine? The architect must design an effective library of spatial parts that embodies both high degrees of flexibility and qualities of space, materiality, and scale aligned with the design problem. Are the currently defined input objectives and constraints enough to define and communicate the context and goals of the design problem, and how well can an architect define "goodness" to the machine? To further improve our method, we continue to add user input constraints and additional analysis methods that yield scoring metrics more closely capturing specific design problems.

CONCLUSION

Through the case study projects, our framework proves to be a powerful tool for architects to develop novel architectural languages with embedded principles of prefabrication and reversible assembly within different contexts and scales while assisted by an AI agent to search the combinatorial design space for the most effective assemblies. It offers customization and classification within spatial parts libraries combined with controlled and repeatable assembly logics, enabling diversity in the range of design solutions and compatibility between parts as reconfigurable building elements.

Our main challenge lies in continuing to improve the designer's ability to communicate their design intent and the context of the design problem more effectively to the AI agent. We continue to build more robust methods for defining and evaluating design goals and making them more customizable for the user for specific design problems.

There is potential for this as a platform to enable new socioeconomic models of shared living through concepts of digital ownership and distributed supply and manufacturing chains. Such a platform is highly dependent on negotiating competing objectives, incentives, and contextual constraints of multiple users. Reinforcement learning with self-play is able to learn these adaptive policies as well as novel policies aligned with future unforeseen goals.

18 Spatial assembly rendered outcome (*IRSILA* 2020).

The framework also enables users to develop spatial parts that organize reconfigurable material strategies integrated with robotic assembly systems such as the one prototyped in the *IRSILA* project (Fig. 17). As distributed robotics become more sophisticated, this opens a great opportunity to move toward robotic building strategies that autonomously adapt assemblies to our changing future needs.

ACKNOWLEDGMENTS

Living Architecture Lab, The Bartlett AD Research Cluster 3 (RC3)
Studio masters: Tyson Hosmer, Octavian Gheorghiu, Valentina Soana (2019–2020), David Reeves (2017–2019).
Machine learning tutor: Panagiotis Tigas.
Theory tutor: Jordi Vivaldi Piera.
Technical tutor: Ziming He.
Robotics tutor: Justin Moon (2019–2020).
ArchiGo (2017–2018) team: Jelena Peljevic, Yekta Tehrani, Shahrzad Fereidouni, Noura Alkhaja.
NoMAS (2018–2019) team: Athina Athiana, Evangelia Triantafylla, Ming Liu.
IRSILA (2019–2020) team: Elahe Arab, Barış Erdinçer, Yifei Jia, Georgia Kolokoudia.
The Bartlett AD director: Gilles Retsin.
The Bartlett BPro director: Professor Frédéric Migayrou.

REFERENCES

Brand, Stewart. 1995. *How Buildings Learn: What Happens after They're Built*. Penguin.

Chaillou, Stanislas. 2019a. "AI + Architecture: Towards a New Approach." Master's thesis. Harvard School of Design.

Chaillou, Stanislas. 2019b. "Archigan: A Generative Stack for Apartment Building Design." Nvidia Develop blog, July 17. https://developer.nvidia.com/blog/archigan-generative-stack-apartment-building-design/.

Chaillou, Stanislas. 2019c. "The Advent of Architectural AI: A Historic Perspective." Built Horizons blog, January 27. https://medium.com/built-horizons/the-advent-of-architectural-ai-2fb6b6d0c0a8

Chaslot, G., S. Bakkes, I. Szita, and P. Spronck. 2008. "Monte-Carlo Tree Search: A New Framework for Game AI." In *Proceedings of the Fourth Artificial Intelligence and Interactive Digital Entertainment Conference*, Stanford, CA, 22–24 October 2008, edited by Chris Darken and Michael Mateas, 216–217. AAAI Press.

Gershenfeld, Neil, Matthew Carney, Benjamin Jenett, Sam Calisch, and Spencer Wilson. 2015. "Macrofabrication with Digital Materials: Robotic Assembly." *Architectural Design* 85: 122–127.

GlobalData. 2018. "Global Construction Outlook to 2022-Q4 2018 Update." https://www.orbisresearch.com/reports/index/global-construction-outlook-to-2022-q4-2018-update.

Goodfellow, Ian, J. Pouget-Abadie, M. Mirza, et al. 2014. "Generative Adversarial Networks." In *Proceedings of the 27th International Conference on Neural Information Processing Systems*, 2672–2680. Cambridge, MA: MIT Press.

Gumin, Maxim. 2016a. *Wave Function Collapse*. https://github.com/mxgmn/WaveFunctionCollapse GitHub repository.

Gumin, Maxim. 2016b. *ConvChain*. https://github.com/mxgmn/ConvChain. GitHub repository.

Gumin, Maxim. 2016c. *SynTex*. https://github.com/mxgmn/SynTex. GitHub repository.

Haarnoja, Tuomas, et al. 2018. "Soft Actor-Critic Algorithms and Applications." arXiv preprint. arXiv:1812.05905.

Hosmer, Tyson, and Tigas Panagiotis. 2019. "Towards an Autonomous Architecture: Deep Reinforcement Learning for Autonomous Robotic Tensegrity (ART)." In *ACADIA 19: Ubiquity and Autonomy [Proceedings of the 39th Annual Conference of the Association for Computer Aided Design in Architecture (ACADIA)]*, Austin, TX, 21–26 October 2019, edited by K. Bieg, D. Briscoe, and C. Odom, 16–29. CUMINCAD.

Isola, Phillip, Jun-Yan Zhu, Tinghui Zhou, and Alexei A. Efros. 2017. "Image-to-Image Translation with Conditional Adversarial Networks." *CVPR*. arXiv:1611.07004.

Karth, Isaac, and Adam M. Smith. 2017. "Wave Function Collapse Is Constraint Solving in the Wild." In *Proceedings of FDG'17, Hyannis, MA, USA*, August 14–17, 2017. https://doi.org/10.1145/3102071.3110566.

Killian, Axel. 2006a. "Design Exploration through Bidirectional Modeling of Constraints." PhD thesis, MIT, Cambridge, MA.

Killian, Axel. 2006b. "Design Innovation Through Constraint Modeling." *International Journal of Architectural Computing* 4 (1): 87–105.

Killian, Axel. 2014. "Design Exploration and Steering of Design." In *Inside Smartgeometry*, 122–129. John Wiley & Sons, Ltd.

Kirschner, Marc. Variations in Evolutionary Biology. Spuybroek, Lars. "The Architecture of Variation." London : Thames and Hudson, 2009. 26-33.

Koehler, Daniel. 2019. "Mereological Thinking: Figuring Realities within Urban Form." *Architectural Design 89* (2): 30-37.

Krzysztof, A. 2003. *Principles of Constraint Programming*. Cambridge: Cambridge University Press.

Merrell, Paul C. 2009. "Model synthesis." PhD dissertation. University of North Carolina at Chapel Hill.

Miguel, Ian. July 2001. "Dynamic Flexible Constraint Satisfaction and Its Application to AI Planning." PhD thesis. Edinburgh University.

Modi, P. J., H. Jung, M. Tambe, W. M. Shen, and S. Kulkarni. 2001. "A Dynamic Distributed Constraint Satisfaction Approach to Resource Allocation." In *International Conference on Principles and Practice of Constraint Programming*, 26 November 2001, 685-700. Berlin, Heidelberg: Springer.

Ngwepe, Lusca, and Clinton Aigbavboa. 2015. "A Theoretical Review of Building Life Cycle Stages and Their Related Environmental Impacts." *Journal of Civil Engineering and Environmental Technology*, 2 (13): 7–15. http://hdl.handle.net/10210/69042.

Negroponte, N. 1970. *The Architecture Machine*. Cambridge, MA: MIT Press.

Parter, Merav, Nadav Kashtan, and Uri Alon. 2008. "Facilitated Variation: How Evolution Learns from Past Environments to Generalize to New Environments." *PLoS Computational Biology* 4 (11): e1000206.

Popescu, George A., Tushar Mahale, and Neil Gershenfeld. 2006. "Digital Materials for Digital Printing." In *Digital Fabrication 2006 [Proceedings of the International Conference on Digital Printing Technologies (NIP)]*, Denver, CO, 17–22 September 2006, 58–61. Society for Imaging Science and Technology.

Retsin, Gilles. 2019. "Bits and Pieces: Digital Assemblies: From Craft to Automation." *Architectural Design* 89 (2): 38–45.

Schulman, John, et al. 2017. "Proximal Policy Optimization Algorithms." arXiv preprint. arXiv:1707.06347.

Silver, D., J. Schrittwieser, K. Simonyan, I. Antonoglou, A. Huang, A. Guez, T. Hubert, L. Baker, M. Lai, A. Bolton, and Y. Chen. 2017. "Mastering the Game of go Without Human Knowledge." *Nature* 550 (7676): 354–359.

Simonis, H. 2005. "Sudoku as a Constraint Problem." In *CP Workshop on modeling and reformulating Constraint Satisfaction Problems* 12: 13–27. Citeseer.

Sutton, R.S. and Barto, A.G. 1998. *Introduction to Reinforcement Learning*. Cambridge, MA: MIT Press.

Sutton, Richard S., and Andrew G. Barto. 2018. *Reinforcement Learning: An Introduction*. Cambridge, MA: MIT Press.

Wang, Ting-Chun, Ming-Yu Liu, Jun-Yan Zhu, Andrew Tao, Jan Kautz, and Bryan Catanzaro. 2018. "High-Resolution Image Synthesis and Semantic Manipulation with Conditional GANs." *CVPR*. arXiv: 1711.11585v2.

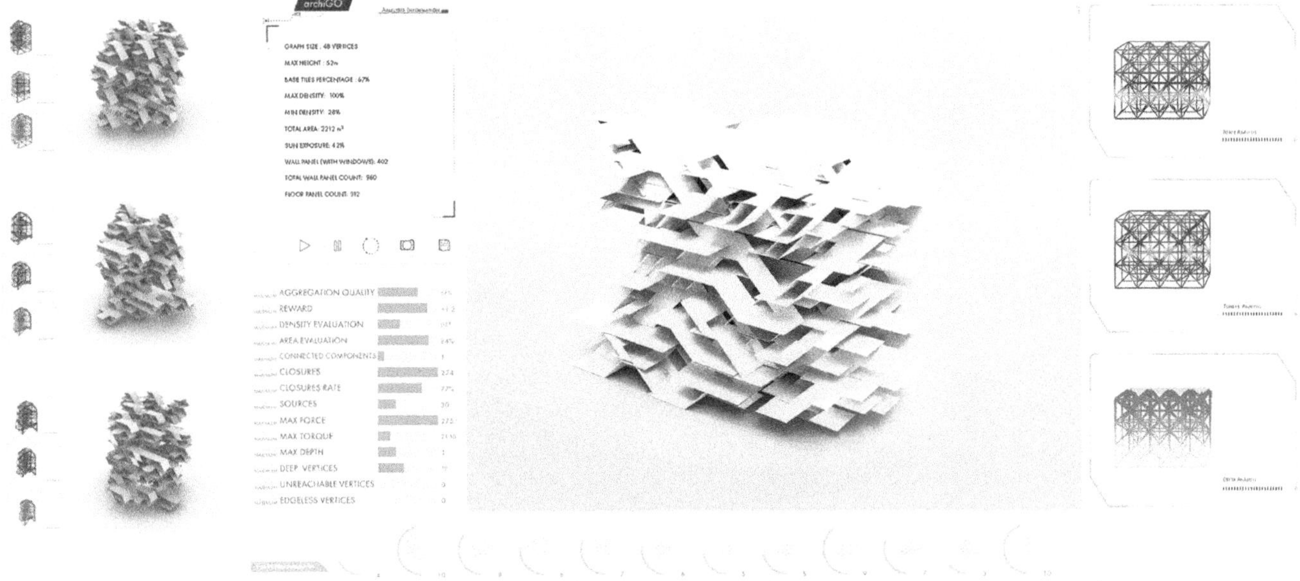

20 *ArchiGo* interface, spatial assemblies, and graph analysis methods (*ArchiGo* 2018).

Wu, Jiajun, Chengkai Zhang, Tianfan Xue, William Freeman, and Joshua Tenenbaum. 2016. "Learning a Probabilistic Latent Space of Object Shapes via 3D Generative-Adversarial Modeling." In *NIPS 2016 [30th Conference on Neural Information Processing Systems]*, Barcelona, Spain, 5–10 December 2016, edited by Daniel D. Lee, Ulrike von Luxburg, Roman Garnett, Masashi Sugiyama, and Isabelle Guyon, 82–90. Curran Associates Inc.

Unity Technologies. 2019. *Unity engine*. Version 2019.3.5f. http://www.unity.com.

Zheng, Hao, and Weixin Huang. 2018. "Architectural Drawings Recognition and Generation through Machine Learning." In *ACADIA 2018: Recalibration: On Imprecision and Infidelity [Proceedings of the 38th Annual Conference of the Association for Computer Aided Design in Architecture (ACADIA)]*, Mexico City, Mexico, 18–20 October 2018, edited by P. Anzalone, M. del Signore, and A. J. Wit, 156–165. CUMINCAD.

IMAGE CREDITS

All images by the authors. Living Architecture Lab, The Bartlett BPro RC3, and the following students:
Figures 1, 3, 4–11, 19: Team *NoMAS*: Athina Athiana, Evangelia Triantafylla, Ming Liu.
Figures 12–18: Team *IRSILA*: Elahe Arab, Barış Erdinçer, Yifei Jia, Georgia Kolokoudia.
Figure 20: Team *ArchiGo*: Jelena Peljevic, Yekta Tehrani, Shahrzad Fereidouni, Noura Alkhaja.

Tyson Hosmer is an architect, researcher, and software developer working at the intersection of design, computation, AI, and robotics. He is a Lecturer at UCL Bartlett BPro in London, where he directs the Living Architecture Lab (RC3). He is an associate researcher with Zaha Hadid Architects, leading grant-funded research development of cognitive agent-based technologies and machine learning for design. His 13 years of experience in practice include working in Asymptote Architecture, Kokkugia, AXI:OME, and serving as research director with Cecil Balmond Studio for six years. Tyson was previously a Course tutor with the AADRL for seven years and has been a visiting professor in several institutions internationally.

Panagiotis Tigas is a PhD student and researcher at the University of Oxford, focusing on artificial intelligence, generative design, and robotics. He has worked for Microsoft, Autodesk Research, and several startups.

David Reeves is a software developer specializing in computational design, geometry processing, and computer graphics. He is currently working on the Frostbite game engine at Electronic Arts, developing tools for procedural asset creation. Previously, he worked in animation and VFX (DNEG) developing shape deformation tools for character animation, and in the AEC industry (Zaha Hadid Architects, Amanda Levete Architects) developing design tools for shape exploration and optimization.

Ziming He is a senior designer and a software developer focusing on computational design, generative design, architectural visualization, and robotics. He is currently working as a senior designer in Zaha Hadid Architects and is a technical tutor with RC3, Bartlett School of Architecture, UCL.

KEYNOTE CONVERSATION

CULTURE AND ACCESS

KEYNOTE EVENT

A Conversation on Culture and Access

Kate Hartman
OCAD University

Vernelle A.A. Noel, PhD
University of Florida

Laura Devendorf
University of Colorado, Boulder

Computational design and data impact nearly every aspect of contemporary life as well as architecture and design practices. Ranging in accessibility from user-friendly social media to highly skilled programming, these technologies are informed by the exchange between a technology's end user and its author(s). In this context, what is a computational public? Who is the audience for computational design? How might computational design practices resonate beyond the academy or rarefied audiences? How can computational designers facilitate access to their work and understanding of its impact on the built environment? In this keynote conversation, three designers and scholars whose work deals critically with questions of computation, craft, and public engagement gathered to share their work and discuss these important questions.

Kate Hartman, Associate Professor at OCAD University and director of the Social Body Lab, began the event with a presentation of her work with wearable technology and electronic textiles. In her talk, Hartman described her work as exploring "how the devices we wear affect the ways in which we relate to ourselves, each other, and the world around us." She presented a number of projects that instigate a sense of shared collectivity both in their processes of making and in their social effects as interactive prosthetics.

Vernelle A. A. Noel, Assistant Professor at the University of Florida, followed with a presentation on her work with community engagement, craft practices, and what she calls "situated computations": an expanded approach to computational design that "acknowledges the historical, cultural, and material contexts of design and making." By studying the traditional craft of wire-bending with artisans in Trinidad and Tobago and melding this knowledge with computational tools, Noel's work positions digital workflows as a mechanism for repair: computation and craft learn from each other, preserve traditional knowledge, and engage a broader public.

Laura Devendorf, Assistant Professor at the University of Colorado, Boulder, and director of the Unstable Design Lab, responded with a reminder that tools are never neutral; their

1 "Tools shape action and perception.... Within this broad ecology, designers are in a unique position to be both using tools and making tools—to moderate the resonance between different actors—both human and non-human—different cultures, different histories, different stories.... How has your making practice shaped who and what you listen to?" —Laura Devendorf
(Image: Laura Devendorf)

biases shape action and perception, and therefore they are always political in nature. A lively conversation followed, with the participants discussing ways in which design technology might enable new forms of inclusivity, participation, and community, pointing towards what Devendorf referred to as a "broad ecology" of tools for both acting and listening. The conversation is reproduced below in edited form.

For a recording of the entire event, please see this link: **https://www.youtube.com/watch?v=W83McyRQ2JI**

Laura Devendorf (LD): A making practice is not only about what you make but what kinds of things you learn, the materials and people you collaborate with, and who you're able to listen to along the way. I am curious if you could share how engaging in making has enabled you to listen differently. In the context of Vernelle's work, why ethnography *and* tool building, and not just ethnography?

Vernelle A. A. Noel (VN): I enjoy making, and it's the way I grew up understanding and making sense of the world. While certain things might seem too abstract, I understand aspects of the world, and even abstract theory, through hands-on making and digging into the realness of the work. As for ethnography, I am not attempting to be the savior for anyone. I am there to understand a specific culture, understand its people, and part of this is validating their story. People are just happy to tell their stories, to be validated, and to be listened to. Seeing how people interact with the humanity of the design is important, especially when we're talking about such abstract things like computation. So for me, that's why I engage in both ethnography and the making. It's in the real world.

LD: Kate, releasing products is a really important part of your practice. Yet, in academia, we are often not required to go that extra mile and fully document or release the innovations we make. How do you think your practice would be different if you didn't release these projects as products?

Kate Hartman (KH): For me, one thing that's exciting and also important is moving beyond my own sphere and getting outside of my own communities. I'm always trying to mix it up, meet new people, and expand my networks, and it doesn't have to be only through products. It just happens to be that in some ways, making something a product lowers

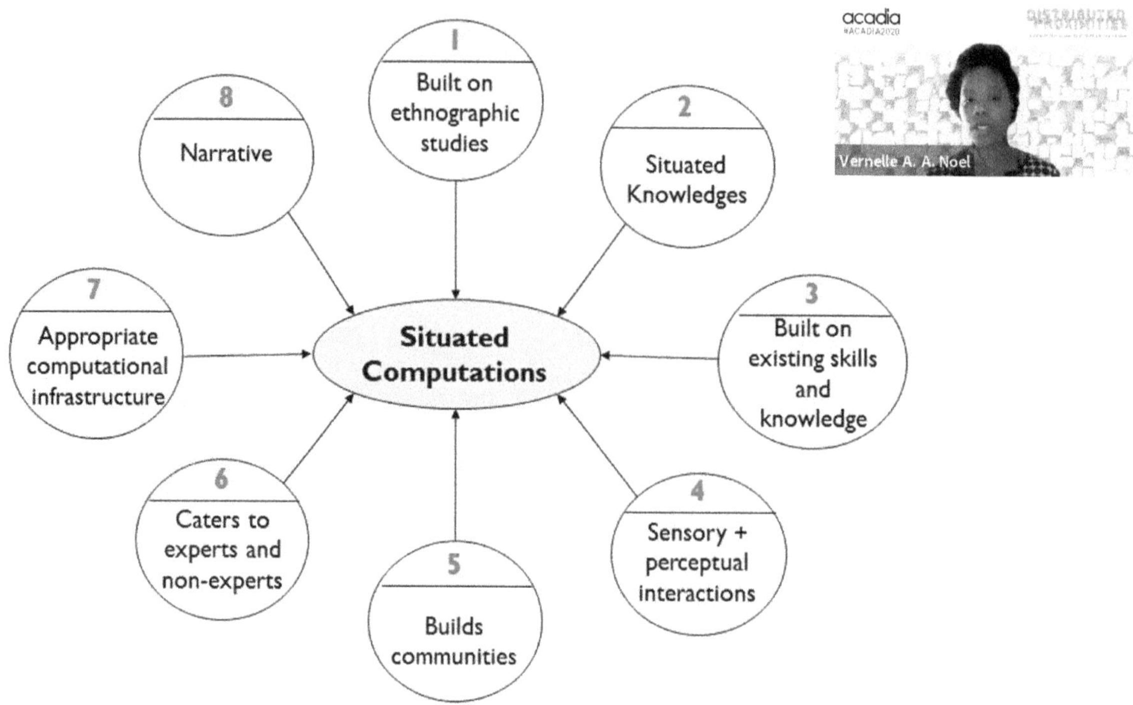

2 "Situated Computations grounds our technologies or methods and our work in the social world by acknowledging the historical, cultural, and material contexts of design and making. It acknowledges and responds to a setting's social and technological infrastructure, and it asks that we refuse to remain ignorant of social and political structures that shape our field and our work." —Vernelle A. A. Noel

the barrier to entry. So, publishing an Open Hardware circuit board design doesn't necessarily make it easy for everyone to use. Not that buying any circuit board makes it easy for everyone to use. But there's a difference between the complex process of having to order something from a printed circuit board manufacturer versus something that's off the shelf, or can be purchased easily from an online retailer. So that's been a really interesting process for me. Both through the products and in working on other open-source tools, it has been neat to connect to different communities and see how these things get used in different ways.

LD: What do you say to people when they say, "Oh, isn't craft romantic?"—that this kind of work is sort of a doomed endeavor, that it's not realistic to use in the "real world"? What's your response to something like that?

KH: I have definitely had these experiences in my lab, Social Body Lab, in terms of both gendering and deviating the work towards what it might be considered more useful for. Sometimes these comments are really great, meaningful suggestions. My work is particularly playful, and I think sometimes that causes people to think that it's not serious. But I like to describe it as seriously playful. I think play is incredibly important in terms of how we relate as human beings. Our social interactions and understandings affect how we connect or how rifts grow between us.

But how do I respond to people who say that craft is not real? You referenced in your presentation the book *Critical Fabulations: Reworking the Methods and Margins of Design*, which I think covers some really great examples of how craft in its own right is important and meaningful, and how we create it.[1] Craft facilitates not only the obvious, such as the clothing that we wear, but also things like space travel and important industrial processes. It's not necessarily limited to hobbyist pursuits.

VN: My response to that would be that *everything* is romanticized. We romanticized the maker movement. We romanticize robots. We romanticize drones. Everything is romanticized.

LD: Maybe what's romanticized is always what doesn't seem possible or worthwhile, and that doesn't break along

Kinetic Wearables Toolkit
with Chris Luginbuhl

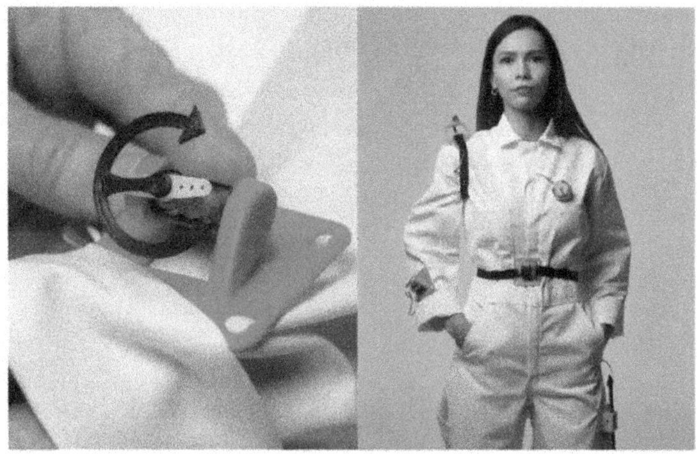

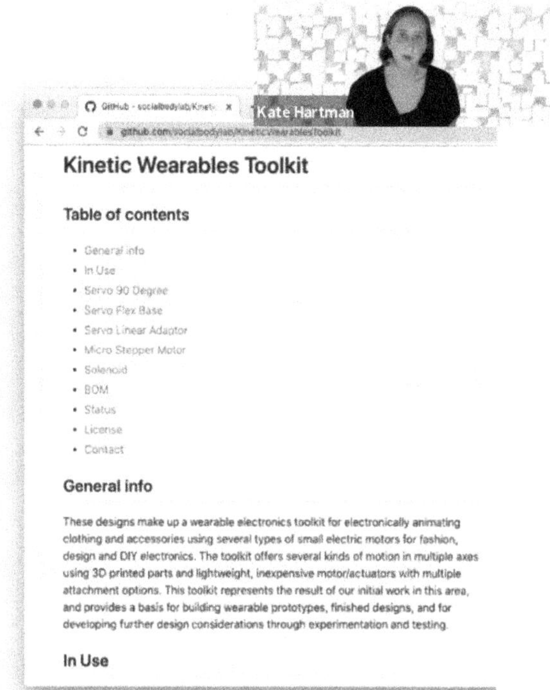

3 "The toolkit model provides a way to look at electronics through a design-oriented lens as something that people can plug and play into their own making and crafting processes." —Kate Hartman

equal lines. There are certain kinds of technical practices, processes, or tools that are immediately going to be taken more seriously than maybe something made out of, say, cardboard, or something that's not made in order to fit a certain kind of aesthetic profile. I'm wondering if you can reflect on how that's affected your work. How do you navigate that tension between presenting something as new, while still holding true to the histories?

KH: Technology so often gets presented as new, and there are waves of interest and awareness that constantly shift as things enter the public sphere. We see this now in wearable technologies and electronic textiles. It's important to look back and recognize that people have been doing this for decades, or even centuries. Obviously, certain aspects of computation are quite new, but computation itself is not new, and it ties back to these practices and traditions. Your work, Laura, with weaving as a technology in relation to computation is a great example of this. In my teaching, I often remind my students that this kind of work is not cutting-edge, and that's okay.

VN: I think we need to open up how we define what is new. We have all these new technologies that many times continue to reinforce terrible social issues that have existed for years. How can we think beyond the technologies that we develop and look into practices that are socially and culturally rich, that form communities and bring them together? We need to think about "new" beyond the technology itself and think about "new" as including groups and voices who have been left out or marginalized, including other ways of thinking, including other knowledges and communities.

LD: I'm curious how your practices affect your teaching. Who do you consider to be students, and who do you consider to be teachers?

VN: For me, I teach architectural studio and seminars. Studio is very much focused around making. As architects and architecture students, that's what we do. But even in my seminars, we unpack those theoretical concepts through making. In both types of classes, I try to cater to the different ways that people understand. If you didn't grow up reading Roman or Greek stories and theory, it's okay; you can still understand certain concepts by making.

Regarding who's a teacher and who's a student: I know all teachers learn from their students, and some of my best experiences are with my students. We are all learning together and sharing together. For me, that's the fun of this communal hands-on making way of teaching and learning; we all have this mediated space to talk to each other, share, laugh, and work through ideas.

KH: My students are my teachers. I was on a beautiful meet-up call last night with people working on physical computing across several different institutions, and we realized that there were many different generations of teacher-student-teacher-student over two decades on this one call. It was beautiful because I was on there and I brought my students in, but then one of my old teachers was there.

There's a really close relationship between my research and my teaching, and one of the joys of being able to teach in your area of expertise is that you can immediately bring things into the classroom in a meaningful way. The thing that I learn the most from my students is to challenge my assumptions. Related to our earlier conversation about craft and making, I try as much as I can to make alongside my students. Even that makes me challenge the assumption of how long it takes to do something.

I was teaching a weekend workshop a couple weekends ago. It was a new group that I had never worked with before, and they had to sew their first electronic circuits. And so we sat on Zoom together and I sewed with them. After all these years, it blew my mind how long it took us to sew a single circuit.

LD: I would also say I mostly learn from my students. They're not as jaded as I am, which I find really refreshing.

We have a question for Vernelle from Maria Yablonina in the audience: "It seems that the concept of repair is not given as much attention as it deserves in the field of architecture, and, specifically, in computational design and digital fabrication. I was wondering if you could speculate why this is the case, and what we can do as a community to shift the focus towards repair and care in architecture?"

VN: It has a lot to do with funding and what's being prioritized by funders. We know that there is money to support the implementation of robotics and new technologies, and of course that technical knowledge is essential for us to become experts with these tools. But regarding questions of repair and care: I suspect people just don't think these issues are sexy enough. As a field, I think it's a critical question that we should all be asking ourselves.

LD: Kate, how do you see the relationship between repair and documentation, or even documentation and the notion of the "silence of the archives"? When you are making documentation, are you thinking about it as kind of a cultural preservation practice, or more of a means to an end in terms of having somebody replicate something?

KH: It's a critical question: the difference between documenting as a way to show someone what you did, versus documenting in a way to allow that person to make what you made. That extends to repair, because if you understand how something is made, then you understand how to repair it. Vernelle's work is so important in this regard. I think there's more movement towards this alternate form of documentation, including emerging tools, some of which are very much discipline-specific. For instance, we had a student, Omid Ettehadi, who just finished the OCADU Digital Futures graduate program, and his research looked at 3D printing and augmenting the 3D printed design as a way to share not just the file, but the minute decisions made along the way in the process of actually making the print.[2]

VN: Documentation is important. In my work, though, I think less about the artifact and more about the broader process of computational design. The end result, the product, is not the goal. The important thing is all the "meat" in between: the social interactions, the conversations, the things that people learn. That is the main part of the work, so that these people, these stories, these skills can be translated through the product. The artifact just facilitates that process.

LD: This brings up some interesting points around care and working with communities. It is quite interesting that in both of your practices, you're really deeply engaged with an audience or with a community, in slightly different ways. I'm wondering, for others who might be interested in cultivating these kinds of relationships, how do you build them and how do you sustain a fruitful, collaborative, craft relationship in your research?

KH: I have worked among different communities for a long time, but my more recent work with *Textile Game Controllers* is my first durational, embedded contact with a community that is different from my own. One of the organizers from our partner organization Dames Making

Hand, Material, Mind

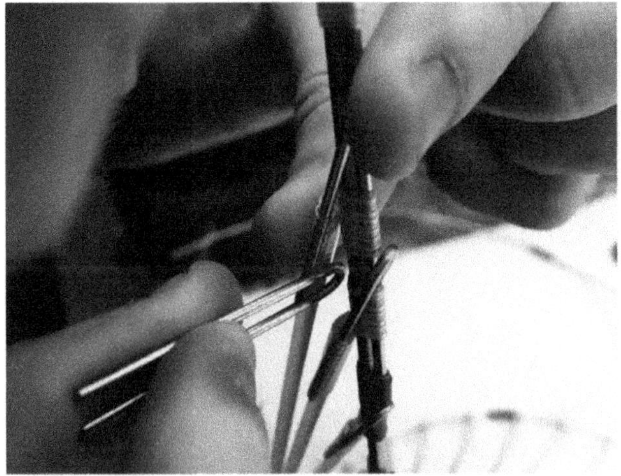

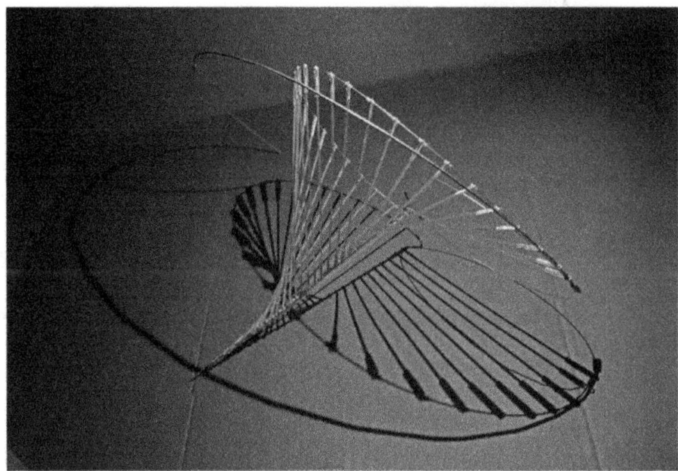

4 "By engaging multiple ways of seeing, knowing, and doing—and by amplifying the stories of marginalized groups by deploying their stories in our research, design practices, and education." —Vernelle A. A. Noel
[Left image: Phuong 'Karen' Tran; right image: Phuong 'Karen' Tran and Jamieson Pye; photography by Vernelle A. A. Noel]

Games[3] was a former member of my lab, so we have a deeper, longer personal connection that we've been building over time. The trust built through collaboration and co-working allowed us to bridge our two organizations, collaborate over the course of two years, and conduct several workshops that led to an even larger event that connected with the community in a deeper way. And now we're looking at what we can do next. It's not just a matter of doing the project and then dropping it and moving on, but instead having a more sustained connection and working together in a more sustained way.

VN: With regard to my work in Trinidad and Tobago, I'm from Trinidad and Tobago, so that cultural connection already existed. However, I was not a part of the specific Carnival community, and I had to find someone to introduce me to that community. Research takes time, especially research that is with humans. Yes, I interview and observe, but I'm sure people are also gauging me. Trust is important in these practices; it determines what people also share with you. And to form these kinds of relationships requires the same commitments essential for any human relationship: constant conversations, cooking together, eating together, and so on. These very social and real, embedded ways of how humans interact are part of the research process. It's a sustained relationship that takes time.

LD: I was asked once what I could do to bring more collaboration to a space I was working in, and I thought back to examples like Autodesk's Pier 9 Workshop, where the kitchen exists within the lab. If you bring a kitchen in, somehow different things start to emerge, which I think resonates with your comments.

Another question from the audience, from Rebecca Duque Estrada: "How do you bring playfulness, openness, and chances to make mistakes to academia?"

KH: I can say that my mistakes came first, and academia came second. I like awkwardness, weirdness, and a "guts out" approach. That's always how I've approached things through my art-making and my research. Part of making things that have a playful edge to them is about creating space for other people to be playful. One of the reasons I really like working in wearables is the potential to enable people to transform even just a little bit through embodying a different space or a different identity. This allows people to distance themselves a bit from their self-conscious natures, and release in a way that wouldn't be possible in their everyday format.

VN: One of my dreams in life is to have grandkids who say, "Grandma, you play too much!" I just like to play. The culture

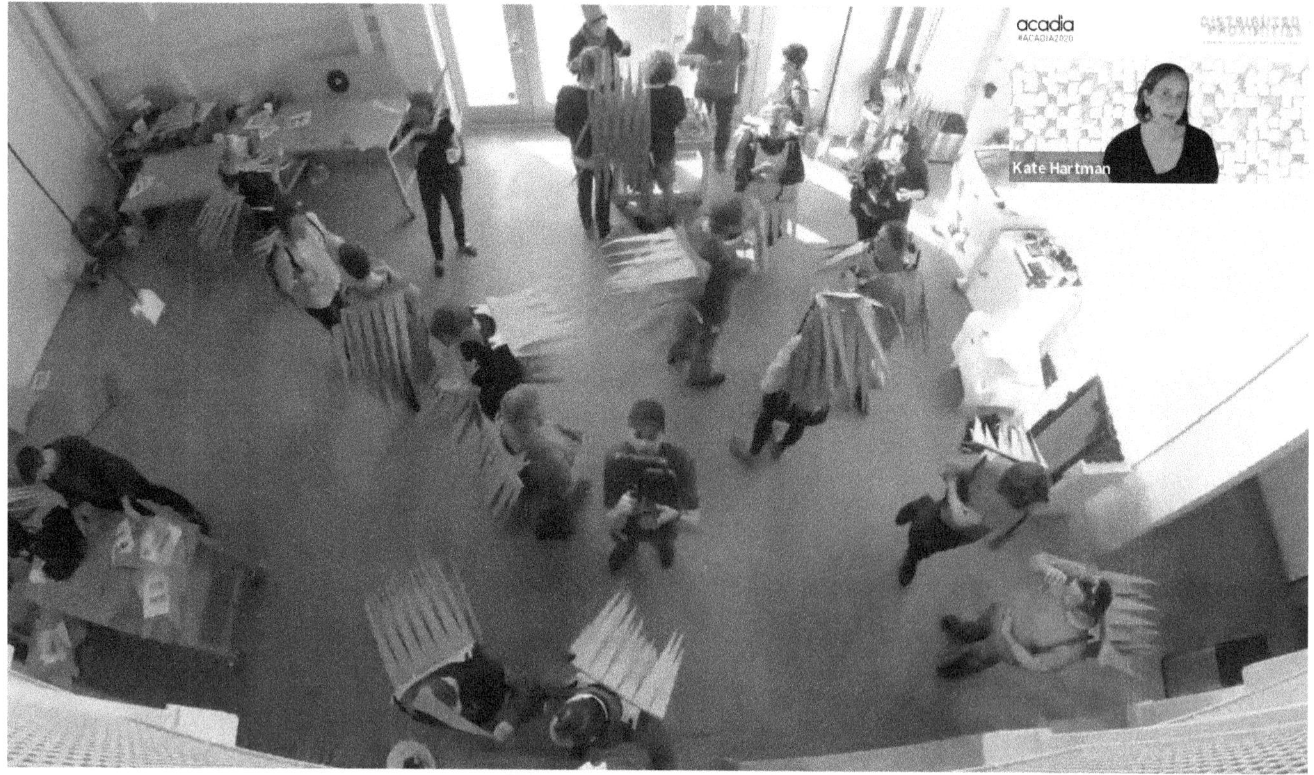

5 "When we shift our physical envelopes, when we change our sense of embodiment, it changes how we move through the world and how we relate to each other.." —Kate Hartman

I come from is a playful one. I've been blessed enough to play when I was young, and so my approach to teaching studio is to take play seriously. If my students aren't having fun, we need to rethink this, because I believe that's where creative juices really come forward—by giving everyone the space to fail. The more you fail, the closer you are to figuring something out.

LD: You may be familiar with Sister Corita Kent's "Ten Rules." One of them is: "Don't try to create and analyze at the same time. They're different processes."[4] When I'm making, I've always found resisting that critical impulse to be really freeing. If you're going to truly make something, you have to create a space for something unexpected to happen.

Another audience question from Shelby Doyle: "For there to be access, I think there needs to be a public. Who is the computational public? Where do these ideas escape the academy or seemingly esoteric practices, and why is craft an effective way to engage with this computational public? Are there other methods available, or is craft unique?"

VN: Everyone is a computational public. We are all computational publics. From the very moment we started counting and using data to make decisions, humanity became a computational public. This is why it's important that we as a field work with those outside of our bubble to show people how they are part of a computational public. I think it's important that we remind ourselves that we have a responsibility to engage with people, to learn from them, and for them to learn from us how computation changes and affects our society.

KH: Regarding how craft can be an effective way to engage the computational public, I am a big fan of embodiment and physicality. Even now, in the midst of the pandemic, it's still important; we still have these bodies, even though we're sharing a virtual space. One of the things that I love about craft, which isn't limited to craft, is its engagement with the body and an embodied knowledge. Embodied knowledge is knowledge that has been around for as long as we've existed, and it acknowledges all of these practices that have come before us. I think physical and embodied engagement is a way to break down barriers in terms of helping people feel included and engaged in learning particular material.

Craft can serve as an on-ramp for novices, but it's also important to understand that craft is not simple. It is terrific that there are aspects of craft that are very accessible, but there are also aspects of craft that are extremely advanced and deeply technical, requiring apprenticeships or significant time investment.

LD: How do we create inclusion? How do we make our teaching more inclusive? And what advice would you give to somebody who said, "I want to make my research more inclusive"? Where would you tell them to start?

VN: I would say, start by looking and paying attention to who is not there. Who is not there in your research? Who is not there in what you're reading? Who is not there in your school or your classroom?

KH: I would say it's important to include more people, to include different people, and to challenge our own notions of what "different" is. The sharing of process is important in my work—as a method of being inclusive and as a way to get people more involved in and more aware of how things are made. It opens opportunities and reveals new perspectives, helping us to challenge our assumptions in what and how we make.

LD: Your comments remind me of Donna Haraway, who encourages us to attend to the differences that make a difference.[5] By this, Haraway means not considering differences as such, but rather how they are constructed and maintained. Thank you both for a wonderful conversation and for sharing work that demonstrates this deeper understanding of difference. I hope it gives us all a provocation to consider how each of us interprets and assigns labels to categories like craft, culture, and technology.

NOTES

1. Daniela K. Rosner, *Critical Fabulations: Reworking the Methods and Margins of Design* (Cambridge, MA: MIT Press, 2018).
2. Omid Ettehadi, "Documented: Embedding and Retrieving Information from 3D Printed Objects" (master's thesis, OCAD University, 2020).
3. DMG, https://dmg.to/.
4. Corita Kent and Jan Steward, *Learning by Heart: Teachings to Free the Creative Spirit* (New York: Simon and Schuster, 2008).
5. Donna J. Haraway, *Staying with the Trouble: Making Kin in the Chthulucene* (Durham, NC: Duke University Press, 2016).

Kate Hartman is an Associate Professor at OCAD University in Toronto, where she is Graduate Program Director of Digital Futures and the founding Director of Social Body Lab, a research and development team dedicated to exploring body-centric technologies in the social context. She is also an Adjunct Instructor and Director of ITP Camp at the Interactive Telecommunications Program at New York University. She is the author of the book *Make: Wearable Electronics* (Maker Media, 2014), was an artist-in-iresidence at Autodesk's Pier 9, and has work that is included in the permanent collection of the Museum of Modern Art in New York. Hartman is interested in people and the nuances and awkward bits of their social interactions. Through the use of wearable technologies, electronic textiles, and digital fabrication techniques, she explores new possibilities for expressive, tangible, and embodied interactions.

Vernelle A.A. Noel PhD is a computational design scholar, architect, TED Speaker, and artist. She is currently an Assistant Professor of Architecture + Computational Design at the University of Florida, and Founding Director of the Situated Computation + Design Lab. Her research in design and computation investigates traditional and digital ways of making, emerging technologies, and their intersections with society to build new expressions, methodologies, and theories in design. She holds a PhD in Architecture (Design Computing) from the Pennsylvania State University, a Master of Science in Architectural Studies (Design + Computation) from MIT, a BArch from Howard University, and a Diploma in Civil Engineering from the John S. Donaldson Technical Institute in Trinidad and Tobago. Noel has taught courses and conducted research in Design Computation and Architecture at the Georgia Institute of Technology, Pennsylvania State University, the Singapore University of Technology and Design (SUTD), and MIT, and has practiced as an architect in the USA, India, and Trinidad and Tobago.

Laura Devendorf is a design researcher and technologist working at the intersection of textiles, electronics, and digital fabrication. She is currently Assistant Professor of Information Science, ATLAS Institute Fellow, and director of the Unstable Design Lab at the University of Colorado, Boulder, where she and her students collaborate with machines and develop design workflows and artifacts that envision more playful and sustainable futures. Her research has been supported by the Center for Craft and National Science Foundation. She has received multiple best paper awards at top conferences in the field of human-computer interaction.

PEER-REVIEWED PAPERS

CULTURE AND ACCESS

"How can we think beyond the technologies that we develop and look into practices that are socially and culturally rich, that form communities and bring them together? We need to think about 'new' beyond the technology itself and think about 'new' as including groups and voices who have been left out or marginalized, including other ways of thinking, including other knowledges and communities."

—Vernelle A. A. Noel, "A Conversation on Culture and Access"

This section begins with a project to counteract insipid social media filters through the implementation of spatial practice in order "to present [it] from a collective viewpoint rather than a personalized one." Seen through this lens, each of the papers that follow also privileges the collective in its own subtle ways, situating more technically oriented research within broader craft traditions that link social, material, and computational cultures and lowering barriers to access.

Engelbart

An Agent-Based Interface for Exploring Beyond the Social Media Filter Bubble

Eric Duong*
Garrett Vercoe*
Ehsan Baharlou
University of Virginia School of Architecture
*Authors contributed equally to the research

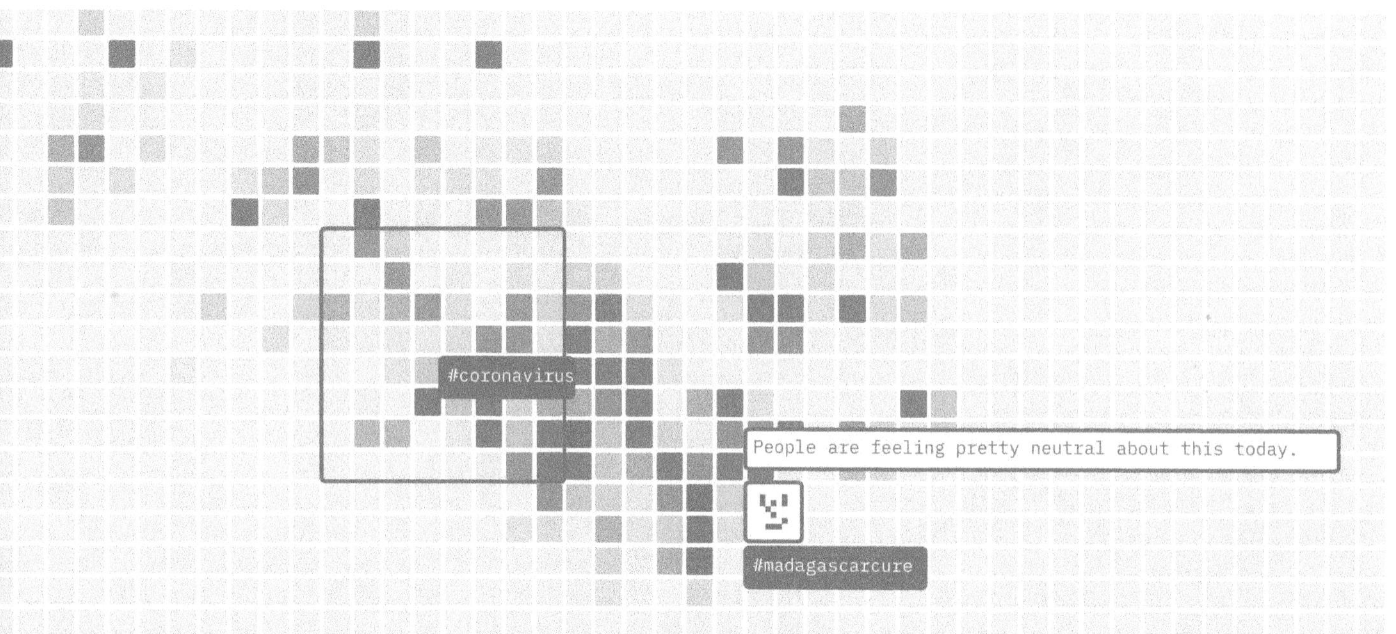

1

1 Engelbart, the autonomous agent, approaches a topic discussion and summarizes what people are saying and feeling about it.

ABSTRACT

The internet has long been viewed as a cyberspace of free and collective information, allowing for an increase in the diversity of ideas and viewpoints available to the general public. However, critics argue that the emergence of personalization algorithms on social media and other internet platforms instead reduces information diversity by forming "filter bubbles" of viewpoints similar to the user's own. The adoption of these personalization algorithms is due in part to advancements in natural language processing, which allow for textual analysis at unprecedented scales.

This paper aims to utilize natural language processing and architectural spatial principles to present social media from a collective viewpoint rather than a personalized one. To accomplish this, the paper introduces Engelbart, a data-driven agent-based system, where real-time Twitter conversations are visualized within a two-dimensional environment. This environment is interacted with by the artificial intelligence (AI) agent, Engelbart, which summarizes crowdsourced thoughts and feelings about current trending topics. The functionality of this web application comes from the natural language processing of thousands of tweets per minute throughout several layers of operations, including sentiment analysis and word embeddings. Presented as an understandable interface, it incorporates the values of cybernetics, cyberspace, agent-based modeling, and data ethics to show the potential for social media to become a more transparent space for collective discussion.

INTRODUCTION

Personalization algorithms are increasingly deciding what content users see online (Hannak et al. 2013). Without their approval, users are becoming isolated in ideologically segregated "filter bubbles" (Pariser 2011) that selectively expose content intended to keep their attention (Bakshy, Messing, and Adamic 2015). These filter bubbles have garnered concern as they form echo chambers that amplify viewpoints and limit the breadth of discussion (Sunstein 2017). Social media now resembles a "Daily Me" (Negroponte 1995) platform where users live in a private, personalized network of information. In this age of social isolation, there is a growing need for a "Daily Us" (Negroponte 1995), a place to engage with the distributed public network. Progress in natural language processing (NLP) (Joulin et al. 2017) allows for this unrestricted public view of information, yet there are inherent difficulties in visualizing and interfacing with the scale of these networks (Rafiei and Curial 2005). The predominant social media interface of the linear feed is not able to show this holistic view of the wider network, and while conducted research has explored methods of visualizing and communicating at the network scale (Correa and Ma 2011; Kitchin 1998), development is lacking in translating these networks into understandable interfaces.

This paper introduces Engelbart,[1] a real-time web application that presents the Twitter content network through an agent-based system. The goal of this spatial interface is to create a digital public space that promotes discovery of new and diverse content, providing an alternative to the informational echo chambers that often occur in linear feeds.

BACKGROUND

Understanding Cyberspace

Engelbart views Twitter as a "cyberspace" (Gibson 1984) unconstrained by the algorithmic content recommendations that form filter bubbles. At the beginning of the internet, this metaphor of cyberspace emerged as a conceptualization of a new information-based space that transcended physical boundaries (Benedikt 1991). Composed of the flow of data between computers, cyberspace is simultaneously virtual and real as a construct of thought (Novak 1991). For instance, a message sent from one user to another is said to exist in cyberspace but cannot be located as a tangible object. This ambiguity does not mean that cyberspace is unable to be scrutinized—quite the opposite. Because data is the fundamental building block of cyberspace, its information can be processed quickly and efficiently. In doing so, it is possible to uncover invisible relations through the mapping from data to representation (Novak 1991).

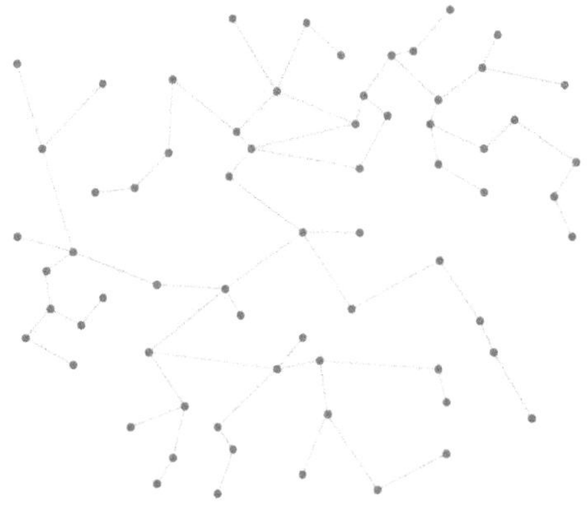

2 Node-edge graph.

Advances in NLP (Joulin et al. 2017) have accelerated efforts to analyze human language data at scale. Recent studies have explored ways to represent larger cyberspatial networks built from rich data (Chen et al. 2018; Correa and Ma 2011; Ma and Muelder 2013), but they often resemble the established form of a node-edge graph (Fig. 2) (Battiston et al. 2020). Within the context of cyberspace, nodes represent individual units such as computers or users while the edges that connect them represent the transfer of data (Boccaletti 2006). Projects like Social Mirror (Gillani et al. 2018) have been able to use this layout to effectively show the exacerbation of political polarization online, but are unable to show higher-order interactions. Because edges can only connect pairs of nodes, the node-edge graph cannot represent real social systems where interactions regularly occur in groups of three or more nodes (Battiston et al. 2020). This feature of node-edge graphs makes them difficult to scale for the representation of larger networks (Correa and Ma 2011).

The computational landscape today has shifted toward enabling computers to solve problems in their own way. As data becomes more abundant and rich, this approach has become not only more effective but even necessary. Just as architects are beginning to employ machine intelligence for form-finding (Carpo 2017), this research uses it to build a dynamic representation of cyberspace that shows higher-order interactions of Twitter as a whole. This allows for it to act as a space of its own, and presents the opportunity to introduce an occupant that offers more detailed information from cyberspace. This translation of cyberspace into an occupiable space becomes an agent-based model—a series of simulated interactions between an autonomous entity and its environment (Jennings 2000).

Agent-Environment Interaction

Agent-based modeling is the computational simulation of the interactions between one or more autonomous entities and their rule-based environment (Jennings 2000). Engelbart uses this approach to create an interface that delivers information from two scales: the individual agent and the collective environment. As a social media alternative, both the agent and the environment are designed to be understandable for the end user.

For the agent, this project looks to cybernetics to inform the way it negotiates the environment and relates to the user. As the study of communication between human and machine, the field of cybernetics has long been experimenting with developing and using AI to solve complex design problems. Yet, despite their focus on the leading edge of technology, cyberneticists hold to a philosophy of humanism through machines—believing that machines should not only solve problems but also rationalize and relate to them (Negroponte 1973). Despite decades of technological advances since the first cyberneticists, the field has remained relevant because of this central tenet of humanism. The early cyberneticist Gordon Pask (1962) maintained that the act of conversation is enough to be a meaningful cybernetic interaction, which has become a point of inspiration for the interaction between agent and user.

For the environment, psychogeography is foundational to visualize the high-order network of cyberspace. In the same way that city plans do not reveal the social complexities of a community, the objective mapping of networks in node-edge graphs limits the view of collective interactions. In the Naked City (Debord 1955), Guy Debord explores how the city plan can be deconstructed and layered with subjective interpretations of space. The result is a map that views Paris from an experiential lens that focuses on the social centers of the city. With NLP, this same approach can be applied to understand the social dynamics of the web and create a human-readable subjective mapping.

The Ethics of Cyberspace

Cyberspace is not only a metaphor for the internet but also an ideology. Alongside the idea of cyberspace came ideas for how it should be governed. At its inception, the complete freedom of the internet encouraged ideals of equal access to information. The 1996 Declaration of the Independence of Cyberspace reflected this belief, calling for the civilization of cyberspace to be "more humane and fair than the world your governments have made before" (Barlow 1996, 7). Yet the modern internet has only become more locked down as companies consolidate control over

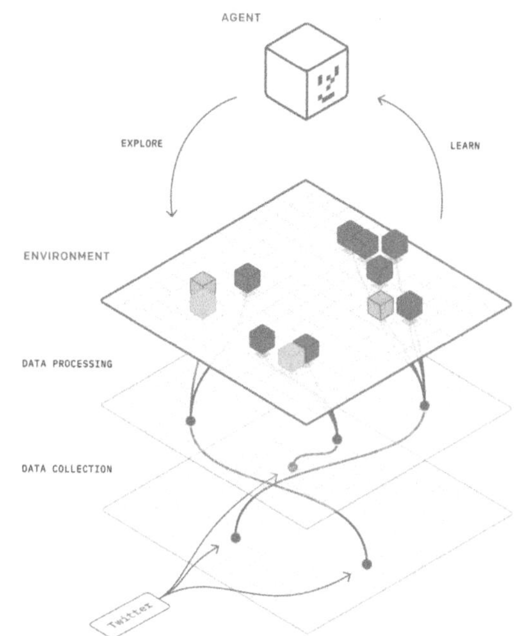

3 The framework for construction of the agent-based model.

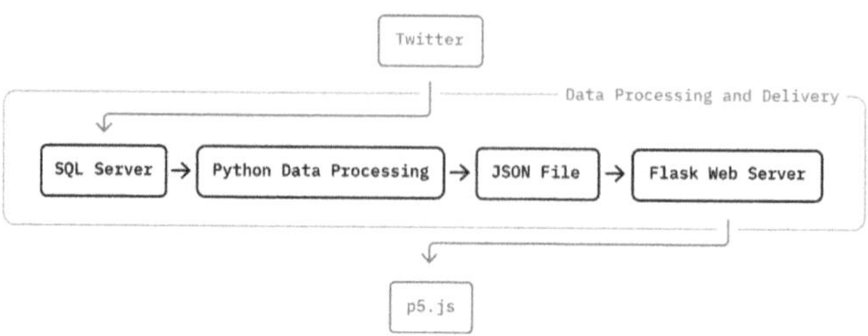

4 Technical system diagram of the web application.

communication, commerce, and search (Patelis 2013). In the social media sector, projects like Civic Signals (Pariser 2019) are working to rebuild platforms as true public spaces. Principles of urban planning are central to their proposals and include ideas like online parks or digital cities (Pariser 2019) free from the algorithms that lock users into filter bubbles. This project upholds the original promise of a humane cyberspace while also looking toward these spatial models for transparent and open online spaces. In combination with agent-based modeling, Engelbart presents a more equitable and understandable cyberspace.

METHODS

Design Framework

Personalization algorithms cause users on social platforms such as Twitter to engage with the app for longer, with the downside of forming narrow filter bubbles of information. To provide an alternative to a user's filter bubble, the Engelbart web application shows the collective content on the Twitter platform rather than a select

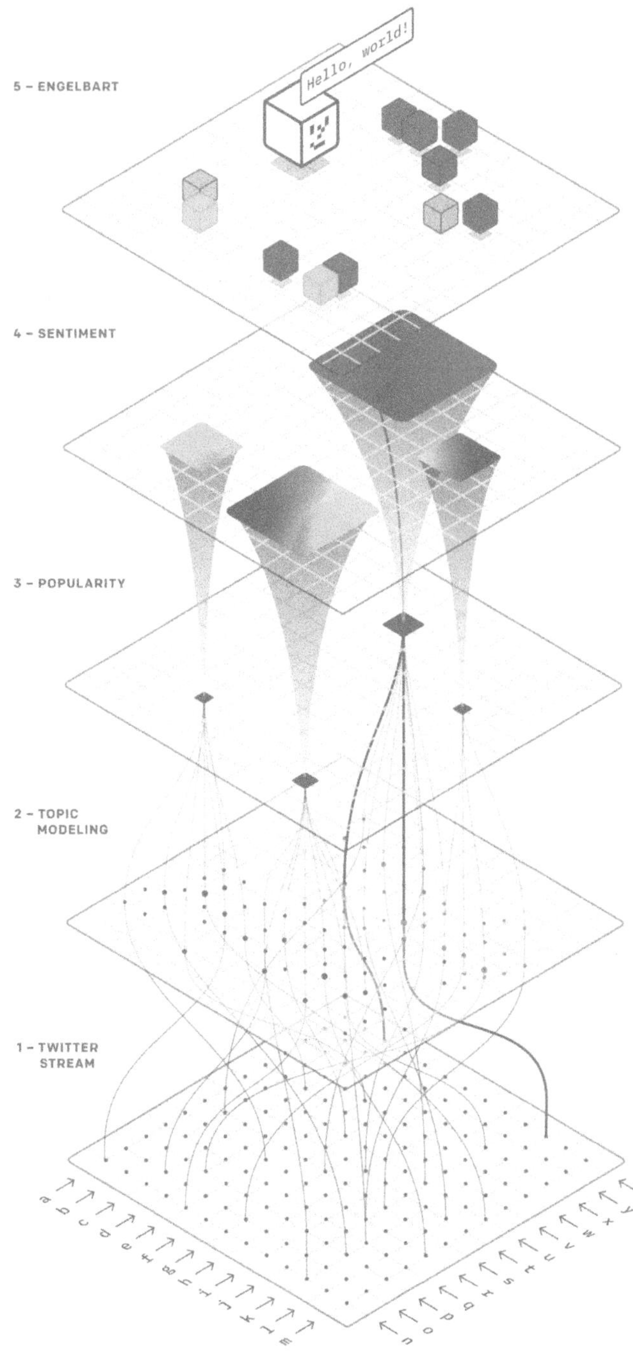

5 (1) The bottom layer represents the raw data capture from a live Twitter stream. On the way to the next layer, sentences are divided into words in preparation for further processing. (2) Words are vectorized and rearranged within multidimensional space based on topic similarity. (3) The vector space is flattened to reveal dense clusters of varying size. (4) Sentiment analysis visualizes topic opinions through color. (5) Topic clusters become squares in the grid interface that reflect the sentiment of the tweets that make them up. Engelbart studies each topic and relays what it has learned to the user.

slice. However, the collective content of a platform as large as Twitter becomes quickly incomprehensible. To aid in human understanding, the system is structured as an agent-environment model to reflect the mental model of an in-person communication network (Fig. 3).

As this research was conducted during COVID-19 in 2020, the project is designed as an open-source web application[2] so that it can be accessible to distributed audiences and reflect the medium of social media that it pulls from. Because of the dynamic nature of social media, a primary design consideration is to show emerging conversations in real time.[3] The interface is built in Processing and Javascript, while the data collection and processing uses Python and NLP packages to aggregate and summarize the data (Fig. 4).

Aesthetics and Experience

The primary context for understanding this collective view of Twitter for this project is the mapping of multidimensional Twitter data onto a two-dimensional rectangular grid. This superimposition is influenced by the von Neumann neighborhood model for cellular automata (von Neumann 1966) and the traditional checkerboard visualization often used for social dynamic modeling (Hegselmann 2017). This allows for the drawing of higher-order relationships simply through the proximity of cells to one another. The model is also conceptually influenced by the architectural public square (Mattson 1999), providing a structured yet open space for public discourse to be viewed. Within this environment, the agent personifies the Twitter data to form a 1:1 connection between the user and the collective data. This creates a flow of information that is done conversationally by the agent over time, helping to reduce the cognitive load of the user.

Layering System

The agent-environment model is composed of five separate layers: (1) collection and cleaning of Twitter data; (2) topic modeling of categorical clusters; (3) popularity; (4) sentiment; and (5) Engelbart, the agent that visualizes and interfaces with the topical categories. Figure 5 is a process diagram of this system.

Layer 1: Collecting Twitter Data

The first layer and foundation of the system is the data collection layer. This layer utilizes Tweepy (Roesslein 2020), an API to access Twitter, and captures the stream of tweets as they are posted in real time. Tweets are collected in a 10% random sample of overall Twitter activity. Three fields are captured: (1) tweet message;

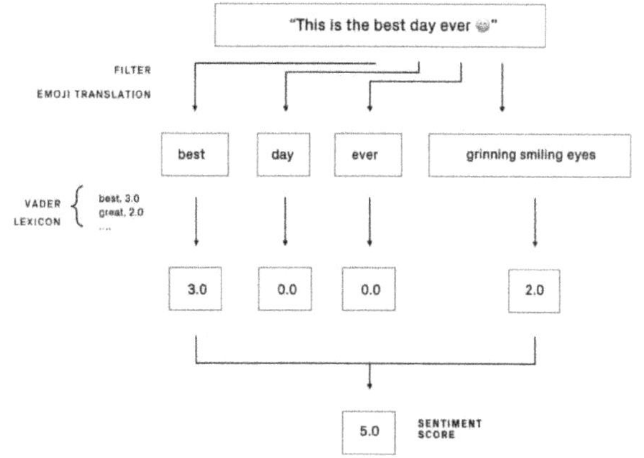

6

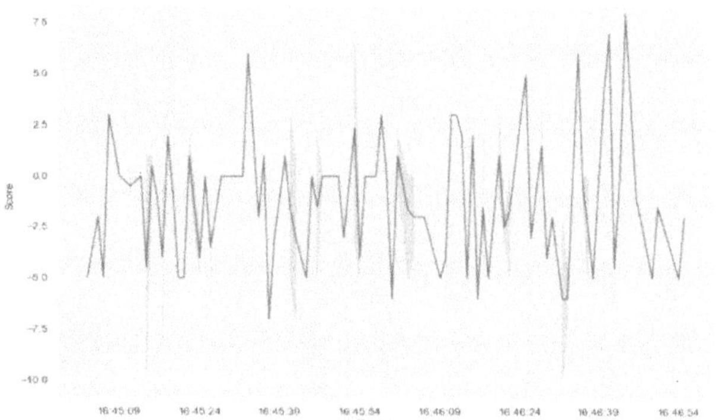

7

6 Tweet sentiment deconstruction by the VADER algorithm.

7 Sentiment score variation of collected tweets over a two-minute period.

8

9

8 Vectorized 3D word embeddings from 10,000 tweets, captured in March 2020 in a 20-minute window.

9 Topic clusters placed within the 2D grid, where closer distance equates to closer topic similarity. #covid19 and #china are shown as neighbors while #saynotoalcohol is farther away.

(2) post time; and (3) sentiment, which is calculated by the VADER algorithm (Hutto and Gilbert 2014). The VADER algorithm is a sentiment lexicon library specifically attuned to social media (Fig. 6). No other content is recorded, to protect the privacy of users.

Before this data is piped to the rest of the system, the tweets are tokenized and stemmed with the Natural Language Toolkit (NLTK) package so that they can work with NLP libraries in the following layers. As the stream is taking in tweets globally, tweets are filtered to include only messages written in English. The database is sent to the rest of the system every 15 minutes for processing.

Layer 2: Topic Clustering with Deep-Word Embeddings

The content discussed on Twitter is varied and broad. Spatializing tweets on a 1:1 basis quickly becomes incomprehensible. To help make sense of the larger picture, tweets are aggregated into groups based on their hashtag and keyword usage. These groups are then given a multidimensional vector based on their content similarity to other tweets and clustered by FastText (Mikolov et al. 2013), a nearest-neighbors word embedding algorithm. The result is a series of topic clusters positioned in space relative to how similar they are to each other (Fig. 8).

The nature of these deep-word embeddings of topic clusters is that their vectors are highly dimensional (n = 100) and impossible to visualize in their original form. To make them understandable to the user, singular value decomposition is used to translate this high-dimensional space into a 2D field that is overlaid and scaled responsively onto the environment's grid system (Fig. 9). This 2D coordinate system allows for a clearer organization of topic clusters to the end user compared to a 3D coordinate system, which creates difficulty in measuring the distance, and thus the similarity, between clusters.

Layer 3: Topic Popularity

Alongside topic distribution, the size of each topic cluster corresponds to the amount of user activity within the topic, rather than tokenized measures such as likes or retweets. The more tweets that mention a particular topic, the wider the area of squares covered on the grid environment (Fig.

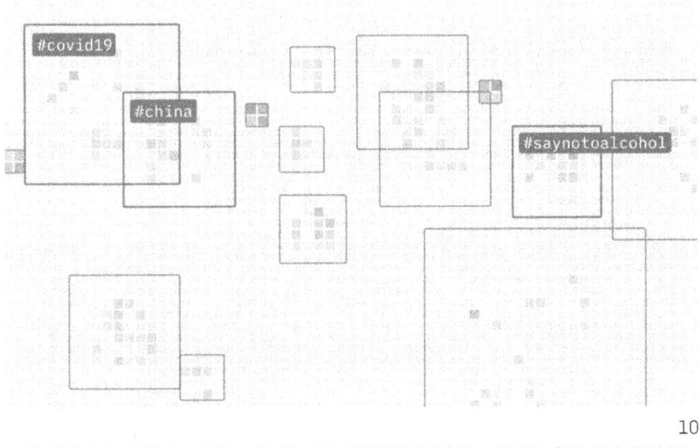

10

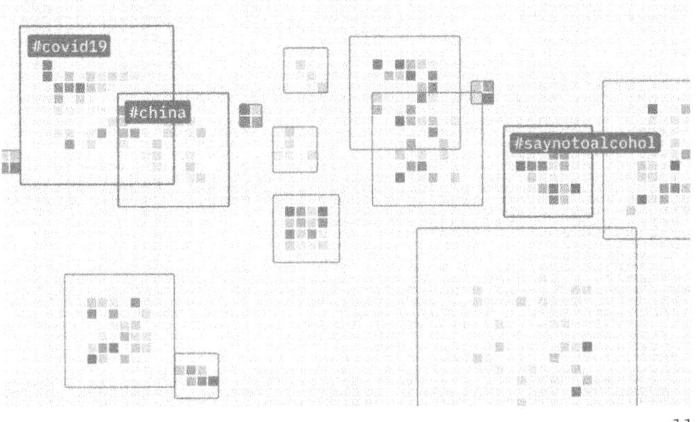

11

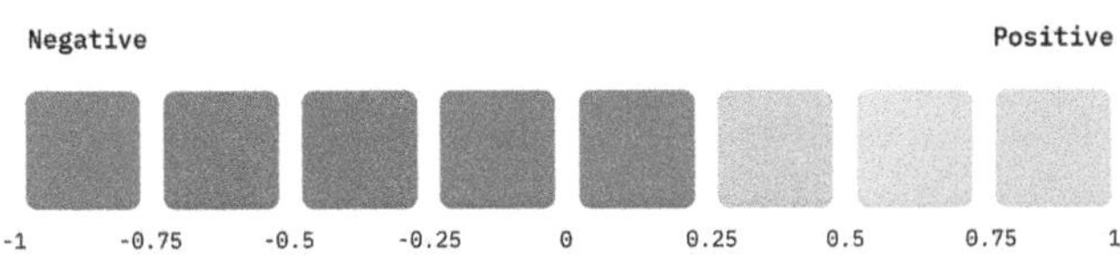

12

10 Topic clusters are scaled based on their popularity. Due to #covid19 being a popular discussion, it is one of the largest topic areas.

11 Topics with sentiment data mapped to their squares. Sentiment regarding #covid19 is mixed, while #saynotoalcohol is entirely negative.

12 The sentiment color scale from most negatively charged tweets to most positively charged. Sentiment scores of tweets in topic are normalized and bucketed onto a -1 to 1 scale.

10). To show the dynamism of conversations happening in real time, squares pulsate and reposition within the topic cluster area.

Layer 4: Sentiment Diversity

Though many people may be conversing about the same topic online, these individual voices often form a diverse array of opinions and feelings in the discussion. To account for these individual voices, when a new conversation topic appears in the application, its sentiment variety is shown through the proportion of colored squares within the topic cluster (Fig. 11). This differentiation is determined by a colored scale of sentiment polarity for the given topic (Fig. 12).

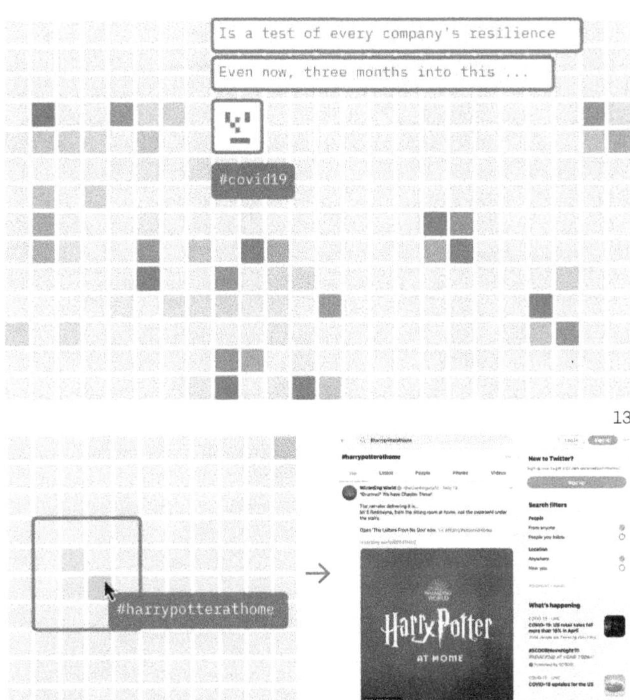

13

14

13 Engelbart reveals the topic cluster of #covid19 with diverse sentiment. He comments on company resilience during COVID-19.

14 User hovers over topic #harrypotterathome. Upon clicking, they are directed to the Twitter page of that discussion.

Layer 5: Interactive Agent

Engelbart, the intelligent agent, learns what people are talking about in the environment and returns a concise summary (Fig. 13). This provides a direct connection between the individual user and the collective user base of Twitter.

On initial load, the only information visible to the user is the location of topic clusters and their popularity. Engelbart must explore the environment to reveal further information about the Twitter topic clusters. To do this, Engelbart approaches the closest unvisited clusters one at a time based on a nearest neighbor search algorithm. Once Engelbart arrives at a cluster, it reveals the summary, sentiment, and hashtag of the topic.

Engelbart's summaries are constructed by utilizing a term frequency-inverse document frequency (TF-IDF) summary algorithm (Bun and Ishizuka 2001), which strings together the most frequently used phrases for the given topic. During its summary, Engelbart interjects emotive language and changes its facial expression in reaction to the overall sentiment of the topic cluster.

After summarizing, Engelbart reveals the sentiment and color diversity of the topic to the user. The user can then

15

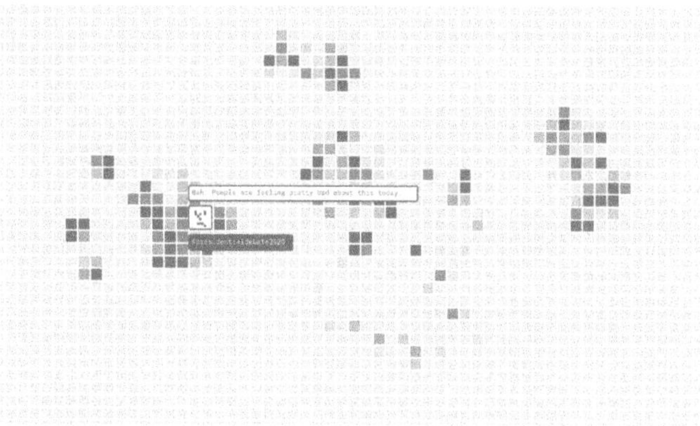

17

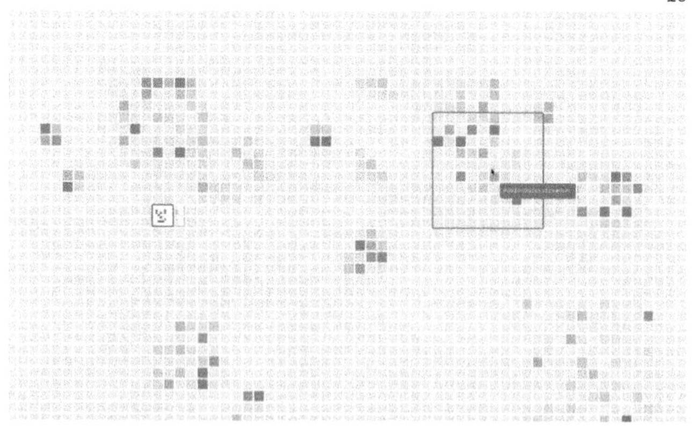

16

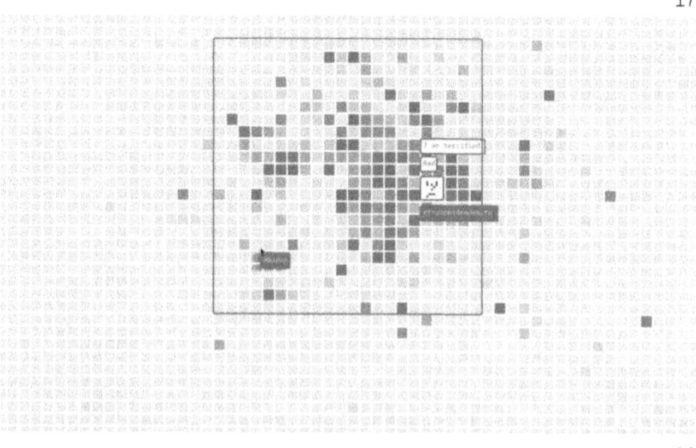

18

15 May 5, 2020, 11:00 am ET. Engelbart reveals the first topic cluster, #covid19, in the environment.

16 May 5, 2020, 11:05 am ET. Engelbart after revealing all of the topic clusters, with #defendpressfreedom highlighted.

17 Sept 29, 2020, 3:30 pm ET. Engelbart with revealed environment, hours before a major presidential debate between Donald Trump and Joe Biden. Several topic clusters of low relativity are apparent, with #presidentialdebate2020 exhibiting mostly negative sentiment.

18 Sept 29, 2020, 9:00 pm ET. Engelbart with revealed environment during the presidential debate. Topic clusters show most all tweets are negatively charged and center around one category: the debate. Engelbart comments on #trumpbiden-debate, "Sad. I am terrified."

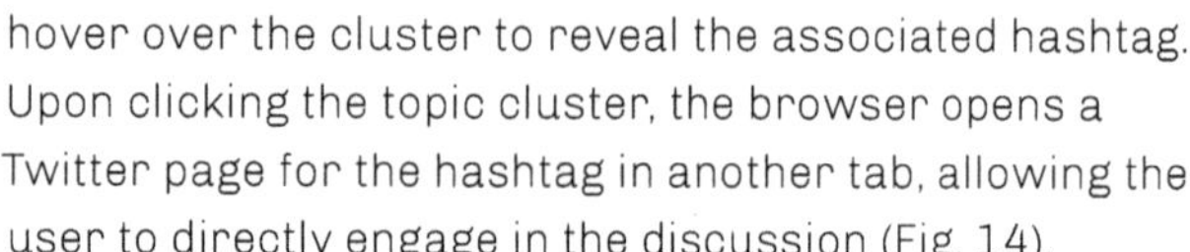

hover over the cluster to reveal the associated hashtag. Upon clicking the topic cluster, the browser opens a Twitter page for the hashtag in another tab, allowing the user to directly engage in the discussion (Fig. 14).

Engelbart then moves through the environment to the next topic cluster, where it will again reveal hidden information about the topic. This process repeats until all topics have been visited.

RESULTS

Reflection

In its holistic view of Twitter, Engelbart helps users see past their filter bubbles by presenting the collective discussion in its entirety. Its indiscriminate approach to data collection ensures that the diverse opinions of Twitter users are represented in both the agent and the environment. Though the scale of the collected data would be unreadable on its own, visual abstraction and layering of information allows for the interface to embrace the topical complexity of Twitter without misrepresenting its data.

To break the filter bubble, users must be able to listen and relate to the views of others. However, to a user who has been within a filter bubble, the collective discussion is likely to be unfamiliar. Engelbart walks the user through the environment and delivers in-depth summaries after processing topic information (Fig. 15). Though Engelbart is unfamiliar with its environment at first, it eventually reveals all topic clusters to present a comprehensive view of the current discussion. Within this view, users are able to revisit topics of interest (Fig. 16) and navigate directly to Twitter in order to become a part of the conversation.

By disrupting the conventional interface of a linear feed, Engelbart presents a different view of social media. Zooming out to a large scale of information removes references to any one Twitter user and promotes a slower-paced browsing of the site. The translation from data to space becomes a visual language that comes closer to the vision of cyberspace: a virtual public square where topics occupy space and take the shape of the discussion going on within them. When observed at different times, each environment captures a moment on Twitter that can reveal shifting conversations when compared to other moments in time (Figs. 17–18).

Limitations

Engelbart should not be used as a representation of online discussion and society as a whole. Though Engelbart treats data fairly in the collection process, the inherent biases of Twitter itself are reflected in Engelbart and the environment. For instance, the character limit does not allow for long-form expressions of opinion, while the political leanings of the platform may not accurately reflect public viewpoints.

As a hybrid between an agent-based model and user interface, Engelbart should be evaluated in the context of both. The model itself is only able to make a new data pull on a new load, making it unable to change over the course of a single instance. In addition to the limited ways in which Engelbart can change the environment, the agent-environment interaction has been simplified compared to other agent-based modeling research.

Engelbart also has its limitations as an interface. In its current state, the conversational component is a one-way flow of information from computer to user. Users have no part in the dialogue-driven interaction, limiting the depth of the information to the summaries that Engelbart provides. By opening this interaction to user inquiry, Engelbart could provide more specific information relating to the topic and become a more robust tool for learning.

The meshing of agent-based model and interface has allowed for a view past the filter bubble, but there is room for the application to develop as a more comprehensive interactive system. In the exploration of these possibilities, continued research can explore emerging modalities of interaction between model and interface.

CONCLUSION

Building on research of cybernetics, agent-based modeling, and cyberspace, Engelbart posits a transparency of social media through its spatial data interface. The Engelbart web application integrates several layers of data processing of the real-time collective discussion of Twitter and presents it as a 2D agent-environment model. The conceptual framework serves as an early prototype for applying architectural spatial principles towards datacentric online spaces. With Engelbart, users can discover topics and opinions that are not represented in the filter bubbles of their own personal feeds, and be pointed to conversations to which they would not have otherwise contributed.

Future Directions

Further iterations could begin to provide users with more direct control of information retrieval. The ability to manipulate the time of the environment would let users observe changes as topics form and change, acting as a quasi-historical method for understanding tipping points of larger movements or societal thought patterns (Fig. 19). Additionally, incorporating a flexible zoom functionality would allow users to view the data of each cluster with more granularity (Fig. 20). The project demonstrates the potential at a grander scale for self-learning and emergent spatial systems that can catalog and adapt their structure to fit online social media content. Further developments of the system could see Engelbart acting on the form of the environment as it simultaneously changes with the data,

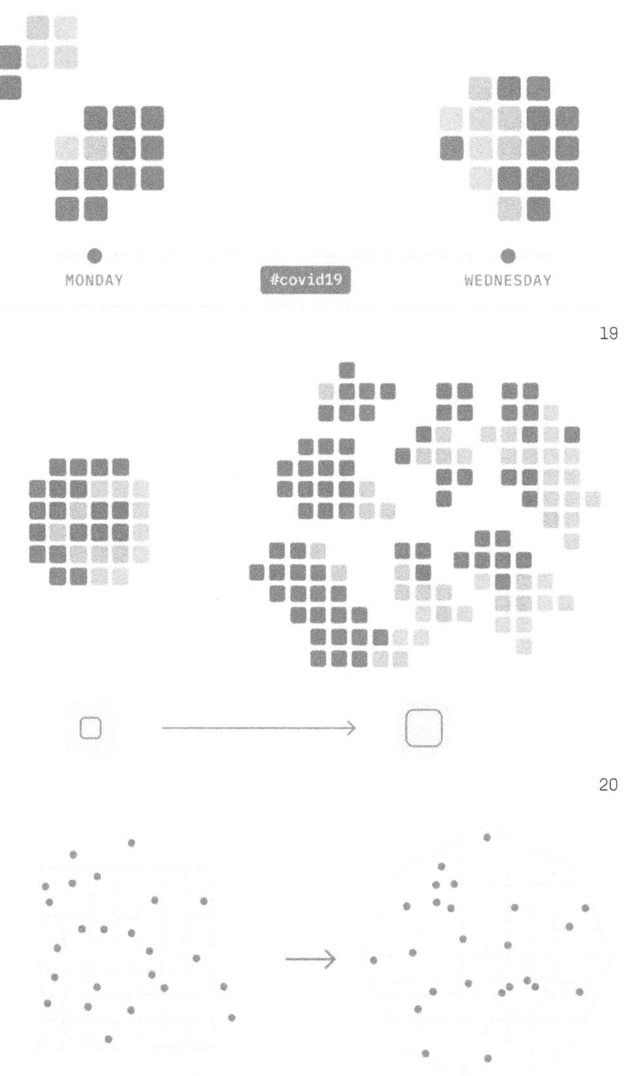

21 In addition to improving the learning potential of the agent in the system for better summarizing of collective topics, there is potential for the spatial environment to be architecturally malleable based on the manifold structure of the word embeddings. This would result in cyberspatial cities of content.

allowing for the emergence of entirely new self-organizing or predictive compositions of cyberspace (Fig. 21). As more of the world goes online, distributed information networks will simultaneously grow in scale and accessibility. This agent-environment model for interfacing with scaling networks allows for an unprecedented ability to discover information from multiple viewpoints, helping to promote equal and ethical online spaces not constrained by the algorithms within which they operate.

ACKNOWLEDGMENTS

This research was completed under the Advanced Technologies undergraduate thesis studio during spring 2020 at the University of Virginia School of Architecture. The primary aim of this studio is to explore different agencies, such as design agency, material agency, and fabrication agency.

The research team would like to thank the following people for helping to improve this research: John Comazzi, Leena Cho, Robin Dripps, Ali Fard, Melissa Goldman, Zaneta Hong, Ryan Shih, and Katelyn Stenger.

NOTES

1. Engelbart is named after Douglas Engelbart, a pioneer in the field of human-computer interaction (Markoff 2013).
2. Open-source code repository available for research at https://github.com/garrettvercoe/Engelbart-Public.
3. A two-minute demo of the application is viewable at https://vimeo.com/411441564.
4. The real-time nature of the application is a primary constraint for the technology stack and allowed data complexity. In all cases, the favored methods and technologies are those that have the quickest processing time. This is why TF-IDF is implemented over GPT-3, FastText over more modern transformers like BERT or ELMo, and singular value decomposition over deep manifold learning.

REFERENCES

Bakshy, Eytan, Solomon Messing, and Lada A. Adamic. 2015. "Exposure to Ideologically Diverse News and Opinion on Facebook." In *Science* 348 (6239): 1130–1132.

Barlow, John Perry. 1996. "A Declaration of the Independence of Cyberspace." *Duke Law and Technology Review* 18: 5–7. https://doi.org/10.7551/mitpress/2229.003.0006.

Battiston, Federico, Giulia Cencetti, Iacopo Iacopini, Vito Latora, Maxime Lucas, Alice Patania, Jean-Gabriel Young, and Giovanni Petri. 2020. "Networks beyond Pairwise Interactions: Structure and Dynamics." *Physics Reports* 874 (August): 1–92.

Benedikt, Michael. 1991. "Introduction." In *Cyberspace: First Steps*. Cambridge, MA: MIT Press.

Boccaletti, Stefano, Vito Latora, Yamir Moreno, Dong-Uk Hwang, and Mario Chavez. 2006. "Complex Networks: Structure and Dynamics." *Physics Reports* 424 (4–5): 175–305.

Bun, Khoo Khyou, and Mitsuru Ishizuka. 2001. "Emerging Topic Tracking System." In *Proceedings Third International Workshop on Advanced Issues of E-Commerce and Web-Based Information Systems (WECWIS)*, San Juan, CA, 21–22 June 2001, 2–11. IEEE.

Camp, Jean, and Y.T.- Chien. 2000. "The Internet as Public Space: Concepts, Issues, and Implications in Public Policy." *ACM SIGCAS Computers and Society 30 (3)*: 13-19. DOI:10.1145/572241.572244.

Carpo, Mario. 2017. *The Second Digital Turn: Design Beyond Intelligence*. Cambridge, MA: MIT Press.

Chen, Wei, Fangzhou Guo, Dongming Han, Jacheng Pan, Xiaotao Nie, Jiazhi Xia, and Xiaolong Zhang. 2018. "Structure-Based Suggestive Exploration: A New Approach for Effective Exploration of Large Networks." *IEEE Transactions on Visualization and Computer Graphics* 25 (1): 555–565.

Correa, Carlos, and Kwan-Liu Ma. 2011. "Visualizing Social Networks". In *Social Network Data Analytics*, edited C. Aggarwal, 307–326. Boston: Springer.

Debord, Guy. 1955. "Introduction to a Critique of Urban Geography." Translated by Ken Knabb. *Les Lèvres Nues 6* (September): 95–109. https://www.cddc.vt.edu/sionline/presitu/geography.html.

Gibson, William. 1984. *Neuromancer*. New York: Berkley.

Gillani, Nabeel, Ann Yuan, Martin Saveski, Soroush Vosoughi, and Deb Roy. 2018. "Me, My Echo Chamber, and I: Introspection on Social Media Polarization." In *WWW 2018 [Proceedings of the 2018 World Wide Web Conference]*, Lyon, France, 23–27 April 2018, 823–831. International World Wide Web Conferences Steering Committee.

Graham, Stephen. 1998. "The End of Geography or the Explosion of Place? Conceptualizing Space, Place and Information Technology." *Progress in Human Geography* 22 (2): 165–185.

Hannak, Aniko, Piotr Sapiezynski, Arash Molavi Kakhki, Balachander Krishnamurthy, David Lazer, Alan Mislove, and Christo Wilson. 2013. "Measuring Personalization of Web Search." In *WWW 2013 [Proceedings of the 22nd international conference on World Wide Web]*, Rio de Janeiro, Brazil, 13–17 May 2013, 527–538. Association for Computing Machinery.

Hegselmann, Rainer. 2017. "Thomas C. Schelling and James M. Sakoda: The Intellectual, Technical, and Social History of a Model." *Journal of Artificial Societies and Social Simulation* 20 (3): 15.

Hutto, Clayton, and Eric Gilbert. 2014. "Vader: A Parsimonious Rule-Based Model for Sentiment Analysis of Social Media Text." In *Proceedings of the International AAAI Conference on Weblogs and Social Media (ICWSM)*, Ann Arbor, Michigan, 1–4 July 2014. AAAI.

Jain, Shikha, and Krishna Asawa. 2015. "EMIA: Emotion Model for Intelligent Agent." *Journal of Intelligent Systems* 24 (4): 449–465.

Jennings, Nicholas. 2000. "On Agent-Based Software Engineering." *Artificial Intelligence* 117 (2): 277–296.

Joulin, Armand, Edouard Grave, Piotr Bojanowski, and Tomas Mikolov. 2017. "Bag of Tricks for Efficient Text Classification." In *Proceedings of the 15th Conference of the European Chapter of the Association for Computational Linguistics*, Valencia, Spain, April 2017, 427–431. Association for Computational Linguistics.

Kitchin, Robert. 1998. "Towards Geographies of Cyberspace." *Progress in Human Geography* 22 (3): 385–406.

Ma, Kwan-Liu, and Chris Muelder. 2013. "Large-Scale Graph Visualization and Analytics." *Computer* 46 (7): 39–46.

Markoff, John. 2013. "Computer Visionary Who Invented the Mouse." New York Times, July 3, 2013. https://www.nytimes.com/2013/07/04/technology/douglas-c-engelbart-inventor-of-the-computer-mouse-dies-at-88.html.

Mattson, K. 1999. "Reclaiming and Remaking Public Space: Toward an Architecture for American Democracy." *Nat Civic Rev* 88: 133–144.

Mikolov, Tomas, Kai Chen, Greg Corrado, and Jeffrey Dean. 2013. "Efficient Estimation of Word Representations in Vector Space." In *Workshop Track Proceedings of the 1st International Conference on Learning Representations*, Scottsdale, Arizona, 2–4 May 2013. ICLR.

Negroponte, Nicholas. 1973. *The Architecture Machine*. Cambridge, MA: MIT Press.

Negroponte, Nicholas. 1995. *Being Digital*. New York: Knopf.

Novak, Marcos. 1991. "Liquid Architectures in Cyberspaces." In *Cyberspace: First Steps*, edited by Michael Benedikt, 225–254. Cambridge, MA: MIT Press.

Pariser, Eli. 2011. *The Filter Bubble: How the New Personalized Web Is Changing What We Read and How We Think*. New York: Penguin Publishing Group.

Pariser, Eli. 2019. "'Filter Bubble' Author Eli Pariser on Why We Need Publicly Owned Social Networks." *The Verge*, November 12. https://www.theverge.com/interface/2019/11/12/20959479/eli-pariser-civic-signals-filter-bubble-q-a.

Pask, Gordon. 1962. *An Approach to Cybernetics*. London: Hutchinson & Co.

Patelis, Korinna. 2013. "Political Economy and Monopoly Abstractions: What Social Media Demand." In *Unlike Us Reader: Social Media Monopolies and Their Alternatives*, edited by Geert Lovnik and Miriam Rasch, 117–127. Amsterdam: Institute of Network Cultures.

Rafiei, Davood, and Stephen Curial. 2005. "Effectively Visualizing Large Networks Through Sampling." In *VIS 05. IEEE Visualization*, 375–382. Minneapolis.

Roesslein, J., 2020. *Tweepy: Twitter for Python!* https://github.com/tweepy/tweepy.

Slovic, Paul. 2007. "'If I Look at the Mass I Will Never Act': Psychic Numbing and Genocide." *Judgment and Decision Making* 2 (2): 79–95.

Sunstein, Cass. 2017. *#Republic: Divided Democracy in the Age of Social Media*. Princeton, NJ: Princeton University Press.

Von Neumann, John. 1966. *Theory of Self-Reproducing Automata*. Urbana: University of Illinois Press.

Eric Duong is a computational designer currently working on research related to COVID-19 and shared spaces. Duong recently completed undergraduate studies at the University of Virginia School of Architecture with a secondary major in computer science.

Garrett Vercoe's work specializes in the building of humane technology that expands what people can think and do. Vercoe recently completed undergraduate studies at the University of Virginia School of Architecture with a secondary major in cognitive science, and an additional computer science concentration.

Ehsan Baharlou is an Assistant Professor of Architecture at the University of Virginia. He also worked as a postdoctoral associate at the Department of Architecture at the Massachusetts Institute of Technology (MIT). Ehsan holds a doctoral title from the Institute of Computational Design and Construction (ICD) at the University of Stuttgart. His work focuses on advanced technology to develop novel approaches to design computation and digital fabrication.

Discrete Continuity in the Urban Architectures of H. Hara & K. Kuma

Ariel Genadt
University of Pennsylvania
Weitzman School of Design

1 Kengo Kuma & Associates, Daiwa Ubiquitous Computing Center, Tokyo University. 2013. Ceiling of the urban porch.

ABSTRACT

The 2020 pandemic has laid bare the ambiguous value of the virtual proximity that distributed computing enables. The remote interaction it ushered in at an unprecedented scale also spawned social isolation, which is symbolically underscored by the reliance of this form of connectivity on individuals' discrete digital identification. This cyber-spatial dualism may be called 'discrete continuity,' and it already appeared in architectural thought in the 1960s with the advent of cybernetics and the first computers. The duality resurfaced in the 1990s in virtual projects, when architectural software was first widely commercialized, and it reappeared in built form in the past decade. This paper sheds light on the architectural aspects of this conceptual duality by identifying the use of discreteness and continuity in the theories of two Japanese architects, Hiroshi Hara (b.1936) and his former student, Kengo Kuma (b.1954), in their attempts to combine the two topological conditions as metaphors of societal structures. They demonstrate that the onset of the current condition, while new in its pervasiveness, has been latent in architectural thinking for several decades. This paper examines Hara's and Kuma's theories in light of the author's interviews with the architects, their writings, and specific projects that illustrate metaphoric translations of topological terms into social structures, reflected in turn in the organization of urban schemes and building parts. While Hara's and Kuma's respective implementations are poles apart visually and materially, they share the idea that the discrete continuity of contemporary urban experience ought to be reflected in architecture. This link between their ideas has previously been overlooked.

INTRODUCTION

The 2020 pandemic has laid bare the ambiguous value of the virtual proximity that distributed computing enables. The remote interaction it ushered in at an unprecedented scale also spawned social isolation, which is symbolically underscored by the reliance of this form of connectivity on individuals' discrete digital identification. This cyber-spatial duality may be called 'discrete continuity,' and it already appeared in utopian architectural thought in the late 1960s with the advent of cybernetics and the first computers. The duality resurfaced in the 1990s in virtual projects, when architectural software was first widely commercialized, and it reappeared again, this time in built form, in the past decade. This paper unfolds the architectural aspects of this conceptual duality by identifying the use of discreteness and continuity in the theories of architect Hiroshi Hara, born in 1936, and his former student, Kengo Kuma, born in 1954. In their respective attempts to combine the two topological conditions as metaphors of societal structures, they have linked their design principles to computational modalities and to modern mathematical and topological models. In so doing, they have demonstrated that the onset of the current condition, while new in its pervasiveness, has been latent in architectural thinking for several decades. I examine Hara's and Kuma's theories in light of my interviews with them, their writings, and their projects, which illustrate their translations of topological concepts into social structures and the organization of urban architecture and building parts. Although Hara's and Kuma's respective implementations are poles apart visually and materially, they share the idea that what I call discrete continuity in contemporary urban experience ought to be reflected in architecture. This link between their ideas has previously been overlooked.

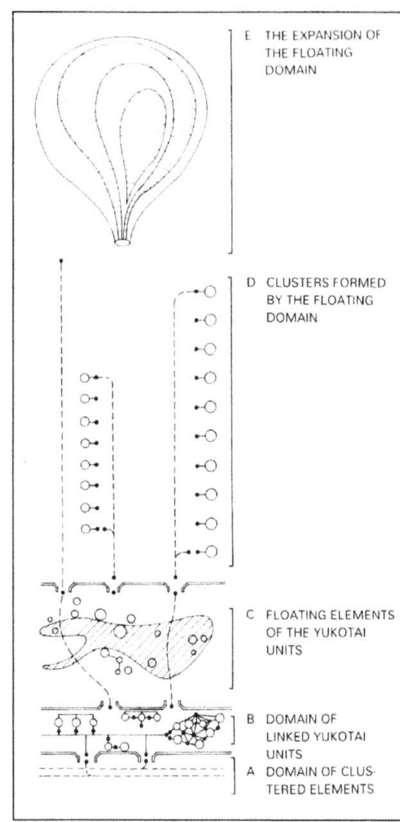

2

3

4

Hiroshi Hara—A Discrete Society

From his first architectural explorations in the 1960s, Hara's theory revolved around the relationships between parts and their aggregations into wholes. His Yūkōtai, or "Perforated Bodies," theory of 1968 rejected what he termed "the a-priori definition of an architectural whole" and "the homogenization of parts or details" in favor of "a process in which a whole is composed from the bottom-up and an autonomy of parts, encouraging logical diversity, [which] . . . anticipates an optimal environmental fit equivalent to the ideals of social structure" (Hara et al. 1993, 32). Another concept he coined—"drift"—similarly implied an aggregation of particles into a fluid or amorphous, changing constellation. He then imagined diagrammatically how this principle might apply to a city where Yūkōtai elements are in constant flux (Fig. 2).

2 Hiroshi Hara. "City diagram based on the concept of drift." 1968.

3 Nicholas Negroponte. 1970. Student project called "LEARN," two iterations of cube arrangements.

4 The Italian village Positano as featured in Nicholas Negroponte's *The Architecture Machine* (1970).

He developed these principles in the 1970s at Tokyo University's Institute of Industrial Science, where he used topology for studying urban and rural settlement patterns. He elaborated a method he called "Activity Contour," using Jordan curves (topologically equivalent to a simple and closed unit circle) to produce "topographical maps" of urban data, such as building volumes, population density, telephone distribution, and so forth. His assistant Akira Fujii wrote a computer program to help draw these maps (Hara 2019).

Hara continued to analyze the relations between individuals and their grouping into communities through direct observation between 1972 and 1978, when he traveled with his students to over 200 villages in 40 countries. In those trips he explored alternatives to what he saw as the rigid framework of modernist urbanism—namely, the idea of a uniform universal space—in vernacular communal habitations (Hara 1987). The ensuing Dwelling Group Domain Theory (*Jūkyo shūgōron*) joined similar ekistical studies including Fumihiko Maki's Investigations in Collective Form and Bernard Rudofsky's Architecture without Architects both of 1964, and Nicholas Negroponte's studies at MIT. Negroponte's Architecture Machine Group used code based-programs to generate discrete organizational principles for settlements, attempting to robotically replicate vernacular settlement patterns (Negroponte 1970). His students wrote such sets of principles that fed various computer programs that generated "automatic" aggregations (Fig. 3). Citing Rudofsky, Negroponte critiqued the rigidity and soullessness of Brasília as an epitome of modernist urbanism, contrasting it to the Amalfian hilltown of Positano, where the houses' spatial arrangement grows from local conditions (Fig. 4). He assumed that the design principles that made towns like Positano picturesque and collectively desirable can be distilled to a combination of uniformity and variegation of discrete components.

Thus, on both sides of the Pacific, vernacular studies coincided with the application of robotics to architectural design. Hara's ideas coincided with Negroponte's, even though he maintains being unaware of them at the time (Hara 2019). Similarly, he imagined a robot he called ARCHITECT that would generate optimal configurations of urban elements, inspired by software playing *shōgi* (Japanese chess) (Bognar and Hara 2001, 123). But unlike Negroponte, he never proceeded to build that robot. Still, it was his sound understanding of topology and group theory that made him both curious and able to grasp how digital technology could one day inform architecture and urban design, namely in finding optimal configurations among many options.

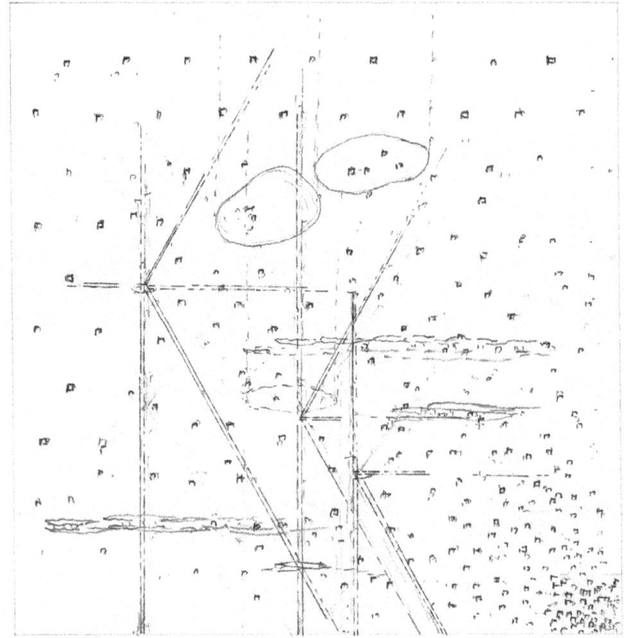

5 Hiroshi Hara, Discrete City – Sketch, 1997.

5

The humanist interest in the vernacular and the new potential of robotics coincided with the appearance of personal computers and color television. Together these informed the way Hara understood and visualized new urban structures. In Dwelling Group Domain Theory, Hara concluded that "the foundation of this world of inter-subjectivity [is that] all must create together. Each one should also create individually." (Hara 1987). And he later added, "the world is a continuum, and simultaneously a set of individuum . . . In architecture and the city we are always facing these two concepts . . . because the human body is an individuum, and consciousness is a continuum" (Hara 2009, 212). Thus, while sharing with Negroponte a humanist concern, Hara equally considered perception, phenomenology and semiotics, which he attempted to integrate with the way the individual elements of urban architecture relate to one another.

Hara borrowed the terms *continuum* and *individuum* from Bernhard Riemann's mathematics, which he first read in 1970 in Japanese, being struck by the latter's idea that topological concepts can help interpret the real world "conveniently" (Hara 2019). Riemann spoke of continuous (*stetig*) and discrete (*discret*) manifolds (Riemann [1854] 1998). Accordingly, Hara developed a mathematical model using points, groups, neighborhoods, subsets, and topological spaces, in an attempt to unite in one model the discrete and the continuous as social-structural qualities (Hara 2004, 7).

Key to the possibility to unite these poles through what I have termed discrete continuity is his desire to eschew Hegelian dialectics to "resolve" the apparent conflict between

6

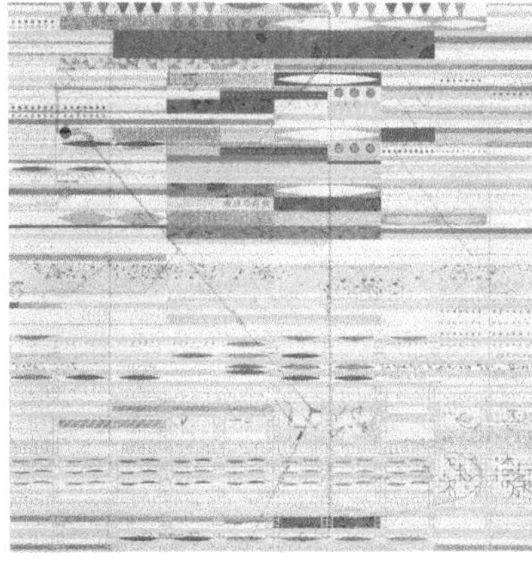

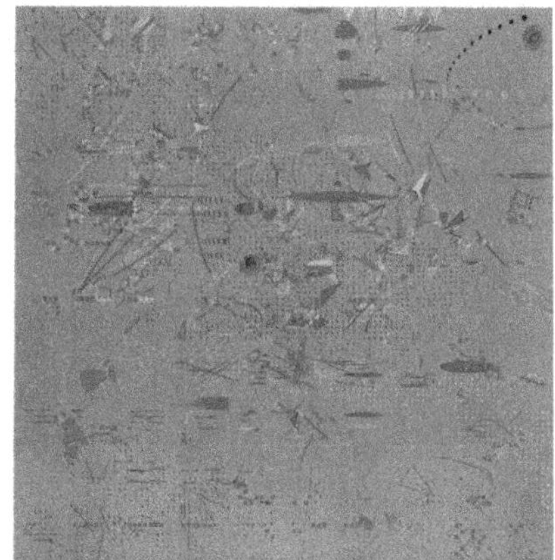

7

6 Hiroshi Hara, 500x500x500 Cube – Model, 1995.

7 Hiroshi Hara, 500x500x500 Cube – Plans and Elevations, 1995.

individuum and continuum. Hara proposed to do so using the Daoist concept *arazu-arazu* (not-not). As he explains: "whereas in dialectics a solution always exists, in arazu-arazu there is never a solution . . . dialectics incorporates a concept of order, [while in] 'not-not' . . . this is substituted with a concept of parallelism and simultaneous existence" (Hara 2009, 13). Hegelian dialectics imply progress, while arazu-arazu allows for diversity without hierarchy. This understanding led Hara to search for topological models that translate 'not-not' into architectural relations. In so doing, he endeavored to rekindle modernist ideals of community, but short-circuiting its reliance on progress through synthesis and allowing more individual diversity in the electronic age.

In the following years, in parallel to his practice in the built realm of Japan's bubble economy, he focused his theoretical concerns on testing his logic at the extra-large scale of the city. In his essay "On Discreteness," he distinguished the functionalist logic of machines—where parts must be connected in order to operate—from that of electronic devices—where parts are spatially separate but connected by invisible electromagnetic flows (Hara 2004, 39–40, 56).

His theoretical project Discrete City was initiated circa 1992 and continued to evolve for over a decade (Fig. 5). It sought to afford "every possibility of connectability and separability. In this sense, 'discrete' is a theory between individuum and continuum" (Hara 2009, 176). This model he proposed as a response to the modernist universal homogenous space, similar to Negroponte's critique. Discrete City represented Hara's conviction that architecture should both enable and express conditions for people to collaborate while keeping their individuality and freedom. He thought new telecommunication would facilitate this, notably the internet, invented only a decade earlier in 1983.

Central to Discrete City was the notion of "floating" (*fuyū*), which Hara understood to mean individual freedom of movement and identity, allowing the city to change and "self-repair" its organizational structure, thus being resilient to changing needs. Similar ideas had already appeared in Hara's theoretical projects Stochastic City and Induction House, both of 1968. Then, he was critical of design based on random probability, and instead believed that to achieve optimal configurations, cities must recombine over and over again. This was a lesson he said he learned particularly from Mexican and Guatemalan villages (Hara 2004, 1). These urban spatial models were to cater to his ideal "discrete society," which he defined as one that displays "maximal multiplicity in people's allegiance and rupture," where "all individuals have complete separability and connectability at the same time . . . a utopian society [with] . . . the most diverse groups of individuals" (Hara 2004, 51, 49). Hara explained that this social ideal was informed by Leibniz's *Monadology*, which he saw as one of the key theories that affected modernist thought. He borrowed from Leibniz two principles: that all monads are independent and different, and, that since each monad is a mirror of the universe, they are ordered by preestablished harmony and communication (Hara 2004, 40).

Hara's 500x500x500m Cube theoretical project (1992–93) was an early study of Discrete City for a Discrete Society (Fig. 5). The Cube was based on a continuous rectangular grid deployed in three dimensions as a frame and then gradually invaded and erased by floating discrete elements, changing position over time. The project's representation in Plexiglas models and a sequence of plans and elevations depicted the

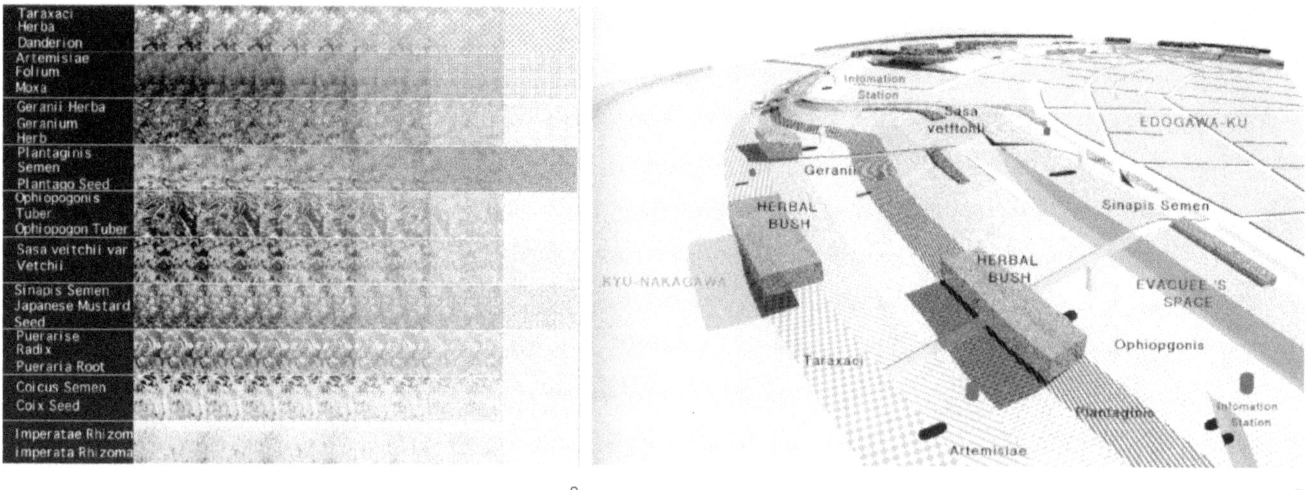

8 9

8–9 Kengo Kuma, Grassnet Project, for Downtown Tokyo, 1996. Plant species pixelated into patterns.

city's possible evolutions over the 21st century. Of the hand-made graphics representing a discrete urban space inspired by integrated circuits, Hara has said: "this expressive technique was able to suggest a computer-like expression just before the computer [graphics] appeared" (Hara 2009, 310). And he was likely well aware of Toyo Ito's text of 1993, *A Garden of Microchips*, that referenced the MoMA exhibition of 1990 (Ito 1993). At the same time, equally striking is the semblance of Hara's representations to Liebniz's landscape metaphor, when he wrote: "Each portion of matter can be conceived as a garden full of plants, or like a pond full of fish. But each branch of a plant, each organ of an animal, each drop of its bodily fluids is also a similar garden or a similar pond" (Liebniz [1714] 1989, §67) (Fig. 6).

Meanwhile, after numerous studies, Hara said he has been unsuccessful in developing a truly new architectural incarnation of the arazu-arazu model for the city. And given the topological particularity of this model, the NURBS-based software of the 1990s that allowed modeling continuous surfaces was unhelpful for Hara, since it could not express his idea of duality between discrete and continuous manifolds. At that, he was, so to speak, ahead of the curve, since this computational capacity has been achieved in "the Second Digital Turn" as Mario Carpo (2018) has explained, when computers can handle discreteness and discontinuity well, processing Big Data without the need for a unifying structure. What I have called discrete continuity can today be calculated, modeled, and expressed in mass customization. Meanwhile, now in the ninth decade of his life, Hara has avowed that to this day he has no mastery of digital algorithms, and that he uses computers only to perform Google searches and to play mahjong (Hara 2019).

Kengo Kuma—Rehumanizing the City

Some avenues for implementing Hara's concepts relating to discrete continuity appeared in the work of his former student Kengo Kuma, around 1997, when Hara sensei gave his retirement lecture "Discrete City" at Tokyo University. By then, Kuma was in his second decade of independent practice. The mid-1990s marked his shift to an interest in what he called "particlization" of architecture. He began with several unsuccessful proposals that used digital graphics to illustrate "digital landscapes" (Kuma 2019). Kuma aimed to transgress what he considered to be a modern and postmodern obsession with clearly delineated "objects," treated as commodities, proposing instead indeterminate "conditions" that grow from an inductive, part-to-whole compositional process, much like Hara's Yūkōtai theory of 1968. Kuma was interested in the digital's possibility of both representing and enabling the translation of the idea of discrete particles into architecture. Unlike Hara, he never spoke of emulating in architecture the structure of electronic devices, but he has adopted terms such as "operating system" and "floating pixels" to refer to the parts that compose the building. Coincidentally, the burst of Japan's bubble economy drove him to take projects in the countryside, thereby reconnecting to natural landscapes, organic materials, and regional craft.

Looking back in 2018, Kuma evoked his trip with Hara sensei to West Africa in 1978. He distinguished himself from his sensei, noting that where Hara studied the relationship between individual lifestyles and communal forms of dwellings, the 24-year-old Kuma was struck by his sensorial discovery of the villages and the aggregated nature of the materials used to build them, namely earth, brick, timber, cane, and thatch (Kuma 2017). In the two decades that followed, the infinitely small and the virtual

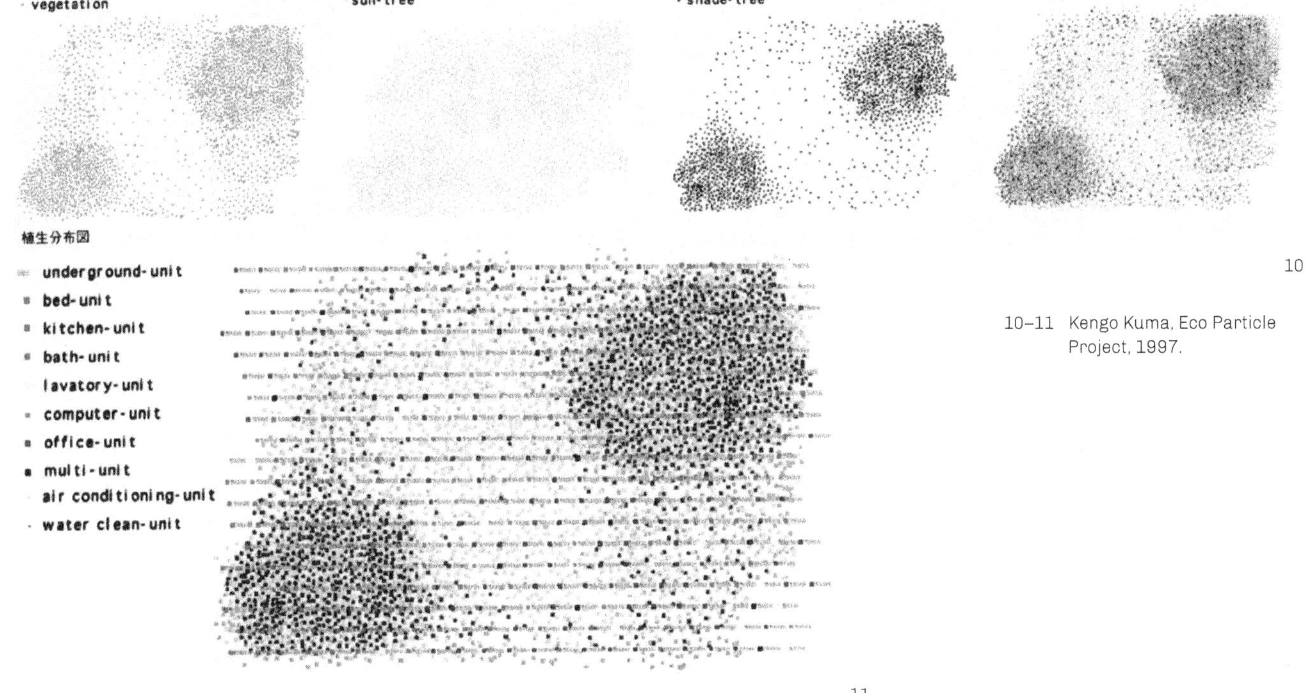

10–11 Kengo Kuma, Eco Particle Project, 1997.

fragment, as represented by pixels on screen, became his kit of parts for design.

The concepts Hara had developed appeared in Kuma's work circa 1996, first at the urban scale and then at the scale of individual buildings' parts. The Grassnet project of 1996, for example (Figs. 8–9), proposed a network of parks in downtown Tokyo that would function as temporary disaster shelter. It expressed Kuma's prediction that the internet, then in its second decade, has the potential to free people from dependence on architectural objects, aiming "to construct a built-form similar to an Internet network that is shapeless yet ubiquitous. An Internet expands thinking capacity by linkage of numerous brains . . . Similarly, Grassnet expands [people's] physical capacity by linkage of numerous bodies" (Kuma 1997, 100–101). This analogy Kuma makes between the Web and the city echoes Hara's earlier conviction that continuity can be achieved simultaneously with a sense of individuality, where experience is no longer defined solely by physical contiguities.

That Kuma too sought a topology (albeit without using mathematical concepts) that would allow for discrete continuity as a social structure can be gleaned from the Eco Particle project of 1997, for the Okinawan island Miyakojima (Figs. 10–11). He proposed that the structures of the religious institution would be "grained into fine particles that contain meaning not in their independence but in their association with the wholeness" (Kuma 1997, 97). Of this project, Greg Lynn has noted, "Here, point, line and plane are not distinct spatial types . . . Instead, points collect along flexible surfaces to make meshworks of varying density . . . [a] topological concept of landscapes" (Lynn 1997, 47). This observation recalls Hara's use of the topological subsets, groups, and so forth to arrive at relations of discrete continuity.

After these abstract projects, Kuma proceeded to apply discrete continuity to construction materials. At that he drew on Leibniz's idea that "matter is . . . the product of pressure applied to aggregation" as Kuma summarized it (Kuma 2006, 67). Among the many projects where he tested the expression of that theoretical possibility, the Daiwa Ubiquitous Computing Center of 2014 has an additional symbolic dimension related to the building's function as suggested by its name. There, Kuma has designed the discrete-continuous aggregation of building parts as a reflection of a "ubiquitous society," a term coined by Ken Sakamura, director of the building and founder of the TRON project at Tokyo University (Watanabe 2019).[1] In such a society, individual computers are "unique and free-floating" but give users "a feeling of being socially connected" (Watanabe 2019). This idea was represented in the pattern of the main façade and the porch's underside, which seems at once continuous as a woven fabric and discrete in its irregularities and material grain (Figs. 1, 12). The design process began by digitally modeling four groups of slats with varying widths and pitch, combining them into a Grasshopper model, and producing multiple iterations (Figs. 13–14). Among those, Kuma chose the one that appeared to be representing both discreteness and a sense of flow. The final adjustments were made using a physical 1:10 scale model and then a full-size mock-up of the façade.

While this kind of expression in construction of discrete continuity is meant to represent the freedom of end users in a loosely meshed social network, the building's digitally crafted envelope is expressive of more than the computational logic of its function. Asked how he uses parametric tools, Kuma replied, "We use algorithms to seek the best pattern for the architecture, taking an account of its environment, location and so on, but to determine [the suitable option] we use our own eyes and hands" (Kuma 2019). Considering Kuma's haptic sensitivity and his rejection of the dichotomy of building and environment, the Daiwa envelope also expresses an attempt to harmonize architecture with its surrounds by mimicking the infinite variations in organic patterns in the natural world, but also Tokyo's urban chaos.

Since the Daiwa project, it appears Kuma has become wary of the effects of digital technology on urban life. In a 2015 essay, he references the parallel drawn by Arata Isozaki (1968) between phases in the evolution of cities and states of individual consciousness, borrowed from Ernst Cassirer's theory: (1) Realism; (2) Functionalism; (3) Structuralism; and (4) Symbolism. Kuma compares these stages to the preindustrial age, the industrial revolution and modernism, a capitalist economy, and postmodernism. In the final stage, he says, "principles of financial fluidity divorced from physical lines and planes dissolved urban space into concentrations of data points . . . the most overlooked, rejected element in the whole process has been people" (Kuma, Jinnai, and Suzuki 2015, 7). Kuma notes that contrary to Isozaki's prophecy that the city will continue to dissolve into "soft" media and invisible telecommunication networks, the digital frenzy of the turn of the 21st century was followed by a return to "urban reality." People are again keen on occupying public spaces that appeal to their haptic sense through warm materiality, regardless of the simultaneous existence of cyberspace.

Further, Kuma continues, a process of "rehumanizing the city" has been ongoing, thanks to the advent of new techniques for fireproofing and strengthening natural materials such as wood, allowing their reintroduction into the public realm. In what seems to be an about-face in relation to his projects of the 1990s, he holds that "there exist things that cannot be experienced virtually via the Internet. . . . The more everything goes digital, the more we're rediscovering . . . just how vital real things are. Computer technology has paradoxically breathed new life into the good old physical city" (Kuma, Jinnai, Suzuki 2015, 8). While these reflections seem to rekindle Hara's phenomenological sensibilities, Kuma has given them an entirely different manifestation in his built work. Meanwhile, his affirmation inadvertently hints to the principle of arazu-arazu, whereby the real and the virtual exist side by side as diverse dimensions of public space, and there is no indication that cyberspace will ever satisfy people's desire for "real" space of interaction.

12

CONCLUSION

While Hara's and Kuma's urban architecture models seemed abstract and futuristic in their time, today they appear to have been clairvoyant in describing the ambiguous discrete continuity of our current state of living. Since the 2020 pandemic has dealt a blow to public space, what Hannah Arendt (1958) called the "public space of appearance" has dissolved almost overnight into cyberspace. But it soon became clear that virtually continuous space falls short of providing room for most of our social interactions

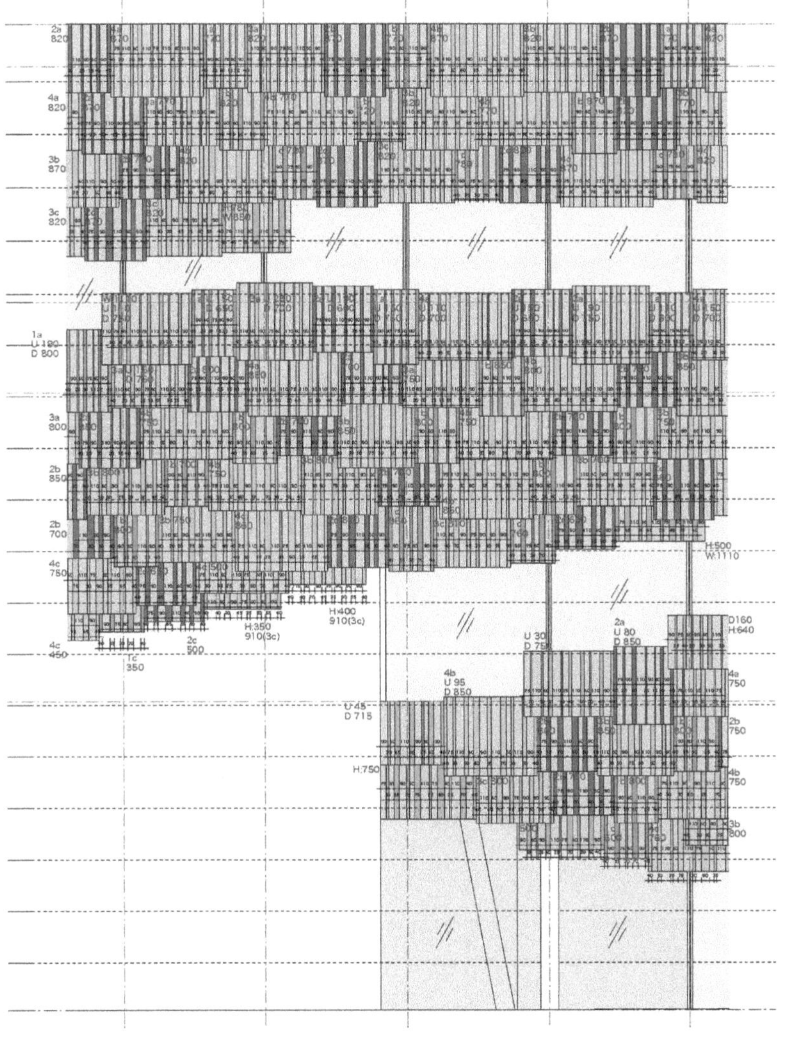

13

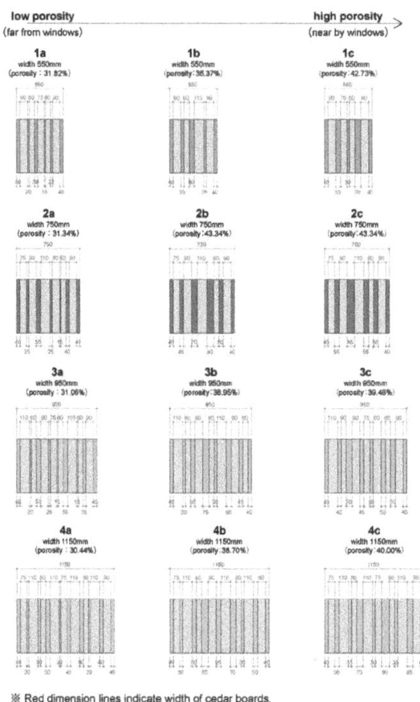

14

12 Kengo Kuma & Associates, Daiwa Ubiquitous Computing Center, Tokyo University, 2013. View of the main façade.

13 Kengo Kuma & Associates, Daiwa Ubiquitous Computing Center, Tokyo University. 2013. Main elevation drawing with color coding of the various groups of slats.

14 Kengo Kuma & Associates, Daiwa Ubiquitous Computing Center, Tokyo University. 2013. Drawing of the various groups of slats.

and sensual needs. Hara's concept of floating individuals connected through electromagnetic steams across the globe is now reality, but the various telecommunication tools available are still manifestly primitive in their capacity to connect us beyond distorted images and sounds. Deprivation has fueled our urge to return to physical public space. It seems that Hara has underestimated the psychological challenges of social isolation and even the technological problems that ensue from reliance on remote interaction. Meanwhile, Kuma's about-face with regard to his earlier excitement about the potential of the internet resonates loudly today.

Discrete continuity is likely to become an integral characteristic of urban architecture in the coming years. The ongoing development and dissemination of dematerialized telecommunication interfaces, targeted advertising in public space (of the kind seen in the 2002 film *Minority Report*), spatial fencing based on face recognition and biometric screening—these and other technologies are likely to be central to the way we perceive and use public space as discrete and continuous simultaneously. These developments present an urgent topic for further research in a postpandemic world. One may hope that the insight gained in 2020 would be used to fix some of the bugs in the current beta version of our cyber-spatial architecture.

ACKNOWLEDGMENTS

I sincerely thank architects Hiroshi Hara, Kengo Kuma, and Suguru Watanabe for kindly responding to my questions and providing new insight into their fascinating work. Many thanks also to the ACADIA peer reviewers for their constructive comments.

NOTES

1. As explained by Suguru Watanabe, project architect for the Daiwa building.

REFERENCES

Arendt, Hannah. 1958. *The Human Condition*. Chicago: University of Chicago Press.

Bognar, Botond, and Hiroshi Hara. 2001. *Hiroshi Hara: The Floating World of His Architecture*. West Sussex: Wiley-Academy.

Carpo, Mario. 2018. "Particlized: The New Arts and Sciences of Particles." *JA: The Japan Architect (109)*: 16–17.

Hara, Hiroshi. 1987. "Learning from the Villages: 100 Lessons." *SD*. Reprinted in *GA Architect 13: Hiroshi Hara*, by Hiroshi Hara, Yukio Futagawa, and David B. Stewart. Tokyo: A.D.A. EDITA, 1993.

Hara, Hiroshi. 2004. *Discrete City. Vol. 1: Essay. On Discreteness. An Essay on Connectability and Separability*. Tokyo: TOTO Shuppan.

Hara, Hiroshi. 2009. *Yet: Hiroshi Hara*. Tokyo, Japan: TOTO Pub.

Hara, Hiroshi. 2019. Interview with the author, September 26, 2019.

Hara, Hiroshi, Yukio Futagawa, and David B. Stewart. 1993. *GA Architect 13: Hiroshi Hara*. Tokyo: A.D.A. EDITA.

Isozaki, Arata, 1968. *Nippon no toshi kukan [Japanese Urban Space]*. Tokyo: Shokokusha,

Ito, Toyo, 1993. "A Garden of Microchips: The Architectural Image of the Microelectronic Age." *JA Library* 2 (Summer): 13.

Kuma, Kengo. 1997. "Grassnet." *SD* 9711 (398): 100–101.

Kuma, Kengo. 2006. *Anti-object: The Dissolution and Disintegration of Architecture*. London: Architectural Association.

Kuma, Kengo. 2017. Interview with Yosuke Obuchi. In "Four Facets of Contemporary Japanese architecture: Theory." Tokyo University course on edX. https://www.edx.org. Accessed 2020-12-01.

Kuma, Kengo. 2019. Interview with the author, September 2019.

Kuma, Kengo, Hidenobu Jinnai, and Tomoyuki Suzuki. 2015. *Hiroba: All About "Public Spaces" in Japan*. Kyōto: Tankōsha.

Leibniz, Gottfried Wilhelm. [1714] 1898. *The Monadology and Other Philosophical Writings*. London: Oxford University Press.

Lynn, Greg. 1997. "Pointillism." *SD* 9711 (398): 47.

Negroponte, Nicholas. 1970. *The Architecture Machine: Toward a More Human Environment*. Cambridge, MA: MIT Press.

Riemann, Bernhard. [1854] 1998. "On the Hypotheses which lie at the Bases of Geometry." *Nature* 8 (183, 184).

Watanabe, Suguru. 2019. Interview with the author, September 2019.

IMAGE CREDITS

Figures 1, 12: © SS Tokyo.
Figures 2, 5–7: © Hiroshi Hara, Atelier Phi.
Figure 3: Platt, Anthony, Peter Bailey, Gary Ridgdill, and William Hurst. In Negroponte 1970.
Figure 4: Gabinetto Fotografico Nazionale. In Negroponte 1970.
Figures 8–11, 13, 14: © Kengo Kuma and Associates.

Ariel Genadt is an architect, lecturer, and scholar. His research focuses on the design and construction of architectural envelopes and their capacity to express cultural and environmental aspects. He further specializes in the history and theory of 20th-century architecture in Japan. Genadt holds a PhD in Architecture (University of Pennsylvania, 2016), an MA (AA School, 2004) and a BArch cum laude (Technion, Israel, 1997). He has collaborated on a wide range of buildings and urban design projects in Europe and Asia, and has taught at University of Pennsylvania, Swarthmore College, and the Technion. In 2012 he was a Fellow Researcher of the Japan Society for the Promotion of Science at the Kuma Lab, Tokyo University, and in 2013, a visiting scholar at the Fondazione Renzo Piano, Genoa. He has published scholarly articles in several distinguished journals.

An AI Lens on Historic Cairo

A Deep Learning Application for Minaret Classification

Islam Zohier
Arab Academy for Science and Technology and Maritime Transport

Ahmed El Antably
Arab Academy for Science and Technology and Maritime Transport

Ahmed S. Madani
Arab Academy for Science and Technology and Maritime Transport

1

1 A sample of minaret data set ground-truth labels for semantic segmentation model training.

ABSTRACT

Reports show that numerous heritage sites are in danger due to conflicts and heritage mismanagement in many parts of the world. Experts have resorted to digital tools to attempt to conserve and preserve endangered and damaged sites. To that end, in this applied research, we aim to develop a deep learning framework applied to the decaying tangible heritage of Historic Cairo, known as "The City of a Thousand Minarets." The proposed framework targets Cairo's historic minaret styles as a test case study for the broader applications of deep learning in digital heritage. It comprises recognition and segmentation tasks, which use a deep learning semantic segmentation model trained on two data sets representing the two most dominant minaret styles in the city, Mamluk (1250–1517 CE) and Ottoman (1517–1952 CE). The proposed framework aims to classify these two types using images. It can help create a multidimensional model from just a photograph of a historic building, which can quickly catalog and document a historic building or element. The study also sheds light on the obstacles preventing the exploration and implementation of deep learning techniques in digital heritage. The research presented in this paper is a work-in-progress of a larger applied research concerned with implementing deep learning techniques in the digital heritage domain.

MOTIVATION

Endangered Heritage and Poor Management

Numerous heritage sites suffer from poor management, extensive new urban development, and general neglect over the past decades. Three international organizations periodically track endangered cultural heritage properties around the world. The UNESCO has its List of World Heritage in Danger (UNESCO World Heritage Centre n.d.), ICOMOS its Heritage at Risk (ICOMOS World Reports 2011), and the World Monuments Fund its World Monuments Watch (World Monuments Fund n.d.). According to UNESCO, there are currently 21 heritage sites in danger in the Middle East. The number of sites is increasing due to heritage mismanagement and conflict in the region (Warren 2005).

There are only a few memories and images left of demolished heritage buildings due to development and poor management over the past decades. For example, in Cairo, El-Dardiry and El Antably (2020) investigated the demolition of Wikālit al-'Anbariyin and its dwellers' associated memories. The building was constructed by Sultan Qalāwun (1290 CE) during the Mamluk period as an amber market (Al Maqrizi 1998). The building was the victim of poor management and neglect, which resulted in its demolition in 2019, after over 750 years of operation.

Digital Heritage Attempts

Experts have resorted to digital tools to attempt to conserve and preserve endangered and damaged sites. For example, Levin et al. (2019) used remote sensing and big data to discover, in real-time, heritage sites affected by armed conflicts through sensing nightlights near these sites and news-mining big data. Tolba (2007) proposed a geographic information system (GIS) method for urban conservation planning that documents existing monument structures in Bahrain's historical cities and their present conditions. That system aims to assist in decisions regarding these structures' preservation, restoration, and possible reuse. Other attempts include attempting to reconstruct lost cultural heritage, like the 3D-printed replica of Palmyra's Arch of Triumph in Syria destroyed by ISIS on October 5, 2015.

These attempts were facilitated by the availability of data and documentation. Therefore, this research's primary motivation was to develop a framework pipeline using the deep learning method to quickly catalog and document historic buildings or elements and contribute new data sets to the field.

AI and Deep Learning

Artificial intelligence (AI) applications have recently disrupted many domains, bringing means and methods to

2

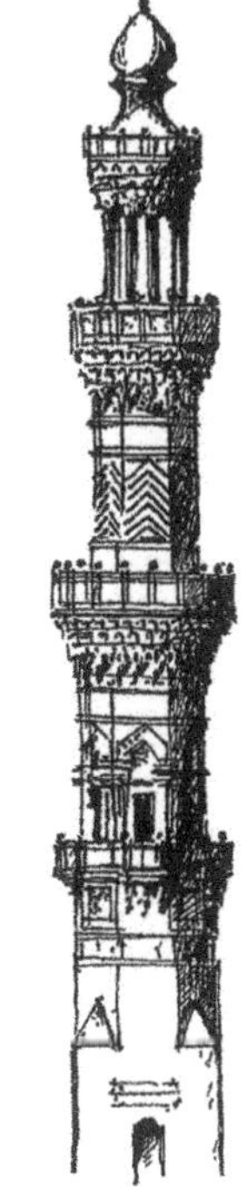
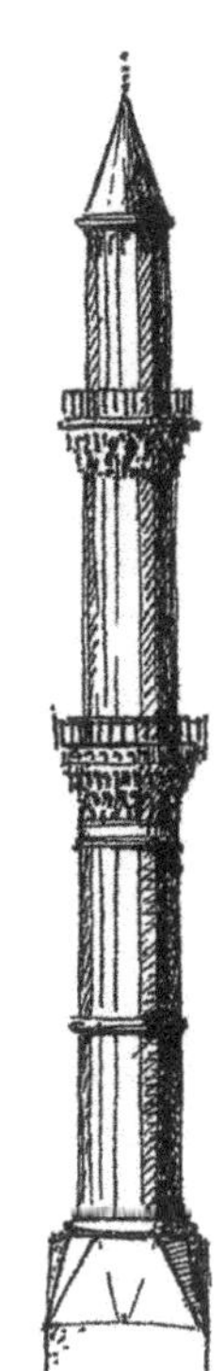

3

2 Parts of Mamluk cemeteries were demolished in 2020 for urban development and highway extensions.

3 From left to right: Mamluk versus Ottoman minaret sketches that form the test case in this study.

4

4 Different building typologies in Historic Cairo.

5 Stage 1: random minaret-detection training data set ground truth samples.

6 Stage 2: minaret type classification training data set ground truth samples: The annotated training data set using a semantic pixel-level segmentation approach.

7 The proposed framework development stages.

previously unresolved challenges across industries. Unlike classical machine learning models, deep learning models do not need a layer of engineered features designed by humans; they can be fed with raw data and automatically discover different levels of representations of the key features found in that raw data. These models managed to perform intricate structures in high-dimensional data such as a multiclass RGB image data set like ImageNet (Deng et al. 2009) and recognize different patterns and structures of features in the given data set. These models have made a significant breakthrough in solving problems that have resisted the AI community and machine learning scientists for many years (LeCun, Bengio, and Hinton 2015).

LeCun, Bengio, and Hinton (2015) mentioned different types of neural networks and their underlying concepts. This research is concerned with two types of neural networks: convolutional neural networks (CNN) and semantic segmentation neural networks (SegNet).

AI Applications in Digital Heritage

In digital heritage, there is an increasing body of work investigating the applications of deep learning techniques. Ćosović, Amelio, and Junuz (2019) surveyed classification methods applied to the cultural heritage context. They did a taxonomy for the classification method used in different cultural heritage categories, whether tangible or intangible, and whether the classified object is movable or not.

There are also other applications of deep learning techniques. For example, classifying cultural heritage images using CNN models (Ćosović and Jankovic 2020; Llamas et al. 2017) or classifying 3D heritage data using either 3D geometry or point clouds, or working on the object scanned texture directly (Grilli and Remondino 2019). On the other hand, there are research attempts applied using generative adversarial networks (GAN) models to reconstruct heritage objects or artifacts using single image or depth maps (Hermoza and Sipiran 2018; Kniaz, Remondino, and Knyaz 2019; Pan et al. 2018).

It is worth mentioning that the Venice Time Machine project uses deep learning techniques in automatic handwriting recognition and painting classification. The project aims to build a multidimensional model of Venice and its evolution covering more than 1,000 years, creating "Big Data of the Past" (Kaplan 2015). It will make the city's archival data accessible via a search engine to interpret the city better and conserve/document its current state (Kaplan 2020).

In this applied research, we propose a framework to implement a deep learning method on the tangible heritage of Historic Cairo. Specifically, we target Cairo's historic minaret styles. The framework proposes a pipeline using a SegNet model to create a multidimensional model from just an image of a minaret. We will test the framework by performing a classification task of two types of minarets, Mamluk and Ottoman.

TEST CASE STUDY

To test the proposed framework, we apply it to the decaying tangible heritage of Historic Cairo, known as "The City of

5

6

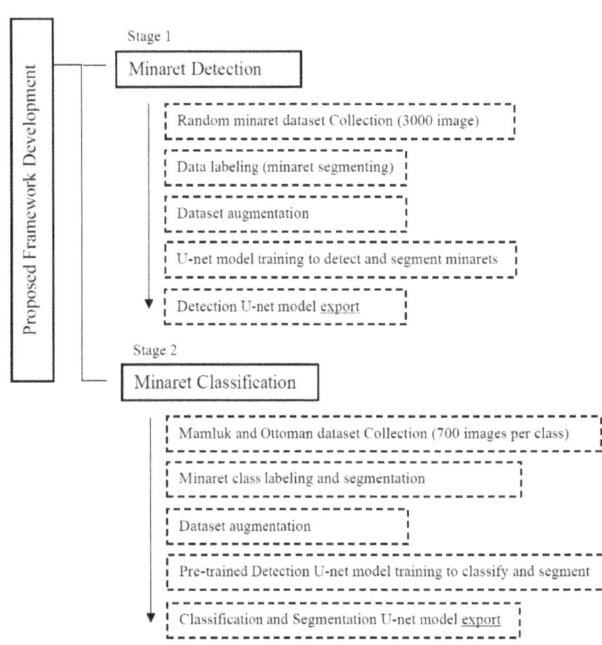

7

a Thousand Minarets." Specifically, the framework targets Cairo's historic minaret styles as a test case study. To our knowledge, there exists no literature on applying deep learning techniques in the proposed context.

Historic Cairo

"Historic Cairo is an unequaled treasure house of Islamic architecture. Built over a span of a thousand years, Cairo's historic center contains the most concentrated, the most numerous, the most varied collection of monuments in the Islamic world" (Williams, Dobrowolski, and Seif 2018, 6). The city has many monuments left from the consecutive dynasties that ruled Egypt. The first started in 641 CE when Amr ibn al-As, during the Rashidun Caliphate, conquered Egypt, built his mosque, and established al-Fustat. The last is the Muhammad Ali dynasty between 1805 and 1952 CE. Each period left its own architectural monuments and style. Some of the remaining monuments are religious, like mosques and religious complexes, and others are secular, like city walls, commercial inns, and houses (Williams, Dobrowolski, and Seif 2018). That immense heritage was preserved through hundreds of years by the Waqf Preservation System and its laws (El-Habashi 2008). Mosques and minarets saw a remarkable evolution through these dynasties. Specific characteristics and features signified each period's minaret. Each period had its own politics of style, building traditions, and decorations, which were at some point imported from or following the Caliphate's capitals (Behrens-Abouseif, O'Kane, and Werner 2010).

The former argument urges Historic Cairo's exploration, with its rich context, using AI and deep learning techniques. This exploration will potentially aid in documenting the city's heritage. Furthermore, it will provide digital accessible knowledge for further investigation and cross-referencing.

METHODOLOGY

The proposed framework for minaret-type classification will detect and segment minarets from a random image and classify its type. The framework will be tested on two types of minarets: Mamluk (1250–1517 CE) and Ottoman (1517–1952 CE) (Fig. 3). Due to the lack of available training data for each minaret type and to avoid training model overfitting, the framework development will be in two stages (Fig. 7). Stage one is minaret detection, where we will train a segmentation model on a random minaret type data set. In this stage, we will detect any minaret object regardless of its type and segment it. As shown in (Fig. 5), this is a sample of minaret training data set "ground truth" to train the semantic segmentation model on minaret detection. Stage two is minaret type classification, where we will train the segmentation model on a minaret data set with the two classes: Mamluk and Ottoman, to classify each segmented minaret object according to its class. Figure 6 shows a sample of minaret type training data set ground truth to train the semantic segmentation model on minaret type classification.

The Problem

To clarify the needed task, we need a pipeline not just to classify or detect minaret types but also to segment and

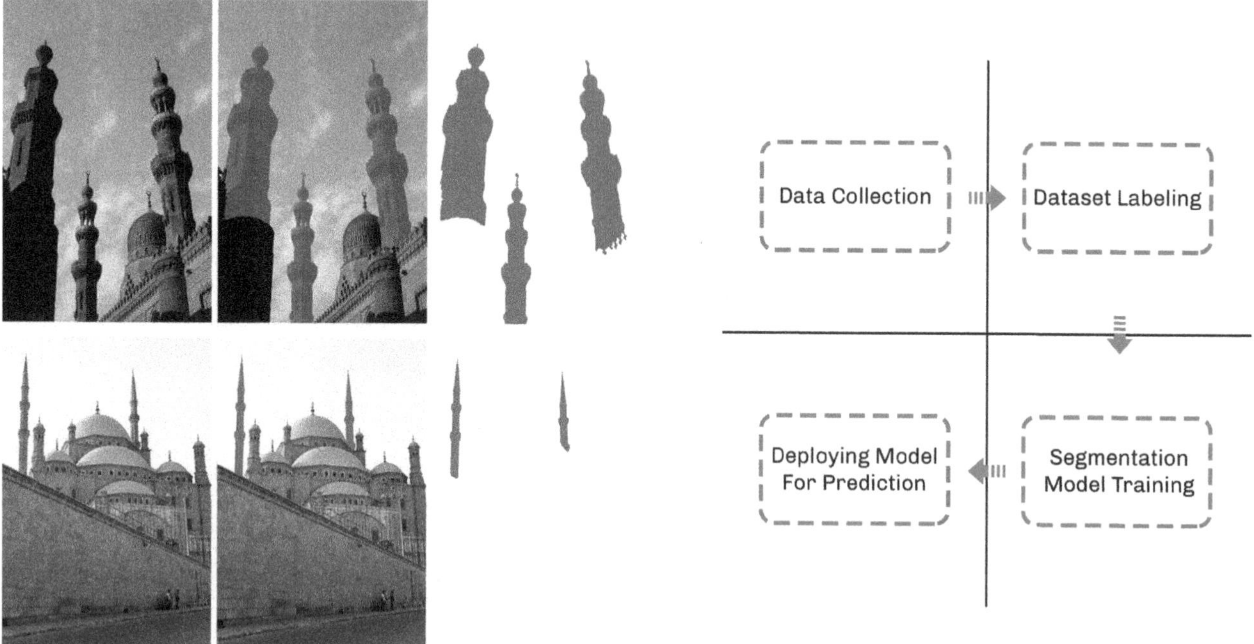

8

9

localize each minaret in the given image input (Fig. 8). It is a common supervised learning task where a semantic segmentation model trains on labeled training data set examples and maps an input to an output based on the given example of input-output pairs. The output of this training process is a prediction function that represents the training data set features. After training, the model is tested on a test data set with new input to test its generalization ability in predicting new outputs. "Generalization" in machine learning is the ability of the model to come up with sensible output predictions on new inputs that it has never seen during training (LeCun, Bengio, and Hinton 2015).

In Figure 9, we illustrate the four stages of applying the deep learning method. First, we collect data. Second, we generate a training data set. Third, we train the selected network (we select the best network architecture and implementation for our task). Fourth and finally, we use the trained model for prediction on new inputs. In the present research, we are still progressing at the third stage, "Segmentation Model Training."

Data Collection

Approaching these tasks, we face a common critical issue while using deep learning applications: data sets. Data collection is a major bottleneck in deep learning applications and a big active topic of research. For example, Roh, Heo, and Whang (2019) researched data collection techniques from a data management perspective. There are specific tasks or applications in machine and deep learning that enjoy massive amounts of training data that have been accumulated for decades. However, more recent tasks or tailored tasks have relatively no training data (Roh, Heo, and Whang 2019).

There was no available minaret data set for semantic segmentation model training after exploring available datasets and online resources. So, we moved to data collection techniques. Data collection was from online image search engines and websites like Google Images, Getty Images, Flickr, and 500px using scraping tools (Fig. 10). Also, we benefited from some websites' APIs to collect images with specific tags. For example, using Python and Flickr APIs, we managed to download images tagged with "minaret," "Historic Cairo," "Mamluk minaret," and "Ottoman minaret." Another way of collecting data was by asking the public to upload their own minaret images using an online Google Form. Using these three techniques, we managed to obtain more than 8,000 images. The collected minaret data set had many noise images (for example, images with wrong tags or low-resolution images). After filtering, we managed to compile more than 3,500 unique high-resolution random minaret image data sets.

Data Set Labeling (Ground Truth)

In labeling this data set, we benefited from auto-selection tools provided by different applications (for example, Photoshop 2020 object select tool). These tools made selection easier and precise on a pixel level. Also, to enlarge the available training data set, we used image augmentation techniques with ImageDataGenerator in the Keras API (Chollet 2020).

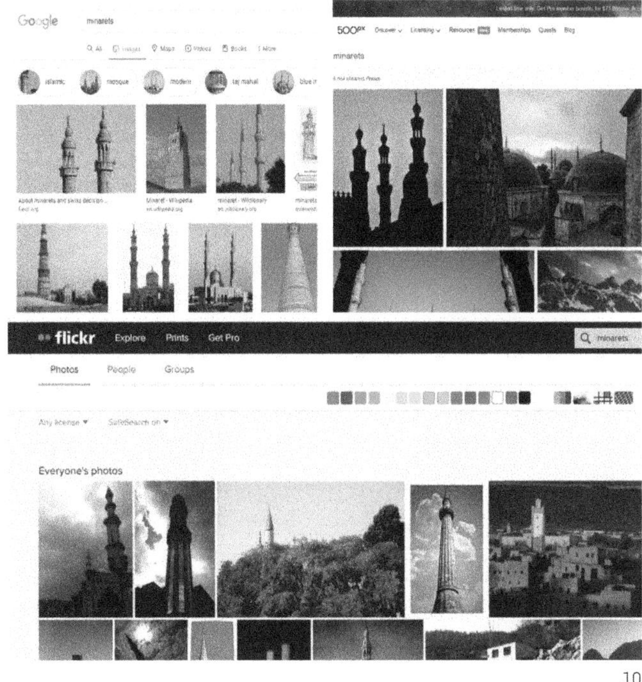

10

11

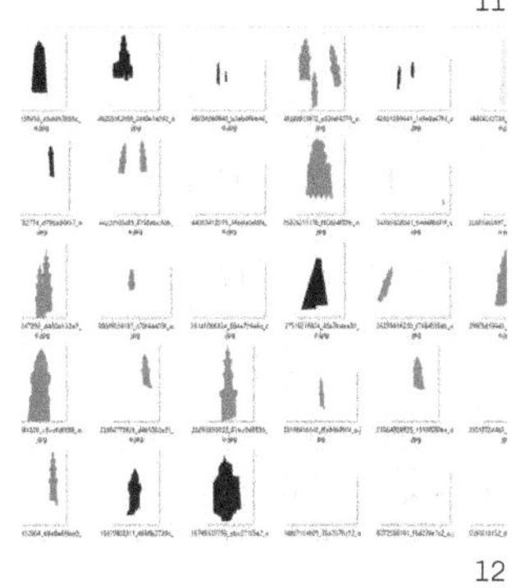
12

8 Localization and segmentation of the minaret in the given input images.

9 An illustration of the four stages of applying the deep learning technique.

10 Data collection from online resources.

11 A sample of the collected minaret data sets.

12 A sample of minaret data set ground truth labels for semantic segmentation model training.

Segmentation Model Network Architecture and Implementation

Image segmentation is a computer vision task in which we link each pixel in an image to a class label. We can think of a semantic segmentation task as an image classification at a pixel level. Semantic segmentation is the state-of-the-art technology with hundreds of papers published every year to solve different computer vision tasks and issues. It is widely used in medical diagnosis and autonomous driving applications to define self-driving cars' surrounding environment (Sultana, Sufian, and Dutta 2020). The segmentation model consists of two parts: an encoder and a decoder. These parts are typical convolutional models (Alom et al. 2019). One approach is to use a fully convolutional network (CNN) model as the encoder module. The decoder module transposes CNN layers to upsample the feature maps into a full-resolution segmentation map (Long, Shelhamer, and Darrell 2017). Building on that approach, Ronneberger, Fischer, and Brox (2015) propose the U-Net architecture to solve two main issues: reaching better results in precise segmentation and localization and performing a segmentation task with a small dataset.

According to Iglovikov and Shvets (2018), due to the lack of training data, transferring initialization weights from a network pretrained on a large data set like ImageNet (Deng et al. 2009) shows better performance compared to CNN models trained from scratch on a small data set. Trained networks on the ImageNet (Deng et al. 2009) data set are commonly used for weight initialization for network weights in other tasks.

Our study uses a semantic segmentation model with a U-Net architecture with a pretrained ResNet model (He et al. 2016) as an encoder CNN model. Training the model was on SageMaker online platform provided by Amazon (Joshi 2020) to overcome computation limitations.

RESULTS AND DISCUSSION

One of our research goals was to propose a framework using deep learning methods that aids in creating a multidimensional model from just an image of a historic building. The proposed framework can potentially help digitize and document the heritage of the context to which it is applied. Our research's other goal was to shed light on the obstacles preventing the exploration and implementation of deep learning techniques within the architectural heritage domain. In that context, the study introduced a large, richly annotated minaret data set to push this field of study further. In this research, we picked up the decaying tangible heritage of Historic Cairo as a case study on which to test the proposed framework. Specifically, the framework targeted Cairo's historic minaret styles as a test case. Historic Cairo is a very rich context to explore using AI and deep learning techniques. The expected output results of the prediction model are shown in Figure 13.

During the study, we faced a big problem with data set availability. There was no access to good data quality in sufficient quantities. It is important to start providing data sets for heritage buildings, as the available data sets in the digital heritage domain are very limited.

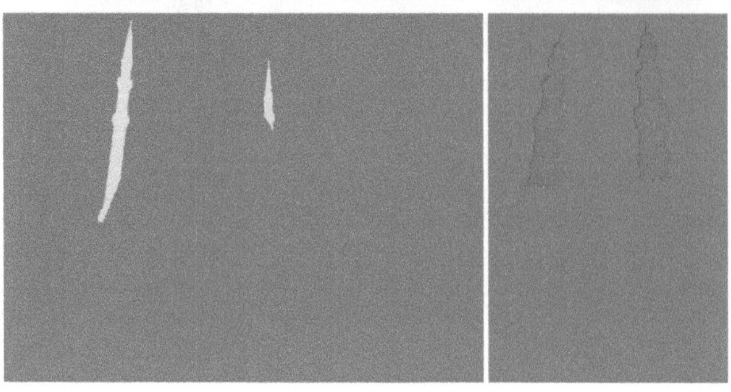

13

13 Our expected result after prediction on the semantic segmentation model: The top images represent input images, and the bottom ones expected masked results.

One of the proposed framework's current limitations is that it runs on only two data sets of ideal historical prototypes (edge cases): It can only identify a minaret's image if it shows the ideal features of either a Mamluk or an Ottoman style. The addition of more data sets can help identify more prototypes but not hybrid styles. Once the framework becomes available to the public and users can upload their own photographs for classification, the data sets will grow. With larger data sets, we hope to train the framework to identify a minaret based on a spectrum of less discrete historical styles.

We benefited from the available advances in the deep learning models and their ability to understand the given image input. Also, we benefited from transferred learning in the pretrained models trained on larger data sets like the MS COCO dataset (Lin et al. 2014) or the ImageNet data set (Deng et al. 2009) that made these models robust enough to generalize and understand new class inputs.

Challenges nowadays in the computer vision domain are more complex than just detection or classification tasks. Some of the emerging research in this field is concerned with, for example, stable continuous interpretation of the dynamic world in a self-driving car that needs to act on a situation in milliseconds (Li, Wang, and Ramanan 2020) or with explicit vision tasks (Zhou, Krähenbühl, and Koltun 2019). These tasks could never reach this level of complexity and demand without building on the continuous exploration, improvement, and advances in these domains. The continuous exploration of the digital heritage domain using these techniques will help solve more complex ideas and tasks.

The proposed framework execution will be an application interface that receives an image from the user and classifies the minaret type. In this case, the proposed framework will help classify and update metadata about the minaret from the uploaded new images, and possibly reconstruct missing or damaged minarets due to the available documentation. It is expected in the future, and when the framework is generalizing, that the application can potentially aid in better interpreting the monument and its political and sociocultural context, and document its current state. It potentially will provide digital accessible knowledge for further investigation and cross-referencing.

CONCLUSION

This research proposes a framework pipeline to collect a data set and train a deep learning model to detect and identify a historical element. This framework's importance is discussed in the context of digitizing heritage, heritage documentation, and interpretation. The paper sheds light on the problem of the lack of training data sets and shows how to overcome such obstacles in the context of training data set harvesting and deep learning model supervised training on such a small data set to perform classification and segmentation tasks. It is predicted that through that framework the deep learning model can identify and segment the minaret style image input.

ACKNOWLEDGMENTS

We are deeply saddened by Professor A. S. Madani's passing away a couple of months ago. Professor Madani inspired this research with great ideas and developed its direction.

REFERENCES

Al Maqrizi, Taqi-ad-Din Ahmad Ibn-Ali. 1998. *al-Mawa'iz wa-'l-i'tibar bi-dikr al-hitat wa-'l-atar al-ma'ruf bi-'l-Hitat al-maqriziya*. Cairo, Egypt: Madbuli.

Alom, Md Zahangir, Chris Yakopcic, Mahmudul Hasan, Tarek Taha, and Vijayan Asari. 2019. "Recurrent Residual U-Net for Medical Image Segmentation." *Journal of Medical Imaging* 6 (1): 014006. https://doi.org/10.1117/1.JMI.6.1.014006.

Behrens-Abouseif, Doris, Bernard O'Kane, and Nicolas Werner. 2010. *The Minarets of Cairo*. Cairo, Egypt: American University in Cairo Press.

Chollet, François, et al. 2020. *Keras*. V.2.4.0. http://keras.io.

Ćosović, Marijana, Alessia Amelio, and Emina Junuz. 2019. "Classification Methods in Cultural Heritage." In *1st International Workshop on Visual Pattern Extraction and Recognition for Cultural Heritage Understanding (VIPERC 2019), Pisa, Italy*. http://ceur-ws.org/Vol-2320/paper3.pdf.

Ćosović, Marijana, and Radmila Janković. 2020. "CNN Classification of the Cultural Heritage Images." *2020 19th International Symposium INFOTEH-JAHORINA (INFOTEH)*: 1–6. https://doi.org/10.1109/INFOTEH48170.2020.9066300.

Deng, J., Wei Dong, R. Socher, Li-Jia Li, Kai Li, and Li Fei-Fei. 2009. "ImageNet: A Large-Scale Hierarchical Image Database." *2009 IEEE Conference on Computer Vision and Pattern Recognition*: 248–255. https://doi.org/10.1109/CVPR.2009.5206848.

El-Dardiry, Aliaa, and Ahmed El Antably. 2020. "Farewell al-'Anbariyin." *International Journal of Environmental Science & Sustainable Development* 5 (1): 1–13. https://doi.org/10.21625/essd.v5i1.713.

El Habashi, Alaa. 2008. "Monuments or Functioning Buildings: Legal Protection over Five Case-Study Historic Hammāms in the Mediterranean." *ArchNet-IJAR: International Journal of Architectural Research* 2 (3): 42–55. https://www.archnet.org/publications/5171.

Grilli, Eleonora, and Fabio Remondino. 2019. "Classification of 3D Digital Heritage." *Remote Sensing* 11 (7): 847. https://doi.org/10.3390/rs11070847.

He, Kaiming, Xiangyu Zhang, Shaoqing Ren, and Jian Sun. 2016. "Deep Residual Learning for Image Recognition." *Proceedings of the IEEE Conference on Computer Vision and Pattern Recognition*: 770–778. https://doi.org/10.1109/CVPR.2016.90.

Hermoza, Renato, and Ivan Sipiran. 2018. "3D Reconstruction of Incomplete Archaeological Objects Using a Generative Adversarial Network." *Proceedings of Computer Graphics International 2018*, Bintan Island, Indonesia. https://doi.org/10.1145/3208159.3208173.

Iglovikov, Vladimir, and Alexey Shvets. 2018. "Ternausnet: U-Net with VGG11 encoder pre-trained on ImageNet for image segmentation." arXiv preprint. arXiv:1801.05746.

International Council on Monuments and Sites (ICOMOS). 2011. *Heritage@Risk reports*. November 14. https://www.icomos.org/en/what-we-do/risk-preparedness/heritage-at-risk-reports.

Joshi, Ameet V. 2020. "Amazon's Machine Learning Toolkit: Sagemaker." In *Machine Learning and Artificial Intelligence*, 233–243. Cham: Springer International Publishing.

Kaplan, Frédéric. 2015. "The Venice Time Machine." *Proceedings of the 2015 ACM Symposium on Document Engineering*: 73. https://doi.org/10.1145/2682571.2797071.

Kaplan, Frédéric. 2020. "Big Data of the Past, from Venice to Europe." *Proceedings of the Twenty-Fifth International Conference on Architectural Support for Programming Languages and Operating Systems*: 1. https://doi.org/10.1145/3373376.3380611.

Kniaz, V. V., Fabio Remondino, and V. A. Knyaz. 2019. "Generative Adversarial Networks for Single Photo 3D Reconstruction." *ISPRS—International Archives of the Photogrammetry, Remote Sensing and Spatial Information Sciences* 42W9: 403. https://doi.org/10.5194/isprs-archives-XLII-2-W9-403-2019.

LeCun, Yann, Yoshua Bengio, and Geoffrey Hinton. 2015. "Deep Learning." *Nature* 521 (7553): 436–444. https://doi.org/10.1038/nature14539.

Levin, Noam, Saleem Ali, David Crandall, and Salit Kark. 2019. "World Heritage in Danger: Big Data and Remote Sensing can Help Protect Sites in Conflict Zones." *Global Environmental Change* 55: 97–104. https://doi.org/https://doi.org/10.1016/j.gloenvcha.2019.02.001.

Li, Mengtian, Yu-Xiong Wang, and Deva Ramanan. 2020. "Towards Streaming Perception." *Lecture Notes in Computer Science* 12347: 473–88. https://doi.org/10.1007/978-3-030-58536-5_28.

Lin, Tsung-Yi, Michael Maire, Serge Belongie, James Hays, Pietro Perona, Deva Ramanan, Piotr Dollár, and C. Lawrence Zitnick. 2014. "Microsoft COCO: Common Objects in Context." In *Computer Vision – ECCV 2014. ECCV 2014. Lecture Notes in Computer Science*, edited by D. Fleet, T. Pajdla, B. Schiele, and T. Tuytelaars, 740–755. https://doi.org/10.1007/978-3-319-10602-1_48.

Llamas, Jose, Pedro M. Lerones, Roberto Medina, Eduardo Zalama, and Jaime Gómez-García-Bermejo. 2017. "Classification of Architectural Heritage Images Using Deep Learning Techniques." *Applied Sciences* 7 (10): 992. https://doi.org/doi:10.3390/app7100992.

Pan, Jiao, Liang Li, Hiroshi Yamaguchi, Kyoko Hasegawa, Fadjar I Thufail, Bra Mantara, and Satoshi Tanaka. 2018. "3D Reconstruction and Transparent Visualization of Indonesian Cultural Heritage from a Single Image." *Eurographics Workshop on Graphics and Cultural Heritage*. https://doi.org/10.2312/gch.20181363.

Roh, Yuji, Geon Heo, and Steven Euijong Whang. 2019. "A Survey on Data Collection for Machine Learning: A Big Data–AI Integration Perspective." *IEEE Transactions on Knowledge and Data Engineering*: 1–1. https://doi.org/10.1109/TKDE.2019.2946162.

Ronneberger, Olaf, Philipp Fischer, and Thomas Brox. 2015. "U-Net: Convolutional Networks for Biomedical Image Segmentation." *Medical Image Computing and Computer-Assisted Intervention—MICCAI 2015*: 234–41. https://doi.org/10.1007/978-3-319-24574-4_28.

Shelhamer, Evan, Jonathan Long, and Trevor Darrell. 2017. "Fully Convolutional Networks for Semantic Segmentation." *IEEE Transactions on Pattern Analysis and Machine Intelligence* 39 (4): 640–651. https://doi.org/10.1109/TPAMI.2016.2572683.

Sultana, Farhana, Abu Sufian, and Paramartha Dutta. 2020. "Evolution of Image Segmentation Using Deep Convolutional Neural Network: A Survey." *Knowledge-Based Systems* 201–202: 106062. https://doi.org/https://doi.org/10.1016/j.knosys.2020.106062.

Tolba, Osama. 2007. "The Role of GIS in Documenting Bahrain's Historic Cities." *Em'body'ing Virtual Architecture: The Third International Conference of the Arab Society for Computer Aided Architectural Design (ASCAAD 2007)*. Alexandria, Egypt, November 28–30. http://cumincad.scix.net/cgi-bin/works/Show?ascaad2007_041.

UNESCO World Heritage Convention. n.d. "List of World Heritage in Danger." Accessed December 11, 2020. https://whc.unesco.org/en/danger.

Warren, John. 2005. "War and the Cultural Heritage of Iraq: A Sadly Mismanaged Affair." *Third World Quarterly* 26 (4–5): 815–830. https://doi.org/10.1080/01436590500128048.

Williams, Caroline, Jarosław Dobrowolski, and Ola Seif. 2018. *Islamic Monuments in Cairo: The Practical Guide*. 7th ed. Cairo, Egypt: The American University in Cairo Press.

World Monuments Fund. n.d. "World Monuments Watch." Accessed December 11, 2020. https://www.wmf.org/watch.

Zhou, Brady, Philipp Krähenbühl, and Vladlen Koltun. 2019. "Does Computer Vision Matter for Action?" *Science Robotics* 4 (30). https://doi.org/10.1126/scirobotics.aaw6661.

IMAGE CREDITS

Figure 2: © Youssof Osama
Figure 3: © Williams, Dobrowolski, and Seif
Figure 4: © UNESCO, Véronique Dauge

All other drawings and images by the authors.

Islam Zohier is currently an MSc student at the Department of Architectural Engineering, the Arab Academy for Science, Technology & Maritime Transport and a professional practitioner with eight years of experience in the field. He is interested in AI and its applications in architecture and digital heritage.

Ahmed El Antably is currently an Associate Professor at the Department of Architectural Engineering, the Arab Academy for Science, Technology & Maritime Transport. He is interested in design media and the ways in which they are socially deployed in design discourse and the effects they introduce in design practice. He is also interested in issues of (re)mediation and perception in virtually (re)constructed places. El Antably received his doctoral degree in architecture from the University of California, Berkeley, with a designated emphasis in new media.

Ahmed S. Madani passed away in a car accident in September 2020. He was an Assistant Professor at the Department of Computer Engineering, the Arab Academy for Science, Technology & Maritime Transport. His research interests were in artificial neural networks, human-computer interaction, and computer security and reliability. The late Professor Madani received his PhD from Malaysia-Japan International Institute of Technology (MJIIT).

Augmenting Craft with Mixed Reality

A Case Study Project of AR-Driven Analog Clay Modeling

Jacky Chun Hin Fong
The Chinese University of Hong Kong, School of Architecture

Adabelle Long Wun Poon
The Chinese University of Hong Kong, School of Architecture

Wing Sze Ngan
The Chinese University of Hong Kong, School of Architecture

Chung Hei Ho
The Chinese University of Hong Kong, School of Architecture

Garvin Goepel
The Chinese University of Hong Kong, School of Architecture

Kristof Crolla
The University of Hong Kong, Departments of Architecture & Civil Engineering

1

ABSTRACT

This paper discusses novel methods for and advantages of integrating augmented reality (AR) and photogrammetry in hand clay-sculpting workflows. These techniques permit nontrained users to achieve higher precision during the sculpting process by holographically overlaying instructions from digital 3D source geometry on top of the sculpting material. By employing alternative notational systems in design implementation methods, the research positions itself in a postdigital context aimed at humanizing digital technologies. Throughout history, devices have been developed to increase production, such as Henry Dexter's 1842 "Apparatus for Sculptors" for marble sculpting. Extrapolating from this, the workflow presented in this paper uses AR to overlay extracted information from 3D models directly onto the sculptor's field of vision. This information can then become an AR-driven guidance system that assists the sculptor. Using the Microsoft HoloLens, holographic instructions are introduced in the production sequence, connecting the analog sculpture fabrication directly with a digital environment, thus augmenting the craftspeople's agency. A series of AR-aided sculpting methods were developed and tested in a demonstrator case study project that created a small-scale clay copy of Henry Moore's *Sheep Piece* (1971–1972). This paper demonstrates how user-friendly software and hardware tools have lowered the threshold for end users to develop new methods that straightforwardly facilitate and improve their crafts' effectiveness and agency. This shows that the fusion of computational design technology and AR visualization technology can innovate a specific craft's design and production workflow, opening the door for further application developments in more architecture-specific fabrication contexts.

1 Postdigital "Apparatus for Sculptors," using augmented reality to overlay 3D digital modeling information onto the analog material.

INTRODUCTION

"Every block of stone has a statue inside it and it is the task of the sculptor to discover it. I saw the angel in the marble and carved until I set him free." —Michelangelo

The Italian Renaissance architect, sculptor, and painter Michelangelo claimed that he could see "David" inside the uncarved marble before he created the masterpiece (Perkin 2018) (Fig. 2). Very few gifted people presumably have the ability to imagine a completed product within an uncarved object. However, with the advancement of AR technology, the overlay of a virtual object onto a material reality has become possible. With a digitally built 3D model, and through apps for Smart Glasses, such as the Microsoft HoloLens, or Smart Mobile Devices, one can visualize a finished product inside uncarved material as if one possessed the talent described in Michelangelo's quote (Fig. 1).

This study aims to make carving and sculpting more approachable to laypeople through the aid of holographic instructions. The workflow presented in this paper uses AR to overlay extracted information from 3D models directly onto the sculptor's field of vision. This information can then become an AR-driven guidance system that assists the sculptor in their actions. Using the Microsoft HoloLens, holographic instructions are introduced in the production sequence, connecting the analog sculpture fabrication directly with a digital environment, thus augmenting craftspeople's agency. A series of AR-aided sculpting methods were developed and tested in a demonstrator case study project that created a small-scale clay copy of Henry Moore's *Sheep Piece* (1971–1972).

Contextualizing this in the world of modern architecture construction, the possibility is proposed that a wider scope of workers can participate in complex crafting work, without the need of extensive prior craft-specific skills. This study explores the augmentation of craft by combining art, technology, and production.

BACKGROUND

Sculpting

This paper challenges the historical reliance of sculpting on skilled crafting. Since the start of human civilization, sculptures have evolved from representing mythical gods, ancient rulers, and religious characters to the worshipping of socially and politically respected individuals. Transcendentally, pieces of craft appear in the form of artistic expressions, realistic human figures, as well as architectural elements (Palagia 2006). Basic traditional

2 *David* (Michelangelo, 1504).

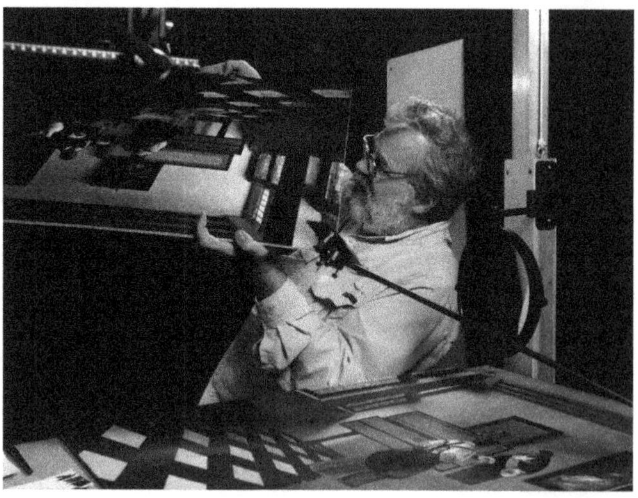

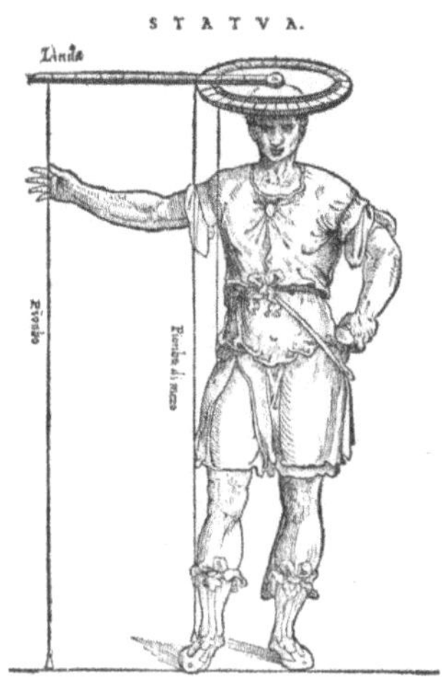

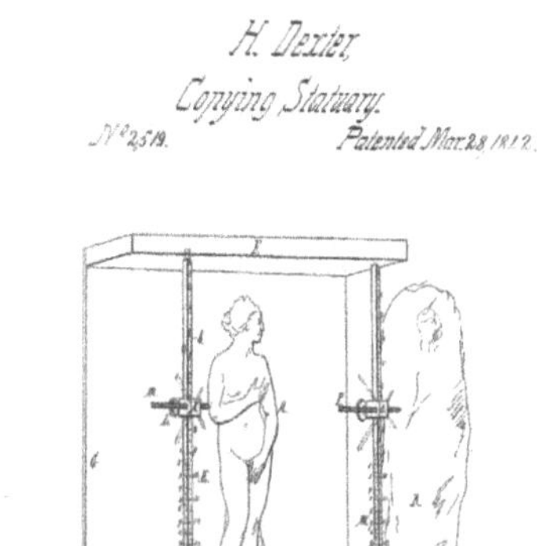

3 Tim Jenison duplicating *The Music Lesson* by Johannes Vermeer.

4 Leon Battista Alberti's device for 3D referencing by measuring spatial coordinates (15th century).

5 Henry Dexter's "Apparatus for Sculptors" to duplicate sculpture (1842).

sculpting techniques include carving and modeling through addition. They can be applied to stone, metal, ceramics, wood, and other materials. The difference in materiality leads to the use of different tools. Metal sculptures, especially bronze, are usually duplicated from an existing model using a lost-wax casting method. For clay and other similar softer mediums, human hands are the tools to shape matter at the stage of modeling when malleable parts are added and smudged to desired forms. In addition, small wooden tools can be helpful, some of which commonly have strong wire curves at the extremities (Lanteri 2018). For harder materials like stone and marble, the techniques and procedures will be different: chisels of various sizes and end shapes are used, and a mallet is essential to strike the other tools against the stone. Due to the irreversibility of sculpting on these materials, drills and bouchardes are used in critical carvings as tools suitable to carve at right angles (Palagia 2006).

Although the tools and detailed techniques vary for different sculptures, their processes share some commonalities. In general, the uncarved material is first fixed onto a working base as preparation, often holes are drilled, or a penetration through the material is needed to join it to a base (Lanteri 2018). Next, wide planar areas are removed using coarser tools to achieve a rough form. Finer modeling is then done by smaller tools with fewer claws or curves. After this modeling stage is completed, tool marks are removed using any means suitable to the material (Palagia 2006).

This raises the question of whether people must receive extensive artistic training before being able to use these tools to create sculptures. A similar question was central to the 2013 documentary film *Tim's Vermeer*, in which Tim Jenison investigated a possible methodology the Dutch painter Johannes Vermeer (1632–1675) could have used to create his paintings, which are typified by the hyperaccurate and realistic depiction of light and color, including chromatic aberrations and depth of field normally impossible to perceive with the naked eye alone (Fig. 3). Jenison discovered that using a rather ingenious small device with a particularly placed mirror allowed him to recreate quasi-identical realism, despite not having any background in painting (Kenny 2014). In doing so, an argument is made for clever tinkering and creative engineering as being an essential and integral part of art production—an argument this paper takes into today's context where augmented reality (AR) and mixed reality (MR) technology are becoming part of readily available and everyday means.

3D Referencing and Photogrammetry

The methodology presented in this paper relies extensively on 3D referencing. The concept of 3D referencing already appeared during the Renaissance, where a form of it was implemented by architect Leon Battista Alberti (1404–1472). Alberti proposed a revolutionary 3D fabrication and design method based on digital data that excluded conventional drawings. He invented a measuring device that was to be positioned on top of the body to be measured (Fig. 4). Then, sculptors were to mark down the spatial coordinates of as many different points of the body as possible and

6

6 Left: Clay scale model copy (authors, 2019). Right: *Sheep Piece* (Henry Moore, 1971–1972).

use this numeric data to create copies (Carpo 2017). With this method, Alberti in principle enabled multiple studios in different places to reproduce different parts of the same statue, which could then be reassembled perfectly (Grayson 1972).

This method, however, was never widely implemented, as Alberti allegedly failed to explain clearly how the spatial coordinates recorded could have been used to execute a sculpture (Wrobel 1987). Nonetheless, Alberti's proposal provided the necessary insights for following generations to develop a machine to replicate "perfect copies of any model." In 1842, American sculptor Henry Dexter (1806–1876) developed the "Apparatus for Sculptors," which guided the sculpting of uncarved marble by measuring the same distances from a finished marble product (Wrobel 1987) (Fig. 5). Such appliances increased the control of less-specialized craftspeople over their work. Yet mass production was still only possible after a first master sculpture was completed, requiring an expert sculptor.

This study uses photogrammetry as a 3D referencing tool. By scanning the gradually transforming sculpture in between carving sequences and comparing it to the digital target sculpture, instructions can be updated at the beginning of each iteration. This allows the sculptor to carve repeatedly through the iterations until the discrepancies between the physical object's scan and the digital base model are acceptable.

Augmented Reality (AR)

The third main component of this study addresses the increasing ability for nonspecialist users to integrate augmented reality into creative design and production. AR technology applications are developing exponentially as more and more software and hardware tools and techniques are becoming available in the market. Today, architectural and engineering applications generally facilitate information extraction from design information models to improve the efficiency and effectiveness of workers' tasks (Chi, Kang, and Wang 2013; Chu, Matthews, and Love 2018). These include onsite applications where AR can be seen implemented in smart helmets and tablets, primarily to help engineers make more accurate and rapid judgments for construction review tasks (Ren, Liu, and Ruan 2017). In industrial settings, case studies of AR systems' user experiences have demonstrated their potential to reduce errors in assembly and improve the quality of maintenance work (Aromaa et al. 2018). A wide range of AR applications can be found in medicine, art, marketing, communication, etc.

This study focuses on the implementation of commonly available AR and photogrammetry techniques in sculpture production. It uses them to develop a method that permits nontrained users to achieve higher precision during the sculpting process. For this, it holographically overlays instructions from digital 3D source geometry on top of the sculpting material using smart glasses and mobile devices like smartphones and tablets, and uses these same devices for iterative 3D referencing through photogrammetry.

OBJECTIVE

The objective of this study is to iteratively develop and test clay modeling methods that incorporate augmented reality to increase a layperson's craft, agency, and opportunities, and to validate the method's effectiveness through a demonstrator. For this, the study utilizes digital sculpture models and holographic projections to create a novel AR-driven guidance system, building on

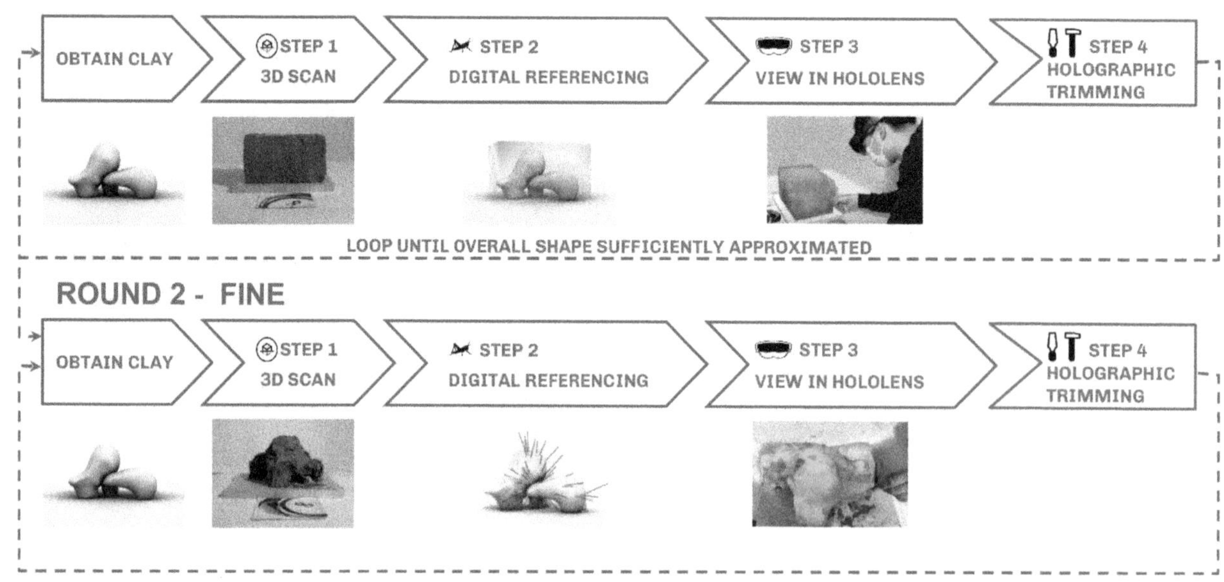

7 Workflow diagram.

fabrication concepts initiated by Alberti and Dexter. With Microsoft's HoloLens as a central tool, mixed-reality holographic instructions are introduced to augment and connect analog sculpture fabrication directly with a digital environment.

One limitation of Henry Dexter's "Apparatus for Sculptors" lies in the difficulty of producing the initial reference model. However, with the ability to replace this with a virtual model, either newly digitally modeled or 3D-scanned by the user, or obtained from online resources, the procedure to carve or replicate a sculpture can be dramatically simplified. In doing so, the proposed postdigital "Apparatus for Sculptors" allows unskilled workers to "see" the virtual model together with the analog sculpting material and create a precise replica accordingly.

METHOD

A series of AR-aided sculpting techniques were developed and tested, using as a case study the creation of a small-scale clay copy of Henry Moore's *Sheep Piece* (1971–1972) (Fig. 7). For this, we used the software platform Fologram (Fologram 2020), an add-on to McNeel's Rhinoceros procedural modeler Grasshopper that allows for real-time streaming of digital data to the Microsoft HoloLens. Currently, the built-in capacity of the HoloLens to automatically scan its surrounding is still too rough and imprecise to permit its direct use in our workflow. Therefore, open-source photogrammetry software Meshroom (AliceVision 2021) was used in combination with high-definition photo cameras from handheld smartphone devices to carry out 3D scanning of the sculpture and derive a digital mesh from the physical sculpted matter.

The overall method contained two major processes, with first an iterative "rough cutting" process to get a relatively precise overall shape approximation in the clay block, and then a "fine cutting" process in which wooden sticks were used to guide further carving (Fig. 7). Photogrammetry was used in both to iteratively measure and visualize the differences between actual modeled clay geometry and the target digital model file, thus providing a feedback loop between the physical model and the digital source file.

The first step of rough cutting visualizes the distance between the 3D-scanned actual clay block and the virtual model by overlaying a predefined color spectrum onto the clay block. This holographic instruction helps determine where large areas of the clay block are to be trimmed (Fig. 8). The setup starts with the acquisition or creation of a digital mesh model of the desired sculpture—for our demonstrator, an open-source model of *Sheep Piece*. This model is scaled down and placed to fit within a bounding box with the dimensions of the to-be-sculpted material block—here, a block of pottery clay measuring roughly 400 mm x 300 mm x 300mm. This block is 3D-scanned and brought into the digital working environment. There, a sphere is digitally centered on the sculpture model geometry and clay block scan with a radius big enough to encompass both. On this sphere, numerous points are

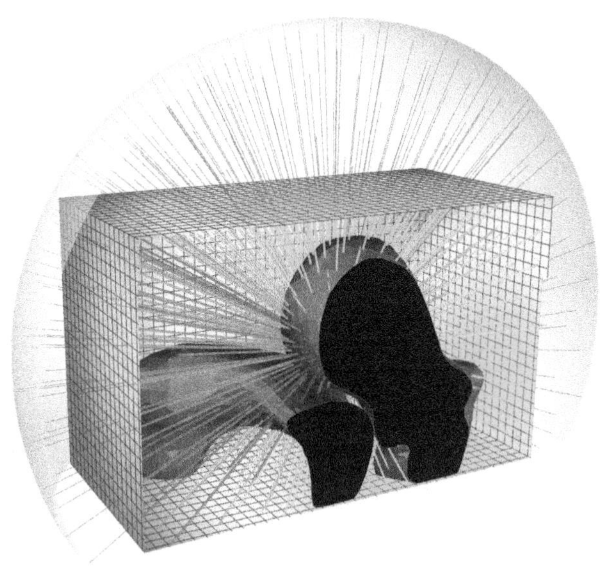

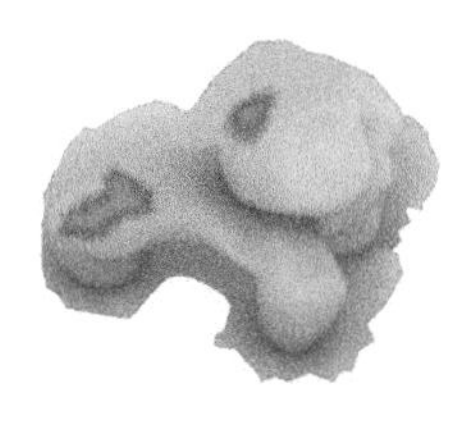

9

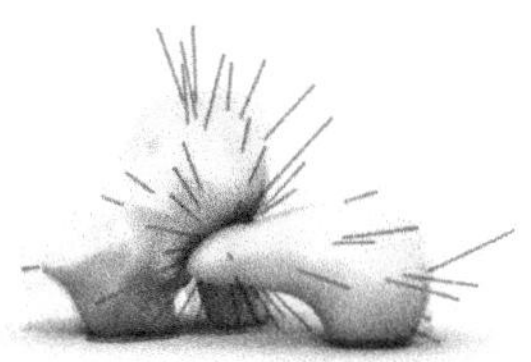

8

10

8 Round 1—rough cutting: model differences are visualized by overlaying color information onto the clay block.

9 Overcarved areas are highlighted in red.

10 Round 2—fine cutting: wooden sticks are inserted according to the model differences.

evenly populated and connected to the center through a line. This line is trimmed at both the clay bounding box and the sculpture's model geometry. The remainders' lengths define the required carving depth. A mesh of the clay bounding box is then colored at intersection points with these remainders according to their lengths, with red to green zones indicating greater to smaller proximity to the sculpture (Fig. 8). Using the HoloLens, this information is then holographically overlaid on top of the physical clay block, indicating areas where material removal is needed. The edited clay block is then rescanned and its geometry replaces the previous digital model of the clay block, with the script instantly updating its color-coded mesh for streaming to the HoloLens. Upon updating the data, the sculptor can repeat the carving process guided by a new spectrum of color codes again. A built-in warning system automatically informs the sculptor of overcarving, as those areas will be indicated in red (Fig. 9).

Once the overall shape is sufficiently approximated, a second tool guides the finer finishing touches. In detailed areas with only minimal distance between the physical clay surfaces and the digital targeted sculpture, the previously derived trimmed lines with distance information are isolated and displayed on the HoloLens. These lines now precisely and directly operate as guides for the insertion of wooden sticks into the clay mass to identify how deep the remaining carving must go. Once all distances and angles of the physical sticks match the digital measurements, the sculptor removes the sticks, and the holes left behind provide the sculptor the reference needed to carve until their imprint can no longer be seen on the clay surface (Fig. 10).

OBSERVATIONS

Efficiency and Accuracy

The production of our demonstrator combined the effort of four laypeople. Once the digital workflow was specified, the fabrication of the sculpture copy, involving three rounds of rough carving and one of fine carving, took the team around 12 hours. The fidelity of the analog replication of the digital model can be evaluated by comparing the 3D scan of the clay model with the digital model. Our final sculpture was estimated by the system to be largely within the 5 mm accuracy range.

Alternative Measuring Methods to Increase Accuracy

In the process of visualizing the measured distances between scanned object and target object, two coloration methods were tested: relative or absolute value visualization. Absolute distance visualizations used the actual distance between the two objects over the color spectrum

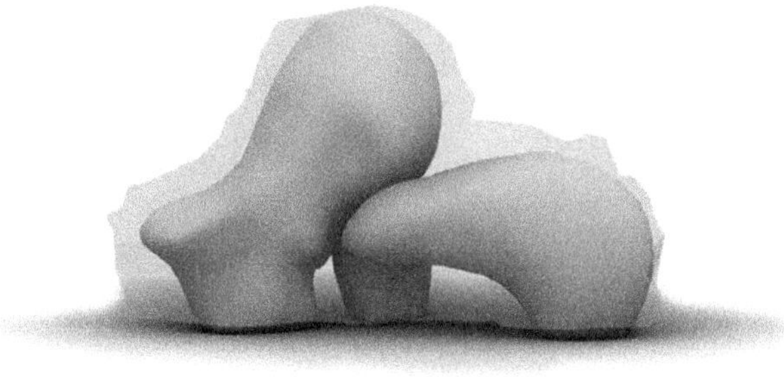

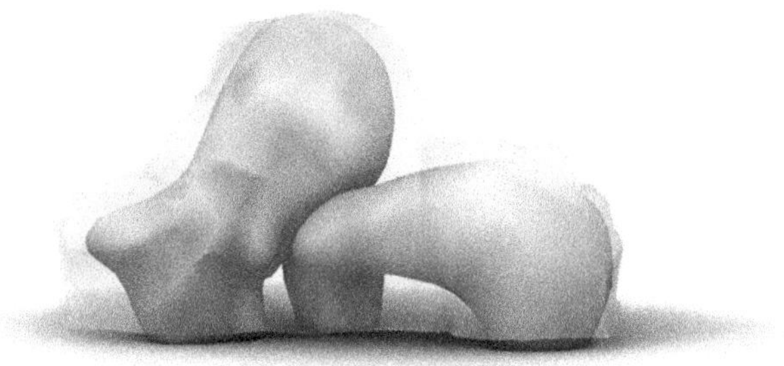

11

11 Absolute (left) versus relative (right) distance value visualization.

and proved to be a great tool early on in round 1 of the process to gauge when larger parts of the massing need to be removed. Relative distance visualization provides color information in relation to the observed range of lengths, and is useful to more clearly identify and highlight the extremities and the finer discrepancy distribution throughout the sculpture (Fig 11).

In round 2, when wooden sticks are inserted in the clay, two ways of measuring distances were also tested. Lines could either be placed between the surfaces of the scanned object and the target object according to the normal vectors of the scanned object surface, or radially from the centroid of the target object. The latter allowed the lines to look more organized and be installed slightly easier, but didn't allow for the capturing of more intricate and detailed surface orientations.

Alternative Photogrammetry Tools

Several 3D-scanning tools and techniques were tested in this research. In addition to using 3D cameras, many open-source 3D scanning software platforms were available online for our use. In this research, we tested the limitations and advantages of three selected 3D-scanning platforms: Meshroom, 3DF Zephyr, and Colmap. All of these work by using snapshots taken from a camera circulating around the material to reconstruct a solid shape through computational triangulation. Meshroom provided the most control options for the final product and gave the most precise results. Comparatively, however, it required relatively long generation times. 3DF Zephyr has fewer options to customize and edit the outcome but was the quickest to produce 3D-scanned objects of acceptable resolution. Therefore, if a high-quality 3D scan of the object is required, like during the final stages of sculpting, Meshroom is recommended. During earlier, more rough carving processes, 3DF Zephyr is recommended as it takes less time and allows for faster iterations.

(Ir)reversibility

We opted to use clay for our demonstrator project, which as a material is highly controllable. Its sculpting method using carving wires, scrapers, and spatulas is relatively flexible, and mistakes are reversible, making it a very suitable first study material. Other materials and techniques, like stone or wood carving, are not as forgiving, and further testing of the workflow in these contexts is needed. For hard or brittle sculpting materials, chiseling techniques should be employed, which can be incorporated in an adaptation of the workflow now that the data feedback system between the virtual and physical model is in place.

DISCUSSION

The study shows how a workflow augmented by AR technology can facilitate and improve end user's effectiveness and agency and allow laypeople to engage with an otherwise prohibitively challenging trade. In doing so, this pragmatic evolution of a manual craft might help increase its competitiveness when pressured by mechanical automation.

As demonstrated by work from peers, applications can easily be diversified to other trades, such as bricklaying (Franco 2019), plywood construction (Jahn, Wit, and Pazzi 2019), steel artwork production (Jahn et al. 2018), bamboo construction (Goepel and Crolla 2020), and many more, indicating that a paradigm shift in manual production has been set in motion. Rather than surrendering human skill to automation in manufacturing, AR enhances human capacities to participate in complex processes through simplified instructions (Goepel 2019).

Bottlenecks for this shift are largely hardware-based. In our example here, the integration in the workflow of accurate real-time environment scanning could remove the necessary tedious step of photogrammetry. These challenges can be presumed to be solved soon, as research by, for example, Microsoft's Mixed Reality Capture Studios is rapidly advancing (Roettgers 2018). Future generations of mixed reality headsets will likely improve their 3D-scanning functionality, allowing processed scanned data to be fed back to the craftspeople synchronously with their manual actions, allowing for even smoother real-time sculpting.

CONCLUSION

This study demonstrates how the fusion of computational design technology and AR visualization technology can bring innovative solutions to a specific analog craft's design and production workflows. User-friendly software and hardware tools have lowered the threshold to a point where end users can practically facilitate and improve their effectiveness and agency. Here, through the aid of holographic instructions, amateur sculptors succeeded in replicating complex sculpture geometry with sufficient accuracy without prior training. These and similar tools facilitate democratizing computational design and fabrication techniques beyond the typical applications in CNC or robotic fabrication. This paradigm shift in manual crafting has the potential to profoundly impact the future of manual trades, often under pressure from automation, suggesting opportunities for substantially widening their practically feasible implementation solution space.

ACKNOWLEDGMENTS

This project was developed by Jacky Chun Hin Fong, Adabelle Long Wun Poon, Wing Sze Ngan, and Chung Hei Ho under the supervision of Garvin Goepel and Dr. Kristof Crolla as part of a computational design course at the Chinese University of Hong Kong (CUHK) School of Architecture.

REFERENCES

AliceVision. 2021. *Meshroom*. V.2021.1.0. AliceVision. PC.

Aromaa, S., A. Väätänen, E. Kaasinen, M. Uimonen, and S. Siltanen. 2018. "Human Factors and Ergonomics Evaluation of a Tablet Based Augmented Reality System in Maintenance Work." In *Mindtrek '18 [Proceedings of the 22nd International Academic Mindtrek Conference]*, Tampere, Finland, 10–11 October *2018*, 118–125. Association for Computing Machinery

Carpo, Mario. 2017. *The Second Digital Turn: Design beyond Intelligence*. Cambridge, MA: MIT Press.

Chi, H.-L., S.-C. Kang, and X. Wang. 2013. "Research Trends and Opportunities of Augmented Reality Applications in Architecture, Engineering, and Construction." *Automation in Construction* 33: 116–122.

Chu, M., J. Matthews, and P. E. D. Love. 2018. "Integrating Mobile Building Information Modelling and Augmented Reality Systems: An Experimental Study." *Automation in Construction* 85: 305–316.

Crolla, Kristof. 2018. "Building Simplexity: The 'more or less' of post-digital architecture practice." PhD diss., RMIT University.

Fologram. 2020. *Fologram*. V.2020.3.23. Fologram Pty Ltd. PC.

Franco, José Tomás. 2019. "This Is How a Complex Brick Wall Is Built Using Augmented Reality." *ArchDaily*, January 25. https://www.archdaily.com/908618/this-is-how-a-complex-brick-wall-is-built-using-augmented-reality.

Goepel, Garvin. 2019. "Augmented Construction: Impact and Opportunity of Mixed Reality Integration in Architectural Design Implementation." In *ACADIA 19: Ubiquity and Autonomy [Proceedings of the 39th Annual Conference of the Association for Computer Aided Design in Architecture (ACADIA)]*, Austin, TX, 21–26 October 2019, edited by K. Bieg, D. Briscoe, and C. Odom, 430–437. CUMINCAD.

Goepel, Garvin, and Kristof Crolla. 2020. "Augmented Reality-Based Collaboration—ARgan, a bamboo art installation case study." In *Anthropocene [Proceedings of the 25th International Conference of the Association for Computer-Aided Architectural Design Research in Asia (CAADRIA)], Bangkok, Thailand, 5–6 August 2020, 313–322. CAADRIA.*

Grayson, Cecil. 1972. *Leon Battista Alberti: On Painting and On Sculpture*. London: Phaidon Press Limited.

Jahn, Gwyllim, Cameron Newnham, Nicholas van den Berg, and Matthew Beanland. 2018. "Making in Mixed Reality: Holographic Design, Fabrication, Assembly and Analysis Of Woven Steel Structures." In *ACADIA 2018: Recalibration: On Imprecision and Infidelity [Proceedings of the 38th Annual Conference of the Association for Computer Aided Design in Architecture (ACADIA)]*, Mexico City, Mexico, 18–20 October 2018, edited by P. Anzalone, M. del Signore, and A. J. Wit, 88–97. CUMINCAD.

Jahn, Gwyllim, Andrew Wit, and James Pazzi. 2019. "[BENT] Holographic Handcraft in Large-Scale Steam-Bent Timber Structures." In *ACADIA 19: Ubiquity and Autonomy [Proceedings of the 39th Annual Conference of the Association for Computer Aided Design in Architecture (ACADIA)]*, Austin, TX, 21–26 October 2019, edited by K. Bieg, D. Briscoe, and C. Odom, 438–447. CUMINCAD.

Kenny, Glenn. 2014. "Tim's Vermeer." Roger Ebert.com, January 31. https://www.rogerebert.com/reviews/tims-vermeer-2013.

Lanteri, Edward. 2018. *Modelling: A Guide for Teachers and Students*. California: Palala Press.

Palagia, Olga. 2006. *Greek Sculpture: Function, Materials, and Techniques in the Archaic and Classical Periods*. Cambridge: Cambridge University Press.

Perkin, Neil. 2018. "The Angel in the Marble." Only Dead Fish (blog), August 24. https://www.onlydeadfish.co.uk/only_dead_fish/2018/08/the-angel-in-the-marble.html.

Ren, J., Y. Liu, and Z. Ruan. 2016. "Architecture in an Age of Augmented Reality: Applications and Practices for Mobile Intelligence BIM-based AR in the Entire Lifecycle." In *International Conference on Electronic Information Technology and Intellectualization 2016*, Guangzhou, China, 18–19 June 2016, 664–665. DEStech Publications.

Roettgers, Janko. 2018. "106 Cameras, Holograms and Sticky Tape: Inside Microsoft's Mixed Reality Capture Studios." *Variety*, April 24. https://variety.com/2018/digital/features/microsoft-mixed-reality-capture-behind-the-scenes-1202784950/.

Wrobel, Arthur. 1987. *Pseudo-Science and Society in 19th-Century America*. Lexington: University Press of Kentucky.

IMAGE CREDITS

Figure 2: © Jörg Bittner Unna, 2008.
Figure 3: © The Washington Post, 2014.
Figures 4–5: © *The Second Digital Turn: Design Beyond Intelligence*, 2017.
Figure 6 (right): © The Nelson-Atkins Museum of Art.

All other drawings and images by the authors.

Chun Hin Jacky Fong is a Master of Architecture graduate from The Chinese University of Hong Kong (CUHK) School of Architecture (SoA). He is the recent president of the Graduation Show 2020 Committee. His master's thesis was nominated to participate in the ARCASIA Thesis of the Year Awards 2020 and explored the relationship between the Cantonese language and architecture through bamboo theaters as traditional spaces for performing arts in Hong Kong. His research in AR technology received the CUHK CAADRIA Student Award 2020—commendation.

Long Wun Adabelle Poon is a CUHK SoA Master of Architecture student. She worked previously on East Kowloon Cultural Centre and its theater spaces as a year-out in a local firm. Prior to her postgraduate study, her collaborative project, Experiential Food Arcadia, was shortlisted in a competition by Unfuse. Her master's thesis explores methods to deal with negative emotions through sensory experiences and body architecture in Hong Kong's urban setting. Her research in AR technology received the CUHK CAADRIA Student Award 2020—commendation.

Wing Sze Ngan is a CUHK SoA Master of Architecture graduate who was nominated by the social science faculty to be the recipient of Lion Dr. Francis K. Pan Scholarship 2019/20. Her master's thesis, selected by the school as one of the best works of the year, explores an open-source design framework that preserves the bottom-up construction technique and spirits of Dai Pai Dong, an important cultural asset of Hong Kong. Her research in AR technology received the CUHK CAADRIA Student Award 2020—commendation.

Chung Hei Ho is a CUHK SoA undergraduate who works in a local Hong Kong architecture firm on projects combining Modular Integrated Construction (MIC) and BIM modeling. His research in AR technology received the CUHK CAADRIA Student Award 2020—commendation.

Garvin Goepel is a PhD researcher at CUHK specializing in augmented reality (AR) implementation in fabrication and design processes. He received his Master of Architecture degree with distinction from die Angewandte Studio Greg Lynn, with his thesis "AUGSTRUCTION." He has taught AR and design workshops at multiple international institutions and gained academic experience by researching at CUHK, with Kristof Crolla, focusing on bending active bamboo grid shells and collaborative holographic fabrication techniques. From spring to summer 2020, he joined the ETH's Block Research Group.

Kristof Crolla PhD is an architect who combines his architectural practice, Laboratory for Explorative Architecture & Design Ltd. (LEAD), with an Associate Professorship at the University of Hong Kong's Departments of Architecture & Civil Engineering. His work on the strategic integration of latest technologies in the architectural design and implementation process has received numerous design, research, and teaching awards and accolades, including the RMIT Vice-Chancellor's Prize for Research Impact—Higher Degree by Research. He is best known for the projects "Golden Moon" and "ZCB Bamboo Pavilion," for which he received the World Architecture Festival Small Project of the Year 2016 award.

Completions

Reuse and Object Representations

Daniel Norell
Chalmers University of Technology, Norell/Rodhe

Einar Rodhe
Konstfack University of Arts, Crafts, and Design; Norell/Rodhe

Karin Hedlund
Chalmers University of Technology

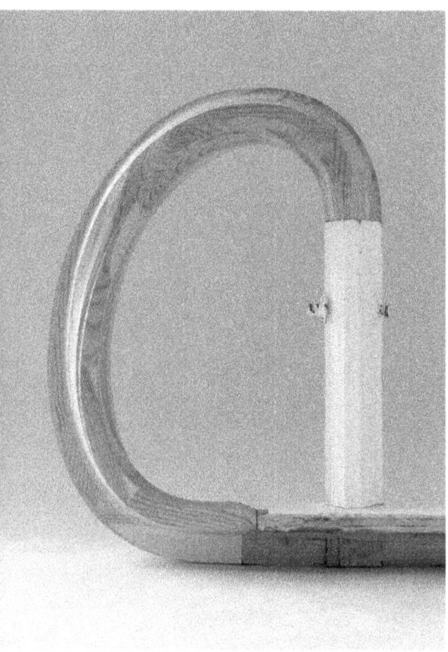

1

1 Completions of salvaged building elements and materials. Window frame (left), door panel (middle), and mantelpiece (right).

ABSTRACT

Reuse of construction and demolition waste tends to be exceptional rather than systemic, despite the fact that such waste exists in excess. One of the challenges in handling used elements and materials is integrating them into a digital workflow through means of survey and representation. Techniques such as 3D scanning and robotic fabrication have been used to target irregular geometries of such extant material. Scanning can be applied to digitally define a unique rather than standard stock of materials or, as in the field of preservation, to transfer specific forms and qualities onto a new stock. This paper melds these two approaches through *Completions*, a project that promotes reuse by integrating salvaged elements and materials into new assemblies. Drawing from the ancient practice of reuse known as *spolia*, the work develops from the identification and documentation of a varied set of used entities that become points of departure for subsequent design and production of new entities. This involves multiple steps, from locating and selecting used elements to scanning and fabrication. Three assemblies based on salvaged objects are produced: a window frame, a door panel, and a mantelpiece. Different means of documentation are outlined in relation to specific qualities of these objects, from photogrammetry to image and mesh-based tracing. Authentic qualities belonging to these elements, such as wear and patina, are coupled with more ambiguous forms and materialities only attainable through digital survey and fabrication. Finally, *Completions* speculates on how more automated workflows might make it feasible to develop extensive virtual catalogs of used objects that designers could interact with remotely.

INTRODUCTION

Construction and demolition waste makes up approximately one-third of all the waste generated in the European Union (EU). According to the EU Waste Framework Directive, member states shall ensure that 70% of all such nonhazardous waste is reused, recycled, or recovered (Directive 2008/98/EC). The aim is to reuse as much as possible, as reuse has an environmental advantage over recycling or recovery. Recently issued guidelines concerning demolition stress the importance of dismantling strategies to enable reuse of, for example, steel, glass, marble, wood, and window frames (European Commission 2016). Valuable elements or materials such as these should be removed before demolition, while usable but less valuable entities might be identified after demolition. Ideally, the process of reuse starts with a waste audit in which elements and materials in an existing building are inventoried. Reuse of elements is preferred over reuse of materials, as elements are of a higher order than materials. A dismantled element that cannot be reused is broken down into its constituent materials. Similarly, reuse is preferred over recycling as recycling involves wasting and reprocessing of materials. Construction waste is in this sense of a lower order, as it often consists of cutoffs and packaging.

Historically, reuse of building elements has been prompted by a scarcity of resources, as the supply of materials was conditioned by means of transport and capabilities of local craft. To reuse simply required less effort than to extract. Today, the world is full of buildings, elements, and materials. Yet reuse is still largely exceptional. One among many factors that currently conditions reuse in architecture and construction is means of representation. Methods for digital survey such as scanning make it possible to integrate an irregular stock of entities into a digital workflow for design and fabrication. Further, such means of representation grant a designer remote access to the often-unique qualities that belong to used elements and materials.

In targeting issues of reuse and representation, this paper brings together methods from two lines of research. First, digital survey and fabrication of nonstandard materials, and second, experimental preservation of artefacts. Through the design project *Completions*, the paper proposes an approach to reuse where building elements and materials are integrated into new assemblies by means of 3D scanning and computer numerically controlled (CNC) fabrication. By surveying and "completing" elements and materials found in a state of disrepair with adjoining parts, the research focuses on two aspects: first, the fidelity as well as the residual effects of scanning as a means of survey, and second, the pairing of used and adjoining elements, including fabrication as well as the transfer of qualities between them. Drawing from the ancient practice of reuse known as *spolia*, the work develops from the identification and documentation of a varied set of objects that later become points of departure for subsequent design and production of new entities.

NONSTANDARD MATERIALS AND REMATERIALIZATION

Standard materials as well as readily available products are typically made available to a designer through online catalogs. The catalog grants remote access to entities in it through images, graphics, and data, and these allow an architect to integrate qualitative as well as quantitative aspects of objects into drawings and models, often including digital models complete with material finishes. Similarly, a building element for reuse must be surveyed and documented before it can be incorporated into a digital workflow. Its dimensions are typically both given and nonstandard, and additionally, its architectural qualities may go beyond what can be captured with conventional digital modeling.

The challenges that pertain to material standards have not gone unnoticed within the realm of digital practice. A large swath of work has focused on overcoming limitations of a standardized stock of materials by using fabrication to produce "nonstandard architectures" from standard materials such as bricks, lumber, or sheet materials. More recently, architects have turned representation and fabrication processes onto extant and nonstandard materials, often with the aim of harvesting and manipulating specific qualities that such material may possess. This entails a larger shift in mindset, from considering materials as an abundant and malleable resource to considering them as a limited and specific set of entities that come with properties and character. Two approaches can be outlined in relation to these recent developments.

One line of inquiry seeks to expand the repertoire of materials and effects available by integrating a unique and often irregular stock of materials into a digital workflow. Greg Lynn's pioneering "Recycled Toy Furniture" used 3D scanning to capture a stock of used plastic toys (Lynn 2009). The scanned toys were assembled by digitally positioning and rotating them in relation to each other so that intersections could be obtained, and fits between entities were accommodated through Boolean operations and robotic carving (Fig. 2). Several recent projects have similarly used structured light scanning or photogrammetry to document entities such as tree branches (Devadass et al. 2016), concrete rubble (Clifford and McGee 2018), or bamboo sticks (MacDonald, Schumann, and Hauptman 2019) for the purpose of fitting them to each other. Such workflows tend to be optimized in relation to a particular logic of fabrication and assembly, based on, for example, nodal joints or masonry logics. While these projects all have advanced the use of scanning in relation to a unique stock of materials, none of them target reuse of building elements or materials.

The scanning process's ability to capture and transfer finer nuances in form, texture, and color is of varying relevance in this type of work. In Lynn's project, scanning is used to mine and expose formal features belonging to the toys. In Brandon Clifford's and Wes McGee's "Cyclopean Cannibalism" masonry wall, on the other hand, scanning is used to define a stock geometry based on concrete rubble into which a new geometry can be fitted. This results in all surfaces of the rubble being carved, thus limiting the visual impact of captured forms on the end result.

Particular techniques for representation can be leveraged against the need for visual and dimensional apprehension and a specific fabrication process. Photogrammetry, the technique used in the research presented here, captures overall geometry as well as texture and color, making it ideal for identifying marks and signs of age. However, the resulting geometry does not come with a set scale, and it tends to be slightly less reliable in its overall measurements compared to laser scanning. Further, specifics of geometry, surface finish, or just the sheer quantity of material might make scanning impractical or too data intensive to use. For planar elements such as sheets, or linear elements such as sticks (MacDonald, Schumann, and Hauptman 2019), photography and edge detection through image processing have instead been used to obtain a two-dimensional outline of an element.

Another line of inquiry involves scanning for rematerialization, or transfer, of forms and qualities from an existing entity onto a new stock. In adaptive reuse, laser scanning is typically used to acquire a model of buildings for the purpose of fitting new elements to unique existing elements through fabrication (Buthke et al. 2020). Recent examples of experimental preservation, such as work in the exhibition *A World of Fragile Parts*, curated by Brendan Cormier (Cormier and Thom 2016), use scanning and fabrication to document and reproduce significant artefacts. Work by David Gissen or Factum Arte complements traditional conservation of such artefacts with the production of replicas. These projects employ techniques and methods that can be used towards representing, mending, or extending used elements and materials. The scanning process's ability to capture and transfer finer nuances of form, texture, and color is essential to this category of work.

While informed by both categories, our work takes a different approach, in which the identification and scanning of a varied set of used elements and materials becomes a point of departure for subsequent design and fabrication of new entities that are combined with the used ones. Our focus has not been on developing a system for a specific type of element or material but rather on developing a workflow that can harvest a multitude of qualities of used entities.

2

3

2 Greg Lynn FORM, Recycled Toy Furniture, 2008.

3 Spolia columns and entablature in Santa Maria in Trastevere, Rome, 1140–1148.

SPOLIA: INCONGRUOUS ASSEMBLIES

The practice of reuse can involve an opportunistic outlook in which used building elements and materials are explored for qualities that may go beyond their intended use. Such "creative" reuse of building elements and materials may not be systemic or institutionalized today, but this has not always been the case. In the late Roman Empire, marked by economic downturn, a practice of reuse emerged that came to be known as *spoliation*. Spolia were building elements sourced from antique buildings in a state of disrepair that were fitted with other parts in the construction of a building on a different site. As Maria Fabricius Hansen (2015) explains, this resulted in a peculiar synthesis of old and new where aesthetic variation was favored over uniformity. Surprising and sometimes incongruous combinations of pieces from different sources were assembled intentionally, and the design and crafting of new pieces were often influenced by the characteristics of the spoliated ones (Fig. 3).

Remarkably, this practice of reuse was state-sanctioned, and legislation suggests that Romans viewed the city as a common material repository, where materials would circulate between buildings. Reuse was regulated based on civic needs with the aim of making the most of material resources and minimizing the need for transportation. According to Joseph Alchermes (1994), The Code of Theodosian (389 AD), for example, protected public buildings from ruination for private purposes. Other laws limited new construction if there was a need to repair old but well-functioning public buildings. When new construction was necessary, the state would often allocate materials for reuse rather than allocate funds. Sourcing of elements and materials within local geographical regions was supported with storage facilities that could house significant structural or decorative elements in transit between buildings (Alchermes 1994).

The technical challenges involved in spoliation included transport and handling, and machinery for lifting and transporting massive blocks of stone had to be invented. The structural integrity of the stone was an issue, but mostly in relation to handling during construction, when fracturing might occur. Spolia is noteworthy in the context of digitally enabled reuse because of the pairing of playful, ad hoc aesthetics with the implementation of systems for sourcing, distributing, and assembling used elements and materials. The inventive combinations of found and new entities promoted through spoliation point to new and untapped opportunities for reuse offered by means of digital survey and production.

STOCK VISITS
Stripping, scavenging, by-products

SURVEY AND POST-PROCESSING
Photogrammetry, photography, flatbed scanning, tracing

DIGITAL MODELING
Repair, adjust, assemble

FABRICATION
CNC-routing, waterjet cutting, etc.

4

5

6

4 Suggested workflow for reuse of building elements and materials.

5 Fragments of window frames at demolition site.

6 Door panel on display at reuse market.

COMPLETIONS

Completions is a response to technical as well as aesthetic issues surrounding contemporary reuse of building elements and materials. While the project promotes a systematic workflow, it challenges a prevailing systems aesthetic in digital practice that relies on repetition of self-similar components. It develops an alternative design position based on the act of repairing, adjusting, and assembling—a formal and material vocabulary that can negotiate fractures, missing parts, patina, misalignment, and abrupt cuts, etc. The three *Completions* pieces described in this section were conceived to reflect this position.

The process of reuse amounts to a workflow (Fig. 4) with an extended engagement with a stock of materials, often beginning with visits to local outlets for used or wasted materials (Figs. 5, 6). Once a stock has been defined, methods for survey and fabrication need to be continuously tuned in relation to varying forms and qualities. The stock establishes an economy of means as well as an element of serendipity that conditions much of the subsequent work.

7

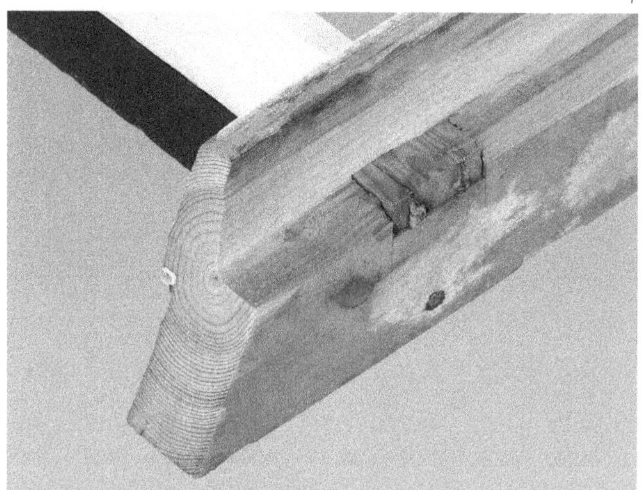

8

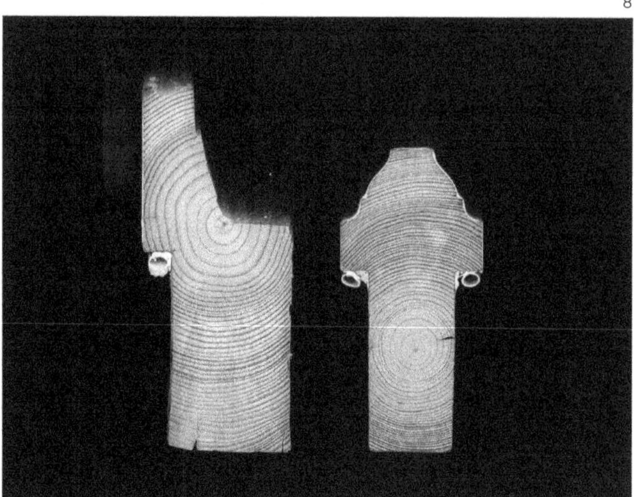

9

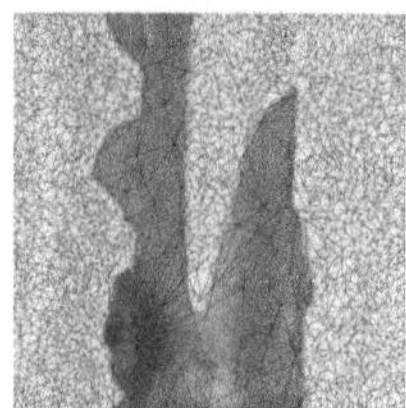

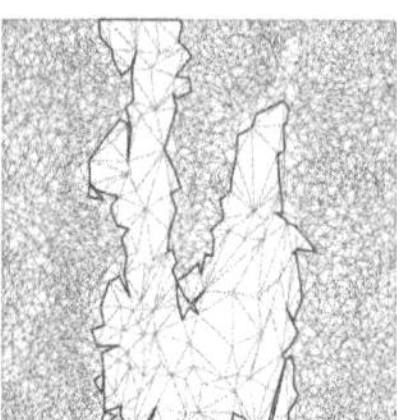

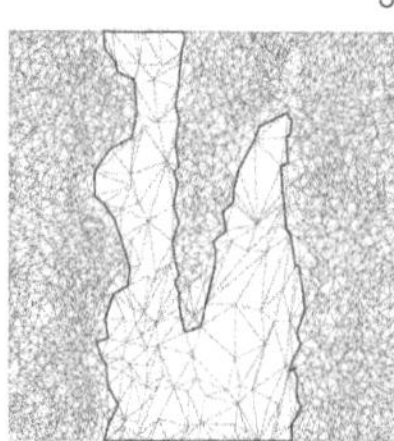

10

7 Photogrammetry scanning process to obtain a closed mesh model. Greenscreen photograph of window frame.

8 Geometry of window frame obtained with photogrammetry (cropped). Closed mesh model with image map.

9 Flatbed scanning of sawn-off ends of window frame for extraction of profile vector drawings.

10 Polygonal face selection methods for tracing of boundaries on door panel: Reduced colored mesh obtained with photogrammetry (left). Selection of faces based on face area (middle). Selection of faces based on color (right).

Stocking Up

Collecting a stock of used or discarded materials and building elements is not trivial, since reuse in the design or building industry is not generally implemented and relies on a variety of independent actors. Generally speaking, three categories of entities can be defined in relation to how construction and demolition waste is handled (European Commission 2016). Each category was considered in the sourcing of material for *Completions*. *Stripping* is the dismantling of more valuable elements and materials before demolition, and such elements may end up for sale in various local outlets. *Scavenging* is the separation of less valuable elements and materials after demolition, and this kind of waste typically goes to recycling stations. *By-products* are leftover materials from manufacturing and construction processes, such as cutoffs and packaging. By-products or elements that are located through scavenging are often damaged and destined for lower-order recycling, recovery, or landfill.

Used objects for completion were located through a series of stock visits to different outlets (Figs. 5, 6). Objects were selected based on qualities such as size (manageability), form (linear, surface, mass), materiality (texture, color, signs of age), and identity (recognizable as a particular material or type of element). One side of a door panel with panel moldings was bought from a reuse market. Part of a wooden window frame was salvaged from a demolition site. A visit to a stone manufacturer gave access to fractured cutoffs from marble sheets. The selected pieces were understood as incomplete fragments rather than as whole objects.

Survey and Postprocessing

Different approaches to documenting each piece were taken depending on the condition it was in, and on its overall geometry, from 3D scanning with photogrammetry to 2D tracing.

For the purposes of scanning, objects were photographed against a green screen and rotated incrementally to achieve

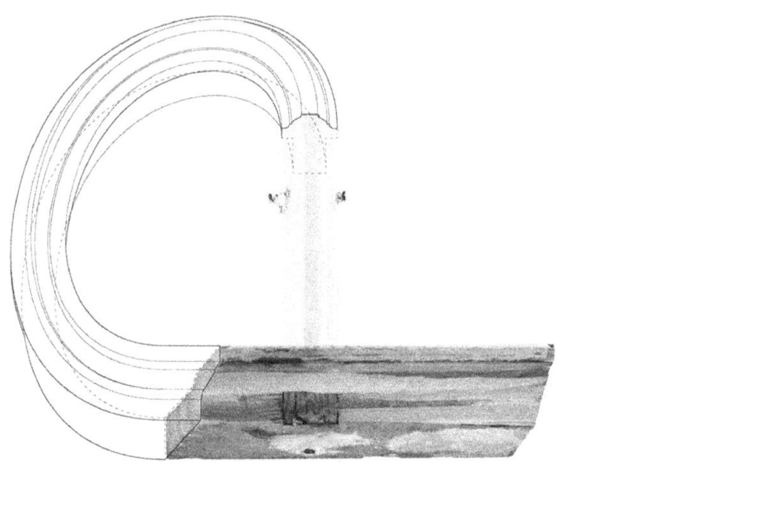

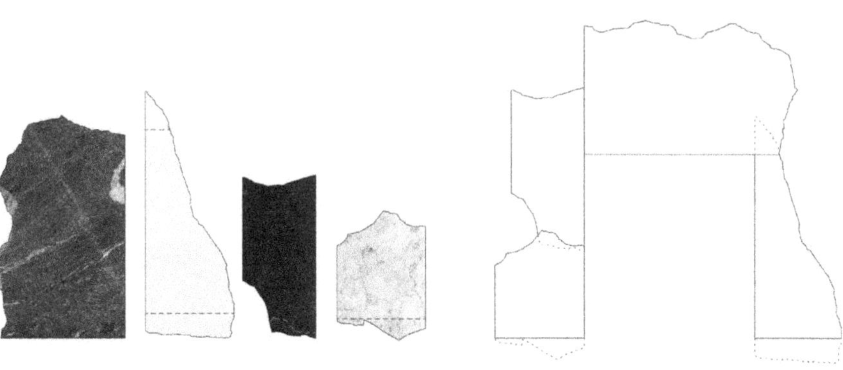

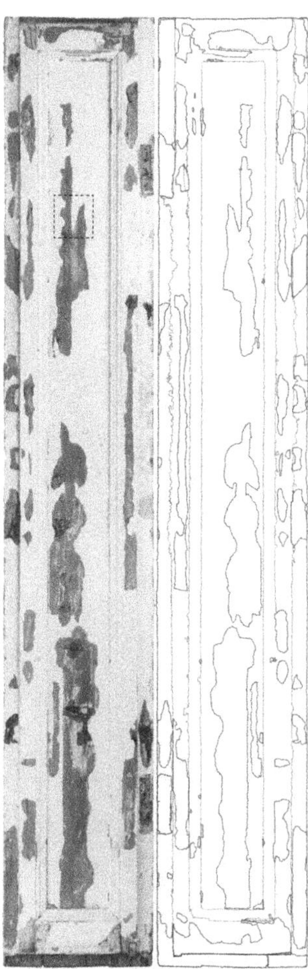

11 Window frame: Isometric of digital model obtained with photogrammetry (top left). Door panel: Elevation of digital model obtained with photogrammetry (right). Marble sheets: Elevation of photographed sheets assembled into mantelpiece, with trimmed parts indicated with dashed lines (bottom left).

a set of images that covered all areas of their surface (Fig. 7). Prior to photogrammetric processing, the green pixels were removed from each image through semi-automatic masking. This method meant that entire objects could be scanned in one session, eliminating the need to combine point clouds that result from scans of different sides of objects (front, back, top, bottom). In addition, it eliminated the typical interference from the background surface that objects are resting on, making it possible to process the point cloud into a closed mesh geometry (Fig. 8).

For some entities, such as the cutoff marble sheets, 3D scanning proved to be cumbersome. While photogrammetry can aptly capture the coarsely textured surface of a fractured edge, the smooth planar surfaces might have problems registering accurately due to glare. In these cases, more appropriate and resource-efficient methods for documentation were considered. Marble sheets were photographed in an elevational view and edges were subsequently extracted as vector drawings with image processing. Similarly, dimensions and profiles of the sawn-off ends of the window frame were obtained using flatbed scanning (Fig. 9).

In other cases, fabrication and finishing processes required that visually distinct regions on surfaces were identified. Dark areas of worn-off paint on the door panel could be separated from the scanned mesh using polygonal face selection methods (Fig. 10). Initial tests using area-based selection of faces in the scanned mesh were abandoned in favor of color-based selection that produced more accurate results. Using these techniques, locally damaged, blemished, or otherwise distinct regions could be identified and taken into consideration in further work.

These ways of representing objects couple visual and dimensional aspects, thereby forming a basis for both design and fabrication. They grant remote access to qualities such as materiality and patina that otherwise tend to elude standard means of architectural representation.

12 Completion of salvaged window frame. CNC-routed solid pine wood.

Modeling and Fabrication

Three pieces were developed based on the window frame, the door panel, and the marble sheets. The design of these pieces was guided by the identity and the state of disrepair that the collected pieces were in. Taking cues from spolia, the completions balanced dutiful mending with add-ons playfully conceived in the manner of an exquisite corpse.

A set of curves derived by connecting edges on two of the window frame's sawn-off ends created a sweeping figure that seamlessly bridged between those ends (Fig. 11). Some of the edges stemmed from the original profile of moldings, while others came from intersections with random fractures where the piece had broken during dismantling. The smooth, interpolated surfaces of the completing piece were both continuous and at odds with the rough materiality of the reclaimed piece (Figs. 1, 12).

The other, missing side of the door panel was added by creating a mirrored replica of the original (Fig. 11). Using the mesh geometry acquired with scanning, a new door panel was fabricated that included worn-off paint and other damages inflicted on the original during its past life. As a residual result of the scanning process, a slight geometrical noise traveled across its smooth white surfaces, making them less crisp and legible than on the original. Because of the symmetry with the completing piece, the status of the spots with worn-off paint seemed to shift, from accidental marks to intentional and ordered articulation (Figs. 1, 13).

The marble sheet cutoffs amounted to a collection of fragments that did not suggest a specific object. By considering straight edges and fractured edges of the sheets, a puzzle of matching edges was created in the form of a mantelpiece (Fig. 11). A few cuts were placed in order to improve the fit between adjacent pieces. Some cuts were straight, while others followed the irregular edge of an existing crack so that a tight fit with a fractured edge of another sheet could be obtained (Figs. 1, 14, 15).

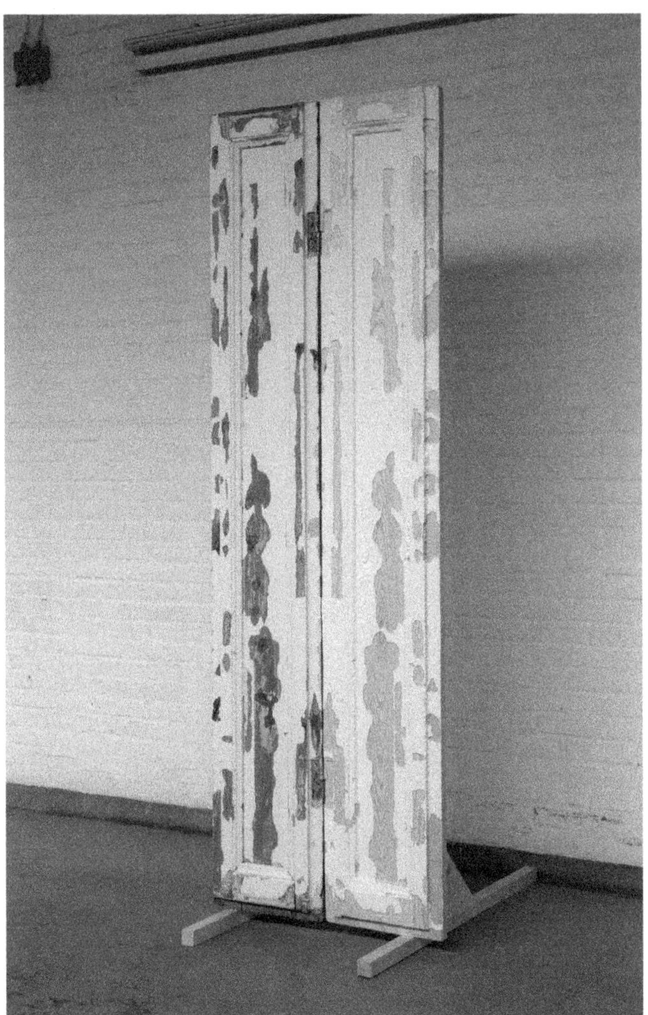

13 Completion of salvaged door panel. CNC-routed solid pine wood.

The process of survey and fabrication made it possible to create seams and formal continuities between and across pieces, and in addition to create new pieces that mimicked the found ones by using the scanned mesh as a basis for fabrication. Materials and fabrication principles were kept consistent within each of the three completed pieces. CNC-routed massive pinewood was used for the window frame and the door panel, and the stone fragments were cut with a waterjet.

By completing it, a used or salvaged object is turned into a new enigmatic entity that seems to be neither wholly repurposed nor newly manufactured. The authentic qualities belonging to these objects, such as materiality, wear, and craft, are paired with more ambiguous forms and materialities only attainable through digital survey and fabrication. The completions playfully adopt the identity or function of a found object while simultaneously suggesting new unexpected possibilities. They depart from a selection of objects but do not end in readymades or as mere agglomerations of such objects.

RESULTS AND DISCUSSION

The results of the *Completions* project form a basis for further research on productive means of representation for integrating extant material into digital workflows.

While *Completions* promotes reuse of building elements, it simultaneously recognizes difficulties associated with such practice. In principle, if an element is reused repeatedly, it will slowly be exhausted to a point where it is reduced to its material. Wear as well as damage inflicted during stripping or demolition will eventually cause deterioration. A completion can make it possible to reuse an element or piece of material that would otherwise go to lower-level recycling, recovery, or landfill. Such a process might require the injection of new material into the stream, but this injection can be weighed against the amount of material that would otherwise have been wasted.

The exactitude and rich materiality of models obtained with scanning can provide an alternative to the "layers of abstraction" that, according to Maarten Gielen of reuse practice Rotor, come with typical CAD drawings (Borasi, Gielen, and Pantazis 2018). The scanning process, unlike the eye of a human conducting a survey, does not discriminate between categories of objects or between what has been intentionally designed and what is circumstantial. It simply captures an object in the state in which it is found, including color and texture. This ability to "see" objects devoid of human preconception resonates with a speculative reuse practice that seeks to go beyond the reduction of waste by mining used objects for their qualities and transferring these qualities into new entities. In addition, scanning can distance an object from its original context and function, thereby opening up alternative possibilities for use and interpretation.

Further research will combine visual qualities acquired with photogrammetry with cross-sectional assessment in order to detect fractures or other defects that could affect structural capacity. Examples of nondestructive assessment methods used today include industrial radiography and ultrasonic testing (mainly for steel constructions) and resistograph inspections (for wood). The virtual model of a salvaged object could be informed by this kind of data in order to simulate its structural capacities.

The research presented here amounts to an approach and a workflow as well as a few design pieces. A systemic application of principles outlined in this paper will require further research regarding the representation and indexing of used entities. Developing more robust workflows for scanning could make it feasible to develop

14 Marble sheet cutoffs assembled into mantelpiece.

15 Detail of fit between fractured edge (white) and edge cut with waterjet (black).

extensive virtual catalogs of used elements that architects could interact with remotely during the design process. In order to be searchable, such catalogs might benefit from the automatic recognition of different types of objects, their features, and constituent materials. Deep learning is currently applied to classify images and video based on architectural elements that they depict (e.g., Kim, Song, and Lee 2019). Overall, these further developments might in turn allow for the design and coordination of larger assemblies where a multitude of elements and materials are combined.

CONCLUSIONS

Completions explores the potential of digital technology for reuse by coupling photogrammetry with fabrication. The aim is twofold: to reduce waste by intercepting existing streams of elements and materials, and to mine such elements for their architectural qualities. The project targets three categories of entities from construction and demolition processes, including elements and materials that result from stripping and scavenging, as well as manufacturing by-products. Methods for representation and fabrication are adopted and fine-tuned in relation to the specific geometries, features, and state of each type of element or material. The work presented is a first test of an approach that brings together methods and thinking from digitally enabled reuse as well as from experimental preservation of artefacts.

Targeting reuse through means of representation can be viewed as an attempt to challenge larger ingrained habits of architectural design. Point clouds, meshes, and image maps obtained with scanning place unique characteristics of objects at the center of the designer's attention. These means of representation assign as much weight to qualities such as materiality, texture, and color as they do to overall form or proportion, properties that architectural representations normally foreground.

ACKNOWLEDGMENTS

This research is funded by the ARQ Foundation, C-ARC at Chalmers University of Technology, and Konstfack University of Arts, Crafts and Design. *Completions* was designed by Daniel Norell and Einar Rodhe, in collaboration with Karin Hedlund. The project was fabricated with the support of workshops at Chalmers and Konstfack. The authors wish to thank the anonymous reviewers for valuable comments.

REFERENCES

Alchermes, Joseph. 1994. "Spolia in Roman Cities of the Late Empire: Legislative Rationales and Architectural Reuse." *Dumbarton Oaks Papers* 48: 167–178.

Borasi, Giovanna, Maarten Gielen, and Konstantinos Pantazis. 2018. "Specifying from a Broader Catalogue." Canadian Centre for Architecture, September 19, 2018. https://www.cca.qc.ca/en/articles/issues/24/into-the-material-world/53665/specifying-from-a-broader-catalogue.

Buthke, Jan, Niels Martin Larsen, Simon Ostenfeld Pedersen, and Charlotte Bundgaard. 2020. "Adaptive Reuse of Architectural Heritage." In *Impact: Design With All Senses, Proceedings of the Design Modelling Symposium* (Berlin 2019), 59–68.

Clifford, Brandon, and Wes McGee. 2018. "Cyclopean Cannibalism: A Method for Recycling Rubble." In *ACADIA 2018: Recalibration: On Imprecision and Infidelity [Proceedings of the 38th Annual Conference of the Association for Computer Aided Design in Architecture (ACADIA)]*, Mexico City, Mexico, 18–20 October 2018, edited by P. Anzalone, M. del Signore, and A. J. Wit, 404–413. CUMINCAD.

Cormier, Brendan, and Danielle Thom, eds. 2016. *A World of Fragile Parts*. London: V&A Publishing.

Devadass, Pradeep, Farid Dailami, Zachary Mollica, and Martin Self. 2016. "Robotic Fabrication of Non-Standard Material." In *ACADIA 2016: Posthuman Frontiers: Data, Designers, and Cognitive Machines [Proceedings of the 36th Annual Conference of the Association for Computer Aided Design in Architecture (ACADIA)]*, Ann Arbor, MI, 27–29 October 2016, edited by K. Velikov, S. Ahlquist, M. del Campo, and G. Thün, 206–213. CUMINCAD.

Directive 2008/98/EC. The European Parliament, Council of the European Union. Article 11.2. https://eur-lex.europa.eu/legal-content/EN/TXT/PDF/?uri=CELEX:32008L0098&from=EN.

European Commission. 2016. EU Construction & Demolition Waste Management Protocol. https://ec.europa.eu/docsroom/documents/20509/attachments/1/translations/en/renditions/native.

Fabricius Hansen, Maria. 2015. *The Spolia Churches of Rome*. Translated by Barbara J. Haveland. Aarhus: Aarhus University Press.

Kim, Jinsung, Jaeyeol Song, and Jin-Kook Lee. 2019. "Approach to Auto-Recognition of Design Elements for the Intelligent Management of Interior Pictures." In *CAADRIA 2019: Intelligent & Informed, Proceedings of the 24th Conference for Computer-Aided Architectural Design Research in Asia* - Volume 2, 785–794.

Lynn, Greg. 2009. "Recycled Toy Furniture." *Architectural Design* 79 (2): 94-95.

MacDonald, Katie, Kyle Schumann, and Jonas Hauptman. 2019. "Digital Fabrication of Standardless Materials." In *ACADIA 19: Ubiquity and Autonomy [Proceedings of the 39th Annual Conference of the Association for Computer Aided Design in Architecture (ACADIA)]*, Austin, TX, 21–26 October 2019, edited by K. Bieg, D. Briscoe, and C. Odom, 266–275. CUMINCAD.

IMAGE CREDITS

Figure 2: © Greg Lynn FORM.
Figure 3: © Camilla Borghese.

All other drawings and images by the authors.

Daniel Norell is Senior Lecturer in architecture at Chalmers University of Technology and cofounder of Norell/Rodhe. His design work and research, often undertaken with Einar Rodhe, focus on reuse, representation, and material agency. Their research has received support from the Swedish Research Council, C-ARC, and Architecture in the Making at Chalmers, the ARQ Foundation, and the Swedish Arts Grants Committee.

Einar Rodhe is an architect and Senior Lecturer in interior architecture and furniture design at Konstfack University of Arts, Crafts and Design, and cofounder of Norell/Rodhe. The work of Norell/Rodhe has been exhibited at Venice Architecture Biennale, Yale University School of Architecture, Oslo Architecture Triennale, and Arkdes, Sweden's National Centre for Architecture and Design.

Karin Hedlund is a member of the research group Chalmers Architecture + Computation, cofounder of hedlund/ekenstam, architect at White Arkitekter and a returning workshop leader at the Architectural Association. Hedlund has received funding from the ARQ Foundation, Barbro Osher Pro Suecia Foundation, Carl Larsson Foundation, and FFNS SWECO Foundation. Her design work and research focus on reuse, representation, robotics, and material agency.

Casting on a Dump

Using Sand as a Form-Generating Formwork

Jiries Alali
California College of the Arts (CCA)

Dr. Negar Kalantar
California College of the Arts (CCA)

Alireza Borhani
California College of the Arts (CCA)

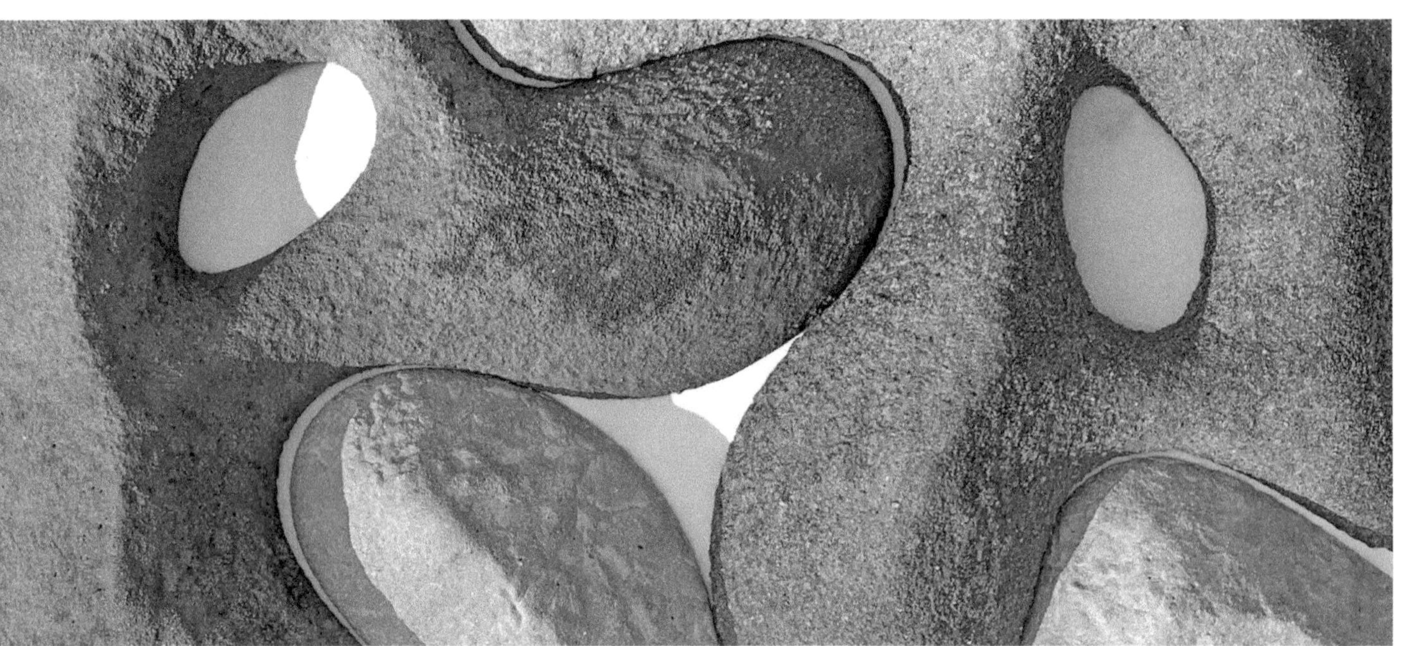

1 Tessellated panels produced with the proposed technique.

ABSTRACT

"Casting on a dump" focuses on finding accessible, low-tech fabrication methodologies that allow for the construction of parametrically designed nonstandard modular cast panels. Such an approach adopts a computational design framework using a single low-tech and low-energy fabrication device to create nonrepetitive volumetric panels cast in situ. The design input for these panels is derived from design preferences and environmental control data. The technique expands upon easy to fabricate and cast methods, targeting less-developed logistical settings worldwide, and thus responding to imminent needs related to climate, available resources, and the economy.

INTRODUCTION

"The future is curved" (Eliasson 2014). Construction techniques for creating freeform architecture are progressing at a relatively slower pace than are the capabilities of computational design tools. The formwork used to create freeform designs with concrete remains problematic, as current construction methods continue to rely on expensive techniques involving costly fabrication technology.

Among the many methods for freeform concrete construction, sand has frequently been highlighted as a zero-waste formwork material, such as in Gericke et al.'s "Fabrication of Concrete Parts Using a Frozen Sand Formwork" (2016) (Fig. 2) and "Procedural Landscapes 2" by Gramazio Kohler Research, ETH Zurich (2011) (Fig. 3). However, this research challenge is addressing the accessibility of a method of construction in underprivileged contexts.

Formerly, architects and designers like Brunelleschi designed not just buildings but also the tools used to construct them (Piano 1998). "Casting on a dump" is proposed as a computational design framework that uses low-tech fabrication tools to construct nonrepetitive volumetric panels cast in situ. This zero-waste fabrication framework generates adaptive forms via a single device and the same material, potentially minimizing the use of cast-in-place materials such as concrete.

Sand's availability, affordability, liquidity, and behavioral predictability make it a promising potential formwork for creating numerous geometric iterations with the same material body. "Casting on a dump" proposes a tool for 3D realization from 2D cutouts that can be achieved with low-skill labor.

METHODS

This research method is inspired by Heinz Isler's freely shaped hill (Chilton 2009) (Fig. 4) and Frei Otto's container of dump test (Vrachliotis et al. 2017). Otto looked at sand dumps as form generators in his form-finding experiments (Fig. 5). And Isler used earth as a formwork material to produce cast-in-situ shelters with a minimum amount of cast materials. The method allows for the application of cast material to sand dump surfaces. The dump's morphology relies on the sand material's property of angle of repose[1] which traces coarse materials' micro-mechanical behavior.

This research was conducted in three main stages. First, experimentation was done with the casting techniques. Second, initial prototyping was conducted to test the feasibility of the fabrication process. Finally, the design computations were completed.

2

3

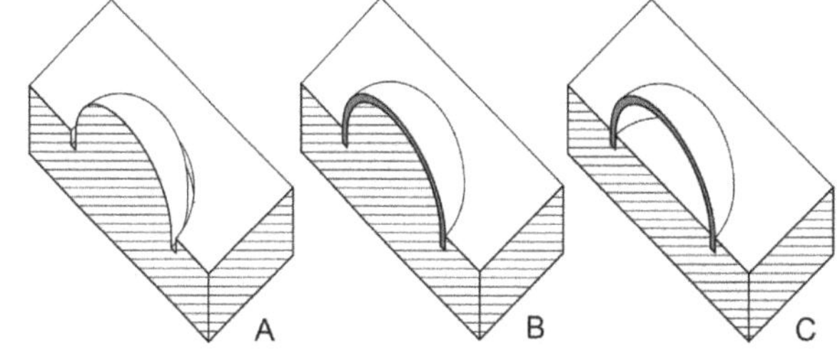

4

5

2 Fabrication of concrete parts using a frozen sand formwork.

3 "Procedural Landscapes 2," Gramazio Kohler Research, ETH Zurich, 2011.

4 Diagram illustrates Isler's freely shaped hill formwork.

5 Experiment based on Frei Otto's container of dump test.

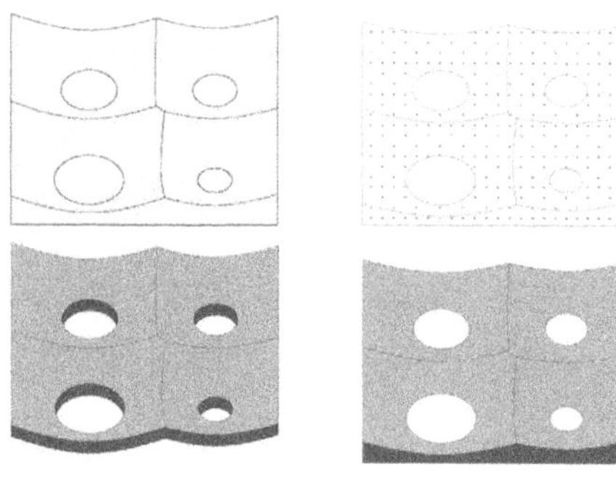

6

7

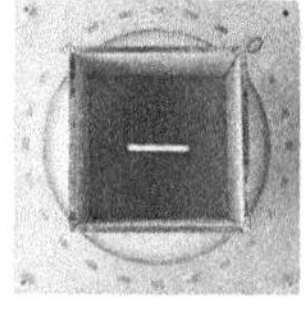

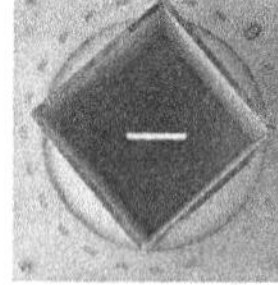

8

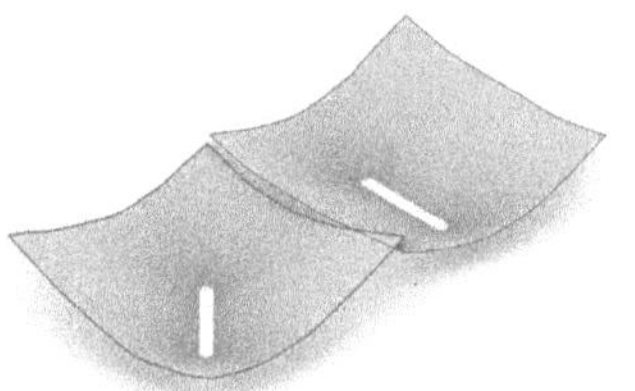

9

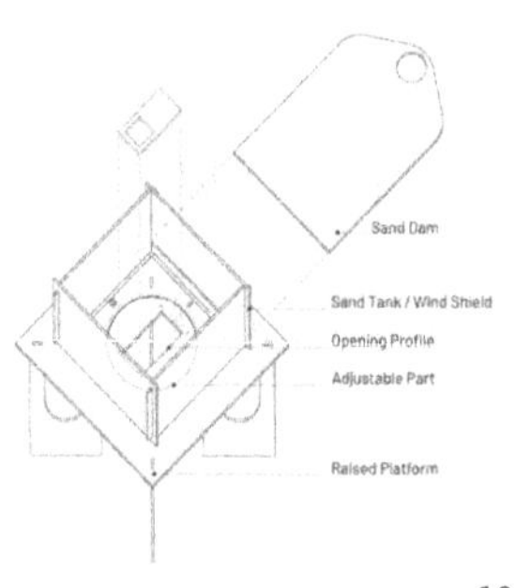

10

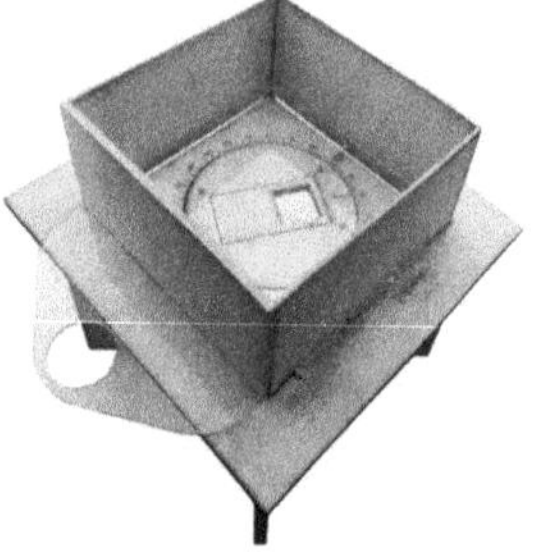

11

6 Diagrams of the first (left) and second (right) casting techniques.

7 Casts of the first (left) and second (right) casting techniques.

8 First prototype formwork device (left) and different shells produced (right).

9 Diagram illustrates the initial prototype of two cast panels with non-matching parabolic profile edges.

10 Illustration for the second prototype components.

11 Second prototype used to provide straight flat-edged casts.

CASTING TECHNIQUES

This research began with identifying a casting technique that would allow for cloning of the dumped sand's surface geometry. In this stage, a wooden box with multiple fixed drains in its base was used for experimentation purposes, with two approaches being the main focus of the investigation. The first approach involved layering concrete gradually over the sand body, preserving its geometry by exerting minimal pressure. The exposed sand surface was stabilized with a water spray. Using water as a temporary binding medium allowed us to reuse the sand for multiple casts. After stabilization, several thin layers of dry concrete mix were added and gradually hydrated. The advantage of this approach was the ability to clone the sand geometry on the two surfaces of the cast panel, using a minimal amount of material.

The second approach explored mixing materials, with the goal of designing the granule material's angle of repose; the cast material was at the same moment the form-generating agent. This advantage of this technique was time efficiency, where the process dumped the material mixture in a draining container in a single step and watered the mix in a second action. The benefits to using this method included increased casting process speed and production of thicker blocks for easier assembly. Although the technique looked promising, it required additional investigation to produce a robust mixture with material science applications (Figs. 6–7).

In this study, the experiments tested prototypes using a gradual layering technique to cast material, where a distinction was retained between the two mediums of sand and cement.

PROTOTYPE DEVELOPMENT

In this fabrication method, sand controlled by an adjustable device served as a form-generating medium, achieving a set of cast panels. These nonstandard panels were then computationally simulated. This approach produced volumetric panels by inputting two-dimensional parameters and relying on the sand's physical properties to find the volumetric panel geometry.

The second stage explored three prototype options: rotational boundary, free edges, and tessellation.

The initial prototype was a raised box with a fixed opening in its base and rotating boundaries, as shown in Figure 8. The rotation changed the positioning of the sand drain cutout in relation to its outer edge.

After positioning, the device was filled to overflowing with sand before draining was initiated. Prior to the casting process, the exposed sand surface was temporarily stabilized with a water spray. While the water worked as a bonding agent between the surface sand grains, the exterior was still too fragile to handle the force of poured wet cement. For this reason, the casting technique was designed to exert minimal pressure on the surface of the sandpile, retaining the overall form and preventing deformation. The products cast using this prototype had multiple parabolic profile edges (Fig. 9).

Learning from the initial prototype findings, the researchers designed a second prototype to further develop discretization. In this device, the sand particles receiving platform edges were freed to keep the panel edges flat, allowing for sealed joinery in the paneling process (Figs. 10–12). Moreover, this offered a slot for replacing the sand drain's opening, which allowed for the production of different geometries using the same device (Fig. 13).

TESSELLATED PANELING

Additional prototypes were tested to produce tessellated paneling; the prototypes demonstrated multiple openings and different movement types. The prototypes demonstrated the accuracy of the edges of the panel, an outcome of raising the material's receiving platform to leave space for gravity to dispose of anything unnecessary (Figs. 14–16).

COMPUTATIONAL APPROACH

The third stage involved a computational design approach using Rhinoceros 3D (McNeel et al. 2019) and Grasshopper 3D (Rutten, 2020). This allowed for visualization of the sand dump's geometry and the design of additional iterations. From two-dimensional outlines to three-dimensional volume, the approach simulated the sand's geometry based mainly on the device's adjustable positioning. Parameters included the base panels' shape, the base cutout's location, and the sand's angle of repose.

The prototype's design took into account the ease of shipping and assembly to ensure the formwork device's ability to reach the construction site for casting in situ. The final prototype elements are shown in Figure 10. An additional computational approach was developed to provide cut sheets of formwork for design customization (Fig. 17).

This research also evaluated the computational approach's precision by using CloudCompare software (Girardeau-Montaut 2020) to compare the digital

12

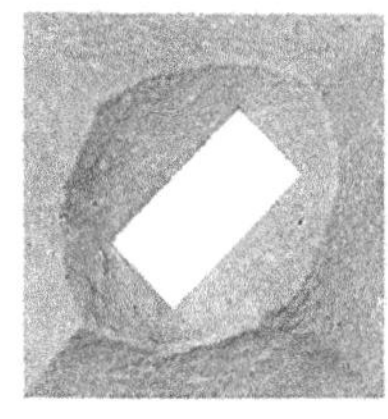
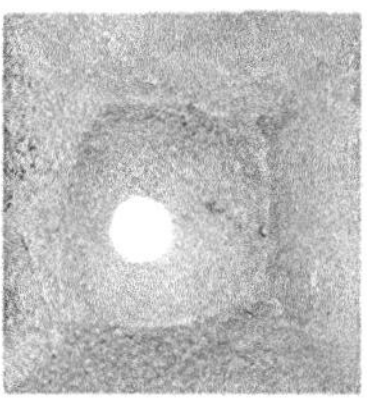

13

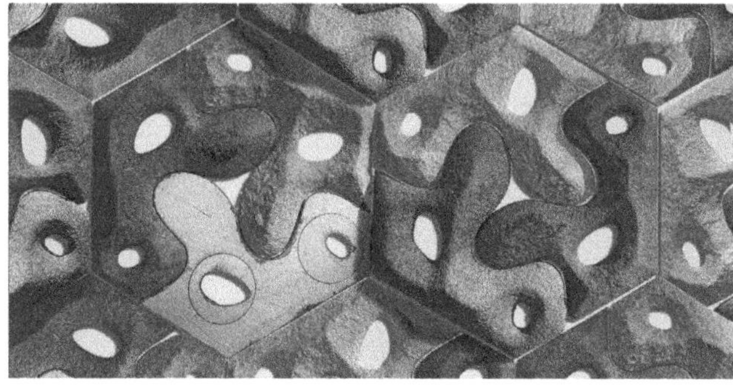

14

15

16

12 Casting process using the second prototype.

13 Three casts produced by using the second prototype.

14 Tessellated panels produced by a prototype with 2 rotational cutouts.

15 Tessellated panels produced by a prototype with axial moving cutout.

16 Escher lizards representation using the proposed technique.

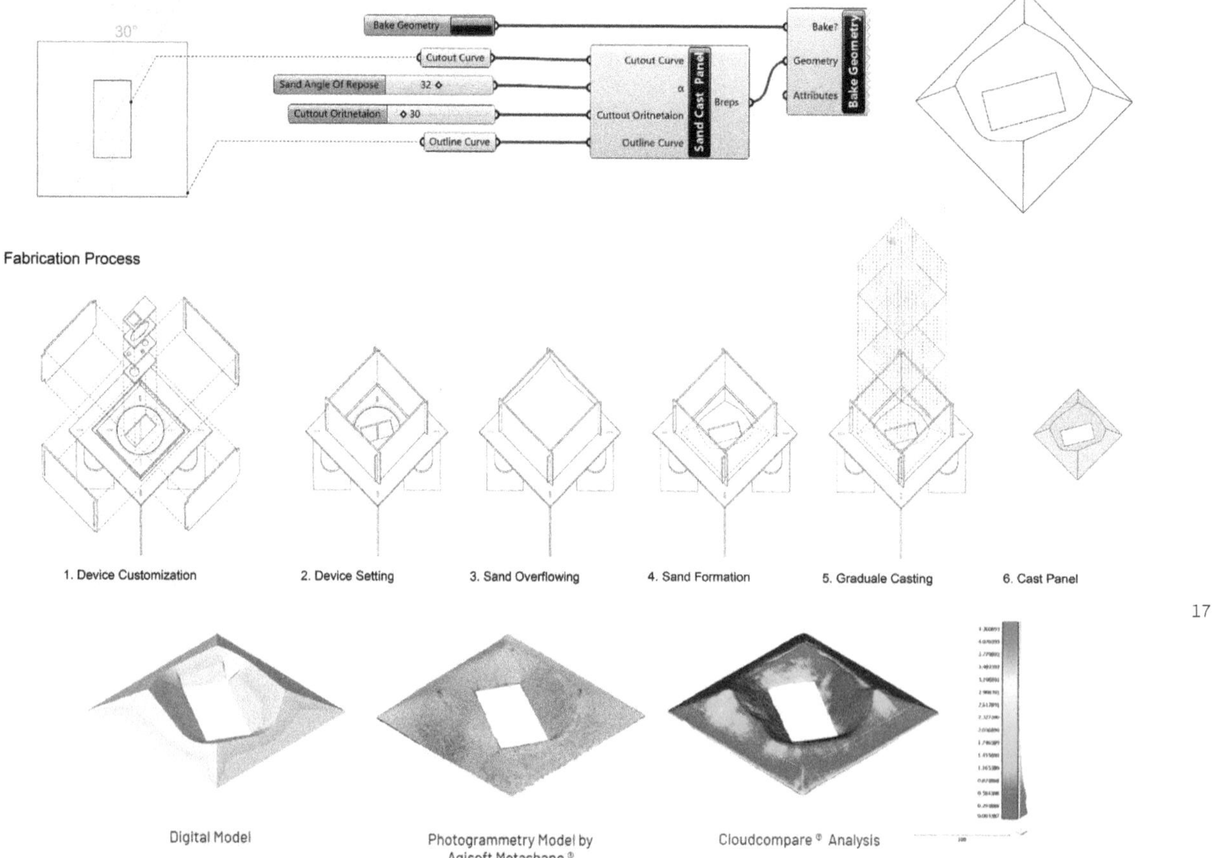

17

18

Rhinoceros 3D model to an Agisoft Metashape photogrammetry scan (Agisoft LLC 2019) of a sand pile in the same position. As shown in the figure, there is minimal deviation between the digital and physical outcomes (Fig. 18).

To assess the structural performance of the cast geometries (the generation of which depended on the angle of repose of the sand), this research used a compression test to roughly evaluate two panels' structural performance. The casting process employed a high-performance anchoring of the cement to make the tested tiles, with an average of 7 mm and 12 mm. While the 7 mm panel broke at 22 PSI, the 12 mm panel broke at 32 PSI, as shown in Figures 19–20.

The process was carried out on a panel of 60 × 60 cm^2. A 19 mm volume of chopped fiberglass was mixed with the dry cement at a 7:100 volume ratio for reinforcement purposes. This prototype introduced several nearby openings that served as corners for mechanical fixation purposes, allowing the panels to be affixed to mass-produced metal plates and dowels on studs, a step towards a more affordable concrete screening system (Figs. 21–22).

RESULTS AND DISCUSSION

This research's findings propose a set of affordable digital and physical tools for designing and executing nonstandard paneling facades with one formwork device. This experiment is a potential avenue for constructing parametrically designed facade systems, where the input parameters include quantitative environmental information such as light. This research's outcomes are twofold: (1) a visual programming design for envisaging complex shell surfaces from different outlines and cutouts, and (2) prototyping devices for panel fabrication. This method offers a high-tech/low-tech process that ensures production consistency because the morphing process depends mainly on gravity.

Adding to the fact that it minimizes the waste of formwork material, the research process provides a time-efficient experimental design tool for generating complex geometries. Also, it allows users with limited design and construction expertise to create customized objects.

Even though this method works with various shapes and sizes of openings, restricting the openings to a fixed size

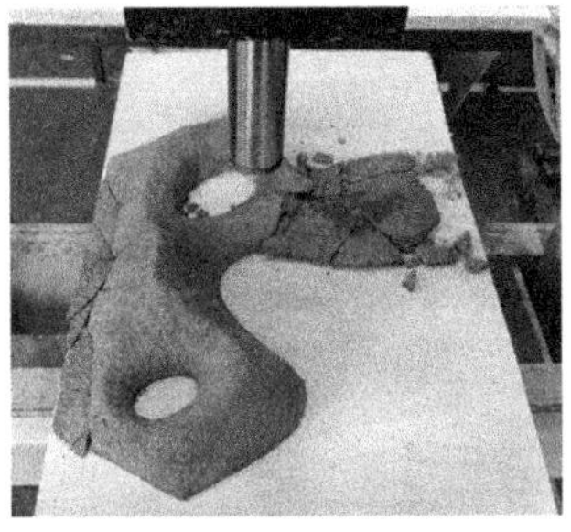

19

20

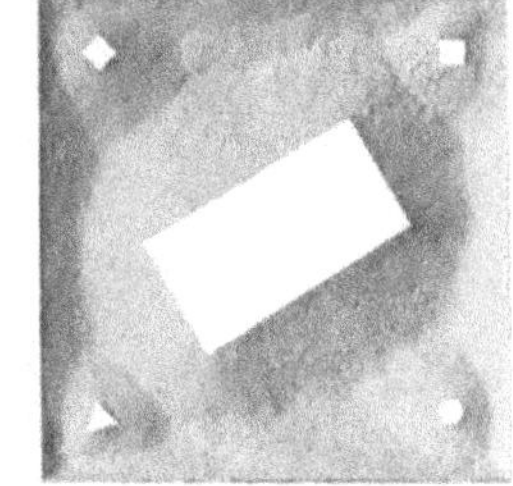

21

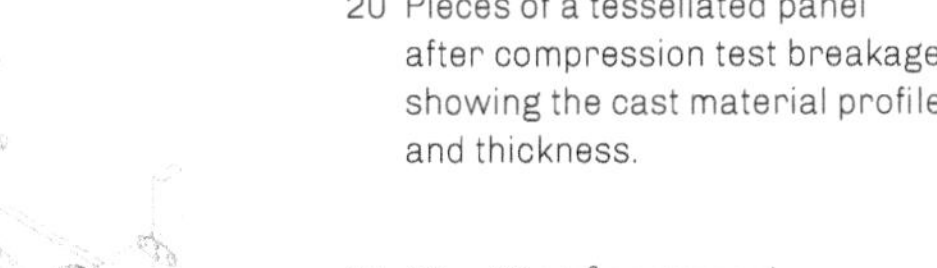

22

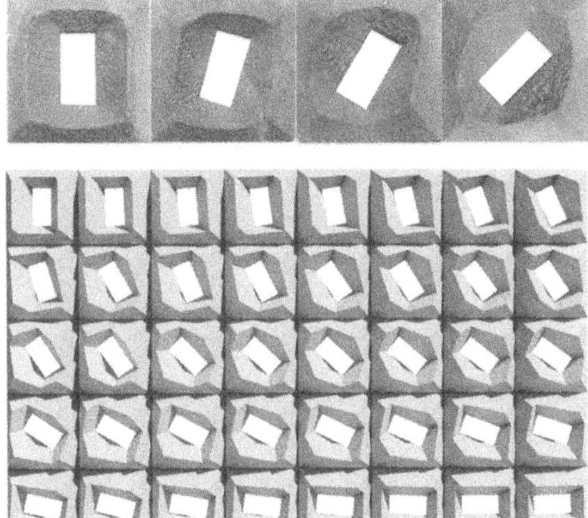

23

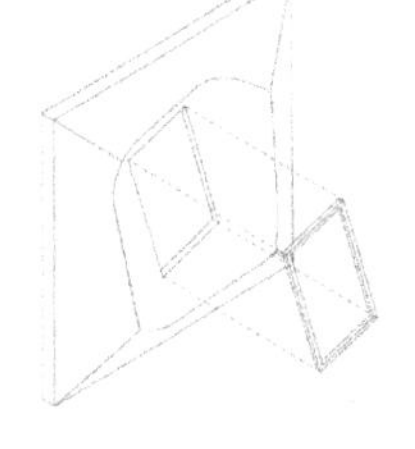

24

17 Computational design approaches and fabrication process.

18 Comparison of the digital Rhino 3D model with photogrammetry of a sand pile in the same position.

19 Compression test for 7 mm panel failed at 22 PSI.

20 Pieces of a tessellated panel after compression test breakage showing the cast material profile and thickness.

21 60 × 60 cm² cast panel.

22 Mechanical fixation proposal.

23 Four panels produced with the second prototype tool (top); rendering of tiles that can be produced with the same device (bottom).

24 Illustration for mass-produced glazing designed for openings in the mass-customized panels.

and arranging them with different orientations allows for the fabrication of parametric design facade panels that can be glazed and mass-produced, keeping the end product economical (Figs. 23–24).

The technique can be used to create a rippled surface by introducing multiple microsize sand drains, creating a surface geometry that enhances the casted panel's structural performance while using a minimal amount of material (Figs. 25–26).

Moreover, the process can be employed to produce feasible architectural elements for environment control by integrating quantitative environmental information such as light and acoustics into the panel design.

LIMITATIONS AND FUTURE DEVELOPMENTS

This research produced an array of tools for fabricating concrete panels, but many challenges were faced. The low-tech process is still time- and labor-intensive. Thus, the study is ongoing. Control of the cast panel's thickness requires further development. The computational portion is limited to simulating the form of the panels, without reflecting structural performance. Additionally, the challenge of creating double-curved surfaces with the given panel rigidity needs to be resolved.

Although this study has shown the potential of sand formwork, there are still many aspects that must be explored in future work. Thus, multiple explorations are presented as suggestions for future research. Scaling up the panel size, patterning, and thickness is a priority because doing so will be useful in proving the fabrication tool's feasibility and optimizing the device for additional parameters such as adapting it to a nonplanar base. Structurally, performance enhancement would be accomplished either by reinforcing the concrete panels with fibers or by experimenting with geometries. On the materials side, developing the concrete mix and testing it with other casting material is essential. Last, introducing automation at different stages and on many levels is a priority.

CONCLUSION

This research describes a threefold fast-track experiment involving materials, computation, and fabrication. Intuitively, the findings of one field shape the others. The findings for

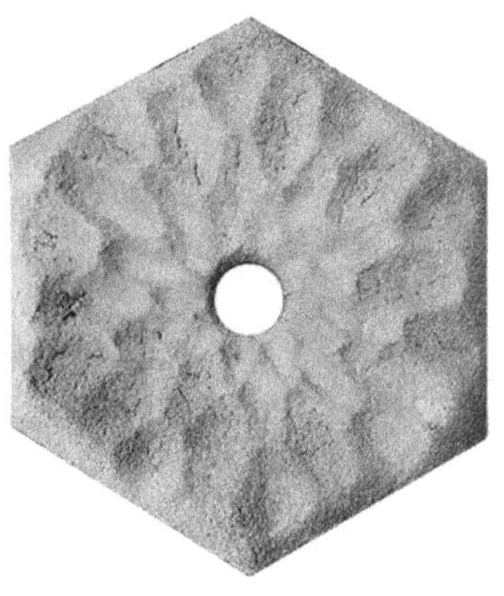

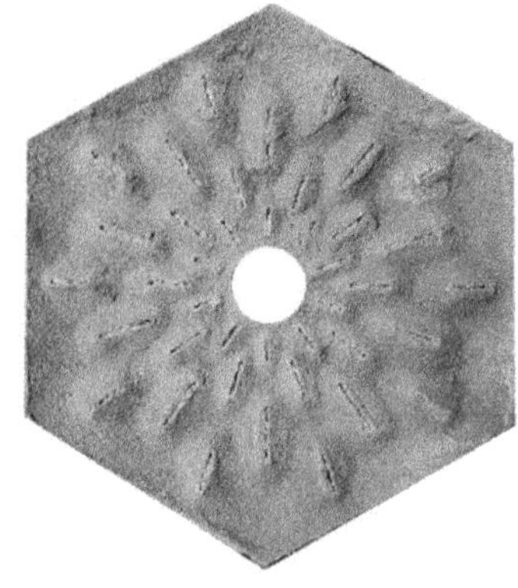

25 Front side of a panel with a rippled surface that enhances structural performance with a minimal amount of material.

26 Back side of a panel with a rippled surface that enhances structural performance with a minimal amount of material.

each were tested through digital simulation and physical prototyping, indicating that the developed system is ready for full-scale upgrading. The ultimate goal is easy fabrication and casting techniques, targeting less-developed settings worldwide and hopefully responding to imminent needs related to climate, available resources, and the economy.

ACKNOWLEDGMENTS

The authors would like to express their gratitude to Autodesk Technology Center in San Francisco. Their Residency Program provided a creative environment, training, technologies, and materials that further pushed this research. Furthermore, the authors extend their thanks to Fulbright Graduate Foreign Exchange Program for sponsoring Jiries's graduate studies and stay in the US.

NOTES

1. Angle of repose refers to the maximum angle at which an object cannot rest on an inclined plane without sliding down.

REFERENCES

Agisoft LLC. 2019. *Agisoft Metashape Standard*. V.1505 build 9097. Windows 64-bit.

Chilton, J. 2009. "39 etc...: Heinz Isler's Infinite Spectrum of New Shapes for Shells." In *Evolution and Trends in Design, Analysis and Construction of Shell and Spatial Structures [Proceedings of the International Association for Shell and Spatial Structures (IASS) Symposium 2009], Valencia, Spain, 28 September–2 October 2009*, edited by Alberto Doming and Carlos Lazaro, 51–62. Universidad Politécnica de Valencia.

Eliasson, Olafur. 2014. "The Future Is Curved." *Architectural Design* 84: 86–93. https://www.doi.org/10.1002/ad.1813.

Gericke, Oliver, Daria Kovaleva, and Werner Sobek. 2016. "Fabrication of Concrete Parts using a Frozen Sand Formwork." In *Proceedings of the IASS Annual Symposium 2016 Spatial Structures in the 21st Century 26–30 September 2016*, edited by K. Kawaguchi, M. Ohsaki, and T. Takeuchi. Tokyo, Japan.

Girardeau-Montaut, Daniel. 2020. *CloudCompare*. V. 2.11.3 (Anoia). Daniel Girardeau-Montaut. Windows 64-bit.

Gramazio Kohler Research, and ETH Zurich. 2011. "Procedural Landscapes 2." Gramazio Kohler Research. Accessed December 6, 2020. https://gramaziokohler.arch.ethz.ch/web/e/lehre/211.html.

McNeel, Robert, at al. 2019. *Rhinoceros 3D*. V.6.0. Robert McNeel & Associates, Seattle, WA. Windows 64-bit.

Piano, Renzo. 1998. "Renzo Piano Acceptance Speech," Transcript of speech delivered at the Pritzker Architecture Prize Ceremony, Washington, DC. June 17, 1998. https://www.pritzkerprize.com/sites/default/files/inline-files/1998_Acceptance_Speech.pdf.

Vrachliotis, Georg, Joachim Kleinmanns, Martin Kunz, Philip Kurz, Irene Meissner, Cornelia Escher, Holger Hanselka, et al. 2017. "Essay." In *Frei Otto: Thinking by Modeling*, 274. Leipzig: Spector Books.

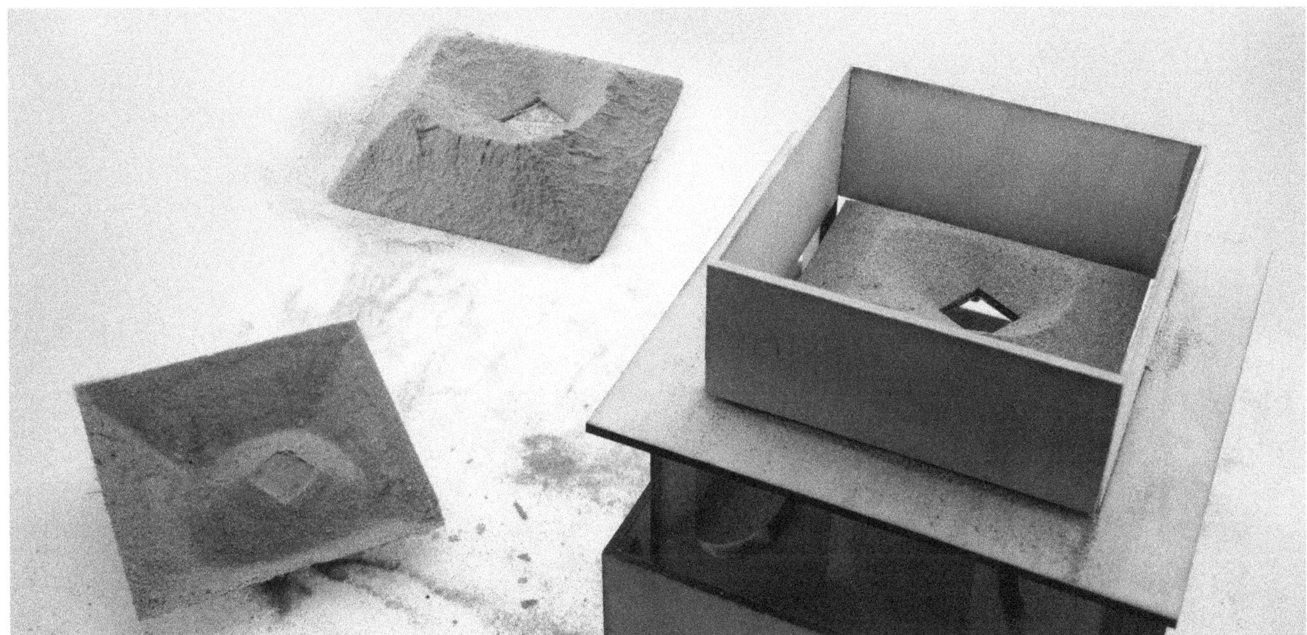

27 Free edges prototype filled with sand with two cast panels.

IMAGE CREDITS

Figure 2: © Gericke, Oliver, Daria Kovaleva, and Werner Sobek, 2016.
Figure 3: © Gramazio Kohler Research, and ETH Zurich, 2011.

All other drawings and images by the authors.

Jiries Alali is a practicing architect experienced in designing buildings with attention to context. During his professional experience, he has worked on a multitude of projects of various scales in vibrant locations of the Middle East and North Africa (MENA) region. Alali is a Fulbright Grantee at California College of the Arts (CCA) in San Francisco, where he finished his master's of advanced architecture design with a focus on design computation and digital fabrication and worked as a research assistant at the Digital Crafts Lab. During his studies, Alali explored low-tech affordable means of fabrication informed by computational design.

Negar Kalantar PhD is an Associate Professor of Architecture and a co-director of the Digital Craft Lab at California College of the Arts (CCA) in San Francisco. Her cross-disciplinary research focuses on materials exploration and robotic and additive manufacturing technologies to engage architecture, science, and engineering as platforms for examining the critical role of design in global issues and built environments. Kalantar is the recipient of several awards and grants, including the Dornfeld Manufacturing Vision Award 2018, the National Science Foundation, Autodesk Technology Center Grant, and X-Grant 2018 from the Texas A&M President's Excellence Fund on developing sustainable material for 3D-printed buildings.

Alireza Borhani is an innovator, architect, educator, and co-principal of the transLAB. His interdisciplinary experience has allowed him to expand his career into a broad scale and type of projects at the intersection of design computation, emerging material systems, additive manufacturing workflows, and robotics. At the forefront of kinematic structures, ranging from architectural-scale shelters to small products, Borhani has been immersed in the world of transformable and adaptive design for the past 20 years. At the California College of the Arts (CCA), Texas A&M, and Virginia Tech, Borhani has taught architecture studio, concurrent with research and practice, for over a decade.

A Case for Lace

Braided Textiles for Architectural Fabrication

Nathaniel Elberfeld*
Massachusetts Institute of Technology, TELTTA

Lavender Tessmer*
Massachusetts Institute of Technology, TELTTA

Alexandra Waller*
Massachusetts Institute of Technology, TELTTA

*Authors contributed equally to the research

1 Detail photograph of *Concrete Tapestry*.

ABSTRACT

Textiles and architecture share a long, intertwined history from the earliest enclosures to contemporary high-tech tensile structures. In the Four Elements of Architecture, Gottfried Semper (2010) posited wickerwork and carpet enclosures to be the essential origins of architectural space. More recently, architectural designers are capitalizing on the characteristics of textiles that are difficult or impossible to reproduce with other material systems: textiles are pliable, scalable, and materially efficient.

As industrial knitting machines join robotic systems in architecture schools with fabrication-forward agendas, much of the recent developments in textile-based projects make use of knitting. In this paper, we propose an alternative textile technique, lacemaking, for architectural fabrication. We present a method for translating traditional lacemaking techniques to an architectural scale and explore its relative advantages over other textiles. In particular, we introduce bobbin lace and describe its steps both in traditional production and at an architectural scale. We use the unique properties of bobbin lace to form workflows for fabrication and computational analysis. An example of computational analysis demonstrates the ability to optimize lace-based designs towards particular labor objectives.

We discuss opportunities for automation and consider the broader implications of understanding a material system relative to the cost of labor to produce designs using it.

INTRODUCTION

Recently, textiles have enjoyed an increasingly prominent role in new directions for architectural fabrication. Designers recognize the unique material characteristics of textiles that are difficult to replicate with any other material system and have integrated textiles into increasingly complex assemblies. Among these characteristics, textiles permit control over material behavior through localized stitch selection (Ahlquist and Menges 2013), support structural integrity through embedded cross-sectional shaping and compositing of multiple layers (Popescu et al. 2018a, 2020), and are expressive through emotional and tactile feedback systems (Davis 2019; Ahlquist 2015).

Much of this recent work uses industrial knitting as the primary method of textile production and demonstrates methods for integrating textiles with architectural tools and workflows such as 3D modeling, simulation, and fabrication. By contrast, our research seeks to demonstrate how techniques from lacemaking, a lesser-used method of textile construction, offers distinct advantages in fabrication workflows with architectural tools.

We have identified three categories in the design and production of architectural textiles in which working with lace is advantageous: (1) fabrication workflow, (2) computational analysis, and (3) strategic material configuration. To support this claim, this paper presents original research in the form of two recent architectural installations that use lace as a primary tectonic as well as multiple investigations into the applications of the lace technique at an architectural scale.

BACKGROUND

A *textile* is a pliable material constructed from a network of intertwining fibers. There are many techniques to form a textile, including *weaving*, *knitting*, *crocheting*, and of interest to this paper, *braiding*. These categories of textile production are characterized by how the fibers interact. Braiding involves twisting two or more threads together. There has been some preliminary research into the computational modeling and fabrication of braided forms (Gmachl and Wingfield 2014; Marks 2017; Zwierzycki et al. 2017).

Lace is a braided textile characterized by its delicate, web-like form. In *bobbin lacemaking* each vertex of a pattern is located before braiding and pinned directly in place during production. Traditional bobbin lace is made in three phases: preparation, working, and finishing (Edkins 2017).

Preparation

Long fibers are first wound from each end onto pairs of handheld spools called bobbins (Fig. 2a). Pattern designs are transferred onto sturdy paper called *prickings*, which are perforated at the locations where pins will be secured into a backing cushion to hold braided threads in place. Bobbins are suspended in pairs from pins in the top of the pricking.

Working

After preparation, the lacemaker proceeds to work the lace by braiding two adjacent pairs of fibers together. There are only two valid operations for this braiding: the *cross* (Fig. 2b) and the *twist* (Fig. 2c). The cross consists of moving the right-hand thread of the left-hand pair over the left-hand thread of the right-hand pair. The twist consists of moving the right-hand threads of each pair over the left-hand threads of its own pair. A slight variation of the twist is occasionally used in which only one of the pairs is twisted (right-twist or left-twist).

During a braiding sequence, the lacemaker might also *pin* (Fig. 2d) between two pairs in order to tension individual fibers without affecting those nearby. The pin may occur in the middle of the braiding sequence (closed pin) or at the end of the sequence (open pin) and is inserted into the pricking pattern through a perforation in the pricking. Some grounds can be worked without pins, while other grounds require pins to secure the braids in place.

After a sequence is completed on four threads, a new set is selected and a sequence is applied. The new set may contain one of the previous pairs, but may also consist of two new pairs depending on the pattern and how the lace is worked. The cycle of selection and braiding continues until the pattern is completed.

Finishing

When a pattern is completed, the fibers are tied off or woven back into the design and the bobbins are cut from them. The pins are removed and the lace is complete.

METHOD

Our research adapts this traditional lacemaking workflow to an architectural scale. In the 3D modeling environment, this includes generating and evaluating patterns and sorting and outputting geometric information such as edges and vertices so it can be physically worked in the correct order. In the physical environment, our process translates the traditional tools of lacemaking, such as bobbins, pricking patterns, and pinning cushions, into larger-scale operations for architectural assembly that can be precisely represented by digital models. In doing so, we circumvent some of the fundamental challenges associated with knitting and weaving.

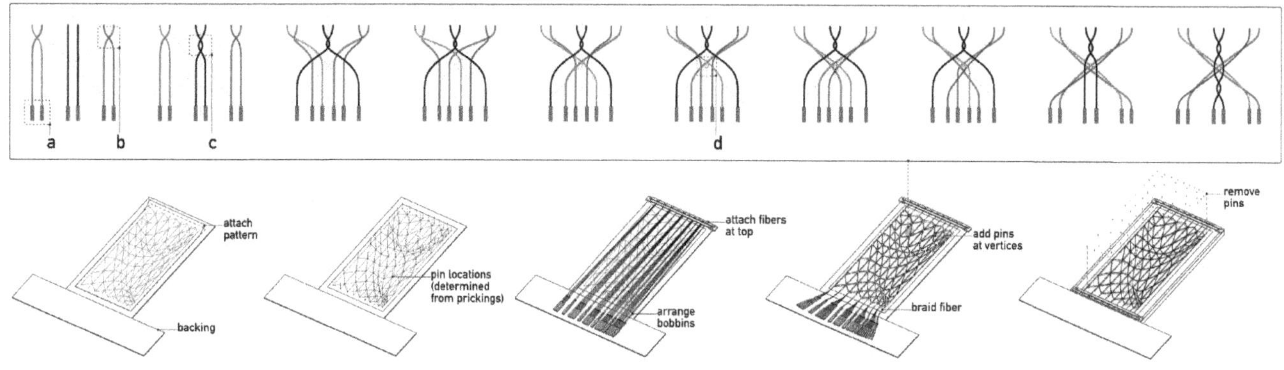

2 Process of forming a lace stitch with bobbins.

Fabrication Workflow

In a computational workflow typical for textile-based architectural fabrication with industrial knitting, geometry is initially modeled as surfaces (e.g., NURBS or mesh patches) and then converted to a stitch mesh subdivision for simulation and form finding (Popescu et al. 2018b). In a separate process, the 3D model must be converted into properly gauged stitch matrices for textile machines in a process analogous to vector-to-raster conversion (McCann et al. 2016; Narayanan et al. 2018). As a result, there can be an extensive process of developing reliable approximations between digital and physical models in architectural workflows (Sabin 2013; Sabin and Pranger 2018).

These challenges originate in a fundamental characteristic of knit and woven textiles: they are composed of aggregations of single stitches, which are individually unit-less and unpredictable, similar to digital pixels. The size of a basic unit of knitting—a single stitch—is difficult to estimate, since it is affected by numerous variables that can affect the length and geometry This results in complex methods necessary to estimate the size of each stitch (Ramgulam 2011). Physical dimensions are manipulated through adding or subtracting individual stitches, or by changing the operation of the machine to adjust the relative size of each individual loop. In the creation of three-dimensional textiles, this process reflects the contrasts between path-based information that exists in 3D models in comparison to two-dimensional rastering of stitches, where path-based shapes must be approximated by whole numbers of pixels (Lourie 1973).

Alternatively, braiding offers a method for physically constructing the textile from its literal representation in the digital modeling interface, which is not subject to the same challenges as knitting or weaving. Lace is directly constructed from a set of edges and vertices, and the digital representation is identical to the physical output and may be described by a mesh. 3D meshes can be used simultaneously for digital processes and physical fabrication without extensive geometric conversion.

Existing research examines a similar relationship between the production of complex form and traditional braiding techniques, showing how current computational tools for textile design are limited by matrix-based stitch control systems. Here, some work has also been done to develop methods of digitally generating braid structures that can cover complex surfaces, showing the possibility for textile production related to three-dimensional form (Győry 2016). In another vein of computational research related to braiding, computer scientists have developed a computational tool for generating geometric variety in braiding patterns, showing that stitch-level pattern control can exist for this textile production method as well (Irvine and Ruskey 2014). Traditional techniques show both complex three-dimensional form as well as spatial control of physical location of individual patterns. In particular, traditional bobbin lace allows intricate construction of detailed imagery along with physical integrity produced through intertwined fibers (Dillmont 1924). The proposed workflow explores braiding—influenced by traditional lacemaking techniques—as a textile production method that has potential for dimensional precision in textile components.

Braiding Workflow for Three-Dimensional Surfaces

Our three-dimensional lace workflow consists of three steps: first, a 3D digital model of a surface is converted to a fiber stitch pattern; second, the vertices from the pattern are output into instructions for a rudimentary "machine"; third, a physical object is constructed by hand using the three-dimensional information generated by the machine instructions.

In the first step, a "braidable" pattern of ordered lines is applied to a 3D surface. There are numerous existing patterns that could be used for this purpose, but the "eight-thread armure" pattern is selected because of the simple fiber intersections at vertices, enabling a first step of integrating the traditional technique with a new process (Fig. 3).

The workflow allows the input of a user-generated three-dimensional surface to which a braiding pattern is applied. There is also a series of user inputs that allow for selection of density and proportion of the textile patterning. The pattern is visualized as a set of continuous strands that are to be physically intertwined during the production process. From these, a set of X, Y, and Z coordinates are located and assigned an order according to the process by which the braiding technique will be applied to each fiber. This information is then separated into coordinates in the X-Y plane, and a set of Z axis positions (Fig. 4).

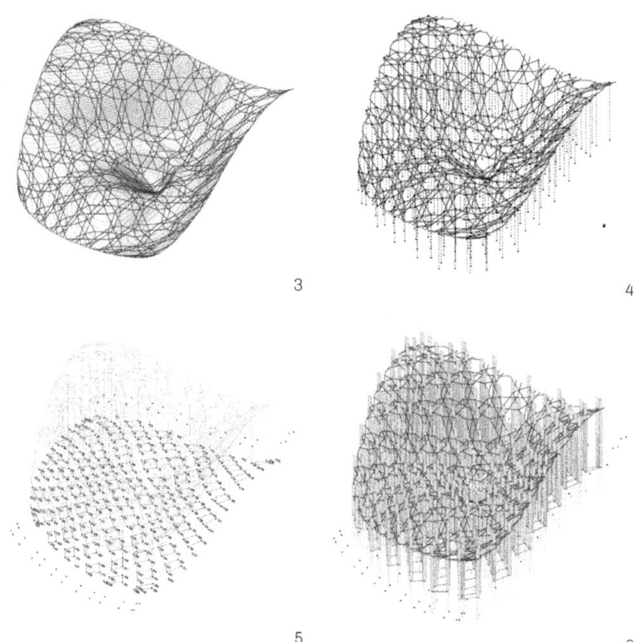

3 Braiding pattern applied to curved surface.

4 Pattern projected to X-Y plane.

5 Ordered set of X-Y vertices for braiding.

6 Z axis pin parts match surface curvature.

The coordinates in the X-Y plane are used to generate a 2D pattern that records both the order and physical location of braided vertices. The sequence of vertices represents the order in which each fiber vertex is physically intersected and fixed in place by its Z axis pin. For the pattern used here, the vertices are constructed in sets of four, which are then organized into rows that are fabricated sequentially (Fig. 5).

In the Z axis, there are two pieces of information that transfer from the digital model to the device for fabrication: first, the height of each vertex is used to determine the location of a hook on each pin; second, the curvature of the input surface is analyzed to generate a selection of hook detail. Depending on the location of the vertex within the curvature of the surface, the hook will either tension the fiber upwards or work to fix it down. The Z axis dimensions, along with the selection of hook detail, are output to fabrication drawings for a set of unique pins that match the height of each vertex location in the braiding pattern (Fig. 6).

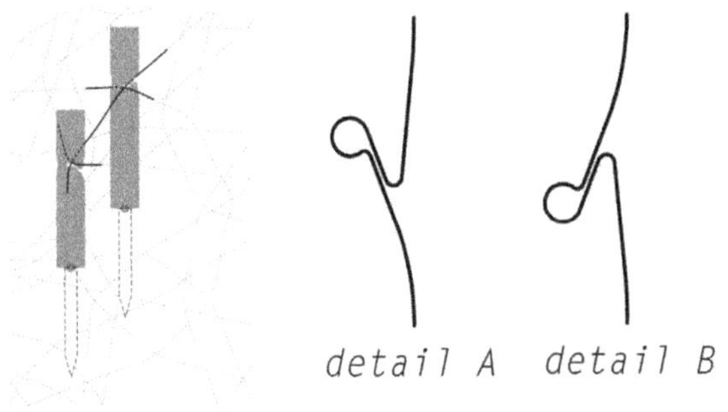

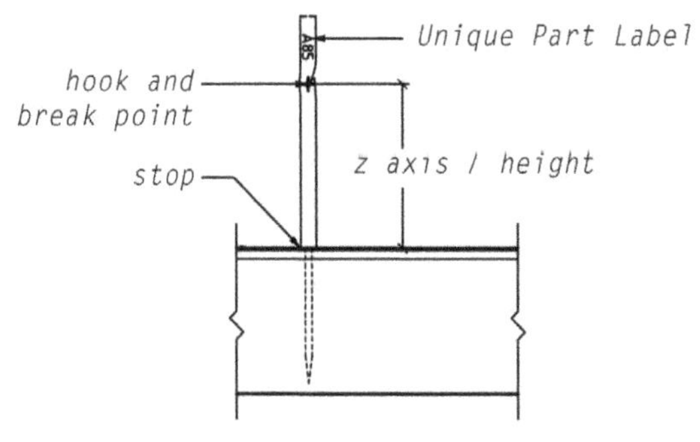

7 Curvature-sensitive pin detail registers Z axis position of lace.

The method of Z axis construction reflects the most significant difference between the proposed method and the traditional method of producing the textile; traditional techniques for producing three-dimensional lace objects typically use a solid three-dimensional form with a generic pin (Fig. 7).

In Figure 8, a series of small-scale studies show that edge-and-vertex patterning of a doubly curved surface can be fabricated as a continuous linear network by braiding fibers. The physical models are constructed from ordered vertices directly outputted from the digital model and that correspond to the assembly of braided fibers.

Translation to Architectural Scale

The project *HEDGE* (Fig. 9) demonstrates that lacemaking for architectural fabrication permits a direct correlation between digital modeling and textile fabrication at a large scale. *HEDGE* is a braided carbon fiber screen adorned with 2,000 pounds of plastic parts that are the repurposed byproducts of a local industrial process. The installation creates a synthetic spatial "vegetation" in the exterior courtyard of the Contemporary Art Museum St. Louis, demonstrating a hybrid of digital and analog craft processes that capitalizes on the efficiency of digital design dexterity of handcrafted work. The plastic parts are suspended by an ultra-light netting of resin-impregnated carbon fiber strands. The technique offers a method for fabricating a high-tensile-strength armature without knots or fasteners. The digitally optimized morphing diagrid responds dimensionally to the site context, desired visual densities, and structural considerations; the pattern is manually traced onto plywood panels and hand-braided using bobbins wound with carbon fiber. Thirty hand-braided panels arranged in two rows covered an area of approximately 38 feet by 10.5 feet and were designed with a parametric model.

Computational Analysis of Embodied Labor and Structural Performance

The flexibility and large design space associated with bobbin lacemaking challenges the designer to balance competing forces: pattern density vs. labor cost, load density vs. structural performance, and the interconnected nature of any such decisions. The precise digital representation of textile vertices permits the application of optimization tools for managing these trade-offs.

Historically, great value has been attributed to lace based on the fact that it is labor intensive, and thus rare and exclusive. Working towards an architectural scale only compounds this problem.

Producing lace involves several labor-intensive steps. At the same time, the geometry of the lace is encoded with information about the labor, or effort, required to produce it. For example, adding additional columns to a lace pattern will require more effort than adding the same amount of rows because it requires more effort to prepare and mount the bobbins needed to produce the extra width whereas extra length is achieved with the same number of bobbins. Even more effort is required to introduce subdivision patterns to the lace, again requiring extra bobbins for the extra threads, but also requiring extra cognitive effort to manage the additional threads as they propagate through the design.

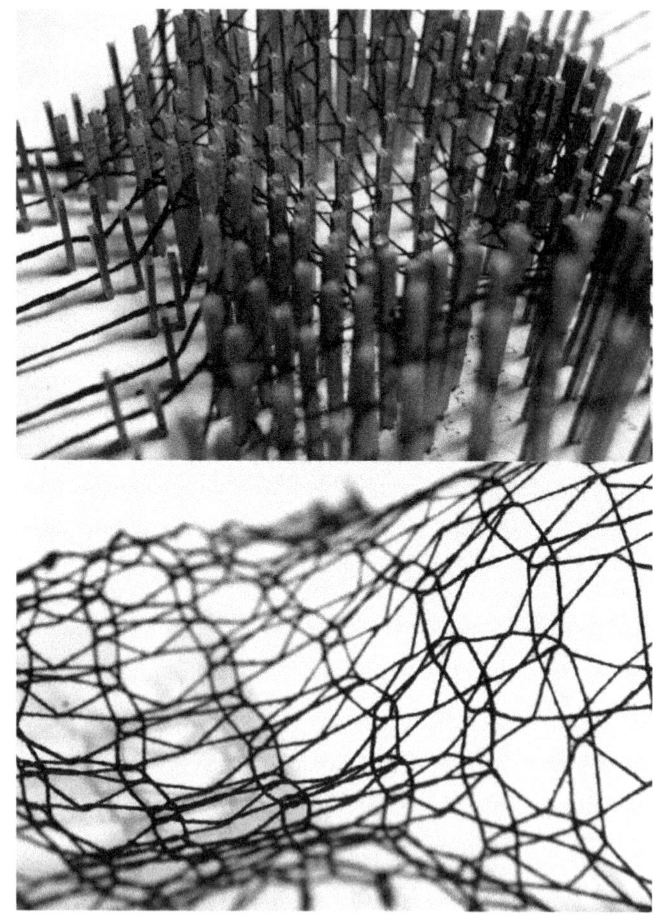

8

8 Small-scale study of fabrication workflow for a doubly curved lace surface.

In a load-bearing application of lace such as *HEDGE*, the trade-off between the effort required to make the lace and its structural performance can be explored. Here, an analytical workflow is presented that optimizes the shape of the lace by reducing the highest contribution to labor—subdivision—only where it will reduce the overall stress in the structure. The specificity in steps to make lace, coupled with a mesh representation, allows designers to optimize labor resources relative to performance criteria.

Computational Model

A computational model needs to consider the following labor-important variables: the number of vertices in the design and the number of bobbins required for pattern. Additional labor includes the embodied cognition of managing the complexity of deploying bobbins and managing them as they move through the pattern. The following equation summarizes the embodied labor of particular design:

$$L=V+B$$

9 *HEDGE* installation in the exterior courtyard of Contemporary Art Museum St. Louis, showing the panel elevation diagram, fabrication armature, and full-scale installation.

where *L* is the total embodied labor, V is the embodied labor contributed from vertices, and B is the embodied labor contributed from bobbins.

If visual variety achieved by varying density of a pattern is the strength of bobbin lacemaking, it is also the challenge for the designer balancing competing forces of labor with visual complexity. Density may be introduced to a pattern by four methods, or any combination thereof:

1. Bunching vertices together
2. Adding rows
3. Adding columns
4. Local subdivisions

Each strategy is associated with a different cost of embodied labor. Topology-preserving translation of vertices adds no extra labor because the vertex count and required amount of bobbins are unchanged. Adding rows only adds vertices, as bobbins are mounted at the top of each column, irrespective of how many rows are in the pattern. Adding columns, however, will increase the vertex count and the required number of bobbins. Finally, local subdivisions add both vertices and bobbins, as extra bobbins are required to be mounted at the top of any column that contains a subdivision. The net changes in required vertex labor (V) and bobbin labor (B) under the above conditions is summarized below:

1. $\Delta V=0;\Delta B=0$
2. $\Delta V>0;\Delta B=0$
3. $\Delta V>0;\Delta B>0$
4. $\Delta V>0;\Delta B>>0$

In structural bobbin lace, as in *HEDGE*, the designer might also introduce applied loads to vertices, treating the lace as a lattice on which to suspend other elements contributing to visual density.

Density in structural bobbin lace is achieved by a variety of methods and in response to a variety of factors. A designer must balance these considerations together in order to make the most of materials and labor. A computational model in the service of structural bobbin lace will address the following questions:

a. How dense is the pattern overall?
b. Where are the vertices located?
c. Is subdivision allowed?
d. What visual effect will adding external loads have?
e. What is the structural effect of the combined density methods?
f. Can these cause-and-effect relationships be visualized to generate a catalogue of design options?

Answering these questions requires the following corresponding parameters, subroutines, and outputs:

a. Row count, Column count;
b. Subroutine for moving vertices without breaking topology;
c. Domain(s) where subdivision is allowed;
d. Subroutine for adding external loads;

e. Subroutine for structural analysis; and
f. Visualization of all criteria

With the designer's questions reformulated or addressed as series of parameters, subroutines, and outputs, a hybrid computational and human workflow model is outlined below:

1. A parametric model in *Grasshopper* will initiate a base line Torchon ground tiling of a rectangular surface in the XZ plane. The density of the initial grid will be controlled by the u and v density of tiling, and corresponding to density methods (2) and (3), the rows and columns of the pattern respectively (Rutten 2018).
2. The designer decides if B, embodied bobbin labor, is sufficiently low (e.g., requiring a quantity of bobbins that is acceptable or available)
3. The designer chooses or generates a grayscale image that corresponds to desired density through method (1), "bunching."
4. The grayscale image locating areas with greater desired density is used with *Kangaroo3D* (Piker 2017) to shorten mesh edges near corresponding values of 0 (black) and to be unaffected by values of 255 (white).
5. The designer chooses or generates a grayscale image that corresponds to the distribution of load and sets an upper and lower limit of allowable point loads.
6. The grayscale image locating load distribution is used with *Karamba3D* (Preisinger 2013) and assigns the upper domain value of allowable loads to vertices with sample values of 0 and the lower domain value to vertices with sample values of 255.
7. The system is modeled with supports at the vertices coincident with the top edge of the initial rectangle from step 1 and load forces pointing down in the z axis.
8. The designer sets allowable domain(s) for subdivision. For example, if the loading image from step 5 contains one contiguous region of load density, the designer may choose to search the full domain. Alternatively, if the loading image contains three separate areas of density, the designer may choose to divide the full domain into three discrete zones for subdivision search.
9. *Goat* (Rechenraum GmbH 2016) searches the domain(s) of allowable subdivision to minimize $\Sigma_i\ |F_i|L_i$, a value proportional to structural weight and an output from *Karamba*'s structural analysis.
10. The final design is visually inspected and analyzed for total number of vertices and total number of bobbins, including those contributed from subdivision, and entered into a design catalogue for comparison.

From the outline above, the manual inputs and computational optimization variables and objective may be summarized as follows:

Inputs:

Number of rows
Number of columns
Image describing bunching of vertices
Image describing loading of vertices
Number of discrete, contiguous domain(s) for subdivision

Variables:

X_1^n: Lower boundary in domain *n*
X_2^n: Upper boundary in domain *n*

Objective:

Minimize $\Sigma_i\ |F_i|L_i$

Figure 10 shows the workflow described in steps 1–10 above.

The method described here does not use optimization algorithms to minimize V or B directly, but rather uses structural analysis to generate subdivisions, with the highest contribution of embodied labor, only where it is structurally effective given the designer inputs. This solution gives the density methods with lower embodied labor priority in configuring the final output. The designer can produce a catalogue of results and decide which will best be suited for production.

A small catalogue of designs was created to test the efficacy of the method described above. The row count and column count was kept constant at 20 and 25, respectively, and a bank of grayscale images was created and used for the image sampling routines (Fig. 3). A selection from the catalogue is shown in Figure 12.

Strategic Material Configuration

Lace permits a wide spectrum of material characteristics. Other textiles almost exclusively act as membranes in tension (à la Frei Otto) rather than finite elements in either tension or compression. While similar polygonal shapes can be cut by CNC, there are two undesirable costs to that method: (1) material waste between the linear elements and (2) inaccessible high-performance composite material palettes.

In the project *Concrete Tapestry* (Figs. 1, 13), we applied a coating of concrete to four large, laced panels approximately 3' x 7' that were similarly prepared as in *HEDGE*, but introduced localized subdivisions within the lace to give greater density, and structural integrity, in the self-supporting panels.

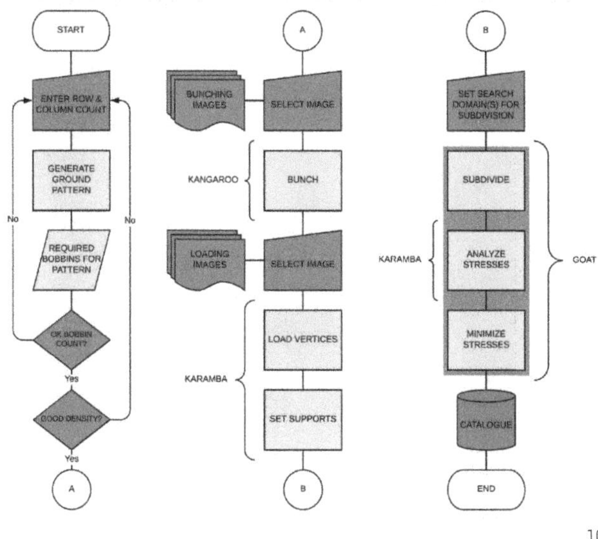

10

Smile | Abstract 1 | Abstract 2

Columns | Center Dot | Left Dot

Dot Dot Dot | Right Dot | Triple Dot

11

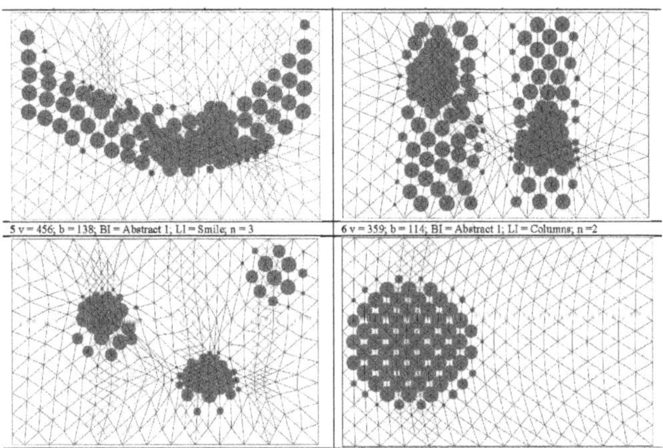

5 v = 456; b = 138; BI = Abstract 1; LI = Smile; n = 3
6 v = 359; b = 114; BI = Abstract 1; LI = Columns; n =2

12

10 Flowchart showing a *Grasshopper* workflow with human interaction (red) and computational processes (blue) to iteratively minimize labor (purple).

11 Selection of images controlling lace bunching and load density in optimization routine.

12 Selected designs from the optimization. Note that subdivision, the most labor-intensive process, only occurs near the applied loads.

At various stages in the fabrication process, the lace pattern enables the panels to perform in various roles: in tension during the braiding, coating, and curing stages, and predominantly in compression while cured and displayed.

DISCUSSION

We have shown that lace has certain advantageous properties when using textiles at an architectural scale. While not intended to replace applications where high-density or sheet-like textiles are preferred, and for which it would be hard to justify the labor-intensive process of making lace relative to established industrial processes, specific cases where there is a desire for large cellular spacing or linear networks of varying density support the choice of lace within the field of architectural textiles.

This body of work can be understood as the foundation for multiple modes of exploration. Now that we have identified the manual tools and computational steps for producing architectural lace, we can move towards automating parts of this process such as placing the pins in precise and customizable locations. This trajectory can lead to systems capable of generating machine instructions for textile and nontextile parts from the same 3D model using the same coordinate information. Ultimately, this body of research could develop towards applications in mainstream construction in which quality, consistency, and economy are prerequisites for widespread adoption.

Another way to continue this work is to focus on extending the methodologies of labor optimization to other material systems and to further develop a computational understanding of design criteria relative to labor consequences. Lace has provided an opportunity to study this interplay of constraints because the required labor to make it is directly related to its form and process of making. However, this line of thinking can extend to other methods of designing and making.

ACKNOWLEDGMENTS

The authors would like to acknowledge the cognitive and physical labor of the faculty and students that supported the projects presented here:

HEDGE
DESIGN: Jason Butz, Lavender Tessmer, Nathaniel Elberfeld
PROJECT TEAM: Evan Bobrow, Marija Draškić, Yuchen Song, Michael Zhou
FABRICATION ASSISTANTS: Sam Bell-Hart, Finnegan Roy-Nyline, Greg Smolkovich
WITH SUPPORT FROM: PolyOne

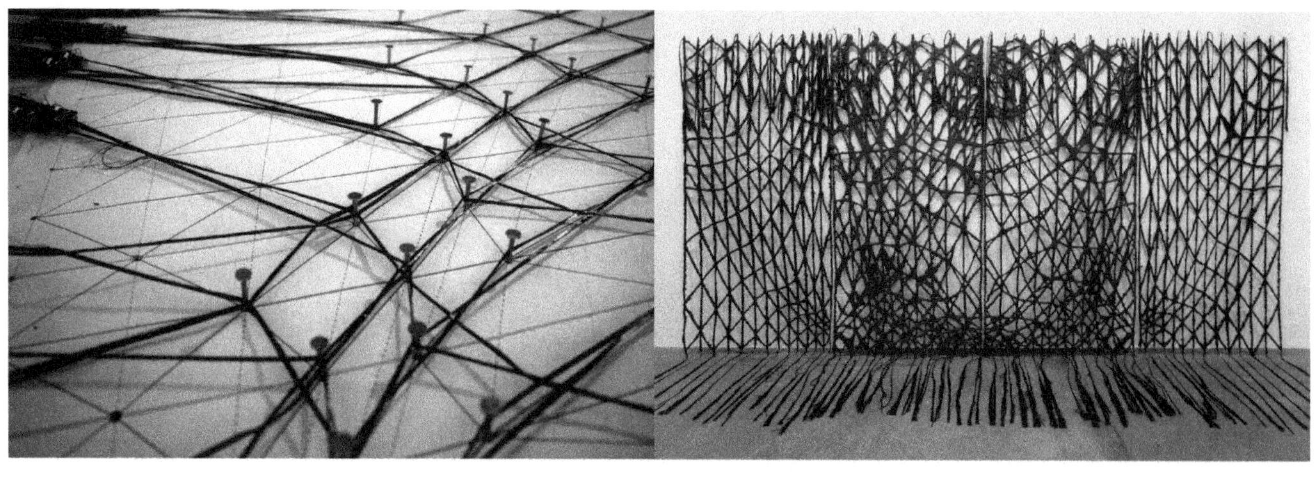

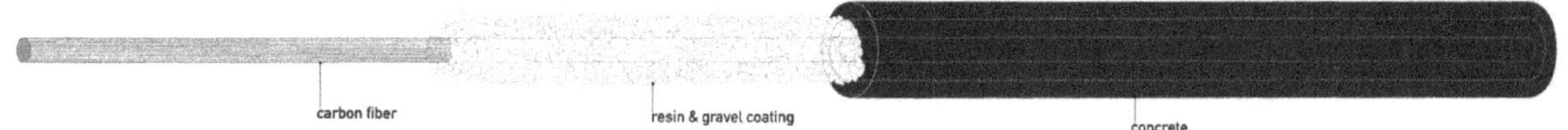

13

13 Fabrication process, coatings diagram, and final installation of *Concrete Tapestry*.

Concrete Tapestry
DESIGN: Lavender Tessmer, Nathaniel Elberfeld, Alexandra Waller
FABRICATION ASSISTANT: Sam Bell-Hart
WITH SUPPORT FROM: Regional Arts Commission of St. Louis

Faculty and teaching assistants at the Massachusetts Institute of Technology who advised our bobbin lace research:
Caitlin Mueller, Pierre Cuvilliers, and Skylar Tibbits.

REFERENCES

Ahlquist, Sean. 2015. "Social Sensory Architectures: Articulating Textile Hybrid Structures for Multi-Sensory Responsiveness and Collaborative Play." In *ACADIA 2015: Computational Ecologies: Design in the Anthropocene [Proceedings of the 35th Annual Conference of the Association for Computer Aided Design in Architecture (ACADIA)]*, Cincinnati, OH, 19–25 October 2015, edited by L. Combs and C. Perry, 263–273. CUMINCAD.

Ahlquist, Sean, and Achim Menges. 2013. "Frameworks for Computational Design of Textile Micro-Architectures and Material Behavior in Forming Complex Force-Active Structures." In *ACADIA 13: Adaptive Architecture [Proceedings of the 33rd Annual Conference of the Association for Computer Aided Design in Architecture (ACADIA)]*, Cambridge, ON, Canada, 24–26 October 2013, edited by P. Beesley, O. Khan, and M. Stacey, 281–292. CUMINCAD.

Davis, Felecia. 2019. "FELT: Communicating Emotion Through Textile Expression." *Technology|Architecture + Design 3* (2): 146–149.

Dillmont, Thérèse de. 1924. *Encyclopedia of Needlework* (*Encyclopédie Des Ouvrages Des Dames*). Mulhouse, Alsace: Th. De Dillmont.

Edkins, Jo. 2017. "Jo Edkins' Bobbin Lace School." https://www.theedkins.co.uk/jo/lace/.

Gmachl, Mathias, and Rachel Wingfield. 2014. "Loop.PH." Kensington Archilace. January 16, 2014. http://loop.ph/portfolio/kensington-archilace.

Győry, Georges. 2016. "Modelling Complex Non-Rectilinear Textile Structures." *International Journal of Humanities & Arts Computing: A Journal of Digital Humanities* 10 (2): 145–178.

Irvine, Veronika, and Frank Ruskey. 2014. "Developing a Mathematical Model for Bobbin Lace." *Journal of Mathematics & the Arts* 8 (3/4): 95–110.

Kyosev, Yordan. 2019. "Topology Based Models of Tubular and Flat Braided Structures." In *Topology-Based Modeling of Textile Structures and Their Joint Assemblies: Principles, Algorithms and Limitations*, edited by Yordan Kyosev, 13–35. Cham: Springer International Publishing.

Lourie, Janice R. 1973. *Textile Graphics/Computer Aided*. Fairchild Publications.

Marks, Lisa. 2017. "Parametric Craft Techniques: Design Methodology for Building on Embodied Cultural Knowledge." Unpublished manuscript, August 17, typescript.

McCann, James, Lea Albaugh, Vidya Narayanan, April Grow, Wojciech Matusik, Jen Mankoff, and Jessica Hodgins. 2016. "A Compiler for 3D Machine Knitting." *ACM Transactions on Graphics* 35 (4): 1–11.

Narayanan, Vidya, Lea Albaugh, Jessica Hodgins, Stelian Coros, and James McCann. 2018. "Automatic Machine Knitting of 3D Meshes." ACM *Transactions on Graphics* 37 (3): 35:1–35:15.

Piker, Daniel. 2017. *Kangaroo Physics*. V.2.42. https://www.food4rhino.com/en/app/kangaroo-physics.

Popescu, M., L. Reiter, A. Liew, T. Van Mele, R.J. Flatt, and P. Block. 2018a. "Building in Concrete with an Ultra-Lightweight Knitted Stay-in-Place Formwork: Prototype of a Concrete Shell Bridge." *Structures* 14 (June): 322–332.

Popescu, Mariana, Matthias Rippmann, Tom Van Mele, and Philippe Block. 2018b. "Automated Generation of Knit Patterns for Non-Developable Surfaces." In *Humanizing Digital Reality*, edited by Klaas De Rycke, Christoph Gengnagel, Olivier Baverel, Jane Burry, Caitlin Mueller, Minh Man Nguyen, Philippe Rahm, and Mette Ramsgaard Thomsen, 271–284. Singapore: Springer Singapore.

Popescu, Mariana, Matthias Rippmann, Andrew Liew, Lex Reiter, Robert J. Flatt, Tom Van Mele, and Philippe Block. 2020. "Structural Design, Digital Fabrication and Construction of the Cable-Net and Knitted Formwork of the KnitCandela Concrete Shell." *Structures* 31 (June): 1287–1299. https://doi.org/10.1016/j.istruc.2020.02.013

Preisinger, C. 2013. "Linking Structure and Parametric Geometry," *Architectural Design* 83: 110-113. doi: 10.1002/ad.1564.

Ramgulam, R.B. 2011. "Modelling of Knitting." In *Advances in Knitting Technology*, edited by K.F. Au, 48–85. Cambridge, England: Woodhead Publishing.

Rechenraum GmbH. 2016. *Goat.* V.3.0. Rechenraum GmbH. https://www.rechenraum.com/en/goat.html.

Rutten, D. 2018. *Grasshopper 3d.* V.1.0.0. Robert McNeel & Associates. https://www.rhino3d.com/.

Sabin, Jenny E. 2013. "MyThread Pavilion: Generative Fabrication in Knitting Processes." In *ACADIA 13: Adaptive Architecture [Proceedings of the 33rd Annual Conference of the Association for Computer Aided Design in Architecture (ACADIA)]*, Cambridge, ON, Canada, 24–26 October 2013, edited by P. Beesley, O. Khan, and M. Stacey, 347–354. CUMINCAD.

Sabin, Jenny, Dillon Pranger, Clayton Binkley, Kristen Strobel, Jingyan (Leo) Liu. 2018. "Lumen." In *ACADIA 2018: Recalibration: On Imprecision and Infidelity [Proceedings of the 38th Annual Conference of the Association for Computer Aided Design in Architecture (ACADIA)]*, Mexico City, Mexico, 18–20 October 2018, edited by P. Anzalone, M. del Signore, and A. J. Wit, 444–455. CUMINCAD.

Semper, Gottfried. 2010. *The Four Elements of Architecture*. Trans. Harry Francis Mallgrave and Wolfang Hermann. Cambridge: Cambridge University Press.

Zwierzycki, Mateusz; Vestartas. 2017. "High Resolution Representation and Simulation of Braiding Patterns." In *ACADIA 2017: Disciplines and Disruption [Proceedings of the 37th Annual Conference of the Association for Computer Aided Design in Architecture (ACADIA)]*, Cambridge, MA, 2–4 November 2017, edited by T. Nagakura, S. Tibbits, M. Ibañez, and C. Mueller, 670–679. CUMINCAD.

IMAGE CREDITS

All drawings and images by the authors.

Nathaniel Elberfeld, Alexandra Waller, and Lavender Tessmer are founding partners of the computational design and research studio TELTTA. Sharing interest and scholarship in material and labor economy, workflow optimization, and customized assemblies, their work confronts the complexities of design through comprehensive engagement with means of production, contexts, and aesthetics. They employ computational models to design processes that address the interaction of competing forces in cultural production.

Each of the trio received a Master of Architecture from Washington University in St. Louis in 2011, to which they all returned and served as faculty, teaching design studios and courses in architectural representation, design research, and digital fabrication. Alexandra, Nathaniel, and Lavender are affiliated with the Design and Computation group at the Massachusetts Institute of Technology, where they are currently pursuing or recent recipients of degrees: SMArchS ('21), SMArchS ('20), and SMArchS ('19)/PhD ('24), respectively.

In addition to publishing research, they exhibit their work in galleries, museums, and public spaces.

Design-to-Manufacture Workflows of Sound-Scattering Acoustic Brick Walls

Gabriella Rossi
James Walker
Asbjørn Søndergaard
Odico

Isak Worre Foged
Anke Pasold
Studio Area

Jakob Hilmer
Jacob Hilmer Architecture

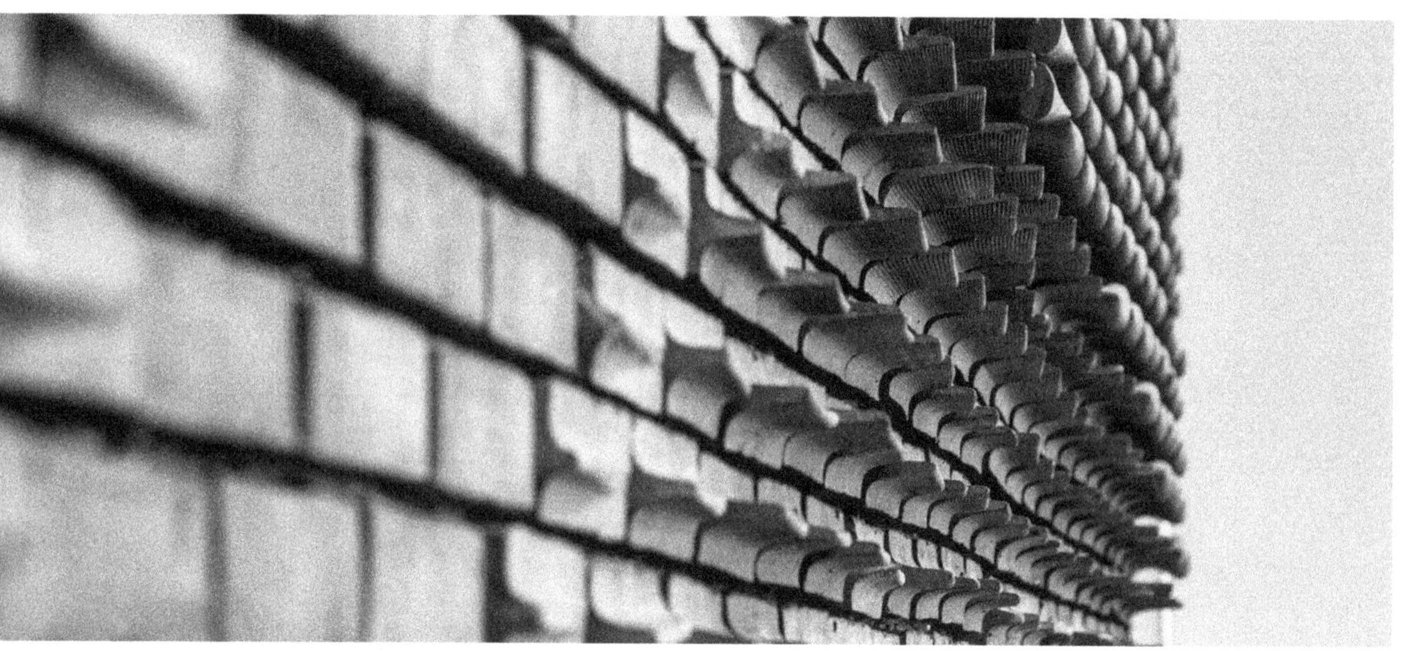

1 Close-up of the full-scale demonstrator with the Cusp brick family variants in focus.

ABSTRACT

Improving speech intelligibility in classrooms enhances information dissemination, institutional knowledge capture, and quality of learning experience. While off-the-shelf solutions are available for acoustically retrofitting existing learning spaces, they do not allow for a fine-tuned context-specific intervention. However, this possibility is enabled through bespoke digital manufacturing informed by advanced digital simulations. In this research we explore and synchronize architecture, acoustics, computation, and fabrication for the making of better sound environments.

We present performance-driven design-to-manufacture (DTM) workflows for sound-scattering brick elements. We reimagine the brick as an acoustically active geometry capable of modulating the sound experience in a university classroom by improving speech intelligibility. We contextualize our research within existing methods of digital performance-based design and robotic fabrication processes, namely wire cutting and pick-and-place applications. We then detail digital methods that combine heuristics and acoustic simulation to design the bricks within the 3D modeling environment, as well as describe the processes of robotic oscillating wire cutting and adaptive pick-and-place developed for the execution of the full-scale demonstrator. Finally, we report on the results of the acoustic analysis performed on the full-scale demonstrator in situ and laboratory measurements of a representative demonstrator which validates our design hypothesis.

INTRODUCTION

The use of earthen bricks in architecture is a millenary craft. In the preindustrial era, the adoption of mud bricks to build simple stacked architectural enclosures was limited to hot climate areas, since they were hand-molded and air-dried. The discovery of firebricks in Roman times led to the proliferation of the fired brick as a building material. Firing allowed the material to acquire a better compressive strength from its unfired counterparts, which led to the development of new structural forms such as arches and domes previously impossible with mud bricks. With the advent of industrialization, brick manufacturing lent itself well to large-scale production chains. Wet clay could be continuously extruded through a die, and the development of new kilns such as the Hoffman kiln or the Tunnel kiln guaranteed a continuous firing production line. These advancements made bricks an affordable construction material that leveraged handcraft knowledge to produce beautiful buildings (Campbell and Pryce 2016). Historically, the main driver for the shape of the brick, beyond its structural function, was the size of the human hand and the weight it could comfortably carry, considering all bricklaying was performed manually. Bricks are sized so that their lateral dimensions, with the inclusion of a mortar joint, are multiples of each other. This allows for the bricks to be arranged in interlocking patterns, known as bonds, which have both a structural performance as well as an aesthetic expression (Hall and Cruickshank 2019). Yet, since the postwar era and with the rise of the cost of handcraft, we see less and less on-site building of masonry walls. In fact, most contemporary facades that include bricks are prefabricated (Krechting 2004). These systems favor efficiency and cost reduction to the detriment of tectonics and aesthetics.

This project looks at the humble brick from a distinct perspective. Rather than thinking of the brick as a structural module, we assign to it a different performance: that of acoustic modulation. By doing so, we examine the intimate relationship between design, performance, and manufacturing in the age of digital simulation and robotics. In fact, bricks could be well-suited to bespoke acoustic treatments: they are cheap to produce and relatively lightweight, and their porous texture can provide sound modulating qualities on a micro scale. However, to be diffusive at a macro scale, bricks must move away from a prismatic profile to new custom shapes that better respond to the acoustic setting of their environment. This cannot be achieved via die extrusion, considering changes in design can become very costly and nonscalable. However, it could be achieved by leveraging digital 4.0 technology with existing industrial-scale manufacturing.

We propose novel design-to-manufacture workflows that embed acoustic performance, a clay material system, and robotic fabrication limits within the design of the brick. We demonstrate the deployment of this workflow with our industrial partner, Strøjer Tegl, in the making of a full-scale acoustic wall demonstrator. We first review examples of state-of-the-art performance-driven brick design and manufacture. Then we unpack our methodology for the design of the bricks using acoustic simulation software and their manufacture combining novel robotic oscillating wire cutting and adaptive robotic pick-and-place methods. Finally, we evaluate the acoustic performance of our wall and its tectonic qualities, discussing the advantages and limits of our methods.

PERFORMANCE-DRIVEN BRICK DESIGN

In this section we examine the added value of new synergies between digital design and manufacturing, which can not only achieve complex forms of architectural elements but also embed specific qualities through designed performance (Hensel and Menges 2008; Kolarevic 2005). We focus specifically on performance-driven ceramic bricks within the body of computational design research.

The most common performance criterion for bricks is naturally mechanical. This is exemplified by the early works at ETH Zurich of Gramazio and Kohler's programmed walls and columns, where robotic pick-and-place workflows were established, leveraging digital design information pipelines with the robot's capacity to precisely position bricks to produce bespoke statically stable curved walls (Bonwetsch 2012; Gramazio and Kohler 2008). Here, bricks are in their standard prismatic or perforated shape and are grabbed by either vacuum or spike end effectors and stabilized using glue applied by either a human operator or a static dispenser. In the subsequent iteration of the work, the focus has been on the development of a digital twin via lidar scanning to ensure the precision of the assembly (Dörfler 2018). A by-product of the systems' structural performance is an aesthetic quality, which is present in the robotically assembled facade of recycled bricks at the Chi Sho gallery (Archi-Union 2010) or in the Gantenbein Winery (Bonwetsch 2015). The latter not only aims to provide a playful "bubble" pattern to the prefabricated brick panels but also programs the space with specific requirements for shading and ventilation of the wine barrels.

While the above examples focus on the assembly of standard bricks, the following examples go beyond prismatic geometry towards free-form performance-driven shaping using various fabrication methods. The first is robotic static wire cutting. In the case of the Revolving brick project

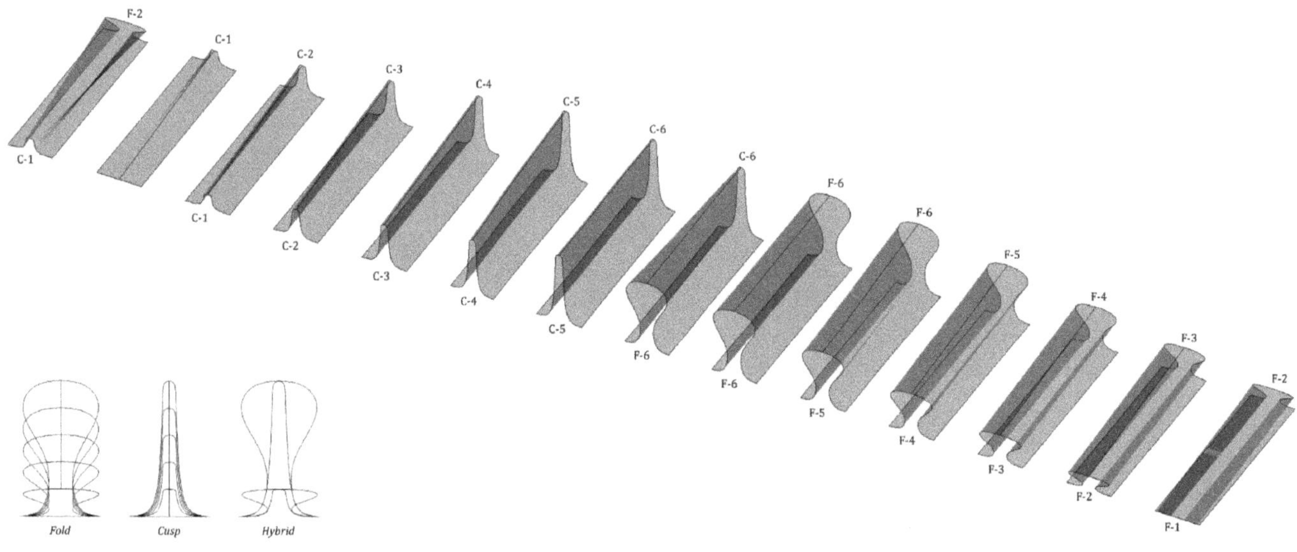

2

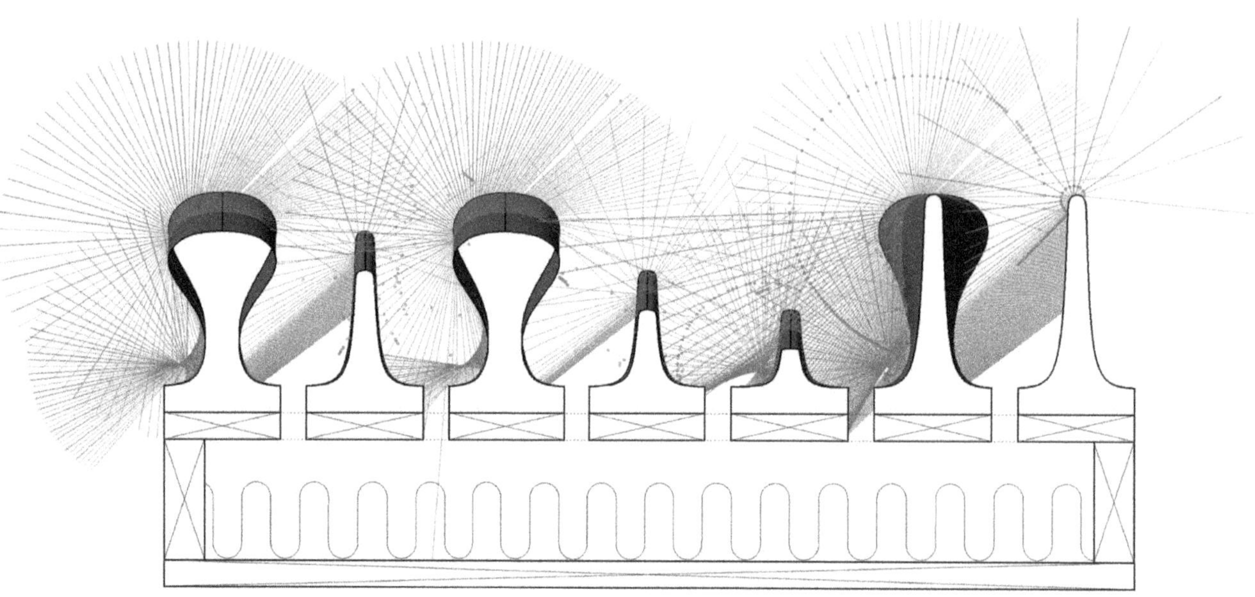

3

2 The 14 families of acoustic-driven brick design (left to right), Fold and Cusp transitioning into flat tile, Cusp family, Cusp to Fold, and Fold family.

3 Cross-section showing the variable scattering qualities of the tiles and how their sequence creates complimentary interactions.

(Andreani and Bechtold 2014), wet clay bricks are cut using a robot-held end effector with a tensioned metal wire. This produces truncated volumes, which create a shading effect and presents a dynamic texturing of the façade. The geometries produced by this method are limited to shallow curvatures. 3D printing, on the other hand, allows for more geometric freedom in the brick, which is crucial for modulating thermal performance through porosity and mass distribution. This is exemplified through the work of Foged and Jensen (2018), where an energy model, thermal model, and fabrication model drive the shaping of 3D-printed thermal-based building blocks, where the mass distribution provides passive thermal effects for occupants. Another example is the Cool Brick (Rael and San Fratello 2015), which is a porous brick that absorbs water and slowly releases it into the interior environment as air moves through, providing a cooling effect via evaporation. Furthermore, the geometry of the brick is self-shading,

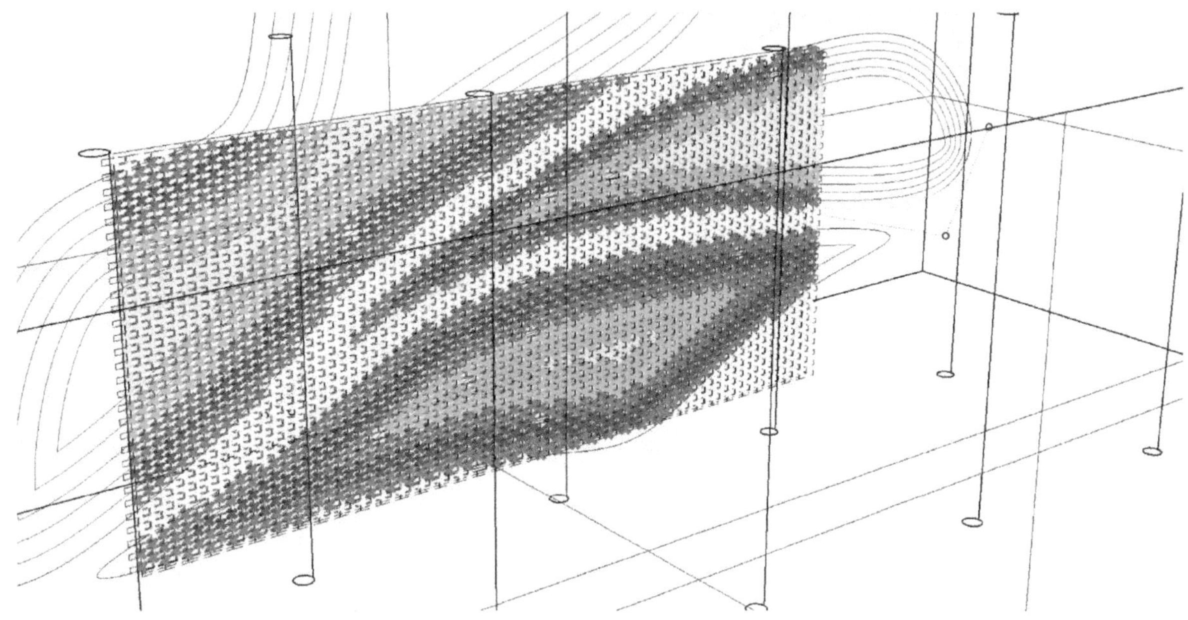

4 Acoustic testing of the full scale demonstrator in Rhino using Pachyderm, with the implementation of a sound source and receiver setup.

which adds to the wall's performance. In contrast, the example of the PolyBrick H20 (Zhang, Qian, and Sabin 2019) uses the shape of the brick to retain water. In fact, the programmable microtexturing from the 3D printing, combined with a specific glazing technique, can steer the water flow on the surface of the brick.

PROJECT BACKGROUND

Looking beyond the ceramic brick, digital simulation and fabrication have been used to create custom modules, arrayed in periodic patterns, to enhance acoustic performance of existing spaces. There are examples of full-scale demonstrators such as robotically pick-and-placed plastic extrusions (Vomhof et al. 2014) and robotically 3D-printed polyurethane (Bonswetch et al. 2008) or examples of 1:10 scaled samples such as robotically carved foam panels (Reindhart and Cabrera 2017) and 3D-printed hexagonal scattering patterns (Peters and Olesen 2010). While these projects primarily focus on the overall placement of materials, they do not address the specific design of the modular unit geometry. We believe that by combining the steering of local module geometry with the global pattern distribution, we can not only achieve a finer-tuned acoustic performance but also address pragmatic issues of fabrication and assembly.

In our intervention for the design of an acoustic partition to improve speech intelligibility in a university lecture hall, we design novel brick geometries driven by acoustic performance, specifically sound scattering, and limited by their manufacturing and assembly possibilities, specifically a ruled surface geometry and a grippable base. While the project could be considered a small-to-medium-scale intervention, it still comprised of 2,200 bricks arranged on a 30 m^2 wall. This marked the need for a comprehensive design-to-manufacturing workflow, beyond the lab setting. In fact, the only way to guarantee the humidity content of the bricks while cutting is by operating within the brick factory itself. We deploy our containerized robotic cell at the facilities of our industry partner, customizing our bricks directly on the production chain, as we detail below.

ACOUSTIC-DRIVEN BRICK DESIGN

The design research methods used are specifically focused on acoustics and include geometric, assembly, and spatial considerations. Initiating-- studies are conducted through geometric versioning paired with acoustic sound scattering properties, based on two primary forms, defined as Cusp and Fold surface definitions (McRobie 2017). The two base forms are selected from their different surface characteristics, with the Cusp defined by two opposing concave curves creating a pointy element, and the Fold defined by two opposing concave curves creating a convex broad curvature element (Fig. 2). Both geometries are maintained within the Danish Standard Brick dimensions (228 × 108 × 54 mm), which enable the elements to be nested as a modular brick system. Six variations of both Cusp and Fold geometries are then parametrically created to increase/decrease the geometric definition, also including two hybrids that combine the Cusp and Fold geometries.

5

6

7

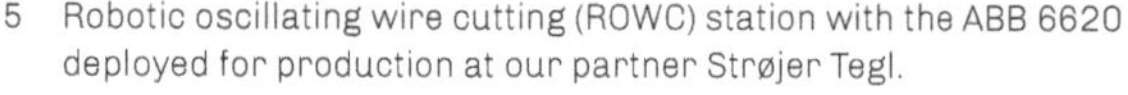

5 Robotic oscillating wire cutting (ROWC) station with the ABB 6620 deployed for production at our partner Strøjer Tegl.

6 Ribbed texture acquired by the cut brick, a unique characteristic of the ROWC (left). Cut bricks brought into the drying chambers (right).

7 ROWC's oscillating frame in the process of cutting a Fold family brick.

This creates a set of 14 unique yet combinable geometries, which enable making and studies of complex surfaces compositions that can be developed to act in respect to periodicity and modulation for specific sound frequencies (Cox and D'Antonio 2017).

Through a parametric design model, sound scattering of element compositions are then modeled with a specular ray-tracing method to understand the behavior of rays in relation to sectional configurations (Fig. 3). The alternation between Cusp and Fold allows the composition to steer the spreading of sound waves in relation to incidence wavelengths, and thereby add design instrumentality across frequencies. With the tiles mounted on a base plate with perforations (that can be varied in the design model), sound energy can also be reflected into deeper structural layers containing porous material (stone wool insulation), allowing

8

9

8 Robotic adaptive pick-and-place ABB 1600 station. An optical sensor adapts the tool path based on brick tolerance through online feedback.

9 Close-up details of the assembled wall. The bricks are fixed with mortar onto CNC-milled plywood panels incorporating an acoustically absorbent cavity.

a dual acoustic design strategy of both scattering and absorption properties.

Similarly, sound scattering of different compositions are assessed by a finite volume method using Pachyderm Acoustical Simulation (van der Harten 2013), where simulated tile sample compositions span 2 × 2 m. Based on computational studies, combining topological versioning of Cusp and Fold geometries with sound scattering assessment through simulations, a final design model is developed, where the understanding of the sound spreading is embedded into the model where the designer intuitively can "sketch" design curves on a 30 m^2 canvas, to have the tiles distributed automatically according to acoustic and visual expressive characteristics (Fig. 4). In the built demonstrator, the pattern comprises a central vein of flat bricks and a gradient concentric distribution of the 14 families from flat to full height, alternating between Cusp and Fold families. This responds to a tile organization that aims to scatter sound at both higher and lower frequencies, and to illustrate the capacity of the tiles to create varied yet holistic articulations across the design system.

ROBOTIC BRICK MANUFACTURING

The acoustic-driven design of our bricks presents two challenges: the brick geometries are nonextrudable and the variation in their profile causes a different shrinkage ratio during firing, which means that the bricks come with a significant tolerance and are difficult to grip. We address these challenges by implementing novel robotic manufacturing workflows that build upon the state-of-the-art: robotic oscillating wire cutting and adaptive pick-and-place, which we describe below and in further detail in another publication (Rossi, Walker, and Søndergaard 2021).

10 The acoustic testing of the full-scale demonstrator that was measured with and without its presence to discern the effect.

Initial Prototypes

Early prototyping tests of Cusp-type bricks revealed problems with fabricating the complex geometries when considering the manufacturing chain of robotic-based oscillation cutting, drying, kiln burning, and transporting the sharp edges. Through iterative testing, the geometries were gradually adapted between both material and manufacturing performance with designed acoustic and visual properties. This required the inclusion of a minimum radius at the edges, without losing the intended geometry of the tiles.

Robotic Oscillating Wire Cutting (ROWC)

While static wire cutting of wet clay has proven effective for the truncated cutting of wet clay blocks, it has an exceptionally large failure rate when dealing with longer surface cuts, especially if they present tight curvatures and changes in direction like in our 14-brick family design. We have found that by introducing an oscillating motion to the wire, we are able to produce these geometries at a low failure rate and a high cutting speed of 4.5 mm/s (compared to 1 mm/s for a static wire). In fact, the reciprocating motion of the wire reduces the friction it encounters while cutting through the block of clay. By tuning the oscillation frequency, we can obtain a texture on the brick that also contributes to its acoustic properties (Fig. 6). We term the manufacturing process robotic oscillating wire cutting, and we design a proprietary end effector combining an electrical engine and wire frame. We deploy a robotic cell with an ABB 6620 (Figs. 5, 7) at our industrial partner facilities, where the bricks are cut in batches of 50 taken from the production chain. Fabrication time of the 2,000+ bricks, with the robot cell operated by two people, lasted 10 days. The cut bricks are left to dry in a humidity buffer zone for two weeks, then enter the drying chambers for a day and are subsequently taken on automatic carts into a tunnel kiln, where they are fired at 1200°C overnight.

Robotic Adaptive Pick-and-Place (APnP)

While our bricks have varying cross-sections, they share a common 25 mm high base, which is used by the gripper in assembly. We designed a custom finger-actuated gripper and attached it to an ABB 1600. The station also features a passive conveyor system for the different families that is manually restocked during the assembly process. An integrated computational workflow, from brick pattern design to robotic production, was developed in Rhino/Grasshopper to assemble 135 unique panels (Robert McNeel & Associates 2020; Rutten 2020). The outputs were ABB RAPID code informing the robot of the conveyance roller sequence from which it is to pick each brick and its ideal target location on the panel, which is adapted to brick tolerance using sensor feedback. As mentioned, the bricks come with a problematic varying tolerance of 2–8 mm due to differential shrinkage. Since it would be cumbersome for all 2,200 bricks to be scanned a priori and best fitted

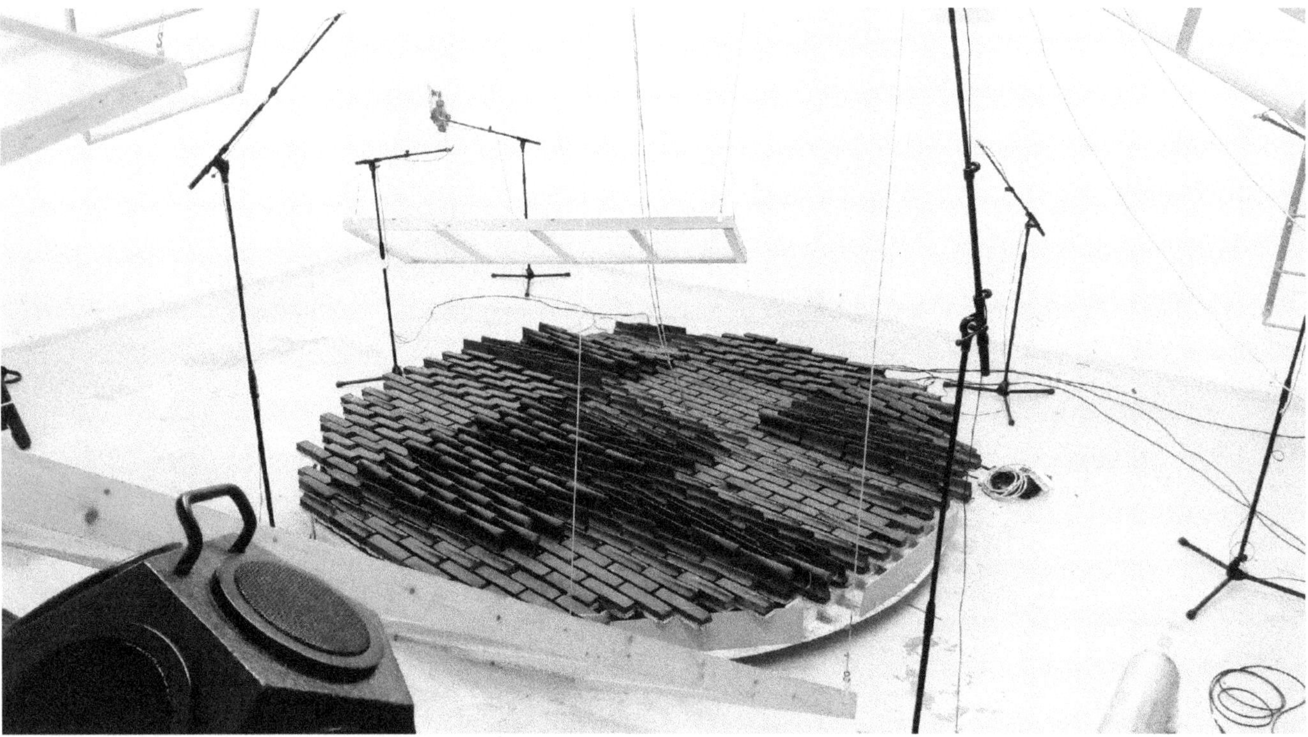

11 Circular sample of the wall tested in a university lab.

according to their tolerance, we developed a hands-off online feedback approach that embraces the tolerance of the bricks and adapts the previously generated robotic pick-and-place tool path to the real dimension of the brick read via an optical fork sensor (Fig. 8), on the fly without designer or robot operator intervention. The robot operator applies a mortar mix to the substrate panels, after which the robot commences the assembly, each panel taking 10 minutes.

On-Site Assembly

The 135 panels are designed with a carrying weight that is below 23 kg so they can be easily handled. The wall was assembled in the auditorium within half a day by 10 people. The substructure is composed of a platform reinforced with metal brackets, four structural timber columns, and stone wool insulation placed in between. The wall provides the room with a unique tectonic expression (Fig. 9).

VALIDATION OF ACOUSTIC PERFORMANCE

The acoustic tiles were subject to measurement both on site and in the laboratory. Spatial acoustic analysis (room analysis) was conducted in the lecture hall in which the demonstrator stood, following the ISO 3382:2008 acoustic room analysis standard. For a comprehensive acoustic analysis, a frequency sweep was conducted using the FuzzMeasure acoustic measurement software (RØDE Microphones 2020), with a focus on evaluating the reverberation time (T30) and definition (D50) of the lecture hall (Fig. 10). The general finding is that there is an improved speech intelligibility due to an increase of the definition. In the university laboratory reverberation test chamber, absorption and scattering measurements are conducted with a static 12 m^2 rectangular sample and a rotating circular sample, respectively, following the ISO methods for measurements (ISO:354:2003/2005) (Fig. 11). The measured samples are composed by a variation of tiles in segments of Cusp and Fold geometries to convey an understanding of the acoustic phenomena that can be created through such applications.

The results of the acoustic measurements in laboratory and field conditions illustrate that the tiles can be composed to scatter sound strategically in relation to the composition of the assembly, and in respect to specific frequencies. The results reflect the specific samples measured. It should be noted that the results are obtained in both laboratory and field conditions from planar compositions, which isolate sound scattering to be based entirely on the tile geometries and their collective planar distribution, resulting in higher scattering coefficients at higher frequencies. The scale and modularity of the tile system, however, enables the tiles to be mounted on a curved wall geometry, which theoretically will increase the sound scattering at lower frequencies due to longer wavelengths. The acoustic design and development could thereby enable an even greater variation in sound scattering effects with such geometric additions to the design system.

CONCLUSION

This paper presented a novel integrated design-to-manufacture workflow for custom sound-scattering brick walls. We developed a simulation-based form-finding technique for performance-driven brick design, custom data management pipelines from design to production, and novel robotic fabrication methods, namely oscillating wire cutting and adaptive pick-and-place. We show the possibilities of using this workflow for improving sound qualities in buildings through the fabrication of a full-scale demonstrator, and we detail the acoustic results of our laboratory and field tests.

This project reveals the synergetic relations between material, form, fabrication technique, acoustics, and visual effects. These relations illustrate the necessity to investigate factors through an integrated design approach and to uncover interrelated features that contribute to a holistic and buildable design performance, as demonstrated. The strategic combination of modularity and in-element versatility is pivotal in allowing the acoustic variation properties, and thereby enabling the design system to be adapted to specific contexts, performances, and spatial intentions. While in this initial demonstrator we have focused our design effort on the brick family modules and their distribution on a planar substrate, future efforts will address the overall design of the partition. In fact, this system could be further extended by arraying the bricks over a curved substrate, which would contribute to an improved response in diffusing larger wavelengths at lower frequencies.

ACKNOWLEDGMENTS

This research was funded by Realdania. The authors thank Frederik Vinter-Hviid, Mads Alber, and Mikkel Heebøll Callesen at Odico Construction Robotics for their help.

REFERENCES

Archi-Union, Fab-Union. 2016. "Chi She." Accessed September 2020. http://www.fab-union.com/en/nd.jsp?id=19#_jcp=1.

Andreani, S., and M. Bechthold. 2014. "[R]evolving Brick: Geometry and Performance Innovation in Ceramic Building Systems Through Design Robotics." *Fabricate 2014 Proceedings. Fabricate 2014 Negotiating Design & Making*, edited by Fabio Gramazio, Matthias Kohler, and Silke Langenberg ISBN: 9781787352148

Bonwetsch, T. 2012. "Robotic Assembly Processes as a Driver in Architectural Design." *Nexus Network Journal* 14 (3): 483–494.

Bonwetsch, T. 2015. "Robotically Assembled Brickwork: Manipulating Assembly Processes of Discrete Elements." PhD dissertation, ETH Zurich.

Bonwetsch, T., R. Baertschi, and S. Oesterle. 2008. "Adding Performance Criteria to Digital Fabrication: Room-Acoustical Information of Diffuse Respondent Panels." In *ACADIA 08: Silicon + Skin: Biological Processes and Computation, [Proceedings of the 28th Annual Conference of the Association for Computer Aided Design in Architecture (ACADIA)]*, Minneapolis, MN, 16–19 October 2008, edited by A. Kudless, N. Oxman, and M. Swackhamer, 364–369. CUMINCAD.

Campbell, J. W., and W. Pryce. 2016. *Brick: A World History*. London: Thames & Hudson.

Cox, T.J., and P. D'Antonio. 2017. *Acoustic Absorbers and Diffusers: Theory, Design and Application*. 3rd ed. CRC Press, Taylor & Francis.

Dörfler, K. 2018. "Strategies for Robotic In Situ Fabrication." PhD dissertation. ETH Zurich.

Foged, I. W., and M. B. Jensen. 2018. "Thermal Compositions Through Robot Based Thermal Mass Distribution." In *Education and Research in Computer Aided Architectural Design in Europe (eCAADe 2018)*, 783–790. eCAADe.

Gramazio, F., and M. Kohler. 2018. *Digital Materiality in Architecture*. Baden: Lars Muller.

Hall, W., and D. Cruickshank. 2019. *Brick*. London: Phaidon.

Hensel, M., and A. Menges. 2008. "Manufacturing Performance." *Architectural Design* 78 (2).

Kolarevic, B. 2005. *Performative Architecture: Beyond Instrumentality*. New York: Routledge Chapman & Hall.

Krechting, A. 2004. "Prefabrication in the Brick Industry." In *Proceedings of the 13th International Brick/Block Masonry Conference, Amsterdam*, 4–7 July 2004, edited by D.R.W. Martens and A.T. Vermeltfoort. Technische Universiteit Eindhoven.

McRobie, A. 2017. *The Seduction of Curves*. Princeton, NJ: Princeton University Press.

Peters, B., and T. S. Olesen. 2010. "Integrating Sound Scattering Measurements in the Design of Complex Architectural Surfaces: Informing a parametric design strategy with acoustic measurements from rapid prototype scale models." In *FUTURE CITIES: 28th eCAADe Conference Proceedings*, edited by Gerhard Schmitt et al., 481–491. ETH Zurich.

Rael, R., and V. San Fratello. 2015. "Cool Brick." *Emerging Objects*, March 3. http://emergingobjects.com/2015/03/07/cool-brick/.

Reinhardt, D., and D. Cabrera. 2017. "Randomness in Robotically Fabricated Micro-Acoustic Patterns." In *Protocols, Flows, and Glitches: Proceedings of the 22nd CAADRIA Conference*, edited by Patrick Janssen, 853–862. Association for Computer-Aided Architectural Design Research in Asia (CAADRIA).

Robert McNeel & Associates. 2020. *Rhinoceros*. V.6.0. Robert McNeel & Associates. PC.

RØDE Microphones. 2020. *FuzzMeasure*. V.4. RØDE Microphones. PC.

Rossi, G., J. Walker, A. Søndergaard, et al. 2021. "Oscillating Wire Cutting and Robotic Assembly of Bespoke Acoustic Tile Systems." *Construction Robotics* 5: 63–72. https://doi.org/10.1007/s41693-020-00051-8.

Rutten, David. *Grasshopper*. V.1.0.0007. Robert McNeel & Associates. PC. 2020.

van der Harten, Arthur. 2013. "Pachyderm Acoustical Simulation: Towards Open-Source Sound Analysis." *Architectural Design* 83 138-139. DOI:10.1002/ad.1570.

Vomhof, M., L. Vasey, S. Brauer, K. Eggenschwiler, J. Strauss, F. Gramazio, and M. Kohler. 2014. "Robotic Fabrication of Acoustic Brick Walls." In *ACADIA 14: Design Agency [Proceedings of the 34th Annual Conference of the Association for Computer Aided Design in Architecture (ACADIA)]*, Los Angeles, CA, 23–25 October 2014, edited by D. Gerber, A. Huang, and J. Sanchez, 555–564. CUMINCAD.

Zhang, V., W. Qian, and J. Sabin. 2019. "PolyBrick H2.0." In *ACADIA 19: Ubiquity and Autonomy [Proceedings of the 39th Annual Conference of the Association for Computer Aided Design in Architecture (ACADIA)]*, Austin, TX, 21–26 October 2019, edited by K. Bieg, D. Briscoe, and C. Odom, 246–257. CUMINCAD.

IMAGE CREDITS

Figures 1–4, 9–11: © Studio AREA.
Figures 5–8: © Odico Construction Robotics.

Gabriella Rossi is a PhD Fellow at CITA, Royal Danish Academy. Her work focuses on the intersection between machine learning and robotics, exploring novel materialities and manufacturing workflows applied to architecture. She teaches in the master's program Computation in Architecture at the Royal Danish Academy, and has guest-taught at the University of Technology Sydney and Southeast University in Nanjing. Previously, she worked as a computational design specialist at Odico Construction Robotics. She is member of the Danish Association of Architects.

James Walker is a registered architect (MAA & ARB) and a Design Specialist at HD Lab in Copenhagen. Previously, he worked as a computational design specialist at Odico Construction Robotics. His research has investigated the robotic fabrication of performance-optimized geometries, and currently explores the application of environmental simulation and design optimization methods in practice.

Asbjørn Søndergaard is founding partner and Chief Technology Officer in Odico Construction Robotics, a technology enterprise dedicated to large-scale architectural robotic formwork fabrication. Founded in 2012 through a joining of research trajectories following the Fabricate 2011 conference, Odico Construction Robotics has embarked on a mission to revolutionize global construction. Søndergaard heads the software development and industrial research and development within the company. This work entails several high-profile research efforts to develop novel fabrication technologies within architectural construction, such as robotic hot-blade cutting, abrasive wire-cutting of EPS-optimized formwork, and automation of nonrepetitive robotic manufacturing.

Isak Worre Foged is a trained architect (MAA), civil engineer (IDA), and researcher (PhD), and a Professor with specific responsibilities at the Royal Danish Academy, focusing on synergetic studies between materials, technology, and sustainability across design scales. His studies are tied closely with human sensations through thermal, acoustic, and visual phenomena integrated into bespoke design models. In parallel, Isak is the cofounding partner of AREA Architects, established in 2010 with Anke Pasold, to strategically develop innovation projects in the intersection between academia and industry, with the aim to accelerate ideas, methods, and designs that drive an environmental sustainable future.

Anke Pasold is an architect, designer, and cofounder and partner of the architectural practice AREA. She is an Associate Professor at Material Design Lab at KEA Copenhagen.

Jacob Hilmer is an architect and founder of Jacob Hilmer Architecture in Copenhagen.

Parametric Photo V-Carve for Variable Surfaces

Computational Design for a Cultural Application

Namjoo Kim*
Höweler + Yoon Architecture

Eto Otitigbe*
Artist

Caroline Shannon*
Höweler + Yoon Architecture

Brian Smith*
Quarra Stone Company

Alireza Seyedahmadian*
Quarra Stone Company

Eric Höweler
Höweler + Yoon Architecture

J. Meejin Yoon
Höweler + Yoon Architecture

Alex Marshall
Quarra Stone Company

James Durham
Quarra Stone Company

*Authors contributed equally to the research.

1 Completed construction of the Memorial to Enslaved Laborers at the University of Virginia.

ABSTRACT

This research project was part of the design and construction of the Memorial to Enslaved Laborers (MEL) at the University of Virginia (UVA). The MEL was dedicated to an estimated 4,000 enslaved persons who worked at UVA between 1817 and 1865. The 80-foot-diameter memorial is a tapered toroidal shape composed of 75 stone blocks. This project demonstrates how computational design tools along with robotic digital fabrication can be used to achieve unique social and experiential effects in an architectural application.

The memorial's design was informed by an extensive community engagement process that clarified the importance of including a visual representation of enslaved people on the memorial. With this input, the eyes of Isabella Gibbons were selected to be used as a symbolic representation of triumph on the outer wall of the memorial. The MEL project could not rely solely on prior methods or existing software applications to design and fabricate this portrait due to four particularities of the project: material, geometry, representation, and scale.

To address these challenges, the MEL design team employed an interdisciplinary collaborative process to develop an innovative parametric design technique: parametric photo V-carve. This technique allowed the MEL design team to render a large-scale photo-realistic portrait into stone. This project demonstrates how the synthesis of artistic motivations, computational design, and robotic digital fabrication can develop unique expressions that shape personal and cultural experiences.

INTRODUCTION

Computational design tools and robotic digital fabrication are often disconnected from discussions of social experience in architectural applications. This paper describes elements of the design and fabrication of the Memorial to Enslaved Laborers (MEL) at the University of Virginia (UVA), completed in 2020. The MEL design team employed an interdisciplinary collaborative process to develop an innovative parametric design technique: parametric photo V-carve. This technique allowed the MEL design team to render a large-scale photo-realistic portrait into stone. This project demonstrates how the synthesis of artistic motivations, computational design, and robotic digital fabrication can develop unique expressions that shape personal and cultural experiences. The collaboration resulted in a highly calibrated photo-realistic representation of a historical figure layered with symbolism from a complex cultural context.

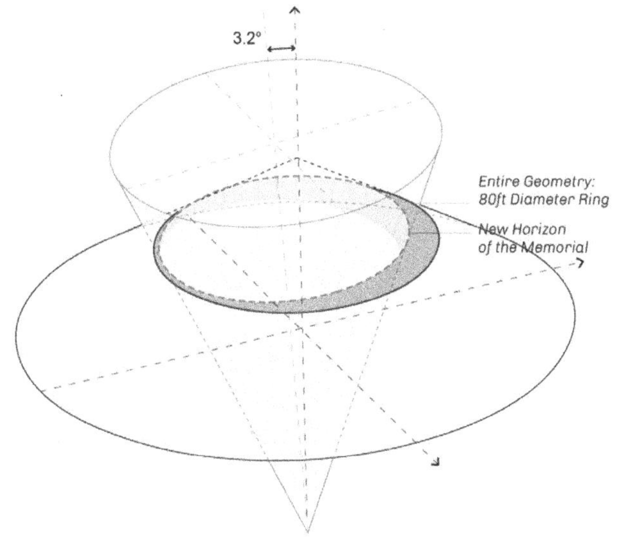

2 Geometry of the memorial: Intersection of two cones.

Historical Context

The MEL honors over 4,000 persons who were enslaved at UVA between 1817 and 1865. Over 75 stone blocks were used in the memorial's construction to create a tapered toroidal form that is approximately 80 feet in diameter. The volume can be understood geometrically as the intersection of two cones. The form gently tapers into the ground at one side, creating a point of entry into a space that could function as a meeting ground for commemoration, education, or cultural interaction (Fig. 2).

The MEL design team was led by Höweler + Yoon Architecture along with Dr. Mabel O. Wilson, Dr. Frank Dukes, and landscape architect Gregg Bleam. Quarra Stone Company was the MEL's official stone fabricator. The final design was informed by an extensive community engagement process that took place at UVA and around Charlottesville and Albemarle County in places such as the Ebenezer Baptist Church, The Jefferson School, Charlottesville High School, the Monticello plantation, and the Montpelier plantation. Conversations at these sites involved community stakeholders and members of genealogical groups who could trace their ancestry to people who were enslaved in Charlottesville and by UVA. During these conversations, community members articulated a desire for integrating imagery that portrayed triumph over despair along with visual cues to suggest who the enslaved people were and how they lived into the memorial's design.

Given the importance of the representational aspects of the memorial, the design team engaged artist Eto Otitigbe as a collaborator. Otitigbe sought to layer the information gleaned from conversations, historic sites, and archives to develop an expression for the memorial's exterior surface that would complement key design elements on the MEL's interior—memory marks representative of each enslaved person, a timeline that chronicled historic events during the years of slavery at UVA, and a water feature as a symbol for libation.

Some of the imagery was inspired by gouge patterns in rough-hewn tombstones from the Daughters of Zion African American burial ground in Charlottesville (Fig. 3). Another visual signifier was influenced by vertical grooves found in newly quarried stone that would eventually be worked away at the hands of skilled masons.

To achieve the desired representational expression, the artist proposed carving two large eyes across several textured stone blocks on the memorial's exterior surface with overall dimensions of approximately 8 feet by 39 feet. The eyes were sampled from a rare photograph of Isabella Gibbons (Fig. 4), a woman who had once been enslaved at UVA, where she worked for William Barton Rogers, who later became the founder of the Massachusetts Institute of Technology (Harrison 1853). Gibbons, who learned to read and write while she was enslaved, remained in the area around Charlottesville after emancipation and became a teacher at the Freedman School until her death. Through Gibbons's figurative presence, the MEL's exterior surface was transformed into a sculpted portrait that symbolized a welcoming gaze for visitors and a watchful presence to commemorate those who were enslaved.

3

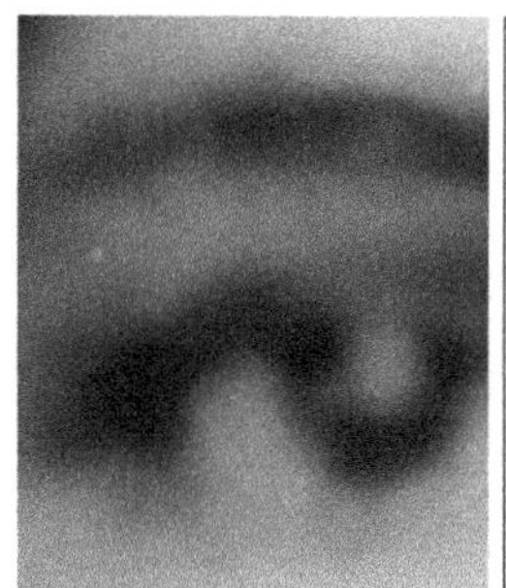

4

3 Daughters of Zion African American Burial Ground.

4 Isabella Gibbons. Photo courtesy of Boston Public Library.

5 Reference image (left); PhotoVCarve user interface (center); detail of PhotoVCarve simulation (right).

BACKGROUND

Creating Parametric Photo V-Carve

The design team was interested in applying a photo V-carve technique to render the portrait in stone. Photo V-carve is a computer-aided manufacturing (CAM) process that is used to engrave imagery in solid substrates. The process generates a series of parallel linear grooves with variations in depth and width produced by a V-shaped carving tool. The combination of cutting depth and groove width simulate intensity values from a reference image. There has been much research dedicated to the study of techniques for the construction of 3D objects from 2D image inputs, and the team reviewed prior research efforts and software options to develop the parametric photo V-carve technique.

Rockwood and Winget (1997) proposed techniques to construct a 3D model from 2D images through the repeated adjustment of a mesh. Other researchers extended this method through an investigation of reconstructing a surface from multiple images by combining several patches (Zeng et al. 2007).

Researchers in the technical sciences at the University of Novi Sad (Serbia) developed a novel approach for generating anamorphic sculpture based on parametric design tools, robotic fabrication, and stick placement. The process relies on gray-scale images as an input to determine the placement of cylindrical sticks into predrilled holes in a board (Jovanović et al. 2017). While this process results in a unique sculpture form that is based on an image, it does not apply to the intended materials or method of representation for the MEL project.

Laser scanning and photogrammetry are often used to generate 3D digital models from physical 3D forms for heritage and conservation projects. These models are then realized as physical forms using additive or subtractive digital fabrication processes. A collaboration between the Carleton Immersive Media Studio (CIMS), the Dominion Sculptor of Canada, and the Heritage Conservation Directorate (HCD) of Public Works and Government Services Canada (PWGSC) resulted in the creation of a sculptural element to repair a physical detail in a historical architecture. The process was useful for a 1:1 translation of physical model to digital model and vice versa (Hayes 2015).

For manufacturing and production, a postprocessor is required to translate numeric information from 3D surfaces that are constructed from 2D images into a useful format for CNC machines or fabrication robots. Sood et al. (2018) presented an approach that resulted in a tool path based on a 2D image by generating a 3D point cloud from the digital image. This study was for a small-scale application on a flat surface, unlike the proposed application for a large-scale representation on a convex, textured surface.

Independent software developer Franklin Wei developed RasterCarve, an open source, web-based CNC photo V-carving application in response to a fee-based commercially available software from Vectric. This software allows users to generate G-Codes for CNC tool paths using a web browser as an interface (Wei 2019). The software allows a user to upload a photograph, then adjust certain image viewing parameters. The application then generates a tool path consisting of a series of parallel lines, each based on "varying depth to convey brightness information of the input image" (Wei 2020).

The most relevant technology was the PhotoVCarve Version 1.1.02 software developed by Vectric LTD. The PhotoVCarve process requires a reference image as an input (Fig. 5). Then the application allows the user to set parameters such as material size, line spacing, line angle, carving depth, and image contrast. After these parameters are set, the

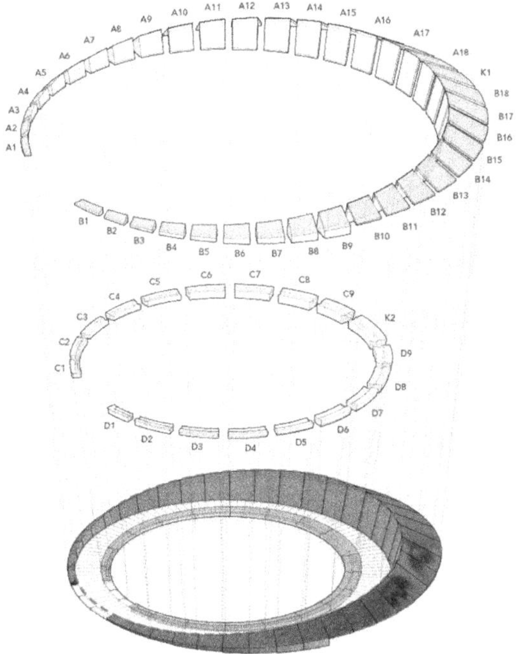

6 Exploded axon: 18 solid stone blocks and 38 built-up stone blocks. 6

application generates a simulation of the final 3D carving along G-Code for CNC milling.

Otitigbe had experience applying PhotoVCarve software to make 2D art. In 2012 the artist created a series of CNC-carved photo-realistic self-portraits called *Becoming Visible*. The series paid homage to Trayvon Martin and was inspired by historical wood carvings and bronze statues from Benin, in West Africa. PhotoVCarve was integrated into the design process for the memorial's exterior surface; however, the typical outputs of this application had to be augmented using parametric modeling to meet the specific constraints and requirements of the project.

Memorial Geometry

The memorial forms two concentric rings, nested in the sloping landscape. The base geometry of the outer ring emerges from the intersection of two cones, creating an inclined wall that rises to 8 feet on the inner wall and 5 feet on the outer wall. After considering factors such as the size limitations of the quarried stone, transportation efficiency, and machining efficiency, the memorial's 80-foot-diameter outer ring was divided into 37 sections: 18 solid stone blocks and 38 built-up stone panels (two panels per section), composed of two blocks, one inner wall block and one outer wall block (Fig. 6).

Extremely tight construction tolerances, less than 1/16", were required to achieve the overall circular geometry. To accommodate these functional requirements, the project required advanced computational design and digital robotic fabrication techniques along with a precise installation plan.

This paper focuses on several of the panelized stone blocks on the outer wall, designated B12 to B17, where the partial portrait of Isabella Gibbons is located (Fig. 7).

METHODS

Challenges

A typical photo V-carve process could not be used to produce the portrait for the MEL because of four design-related particularities: material, geometry, scale, and representation.

The first challenge was caused by the selected material, Virginia Mist granite. The stone's surface, which ranges in color from light gray to near black, contains white and light gray veins throughout. The stone's surface reflectivity varies significantly according to how it is cut and finished. This particular granite was sourced from a quarry in Culpepper, Virginia, close to UVA. The MEL design team traveled to the quarry on several occasions to inspect and select stone blocks. The appearance of each block needed to meet specific visual criteria related to veining patterns. To minimize interference with the imagery, only stones with wispy vertical vein patterns were used for the portrait stones B12 to B17 (Fig. 8).

The second challenge was related to the overall geometry of the memorial. Typically, photo V-carve is applied to a material with a flat surface uniform thickness. For the MEL, the image needed to be placed on a trapezoidal, convex textured surface. Each V-groove used to represent the image needed to be parametrically corrected to account for surface curvature, variable material thickness, and nonuniform texture. These factors necessitated the development of a new process, including a series of inputs, scripts, and tool

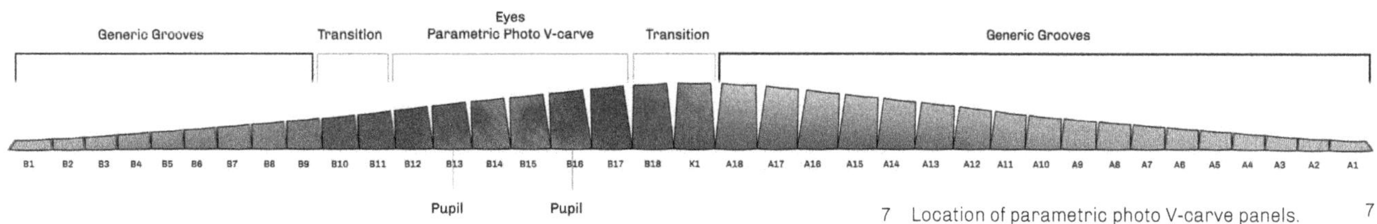

7 Location of parametric photo V-carve panels. 7

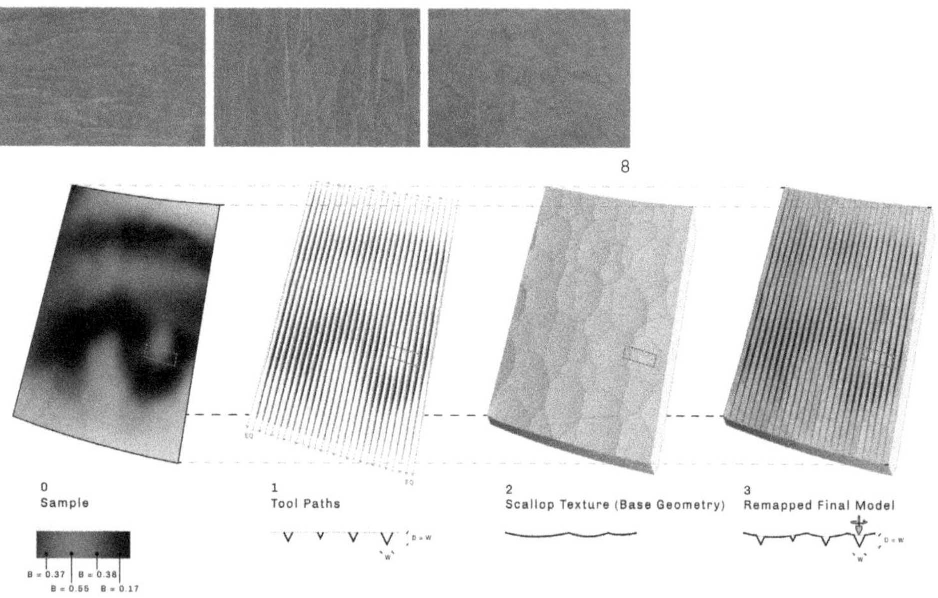

8 Stone veining, wispy linear veining horizontal (left); wispy linear veining vertical for the portrait stones (center); nondirectional veining (right).

9 Software workflow: (0) reference image for intensity values; (1) tool paths (G-Code) produced based on image sampling; (2) scallop texture (base geometry) generated by parametric tool; (3) final 3D model, parametrically remapped on base geometry.

pathing strategies to ensure that the image was legible and not confounded by geometric variables.

The third challenge involved the portrait's scale and tooling. Standard V-shaped cutting tools are used for typical photo V-carve projects to cut individual grooves in a single pass or multiple passes where only the depth of cut is increased. These cutting tools may range from 1/4" to 4" in diameter with a 30° to 120° taper. The desired MEL portrait was approximately 8 feet high by 39 feet long. The image generated by the parametric photo V-carve lines was wider than those generated by a typical photo V-carve process. A standard V-shaped cutting tool would not deliver the most optimal results.

A method to transition from figurative representation to graphic design elements was the fourth challenge to the MEL design. The team needed to develop a system for differentiating grooves that displayed photographic content (parametric photo V-carve) from those that did not (parametric V-carve) and seamlessly transition between them. The team identified six blocks as "portrait blocks" to be designed and fabricated with the parametric photo V-carve technique. Two blocks on either side of the series of portrait blocks would be designated as "transition blocks." The remaining 27 blocks would be textured without any embedded imagery using a parametric V-carve process. Every V-groove, regardless of the type of block it was on, needed to be tapered at the top and bottom to maintain a consistent visually clean edge. The PhotoVCarve software could not be used to meet these design requirements since it can only translate images to cut files and does not allow for customizing each V-groove.

Computational Design

To address the primary design challenges, the MEL design team divided the computational design into three distinct layers (Fig. 9).

- Layer 1: The first layer was used to reinterpret the image of Isabella Gibbons's eyes. First the artist used Adobe Photoshop to adjust the brightness and contrast of the photographic source image. Then Adobe Illustrator was used to align the image to the geometry of each stone block. The location of the eyes was influenced by the anticipated view corridor from outside of UVA's campus to the memorial and by their position relative to an observer standing close by. The eyes also needed to be level relative to the elevation of the site. The eyes were cropped from the photograph and sliced into six sections. Each section was resized and scaled to correspond with the designated portrait blocks (Fig. 10). Then each image was processed separately in PhotoVCarve. A project folder containing the PhotoVCarve project file, G-Code cut file, and a reference image of the simulation was created for each image. Each project folder was sent to the stone fabricator for further processing.
- Layer 2: The architect developed a custom Grasshopper script to produce a scalloped texture over the entire outer wall of the MEL's base geometry. This script was designed to vary parameters between stone panels as the stone panels diminish in height from the center stone to the entrance stones. The parameters included size of the scallop, depth of the scallop, and distance between each scallop. Each scallop shared an imaginary bottom surface to maintain the original concavity of the geometry. The scalloped texture was shallow on the portrait blocks and deeper on the transition and generic blocks.

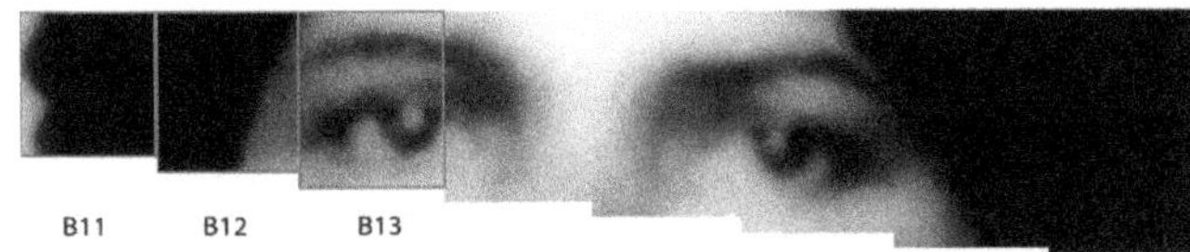

10

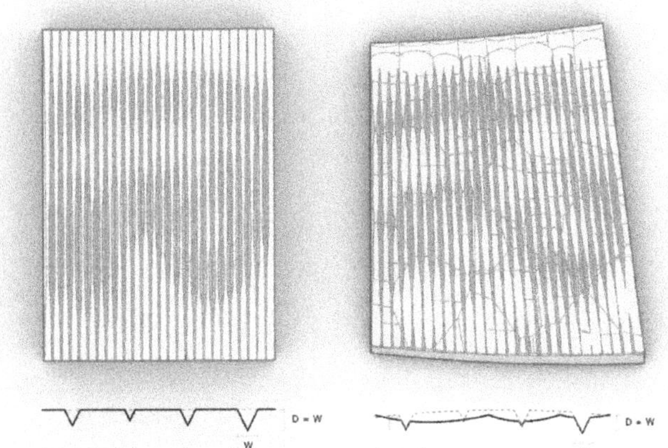

11

10 Scaling image across stone blocks.

11 Parametric photo V-Carve remapping progress, 1 - Photo V-Carve on flat surface: remapping is not required; 2 - Parametric photo V-carve (in progress) : G-code remapped on the curved surface only. Scalloped texture cancels out the V-Carve; 3 - Parametric photo V-carve on scalloped surface (final) : G-code remapped on the curved scalloped surface. Remapped points maintain a z-depth relative to the scalloped surface.

Within a block, the texture's depth decreases moving towards the top edge to maintain the sharpness of the quirk miter joint.

- Layer 3: The stone fabrication researchers developed a Grasshopper script to parametrically combine layers 1 and 2 and generate the CAM tool path for fabrication. Taking the G-Code that was generated for a flat V-carve surface in layer 1, the script parsed the tool path coordinate data to generate scaleless reference points. These points were then scaled and remapped by evaluating the UV coordinates of the flat base surface onto the convex reference surface. Through some early studies in the process, it was found that the image's legibility would be preserved only if the remapped points maintained a predetermined z-depth relative to the scalloped surface (Fig. 11). In doing so the shadows generated were able to overcome the scalloped texture of the surface, enabling the image of the eye to be visible. The final step was to generate tool paths for production on a Kuka KR480-MT CNC robot and other large CNCs that used diamond-segmented saw blades to machine the complex surfaces.

Material and CAM Process

The material properties of Virginia Mist make it impractical to machine with traditional V-shaped cutting tools. These tools are often used for cutting metal and smaller applications. Some V-shaped tools are used for stone cutting processes but they were inefficient for this application due to the prolonged machining times and large surface area. Instead, the stone fabricators used industrial diamond-segmented end mills, and large-diameter stone-cutting saw blades were used for the MEL.

The stone fabricators created a "virtual tool" in CAM software to machine simulated material stock into digital models to help visualize the machining process. Real-time visualization of production-ready 3D surface models facilitated easier preparation, setup, and multiaxis tool path generation of real-world stone machining centers. Large-diameter saw blades and parametric radial CAM tool path strategies were used to realize the large-scale portrait in stone. This efficient machining strategy resulted in an "as-cut" surface finish more in tune with the digital design of the panels and reduced time for manual finishing.

To prevent any discontinuities caused by seams between stone blocks across the carved portrait, the custom Grasshopper script included a feature that centered V-carve lines on stone seams (Fig. 12).

Mock-up

Once the design and fabrication methodology were established, the team identified several key variables for the legibility of the final image in stone. These included groove spacing, groove depth, scallop depth in the base geometry, and stone finish. Additional considerations were made for environmental conditions such as lighting and moisture, which could affect the overall legibility of the image.

The artist intended to achieve an image that flickered between visibility and invisibility (Fig. 13). The areas where the portrait was located needed to have a reduced visual presence of the scalloped surface texture—and vice versa. Achieving this delicate balance of perception and experience based on the environment and the position of the viewer would determine the project's success. To generate

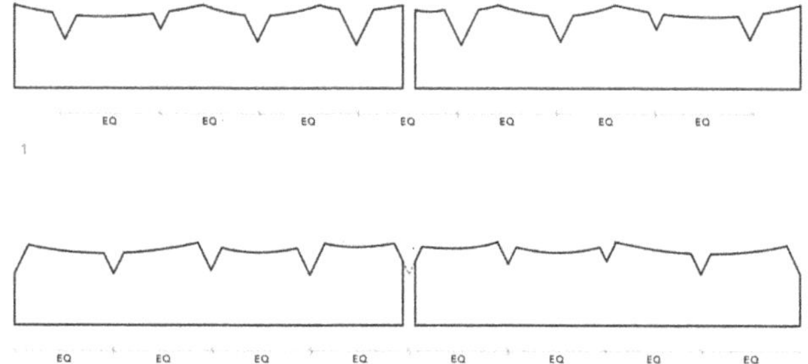

12

13

Left (Selected)
Groove - Sand Blasted
Scallop Surface - Honed

Middle
Groove&Surface -
Grind

Right
Machine Finish

14

a range of mock-up options, a custom Grasshopper script was developed using the depth, width, spacing, and angle of the grooves along with the shape and depth of the scallops on the surface as design parameters. After exploring the various combinations of the parameters in the digital model, several iterations were selected to be fabricated as physical mock-ups to test the visual qualities and legibility of the image. Through these studies it was found that the depth had a large impact on the intensity of the image, and the spacing determined the resolution of the image.

There were three stages in the mock-up process: pre-mock-up, EPS foam mock-up, and full-scale stone mock-up.

Physical models in the pre-mock-up stage were produced to the following critical variables: groove density on portrait panels, visual harmony of transition panels and generic grooves, and the legibility of the portrait (Fig. 15). Two different settings for groove density were used, center-to-center spacing at 3 1/16" and then 3 5/8". The pre-mock-up results were inconclusive, and the team needed more information to better understand the relationship between the critical variables and design/machining strategy.

The team created new models using expanded polystyrene (EPS) foam to refine the solution. Six different groove

Mock-up area
Selected

Pupil Pupil

M1 M2 M3

B9 B10 B11 B12 B13

	M1	M2	M3-01 Opt 1	M3-02 Opt 2
Groove Spacing (Digital Model)	3 5/8"	3 5/8"	3 5/8" At 1" Depth	3 1/16" At 1" Depth

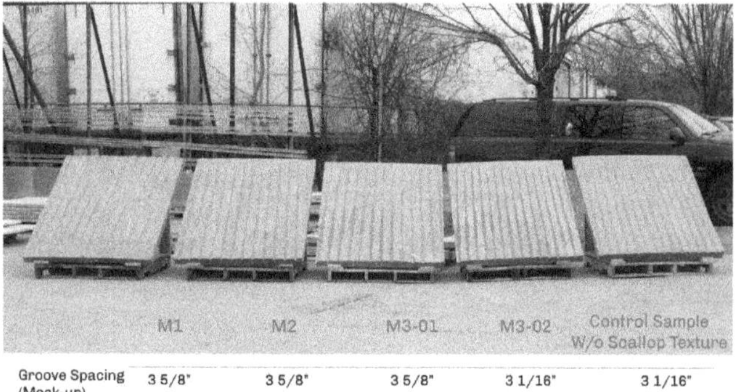

	M1	M2	M3-01	M3-02	Control Sample
Groove Spacing (Mock-up)	3 5/8"	3 5/8"	3 5/8"	3 1/16"	3 1/16"
Tested Finish	Machine Finish	Machine Finish	Various	Sand Blasted+honed	Machine Finish

15

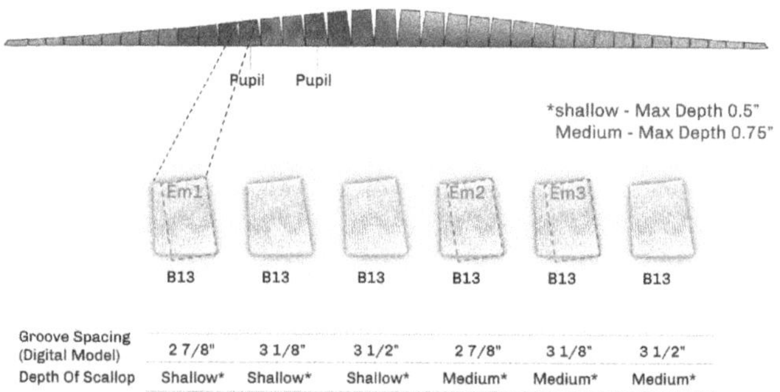

Groove Spacing (Digital Model)	2 7/8"	3 1/8"	3 1/2"	2 7/8"	3 1/8"	3 1/2"
Depth Of Scallop	Shallow*	Shallow*	Shallow*	Medium*	Medium*	Medium*

	Em1	Em2	Em3
Groove Spacing (Mock-up)	2 7/8"	2 7/8"	3 1/8"
Depth Of Scallop	Shallow*	Medium*	Medium*

16

densities and two scallop depths were tested in a 3D computer model. Then three options were selected for full-scale prototyping. These physical models were viewed under a range of natural lighting conditions (Fig. 16).

Finally, a series of full-scale mock-ups were prepared in stone (Fig. 17). Finishing techniques had a significant effect on the stone's final color and appearance. The team needed to determine the best combination of techniques to enhance the legibility and interplay between the portrait and scalloped texture. Various sand-blasting, honing, and grinding treatments were applied to both the surface and machined grooves of the stone (Fig. 14). A combination of sand-blasting and honed finish were selected since they resulted in the best image legibility and contrast between the grooves and scalloped surface.

RESULTS

After refining the parametric digital modeling strategy, exploring various digital workflows, iterating process parameters, and creating a series of physical mock-ups, the design team was able to establish a final set of parameters for the fabrication of the stone blocks. The parametric photo V-carve panels required a groove density based on 2 7/8" center-to-center spacing with a groove depth of 1". The transition panels required a groove density based on 3 3/8" center-to-center spacing. The generic panels required the groove density to gradually increase from 3 3/8" to 5 1/2". The scallop texture depth ranged between three levels: 1/2" for parametric photo V-carve panels, 3/4" for transition panels, and 1 ¼" for generic parametric V-carve panels. Sand blasting was used as a final finishing specification for the inner surface of the V-grooves while the scalloped surface was honed. These parameters resulted in a portrait that was most visible from certain oblique angles and under certain lighting conditions.

The final blocks were installed on the grounds at the University of Virginia in the spring of 2020. Although the site conditions were difficult to predict, the final installation yielded the intended perceptual effects as the image of Isabella Gibbons's eyes appeared and vanished depending on the viewing angle and environmental conditions.

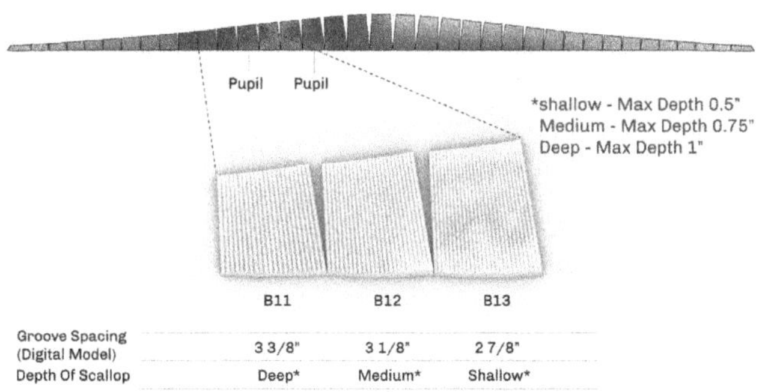

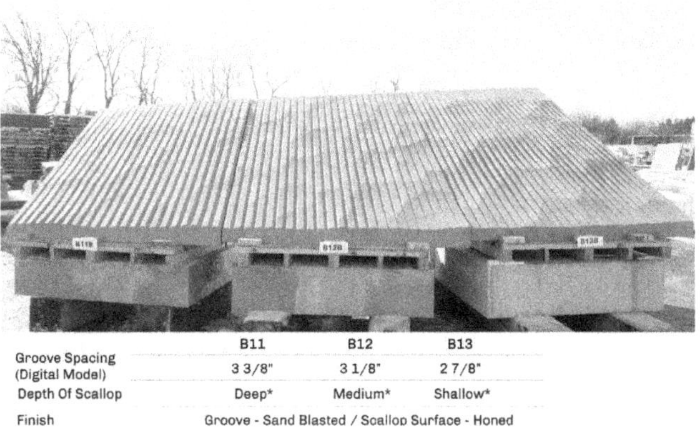

B11
B12
B13
Groove Spacing (Digital Model)
3 3/8"
3 1/8"
2 7/8"
Depth Of Scallop
Deep*
Medium*
Shallow*
Finish
Groove - Sand Blasted / Scallop Surface - Honed

17

Table No. 01: Photo V Carve and Parametric V Carve

Factors	Photo V Carve	Parametric V Carve
Transition	Raster Image to Toolpath	Raster - Parametric tool - Toolpath
Tool	V-bit	32" Diamond CNC Saw Blade
Toolpathing Strategy	Single Line Machining	Surface Machining
	Creates toolpaths from images to carve grooves which vary in depth and width to render the input image. The overall image is visible only after the grooves are carved at the required depth/width and spacing with the corresponding tool. Stock model simulation tools typical in CAM software provide a visual representation of the final product.	The process simulates the Photo V Carve workflow within grasshopper. This workflow is not limited to planar stock/surfaces and can be applied to complex surfaces. This workflow results in a real-time visualization of production ready 3d surface models that is machined using multiple passes. The photo-realistic effect is embedded in the 3d model that is generated by the grasshopper script.

12 Joint condition: (1) V-grooves only on surfaces; (2) V-grooves at the joint.

13 Sunny (left); overcast (right).

14 Stone finish test.

15 Pre-mock-up 3D model (top) and physical mock-up (bottom).

16 EPS mock-up 3D model (top) and physical mock-up (bottom).

17 Final mock-up 3D model (top) and physical mock-up (bottom).

18 Final installation.

DISCUSSION

Through the coordinated efforts of the interdisciplinary MEL design team, the design process, artistic intent, and fabrication methodology intersected and informed one another to produce the desired effect. Rather than the design team transferring a drawing or 3D model to the fabrication team, the final parametric photo V-carve solution was achieved through iterative testing and problem solving by the multidisciplinary team (Table 1)

The iterative and interdisciplinary workflow from the start ensured the project's success. By working closely together to incorporate fabrication knowledge with the design intent from the beginning, we were able to avoid a common problem of a compelling design concept that can't be fabricated. Mock-ups played a critical role in the success of the final parametric V-carve image. We learned that there were limitations to evaluating the visual effects of the digital models; it was only possible to accurately evaluate them in real lighting conditions with stone material properties.

In future applications, improvements could be made to streamline the image generation process. What is currently a multistep process using multiple softwares and is specific to the geometry of this memorial could be developed into a more automated workflow entirely within Grasshopper. Doing so would eliminate several manual steps in the process and open up the workflow to become geometry-agnostic and simple to apply in other use cases.

CONCLUSION

The MEL project was meant to address a combination of sensitive cultural and historical issues at a critical point in history for public monuments and discussions about race in the United States of America. Input from community stakeholders at UVA and Charlottesville regarding the MEL design was a fundamental part of the design process. The parametric photo V-carve technique allowed the MEL design team to address the community's request for the inclusion of figurative representation on the memorial's exterior surface. Meeting the specific representational goals and material constraints of the project was essential to its success. The design team's iterative and collaborative workflow and prototyping processes allowed for careful calibration of the perceptual range of the image so that it appeared and disappeared depending on variations in the viewer's position, lighting, and weather. This effect, made possible by parametric design, allows visitors to discover it throughout their experience of the memorial—inviting reflection on the layers of history embedded in the university's grounds (Fig. 18).

ACKNOWLEDGMENTS

The Memorial to Enslaved Laborers was designed by Höweler + Yoon Architecture (Eric Höweler, professor at the Harvard GSD, and Meejin Yoon, dean at Cornell AAP) in collaboration with historian and designer Dr. Mabel O. Wilson (professor at Columbia GSAPP and founder of Studio&), Gregg Bleam Landscape Architect, community facilitator Dr. Frank Dukes, and artist Eto Otitigbe (professor at Brooklyn College, Art Department, and director of Turnbull Gallery). The authors would like to acknowledge the entire design and construction team, including Team Henry Enterprises (general contractor) and Quarra Stone (stone fabrication and installation). The Memorial to Enslaved Laborers represents the culmination of years of community engagement by the President's Commission on Slavery and the University and by the memorial design team. Many valued partners were critical to the commission's work and deeply informed the memorial's design.

We acknowledge the use of Rhinoceros (www.rhino3d.com), a program developed by Robert McNeil, and Grasshopper (www.grasshopper3d.com), a plug-in developed by David Rutten for Rhinoceros for form generation. We acknowledge the use of PhotoVCarve (www.vectric.com/products/photovcarve), a program developed by Vectric LTD for image manipulation and form generation. We acknowledge the use of Autodesk's Powermill (www.autodesk.com/products/powermill/overview) for programming the CNC and robotic tool paths for stone machining.

REFERENCES

Harrison, Smith. 1853. Tucker papers, December 20. W. B. Rogers, Boston, to Prof F. A. Smith.

Hayes, Fai. 2015. "Digitally-Assisted Stone Carving of a Relief Sculpture for the Parliament Buildings National Historic Site of Canada." *ISPRS Annals of the Photogrammetry, Remote Sensing and Spatial Information Sciences II-5/W3*, no. 5 (August 11): 97–103.

Jovanović, M., J. Tasevski, B. Tepavčević, M. Raković, D. Mitov, and B. Borovac. 2017. "Fabrication of Digital Anamorphic Sculptures with Industrial Robot." In *Advances in Robot Design and Intelligent Control*, edited by A. Rodić and T. Borangiu. Cham: Springer. https://doi.org/10.1007/978-3-319-49058-8_62.

Rockwood, Alyn, and Jim Winget. 1997. "Three-Dimensional Object Reconstruction from Two-Dimensional Images." *Computer-Aided Design* 29: 279–285.

Sood, Sumit, Ravinder Kumar Duvedi, Sanjeev Bedi, and Stephen Mann. 2018. "3D Representation and CNC Machining of 2D Digital Images." *Procedia Manufacturing* 26 (January): 10–20. https://doi.org/10.1016/j.promfg.2018.07.001.

Wei, Franklin. 2019. "On Opening Black Boxes or: How I Learned to Stop Worrying and Love G-Code." Franklin Wei's Webspace, November 28. https://www.fwei.tk/blog/opening-black-boxes.html.

Wei, Franklin. 2020. *RasterCarve Live*. V.1.4.2. RasterCarve Live. Accessed December 6, 2020. https://rastercarve.live/.

Zeng, G., S. Paris, L. Quan, and F. Sillion. 2007. "Accurate and Scalable Surface Representation and Reconstruction from Images." *IEEE Transactions on Pattern Analysis and Machine Intelligence* 29 (1): 141–158. https://doi.org/10.1109/TPAMI.2007.250605.

IMAGE CREDITS

Figure 1, 18: © Sanjay Suchak.
Figure 4: © Boston Public Library.
All other drawings and images by the authors.

Namjoo Kim, AIA, received her MArch from Massachusetts Institute of Technology in 2016. She has worked on various scale projects that required sophisticated design skills and coordination effort. She served as a project manager of the Memorial to Enslaved Laborers at the University of Virginia, producing the complicated 3D model and coordinating the cutting-edge digital fabrication.

Eto Otitigbe is a polymedia artist whose practices explore sculpture, performance, and installations that set alternative narratives in motion. He is an Assistant Professor of Sculpture in the Art Department at Brooklyn College. He contributed to the creative expression on the exterior surface of the Memorial to Enslaved Laborers. He received his MS in Product Design from Stanford University and his MFA in Creative Practice from the University of Plymouth.

Caroline Shannon, AIA, LEED AP, is an Associate at Höweler + Yoon Architecture. Her practice as an architect and researcher is focused on health, equity, and social justice in the design of the built environment. She received her MArch from the Harvard Graduate School of Design with distinction and was awarded the AIA Henry Adams Medal and Julia Amory Appleton Traveling Fellowship.

Brian Smith is a designer and fabricator. He is the Director of Quarra Stone's robotic and digital fabrication department (QLAB). He has a Bachelor in Architecture and a Master of Science in Computational Design, and his work has focused on the intersection of high-skill handcraft and advanced fabrication technologies.

Eric Höweler, AIA, LEED AP, is an architect, designer, and educator. He is an Associate Professor in Architecture at the Harvard Graduate School of Design, where he has taught since 2008. Eric's research focuses on building technology integration and material systems. Eric is cofounding Principal of Höweler + Yoon Architecture LLP. Prior to HYA, Höweler was a senior designer at Diller Scofidio + Renfro in New York and an Associate Principal at Kohn Pedersen Fox Associates.

J. Meejin Yoon, AIA, is an architect, designer, and educator. She is the Gale and Ira Drukier Dean of Cornell University's College of Architecture, Art, and Planning, and was previously Professor and Head of the Department of Architecture at MIT, where she began teaching in 2001. Yoon is cofounding Principal of Höweler + Yoon Architecture. Her work investigates the intersections between architecture, technology, and public space.

Alex Marshall, AIA, LEED AP is an architect, designer, and fabricator. He currently is the Senior Director—Technical Operations at Quarra Stone. He holds a Master of Architecture from MIT and has previously worked at Höweler + Yoon Architecture LLP. He directed and was actively involved with the memorial's installation.

James Durham founded Quarra Stone in 1989. He has served as stone consultant to the Smithsonian and coauthored several research papers on stone milling. In 2012, he received an Honorary Master Stone Carver designation from The German State School for Stone Working.

Alireza Seyedahmadian is a designer and digital fabricator. He holds a Masters in Architecture from the University of Michigan. Currently, he is a senior design engineer at Eventscape, a custom art and architectural fabrication company, where he leads the company's New York advanced manufacturing department. Previously, he was a project engineer and the codirector of QLAB, Quarra Stone's robotic and digital fabrication department.

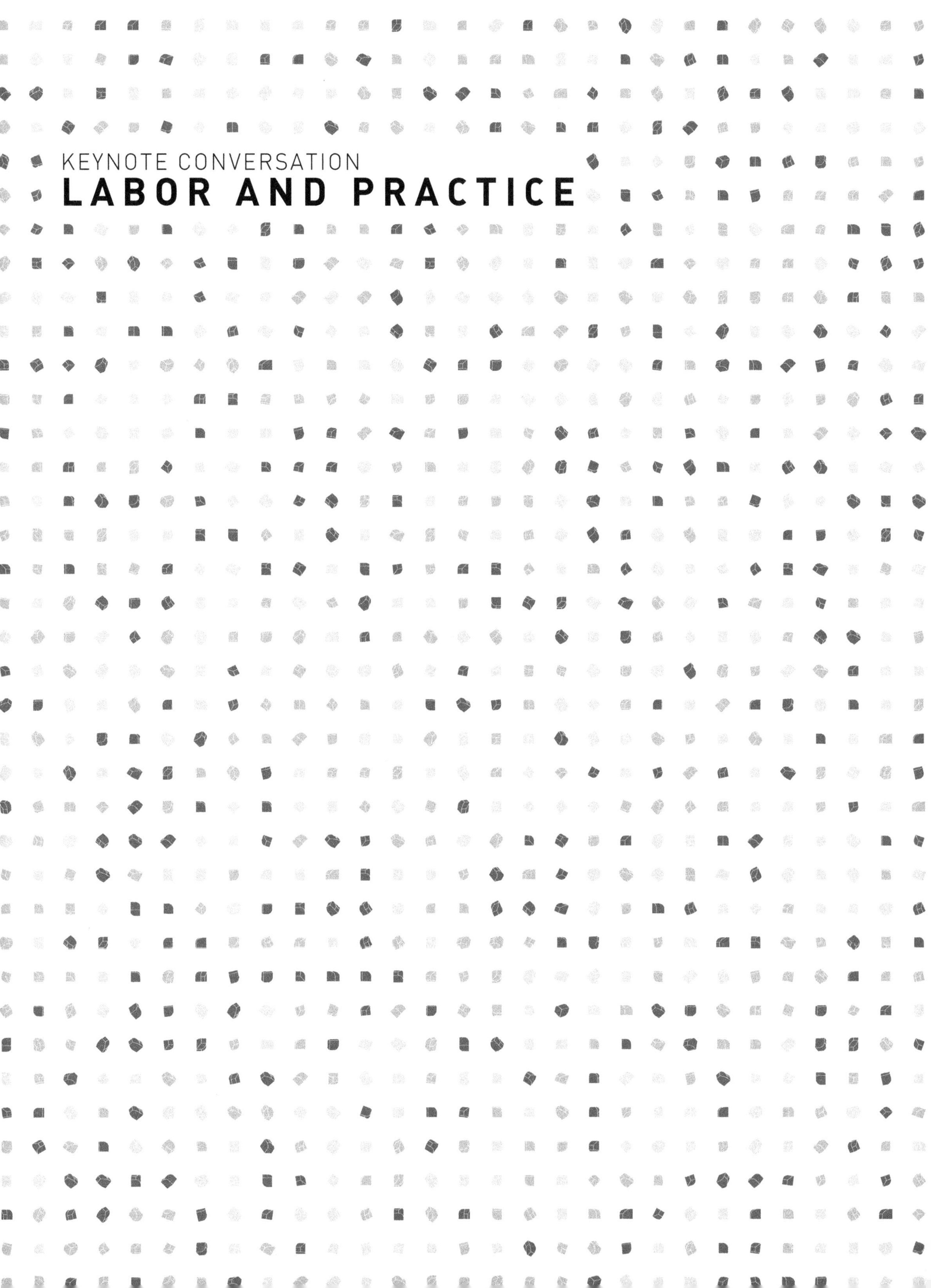

KEYNOTE CONVERSATION

LABOR AND PRACTICE

KEYNOTE EVENT

A Conversation on Labor and Practice

Peggy Deamer
Yale University

Billie Faircloth
KieranTimberlake

Mollie Claypool
AUAR / The Bartlett, UCL

Automated approaches to design, fabrication, and construction present disruptive and potentially transformative challenges to the conventional practice of architecture, as computational workflows recalibrate traditional roles and responsibilities in the production of buildings. How does computational design change how labor is defined and enacted in architectural and construction practice? What ethical implications and questions arise in this context, particularly as we consider the implications of the uncompensated or under-compensated labor of those doing computational work? In this keynote conversation, three architects and thinkers convened to critically explore the intersections between computation, labor, and practice.

Peggy Deamer, Professor Emerita of Yale University's School of Architecture and a founding member of the Architecture Lobby, began the event with a polemical call for the computational design community to radically reassess its existing labor practices in both academic and professional settings. Addressing what she sees as the "latent animosity between automation and labor," Deamer argued that computational workers should embrace their autonomy in the labor force and increase efforts to support each other, organize collectively, and advocate for the value of their work.

Billie Faircloth, partner at KieranTimberlake, followed with a presentation of her firm's efforts to situate computational design and automation within the broader context of what Howard Davis has called the "culture of building,"[1] developing strategies to leverage computation to increase the value and agency of architectural labor. As an example, Faircloth discussed how Tally®, the firm's life-cycle assessment software plugin, enables architects to calculate embodied carbon, better analyze and understand a building's environmental footprint, and take on expanded agency in addressing architecture's role in climate change.

Mollie Claypool, an architecture theorist and activist at AUAR and UCL Bartlett, concluded with a presentation of her work developing critical approaches to automation in relation

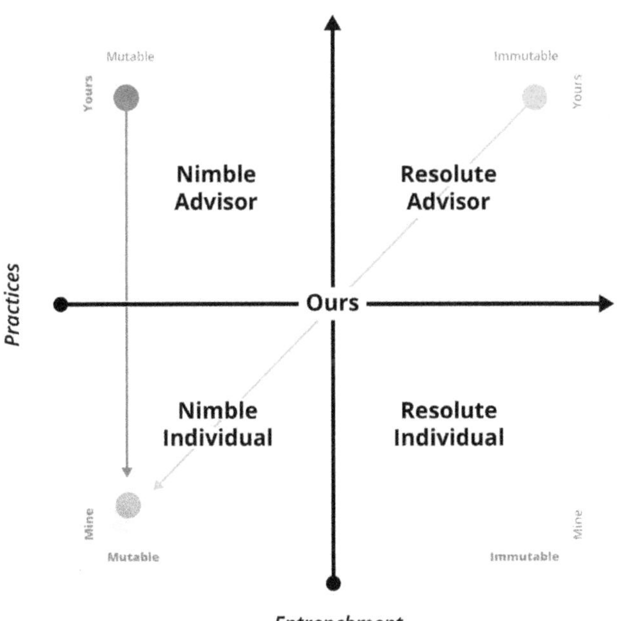

1 "Only when we examine who and what we are laboring for can we begin to approach the question of computational design labor. [...] By mapping the perception of our agency, we can also recognize that there is not one source of agency when it comes to building culture. There are competing agencies." —Billie Faircloth
(Image: Billie Faircloth / KieranTimberlake)

to housing production and models for localized manufacturing. Claypool's work resists automation's extractive tendencies, instead advocating a distributed approach to automation as an empowering force to bring architects and communities together to realize new housing prototypes. A conversation on the politics of computational labor followed, and is reproduced below in edited form.

For a recording of the entire event, please see this link: **https://www.youtube.com/watch?v=F0Gsrn-p_fo**

Mollie Claypool (MC): We can't really talk about labor and practice without recognizing that computational design labor has predominantly been done by white men. And the rise of automation means that those roles are going to be increasingly at risk. To what extent do you see this as a chance to begin to expand and reorganize the nature of this labor for radical inclusion and greater equity among BIPOC and womxn? As we've seen earlier this week in Ruha Benjamin's talk[2], BIPOC are more largely affected by automation already, and womxn and BIPOC are most marginalized in the discipline. What opportunities are there, and what challenges do you see in addressing this inequity?

Billie Faircloth (BF): We are not going to be able to address this unless we explicitly state equity and inclusion goals for building culture. Without these being stated, we're not actively addressing equity. Without goals, how do we know what we're aiming for? There needs to be a process for setting goals. I've seen some examples within the building industry, but at present they are exceptions. The question that you're asking is one of outcomes. We should also ask: What will our industry look like in the future? What should it look like? Whose vision is it, and why? One of the things that's missing is the capacity to measure and understand social outcomes. Although we start projects with deep aspirations for practice transformation and advocacy, there is still this larger issue of knowing how to evaluate whether or not our tactics are working. This is a time to learn how to measure and evaluate these other things.

MC: I completely agree with you. Where are we measuring social-value impact? Other disciplines have ways of doing this. I think this goes back to what Peggy talked about at the beginning of her presentation: the devaluing of the humanities within the architectural discipline. The humanities have more ingrained practices of how to value social impact.

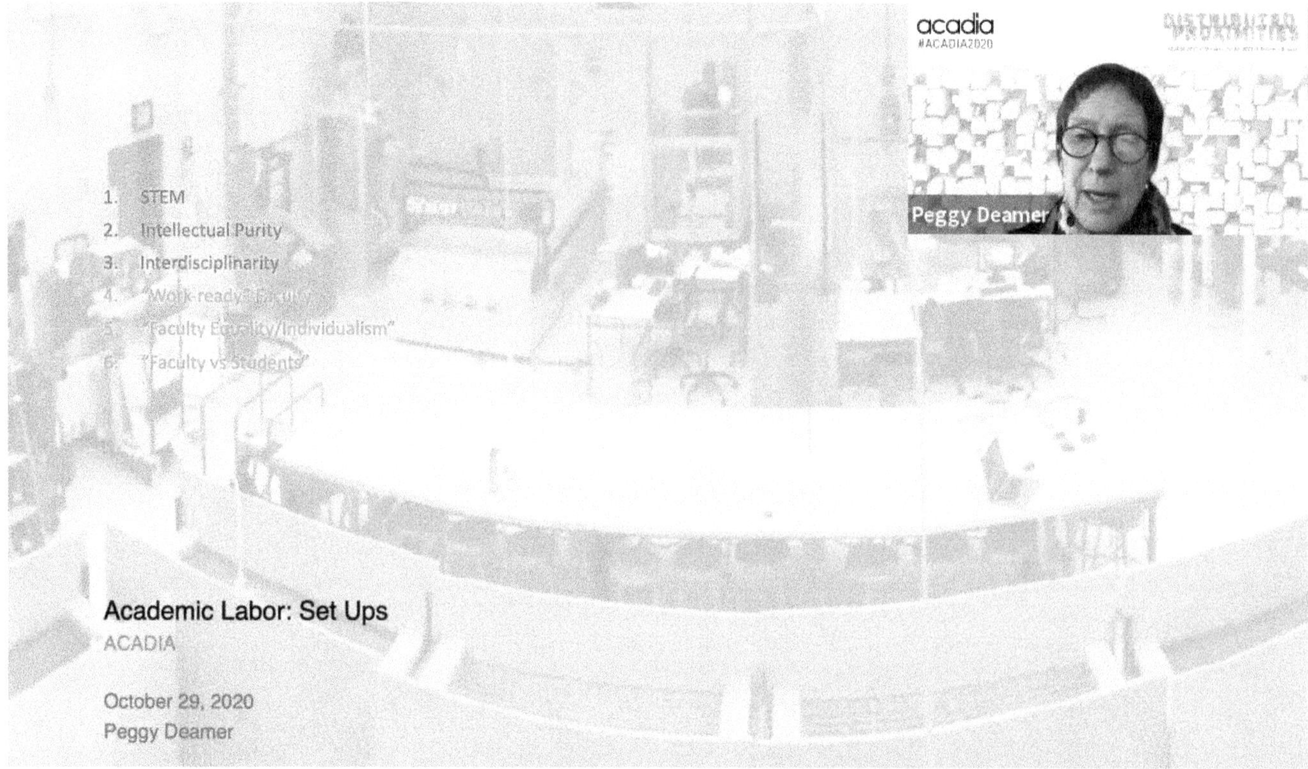

acadia
#ACADIA2020
Peggy Deamer
1. STEM
2. Intellectual Purity
3. Interdisciplinarity
Academic Labor: Set Ups
ACADIA
October 29, 2020
Peggy Deamer

2 "The university assumes, and profits from, our atomized individuality in a meritocracy, leading us to believe that if we just work hard enough, publish enough, get good enough teaching evaluations, and so on, we will be protected from precarity." —Peggy Deamer (Image: Peggy Deamer)

Peggy Deamer (PD): Yes. But I think we also have to address the fundamental condition of how expensive our education is, and how little reward people who might go into it are going to get. And so people who are the first in their family to go to college, or who are looking at professionalization for the first time, will look at architecture, the expensiveness of its education, the length of its education, what they're going to make, and basically the precarity of of the business that they're going into, and just think, "No thank you." It's a real barrier for getting people of color or people from disadvantaged social circumstances to enter into the profession. This certainly includes gender issues, racial issues, and economic issues. Until we can figure out a better way of having the reward, it's going to be a problem.

This is where I do want to link up with what Billie is talking about. One way that our architectural offices or the profession can actually indicate that we deserve more value is to be able to prove that our outcomes from this knowledge-gathering makes better buildings. Until we can measure and articulate that kind of data, I think our services are going to continue to be undervalued. If you can't actually prove that this knowledge makes buildings perform better in the long term, it's going to be hard.

I also think that in some way, questions of value and social impact relate to what architecture's relationship is to construction. The work that both of you showed is beginning to redefine this relationship. The construction industry and labor unions need to be brought on board. We can't continue to talk about inequity within the architecture profession and have projections into how the construction industry and labor unions might accept new models of practice and collaboration, while leaving them out of that discussion. I think that's absolutely essential to the question that you're asking: how we begin to change on that side and bring them on board with our different aspirations.

BF: Peggy, you have spoken about the limits of our educational models, and I'm wondering, are you suggesting that we should be exploring other methods of education?

PD: Yes. In my critique of the profession, I think we should develop educational models that don't subscribe to NAAB (National Architectural Accreditation Board) and NCARB

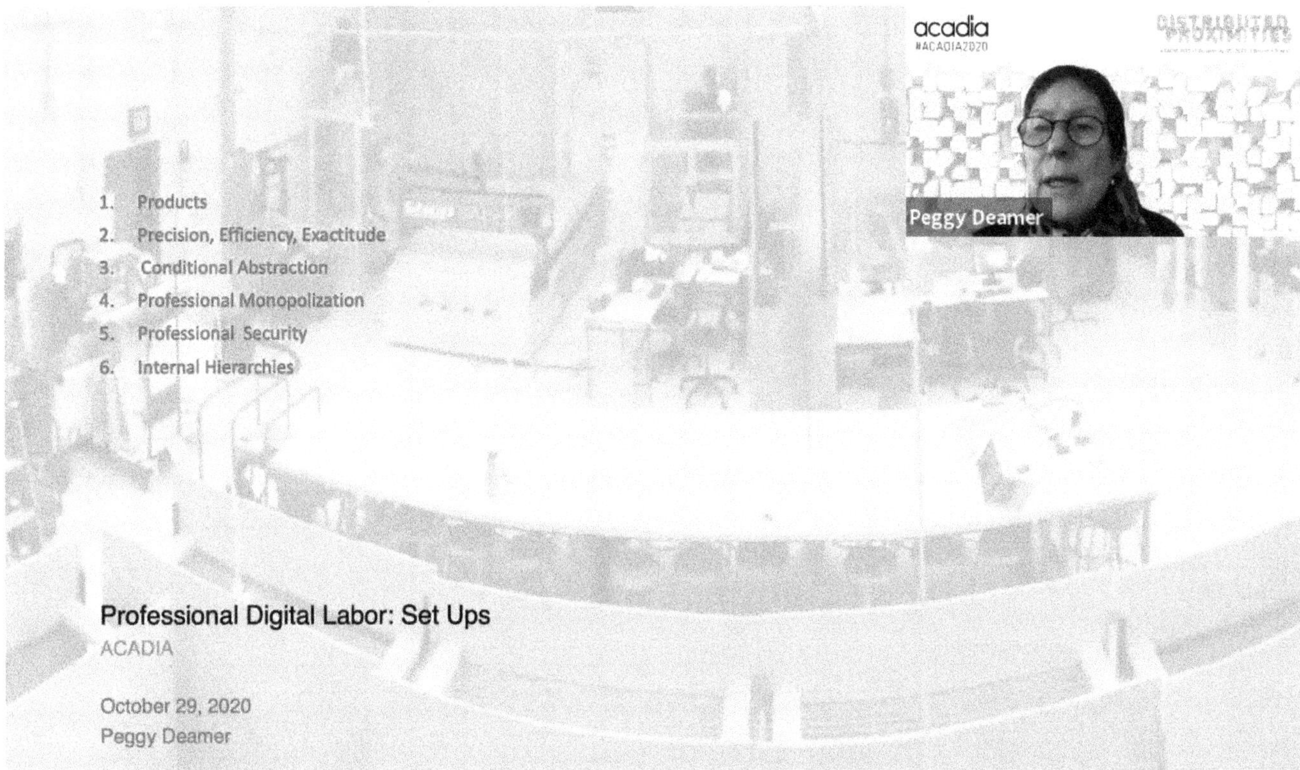
acadia
#ACADIA2020
Peggy Deamer
1. Products
2. Precision, Efficiency, Exactitude
3. Conditional Abstraction
4. Professional Monopolization
5. Professional Security
6. Internal Hierarchies
Professional Digital Labor: Set Ups
ACADIA
October 29, 2020
Peggy Deamer

3 "One does not want to contribute to a world that may be smart and well controlled but allows no room for the ad hoc, the deviant, or the creative." —Peggy Deamer (Image: Peggy Deamer)

(National Council of Architectural Registration Boards). I think there's a construct there that prevents us from making significant progress on the issues of labor, representation, and value that we have been discussing. The Architecture Lobby is putting together a summer school that might model what that new kind of education will be. Entitled Architecture Beyond Capitalism (ABC), the "classes" will cover three main topics—Unlearning Capitalist Architecture; Capital, Labor, and Product in Architectural Design; and Changing Procurement/Alternative Forms of Cooperation—over six weeks in June and July of 2021. We see this as a beta test not just for future summer schools, but a new form of architectural education.

MC: Let's hone in a little bit more on education. One of the core elements of architectural education is the design studio. The design studio, or unit, still establishes a kind of power structure or hierarchy that perpetuates the notion of the "master" architect. What ways do you think digital labor and automation can help rethink or catalyze a rethinking of the power structures of the studio? What kinds of studio practices could be constructed or reconstructed, and which ones could be completely abandoned?

PD: I think that computational design is a big disrupter, and that's what we need. The kinds of issues that computational design can enable architects to address—better performance, better carbon footprints, a certain "do it yourself"-ness that communities can engage with—these are the issues that continue to be left out of normal studio discourse, but become foregrounded in computational design. Another way of saying that is, computational design and digital labor at least talks about labor. They put labor—what we as designers actually do—on the table in a way that a normal design studio doesn't. Computational design foregrounds the process in lieu of the product.

At the same time, I would just say that I've been to conferences for digital computation that are all about a kind of digital utopia. At these events, there is zero discussion of things that we have learned that we need to worry about, such as Taylorization. So that's one place where, in the academy, I think we do need to make sure that the humanities are talked about in the studio at the same time as making and procurement. All of those different things need to be thought about together.

MC: The people who are just beginning their architectural studies now, and entering their first studio, will typically find that it follows a Beaux Arts traditional model. They are immediately confronted with a structure of the relationship between labor, knowledge, and expertise that sets them up for the expectation that such a structure can't be unwritten.

This is something that needs to be looked at urgently in architecture education. This is also very difficult because that first studio is also inherently the hardest year to teach. And it's not just a change in a way of thinking, a way of drawing, and a way of looking at the world; it's also an unraveling of all the other practices that came before.

If we were beginning to rethink what a good hierarchy of the first studio would look like, we would talk much more explicitly about the contexts that people come from, the labor that it takes for them to even get there, the situations that they might have at home that brings constraints into their ability to work—all the things that have been brought to the fore now with Covid-19. I hope that this discussion becomes more integrated into our practices as we shift towards more student-centered education.

BF: One thing that you just demonstrated really well is that pedagogy shapes the perception of our design agency very early on. It's one of the central roles of pedagogy. One of the things we have to do as educators is step back and ask ourselves: what perception of agency are we creating, and how are we structuring education differently?

The work of AUAR exemplifies some of the threads that Peggy and I were talking about around this notion of distributed knowledge. Clearly, the work that you're doing is trying to distribute knowledge and to show that there's value in distributed knowledge models. There's another perception or pedagogy that says that others create knowledge for architecture; therefore, we do not have the agency to study and understand outcomes. We legally delimit where our responsibility begins and ends, and therefore we actually hamper our efforts to understand the large systems and facts that our work actually creates. So pedagogy needs to be fundamentally rethought, I believe, through the point of view of agency.

PD: I think it's important to note that the students that come to first year studio don't just need another pedagogy, but we need to recognize the individuality and the intersectionality and the differences that they bring to the table, as opposed to thinking of a new pedagogy as "wipe the slate clean" from who they are, what they've known, and what they bring. We need to think about those differences and the individual contributions that can be made to that pedagogical discussion.

MC: An obstacle to this is that higher education has been marketized. One of the core challenges with being able to actually amplify that intersectionality is the exchange-based structure of education, in which schools sell services to students.

This touches on one other thing I wanted to talk to you both about: notions of capital, money, and wealth. Digital labor really goes hand in hand with extractive practices, productivity, and infinite growth, which is constructed. I think that all of these practices are designed to be at the expense of social value. What do you think is the starting point for practices and the discipline to begin to rethink our relationship to capital?

BF: One of the ways that we've tried to rethink our relationship to capital and, more specifically, to these extractive practices began by trying to expand the system boundary of architecture. For instance, a life-cycle thinking framework causes us to immediately question where to act and why. What we're up against is a fundamental shift in our design agency, as well as understanding that the decisions we make are connected directly and deeply to communities and neighborhoods. We can no longer pretend to be the customer at the end of a supply chain. We have to do the work to connect one end of the supply chain to the other; we need to build conversations, discourse, and commitments broadly. I think the other place to begin is to simply try to integrate this kind of thinking into our design practice—to try to model what's happening, especially with extractive practices.

PD: Part of what I want to emphasize is that it's not just about being better business people and understanding precisely where your project fits into a larger discourse of real estate value and ownership gain and all of that (which, if you're a good business architect, you'll do). But we must also understand where this fits in that larger discourse—where architecture relates to construction, material goods, global exchange, and the whole procurement network. Until we do that, as students or practitioners, we're not going to have a sense of our responsibility. Without a sense of responsibility, there will be no call to agency.

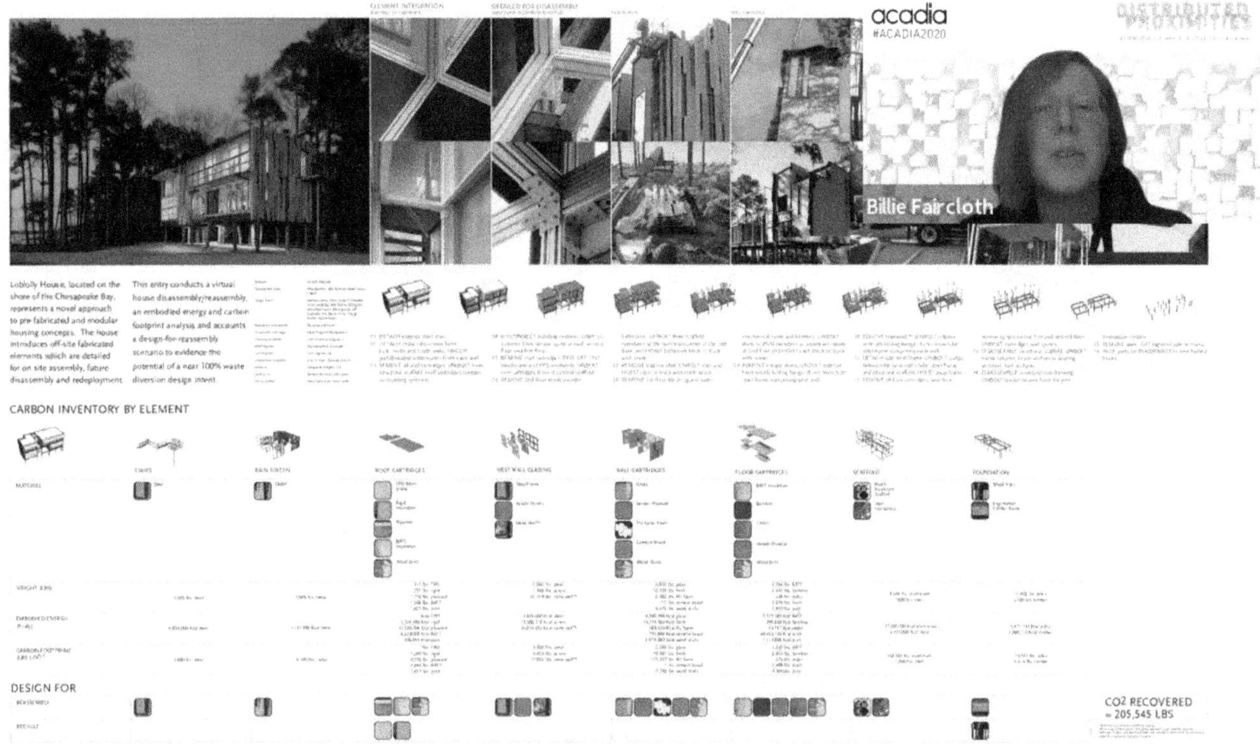

4 "I want to leave us with three questions. What are the outcomes of designed computation labor and who benefits from it? What are the current barriers in our work and where are the gaps in our understanding? And who do we need to be in conversation with now?" —Billie Faircloth (Image: KieranTimberlake)

I believe as long as this is taken on at the level of each individual office, no headway is going to be made. This is where I really want to advocate for architecture offices to work together and to work collaboratively, in order to make a united voice for the profession of architecture that isn't divided and isn't competitive with each other, but really just makes a stand in the whole process around a healthy planet. We need a clear statement that we refuse to do work that continues with extractive practices. Not competition; collaboration, united voice, and real, strong ethical statements.

BF: I appreciate this, Peggy, and agree. We've experienced this through our work on Tally.[3] We are one small voice that is part of a much larger movement within the profession, inclusive of architects, engineers, contractors, manufacturers, building owners, and policy makers. It's been an unexpected outcome, but it was certainly what we had dreamt would happen. Ours is one tool within a sea of other tools, but the discourse and movement across the industry has been where the real value is.

MC: Where can this kind of work interface with governance and governing bodies? Here I'm thinking of governance in the sense of planning and policy making, rather than professionalization.

BF: Regarding Tally: early on, the practice of design integrated life-cycle assessment, and carbon modeling quickly began to intersect with efforts of city-level policy makers who sought to mandate embodied carbon benchmarks for new construction. There are now country- and city-level efforts alongside other organizations, saying "Let's draw a line here."

In terms of governance in general, I think we need to look at how codes are made. Let's look at who lobbies for changes in code, and who has the power to lobby for changing code. That is an entirely other part of this issue that plays a huge role in everything that we're talking about. If we want to transform building culture and building practices, we can't leave governance off the table. But we also have to look at how that lobbying happens right now.

PD: The issue of governance makes me think about two different scales. One is bottom-up and the other is top-down. The bottom-up is in the work that we all want to be doing—that the two of you are doing—which is very

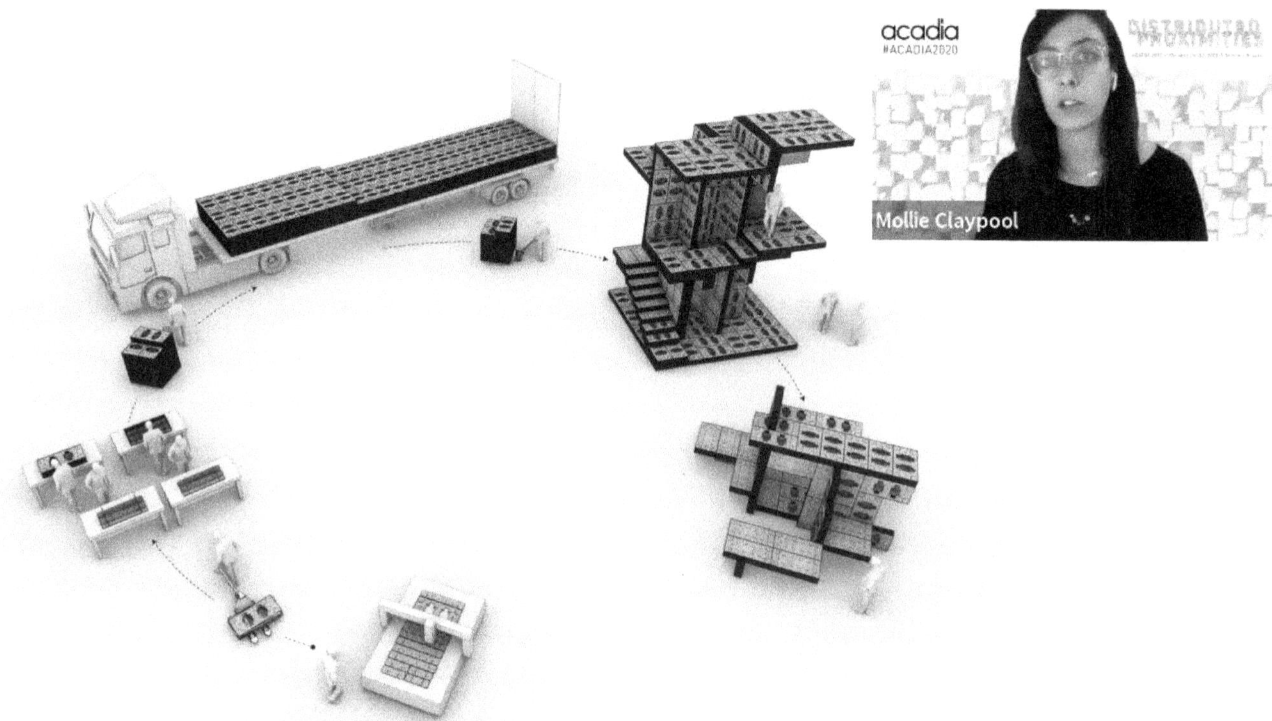

5 "We don't yet have the right kind of architectural syntax or production chain that can enable both increasing automation and community level engagement. We have a construction industry that's highly ineffective with productivity flatlined since the middle of the 20th century, a highly precarious workforce in short supply, and construction is one of the least digitized industries worldwide. Automation is largely centralized and extractive, creating more wealth for only the top 0.1%. [...] In this context, the work of AUAR is focused around issues of social justice. Our core belief is in the potential of increasing automation in our potential production to provide better opportunities and more housing for more people." —Mollie Claypool
(Image: Automated Architecture - AUAR)

integrated with the communities. It's not a traditional client. The more on-the-ground work one is doing, the more you then deal with governance, real estate, codes, policies that affect that neighborhood, redlining, all those things, the more you kind of can't avoid governance at that level.

One gets one's hands dirty, and one's knowledge is amplified by that. The real work gets us there in some way and educates us.

The top-down really has to do with the institutional nature. It isn't just our individual agency or the individual agency of a firm, but we operate in institutions that should be doing much more around governance. For example, I think we architects at the Yale School of Architecture should be putting pressure on Yale University around their endowments, what they're invested in, and the governance that is basically real-estate driven. We could also say that the AIA might actually begin to take a stance and use their lobbying power, limited as it is, to talk about issues of governance that I don't think they're willing to touch with a 10-foot pole. We need our institutions to amplify our concerns.

MC: In an event with Amahra Spence of MAIA, she used the term "amplifying our interdependence"—which I think is a great way of capturing what we've been talking about today. Thank you again, Peggy and Billie, for taking the time to be here with us today.

NOTES

1. Howard Davis, *The Culture of Building* (Oxford: Oxford University Press, 1999).
2. See "A Conversation on Data and Bias" in this volume.
3. For more information on Tally, see https://kierantimberlake.com/page/tally.

Peggy Deamer is Professor Emerita of Yale University's School of Architecture and principal in the firm of Deamer, Studio. She is the founding member of the Architecture Lobby, a group advocating for the value of architectural design and labor. She is the editor of *Architecture and Capitalism: 1845 to the Present* (Routledge, 2014) and *The Architect as Worker: Immaterial Labor, the Creative Class, and the Politics of Design* (Bloomsbury, 2015), as well as *Architecture and Labor* (Routledge, 2020). Articles by her have appeared in *Log*, *Avery Review*, *e-Flux*, and *Harvard Design Magazine*, among other journals. Her theory work explores the relationship between subjectivity, design, and labor in the current economy. Her design work has appeared in *HOME*, *Home and Garden*, *Progressive Architecture*, and the *New York Times*, among other journals and periodicals. She received *Architectural Record*'s 2018 Women in Architecture Activist Award.

Billie Faircloth is a Partner at KieranTimberlake, where she leads a transdisciplinary group leveraging research, design, and problem-solving processes across fields including environmental management, chemical physics, materials science, and architecture. She fosters collaboration between disciplines, trades, academies, and industries to define a relevant problem-solving boundary for the built environment. Billie has published and lectured internationally on themes including research methods for a transdisciplinary and transscalar design practice; the production of new knowledge on materials, climate, and thermodynamic phenomena through the design of novel methods, tools, and workflows; and the history of plastics in architecture to demonstrate how architecture's "posture" towards transdisciplinary practices and new knowledge has changed over time.

She is an Adjunct Professor at the University of Pennsylvania Weitzman School of Design and has served as the BarberMcMurry Professor at the University of Tennessee, Knoxville, and VELUX Visiting Professor at the Royal Danish Academy of Fine Arts. She is the author of *Plastics Now: On Architecture's Relationship to a Continuously Emerging Material* (Routledge, 2015), and she received *Architectural Record*'s Women in Architecture Innovator Award in 2017. Billie is recognized as a Fellow at the American Institute of Architects, an honor bestowed on those who create exceptional work and contributions to architecture and society.

Mollie Claypool is an architecture theorist and activist. She is Director of Automated Architecture Ltd (AUAR), a design and technology studio in the UK, and Co-Director of Automated Architecture (AUAR) Labs at The Bartlett School of Architecture, UCL, where she is History and Theory Coordinator in MArch Architectural Design in B-Pro. Her work broadly focuses on issues of social justice highlighted by the increasing automation in architecture and design production, such as the future of work, housing, platforms, localized manufacturing, and circular economies. She is the Managing Editor of *Prospectives*, a new open-source peer-reviewed journal supported by The Bartlett. Mollie has studied at Pratt Institute, AA School of Architecture, and The Bartlett. In parallel to her work in architecture, she is also a trade unionist, an environmental activist, and a birth worker.

PEER-REVIEWED PAPERS

LABOR AND PRACTICE

"The kinds of issues that computational design can enable architects to address—better performance, better carbon footprints, a certain 'do it yourself'-ness that communities can engage with—these are the issues that continue to be left out of normal studio discourse, but become foregrounded in computational design. Another way of saying that is, computational design and digital labor at least talks about labor. They put labor—what we as designers actually do—on the table in a way that a normal design studio doesn't. Computational design foregrounds the process in lieu of the product."

—Peggy Deamer, "A Conversation on Labor and Practice"

Deamer's "digital labor" forms the heart of this collection of papers, foregrounding "process in lieu of the product." With topics ranging from material research, fabrication techniques, and issues of construction labor, these processes also demonstrate the type of "interdependence"—beyond collaboration—that concluded the discussion.

Con-Create

A Geometrical Approach to Mitigate High-Tech Machinery Requirements for Construction of Irregular Concrete Structures

Arman KhalilBeigi Khameneh*
University of Tehran

Esmaeil Mottaghi*
University of Tehran

Ali Ghazvinian
Penn State University

Saeede Kalantari
Tarbiat Modares University

*Authors contributed equally to the research.

1

1 Completed architectural-scale pavilion as a proof of concept.

ABSTRACT

Net structures, because of their minimal material waste and intuitive aesthetics, are gaining more interest recently. There are various efforts to redesign the tensile- and compression-only structures, as the computational tools and novel materials have broadened the scope of geometries possible to construct. However, the fabrication process of these structures faces different challenges, especially for mass construction. Some of these challenges are related to the technology and equipment utilized for materializing these complicated forms and geometries. Working with concrete as a quickly forming material for these irregular forms seems promising. Nevertheless, using this material has difficulties, including the preparation of formworks and joints, material reinforcement, structural behavior in the fresh state, and the assembly procedure. This paper introduces a method based on computational design and geometrical solutions to address some of these challenges. The goal is to shift the complexity of construction from the high-tech equipment used in the fabrication stage to integrating design and fabrication through a hierarchical system made entirely by affordable 2D CNC laser cutters. The stages of developing the method and the process of designing and building an architectural size proof-of-concept prototype by the proposed method are discussed. The efficiency of the method has been shown by comparing the designed prototype with the Con-Create Pavilion.

INTRODUCTION

There has been growing interest in the construction of net structures recently. These are structures that bear a single kind of stress, like tensile- or compression-only structures. By avoiding the use of materials in unnecessary points of structural elements, these structures reduce material waste and suggest more intuitive aesthetic forms (Rippmann and Block 2013).

Compression-only structures have been the dominant method of building roofs in the shape of vaults and domes for centuries (Block et al. 2010). After the invention of high-strength materials such as concrete and steel, the compression-only structures were replaced by flexural structures like frames. Recently, problems such as the depletion of natural resources and the increasing emission of greenhouse gases in the construction industry have led designers to reconsider net structures. Efforts of scholars from Block Research Group (Oval et al. 2019; Bhooshan et al. 2018; Heisel et al. 2017) and Polyhedral Structures Laboratory (Bolhassani et al. 2018) are examples of this kind of structure. However, these novel structures are facing unsolved technical challenges to be used for mass construction.

The major problem in the mass construction of these structures is the availability of the technologies needed for the formworks and assembly. Most similar projects have used complex CNC milling machinery, negative/additive molds, or robotic arms for formworks. Sarafian, Culver, and Lewis (2017) have used the idea of cooperative robotic fabrication to keep the geometry of elements accurate during the casting and curing process. Parascho et al. (2017) applied the same idea of using two articulated robotic arms on a more extensive gantry system to accurately position elements in 3D space. These approaches offer higher precision in fabrication.

Nevertheless, these methods are dependent on the machinery involved. This high-tech equipment is quite expensive, not widely accessible, and requires extensive preprogramming, knowledgeable labor, and special tools. Another solution is to use subtractive manufacturing to fabricate negative molds. Negative molds also require high accuracy and use specific machinery, which is more accessible than robotic arms. However, there are two bottlenecks with this method. First, due to the nature of high-axis milling, complicated parts may need to be fabricated from more than one piece of mold. Besides, there is a considerable amount of material required for molds, engraved in a time- and energy-consuming process. These extra materials are mostly expanded-foams or resin

2

2 Exemplary elements of the structure, fabricated via the proposed system of elements.

and fiberglass, which are not environmentally friendly. Moreover, while assembling parts of spatial structure, a system of scaffolding or falsework is needed to support the structure. This vital support is because the structures are designed for the entire dead-load exerted by their weight. As another solution, additive manufacturing (AM) is a more sustainable method. Nevertheless, AM also faces limitations for material choice and durability (Li et al. 2020). In this paper, we are introducing a solution to address these problems.

In the proposed system, we have tried to define a method for designing, fabricating, and constructing a funicular manifold concrete structure. No high-tech machinery and extra elements such as falsework or scaffolding system are needed. As they have dry joints, elements can be dismantled, used again, and maneuvered by two amateur workers. The proposed method integrates parts and performs so that each element has a crucial role in solidifying and controlling the geometry and contributing to structural behavior and assembly needs. Considering all these, the proposed method is more sustainable than the typical methods in several aspects. While implementing the method, more advantages in the structural behavior and concrete curing process have been found, covered in the following.

METHODOLOGY

There is still a considerable gap between the design tools and methods, and the level of complexity that they offer, and the extent of our use of them (Pottmann 2007). Novel computer-aided design (CAD) tools enable designers to design intricate forms that may not be fully fabrication-aware. Nevertheless, 'fabrication intelligence' is bridged by the help of cutting-edge machinery. Using this high-tech equipment results in either a considerable amount of postprocessing or postrationalization or is covered by machining solutions. Methodologies that use computational geometry are beneficial as they embed the fabrication and

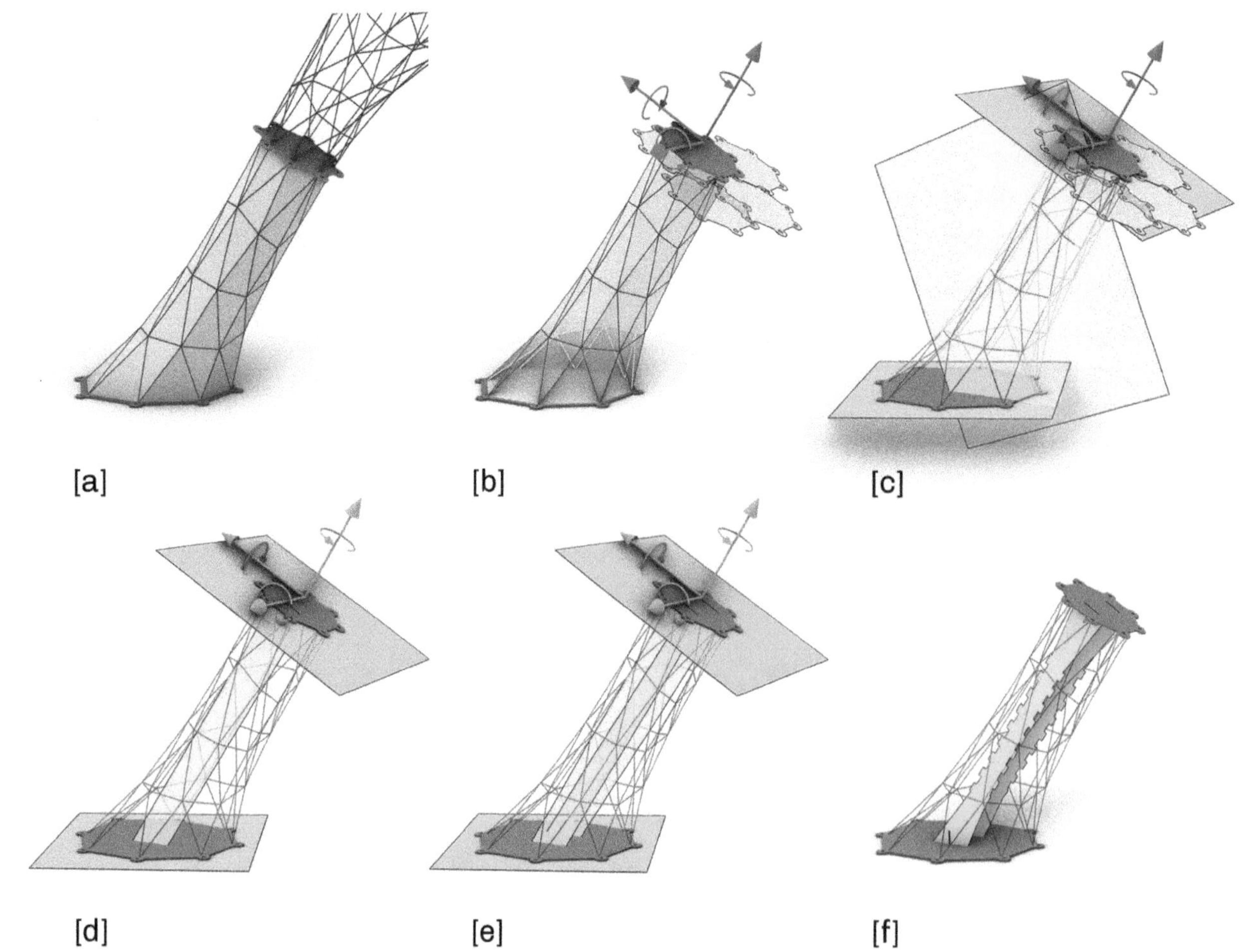

3 The geometrical approach to design two-valence elements of the system.

construction data within the design process in a more efficient way to save more time and energy.

In the proposed method, the structural elements of the net structures can be designed and built by 2D CNCs (in our case, laser cutting) while the complexity shifts towards the geometrical and computational solutions. This shift means that the accuracy obtained by cutting-edge machinery can be replaced with a procedure of integrated design and fabrication solutions.

In this system's first stage, a data-driven geometry is designed and optimized to relax the geometry and regulate the base network's stress flow utilizing a customized dynamic force density equation (Schek 1974) and its application with computational geometry. Then, considering the structure's requirements, elements are shaped and prepared to be fabricated with the conventional laser cutting CNC. Furthermore, to make the system more applicable, the material for filling the formworks is studied and enhanced. Finally, a prototype to show the proof of concept has been designed and built (Fig. 1). The details of each stage of designing and building are discussed in the following steps. The critical value in this method is that by losing all the negative molds, falsework, and 3D milling, the accuracy of the system in assembly tends to drop critically. Nevertheless, in the proposed method, a hierarchical system of elements is proposed to support and correct the geometry and minimize possible errors throughout casting and assembling (Fig. 2).

Method Implementation

The structural elements must address precision and efficiency, which means minimal deviation in molding and assembly. The goal is to eliminate the need for high-tech machinery. Besides, elements must be designed to tolerate the fresh concrete weight and the stresses while assembling the structure, with minimum deformation. To do so, we have taken advantage of a steel skeleton system, made with

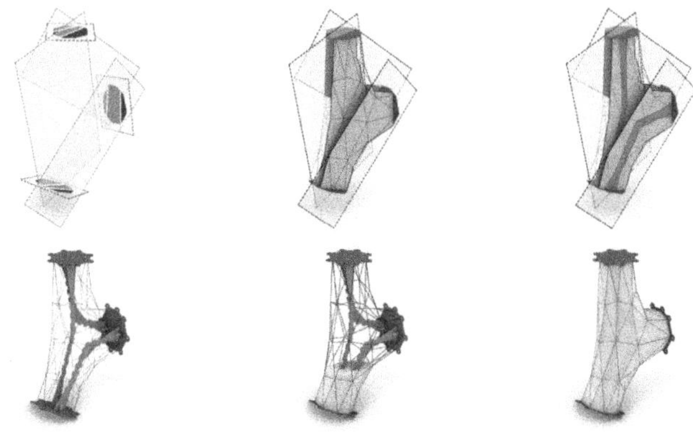

4 The geometrical approach to design three-valence elements of the system.

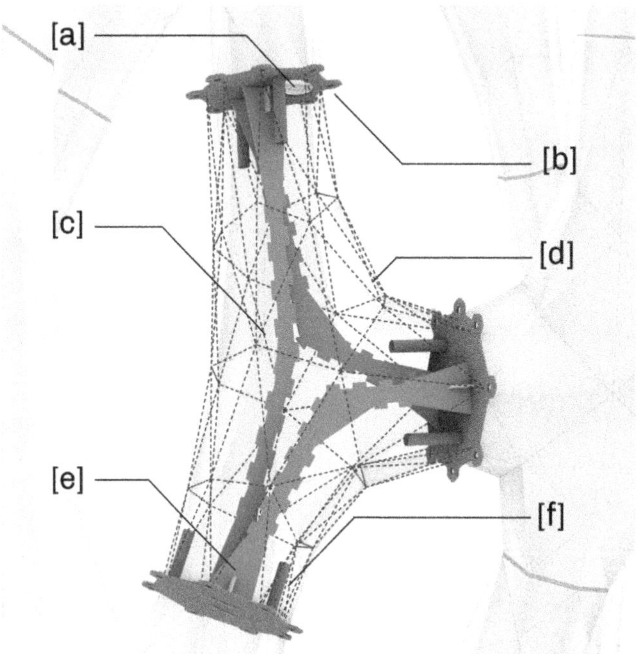

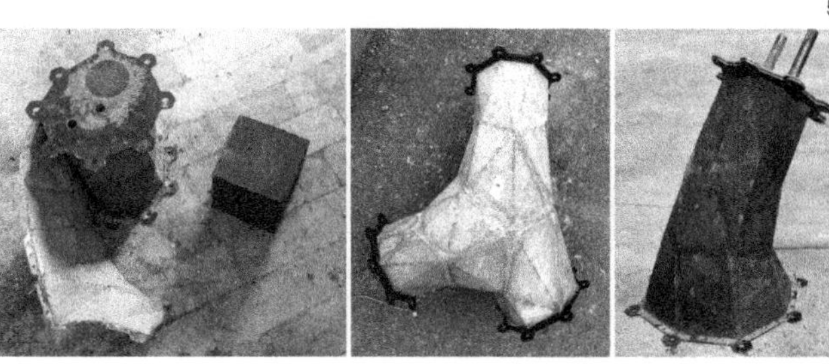

5 Parts of the hierarchical system of structure.

6 The unmolded element of the system.

two-dimensional elements, which serve multiple purposes. The elements of the system are from different valences. To show the application of the system, we scrutinize a two-valance element because of its simplicity (Fig. 3a). Each element includes an envelope mesh, connecting endplates, and the skeleton system details.

The most critical challenge in each element is orienting and locating the connecting plates precisely, as they have a crucial role in the fabrication of the elements. Supposing one end is set, the other connecting endplate(s) must be kept in the proper location(s) with no relative transition (Fig. 3b). To do so, we can add an element in the plane perpendicular to both connecting plates. This plane needs to comply with several criteria (Fig. 3c). First, these skeletal elements must be adequately distant from the outer shell to be covered by concrete. In addition, the other criterion is the relative distance between the endpoints, since this distance is the critical parameter of slenderness ratio to avoid local buckling. Next, these skeletal elements are sought to be in tensile stress regions. Finally, in more complex elements, such as three or four valences, these inner parts might collide with other parts. Thus, we defined a recursive procedure between each element's overall geometry and the discretization method of designing the inner skeleton. All four criteria need to be fulfilled unless the segmentation changes recursively.

After finding the proper plane fulfilling the above-mentioned criteria, we locate the guide strap (Fig. 3d). Additionally, we need to hinder the relative rotation, too. For this purpose, another guide strap with the same conditions is added (Fig. 3e). This time, all the required criteria are subject to the distance between two straps. To control the rotation better, each end of the straps is thicker. For a better adhesion between steel and concrete, the straps are ribbed (Fig. 3f). Hence, the bars' indentations provide more bond with the concrete to transmit the bars' force to the concrete following simple geometric details. These details are discussed below in "Structural Analysis." In this stage, relative transition is impeded. We then added secondary stiffeners to connect plates and straps to enhance the joints. The process is repeated for higher valences with the same criteria (Fig. 4).

In summary, each element includes connection plates (Fig. 5b), which are the dry joints among elements, guide straps that orient and locate these plates in their precise locations (Fig. 5c), stiffeners that enhance the connection between those two (Fig. 5e), and outer shells as reusable formwork for fresh concrete (Fig. 5d). The constraints of distance, maneuverability, and avoiding collisions are more difficult in complex elements than two-valence elements. This complexity requires more iterations in the recursive procedure for each element. In the fabrication process, we added other details such as holes for pouring concrete, openings for air evacuation throughout vibration (Fig. 5a), and spike

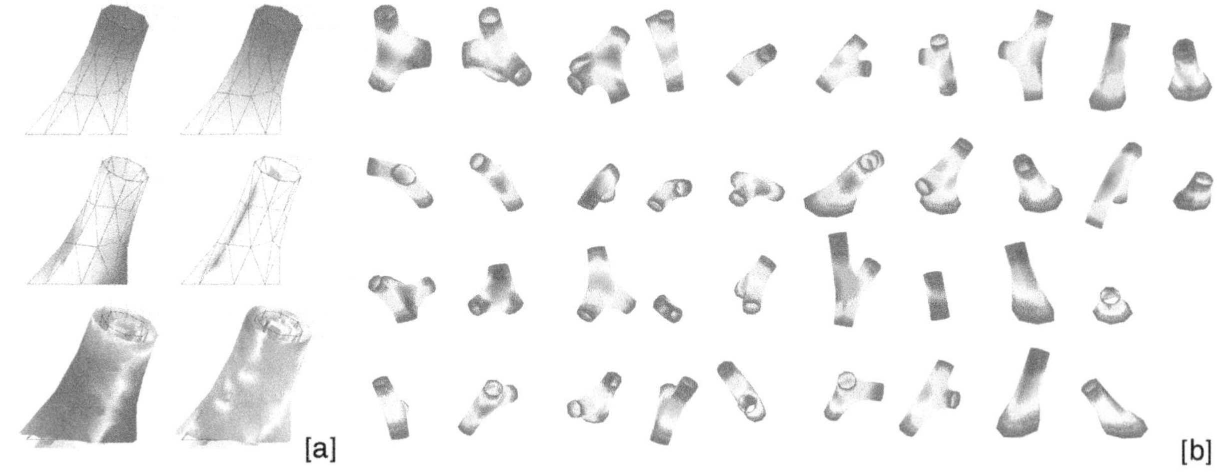

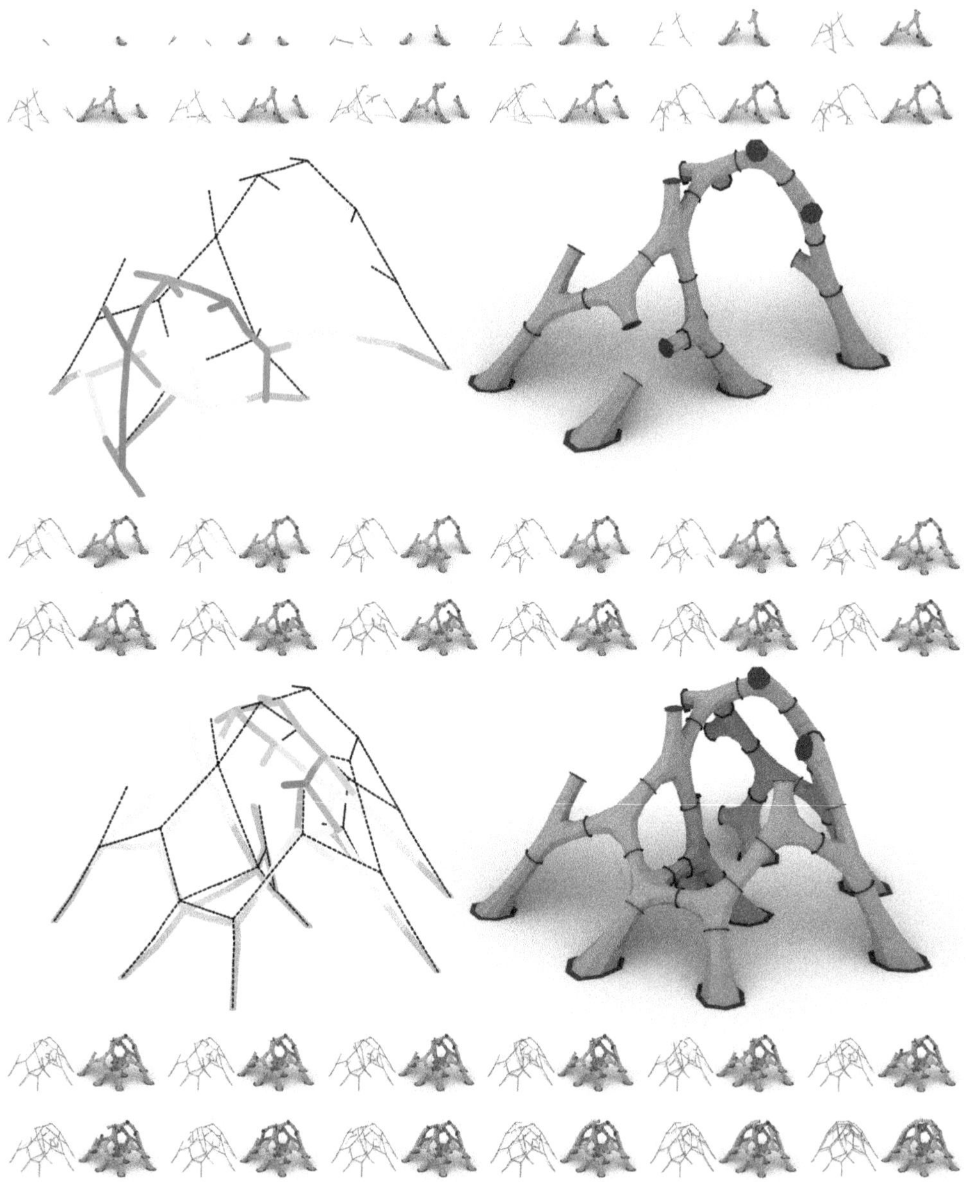

7

8

7 [a] FEM Analysis to study the structural rigidity and capacity with and without the guide straps. The first column depicts displacement, principal stresses, and utilization ratio, respectively, without utilizing guide straps. The second column shows the mentioned three criteria after using guide straps. [b] FEM Analysis for each element.

8 The procedural analysis and optimization of the assembly process of the Con-Create Pavilion.

Table 1. Structural and mechanical properties of the concrete mix.

Concrete Mix Properties	
Average Compressive Strength (Mpa)	22.5
Average Tensile Strength (Mpa)	2.8
Dry Density (Kg/m3)	1400
Wet Density (Kg/m3)	1540
Modulus of elasticity (g/m3)	119500
Slump Test (cm)	≥20
Slump Flow Test (cm)	40-50

bars to control adjacent elements' shear load (Fig. 5f). These spike bars also work as guides for assembly.

FABRICATION DEVELOPMENT

The proposed method results in parts that shape the elements fulfilling all the mentioned criteria. To materialize the outcome, more challenges need to be addressed. The filling material, the structural behavior, and the assembly strategy are the most crucial challenges discussed in this part.

Material Study

One of the essential parameters of the system is the filling material, in this case, concrete. The material exploration in this research is concentrated on enhancing concrete to be used with the proposed system. In this sense, lightweight and workable concrete are desired. Expanded light aggregations have been used to decrease the density of the final concrete. The additives of the concrete mixture are fibers and superplasticizers. Enhancing the concrete's mechanical behavior, fibers of steel and polypropylene microfibers have been added to the mixture. The superplasticizers are used because of the small diameter of elements, which are about 15 centimeters, and the steel skeleton's complexity. This complexity requires a workable concrete with high viscosity. After examining different vibration methods, we decided to add 0.5% superplasticizers to make the concrete self-compacted. On the one hand, because of the dense inner skeleton, motorized vibration from inside does not work. On the other hand, vibration tables separate the water and cement and work poorly for this system, so mechanical surface vibration was used. Finally, we used a lightweight, workable mixture. The 0.5 water-to-cement ratio of the concrete is strong enough for the proposed system (Table 1). Our tests found that the outer shell can save the water in the fresh concrete and help with the curing process. After unfolding the outer shells, spike bars are added, and parts are ready to be assembled (Fig. 6).

Structural Analysis

For such an innovative fabrication method, a novel reinforcement method that is more compatible with the entire system works better. The most critical requirement of such a method is a high degree of freedom regarding complicated shapes. Asprone et al. (2018) classify possible approaches of reinforcing concrete into six various methods or a hybrid solution including more than one. Regarding the classification, we used a hybrid method with arrangement and placement of configurations inside the concrete before casting with the ribbed strap guides and addition of reinforcement agents to the material itself. For

9

9 The Con-Create Pavilion.

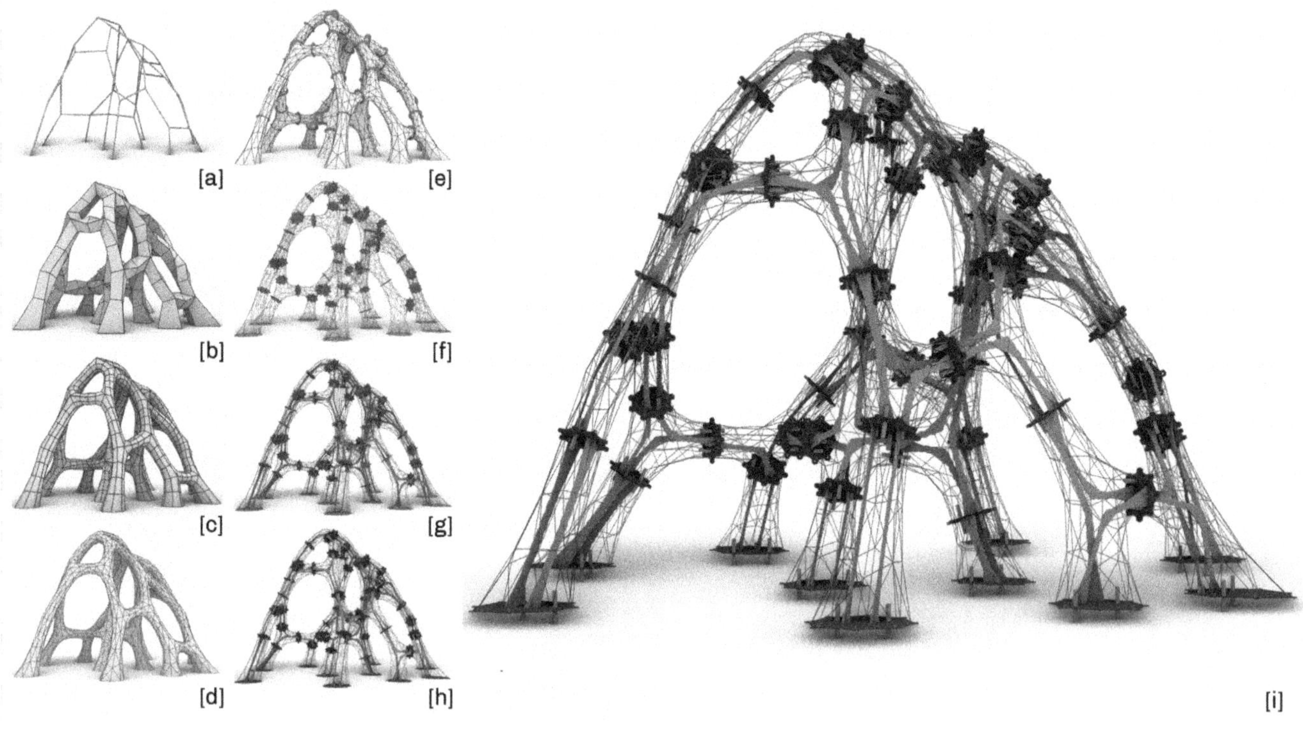

10 Stages of development of the segmented model form via the recursive method and details of the hierarchical skeleton system for the pavilion.

the latter, as mentioned, we have added steel and glass microfibers to the mixture to compensate for lightweight aggregates' natural weakness.

One question regarding the proposed system is if the ribbed guide straps can reinforce the concrete adequately so that we no longer need to use steel bars and enhance the system's structural behavior. To answer this question, we evaluated the displacement as stiffness criterion and stress utilization in each element (Fig. 7). We found that straps actively absorb tensile stress so that the concrete remains in compressive stress. Further, the guide straps suitably increase the stiffness. Numeric FEM analysis confirms that adding guide straps reduces displacement. After adding the ribbed guide straps, maximum displacement, under self-weight and lateral load, decreased by 82%. Maximum compressive stress decreased by 32.2%, and tensile stress was reduced by 52%. These results verify the fact that the ribbed guide straps have been engaged in the tensile load-bearing system. Thus, they effectively play the role of reinforcement in the concrete structure.

Assembly

The assembly process is a critical stage in the fabrication of compressive-only structures (Beyeler, Bazin, and Whiting 2015; Kao et al. 2017) since elements are designed to bear compressive stresses under dead load. However, during assembly, elements undergo bending stresses as there is not enough support. Thus, it is of great importance to optimize this stage to minimize the unpredicted imposed stresses. To study the assembling pattern, a procedural analytic process is used (Fig. 8). We reversed the process and supposed the structure was fully assembled. Then we excluded parts one at a time to determine the relative effects of their elimination on the stability of the incomplete structure. To evaluate, the criterion is the lower displacement and residual energy in the remaining model. The part with the least effect on the stability, P_0, will be the last to assemble. The procedure proceeds by determining the second-to-last element, P_1. The topological connectivity of the entire structure inquires that by eliminating which element, the structure is less stressed among the neighbors of P_0. Next, the neighbors of both P_0 and P_1 are examined for the next stage, and the process iterates as needed to ultimately determine the assembly sequence. The reverse approach in the proposed method is crucial, as the direct method seems more time-consuming in terms of computation time and capacity, especially in structures with more elements.

ARCHITECTURAL-SCALE PROOF OF CONCEPT

To ensure the efficiency of the proposed method, a large

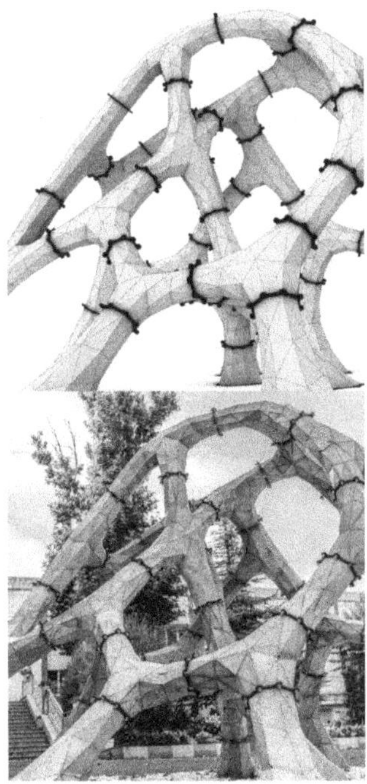

11 Comparison of the designed and the built pavilion.

12 The Con-Create Pavilion.

scale pavilion was designed and fabricated that inscribes a 5 x 4 x 3 cube as its bounding box (Fig. 9).

The work's overall geometry is created regarding a base network derived from the heatmap of the people commuting on the site of the project. We created an interconnecting network by a set of points extracted from the heatmap. Then, through a physical implementation of force density relaxation, similar to a particle-mass spring system, the primary network emerges. Followed by a secondary relaxation process, the 3D network is processed, which relaxes nodes and moderates the elements' angles. In this system, the springs' stiffness, the particles' masses, and the distances were adjusted based on the corresponding stresses that each element bears. Together, these enable control of geometry intuitively to comply with architectural requirements. This form-finding process ensures that the resulting form will only undergo compressive forces with complex-shaped load-bearing elements.

With all of the previously mentioned outcomes, we started materializing the concept in a real-scale pavilion. In this stage, the previously created network (Fig. 10a) undergoes volumetric modeling to create a thickened mesh (Fig. 10b). The thickness for each element is dependent on its stress. As the tests showed that circular convex sections tend to be less deformed under freshly poured concrete pressure, the base mesh was relaxed and smoothened (Fig. 10c, 10d). Thicknesses of the mesh that reflect the corresponding stresses eventually varied between 15 and 45 centimeters. Naturally, the thicker parts are in the elements closer to the ground, and the thinner ones are in the upper layers.

At this stage, the final mesh needs to be segmented regarding the criteria of the system. For the segmentation procedure, a fitness function was defined, depending on three main goals: fulfilling the criteria for each element, structural behavior, and the total number of parts. This procedure results in an explicit segmented form (Fig. 10e). In the next step, endplates are shaped (Fig. 10f) and the details of dry joints are added. Then, the guide straps are located (Fig. 10g). In this step, if we cannot find a fulfilling guide strap, the segmentation starts to be modified. Afterward, secondary stiffeners are added to solidify the system, and finally, spike bars are placed (Fig. 10h). The outcome of this recursive system is the final form of the structure (Fig. 10i). Comparing the designed geometry and the fabricated pavilion confirms the efficiency of the proposed method. (Fig. 11). The Con-Create Pavilion (Fig. 12) comprises 38 elements resulting from the application of the aforementioned criteria. The final product was constructed with less than 1.4 cubic meters of concrete and assembled by a team of amateur workers.

CONCLUSION

A geometry-based system for designing and building irregular concrete structures has been introduced, and a proof-of-concept architecture scale prototype discussed.

All the structural connections are dry joints, making it possible to dismantle and reassemble the structure in another location.

The core value of the system resides in the fabrication system. An interconnected system of two-dimensional elements has been proposed with two significant advantages. First, the proper fabrication of the elements is ensured by the computational application of geometrical procedures in lieu of high-tech machinery. This approach mitigates the necessity of using complex machinery that is not widely accessible and requires excessive preprogramming. Furthermore, through computational geometry this method is more efficient than similar methods in cost, time, and material. Second, as our analyses verify, the internal network of elements in the skeleton also serves as reinforcement in the concrete. This result integrates the reinforcement system with the entire fabrication method. In addition to these, the assembly process has been modeled and simulated with minimal support needed during construction.

ACKNOWLEDGMENTS
The Pavilion was built through a cooperation between the University of Tehran's architecture faculty, the Center of Excellence in Architectural Technology (CEAT), and the University of Tehran Science and Technology Park. The authors would like to thank the students of the Architecture Technology MA class of 2021.

REFERENCES

Asprone, Domenico, Costantino Menna, Freek P. Bos, Theo A.M. Salet, Jaime Mata-Falcón, and Walter Kaufmann. 2018. "Rethinking Reinforcement for Digital Fabrication with Concrete." *Cement and Concrete Research* 112: 111–121. https://doi.org/10.1016/j.cemconres.2018.05.020.

Beyeler, Lukas, Jean-Charles Bazin, and Emily Whiting. 2015. "A Graph-Based Approach for Discovery of Stable Deconstruction Sequences." In *Advances in Architectural Geometry 2014*, edited by P. Block, J. Knippers, N. J. Mitra, and W. Wang, 145–157. Springer.

Bhooshan, Vishu, David Reeves, Shajay Bhooshan, and Philippe Block. 2018. "MayaVault—a Mesh Modelling Environment for Discrete Funicular Structures." *Nexus Network Journal* 20 (3): 567–582. https://doi.org/10.1007/s00004-018-0402-z.

Block, Philippe, Lorenz Lachauer, and Matthias Rippmann. 2010. "Validating Thrust Network Analysis Using 3D-Printed, Structural Models." In *Proceedings of the International Association for Shell and Spatial Structures Symposium*, November 8-12 2010, Shangai, China.

Bolhassani, Mohammad, Masoud Akbarzadeh, Mehrad Mahnia, and Ramtin Taherian. 2018. "On Structural Behavior of a Funicular Concrete Polyhedral Frame Designed by 3D Graphic Statics." *Structures* 14: 56–68. https://doi.org/10.1016/j.istruc.2018.02.002.

Heisel, Felix, Juney Lee, Karsten Schlesier, Matthias Rippmann, Nazanin Saeidi, Alireza Javadian, Adi Reza Nugroho, Tom Van Mele, Philippe Block, and Dirk E Hebel. 2017. "Design, Cultivation and Application of Load-Bearing Mycelium Components: The MycoTree at the 2017 Seoul Biennale of Architecture and Urbanism." *International Journal of Sustainable Energy Development* 6 (1): 296–303. https://doi.org/10.20533/ijsed.2046.3707.2017.0039.

Kao, Gene T C, Axel Körner, Daniel Sonntag, Long Nguyen, Achim Menges, and Jan Knippers. 2017. "Assembly-Aware Design of Masonry Shell Structures: A Computational Approach." In *Proceedings of the International Association for Shell and Spatial Structures Symposium*, 2017, Hamburg, Germany, 1-10.

Li, Zhanzhao, Maryam Hojati, Zhengyu Wu, Jonathon Piasente, Negar Ashrafi, José P. Duarte, Shadi Nazarian, Sven G. Bilén, Ali M. Memari, and Aleksandra Radlińska. 2020. "Fresh and Hardened Properties of Extrusion-Based 3D-Printed Cementitious Materials: A Review." *Sustainability* 12 (14): 5628. https://doi.org/10.3390/su12145628.

Oval, R., M. Rippmann, R. Mesnil, T. Van Mele, O. Baverel, and P. Block. 2019. "Feature-Based Topology Finding of Patterns for Shell Structures." *Automation in Construction* 103: 185–201. https://doi.org/10.1016/j.autcon.2019.02.008.

Parascho, Stefana, Augusto Gandia, Ammar Mirjan, Fabio Gramazio, and Matthias Kohler. 2017. "Cooperative Fabrication of Spatial Metal Structures." In *Fabricate*, edited by Menges Achim, Sheil Bob, Glynn Ruairi, and Skavara Marilena, 24–29. London: UCL Press.

Pottmann, Helmut. 2007. *Architectural Geometry. Vol. 10.* Bentley Institute Press.

Rippmann, Matthias, and Philippe Block. 2013. "Funicular Shell Design Exploration." In *ACADIA 13: Adaptive Architecture [Proceedings of the 33rd Annual Conference of the Association for Computer Aided Design in Architecture (ACADIA)]*, Cambridge, ON, Canada, 24–26 October 2013, edited by P. Beesley, O. Khan, and M. Stacey, 337–346. CUMINCAD.

Sarafian, Joseph, Ronald Culver, and Trevor S. Lewis. 2017. "Robotic Formwork in the MARS Pavilion Joseph Form Found Design Towards the Creation of Programmable Matter." In *ACADIA 2017: Disciplines and Disruption [Proceedings of the*

37th Annual Conference of the Association for Computer Aided Design in Architecture (ACADIA)], Cambridge, MA, 2–4 November 2017, edited by T. Nagakura, S. Tibbits, M. Ibañez, and C. Mueller, 522–533. CUMINCAD.

Schek, H-J. 1974. "The Force Density Method for Form Finding and Computation of General Networks." *Computer Methods in Applied Mechanics and Engineering* 3 (1): 115–134.

IMAGE CREDITS

All drawings and images by the authors.

Arman KhalilBeigi Khameneh is a digital architect. He holds a Master's degree in Architectural Technologies. He is a design technician and his career and teaching are focused on design computation and integration of cutting-edge or customized fabrication technologies into the design process. He pushes the boundaries of his designs to the intersection of computational geometry, digital fabrication, and material technologies.

Esmaeil Mottaghi is a computational designer, architect, and computational geometry researcher based in Tehran, Iran. He graduated with a master's degree in computational design from the University of Tehran and has several experiences as an expert for digital manufacturing and as a computational design tutor. He has also directed multiple digital fabrication and algorithmic design workshops organized by Tehran University and other architectural centers.

Ali Ghazvinian is a civil and architectural engineer interested in integrative design among different disciplines. He works on the border of computational design, biodesign, and material tinkering. After finishing his Bachelor's and Master's studies at the University of Tehran, Iran, he began his PhD studies at Penn State University.

Saeede Kalantari is a PhD researcher in architecture at Tarbiat Modares University (TMU). Her focus is on AI and ANN applications in architecture. She has two Bachelor's degrees in Computer Engineering and Architecture from the University of Tehran. Before starting her PhD, she finished her master's in Architectural Technologies from IUST. She has been assigned as a teaching and training assistant in the fields of fabrication, computational design, and smart materials at IUST and the University of Tehran.

Additive Thermoplastic Formwork for Freeform Concrete Columns

Mania Aghaei Meibodi
University of Michigan

Christopher Voltl
University of Michigan

Ryan Craney
University of Michigan

1 PLA thermoplastic formwork fabricated with FDM 3D printing.

ABSTRACT

The degree of geometric complexity a concrete element can assume is directly linked to our ability to fabricate its formwork. Additive manufacturing allows fabrication of freeform formwork and expands the design possibilities for concrete elements. In particular, fused deposition modeling (FDM) 3D printing of thermoplastic is a useful method of formwork fabrication due to the lightweight properties of the resulting formwork and the accessibility of FDM 3D printing technology. The research in this area is in early stages of development, including several existing efforts examining the 3D printing of a single material for formwork—including two medium-scale projects using PLA and PVA. However, the performance of 3D printed formwork and its geometric complexity varies, depending on the material used for 3D printing the formwork. To expand the existing research, this paper reviews the opportunities and challenges of using 3D printed thermoplastic formwork for fabricating custom concrete elements using multiple thermoplastic materials.

This research cross-references and investigates PLA, PVA, PETG, and the combination of PLA-PVA as formwork material, through the design and fabrication of nonstandard structural concrete columns. The formwork was produced using robotic pellet extrusion and filament-based 3D printing. A series of case studies showcase the increased geometric freedom achievable in formwork when 3D printing with multiple materials. They investigate the potential variations in fabrication methods and their print characteristics when using different 3D printing technologies and printing materials. Additionally, the research compares speed, cost, geometric freedom, and surface resolution.

INTRODUCTION

Concrete is the second most used material in the world, preceded only by drinking water, and is responsible for 8% of the world's carbon emissions. According to material chemist Karen Scrivener, the high consumption of concrete results from the fact that it is a very "low impact material" and replacing it with another material would ultimately increase the carbon footprint of the structure (Crow 2008, 63). In construction, concrete is a versatile and ubiquitous building material with structural integrity and the convenient ability to assume any shape and surface detailing. Yet the architectural potential of a concrete element is largely limited by our ability to fabricate its formwork.

Traditional methods used in formwork production are geometrically constraining, labor-intensive, and materially expensive. In fact, the cost of formwork can amount from 40% to 60% of the overall construction cost of a building, exceeding the combined total cost of concrete mixture, reinforcement materials, and labor (Lab 2007).

Additive manufacturing of formwork has expanded the geometric vocabulary of concrete design and enabled several new approaches to the manufacturing of concrete formwork. For example, binder jet 3D printing (BJP) was used in the production of a lightweight concrete slab in *Smart Slab* (Aghaei Meibodi et al. 2018), a concrete truss (Morel 2014), and the sprayed thin shell of the Swiss Pavilion at the Venice Biennale (Dillenburger 2016). While the BJP method offers a high level of geometric freedom, detailed resolution, and geometric precision of fabricated parts when compared to other 3D printing techniques, our research explores alternative methods of fabrication—using fused deposition modeling (FDM) technology—to fabricate thermoplastic formwork.

Compared to BJP, FDM 3D printing is widely accessible, can be used at a variety of scales, requires less postprocessing, uses less expensive printing materials, and requires less energy. The thermoplastic formwork manufactured using FDM is also lightweight, easy to transport, recyclable, reusable, and removable. For these reasons, FDM 3D printing of concrete formwork shows significant potential for its use in the construction industry.

There are several examples of research showcasing the benefits of FDM applications in concrete formwork; Peters (2015) presented small-scale flexible formwork based on FDM technology, Gardiner, Janssen, and Kirchner (2016) presented 3D printed wax formwork, thin-shell PLA formwork was used for a concrete canoe (Jipa et al. 2019), and dissolvable PVA was applied in a 900 mm high capital formwork (Leschok and Dillenburger 2019) and a 115 mm scaled-down column (Doyle and Hunt 2019). The body of research exploring adaptations of FDM in large-scale concrete construction is at an early stage of development, and the existing efforts are limited to the additive manufacturing of a single-material formwork—namely PLA, wax, and two medium-scale projects in PVA.

Employment of any technology for construction should allow fabrication of large-scale formwork in a timely and economical manner. Adapting FDM 3D printing methods, which have primarily been used for small-scale prototypical parts, to meet the scale and criteria of architectural construction introduces many challenges:

- FDM is a relatively slow 3D printing process, and speeding up the printing time has a negative impact on the precision and resolution of printed parts. Printing speed varies largely depending on the printing material, technique (robotic vs. desktop printer), and the geometry being printed (for example, branching geometries would require multiple start and stop points throughout the printing process).
- Conventional 3D printing of certain geometric features, such as overhangs and cantilevers, requires auxiliary support structures that significantly increase the fabrication time and the material waste when fabricating formwork with complex geometries.
- The interface between 3D printed layers is prone to delamination due to hydrostatic pressure of concrete against the formwork.
- Formwork removal is challenging for complex geometries with undercuts and small pockets. Care must be taken to ensure proper formwork draft angles and eliminate chipping on the concrete surface.
- Unavailability of design tools that enable precast and its formwork design with respect to the fabrication constraints of FDM 3D printing.

METHOD

This research project expands on the existing field of FDM 3D printed concrete formwork by investigating the degree of geometric freedom achievable in concrete formwork when printing with different materials—namely PLA, PVA, and PETG—and different FDM printing techniques—namely robotic pellet extrusion and filament-based Cartesian machines.

2 Robotic arm fitted with a custom-fabricated pellet extrusion end-effector.

PLA, PVA, PETG, and Multimaterial

This research seeks to achieve formal complexity in concrete by cross-referencing and investigating PLA, PVA, and PETG print materials, as well as a combination of PLA-PVA formwork. PLA (polylactic acid) is a common plastic material in the 3D printing industry, being both biodegradable and produced from renewable organic starches (Grossman and Nwabunma 2011). PVA (polyvinyl acetate) is a water-soluble synthetic polymer often used for support material on complex 3D prints due to its ease of removal when in direct contact with water. This research uses PVA to directly 3D print the formwork parts. Due to its high sensitivity to moisture, PVA requires airtight storage containers, and because of the material's sensitivity, PLA can clog the nozzle if it is left slightly hot or cold when not extruding. PETG (polyethylene terephthalate glycol) is a thermoplastic copolyester with high chemical resistance, durability, and ductility. It is also fully recyclable. This research hypothesizes that combinatory additive manufacturing of multimaterial formwork as a new approach will expand the geometric freedom of formwork in an economical manner.

Pellet Extrusion vs. Filament-Based Extrusion

Pellet-based and filament-based extrusion methods of 3D printing are both valid approaches to geometric complexity and are examined against each other in this research. In filament-based extrusion, thermoplastic filament is fed through a geared extruder that pushes it into a heat block, which melts and extrudes the polymer through a nozzle. In pellet-based extrusion, granules of material are fed through a hopper into a barrel with multiple heat zones. A motor-driven screw pushes the molten plastic through the barrel and out of a nozzle. Pellet-based extrusion has the following advantages over filament-based extrusion in the context of large-scale production in construction:

- Pellets come in a much greater variety of material choices. There are many pellets with high levels of carbon fiber that could not be produced in the form of filament, as it would be too brittle to wind onto a spool.
- Pellets can cost up to 10 times less than their filament counterparts.
- Pellet extruders can extrude significantly faster than filament-based extruders, since the pellet extruder's flow rate is only limited by the size and speed of the screw inside the barrel. In filament-based extrusion, flow rate is limited to speed of the filament drive wheel and the diameter of the nozzle, which must be smaller than the diameter of the filament to maintain the pressure and melt consistency needed for a quality print.
- Two advantages of pellets are the portability of the material and the ability to continuously dry and load the material into the end effector. When printing a 30 kg part with filament, the spool containing the filament would need to be replaced up to seven times.

Robotic vs. Desktop Printer

In this research, pellet extrusion was investigated using a six-axis robotic arm fitted with a custom-built pellet extruder end effector (Fig. 2). The pellet extruder was fitted with a 2 mm diameter print nozzle and integrated air cooling. The filament-based extrusion was explored using a large-format 3D printer with a build volume of 305 × 305 × 605 mm and a three-axis Cartesian system featuring a 0.4 mm diameter nozzle.

Computational Design

A synergy between FDM 3D printing of formwork and computational design is important in order to fully utilize the geometric freedom offered with 3D printing, achieve a high degree of customization, materialize the geometric complexity offered by algorithmic design, and reveal a new set of formal and topological possibilities.

In this research, computational design, material, and fabrication experiments are synchronized to create a feedback loop between them. Because of the flexibility offered by algorithmic and computational design, the design can be constantly reformed by feedback received from material and fabrication experiments.

CASE STUDY

To examine these approaches against the contextual requirements of architecture and construction—scale, production speed, cost, and structural performance—three concrete columns were designed and fabricated with identical bounding dimensions (1.00 m height x 0.35 m diameter), and a framework was developed for the exploring different methods.

The column is an ideal building element to express the geometric freedom offered by computational design and additive manufacturing. While the primary function of columns is to transfer the structural loads of a building, they also contribute to the aesthetic look of a building and their evolution expresses the technological capability of their time. Three case studies showcase the potential of FDM 3D printing for freeform formwork, with a variety of materials, to exceed what is possible through conventional formwork making methods.

FDM Printing of PLA and Agent-Based Computing of Slender Load-Bearing Ribs

The first column expands upon existing research into ultra-thin-shell concrete formwork by increasing the dimensions of the 3D printed formwork, examining its ability to resist hydrostatic pressure, casting slender concrete elements of varying diameters (10–50 mm), and enabling geometric and functional complexity. The 1 m tall, ultrathin 3D printed formwork—with a wall thickness of only 0.8 mm—was printed in 122 hours and used only 1.42 kg of PLA filament (Figs. 3, 4).

The computational design framework of this column was developed on the logic of swarm intelligence (Bonabeau, Theraulaz, and Dorigo 1999) and was employed using multiagent algorithms (Snooks 2018 and 2020). In a swarm-intelligent system, complex collective behavior emerges from interactions among individuals that exhibit simple behavior (Bonabeau, Theraulaz, and Dorigo 1999). Here, the design solution space is not predefined but emerges as a result of the interactions among and between individuals and their environment, as much as from the behaviors of the individuals themselves.

In this case study, a multiagent based algorithm was developed to connect the concrete rheology, structural

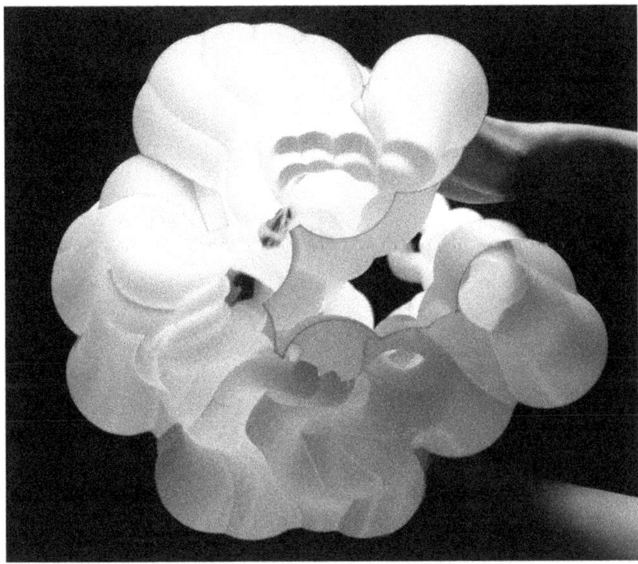

3 Ultrathin 3D printed PLA formwork with a 0.8 mm wall thickness.

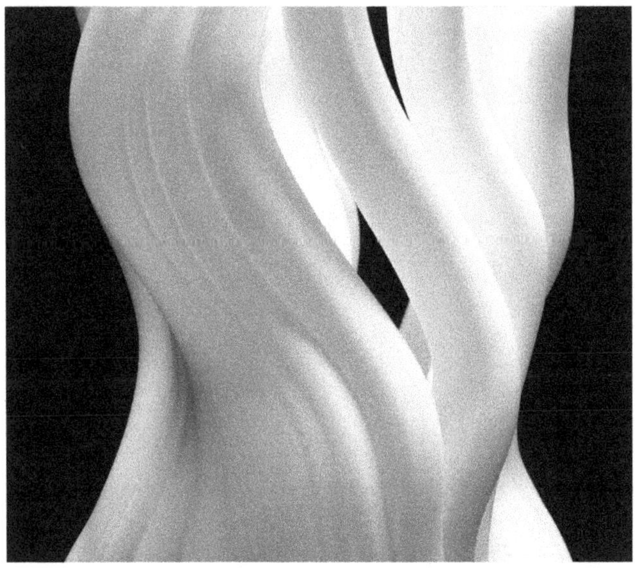

4 Detail of the layer resolution used for ultrathin 3D printed PLA formwork.

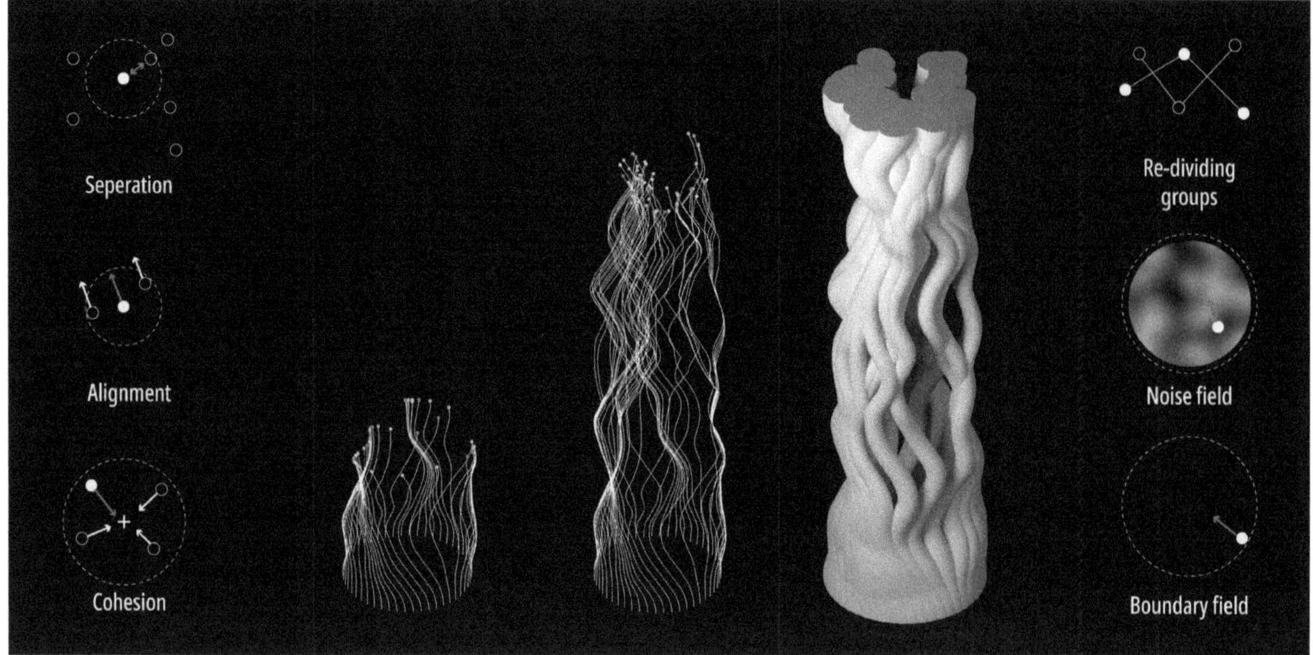

5 Visualization of the agent-based computational design process.

stability under dead load, material reduction, ornamentation, and castability. The geometry of the column emerges from the paths generated as a result of the interaction between agents representing the gravitational flow of fluid concrete (simulation of gravity forces) and their cohesion and alignment behaviors, informed by aesthetic and structural performance (Fig. 5).

This experiment opens the door to a novel hybrid design approach between the fields of agent-based design and computational fluid dynamics as they relate to the 3D printing of complex formwork. The question is: How does the method connect and enable cooperation between these various individual fields with collective performance? What interactions are needed to produce a formwork with minimal material that is stable throughout casting?

From the same model, the formwork parts and their detailing were generated automatically using the embedded fabrication logic built into an algorithm. Design model and fabrication techniques coevolve through a feedback loop between the generative design processes, refining the process of large-scale fused deposition modeling and prototypical casting. To counterbalance the hydrostatic pressure applied to the ultrathin formwork when casting, the formwork was placed into a reusable sandbox.

FDM Printing of PVA and Computing of the Inner Voids

The second column expands on existing research into water-soluble formwork by examining the performance of large-scale PVA formwork (1 m height) and strategically combining PVA and PLA prints into a single formwork. PVA dissolves in a high-moisture environment (Fig. 6); therefore, a formwork application enabled new design features for concrete elements with complex geometry, including inner voids, undercuts, long tubular voids, and deep hollow areas. However, the print speed of PVA was limited to ensure proper layer adhesion and required careful moisture control. By combining PVA and PLA, PVA was selectively applied to locations of geometric complexity and later washed away. The remainder of the formwork was printed in PLA, where formwork removal was not a constraint.

The multimaterial formwork consists of one PVA and two

6

PLA parts, printed using 1.75 mm diameter filament. The PVA filament required special considerations to prevent it from reacting with the water content present in the air, thus degrading the quality of the filament by producing air pockets in the material. This issue was mitigated by providing a controlled printing environment using desiccant and an airtight enclosure to dehumidify the material sealed inside. Also, the initial PVA printing tests did not properly adhere to the printing bed. This was resolved with a textured tape placed on the bed, an increased first layer extrusion rate (150%) and a decreased print speed (35 mm/s).

Print time was a major consideration in the production of the formwork. To accelerate the printing process, the print was split into PVA and PLA material sections, because printing with PLA is faster than PVA for the same geometry. The 640 mm high PLA parts were printed in 26h20m and the 360 mm high PVA part was printed in 37h30m.

The design of the geometry evolved along with material experimentation. PVA allowed for easy removal of formwork with undercuts and pockets, while the removal of the PLA was much more challenging and cumbersome with these features. Although PVA was initially chosen for its desirable water-soluble properties to ease the formwork removal, the first test showed that the water content in the concrete mixture weakens the structural performance of the PVA formwork. The wall thickness in this early prototype consisted of 2 shells with 0.4 mm width for each shell (0.8 mm in total). Because the PVA formwork would be exposed to a much higher moisture content in the full-scale cast, an additional layer was added to the shell, making the wall 1.2 mm thick.

Robotic Pellet Extrusion of PETG Formwork with Fabrication-Informed Computational Design

The third column design explores the robotic pellet extrusion of PETG formwork and addresses the demand for self-supporting reusable formwork that can be assembled on-site and withstand the hydrostatic pressure of cast-in-place concrete construction. The resulting 1 m tall, 6 kg, clear PETG thermoplastic formwork was printed with a 1 mm layer height and 3 mm wall thickness in eight hours. The robotic printing process was developed based on the following criteria: print speed, printable volume, layer height, wall thickness, degree of overhang, and the surface resolution. These performance criteria were selected for their impact on the overall fabrication time, print quality, and degree of geometric complexity in the fabricated formwork. Several permutations of these criteria were tested through an iterative prototyping process, thus identifying the constraints of the robotic printing setup. For example, it was found that the optimal print speed, layer height, and wall thickness to be 35 mm/sec, 1 mm, and 3 mm, respectively. These constraints define an ideal set of printing standards that could be applied to the final formwork print.

The iterative prototyping process revealed specific geometric constraints related to toolpath overhang between layers. Overhangs occur when the input geometry has a surface curvature in the vertical plane (Fig. 7a). When printing at 35 mm/s with a 3 mm extrusion width and 1 mm extrusion height, tests show that this overhang value is constrained to a maximum overhang angle of 33° between layers. Any surface curvature beyond this angle will cause significant surface deformation and eventual failure in layer adhesion. This type of failure would create

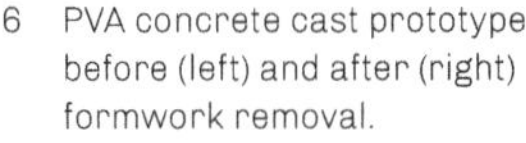

6 PVA concrete cast prototype, before (left) and after (right) formwork removal.

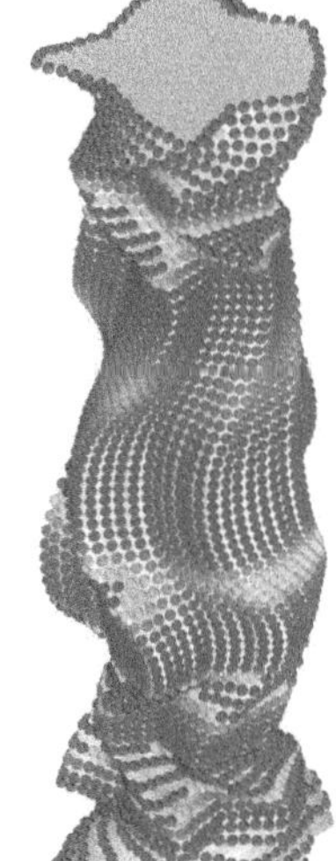

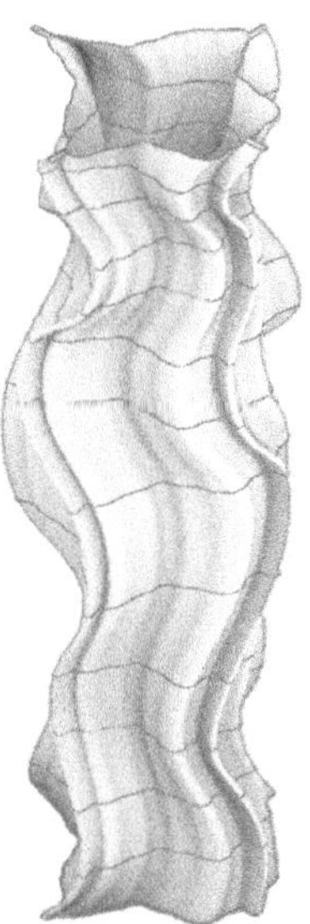

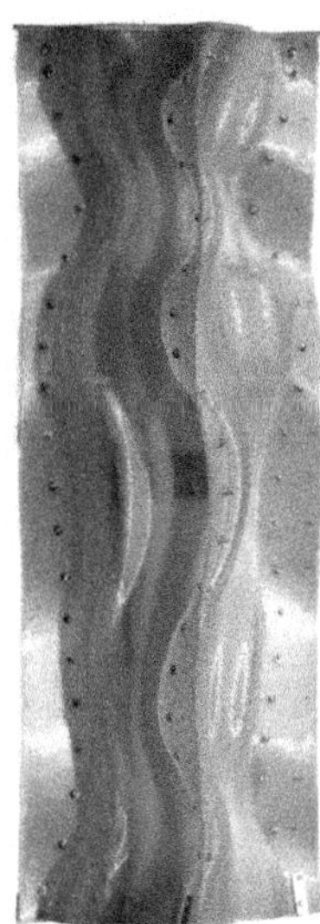

7 Robotic pellet extrusion case study, from left to right:

(a) Geometric analysis of print overhangs, as constrained by robotic pellet extrusion.

(b) Parametric model of the formwork.

(c) 3D printed PLA core (red) embedded within the transparent PETG formwork to reduce concrete use.

(d) PETG formwork capable of resisting the hydrostatic pressure of wet concrete without the need for additional support.

large openings in the formwork surface, leaving it unable to contain the concrete mixture.

To prevent overhang failure during the print, a Python script was developed to simulate and identify areas of the input geometry that exceed the limits of the robotic setup (Figs. 7a and 7b). Using this script, we were able to analyze and modify the surface geometry to meet the constraints prior to the actual print. Failure toward the end of a large-scale robotic print operation is both costly in terms of time and material. Thus, this fabrication-informed computational process increases the likelihood of a successful print and the efficiency of the printing process.

Once printing was completed, and the formwork panels were assembled, the formwork was prepared for concrete casting (Fig. 7c). A PVA-based mold release was painted onto the casting surfaces and silicone sealant was applied to the seam between each panel. A 3D printed PLA core element was placed in the center of the formwork to reduce concrete use and provide a functional core within the column to allow for integrated building services, such as electrical conduct, plumbing, air ducts, etc. An ultra-high-performance, fiber-reinforced concrete mixture was poured into the cavity of the formwork (Fig. 7d), and the concrete was visually inspected for air pockets through the transparent formwork. Once cured, the formwork was unbolted and removed, and the PVA mold release was rinsed from the concrete surface.

Hydrostatic pressure is the main force that the PETG formwork must resist during the casting process. The ductile nature of PETG increases its strength, but also results in deformation under load. It was observed that a deformation of up to 10 mm could occur without stress failure in the formwork. Tests performed with base attachment methods (securing the formwork to the base) that do not allow for this lateral movement resulted in formwork cracking and concrete leakage. Thus, care must be taken to design connections that can allow sufficient deformation.

RESULTS AND DISCUSSION

The results of the research are three different approaches to the design and fabrication of 3D printed thermoplastic formwork for concrete columns (Figs. 8, 9). Each method explores the ability to FDM print large-scale formwork using a different process. The following data was documented from each process for examination and comparison: print speed, geometrical freedom, formwork strength, and formwork removal. A summary of these results is presented in Figure 10 and in the following comparisons:

1. There were large variations in print speed between the printing processes, with the robotic pellet extrusion of PETG effectively printing each layer three times faster than PVA and 27% faster than PLA. Although the actual speed of the nozzle is sometimes faster in Cartesian printing, the increased volume of material flowing through the pellet extruder saves time by producing a sufficient wall thickness without the need for multiple passes.

2. The allowable geometrical complexity is heavily dependent on the material properties of the thermoplastic and the printing process. Robotically printed PETG was unable to reach the same overhangs as seen in the Cartesian methods (33 degrees vs. 45 degrees). In contrast, PVA was ideal for complex geometric forms (including narrow pipes, undercuts, and unreachable voids) due to its water-soluble properties. The PLA prints were capable of the same level of geometric complexity as the PVA counterparts; however, consideration must be made regarding the formwork removal.

3. PVA was the weakest of the formwork materials. Its water-soluble properties left it susceptible to degradation when left in a typical construction environment, which was worsened by the addition of water from the concrete. The PLA, although stronger than PVA, still required the support of a sandbox during the concrete casting process due to its thin wall thickness (0.8 mm). The much thicker PETG formwork (3 mm) was capable of resisting the hydrostatic forces of the concrete mixture without need for a sandbox.

4. The formwork removal process was conceptually unique for each case study. The PETG formwork, with its 3 mm wall thickness, was easily removed from the cured concrete and could be reassembled and reused in other concrete pours. However, the increased layer height of the robotic printing process left a noticeable texture on the concrete that may not be desired in certain situations. The PLA formwork removal process required cutting off the PLA in small pieces, a process that is both labor-intensive and destructive to the formwork. The PVA was the easiest to remove, as it could simply be rinsed or brushed off.

None of the thermoplastic materials outperformed the others in all categories; rather, each material has its unique strengths to be applied as necessary to achieve the desired result. This is exhibited most clearly in the hybrid approach of the PVA-PLA case study (Fig. 11). The addition of PLA decreased printing times (up to 50% less) and added cost

8 Three case studies of thermoplastic formwork enabled by FDM 3D printing: (a) PVA-PLA formwork for branched and twisted columns with inaccessible void in center; (b) PETG formwork produced through robotic pellet extrusion; (c) PLA formwork generated using agent-based computation print.

9 Resulting fiber-reinforced concrete columns.

Print Material	PLA	PVA	PETG
Material Format	1.75 mm filament	1.75 mm filament	Pellet
Printer Type	Enclosed Cartesian FDM printer	Enclosed Cartesian FDM printer w/ filament dry box	Pellet extruder end-effector on robotic arm
Nozzle Size (mm)	0.40	0.40	2.00
Nozzle Temp (C)	205	200	220
Print Speed (mm/s)	40.00 inner shell 70.00 outer shell	30.00	35.00
Extrusion Layer Width (mm)	0.40	0.40	3.00
Layer Height (mm)	0.25	0.40	3.00
Formwork Wall Thickness (mm)	0.80	1.13	3.00
Formwork Wall Layers	2	3	1
Effective Print Speed (Print Speed / # of Wall Layers) (mm/s)	27.50	10.00	35.00
Geometric Features (Undercuts, Inner Voids, and Narrow Long Tubes)	Branched and narrow long tubes (10–50 mm diameter), accessible for formwork removal	Branched and narrow twisted tubes (30–50 mm diameter) with unreachable voids and inner core	Freeform surface with undulating details. Inner formwork insert creates a voided core.

10

11

10 Matrix detailing the material, print setup, and formwork geometry developed through prototyping, which allows for successful 3D printing of formworks and cross-referencing between different formwork systems.

11 Intersection of PLA and PVA materials on a case study column formwork.

savings in areas where inner voids and undercuts are not present. The use of PVA shows promise in areas in which geometric complexity is present and a solution for fast and efficient formwork removal is needed.

CONCLUSION

This project demonstrates the production of lightweight concrete formwork—using PLA, PVA, and PETG—for the construction of structural concrete columns. FDM 3D printing of PLA thin-shell formwork can be used for extremely complex geometric features, including long tubular structures, but access for formwork removal should always be provided; FDM 3D printing of PVA is a great approach for higher-geometric complexity where access for formwork removal is limited. The PVA-PLA formwork can be a solution to a diversified complexity in concrete elements while keeping up with the speed and economy of production. Finally, robotic pellet extrusion of PETG is fast and efficient, and enables production of larger durable parts in a single print. In conclusion, this research shows that a hybrid and combinatorial approach to additive manufacturing can be more economical and efficient while enabling a high degree of geometric complexity.

ACKNOWLEDGMENTS

The presented case studies were designed and fabricated as part of the Materials Engagement course instructed by Dr. Mania Aghaei Meibodi at Taubman College of Architecture and Urban Planning, University of Michigan. A special thanks to the following students who worked on design and fabrication of these columns: Han-Yuan Chang, Carl Eppinger, Monik Gada, Chih-Jou Lin, Feras Nour, Aaron Weaver, and Chia-Ching Yen.

REFERENCES

Aghaei Meibodi, Mania, Andrei Jipa, Rena Giesecke, Demetris Shammas, Mathias Bernhard, Matthias Leschok, Konrad Graser, et al. 2018. "Smart Slab." In *ACADIA 2018: Recalibration: On Imprecision and Infidelity [Proceedings of the 38th Annual Conference of the Association for Computer Aided Design in Architecture (ACADIA)]*, Mexico City, Mexico, 18–20 October 2018, edited by P. Anzalone, M. del Signore, and A. J. Wit, 320–327. CUMINCAD.

Bonabeau. Erik, Guy Theraulaz, and Marco Dorigo. 1999. *Swarm Intelligence: From Natural to Artificial Systems*. Oxford: Oxford University Press.

Crow, James Mitchell. 2008. "The Concrete Conundrum." *Chemistry World* 5 (3): 62–66.

Dillenburger, Benjamin. 2016. "Maschinelle Übersetzungen." *Tech21* 23 (June): 24–27.

Doyle, Shelby E., and Erin L. Hunt. 2019. "Dissolvable 3D Printed Formwork." *In ACADIA 19: Ubiquity and Autonomy [Proceedings of the 39th Annual Conference of the Association for Computer Aided Design in Architecture (ACADIA)]*, Austin, TX, 21–26 October 2019, edited by K. Bieg, D. Briscoe, and C. Odom, 179–187. CUMINCAD.

Gardiner, J. B., S. Janssen, and N. Kirchner. 2016. "A Realisation of a Construction Scale Robotic System for 3D Printing of Complex Formwork." In *33rd International Symposium on Automation and Robotics in Construction*, 515–521. Auburn: ISARC.

Grossman, Richard F., and Domasius Nwabunma. 2011. *Poly(lactic acid): Synthesis, Structures, Properties, Processing, and Applications*. New Jersey: John Wiley & Sons.

Jipa, Andrei, Mathias Bernhard, Nicolas Ruffray, Timothy Wangler, Robert Flatt, and Benjamin Dillenburger. 2019. "Formwork Fabrication Freedom for a Concrete Canoe." *Gestão & Tecnologia De Projetos (Design Management and Technology)* 14 (1): 25–44.

Lab, Robert H. 2007. "Think Formwork—Reduce Costs." *Structure magazine* (April): 12–14

Leschok, Matthias, and Benjamin Dillenburger. 2019. "Dissolvable 3DP Formwork." In *ACADIA 19: Ubiquity and Autonomy [Proceedings of the 39th Annual Conference of the Association for Computer Aided Design in Architecture (ACADIA)]*, Austin, TX, 21–26 October 2019, edited by K. Bieg, D. Briscoe, and C. Odom, 188–197. CUMINCAD.

Morel, Philippe. 2014. "Sand Molds for Ultra-High-Performance Concrete." Architecture trade fair in FRAC Centre in Orléans.

Peters, Brian. 2015. Formwork for Architectural Applications and Methods. US Patent 20150336297, filed May 21, 2015.

Snooks, Roland. 2018. "Sacrificial Formation." In *Towards a Robotic Architecture*, edited by A. Wit and M. Daas, 100–113. Novato, CA: Oro Editions.

Snooks, Roland. 2020. *Behavioral Formation: Volatile Design Processes and the Emergence of a Strange Specificity*. New York: ACTAR.

IMAGE CREDITS

Mania Aghaei Meibodi PhD is an Assistant Professor of Architecture at Taubman College. She has been a leader in computational design and digital fabrication methods suitable for large-scale manufacturing in the building industry.

Christopher Voltl is a PhD student of computational design and digital fabrication at Taubman College.

Ryan Craney is a research assistant at Taubman College, where he recently completed a Master's of Science in Digital and Material Technologies.

FORM{less}

Robotically Thermoformed Molds for Concrete Casting

Mackenzie Bruce*
University of Michigan

Gabrielle Clune*
University of Michigan

Ryan Culligan
Skidmore, Owings and Merrill

Kyle Vansice
Skidmore, Owings and Merrill

Rahul Attray
Skidmore, Owings and Merrill

Wes McGee
University of Michigan

Tsz Yan Ng
University of Michigan

*Authors contributed equally to the research.

1 Thin-shell concrete cast using robotically thermoformed nested molds displays the range of potential geometries and orientations achievable through this process.

ABSTRACT

Form{less} focuses on the creation of complex thin-shell concrete forms using robotically thermoformed plastic molds. Typically, similar molds would be created using the vacuum forming process, producing direct replications of the pattern. Creating molds with this process is not only time- and material-intensive but also costly if customization is involved. Thin-shell concrete forms often require a labor-intensive process of manually finishing the open-face surface. The devised process of thermoforming two nested molds allows the concrete to be cast in between, with finished surfaces on both sides. Molds made with polyethylene terephthalate glycol (PETG) allow the formwork to be reused and recycled. The research and fabrication work include the development of heating elements and the creation of the robotic process for forming the PETG. The PETG is manipulated via a robotic arm, with a custom magnetic end effector. The integration of robotics not only enables precision for manufacturing but also allows for replicability with unrestricted three-dimensional deformation. The repeatable process allows for rapid prototyping and geometric customization. Design options are then simulated computationally using *SuperMatterTools*, enabling further design exploration of this process without the need for extensive physical prototyping. This research aims to develop a process that allows for the creation of complex geometries while reducing the amount of material waste used for concrete casting. The novelty of the process created by dynamically forming PETG allows for quick production of formwork that is both customizable and replicable. This method of creating double-sided building components is simulated at various scales of implementation.

INTRODUCTION

Form{less} seeks to advance manufacturing processes of thermoforming PETG to create complex geometries for thin-shell concrete casting by integrating robotics using a magnetic end effector to give unrestricted opportunity in 3D deformation. The research aims to advance the process of thermoforming to manufacture components at the architectural scale. The developed process brings together diverse manufacturing processes, from thermoforming, robotics, and PETG molds production, to develop formworks for casting concrete elements with complex geometries.

Concrete is widely used in the architecture construction industry for its low cost and considerable strength as a composite building material. The material's fluidity, innate to its fabrication process, creates monolithic geometries that allow designers to work with nearly any form imaginable, if the technology to build the formwork is possible. The introduction of reinforcement, often using steel rebar or fibers, improved concrete's weakness in tension and, when combined, created a key building material for the architecture construction industry for the last hundred years. It is now the second most consumed material on earth, second only to water. Concrete contributes to 8% of global human-made carbon emissions (Lehne 2018). While it is widely known that concrete has harmful effects on the environment, reducing its use in buildings proves difficult. This research seeks to advance concrete construction by reducing the amount needed in construction through the examination of geometric forms and their creation.

Since concrete performs best in compression, a thin-shell form allows for the reduction in concrete and steel reinforcement by using the material only where it is needed based on its stress loading. Often seen as the father of reinforced thin-shell concrete construction, Felix Candela gained international fame for his elegant structural forms. Although the monolithic structures still stand today, the question of unsafe labor practices and extraordinary use of lumber in the falsework made this building technique unsustainable (Pendas 2018). Thin-shell forms enable complex geometries to work more efficiently but require complex formwork. Thus, this construction method does not wholly address environmental impact or labor practices, as it requires extensive formwork that is material- and labor-intensive. Thin-shell forms can reduce the amount of concrete necessary; however, the formworks are difficult to manufacture and contribute to construction waste. The method researched tackles the issue of creating complex geometry with minimal formwork for casting as well as devising designs using component systems for construction.

2

3

2 PETG is attached to the frame and pulled by using the magnetic end effector. The robotic arm enables unrestricted three-dimensional deformation—challenging if not impossible through other processes.

3 Resultant thin-shell concrete cast demonstrating the incredibly thin edge condition achievable through this process.

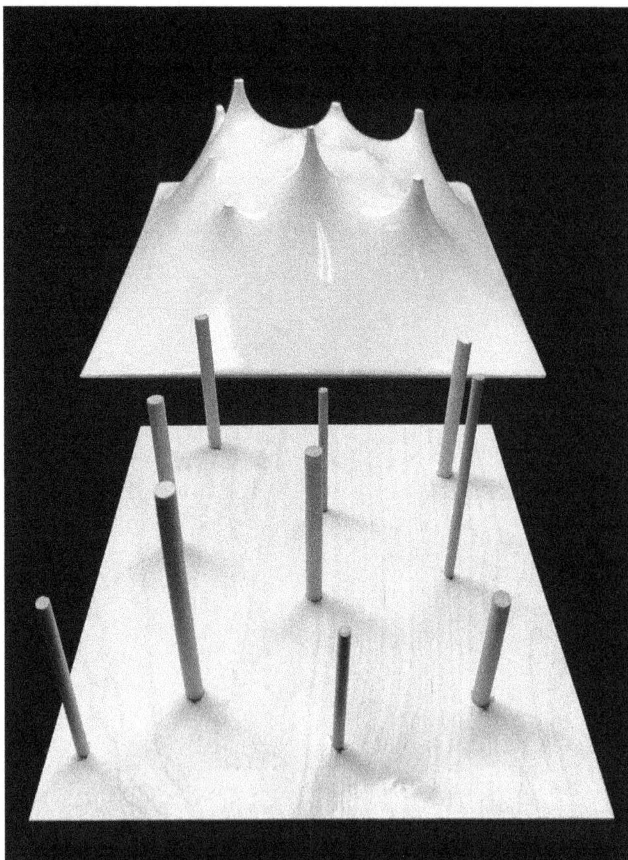

4 The devised modified vacuum forming process uses a jig to create surface conditions without directly replicating the pattern below.

5 The resulting cast required no postfinishing, creating a porcelain finish to the concrete.

In 2011, Ole Egholm Pedersen (2013) created a concrete pavilion using polyethylene terephthalate glycol (PETG) formwork that was quickly constructed with a small budget using relatively unskilled labor. The PETG sheets were laser-cut and folded to create 3D formwork. This project highlights PETG as a lightweight, easily deployable formwork for concrete casting. A significant advantage of using PETG as formwork is that there is no surface preparation of the formwork for casting and no postfinishing for the part as the concrete has a mirror finish cast against the PETG.

The project *Thick Nest* by Tristan Al-Haddad (2007) investigates how thermoforming can be used to stretch plastic into 3D spatial structures. In this manual process, the plastic is heated and pulled from a frame to the base, where it is secured in the desired position. The project demonstrates PETG's malleable thermoplastic properties to create complex geometries with unrestricted deformation when heated and cooled. This shows the plastic's ability to significantly deform, especially when apertures are cut into the sheet before deformation. The results are highly expressive, giving insight to the potential for PETG to be stretched into spatial forms. *FORM{less}* capitalizes on PETG's malleability, linking digital robotic automation processes to manufacture lightweight formworks for concrete casting. The project includes custom manufacturing of robotic end effector, heat table and workflow process for forming, as well as designs and prototypes of thin-shell concrete components.

BACKGROUND

Industrial thermoforming processes such as mechanical, vacuum, pressure, and drape forming are efficient manufacturing methods for PETG and have been used with a variety of applications, from small-scale product packaging to larger-scale bathtubs and architectural-scaled aircraft canopies. Thermoforming has been widely used due to its low equipment and tooling costs, ease in prototyping and manufacturing, and low overall material cost based on surface-to-thinness ratios (Klein 2009). Low-volume patterns for forming can be quickly and efficiently produced through CNC milling and 3D printing but have geometric limitations such as draft angles and undercuts. While unique thermoform patterns allow for repeatable mass production of parts with consistent results, they are not customizable without creating new patterns. Architecture designs often require customization to adapt to specific project needs, a limiting factor in architecture-scale assemblies when using thermoforming as part of the manufacturing process. *FORM{less}* seeks to advance industrial thermoforming processes, enabling the creation of customizable forms without the need for the manufacturing of unique patterns for PETG forming.

Reimagining thermoforming processes by incorporating robotics allows for exploration into precision, replicability, and customization. The project *Robotic Forming* uses a spherical tool to shape 1 mm PETG sheets (Lublasser et al. 2016). The plastic is incrementally "pushed" using a robotic arm to create controlled manipulation. The research, showcased as an installation at Ars Electronica Festival 2015, enables PETG deformation by gradually moving deeper into the material and shaping incrementally without the need for heating. Incremental forming, typically used for sheet metal work, here applied to PETG forming, is slow. There's a limit to the extent of 3D deformation possible, and it does not leverage thermoplastic's material properties in shaping deformation through heating and cooling. *D-FORM*, another robotic process with PETG, does utilize heat but is deformed over a fixed form (Weissenböck 2014). *D-FORM* explores the use of laser-cut geometric patterns on PETG sheets. The process includes attaching the frame for the plastic to a robotic arm, moving the plastic over a fixed heat gun, and forming the plastic over a fixed tool. This allows the robot to precisely deform the plastic in specific areas of the sheet,

5

allowing for quick control over deformation. However, it still requires a fixed form to shape the deformation. The advancements made in this work set the stage for further research into robotic thermoforming plastic. The approach for *Form{less}* includes developing the process for heating the PETG to achieve deformation, but instead of pushing against a fixed pattern or tool to shape the PETG, the robotic process pulls the heated PETG in preprogrammed paths that are repeatable and customizable. Also, by doing away with a pattern to mold against for deformation, less material is used for the PETG formwork production.

Typical vacuum-forming machines only allow Z-axis deformation, with size limited by the height of the machine. While it might be possible for undercuts to occur due to the suction of the malleable PETG, the limitation of this singular direction enables only specific types of deformation. *Thick Nest* pushes against the limits of traditional thermoforming methods, locally pulling the heated plastic while using perforations in the plastic to achieve greater deformation while maintaining structural thickness of the PETG and reducing the material required to create the deformation. *D-FORM* uses localized heating methods, requiring the PETG to be attached to the robot, allowing for the control of the desired heating area before pressing the PETG over a fixed form but limiting the deformation of the plastic. Through the use of a magnetic end effector in *FORM{less}*, PETG can be thermoformed from a fixed frame attached to a heating table, allowing the 7-axis Kuka robotic arm to pull the heated PETG multidirectionally (Fig. 2). This presents the opportunity for complex geometric PETG deformation previously difficult to achieve. By employing robotic processes for pulling, PETG deformation does not have to be bounded by a single I axis and the formwork could be customizable, such as for the production of nested molds with offsets for uniform concrete thickness when cast. The freedom afforded by multidirectional PETG deformation opens up design opportunities for customizable cast-concrete components. The novelty of the process leverages PETG's material properties with multidirectional deformation through robotic processes to create customizable PETG formworks for concrete casting.

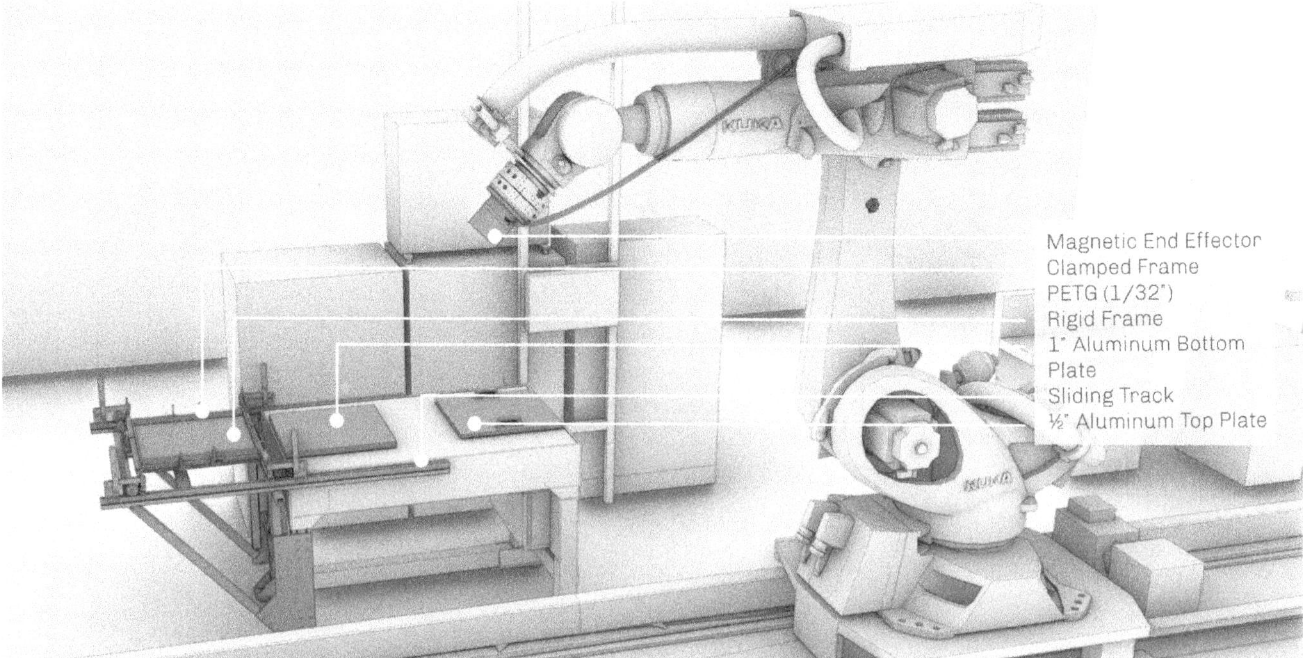

6

METHODS

Initial experiments were tested through a modified vacuum forming technique where the PETG is pushed against a set of minimum restrictions to create surface topologies that are not direct replications of the pattern below (Fig. 4). This process allows for the creation of complex formwork that is quick to produce and stiff enough for concrete casting while reducing the material required to create the geometry. Resultant forms have the potential to move to a more 3D spatial form, questioning whether a pattern is required for manipulating PETG while thermoforming. When looking to replicate these thermoformed molds, limitations to this process were observed, whereby it is impossible to replicate the forms due to inconsistencies in the exact airflow of the vacuum for each mold. The desired level of precision was not achievable on the vacuum-forming machines; thus, a shift in methodology was required to both push the PETG forming process and achieve repeatability.

The devised setup involves the PETG sheet sandwiched between two aluminum plates with a frame attached to a heat table (Fig. 6). It is necessary to have both a top and bottom metal plate to ensure even heating, which allows for maximum level of deformation. This system concentrates the heating directly on the PETG sheet rather than the use of a kiln or oven, which heats the air around it. The PETG is inserted between the heated plates of aluminum and secured in place using a metal frame, which is attached to a slider to manage the short window between heating the PETG and immediate manipulation. Given this short window, the setup is situated next to the robot to take advantage of the moment when the PETG is most malleable.

To create offset formwork, a smaller metal plate for pulling was used to account for interior nested formwork dimension. One modification was necessary—the size of the metal plate pulled (Fig. 7). To expand on types of deformation controlled by the contours of the steel plate, a series of tests were done with different geometries such as different rectangular bars as well as dual magnetic heads for double deformation at the same time (Fig. 8). Additionally, after achieving repeatable results with orthogonal axis pulls, multiaxis directional pulls were explored, possible only with this thermoforming process.

To assess the ability to create thin-shell concrete formwork using this process, two-part nested molds were visualized three-dimensionally using Rhinoceros (Robert McNeel & Associates 2020) and the Grasshopper plugin Kangaroo (Rutten 2018; Piker 2013). Tests were conducted to find how far a 1/32" PETG could be stretched. The results of the physical prototyping informed computational processes for both design and robotics control using SuperMatterTools (SMT) (McGee and Pigram 2011). SMT includes simulation capabilities, ensuring that there is no physical collision during the deformation process as well as a smooth workflow (Fig. 11). This is especially necessary for safety reasons since the deformation process is a choreographed human-robot interaction, requiring manual positioning of the heated PETG sheet and positioning of a steel plate under the PETG that is then magnetically picked up by the end effector for pulling. The simulations helped inform the physical prototyping, allowing further exploration of the process without the need for extensive physical prototyping. By controlling the pulls, formwork can be manipulated to create elements with uniform or variable thickness.

These prototypes show the potential for creating repeatable, customized PETG formwork that is geometrically complex. The casting process involves a rigid frame for the outer piece of PETG to attach (Fig. 12). Concrete is poured into the mold, and the inner nested piece is inserted. Sand is added to offset the pressure, creating thin concrete walls with uniform thickness. The two-part formwork results in a concrete shell with double-sided porcelain-like finish.

The integration of robotics allows for the prospect of replicability for manufacturing the formwork and gives unrestricted opportunity for deformation. This enables complex geometries for thin-shell casting that is challenging if not impossible through other processes. The repeatability of the process allows for rapid prototyping and geometric customization that brings promising opportunities to analyze the precision and replicability of the formwork. The forms themselves have inherent structural properties and resemble catenary structural forms. Axial symmetry gives strength to the cast as the hydrostatic pressure is evenly distributed throughout the formwork.

RESULTS AND DISCUSSION

While 1/32" PETG was used in all successful pulls, tests with 1/8" PETG were conducted with the anticipation of greater deformation. Failure was observed in the disengagement of the steel and the magnet with the thicker PETG. Factors influencing this failure may include the thickness of plastic weakening the strength of the magnet bond. Thicker-gauge PETG also required greater heating time, with a higher temperature as the plate met the magnet. The higher temperatures can cause the magnet to release. The magnet's failure therefore was not able to deform the 1/8" PETG to its full potential. Future work with thicker PETG will require a stronger magnet that can withstand higher temperature for better hold.

The 1/32" PETG sheets consistently provided a maximum height of 29" without any visible distortion and before the forces on the magnet were too strong. Testing with the dual magnetic end effector offered the possibility for branching structures using multiple robots for simultaneous pulls. This can allow the forms to be connected for spatial components, creating a new typology. With the implementation of multiple magnetic end effectors and custom steel plates, further exploration of the setup is necessary for accurate results.

Integrating an electromagnet to the steel plate's placement process would allow for accuracy of the pickup location.

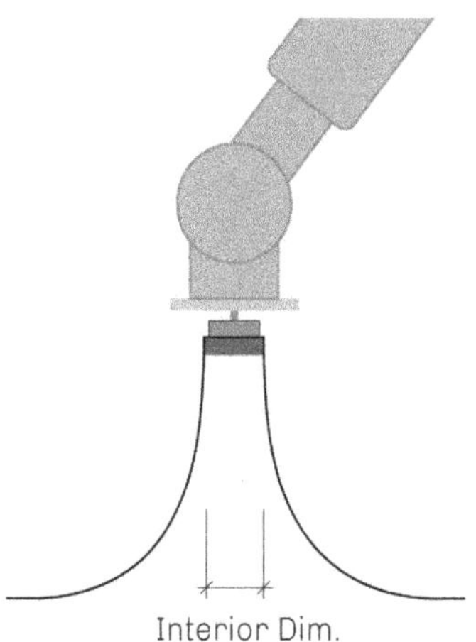

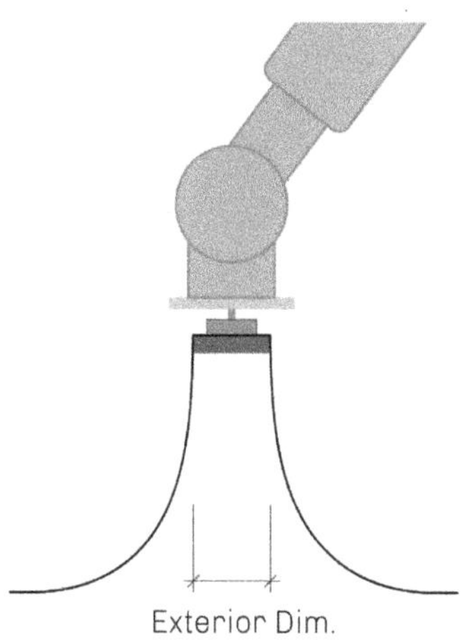

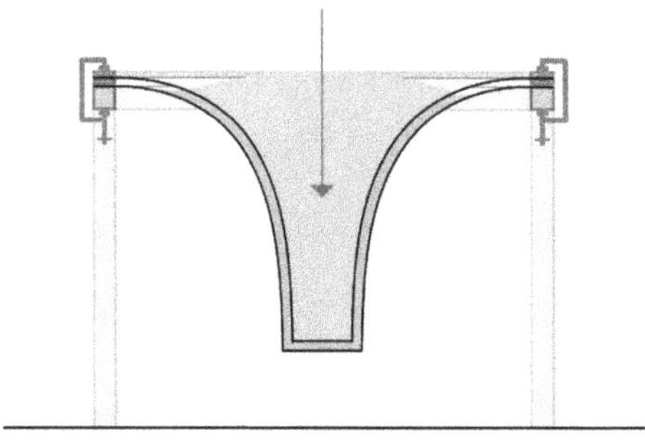

7

6 The devised setup of the thermoforming process included the creation of heating elements, a rigid frame, and magnetic end effector.

7 Steel picked up by the magnetic end effector creates the interior dimension of the formwork. The exterior dimension of the formwork is formed by offsetting the PETG creating nested molds determining the thickness of the concrete. The two thermoformed molds are attached to a frame, suspending the cast.

8

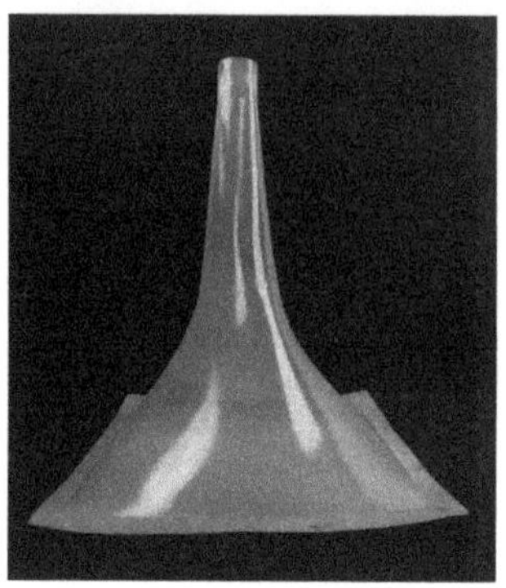

9

10

11

8 Dual magnetic end effector resultant pull. When the PETG is cooled, the end effector is retracted and the magnets release.

9 Resultant thermoformed plastic vertical pull with 29" deformation is the greatest height achievable without deformation after magnet is released

10 Resultant thermoformed plastic diagonal pull.

11 Using SuperMatterTools, resulting forms are simulated, allowing for an iterative process without extensive physical prototyping.

12 The casting process includes a rigid frame to suspend the PETG formwork. Concrete is added to the exterior mold. The interior mold is then placed on top using sand to maintain the structure of the mold.

Greater precision in the position of the steel plate prior to heating the PETG would help prevent inconsistencies in the offset formwork while also enabling the formwork to grow in complexity. This would allow for a more automated and precise process where the steel is retrieved from a pickup station and placed within the boundaries of the frame. Once the PETG is heated and locked into the frame, the robotic arm can retrieve the steel plate.

The form-finding process allowed for exploration of how the PETG reacts when heated and pulled between two control points, the fixed and the activated steel plate. The steel frame not only ensures the PETG is secured but also provides consistent edges that aid in the casting and analysis of molds. Some failures during the casting process include blowout of the PETG because of the thinness of the mold when deformed past 18". To achieve consistent edge thickness and promote reusability, a minimal frame was used to suspend the form-work. Further investigation will include fabricating a spacer to be inserted between the nested PETG for consistent thickness. The resulting cast shows the ability to create a double surface finished thin-shell concrete structure.

FUTURE WORK

In-depth performance analysis of the casts is required to fully understand the potential of this investigation. The precision of the robotically thermoformed molds may be measured using photogrammetry or 3D scanning technologies. The formwork pieces must be painted with a matte paint to allow for accurate analysis. After casting, concrete pieces should be studied for any distortion between the mold and the concrete components. Both physical load testing and analysis of the catenary profile can give insights to the structural capacity. Controlled variable thickness of the casts can be explored as a way to enhance structural properties. The forms appear to have distinct acoustical properties by the nature of the resultant geometries. An investigation into the acoustical properties of the cast may help inform further investigations and architectural applications. The unique double-sidedness of the casts creates multifaceted forms that, when scaled up for construction, will have enormous potential for application.

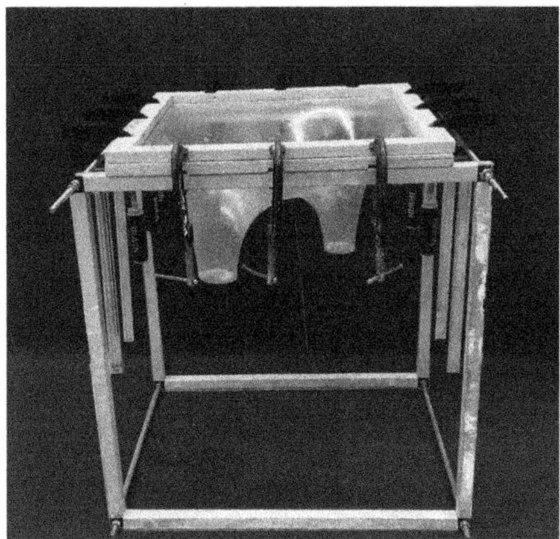
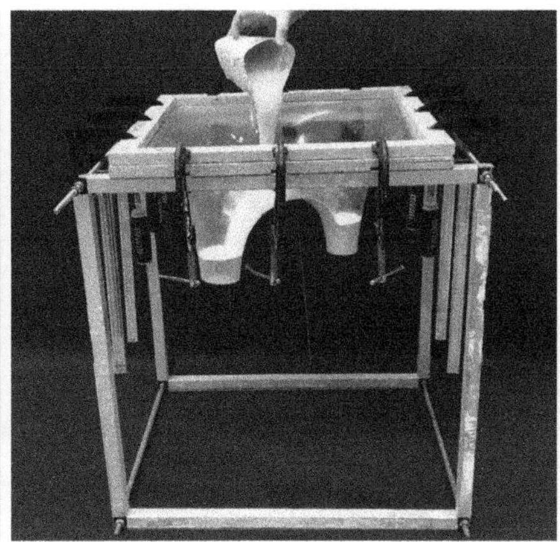
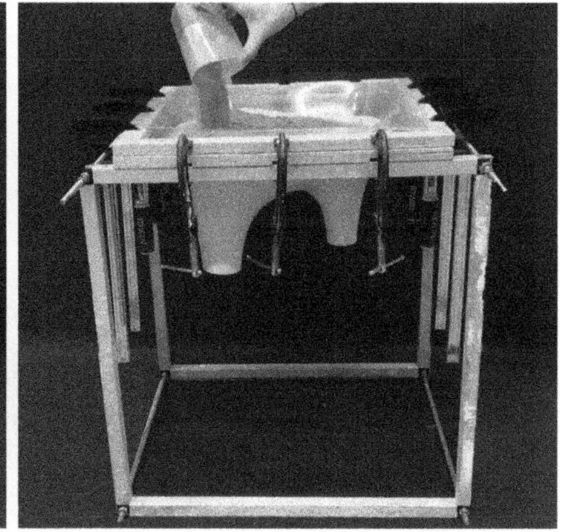

12

The research is currently limited by the strength of the magnet and the size of the heat table setup. Scaling up the process will require stronger magnets, a larger heat table setup, and more automated processes. A robot attached to a larger gantry system would allow the forms to take on a more architectural scale, increasing the impact of this process. Initial investigations would start by testing the magnet with a thicker material such as 1/16" PETG. It is critical to observe the limits of both the magnet and the material. Understanding the relationship between material thickness, pull height, and magnet strength is the next step, as only one gauge of PETG was successfully tested. Increasing magnet strength may also create greater challenges to the release process. Implementing an electromagnet to both the steel plate's placement and pickup creates a seamless release process, preventing the formwork from becoming damaged.

Although *Form{less}* significantly reduces the amount of formwork needed for casting complex concrete components, PETG is often hard to recycle and takes thousands of years to decompose. Replacing PETG with a more sustainable material could reduce the environmental impact. Research into recycled PETG and bioplastics for this thermoforming process could be tested as it would allow the process to be more environmentally friendly. Bioplastics with thermoforming capabilities are widely available today and used already in the production of sustainable thermoformed lids for drinking cups (Barrett 2019). Although PETG allowed the formwork to be reused, the potential of using bioplastics reinforces the ethos of reducing material waste and sustainability for manufacturing.

CONCLUSION

Form{less} investigated 3D deformation of PETG to create formwork for concrete casting. PETG formwork eliminates the labor-intensive process of manually finishing formwork or the need for a release agent. The devised process of thermoforming two-nested molds allows the concrete to be cast in between, creating a finished surface on both sides. The molds made with PETG allow the formwork to be reused and recycled, investigating the fabrication of thin-shell concrete forms with minimal formwork and falsework. The formation of catenary-like geometries along with fiberglass reinforcement allows the concrete to perform mostly in compression, reducing the amount of concrete structurally necessary. This method of creating double-sided components is simulated at various scales of implementation. Through rapid prototyping, form-finding, and simulation using SuperMatterTools and Kangaroo, the study creates an iterative process for design and development.

Due to the modular nature of the components, aggregation for larger building systems is possible as panelized units can create an interlocking wall system. Through the lens of labor, the work situates itself in a position that directs all computational and specialized labor to the formwork-making process while using traditional casting methods. Components can be designed, tested, and manufactured through computational simulations and thermoforming processes developed in this research. The molds can then be deployed on the construction site to be cast by local labor.

The novelty of the process created by dynamically forming PETG using the robotic arm allows for quick production of formwork that is both customizable and replicable. *FORM{less}* seeks to advance thermoforming manufacturing processes, allowing the process to take on the architectural scale. The integration of robotics not only enables manufacturing precision but also replicability with unrestricted three-dimensional deformation. This process studies material manipulation that creates increased order and enables the creation of complex geometries for thin-shell casting that cannot be replicated through other processes.

ACKNOWLEDGMENTS

The project was generously supported by Skidmore, Owings and Merrill (SOM). The gift supported the studio Topology+ at the University of Michigan Taubman College of Architecture and Urban

13

14

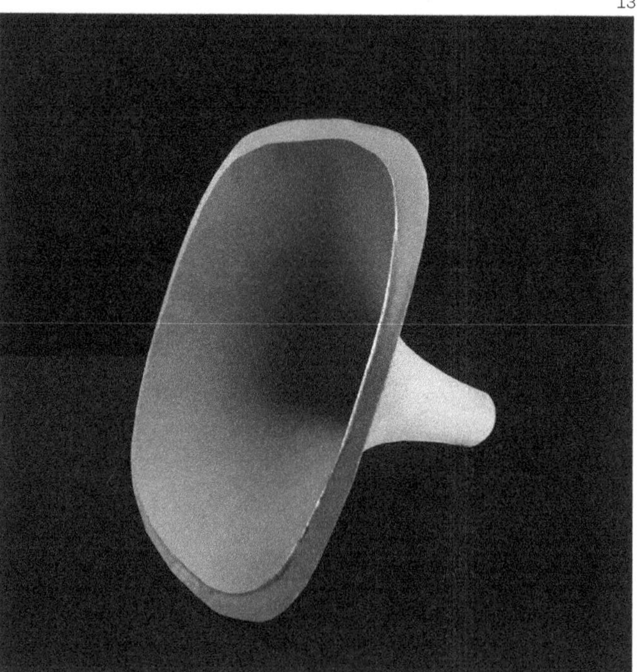

15

Planning, which focused on advanced computational design and fabrication for concrete forming.

REFERENCES

Al Haddad, Tristan. 2007. "WORK." formations studio. http://formations-studio.com/work.

Barrett, Axel. 2019. "Thermoforming With Biobased Plastics for Greater Sustainability." *Bioplastics News*, May 4. https://bioplasticsnews.com/2019/05/04/thermoforming-with-biobased-plastics-for-greater-sustainability/.

Burry, Jane, Jenny E. Sabin, Bob Sheil, and Marilena Skavara. 2020. "The Design and Fabrication of Confluence Park." In *Fabricate 2020: Making Resilient Architecture*, 28–34. London: UCL Press.

Chang, Yuan, Xiaodong Li, Eric Masanet, Lixiao Zhang, Zhiye Huang, and Robert Ries. 2018. "Unlocking the Green Opportunity for Prefabricated Buildings and Construction in China." *Resources, Conservation and Recycling* 139: 259–261. https://doi.org/10.1016/j.resconrec.2018.08.025.

Klein, Peter W. 2009. *Fundamentals of Plastics Thermoforming*. San Rafael, CA: Morgan & Claypool Publishers.

Lehne, Johanna. 2018. "Making Concrete Change: Innovation in Low-Carbon Cement and Concrete." Chatham House, June 13. https://www.chathamhouse.org/2018/06/making-concrete-change-innovation-low-carbon-cement-and-concrete.

Lublasser, E., J. Braumann, D. Goldbach, and S. Brell-Cokcan. 2016. "Robotic Forming: Rapidly Generating 3d Forms and Structures Through Incremental Forming." In *Living Systems and Micro-Utopias: Towards a Continuous Designing [Proceedings of the 21st International Conference of the Association for Computer-Aided Architectural Design Research in Asia (CAADRIA 2016)]*, Melbourne, Australia, 30 March–2 April, edited by S. Chien, S. Choo, M. A. Schnabel, W. Nakapan, M. J. Kim, and S. Roudavski, 539–548. CAADRIA.

McGee, Wesley, and David Pigram. 2011. "Formation Embedded Design: A Method for the Integration of Fabrication Constraints into Architectural Design." In *ACADIA 11: Integration through Computation [Proceedings of the 31st Annual Conference of the Association for Computer Aided Design in Architecture (ACADIA)]*, Banff, AB, Canada, 13–16 October 2011, edited by J. S. Johnson, J. Taron, V. Parlac, and B. Kolarevic, 122–131. CUMINCAD.

Pedersen, Ole Egholm. 2013. "Tectonic Potentials of Concrete." PhD thesis, Århus School of Architecture, Denmark.

Pendas, Maria Gonzales. 2018. "Fifty Cents a Foot, 14,500 Buckets: Concrete Numbers and the Illusory Shells of Mexican Economy." *Grey Room* 71: 14–39. https://doi.org/10.1162/grey_a_00240.

Piker, Daniel. 2013. "Kangaroo—Form Finding with Computational Physics." *Architectural Design* 83 (2): 136–137.

Robert McNeel & Associates. 2020. *Rhinoceros*. V.6.0. Robert McNeel & Associates. PC.

Rutten, David. 2018. *Grasshopper 3d*. V.1.0.0. Robert McNeel & Associates. https://www.rhino3d.com/.

Weissenböck, Renate. 2014. "D-FORM." In *Robotic Fabrication in Architecture, Art and Design 2014*, edited by W. McGee and M. Ponce de Leon, 249–260. Cham: Springer. https://doi.org/10.1007/978-3-319-04663-1_17.

Mackenzie Bruce holds a Bachelor of Fine Arts in Architecture from the University of Massachusetts Amherst and a Master of Architecture from Taubman College of Architecture and Urban planning at the University of Michigan. She has continued her education and research by pursuing a Master of Science in Digital and Material Technologies at the University of Michigan. Her research focuses on the development of material processes that question traditional methods of construction, working with material behavior to inform design.

Gabrielle Clune holds a Bachelor of Design in Architecture from the University of Florida and a Master of Architecture from Taubman College. After completing her master's, she has continued her education and research at the University of Michigan by pursuing a Master of Science in Digital. Her research focuses on material-based design, aspiring to advance the architecture and construction industry by expanding the use of advanced digital technologies, novel processes, and material manipulation.

Ryan Culligan, AIA, is an Associate Director at Skidmore Owings and Merrill (SOM).

Rahul Attray is an Architectural Professional at SOM.

Kyle Vansice is an Architectural Designer at SOM.

Wesley McGee is an Associate Professor and the Director of the FABLab at the University of Michigan Taubman College of Architecture and Urban Planning. His work revolves around the interrogation of the means and methods of material production in the digital era, through research focused on developing new connections between design, engineering, materials, and manufacturing processes as they relate to the built environment.

Tsz Yan Ng is an Assistant Professor in Architecture at Taubman College, University of Michigan. Ng's material-based research and design primarily focus on experimental concrete forming (hard) and textile manipulation (soft), oftentimes in direct exchange and incorporating contemporary technologies to develop novel designs for building and manufacturing. A common thread to her work investigates questions of labor in various facets and forms—underscoring broader issues of industrial manufacturing innovation, human labor, crafting, and aesthetics.

Structural Papercuts

Nicholas Bruscia
University at Buffalo, State University of New York

Scaling Disclinations in Self-Reactive Surfaces

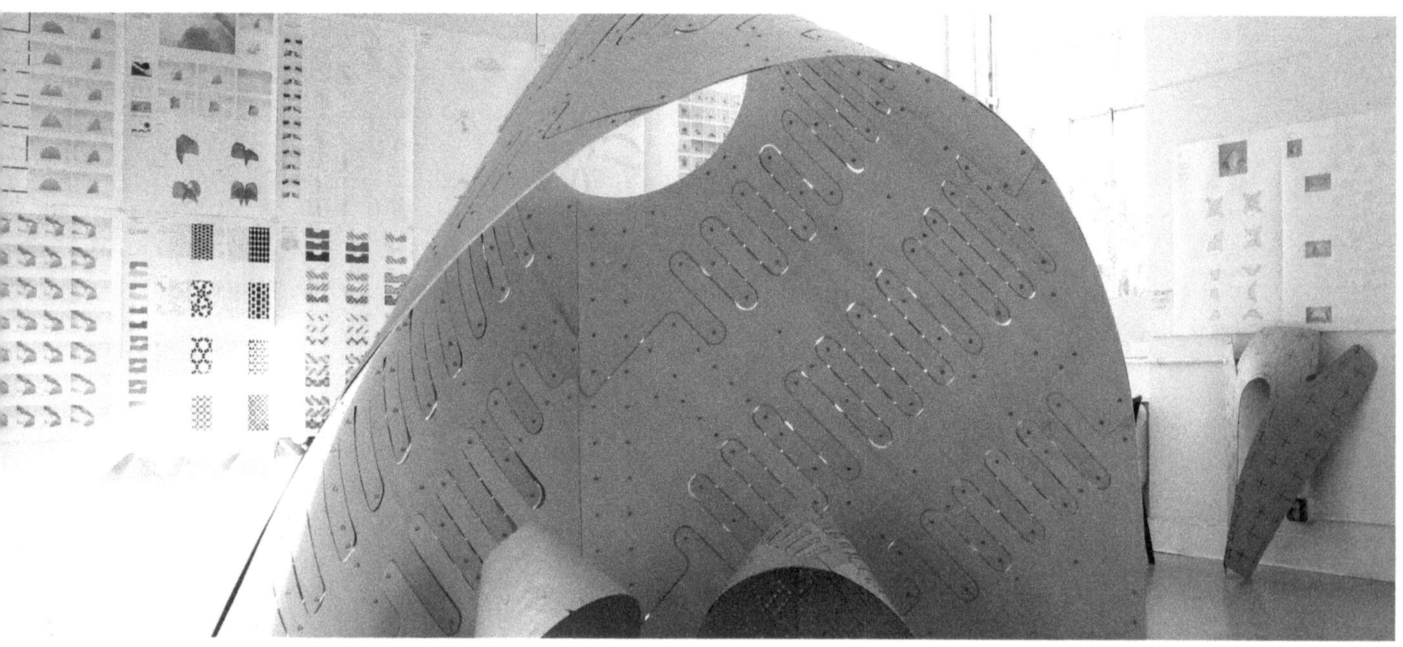

1 [+x°] wedge disclination prototype.

ABSTRACT

This paper reviews and explores the topological properties of surface disclinations applied to elastic sheets and suggests how these properties may be reproduced at an architectural scale. A variety of surface disclinations and their translation from digital and physical form-finding processes to thin plywood prototypes are discussed. Initial phases of this research have been focused on the bending behavior of various sheet disclination types and have studied a variety of computational form-finding techniques that demonstrate this behavior in an architectural workflow. Several large-scale prototypes of architectural disclinations were produced to test the scalability of topologically induced surface curvature, discussed within the context of bending-active plate structures.

INTRODUCTION

The basic topological concept of a disclination acknowledges the role of the "defect" in the composition of a material structure. However, the basic principles of disclinations can be applied to material systems at multiple scales. For example, the process of strategically inserting geometric disclinations in woven lattices results in out-of-plane buckling, producing concentrations of either positive or negative curvature (Martin 2015) (Fig. 2a). Similarly, thin sheets absorb the strain induced by disclinations by buckling into repeatable, complex forms (Harris 1977). Since complex surfaces must often be postrationalized with a geometry-based approach prior to construction, it is useful to investigate approaches that are directly related to material properties that reinforce rationality from the start, helping to define alternative and more efficient design processes and fabrication techniques.

Surface Disclinations

Disclinations depend on rotational symmetry, usually around the center axis of a torus or a sphere. This differs from dislocations and dispirations, which rely on translational and screw symmetry, respectively (Harris 1978). The work in this paper focuses specifically on compact disclinations of rotational movement to force out-of-plane bucking in thin sheets. For example, *wedge disclinations* in flexible sheet materials can be built to conceal the topological condition that creates curvature through self-reaction, a rather elegant construction technique (Fig. 2b). The strain applied to the material during assembly is eventually distributed smoothly (Harris 1977), and it has been empirically observed via physical models that some surfaces resulting from wedge disclinations are bi-stable since the surface exhibits snap-through buckling as it is forced to move between two stable positions. When stable, the surface remains in a state of self-reaction where strain is distributed smoothly (Kroner and Anthony 1975).

Disclinations in sheet materials can be created with a simple procedure. By slicing through the material along a straight line but not entirely across, one can choose how to reconnect the surface ends in order to induce self-reactive curvature. By removing material prior to reconnection, positive curvature is created. By adding material prior to reconnection, negative curvature is created as the surface reacts by buckling into a [-x°] wedge disclination. For example, a [-360°] wedge disclination performed on a circular sheet gives rise to severe deformation resulting in a saddle-like surface (Fig. 2d). Formally, this results in a surface drawn from two double cones, as the surface can be generated by moving a straight line fixed at one end (Harris 1977).

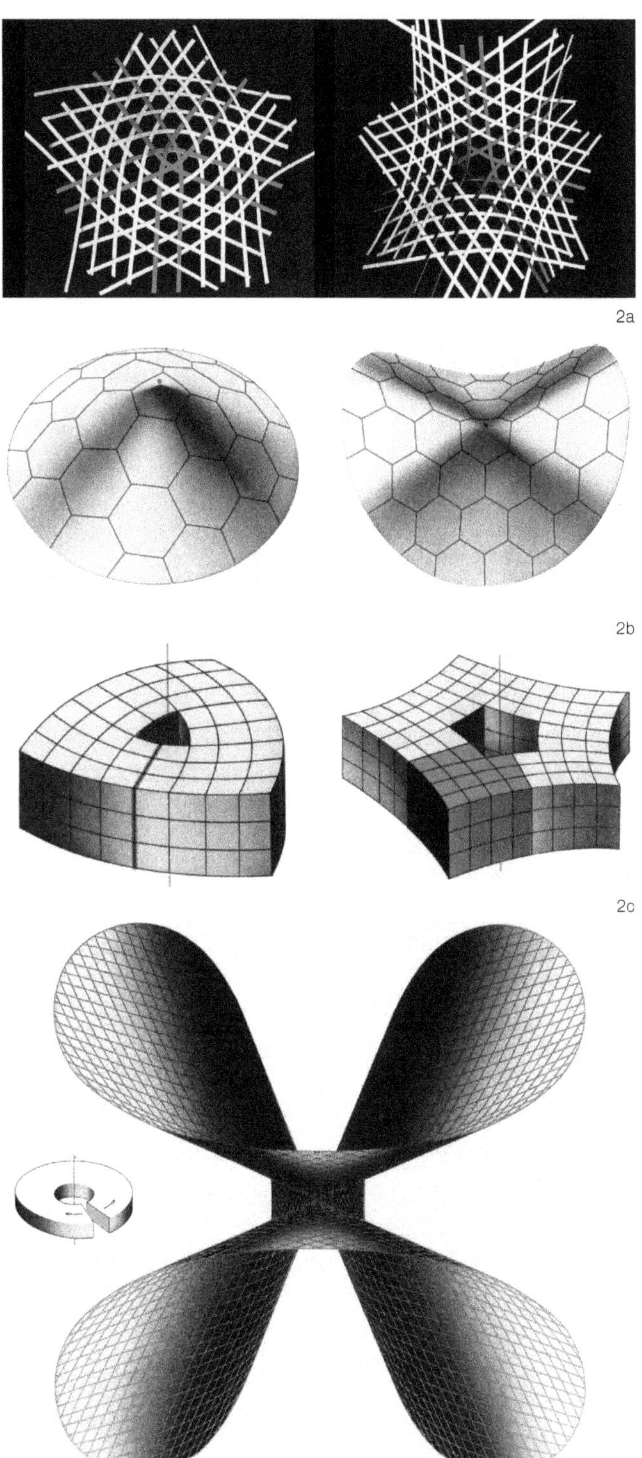

2a <6 and >6 edge count polygons introduced to the regular lattice produce positive and negative Gaussian curvature (Ayres et al. 2018).

2b [+60°] and [-60°] wedge disclinations: a 60° sector is removed to form a cone or added to the disk to form a saddle-like surface (Harris 1977).

2c [+90°] and [-90°] wedge disclinations illustrated as cubic lattices, shown here in comparison to similar topologically induced bends in woven lattices and thin sheets (Harris 1977).

2d Top-down view: [-360°] wedge disclination creates extreme buckling. The inserted "wedge" itself is a full circle (Harris 1977).

3a Josef Albers, curved-crease sculpture.

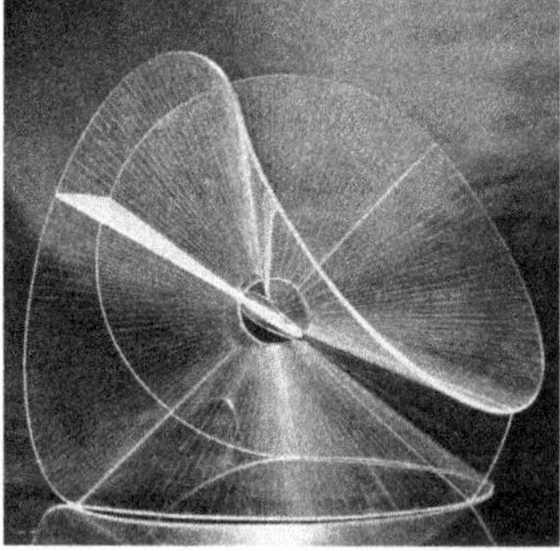
3b Naum Gabo, Spheric Theme.

3c 2-circle [-x°] disclination.

3d 3-circle [-x°] disclination.

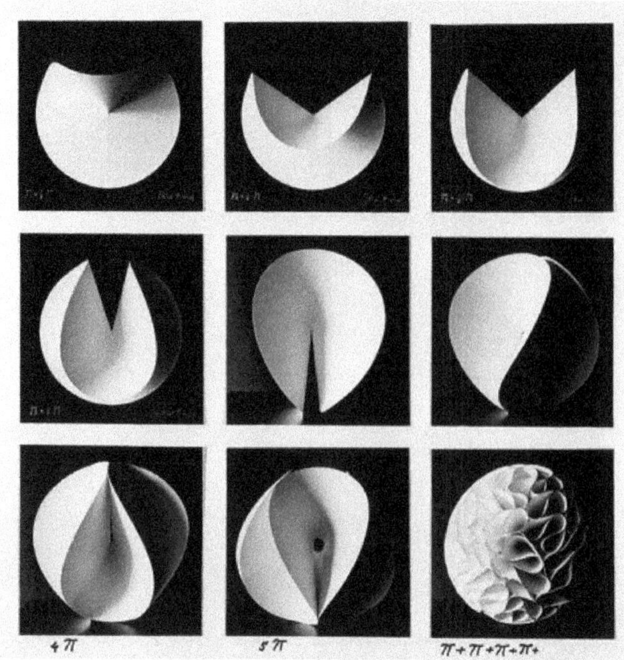

4 Ilhan Koman, π+π+π+... sculptures.

Naum Gabo was perhaps the first to document this technique in built form in the 1930s, but it was later discussed as a wedge disclination by crystallographer William Harris who characterized them with negative or positive angle measures, which is the notation adopted in this paper (Harris 1977). Similarly, Turkish sculptor Ilhan Koman cataloged the various surface variants as factors of pi (Akgün, Koman, and Akleman 2006). In both instances, the degree of rotational movement and the amount of material inserted into (or removed from) a single disk is made explicit. Another way to describe surface disclinations may be possible with the Gauss-Bonnett theorem that relates a surface's geometric curvature to its topological Euler characteristic. While a proper investigation into this relationship is beyond the scope of this paper, its relevance to this work is illustrated by mathematician Edmund Harriss's *Curvahedra* system and its application to large sheet metal sculptures (Harriss 2020).

BACKGROUND AND RELATED WORK

This paper borrows its title from László Moholy-Nagy, who in *Vision in Motion* described beginning design exercises of manipulating flat sheet materials into three-dimensional structures (1947). Paper cutting and bending is an effective form-finding process since some basic understanding of the strength of materials, role of grain direction, and the varying tension and compression forces can be inferred from small-scale models. For example, both grain direction and slight overlapping of material can determine in which of the two stable states the model will tend to rest. If unintended, this may bias the bending behavior and affect the evaluation of the model. Building on the origins of foundational design exercises of the Bauhaus and later at the Hochschule für Gestaltung Ulm (Ulm School of Design), it is useful here to recall the pedagogical work of Josef Albers that produced the first account of a curved crease model (Fig. 3a) consisting of concentric circles (Demaine et al. 2011). The alternating concentric mountain and valley folds along the curved creases results in a saddle-like form quite similar to Naum Gabo's *Variation on a Spheric Theme* (Fig. 3b), and Harris's [-x°] wedge disclination in a circular disk (Figs. 3c, 3d). In comparison, the [-x°] wedge disclination can also produce a wide variety of results since it is not limited to the surface area of a single circle. This is demonstrated by Ilhan Koman's developable sculptures in [π+π+π+....] form, which clearly illustrate the variety of distinct surface types that emerge from this process (Akgün, Koman, and Akleman 2006) (Fig. 4). These examples and their history of multidisciplinary exploration help demonstrate that working with paper leads to a fundamental understanding of form making and efficiency of means. Since the material will be utilized to its maximum potential, complex design proposals with little waste result from a simple material process (Demaine et al. 2011).

While the primary motivation driving the research is to explore surface disclinations at an architectural scale, the work takes inspiration from several case studies that have either directly or indirectly influenced the results to date. An appreciation for thin sheets formed within the limitations of their material characteristics is inspired by the Plyform work of Charles and Ray Eames in conjunction with the Molded Plywood Division of Evans Products in 1943. The Eameses constructed a variety of large-scale molded plywood parts

5 Charles and Ray Eames, airplane fuselage, 1943.

for the U.S. Navy, built from enormous pieces of wood veneer and pressed into doubly curved aircraft sections. The scale at which they managed to mold plywood components and the pinch-forming techniques they devised to hold specific curves may be best exemplified by their airplane stabilizer tail and airplane fuselage (Fig. 5). A similar source of inspiration comes from the construction of early wooden monocoque shells built for racing airplanes in the early 1900s, specifically because the fuselage was constructed from multiple layers over a removable framework. For example, the Deperdussin monoplane was constructed of three 1/16 inch layers of tulip wood glued over a mold (Hoff 1946). The prototypes discussed in this paper were built to a similar thickness, but from two layers of 3 mm bendable poplar plywood without a mold or supporting framework.

Various early paper models and the finished prototype of the [+x°] wedge disclination share a likeness to Skating Shelters by Patkau Architects. The standard 4 × 8 ft dimension of plywood sheets was a limitation to overcome, resulting in the assembly of larger panels consisting of lapped layers. The layers were cut to a pattern specific to a recipe of grain orientation and bending bias (Patkau Architects 2017). The shelters are constructed from bendable anisotropic plywood designed to bend along one axis relative to the sheet proportions, which are made of a single veneer core and two thicker outer layers with grain orientation in the same direction. The prototypes discussed adopt the double-layer approach to scalability and make use of a bendable poplar plywood with grain orientation in either the short direction (barrel grain) or the long direction (column grain). Similar in spirit and in materiality, perhaps surface disclinations may also be seen as an elegant combination of the structural and geometric qualities of bent surfaces.

This work also takes inspiration from prior research on bending-active plate structures, a structural system that is characterized by the use of large elastic deformations of initially flat planar materials (Knippers et al. 2011). These systems use bending to enhance their structural properties, as opposed to traditional building structures that aim to limit the amount of bending. Controlling a material's flexibility to produce self-stabilizing potential energy has proven to be a versatile approach to designing lightweight shell structures (Schleicher and La Magna 2016). Prominent examples include Buckminster Fuller's plydomes, the 2010 and 2015–16 Research Pavilions by the ICD/ITKE at the University of Stuttgart, as well as the Berkeley Weave and Bend9 installations at UC Berkeley's College of Environmental Design.

METHODS

In order to demonstrate the potential application of surface disclinations in an architectural context, it is necessary to understand their topological and geometric nature. While it is possible to approximate surface disclinations with manually constructed conic sections, the natural surface curvature created by bending against restrictive material constraints is seen as an opportunity for nuanced formal variation and control via computational simulation. The geometric construction of the approximated topology prepares the physics-based simulations that are explored alongside paper model bending. An iterative physical modeling process using paper stock assists, and in specific cases provides an alternative to, the computational form-finding techniques developed in this phase. For example, it was empirically observed that how the paper stock is reconnected (the sidedness of the material overlap) will determine which of the two stable states the model will tend toward. Reproducing this behavior digitally is interesting territory to explore. At this stage, however, the simulations are intended to approximate either of the two stable states that are revealed by the paper models. This seemingly inherent characteristic of bi-stability has inspired future work toward large-scale components designed to counteract one another as they are forced to connect between stable states. The opposing potential energies may find a productive equilibrium, suggesting the possibility for larger structures.

Acknowledging the role of the paper models and their ability to demonstrate interesting topological behavior, a materials-based form-finding approach is preferred over a top-down approach to form-conversion in this phase, although the latter may become a useful technique for more

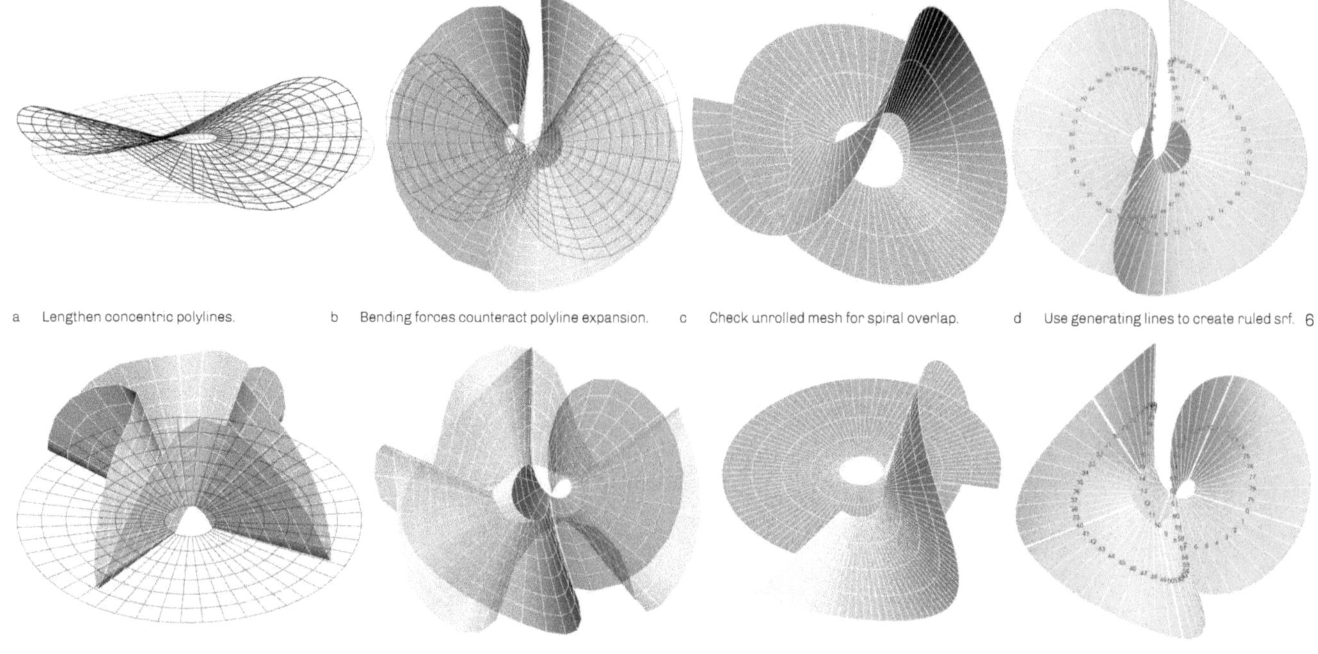

a Lengthen concentric polylines. b Bending forces counteract polyline expansion. c Check unrolled mesh for spiral overlap. d Use generating lines to create ruled srf. 6

a Fold base mesh to increase srf area. b Apply bending forces, allow mesh to take shape. c Check unrolled mesh for spiral overlap. d Use generating lines to create ruled srf. 7

complex assemblies that require an array of embedded disclinations. To date, [-x°] disclinations have been of particular interest since their resultant form cannot be fully predetermined through explicit 3D modeling. As mentioned previously, the material is self-reactive in the forming process (physical models benefit from surface self-collision), the simulation of which has proven to be a challenge worthy of pursuit.

Computational Form Finding

This section describes the computational form-finding techniques carried out in this research to date, in comparison to other known approaches to similar modeling problems. The multistep form-finding techniques described below utilize physics-based dynamic relaxation techniques in Kangaroo2 (Piker 2013), and are consciously developed within the tradition of form-finding strategies of architects and engineers from the 1950s onward that incorporated materials and forces in the systematic exploration of lightweight structures (Schleicher and La Magna 2016). Now a common tool in architectural design and research, Kangaroo2 has played an important role in visualizing the resultant geometry of surface disclinations based on the application of forces and counterforces in meshes drawn specifically for this purpose. In addition, the real-time feedback allows for simple numeric input to control the outcome. For example, a single simulation can very quickly produce [-x°] wedge disclinations from very small fractions of π, up to or nearing a full π insertion ([-360°]). Multiple π insertions are possible if surface self-collisions are solved or if a different approach is taken to model the initial topology. However, the exact amount of π inserted into a flat disk need not be predetermined if the simulation accounts for self-reactive bending; the user simply increases or decreases a number slider to achieve more or less curvature in the surface. In this example, the numeric input is not entirely abstract; the number slider domain is set between 1.0 and 2.0, which is a multiplying factor of the concentric mesh edge lengths that relate directly to real-world dimensions.

Digitally "inserting" material into the disk through differential edge expansion is comparable to predetermined paper stock insertions and mathematical insertions of factors of π since the formal result is the same. This is perhaps equally intuitive, since one can first use visual judgment to confirm the desired outcome and extract specific dimensions and the amount of surface area addition later, postsimulation in a multipart workflow. In summary, a topology approximation is modeled using line and mesh elements that organize the applied forces with the goal of finding an accurate, developable surface that can be unrolled within a very small percentage of dimensional and area deviation (<0.5%, as determined by Rhinoceros 3D ruled NURBS surface creation and unrolling in dozens of trials) (Robert McNeel & Associates 2020). The unrolled surface is then discretized into parts that fit onto standard plywood sheet sizes for CNC fabrication.

Technique 1—Expanded Concentric Polylines: The [-x°] wedge disclination is created by inserting a wedge of material into a circular disk. When reconnected, the increased surface area is forced within the original dimensional boundary,

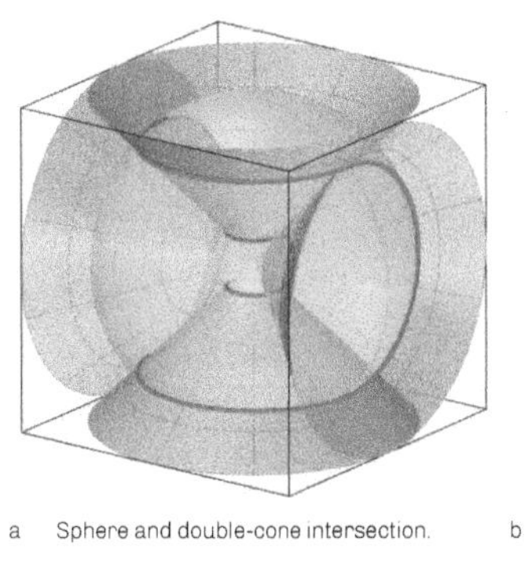
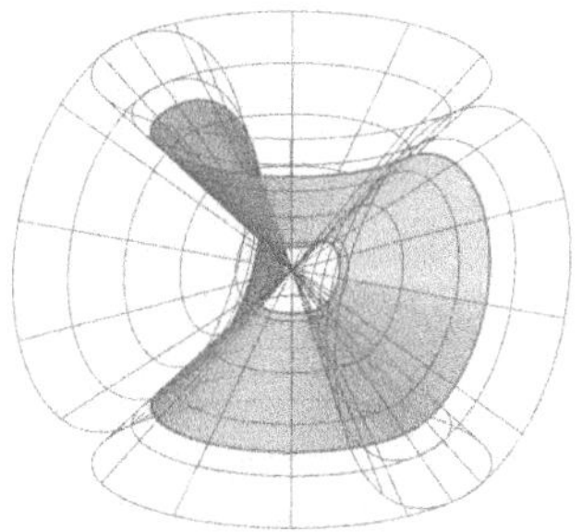
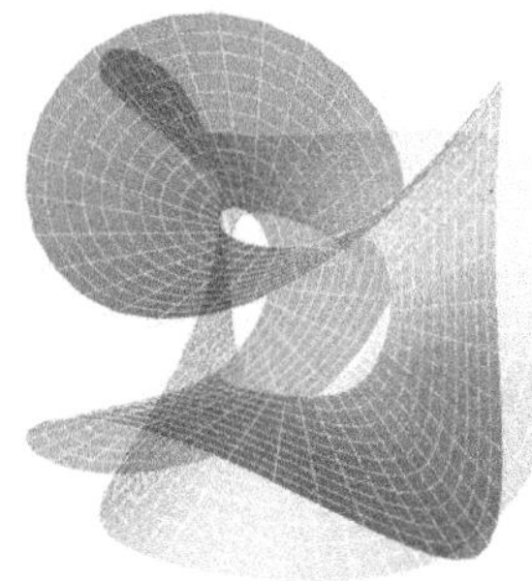

a Sphere and double-cone intersection. b Trim/join alternating conic sects. at tangents. c Create mesh and expand concentric mesh edges. d Use generating lines to create ruled srf. 8

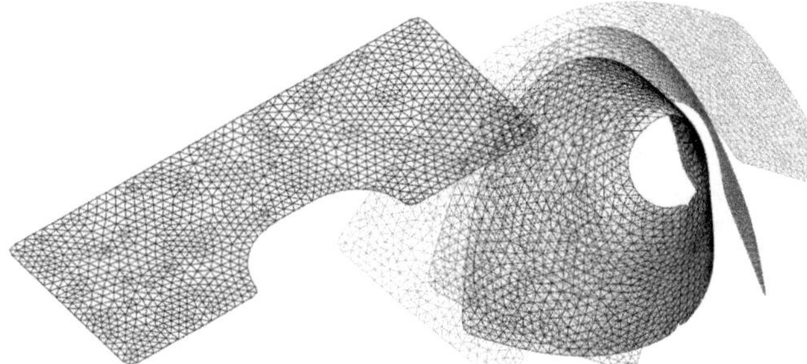
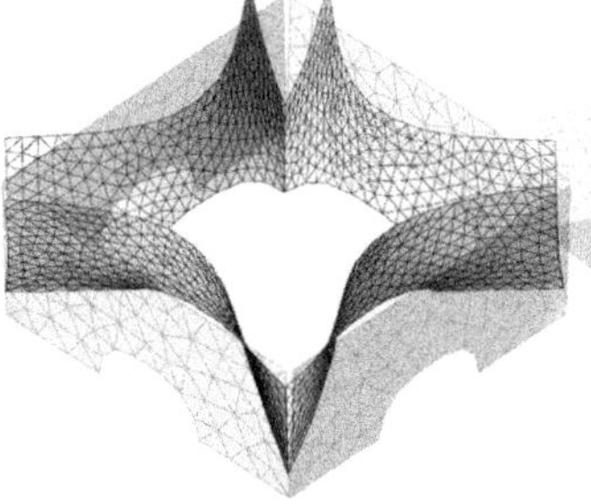
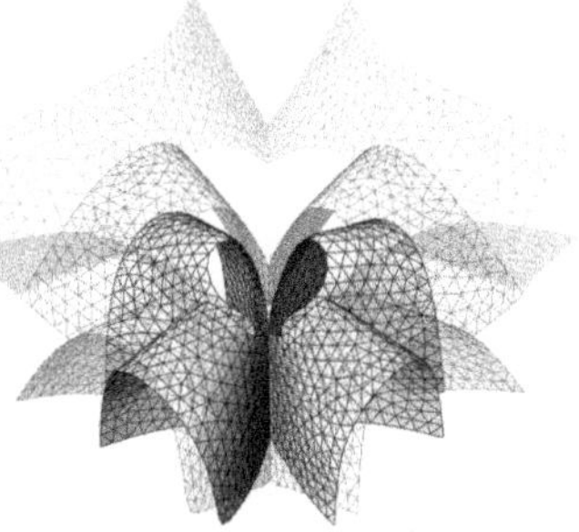

a Pull together selected mesh vertices. b Weld mesh to align vertices and continue bending across seam. c Snap together lower mesh anchoring vertices. d Rotate folds toward vert. center axis. 9

forcing out-of-plane buckling. To simulate the expansion of surface area, a simple quad mesh is produced as a control polygon. The concentric polylines are extracted and forced to expand while the radial polylines are forced to maintain their starting lengths. The factoral input of linear expansion can be converted to document the increase in rotational degrees (the starting point being 360° for a flat disk). Bending forces counteract the expansion within the constant diameter, forcing an out-of-plane reaction (Fig. 6). In this and the following examples, the mesh is tested for unroll planarity, and radial polylines are straightened in place upon convergence and used to produce a ruled NURBS surface for further discretization into smaller parts, which are detailed for full-scale assembly.

Technique 2—Relaxed Folded Mesh: A circular boundary surface is separated into four quadrants. Each surface is rotated along its two bounding radii, forming two intersecting surfaces within each quadrant. The line of intersection is used to create new surfaces resembling a series of accordion folds. The polysurface is converted into an evenly distributed, quad-dependent triangle mesh with up to twice as much surface area as the original circle but maintains its original diameter. Bending forces applied to the mesh allow it to relax naturally into the expected saddle-like form (Figs. 7, 10a).

Technique 3—Double-Cone Intersection: To demonstrate the [-x°] wedge disclination's conic geometry, a simple approximation is produced by intersecting a set of two opposing double cones with a large and small sphere, all of which share a common center point (Fig. 8). The intersection between the cones and spheres creates circles that can be split into continuous curves that form the outer and inner surface profiles. A ruled surface is drawn between the profiles and subdivided into an evenly distributed, quad-dependent triangle mesh. One could also simply trim the cones using the intersecting circles and the tangent lines between the cones, producing congruent conic sections that can be combined to form the approximated surface. The mesh is relaxed and bending forces are applied, resulting in a more natural saddle-like form, and the concentric mesh edges are expanded or contracted to control the surface geometry. Note that this technique of inscribing cones into the cube is useful to create initial surfaces of [-720°] (4π) by adding a third double cone between the remaining two opposite faces of the cube followed by the previous steps. For a clear example, and a technique to account for formal variation by adjusting cone apertures and inscribing their base circles in n-gonal polyhedra, see Verhoeff and Verhoeff's (2014) modeling of their *Lobke* sculptures.

These techniques result in near identical surfaces. This is intentional and highlights that while the base topology and simulation strategy are devised with a particular disclination variant in mind, the result is a reliable approximation suitable for the transition to larger scales.

Additional Approaches

In addition to the above, other digital form-finding techniques were used to simulate [+x°] wedge disclinations. The development of the base topology as well as the controlled motion to induce bending were directly related to the way in which the

10a Folded mesh bending with polygonal profile.

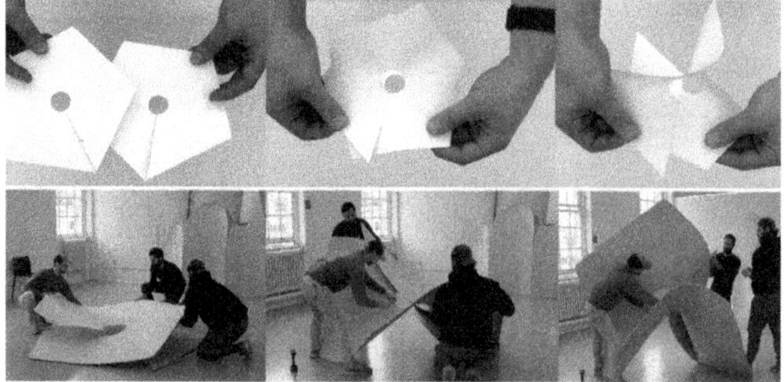

10b 2-pentagons with 72° overlap.

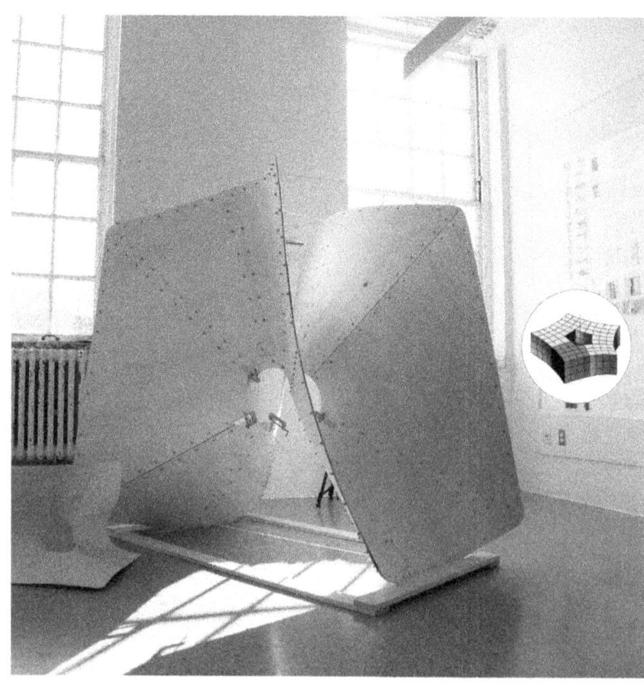

10c [-288°] wedge disclination prototype.

paper models were formed. This technique is more straightforward since these particular interpretations of the [+x°] wedge disclination do not involve the addition (or lengthening) of material. Rather, they are designed with the removal of material in mind, and are digitally pinched together to form single conic shells as well as small clusters of two, three, and four connected conic shells (Fig. 9). This is similar in setup to the "effective pinching" technique demonstrated by Schleicher et al. (2015), and similar in practice to the simulation techniques demonstrated by Soriano et al. (2015). While the former example is not defined as a disclination, since a rotational transformation is not required, the latter does exhibit the result of rotational movement in the mesh after a wedge of material is removed in order to simulate positive curvature in an elastically bent sheet. Methods described in Soriano et al. for modeling the effect of mesh singularities on elastic planar meshes toward negative curvature may be compared to the techniques described above. Specifically, a separate square mesh portion is inserted into a half-length cut within a larger square mesh, forcing the mesh to curve into a saddle-like form; a process that compares to technique 2. Second, their "plate network" simulation process is similar to technique 1 in that the base topology begins flat until a change in the topology forces the buckling, and because material overlap that occurs in reality is avoided in favor of a faster and more reliable digital simulation (Soriano et al. 2015). Another comparable technique is demonstrated by Ayres, Martin, and Zwierzycki (2018) that uses a variety of adjustments to low-polygon meshes in order to establish an appropriate valence structure required for a triaxial woven pattern prior to relaxing the form into a more accurate depiction of the woven lattice. Technique 3 may be comparable, as the crude base mesh is developed with a predetermined disclination form, which is then relaxed to approximate the bending behavior.

Finally, some paper modeling exercises have helped define the physical vs. digital modeling relationship. The [-x°] wedge disclination prototype above was designed with two pentagons that overlap 72° (sharing one edge) at the start and end of the bending sequence (Figs. 10b, 10c). The full face overlap specifies the amount of material insertion by degree, in this case creating a [-288°] wedge disclination with a polygonal outer profile, and sets the appropriate amount of layer overlap needed for consistent bending across seams. Since the paper model dictates the limits of form finding by virtue of the number of polygonal faces, a variety of digital modeling techniques could apply so long as they satisfy the intended degree of rotational bending and material overlap.

RESULTS AND DISCUSSION

The challenges of scaling self-reactive surfaces are partially due to the dimensional limitations in sheet materials (Leinhard and Knippers 2013). A common approach to scaling the bending active technique has been to localize the bending forces into smaller parts within an aggregate assembly (Schleicher et al. 2015). Instead, this phase of the work opted to build large, flat two-layer plywood sheets. The sheet, shaped specifically to accommodate the desired finished form, is itself discretized prior to bending. To test the scalability of the surface disclination workflow described previously, a series of plywood prototypes onto which a partial fiberglass

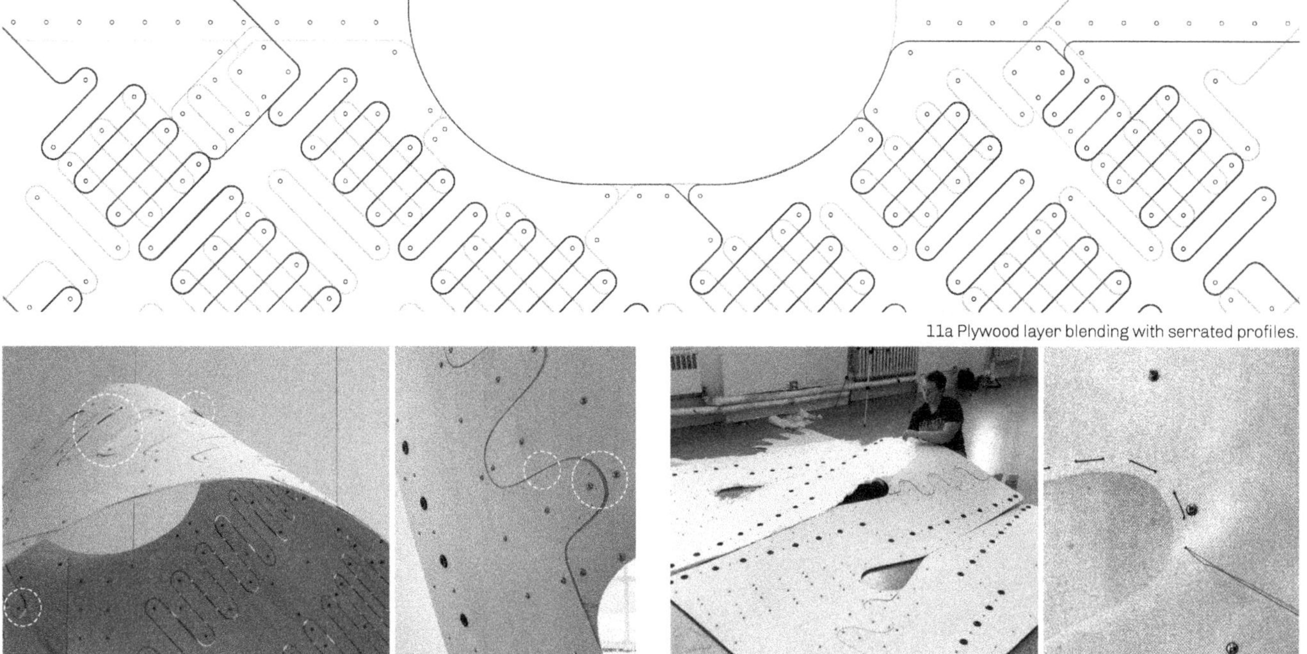

11a Plywood layer blending with serrated profiles.

11b Expansion and contraction in joints.

11c Fiberglass sew-up.

layer was tailored, stitched, and cured with epoxy resin were constructed. Each utilized a similar technique to overcome the dimensional limitations of plywood sheets by interlocking serrated profiles, allowing continuous bending across panel seams. New connection types have proven necessary as thin materials have become more common in research on timber shell construction. Typical jointing techniques that are optimized for thicker materials do not account for consistent bending across ultra-thin materials (Schwinn, Krieg, and Menges 2016). In order for the assembled flat sheet to bend across seams evenly and without concentrating the stresses to a single layer, a deeply serrated edge profile for each layer part was devised (Fig. 11a). The layers blend into one another, thereby avoiding a continuous split in the two-layer sandwich. In other words, the seam is never perpendicular to the bending direction (or parallel to the bending axis), and the two-layer thickness is maintained across the vast majority of the seam. As prototyped from 3 mm thick plywood with uniform grain direction, the two-layer serrated seam technique performs very well for bending across surfaces with dimensions larger than stock material constraints, although in some cases a considerable reduction in bending resistance was observed.

There are added benefits to the double-layer construction, for example, the ability to orient grain directions to influence the local bending behavior, as demonstrated in the ICD/ITKE 2015-16 Research Pavilion (Schwinn, Krieg, and Menges 2016). Also, the double-layer construction allows for lapping across large dimensions that avoid the awkward accumulation of material and consistency of thickness throughout. A drawback is that the layers need to be joined while in a deformed state, making a glued connection difficult and increasing the chances of delamination (Bechert et al. 2016).

An additional challenge is that due to material thickness, the layers slide as they bend at different rates. Tolerance is achieved by fitting M3 bolts and nylon-inserted locknuts, which act to set the position of each part within their respective layers but allow 1–2 mm of movement during the bending process (Fig. 11b). Bending occurs prior to the tightening of the bolts, which locks the layers and sets the form. In this phase of the research, the bolts remain during and after the composite lay-up, an area of necessary improvement (Fig. 11c). To follow, a fiberglass "jacket" was added to provide stiffness and protection from the elements. The textile was cut to match the surface profiles, manually sewn onto the pre-bent plywood assembly through CNC-machined holes along the edges. This is also an area of intended improvement, and will likely be substituted with the application of preimpregnated composite strips. The layup sequence and geodesic patterning as they may relate to the analysis of surface stresses and areas of weakness are seen as necessary steps toward realizing surface disclinations at an architectural scale.

OUTLOOK AND CONCLUSION

The work outlined in this paper is intended to demonstrate the potential of surface disclinations at a large scale, and is proposed as the preliminary step toward a more robust fabrication technique and associated computational workflow. A wider range of surface disclination strategies and how they may combine to form larger aggregate constructs is currently being developed in parallel with new

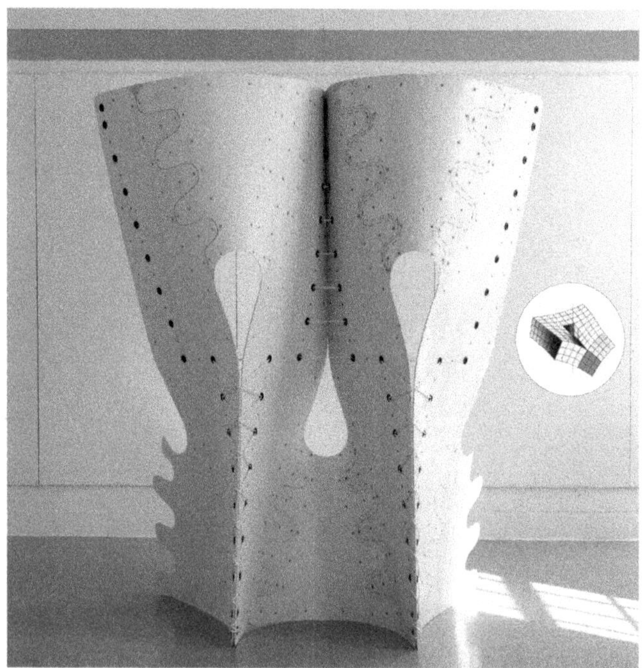

12 [+/-90°] twist disclination prototype.

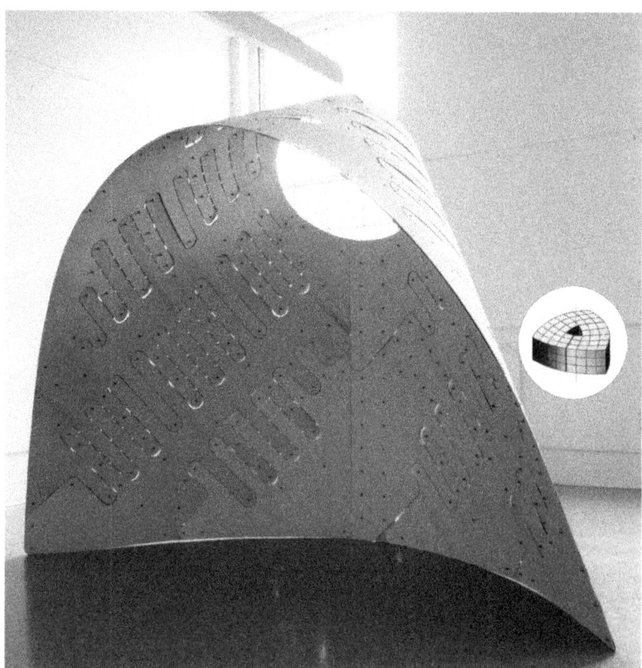

13 [+180°] wedge disclination prototype.

developments in the form-finding process and simulation approaches. A more direct connection between the composite lay-up process and simulation is seen as an important step to directly connect the on- and off-screen work. This includes finite element methods for analyzing potential bending stresses both during assembly and under loading to help predetermine fiber directions along the surfaces for increased structural stability. Using holographic guides to assist with the manual application of preimpregnated composite strips to the plywood core is a future goal and an interesting challenge, as this would further necessitate precise calibration between paper models, simulations, and construction. Another important improvement to the fabrication process will be to drastically reduce the number of temporary fasteners to prevent fiber lay-up interference, if and when the plywood surfaces are intended to act as cores in a moldless composite construction process. Finally, further work to determine the scalability of the inherent snap-through buckling behavior holds exciting potential for the application of self-reactive surface disclinations at an architectural scale.

ACKNOWLEDGMENTS

The work presented in this paper was funded by the Nohmura Foundation for Membrane Structure's Technology and was conducted at the intersection between research and teaching together with students from the Situated Technologies Research Group at the University at Buffalo, State University of New York. The author would like to express their gratitude towards Heidi Flores, Rossella Giangreco-Marotta, James Hedger, Russ Kolker, Rania Moussa, Rebecca Flanagan, Stanicka Mathurin, Mehrad Naghizadeh, Kajal Patel, Yogesh Ravichandar, and Timothy Zeng for their contributing work as part of the fall 2019 STRG design studio. The author would also like to thank the peer reviewers for their extremely helpful comments and suggestions.

REFERENCES

Akgün, Tevfik, Ahmet Koman, and Ergun Akleman. 2006. "Developable Sculptural Forms of Ilhan Koman." In *Proceedings of the Bridges Conference*, 343–350. London: Tarquin Publications.

Ayres, Phil, Alison Grace Martin, and Mateusz Zwierzycki. 2018. "Beyond the Basket Case: A Principled Approach to the Modelling of Kagome Weave Patterns for the Fabrication of Interlaced Lattice Structures Using Straight Strips." In *Advances in Architectural Geometry 2018*, edited by L. Hasselgren et al., 72–91. Vienna: Chalmers University of Technology.

Bechert, Simon, Jan Knippers, Oliver David Krieg, Achim Menges, Tobias Schwinn, and Daniel Sonntag. 2016. "Textile Fabrication Techniques for Timber Shells. Elastic Bending of Custom-Laminated Veneer for Segmented Shell Construction Systems." In *Advances in Architectural Geometry 2016*, edited by S. Adriaenssens et al., 154–169. Zurich: vdf Hochschulverlag AG an der ETH Zurich.

Demaine, Erik D., Martin L. Demaine, Duks Koschitz, and Tomohiro Tachi. 2011. "Curved Crease Folding: a Review on Art, Design and Mathematics." In *Proceedings of the IABSE-IASS Symposium 2011: Taller, Longer, Lighter*, 145–161. London: International Association for Bridge and Structural Engineering (IABSE) / IASS.

Harris, William F. 1977. "Disclinations." *Scientific American* 237 (6): 130–145.

Harris, William F. 1978. "Dislocations, Disclinations and Dispirations: Distractions in Very Naughty Crystals." *South African Journal of Science* 74: 332–338.

Harriss, Edmund. 2020. "Gauss-Bonnet Sculpting." In *Bridges 2020 Conference Proceedings*, 137–144. Phoenix, AZ: Tessellations Publishing.

Hoff, N.J. 1946. "A Short History on the Development of Airplane Structures." *American Scientist* 34 (3): 370–388.

Knippers, Jan, Jan Cremers, Markus Gabler, and Julian Lienhard. 2011. Construction Manual for Polymers + Membranes. Basel: Birkhauser.

Kroner, E., and K. H. Anthony. 1975. "Dislocations and Disclinations in Material Structures: The Basic Topological Concepts." *Annual Review of Materials Science* 5: 43–72.

Lienhard, Julian and Jan Knippers. 2013. "Considerations on the Scaling of Bending-Active Structures." *International Journal of Space Structures* 28 (3–4): 137–147.

Martin, Alison G. 2015. "A Basketmaker's Approach to Structural Morphology." In *Proceedings of the International Association for Shell and Spatial Structures (IASS) Symposium 2015: Future Visions, 1-8.* Amsterdam: International Association for Shell and Spatial Structures (IASS).

Moholy-Nagy, László. 1947. *Vision in Motion.* Paul Theobald & Co.

Patkau Architects. 2017. *Patkau Architects Material Operations*. New York: Princeton Architectural Press

Piker, Daniel. 2013. "Kangaroo—Form Finding with Computational Physics." *Architectural Design* 83 (2): 136–137.

Robert McNeel & Associates. *Rhinoceros*. V.6.0. Robert McNeel & Associates. PC. 2020.

Schleicher, Simon, and Riccardo La Magna. 2016. "Bending-Active Plates. Form-Finding and Form-Conversion." In *ACADIA 2016: Posthuman Frontiers: Data, Designers, and Cognitive Machines [Proceedings of the 36th Annual Conference of the Association for Computer Aided Design in Architecture (ACADIA)]*, Ann Arbor, MI, 27–29 October 2016, edited by K. Velikov, S. Ahlquist, M. del Campo, and G. Thün, 260–269. CUMINCAD.

Schleicher, Simon, Andrew Rastetter, Riccardo La Magna, Andreas Schönbrunner, Nicola Haberbosch, and Jan Knippers. 2015. "Form-Finding and Design Potentials of Bending-Active Plate Structures." In *Modelling Behaviour. Design Modelling Symposium 2015*, edited by M. Ramsgaard Thomsen et al., 53–63. Cham: Springer International Publishing.

Schwinn, Tobias, Oliver David Krieg, and Achim Menges. 2016. "Robotic Sewing. A Textile Approach Towards the Computational Design and Fabrication of Lightweight Timber Shells." In *ACADIA 2016: Posthuman Frontiers: Data, Designers, and Cognitive Machines [Proceedings of the 36th Annual Conference of the Association for Computer Aided Design in Architecture (ACADIA)]*, Ann Arbor, MI, 27–29 October 2016, edited by K. Velikov, S. Ahlquist, M. del Campo, and G. Thün, 224–233. CUMINCAD.

Soriano, Enrique, Pep Tornabell, Dragos I. Naicu, and Gunther H. Filz. 2015. "Topologically-Based Curvature in Thin Elastic Shell Networks." In *VII International Conference on Textile Composites and Inflatable Structures: Structural Membranes 2015*, edited by E. Onate, K-U. Bletzinger, and B. Kroplin, 167-176. Barcelona: International Center for Numerical Methods in Engineering (CIMNE).

Verhoeff, Tom and Koos Verhoeff. 2014. "Lobke, and Other Constructions from Conical Segments." In *Proceedings of the Bridges Conference 2014*, 309–316. Phoenix, AZ: Tessellations Publishing.

IMAGE CREDITS

Figures 1, 10c: He 2019.
Figure 2a: Ayres et al. 2018.
Figures 2b, 2c, 2d: Harris 1977.
Figure 3a: Koch, Conrad. © HfG-Archiv/Ulmer Museum.
Figure 3b: Naum Gabo, The Museum of Modern Art.
Figure 4: Tuncelli, in Akgün 2006 .
Figure 5: © Eames Office.
Figures 10b, 10c: Hedger and Kolker 2019.
Figures 9, 11a: Flores and Moussa 2019.

All other drawings and images by the author.

Nicholas Bruscia is an Assistant Professor in the Department of Architecture at the University at Buffalo, State University of New York, where he is also a researcher in the Sustainable Manufacturing and Advanced Robotics Technology (SMART) Community of Excellence. A strong interest in architectural geometry and enthusiasm for calculated formal and structural elegance informs much of his work with materials and fabrication processes. He has over a decade of experience in applied digital design media, and his primary role in collaborative projects has focused on the workflow associated with the design and realization of large-scale prototypes.

Active-Casting

Functionally Graded Knits for Volumetric Concrete Casting

Tsz Yan Ng
Taubman College,
University of Michigan

Sean Ahlquist
Taubman College,
University of Michigan

Evgueni Filipov
Department of Civil and
Environmental Engineering,
University of Michigan

Tracey Weisman
Taubman College,
University of Michigan

1 Detail of drupelet texture cast.

ABSTRACT

Active-Casting explores the use of bespoke computer numerical controlled (CNC) manufactured knits to produce volumetric textile formwork for casting glass-fiber-reinforced concrete (GFRC). As a collaboration between experts in architecture, textile fabrication, and civil engineering, the research investigates multimaterial, functionally graded knit formwork as a fully seamless system to cast concrete. Working with controlled characteristics such as elasticity and stiffness of yarn type and knit structure, the soft textile is conceived as the vessel that defines the performative characteristics of volume, geometry, and surface detail. With only a minimal frame to suspend the volumetric cast, hydrostatic pressure "inflates" the fabric formwork, creating a dynamic form-finding process that eliminates the need for typical molding materials such as wood or foam. While active form-finding processes for CNC knit casting have been explored as an open-face, GFRC-sprayed system, the Active-Casting process produces a finished surface on all faces, embedded with expressions in form and surface detail from the knitted formwork. The precast units using this process reduce the amount of construction waste for formwork production, proposes a more automated fashion for manufacturing the formwork, and produces casts with complex geometries difficult to accomplish with traditional casting methods.

INTRODUCTION

Fabric casting has been extensively explored (Veenendaal et al. 2011) with more recent development by Mark West (2016), using advanced computational design and fabrication techniques by the Block Research Group (BRG) with *KnitCrete* (Popescu 2019), and more collaboratively with Zaha Hadid Architects Computation Design Group for *KnitCandela* (Popescu et al. 2021). Building from Ahlquist's work on functionally graded form-active knits (Ahlquist 2015; Ahlquist et al. 2017), our research investigates the dynamic interaction of casting where weight and hydrostatic pressure of the fresh concrete is restrained by a customized 3D-knitted formwork. This deviates from BRG's approach of using knits as explicitly stiffened formwork (imbued with a hardening agent) or as an open-face formwork with a combination of predetermined stretch and form-finding for concrete spraying (Wen et al. 2019). As a result, the final cast volume is not a direct negative of the knitted formwork, but rather the cast is uniquely shaped, derived from the behavior of the knit in direct interaction with the concrete's rheological properties as a poured volume.

The motivation of the research stems from using soft CNC-knitted formwork that could be customized in terms of yarn type, knit structure, and overall geometric form. As opposed to rigid sheet material used in typical concrete construction, the soft multimaterial and functionally graded textile could incorporate local and global controls, producing complex geometries that are difficult to achieve with standard flat and rigid stock material. Due to the knit's elastic characteristic and the ability to control various performative behavior under tension, knits as formworks offer alternative means to cast concrete where the knit is lightweight and transportable, and does not require extensive falsework. This investigation outlines initial research to develop the methods necessary to achieve cast concrete components and test the viability of the process in relation to the different stages of concrete forming and construction. More than "filling a bag" with concrete, the customized knits are designed and fabricated to produce architectural components with a range of typologies to inform designs for potential architectural systems. This includes in-plane and out-of-plane panels, diagrid frame components, and thin-shell double-curve funnels. The aim is to reconsider textile concrete forming using nontraditional formwork through the lens of contemporary CNC technologies and computational modeling, enabling not only construction efficiencies such as time, material, and labor, which translate to overall cost reduction, but also emergent architectural designs previously difficult to achieve.

BACKGROUND

The interaction between the textile industry and architecture has predominantly been focused on product development such as interior tactile surface treatments,

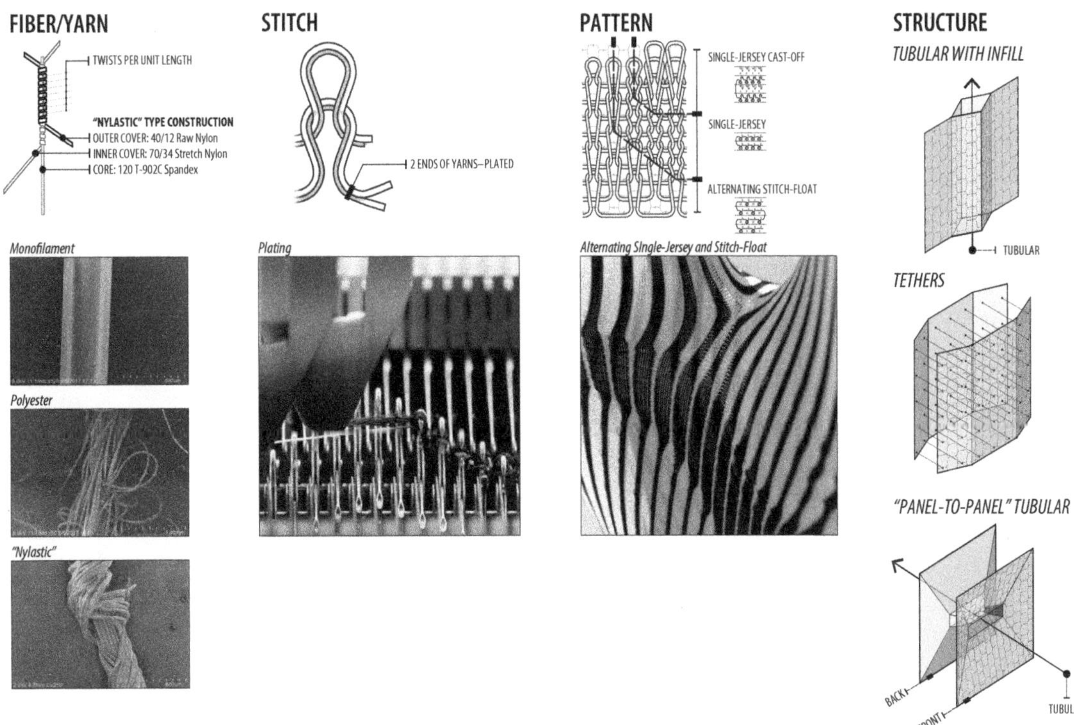

2 Knitting parameters that affect overall textile behavior: fiber/yarn, stitch, and pattern. The column on the right identifies the three knit types used in this investigation: (from top to bottom) 1–tubular pockets with single layer infill, 2–tethers, and 3–apertures or "panel-to-panel tubular." 2

furniture, or membranes such as vapor barriers or geotextiles. In terms of integrating manufacturing processes, especially ones that are automated, there are fewer instances where textile manufacturing processes contribute directly to construction. The automation of CNC knitting to create formwork for casting concrete is unique in this respect. The proposed convergence of textile manufacturing and construction in this project directly addresses the call for the architecture, engineering, and construction (AEC) industry to catch up to other manufacturing industries and increase productivity through automation (Barbosa et al. 2017). Two key factors that contribute to productivity—time and labor—are especially pronounced in concrete construction, whereby formwork and falsework manufacturing is time- and labor-intensive, covering anywhere between 60–70% (this includes material cost) of the overall construction budget depending on the formwork's geometric complexity (García de Soto et al. 2018; Hurd 2005). Thus, yoking of automated processes for formwork production, in this case, using CNC knitting technology, proves promising not only to address productivity for the construction industry but more directly for concrete construction. In co-opting an already robust industry in CNC knitting (fashion, furniture, auto manufacturing), production facilities are available around the world, making it potentially a unique opportunity for wide adoption as well as drawing from skilled labor markets previously untapped. Additionally, the lightweight quality of the textile for transport is particularly advantageous in the context of the overall embodied energy calculation for building construction.

Flexible formwork for concrete casting, especially at the building scale, has been explored extensively, with the earliest patent filed in 1899 by Gustav Lilienthal for a floor system (Hawkins et al. 2016). Most flexible formwork utilizes premanufactured textiles, mainly out of woven material, with different yarn types. These formworks are typically patterned, assembled by sewing, or serged together to create the overall formwork. Fabric casting may be used for form-finding possibilities as the soft textile drapes or reacts to the weight and hydrostatic pressure of the concrete. The natural draping, in catenary form, has also been explored for its structural efficiency, leading to reduction in material use, where material is used only where it is needed (West 2016).

Recent renewed interest in flexible formwork, especially CNC-knitted formwork, is driven by computational processes for structural and material optimization as well as widely available digital fabrication technologies that challenge traditional building processes and existing built form (Hawkins et al. 2016). CNC knits explored in this research have customized multifunctional properties controlling characteristics such as elasticity and stiffness, offering a variety of topological features. Explicitly focusing on filled molds rather than open-face pre-stretched molds, concrete's fluidity is leveraged for form-finding capacity, especially complex geometries. With minimum postprocessing, as soon as they are knitted, the formworks are ready for casting. Beyond material and time/labor reduction in mold making, the fillable flexible formworks present other advantages for casting such as finished surfaces on all sides (as opposed to single-sided for open molds), the prospect of having undercut geometries, and embedding textured impressions from the knit directly onto the concrete surface.

FORMWORK AND CONCRETE CASTING

The stages of the work can be broken down into CNC knit formwork design and production, concrete casting, and computational analytic models to inform the behavior of the knit under stress loads, namely concrete's self-weight and hydrostatic pressure.

CNC-Knitted Formwork

The formworks in this research are knitted on the Stoll CMS 7.2-gauge 822 HP machine. The manufactured knits have tailored performance properties through the specification of fiber and yarn type, stitch type, and stitch patterns within a single knitted textile. The yarn specification for the different formworks in this study includes polyester (720 denier), nylon monofilament (Tex 35), and thermoplastic elastomer monofilament, which does not absorb water and has high tensile capacity, or a combination of elastane core with nylon wrapper called nylastic, which is very stretchy. The double bed of the Stoll machine enables the production of the double layer needed for fillable formwork, closing the sides to effectively create a "pouch." The knit types are categorized as 1-tubular pockets, 2-tethers as an expanded version of the spacer, and 3-apertures (Fig. 2). The tubular pockets are created by interconnecting specific regions of the tube into a single layer, effectively closing off those areas and resulting in a network of open tubes where the concrete will eventually be cast. The tethers connect the two layers with a yarn that zigzags perpendicularly to the knitting direction, controlling the gap between the layers with specific distances. The lengths of the tethers are customizable, as is the frequency throughout the knit. The apertures are described in knitting terms as "panel-to-panel" tubulars, created as a slit between two layers through a combination of bind-off and cast-on techniques that define the size and volume of the aperture.

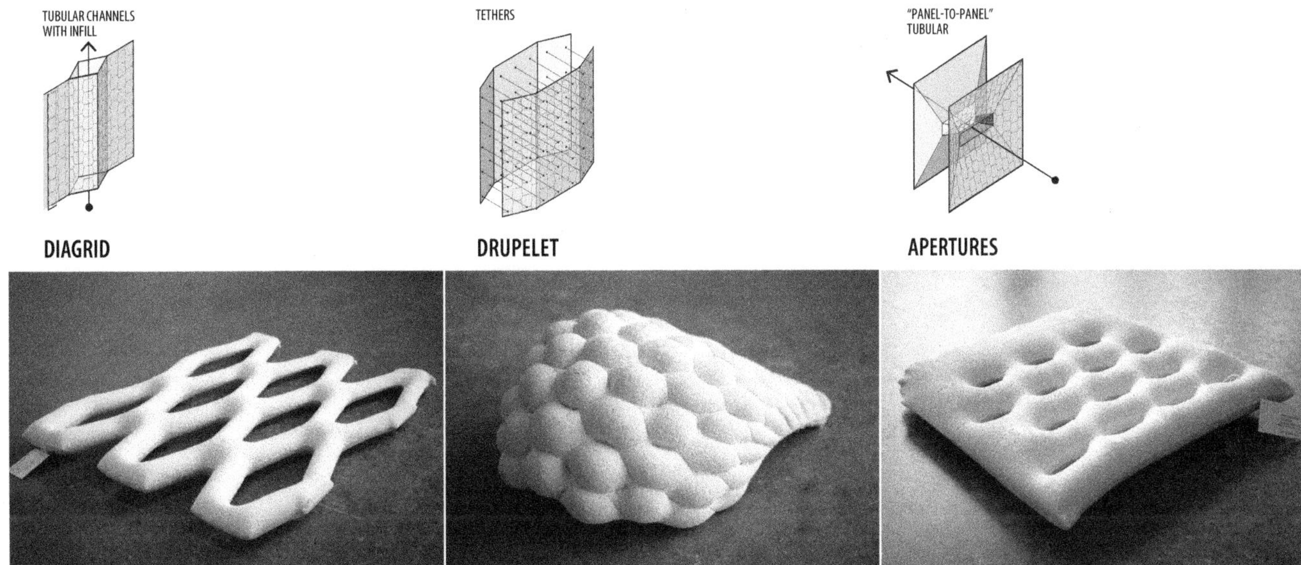

3

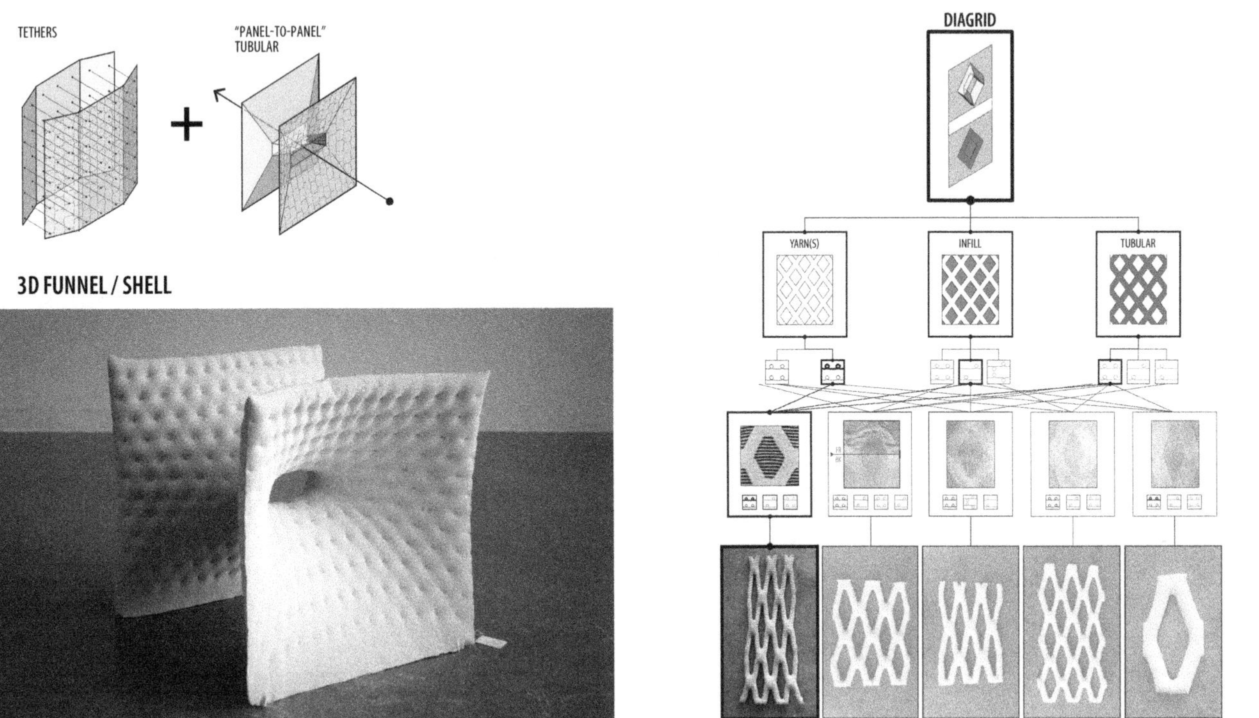

4

5

3 Three of the four typologies developed leveraging knit's manufacturing logic to create fillable formwork: diagrid, drupelet texture, and apertures.

4 The fourth typology, 3D funnel shell, which combines tethers and panel-to-panel tubular knit types.

5 Diagrid knit in detail showing the knit structures and the single-layer infill tailored for multiaxial stretch to control the proportion of the diagrid cells.

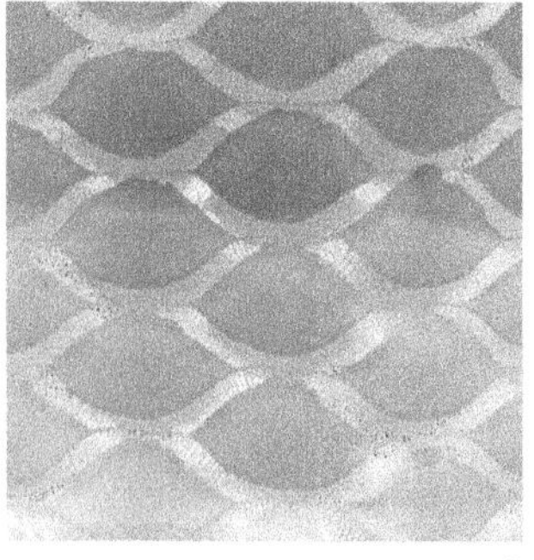

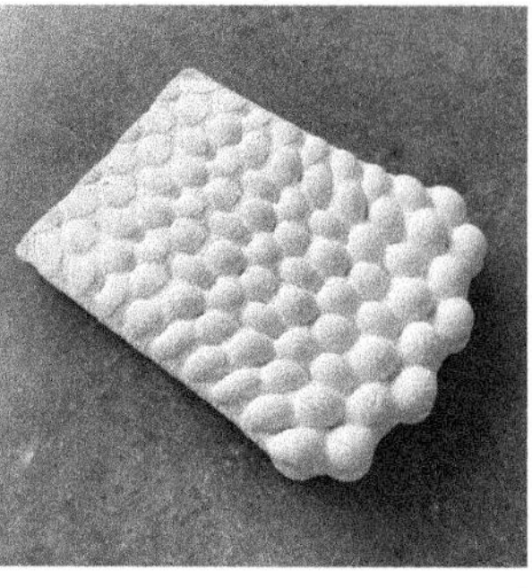

6 Detail of drupelet texture formwork with polyester yarn web and nylastic yarn infill.

7 Resultant cast using the knit shown in Figure 6.

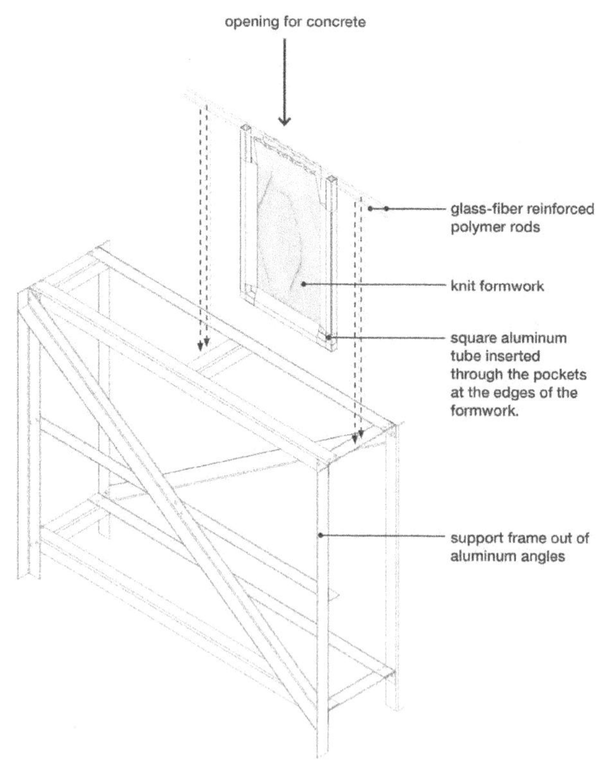

8 Exploded diagram of the casting setup.

The formwork manufactured leverages many combinations of yarn types, knit structures, and patterns, producing four distinct typologies for concrete casting: diagrid, drupelet texture, apertures, and 3D funnel shell (Figs. 3, 4). The diagrid typology utilizes continuous pockets that intersect, where single-layered fields or cells are produced in-between. Figure 5 shows the diagrid knits in detail where the knit structures of the cells are tailored to constrain multiaxial stretch, helping to control the proportion of the diagrid cells. When the knit is removed after casting, the cells between the tubular volumes produce openings in the concrete cast. Typically, including openings within the textile itself can be extremely time-consuming to knit. This method of designing a solid knit with nonfilled regions is very efficient. The drupelet prototype involves constraining a web of polyester with highly extensible infills of nylastic yarn. While it looks as if the polyester is knitted in a wavy pattern, it is actually complete horizontal stripes with diamond-shaped regions of nylastic short rows inserted in-between, distorting the shape. This means that some columns only contain polyester stitches while others are mostly nylastic, causing the polyester stripes to act as the constraining mechanism. The significant difference in stretch, stitch structure, and amount of material between the two patterns offer varying levels of restraint for the mold's surface, thus creating the protrusions under the hydrostatic pressure of the fresh concrete (Figs. 6, 7). The drupelet panels also include the use of tethers to maintain the relative distance between the two layers of knits, allowing the nylastic drupelets to be activated. The apertures typology utilizes the knit type of the same name, whereby openings are created throughout the panel. The size of the openings, the geometry, and their relative positions are all customizable within reason to the knitting parameters. The last typology, 3D funnel shell, employs the combination of apertures and tether knit types, whereby two knits are combined at the aperture (funnel end) to form a single monolithic cast (Fig. 4). The shell thickness is constrained by the tether knits. This is the only typology that requires postproduction, serging the two knits together at the aperture end to create the necessary four-layer textile system.

Casting Setup and Process

Each typology is explored at different scales, developing control and variations through refined casting processes and specific GFRC mix design. The casting setup involves an aluminum frame by which the knit is minimally hung at the top (Fig. 8). The formwork includes knitted eyelets at the top to allow two glass-fiber-reinforced rods (GFRP) to be threaded through horizontally. The rods are then rested on the aluminum frame with zip ties added to keep the GFRP rods from deforming from the weight of the concrete. This opening is where the concrete is poured. The connections for the frame are not rigidly tightened to allow the entire frame to wobble during casting. The frame is agitated to wobble during the casting process to help the flow of the GFRC without tugging at the knit, which may cause unintended deformation. This helps to isolate as much as possible the forces, concrete's self-weight/ gravity and hydrostatic pressure, to interact with the knit

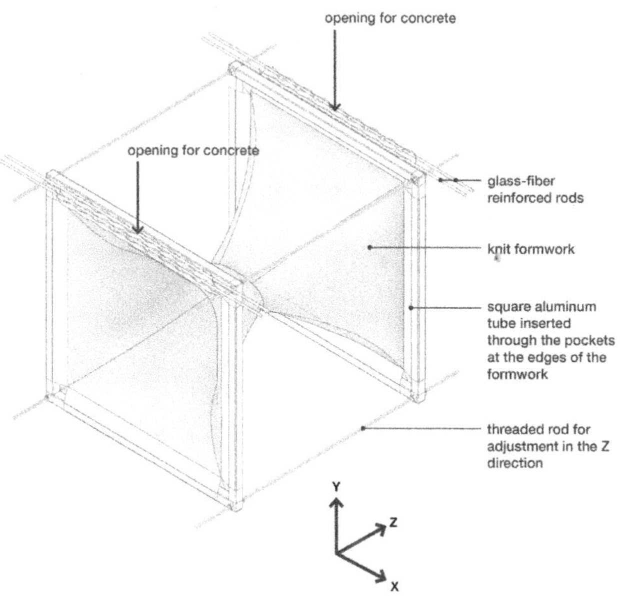

9 Exploded diagram showing 3D funnel shell casting setup.

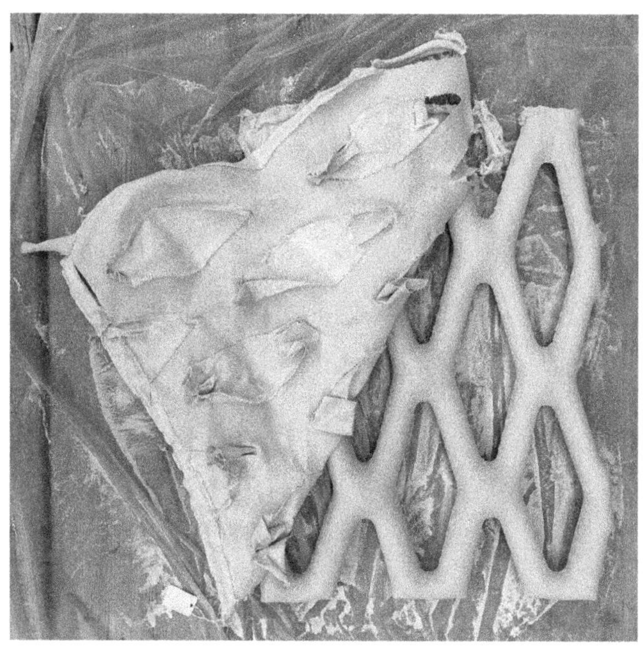

10 Demolding process for a diagrid panel. Due to the single-layer cells, one side is demolded first and then flipped to remove the other side.

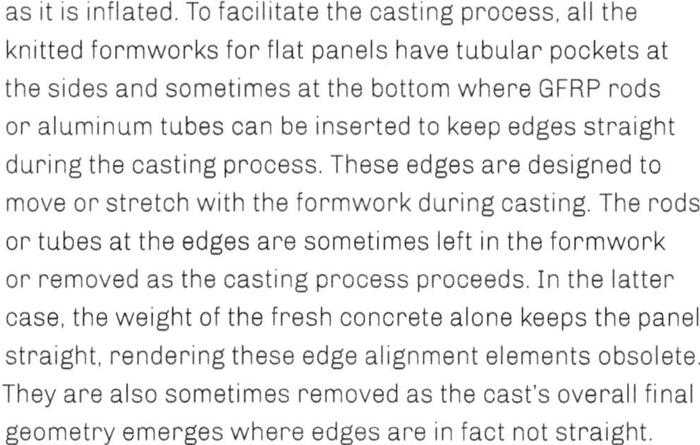

as it is inflated. To facilitate the casting process, all the knitted formworks for flat panels have tubular pockets at the sides and sometimes at the bottom where GFRP rods or aluminum tubes can be inserted to keep edges straight during the casting process. These edges are designed to move or stretch with the formwork during casting. The rods or tubes at the edges are sometimes left in the formwork or removed as the casting process proceeds. In the latter case, the weight of the fresh concrete alone keeps the panel straight, rendering these edge alignment elements obsolete. They are also sometimes removed as the cast's overall final geometry emerges where edges are in fact not straight.

The 3D funnel typology is the only one that is pre-stretched and constrained against the frame due to the nature of the geometry (Fig. 9). In this case, the pour openings are designed along the top edge of both funnels with the concrete being filled from both sides simultaneously. This ensures even distribution of the concrete as it meets at the joined apertures. The frame is composed of 1-inch square aluminum tubes, with L corner caps. The frame size in the x and y direction are adjustable by using different tube lengths. The aluminum tubes thread through the knitted pockets along the edges of the formwork. The frame is adjustable in the z direction as the funnels stretch, aided by four threaded rods serving as compression elements connected at the corners of the frame.

Once the formwork is set up, the knit is saturated with water before casting to ensure that the knit won't draw moisture from the fresh concrete, affecting the hydration process. The devised GFRC ratio most conducive to casting is 35.5% by weight cement, 4.7% silica fume, 9.5% ground silica, 35.5% fine sand, 1.1% superplasticizer, 2.4% polymer, 0.9% glass fiber, and 11.1% water. This roughly works out to 27.65% water-to-cementitious ratio. Depending on the part, if the formwork has small tubular pockets or if panel thickness is thin, which makes flow difficult, the superplasticizer is adjusted. 1.1% superplasticizer is the maximum amount used as the "stiffness" of the GFRC has to be calibrated in order to control seepage through the knit. The balance was struck between minimizing seepage but fluid enough for flow during the casting process. If seepage is extensive, encasing the knit completely, the demolding process will be difficult. This is of special concern for the drupelet casts, as the nylastic yarns are stretched extensively, opening up more gaps between the stitches for fresh concrete to seep through. After filling, the entire cast is wrapped in plastic to keep the surfaces of the cast from drying out, maintaining a steady hydration level as much as possible to avoid adverse effects on the strength of the GFRC. After two days, the demolding process involves simply cutting the knit formwork and pulling the knit off the concrete surface (Fig. 10). Depending on the level of seepage, power washing the surface helps to remove encased yarn.

Predictive Modeling/Simulations

In order to understand the effects of the knit in relation to the hydrostatic pressure of the concrete, simple cylinders were cast to isolate the behavior of the forces (Fig. 11a–b), and computational analytical models were created to predict the shape. For the analytical models, cylinder casts were discretized, where the height of the cylinder was marked into half-inch segments h, and for each segment, we compute the vertical concrete pressure generated during casting σ_v. The hoop stress equation is used to compute the horizontal stress in the knit as $\sigma_x=\sigma_h=(\sigma_v*r)/t$, where r is the radius of the segment, and t is the thickness of the knit (Fig. 11c). The vertical stress of the knit σ_y is found by integrating the weight of concrete supported underneath each segment and dividing by the cross-sectional area of the knit (i.e., the top segment has the largest σ_y). The matrix in Figure 11d relates the anisotropic stresses to strains within the fabric. An iterative procedure steps through the deformations, until a converged result is obtained for the shape (Fig. 11e).

RESULTS AND DISCUSSION

The prototypes produced from the four typologies have highlighted specific areas to develop further based on the initial findings. Of the four typologies, the diagrid was explored most at different scales, between grid and tube sizes, as well as the number of intersections. The largest panel produced thus far measures over 7 ft high (Fig. 12), cast from a multimaterial (monofilament and nylastic yarns) striped knit that stretched about four times its original length during casting, and produced deep undulating ribbed textures on the surface (Fig. 13). Compared to other smaller diagrid casts, it was evident that the knit was able to withstand the weight and hydrostatic pressure at this larger scale. Stitch density and integration of the monofilament yarn aided in the tensile strength of the knit. However, because of the height (cast vertically), the hydrostatic pressure, especially at the base, forced concrete to seep through much more, which made demolding difficult. An option to consider in the future is to cast from the side (changing the orientation) to reduce the height, which proportionally will reduce the hydrostatic pressure. The striped knit out of all the knit types had the most overall stretch. This is due to the inherent welt-wise curling in the stripes of the elastomeric monofilament, shortening the height of the knit when in its static state. When concrete is cast into these knits, the weight and hydrostatic pressure is enough to overpower the curling, causing the yarn to straighten.

Similar to the diagrid, the drupelet casts had a fairly large amount of deformation globally (almost double in length) and locally on the surface. Initial tests using a singular yarn type but different knit structure did not yield the protrusions. Nylastic yarn worked best for the infill pattern since the elasticity of the yarn allowed the pressure from the fresh concrete to push farther from the surface. However, as mentioned, the seepage through the stitching made demolding difficult. Unlike other yarns with more tensile strength, which enabled the yarn to crack the cement-encased surface when pulled, the nylastic yarn breaks easily, leaving the yarn embedded. To create more bulk in the nylastic region, two ends of nylastic were used to make the gaps between the stitches tighter. This helped to a certain degree to reduce seepage, and more tests will be needed to refine the process. A high viscous mix may be used in this case, since these panels are easier to cast than thin tubular knits.

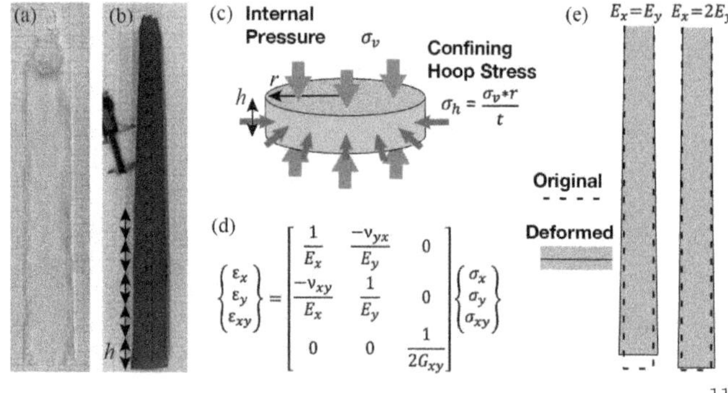

11

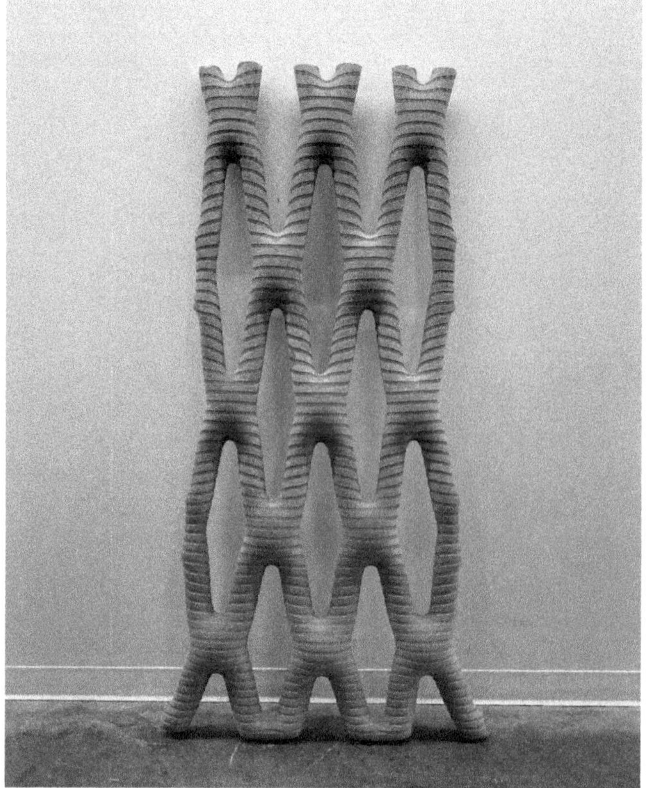
12

11 Analytic modeling study with isolated forces between the knit and the fresh concrete.

12 Cast full-scale diagrid panel, measuring over 7 ft high and 3 ft wide, using a combination of monofilament and nylastic yarns.

13 Deep undulating textures with alternating rows of different yarns indexing the complex geometric surface deformation during casting.

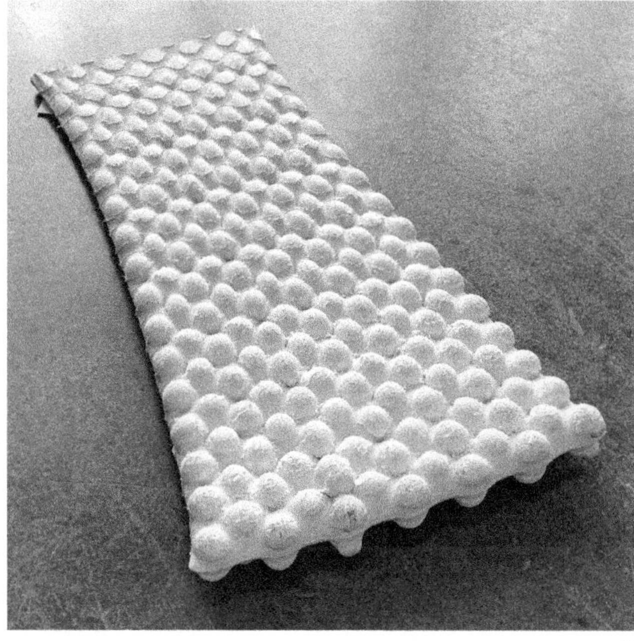

14 A drupelet cast showing the drastic tapering effects as the knit undergoes deformation with the bottom wider and thicker than the top. This is due to more weight and pressure at the bottom from the fresh concrete.

As mentioned above, the 3D funnel typology is the most restrained of all the casts. Yet there are still noticeable differences between the top and the bottom of the cast due to the weight and pressure of the concrete. Given the three-dimensional complexity of the funnel geometry, the overall shaping of the knit is more difficult to control. In fact, when the formwork is stretched more tautly, leaving less give to the knit, the deformation created pinch points between the formwork's inside and outside surface where concrete did not fill. This created openings at the aperture connection. Further studies will inform the relationship of the knitted formwork in context to the concrete's deformation for this typology.

An expected phenomenon in each prototype (Fig. 14) was observed where the bottom of the cast is deformed wider and thicker than the top. This is due to the fact that the bottom receives the most weight and pressure. One can either work with this phenomenon or try to counteract the effects either in the knit design (such as shaping) or to use constraining measures such as rigidly held frames. Depending on the application and designs of the architectural system, these approaches will be weighed. For instance, the edge constraints might be needed if the panels have to meet side-by-side, where a straight edge is necessary for alignment and connection. One of the key motivations for the development of the computational analytic models is to predict the knit's behavior so that shaping of the knit does not need to be derived through multiple iterations of extensive physical prototyping. The analytical model shows correlation with simple tubular casts. The current simulation methods will also be extended to capture more complex geometries such as diagrid and nonplanar geometries, exemplified by the drupelet cast (Fig. 15), where the side edges are restrained to allow more material surface to stretch and drop in a nonplanar fashion.

While the formwork could be left in place after casting, the prototypes produced in this investigation are demolded to gauge where manual labor, in the entire process, could be kept to a minimum. This ensures the practicality of the proposed method to be not just comparable but more advantageous than existing casting methods. The current scale of production due to limitation of the research lab remains as prefabricated units. Large-scale prototypes or monolithic constructs will be developed along with practices that will enable the technique to be readily deployed for typical on-site construction settings. In order to bring this investigation to scale, testing to characterize the results using this casting technique will be necessary. This includes specimen testing of the GFRC's strength capacity in comparison to other casting methods as well as destructive testing of cast components.

Future investigation will further refine the casting techniques in relation to the formwork's behavior to best harness design potentials for architectural production. For instance, after the formwork is filled, the cast could

15 Nonplanar deformation of a drupelet cast when the sides of the knit are left unconstrained.

16 Multimaterial system of a diagrid cast with slumped acrylic filling the cells to create a completely sealed surface. Note the slightly flattened diagrid members from lying flat on a horizontal surface during the curing process.

lie flat on a horizontal surface to cure. Doing so allows the hydrostatic pressure to distribute evenly across the entire panel. However, this process creates flat bottoms against the surface as can be seen in the diagrid cast in Figure 16. Depending on the application, different processes will be considered and adjusted. Additionally, beyond GFRC casting, postproduction with multimaterial systems will be explored. As shown in Figure 16, slumped acrylic is vacuum set directly on top of the diagrid to provide a sealed surface. The complex geometries of the acrylic in the cell region could also offer acoustic control properties. By replacing regular Portland cement with refractory cement, glass could be slumped instead of acrylic in a kiln. Other multimaterial systems include reinforcement insertion, where the formwork has preknitted positioning holes to insert reinforcement or jointing connections. The reinforcement could be pre-bent and inserted before casting. This takes advantage of the soft textile, which allows it to flex around the rigid insertions, especially when the reinforcement changes direction but remains continuous, following the panel's geometry. Reinforcement will be critical for full-scale designs where GFRC's tensile capacity may not be sufficient for loading conditions that are more demanding.

Integrated characteristics of this nontraditional casting method will be harnessed for various design applications. This includes the textural effects such as the "tufted" soft look when the tether knits create dimples from the tethers' restrain on the surface (Fig. 5). While the rib knits are designed for strength and stretch, the alternating rows not only index the complex geometric deformation but could also be used for aesthetic or practical purposes such as underfoot traction and novel tactile expression (Fig. 13). Typically, textures like these are cast with a liner insert. Here, it is an integral part of the knitted formwork, conforming to complex geometries of the cast form.

CONCLUSION

The present research consists of the design and manufacture of customized CNC-knitted formwork, working with limitations and parameters inherent to industrial knitting processes as well as concrete casting techniques, which required rheological calibration. This research is investigated through prototypes and analytical models. As an initial exploration, the prototypes produced in this paper focus on the material behavior of the dynamic relationship between the knitted formwork and fresh concrete. The discussion outlined results and challenges that emerged in relation to constructability and broader trajectories for refined investigation in relation to formwork design, construction, material behavior (of knit and fresh concrete), and architectural componentry systems with integrated structural and performative capacities. Future work will be both bracketed along specific trajectories (e.g., computational simulation) and will intersect and inform further explorations jointly to advance this research. The project holds tremendous potential for recalibrating how concrete is spatially, formally, and constructively conceived, developing emergent designs that were previously prohibitive due to cost in labor, material, and time in construction.

ACKNOWLEDGMENTS

This work is generously supported through the Prototyping Tomorrow Grant Initiative from Taubman College of Architecture and Urban Planning, University of Michigan, as well as a Small Project Grant from the University of Michigan Office of Research (UMOR).

Principal Investigators: Tsz Yan Ng, Sean Ahlquist, and Evgueni Filipov.
Technical knitting: Tracey Weisman.
Research Assistants: Mackenzie Bruce, Gabrielle Clune, and Jeffrey Richmond.

REFERENCES

Ahlquist, S. 2015. "Integrating Differentiated Knit Logics and Pre-Stress in Textile Hybrid Structures." In *Modelling Behaviour: Design Modeling Symposium 2015*, edited by M. Thomsen, M. Tamke, C. Gengnagel, B. Faircloth, and F. Scheurer, 101–111. Cham, Switzerland: Springer.

Ahlquist, S., W. McGee, and S. Sharmin. 2017. "Pneumaknit: Actuated Architectures Through Wale- and Course-Wise Tubular Knit-Constrained Pneumatic Systems." In *ACADIA 2017: Disciplines and Disruption [Proceedings of the 37th Annual Conference of the Association for Computer Aided Design in Architecture (ACADIA)]*, Cambridge, MA, 2–4 November 2017, edited by T. Nagakura, S. Tibbits, M. Ibañez, and C. Mueller, 39–51. CUMINCAD.

Barbosa., F., J. Mischke, and M. Parson. 2017. "Improving Construction Productivity." McKinsey & Company, July 18. https://www.mckinsey.com/business-functions/operations/our-insights/improving-construction-productivity.

García de Soto, B., I. Agustí-Juan, J. Hunhevicz, S. Joss, K. Graser, G. Habert, and B. T. Adey. 2018. "Productivity of Digital Fabrication in Construction: Cost and Time Analysis of a Robotically Built Wall." *Automation in Construction* 92: 297–311.

Hawkins, W. J., M. Herrmann, T. J. Ibell, B. Kromoser, A. Michaelski, J. Orr, R. Pedreschi, A. Pronk, R. Schipper, P. Shepherd, D. Veenendaal, R. Wansdronk, and M. West. 2016. "Flexible Formwork Technologies – A State of the Art Review." *Structural Concrete* 17 (6): 911–935.

Hurd, M. 2005. *Formwork for Concrete (SP4)*. 7th ed. Michigan: American Concrete Institute.

Popescu, Mariana. 2019. "KnitCrete: Stay-in-place Knitted Fabric Formwork for Complex Concrete Structures." PhD thesis, Department of Architecture, ETH, Zurich.

Popescu, Mariana, Matthias Rippmann, Tom Van Mele, and Philippe Block. 2020. "KnitCandela, Challenging the Construction, Logistics, Waste and Economy of Concrete-Shell Formworks." In *FABRICATE 2020*, edited by J. Burry, J. Sabin, B. Sheil, and M. Skavara, 194–201. London: UCL.

Popescu, Mariana, Matthias Rippmann, Andrew Liew, Lex Reiter, Robert J. Flatt, Tom Van Mele, and Philippe Block. 2021. "Structural Design, Digital Fabrication and Construction of the Cable-Net-and Knitted Formwork of the KnitCandela Concrete Shell." *Structures* 31: 1287–1299. http://www.doi.org/https://doi.org/10.1016/j.istruc.2020.02.013.

Veenendaal, Diederik, Mark West, and Philippe Block. 2011. "History and Overview of Fabric Formwork: Using Fabrics for Concrete Casting." *Structural Concrete* 12 (3): 164–177.

Wen, S.C., M. Aljomairi, and M. Patel. 2019. "Kneucrete, CNC Knits for Programmable Hybrid Formworks." In *ACADIA 19: Ubiquity and Autonomy [Project Catalog of the 39th Annual Conference of the Association for Computer Aided Design in Architecture (ACADIA)]*, Austin, TX, 21–26 October 2019, edited by K. Bieg, D. Briscoe, and C. Odom, 74–79. ACADIA.

West, Mark, 2016. *The Fabric Formwork Book: Methods for Building New Architectural and Structural Forms In Concrete*. London: Routledge.

IMAGE CREDITS

All drawings and images by the authors.

Tsz Yan Ng is Assistant Professor in Architecture at Taubman College of Architecture & Urban Planning, University of Michigan.

Sean Ahlquist is Associate Professor in Architecture at Taubman College of Architecture & Urban Planning, University of Michigan.

Evgueni Filipov is Assistant Professor in the Department of Civil and Environmental Engineering, University of Michigan.

Tracey Weisman is a technical knitting expert and research assistant at Taubman College, University of Michigan.

Computational Design of Fiber Composite Tower Structures

Marshall Prado
University of Tennessee

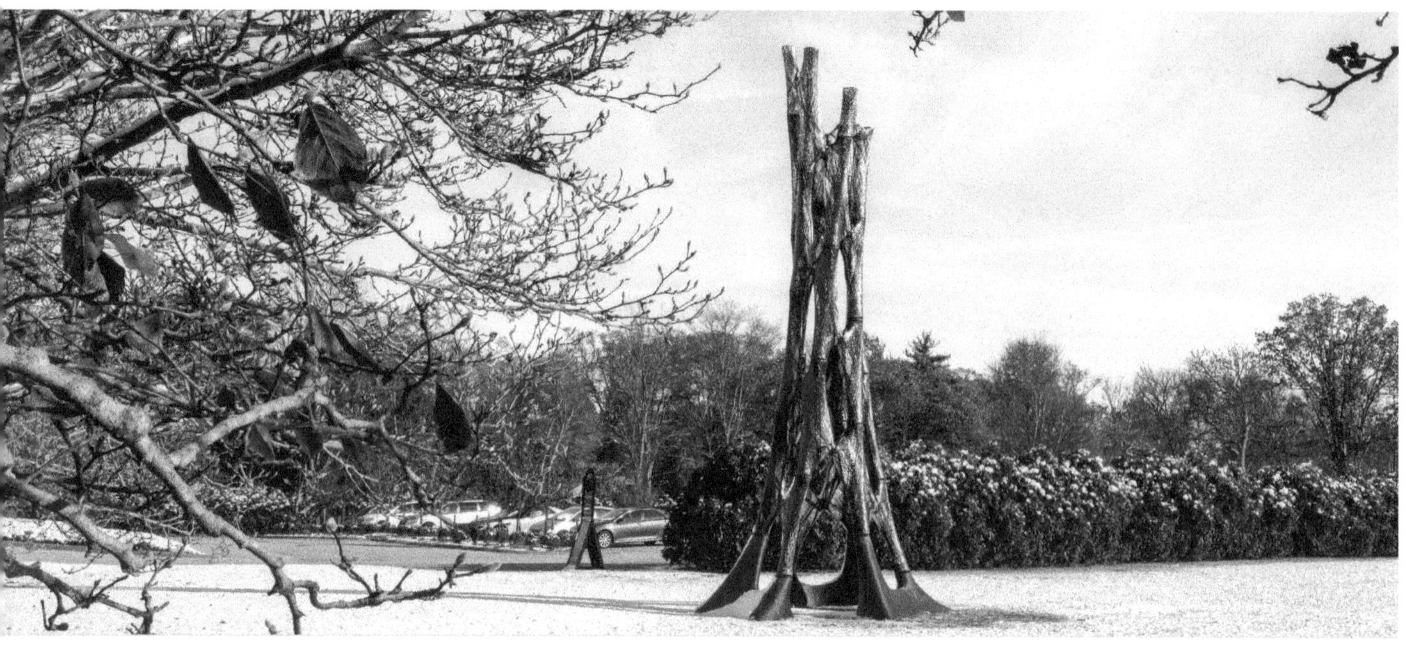

1 Full-scale demonstrator of composite tower.

ABSTRACT

This paper describes the computational design aspects of large-scale fiber composite tower structures that are fabricated using novel coreless filament winding processes. Current research on coreless filament winding has shown how high-performance composite materials can be used for many architectural scenarios; however, structural typologies for towers have never been tested. Additionally, biomimetic research on the lightweight lattice systems of cactus skeletons has demonstrated the potential for using interconnected multinodal component geometries to make efficient, tall structures. New integrated computational design and fabrication processes are required to utilize multi-nodal components in composite towers. These processes integrate biomimetic principles, structural performance, material organization, and fabrication logic. The goal of this research is to streamline the form-finding process, to more accurately simulate coreless wound geometries, and to develop adaptive fiber simulation processes for winding syntax development and robotic fiber winding. These techniques improved accuracy and control over existing methods of fabrication for coreless wound structures while simultaneously making the process more efficient. The research presented here will describe and showcase the key improvements used in the design and fabrication of a full-scale architectural demonstrator.

INTRODUCTION

Tall structures, such as skyscrapers, wind turbines, and electrical or communication towers, have demanding structural requirements. It is advantageous for structures like these to have low self-weight while maintaining high strength and stiffness (Schlaich and Schlaich 2000). Composite materials are uniquely suited for these challenging applications. By controlling material density and fiber orientations, the structural performance and material properties can easily be tuned. Composites are lightweight, easily formed through a variety of processes, corrosion-resistant, and may provide significant cost savings over traditional building materials (Kreysler 2017). Despite many advantages of fiber composite materials, they are rarely used structurally in building construction. Many factors that contribute to this, however, are beginning to change. The building industry is becoming more familiar with composite materials as they are more regularly used in construction and international building codes are adapting to the use of fiber-reinforced polymers (ICC 2018). Implementing composites into building systems still poses some challenges. Working with composites means designing at the material level. Structural performance is linked to the organization of the fibers in the composite, which is tied to fabrication strategies and formal design decisions. These systems cannot be disassociated. Integrated design and production strategies are needed to implement composites into building construction (Green 1987). Bottom-up design processes that synthesize biological principles, structural performance, material properties, and fabrication logics have proven to be useful in this regard (Parascho et al. 2015; Reichert et al. 2014).

Composite design and production have traditionally been utilized in performative engineering applications such as in the aerospace, automotive, and marine industries. Wind turbine blades and fuselages are already produced at an architectural scale. However, many of these composite structures are made with traditional processes that require full surface molds or winding mandrels. This can be a tremendous cost and material investment that is often offset by the logic of mass production and reusable tooling. Though the architecture industry has explored the idea of mass production and composite buildings before, for example, Mansato House (1957) or the Futuro House (1968), most buildings are custom designed and fabricated. This is a major barrier to the use of standard composite production processes for architectural applications. Novel computational design and fabrication processes for coreless filament winding have eliminated the need for large surface molds and have enabled more adaptive customizable production. Without a form-defining mold, the complex and highly orchestrated fiber-laying process is required to generate a structured composite surface (Knippers et al. 2016; Prado et al. 2014). This process builds on previous research and related projects at the Institute for Computational Design and Construction at the University of Stuttgart. This research explored the design and production of large roof structures, domes, and cantilevers with differentiated fiber morphologies (Doerstelmann and Prado 2017). In a recent project, the BUGA Fiber Pavilion, a composite lattice structure was developed (Zechmeister et al. 2019). Lattice

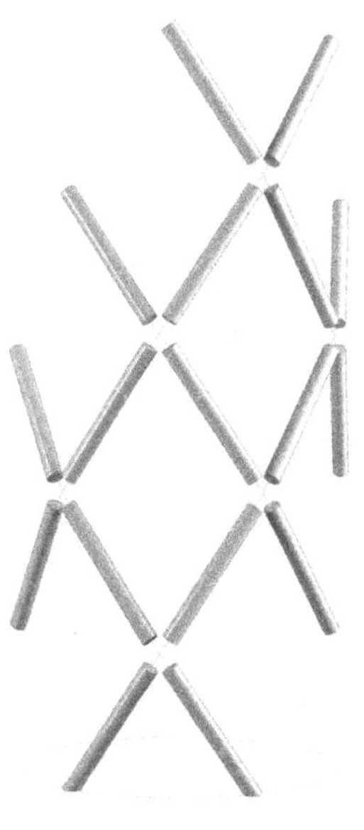

2

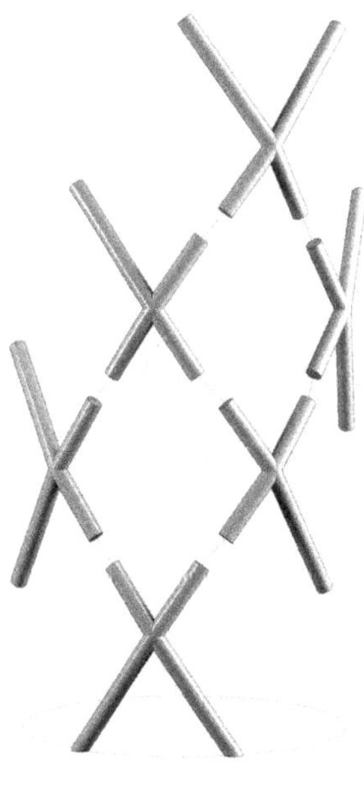

3

2 Strut lattice system: 17 linear components; 4 unique connections per joint; nonplanar connections; discontinuous intersections.

3 Multinodal system: 6 unique components; uniform connections; planar connections; continuous intersections.

structures offer new opportunities in composite construction. Using surface molds typically results in a continuous monocoque composite. By utilizing lattice structures, less material is needed. Coreless filament wound structures also require fewer winding points and less time to fabricate. Lattice structures are typically built from a series of struts connected at nodes (Fig. 2). When a lattice structure has a nonuniform shape, the nodes become more complex, adapting to various angles or strut connections. The intersections of the lattice become weak points where the strut material is discontinuous. An alternative, multi-nodal approach to lattice construction is proposed that is enabled by the affordances of composite materials (Fig. 3). Fiber wound components are not limited by linear stock or sheet materials like many traditional building systems. By creating multinodal components, many of the limitations of strut-based lattices can be overcome. Geometric complexity is embedded in the component geometry rather than complex joints. Connections can be planar and uniform, which simplifies aspects of fabrication and assembly. The same lattice structure also requires the fabrication of fewer components. This shift in concept introduces new challenges for the design of the form, development of the production process, structural simulation, and material performance. A refined computational design approach was needed to explore solutions. The proposed research describes the computational strategies for the design and production of a large-scale composite tower that implements alternative strategies for multinodal lattice structures. This includes advancements made towards more accurate form generation, simulation of fiber interaction, and robotic production.

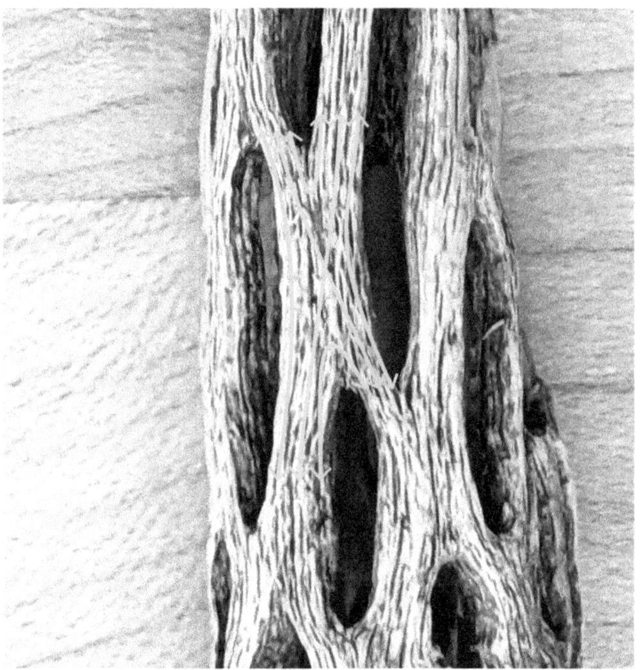

4

METHODS

Biomimetic Investigation

New design strategies are needed to implement coreless filament winding in architectural design. Structural logics and material organization principles found in natural biological specimens offer innovative potentials for architectural applications. Most biological structures are fibrous in nature, that is, made of fibers such as cellulose, chitin, or collagen. These natural fibrous materials are functionally similar to the technical fibers utilized in engineering-based applications such as carbon or glass. By analyzing, abstracting, and transferring biological principles found in natural

4 Biomimetic investigation: cholla cactus skeleton.

5 Diagram of geometric development of the tower structure.

5

specimens, integrated computational design solutions can be developed with higher material efficiency, increased structural performance, and novel architectural design principles. For this research, the skeleton of the cholla cactus, *Cylindropuntia*, was investigated (Fig. 4).This species has a wood-like branching structure that enables the skeleton to be both lightweight and rigid while growing upwards of 13 ft tall (Bobich and North 2009). The microstructure of the skeleton is formed by fiber bundles that are arranged in an interconnected biaxial lattice tube. Several abstracted biological principles were transferred into the design and fabrication of an architectural demonstrator. These include the hierarchical fiber arrangements, differentiated geometries, multidirectional branching structure, fiber continuity, and the tubular macro form.

Tower Development

A custom computational design process was developed to integrate biological design principles, material properties, structural performance, fabrication logics, and architectural design constraints into a large-scale composite lattice tower. Hierarchical form-finding strategies were implemented to shape the tower, represent structural components' geometries, and simulate fiber arrangements. Basic design constraints for size, number of components, structural topology, and site-specificity were used to generate a skeletal lattice of interconnected lines. These lines formed six major columns with secondary connections. This lattice was used as a framework for the geometric development of the tower (Fig. 5). A topological mesh surface was constructed on the lattice that was relaxed using a physics-based particle spring system (Piker 2016). The relaxed mesh was split into a checkerboard pattern and organized into solid faces and void areas of the structure. Quad faces were used to generate four-node components while triangular faces were used to generate three-node components. Connection planes were constructed at the shared vertices of adjoining components and were used to determine the orientation of each node. Major nodes, positioned along the columns, could be uniformly horizontal. Minor nodes, which create cross-column connections at various angles, required some consideration of the winding process to determine their orientation. The planes connecting components could not intersect either form without limiting the windability of the node. An average alignment vector was determined for each plane using the adjoining vertices. Rough quad mesh representations of each component were computationally modeled from the solid face vertices, centroids, edge midpoints, and connection planes (Fig. 6). The simplified component forms were initially subdivided and relaxed as well to create smooth mesh forms that minimally represented the hyperbolic geometries created from the coreless winding process. However, isotropic relaxation, which was previously utilized to simulate two-node composite geometries (Prado et al. 2014, 2017), did not accurately represent the multinodal components. Significant constraints on the fabrication process required iteratively refining the component simulation to more accurately predict the geometry of the finished components. This required considering both the directionality of the fibers and nonuniform tension in the winding process. Additional mesh faces were added to the rough mesh components to simulate fiber directionalities specific to the multinodal components (Fig. 6). Due to the curvature of the tower, the inserted mesh faces on the

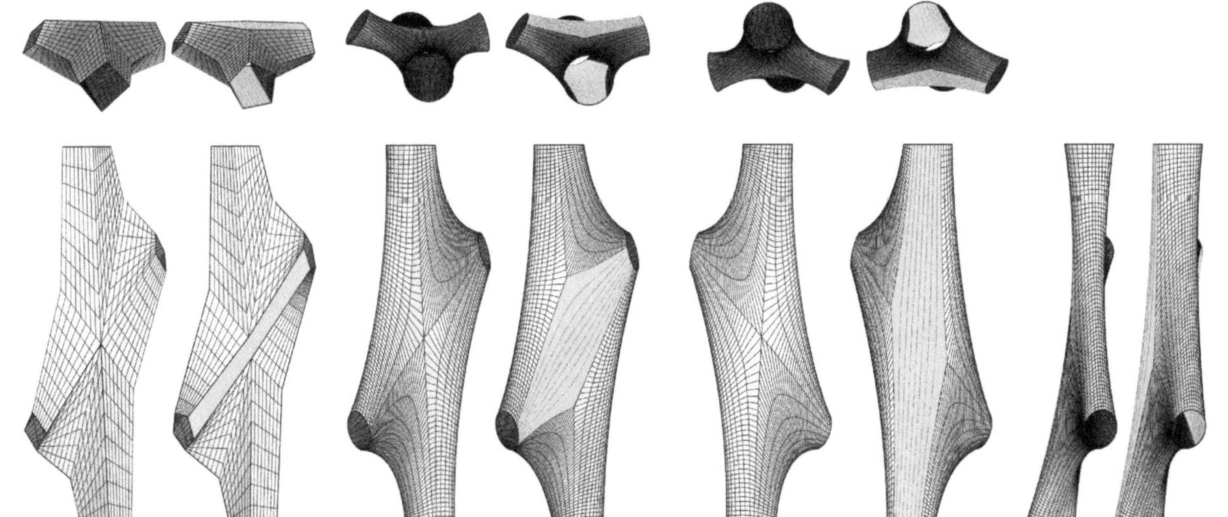

6 Isotropic relaxation simulation with generic mesh topology vs. anisotropic relaxation simulation with customized mesh orientations.

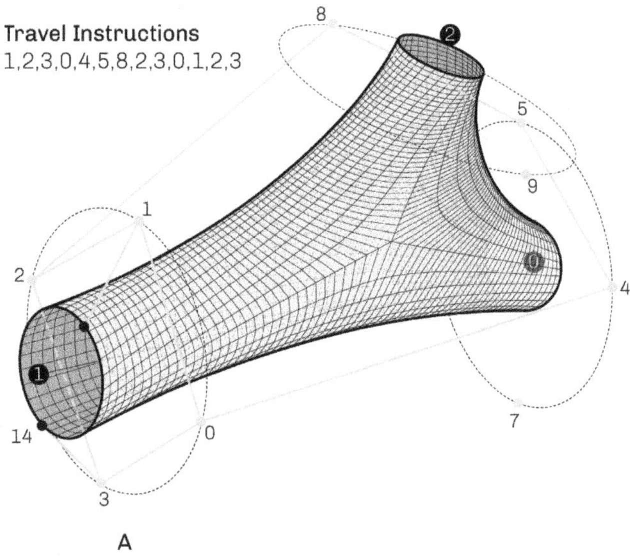

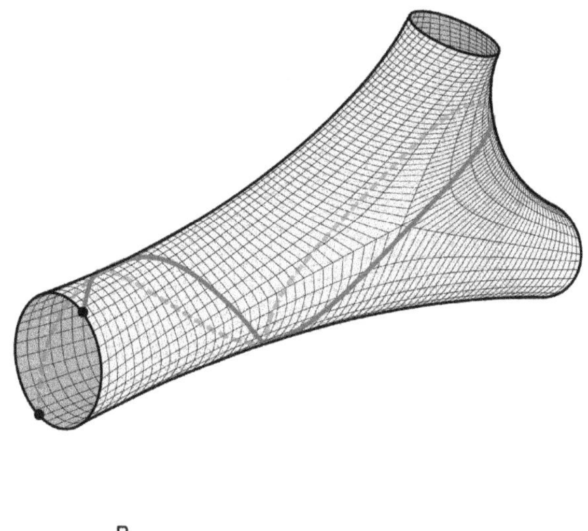

7 (a) Diagram of winding instructions; (b) diagram of the simulated path.

outside of the components aligned with the major column directions and mesh faces on the inside of the components aligned with the secondary connections. Anisotropic relaxation was applied to the revised mesh so that mesh edges that continuously connected two nodes of the component would be more tensioned. This decreased the curvature of the component along these directions and more accurately represented the composite material, variable tension states, and sequential fabrication process in the multinodal geometries (Fig. 6).

Syntax Development

Coreless filament winding requires precise control of fiber placement as well as the sequenced build-up of individual fibers into a structured composite surface. Topological variations in component geometries require customized syntax development (Kauffman and Mballa-Ekobena 2016). This often begins by manually test-winding string on generic frames to understand fiber orientation as well as geometric constraints. In previous research projects, the cellular components or linear struts could be wound with two frames. Fibers could be wound from winding point to winding point on opposite frames or across the composite surface to a winding point on the same frame. The winding syntax could be simplified to a list of sequential winding points and a positive or negative value for winding direction. This could be articulated algorithmically and adaptively once the process was understood. The development of multinodal components provided new scenarios for syntax development. Instead of two frames, a component had three or four nodes. This reduced the number of winding points but also increased the potential winding paths. A fiber can be wound across the composite surface between the nodes and in different directions. In Figure 7b, you can see how a fiber path can become quite complex while only connecting winding points on the same node. This increased complexity could not be articulated with a list of sequential winding points but required a more robust method of describing the fiber travel instructions. New processes of codification were developed to enable more complex winding syntaxes. Using a set of numbered reference points around each node, unambiguous travel instructions could be determined and represented as a simple polyline (Fig. 7a). By relaxing the polyline on the mesh surface, an accurate fiber simulation could also be generated. Though the same particle-spring systems could be used to simulate a single relaxed fiber, the complexity of hundreds or thousands of fiber paths in a component made this method computationally inefficient. A custom Laplacian/Gaussian smoothing algorithm was utilized instead (Ekdemir 2011; Lawoon et al. 2014). By subdividing the polyline and averaging adjacent vertices, a relaxed approximation of the fiber was generated without negotiating forces in a particle-spring system. The algorithm iteratively smoothed the curve until it intersected the mesh surface. The curve then continued to tighten, traveling along the mesh until it found a geodesic path. This method could quickly simulate all the fibers on a component. It also was accurate enough to simulated fiber behaviors, such as spanning or slippage, that previously would have only been apparent through physical testing. This provided a useful tool for simulating various winding syntaxes, testing design iterations, and generating robotic fabrication data (Prado 2020). Finite element analysis

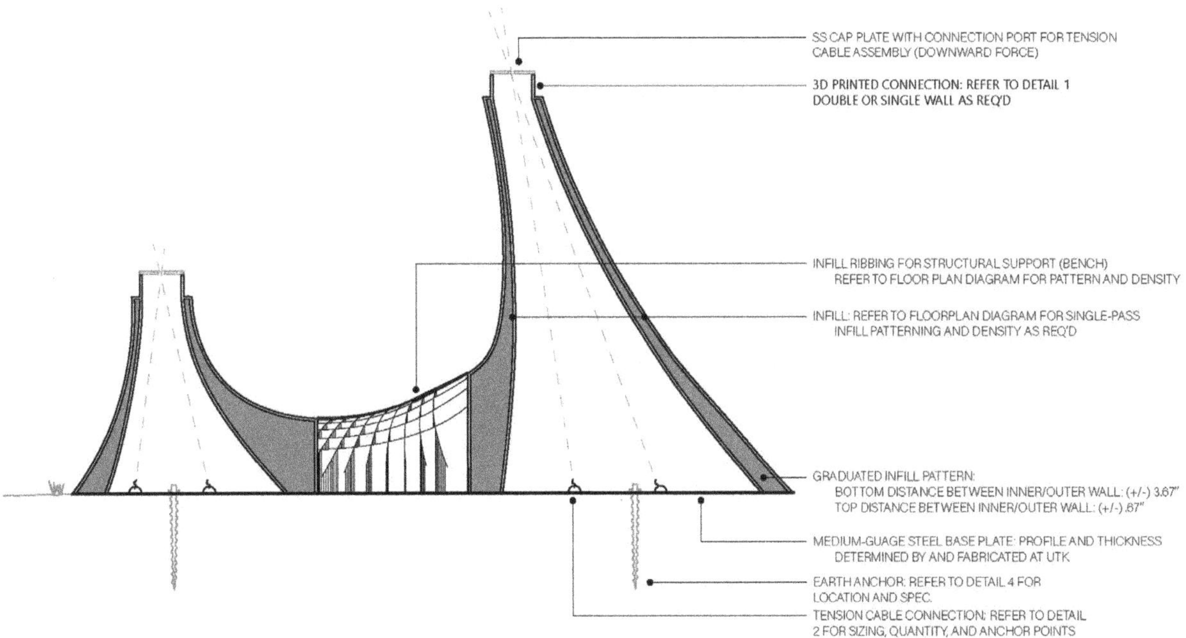

8 Section of 3D-printed base geometry.

was used to further understand the structural requirements across the tower and the specific material densities needed for each component. The fiber simulation method was used to generate a high-resolution beam model of the proposed winding syntax and iteratively test structural fiber densities. This fed back into design iterations and winding syntax development.

Base Development

Three base components were developed to anchor the tower to the ground, forming the ballast and foundation of the structure. Each base connected two main columns, provided visitor seating, and framed entrances to the interior of the tower. Unlike the lightweight fiber composite components, the bases needed to be heavy and did not rely on coreless filament winding. Alternative strategies were developed to design and fabricate the bases to take advantage of carbon-fiber-reinforced acrylonitrile butadiene styrene (CF-ABS) and large-scale additive manufacturing (Love et al., 2014). Similar methodologies for digital form-finding and simulation were used to create the base geometries in order to provide a continuous surface from the fiber composite components. However, since the forms were not constrained by the same fabrication logics, these methodologies were adapted to other constraints. Like the fiber composite components, a simplified quad mesh representation of each base was developed. Anisotropic variation in the mesh relaxation was used to sculpt the geometry and constrain the bench rather than simulate fiber tension. Additional postprocessing and analysis were needed to adapt the form for manufacturing. Slope analysis was used to determine what areas of the mesh exceeded overhang limitations and needed structural reinforcing during fabrication. Variable wall thickness was added to adapt to structural requirements and connections to the composite components (Fig. 8). The base components were fabricated in collaboration with Oak Ridge National Laboratory (ORNL) in the Manufacturing Demonstration Facility. A big area additive manufacturing (BAAM) printer was used (Biswas 2016). Further machine-specific requirements were implemented into the design of the bases by ORNL researchers through the use of custom fabrication software and slicers (Roschli et al. 2019).

RESULTS AND DISCUSSION

The computational processes developed for this research enabled the production of a 30 ft tall composite tower to be manufactured, including 27 geometrically unique multinodal structural components with adaptive fiber layouts (Fig. 9). Each component weighed between 5 and 30 lbs and was up to 7 ft in length. The lattice structure covered an area of 85 ft^2, weighed roughly 340 lbs, and consisted of over 50 miles of glass and carbon fiber. The form-finding strategies were iteratively refined and improved to have more accurate geometric representations of the self-forming material system. Integrating specificity in the mesh topology and anisotropic tension were key aspects of this improvement. The design simulation provided a quick iterative tool that did not rely on computationally heavy material modeling. The sequential simulation of the fiber interaction throughout the winding process greatly improved the control of the fiber placement and path planning for robotic production. Despite having a more refined simulation tool, many complex fiber reactions are not integrated into the process. Each fiber is currently simulated independently of the others. More complex interactions that happen throughout component production are not currently feasible. This is perhaps a limitation of the system, as failures in composite surface quality due to tightening or loosening of previously laid fibers are not predictable. Codification of the winding syntax enabled more complex fiber-laying procedures and multi-nodal component configurations that were not previously possible. Though the translation from syntax to winding code was streamlined, and the fiber simulation tool aided in the generation of the adaptive winding codes, the generation of the travel instructions that enabled these was still an analog process. In future iterations, this tedious and error-prone step can be augmented with a more robust computational fiber simulation tool.

CONCLUSION

The developed processes show continued improvement towards the use of structural composites in architectural building scenarios. Further exploration is needed for testing multistory or load-bearing structures. The integration of more building systems, including enclosure, insulation, and floor slabs, is also needed to show the potential of composites in various architectural uses. The computational tools needed for design, simulation, planning, and production should continue to develop with each new application. With the increase in the geometric complexity of the multinodal components, further development of syntax generation is required for topological variants. Automated strategies are not currently adaptable to components with more than four connections or for nonlinear topologies. Algorithmic development of this process can build from the computational tools shown here to have a broader impact on the production process and streamline the design generation of new architectural models.

ACKNOWLEDGMENTS

The author would like to acknowledge the help and support from the many research assistants and students that contributed to the design and production of the research demonstrator. Development, fabrication and construction: Shane Principe, Sarah Wheeler, Courtney St. John, Alex Stiles, Nadin Jabri, Geng Liu, Pete Paueksakon, Tyler Sanford, Michaela Stanfill, Michael Mckever, Michael Swartz, Hollywood Conrad, Teig Dryden, Howard Fugitt, Kristia Bravo, Bridget Ash, Kevin Saslawsky, Michael Vineyard, Zane Smith, Josh Mangers, Patrick Dobronski, Joe Gauspohl, and with the support of Craig Gillam and the UTK Fablab. The author would also like to acknowledge the research collaborators that enabled the conceptual development, engineering and production of the research demonstrator. In collaboration with Oak Ridge National Laboratory—Manufacturing Demonstration Facility Format Engineers Ltd., Fiber and Composite Manufacturing Facility, Entomology and Plant Pathology.

REFERENCES

Biswas, Kaushik, Randall Lind, Brian Post, Roderick Jackson, Lonnie Love, Johney Green Jr, and A. M. Guerguis. 2016. "Big Area Additive Manufacturing Applied to Buildings." In *Thermal Performance of the Exterior Envelopes of Whole Buildings XIII International Conference*, Clearwater, FL, 4–8 December 2006, 583-590. Curran Associates.

Bobich, Edward G., and Gretchen B. North. 2009. "Structural Implications of Succulence: Architecture, Anatomy, and Mechanics of Photosynthetic Stem Succulents, Pachycauls, and Leaf Succulents." In *Perspectives in Biophysical Plant Ecophysiology, A Tribute to Park S. Nobel*, edited by Erick de la Barrera and William K. Smith, 3–37. Mexico City: Universidad Nacional Autónoma de México.

Doerstelmann, Moritz, and Marhsall Prado. 2018. "Explorative Design and Fabrication Strategies for Fibrous Morphologies in Architecture." In *Digital Fabrication*, edited by Philip Yuan, Achim

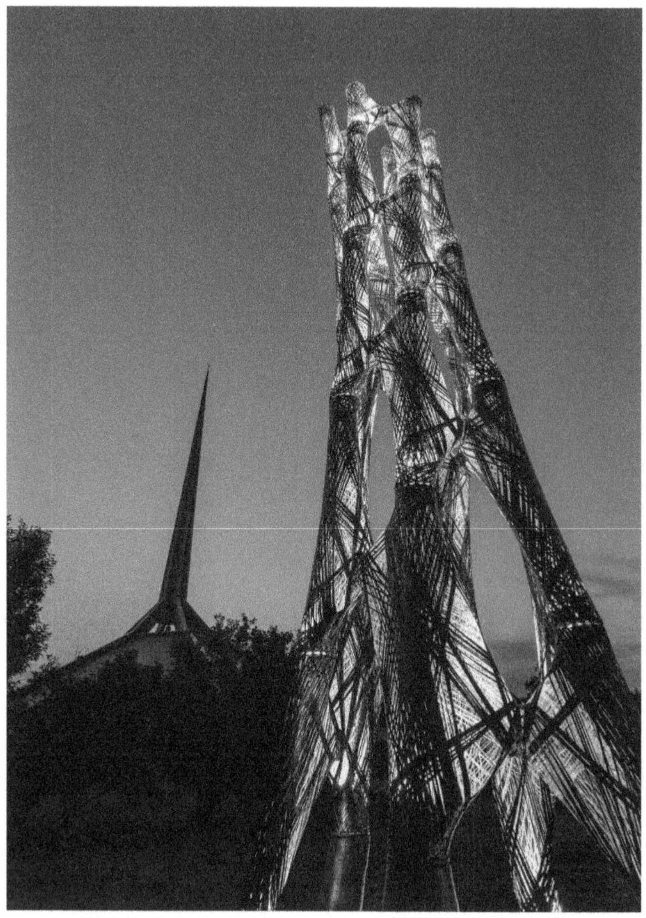

9

9 Photo of the UTK Filament Tower at night.

Menges, and Neal Leach, 170–181. Shanghai: Tongji University Press.

Ekdemir, Şadan. 2011. "Efficient Implementation of Polyline Simplification for Large Datasets and Usability Evaluation." PhD Diss., Uppsala University.

Green, Andrew. 1987. "Glass-Fiber-Reinforced Composites in Building Construction." *Transportation Research Record* 1118: 73–76.

International Code Council (ICC). 2018. *International Building Code 2018*.

Kauffman, André, and Alexandre Mballa-Ekobena. 2016. "A Fabrication Process for a 3d Modular Fiber Composite Architecture System." ITECH MSc Master's thesis, University of Stuttgart.

Knippers, Jan, Valentin Koslowski, James Solly, and Thiemo Fildhuth. 2016. "Modular Coreless Filament Winding for Lightweight Systems in Architecture." In *Proceedings of the 8th International Conference on FRP Composites in Civil Engineering, CICE*, Hong Kong, 14–16 December 2016, edited by J.G. Teng and J.G. Dai, 1424–1429. IIFC.

Kreysler, William. 2017. "Qualifying Frp Composites for High-Rise Building Facades." In *Fabricate: Rethinking Design and Construction*, edited by Achim Menges, Bob Sheil, Ruairi Glynn, and Marilena Skavara, 130–137. London: UCL Press.

Lawonn, Kai, Rocco Gasteiger, Christian Rössl, and Bernhard Preim. 2014. "Adaptive and Robust Curve Smoothing on Surface Meshes." *Computers & Graphics* 40: 22–35.

Love, Lonnie J., Vlastamil Kunc, Orlando Rios, Chad E. Duty, Amelia M. Elliott, Brian K. Post, Rachel J. Smith, and Craig A. Blue. 2014. "The Importance of Carbon Fiber to Polymer Additive Manufacturing." *Journal of Materials Research* 29 (17): 1893.

Parascho, Stefana, Jan Knippers, Moritz Dörstelmann, Marshall Prado, and Achim Menges. 2015. "Modular Fibrous Morphologies: Computational Design, Simulation, and Fabrication of Differentiated Fibre Composite Building Components." In *Advances in Architectural Geometry 2014*, 29–45. Cham: Springer.

Piker, Daniel. 2016. "Kangaroo Physics." http://www.food4rhino.com/app/kangaroo-physics.

Prado, Marshall. 2020. "Skeletal Composites: Robotic Fabrication Processes for Lightweight Multi-Nodal Structural Components." *Construction Robotics* 4, no. 3 (November): 217-226.

Prado, Marshall, Moritz Dörstelmann, Tobias Schwinn, Achim Menges, and Jan Knippers. 2014. "Core-Less Filament Winding." In *Robotic Fabrication in Architecture, Art and Design 2014*, 275–289. Cham: Springer.

Prado, Marshall, Moritz Doerstelmann, James Solly, Achim Menges, and Jan Knippers. 2017. "Elytra Filament Pavilion: Robotic Filament Winding for Structural Composite Building Systems." In *Fabricate: Rethinking Design and Construction*, edited by Achim Menges, Bob Sheil, Ruairi Glynn, and Marilena Skavara, 224–231. London: UCL Press.

Reichert, Steffen, Tobias Schwinn, Riccardo La Magna, Frédéric Waimer, Jan Knippers, and Achim Menges. 2014. "Fibrous Structures: An Integrative Approach to Design Computation, Simulation and Fabrication for Lightweight, Glass and Carbon Fibre Composite Structures in Architecture Based on Biomimetic Design Principles." *Computer-Aided Design* 52: 27–39.

Roschli, Alex, Katherine T. Gaul, Alex M. Boulger, Brian K. Post, Phillip C. Chesser, Lonnie J. Love, Fletcher Blue, and Michael Borish. 2019. "Designing for Big Area Additive Manufacturing." *Additive Manufacturing* 25: 275–285.

Schlaich, Jörg, and Mike Schlaich. 2000. "Lightweight Structures." In *Widespan Roof Structures*, edited by Michael Barnes and Michael Dickson, 177–188. London: Thomas Telford.

Zechmeister, Christoph, Serban Bodea, Niccolo Dambrosio, and Achim Menges. 2019. "Design for Long-Span Core-Less Wound, Structural Composite Building Elements." In *Impact: Design With All Senses [Proceedings of the Design Modelling Symposium]*, Berlin, Germany, 23–25 September 2019, edited by Christoph Gengnagel, Olivier Baverel, Jane Burry, Mette Ramsgaard Thomsen, and Stefan Weinzierl, 401–415. Springer.

IMAGE CREDITS

Figures 1, 9: © Hadley Fruits, 2019.

All other drawings and images by the author.

Marshall Prado is an Assistant Professor of Design and Structural Technology at the University of Tennessee. He holds a Bachelor of Architecture from North Carolina State University, a Master of Architecture and a Master of Design Studies in Technology from the Harvard University Graduate School of Design. Marshall has previously taught at the Institute for Computational Design and Construction in Stuttgart and the University of Hawaii. He has led several workshops on digital design and fabrication techniques. His current research interests include integrated computational design and robotic fabrication of lightweight fiber composite systems for architectural applications and spatial design strategies.

Towards Modular Natural Fiber-Reinforced Polymer Architecture

An Integrative Approach to Moldless Fabrication with Tailored Fiber Placement (TFP) and Coreless Filament Winding (CFW) Techniques

Sacha Cutajar*
ITECH/University of Stuttgart
Vanessa Costalonga Martins*
ITECH/University of Stuttgart
Christo van der Hoven*
ITECH/University of Stuttgart
Piotr Baszyński
BioMat/University of Stuttgart
Hanaa Dahy
BioMat/University of Stuttgart
FEDA/Ain Shams University Cairo
*Authors contributed equally to the research.

1 Interior of a modular natural fiber-reinforced polymer spatial structure.

ABSTRACT

Driven by the ecological crisis looming over the 21st century, the construction sector must urgently seek alternative design solutions to current building practices. In the wake of emergent digital technologies and novel material strategies, this research proposes a lightweight architectural solution using natural fiber-reinforced polymers (NFRP), which elicit interest for their inherent renewability as compared to high-performance yarns. Two associated fabrication techniques are deployed: tailored fiber placement (TFP) and coreless filament winding (CFW), both favored for their additive efficiencies granted by strategic material placement. A hypothesis is formed, postulating that their combination can leverage the standalone complexities of molds and frames by integrating them as active structural elements. Consequently, the TFP enables the creation of a 2D stiffness-controlled preform to be bent into a permanent scaffold for winding rigid 3D fiber bodies via CFW. A proof of concept is generated via the small-scale prototyping and testing of a stool, with results yielding a design of 1 kg capable of carrying 100 times its weight. Laying the groundwork for a scaled-up architectural proposal, the prototype instigates alterations to the process, most notably the favoring of a modular global design and lapped preform technique. The research concludes with a discussion on the resulting techno-implications for automation, deployment, material life cycle, and aesthetics, rekindling optimism towards future sustainable practices.

INTRODUCTION

The adverse environmental impact of the built environment has been well documented. This footprint may lie in the quantity of material used and its embodied energy, the waste created during construction, or in the production infrastructure itself (Abergel, Dean, and Dulac 2017). This is not a new problem in architecture, but one that can benefit from different design attitudes, which could translate into more harmonious built solutions.

Fiber-reinforced polymers (FRPs) represent an alternative material approach for construction. Composites, and the growing variety of technologies that enable their additive production, make them attractive to applications that necessitate strategic material placement to create differentiated structure and geometry (Menges and Knippers 2015). These design benefits additionally predispose them to produce far less waste than conventional construction practices (Prado et al. 2014). By placing material only where it is needed, this can result in high specific strength. A high strength-to-weight ratio allows for reduced material use and, in turn, reductions in material quantities (cement, metals, etc.) for the subsidiary structures that often support them (Dahy, Petrš, and Baszyński 2020).

Two novel fabrication methods for FRPs emerging for the architectural scale are coreless filament winding (CFW) and tailored fiber placement (TFP). These techniques employ digital design-to-production workflows for precision, efficiency, and mass-customization. Both CFW and TFP, however, usually require complicated and resource-intensive fabrication frames or molds during production. Coming from research, there are a variety of approaches for moving CFW and TFP towards moldless composite fabrication. Of particular interest are the ICD/ITKE Research Pavilion 2016–17 (Felbrich et al. 2017), the project "Tailoring Self Formations" (Aldinger et al. 2018), and the *Biomat Flat to Spatial Mock-up* (BioMat at ITKE 2020).

In the first precedent, the complexity of production is reduced with an embedded bending active winding frame. This project utilizes a 2D filament-wound preform that is arched into shape, becoming the production scaffold that receives and holds the main layers of structural filaments during the robotic winding process. This means a substantial portion of the fabrication setup remains embedded within the structure, taking on an additional function (Felbrich et al. 2017). 2D filament winding, nonetheless, is prone to delamination due to poor fiber-to-fiber interaction. Moreover, this bending active mesh requires its very own winding frame, effectively serializing, rather than eliminating, producing infrastructure. These

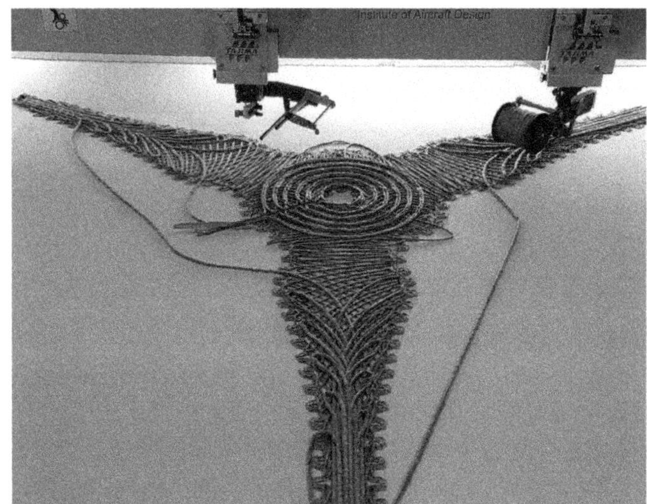

2

3

4

2 Stitch: Tailored placement of annually renewable natural fiber yarns.

3 Bend: Active bending of a natural fiber-reinforced polymer preform.

4 Weave: Coreless filament winding of resin-impregnated natural fibers.

limitations invite a different approach to the materialization of the integrated preform.

"Tailoring Self-Formations" explores carbon-fiber-reinforced polymer (CFRP) bending elements sewn onto a prestressed membrane substrate. Tension in the textile actuates and drives the CFRP elements into bending, determined by specific predefined geometric patterns. This project illustrates bent forms in states of compound Gaussian curvature with mold-less tailored fiber placement fabrication, enabled by regions of variably tailored stiffness and elasticity (Aldinger et al. 2018). The deployment of the membranes from 2D to 3D, however, requires careful calibration between tension in the membrane and stiffness of the CFRP pattern. Consequently, an inherently unstable system is produced regardless of any required structural capacity or expected dynamic loads. This prompts the introduction of a supplementary structural system to lock the geometry in a stable configuration, after bending.

Finally, the *Biomat Flat to Spatial Mock-up* demonstrates a vision for modular sustainable composite architecture, where annually renewable biomaterials are used for topologically optimized tailored fiber placement fabrication. This allows for simple and intuitive assembly of lightweight modules, as well as their later disassembly, transport to a new location, and reassembly (BioMat at ITKE 2020). Initially designed for the sewn textile to be suspended in an adaptable scaffold for matrix impregnation and curing, the pursuit of a simple reconfigurable fabrication remains a relevant realm of inquiry.

As such, this research aimed to develop an approach for a complex NFRP spatial structure combining coreless filament winding and tailored fiber placement techniques, without the use of a complicated static frame or mold. Through an integrative approach, this project sought to co-design a new materialization process by interconnecting the development of design objectives, engineering systems, and fabrication processes (Knippers et al. 2018).

METHODS

Conceptual Framework

This project synergizes with the growing body of research on sustainable bio-based alternatives to synthetic composites by exploring flax fiber as a building material for full-scale architectural applications (Pickering, Efendy, and Le 2016). The investigation was undertaken through a bespoke computational toolkit, comprising three conceptual stages: Stitch (Step 1), Bend (Step 2), and Weave (Step 3). In Stitch, a tailored natural fiber textile is designed and produced in its flat form. This textile is infused with resin to create a fiber composite preform (Fig. 2). With Bend, the preform is activated into shape, which is enabled by specific fiber bending patterns created in the TFP design (Fig. 3). Finally, in Weave, the preform becomes a permanent winding frame upon which natural fibers are placed through coreless filament winding (Fig. 4). Once cured, the tailored fiber placement and coreless filament winding elements become a codependent functional and structural system.

The digital design process adopted by the research draws on an analysis of the above techniques, both of which are deeply rooted in computational methods of production. Layups for tailored fiber placement and coreless filament winding processes are both numerically controlled, relying on the input of polyline-based data generated in CAD software such as Rhinoceros3D and Grasshopper3D (Robert McNeel & Associates 2020; Rutten 2020).

Tailored Fiber Placement: Stitch & Bend

The Stitch and Bend phases are characterized primarily by the design and fabrication of the TFP preform. The TFP process allows a vast arrangement of 2D fiber layups using an industrial machine that continuously lays the flax fiber and stitches it to a textile substrate over a flat movable frame via fixed needle and bobbin (Aschenbrenner, Temmen, and Degenhardt 2007). Primary fabrication parameters of the setup include the "stitch length" and "stitch width" for threaded yarns of variable cross-sections, which impact pattern resolution.

In terms of the pattern design, since this technique can provide an infinite set of customizable arrangements, a subhypothesis was formulated as to whether the tailored orientation of fibers in a cured state could allow for a controlled ability to bend a surface and achieve specific geometries. Therefore, the goal for the TFP pattern design was to create regions of differentiated strength and stiffness within the preform. To achieve this, an interpretation of classical lamination theory was used to inform the fiber pattern. This theory equates the inherent mechanical stiffness of 2D composite laminates to be a product of the general orientation of the constituent fiber reinforcement (Herakovich 2012).

When paired with a topological optimization tool, this theory helps orient the fibers on the pattern to respond to specific structural or functional needs. For instance, fiber paths oriented at -45°, 0°, and 45° to the edge aim to create a quasi-isotropic layup sequence, resulting in constant stiffness of the material regardless of the force direction. Laying the fibers at an angle close to parallel to the edge creates directional behavior. To generate a flexible hinge zone, fiber paths are oriented at -15° and 15°. The application of these interpretations is directly related to structural requirements and material usage and can vary depending on the boundary geometry and desired preform behavior.

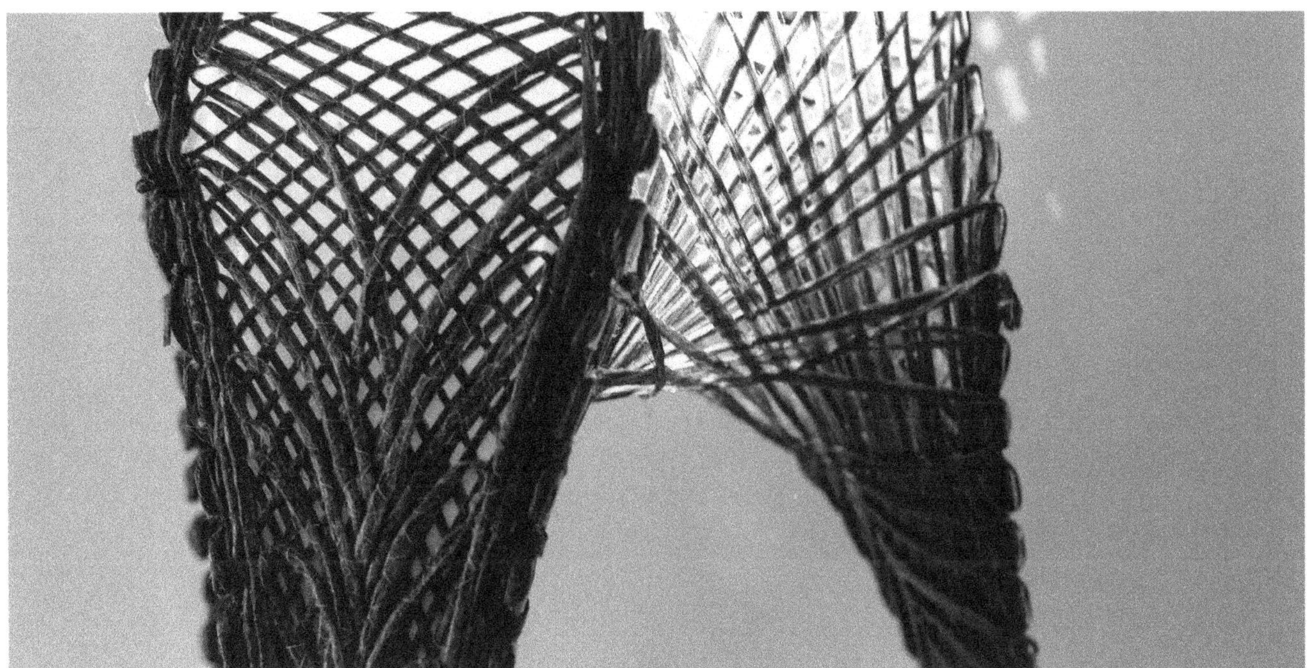

5 System prototype: stool as demonstrator.

Once a determined pattern has been stitched on the tailored fiber placement machine, the preform needs to be resin impregnated, since the mechanical properties of fiber composites are heavily influenced by their matrix (Rana and Fangueiro 2016). Vacuum infusion is a process that produces uniform fiber impregnation. The preform is placed into an airtight bag, and a precalculated amount of resin is poured onto it. A vacuum pump applies negative pressure, causing the resin to disperse throughout the preform. Once full infusion is achieved, the preform is removed from the bag and left to cure, after which it is activated with simple clamps that vary according to the scale of the final element and available robotic setup. The activated preform constitutes the frame for the Weave phase.

Coreless Filament Winding: Weave

CFW entails the continuous winding of resin-impregnated fiber layups in 3D space using an appropriate scaffold, typically via robotic automation (Prado et al. 2014). The numeric or indexed sequence in which a continuous fiber is wound, resulting in a desired geometric arrangement, is termed syntax (Zechmeister et al. 2019). Since this method allows for localized material placement, the syntaxes can be tailored to specific structural and fabrication requirements.

During this process, the fibers are continuously passed through a custom-built resin bath to absorb sufficient resin throughout the winding process. Upon completion, the element is left to cure completely and can only then be released from the fabrication clamps.

STOOL AS A DEMONSTRATOR

To test this production method, the design and prototyping of a stool were used as an analog for the functional and structural requirements of an architectural system (Figs. 5 and 6). As a means to analyze the outcome of this phase, functional and performative criteria were established. The stool had to sustain a minimum of 80 kg while having a high strength-to-weight ratio. The three steps (Stitch, Bend, and Weave) were then applied accordingly.

The global shape of the stool was designed based on the hallmark three-legged configuration, chosen for its efficiency and elegance. To achieve the desired shape, three important pattern regions were identified: the seat, the legs, and a hinge area between the two. Each region had different functional and performative requirements.

For the seat, the fibers were oriented at -45°, 0°, and 45° degrees. This layup resulted in uniform stiffness with minimal elasticity for seating comfort. In the legs, the fiber path was almost parallel to the leg axis (-75°,75°), thus creating stiff regions where the stool meets the ground and providing directionality to the force transfer. The hinge zones were the most critical areas, as the pattern had to provide enough flexibility for the stool to activate from 2D to 3D while not failing in the process. The balance between flexibility and strength was achieved with a more perpendicular pattern orientation, reaching -15° and 15° in the center of the hinge areas. Finally, the edges were laced with a series of winding pins designed to receive the wound fiber rovings. Their 'T' profile ensures no slippage of fibers in the Weave stage (Fig. 7).

6

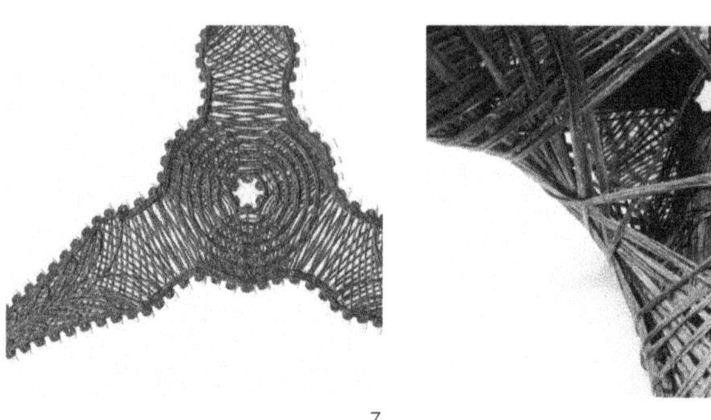

7

8

6 Demonstrator stool.

7 Prototype tailored fiber placement preform.

8 Prototype coreless filament winding layup.

Once stitched, the textile was resin-infused and cured flat. The tailored fiber placement preform predictably activated into regions of single curvature using a simple tripod clamp. This bending active surface served as an embedded winding frame for the coreless filament winding process. A syntax consisting of three layers was subsequently wound, providing geometric depth to the structure in an evocative anticlastic shape; a geometry that is difficult and costly to create using traditional fabrication methods. Each layer served a unique purpose: the Spine transfers forces from the center of the seat to each leg, locking the bending zones; the Bracing sequence ensures fiber interaction; and the Locking layer prevents the stool from opening up by linking the legs together (Fig. 8).

The structural performance assessment of the stool was conducted via a series of seating tests, with participants of different weights.[1] The completed prototype weighed 1.08 kg. Despite its low mass, the stool successfully supported loads from 55 kg to 85 kg. Only a slight elastic deflection (3.5 mm on each leg) was observed for the highest load. Both the global shape of the stool and the span between legs was sufficient to provide stability during the test. As designed, the seating area presented satisfactory elasticity for comfort while the legs remained stiff.

These results hint at the potential of the system at the larger architectural scale. Such low deflection in the test indicated that the stool could potentially withstand higher loads before failing. However, to date, a destructive test was not performed to validate this hypothesis. Nonetheless, the stool can be seen as a successful initial demonstrator for the proposed fabrication process.

UPSCALING FRAMEWORK

Two ways of propagating larger spaces were considered:

- Continuously, by using a large scale TFP scaffold that gets wound. *Tailored Biocomposite Mock-up of BioMat 2019* (Dahy, Petrš, and Baszyński 2020), a monolithic single-curved canopy of approximately 225 cm high and 125 cm wide, is an example of large-scale TFP implementation. This workflow would be extended with continuous on-site winding, allowing for larger building elements with fewer connectors in between.
- Discretely, where we can use smaller components to form complex surfaces. This is exemplified in the *Biomat Flat to Spatial Mock-up* (BioMat at ITKE 2020). A controlled prefabrication environment could help with material fabrication constraints while the light weight of the modules makes them easier to assemble, transport, and handle.

Challenges to scaling up include requirements for building enclosure, material interfaces, and complex structural behaviors. However, the most limiting of these challenges relates to physical constraints in the fabrication setup. Both tailored fiber placement and coreless filament winding processes have physical constraints, especially when considering typical setups. The type and size of the TFP machine determine the size and thickness of the resulting preform. This could be circumvented by laminating or stitching preforms together for larger geometries (Rihaczek et al. 2020). Similarly, robotic filament winding is subject to geometric and kinematic constraints determined by the robotic cell. While large-scale continuous winding could be achieved with the use of mobile robots (Yablonina and Menges 2019), the activation of a large-scale preform on-site would require the use of a large frame, which diverges from the research's aim.

These restrictions suggest that this method is better suited to lightweight small-scale components that can be easily prefabricated and then assembled into full-size building structures. Such an application strategy would also allow for integrating design-for-disassembly scenarios, already at the design phase, in which modular structures, at their end of life, are reconfigured or disassembled and reused in different locations and/or constellations, guaranteeing a closed-material cycle of the building structure (Dahy, Petrš, and Baszyński 2020).

A MODULAR NFRP PROTO-ARCHITECTURE

To further explore the implications of upscaling the production technique, a simple architectural-scale spatial structure is developed. This investigation articulates the discrete upscaling approach, speculating on a possible expression this approach may take. In doing so, insight is provided into the spatial quality that this system can achieve, the specific technical requirements to produce such a structure, and how the conceptual framework is expanded to meet the challenges of an architectural application.

Stitch: For conceptual translation, the triangular base geometry of the prototype is maintained, albeit significantly modified in size and morphology to produce a typical component. As before, the boundary and interior of the preform are articulated with winding and connection points. To produce a continuous surface when aggregated, the triangular components present an elongated bending zone (Fig. 9). Adequate structural depth and good CFW fiber-to-fiber interaction further inform the petal-like expression of each of the edges.

As the scale of a preform would exceed the 1.4 m x 1 m limits of typical TFP production, a further discretization strategy is developed. Each piece is subdivided into parts that can be efficiently sewn. These subgeometries are then lapped and stitched together via an additional textile layer to produce the desired shape. Capitalizing on this layering process, the outer layer is intentionally oversized, creating a weatherproofing skin. Finally, the generatively designed TFP pattern is applied to the surface, producing the required variable fiber sewing patterns to create the stiffened faces and bending regions.

Bend: Once tailored, the patterned textile is resin-infused and cured. The activated composite preform can then be actively bent into shape in preparation for the robotic filament winding process; the supplementary load-bearing sequence complements the TFP structure and locks the component into its required form. For this, the tailored fiber placement surface is temporarily mechanically fixed into the coreless filament winding cell. These embedded connection positions are later reutilized to join individual components together in a global geometry. The combination of the internal structure of the preform and support of the winding cell sufficiently stabilizes the surface edges and embedded winding points for the unique stresses induced by the various hooking and winding robot kinematics.

To create the geometrically diverse components, a hypothetical production cell would consist of a six-axis robot, a fiber impregnation station, and adjustable clamps—internal and external—on a reconfigurable base that delineates the fabrication limits. Important is the scaled-up clamp; like its smaller counterpart, this simple stabilizing apparatus can be reconfigured within several degrees of movement and rotation, thereby enabling component mass customization.

Weave: The component syntax builds upon the three-layer approach developed for the prototype. Navigating between the embedded winding points, encoded along the edge of the bent preform, each syntax takes on a distinct function. These roles are as follows:

- The first layer, the Body, connects the petal-like edges to one another and stabilizes the hinge. This layup creates the initial hollow surface-like fiber lattice which provides geometric structural depth (Fig. 10).
- The second layer, the Spine, transfers forces from the center of the component to each leg, and braces the first layer by reducing the buckling length of filament bundles through fiber-to-fiber interaction (Fig. 11).
- The Bracing reinforces each edge individually, locking the coreless fiber lattices in shape and bearing stresses perpendicular to the first two syntaxes (Fig. 12).

In addition to these local performances, the filaments satisfy broader structural and aesthetic requirements. Global structural behaviors can then be tuned by using the anisotropic nature of the fiber bundles to direct force flows. The visual impact of these bundles and the graphic quality they produce can then be delineated through the selection and variation of individual bundle cross-section. In this manner, individual components are customized to meet local and global requirements. Within the tailored fiber placement and coreless filament winding fabrication limits, then, an almost unlimited range of geometric, structural, and aesthetic variations is possible (Fig. 13).

DISCUSSION AND CONCLUSION

Explored Aims and Results

This research is driven by the hypothesis that the symbiosis of tailored fiber placement and coreless filament winding

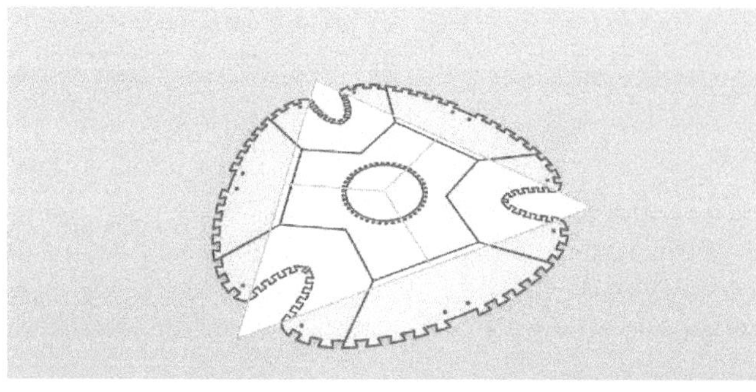

9

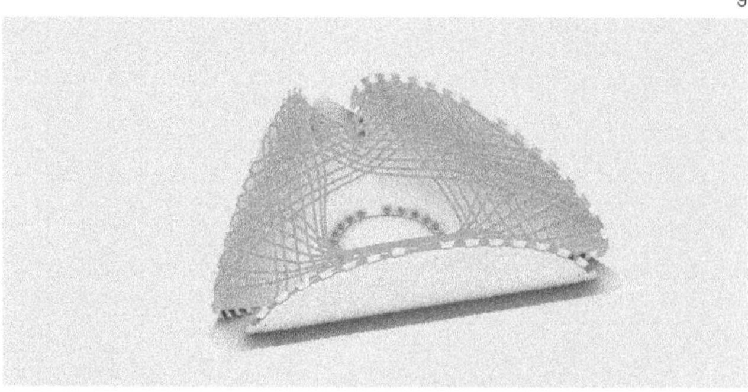

10

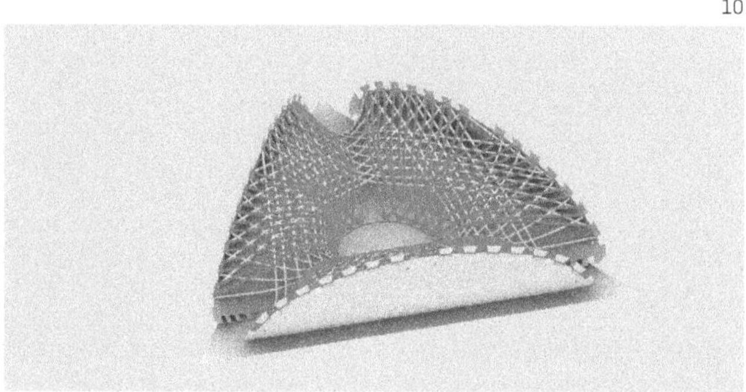

11

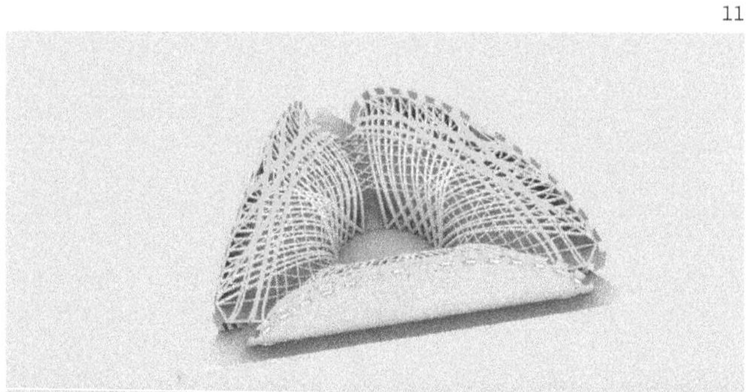

12

9 Proto-architectural component: internal tailored fiber placement preform and external tailored fiber placement skin.

10 Proto-architectural component: coreless filament winding body syntax.

11 Proto-architectural component: coreless filament winding spine syntax.

12 Proto-architectural component: coreless filament winding bracing syntax.

could help to alleviate each others' standalone limitations to create an architectural product greater than the sum of its parts. As explored through case studies, the most pressing of these restrictions lie in eliminating typical needs for complex winding frames in CFW as well as scaffolds for TFP preform shaping, both of which are complex, laborious, and costly to create. Consequently, the investigation becomes concerned with an exploration of two aspects related to moldless NFRP components, namely: the implications of combining tailored fiber placement and coreless filament winding techniques, previously deployed as uniquely separate production methods within the design process, and that of bringing such techniques to the architectural scale.

As demonstrated, the TFP preform behaves predictably as an embedded frame, while the CFW syntax provides a complementary layer of formal complexity and structure. Furthermore, material and structural efficiency were validated, with the demonstrator carrying more than 80 times its weight. Due to the anisotropic nature of fiber composites, computational tools were instrumental in creating an integrative design and simulation framework to navigate the complex and interrelated terrains of material, geometry, structure, and fabrication.

Fabrication, Assembly, and Sustainability

The combination of the two fabrication techniques not only circumvents the pervasive limitations of CFW in generating weathertight surfaces but also unlocks possibilities to structurally tailor both the component's volumetric body and its integrated skin. This opens new efficiencies in regulating material deployment in the skin, which may cater to the complex networks of induced planar stresses, along with varying light-filtering qualities into the interior space. With respect to workflow efficiencies, there remains an inherent drawback to the system insofar that a component must undergo two separate instances of resin-curing. In this instance, consideration of the use of sewn/wound preimpregnated fibers for both techniques are increasingly pertinent to streamline current production. A study on the consequential changes to the TFP preform's behavior is merited here since the substrate and stitching would remain largely "dry" in the finished state.

It was observed that the proposed methods pose new implications for scaling and assembly. The adopted lapping technique assists in bypassing the machine limits for the TFP preform, shifting production constraints away from the machine's build space to that of the robotic cell used during winding. Consequently, the assembly and transport limits that constrict previous CFW projects remain pertinent challenges to this approach. Opportunities arise, however, via the integrated

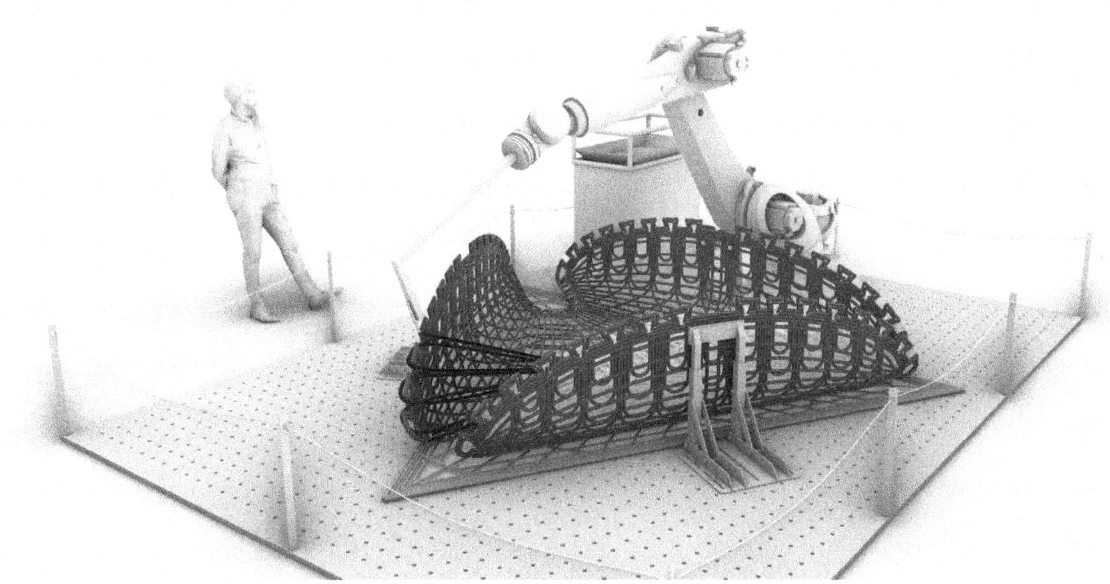

13 Robotic filament winding production cell.

frame, now being a flat-packable element and thus more amenable to on-site production methods.

Within the broader ecological discourse, the proposed hybrid fabrication appears promising insofar that the sum of two additive techniques produces virtually negligible material waste under controlled laboratory conditions. Conversely, the greatest impacts generated by natural fiber-reinforced polymers may be tackled on two levels: first, in material selection, whereby current thermoset resins may be swapped out for bio-based alternatives, along with the use of organic textile substitutes for the TFP stitching substrate; second, on a morphological level, wherein modular strategies provide ample benefits in establishing designs for disassembly, thus becoming amenable to more closed-loop lifecycles.

Techno-Aesthetic Implications

From a sociocultural perspective, this work builds on the semiotic framework put forth by scholars such as Gottfried Semper (2004) on materializing tectonics and, more aptly, Lars Spuybroek (2016) on the transforming gothic as an organic precursor to today's applied computational logic. These theoretical precedents pave the way to facilitate the introduction of an entire novel body of digitally enabled experimentation, to which this research contributes.

Architecturally, the fiber pattern design recalls vernacular woven structures and textiles (Fig. 14), in contrast to high-performance yarns like carbon and glass, which are not abundantly present in everyday life (Prado et al. 2014). As one's association with a material relates to one's understanding of its origin, natural fibers invoke their familiar biological roots. So, if fibers are to permeate everyday architecture, it is logical to use a material already present in the collective imaginary (Pallasmaa 2012).

OUTLOOK

Synergizing with the growing concerns to address global environmental challenges, this paper forms part of broader research on the integration of fibrous composites within the architectural realm, thereby challenging conventional construction practices. Further research is merited on these grounds, particularly concerning the new automation opportunities and challenges that the combined techniques and their scaling up entail. With equal capacity, the simulation and physical structural testing of both upscaled components and the global structure at large become the next pressing avenues of investigation. These research developments will provide a crucial tipping point to resume discussions of the richness that new architectural possibilities bring into the fray for truly sustainable building systems in the future.

ACKNOWLEDGMENTS

This project was initially developed in the seminar Material Matter Lab, offered by BioMat at ITKE, with the support of the Institute of Aircraft Design, both at the University of Stuttgart. The research was partially supported by the Deutsche Forschungsgemeinschaft (DFG, German Research Foundation) under Germany's Excellence Strategy EXC 2120/1-390831618, and by the Agency for Renewable Resources (FNR) under the Federal Ministry of Food and Agriculture (BMEL) throughout the research project LeichtPro: Pultruded load-bearing lightweight profiles from natural fiber composites

(FKZ:22027018), managed by Hanaa Dahy. The flax rovings used were courtesy of Group Depestele, France, and the resin courtesy of Hexion Stuttgart GmbH, Germany.

NOTES

1. More information on prototype testing can be found in Costalonga Martins et al. (2020).

REFERENCES

Abergel, Thibaut, Brian Dean, and John Dulac. 2017. *Towards a Zero-Emission, Efficient, and Resilient Buildings and Construction Sector: Global Status Report 2017*. Paris: UN Environment and International Energy Agency.

Aldinger, Lotte, Georgia Margariti, Axel Körner, Seiichi Suzuki, and Jan Knippers. 2018. "Tailoring Self-Formation Fabrication and Simulation of Membrane-Actuated Stiffness Gradient Composites." In *Proceedings of IASS Annual Symposia*, 1–8. International Association for Shell and Spatial Structures (IASS).

Aschenbrenner, Lars, Hubert Temmen, and Richard Degenhardt. 2007. "Tailored Fibre Placement Technology—Optimisation and Computation of CFRP Structures." In *Advances in Design and Analysis of Composite Structures [Proceedings of ESAComp Users' Meeting 2007]*, Braunschweig, Germany, 24–25 April 2007. DLR. https://elib.dlr.de/48326/.

BioMat at ITKE. 2020. *BioMat Flat to Spatial Mockup 2020: Minimal Surface Modular Biocomposite Material*. Stuttgart. http://vimeo.com/468478016.

Costalonga Martins, Vanessa, Sacha Cutajar, Christo van der Hoven, Piotr Baszyński, and Hanaa Dahy. 2020. "FlexFlax Stool: Validation of Moldless Fabrication of Complex Spatial Forms of Natural Fiber-Reinforced Polymer (NFRP) Structures through an Integrative Approach of Tailored Fiber Placement and Coreless Filament Winding Techniques." *Applied Sciences* 10 (9): 3278.

Dahy, Hanaa, Jan Petrš, and Piotr Baszyński. 2020. "Biocomposites from Annually Renewable Resources Displaying Vision of Future Sustainable Architecture Design and Fabrication of Two 1:1 Demonstrators." In *Fabricate 2020: Making Resilient Architecture*, edited by J. Burry, J. Sabin, B. Sheil, and M. Skavara, 66–73. London: UCL Press.

Felbrich, Benjamin, Nikolas Frueh, Marshall Prado, Saman Saffarian, James Solly, Lauren Vasey, Jan Knippers, and Achim Menges. 2017. "Multi-Machine Fabrication: An Integrative Design Process Utilising an Autonomous UAV and Industrial Robots for the Fabrication of Long Span Composite Structures." In *ACADIA 2017: Disciplines and Disruption [Proceedings of the 37th Annual Conference of the Association for Computer Aided Design in Architecture (ACADIA)]*, Cambridge, MA, 2–4 November 2017, edited by T. Nagakura, S. Tibbits, M. Ibañez, and C. Mueller, 248–259. CUMINCAD.

Herakovich, Carl T. 2012. "Composite Materials: Lamination Theory." In *Wiley Encyclopedia of Composites*, edited by L. Nicolais, 1–5. John Wiley & Sons.

Knippers, Jan, Achim Menges, Hanaa Dahy, Nikolas Früh, Abel Groenewolt, Axel Körner, Katja Rinderspacher et al. 2018. "The ITECH Approach: Building (s) to Learn." In *Proceedings of IASS Annual Symposia*, 1–8. International Association for Shell and Spatial Structures (IASS).

Menges, Achim, and Jan Knippers. 2015. "Fibrous Tectonics." *Architectural Design* 85 (5): 40–47.

Pallasmaa, Juhani. 2012. *The Eyes of the Skin: Architecture and the Senses*. John Wiley & Sons.

Pickering, K. L., M. G. Aruan Efendy, and T. M. Le. 2016. "A Review of Recent Developments in Natural Fibre Composites and Their Mechanical Performance." *Composites Part A: Applied Science and Manufacturing*, Special Issue on Biocomposites, 83 (April): 98–112.

Prado, Marshall, Moritz Dorstelmann, Tobias Schwinn, Achim Menges, and Jan Knippers. 2014. "Core-Less Filament Winding: Robotically Fabricated Fiber Composite Building Components." In *Robotic Fabrication in Architecture, Art and Design 2014*, edited by Wes McGee and Monica Ponce de Leon, 275–289. Cham, Switzerland: Springer.

Rana, Sohel, and Raul Fangueiro. 2016. *Fibrous and Textile Materials for Composite Applications*. Cham, Switzerland: Springer.

Rihaczek, Gabriel, Maximilian Klammer, Okan Başnak, Jan Petrš, Benjamin Grisin, Hanaa Dahy, Stefan Carosella, and Peter Middendorf. 2020. "Curved Foldable Tailored Fiber Reinforcements for Moldless Customized Bio-Composite Structures. Proof of Concept: Biomimetic NFRP Stools." *Polymers* 12 (9): 2000.

Robert McNeel & Associates. *Rhinoceros*. V.6.0. Robert McNeel & Associates. PC. 2020.

Rutten, David. *Grasshopper*. V.1.0.0007. Robert McNeel & Associates. PC. 2020.

Semper, Gottfried. 2004. *Style in the Technical and Tectonic Arts, or, Practical Aesthetics*. Getty Publications.

Spuybroek, Lars. 2016. *The Sympathy of Things: Ruskin and the Ecology of Design*. Bloomsbury Publishing.

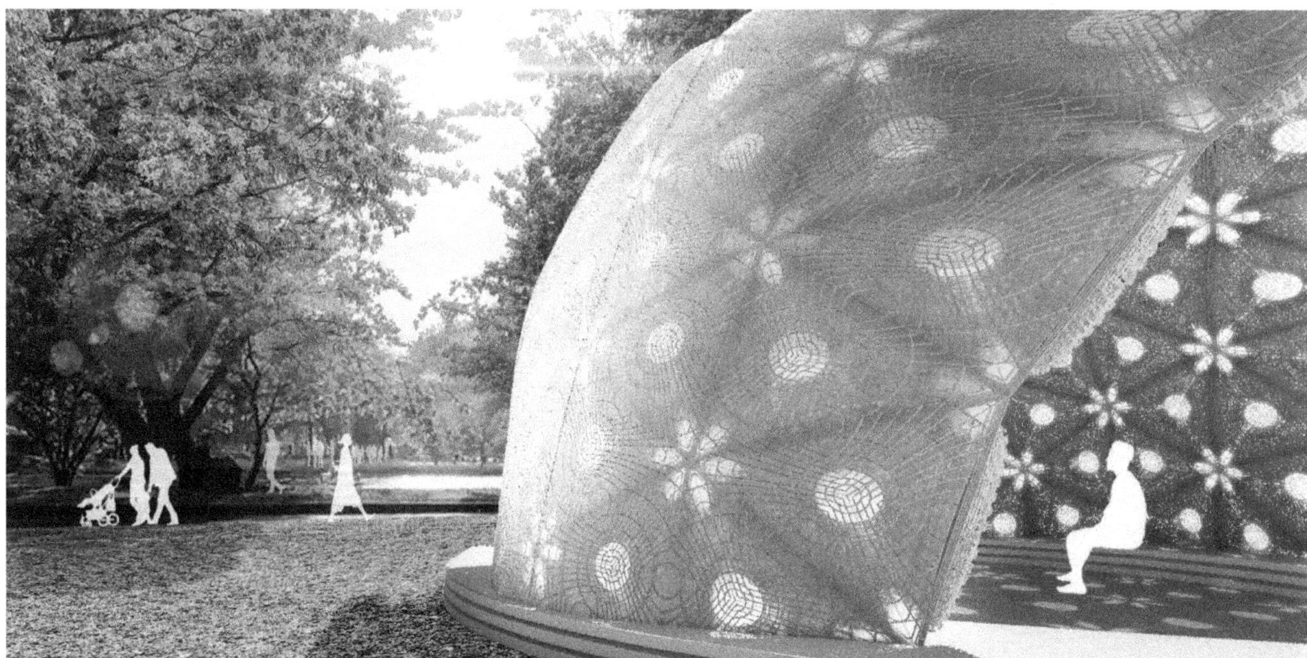

14 Interior of a modular natural-fiber-reinforced polymer spatial structure. 14

Yablonina, Maria, and Achim Menges. 2019. "Towards the Development of Fabrication Machine Species for Filament Materials." In *Robotic Fabrication in Architecture, Art and Design 2018*, edited by Jan Willmann, Philippe Block, Marco Hutter, Kendra Byrne, and Tim Schork, 152–166. Cham: Springer.

Zechmeister, Christoph, Serban Bodea, Niccolo Dambrosio, and Achim Menges. 2019. "Design for Long-Span Core-Less Wound, Structural Composite Building Elements." In *Impact: Design With All Senses*, edited by Christoph Gengnagel, Olivier Baverel, Jane Burry, Mette Ramsgaard Thomsen, and Stefan Weinzierl, 401–415. Cham: Springer.

Vanessa Costalonga Martins is a registered architect and urbanist (University of Brasilia) with a MSc in Integrative Technologies and Architectural Design Research (University of Stuttgart). Based in Germany, she has worked on projects around the world, including Italy (at Renzo Piano Building Workshop), South Africa, and Brazil. Specializing in computational design, digital fabrication, and composites, she is interested in how technology and experimental building materials can be combined to create more sustainable building solutions.

Sacha Cutajar is a registered architect, constantly hung up on the ever-enticing negotiations between design and making, and enthralled by their ties to computational processes and natural phenomena. After acquiring an MArch at the University of Malta in 2016, he worked on residential, commercial, and public projects across the island. Now based in Germany, he is a recent graduate of the ITECH MSc Program at the University of Stuttgart, specializing in computational technologies of construction and their sustainability.

Christo van der Hoven is an architect specializing in computational design, digital fabrication, and the networked knowledge production of rapidly reformulating cross-disciplinary design teams. He holds a BSc(Arch), as well as a BAS and MArch from the University of Cape Town (cum laude). In 2020 he graduated from the ITECH Master's Program. Previously he has practiced in both Europe, at Renzo Piano Building Workshop, and in his native South Africa, completing projects across a range of scales.

Piotr Baszyński is an architect and research associate at the department BioMat/ITKE at the Faculty of Architecture and Urban Planning at the University of Stuttgart. In 2013 he graduated from the Architecture for Society of Knowledge master's program at Warsaw University of Technology. During his professional and academic work, he developed an interest in computational design and digital fabrication combined with biocomposite materials and their applications in building elements and architecture. As a PhD candidate, he focuses on the possibilities of using biocomposite profiles as a replacement of timber elements in modular housing.

Hanaa Dahy is a registered architect, engineer, and material developer who established the research department BioMat (Bio-based Materials and Materials Cycles in Architecture) as a Junior Professor at ITKE (Institute for Building Structures and Structural Design) at the Faculty of Architecture and Urban Planning in the University of Stuttgart. She developed, designed, and manufactured a number of innovative sustainable building products that were presented in international exhibitions and attracted industrial interest. Among other research areas, she is particularly interested in biomimetic principles, sustainability, and their impact on architectural practice and applications.

Computational Fluid Dynamics in Building Design Practice

John Nguyen
University of Toronto

Brady Peters
University of Toronto

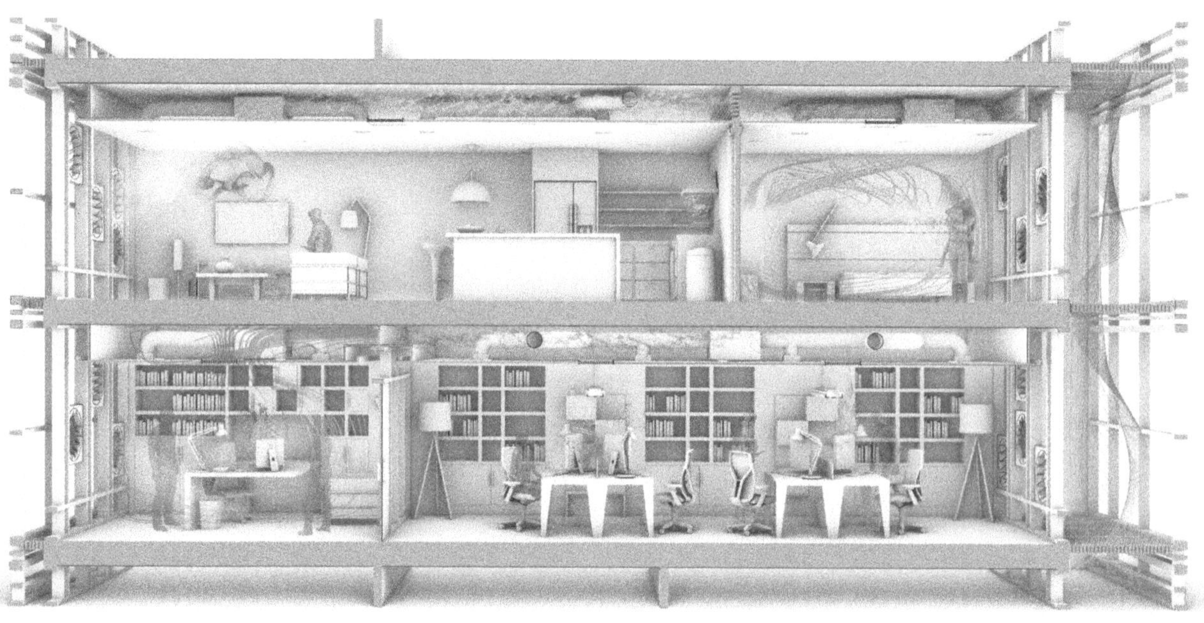

1

1 A sectional rendering showing fluid flow through different spaces.

ABSTRACT

This paper provides a state-of-the-art of computational fluid dynamics (CFD) in the building industry. Two methods were used to find this new knowledge: a series of interviews with leading architecture, engineering, and software professionals; and a series of tests in which CFD software was evaluated using comparable criteria. The paper reports findings in technology, workflows, projects, current unmet needs, and future directions.

In buildings, airflow is fundamental for heating and cooling, as well as occupant comfort and productivity. Despite its importance, the design of airflow systems is outside the realm of much of architectural design practice; but with advances in digital tools, it is now possible for architects to integrate air flow into their building design workflows (Peters and Peters 2018). As Chen (2009) states, "In order to regulate the indoor air parameters, it is essential to have suitable tools to predict ventilation performance in buildings." By enabling scientific data to be conveyed in a visual process that provides useful analytical information to designers (Hartog and Koutamanis 2000), computer performance simulations have opened up new territories for design "by introducing environments in which we can manipulate and observe" (Kaijima et al. 2013). Beyond comfort and productivity, in recent months it has emerged that air flow may also be a matter of life and death. With the current global pandemic of SARS-CoV-2, it is indoor environments where infections most often happen (Qian et al. 2020). To design architecture in a post-COVID-19 environment will require an in-depth understanding of how air flows through space.

METHODS

This experiment came about as part of a search to find computational fluid dynamics (CFD) software that could be used in a generative design process. There were two parts to this study: (1) a series of interviews with architecture, engineering, and software professionals, and (2) an evaluation of several CFD software packages used in the building industry. It should be noted that parts 1 and 2 were not carried out in isolation, and the results from the software investigations helped to inform the interviews questions, and vice versa.

Industry Professionals

In part 1, interviewees (Table 1) were asked about their integration of airflow analysis into their design processes, revealing existing design technology, workflows, and projects. Interviews were conducted in person, using a series of standard questions:

- Does this firm study/analyze airflow?
- If yes, what is the use of air flow analysis at the firm?
- Which CFD softwares are being utilized?
- At which phase of the design process is airflow considered?
- What are common issues involving CFD that arise in practice?
- What are the challenges when working in a collaborative team involving architects and CFD specialist consultants?
- Is there any postoccupancy data being collected?
- What are your future hopes and outlook for CFD applications?

The direction of the conversation was allowed to deviate and new questions were introduced based on the interests and knowledge of the interviewee. In this way, the interview process was both structured and unstructured (Kvale 1996).

CFD Software Packages

In part 2, software was evaluated in terms of accessibility, hardware requirements, costs, learning resources, and the level of difficulty learning the program. The selected software packages (Table 2) were tested through form-finding exercises. These exercises looked at air flow in interior conditions, such as impacts of mechanical ventilation, the effects of elements such as walls, and the influence of furniture layout and floor plan adjustments.

RESULTS

Industry Interviews

One of the key findings of the interviews was that not only

Table 1 Industry professionals.

FIRMS	INDUSTRY	SOFTWARE
BIG IDEAS	ARCHITECTURE	OpenFOAM SWIFT/Butterfly
KPMB ARCHITECTS	ARCHITECTURE	SimScale Autodesk CFD
ERA ARCHITECTS	ARCHITECTURE	N/A
UNITED NATIONS	ARCHITECTURE	Autodesk CFD
ARUP	ENGINEERING	Inhouse Software
RWDI	ENGINEERING	Inhouse Software
AUTODESK	DEVELOPER	Autodesk CFD Flow Design

Table 2 CFD software packages.

SOFTWARE	DIFFICULTY	TUTORIAL	STRENGTH
RHINO CFD	INTERMEDIATE	LIMITED	BUILT FOR RHINO
SIMSCALE	INTERMEDIATE	DETAILED	CLOUD COMPUTING
BUTTERFLY OPENFOAM	INTERMEDIATE	LIMITED	GRASSHOPPER INTEGRATION
OPENFOAM PARAVIEW GMSH	ADVANCED	AVERAGE	OPENSOURCE

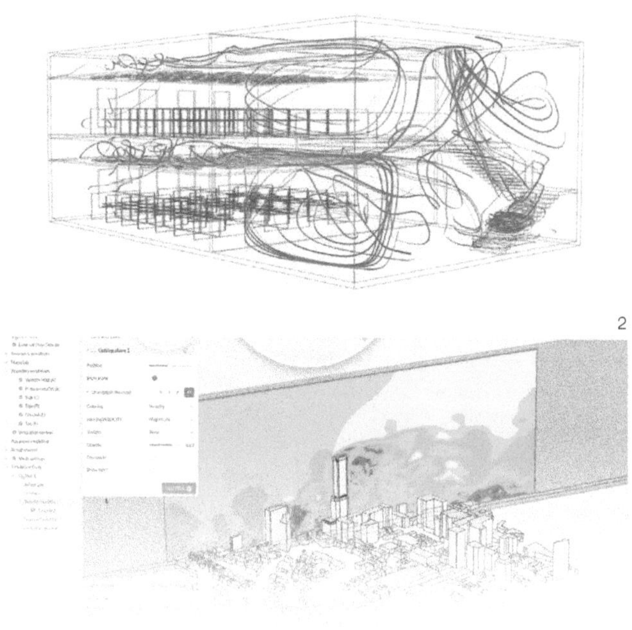

2

3

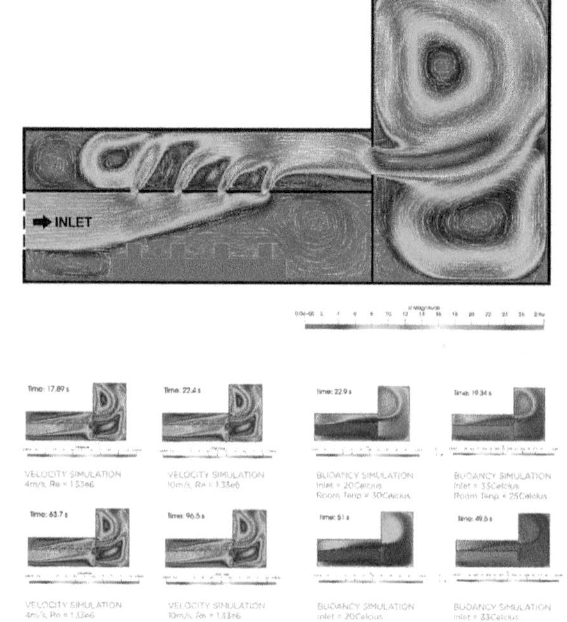

4

are architects aware of CFD and its potentials, but they have clear objectives for its use, and are already using it in multiple ways (Table 1). The interviews reveal a recent interest from architects in CFD, which is attracting the attention of software developers. As a result, software developers are already beginning to target the architecture market with CFD analysis for interior and exterior building elements (Table 2). The answers to the question regarding the role of air flow revealed the wide differences in terms of the analyses being done, which can range in scale, location, program, design stage, and desired results. Although professionals may have different needs for CFD, the underlying consensus is that CFD is a valuable and important tool but needs to become more user-friendly. What was surprising to discover during these interviews is that even though architecture firms are using CFD, no postoccupancy data has been collected to validate its performance.

ERA Architects Inc. is a practice started in 1990 with offices in Toronto, Montreal, and Ottawa. The firm specializes in heritage conservation, architecture, landscape, and planning as they relate to historic places. Their core values are about addressing heritage-related issues to a broader consideration of urban design and city building. ERA often partners with other firms in projects involving city building, conserving heritage architecture, and improving the built environment. Noah McGillivray, a staff member at ERA Architects, states that a lot of their projects involve working on heritage buildings where it is not possible to implement mechanical systems for cooling, leaving only passive ventilation as a viable method. Hence, the factor of airflow analysis is an important element early on in the design process. A common issue is the retrofitting of interior conditions where transom windows have been covered up or the hallway system has changed, impacting the airflow performance of the original design. The firm does not employ anyone with knowledge in the field of CFD. As a result, most of the work gets outsourced to consultants such as RWDI and Arup, incurring extra costs and time. On average, a consultant takes three weeks to return the results of an airflow analysis, by which time the submitted design may have already progressed drastically or been canceled for another option. The postoccupancy data specific to airflow analysis is dependent on the type of project and done by consultants. A basic tool to allow ERA architects to get some in-house feedback regarding airflow analysis in between concept iterations would be of great interest to ERA.[1]

Natalie Sham is an architectural designer specializing in automation at Arup's Toronto location. She was formerly an architect part II working for the United Nations Office in Geneva, where her work involved passive airflow improvement studies through the use of CFD software with genetic algorithms. The research was primarily focused on the conceptual design phase and never published due to its sensitive nature. The scope of the project entailed furniture orientation and wall placements as the driving factors for the generative design constraints. A combination of Revit and Rhino were used to develop 3D models, and Autodesk CFD was the program used to run airflow analysis. As this project was only a study, no postoccupancy data exists.

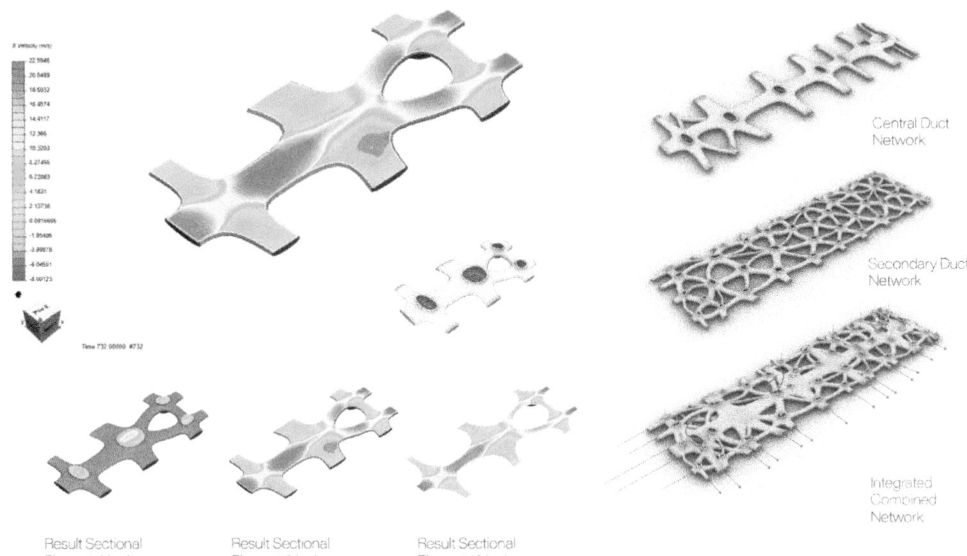

2 A passive ventilation study for an open office floorplan layout simulated in RhinoCFD.

3 SimScale's browser based interphace displaying its new collaboration feature.

4 Buoyancy and velocity studies for an open office floorplan using OpenFOAM, GMSH and Paraview.

5 A study of various ventilation shaft designs done in SimScale.

Sham states that this study highlighted the importance of CFD from the concept phase instead of integrating it towards the end of the design development.[2]

Geoffrey Turnbull is the director of innovation at KPMB Architects in Toronto, one of Canada's leading architecture firms. KPMB's projects encompass all elements of building practice, where, according to Turnbull, the analysis of fluid flow in itself is not of great interest to the firm's workflow in contrast to flow as a factor for microclimates. KPMB's research laboratory is collaborating with Ryerson University to develop tools that allow the firm to understand and analyze the impact of microclimates within buildings so that climate factors can be taken into consideration from the earliest design concepts through to the detailing stage. The objective is to achieve optimized designs that have higher performance levels, lower environmental impact, and increased user comfort. Although KPMB does not have a dedicated CFD specialist, its technical team does utilize Simscale and various CFD applications to the extent of testing initial designs.[3]

BIG IDEAS was founded as a product design firm and branch of the architecture firm Bjarke Ingels Group (BIG) in 2014. Over time, it has transitioned to become an in-house specialist group for the main architecture firm BIG (Maescher 2016). "Its three primary objectives are: simulations, product design and conceptual ideas. The simulations are carried out by a team of experts in computationally derived methods of design. With this close collaboration, they solve the designs from BIG's architectural department while addressing sustainable and environmental needs of a project" (Sayer 2016). Tore Banke is the head of computation, and Alexander Matthias Jacobson is a computational design specialist with a specialty in climate modeling and energy analysis. In our conversation, it was revealed that BIG IDEAS has been working with CFD applications in a substantial manner, where concept sketches are informed by team members' intuition about airflow, which are processed through CFD simulations, and any feedback is iterated back into the design process for further prototyping and repeated until the team is satisfied. This information is then shared with the design team at other BIG offices. BIG IDEAS is currently working on an in-house project called Adele, where three-year-old computers are bridged to create a physical cloud computing network for CFD simulations. The team is developing software that will allow all of BIG's offices to access CFD data, simulation, and updates in real time. Currently, the BIG IDEAS team primarily utilizes ODS Studio and SWIFT for CFD analysis, where SWIFT is used to study multidirectional wind analysis. The results are represented in a multitude of graphical standards in line with the firm guidelines using Paraview and in-house scripts, where data files from OpenFoam are processed and the points are extracted into Rhino/Grasshopper for color adjustments or graphical adjustments. Banke mentions that it is important for the simulation results to be presented legibly so that the resulting data output does not become overwhelming. The preferred way of going about this is to utilize two-dimensional planes that limit the visual information of the results to a specific sectional slice of fluid flow. CFD is now something that more clients are insisting be included as part of the design process, as there is inherent value in maximizing fluid flow performance. Although a lot of the initial stages of CFD analysis are conducted in-house, an external consultant is hired to validate the data at various stages prior to finalizing the documentation. As it stands, all projects inside BIG IDEAS are influenced by CFD analysis in some aspect. Jacobson states that 30 projects with which he has been involved leveraged CFD studies within just the last three months. Banke predicts that in the next five years, all the projects inside the BIG offices will involve CFD as part of design processes, as clients will demand it. According to Alexander, the use of CFD analysis has also allowed the architects to work more closely with landscape architects, as the types of trees and landscape topology can have a major impact on a building's fluid flow performance. Although CFD simulations are prevalent within the BIG IDEAS workflow, no postoccupancy data has been collected on any of the projects to validate these performance metrics produced by the simulation results.[4]

Rowan Williams Davies & Irwin Inc. (RWDI) is an engineering consulting firm founded in 1972, specializing in wind and environmental engineering. The company has offices around the world due to their industry-leading expertise in wind engineering. The firm utilizes in-house wind tunnel testing (WTT) in combination with CFD software to assess various wind conditions (RWDI n.d.). Eric Li is a senior project engineer at RWDI specializing in CFD. He states that when working with architectural firms, each project is often very different due to the constraints that must be specifically tailored to conditions such as offices, hospital, or schools. These spaces have different conditions that impact the level of granularity that needs to be analyzed and the data produced have to be adjusted accordingly. As a firm specializing in wind engineering, RWDI uses different CFD software packages according to the scenario, some of which are developed in-house and use OpenFOAM. Li mentions that there is some interest in looking at Grasshopper workflows for future applications. A combination of data between WTT or water bath modeling (WBM) testing is also utilized to validate or enforce simulation results from CFD simulations. A combination of these varied methods is done based on cost savings benefits and time sensitive cases for data output.[5]

Arup's wind engineers are specialists within the larger multinational consulting service. They specialize in using advanced analysis and design techniques to ensure feasibility, safety, durability, and occupant comfort for structures that go beyond the standard. Arup visualizes wind behavior through WTT and CFD studies along with other alternative methods of analysis. The fluid dynamics group is another specialist subset within Arup that deals with how gases and fluids move and interact in buildings regarding fire engineering and clean water supply. Erthan Hataysal is a senior mechanical tunnel ventilation engineer at Arup London, specializing in CFD for internal and external investigations. He frequently works with architects on projects and states that differences in terminology regarding fluid flow can sometimes result in miscommunication and frustration between architects and engineers. Hataysal thinks that the current state of CFD requires architects to increase their understanding of basic fluid dynamics in order to reduce miscommunications and expectations regarding fluid flow studies. This would also help speed up the setup and processing of simulation studies, as architects can produce 3D models with an understanding of how meshes and boundary conditions are set, so that the CFD team does not need to reconstruct their 3D models, saving time and associated expenses. Arup develops in-house software that runs on OpenFOAM or leverages industry-available CFD packages depending on the situation. Oftentimes, in a city like London, a single new high-rise building requires a majority of the city to be modeled in order to produce the correct granularity level for accurate results. In these types of situations, CFD is extremely useful, as building an entire wind tunnel or water bath model of a city is not only time-consuming but cost-prohibitive. It is up to the team of CFD specialists to decide which approach to take and proceed with the best option.[6]

The Complex Systems Research Group is a specialist team within Autodesk Research that helps designers and researchers develop greater knowledge and understanding of complex systems such as ones found in the biological world. Azam Khan is the head of complex systems research at Autodesk. In our conversation about why CFD has such slow adoption rates within architecture, he recalls that there was a lot of interesting CFD-related work done in the early 2000s but that interest was primarily by the entertainment and gaming industry, while the architectural industry showed little interest. This caused most software developers to focus fluid dynamics simulations towards the gaming and entertainment industry, while any architecture, engineering, and construction (AEC) software focus for CFD was geared towards engineers. However, that is changing, as there is an increasing need to understand data for microclimates as part of the building information modeling (BIM) package. Khan states that Autodesk Research is currently looking at integrating deep learning into its Autodesk CFD solver to speed up the process and reduce the resource intensiveness associated with complex

CFD analysis. This in combination with its SyDevs framework for simulation-based analysis of complex systems involving people, devices, physical elements, and dynamic environments will help make CFD much more accessible to everyone in the future. Khan believes that as the time and resource intensity of CFD simulations are reduced, architects will be more willing to invest resources into learning and using CFD applications. His vision of future workflow for architects is to provide a framework where the designer specifies where and how they want the fluid to flow, and the software will make the necessary modeling changes seamlessly without the need for an engineer. All this can only become feasible if the data sourced and produced for these CFD simulations can be optimized for cloud computing, as the current situation does not allow for this to occur effectively on local desktop systems.[7]

Software Evaluation

How air transverses through a space has direct impact on building performance and occupant health (Wilson 1963). Given the situation of COVID-19, CFD analysis techniques are appropriate for studying infectious pathogen particulate transport. CFD can provide a highly resolved estimate of air and species transport within the region of interest in lieu of obtaining field samples (Richmond-Bryant 2008). The CFD software evaluation used a case study project of a complex ventilation shaft design (Fig. 5) and ceiling opening placements (Figs. 2, 4), and asked how these can impact air movement. Throughout this study of software, a challenge of how to convey and visualize CFD results effectively for different use cases is an evolving pursuit, as different firms have their own stylistic preferences and these may differ from the representation options provided in CFD packages (Fig. 6). Furthermore, the interoperability between these softwares can be challenging, as not all the programs allow for ease of visual data extraction and visualization, such as making animations, or extracting streamlines.

SimScale is a cloud-based CFD platform (Guenther 2020). It is comprehensive in nature, allowing for not just fluid flow analysis but also thermal studies to be conducted. Of particular interest to architects are the options for compressible and incompressible flow analysis, and convective and conjugate heat transfers (e.g., auditorium/ large open office plans). The inclusion of free cloud core hours with options for more to be acquired through fees for larger scenarios make it appealing for architects to invest time into the platform as it does not require new hardware or take away computing resources from other projects. That said, any work performed with a free account is publicly accessible on the online depository that functions similarly to Google SketchUp's Warehouse. The benefit is

SIMSCALE

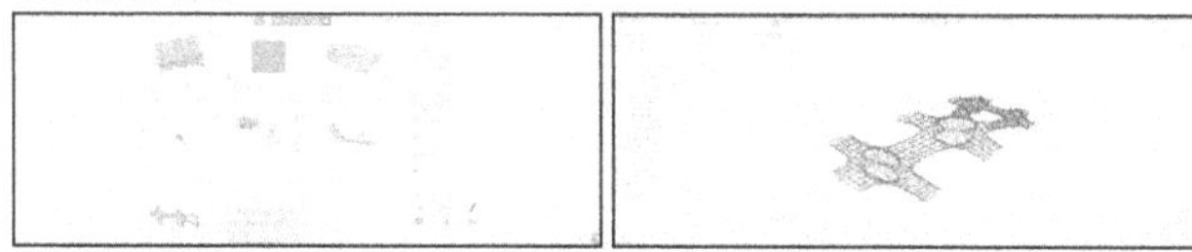

BUTTERFLY

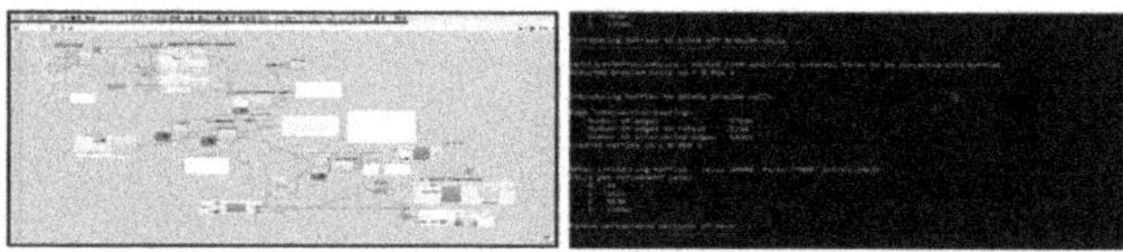

PARAVIEW

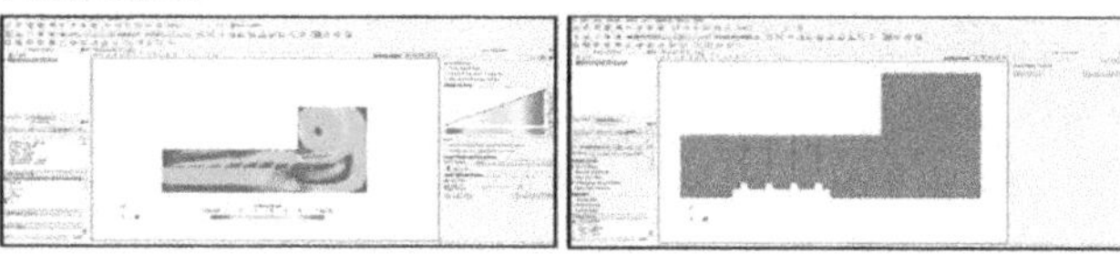

GMSH

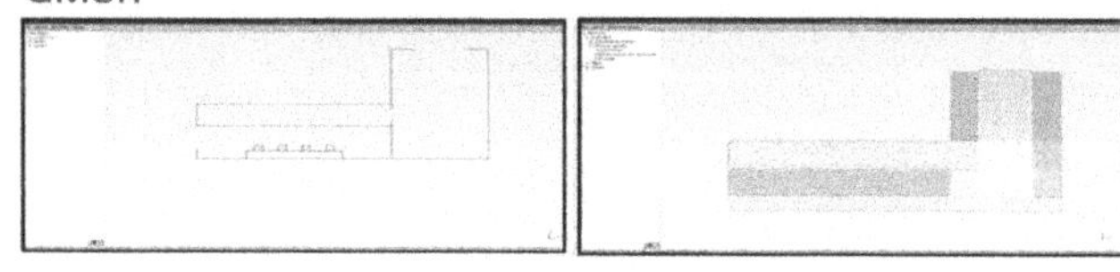

6 CFD software application interfaces.

that it can help users learn by looking at how others have set up their files and access the 3D files without the need to remodel the scenario. A downside is that the settings may be incorrect as data input can be wrong. Furthermore, any testing of unpublished work is exposed to the public, which can prevent firms from testing ongoing projects. A lack of streamlined animation export options is apparent for such a comprehensive platform. However, the files can be downloaded and exported into Paraview as a workaround. SimScale has a great depository of online tutorials on its official blog and a YouTube channel, which is beneficial to new users.

RhinoCFD is a plugin by CHAM's Phoenics that is built for Rhinoceros 3D (Concentration, Heat and Momentum Ltd. 2018). In its framework, an option titled FLAIR allows for the analysis of fluid flow and thermal simulations. It is intuitive for Rhinoceros users to navigate, as modeled objects can be easily converted to meshes for analysis without usual interoperability issues between different software packages where closed boundary errors often arise. An issue that RhinoCFD shares with most other CFD software packages is in its physics settings. A lack of foundation in fluid dynamics makes it difficult for new users to know what physics values to implement. The user interface does not structure the entering of these settings in chronological steps, in contrast to SimScale, which does this exceptionally well. Online resources and tutorials are available, but are limited and sometimes outdated. Official tutorials consist of a handful of short PDF files where external flow around buildings and HVAC tutorials may be of direct interest to

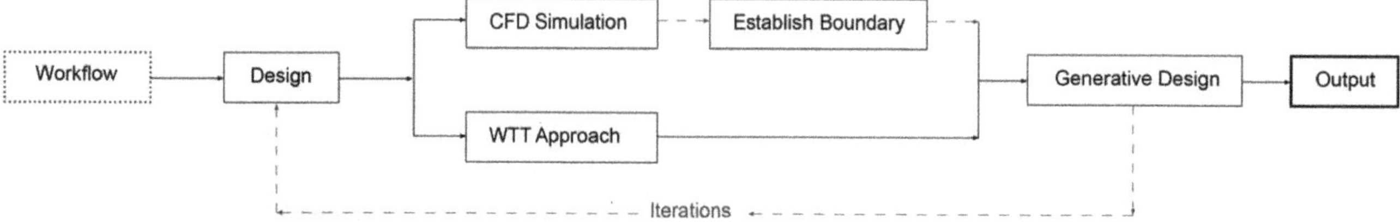

7 Workflow diagram.

architects. Both these tutorial's PDF files were produced in 2017. The official YouTube channel CHAM lacks any in-depth instructional videos that would be of interest to architects. Visualization options are similar to other CFD applications but benefit from the Rhino3D platform by allowing geometry to be directly called into Grasshopper.

OpenFOAM is a free open-source software provided by the OpenFOAM Foundation (2020). It is a powerful platform that is able to run advanced simulations. It has a large user base spanning across industry and academia. However, it requires a foundation in fluid dynamics and C++ abilities due to the lack of a graphical user interface (GUI) that architects are accustomed to. Everything is entered through command lines. As a software development kit, OpenFOAM at its core contains only the basic essentials, where anything more complicated than a simple geometry cannot be processed using blockmesh but instead needs to be combined with external programs such as GMSH for meshing and Paraview for data visualization and animation output. In comparison to other CFD packages on the market, OpenFOAM is the least user-friendly. That said, it is built as a development kit intended for experienced users to develop their own programs or scripts. Online learning resources and tutorials tend to be very topic specific or advanced and not welcoming for architects.

Butterfly is a plugin for Ladybug Tools Suite for Grasshopper in Rhinoceros 3D and Dynamo for Autodesk Revit. It leverages OpenFOAM to run advanced CFD simulations. According to the Ladybug Tools website, "Butterfly is built to quickly export geometry to OpenFOAM and run several common types of airflow simulations that are useful to building design. This includes outdoor simulations to model urban wind patterns, indoor buoyancy-driven simulations to model thermal comfort and ventilation effectiveness" (Ladybug Tools LLC n.d.). From a user's perspective, Butterfly is easy to grasp for anyone with moderate Grasshopper experience. However, an understanding of meshes and fluid dynamics is required. The example Grasshopper scripts provided are helpful in running basic buoyancy and velocity studies for forced air and heat stack scenarios. As Butterfly is a work in progress, some of the online video tutorials are outdated. A new initiative to develop a paid video tutorial platform is mentioned to be in progress. The installation of OpenFOAM in a virtual box environment to run Butterfly was a major problem for many users, as it produced a variety of issues making Butterfly unusable. However, the recent transition to using blueCFD-Core in early 2019 seems to have circumvented this issue. In regards to data output, vector coordinates can be exported, graph charts are built into the example scripts, and the utilization of colored grid cells with directional vector arrows is the primary method of visualization. Unfortunately, results do not allow for streamline extraction at the time of testing, which would be of interest to architects.

WORKFLOW

As a result of the interviews and software experiments conducted, we derived a workflow that utilizes a combination of (1) generative design, (2) CFD simulations, and (3) WTT method (Fig. 7). This approach was based on the information shared by Natalie Sham regarding her research at the United Nations where she used generative design with Autodesk CFD for passive ventilation studies, Erthan Hataysal's expertise at Arup, and Eric Li's specialty at RWDI, where both used either CFD or WTT methods paired together or separately, depending on the project requirements. Although each interviewee mentioned their work involving two of the three methods, none linked all three approaches into one workflow. The benefit of combining all three approaches is that the shortcomings in one method can be addressed by another. WTT studies can be cost-prohibitive and time-consuming to set up, as was made aware in the interview with Erthan Hataysal, where the city of London needed to be physically modeled to conduct a wind flow analysis for one new high-rise building. CFD simulations can address this shortcoming by leveraging 3D modeling and computational power. However, depending on the situation and granularity required, results produced by CFD may need to be validated and can take longer to simulate in contrast to conventional WTT studies. These shortcomings in CFD and WTT can be

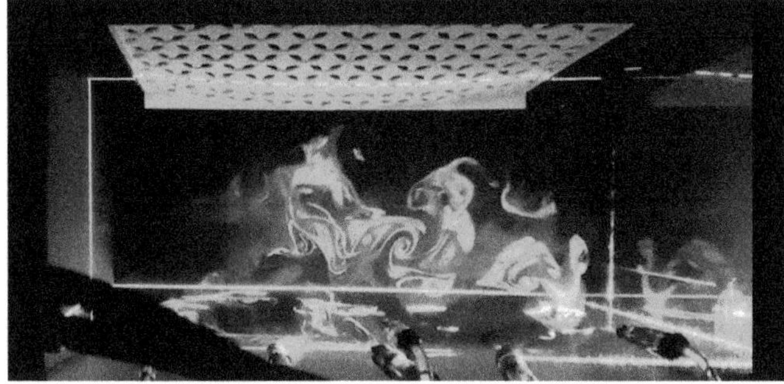

8 WTT study in progress.

disruptive to an architect's design process, where ideas are rapidly evolving through numerous iterations. As Noah McGillivray from ERA Architects mentioned, designs sent to consultants for airflow analysis can take three weeks to complete, by which time the original design may already be obsolete. Generative design can assist in this scenario by providing architects with a tool to create design permutations informed by fluid flow parameters that are established through constraints from existing CFD data. However, initial value ranges for the constraints need to be established and validated through CFD simulations or WTT measurements if scenario-related numerical data does not already exist. In this study, the combination of all three approaches into a workflow begins by running an initial design through several CFD simulations to create a matrix of conditions where elements such as distances between ceiling returns placements can provide the boundary values to be utilized as generative design constraints to create different permutations. Specific results from these permutations can then be individually selected and studied in further detail through the WTT method where a scaled prototype of the model is built and tested in parallel with CFD applications. As seen in Figure 4, a CFD's buoyancy study is used to reveal issues regarding areas within the design where the use of a passive cooling approach does not fully circulate cool air through the entire space, allowing for other studies from the design matrix created to be selected and studied.

WTT METHOD TESTING

This study looked at using the WTT method to validate data derived from CFD simulations by leveraging architects' expertise in building physical scaled models as part of the process. These models were scaled based on matching Reynolds numbers (NASA n.d.). A mixture of distilled water and glycerin filled in modified vape pens was utilized to generate the smoke using remote-controlled activation. The smoke was visualized using wide-angled lasers that can produce vertical and horizontal planes of vision. These lasers were attached to a remote-controlled automated dolly, which allowed the sectional planes of vision to be moved in real time during simulation studies. Different types of mechanical fans were used to produce the necessary cubic feet per minute (CFM) in relation to the matching Reynolds number conversion requirements. Although the initial objective for leveraging this WTT method as a data validation tool for CFD output was inconclusive due to the erratic nature of the eddies produced, it did provide basic information such as the type of flow produced and how this flow is moving through the interconnected spaces within the model. This real-time visualization can help architects understand fluid flow in their designs at a basic level throughout the initial conceptual design phases. This experiment also revealed a need for further investigation into the types of sensors that are required to measure fluid flow within the model for numerical data to be collected, as the images and videos recorded of the experiment were limited to qualitative visualization.

CONCLUSION

The interviews and software evaluation reveal a great interest in, and emergent potential for, CFD in architecture. As a result, software developers are already beginning to target the architecture market with increased CFD analysis resources for interior and exterior building elements. However, throughout this study, it became apparent that before CFD can be used properly, an understanding of the underlying physics is required. Upon being able to produce CFD simulations based on this knowledge, opportunities for leveraging other computational aspects as part of a generative design workflow in combination with WTT methods are discovered. Additional research and laboratory testing needs to be conducted with regards to the WTT approach to establish its purpose as a validation tool. The answers to the question regarding the role of airflow revealed wide differences in terms of the analyses being done, which can range in scale, location, program, design stage, and desired results. Although professionals may have different needs for CFD, the underlying consensus is that CFD is a valuable and important tool but needs to become more user-friendly. What was surprising to discover during these interviews is that even though architecture firms are using CFD, no postoccupancy data has been collected to validate the performance.

NOTES

1. Noah McGillivray. Interview by authors. Personal interview. Toronto, October 9, 2019.
2. Natalie Sham. Interview by authors. Personal interview. Toronto. October 10, 2019.
3. Geoffrey Turnbull. Interview by authors. Personal interview. Toronto. October 24, 2019.
4. Tore Banke and Alexander Jacobson. Interview by authors.

Personal interview. Toronto. October 27, 2019.

5. Eric Li. Interview by authors. Personal interview. Toronto. October 30, 2019.
6. Ertan Hataysal. Interview by authors. Personal interview. Toronto. November 11, 2019.
7. Azam Khan. Interview by authors. Personal interview. Toronto. November 13, 2019.

REFERENCES

Brito, Christopher. 2020. "Coronavirus 'May Never Go Away,' World Health Organization Warns." *CBS News*, May 15.

Bromage, Erin. 2020. "The Risks—Know Them—Avoid Them." Blog, May 20. https://www.erinbromage.com/post/the-risks-know-them-avoid-them.

Chen, Qingyan. 2009. "Ventilation Performance Prediction for Buildings: A Method Overview and Recent Applications." *Building and Environment* 44 (4): 848–858. https://doi.org/10.1016/j.buildenv.2008.05.025.

Concentration, Heat and Momentum Ltd. 2018. *RhinoCFD*. V.1.0. CHAM. http://www.rhinocfd.com.

Guenther, Sebastian. 2020. "SimScale Announces Cloud-Based Collaboration Features." SimScale Blog (blog), April 17. https://www.simscale.com/blog/2020/03/cae-collaboration-features/.

Hamner, Lea, Polly Dubbel, Ian Capron, Andy Ross, Amber Jordan, Jaxon Lee, Joanne Lynn, et al. 2020. "High SARS-CoV-2 Attack Rate Following Exposure at a Choir Practice—Skagit County, Washington, March 2020." *MMWR: Morbidity and Mortality Weekly Report* 69 (19): 606–610. https://doi.org/10.15585/mmwr.mm6919e6.

Hartog, J.P., and A. Koutamanis. 2000. "Teaching Design Simulation." In *Promise and Reality: Proceedings of the 18th Conference on Education in Computer Aided Architectural Design in Europe 2000*, 197–200. Weimar: eCAADe.

Kaijima, Sawako, Roland Bouffanais, Karen Willcox, and Suresh Naidu. 2013. "Computational Fluid Dynamics for Architectural Design." *Architectural Design* 83 (2): 118–123. https://doi.org/10.1002/ad.1566.

Kvale, Steinar. 1996. *Interviews: An Introduction to Qualitative Research Interviewing*. Thousand Oaks, CA: Sage Publications.

Ladybug Tools LLC. n.d. "What Is Ladybug Tools?" Accessed December 10, 2019. https://www.ladybug.tools/.

Lu, Jianyun, Jieni Gu, Kuibiao Li, Conghui Xu, Wenzhe Su, Zhisheng Lai, Deqian Zhou, Chao Yu, Bin Xu, and Zhicong Yang. 2020. "COVID-19 Outbreak Associated with Air Conditioning in Restaurant, Guangzhou, China, 2020." *Emerging Infectious Diseases* 26 (7): 1628–1631. https://doi.org/10.3201/eid2607.200764.

Maescher, Tobias. "Jakob Lange on Founding BIG Ideas and the Diverse Future of Architectural Practice." ArchDaily. January 18, 2016. www.archdaily.com/780533/jakob-lange-on-founding-big-ideas-and-the-diverse-future-of-architectural-practice.

NASA. n.d. "Reynolds Number." NASA Glenn Research Center. Accessed September 5, 2019. https://www.grc.nasa.gov/www/k-12/airplane/reynolds.html.

OpenFOAM Foundation. 2020. *OpenFOAM*. V.8. https://openfoam.org/version/8/.

Park, Shin Young, Young-Man Kim, Seonju Yi, Sangeun Lee, Baeg-Ju Na, Chang Bo Kim, Jung-Il Kim, et al. 2020. "Coronavirus Disease Outbreak in Call Center, South Korea." *Emerging Infectious Diseases* 26 (8). https://doi.org/10.3201/eid2608.201274.

Peters, Brady, and Terri Peters. 2018. *Computing the Environment: Digital Design Tools for Simulation and Visualisation of Sustainable Architecture*. John Wiley & Sons: London.

Qian, Hua, Te Miao, Li Liu, Xiaohong Zheng, Danting Luo, and Yuguo Li. 2020. "Indoor Transmission of SARS-CoV-2." medRxiv. https://doi.org/10.1101/2020.04.04.20053058.

Ramponi, R., and B. Blocken. 2012. "CFD Simulation of Cross-Ventilation for a Generic Isolated Building: Impact of Computational Parameters." *Building and Environment* 53: 34–48. https://doi.org/10.1016/j.buildenv.2012.01.004.

Richmond-Bryant, Jennifer. 2008. "Transport of Exhaled Particulate Matter in Airborne Infection Isolation Rooms." *Building and Environment* 44 (1): 44–55. https://doi.org/10.1016/j.buildenv.2008.01.009.

RWDI, n.d. "Computational Fluid Dynamics (CFD)." RWDI. Rowan Williams Davies & Irwin Inc. Accessed December 4, 2020. www.rwdi.com/en_ca/expertise/building-performance-cfd.

Sayer, Jason. "Inside Bjarke Ingels Group's Own Tech-Driven Think Tank." The Architect's Newspaper, October 3, 2016. www.archpaper.com/2016/09/bjarke-ingels-group-big-ideas-jakob-lange/.

Stadnytskyi, Valentyn, Christina E. Bax, Adriaan Bax, and Philip Anfinrud. 2020. "The Airborne Lifetime of Small Speech Droplets and Their Potential Importance in SARS-CoV-2 Transmission."

Proceedings of the National Academy of Sciences 117 (22): 11875–11877. https://doi.org/10.1073/pnas.2006874117.

Wilson, A. G. 1963. "Air Leakage in Buildings." *Canadian Building Digest* 23. National Research Council of Canada, Ottawa.

IMAGE CREDITS

Figure 3: © Simscale, 10/08/2020,

All other drawings and images by the authors.

John Nguyen is a researcher at the University of Toronto, where he also received his master of architecture degree. He was previously a computational designer at UofT's Platform for Resilient Urbanism working on collaborative projects with MIT's Urban Risk Lab. Prior to this, he was a resident at Autodesk Technology Center in Toronto working on generative design applications for 3D-printed building joinery and landscape redevelopment.

Dr. Brady Peters is an Assistant Professor of architecture at the University of Toronto where he teaches design studio, computation, digital fabrication, and architectural acoustics. He is a director of Smartgeometry, an organization that promotes the use of computation in architecture. After graduating from Dalhousie (MArch 2001), Brady moved to London, England, and worked for Buro Happold and Foster + Partners, where he was an Associate Partner with their research and development team. He received his PhD in architecture from the Royal Danish Academy of Fine Arts in Copenhagen in 2015.

Parametric Model Manipulation in Virtual Reality

Lowering the Barriers of Algorithmic Design in Remote Collaboration

Catarina Brás
INESC-ID, Instituto Superior Técnico, Universidade de Lisboa

Renata Castelo-Branco
INESC-ID, Instituto Superior Técnico, Universidade de Lisboa

António Menezes Leitão
INESC-ID, Instituto Superior Técnico, Universidade de Lisboa

1 Collaborative textual-based algorithmic design in VR mock-up.

ABSTRACT

Algorithmic design (AD) uses algorithms to describe architectural designs, producing results that are visual by nature and greatly benefit from immersive visualization. Having this in mind, several approaches have been developed that allow architects to access and change their AD programs in virtual reality (VR). However, programming in VR introduces a new level of complexity that hinders creative exploration. Solutions based in visual programming offer limited parameter manipulation and do not scale well, particularly when used in a remote collaboration environment, while those based in textual programming struggle to find adequate interaction mechanisms to efficiently modify existing programs in VR.

This research proposes to ease the programming task for architects who wish to develop and experiment with collaborative textual-based AD in VR, by bringing together the user-friendly features of visual programming and the flexibility and scalability of textual programming. We introduce an interface for the most common parametric changes that automatically generates the corresponding code in the AD program, and a hybrid programming solution that allows participants in an immersive collaborative design experience to combine textual programming with this new visual alternative for the parametric manipulation of the design. The proposed workflow aims to foster remote collaborative work in architecture studios, offering professionals of different backgrounds the opportunity to parametrically interact with textual-based AD projects while immersed in them.

VIRTUAL REALITY IN ARCHITECTURE

Virtual reality (VR) is an interaction paradigm where users inhabit a virtual environment (VE), experiencing computer-generated worlds in a deeply immersive manner.

Multiple authors have studied the benefits and challenges of using VR in architecture (Milovanovic et al. 2017; Portman, Natapov, and Fisher-Gewirtzman 2015), generally dividing the range of applications into three main groups: (1) visualization—the ability to create more intuitive and realistic model representations that increase spatial perception (Hermund, Klint, and Bundgård 2018); (2) collaboration—where VR has positive effects in planning time, decision-making, cooperation, and error detection (Drosdol, Kieferle, and Wössner 2003), as well as in long-distance collaborations (Dorta et al. 2011); and (3) the design process itself—where architects enjoy the benefits of VR without having to break the visualization workflow, e.g., virtual reality aided design (VRAD), a design technique that uses VR (Donath and Regenbrecht 1995) for creative ideation (Graessler and Taplick 2019).

Unity Reflect (Unity Technologies n.d.), Twinmotion (Epic Games, Inc. n.d.), and IrisVR Prospect (IrisVR, Inc. n.d.) are examples of tools used for the visualization of realistic models in VR. Even though the first two offer synchronization with 3D models, it is still necessary to remove the VR headset to modify the geometry in the modeling software, or alternatively, have someone operate the software outside VR. Moreover, changes made in VR merely serve visualization purposes, as none are saved to the original model.

Other examples provide live editing options for models in VR. However, most approaches require virtual manual model manipulation (Anderson, Esser, and Interrante 2003; de Klerk et al. 2019) using VR controllers. This modeling workflow tends to be slower than the traditional (digital) one, which in turn is already quite slow and error-prone when systematic changes are needed. There is one design approach, however, that promises to overcome this problem: algorithmic design (AD).

ALGORITHMIC DESIGN

AD is a design process that creates forms through algorithmic descriptions (Caetano, Santos, and Leitão 2020) implemented as computer programs. In practice, AD implies that the architect, instead of modeling a single design solution, creates a design space defined by parameters in the program. Consequently, AD allows for a more flexible design process in which the architect can easily obtain design variations by assigning different values to parameters, causing changes that are automatically propagated through the program (Burry 2011). However, differently from parametric design, AD can go much further by also supporting modifications in the algorithms themselves.

Considering these advantages, many design-oriented programming tools have been developed, and two main paradigms stand out: visual programming (VP) and textual programming (TP).

In VP environments, such as Grasshopper and Dynamo, programs are graphically described. VP simplifies the learning process but lacks scalability (Celani and Vaz 2012), meaning that programs become hard to understand and navigate as they grow in complexity (Janssen 2014). On the other hand, TP languages, like Python or RhinoScript, rely on textual descriptions. In contrast to the former, they support larger-scale projects (Leitão, Santos, and Lopes 2012), although they require more extensive programming knowledge.

In sum, there seems to be no silver bullet, and, as a consequence, this dichotomy is transparently translated in the applications of VR to AD as well.

ALGORITHMIC APPROACHES IN VR

Immersive visualization of models developed through algorithmic processes has been studied in the past (Leitão, Castelo-Branco, and Santos 2019). However, most solutions focus on the visualization of the resulting 3D model, rather than taking advantage of VR as part of the design process. This severely hinders the parametric experimentation process that characterizes AD, forcing users to rely on VR for final showcasing stages only. Furthermore, since we are unable to transport the design workflow to VR, the collaborative potential of the medium is lost.

While inside VR, one serious obstacle to the AD approach comes from the need to modify the program that generates the model, instead of modifying the model itself. While traditional VR experiences may motivate users to manually change the model in front of them, changes to an AD model must be controlled through its algorithmic description or they will be lost upon regeneration of the model. Therefore, the VE should provide adequate mechanisms for this to be possible.

Visual Programming

Within the VP paradigm, there are already solutions for transporting the parametric nature of the design process in the VE. The following ones were implemented on top of Grasshopper: Coppens, Mens, and Gallas (2018)

2

2 Changing the family thickness parameter for all the wall objects: the user adjusts the thickness slider (on the left), saves the changes, and the wall's thickness is updated (on the right).

and Hawton et al.'s (2018) proposals allow users to edit program parameters using sliders. In both cases, sliders are presented in VR through a two-dimensional interface floating in space, where users drag the sliders using VR controllers and immediately visualize the resulting model.

Despite the proven usefulness of parameter calibration in design experimentation, it is frequently necessary to modify the algorithm itself. In the case of Grasshopper, this means changing nodes and connections, which, unfortunately, neither of the previous solutions allow.

Textual Programming

Within the TP paradigm, we can find several solutions for programming in VR. For instance, RiftSketch (Elliott, Peiris, and Parnin 2015) and CodeChisel3D (Krahn 2015) are browser-based live coding environments for VR, where the user can see the graphical results of the program changing alongside it. The application of this concept to architecture was proposed by Castelo-Branco, Leitão, and Santos (2019), with Live Coding in Virtual Reality (LCVR).

In LCVR, architects have access to the entirety of the AD program from the VE, which means they can modify the program's structure just as they could outside the VE. This is achieved by projecting the user's desktop onto the VE, showcasing any programming environment of choice.

Being textual based, however, the LCVR approach has one severe limitation: while changes to visual programs in VR can rely on gripping mechanisms to drag and drop components and wires, changes to textual programs are typically done using a keyboard. Unfortunately, architects find it hard to type in VR with the same performance they would have in the real world, which may compromise the use of this solution as part of the design process after all (Castelo-Branco, Leitão, and Santos 2019).

Considering this analysis, we argue that textual-based AD in VR could benefit from more user-friendly mechanisms for editing AD programs.

PROPOSED SOLUTION

The goal of this research is to incorporate the VR paradigm into the design workflow of textual-based AD, all the while guaranteeing the possibility of remote collaboration, a particularly pressing concern nowadays. We propose an interface for typical parametric manipulations in VR, and its subsequent integration in the collaborative AD workflow. The solution exploits the trade-off required between (1) full control over the program with difficult interaction and (2) a more limited range of action with better interaction. To that end, the proposal is threefold:

1. We introduce a method to support the most common parametric changes that automatically generate the corresponding code in the textual AD program based on the interaction with a graphical user interface (GUI) in VR. This allows users to interact with the program and the model without relying on external equipment for text input.

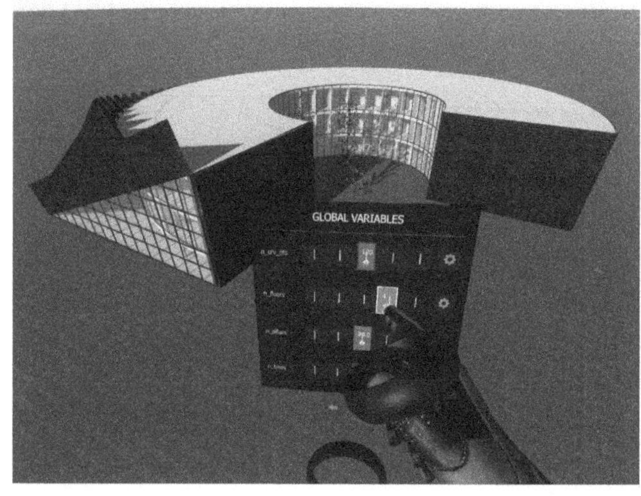

4

3 Adding an object to the scene: the user adds a table object and changes the object's location.

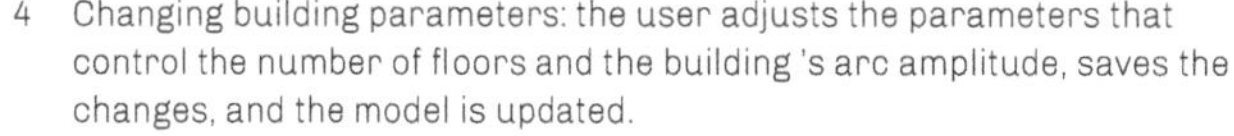
4 Changing building parameters: the user adjusts the parameters that control the number of floors and the building's arc amplitude, saves the changes, and the model is updated.

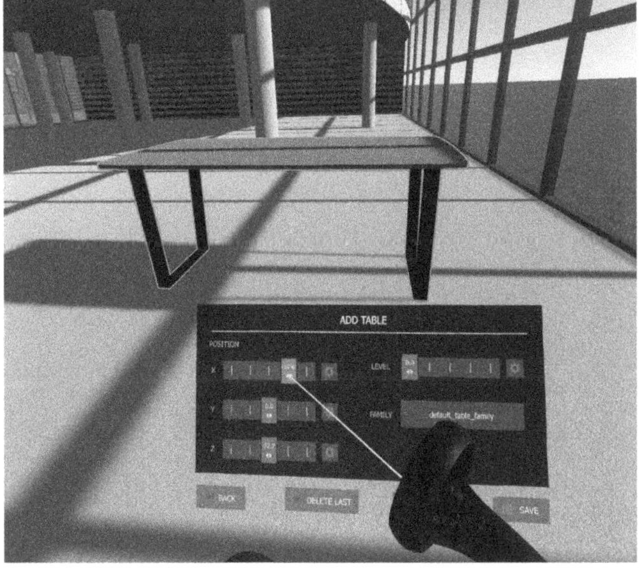

3

2. We explore the potential of a hybrid programming solution that integrates the GUI with an existing workflow for textual-based AD, LCVR, allowing practitioners to access and modify the entirety of their AD programs from VR using a keyboard.

3. We investigate remote collaboration solutions for the hybrid programming approach.

In the following sections we explain the proposal and discuss its applicability, advantages, and limitations.

5 Hybrid workflow: both the interface and the mirrored programming environment are in the user's field of view, so the two can be used.

Graphical User Interface

The first component of the proposed solution aims to ease the task of editing textual AD programs in VR by having architects interact in a more intuitive manner with the design projected around them. The interface allows users to perform common parametric manipulations to the generated objects and their properties without interacting directly with the AD program. For each geometry selected in the VE, the interface presents a range of possible manipulations that can be applied. If any changes are applied to the model, the corresponding code changes are automatically applied in the original AD program in order to guarantee the consistency between program and model. Below, we discuss three common parametric changes architects can perform with the interface. As an example, we use a model inspired by BIG's Business Innovation Hub for the Isenberg School of Management in Amherst, Massachusetts.

1. Object families are a common target for parametric changes, namely their dimensions or materiality. Figure 2 presents an example: the user is immersed in the model and starts by selecting an object, in this case a wall, and a GUI panel with the wall family properties is displayed. Through this panel, the user can modify not only each slider value but also the slider's range and precision. When the new value is chosen and the changes saved, the AD program is updated and the model is rendered anew with the changes applied. Further explanation on the program update process can be found in the "Code Manipulation" section.

2. The GUI also supports adding new objects to the model. We find this to be a common scenario in showcasing or ideation sessions. The opportunity to evaluate the spaces they create in an immersed manner may compel users to fill the space with furniture objects to have a better notion of scale and function (Fig. 3). Alternatively, they may wish to add or manipulate windows or lights to experiment with lighting conditions.

3. To experiment with multiple building variations, it is also possible to adjust parameters that control the model's structure. The interface exposes the current parameter values with sliders so the architect can change them and instantly visualize the outcome. In Figure 4, the user decreases the building's arc amplitude and increases the number of floors. Adjusting these values inside VR provides a better insight for assessing the model's proportions and sizes at full scale.

The presented interface allows users to experiment with different parameters without having to worry about finding the part of the program that needs to be updated, which is especially helpful when the algorithmic description is large and difficult to read. The GUI not only renders the use of keyboards unnecessary but also allows architects to focus exclusively on the task of design experimentation, thus enhancing their creative potential. Furthermore, the use of the GUI can streamline the process in showcasing sessions with clients and other architects who are not familiar with algorithmic approaches, allowing them to visually communicate their ideas to their colleagues directly in the model.

Hybrid Workflow

The presented interface is particularly beneficial to users who are not familiar with programming and to AD practitioners whenever they wish to apply some modification within the scope of the interface. Nevertheless, a programming architect familiar with his program can feel limited by the choices provided.

LCVR's fully textual-based approach, on the other hand, gives access to the entirety of the program from within the VE. With this approach, architects profit from AD's flexibility much like they would while programming outside VR, albeit more slowly, due to the difficulties of keyboard use in VR.

We propose the application of a hybrid workflow, combining the interface with LCVR. Architects can combine both approaches by placing the mirrored programming environment and the interface in different locations of their field of view and switching between one and the other whenever they see fit, as shown in Figure 5.

6

6 Mock-up of the collaborative workflow with a programming architect and a client or a nonprogramming colleague. The former manipulates the program via LCVR and the latter edits it through the interface (top); the architect alone manipulates the program via LCVR or GUI (bottom).

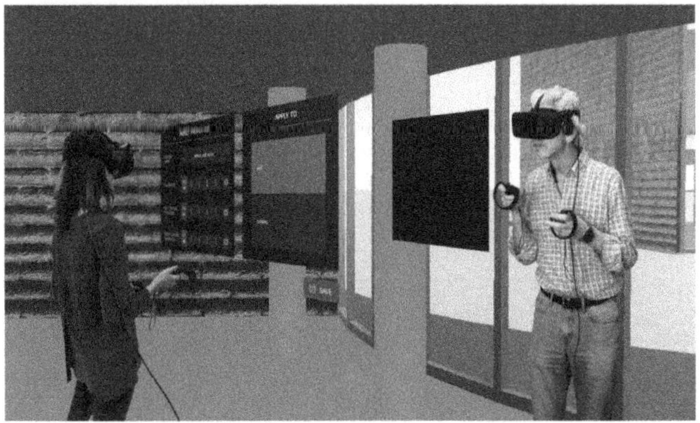

7

7 Mock-up of the collaborative workflow with two or more programming architects using LCVR (top) or the interface (bottom).

Using only LCVR, the user has full control over the program's structure, although this requires setting up a more complex workflow outside VR, namely by sitting down at a desk to access the physical keyboard. With the hybrid approach, the user requires no more setup than the usual VR headset and controllers.

In sum, with this solution, users can choose when they want to interact with the AD program directly, much like the LCVR approach allows, or indirectly, using the interface instead, yet being assured that any indirect changes made are being saved in the program. Architects can also use LCVR to simply visualize the changes in the program caused by the application of a certain modification through the interface.

Collaboration

The proposed workflow supports collaborative scenarios as well. More specifically, we divided them in two, illustrated in Figures 6 and 7, respectively.

In the first one, the programming architect is immersed with the client or any other coworker not skilled in AD. The second participant will likely prefer to use the interface, rather than interacting with the full program (Fig. 6, top), or simply observe and discuss while the architect performs the changes (Fig. 6, bottom).

In the second scenario, we find two or more programming architects working collaboratively, each accessing the AD program through either of the available options. In the case of LCVR (Fig. 7, top), the same program is being showcased in the editor of each participant, and they can track each other in the document, seeing the changes others are making. If they agree to them, they can run them on their side and the model will be rebuilt around them. In this scenario, architects can also use the interface, instead of LCVR, although this is a less collaborative experience (Fig. 7, bottom). Although the AD program is shared among participants, the interfaces are not. Participants are aware of the changes made by others through the code injected in the shared AD program each time a user saves changes using the interface.

IMPLEMENTATION

For the implementation of our solution, we require an AD tool and a visualization tool capable of rendering and providing VR integration. The AD tool chosen was Khepri (Leitão, Castelo-Branco, and Santos 2019), a TP-based tool that offers a direct connection with the game engine Unity, which supports VR. The VR equipment used were the Oculus Quest and the HTC VIVE, both of which include a headset and two controllers.

In order to develop this new approach, three important dimensions of the problem were considered: (1) collaborative programming mechanisms—how the program is shared; (2) interaction design—how the user interacts with the model's design inside the VE; and (3) code manipulation—how the changes made in VR using the GUI are translated to the program.

Collaborative Programming

Typical remote collaboration scenarios in architectural design entail sharing data across the network to ensure all the collaborators are working on the same geometric model. Depending on the tools being used, these models can comprise large amounts of information that will cause inefficient data exchanges and application failure with large data transfers, as reported by Hawton et al. (2018).

The previous problem is solved by collaborative AD, as it only requires sharing the same algorithmic description. The goal is to share the textual AD program that represents the model, instead of the model itself. This not only offers control to all participants but also considerably reduces the data transferred, as AD programs tend to be a lot lighter than the models they generate. To that end, we propose the usage of a programming environment capable of sharing the editor in real time. For this implementation, we chose Atom with the Teletype package (teletype.atom.io 2018).

For safety reasons and to avoid dizziness in VR, we do not automatically run programs on other users' machines. Hence, model updates are not rendered immediately, as it is preferable to have each user decide when to regenerate their version of the model. Therefore, it is useful for participants to share an online conversation throughout this experience, in order to notify each other of changes they may have performed in the program outside the other's view scope. Then both users can reload the program without leaving the VE, using the programming environment (LCVR) or the interface.

Interaction Design

Most literature considers that interaction in VR should feel natural, following metaphors that resemble reality so that the user can quickly learn how the virtual world works. In this sense, it is often advised to avoid the WIMP (Windows, Icons, Menus, Pointer) metaphor commonly found in almost every 2D interface (Nielsen 1993). However, the architectural design domain requires tasks, such as the creation and modification of model elements and the adjustment of numerical values, that cannot be easily mapped onto real-world actions (Bowman and Wingrave 2001). Alternatively, this domain can benefit from simpler techniques such as graphical menus, since users are already familiar with them from the typical software used in the industry.

Taking this into account, we implemented a two-dimensional graphical menu with components for data manipulation using the simple but functional Hover UI Kit (Kinstner 2014). Most parametric manipulations rely on setting numerical values, so sliders are the most frequent components in the interface. Their range and precision are controlled by a submenu that pops up next to the main one. For general system control, such as saving changes and navigating across the interface's menus, buttons were used (Fig. 2).

For input, we took advantage of two-track VR controllers and voice commands. To select model parts, a virtual pointer was implemented using ray-casting (Mine 1995). To interact with the buttons and sliders, the user can either use the virtual pointer (Figs. 2, 3) or the index finger of one of the hands (Fig. 4) holding the controller. The latter option was designed to accommodate other input options, such as hand-tracking devices. Users can also navigate the interface by using voice commands in English. The interface can be placed in a fixed world position or attached to the user's hand.

Code Manipulation

To offer users a way to indirectly apply changes to the AD program, the interface must be capable of inferring the needed changes from the user's interactions and modifying the AD program by carefully injecting additional code in selected places. The flexibility of AD presents a challenge to this approach because there is not just one correct way of solving a problem, hence different programs can produce the same results.

For this implementation, the modifications were restricted to editing object families, adding building elements, and visualizing design variations. The former presents the more complex challenge, which we divided in two phases: (1) locating the part of the program that generated the selected object, and (2) finding the correct scope for the changes, that is, the correct function to update.

To tackle the first problem, we used Khepri's tracing capabilities. Traceability entails the identification of the parts of the program that generated parts of the model. Grasshopper and Dynamo present unidirectional traceability, relating program components to model elements. Khepri, on the other hand, provides bidirectional traceability, meaning users can select program parts and/or model parts and see the corresponding parts highlighted at the other end.

A

```
function first_floor()
  slab(...)
  wall(...)
  wall(...)
  ...
end

function isenberg()
  ground_floor()
  first_floor()
  ...
end

isenberg()
```

B

```
function first_floor()
  slab(...)
  with(wall_thickness=.6)
    wall(...)
  end
  wall(...)
  ...
end

function isenberg()
  ground_floor()
  first_floor()
  ...
end

isenberg()
```

C

```
function first_floor()
  slab(...)
  wall(...)
  wall(...)
  ...
end

function isenberg()
  ground_floor()
  with(wall_thickness=.6)
    first_floor()
  end
  ...
end

isenberg()
```

D

```
function first_floor()
  slab(...)
  wall(...)
  wall(...)
  ...
end

function isenberg()
  ground_floor()
  first_floor()
  ...
end

with(wall_thickness=.6)
 isenberg()
end
```

8 Wall family thickness change listings: (A) original program; (B) change applied to a single wall; (C) change applied to all the walls on the first floor; (D) change applied to all the walls in the building. 8

By selecting a shape in the scene, the traceability module guides us towards the program functions that were invoked to generate that shape. As typically occurs in AD programs, a shape is not the result of a single function call but rather of a sequence of calls. By tracing this sequence back, we find the functions that should be updated.

Functions in AD programs are typically interdependent but also linked in call chains, which means that changing the parameters of an object's family, for instance, can propagate the alteration to other objects of the same family. Depending on the case, this might or might not be the desired result. Therefore, we first present the users with the call chain that created the selected object so that they can choose where the code injection is to be made and, consequently, which parts of the model it affects.

Figure 2 shows an example where the user selected a wall to access its function call. By choosing the *isenberg* function on the right-hand panel, the changes were applied to all the walls in the building. Figure 8 (A) and (D) shows a simplified version of the model's algorithm, before and after this modification, respectively. In this case, the *isenberg* function call is surrounded with code that overrides the value of the default parameters. Figure 8 presents two other possible scenarios where the change affects only the selected wall (B) or all the walls located on the first floor (C). These two scenarios could be achieved by selecting the remaining two options of the right-hand menu shown in Figure 2.

For the creation of objects, the process is simpler: the code for creating the object with the chosen parameters is added to the end of the program. For instance, in Figure 3, the interface simply added a call to the *table* function, with the position values the user chose. The adjustment of parameters is done through the same mechanism as above: the system locates the line where the parameter is defined and updates it with the new value. Seeing design variations implies that the interface prelocates the design's parameters to present them in the VE for the user to manipulate.

CONCLUSION

In this paper, we proposed to support architects who wish to use collaborative textual-based algorithmic design in virtual reality by introducing an interface for the most common changes that automatically generates the corresponding code in the AD program. A hybrid solution was also presented for participants in an immersive collaborative design experience to combine textual programming with a more visual alternative to parametrically manipulate the design.

One of the main benefits of an AD workflow lies on the flexibility architects have when modeling. The Live Coding in Virtual Reality approach (Castelo-Branco, Leitão, and Santos 2019) was intended to transport that same design flexibility into the virtual environment by emulating the textual programming activity in VR. However, it relied on interaction mechanisms outside VR, particularly the usage of a physical keyboard, which is not adequate for this paradigm.

The goal of the proposed solution is to offer a simpler and more user-friendly extension to the LCVR workflow. By using an interface embedded in the VE, users can change the textual algorithmic description of the model around them without having to type in the instructions from the VE. The interface presented does not replace the LCVR approach but rather complements it, since the range of modifications users can apply to their programs is limited to those that benefit from the interface. Limiting the changes made inside the VE can be especially beneficial in contexts where users are not familiar with the program or the textual AD paradigm.

While using an interface in VR is not a novelty, the solution presented here innovates by enabling the use of VR as part of the AD workflow, rather than just a means to evaluate the result. In the end, this approach tries to bring together the user-friendly features of visual programming and the flexibility and scalability of textual programming in a hybrid workflow where users can choose the compromise that best fits each design stage: full control over the program with less adequate interaction mechanisms, or limited control with user-friendly interaction. In both cases, changes applied during design sessions in VR are saved to the AD program.

Despite the advantages of the interface, there is still room for improvement when it comes to interaction mechanisms in VR. More advanced user-interface toolkits that take better advantage of the virtual space can be explored. The implemented ray-casting technique might not be adequate for selecting geometry in large or dense models, as the accuracy decreases when selecting small objects or objects that are far away (Argelaguet and Andujar 2013). Moving objects with sliders in a 3D space can also be replaced with other techniques that take better advantage of the VR paradigm.

While the proposed solution allows users to automatically modify textual AD programs based on adjusting properties and creating new objects, we plan to take this research further by exploring additional mechanisms for VR-based adjustments and by allowing deeper modifications to the program's structure.

Finally, we plan to conduct a formal evaluation to test the usability of this approach and compare it with previous results of both LCVR and traditional coding techniques.

ACKNOWLEDGMENTS

This work was supported by national funds through Fundação para a Ciência e a Tecnologia (FCT) with references UIDB/50021/2020 and PTDC/ART-DAQ/31061/2017.

REFERENCES

Anderson, Lee, James Esser, and Victoria Interrante. 2003. "A Virtual Environment for Conceptual Design in Architecture." In *Proceedings of the Workshop on Virtual Environments*, 57–63. Zurich: ACM.

Argelaguet, Ferran, and Carlos Andujar. 2013. "A Survey of 3D Object Selection Techniques for Virtual Environments." *Computers & Graphics* 37 (3): 121–136.

Bowman, Doug A., and Chadwick A. Wingrave. 2001. "Design and Evaluation of Menu Systems for Immersive Virtual." In *Proceedings of the IEEE Virtual Reality 2001*, 149–156. Yokohama: IEEE Press.

Burry, Mark. 2011. *Scripting Cultures*. United Kingdom: John Wiley & Sons Ltd.

Caetano, Inês, Luís Santos, and António Leitão. 2020. "Computational Design in Architecture: Defining Parametric, Generative, and Algorithmic Design." *Frontiers of Architectural Research* 9 (2): 287–300.

Castelo-Branco, Renata, António Leitão, and Guilherme Santos. 2019. "Immersive Algorithmic Design: Live Coding in Virtual Reality." In *Proceedings of the 37th eCAADe Conference*, 455–464. Porto: eCAADe.

Celani, Gabriela, and Carlos E. V. Vaz. 2012. "CAD Scripting and Visual Programming Languages for Implementing Computational Design Concepts: A Comparison from a Pedagogical Point Of View." *International Journal of Architectural Computing* 10 (1): 121–138.

Coppens, Adrien, Tom Mens, and Mohamed Anis Gallas. 2018. "Parametric Modelling Within Immersive Environments: Building a Bridge Between Existing Tools and Virtual Reality Headsets." In *Proceedings of the 36th eCAADe Conference*, 721–726. Lodz: eCAADe.

Das, Kaushik, and Christoph W. Borst. 2010. "An Evaluation of Menu Properties and Pointing Techniques in a Projection-Based VR Environment." In *Proceedings of the 2010 IEEE Symposium on 3D User Interfaces*, 47–50. Waltham: IEEE Press.

de Klerk, Rui, André M. Duarte, Daniel P. Medeiros, José P. Duarte, Joaquim Jorge, and Daniel S. Lopes. 2019. "Usability Studies on Building Early Stage Architectural Models in Virtual Reality." *Automation in Construction* 103: 104–116.

Donath, Dirk, and Holger Regenbrecht. 1995. "VRAD (Virtual Reality Aided Design) in the Early Phases of the Architectural Design Process." In *Proceedings of the 6th International Conference on CAAD Futures*, 313–322. Singapore: Springer.

Dorta, Tomás, Annemarie Lesage, Edgar Pérez, and J. M. Christian Bastien. 2011. "Signs of Collaborative Ideation and the Hybrid Ideation Space." *Design Creativity 2010*: 199–206.

Drosdol, Johannes, Joachim Kieferle, and Uwe Wössner. 2003. "The Integration of Virtual Reality (VR) into the Architectural Workflow." In *Proceedings of the 21th eCAADe Conference*, 25–28. Graz: eCAADe.

Elliott, Anthony, Brian Peiris, and Chris Parnin. 2015. "Virtual Reality in Software Engineering: Affordances, Applications, and Challenges." In *Proceedings of the 37th IEEE International Conference on Software Engineering*, 547–550. Florence: IEEE Press.

Epic Games, Inc. n.d. *Twinmotion*. Accessed February 15, 2021. https://www.unrealengine.com/en-US/twinmotion.

Graessler, Iris, and Patrick Taplick. 2019. "Supporting Creativity with Virtual Reality Technology." In *Proceedings of the Design Society: International Conference on Engineering Design*, 2011–2020. Delft: Cambridge University Press.

Hawton, Dominic, Ben Cooper-Wooley, Jorke Odolphi, Ben Doherty, Alessandra Fabbri, Nicole Gardner, and M. Hank Haeusler. 2018. "Shared Immersive Environments for Parametric Model Manipulation: Evaluating a Workflow for Parametric Model Manipulation from Within Immersive Virtual Environments." In *Proceedings of the 23rd International CAADRIA Conference*, 483–492. Beijing: CAADRIA.

Hermund, Anders, Lars S. Klint, and Ture S. Bundgård. 2018. "The Perception of Architectural Space in Reality, in Virtual Reality, and through Plan and Section Drawings: A Case Study of the Perception of Architectural Atmosphere." In *Proceedings of the 36th eCAADe Conference*, 735–744. Lodz: eCAADe.

IrisVR, Inc. n.d. *IrisVR Prospect*. Accessed February 15, 2021. https://irisvr.com/prospect/.

Janssen, Patrick. 2014. "Visual Dataflow Modelling: Some thoughts on Complexity." In *Proceedings of the 32nd eCAADe Conference*, 305–314. Newcastle upon Tyne: eCAADe.

Kinstner, Zach. 2014. *Hover-UI-Kit*. Accessed February 15, 2021. https://github.com/aestheticinteractive/Hover-UI-Kit

Krahn, Robert. 2015. "CodeChisel: Live programming with three.js and webVR." Accessed July 12, 2019. https://robert.kra.hn/past-projects/live-programming-with-three-and-webvr.html.

Leitão, António, Renata Castelo-Branco, and Guilherme Santos. 2019. "Game of Renders: The Use of Game Engines for Architectural Visualization." In *Proceedings of the 24th International CAADRIA Conference*, 655–664. Wellington: CAADRIA.

Leitão, António, Luís Santos, and José Lopes. 2012. "Programming Languages for Generative Design: A Comparative Study." *International Journal of Architectural Computing* 10 (1): 139–162.

Milovanovic, Julie, Guillaume Moreau, Daniel Siret, and Francis Miguet. 2017. "Virtual and Augmented Reality in Architectural Design and Education: An Immersive Multimodal Platform to Support Architectural Pedagogy." In *Proceedings of the 17th International Conference on CAAD Futures*, 513–532. Istanbul: Springer.

Mine, Mark R. 1995. "Virtual Environment Interaction Techniques." In *1995 Technical Report*, 1–18. Chapel Hill: University of North Carolina at Chapel Hill.

Nielsen, Jakob. 1993. "Noncommand User Interfaces." *Communications of the ACM* 36 (4): 83–99.

Portman, Michelle E., Asya Natapov, and Dafna Fisher-Gewirtzman. 2015. "To Go Where No Man Has Gone Before: Virtual Reality in Architecture, Landscape Architecture and Environmental Planning." *Computers, Environment and Urban Systems* 54: 376–384.

teletype.atom.io. 2018. *Teletype for Atom*. V.0.13.3. GitHub Inc. https://github.com/atom/teletype.

Unity Technologies. n.d. *Unity Reflect*. Accessed February 15, 2021. https://unity.com/products/unity-reflect.

IMAGE CREDITS

All drawings and images by the authors.

Catarina Brás is a Master's student in Computer Science and Engineering at Instituto Superior Técnico of the University of Lisbon, specializing in Cybersecurity. She is currently an intern at INESC-ID, working with virtual reality for algorithmic design.

Renata Castelo-Branco is a Master's graduate in architecture from Instituto Superior Técnico of the University of Lisbon, a junior researcher at INESC-ID, and a Computer Science and Engineering PhD student at the same university. She also studied at the Technical University of Graz (Austria) during her master's. She is currently researching representation methods for algorithmic design.

António Menezes Leitão has a BSc in Mechanical Engineering, an MSc in Electronics Engineering, and a PhD in Computer Science and Engineering, all from Instituto Superior Técnico of the University of Lisbon. Currently, he is Assistant Professor at the same university, senior researcher at INESC-ID, within the Graphics and Interaction Group, and coordinator of the Algorithmic Design for Architecture (ADA) group, teaching, lecturing, and performing research on bringing together the fields of computer science and architecture.

Impact of Robotic 3D Printing Process Parameters on Bond Strength

A Systematic Analysis Using Clay-Based Materials

Mehdi Farahbakhsh
Texas A&M University

Negar Kalantar
California College of the Arts

Zofia Rybkowski
Texas A&M University

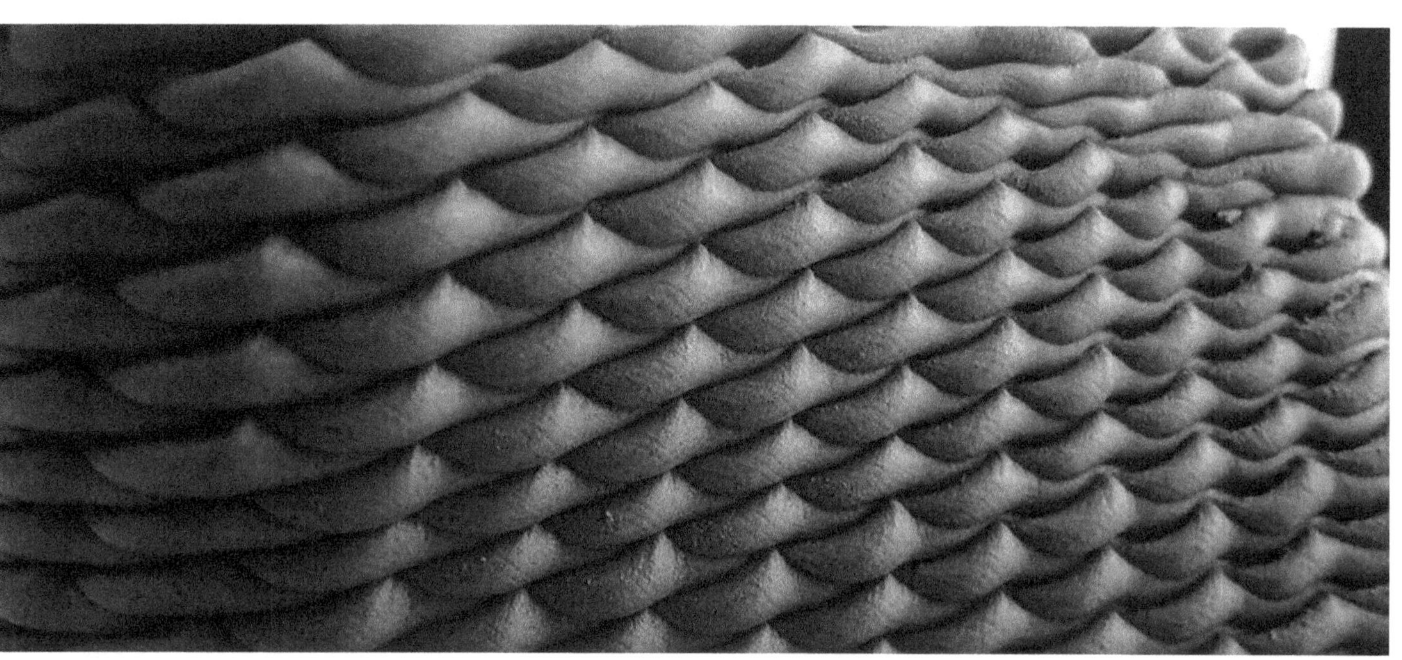

1 A pattern created through the proposed workflow was expected to improve the structural integrity on the mezzo scale.

ABSTRACT

Additive manufacturing (AM), also known as 3D printing, offers advantages over traditional construction technologies, increasing material efficiency, fabrication precision, and speed. However, many AM projects in academia and industrial institutions do not comply with building codes. Consequently, they are not considered safe structures for public utilization and have languished as exhibition prototypes.

While three discrete scales—micro, mezzo, and macro—are investigated for AM with paste in this paper, structural integrity has been tackled on the mezzo scale to investigate the impact of process parameters on the bond strength between layers in an AM process. Real-world material deposition in a robotic-assisted AM process is subject to environmental factors such as temperature, humidity, the load of upper layers, the pressure of the nozzle on printed layers, etc. Those factors add a secondary geometric characteristic to the printed objects that was missing in the initial digital model.

This paper introduces a heuristic workflow for investigating the impacts of three selective process parameters on the bond strength between layers of paste in the robotic-assisted AM of large-scale structures. The workflow includes a method for adding the secondary geometrical characteristic to the initial 3D model by employing X-ray computerized tomography (CT) scanning, digital image processing, and 3D reconstruction. Ultimately, the proposed workflow offers a pattern library that can be used by an architect or artificial intelligence (AI) algorithms in automated AM processes to create robust architectural forms.

INTRODUCTION

There is no doubt that the future of architectural fabrication has strong ties to climate-change concerns and breakthrough technologies and materials for sustainable construction. Thirty-nine percent of global energy-related emissions come from the building industry, and concrete industries are responsible for 8% of all CO_2 emissions (IEA 2019). Therefore, a reliable substitution is urgently needed to address those concerns. On the other hand, despite the advent of a range of new construction materials, the challenges and opportunities of using local materials have become a hot topic again (Bajpayee et al. 2020).

Additive manufacturing (AM), commonly referred to as 3D printing, is the process of constructing objects from three-dimensional model data, in which the material is horizontally extruded and deposited layer by layer (ASTM International 2013; Guo and Leu 2013). The precise, computer-controlled deposition of material has enabled AM processes to reduce resource consumption, speed up construction processes, and reduce total construction costs compared to conventional large-scale construction. Buswell et al. (2007), however, argued that neither speed nor cost are critical reasons for the growing interest in AM for large-scale construction; its popularity is more likely due to enhanced functional performance and geometrically rich building elements.

This paper is part of a more extensive study on robotic-assisted AM of scaffold-free shell structures using a clay-based material. The main research introduces three scales—micro, mezzo, and macro—that are responsible for material properties, binding between layers, and the geometry of architectural forms, respectively (Bajpayee et al. 2020) (Fig. 2). This paper focuses on the mezzo scale (Fig. 3) and introduces a novel workflow to investigate impacts of process parameters on the bond strength between layers of paste in robotic-assisted AM processes, evaluates the results, and creates a reliable benchmark for future research.

The workflow elaborates a process to discover a pattern derived from the manipulations of three selected process parameters and investigate their impacts on the bond strength between layers of paste in AM. Finding such a pattern will facilitate the prediction of the properties of objects printed in similar conditions.

BACKGROUND

During the last decade, AM has greatly improved and found several applications in the jewelry, pottery, aerospace, motor vehicle, medical, and architecture industries, to

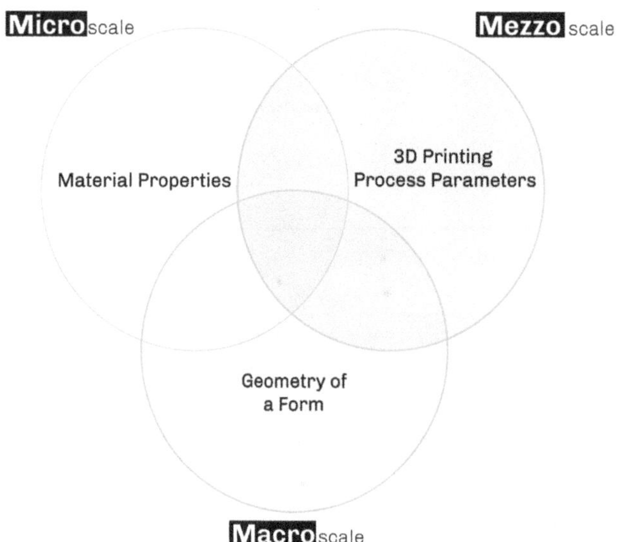

2

3

2 Three major areas for investigating AM with paste: material properties on micro scale; process parameters on mezzo scale; and the geometry of a form on the macro scale.

3 The interface between layers is categorized on the mezzo scale in this research.

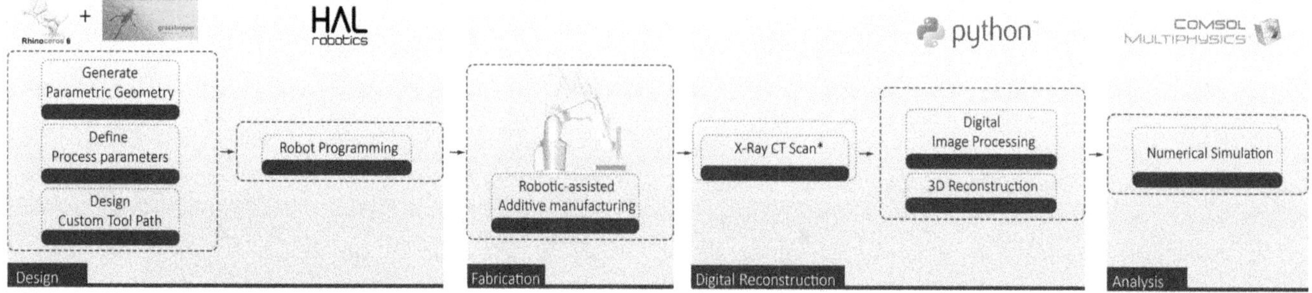

4

name a few (Bhardwaj et al. 2019; Buchanan and Gardner 2019; Gosselin et al. 2016; Khoshnevis 2004). The use of AM in architecture and construction can be summarized in the following three project categories (Gosselin et al. 2016):

1 .The Contour Crafting project, developed by researchers at the University of Southern California (Khoshnevis 2004), utilizes a cementitious material. This project is based on generating a formwork by 3D printing of two layers and then filling the formwork with concrete.

2. The concrete printing project at Loughborough University (Buswell et al. 2007), like the Contour Crafting project, also uses a nozzle mounted on a three-axis crane for material deposition.

3. The D-Shape project by Enrico Dini (Cesaretti et al. 2014) uses binder jetting technology. Binder jetting is an AM process wherein a liquid bonding agent is deposited on a layer of powder (ASTM International 2013).

D-Shape technology also uses a three-axis overhead crane to deposit the binding agent and selectively solidify a large-scale sand bed. In this technique, the powder material serves as additional support to other mentioned technologies. Once the printing process is over, the printed piece is taken out, and the remaining powder material can be used in the process again (Cesaretti et al. 2014; Gosselin et al. 2016). In terms of structural features in an AM process, Zareiyan and Khoshnevis (2017) investigated the role of material in interlayer adhesion and strength in the Contour Crafting process. Gosselin et al. (2016) mentioned the geometric impact of the print strategy and the crucial role of nozzle orientation in the binding between layers.

The binding between horizontal layers has a significant impact on the structural integrity of printed objects. The bond strength between layers can be adjusted by manipulating process parameters (e.g., the speed of the printhead, the rate of material deposition, the distance between the nozzle and the print surface, to name a few). While some of these parameters have been investigated by researchers (Bos et al. 2016; Buswell et al. 2018; Gosselin et al. 2016; Zareiyan and Khoshnevis 2017), the geometry of layers with respect to the binding between them has not yet been sufficiently treated in detail, nor applied to construction projects.

WORKFLOW STEPS

The proposed workflow is an experimental approach that hypothesizes that the manipulations of process parameters impact the bond strength between layers in AM. Three independent process parameters that have not been extensively studied in the literature were systematically manipulated in this paper. The bond strength between layers served as the dependent variable and was measured through the novel digital analysis workflow. The workflow includes four distinct steps: design, fabrication, digital reconstruction, and analysis (Fig. 4).

Design

Eight process parameters in a robotic-assisted AM process were recognized and are elaborated upon in a chart (Fig. 5). Manipulations of the process parameters have geometric impacts on printed objects. Indeed, designing an architectural form to be built with paste in an AM process provides the opportunity to include the process parameters in the design phase. These process parameters consist of parameters related to the programming of the robot, for instance, custom tool pathing and the speed of the robot, as well as

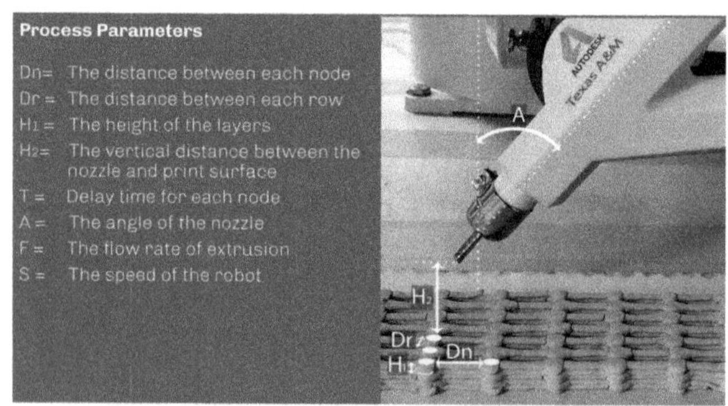

5

6

4 The proposed workflow includes four distinct steps: design, fabrication, digital reconstruction, and analysis.

5 Eight process parameters.

6 Manipulation of only one process parameter, while the other parameters remain constant, is shown in these images. The H_2 parameter (the vertical distance between the nozzle and print surface) is one of the selected process parameters that was studied in this paper.

material deposition considerations such as the extrusion flow rate and the distance between the nozzle and the print surface, to name a few. Among these eight process parameters, five have been comprehensively investigated in prior studies (Bos et al. 2016; Buswell et al. 2018; Wangler et al. 2016) and remained constant values in the current work. The following three selected process parameters (Fig. 6), however, required additional study and have been systematically varied in this research to examine their impact on printed prototypes:

- Dn: Distance between each node
- H_2: Vertical distance between the nozzle and print surface
- T: Delay time at each node

Fabrication

The material deposition process in a real-world environment is subject to environmental factors. Those factors add a secondary geometrical characteristic to the specimens that is missing in the initial digital model. The second step in the workflow is to physically build the digital models designed and programmed in the first step.

While most of the AM projects with concrete use progressive cavity pumps for their material delivery system, the clay-based material used in this research was not a self-flowing material. Therefore, a custom material delivery system consisting of both pneumatic and mechanical pressures was employed to create a linear pressure and to guarantee a consistent flow of material at the extruder head. An ABB robotic arm was programmed for this step, and the selected process parameters were systematically manipulated to study challenges and potentials of each pattern (Fig. 7).

While each parameter has a meaningful range of values, applying values out of that interval would cause undesired irregularities in the printed object (Fig. 8). For instance, the interparticle adhesion of the paste is low. When the H_2 parameter is more than 600% of the nozzle diameter, it leads to filament tears due to the local shear application. On the other hand, when the H_2 parameter is less than 40% of the nozzle diameter, it results in excessive material deposition along the tool path. This happens because the yield stress of the paste material is low while the pressure at the nozzle tip is high. Therefore, values less than the defined minimum value create a pressure gradient and cause the material to squirt. This will cause material accumulation around the nozzle, and when it continues along the tool path, it will decrease the accuracy of material deposition and result in failure of the print process. That means the H_2 parameter is limited to 40% of the nozzle diameter < H_2 < 600% of the nozzle diameter.

Digital Reconstruction

The third step is reconstructing a digital 3D model from the printed objects (Fig. 9). The main challenge here is that initial digital models generated in the software are not adequate for reliable analysis since they lack the impacts

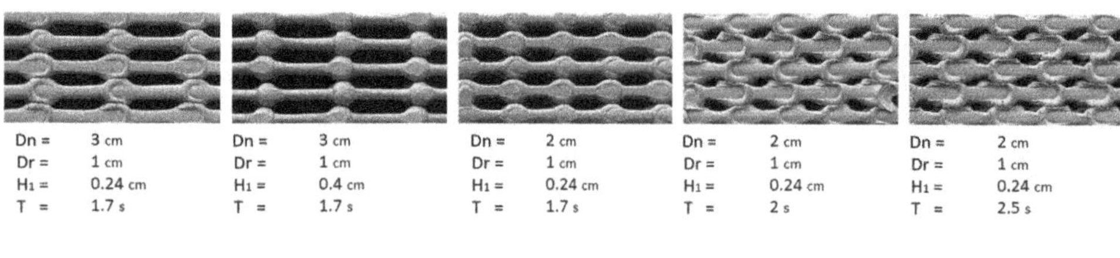

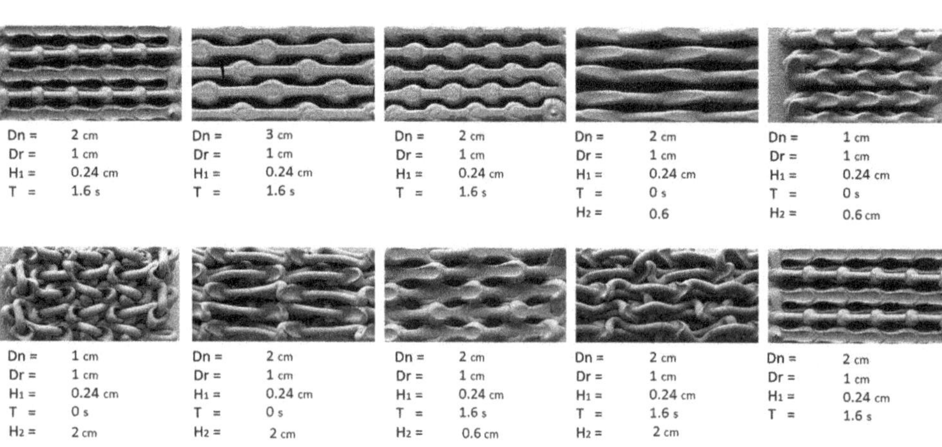

7

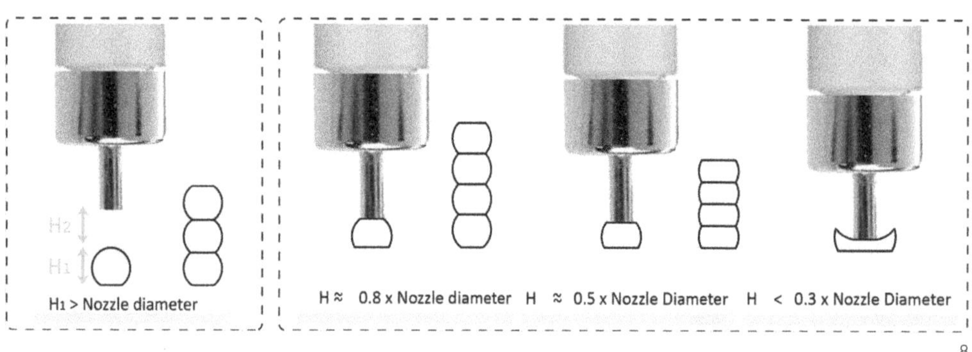

8

7 Manipulations of process parameters have geometrical impacts on the material deposition process and create different patterns.

8 Schematic boundary of the H_1 and H_2 parameters.

of the environmental factors as discussed in the previous step. Accordingly, the digital reconstruction step that includes X-ray CT scanning, digital image processing, and 3D reconstruction was developed to attach the secondary geometrical characteristic to the initial digital model.

- Scanning

There are several techniques for creating a visual representation of an object. While techniques like photogrammetry utilize photographs to visualize the outer surface of an object, other imaging modalities like X-ray CT scanning and magnetic resonance imaging (MRI) use X-ray, magnetic fields, and radio waves to produce more detailed, cross-sectional images of both the inner and outer contours of an object (Kalender 2011). X-ray CT scan technology was used for the 3D reconstruction of the printed objects to create a detailed visualization of each specimen (Fig. 11). The outcome of the X-ray CT scanning is a series of 2D images and almost 1,100 gray-scale images for each specimen in this paper, which were used to create voxel-based 3D models. The axial resolution of the scan (slice thickness) was set to 0.245 mm to create high-resolution images. As a granular material, table sugar was used to improve the accuracy of the scan process and provide a transition from a low-density environment (air) into a dense material (clay) (Fig. 10).

- Digital image processing

An algorithm was developed in Python to extract the object from the 2D images. The algorithm used image segmentation techniques to create a mask that includes the printed object in each image based on a given threshold. In other words, the created mask contains only those pixels of the gray-scale image with a brightness value in the range of the given threshold.

- 3D reconstruction

Ultimately, a 3D mesh of each specimen was calculated from the defined mask. Each pixel of the 2D image in the segmentation step defines a cube in a 3D space called a voxel. The models in this paper had a voxel size of (x/y/z) 0.254/0.254/0.254 mm. The method of creating a polygon

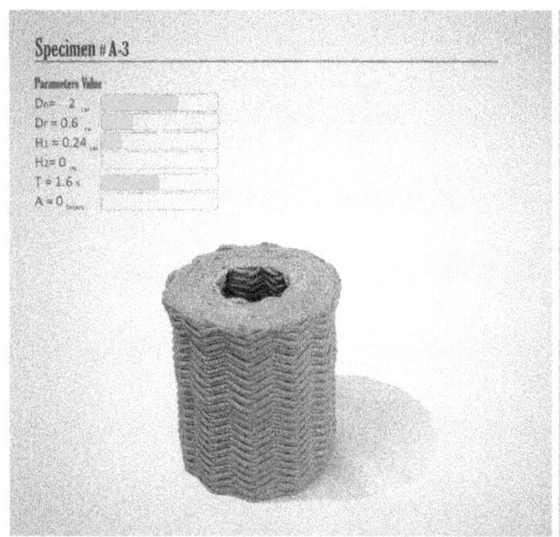

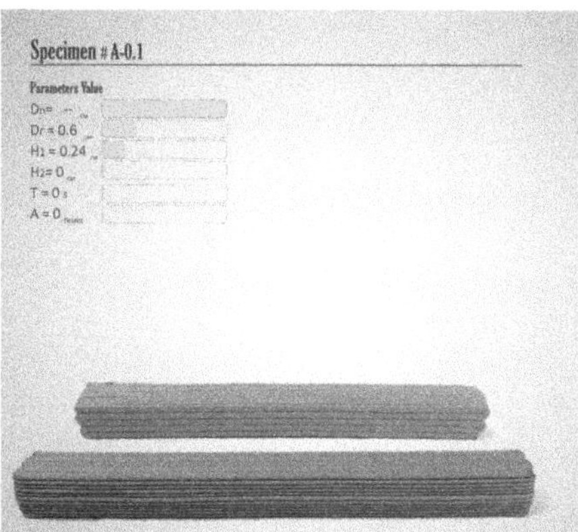

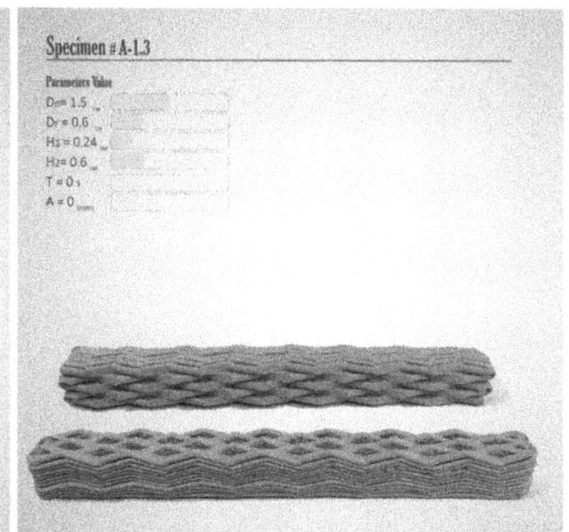

9

10

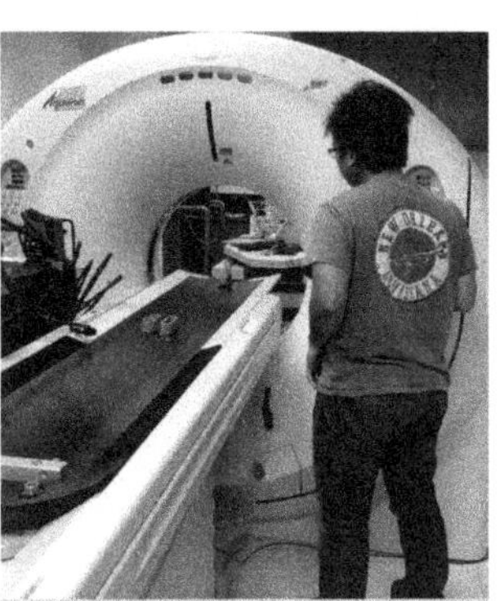

11

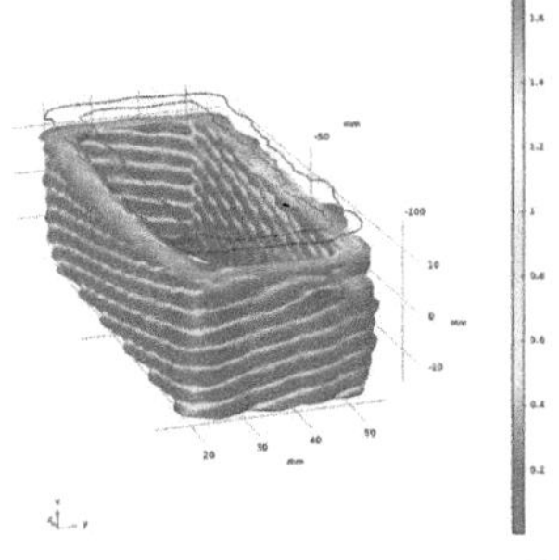

12

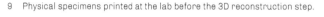

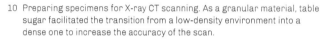

9 Physical specimens printed at the lab before the 3D reconstruction step.

10 Preparing specimens for X-ray CT scanning. As a granular material, table sugar facilitated the transition from a low-density environment into a dense one to increase the accuracy of the scan.

11 X-ray CT scanning for digital reconstruction and analysis.

12 COMSOL Multiphysics, a finite element analysis software, was used for numerical simulations and the final analysis.

mesh from a voxel-based geometry has been explained by Brown et al. (2019) and will be briefly described here. The voxel to mesh conversion algorithm calculates whether a triangular surface passes through a voxel or not. This procedure is also known as the "Marching Cubes" algorithm, where it creates a triangular surface for a 3D model.

Since finite element analysis (FEA), a numerical method for analyzing engineering and mathematical modeling, was performed in this paper, the reconstructed mesh models should be optimized for the analysis step. The triangular surfaces created in this step were slightly modified to fix small inclusions, inverted normals, small gaps, and unconnected and intersecting triangles. Those modifications were necessary toward the FEA, where an enveloping surface is required.

Analysis

What is significant about the final step is the emphasis of the workflow on evaluating the bond strength between layers and creating a library based on the patterns created in the previous steps. COMSOL Multiphysics (COMSOL Inc. 2020), a finite element analysis software, was used for numerical simulations and the final analysis (Fig. 12).

While the research objective is to assess the bond strength between layers, the shear force is the most important area for the investigation. The flexural strength test of concrete and mortar has been adopted to evaluate each pattern. The primary test is the standard test method of ASTM C78 (concrete) and C580 (mortar) (ASTM International 2013) that specifies the modulus of rupture in MPa (Fig. 13).

The flexural test was simulated in COMSOL to evaluate the bond strength between layers for the 3D-reconstructed models. The four-point load condition was simulated, and associated load boundaries were applied to the 3D mesh models. Simulating point forces are possible in COMSOL, where a force is applied to a single point on the surface of the geometry, although point forces do not exist in the real world and result in infinite stresses in theory. In the digital analysis step in this paper, forces are distributed over small patches on the mesh surface instead to simulate what happens in the physical flexural test in the lab.

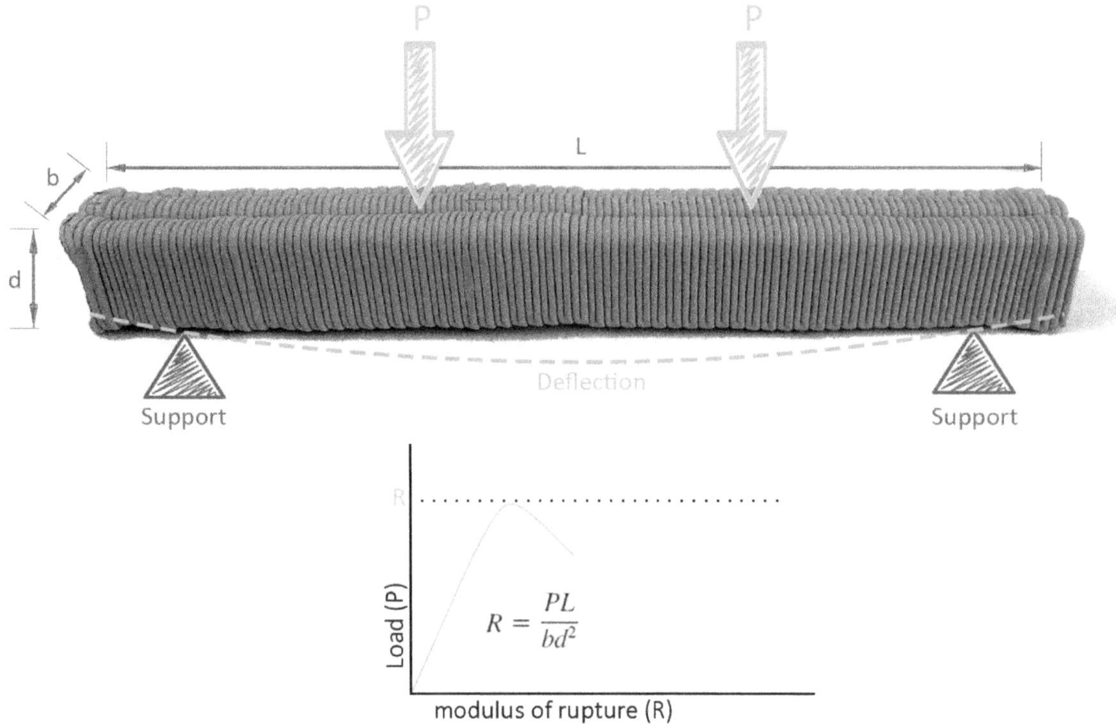

R = modulus of rupture, MPa [psi]
P = maximum applied load indicated by the testing machine, N [lbf]
L = span length, mm [in.]
b = average width of specimen, at the fracture, mm [in.]
d = average depth of specimen, at the fracture, mm [in.]

13 Customized flexural test, ASTM C78 and C580, to evaluate the bond strength between layers of paste in AM. 13

The test provides values for the modulus of rupture for each pattern applied to the specimens.

$$R = PL / bd^2$$

P is the maximum force applied, *L* is the length of the specimen, *b* is the specimen's width, and *d* represents the depth of the specimen. Higher modulus rupture values reflect better bond strength between layers. Each pattern was evaluated based on the given constraints, and a library was created accordingly for use in future research (Fig. 14).

Additional Step

One question remains to be answered: To what extent are the results of the analysis close to reality? Although digital modeling, simulation, and analysis have made it faster and easier to design and make predictions about the results for an architectural fabrication, the accuracy of those predictions needs to be evaluated and generalized for future applications. A series of physical tests were designed based on the four-point flexural strength test to calibrate and evaluate the reliability of the proposed workflow. The various patterns resulting from the three selected process parameters' manipulations were applied to a 2 in × 2 in × 11 in beam-shape geometry to evaluate the bond strength between layers. All the samples were robotically 3D-printed with clay and were used in the physical tests. The comparison between digital and physical tests confirmed, with a small margin of error, the reliability of the workflow.

DISCUSSION

The previous research on improving structural features and expanding architectural applications of large-scale AM processes emphasize different scales of the topic. There is no doubt that paste materials, due to their flexibility, have plenty of potential for creating architectural free forms. However, some issues in using paste materials in AM processes, such as cold joints, reinforcement, and aesthetics, need to be taken into consideration. They can be addressed through approaches like material optimization on the micro scale, and geometrical considerations in design, form optimization, etc., on the mezzo and macro scales. The binding between layers in AM can be improved on both the micro and mezzo scales. The authors have offered a geometric solution for the issue by involving the selected process parameters in the design process. It is worth mentioning that the proposed workflow offers a pattern library, not just a final or ultimate pattern. There is no single best pattern. Rather, there would be an optimum choice that an architect or an AI algorithm can choose based on the given geometry and applied forces. For example, in a surface with dominant shear forces, the optimum pattern would be different from a vertical surface at the corner of a form, where compression forces are most influential. While the current paper focuses on developing the workflow, future publications will elaborate on the results and findings of the digital analysis explained in this paper.

CONCLUSION

The main objective of the current paper is to investigate the structural integrity of an AM process on a mezzo scale through manipulations of process parameters. A novel workflow was presented to include process parameters in the design process and introduced a digital analysis procedure for robotic-assisted AM with paste. In addition to X-ray scanning, image processing techniques have been employed to scrutinize the impacts of environmental stimuli on the printed objects and reconstruct the digital model. The impacts of manipulations of the three selected process parameters on the binding between layers were digitally analyzed, and they indicated that these manipulations did improve the bond strength between layers in AM with paste. Finally, a pattern library was offered for use in robotic-assisted AM processes with paste.

ACKNOWLEDGMENTS

This work was partially funded by the X-Grants Program: A President's Excellence Fund Initiative at Texas A&M University. In addition, the authors appreciate the generous support of Autodesk technology center in San Francisco.

REFERENCES

ASTM International. 2013. *F2792-12a—Standard Terminology for Additive Manufacturing Technologies*. West Conshohocken, PA. Rapid Manufacturing Association. https://doi.org/10.1520/F2792-12A.

Bajpayee, Aayushi, Mehdi Farahbakhsh, Umme Zakira, Aditi Pandey, Lena Abu Ennab, Zofia Rybkowski, Manish Kumar Dixit, et al. 2020. "In Situ Resource Utilization and Reconfiguration of Soils into Construction Materials for the Additive Manufacturing of Buildings." *Frontiers in Materials* 7 (March): 1–12. https://doi.org/10.3389/fmats.2020.00052.

Bhardwaj, Abhinav, Scott Z Jones, Negar Kalantar, Zhijian Pei, John Vickers, Timothy Wangler, Pablo Zavattieri, and Na Zou. 2019. "Additive Manufacturing Processes for Infrastructure Construction: A Review." *Journal of Manufacturing Science and Engineering* 141 (9). https://doi.org/10.1115/1.4044106.

Bos, Freek, Rob Wolfs, Zeeshan Ahmed, and Theo Salet. 2016. "Additive Manufacturing of Concrete in Construction: Potentials and Challenges of 3D Concrete Printing." *Virtual and Physical Prototyping* 11 (3): 209–225. https://doi.org/10.1080/17452759.2016.1209867.

Brown, Justin L, Takuya Furuta, and Wesley E Bolch. 2019. "A Robust Algorithm for Voxel-to-Polygon Mesh Phantom Conversion." In *Brain and Human Body Modeling: Computational Human Modeling at EMBC 2018*, edited by Sergey Makarov, Marc Horner, and Gregory Noetscher, 317–327. Cham: Springer International Publishing. https://doi.org/10.1007/978-3-030-21293-3_17.

Buchanan, C., and L. Gardner. 2019. "Metal 3D Printing in Construction: A Review of Methods, Research, Applications, Opportunities and Challenges." *Engineering Structures* 180: 332–348. https://doi.org/10.1016/j.engstruct.2018.11.045.

Buswell, R. A., W R Leal De Silva, S. Z. Jones, J. Dirrenberger, W. R. Leal de Silva, S. Z. Jones, and J. Dirrenberger. 2018. "3D Printing Using Concrete Extrusion: A Roadmap for Research." *Cement and Concrete Research* 112 (October 2017): 37–49. https://doi.org/10.1016/j.cemconres.2018.05.006.

Buswell, R. A., R. C. Soar, A. G F Gibb, and A. Thorpe. 2007. "Freeform Construction: Mega-Scale Rapid Manufacturing for Construction." *Automation in Construction* 16 (2): 224–231. https://doi.org/10.1016/j.autcon.2006.05.002.

Cesaretti, Giovanni, Enrico Dini, Xavier De Kestelier, Valentina Colla, and Laurent Pambaguian. 2014. "Building Components for an Outpost on the Lunar Soil by Means of a Novel 3D Printing Technology." *Acta Astronautica* 93: 430–450. https://doi.org/10.1016/j.actaastro.2013.07.034.

COMSOL Inc. 2020. *COMSOL Multiphysics*. V.5.6. https://www.comsol.com/comsol-multiphysics.

Gosselin, C., R. Duballet, Ph Roux, N. Gaudillière, J. Dirrenberger, and Ph Morel. 2016. "Large-Scale 3D Printing of Ultra-High Performance Concrete—a New Processing Route for Architects and Builders." *Materials and Design* 100: 102–109. https://doi.org/10.1016/j.matdes.2016.03.097.

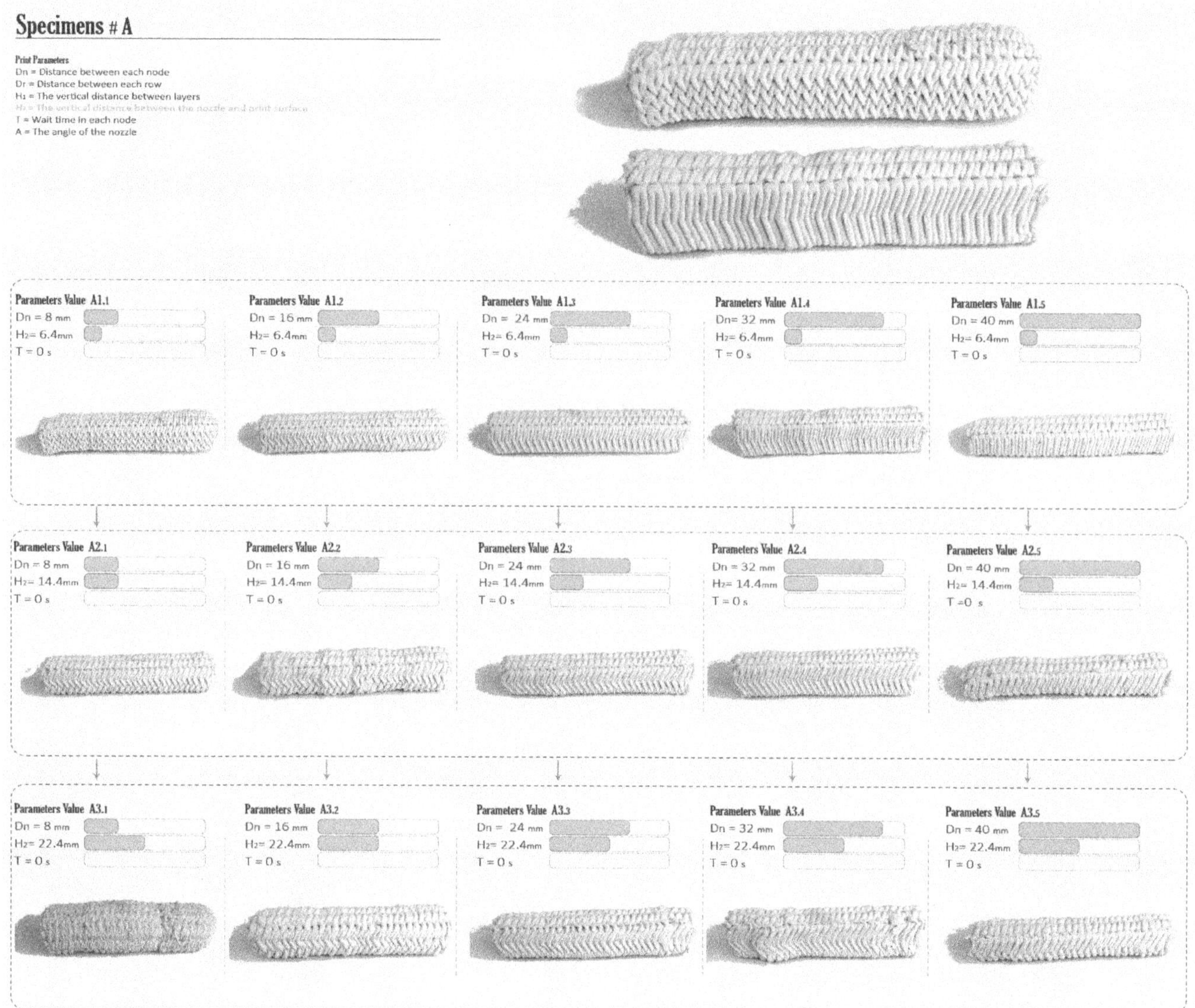

14 The proposed pattern library to be used by an architect or an AI algorithm based on architectural forms and structural requirements.

14

Guo, Nannan, and Ming C. Leu. 2013. "Additive Manufacturing: Technology, Applications and Research Needs." *Frontiers of Mechanical Engineering* 8 (3): 215–243. https://doi.org/10.1007/s11465-013-0248-8.

IEA. 2019. "World Energy Outlook 2019." IEA, Paris. https://www.iea.org/reports/world-energy-outlook-2019.

Kalender, Willi A. 2011. *Computed Tomography: Fundamentals, System Technology, Image Quality, Applications*. Erlangen: Publicis.

Khoshnevis, Behrokh. 2004. "Automated Construction by Contour Crafting, Related Robotics and Information Technologies." *Automation in Construction* 13: 5–19. https://doi.org/10.1016/j.autcon.2003.08.012.

Wangler, Timothy, Ena Lloret, Lex Reiter, Norman Hack, Fabio Gramazio, Matthias Kohler, Mathias Bernhard, et al. 2016. "Digital Concrete: Opportunities and Challenges." *RILEM Technical Letters* 1: 67–75. https://doi.org/10.21809/rilemtechlett.2016.16.

Zareiyan, Babak, and Behrokh Khoshnevis. 2017. "Interlayer Adhesion and Strength of Structures in Contour Crafting: Effects of Aggregate Size, Extrusion Rate, and Layer Thickness." *Automation in Construction* 81: 112–121. https://doi.org/10.1016/j.autcon.2017.06.013.

IMAGE CREDITS

All drawings and photographs were created by the authors.

Mehdi Farahbakhsh is currently a PhD candidate and a lecturer in the College of Architecture and a researcher at the Center for Infrastructure Renewal at Texas A&M University. His research focuses on the robotic-assisted fabrication of scaffold-free shell structures, human-robot collaboration, and digital fabrication technologies. Mehdi holds a master's degree in architecture and worked as an architect for eight years in the Middle East and designed more than one million square feet of commercial and residential buildings.

Negar Kalantar's research and practice lie at the intersection of architecture, science, and engineering. Her current research focuses on applications of additive manufacturing technology and 3D printing as a catalyst for innovation to expand new ways of design in interactive and responsive environments. At Digital Craft Lab, Dr. Kalantar's cross-disciplinary research is to bridge the recent advancements in additive and robotic manufacturing technologies with large-scale structures. She focuses on applications of robots in additive manufacturing technology as a catalyst for shifting not just how infrastructures are constructed today but also transforming the way infrastructures are designed and built in the future from beginning to end.

Zofia Rybkowski is an Associate Professor in the Department of Construction Science of the College of Architecture at Texas A&M University and holds an endowed Harold Adams Interdisciplinary Professorship. Her current research interest on innovations in construction, including automation and 3D printing of large-scale structures in the built environment, is driven by a recognition that industry-wide transformations should be done in alignment with environmental sustainability and social responsibility. Dr. Rybkowski holds degrees from Stanford, Brown, Harvard, the Hong Kong University of Science and Technology, and UC Berkeley, where she earned a PhD. Her interdisciplinary background facilitates system-level research intersecting disciplinary boundaries.

Engrained Performance

Ryan Craney
University of Michigan
Arash Adel
University of Michigan

Performance-Driven Computational Design of a Robotically Assembled Shingle Facade System

1 Performance-driven, fabrication-aware wood shingle facade.

ABSTRACT

This project presents a novel fabrication-aware and performance-driven computational design method that facilitates the design and robotic fabrication of a wood shingle facade system. The research merges computational design, robotic fabrication, and building facade optimization into a seamless digital design-to-fabrication workflow.

The research encompasses the following topics: (1) a constructive system integrating the rules, constraints, and dependencies of conventional shingle facades; (2) an integrative computational design method incorporating material, robotic fabrication, and assembly constraints; (3) an optimization method for facade sun shading; and (4) a digital design-to-fabrication workflow informing the robotic fabrication procedures.

The result is an integrative computational design method for the design of a wood shingle facade. Environmental analysis and multi-objective optimization are coupled with a variable facade surface to produce several optimal design solutions that conform to the constraints of the robotic setup and constructive system. When applied to architectural design, the proposed integrative computational design method demonstrates significant improvements in facade sun-shading performance while also linking the digital design to the fabrication process.

INTRODUCTION

Wood light-frame construction accounts for nearly 95% of single-family homes in the United States, resulting in the construction of over one million new structures each year (United States Census Bureau 2019). Despite their popularity, light-frame structures are still designed using construction conventions that have remained mostly unchanged since the mid-19th century (Schindler 2007). However, recent advances in robotic fabrication, computational design, and environmental analysis provide opportunities to evaluate and rethink framing conventions.

Robotic fabrication technologies offer nonstandard variability for wood construction, as shown in the existing research (Adel et al. 2018; Alvarez et al. 2019; Vercruysse 2020). These projects demonstrated that the use of robotic arms in the production of nonstandard wood structures offers the potential to extend beyond the technical aspects of construction to enable integrative design approaches for creating novel architecture. In this way, nonstandard construction can "close the gap between design and making through assembly, which is enabled by integrative computational design methods and robotic manufacturing technologies" (Adel Ahmadian 2020, 3).

Beyond qualitative design criteria, quantitative metrics—such as material use and structural integrity—can be used to guide the architectural design process, assist the designer in navigating the solution space, and develop design solutions that outperform conventional solutions. This idea has been researched and demonstrated in previous research projects, such as The Sequential Roof (Apolinarska 2018) and the DFAB HOUSE (Adel Ahmadian 2020). Building on the results of these precedents, the research presented in this paper asks: How can nonstandard robotic construction contribute to increased building performance? And how can a prototypical computational design method utilize climate-based performance optimization to accomplish this increase?

To investigate these questions, the research focuses on the building envelope—more specifically, a wood shingle facade system—as a case study. It can be argued that the facade is the most critical component of an architectural design in terms of overall building performance (American Institute of Architects 2019). Thus, the facade can be considered as an ideal application for quantitative performance improvements. MAS House (Eversmann 2017; Eversmann, Gramazio, and Kohler 2017) and Latitudo Borealis (Junghans et al. 2018) are two examples of projects investigating facade performance using nonstandard variability through water-shedding and radiation analyses.

The presented research seeks to further improve the thermal performance of a wood shingle facade system by incorporating sun-shading analysis and multi-objective optimization into a prototypical fabrication-aware computational design method.

Climate-based performance optimization has become increasingly accessible with the emergence of environmental simulation software and multi-objective optimization solvers. Several recent projects have investigated the use of single-objective optimization in facade design (Junghans et al. 2018; Wortmann 2017), yet the complexity of season-based sun-shading analysis might be better suited for a multi-objective optimization workflow. Whereas single-objective optimizations can be used to search for the minima or maxima of a single performance value, a multi-objective optimization is capable of balancing multiple conflicting objectives (i.e., summer and winter performance values) (Kocabay and Alaçam 2017).

When working with optimization workflows and nonstandard construction, an integrative computational design method ensures that the solution space meets the constraints of the fabrication process. As defined by Menges, integrative computational design is "a computational design approach that synthesizes performance-oriented form generation and physical processes of materialization" (Menges 2011, 73). In the context of robotic fabrication, these physical processes must satisfy the robotic constraints such as buildable volume and orientation, as well as the limitations of the materials and constructive systems (Junghans et al. 2018). By integrating these constraints into the computational model, the presented fabrication-aware computational design method is capable of generating forms satisfying the fabrication requirements of a prototypical robotic setup.

The presented literature review covers a wide breadth of research encompassing robotic fabrication, computational design, and climate-based performance optimization. This paper aims to address gaps in the existing research, specific to the design of nonstandard wood shingle facades. This includes the development of a constructive system for nonstandard shingle facade construction, the use of multi-objective climate-based performance optimization, and the integration of a fabrication-aware computational design method. Each of these topics is integral in the development of a prototypical computational design workflow.

Research Objectives

Rather than focusing on the individual areas of research identified in the literature review, the main goal was to

2

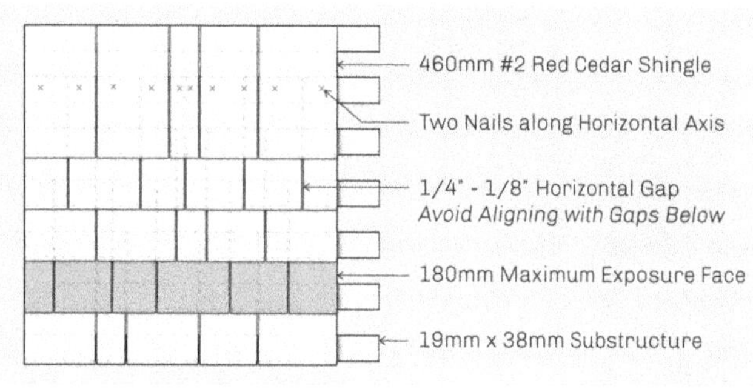

3

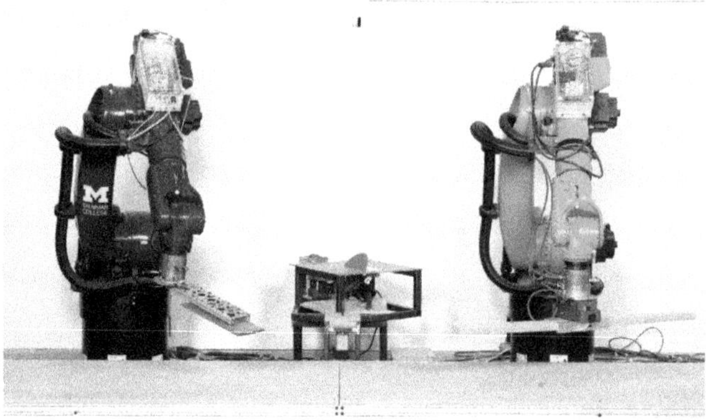

4

2 Four wood shingle design prototypes, exploring different patterns, attachment methods, substructure orientation, and substructure attachment methods.

3 Diagram of the wood shingle constructive system, noting the rules, constraints, and dependencies established during the prototyping process.

4 Prototypical robotic setup, consisting of two robotic arms with grippers, an arbor saw, and a router table, at the Taubman College of Architecture and Urban Planning, University of Michigan.

incorporate the constraints and methods of each into an integrative computational design method and a seamless digital design-to-fabrication workflow. Accordingly, we defined the following research objectives:

- Formalize constraints, rules, and dependencies of a conventional shingle facade system for wood light-frame construction and develop a constructive system suitable for robotic fabrication.
- Develop an integrative computational design method for the generation of a shingle facade system, incorporating material, robotic fabrication, and assembly constraints.
- Extend the functionality of the computational design method by integrating sun-shading analysis and multi-objective optimization of the facade surface to maximize sun exposure in the winter and minimize it in the summer.
- Implement a digital design-to-fabrication workflow to seamlessly transfer design information to robotic fabrication procedures.

METHODS

According to these objectives, the following methods were developed in this research. The first two sections ("Constructive System" and "Fabrication Setup and Process") inform the development of the computational design method and the constraints that need to be integrated into the process. These are then applied in the design of a demonstrator project. Due to the ongoing COVID-19 pandemic, the construction of the demonstrator project has been delayed. However, the validity of this fabrication data was substantiated through virtual simulation of the robotic processes and preliminary physical prototypes.

Constructive System

A constructive system was developed for robotic fabrication from conventional wood shingle-facade construction standards. A shingle-facade constructive system is derived through specific interactions between structure, substructure, and shingle elements. These interactions are defined in conventional facade construction using a series of rules and constraints encompassing substructure placement, shingle lapping, shingle spacing, and attachment methods (Cedar Shake & Shingle Bureau 2020).

To develop, test, and validate the constructive system, the research used an iterative physical prototyping approach (Fig. 2). Several instances of a base unit were prototyped with variations in the shingle placement and substructure attachment rules. We observed and learned the following:

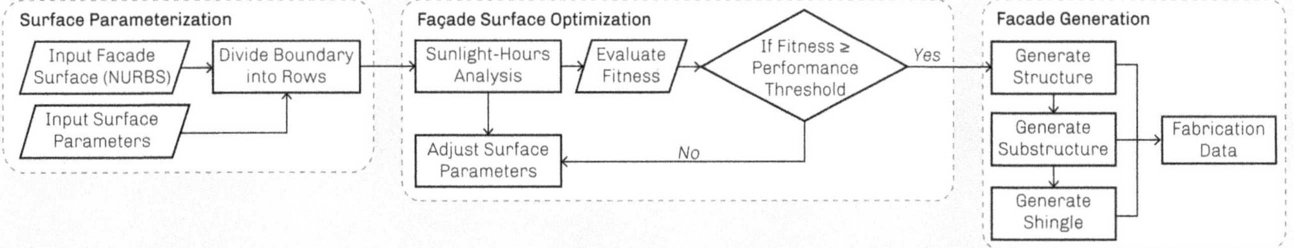

5 Flowchart of the integrative computational design method.

- Methods used for shingle placement require specific positioning relative to the neighboring shingles, as well as the shingles in the course below. Conventional methods dictate an offset of at least 38 mm from the nearest joint below (Cedar Shake & Shingle Bureau 2020).
- Dimensional width of random-width cedar shingles can vary significantly. Further research shows that these widths typically range from 76 mm to 355 mm (Simmons 2007).
- Orientation of the substructure element can lead to unstable shingle courses if the substructure is oriented such that the lower half of the shingle does not contact the course below.
- Substructure elements require a lap joint with the structure elements to maintain their structural integrity. When working with nonplanar elements, the substructure can be notched at attachment points to account for changes in angle and length when spanning between structure elements.

The lessons learned from this iterative approach define the constraints, rules, and dependencies of the shingle facade to be incorporated into the design of the constructive system. This constructive system (Fig. 3) includes details for the shingle type, attachment methods, relative positioning, and maximum exposure face, as well as the sizing and positioning of substructure elements. The robotic setup specified the additional rules and constraints of the tools used for fabrication.

Fabrication Setup and Process

The fabrication sequence follows a just-in-time fabrication method (Adel et al. 2018; Thoma et al. 2018), where individual elements are picked, cut, and placed in a single robotic sequence. This method of fabrication eliminates the need to label and organize nonidentical elements, thus reducing the complexity of the fabrication sequence. This was achieved using a prototypical robotic setup (Fig. 4) consisting of two six-axis industrial robotic arms[1] equipped with pneumatic gripper and vacuum gripper end effectors. Two pickup stations were located on opposite sides of an elevated build platform, while a table saw and stationary router table were positioned between the two robots.

Using this robotic setup and fabrication sequence, several tests were performed to identify the constraints of the fabrication setup. The following constraints were measured and documented: wood elements minimum and maximum profile dimensions (38–89 mm width, 19–89 mm height), minimum and maximum length (400–1300 mm), maximum cut angle (60° off square). These constraints are incorporated into the integrative computational design method, which is described in more detail in the following sections.

Computational Design

The main steps of the developed computational design method are illustrated using the flowchart shown in Figure 5. This method consists of a sequence of three main steps, beginning with the surface parameterization, where the input variables are defined and facade surface generated. Next, the facade surfaces are subjected to sun-shading analysis and iteratively adjusted until a set of optimized design solutions are produced. The selected facade surface is subdivided to derive the attributes necessary to generate structure, substructure, and shingle elements. During this generative process, data regarding the size, shape, and position of each element are stored and referenced for the robotic fabrication process.

Each of these computational design steps was explored in further detail by applying them to a building-scale demonstrator project as a case study.

Demonstrator Project

The demonstrator project consists of a wood light-frame structure sited at the Matthaei Botanical Gardens in Ann Arbor, Michigan. The shingled facade makes up two vertical surfaces, measuring approximately 10 m long and 5 m high, on the north and south faces of the structure.

Situated in a cold-moist climate (Zone 5a), the site is subjected to freezing winters and humid summers (Building

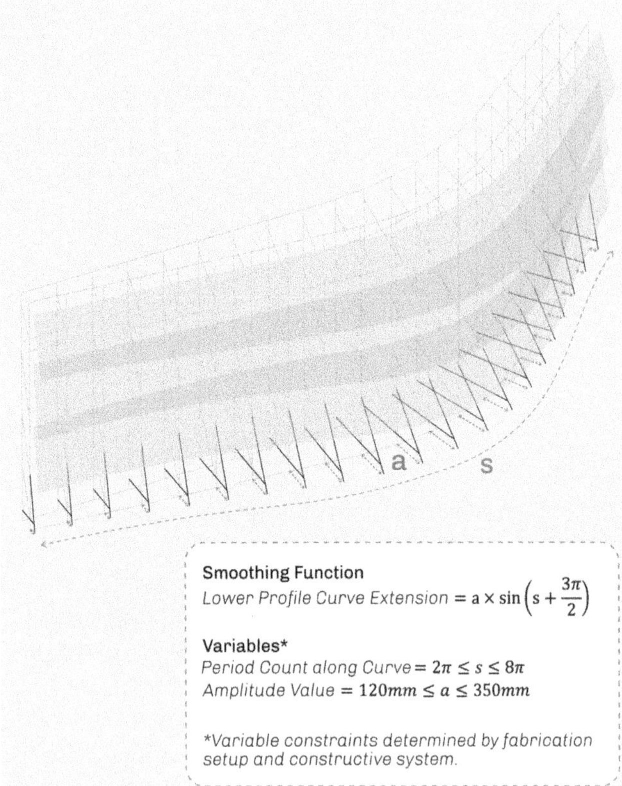

a
s
Smoothing Function
Lower Profile Curve Extension $= a \times \sin\left(s + \frac{3\pi}{2}\right)$
Variables*
Period Count along Curve $= 2\pi \leq s \leq 8\pi$
Amplitude Value $= 120mm \leq a \leq 350mm$
*Variable constraints determined by fabrication setup and constructive system.

6 Visualization of the facade surface parameterization. Variables *a* and *s* control the maximum amplitude and number of undulations on each facade surface.

Technologies Office 2015). In climates with significant annual temperature variation, self-shading strategies can be used to reduce the solar gain of the facade surface in the summer while still allowing the lower angle of the winter sun to heat the facade surface. This design strategy was applied to the facade of the demonstrator project in an attempt to increase the thermal comfort of its interior.

Although this case study was tested for a specific site, the computational design method is transferable to any location or climatic region, provided there is historical weather data accessible for the site in question.

Surface Parameterization

The computational design method begins by defining the facade parameters. A NURBS surface (McNeel 2016), indicating the extents of the shingled facade, is used to generate a set of lofted surfaces spanning the length of the demonstrator project. The angle and height of each surface is constrained by the minimum and maximum element lengths the robot can produce.

The individual surfaces are generated using an upper and lower profile curve. The upper profile remains aligned to the primary structural elements, and the lower profile is offset horizontally from the face of the input NURBS surface to produce a shading effect on the surface below. By adjusting the offset values of the lower profile curve, the self-shading properties of the facade increase or decrease. These offset values are defined using a sinusoidal smoothing function for the lower profile curve of the facade surface (Fig. 6). The number of periods and the maximum amplitude of each sine curve are determined by variables *s* and *a*, respectively. The values for the number of periods (*s*) are constrained by the maximum curvature radius of the shingle constructive system, while the maximum amplitude (*a*) is constrained by the robotic reach specific to the fabrication setup.

In the case of the demonstrator project, the number of periods (*s*) could be an integer between one and four, while the maximum amplitude (*a*) could be an integer between 120 mm and 350 mm. With a total of 16 surfaces, the facade surface had 32 parameters, 16 of each variable, which are utilized in the sun-shading optimization process.

Facade Surface Optimization

The optimization step of the integrative computational design method requires the interaction of several computational tools to produce a sun-shading analysis and optimized solutions (Fig. 7).[2] This process begins by providing the inputs for the facade surface and its parameters. Environmental analysis is then used to generate an average sun exposure value for this input surface for both winter and summer analysis periods (Roudsari and Pak 2013).

Sunlight hours analysis is used to determine the average hours of sun exposure on a facade. Both winter and summer sun exposures are measured to evaluate and compare the sun-shading performance of different facade surface options. To calculate the sunlight hours for the facade, the surfaces are subdivided and a matrix of quad mesh faces is generated. An average quad mesh size of 150 mm × 150 mm was used for the demonstrator project, as determined by a parameter study weighing processing time and mesh resolution. The sun angle is simulated for each hour of the winter (December 21 to March 20) and summer (June 20 to September 22) analysis periods to determine the sun exposure at each mesh face. The sum of these values is then normalized by dividing it with the number of days in each analysis period. The normalized value for each period is fed to the optimization engine.

The optimization is performed using a multi-objective evolutionary algorithm with Pareto optimality[3] (Fonseca and Fleming 1995). Early tests were performed using a single-objective evolutionary algorithm; however, the results were inconsistent, and the algorithm would often get stuck in local optima. Reviewing the literature, we learned that a Pareto-optimal multi-objective method[4] could solve this by removing the search bias that is inherent with using a single weighted-sum objective for both winter and summer performance (Ashour and Kolarevic 2015). Employing the multi-objective approach on the demonstrator project with unique winter and summer objective functions produced several Pareto nondominated solutions—solutions where each objective can only be improved by lowering the other objectives—that vary in performance trade-offs, favoring one objective or the other.

Precise formulation of the objective functions is critical for the optimization to be effective. For the demonstrator project, the overall objective was to improve the thermal performance of the facade using a self-shading design strategy. Therefore, sunlight-hours analysis and local weather data (Energy Plus 2020) were used to formulate two distinct objectives. The first objective was to maximize sunlight hours during the winter, and the second was to minimize sunlight hours during the summer (Fig. 8).

With these equations formalizing the fitness criteria for the evolutionary algorithm, a multitude of facade configurations are evaluated by adjusting the surface parameter variables (*s* and *α*). The optimization uses the following characteristics: population size of 200, 80% elitism, 20% mutation probability, 90% mutation rate, and 80% crossover rate. The optimization of the demonstrator project was run for 24 hours.[5] The solution set was exported from the optimization engine as a text file (consisting of 16 parameter values and two fitness values for each solution) and visualized using a 3D modeler.

The resulting solutions represent the highest-performing design solutions. A design is selected by looking at both the performance impacts of parameter weights and qualitative properties of the facade surface, like surface morphology, formal expression, and aesthetics. Once one of the solutions is selected, its parameter data is passed on to the facade generation process.

Facade Generation

After a facade surface design is selected, the individual elements of the facade are generated algorithmically. The developed constructive system is applied to facade surfaces to generate the topology of the shingle facade. The structure and substructure elements are generated by subdividing the facade surface to derive the attributes necessary for fabrication. Structure elements consist of three data categories: frame at element centroid, cut

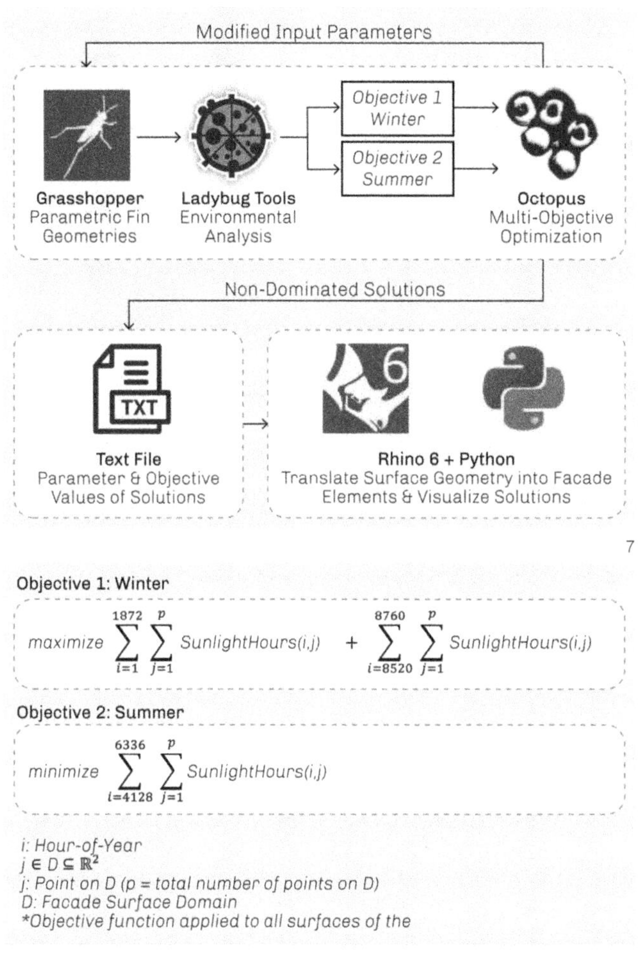

7 Workflow illustrating the sequence, processes, and software used in the multi-objective optimization process.

8 Formulation of two performance objectives that determine the fitness of a specific design solution using sun-shading analysis for the winter and summer seasons.

planes of each end of the element, and frame indicating assembly position and orientation. The substructure also includes these three attributes with the addition of information required for notching the ends of the element. The shingles are positioned onto the substructure elements, completing the facade system (Fig. 9).

RESULTS

When applied to the demonstrator project, the computational design process returned 41 Pareto nondominated solutions derived from 6,000 tested permutations. There was a measurable performance improvement in the solutions as the optimization progressed, with the average ratio of winter sun-hours to summer sun-hours increasing from 0.87 to 0.95. This improvement was mirrored in the result of both performance objectives, with the average summer sun-hours decreasing by 0.21, and the average winter sun-hours increasing by 0.15. These results support

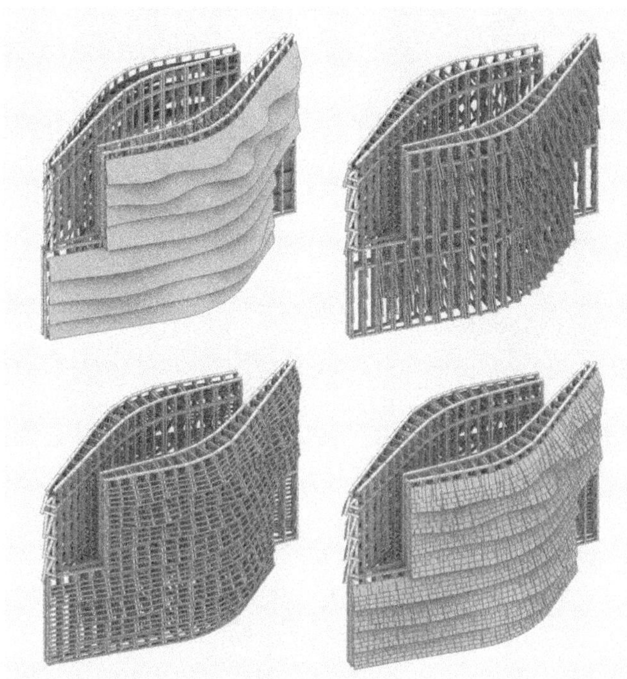

9

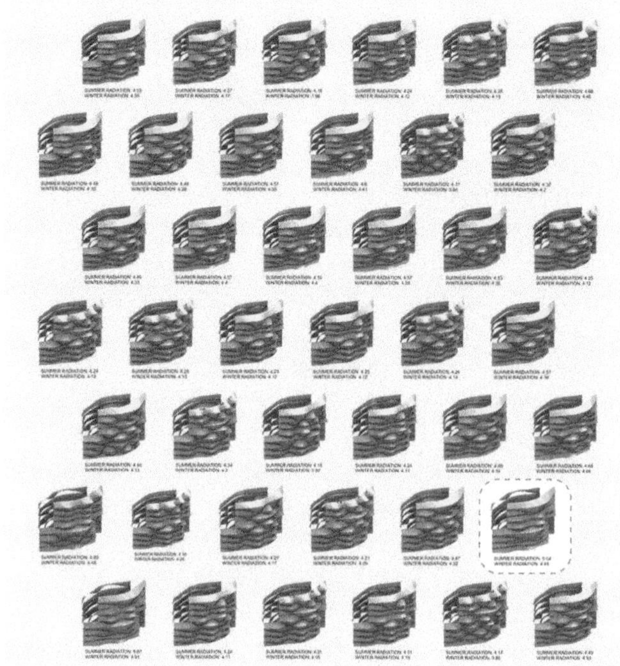

10

the use of Pareto-based multi-objective evolutionary algorithms in season-based shading analysis, even when the solution space is determined by the constraints of the constructive system and robotic setup.

The resulting solution set contained a diverse range of sun-shading performance values. Solutions with a bias towards summer performance achieved sunlight-hours analysis values as low as 4.17 hours per day; solutions prioritizing winter performance achieved values as high as 4.51 hours per day. All solutions fell within a 10% range when comparing their winter-to-summer performance ratios (0.89–0.98). Additionally, the solution set exhibited noticeable variations in formal expression and surface morphologies (Fig. 10).

Upon qualitative evaluation, a shingle facade design solution was selected and applied to the overall design of the demonstrator project. The selected design solution exhibited a 16–17% increase in the ratio of winter to summer sun-shading performance over nonoptimized solutions, with an increase of up to 0.27 sun-hours in the winter and a decrease of up to 0.79 average sun-hours in the summer (Fig. 11).

The generated facade consists of 2,795 wood light-frame elements and 3,371 cedar shingles, and satisfies the robotic fabrication and assembly constraints as these constraints were already integrated into the computational design process.

CONCLUSION

The product of this research is an integrative computational design method for translating NURBS surfaces into a shingle facade system composed of interdependent elements, embedded with the necessary data for robotic fabrication. This paper attempts to further existing research into spatial assemblies and thermal performance optimization by incorporating fabrication-specific constraints into the computational design method. Nonstandard variability and robotic fabrication enable a traditional shingle facade constructive system to be adapted for use on undulating surface geometries. These geometries can provide a self-shading functionality and have the potential to increase thermal performance as illustrated by the demonstrator project. The increase in thermal performance as a result of this integrative method could have a significant impact on energy use in wood light-frame applications. The use of climate-based performance optimization with nonstandard facade geometries is a common design method (Junghans et al. 2018; Wortman 2017). This research adds to existing methods by connecting fabrication criteria, solar analysis, and form-finding into a single design-to-fabrication workflow. This approach establishes a more accurate solution space by eliminating design solutions that do not satisfy the fabrication constraints, reducing the amount of processing required to run an optimization. It can be argued that multi-objective optimization is an effective approach to solving for the conflicting objectives of season-based sun-shading analysis by generating a solution set of

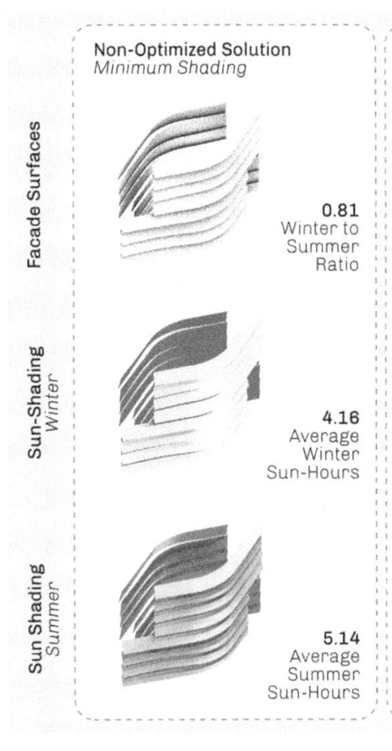

11

9 Sequence showing the generation of the selected facade design solution into structure, substructure, and shingle elements.

10 Visualization of the 41 Pareto nondominated design solutions, with the selected design solution highlighted.

11 Comparison of the selected design solution with nonoptimized alternatives. The gradient mappings in the second and third rows represent the results of the sun-shading analysis.

similar performance values with different fitness biases. From an architectural design standpoint, this method generates several different solutions to the same problem, allowing for subjective input without diminishing the facade performance.

As mentioned at the beginning of this paper, nearly 95% of single-family homes in the United States are fabricated using wood light-frame construction. The presented method could be used to effectively design and fabricate nonstandard shingle facades with a demonstrated increase in sun-shading performance. Such integrative design and fabrication methods could drastically reduce the required energy use for heating and cooling and mark a significant reduction in the carbon footprint of new residential construction.

Future Work

The presented use case—sunlight-hours analysis for self-shading shingle facades—is narrow in scope and may not be applicable in regions where wood shingles are not available or the climate does not support self-shading strategies. The implementation of additional performance objectives into the multi-objective optimization process is a clear next step in the research. New performance criteria, such as daylighting, ventilation, and view studies would further improve the performance of a wood shingle facade and provide additional value to the design.

Additionally, the proposed method was partially limited by the use of ready-made plugins for optimization and environmental analysis. The implementation of custom-made algorithms into the integrative computational design method could provide additional opportunities for designer input and improve upon the environmental performance optimization. For example, the use of a genetic algorithm for multi-objective optimization proved sufficient for the research, yet alternative algorithms (i.e., simulated annealing and Gaussian adaptation) may improve the speed and effectiveness of the optimization process.

ACKNOWLEDGMENTS

The presented research was part of a larger Digital and Material Technologies Capstone project at the Taubman College of Architecture and Urban Planning, University of Michigan. We would like to acknowledge Monik Gada, Chia-Ching Yen, Ying Cai, Han-Yuan Chang, Carl Eppinger, Jessica Lin, Feras Nour, Abhishek Shinde, Thea Thorrell, Christopher Voltl, and Aaron Weaver for their contributions to this project. In addition, we thank Wes McGee for his input and assistance in developing the robotic setup. The research was supported by the Taubman College of Architecture and Urban Planning, as well as the Rackham Graduate School.

NOTES

1. Kuka KR60 robotic arms.
2. The facade surface optimization was performed using Rhinoceros (Robert McNeel & Associates 2018), Grasshopper (Rutten 2018), and Python programming language (Python Software Foundation 2020), in conjunction with the

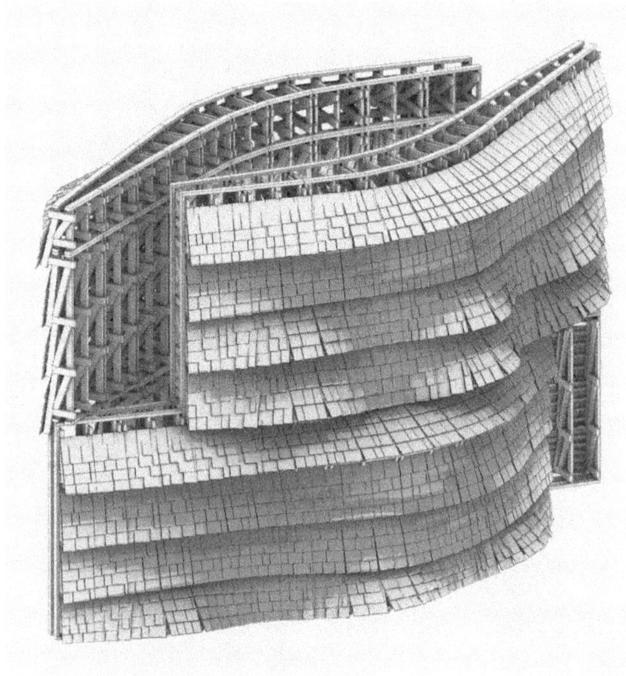

12 Rendering of the optimized wood shingle facade system applied to the building-scale demonstrator project. The summer sun-shading analysis is overlaid, illustrating a gradient of shading values, from heavily shaded areas (blue) to sun exposed areas (yellow).

Grasshopper plugins Octopus (Vierlinger 2020) and Ladybug (Roudsari and Mackey 2017). Weather data for the demonstrator project was obtained from EnergyPlus (Energy Plus 2020).

3. Pareto optimality is a condition where each solution cannot simultaneously improve all of its performance objectives (Fonseca and Fleming 1995).
4. The developed multi-objective optimization process uses HypE (Hypervolume Estimation Algorithm for Multi-Objective Optimization) to obtain a Pareto front consisting of several nondominated solutions (Bader and Zitzler 2008).
5. Optimization was run on a desktop computer (Intel i7-4790K, 16GB DDR3).

REFERENCES

Adel Ahmadian, Arash. 2020. "Computational Design for Cooperative Robotic Assembly of Nonstandard Timber Frame Buildings." PhD thesis, Zurich: ETH.

Adel, Arash, Andreas Thoma, Matthias Helmreich, Fabio Gramazio, and Matthias Kohler. 2018. "Design of Robotically Fabricated Timber Frame Structures." In *ACADIA 2018: Recalibration: On Imprecision and Infidelity [Proceedings of the 38th Annual Conference of the Association for Computer Aided Design in Architecture (ACADIA)]*, Mexico City, Mexico, 18–20 October 2018, edited by P. Anzalone, M. del Signore, and A. J. Wit, 394–403. CUMINCAD.

Alvarez, Martin, Hans Jakob Wagner, Abel Groenewolt, Oliver David Krieg, Ondrej Kyjanek, Daniel Sonntag, Simon Bechert, Lotte Aldinger, Achim Menges, and Jan Knippers. 2019. "The Buga Wood Pavilion." In *ACADIA 19: Ubiquity and Autonomy [Proceedings of the 39th Annual Conference of the Association for Computer Aided Design in Architecture (ACADIA)]*, Austin, TX, 21–26 October 2019, edited by K. Bieg, D. Briscoe, and C. Odom, 490–499. CUMINCAD.

Apolinarska, Aleksandra Anna. 2018. "Complex Timber Structures From Simple Elements." PhD thesis, Zurich: ETH.

Ashour, Yassin, and Branko Kolarevic. 2015. "Heuristic Optimization in Design." In *ACADIA 2015: Computational Ecologies: Design in the Anthropocene [Proceedings of the 35th Annual Conference of the Association for Computer Aided Design in Architecture (ACADIA)]*, Cincinnati, OH, 19–25 October 2015, edited by L. Combs and C. Perry, 357–369. CUMINCAD.

Bader, Johannes, and Eckart Zitzler. 2008. *HypE: An Algorithm for Fast Hypervolume-Based Many-Objective Optimization*. TIK-Report No. 286. Zurich: Computer Engineering and Networks Laboratory, ETH.

Building Technologies Office. 2015. *Guide to Determining Climate Regions by County*. U.S. Department of Energy.

Cedar Shake & Shingle Bureau. 2020. *Exterior and Interior Wall Manual*. Abbotsford: Cedar Shake and Shingle Bureau.

Energy Plus. 2020. "Energy Plus." Weather Data, March 27. Accessed June 20, 2020. https://energyplus.net/weather.

Eversmann, Phillipp. 2017. "Robotic Fabrication Techniques for Material of Unknown Geometry." *Humanizing Digital Reality: Design Modelling Symposium*, 311–322. Paris: Springer.

Eversmann, Philipp, Fabio Gramazio, and Matthias Kohler. 2017. "Robotic Prefabrication of Timber Structures: Toward Automated Large-Scale Spatial Assembly." *Construction Robotics* 1 (2): 49–60.

Fonseca, Carlos M., and Peter J. Fleming. 1995. "An Overview of Evolutionary Algorithms in Multiobjective Optimization." *Evolutionary Computation* 3 (1): 1–16.

Junghans, Lars, Daniel Tish, Dustin Brugmann, Kathy Velikov, and Geoffrey Thün. 2018. "Experiments Toward Hyper-Local Reverse Heat Flow Assemblies." *Technology | Architecture + Design* 2 (2): 218–228.

Kocabay, Serkan, and Sema Alaçam. 2017. "Algorithm Driven Design, Comparison of Single-Objective and Multi-Objective Genetic Algorithms in the Context of Housing Design." *CAADFutures 17*, 492–508. Istanbul: CAAD Futures.

McNeel, Sandy. 2016. "NURBS Surfaces Concepts." McNeel Wiki. Accessed June 20, 2020. https://wiki.mcneel.com/rhino/nurbssurfaces.

Menges, Achim. 2011. "Integrative Design Computation: Integrating Material Behaviour and Robotic Manufacturing Processes in Computational Design for Performative Wood Constructions." In *ACADIA 11: Integration through Computation [Proceedings of the 31st Annual Conference of the Association for Computer Aided Design in Architecture (ACADIA)]*, Banff, AB, Canada, 13–16 October 2011, edited by J. S. Johnson, J. Taron, V. Parlac, and B. Kolarevic, 72–81. CUMINCAD.

Python Software Foundation. 2020. *Python*. V. 2.7.18. https://www.python.org/downloads/release/python-2718/.

Robert McNeel & Associates. 2020. *Rhinoceros*. V.6.0. Robert McNeel & Associates. PC.

Roudsari, Mostapha Sadeghipour, and Chris Mackey. 2020. *Ladybug Tools*. V.1.1.0. Ladybug Tools LLC. PC.

Roudsari, Mostapha Sadeghipour, and Michelle Pak. 2013. "Ladybug: A Parametric Environmental Plugin for Grasshopper to Help Designers Create an Environmentally-Conscious Design." *Proceedings of BS 2013: 13th Conference of the International Building Performance Simulation Association*, 3128–3135. Chambery, France.

Rutten, David. 2020. *Grasshopper*. V.1.0.0007. Robert McNeel & Associates. PC.

Schindler, Christoph. 2007. "Information-Tool-Technology: Contemporary Digital Fabrication as Part of a Continuous Development of Process Technology as Illustrated With the Example of Timber Construction." In *Expanding Bodies [Proceedings of the 27th Annual Conference of the Association for Computer Aided Design in Architecture (ACADIA)]*, Halifax, Canada, 1–7 October 2006, edited by Brian Lilley and Philip Beesley, 1–5. Dalhousie Architectural Press.

Simmons, H. Leslie. 2007. "Wood Shakes and Shingles." In *Olin's Construction: Principles, Materials, and Methods*, 490–502. Hoboken, NJ: John Wiley & Sons.

The American Institute of Architects. 2019. *Architect's Guide to Building Performance: Integrating Performance Simulation in the Design Process*. http://content.aia.org/sites/default/files/2019-06/Energy_Design_Modeling_Guide_v4.pdf.

Thoma, Andreas, Arash Adel, Matthias Helmreich, Thomas Wehrle, Fabio Gramazio, and Matthias Kohler. 2018. "Robotic Fabrication of Bespoke Timber Frame Modules." *Robotic Fabrication in Architecture, Art and Design [Proceedings of Rob|Arch 2018]*, Zürich, Switzerland, 10–14 September, edited by Jan Willmann, Philippe Block, Marco Hutter, Kendra Byrne, and Tim Schork, 447–458. Springer.

United States Census Bureau. 2019. "Annual Characteristics of New Housing." Survey Results.

Vercruysse, Emmanuel. 2020. "The Anatomy of a Skeleton: Hybrid Processes for Large-Scale Robotic Fabrication." *FABRICATE 2020: Making Resilient Architecture*, 226–233. UCL Press.

Vierlinger, Robert. 2018. *Octopus*. V.0.4. University of Applied Arts Vienna. PC.

Wortmann, Thomas. 2017. "Model-Based Optimization for Architectural Design: Optimizing Daylight and Glare in Grasshopper." *Technology | Architecture + Design* 1 (2): 176–185.

IMAGE CREDITS

All drawings and images by the authors.

Ryan Craney is a research assistant at the University of Michigan's Taubman College of Architecture and Urban Planning, where he recently completed a Master of Science in digital and material technologies. His work looks to reevaluate current architectural design practice through the lens of robotic fabrication and computational design in order to develop new tools and methods for the technological advancement of the profession.

Arash Adel is an Assistant Professor of architecture at the University of Michigan's Taubman College of Architecture and Urban Planning. Adel's interdisciplinary research is at the intersection of design, computation, engineering, and robotic construction. He is particularly known for his work with novel integrative computational design methods coupled with robotic assembly techniques for manufacturing nonstandard multistory timber buildings. In his doctoral research at the Swiss Federal Institute of Technology (ETH), he contributed to the widely published *DFAB HOUSE* and led the computational design of its robotically fabricated timber frame structure. Adel received his Master's in Architecture from Harvard University and his doctorate in architecture from ETH.

From Concept to Construction

A Transferable Design and Robotic Fabrication Method for a Building-Scale Vault

Isla Xi Han
CREATE Laboratory/Princeton

Edvard P.G. Bruun
CREATE & Form Finding/Princeton

Stuart Marsh
SOM

Matteo Tavano
SOM

Sigrid Adriaenssens
Form Finding Lab/Princeton

Stefana Parascho
CREATE Laboratory/Princeton

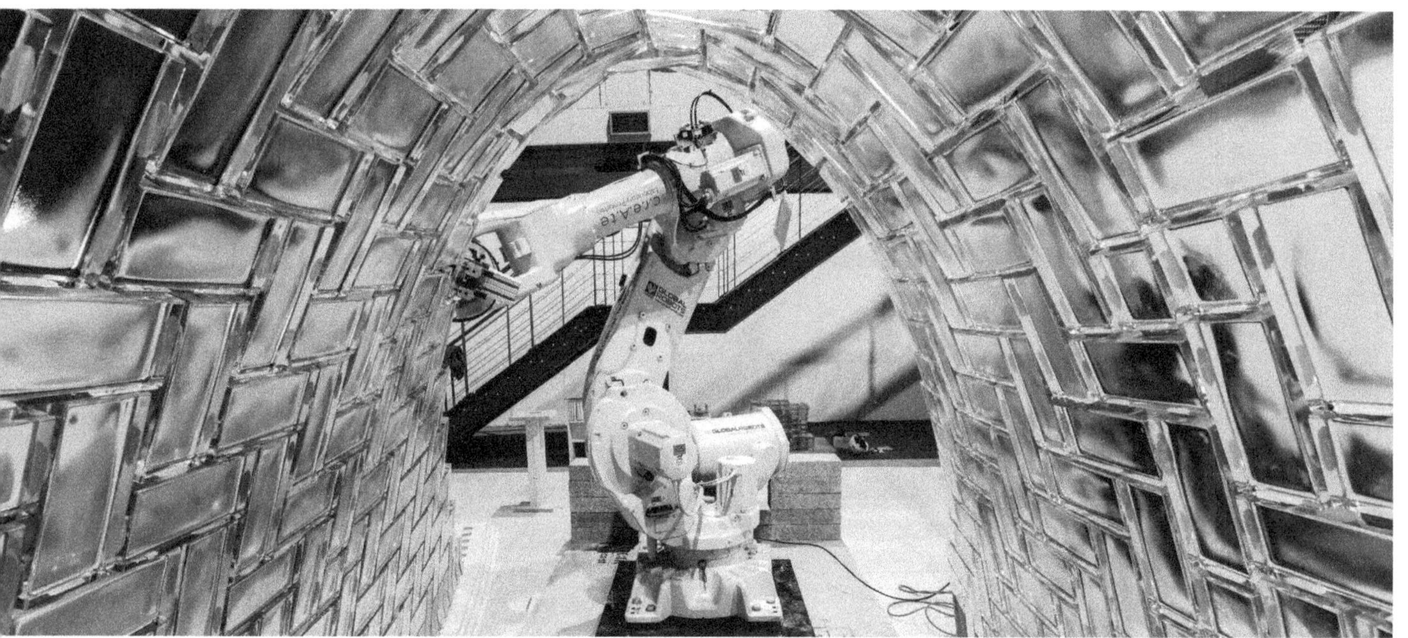

1 The full-scale glass *LightVault* displayed at the "Anatomy of Structure: The Future of Art & Architecture" exhibition at Ambika P3 gallery in London, UK.

ABSTRACT

The *LightVault* project demonstrates a novel robotic construction method for masonry vaults, developed in a joint effort between Princeton University and the global architecture and engineering firm Skidmore, Owings & Merrill (SOM). Using two cooperating robotic arms, a full-scale vault (plan: 3.6 × 6.5 m, height: 2.2 m) made up of 338 glass bricks was built live at the "Anatomy of Structure: The Future of Art + Architecture" exhibition. A major component of the project was developing a fabrication method that could be easily adapted to different robotic setups since the research, prototyping, and final exhibition occurred on different continents. This called for approaches that balanced the generic and the specific, allowing for quick and flexible construction staging and execution.

The paper is structured as follows. First, we introduce the notion of transferability in robotic construction and then elaborate on this concept through the four major challenges in the *LightVault* project development: (1) prototype scalability, (2) end-effector design, (3) path planning and sequencing, and (4) fabrication tolerances. To develop and test solutions for these challenges, we iterated through several prototypes at multiple scales, with different materials for the standardized bricks, and at three distinct locations: Embodied Computation Lab, Princeton, US; Global Robots Ltd., Bedford, UK; and Ambika P3 gallery, London, UK. While this paper is specifically tailored to the construction of masonry structures, our long-term goal is to enable more robotic fabrication projects that consider the topic of transferability as a means to develop more robust and broadly applicable techniques.

INTRODUCTION

The last 10 years have seen significant growth in the use of industrial robots (IFR 2018). In the architecture and construction fields specifically, robotics is most commonly applied to the prefabrication of building elements. However, the disadvantage is that prefabrication cannot occur for structural and material expressions that can only be assembled in situ (e.g., masonry vaults [Davis et al. 2012], cast-in-place concrete structures [Echenagucia et al. 2018; Veenendaal and Block 2014], and sequentially designed structures [Bruun et al. 2020; Parascho et al. 2017]). We believe that more emphasis on developing generalized and transferable on-site methods is necessary to achieve the goal of widening the applicability of robotic fabrication in the construction industry.

On-site robotic technology was first introduced to the construction industry with a patent for an automated brick-laying robot in the early 20th century (Thomson 1904) and a working prototype of such a machine in the 1960s (British Pathé 1967). However, the building sector has generally benefited much less from robotic technology than other fields like the automotive (Bock 2015). Some reasons for this latency in adoption are as follows:

- Technical challenges: Further advancements are necessary in areas such as sensing, path planning, spatial navigation, and communication to ensure a smooth workflow on-site (Petersen et al. 2019)
- Managerial considerations: Efficient and robust robot-human coordination is required to form a safe building environment while maintaining an economic distribution of tasks and decision-making structure between human and robot teams (Cao et al. 1997; Fong et al. 2003; Kangari 1985; Yokota et al. 1994)
- Design philosophy: Robotic fabrication processes are often designed for niche applications, so it can be challenging to adapt techniques for broader applications.

This paper addresses the last point by starting a conversation on how a robotic fabrication process can be designed from the outset to consider broader applicability over specificity. The concept of transferability for a robotic fabrication process is a measure of how readily it can be adapted to alternative sites and setups with little adjustment. In general, a transferability-oriented design paradigm is desirable to facilitate the broader adoption of new methods in the construction industry, as design possibilities are calibrated to the process rather than a specific setup or site. This emphasis on generality will help bring robotic arms from a prefabrication factory environment to construction sites and enable more freedom in architectural articulations.

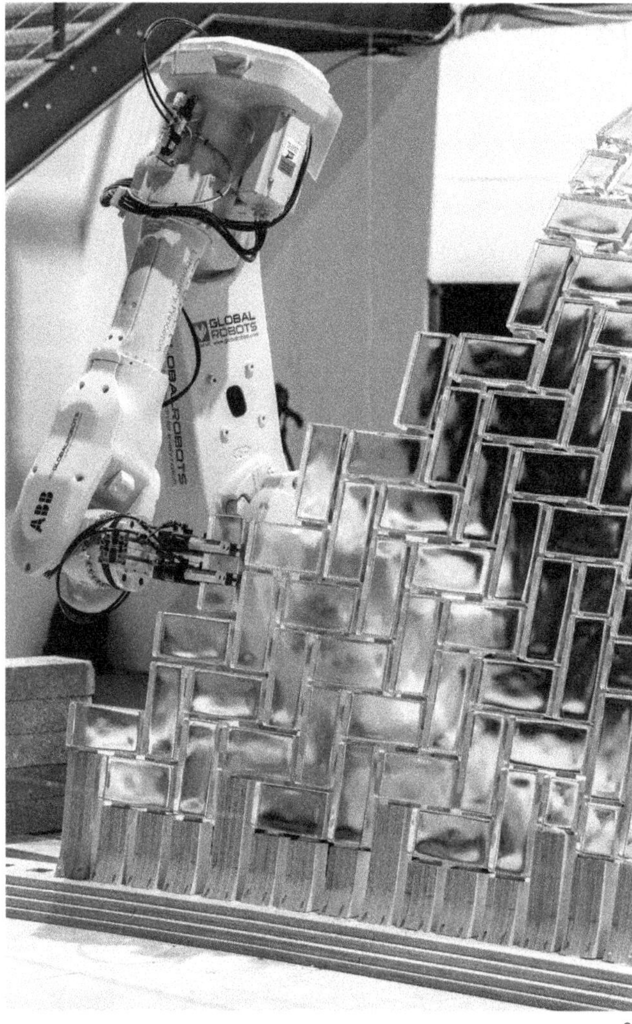

2 Robotic arm placing new brick onto the vault's side extension.

3 Middle arch construction.

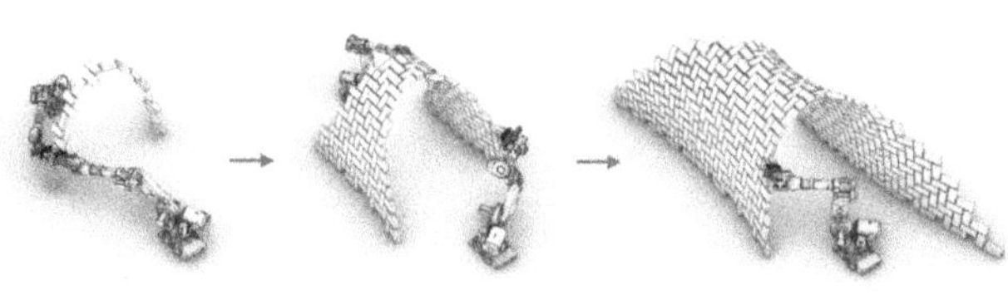

4 Perspective view of final glass *LightVault*.

5 Concept diagram showing the distinct construction phases: (a) middle arch, (b) strengthened middle spine, and (c) full vault.

The proposed method is discussed in the context of *LightVault* (Fig. 1), a building-scale robotic vault where industrial robotic arms alternate between placing bricks and supporting the structure to eliminate the need for formwork or falsework (Parascho et al. 2021). This structure was developed with the specific intention of being built robotically with different construction setups because the nature of the project was such that the development lab, testing site, and exhibition space were all in different locations and partially unknown at the onset of the project. We identified the following four considerations as essential to developing a fabrication method that would achieve this goal: (1) prototype scalability, (2) end-effector design, (3) path planning and sequencing, and (4) fabrication tolerances. The following sections present a general discussion of transferability in the context of these features with specific examples of their implementation in the *LightVault* project. Based on this specific project experience, the scope of the proposed methods is constrained to large-scale robotic assembly processes for vaulted structures.

BACKGROUND

Robotic construction of masonry structures was first performed at the architectural scale in the Gantenbein Winery project, where robots were used to construct the undulating brick walls of the structure (Bonwetsch et al. 2006; Bonwetsch and Kohler 2007). The *LightVault* project builds on this methodology by using standardized construction units, but breaks from the layered vertical construction approach to build a spanning masonry structure out of glass bricks.

Discrete element assembly projects that feature three-dimensional geometric complexity often achieve it through a high level of customization on the local scale (i.e., customization of individual building units is used to achieve complexity globally). For example, in the field of glass construction, Gustave Falconnier (1886) patented an interlocking construction system using blown-glass bricks that could be used as building blocks. Other examples of customization on the local scale are seen in spanning masonry structures such as the Armadillo Vault (Block et al. 2018; Rippmann et al. 2016), or in drone-assisted construction of structures (Goessens, Mueller, and Latteur 2018) as a way to ensure interlocking behavior between units.

Over the past decades, advancements in robotic technology and architectural expression have constantly influenced each other. While novel robotic tools have stimulated new masonry expressions (Bonwetsch et al. 2006; Dörfler et al. 2016) and functional performances (Abdelmohsen et al. 2019) in architecture, masonry construction in return also informed the development of corresponding robotic fabrication processes and machinery (Piškorec et al. 2018). The introduction of integrative design methodologies suggested the co-development of the design formulation, material experimentation, and robotic fabrication strategy to accelerate the iterative progression between tool and design (Parascho et al. 2015). However, tools and techniques developed in such a manner may face difficulties due to overspecialization when applied in contexts outside their original intent. Therefore, a balance between generality and integration is desired in developing a transferable robotic fabrication method.

METHODS AND RESULTS

There are four essential considerations in developing a highly transferable fabrication method. A general discussion of transferability in the context of these features is followed by specific examples of their implementation when developing the *LightVault* project.

Prototype Scalability

Developing new construction methods using robots requires the design team to explore the full range of limitations and abilities of a selected robotic setup for a particular site condition. During the development stages of a robotic fabrication project, it is necessary to verify and solve technical challenges before attempting large-scale construction. As such, it is advisable to aim for a scalable design that does not compromise the overall intent—it allows for both a robust prototyping strategy and final adjustment on-site. In *LightVault*, the structure itself was materially efficient since the shell was form-found to exhibit membrane behavior once fully constructed. The membrane stresses from self-weight in the final state were far below the glass bricks' strength; thus, it was the stability during construction that governed the design. This meant that explorations of stability as a function of sequencing, tessellation, and connection methods could be performed at the smaller scale and then applied to large-scale prototypes.

The development of the *LightVault* project began with three small prototypes built with two UR-5 robots; these prototypes were used to develop the construction sequence logic (i.e., brick tessellation and placement order) and the overall feasible shape based on the robot's position and overlapping reach volume. The next set of prototypes, constructed using two ABB-4600 robots, assessed the overall structural performance at the intended building scale. Figure 5 shows schematically how the final vault was planned around a phased construction approach—alternating segments of the vault were built while maintaining both global and local stability at each phase without the need for temporary scaffolding (for further information on developing a scaffold-free cooperative assembly sequence, see Parascho et al. 2020). The project was then rebuilt with a new setup using two ABB-6640 robots at the final exhibit location. A test construction was first performed at Global Robots Ltd., Bedford, UK, where the grippers and pneumatic systems were assembled and tested within 10 days. The final *LightVault* structure was then assembled live at the "Anatomy of Structure: The Future of Art + Architecture" exhibition in London, UK. Unfortunately, the construction of this final vault was cut short due to the COVID-19 pandemic.

In building the *LightVault* at Ambika P3 gallery in London, we encountered few space and access limitations for on-site masonry construction. While the floor construction was solid reinforced concrete, the gallery operators stipulated that there should be no structural anchoring to the floor, which meant we had to design the robot bases and the arch floor framing with this in mind. The need to prevent movement of the robot bases was of crucial importance. Each robot was bolted down to a relatively heavy (1.8 ton) reinforced concrete base that was strategically arranged to align flush with the arch plinth. The base design was optimized to resist overturning, with appropriate factors

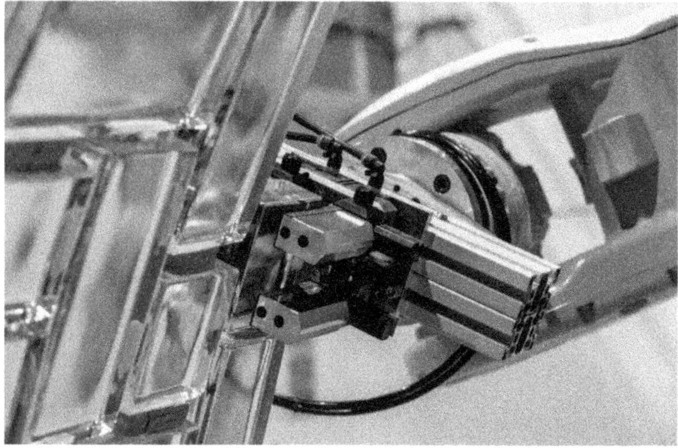

6 End-effector detail.

of safety against the worst-case loading scenarios throughout all building stages. Using conventional timber sections and plywood flooring, we created a raised platform to ensure that the floor was leveled and that the robot arms with attached grippers could reach all areas of the proposed arch geometry. All power cables and air lines were concealed below the floor frame, eliminating potential trip hazards for the operators and ensuring a clean and clutter-free site. Each of these components was developed to be simple to piece together and dismantle, and with sufficient tolerance for a fast in-field and on-the-fly setup.

End-Effector Design

In contrast to a custom-built robot, a robotic arm is a generic tool whose application is mainly defined by the attached end effector. As such, the end-effector design is crucial in determining what types of material manipulations are possible, which in turn shapes and defines the construction procedure. While more complex material processing such as welding and 3D printing might suggest bespoke end-effectors, overcustomization should be avoided, as it can result in low overall transferability of the project. Designing an adjustable end effector that is independent of the robotic system and can accommodate different materials and dimensions has proven advantageous for applications in different environments.

The grippers designed for *LightVault* consisted of a combination of standard products (Fig. 7a, d, f) and customized interfaces (Fig. 7b, c, e). Standardized SCHUNK PGN fingers, and optional quick changers simplified the overall process of assembling new grippers at different sites. Their design also made them transferable across projects, as they were easily adjustable for use with construction units of different dimensions and materials. Specifically for *LightVault*, the

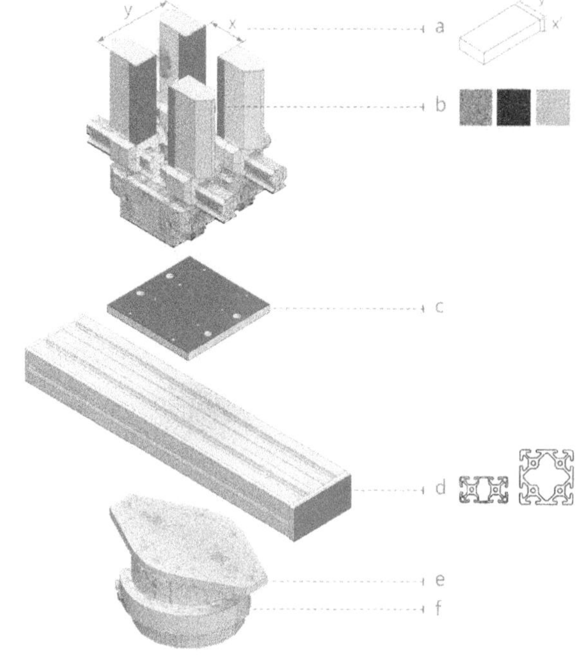

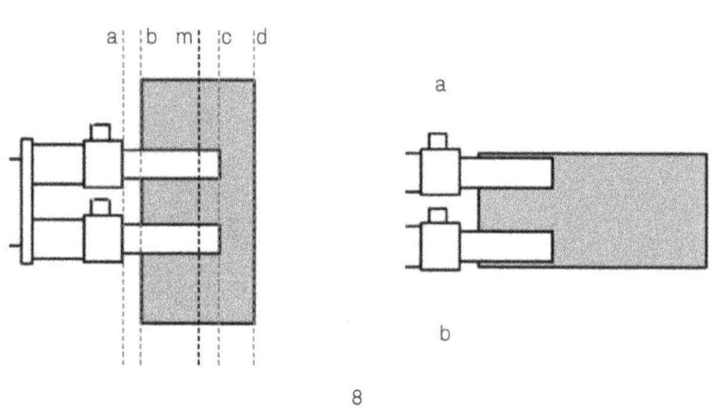

7 Exploded axonometric projection of customized gripper showing: (a) adjustable fingers, (b) replaceable finger surface, (c) customized plate between finger and extrusion material, (d) optional aluminum extrusion to extend reach, and (e–f) quick changer and corresponding plates.

8 End effector dimensional constraints: (a) finger base, (b) brick's inner edge, (m) brick's middle line, (c) finger tip, and (d) brick's outer edge.

9 End effector with asymmetric pneumatic component distribution: (a) the side with pneumatic extrusions and (b) the unobstructed side.

grippers were designed based on the following fabrication-related requirements:

- The finger spacing (Fig. 7 x) shall be constrained by the precision tolerance and gripping power associated with the proposed fabrication method—too narrow a gap between finger spacing and brick thickness (Fig. 7 x and x') can cause collisions, while too wide a distance can result in insufficient gripping power.
- The fingers (Fig. 8a–c) shall be longer than one half brick width (Fig. 8b–m) plus tolerance gap (Fig. 8 a–b) to prevent eccentric loads caused by off-centered gripping. However, long fingers that exceed the brick's outer edge (Fig. 8d) should be avoided due to collision risk between the finger tips (Fig. 8c) and existing vault structure.
- The distance between the two pairs of fingers (Fig. 7 y) shall be as wide as possible for stable gripping without exceeding the brick's width (Fig. 7 y', Fig. 8b–d) to allow the brick to be picked up in different orientations.
- The pneumatic components shall be oriented in such a way that one side of the gripper is left unobstructed (Fig. 9b), which is necessary to avoid collisions in precise placement operations.
- An extension element (e.g., an aluminum profile, Fig. 7d) can be used to prevent collisions in cases where the industrial robot's wrist joint is at high risk of hitting neighboring bricks during construction. However, too long of an extension is not advisable as it results in higher chances of collision during movements and more considerable instability caused by robotic arm deformation.
- The gripper finger surface (Fig. 7b) shall be selected based on the type of brick material used for desired performance (e.g., sandpaper with timber blocks or rubber-based tape with glass bricks).

The design of the proposed end-effector is flexible due to its modularized components. We were thus able to use the same end-effector for wooden, concrete, and glass (both textured and glossy) bricks with minimal adjustment.

Path Planning and Sequencing

Defining the assembly and path planning process parametrically, rather than prescriptively, improves the adaptability of the robotic construction process for complex geometries. But for a construction method to be transferable and robust, it should also take into account that robots are well-suited for a process with repetitive tasks. Therefore, the ideal approach is one that calculates movements parametrically where needed (e.g., for intricate 3D geometric areas) and otherwise relies on predefined repetitive movements.

In *LightVault*, the bricks were added to the vault following an overall diagonal stepping sequence, which was established to maintain global structural stability (Parascho et al. 2020, 2021). Since the general construction sequence was based on growing the vault outwards from the central arch, this allowed for more space to maneuver the robots around the structure without collision. Only when approaching the structure for the final brick placement was it necessary to generate a precise movement path parametrically. This process involved assessing the nearest neighbors for a

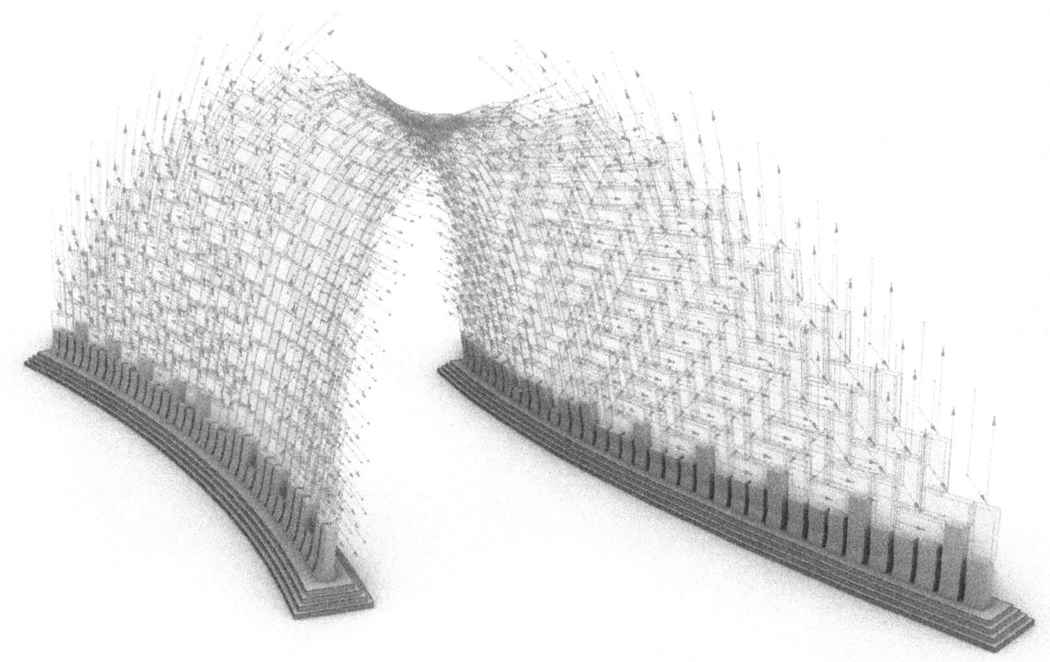

10 Parametric path planning for brick placement.

10

new brick being placed into the structure and then calculating either a diagonal or orthogonal insertion vector to best avoid collisions with the existing structure.

In contrast to the parametric paths determined for the insertion movements, the pickup location and associated motions were discretely categorized based on the brick type (half and full bricks) and gripping orientation (from the shorter or longer edge of brick). The robot then went through a fixed transition pose before moving on to the parametric insertion paths. Making such repetitive movement explicit from a path-planning perspective greatly simplified the computational component of the project. It also gave the user more control over the robot configurations, which helped mitigate the risk of unexpected collision and robotic singularity errors.

In summary, this hybrid path planning approach allocates computational efforts in areas where it's most needed (i.e., around final brick placements) and uses predefined discrete paths in less critical zones (i.e., around pickup station and areas away from the structure). This hybrid approach was computationally efficient and highly predictable from the perspective of human operators, which is particularly important when developing methods that will be transferred to different robots with different kinematic behavior.

Fabrication Tolerances

Differences between the simulated and physical setups are inevitable in any robotic fabrication project. While certain systematic errors can be corrected when working with a constant setup, this is not always possible when a project is applied to a new setup. Therefore, including a certain level of fabrication tolerance as a design feature is a robust way to improve a project's transferability.

To construct *LightVault*, we developed an adaptive mechanism for both the brick-to-brick connections and the vault foundation base. We used a flexible epoxy putty and acrylic shims to account for the different gap sizes and connection angles between the bricks. The epoxy putty was manually mixed and placed by a human, and acrylic shims were additionally used in larger gaps to shorten epoxy curing time and lower material cost. In the final placement step, the robot would move the brick into the correct location, compressing the malleable epoxy layer into the best fitting position, forming a solid connection between bricks.

While the epoxy-shim connection absorbed local-scale imprecision, a series of uniquely designed base shoes offered global-scale tolerance for the entire vault (Fig. 11). These base shoes connected the bottom row of glass bricks with the ground. The tenon and oversized mortise connection (Fig. 12) allowed the base shoes to slide freely in all directions before being anchored with screws into the floor stacks (Fig. 13). The base shoes were prefabricated from high-quality birch plywood with CNC routers.

We performed a few tests before initiating the final

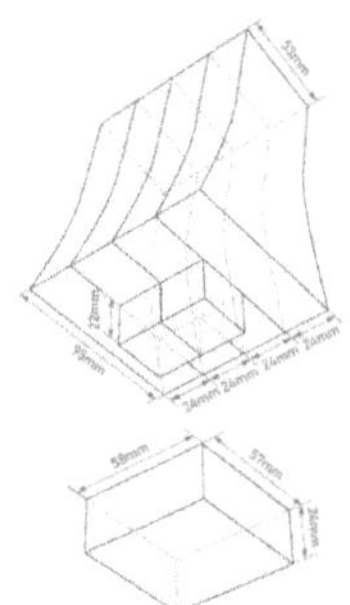

11 Base shoes.

12 Axonometric drawing of one base shoe element showing tenon and oversized mortise connection detail.

13 Base platform setup.

14 Slip test with 35 kg weight at Global Robots Ltd., Bedford, UK.

15 Middle arch prefinal test at Global Robots Ltd., Bedford, UK.

construction to assess whether the robotic tolerances were small enough to be absorbed by our construction method (i.e., offsets less than 5 mm). Gripping strength, brick slipping behavior, and robotic deformation must be checked when a new setup or building unit is adopted. The key parameters for the *LightVault* were (1) evaluating the load capacity of the robots and grippers, and (2) guaranteeing deformations in the setup were minimized and did not lead to collapse during construction.

With respect to the load that the robot would support, the critical stage was reached in the second to last step before completing the middle arch (Fig. 15). At this point, one robot was required to support a load of 32 kg, corresponding to 30% of the partial arch's weight, while the other robot picks up and inserts the last brick to complete the arch.

Several tests were carried out in advance to assess the gripper's ability to hold the required peak load without slip. We conducted these slip tests by hanging a weight on a glass brick that was being held by one robot, as shown in Fig. 14. We identified the air pressure under which the grippers operate to be a significant factor: a minimum air pressure of 7 bar was needed to withstand the required load with no slippage. Therefore, speed of construction, airtight connections with no leaks, and air compressor restart/recharge pressure became essential aspects in the construction sequence planning.

With respect to deflections in the setup, the base structure stiffness and deformability of the robot arms were of paramount importance for global stability during the temporary construction stages of the central arch. As a robot released a brick, there was an instantaneous shift of load from one gripper to another as a new equilibrium configuration was reached. During this dynamic load shift, a deformable base or excessive deformations of robot arms under sustained load may have caused vibration, which could have compromised the structural stability.

CONCLUSION

This paper provides a basic framework for developing robotic fabrication projects that are to be executed at different construction sites and using varying setups. The *LightVault* is an example of such a project, with construction occurring in various locations: several small and large-scale prototypes in Princeton, followed by a test fabrication at the robot factory in Bedford, and the final vault built at a live exhibit in London. This project aims to start a discussion on how to make on-site robotic fabrication more accessible to the construction industry. By invoking a transferability-focused design philosophy and without reverting to using custom, expensive, and time-consuming robotic manipulators, a robotic fabrication project can be explicitly designed to be adaptable to different setups. In developing the *LightVault* project, we found the following to be important considerations: scalable prototypes, end-effector design, path planning and sequencing, and robotic fabrication tolerances.

Future research will aim to expand the design space of cooperative robotic processes and generally increase

16 *LightVault* constructed live during "Anatomy of Structure: The Future of Art + Architecture" exhibition at Ambika P3 gallery in London, UK. 16

the accessibility of robotics in construction. For example, mobile robots could be coupled with stationary industrial robotic arms to expand the application range of cooperative processes to larger fabrication spaces and more complex geometries (i.e., more intricate construction sequences would be possible with an additional robotic agent). To improve the transferability of robotic processes, we aim to address the main challenges that we encountered, namely unpredictable inaccuracies and difficulties in path-planning with a new setup through feedback systems (e.g., force or visual). This information, coupled with results from a structural analysis framework, could be used as the basis for dynamic adjustments to the design and fabrication process to guarantee stability and buildability during construction.

Another approach is to address existing standardized robots themselves by developing new industrial machines based on modularity and standardized components with the potential to customize. Providing easier access to more adjustable machines, rather than more specific ones, could strongly impact the future scale at which robots are employed in architecture and construction. Even though designing and constructing custom robots is an active research field, striving for generality through modular but still ensuring availability through standardized systems would simultaneously provide more freedom of construction and easy implementation and operation.

Similar to hardware requirements, we believe that finding the balance between customization and general validity is key for the software components of a fabrication process. Thus, developing new overall design, structural analysis, end-effector design, and robotic control tools that provide a base of knowledge but allow for quick adaptability is crucial for the successful transferability of robotic fabrication methods. As we experienced firsthand through the COVID-19 shutdown, being able to quickly react to unexpected changes even during the construction process is not only helpful but a necessity to ensure that fabrication processes are successfully advanced.

ACKNOWLEDGMENTS

The construction of the *LightVault* was only feasible through the many people that supported our research through administration, development, and construction. We would like to acknowledge Alessandro Beghini, Samantha Walker, Michael Cascio, David Horos, Mark Sarkisian, Masaaki Miki, Max Cooper, Dimitri Jajich, and Arthur Sauvin (Skidmore, Owings & Merrill), Ian Ting and Lisa Ramsburg (CREATE Lab Princeton), and Grey Wartinger and William Tansley (Princeton School of Architecture).

The project was conducted with support from Faidra Oikonomopoulou and Telesilla Bristogianni from Delft University of Technology and sponsorship from Global Robots Ltd., Poesia Glass Studio, and New Pig Corporation. In addition, the project was made possible through the generous support of the Princeton Metropolis Project and Princeton Catalysis Initiative.

REFERENCES

Abdelmohsen, Sherif Morad, Khaled Aly Tarabieh, Islam Ibrahim Salem, Yomna Saad El-Ghazi, Rana Bahaa El-Dabaa, and Asmaa Gamal Hassan. 2019. "Coupling Parametric Design and Robotic Assembly Simulation to Generate Thermally Responsive Brick Walls." In *Proceedings of the 16th IBPSA Conference*, 3006–3013. Rome, Italy. https://doi.org/10.26868/25222708.2019.210904.

Block, Philippe, Tom Van Mele, Andrew Liew, Matthew DeJong, David Escobedo, and John A. Ochsendorf. 2018. "Structural Design, Fabrication and Construction of the Armadillo Vault." *The Structural Engineer* 96 (5): 10–20.

Bock, Thomas. 2015. "The Future of Construction Automation: Technological Disruption and the Upcoming Ubiquity of Robotics." *Automation in Construction* 59 (November): 113–121. https://doi.org/10.1016/j.autcon.2015.07.022.

Bonwetsch, Tobias, Daniel Kobel, Fabio Gramazio, and Matthias Kohler. 2006. "The Informed Wall: Applying Additive Digital Fabrication Techniques on Architecture." In *ACADIA 06: Synthetic Landscapes, [Proceedings of the 25th Annual Conference of the Association for Computer Aided Design in Architecture (ACADIA)]*, Louisville, KY, 12–15 October 2006, edited by G. Luhan, P. Anzalone, M. Cabrinha, and C. Clarke, 489–495. CUMINCAD.

Bonwetsch, Tobias, and Matthias Kohler. 2007. "Digitally Fabricating Non-Standardised Brick Walls." In *Proceedings from ManuBuild Conference*, 191–196. London, England: CIRIA.

British Pathé. 1967. *Mechanical Bricklayer*. YouTube video. https://www.youtube.com/watch?v=4MWald1Goqk.

Bruun, Edvard P. G., Ian Ting, Sigrid Adriaenssens, and Stefana Parascho. 2020. "Human–Robot Collaboration: A Fabrication Framework for the Sequential Design and Construction of Unplanned Spatial Structures." *Digital Creativity*, November 1–17. https://doi.org/10.1080/14626268.2020.1845214.

Cao, Y. Uny, Andrew B. Kahng, and Alex S. Fukunaga.. 1997. "Cooperative Mobile Robotics: Antecedents and Directions." *Autonomous Robots* 4 (1): 7–27. https://doi.org/10.1023/A:1008855018923.

Davis, Lara, Matthias Rippmann, Tom Pawlofsky, and Philippe Block. 2012. "Innovative Funicular Tile Vaulting: A Prototype in Switzerland." *The Structural Engineer* 90 (11): 46–56.

Dörfler, Kathrin, Timothy Sandy, Markus Giftthaler, Fabio Gramazio, Matthias Kohler, and Jonas Buchli. 2016. "Mobile Robotic Brickwork. Automation of a Discrete Robotic Fabrication Process Using an Autonomous Mobile Robot." In *Robotic Fabrication in Architecture, Art and Design 2016*, 204–217. Sydney, Australia: Springer International Publishing.

Falconnier, Gustave. 1886. Glass Building-Block. Patent #179,595, issued November 11, 1886. https://www.glassian.org/Prism/Patent/402073/page1.html.

Fong, Terrence, Charles Thorpe, and Charles Baur. 2003. "Collaboration, Dialogue, Human-Robot Interaction." In *Robotics Research*, edited by Raymond Austin Jarvis and Alexander Zelinsky, 255–266. Springer Tracts in Advanced Robotics. Berlin, Heidelberg: Springer. https://doi.org/10.1007/3-540-36460-9_17.

Goessens, Sébastien, Caitlin Mueller, and Pierre Latteur. 2018. "Feasibility Study for Drone-Based Masonry Construction of Real-Scale Structures." *Automation in Construction* 94 (October): 458–480. https://doi.org/10.1016/j.autcon.2018.06.015.

IFR. 2018. "World Robotics Report." 2018. https://ifr.org/ifr-press-releases/news/global-industrial-robot-sales-doubled-over-the-past-five-years.

Kangari, Roozbeh. 1985. "Robotics Feasibility in the Construction Industry." In *2nd International Symposium on Automation and Robotics in Construction*. Pittsburgh, PA, USA. https://doi.org/10.22260/ISARC1985/0005.

Méndez Echenagucia, Tomás, D. A. Pigram, Andrew Liew, Tom Van Mele, and Philippe Block. 2018. "Full-Scale Prototype of a Cable-Net and Fabric Formed Concrete Thin-Shell Roof." In *Proceedings of the IASS Symposium 2018*, 20-28. Madrid, Spain: International Association for Shell and Spatial Structures (IASS).

Parascho, Stefana, Jan Knippers, Moritz Dörstelmann, Marshall Prado, and Achim Menges. 2015. "Modular Fibrous Morphologies: Computational Design, Simulation and Fabrication of Differentiated Fibre Composite Building Components." In *Advances in Architectural Geometry 2014*, 29–45. Cham: Springer.

Parascho, Stefana, Augusto Gandia, Ammar Mirjan, Fabio Gramazio, and Matthias Kohler. 2017. "Cooperative Fabrication of Spatial Metal Structures." In *Fabricate* 2017, edited by Achim Menges, Bob Sheil, Ruairi Glynn, and Marilena Skavara, 24–29. London: UCL Press. https://doi.org/10.3929/ethz-b-000219566.

Parascho, Stefana, Isla Xi Han, Samantha Walker, Alessandro Beghini, Edvard P.G. Bruun, and Sigrid Adriaenssens. 2020. "Robotic Vault: A Cooperative Robotic Assembly Method for Brick Vault Construction." *Construction Robotics*. https://doi.org/10.1007/s41693-020-00041-w.

Parascho, Stefana, Isla Xi Han, Alessandro Beghini, Masaaki Miki, Samantha Walker, Edvard P.G. Bruun, and Sigrid Adriaenssens. 2021. "LightVault: A Design and Robotic Fabrication Method for Complex Masonry Structures." In *Advances in Architectural Geometry 2020*, edited by Baverel, Olivier, Cyril Douche, Romain Mesnil, Caitlin Mueller, Helmut Pottmann, and Tomohiro Tachi, 350–375. Paris: Presses des Ponts.

Petersen, Kirstin H., Nils Napp, Robert Stuart-Smith, Daniela Rus, and Mirko Kovac. 2019. "A Review of Collective Robotic Construction." *Science Robotics* 4 (28). https://doi.org/10.1126/scirobotics.aau8479.

Piškorec, Luka, David Jenny, Stefana Parascho, Hannes Mayer, Fabio Gramazio, and Matthias Kohler. 2018. "The Brick Labyrinth." In *Robotic Fabrication in Architecture, Art and Design 2018*, 489–500. Zurich: Springer International Publishing.

Rippmann, Matthias, Tom Van Mele, Mariana Popescu, Edyta Augustynowicz, Tomás Méndez Echenagucia, Cristián Calvo Barentin, Ursula Frick, and Philippe Block. 2016. "Computational Design and Digital Fabrication of a Freeform Stone Shell." In *Advances in Architectural Geometry 2016*, 344–363. Zurich.

Thomson, John. 1904. *Brick-laying machine*. United States US772191A, filed May 9, 1904, and issued October 11, 1904. https://patents.google.com/patent/US772191A/en.

Veenendaal, Diederik, and Philippe Block. 2014. "Design Process for Prototype Concrete Shells Using a Hybrid Cable-Net and Fabric Formwork." *Engineering Structures* 75 (September): 39–50.

Yokota, Kazutaka, Tsuyoshi Suzuki, Hajime Asama, Akihiro Matsumoto, and Isao Endo. 1994. "A Human Interface System for the Multi-Agent Robotic System." In *Proceedings of the 1994 IEEE International Conference on Robotics and Automation*, 1039–1044, vol.2. https://doi.org/10.1109/ROBOT.1994.351220.

IMAGE CREDITS

Figures 1–2, 6, 16: © Maciej Grzeskowiak (SOM), 2020.

All other drawings and images by the authors.

Isla Xi Han is a PhD student in Architecture Technology at CREATE Laboratory at Princeton University. She received her Bachelor's degree in Architecture and Economics from University of Virginia and her MArch from Princeton University's School of Architecture. She worked as a research specialist II in CREATE Laboratory Princeton to develop the *LightVault* project. Her research interests lie in the area of collective robotic construction in architectural contexts, ranging from design to computation to implementation.

Edvard P.G. Bruun is a PhD student working in the Form Finding Lab (Civil and Environmental Engineering Department) and CREATE Laboratory (School of Architecture) at Princeton University. His research interests lie in exploring how industrial robots can be used as the basis for novel design and fabrication processes to build creative but efficient discrete-element structures.

Stuart Marsh helps lead the SOM London structural engineering team to develop and deliver structural designs and documentation for a wide variety of projects along with overseeing and conducting all necessary architectural and services coordination to ensure complete integration of the structural design concepts within project requirements. Stuart's diverse project history includes a range of commercial, residential, and academic developments and cultural and artistic installations throughout Britain, Europe, and further abroad. Throughout his career he has sought to consistently achieve safe, practical, and cost-efficient solutions that enhance the overall design of buildings and their myriad components.

Matteo Tavano is a Senior Structural Engineer in Skidmore, Owings & Merrill's London office. He is responsible for design, analysis, and project coordination on a variety of projects in the residential, commercial, mixed use, and education sectors. Matteo is experienced with the design process from concept to completion, inclusive of early-stage schematic design, advanced design, and site supervision during construction. Throughout his academic and professional career, Matteo specialized in earthquake engineering and high-rise building design. His work reflects the belief that high-quality design can be achieved through creative architectural and engineering solutions.

Sigrid Adriaenssens is an Associate Professor of Civil and Environmental Engineering at Princeton University, where she leads the Form Finding Lab. Her research focuses on lightweight surface systems and how they can be optimized and realized to interact with extreme structural or environmental loading.

Stefana Parascho is an Assistant Professor in the Architecture Department at Princeton University and the director of CREATE Laboratory Princeton. She completed her doctorate at ETH Zurich, Gramazio Kohler Research, and her architectural studies at the University of Stuttgart. Her research interest lies at the intersection of design, structure, and fabrication, with a focus on robotic fabrication processes and fabrication-informed design. In addition to research, she has taught both in Stuttgart and Zurich, in architecture programs as well as specialized programs in computational design and digital fabrication (ITECH Stuttgart, MAS DFAB ETH Zurich).

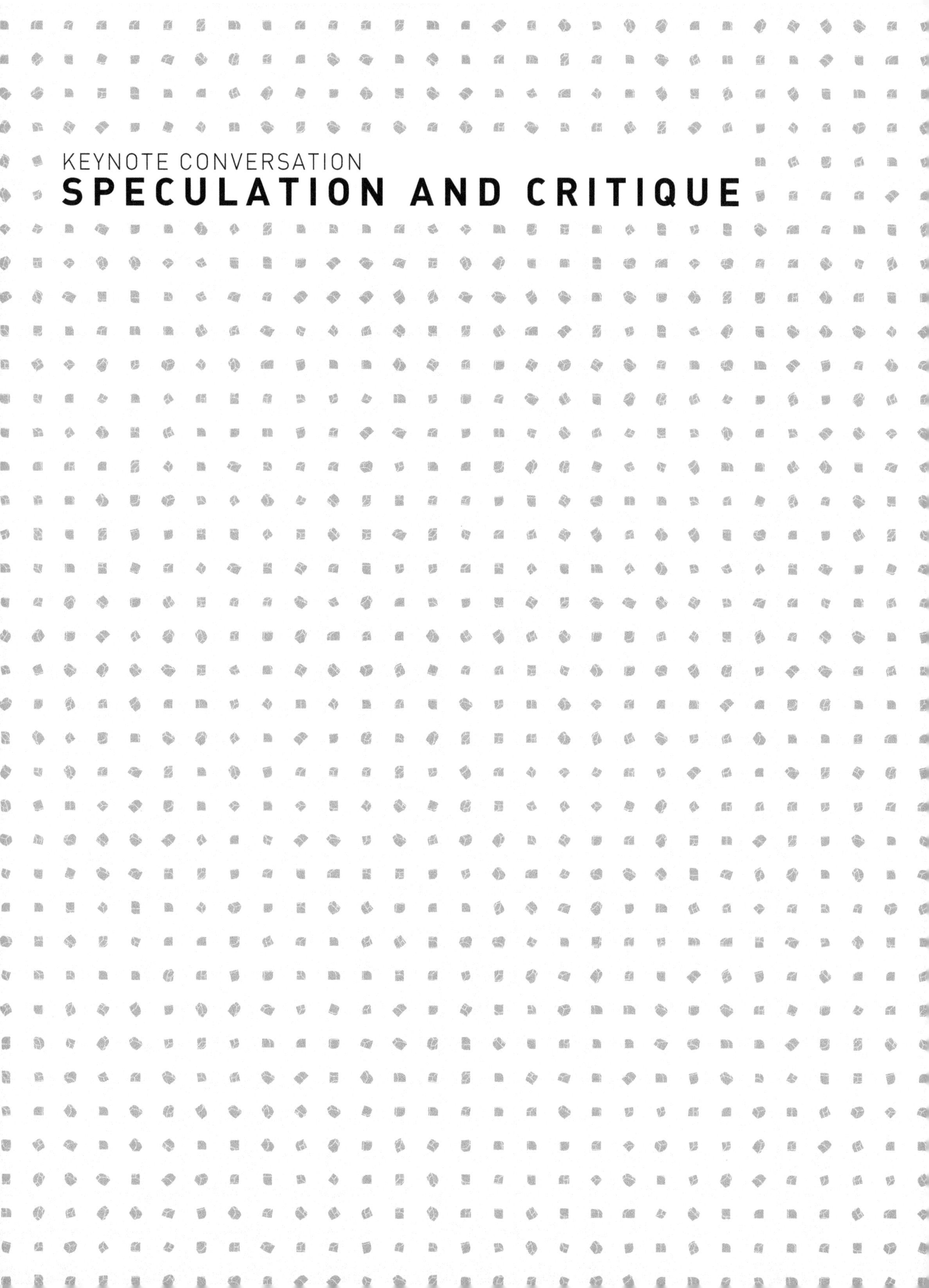

KEYNOTE CONVERSATION

SPECULATION AND CRITIQUE

KEYNOTE EVENT

A Conversation on Speculation and Critique

Hernán Díaz Alonso
SCI-Arc

Winka Dubbeldam
University of Pennsylvania

Nicholas de Monchaux
MIT

Molly Wright Steenson
Carnegie Mellon University

Albena Yaneva
University of Manchester

Kathy Velikov
University of Michigan

This closing conversation convened leaders from academia and practice to reflect on discussions that emerged during the conference, as well as future trajectories for architectural research in design computation. Kathy Velikov, Associate Professor at the University of Michigan Taubman College of Architecture and Urban Planning and Founding Partner of rvtr, began with a prompt inviting the panelists to speculate on how the design computation community might expand its scope beyond the technical to engage more directly in social and cultural discourses.

The panelists—Hernán Díaz Alonso of SCI-Arc, Winka Dubbeldam of the University of Pennsylvania, Nicholas de Monchaux of MIT, Molly Wright Steenson of Carnegie Mellon University, and Albena Yaneva of the University of Manchester—each presented a brief response to this prompt, followed by a wide-ranging discussion moderated by Velikov. The conversation is reproduced below in edited form.

For a recording of the entire event, please see this link:
https://www.youtube.com/watch?v=iT3WzCaok30

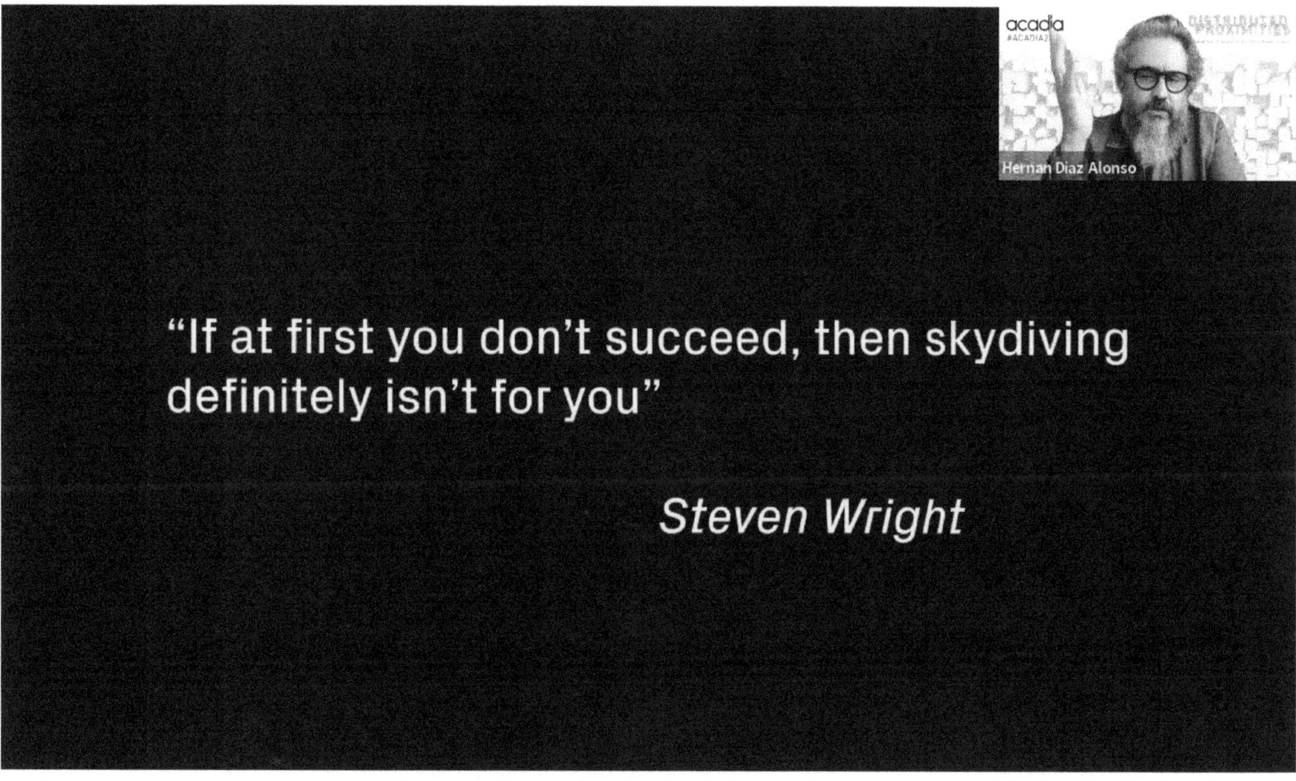

acadia
Hernan Diaz Alonso
“If at first you don’t succeed, then skydiving definitely isn’t for you”
Steven Wright

1 "One of the challenges for us is to speculate how computation can intersect with a social and radical agenda. How can we keep infusing humanism into this work? Speculation can be a really powerful tool to do this." —Hernán Díaz Alonso

Kathy Velikov (KV): I'd like to begin by offering a provisional framing of the topic of speculation and critique. When we are talking about architecture and about technology, there's typically an assumption that we are talking about the future—and all the more so when the word "speculation" comes up. Yet, while speculative works are often situated in a future temporality, they are really less about the future than they are about the present. As authors of speculative fiction argue, the operative role of speculation, even when set in a distant future, is to illuminate and question structures and assumptions of the present. It is about the now. Nor does speculation need to be situated within a future. As my historian colleagues know well, it can just as readily be mobilized with regard to the past in the form of counterfactual speculative histories, whose primary intention is, once again, to ask us to question our present assumptions and the structures and systems of what we believe to be our reality. So the work of speculation explores not only the possibilities of technology, but also the political, social, ideological, and ecological systems within which it is entangled. It is less about experimenting with how things are now or making them better or incrementally different, but more about envisioning other and alternative possibilities and systems altogether. In this way, speculation inherently carries a critical as well as a deeply political dimension in its practice.

I'd like to bring this conversation full circle to the "Data and Bias" keynote conversation, in which Ruha Benjamin so eloquently set up the charge for us as educators in relation to speculation. Ruha argued that education and pedagogy were some of the most important places where we can seed alternatives. In her words, she described it as "plant[ing] seeds in the minds and hearts of students" where "thinking outside the box, thinking beyond certain kinds of boundaries" enables the imagination of sensibilities and attitudes "that have to be fostered in order to transform the ecosystem in which we develop technology."[1] This imagination is required both within the realms of the profession and within grassroots and community organizing.

In this way, how can we recognize our role—again in Ruha's terms—as cultural workers who have the capacity to both "question and create different kinds of norms and values"? How can we challenge ourselves to not just build new versions of the same old thing set within current constraints and systems which only reinforce current structures of power and social dimensions?

2 "We face such complex problems; the only way to address such challenges are with cross-platform, interdisciplinary teams." —Winka Dubbeldam

Speculation is about the ability to operate beyond what we perceive to be the limits of the now and to imagine a different present that may lead to a different future. Computational design has enjoyed a rapid expansion in technological formal and procedural innovation. But what work still needs to be done to cultivate speculative thinking imaginaries as well as tangible practices that might untangle us from perceived restrictions to find alternative relations, vocabularies, aesthetics, and ecosystems? Where do you see the challenges and urgencies for computational design in both academia and in practice relative to broader questions of societal concern and digital culture? Where do you see the role and agency of speculation in computational design, moving forward?

Although each of your presentations has responded to these prompts in very different ways, I've identified a few common threads: Hernán's call for more platforms for flexible and "dirty" computation and agencies of contamination; Winka's discussion of hybrids of complexities and the necessity for collaborations, perhaps messy ones as well; Nicholas's questions about uncertainty and imprecision; Molly's discussion of selves and subjects; and Albena's call for a kind of hybrid social construct that feeds back between the social and the architectural.

In framing this panel (and the conference in general), we've tried to ask, what is missing from current conversations in the ACADIA community? What might the roles of both speculation and critique be in formulating a resistance to, or an alternative to, the precision of our digital tools, given the messiness of the world and the messiness and imprecision of the challenges that we face?

In addition to being practitioners, each of you is also a teacher and pedagogue. In the context of teaching, what are the strategies that you use to introduce some of these ideas and practices to students? How do you start to talk about them? How do you start to cultivate them in the next generation?

Nicholas de Monchaux (NdM): We don't so much try to introduce values in our students. Rather, we hold ourselves accountable for values as a whole community—with learning and teaching happening in both directions between faculty and students. I've only recently arrived at MIT, but already I've learned an enormous amount from my colleagues, from our staff, and our students and our students' challenges. This would be true at any time, but it is especially true in light of the pandemic, the murder of George Floyd and resulting protests, and in the light of our current political crisis. All of these are calls to rethink systems of learning and making and doing. And a way of answering Hernán's wonderful challenge to us; to make today useful to the future versus the other way around.

Winka Dubbeldam (WD): I love the idea of the imperfect or the "other" that emerges from working with computation. If you work in digital design, there is the possibility of testing, looking at iterations, and looking for other kinds of new identities or characteristics that typically wouldn't necessarily emerge. I think this is a huge shift from the past: being able to test designs in real time, and to prototype them both digitally and physically.

I remember in the early 1990s, we were all experimenting with how animation-driven research might result in formal investigations. But in most cases, the work remained purely experimental. What is exciting with this year's ACADIA conference is that technology has been taken out of the box, and we can start to really see its wider impacts beyond form-making. This enables us to ask how architecture can impact the world in a different way. It is interesting to think how ACADIA could really be instrumental in going beyond technology for technology's sake, and considering how we might rethink and change the role of the architect. For our students, this will give them new agency, not only through the way they design and work but also how they implement the knowledge in a much wider field of activities.

Molly Wright Steenson (MWS): I find myself approaching it almost from the other side, with the caveat that I don't have a studio degree in architecture; I have a PhD in architecture. I've been working in the field of interaction design for 25 years, and this is where my home is at Carnegie Mellon in the School of Design. Except for a couple of smaller endeavors, I feel that architects missed out on an opportunity in the late 1990s in the ways that they engaged with the internet. One thing that I find quite interesting about Gen Z students that we're beginning to see as undergraduates is the way that they're taking the digital language of the moment and turning it into material for architecture. I don't know if I want interaction designers to be working more architecturally, or architects to work more at the scale of interaction design. I may have already argued against all of this by reciting the e. e. cummings poem "pity this busy monster, manunkind," which is all about scale—I might challenge that, or want to see it happen differently.

Hernán Díaz Alonso (HDA): One of the things I like the most about architecture and architects is that we basically misuse and misunderstand everything. This extends to technology: whatever role technology takes in architecture, it is a pretty muddy appropriation.

I don't think the question is about what ACADIA is missing; it's about what other layers we can bring to the table. In crises like the current one, which is actually multiple concurrent crises, it's an opportunity for us to rethink that. I am more comfortable if we actually don't make these decisions, and instead embrace the notion of architecture being very elastic. I really believe that in this moment, the architectural discipline is actually one of the most interesting disciplines, because we are experts in being generalists in a culture that is moving differently. In regard to COVID and Black Lives Matter, at least in the context of SCI-Arc, the students were so active in driving that conversation and demanding a different mechanism for how we operate.

I think one of the problems with computation and technology is the idea of decentralization and challenging hierarchies. Sometimes the apparatus of architecture is so heavy that we forget that our authority actually comes from a position of weakness—weakness in a good way, not a bad way. We are a weak discipline; we have allowed ourselves to be contaminated fairly often, by other disciplines like philosophy and science. I think we need to figure out a way to see this as a virtue and not a problem.

When you think about the summer protests following the assassination of George Floyd, they took on a whole other dimension because of the level of interconnectivity that we have. The massive interconnectivity provided by technology lit a spark, a kind of communal rage. And if these things make it into our island of architecture, then those are clues for us to think about. To me, that was always the most exciting thing about technology.

Of course, this is a historical conversation that has been ongoing for 30 years. To me, one of the most interesting moments was in the early 1990s, as Winka referred to, when there was an appetite to break through and break away from things that we knew. But then, very quickly, architects became invested in writing new manifestos and redefining the discipline. There was a desire to get out of the canon, but also a desire to come back and ask permission to be reincorporated into the canon. I wonder if this moment is a moment to revisit that, and exploit that and go beyond that.

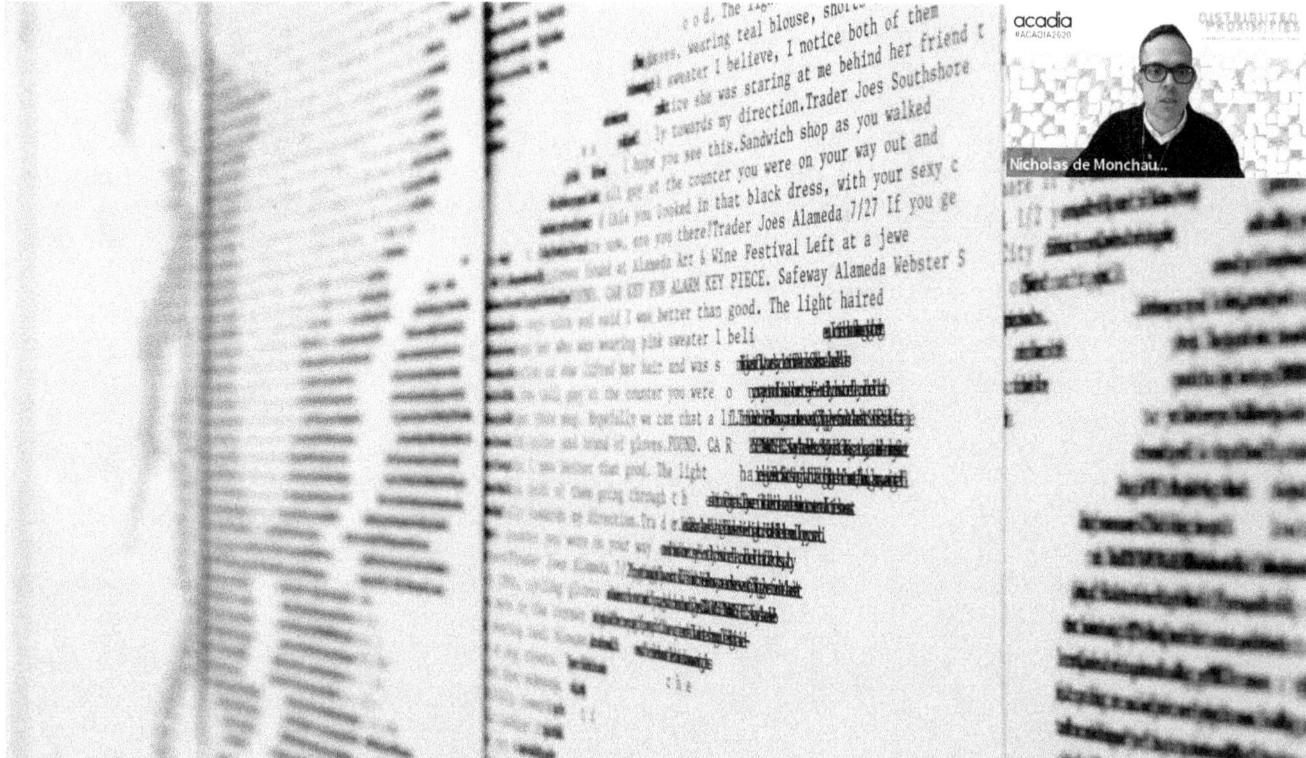

3 "These two ideas of uncertainty and inclusion actually go together. The more uncertain, imprecise, and open-ended a digital process will be—despite its DNA of optimization and precision—the more we leave opportunities for tools and processes of inclusion to shape the solution, and the more we leave the possibility for those two things together to continue to adapt solutions over time in the way that we know the climate crisis will force us to" —Nicholas de Monchaux (Image: modem)

I also want to be clear that I am spitballing most of what I am talking about, because I have no certainty about any of these things. To me, this is very exciting. There is potential in the uncertainty.

KV: A question from Sina Mostafavi in the audience: "Thanks for picking up on the idea of uncertainty and inclusion. It would be great if we could elaborate a bit more on the notion of uncertainty. Is uncertainty about developing and applying uncertain design systems and processes, or is it about the design or team being uncertain about what is going on but staying critical about the system's outcome as long and as much as possible?"

NdM: Uncertainty and its amplification of inclusion, and inclusion and its amplification of uncertainty, is sort of the flip side of technology's own identity as a cultural artifact.

I remember the late 1990s too, and the way in which a kind of retroactive heroism was ascribed to various kinds of software packages for their potential for architectural creation. But those technology packages, of course, came from certain industries—car production, animation, aviation—where there are very narrow bands of social and cultural creation. For example, the ideals for a Boeing airframe are optimization and precision. But when digital tools designed for this outcome are received in a larger culture, particularly in a culture of cities or a culture of ecologies, optimization and precision are very unsuitable values. No matter how much verbiage we stack on top of that software, those goals will be embedded in it, unless we actively work to acknowledge them and undermine them.

I encourage a kind of self-conscious uncertainty about design systems and processes of the sort that Hernán spoke of, as well as an awareness of our tools and our data and where they're coming from. It is important to remain open about the outcome of a process for as long as possible. But the fundamental point I was making about uncertainty and inclusion is that they are deeply interrelated and amplify each other, and therefore should be a kind of shared ideal in a digitally driven process.

KV: Albena, I would love to hear you speak to this, from your perspective, which is both inside and outside of architecture.

Albena Yaneva (AY): The theme of uncertainty is particularly relevant as it connects to climate change; this also came up during some of the other keynote presentations, such as the "Ecology and Ethics" event and the "Data and Bias" event. Orit Halpern, in particular, challenged us to invent new techniques for remapping nature and environmental issues.[2] This makes me think about how computational tools might empower us to address the new climatic regime. Reflecting on the new climatic regime, designers can help better than anyone else, to produce alternative accounts and visualizations to represent environmental issues such as climate change, soil or landscape degradation, biodiversity, and the massive stores of pollution in our atmosphere, sea, and soil. We can address the complexity of these issues in their multiple scales, gravity, and duration. We can provide new representational tools and tactics of representation. The lack of a common visual language hampers the understanding of environmental issues. Conventional cartographic, scientific, and cybernetic images speak of nature in an abstract way, using a top-down aesthetic. The difficulty of visualizing and comprehending the conditions of environmental transformation has led to climate-change skepticism and denial. Thus, computational design can help us to multiply the instruments for data collection and representation, and to rethink the representational techniques that for a long time have shaped how we look at nature.

Designers are in a good place to deal with this kind of uncertainty, and to reinvent the traditional way of looking at nature and talking about climate. We are well-placed to present and analyze this complexity. This new regime of visualization rather suggests that we live *within* nature and interact with it, that we weave a web of connections that might hurt or repair its balance. Instead of acting "against" pollution or deforestation in a blatantly political, militant way, architects can act *from within*, raising awareness and offering new compositions, new local adjustments that would craft the cosmos differently. In this way, we can promote a new role for architectural design: as a powerful apparatus for rethinking, re-diagramming, and reimagining the new cosmopolitical order. How can computational design tools and all the intelligent workflows presented at this conference empower us to do so?

KV: Another question from the audience, from Brandon Clifford: "I'm really curious about higher education and, from your point of view, how we're preparing the architects of the future. If you had a magic wand, what would be the one thing you would shift?"

MWS: More criticality. I'm still struck by things like when I learned that a table of contents is a political statement, and that every word on every page matters, and that, frankly, so does every line and vector. How can we better encourage our students to learn to question everything?

NdM: I would challenge our notion of authorship. Fundamentally, we live in a culture broadly, but a design culture in particular, that likes to ascribe heroic singularity to the work of teams and collaborations. The potential of the digital to forge new kinds of collaborations, as we're doing even here in this event, is actually one of its most promising potentials in the current moment.

AY: I would abolish the division between the humanities and technology. We should stop drawing boundaries between architectural technologies and architectural humanities, between materiality and meaning. The idea of having two libraries—one that deals with the technical and objective aspects of architecture and then another that deals with the symbolic and humanist power of architecture is absolutely unsustainable. In the literature, technology and society are completely disentangled. On one hand we find glossy books on architectural technology, where the skin, the performance, the material properties, and the functionality of building are discussed, and on the other, we learn about social symbolism, politics, and cultural factors impacting architecture. This division, reproduced in different forms, continues to blind architectural studies and by extension, architectural pedagogy.

That is why I would entirely abolish this dichotomy and invite the disciplines to mix their tools, experiment, and enhance synergies at all levels of the curriculum. We need to invent new formats of pedagogy that will mobilize both the humanities and technology in an inventive way. This can result in novel ways of conceptualizing architectural objects and practices that will grasp their sociomaterial complexity without falling into the trap of abstract divides between nature and culture, society and architecture.

WD: I would love to help our students earn their architectural registration upon completing their education, which lasts so long and costs so much. This would mean providing practical training during one's studies, which would allow students to be registered upon graduation.

KV: A question from Rebecca Smith in the audience: "Ruha Benjamin advocates for speculation, but she does so from a very explicitly political framing of abolitionist imaginaries in the context of mass incarceration and centuries of anti-Black racism. Benjamin also cautions that design itself is a form of colonization. This leaves me thinking speculation is great, but I worry that we run the risk of just reproducing existing power relationships through our imaginaries if we're not also critiquing ourselves and the privileged position that many of us operate from. I wonder if we can think of technological uncertainty or completeness or partiality as perhaps being able to aid us in some of that reflexive self-critique or opening up of our discourse?"

NdM: I would say that uncertainty and incompleteness—which is the very appropriate connection you are making—have also a lot to do with this subjectivity and the structure of creativity. In a way, the question presents a better version of my previous comment about authorship. Authorship should remain as an idea, but the essential idea is that it needs to be shared, and designers need to see themselves as facilitators of a process of co-creation. This is true with communities, with those who design affects, and also in more speculative ways; indeed, Albena encouraged us to challenge preconceptions about whom we collaborate with and the lines across which we declare our collaborations crossing.

To really take what Ruha Benjamin is saying seriously, one must recognize the designer's role as a facilitator in a specific kind of interaction in today's global culture: between global, digitally enabled architectures of production and consumption that are virtual, and the creation and the impact of these global supply chains on the real world. Take the iPhone as an example. You have literally enormous structures of labor, and often oppression, in the construction of devices half a world away, in a single building that can contain up to 300,000 workers, many of them hired through conditions and circumstances meeting the definition of slave labor. You have a remarkable physical object that results, that we interact with and purchase digitally, and which is part of a digital universe. But its beauty belies a certain kind of ugliness as well. Its precision, for example, is not the result of robots, even though its contained and sleek form implies the absence of a human hand. Yet it is in fact the result of hundreds and hundreds of individual hands, many of them charged with putting a lot of ever-so-slightly-mismatched parts together to look like no human was ever involved. The object's design is the direct facilitator of the kind of elision, or hiding, of those networks and systems and structures of power. So I think we have a lot to answer for in that regard. Today, there are many possibilities for designers to enter and open up structures of collaborating and making. But, just like the deceptive appearance of a consumer object like the iPhone, dispensing with our preconceptions towards the apparently unitary or singular is an essential step to truly develop our digital practices and professions.

MWS: I think it's important to broaden the range of work that we look to. One example that comes to mind is James Garrett Jr. from the firm 4RM+ULA in St. Paul, Minnesota, who recently keynoted the AIA conference in Minnesota with Rory Hyde from the Victoria and Albert Museum. James is an African American architect and one of fifteen registered African American architects in the state of Minnesota. His practice includes built work, as well as public artwork. I think that when you start to extend slightly beyond the boundaries, you can still stay architectural while operating at different kinds of scales that provide access or interest or mutability from diverse publics—publics that are not the six of us sitting here. Looking at work like his and and others is all the more meaningful in the wake of George Floyd's murder. I think that it makes new possibilities imperative.

WD: I think that we all need to become better listeners, because every time we think we do good, we might do wrong. I think the most important thing for all of us is to listen better, and to listen more. I think now is actually a very beautiful moment to take the time, to stop, and to just really assess where we are. Here we are as students, faculty, citizens, and how can we help and what can we do?

Design is also a great tool where you can be equal and democratic and give people the right to have a beautiful thing. Including people in the design process is very difficult, but it is extremely humbling to realize that people know so much more than you think they do. You learn a lot.

I actually think that in academic environments, we have more power than we think we have. What if we did start to create some havoc, insert ourselves more actively in design and planning processes, and start to be much more proactive in how we can help? Kathy suggested this in her introduction—that we should not be reactive anymore but start to be proactive. This is probably the biggest thing we need to change.

KV: I think that a desire for certainty is probably one of the characteristics of power structures and power regimes, and so cultivating a kind of ambiguity and uncertainty is perhaps a kind of political act as much as it might be a productive one.

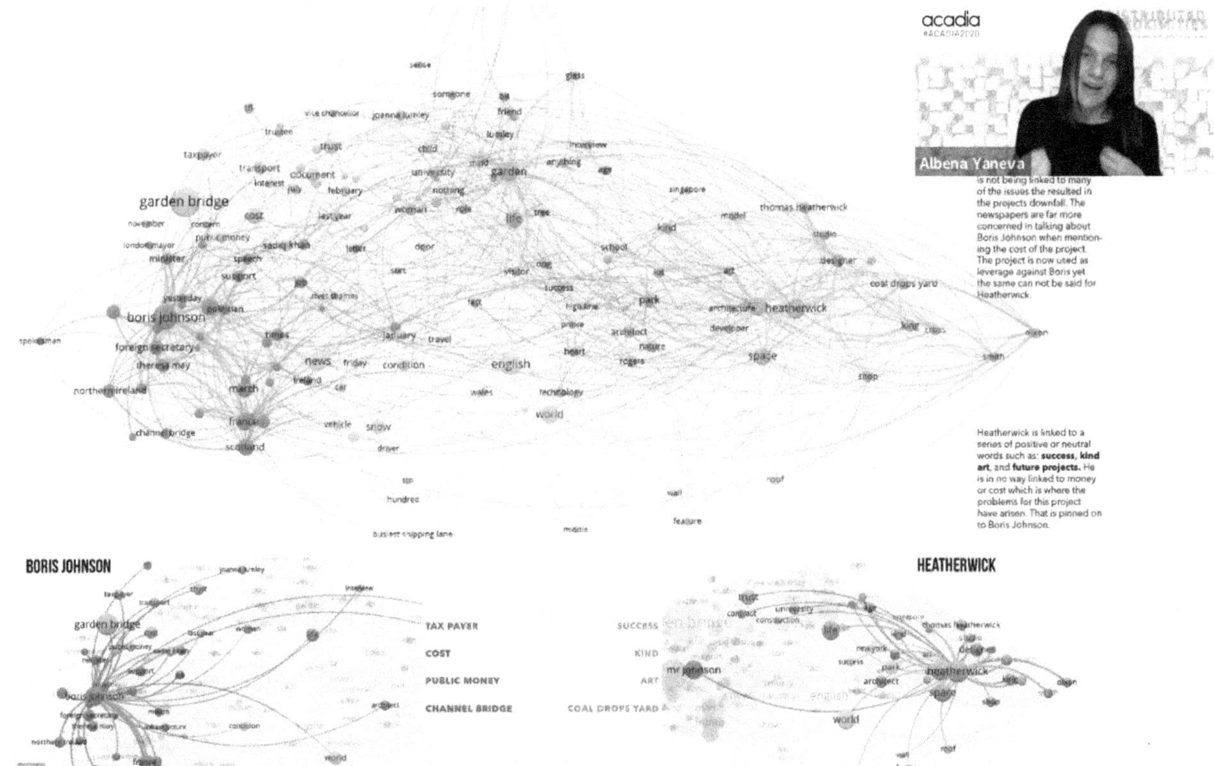

4 "This specific epistemology of computation helps us to develop an analytic method capable of revealing a degree of complexity that we cannot capture with other tools and other methods. The mapping captures, in a way, the fluidity of the social." —Albena Yaneva (Image: The Manchester School of Architecture)

As we bring this conversation to a close, I'd like to put Molly on the spot. Molly, you participated in the conference's opening keynote event as well, and I'm wondering if you'd like to offer any closing reflections?

MWS: We started out with a conversation with Jennifer Gabrys about her work with sensing technology, and her recent book *How to Do Things with Sensors*. What's so neat about that book is that it's a little bit manifesto, a little bit how-to guide, a little bit turning that upside down, and making us ask questions about what it really does mean when there are sensors in the environment and there is a "becoming environmental" around us, and the ecologies are activated in certain kinds of ways.

It was interesting to start with a session titled "Ecology and Ethics," which dealt very much with ways we can act within the world. In many ways, this boils down to morals, and I wondered if maybe we needed to open that up a little bit and look at that a little bit more objectively and differently.

What I think is fascinating about this session is that there have been a number of different ways to look at doing that. From Hernán, we have an idea of dirty computation or flexibility. From Albena, we see the networks come to life, the unseen, and the way of not just mapping, but understanding the discourses that those things are a part of and are unnaturally separate from. Nicholas has raised the notions of uncertainty and inclusion together. And Winka, I'm struck by what you bring to the notion of collaboration and what it takes to do this profession, which is paid less than other design professions and requires a more complete education than ever before. Indeed, this is a matter of collaboration. None of us does any of this alone, and I think that architects always go back and forth between understanding our work as solitary or as collaborative. I wonder if we might think of it as making material for all of us—for productive conversations and future provocations, and another year of ACADIA, and another 60 years of computation.

KV: I love the way this panel embraced the uncertainty about where the conversation could go, and I'm so glad that it ended up where it did. Thank you, everyone, for bringing these kinds of provocations and speculations to the table.

NOTES

1. "A Conversation on Data and Bias," this volume.
2. Ibid.

Hernán Díaz Alonso assumed the role of Director at SCI-Arc beginning in the 2015 academic year. He has been a distinguished faculty member since 2001, serving in several leadership roles, including Coordinator of the graduate thesis program from 2007 to 2010, and Graduate Programs Chair from 2010 to 2015. He is widely credited with spearheading SCI-Arc's transition to digital technologies, and he played a key role in shaping the school's graduate curriculum over the last decade. In 2018, Díaz Alonso ranked among the top 25 Most Admired Educators by DesignIntelligence Rankings. In parallel to his role at SCI-Arc, Díaz Alonso is principal of the Los Angeles–based architecture office HDA-x (formerly Xefirotarch). His multidisciplinary practice is praised for its work at the intersection of design, animation, interactive environments, and radical architectural explorations. Over the course of his career as an architect and educator, Díaz Alonso has earned accolades for his leadership and innovation, as well as his ability to build partnerships among varied constituencies. In 2005 he was the winner of MoMA PS1's Young Architects Program (YAP) competition, and in 2012 he received the Educator of the Year award from the American Institute of Architects (AIA). He won the 2013 AR+D Award for Emerging Architecture and a 2013 Progressive Architecture Award for his design of the Thyssen-Bornemisza Pavilion/Museum in Patagonia, Argentina.

Winka Dubbeldam is the Chair and Miller Professor of Architecture at the University of Pennsylvania's Stuart Weitzman School of Design and the Director of the Advanced Research and Innovation Lab [ARI], and has taught at Columbia, Cornell, and Harvard, among other universities. Dubbeldam was the external examiner for the AA in London (six years), and currently at the Bartlett London. Dubbeldam was named one of the DesignIntelligence 30 Most Admired Educators in 2015. Winka is also the founder/principal of the WBE firm Archi-Tectonics NYC, and is widely known for her award-winning work. Archi-Tectonics recently won the Asian Games 2022 Design Competition in Hangzhou, China (2018), currently under construction. Recent awards include the A+ Award for the Asian Games 2022 masterplan & buildings, the RTF award for the 512GW Townhouse, and recognition for the Inscape project by *Wired* magazine as "one of the 25 best architecture projects in 2019." Publications include the three monographs Winka Dubbeldam, Architect (010, 1996), AT-INdex (Princeton Press, 2006), and Archi-Tectonics (DAAB, 2010); a new book, *Strange Objects*, is planned for 2021 with Actar Spain.

Nicholas de Monchaux is Professor and Head of Architecture at MIT. He is a partner in the architecture practice modem, and a founder of the design technology company Local Software. Until 2020 he was Professor of Architecture and Urban Design, and Craigslist Distinguished Chair in New Media at UC Berkeley. De Monchaux is the author of *Spacesuit: Fashioning Apollo* (MIT Press, 2011), an architectural and urban history of the Apollo Spacesuit, winner of the Eugene Emme award from the American Astronautical Society and shortlisted for the Art Book Prize, as well as *Local Code: 3,659 Proposals about Data, Design, and the Nature of Cities* (Princeton Architectural Press, 2016). His design work has been exhibited widely, including at the Biennial of the Americas, the Venice Architecture Biennale, the Lisbon Architecture Triennale, SFMOMA, the Yerba Buena Center for the Arts, the Storefront for Art and Architecture, and the Museum of Contemporary Art in Chicago. His work has been supported by MacDowell, the Santa Fe Institute, the Smithsonian Institution, the Hellman Fund, and the Bakar Spark Fund. He is a Fellow of the American Academy in Rome.

Molly Wright Steenson is Senior Associate Dean for Research in the College of Fine Arts at Carnegie Mellon University, where she is also the K&L Gates Associate Professor of Ethics & Computational Technologies and Associate Professor in the School of Design. She is the author of *Architectural Intelligence: How Designers and Architects Created the Digital Landscape* (MIT Press, 2017), a history of AI's impact on design and architecture, and the co-editor of *Bauhaus Futures* (MIT Press, 2019). She was previously an assistant professor at the University of Wisconsin–Madison and an associate professor at the Interaction Design Institute Ivrea in Italy, home of the Arduino. She began her tech and design career at groundbreaking studios, consultancies, and Fortune 500 companies in 1995. Steenson holds a PhD in Architecture from Princeton and an MED from the Yale School of Architecture.

Albena Yaneva is Professor of Architectural Theory and Director of the Manchester Architecture Research Group (MARG) at the Manchester Urban Institute. She has been Visiting Professor at Princeton School of Architecture and Parsons, New School. She held the prestigious Lise Meitner Visiting Chair in Architecture at the University of Lund, Sweden (2017–2019). She is the author of several books: *The Making of a Building* (Peter Lang, 2009), *Made by the OMA: An Ethnography of Design* (010 Publishers, 2009), *Mapping Controversies in Architecture* (Routledge, 2012), *Five Ways to Make Architecture Political: An Introduction to the Politics of Design Practice* (Bloomsbury, 2017), *Crafting History: Archiving and the Quest for Architectural Legacy* (Cornell University Press, 2020), and *The New Architecture of Science: Learning from Graphene* (World Scientific, 2020), co-authored with Sir

Kostya S. Novoselov. Her work has been translated into German, Italian, Spanish, French, Portuguese, Thai, Polish, Turkish, and Japanese. Yaneva is the recipient of the RIBA President's award for outstanding research (2010).

Kathy Velikov is an Architect, Associate Professor at University of Michigan's Taubman College, and the current President of ACADIA. She is founding partner of the research-based practice rvtr, which serves as a platform for exploration and experimentation in the intertwinements between architecture, the environment, technology, and sociopolitics. Her work ranges from material prototypes that explore new possibilities for architectural skins that mediate matter, energy, information, space, and atmosphere between bodies and environments, to the investigation of urban infrastructures and territorial practices, working through the techniques of mapping and analysis, speculative design propositions, physical prototyping, exhibitions, and writing. She is a recipient of the Architectural League's Young Architects Award and the Canadian Professional Prix de Rome in Architecture. Kathy is co-author of *Infra Eco Logi Urbanism* (Park Books, 2015) and is currently working on a new book, *Ambiguous Territory: Architecture, Landscape and the Postnatural* (Actar, 2021).

PEER-REVIEWED PAPERS

SPECULATION AND CRITIQUE

"[T]he work of speculation explores not only the possibilities of technology, but also the political, social, ideological, and ecological systems within which it is entangled. It is less about experimenting with how things are now or making them better or incrementally different, but more about envisioning other and alternative possibilities and systems altogether. In this way, speculation inherently carries a critical as well as a deeply political dimension in its practice."

—Kathy Velikov, "A Conversation on Speculation and Critique"

By definition, all of the work included in this volume involves some form of hypothesizing speculation in order to stretch the bounds of the research. This section on "Speculation and Critique" includes a selection of work that exhibits the type of speculation in the service of critique so succinctly defined by Velikov in her introduction to the conference's closing conversation.

Discrete Automation

Community-Led Housing Platforms

Mollie Claypool
Manuel Jimenez Garcia
Gilles Retsin
Clara Jashke
Kevin Saey
Automated Architecture Ltd &
AUAR Labs, The Bartlett, UCL

1 The housing prototype Block West was co-designed and built by the community of Knowle West at the entrance of the Knowle West Media Centre in Bristol, UK.

ABSTRACT

Globally, the built environment is inequitable. And while construction automation is often heralded as the solution to labor shortages and the housing crisis, such methods tend to focus on technology, neglecting the wider socioeconomic contexts. Automated Architecture (AUAR), a spinoff of AUAR Labs at The Bartlett School of Architecture, UCL, asserts that a values-centered, decentralized approach to automation centered around local communities can begin to address this material hegemony. The paper introduces and discusses AUAR's platform-based framework, Discrete Automation, which subverts the status quo of automation that excludes those who are already disadvantaged into an inclusive network capable of providing solutions to both the automation gap and the assembly problem.

Through both the wider context of existing modular housing platforms and issues of the current use of automated technologies in architectural production, Discrete Automation is discussed through the example of Block Type A, a discrete timber building system, which in conjunction with its combinatorial app constitutes the base of a community-led housing platform developed by AUAR. Built case studies are introduced alongside a discussion of the applied methodologies and an outlook on the platform's potential for scalability in an equitable, sustainable manner.

INTRODUCTION

The state of the built environment serves as a tangible example of societal values. Inequity abounds: housing is in crisis (Woloszko and Causa 2020). It is vital to radically rethink what is built, and how. And despite a need to exponentially increase automation in construction due to significant automation gap (Bughin et al. 2016), a labor shortage, and high need for housing, technology alone is not the answer. We must consider the processes and frameworks that are used, and the consequences of these processes more broadly as a representation of societal values. Automated Architecture (AUAR) Ltd, a spinoff of AUAR Labs at The Bartlett School of Architecture, UCL, argues that local communities need to be put at the forefront of the discussion of automation using a values-centered, decentralized approach, particularly because automation tends to further disadvantage those who are already disadvantaged the most (Eubanks 2018; O'Neil 2016). AUAR proposes to do this through a platform-based approach, considering the design production process from end to end. And this is apt timing, as the construction technology ecosystem is shifting towards integrated software platforms, predicting that a combination of multiple platforms will come to coexist (Bartlett et al. 2020).

To frame the platform approach, AUAR utilizes Discrete Automation. As previously explored in the author's work, Discrete Automation considers every element as a piece of data that can be computed (Claypool 2020; Retsin 2020). This enables the design of new frameworks around architectural production that may anticipate full automation, and enabling an "architecture for automation." Discrete Automation is also a system for production with the ability to localize the mass production of self-similar elements. This addresses what has been referred to as the "assembly problem," and enables the anticipation of a vision for full automation where "humans, robots and materials can collectively build structures through local interaction rather than top-down centralized control" (Tibbits 2017).

Discrete Automation can act as a counterpoint to large-volume modular housing platforms such as Bryden Wood, Urban Splash, TopHat, and Katerra, companies funded by significant venture capital investment[1] (see, for example, Sweet 2018). These companies implement automation and prefabrication using modular building systems produced in off-site, centralized factories, disconnected from the contexts in which these systems are deployed. Furthermore, the workers who build these modular housing systems are currently "imported" onto sites from elsewhere, resulting in limited opportunity for modular investment in local employment and economic development. These housing platforms

2 Prototype of the Automated Living System (ALIS) for the BPro Show 2019 at The Bartlett School of Architecture.

3 AUAR Home-Office installation at the Building Centre. This installation reused the blocks from the BPro show installation.

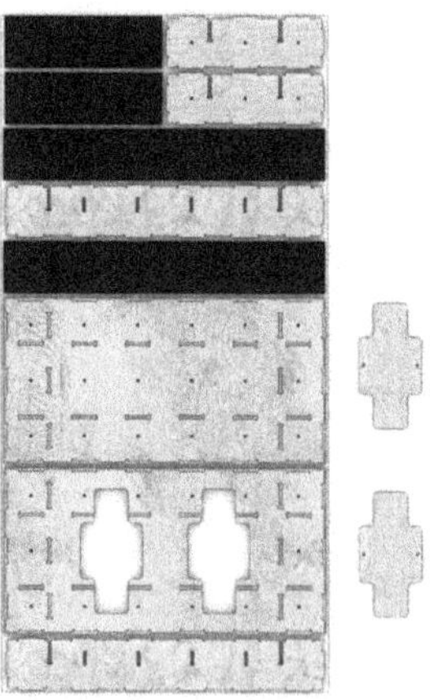

4

are then seen as displacing local jobs, which creates resistance and skepticism among local communities and creates limited localized capacity for these kinds of building systems (Mean et al. 2017). Automation is met with similar resistance amongst local communities, particularly as automation often affects more significantly those who are already disadvantaged (Benjamin 2019).

Decentralizing automation in production begins to unravel the long, widely inefficient production chains that currently exist in design production. However, in this decentralization there must also be a networked approach in order to ensure that knowledge is not lost between localities, guaranteeing knowledge transfer and mutual benefits. To achieve this, new tools must be developed that: (1) enable accessibility to automation and novel building systems for housing to democratize their use and implementation in local settings in ways that empower and enhance collaboration with the community, responding to needs and reducing cultural barriers to new ways of producing housing using automation; (2) consider scalability of the social and technological infrastructure, and how this enables coordination across localities; and (3) provide lifelong learning tools and skills for communities to be empowered in a sustainable and values-centered way in engaging with the production of the built environment.

Key to AUAR's approach is a low-threshold Discrete building system named Block Type A, designed both for collaborative construction and increasing automation, which is embedded with tangible, accessible design intelligence. This sits in contrast to design coordination strategies such as Building Information Modeling (BIM), which leverages digital technologies to generate a centralized shared means of production but still relies on technical drawings, specification text, etc. Block Type A, on the other hand, utilizes an ecology of design, visualization, and assembly tools that act as a platform for interfacing between design and construction, specifically designed for the local communities who will use it to build the homes and spaces they need.

This paper discusses AUAR's platform development as a form of social and technological infrastructure, as well as Block Type A. Several projects by AUAR utilizing Block Type A will be discussed, including Block West in Knowle West, Bristol, UK. Block West was a collaboration with Knowle West Media Centre (KWMC) and social scientist Dr. Claire McAndrew. Other instances of Block Type A will be presented to illustrate the versatility and applicability of the Discrete approach for housing.

METHODS

Equity & Participation

The tools and building systems are developed through an "engaged scholarship," or values-centered, approach. An engaged-scholarship approach addresses "our most pressing social, civic, and ethical problems" (Boyer 1996) and knowledge exchange through participatory approaches to design such as co-design. Co-design at each stage of development of a project is used as a means of providing a value-centered approach. This enables the community users of a design to participate in its process of creation, as a means of "equalizing power relations, democratic practices, situation-based action, mutual learning, tools and techniques, and alternative visions about technology" (van der Velden and Mortberg 2014).

To increase equity in participation by local communities in AUAR projects, AUAR engages with communities of people tied to local organizations, such as Knowle West Media Centre in Bristol, UK. Involving both tradespeople as well as laypeople, AUAR projects include people from a wide range of demographics, including gender, age, race, education, etc., who are paid a daily wage to participate in the projects. The framework that AUAR uses serves as a prototype response to the UK government's Levelling Up

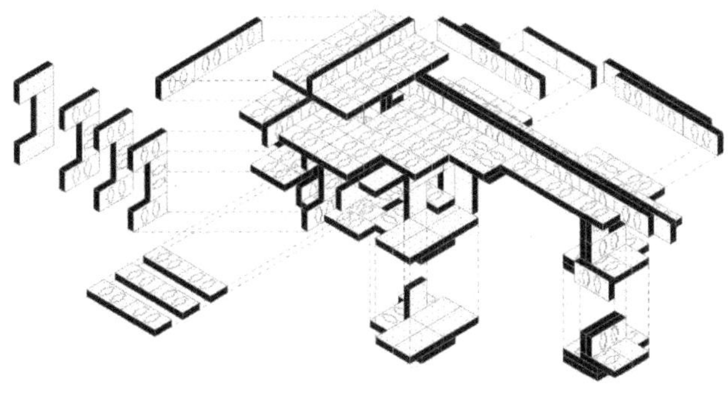

5

4 CNC layout and assembly diagram of the Block Type A system by AUAR Labs.

5 Assembling Block Type A configurations is easy: smaller configurations can be preassembled and combined to make a finished product.

agenda (Sainsbury 2021) as a means for driving investment in local communities in terms of both skills and housing. By engaging with and empowering community users in this way, a values-centered platform emerges that enables an increase in digital construction skills in localized settings.

Block Type A

Drawing on previous work on Discrete architecture (Köhler 2016; Retsin 2016, 2019; Sanchez 2017) and other low-threshold building systems (Parvin 2013), AUAR develops Discrete building systems for housing called kits of parts, consisting of self-similar elements without designated functions. Block Type A is a rectangular box with dimensions of 120 cm × 60 cm × 20 cm. The blocks are fabricated using standardized sheet timber that is processed by CNC milling services. Block Type A is designed to fit exactly on a single standard plywood sheet of 244 cm × 120 cm with a minimum of waste material. The CNC-cut parts are then manually assembled using off-the-shelf tools and materials. The inner frames of the blocks are connected to adjacent blocks using steel rods, which are post-tensioned together. Based on the granularity of the Discrete, the post-tensioning method AUAR is applying uses reversible connections consisting of local Discrete rods that enable blocks to be added to the structure one by one.

Automation

The design of Block Type A enables us to construct a vision for increasing automation. This occurs at several scales: prefabrication of the blocks themselves as well as assembly. Robotic prefabrication of the blocks has been tested in the 2018–2019 project Automated Living System (ALIS) in Research Cluster 4 (RC4) in AUAR Labs at The Bartlett School of Architecture, UCL. Two ABB industrial robot arms were used to assemble building components (Fig. 7). One robot would pick and place the CNC-cut elements on a jig, and hold them in place while the other robot nailed the parts together.

As a digital material, the blocks can be described by 18 cubic voxels with a side dimension of 20 cm (6 voxels × 3 voxels × 1 voxel). With a total of 54 connection points per block, each voxel of Block Type A has the potential to connect to another block in various orientations. As a literal translation of these voxels, the blocks fit within the computational backbone of a voxelgrid. This means that the automation of assembly can be speculated on and simulated. This is possible at two scales: the scale of assembling "chunks" of blocks, as demonstrated in work by AUAR outlined below, as well as a more speculative scale of modular distributed robotic assembly, as demonstrated throughout RC4 projects documented elsewhere by the authors. This speculative vision around the progressive increase of automation in design and construction automation is valuable as it serves as a narrative and speculative device for "holding on" and embedding the potential of, and knowledge about, automation within the local communities learning how to use these tools and building systems for the first time.

Platform & Tools

A combination of digital and physical tools constitute the base for AUAR's housing platform. The platform instrumentalizes the digital structure of the blocks within an ecology of tools that communicate with each other due to the standardization of the digital objects. The voxel-based computational logic is agnostic to scale and geometry. This means that the platform can accommodate the inclusion of multiple modular/discrete building systems of any scale. Due to this system agnosticism, the platform is a suite of tools from design-to-production apps that utilize Discrete systems as well as augmented reality/virtual reality (AR/VR), linking together the various parts of an otherwise fragmented production chain. This continues the tradition of the notion of the systematic, gridded architectural drawing, as seen in historical examples such as Walter Segal, as a means of communication (Hilmer 2020) with nonexpert clients.

The three tools—design, fabrication, and assembly—enable the platform to act as an interface between design and construction. The first app, a combinatorial design app, is geared towards addressing the expertise and steep learning curve in digital design software. It is designed for nonexpert audiences with an intuitive 3D environment and ease of use via both desktop and mobile. This app is

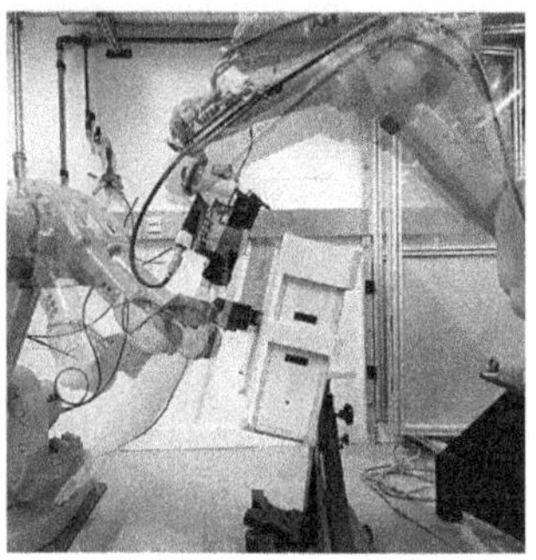

6 Combinatorial app designed for the local community to experiment with the possibilities of the Block Type A system and design their Block West proposal.

7 Two industrial robot arms assemble building blocks as part of the Automated Living System (ALIS) project.

8 Community members and the AUAR team assemble Block West housing prototype at KWMC.

web-based and OS independent, removing an additional user threshold. This application has been continuously evaluated and developed, incrementally incorporating feedback throughout the projects from participants on the ease of use and accessibility as a design communication platform. As an easy and accessible tool that doesn't require extensive training, the combinatorial app is closely linked to the professional CAD tool Rhinoceros 3D, which is used to create a building sequence and a construction manual.

Besides the combinatorial design app, AUAR is also developing a set of VR and AR tools to expand the applicability and accessibility of the construction process and visualization of spaces and structures.

BUILT PROTOTYPES

AUAR, along with its sister lab, AUAR Labs at The Bartlett School of Architecture, UCL, has deployed this ecology alongside the Block Type A system with a number of 1:1 physical prototypes. The first prototype (Fig. 2) was Automated Living System (ALIS), developed in the context of RC4 in the MArch Architectural Design at The Bartlett School of Architecture with students Joana Correia, Evgenia Krassakopoulou, Akhmet Khakimov, Kevin Saey, and Estefania Barrios. A team of three built a 15.8 m^2, 6 m high structure using 60 blocks in five days, later disassembled in two days by two people.

For Home-Office (Fig. 3), a temporary residency space for AUAR at The Building Center, London, 55 blocks were repurposed from the installation of ALIS for a 30 m^2 space that was 3.2 m tall and completed in two days. Home-Office served as a prototype for new models of shared working and living spaces. The project was accompanied by an online booking app with which anyone could reserve a workspace in the installation for a few hours or a day, opening up discussions with those booked around the building system and its spatial potential. These first two projects served as a test for understanding the accessibility of Block Type A. Whereas ALIS was designed and built by architects, Home-Office was partially assembled by nonexpert users encountering Block Type A for the first time.

The third project, Block West (Figs. 1, 5, 8, 11, and 12), was a collaboration with citizen-led digital arts organization Knowle West Media Centre, social scientist Dr. Claire McAndrew, and a group of local Knowle West, Bristol, residents. Using a values-centered approach, AUAR, KWMC, and McAndrew set up a cocreation framework throughout a six-month period. To establish equity between local residents and partners, the project created 25 part-time jobs to be filled by the community throughout the co-designing, fabrication, and assembly processes. This job creation program served as a test and training program for more permanent roles being created by KWMC for their We Can Make project, which takes an arts-led approach to community-led housing. The wages provided for residents to participate is significant in an area like Knowle West, where historically there has been little investment and funds often "wash through" the community. Throughout the project, local residents aged 19 to 76 took part, with a 50/50 male/female cohort, working alongside AUAR and KWMC to level up skills and knowledge within the community. The community co-designed a housing prototype that responded to ideas of what they see missing in their local area: spaces to rest, be together, and work in a safe, outdoor way. The local community of Knowle West learned to use the combinatorial design app alongside automated fabrication technologies in a community digital manufacturing hub, KWMC The Factory, allowing them to think about how to design the homes and community spaces that they need with new tools and technologies. Built out of 145 Block Type A elements, the result of this process—Block West—was prefabricated and assembled by the community in less than two weeks (Fig. 8), and showcases the potential for local communities to

8

take over the future of housing automation by placing their experiences and participation at the heart of local housing production. In 2021 Block West will be dismantled, and the blocks will be dispersed into the community for a second stage of co-design, serving as planters for growing and other smaller community spaces throughout Knowle West.

DISCUSSION

Block West and the other two prototypes begin to set up a framework for innovation in collaborative, cocreated design and construction, while addressing a current tension in digital architectural production. Pointed out by Peggy Deamer (2020), this tension exists in the latent animosity between automation and labor. Instead of using automation to perpetuate a neoliberal attack on collective labor (Deamer 2020), the community-led housing platform using Discrete Automation that AUAR is developing situates itself within a wider paradigm shift in the architectural discipline. Over the last several decades, the discipline has changed in its practices to benefit neoliberalism, which suppresses the strength and power of the local or small-scale. Furthermore, the position of the architect has also become marginalized in this process. A change in architecture is needed both within the discipline and in the ways it engages with other disciplines. This shift can occur through an understanding of automation as a holistic paradigm that can, and should, empower communities instead of suppressing them or being extractive. Through the notion of platforms as distributed architectural vectors, dissemination of knowledge is possible in a way that neoliberal positions so far have prevented digital technologies from achieving. In this, automation itself becomes the primary design project that architecture must confront.

AUAR's Block Type A system sits in a wider technical context of other companies and research laboratories also working on modular housing platforms. However, these systems stop short of integrating their modularity into a wider discussion around the disciplinary culture of the built environment. Modular systems are often considered to be a value-engineered consequence. A radical rethinking of the design production process is needed in order to position them as a starting point for a renewed understanding of the potential of automation in architecture.

Scalability of Parts

Traditionally, "self-build" happens within a DIY atmosphere mostly resulting in localized ad hoc solutions, containing a plethora of parts and procedures that require extensive skill sets, expertise, knowledge, and labor. While this might work as one-off solutions, it is not scalable. Other examples attempting to improve on self-build, such as WikiHouse, have begun to pave the way for a more systematic and digitized approach. As a housing platform, it fails to address the issue of scalability, being stuck with the typology of a single family house with a pitched roof. In addition, WikiHouse was originally conceptualized as a parametric project, yet it is now being pushed towards a modular approach due to costs as it scales up production. WikiHouse is in danger of falling into folk politics—a "politics of immediacy" (Srnicek and Williams 2016)—by not addressing scalability at the very core of the project.

Block Type A in combination with a values-centered approach does not require significant infrastructure when scaling up. The simplicity of the system—using only one block—enables distributed production in localized manufacturing settings (such as KWMC The Factory or

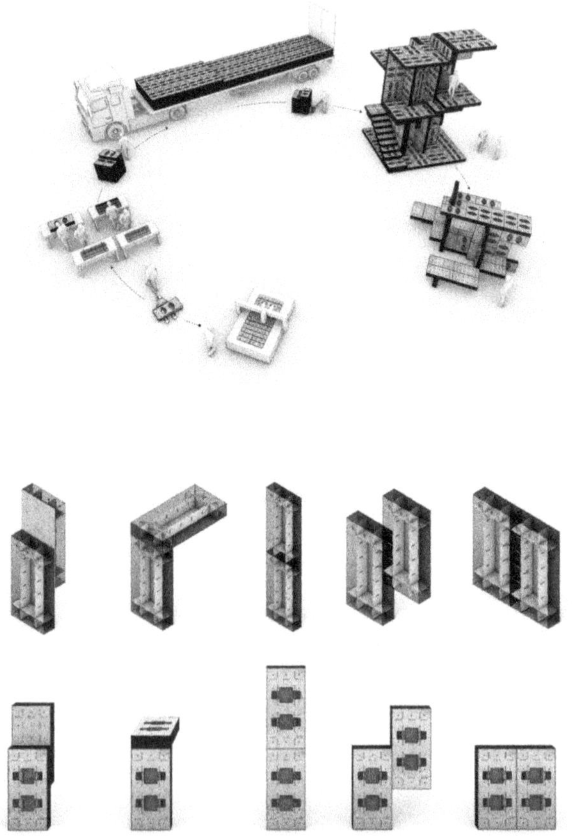

9

10

others operating at the community scale), eliminating the need for a large, centralized factory. The work completed by the community utilizing the combinatorial design app does not lose relevance, as the computational logic based on voxels is agnostic to scale. As a material system, a shift to larger-scale construction can easily be made. Shifting from plywood to, for example, LVL can scale up the system to multistory buildings without overhauling its logic. Furthermore, the connection logic of Block Type A is universal (Fig. 10), translating into a limited set of tasks having to be learned by local people in order to master the system. This also simplifies the communication of the construction logic itself. As an interface, the intuitivity of the combinatorial design app and its 3D workspace directly corresponds with the building system, providing synchronicity between the virtual and the physical at any scale.

Scalability within Communities

AUAR's approach is inherently scalable not only in terms of Block Type A but also due to its project-agnostic virtual-physical interface, which streamlines and facilitates nonhierarchical interaction by a wider set of stakeholders such as local communities of residents who are working together to produce housing. This drives an exponential growth of knowledge and understanding of digital construction skills in the communities. This is especially relevant for communities such as Knowle West, which has high levels of disadvantage and in-work poverty, and a high number of people in traditional construction trades jobs that are at risk from increasing automation. As a community, Knowle West is already actively seeking responses to the socioeconomic issues it is facing via the work of Knowle West Media Centre and other community-led organizations, providing an ideal test bed for the platform. Such communities can grow into hubs of knowledge and expertise and, in doing so, accelerate the power of local "bottom-up" change. This means that hubs of knowledge shift from the silo of academia or the off-site factory to being embedded in communities that previously had little opportunity to access this kind of knowledge, skills, or jobs. Scaling up projects into multiple-story housing blocks increases complexity on many levels, yet taking a values-centered approach means that local communities remain key throughout that scaling process in determining what values should remain at a project's core. The community actors also can have a continued involvement in the platform ranging from inducting and engaging other communities as more projects are developed in other localities, creating a network of mutually beneficial knowledge exchange and transfer. This growing network can function as a social and technological infrastructure within communities that can anticipate and support a change in scales of housing production.

Scalability of Production

Block Type A shares the WikiHouse approach of using modular timber elements consisting of CNC-cut parts with other companies working in housing production such as blokbuild, U-Build, and Mass Bespoke. What distinguishes AUAR's housing platform is the Discrete approach to modularity in the building system, as well as the development of accessible design-to-production tools. Unlike traditional modular systems, which rely on kits of predefined parts (e.g., walls, stairs), the Discrete geometry of Block Type A enables design possibilities to remain open-ended.

As a reversible system, Block Type A can respond to long-term as well as short-term needs. When a structure moves beyond its practicability or prescribed lifetime, the blocks can be repurposed back into the platform as available building materials within certain constraints (Fig. 9). This requires analysis and maintenance of the blocks. The management and upkeep of this afterlife also requires its own logistical application within the platform.

As an extension of the design phase, the combinatorial design app could be further developed to immediately inform the designer about the amount of blocks, the needed materials, and the included costs, as well as performing a

11

9 The Block Type A system is an entirely localized building system. Cutting, prefabrication, and assembly can take place locally. The blocks can be configured and then reconfigured in a variety of ways.

10 Block Type A blocks can be assembled in a variety of ways, making Block Type A a versatile building system.

11 The housing prototype Block West was co-designed and built by the community of Knowle West at the entrance of the Knowle West Media Centre in Bristol, UK.

structural analysis to verify if the proposed design is structurally sound. Additionally, planning of the construction site is presently a predominantly manual task. Future automation could assist in the creation of a building sequence, a construction manual, and a database of materials and machines, tutorials, a network of material suppliers, producers, and collaborators as well as a forum for discussion, available via the software for web/tablet/phone.

In terms of physical automation, automated prefabrication of the building block as demonstrated in the ALIS project should be tested further. In a move to robotic assembly of the building blocks, three potential paradigms are being researched. First, industrial robots, in combination with a human worker and guided by an AR application, could assemble larger chunks that fit standard transportation. These chunks would then be assembled on-site using standardized connections. A second development would be moving this collaboration on-site using existing autonomous robots that assist a team of workers. Finally, on-site assembly could be completely automated using distributed robots designed in-house specifically for the system, as demonstrated by multiple projects in the context of RC4 at The Bartlett School of Architecture, UCL.

CONCLUSION

This work constitutes an effort to break down barriers of privilege, money, and power in the housing system by creating opportunities for communities to engage with Discrete Automation and take their local built environment into their own hands. It serves as an accelerator for a values-centered approach to collaboration using Discrete systems, democratizing and distributing the tools, processes, and technology into communities.

The UK government is now recognizing the social value of this approach. In an effort to support cocreation and design of appropriate digital technologies and services that will support a fairer, more inclusive society, the UK's Engineering and Physical Sciences Research Council (EPSRC) has added "societal and cultural change—managing the disruptive impact of digital technologies" as a core theme that EPSRC-funded work must address (EPSRC 2020). AUAR believes successful situation-based change can be achieved by taking an asset-based approach, assuming 80% of what is needed is already present in a place. The core issue is reframing the process of creation to be more values-centered, focused on identifying what is missing from a place, and designing tools and processes that can begin to support a process of "filling the gaps."

Discrete building systems are adaptive and responsive to different contexts. In combination with placing higher value on cocreation, the generic building blocks, reversible connections, and ease of design and assembly provide a low-threshold system accessible to people who are most vulnerable to social inequity. This enables cocreation of alternative visions of housing and technology.

The scalability of the platform is central to the sustainability of this approach. A growing network of communities have "leveled up," constructing a distributed, cooperative network of skills and knowledge around automation in housing production. Material scalability is achieved through a horizontal distribution of fabrication within the network. AUAR does not sit not at the center of this network but functions as a link and a means of communication and knowledge transfer between local community actors.

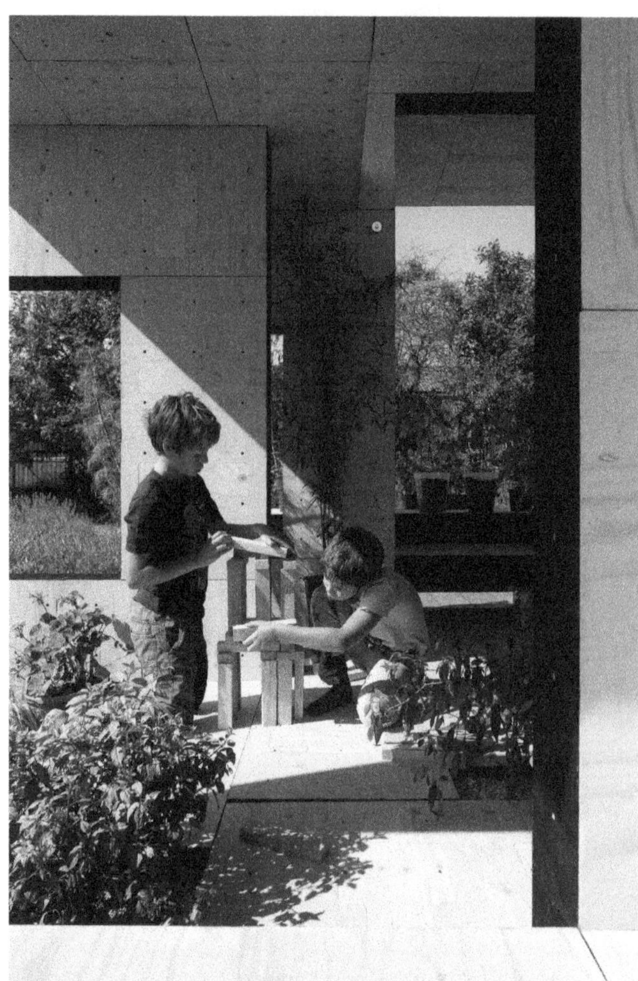

12 The housing prototype Block West was co-designed and built by the community of Knowle West at the entrance of the Knowle West Media Centre in Bristol, UK.

ACKNOWLEDGMENTS

Automated Architecture (AUAR) Ltd and AUAR Labs are directed by Mollie Claypool, Gilles Retsin, and Manuel Jimenez Garcia with Clara Jaschke, Nikolaos Tsikinis, David Doria, Danae Parissi, Tomas Tvarijonas, and Kevin Saey. We express our deepest appreciation to all the people who form the communities at the center of this research for their motivation and input. Special thanks to Dr. Claire McAndrew (The Bartlett) and Melissa Mean (Knowle West Media Centre) for the invaluable collaborations and insights. We are grateful for the structural engineering support by Manja van de Worp of YIP Engineering. The work in this paper would not be possible without the support of Transforming Construction Network Plus, The Bartlett School of Architecture, and the South West Creative Technology Network (SWCTN). Finally, we thank everyone involved in the construction of the prototypes.

NOTES

1. Urban Splash, a modular off-site solution, recently partnered with Japan's biggest house builder, bringing a £90m investment boost to the UK housing market. TopHat, founded in 2016, delivering developments "to a move-in ready standard," received £75m from Goldman Sachs this year despite still being in the process of developing its first scheme. Bryden Wood Technology Ltd., along with its partners, received UKRI funding in 2018 for its SeISmic (Standardization of School Components) project, which allows users to customize the design of a school; Katerra received $865m in a funding round led by Softbank last year.

REFERENCES

Bartlett, Katy, et al. 2020. "Rise of the Platform Era: The Next Chapter in Construction Technology." McKinsey & Company. https://www.mckinsey.com/industries/private-equity-and-principal-investors/our-insights/rise-of-the-platform-era-the-next-chapter-in-construction-technology.

Benjamin, Ruha. 2019. *Race After Technology: Abolitionist Tools for the New Jim Code*. Cambridge: Polity Press.

Boyer, Ernest L. 1996. "The Scholarship of Engagement." *Journal of Public Service & Outreach* 1 (1): 11–20.

Bughin, Jacques, et al. 2016. *Digital Europe: Pushing the Frontier, Capturing the Benefits*. McKinsey Global Institute Report, June 2016. https://www.mckinsey.com/~/media/mckinsey/business%20functions/mckinsey%20digital/our%20insights/digital%20europe%20pushing%20the%20frontier%20capturing%20the%20benefits/digital-europe-full-report-june-2016.ashx.

Claypool, Mollie. 2020. "Discrete Automation." In *FABRICATE 2020: Making Resilient Architecture*, 272–279. London: UCL Press.

Deamer, Peggy. 2020. "ACADIA2020 Keynote: A Conversation on Labor & Practice." ACADIA2020 Conference streamed live, March 29, 2020. YouTube video. https://youtu.be/F0Gsrn-p_fo.

Delgado, Juan M. D., et al.. 2019. "Robotics and Automated Systems in Construction: Understanding Industry-Specific Challenges for Adoption." *Journal of Building Engineering* 26. https://doi.org/10.1016/j.jobe.2019.100868.

EPSRC. 2020. "Engineering and Physical Sciences Research Council—About." https://epsrc.ukri.org/.

Eubanks, Virginia. 2018. *Automating Inequality: How High-Tech Tools Profile, Police and Punish the Poor*. New York: St. Martin's Press.

Hilmer, Luisa. 2020. "Participatory Housing: Segal's Self-build Method." In *16th Participatory Design Conference 2020: Participation(s) Otherwise, PDC'20: Vol. 2, June 15–20, 2020*, 68–71. Manizales, Colombia: Association for Computing Machinery. https://doi.org/10.1145/3384772.3385156.

Köhler, Daniel. 2016. *The Mereological City: A Reading of the Works of Ludwig Hilberseimer*. Bielefeld: transcript Verlag.
Mean, Melissa et. al. 2017. *We Can Make: Civic Innovation in Housing*. https://wecanmake.org/wp-content/uploads/2018/04/We-Can-Make-Report-2018r.pdf.

O'Neil, Cathy. 2016. *Weapons of Math Destruction*. New York: Crown Books.

Parvin, Alistair. 2013. "Architecture for the People by the People." Ted2013 video. https://www.ted.com/talks/alastair_parvin_architecture_for_the_people_by_the_people/up-next.

Retsin, Gilles. 2016. "Discrete and Digital." TxA 2016 (unpublished).

Retsin, Gilles. 2019. "Discrete: Reappraising the Digital in Architecture." *Architectural Design* 89 (2): 6–13. https://doi.org/10.1002/ad.2406.

Retsin, Gilles. 2020. "Discrete Timber Assembly." In *FABRICATE 2020: Making Resilient Architecture*, 264–271. London: UCL Press.

Sainsbury, David. 2021. *Levelling up the UK's Regional Economies*. London: Centre for Cities. https://www.centreforcities.org/wp-content/uploads/2021/03/levelling-up-the-uks-regional-economies.pdf.

Sanchez, Jose. 2017. "Combinatorial Commons: Social Remixing in a Sharing Economy." *Autonomous Assembly: Designing for a New Era of Collective Construction. Architectural Design* 87 (4): 16–21. https://doi.org/10.1002/ad.2190.

Srnicek, Nick, and Williams, Alex. 2016. *Inventing the Future: Postcapitalism and a World Without Work*. London & New York: Verso Books.

Sweet, Rod. 2018. "Avoiding the Revolution: Will Offsite Manufacturing Leave the UK Construction Industry Behind?" *Construction Research and Innovation* 9, no. 4: 99–102.

Tibbits, Skylar. 2017. "From Automated to Autonomous Assembly." *Autonomous Assembly: Designing for a New Era of Collective Construction. Architectural Design* 87 (4): 6–15. https://doi.org/10.1002/ad.2189.

van der Velden, Maja, and Christina Mortberg. 2014. "Participatory Design and Design for Values." In *Handbook of Ethics, Values, and Technological Design*, edited by M. J. van den Hoven, P. E. Vermaas, and I. van de Poel, 1–22. Berlin: Springer Verlag.

Woloszko, Nicolas, and Orsetta Causa. 2020. "Housing and Wealth Inequality: A Story of Policy Trade-Offs." https://voxeu.org/article/housing-and-wealth-inequality-story-policy-trade-offs.

IMAGE CREDITS

Figure 1, 3, 11, 12: © Studio NAARO, 2020.
Figure 8: © Ibolya Feher, 2020.

All other drawings and images by the authors.

Mollie Claypool is a theorist with a focus on computation and automation, and its relationship to contemporary building practices. She has written, edited, or consulted on articles and books on these topics, including *Robotic Building: Architecture in the Age of Automation* (Detail Edition, 2019). She studied at Pratt Institute, the Architectural Association, and is completing her PhD at The Bartlett, UCL. Mollie coordinates architectural theory in M.Arch Architectural Design at The Bartlett School of Architecture, UCL, where she is also Co-Director of Automated Architecture Labs.

Gilles Retsin is an architect, educator, and thinker working at the intersection of computation, fabrication, and architecture. He studied architecture in Belgium, Chile, and the UK, where he graduated from the Architectural Association. He has designed multiple provocative schemes for residential and cultural projects and built experimental installations at some of the world's most renowned museums and institutions. Gilles is the Director of M.Arch Architectural Design and Co-Director of Automated Architecture Labs at The Bartlett School of Architecture, UCL.

Manuel Jimenez Garcia is an architect specializing in design, computation, and fabrication including additive manufacturing. His work is regularly exhibited in galleries, and he lectures and delivers workshops on digital design and manufacturing in architecture schools internationally. In addition to his work in Automated Architecture, Manuel is cofounder of the robotic manufacturing design brand Nagami, and is the Director of MSc Architectural Computation and Co-Director of Automated Architecture Labs at The Bartlett School of Architecture, UCL.

Clara Jashke is an architect and researcher specializing in digital tools and technology. She holds a Master's in Architecture from the University of Innsbruck as well as a MRes in Architecture & Digital Theory from The Bartlett School of Architecture, UCL, where she is now a Teaching Fellow in addition to being a Researcher at AUAR.

Kevin Saey is an architect and researcher at design and technology consultancy Automated Architecture with a focus on digital fabrication and computational design with a background in game design. His collaborative work with Gilles Retsin has been exhibited at renowned institutions. Currently he is an architectural design tutor in the B-Pro Program at the Bartlett. Kevin studied Digital Arts and Entertainment at University College West Flanders, MSci in Architecture at KU Leuven and MArch Architecture at The Bartlett School of Architecture, UCL.

Space Group Symmetry Generation for Design

The HORTA Component Library

Duane McLemore
Mississippi State University

1

1 Aggregation of frames derived from the Wigner-Seitz cell of points in an I4-11 pattern within a [5, 5, 5] orthorhombic lattice.

ABSTRACT

This project proposes to implement space group symmetries as a novel descriptive framework for architectural assemblies. To date there is scant examination within architectural computation of this system used to describe the 230 unique configurations of symmetry elements and operations repeating in three dimensions. This research changes this by developing HORTA, a component library for the application of the space groups within Grasshopper. This ongoing project builds a language of arrangement and connectivity from the unambiguous spatial logic and descriptive efficiency of the space groups. This is particularly useful in defining forms for digital fabrication and autonomous assembly at the scale of a material subunit—broadly defined as "bricks." However, it is not limited to this—HORTA has potential for application across scales, wherever control of repetition and combination with a minimal instruction set is useful. The result is not a tool for a singular design process or specific formal outcomes, but a new system for describing aggregations that inherently balance novelty and predictability. With HORTA, aggregations can be proposed that are composed of a finite but scalable number of possible subunits. Inherently symmetrical, any increase in complexity is realized as an increase in rotations and frequencies of similar subunits rather than an increase in unique unit variants. HORTA theorizes that this previously underexplored area of computation can open sophistication not just in forms but in the description of aggregations with minimal instruction sets, resulting in new methods for the calculation and fabrication of architecture.

INTRODUCTION

Computers excel at processing incremental variations. So much so that in architectural computation, a direct relationship between increases in computing power and increasingly complicated formal morphologies is often assumed. This is seen in projects that use a "deformed" grid or lattice to rationalize a shape imposed in a "top-down" fashion. The unit basis is topologically repetitive, but each dimension of each cell is unique. Engel (1967) provided examples in his landmark *Tragsysteme*, and architects have applied these methods with great success as the structure in projects such as the Heydar Aliyev Center by Zaha Hadid Architects (*GA Document* 2017).

Recently, the so-called "discrete tendency" has put forth alternatives to this paradigm by proposing that these advances in computing power be used to realize morphologically simple units in complex aggregations.[1]

In other words, within discrete computation, the number of morphologically distinct units is few, but their combinations and aggregations are complex. Thus, a challenge arises: if these combinations are to develop sophistication through computation, a system for describing and managing them is needed. An opportunity also arises: a system readable by both humans and computers could allow not just computational efficiency but precision and control in design.

This paper proceeds from the question: rather than formulate a new system which satisfies these criteria, can the existing mathematical concept of space group symmetries be used to systematically describe the aggregation of discrete geometric objects in three-dimensional space within architectural computation?

Historical Background

Since Vitruvius, "symmetry" (speaking broadly) was primarily concerned with the study of the proportions of parts to other parts and to the whole. But with the growth of pure mathematics through the 19th century, the subject came within the purview of group theory.

It was with this formal study of the symmetry operations and symmetry elements as mathematical groups that symmetry came to have utility for systematically describing the continuous repetition of objects in a given dimension.[2] The seven distinct crystal systems that tessellate 3D space continuously have long been known. In 1848, physicist Auguste Bravais codified these in combination with the five[3] varieties of cell centerings into the 14 Bravais lattices (Wondratschek 2006).

In their 1892 correspondence, chemists Schoenflies and Fedorov settled the 230 the unique configurations of repetitive geometries that can arise within these lattices (Wondratschek 2006). These were given the unsurprising name the "space groups." Schoenflies invented the notational system still favored by chemists, and what came to be known as the international system was developed by the crystallographers Hermann and Mauguin in the late 1920s and early 1930s (Wondratschek 2006). Today, within mathematics, crystallography, and solid-state chemistry, there are many programs for viewing the space groups but none are suited for implementation in design.[4]

Within Architecture

To date there has been no focused examination of the space groups as a system for design within architecture. The subdivision of space by the symmetrically simplest unit—cubes—is well-developed. In *Digital Architecture Beyond Computers*, Roberto Botazzi (2018) provides an excellent review of the use of voxels, "cubelets," and "proto-voxels" throughout history, linking the cubic subdivision of space to theories of matter and form as far back as Vitruvius. Botazzi credits civil engineer Albert Farwell Bemis[5] for introducing a system for the aggregation of discrete cubic volumes into built form.[6] Later in the 20th century, designers such as Buckminster Fuller, Keith Crichelow, the Pearces, Robert Williams, and others examined cubes and other space-filling polyhedra and quasiregular honeycombs in search of "ideal" architectural forms. Zvi Hecker was notably successful in realizing buildings designed using aggregated polyhedra. Space frames were used extensively for their economical spanning properties. In fine arts, sculptors Tony Smith, Erwin Hauer, and others explored the spatial and affective qualities of repetitive unit geometries.

In this century, voxel lattices are regularly used in imaging and analysis programs. Tomas Saraceno uses complex aggregations extensively in his sculptures.[7] Henning Larsen Architects and Olafur Eliasson used a 2D slice of a 3D tessellation to design the facade system for the Harpa Concert Hall (Henning Larsen n.d.). While Gramazio and Kohler do not work with uninterrupted tessellations of 3D space, their work includes in-depth examination of configurations of unit cells.

With the advance of architectural computation, many programs and plugins have been written that apply continuous spatial subdivisions, cell centerings, and aggregations of discrete elements.[8] But to date, none have utilized the entire system of the Bravais lattices, the space groups, or a notational system for their rigorous deployment in architecture.

This research addresses this gap by creating HORTA, a computer program for the application of space group symmetries.

Project Background

This project is embedded in a larger body of research on symmetry. This emerged from the observation that this fundamental concept is often taught and used imprecisely within architecture, and seeks to address this gap in the discipline. This observation led to the question: Can the order of the space groups drive a design language built on its logic of order[9] and connection?

The most essential contributions of HORTA are that it:

1. *Implements the space groups:* Any combination of symmetry operations and elements in three dimensions can be described by one of these 230 groups. The "closure" of the system ensures rigor and thoroughness in the description of spatial tessellations.
2. *Uses the international system for notation:* This system is readable by humans and machines. These concise and precise instruction sets provide a direct link between design intention and computational execution.
3. *Is structured:* HORTA maintains the index at which each unit cell, subunit, or transformation can be located throughout all component operations.
4. *Is developed for designers:* HORTA is developed for Grasshopper, a common and easy-to-use programming environment.
5. *Does not require mathematical expertise:* Each description consists only of a crystal system and cell centering, and three-part international system symbol. HORTA provides all of these in readable form, alongside instructions to interpret any information specific to a group. The final program will provide flexible means for selecting or constructing space groups, so time is focused on design, not math. Ample feedback is given by the program so that the designer does not need to be an expert in the space groups to use them.
6. *Is an open-ended toolkit:* As of writing, only HORTA allows for use of any values for the axis dimensions and angles. Exposing all lattice, cell, and symmetry operation input parameters, HORTA can utilize the extensive catalog of other component libraries and plug-ins for Grasshopper and Rhino. The final program will provide tools not only for the generation of these geometries in abstract but for their use in making form and space (see "Future Goals").

Audience and Applications

The intended audience is designers, architects, and students regardless of educational level or computational knowledge. The primary focus of development is the autonomous assembly of building elements. (See "Autonomous Construction.") There is potential for application across scales, wherever control over repetition and combination is desirable. For example, at the micro-scale, the anisotropic properties of specific space groups could be used to construct high-performance materials. At the urban scale, the topology of the graph structures of space groups could be useful in the analysis of infrastructural networks. These uses are beyond the scope described here, but the hope is they will be explored in the near future.

METHODS

As stated, HORTA generates and implements the space groups to manipulate geometric objects. Following is a description of the concepts involved, the processes used, and the specific components created.

Symmetries

Three-dimensional symmetries (Table 1) are generated by three primary symmetry operations. These combine with translation to create three secondary symmetry operations. (Vainshtein 1996). All operations are relative to symmetry elements (Fig. 2).

Table 1 Three Dimensional Symmetries.

Symmetries	*Element*	*Symbol*
Primary Operations		
Inversion	*Point*	$\overline{1}$
Rotations (n – Fold)	*Axis*	n
Mirror (Parallel to Current Axis)	*Plane*	m
Secondary Operations		
Mirror (Perpendicular to Current Axis)	*Plane*	$/m$
n – Fold Improper Rotations (Rotate and Invert)	*Axis and Point*	$\overline{n}$
n – Fold Screw – Axis Rotations (Rotate and Translate)	*Axis*	n_q*
Glide Planes (Mirror and Translate)	*Plane*	$a - e, n*$
**See Vainshtein For Additional Information*		

Structure

HORTA was written in the C# programming language. An object oriented language, it is also strongly and statically typed. The operations and geometries could have been handled procedurally, but this would require the types of input objects (such as different geometries) to remain static (unchanging) for the generation of the entire lattice.

Each node, cell, or the contents of these can be seen as instances of the type to which they belong, similar to the cellular structure of lattices. Since each instance is a separate iteration of the program, the type of each input is only static per node or cell. It is possible to provide different input types to different cells (varying geometries or international system symbols).

With an object oriented structure, the outputs from the Lattice Generator component (Fig. 3) are encapsulated. This

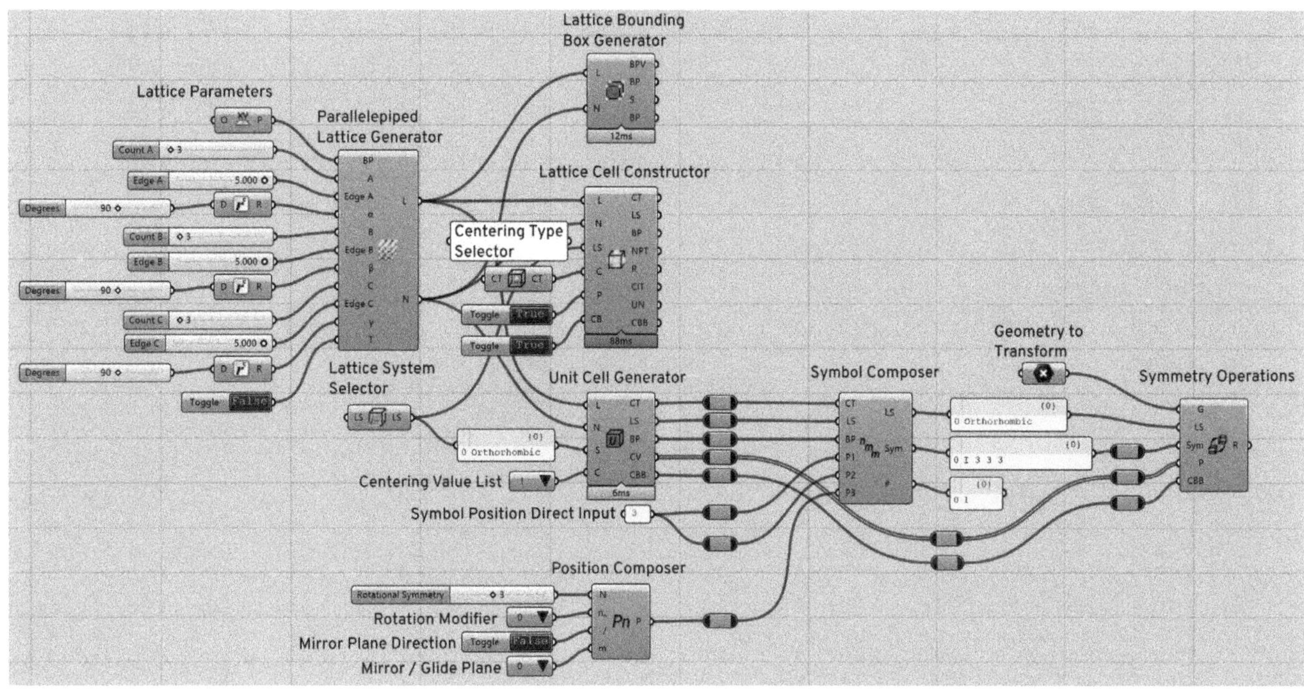

3 Component graph.

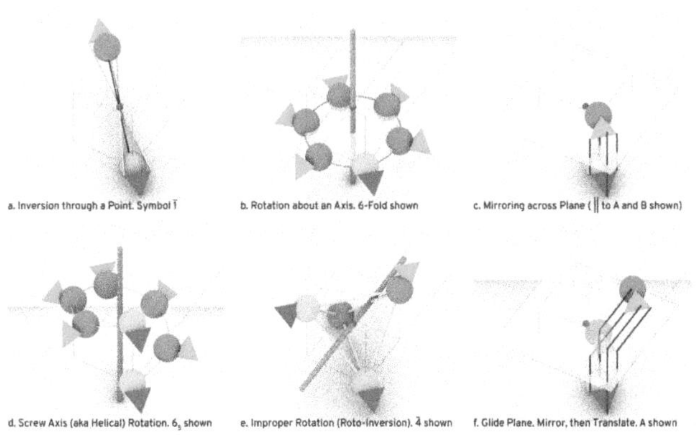

a. Inversion through a Point. Symbol 1̄
b. Rotation about an Axis. 6-Fold shown
c. Mirroring across Plane (|| to A and B shown)
d. Screw Axis (aka Helical) Rotation. 6_1 shown
e. Improper Rotation (Roto-Inversion). 4̄ shown
f. Glide Plane. Mirror, then Translate. A shown

2 Primary and secondary symmetry operations.

way they cannot be connected to components that cannot properly process them, preventing confusing errors, especially among less experienced users.

The strongly and statically typed structure of C# is also computationally efficient. This is important because the program is intended to generate very large sets of geometry. A future goal is to utilize CPU multithreading or GPU processing for faster calculation, which an object oriented structure also makes easier.

Lattice Generation

Using the Parallelepiped Lattice Generator and the Lattice Cell Constructor, HORTA generates the Bravais lattices by applying a cell centering to a crystal system (Vainshtein 1996). The generator takes in a series of parameters (Fig. 4) and procedurally defines:

1. The properties of the whole lattice: (a) basis plane; (b)

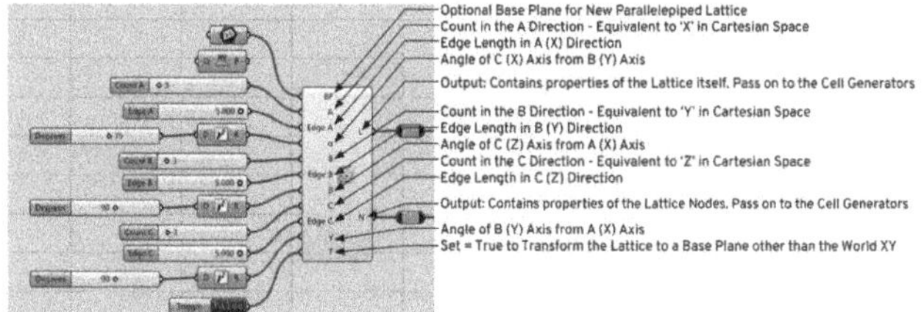

4 Parallelepiped Lattice Generator.

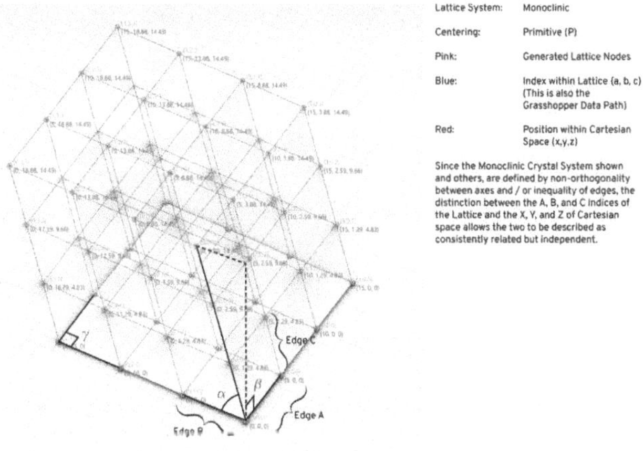

Lattice System: Monoclinic
Centering: Primitive (P)
Pink: Generated Lattice Nodes
Blue: Index within Lattice (a, b, c) (This is also the Grasshopper Data Path)
Red: Position within Cartesian Space (x,y,z)
Since the Monoclinic Crystal System shown and others, are defined by non-orthogonality between axes and / or inequality of edges, the distinction between the A, B, and C indices of the Lattice and the X, Y, and Z of Cartesian space allows the two to be described as consistently related but independent.
Edge C
Edge A
Edge B

5 Monoclinic lattice resulting from generator.

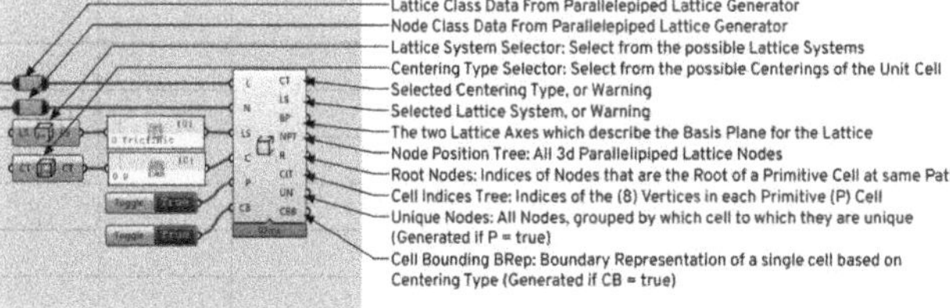

6 Lattice Cell Constructor component.

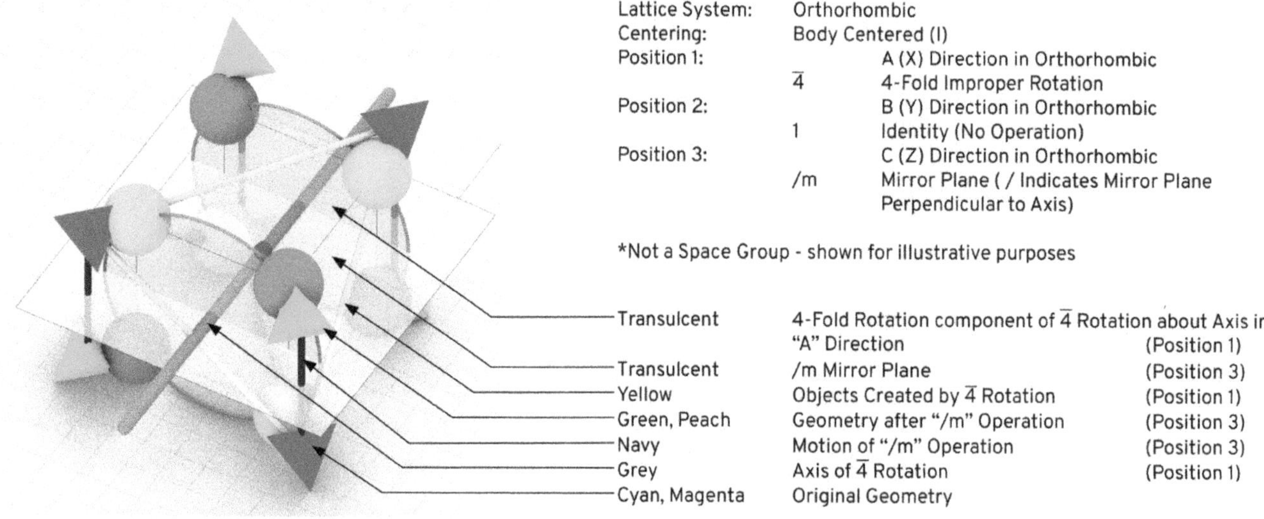

10 Space Group Symmetry operation for *orthorhombic I4-1/m*

Crystal System
Triclinic
Monoclinic
Orthorhombic
Tetragonal
Hexagonal
(Rhombohedral)∗
Cubic
∗Sub – Class of Hexagonal System Identified and Generated Separately here

Table 2

Centering	*Symbol*
Primitive	*P*
Rhombohedral Primitive	*R*
Body	*I*
C – Faces∗	*C∗*
Face – Centered	*F*
∗A and B Face Centerings Allowable Refer to Vainshtein or Wondratschek for Exact Conditions	

Table 3

Number of Elements rotated around Axis at this Position (1-6)
Modifies the Rotational Symmetry provided in N for Screw Axis (n) or Improper Rotations (-)
If Mirror Plane(s) are present from input 'm,' "false" = Planes parallel to Axis
Position Symbol Output to Symbol Composer
Mirror or Glide planes present (m, a, b, c, n, d, or e)
Centering - From Unit Cell or Lattice Cell Generator
Lattice System - From Unit Cell or Lattice Cell Generator
Basis Plane - From Unit Cell or Lattice Cell Generator
Current Lattice System
String containing Long-Form International Symbol for desired Space Group (concatenated from individual Position Symbol inputs)
Number representing desired Space Group from 1-230
String containing all Elements describing Position 1 (example from Position Composer - see Fig. 5)
String containing all Elements describing Position 2 (direct input from Panel)
String containing all Elements describing Position 3 (direct input from Panel)

7 Position and symbol composer components.

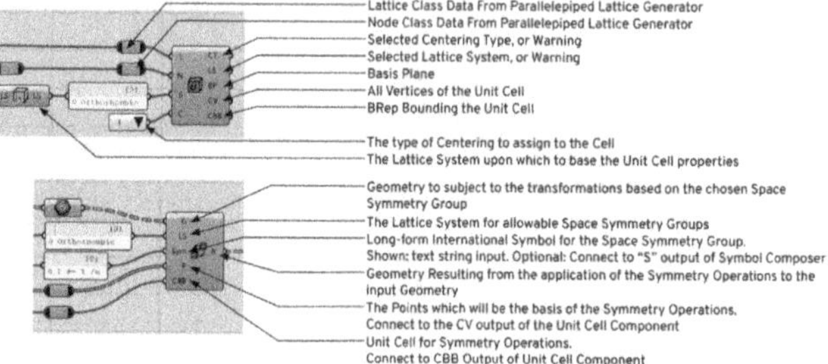

8 & 9 Unit Cell and Symmetry generators.

allowable crystal systems, with allowable centering types and the graph of the lattice expressed in the format *{A, B, C}*. *2. The properties of each node:* (a) the index of the node within the graph expressed in the format *{A, B, C}*, equivalent to the data path at which it can be found; (b) the path of the node and any cells for which it is the primitive root node; (c) a list of paths of all cells to which the node belongs; (d) the coordinates of the node as a point in Cartesian space expressed in the format *(x, y, z)*.

See Figure 5 for an example. These properties are passed to the Lattice Cell Constructor (Fig. 6). Here the intended crystal system and centering are chosen from the lists of those allowable.

This component processes actions over the entire lattice, optimizing by generating only information unique to each cell. For example, instead of creating the node at *{n, p, q}* for each of the eight cells of which it describes a corner, the component creates it only in the cell for which it is the root node and accesses it by reference in the other seven cells.

The Lattice Cell Constructor always passes the unique node and cell information downstream, but the two Boolean toggles can be set to True to expose this information here for use in actions across the entire lattice (for example, to generate geometry packings based only on the Bravais lattices). The root nodes are used in both the Symmetry Operations component and later to translate its results into each cell of the lattice.

International Notation System

As mentioned, the international notation system has potential utility as an instruction set because it is concise and readable by humans and computers. It is composed of only five pieces of information: the crystal system, the centering type, and three positions:

Crystal System | Centering | P_1 | P_2 | P_3 |

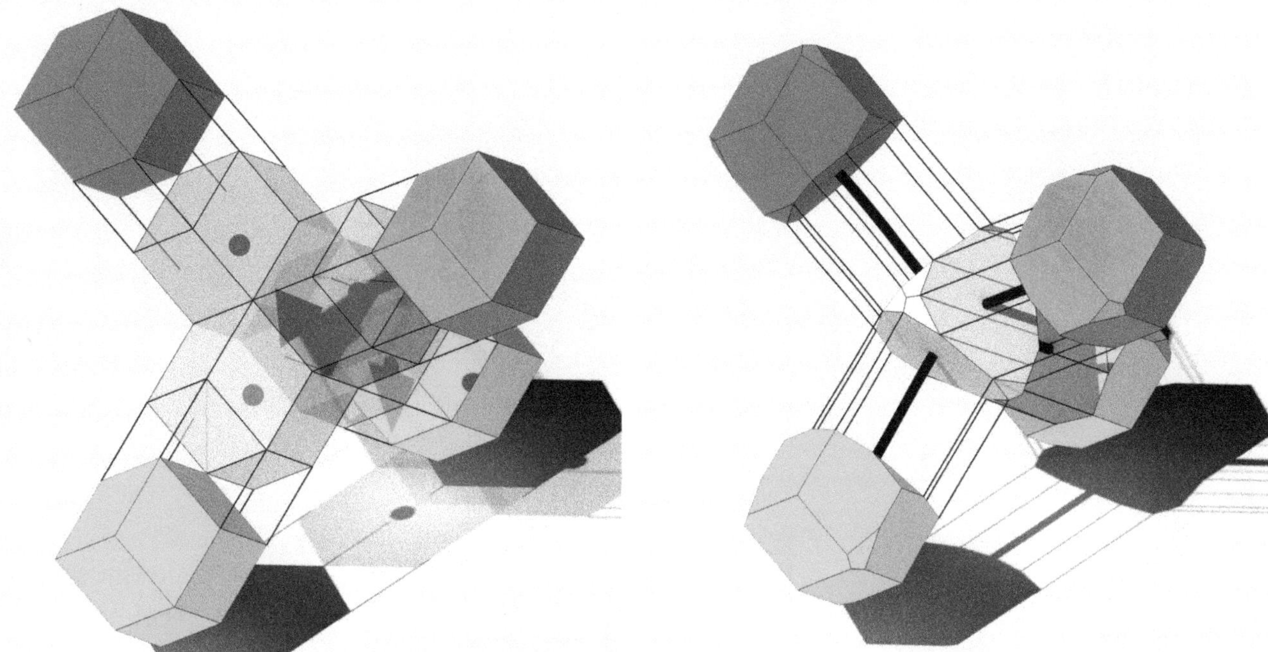

11 Comparison of patterns generated by orthorhombic 1114 without (L) and with (R) the root node of the unit cell included.

A typical symbol reads similar to:
Cubic P 4_2/m 3 2/n (Space Group #223)
Each element has a unique and distinct meaning, as shown in Tables 2 and 3.

In HORTA, the symbol can be provided as a text string or by using the Position Composer and Symbol Composer (Fig. 7). The Position Composer produces a correctly formatted symbol for a single position in the international system. The Symbol Composer aggregates these with the Bravais lattice from Lattice Cell Constructor or Unit Cell Generator to compose an entire symbol. These components prevent the errors resulting from incorrectly formatted text input. If a text string input has an error, a filter is being implemented within the Symbol Composer to return only valid space group symbols and a warning message with how to fix the error. See "Feedback" for an example.

The Unit Cell

The Unit Cell Generator receives the lattice and node information from the Lattice Generator and creates only the node and cell information for a single unit cell for efficiency. It provides this information to the Symmetry Operations component for use as its bases of transformations.[10]

Space Group Symmetry Generation

The unit cell and international system symbol information are passed to the Symmetry Operations component, which transforms the provided geometry with respect to the symmetry elements defined by the symbol (Fig. 9).

The cyan and magenta objects closest to the camera are the original objects (Fig. 10). The P_n transformations are applied in order, so these objects are subjected to a four-fold improper rotation with respect to the axis parallel to A and the point at I. Then, since P_2 is identity, there is no change. Finally, per P_3 they are mirrored across a plane perpendicular to z, as denoted by /.

Geometry Input

Any valid Rhino3D geometry can be subjected to the space group transformations. During development, legibility of results has been a priority. To achieve this:

1. The orthorhombic crystal system has been used, as the *A*, *B*, and *C* axes follow the *x*, *y*, and *z* of Cartesian space.
2. Symmetries have been expressed with respect to the AB plane, rather than the international system standard, which may vary.[11]
3. Geometry input has been limited to point objects. These are then used to determine the Wigner-Seitz cells[12] as a subpattern of the lattice.

Using this method, it has been possible to use Grasshopper's built-in Voronoi cell component to identify and differentiate symmetry patterns as continuous tessellations of 3D space. For example, Figure 11 shows an exploded diagram of the impact of including the root node of the unit cell in the Voronoi calculation.

On the left, the four-bar distribution of points creates a lattice of rhombic dodecahedra, while on the right, a series

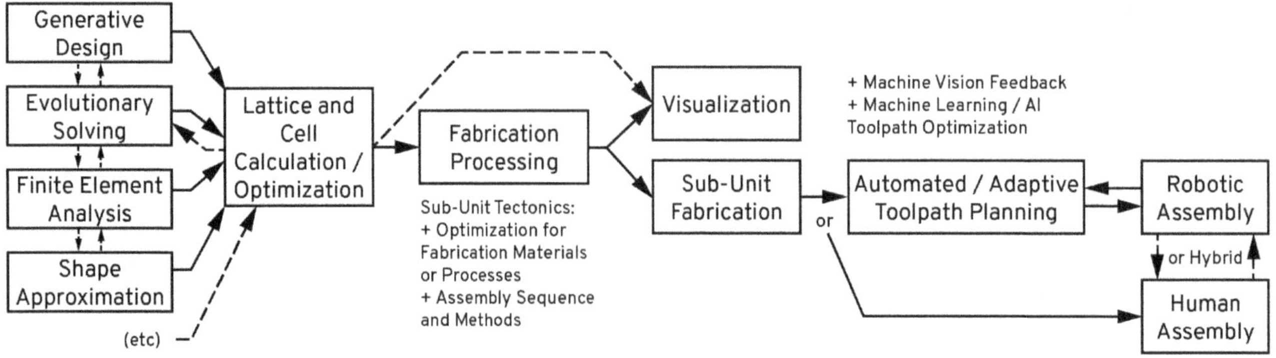

12 Flow chart for an automated construction process using HORTA.

of more complicated pieces is generated by the inclusion of the root node.

In both cases, each of the four subunits created by the symmetrically distributed point is identical, differing only in rotation with respect to the root.[13]

Similarly, more complex space group-generated patterns can be described using the same simple procedural steps. Using the generated Wigner-Seitz cells in the testing process has the advantage that the relationship between the symmetry pattern and the subunits it generates is clearly legible.

Autonomous Construction

Currently under development is an autonomous construction workflow (Fig. 12). The goal is construction without human intervention. The system as designed will use a robotic arm[14] equipped with machine vision to identify, manipulate, and place subunits with no prior tool-path instruction. All vision and control processes in the planned workflow are standard operations. A component to analyze subunit support and adjacency is being written to define assembly and aggregation order.

Feedback

As is standard in Grasshopper, hovering over a component or input/output displays informational text. Here HORTA informs the user about proper implementation of the program and the space groups.

For example, if noncompatible crystal system and centering are entered into the Lattice Cell Generator, the warning reads: "*_ Centering is not possible within the _ Lattice System. It is possible within the _ and _ Systems. P Centering has been provided instead.*"

If the Symbol Composer receives an unprocessable direct text input, it provides this message: "*The input provided for Position is not valid for the _ Crystal System. Refer to a list of the Short Names of the Space Groups for allowable Symbols.*" These are just two of the many messages HORTA generates.

To help familiarize designers with the concepts behind HORTA, the documentation will provide references to source materials in crystallography and mathematics.

RESULTS AND DISCUSSION

Results

All core aspects of HORTA are functional for six of seven lattices classes. Development and expansion are ongoing where identified. The program benefits from the modular structure of Grasshopper: properties for user input can be exposed or obscured as needed, allowing flexibility while minimizing user failure. Development has concentrated on the computational logic behind the system. As stated, only points and the resulting Wigner-Seitz cells have been used in testing for this paper. The results are formally sophisticated, but still preserve the rigor of their conceptual basis. All figures (except Fig. 12) were produced with HORTA.

An advantage of the space groups is that increases in complexity are realized not as an increase in unique singleton unit variants but as an increase in rotations and frequencies of identical subunits. When transforming a single point, the maximum complexity is of eight units in six rotations each or six units in eight rotations each.[15] These transformations are encoded in the international system notation, making HORTA useful for machine instruction.

Discussion

HORTA helps designers better understand and implement discrete concepts by creating a very rigorous system

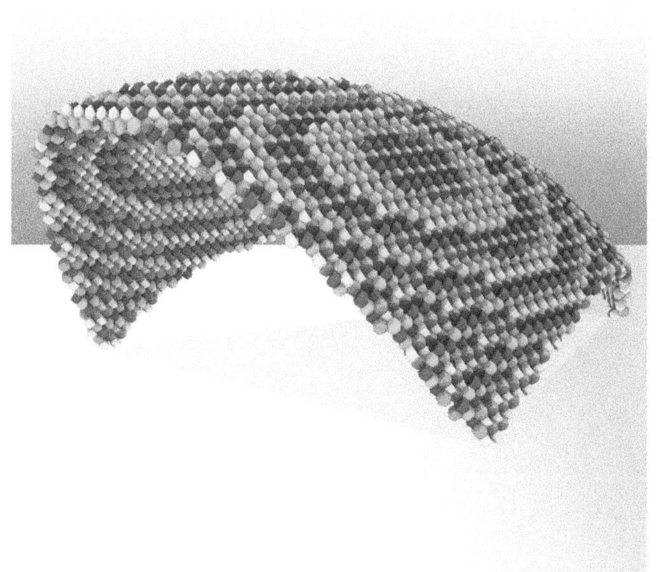

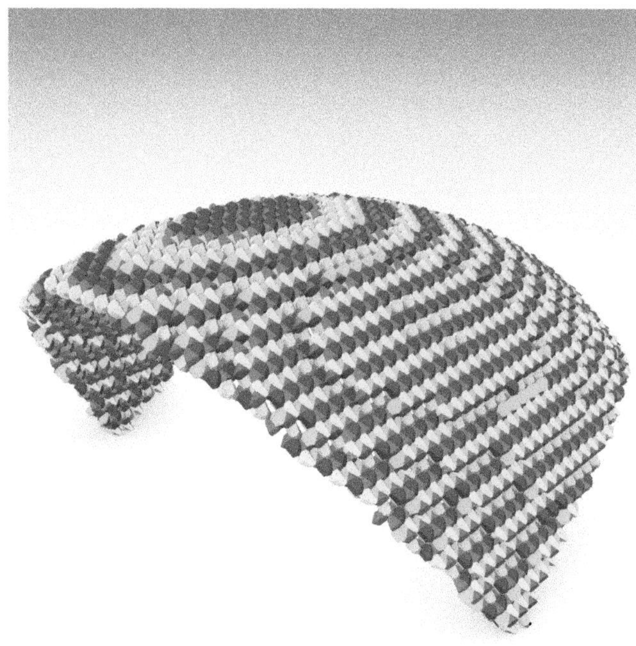

13 Comparison of aggregations of I114- (L) and $I116_1$ (R) cells defining a doubly catenary shell.

for definition of part/part relationships. The hope is this contributes to the understanding of the fundamental taxonomy of discrete aggregations within architectural computation.

A primary goal of the software is to approximate any shape with subunits, and so a Multi-Level Geometry Filter component is being written. This will discard from calculation any cells of the overall lattice the shape does not contact and run again with only the subunits of the remaining cells. The outcome of this is shown in Figure 13 via Grasshopper scripting, but it is being written as a component for optimization. One major concern of HORTA is connectivity, so a component to implement branching and adjacency algorithms to ensure each subunit is supported during autonomous construction.

Challenges and Responses

As significant challenges have been encountered during development, most have been addressed as described. The planned responses for outstanding known issues are:

Challenges: Subdividing an entire lattice with the geometry created using symmetry operations results in excessive file sizes. (The file in Fig. 1 is 687 MB although there are only four unique pieces in a *{5,5,5}* lattice.) But using Grasshopper to translate generated geometry into each cell of the lattice, avoiding the need to "bake" geometry out to Rhino3D, is still extremely computationally intensive.

Responses: In addition to the Multi-Level Geometry Filter, a Transformation Constructor component and Proxy Geometry component are being written. The Transformation Constructor will describe the translation and rotation needed to reorient any single subunit without having to perform the operation geometrically. The Proxy component will allow the geometric translation to be output only when desired—for example, rendering to a viewport, image, or VR environment.

Challenge: The existing Rhino/GH Voronoi cell generator can have unpredictable results. Speed in prototyping has been impeded due to building extensive workarounds in Grasshopper.

Response: A novel computationally efficient method for deriving the subunits has been designed and the custom component is being written.

Challenge: Since they continuously fill space, the results from these space group operations are difficult to visualize.

Response: Thus far, various novel stereographic drawing processes have been implemented to help see "inside" the lattices. While beautiful, they have been of uneven usefulness and require training to read. As the program matures, the goal is to incorporate virtual reality visualizations into the project workflow.

Future Goals

Other future goals for development are:

1. A separate paper on evaluating the results of the space

group generation using Wigner-Seitz cells (in progress).
2. The development of components to extract information for constructing lattices of subunits at architectural scale (fabrication processing in Fig. 12). For example, components to extract and orient edges as struts and vertices as the nodes at which they intersect.
3. Components to help fabricate these by locating and generating the means of attachment, etc.
4. An exciting future direction is to use finite element analysis and other methods for goal-oriented solving and generative design. In both of these methodologies and in traditional shape approximation, the ability to output the best pattern of subunits by cycling through space groups, input geometries and their locations, and lattice resolutions is extremely important. Thus, implementing evolutionary solving is an important future aspect of HORTA. This is easily within reach—all inputs other than the geometry to be manipulated or approximated can be represented numerically or in simple strings with no data loss.
5. Because lattices and object oriented structure are modular (a) multiple space groups can be generated and combined within a single lattice while maintaining coherent organization; and (b) lattices and subunits can be nested recursively or selectively. Both of these are dynamic and robust additions to generative and evolutionary methods.

CONCLUSION

Until recently (Retsin et al. 2019), the popular conception of computation within form-making was as a tool for calculating continuous morphological incrementation (Carpo 2017; Kolarevic 2003) to create variation (Carpo 2013), and thus "complexity" (Jencks 2013).

This project theorizes that by beginning from an earlier architectural competency—the ordering of discrete objects in space (Chiappone-Piriou 2019; March and Steadman 1974; Mitchell 1990; Staal 1999)—implementing space groups allows computation to instead be used to design using novel spatial/formal subdivisions. In turn, this will lead to new methods for calculation and fabrication.

The current outcomes from HORTA show that it can implement the space groups, and they can create spatial aggregations that are novel and sophisticated yet intrinsically highly ordered. As an introduction to the process, simple honeycombs have been shown, but extremely intricate aggregations are also possible, and have been generated. The Space Groups—previously underexplored in architectural computation—have potential open sophistication not just in forms but in the description of aggregations using minimal instruction sets, resulting in new methods for the calculation and fabrication of architecture.

ACKNOWLEDGMENTS

Thank you to interim director Jassen Callender and director emeritus Michael Berk and the Mississippi State University School of Architecture for their support and guidance. Thank you to the paper reviewers for the excellent feedback. Thank you to Joseph Choma for excellent input at a crucial time. Thank you to Jose Sanchez and Ewan Branda for support and input throughout the process. Thank you to Mark Ericson for the same—and for the years of exciting dialog that led to the birth of HORTA. Most of all, thank you to Katherine for your collaboration, inspiration, and patience.

NOTES

1. See *Discrete: Reappraising the Digital in Architecture* (Chiappone-Piriou 2019) for more.
2. For example, wallpaper tilings in two dimensions and sphere packings in three.
3. For simplicity in counting, centerings on a single set of A,B, or C faces are considered as a single "variety."
4. List available upon request.
5. From his 1936 book *The Evolving House* (Bemis 1936).
6. Chapter 8 of Botazzi (2018) and Chapter 1–3 of March and Steadman's (1974) *The Geometry of Environment* are helpful preludes to this paper.
7. For example, the sculptures of his *Cloud City* series.
8. List available upon request.
9. See Wolchover 2017.
10. A geometry filter component is being written to combine this output with the unique nodes from the Lattice Cell Constructor so that the repeating geometry that would be created by the face-based centerings is omitted prior to being distributed across the lattice.
11. Instead of *I4(bar)11* in the *BC Plane*, it is expressed as *I114(bar)* to avoid specifying "*In the AB Plane*" each time.
12. Functionally the same as the Voronoi cell.
13. Due to the rhombic dodecahedron's higher degree of symmetry, it is invariant after the result of the operations.
14. A six-axis robot arm is currently being configured for testing, but this could include other types or combinations of types.
15. The permutations arising from this method are being addressed in depth in a separate paper.

REFERENCES

Bemis, Albert F., and John Burchard. 1936. *The Evolving House, Vol. 3*. Cambridge, MA: MIT Press.

Botazzi, Roberto. 2018. *Digital Architecture Beyond Computers*. London: Bloomsbury Publishing.

Carpo, Mario. 2013. *The Digital Turn in Architecture*. Chichester: Wiley and Sons.

Carpo, Mario. 2017. *The Second Digital Turn*. Cambridge, MA: MIT Press.

Chiappone-Piriou, Emmanuelle. 2019. "Et Alia—A Projective History of the Architectural Discrete." In *Discrete: Reappraising the Digital in Architecture*, edited by G. Retsin, 78–85. Chichester: Wiley and Sons.

Engel, Heino. 1967. *Tragsysteme*. New York: Praeger Publishers.

GA Document no. 140. 2017. "Zaha Hadid: Heydar Aliyev Center." Tokyo: ADA Edita Tokyo.

Jencks, Charles. 2013. "Nonlinear Architecture: New Science = New Architecture?" In *The Digital Turn in Architecture 1992–2012*, edited by M. Carpo, 83–107. Chichester: Wiley and Sons.

Henning Larsen. n.d. "Harpa Concert Hall and Conference Center." https://henninglarsen.com/en/projects/featured/0676-harpa-concert-hall-and-conference-center/.

Kolarevic, Branko. 2003. "Digital Morphogenesis." In *Architecture in the Digital Age*, 13–27. London: Spon Press.

March, Lionel, and Philip Steadman. 1974. *The Geometry of Environment*. Cambridge, MA: MIT Press.

Mitchell, William. 1990. *The Logic of Architecture*. Cambridge, MA: MIT Press.

Retsin, G., ed. 2019. *Discrete – Reappraising the Digital in Architecture*. Chichester: Wiley and Sons.

Staal, Frits. 1999. "Greek and Vedic Geometry." *Journal of Indian Philosophy* 27: 105–127.

Vainshtein, Boris. 1996. *Fundamentals of Crystals: Symmetry and Methods of Structural Crystallography*. Berlin: Springer-Verlag.

Wolchover, Natalie. 2017. "Digital Alchemist Sharon Glotzer Seeks Rules of Emergence." *Quanta Magazine*, March 8. http://www.quantamagazine.org/digital-alchemist-sharon-glotzer-seeks-rules-of-emergence- 20170308.

Wondratschek, Hans. 2006. "1.4.1: Symbols of Space Groups." In. *International Tables for Crystallography, Volume A: Space Group Symmetry*, edited by T. Hahn, 42–48. Hoboken, NJ: Wiley and Sons.

IMAGE CREDITS

All drawings and images by the author.

Duane McLemore AIA is an Assistant Professor at Mississippi State University and a licensed architect in the State of California.

Making a New City Image

Brian Ho
Harvard GSD + SEAS
Sidewalk Labs

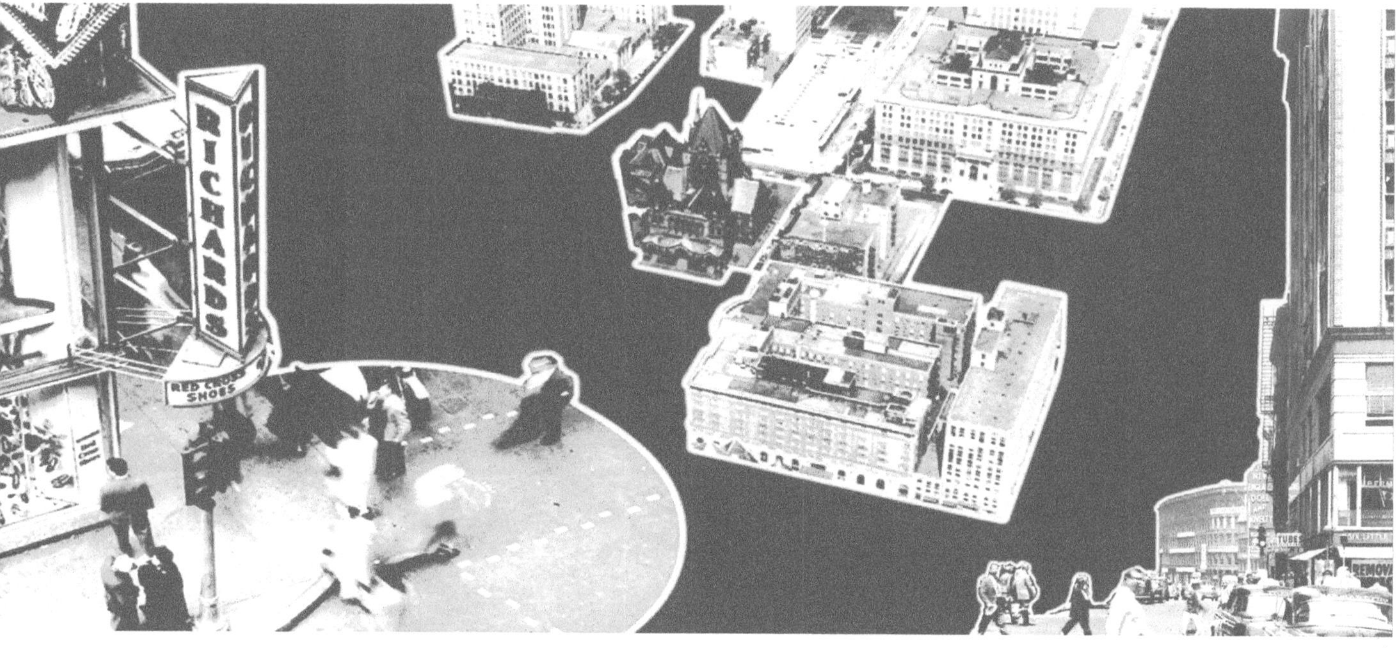

1 The new city image combines historic photographs from Lynch's Image of the City with computer vision and machine learning to predict labels for human experience.

ABSTRACT

This paper explores the application of computer vision and machine learning to street-level imagery of cities, reevaluating past theory linking urban form to human perception. This paper further proposes a new method for design based on the resulting model, where a designer can identify areas of a city tied to certain perceptual qualities and generate speculative street scenes optimized for their predicted saliency on labels of human experience.

This work extends Kevin Lynch's *Image of the City* with deep learning: training an image classification model to recognize Lynch's five elements of the city image, using Lynch's original photographs and diagrams of Boston to construct labeled training data alongside new imagery of the same locations. This new city image revitalizes past attempts to quantify the human perception of urban form and improve urban design. A designer can search and map the data set to understand spatial opportunities and predict the quality of imagined designs through a dynamic process of collage, model inference, and adaptation.

Within a larger practice of design, this work suggests that the curation of archival records, computer science techniques, and theoretical principles of urbanism might be integrated into a single craft. With a new city image, designers might "see" at the scale of the city, as well as focus on the texture, color, and details of urban life.

INTRODUCTION

The way cities are seen changes how they are experienced and designed.

The view from above—the plan view—dominates as the way to see cities at scale. Evolving from early photographs taken at an elevated vantage by pigeon or balloon to remote sensing and geographic information systems (GIS), the plan view has become highly calibrated and engineered. This evolution has driven equally significant changes to urban design and planning. The historical development of SYMAP, and the resulting emergence of ESRI and geospatial software, led to new computational methods for both design practice and urban governance (de Monchaux 2016). The plan view, augmented by pervasive, GPS-enabled digital services and sensor systems (Kurgan 2013) now drives an infrastructural concept of the "smart city" as an objective of urban management and design.

The creation of the plan view, however, requires inherent processes of abstraction and simplification (Scott 1998) that deemphasize the experience and characteristics of urban form. The view from the ground, a perspective that can supply this missing information, has historically been limited to ethnographic or anecdotal approaches within disciplines of urbanism and design. Observation of urban environments from the ground can only be carried out by researchers for a set period of time in a specific area of study (Whyte 1980); other humanistic readings of urban experience are both highly qualitative (Debord 2006) and idiosyncratic (Benjamin 1999).

A key attempt to combine the rigor of a city's plan view with an appreciation for the view from the ground was Kevin Lynch's work on *The Image of the City* (1960). In a five-year study, funded by the Rockefeller Foundation and carried out in partnership with the designer Gyorgy Kepes, Lynch defined urban imageability: the perceptual characteristics of urban form that give "identity, structure and meaning" to a human viewer's mental impression of a city. Lynch sought to document imageability through cartographic investigations of Boston, Jersey City, and Los Angeles, relying on both "systematic field reconnaissance ... by a trained observer" and "lengthy interview[s] ... with a small sample of city residents," all supported by photographs, hand-drawn maps, and transcripts (Lynch 1960, 15).

Lynch practiced a systems approach to cataloging experiential information about an urban environment (Halpern 2019). From his research, he identified common perceptual elements of a city image from the ground view—the path, edge, district, node, and landmark—and mapped them as

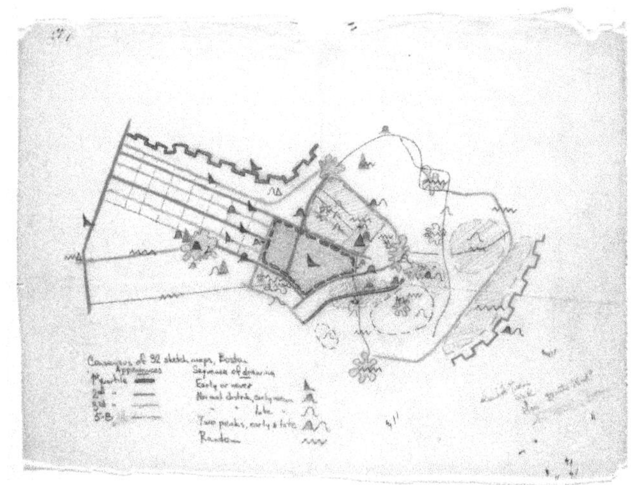

2 Lynch's diagram of the city image of Boston. Areas corresponding to the elements of the city image are abstractly mapped, based on interviews and observation. Diagram from *The Image of the City*.

3 Results of projecting Lynch's diagram of the city image in GIS. The diagram is translated into specific features: e.g., buildings as districts and landmarks, streets as paths, parks and shorelines as edges.

specific physical locations in the city's plan view (Fig. 2). Lynch (1984) would later develop these elements into a generalized theory of urban form, intended to more directly guide urban design.

Lynch's systematic and perceptual description of cities suggests modern equivalents for cities today. This paper proposes a new mode of analysis inspired by Lynch's original approach but updated with current technology to produce a new city image.

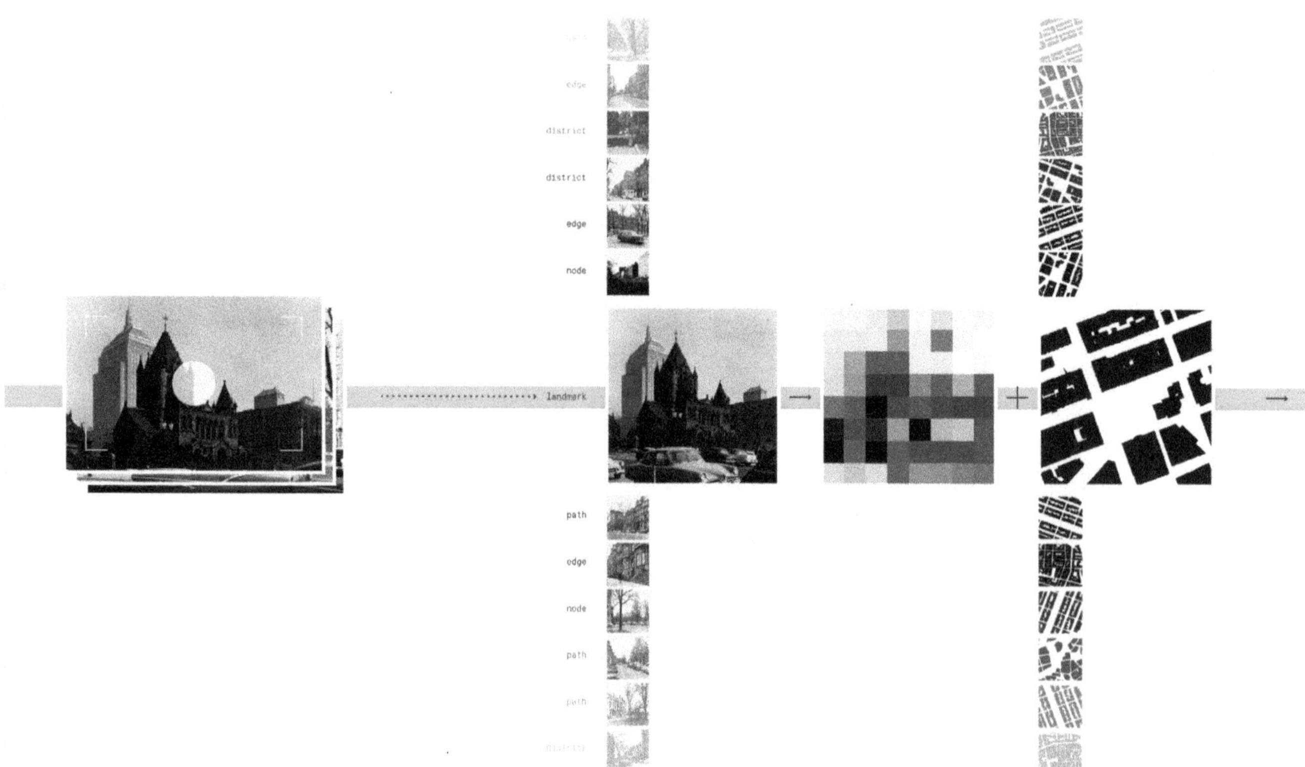

4

BACKGROUND

Precedent for the application of technology to both understand and map the human perception of cities exists in architecture, urbanism, and computer science, with overlaps in cognitive science, behavioral science, and neuroscience.

Early foundational work at MIT linked the ground view of cities to a more comprehensive plan view using digital media. Nicholas Negroponte and the Architecture Machine Group created an interactive experience of an urban environment in the Aspen Movie Map (Mohl 1981), combining ground and plan views in an early precursor to Google Maps and Street View. The Aspen Movie Map did not, however, attempt to model a relationship between visuals and perceptions of urban form; later work on the URBAN2 and URBAN5 software would include machine learning, but shifted emphasis from human experience to human-computer interactions within computer-aided design (Halpern 2019). This paper shares that original interest in merging ground and plan views, and adds the use of machine learning to model perception.

More recent advances use computer vision to classify and predict images of cities from the ground view. The Streetscore project used Google Street View imagery and Support Vector Machine (SVM) methods to build localized "evaluative maps" of perceived safety (Naik, Raskar, and Hidalgo 2016); the same researchers later applied deep learning—convolutional neural networks—to predict additional qualitative labels on ground views from cities around the world (Dubey 2016). These perceptual labels apply to the entire scene and are based on training data annotated by systems for crowdsourcing and social computation. This research applies similar neural network architectures to classify ground view images but uses historical images with labels derived from urban theory, and adds plan views to the input.

A specific interest of this research is the automated detection of features of the built environment significant to humans within a larger ground view image. The *Tohme* project detected curb ramps on sidewalks within Street View imagery, using models trained on crowdsourced labeled data to promote physical accessibility (Hara et al. 2014). Doersch et al. (2012) found key visual elements of architecture and urban form that helped identify a city, using SVMs to determine if smaller tiles of a Street View image were significant to classification of the image as being "in Paris."

Making new city images builds on this precedent, with an aim to bridge the technical and theoretical to develop a new approach with applications for urban design.

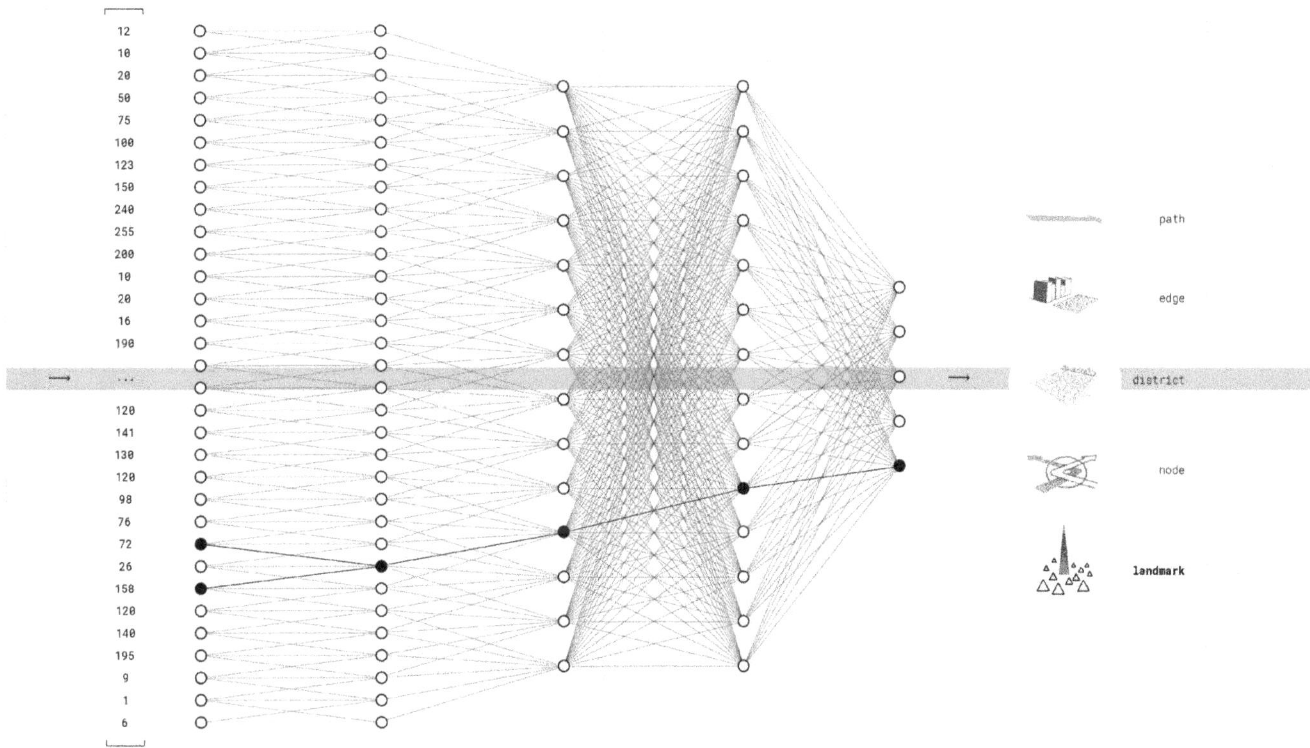

METHODS

Creating the Data Set

The creation of the new city image began with the development of a labeled data set of urban imagery suitable for training an image classification model (Fig. 4). This training data set required sufficient images that could serve as examples of each class intended to be a predicted output of the model.

This research reconsidered the work of Kevin Lynch by directly using images from his archives of The Image of the City to create the initial data set (Lynch 1988). A total 1,908 original photos of Boston from Lynch's research, taken by Nishan Bichajian, were downloaded from the publicly accessible Flickr gallery of the MIT Lynch-Kepes collection using the Flickr API. Each downloaded photo had basic metadata and a short description but no precise geolocation information or annotation marking the image as belonging to a specific element of the city image.

Geolocation and Labeling

Geolocation was performed in two steps to label the images. First, the metadata associated with each image was used to geocode the images with the Google Maps API. Second, the results were fine-tuned in an interactive web interface for comparison.

4 The creation of the new city image begins with Lynch's original images from his research archive. Labels corresponding to the elements of the city image were applied to the images and the images were joined with matched plan views.

5 The resulting data set of labeled and concatenated ground- and plan-view images were used as training data for an image classification model. The model learned to predict a label for a specific city image element.

An initial geolocation was performed using the metadata associated with each image. The description text was submitted as a query to the Google Maps API for Place Search. The resulting latitude and longitude coordinates provided an approximate location for each image. This approximate location was then displayed in a custom interface with side-by-side Maps and Street View windows, alongside the original downloaded image (Fig. 10). Clicking on the Maps window and adjusting the Street View until it matched the downloaded image allowed more precise latitude and longitude, as well as heading and pitch information, to be added to each.

The geolocated Lynch images were then labeled as belonging to one or more of Lynch's elements of the city image. This required using ArcGIS Pro (ESRI Inc. 2018) to project a digital image of Lynch's city image diagram of Boston, creating a raster layer in a standard coordinate reference system. The raster layer was traced in ArcGIS Pro to produce custom polygon vector shapefiles, one for

6 Model prediction results on unseen test data for the label of "district." Black dots are correct guesses, and white dots are incorrect guesses.

7 Model prediction results on unseen test data for the label of "landmark." Results are overlaid on a map based on Lynch's projected diagram.

each element of the city image: path, edge, node, landmark, and district (Fig. 3). A spatial join then associated points representing each geolocated image with specific elements of the city image, providing training labels for the data set. Given the spatial overlaps in Lynch's original diagram, the images could end up with multiple labels: for example, one image might be both a district and a landmark.

After the images were geolocated, they were mapped on an interactive web map that displayed each image from the data set as a point on top of the original diagram used for labeling (Fig. 11), for both validation and communication of the results.

Data Augmentation

The final step in creating the labeled training data set was concatenating the ground view images with an additional plan view of the corresponding area (Fig.4).

The plan view was generated by providing the geolocated latitude and longitude coordinates of each image to the Mapbox API, specifying a custom Mapbox style designed to depict buildings and the ground as a simple black-and-white figure-ground drawing. Each resulting map tile was rotated based on the heading information created by the geolocation process, allowing for consistent orientation of the plan views with respect to the ground view. Every square map tile was then joined to its associated square image to create a hybrid image of a 2:1 aspect ratio, which would serve as a combined input array for the classification model.

Model Training and Use

The original data set of 1,908 hybrid image inputs was preprocessed from RGB to grayscale representation, and multiple versions of each original image were created with slight augmentation (affine transformations) to better generalize the model. A convolutional neural net, written in Keras (Chollet et al. 2018), was trained to learn the relationship between the hybrid input imagery and an output label corresponding to one of Lynch's elements of the city image in binary classification (Fig. 5). After training, the model demonstrated accuracy rates of up to 70% on unseen validation data for the landmark and district elements in a binary classification setting. The other categories demonstrated poor results and behavior indicating overfitting.

After training, results from the model (predictions on unseen data from the original data set) were mapped. Visualizations for each label of the city image were analyzed for areas of local density and sparseness (Figs. 6, 7).

Speculative scenes of hypothetical urban intervention were then created and tested using the classification model. Suitable examples from the data set that did not receive a predicted label were chosen as the "site" for the design,

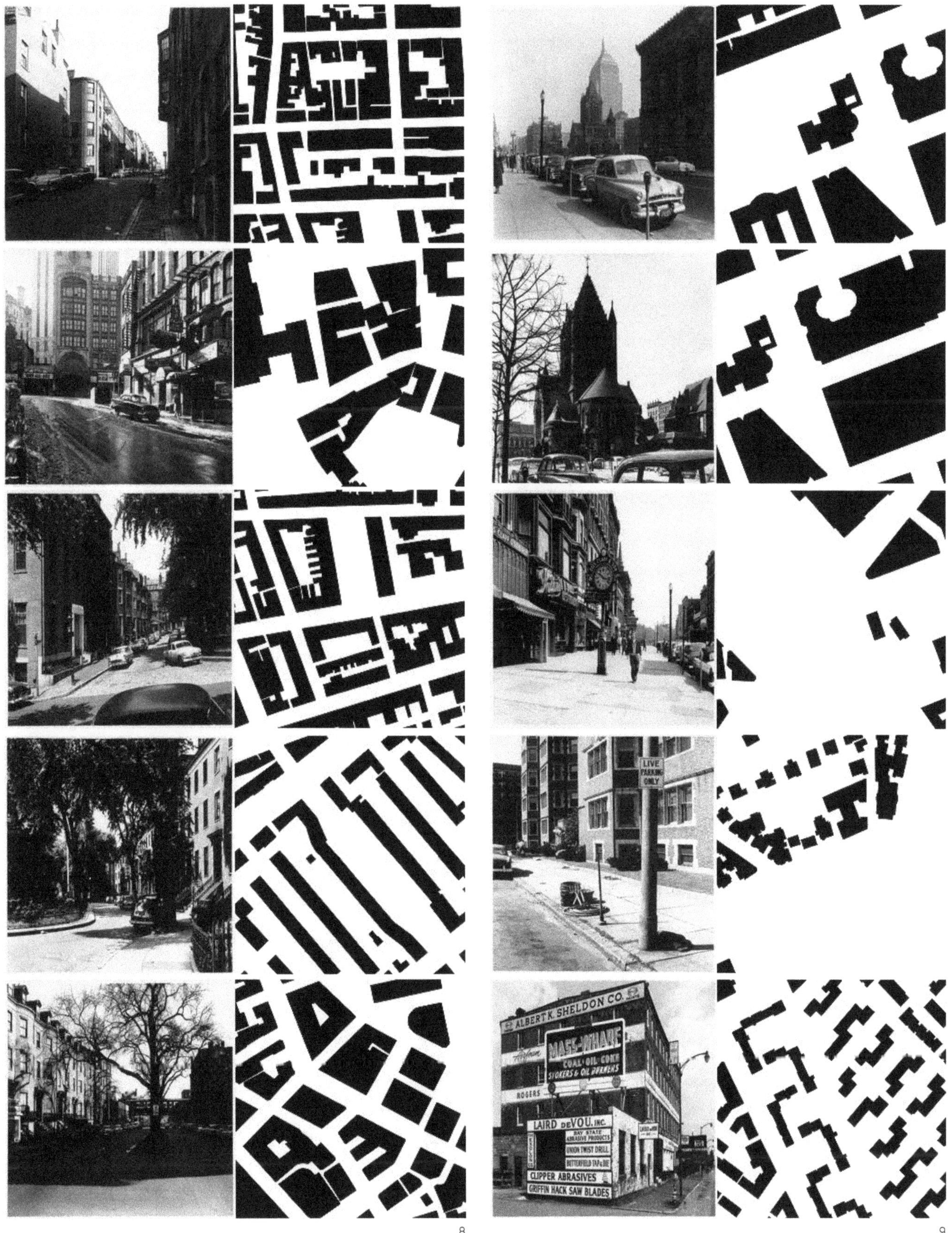

8 Examples of images labeled as "district" in binary classification. Plan views tend to have more regular blocks and built density; ground views have more street wall and facade, usually in perspective.

9 Examples of images not labeled as "district." Plan views have sparser context. In the third example, an image with the same plan view can have a different label.

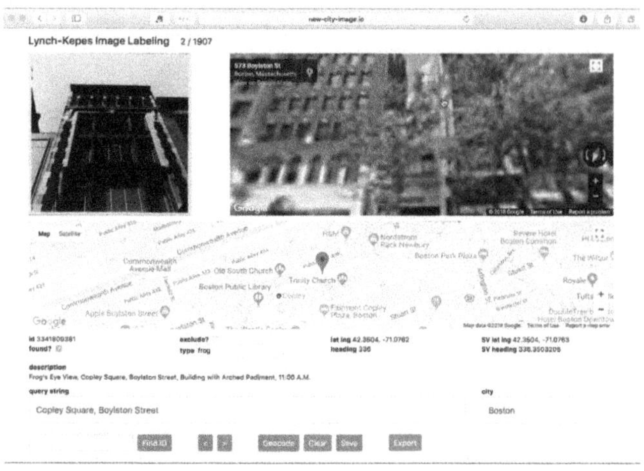

10

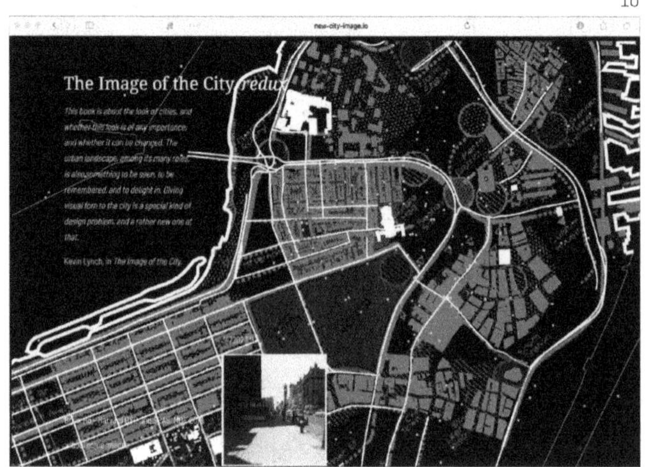

11

10 Interface for labeling images. A matched Google Street View, map, and original image are shown so a user can align the perspective and find a more precise location.

11 Visualization of labeled images in a web interface.

such as an image with the Charles River or a lumberyard in the foreground. Then, portions of original Lynch imagery were collaged on top of the "site" image, and invented urban plan-form schemes were simultaneously drawn alongside (Figs. 12–15). Model predictions based on these collages were applied sequentially as the collages were being created, with design continuing until a desired label was achieved through model inference on the result. Negative predictions from the model were used as feedback to adjust a collage that would otherwise be considered complete, prompting the creator to try alternative designs.

RESULTS AND DISCUSSION

As a means of comparing predicted results to actual labels, the output of the classification model on unseen images from the created data set were visualized against the original diagram of the city elements on a map of Boston. While preliminary, the resulting artifacts (a map for each element of the city image) indicated that this method can produce unique plan view diagrams that reveal perceptual information about a specific city, based on both historic imagery and theory. One example were images that were taken in areas to the west of the Back Bay, outside of Lynch's original zone for a "district" quality. In this case, these images were also classified as districts.

The creation of speculative street scenes with the model also demonstrated how a new city image might inform design practice. In several cases, attempts to create a "district" scene by combining specific ground view elements and plan forms did not result in the desired prediction from the model. In these instances, increasing the number of elements in the ground view and reducing the interval of the street grid in the plan view led to the desired outcome. This pattern of interaction—using a machine learning result to guide a design process—suggests a new pattern for urban design for perceptual goals, assisted by technology.

More broadly, this work suggests that within a holistic process of urban design, disparate methods from planning, theory, and the humanities might be integrated through machine learning. As demonstrated by this work, deep learning and image classification trained on curated archival imagery can empower designers to generate new images in response to historical precedent—not on the superficial basis of visual similarity but in alignment with previous observations and studies of perceived experience.

This process revitalizes archival imagery of cities by using it as training data for machine learning and computer vision techniques. In addition, this process explores the creative augmentation of training data by hybridizing inputs to combine both ground and plan views of a specific area into a single image. By linking technological methods to historic literature on the experience of cities, this method provides a framework for designers to apply a theory of perception to their creation of new urban form.

CONCLUSION

The work in this paper indicates a number of future directions for exploring design possibilities for understanding and mapping the perception of the built environment in cities.

Technical refinements to the method could include multiclass and multilabel classification, allowing a single image to be predicted against multiple classes, or predicted as being part of multiple classes. This would increase the corresponding sophistication of model outputs. The model

12

12 Start and end state for a collage of a speculative street scenes. The start (above) was example image labeled as "not district"; the resulting image was labeled as a "district."

13 Sequential stages of the collage. At each stage, the image was provided to the model for prediction. In some cases, the label of "district" was achieved before the end state.

13

itself could be created through transfer learning, where a pretrained model with demonstrated performance on similar tasks is retrained on a specific target data set.

The labeled data set itself could be expanded with other historical imagery from relevant time periods and geographic areas. The plan view images used to create the hybrid inputs could be derived from geolocated archival maps and documents, rather than contemporary digital files produced by online maps services.

In terms of applications, the trained model could also be used directly within a generative design system, as an objective (cost) function for optimizing collages to produce synthetic views of the city image. This application might in turn necessitate a more complex model that labels with confidence or probabilistic values, to support optimization and learning.

Finally, further exploration of Lynch's theories through machine learning could be done by applying a model trained in one city to another. In particular, the model was trained on images of Boston; Lynch's work in the *Image of the City* was also applied to Jersey City and Los Angeles. Testing the performance of a model across multiple cities might provide insight on whether the city elements in one translate to another. Additional work could examine Lynch's research in *The View from the Road* (Appleyard, Lynch and Myer 1964), leveraging a linear series of images as training data for machine learning sequence models.

ACKNOWLEDGMENTS

The author would like to thank and credit Robert Pietrusko, associate professor of landscape architecture at the Harvard Graduate School of Design, and Krzysztof Gajos, the Gordon McKay Professor of Computer Science at the Harvard Paulson School of Engineering and Applied Sciences for their role as indispensable advisors to this project. This work was funded in part by the master in design engineering program at Harvard University.

REFERENCES

Appleyard, Donald, Kevin Lynch, and John R. Myer. 1964. *The View from the Road*. Cambridge, MA: MIT Press.

Benjamin, Walter. 1999. *The Arcades Project*. Cambridge, MA: Harvard University Press.

Chollet, François, et al. 2018. *Keras*. V.2.2.0. http://keras.io.

De Monchaux, Nicholas. 2016. *Local Code: 3,659 Proposals About Data, Design & the Nature of Cities*. New York: Princeton Architectural Press.

Debord, Guy. 2006. "Theory of the Dérive, Internationale Situationniste# 2." In *Situationist International Anthology*, edited by Ken Knabb. Berkeley, CA: Bureau of Public Secrets.

Doersch, Carl, Saurabh Singh, Abhinav Gupta, Josef Sivic, and Alexei Efros. 2012. "What Makes Paris Look Like Paris?" *ACM Transactions on Graphics* 31 (4).

Dubey, Abhimanyu, Nikhil Naik, Devi Parikh, Ramesh Raskar, and César A. Hidalgo. 2016. "Deep Learning the City: Quantifying Urban Perception at a Global Scale." In *European Conference on Computer Vision*, pp. 196-212. Cham: Springer.

ESRI Inc. 2018. *ArcGIS Pro*. V.2.0. PC.

Halpern, Orit. 2019. "Architecture as Machine: A Brief History of the Smart City, Design and Cybernetics." In *When Is the Digital in Architecture*, edited by Andrew Goodhouse. London: Sternberg.

Hara, Kotaro, Jin Sun, Robert Moore, David Jacobs, and Jon Froehlich. 2014. "Tohme: Detecting Curb Ramps in Google Street view Using Crowdsourcing, Computer Vision, and Machine Learning." In *Proceedings of the 27th Annual ACM Symposium on User Interface Software and Technology*, 189–204. ACM.

Kurgan, Laura. 2013. *Close Up at a Distance: Mapping, Technology, and Politics*. Cambridge, MA: MIT Press.

Lynch, Kevin. 1960. *The Image of the City*. Cambridge, MA: MIT Press.

Lynch, Kevin. 1984. *Good City Form*. Cambridge, MA: MIT Press.

Lynch, Kevin. 1998. Kevin Lynch papers, MC 208, box X. Massachusetts Institute of Technology Institute Archives and Special Collections, Cambridge, Massachusetts.

Mohl, Robert. 1981. "Cognitive Space in the Interactive Movie Map: An Investigation of Spatial Learning in Virtual Environments." PhD dissertation, Massachusetts Institute of Technology.

Naik, Nikhil, Ramesh Raskar, and César A. Hidalgo. 2016. "Cities Are Physical Too: Using Computer Vision to Measure the Quality and Impact of Urban Appearance." *American Economic Review* 106 (5): 128–132.

Scott, James C. 1998. *Seeing Like A State: How Certain Schemes to Improve the Human Condition Have Failed*. New Haven, CT: Yale University Press.

Whyte, William Hollingsworth. 1980. *The Social Life Of Small Urban Spaces*. Washington, D.C.: Conservation Foundation.

IMAGE CREDITS

Figure 2: © Kevin Lynch, 1964

All other drawings and images by the author. Some images use data from the MIT Lynch-Kepes collection on Flickr, under Creative Commons Attribution-NonCommercial 3.0 license.

14

15

Brian Ho is a senior design lead at Sidewalk Labs for its generative urban design product (Delve). Brian has worked previously at the Center for Green Buildings and Cities, the Boston Mayor's Office of New Urban Mechanics, Leroy Street Studio, and Waggonner & Ball Architects on digital and physical projects in civic technology, architecture, and urban planning. Brian teaches in urbanism and urban studies at the Yale School of Architecture and the Youth Design Center. He received a Master in Design Engineering with distinction from Harvard University's Graduate School of Design and School of Engineering and Applied Sciences, and a BA in Architecture with distinction from Yale University.

14 Start and end state for another collage. The start (above) was example image labeled as "not district"; the resulting image was labeled as a "district."

15 Sequential stages of the collage. In some cases, the label of "not district" was not achieved at the end, and the collage was revised.

DeepGreen

Coupling Biological and Artificial Intelligence in Urban Design

Claudia Pasquero
Innsbruck University;
The Bartlett UCL

Marco Poletto
ecoLogicStudio

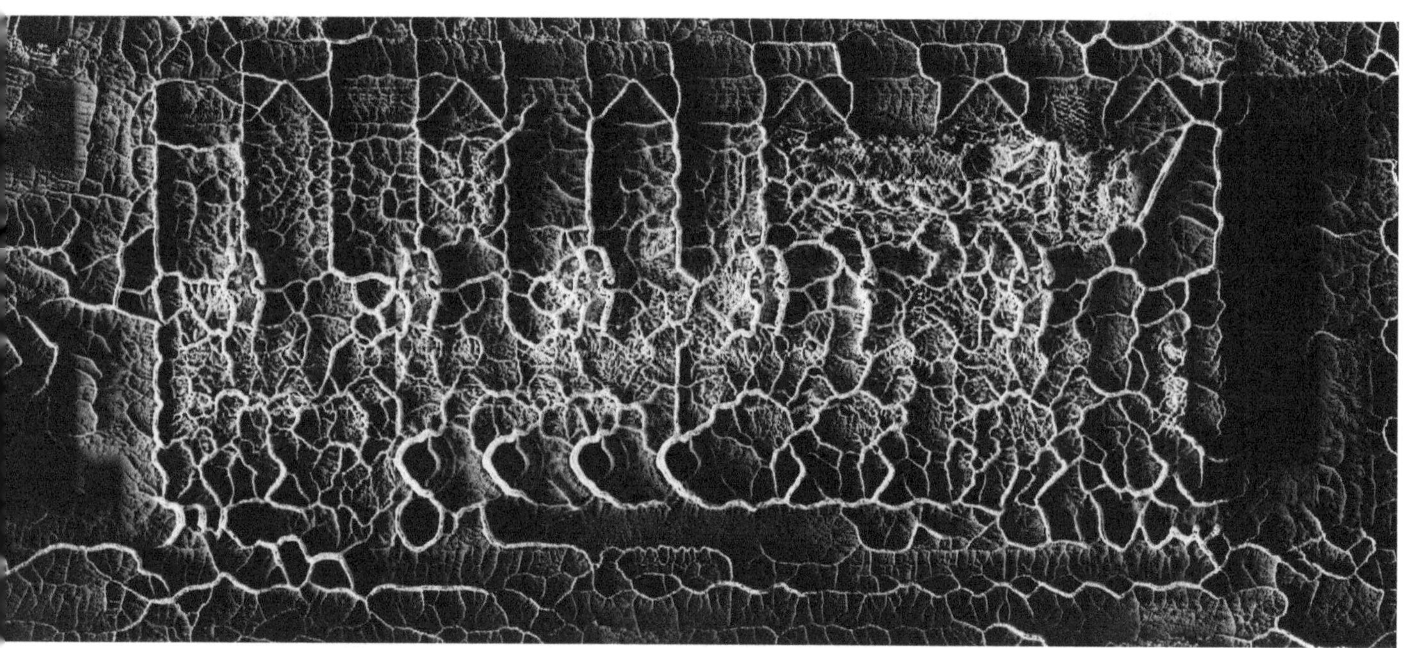

1 Translation of the Centre Pompidou based on the GAN_Physarum algorithm.

ABSTRACT

Ubiquitous computing enables us to decipher the biosphere's anthropogenic dimension, what we call the Urbansphere (Pasquero and Poletto 2020). This machinic perspective unveils a new postanthropocentric reality, where the impact of artificial systems on the natural biosphere is indeed global, but their agency is no longer entirely human.

This paper explores a protocol to design the Urbansphere, or what we may call the urbanization of the nonhuman, titled DeepGreen. With the development of DeepGreen, we are testing the potential to bring the interdependence of digital and biological intelligence to the core of architectural and urban design research.

This is achieved by developing a new biocomputational design workflow that enables the pairing of what is algorithmically drawn with what is biologically grown (Pasquero and Poletto 2016). In other words, and more in detail, the paper will illustrate how generative adversarial network (GAN) algorithms (Radford, Metz, and Soumith 2015) can be trained to "behave" like a *Physarum polycephalum*, a unicellular organism endowed with surprising computational abilities and self-organizing behaviors that have made it popular among scientist and engineers alike (Adamatzky 2010) (Fig. 1).

The trained GAN_Physarum is deployed as an urban design technique to test the potential of *polycephalum* intelligence in solving problems of urban remetabolization and in computing scenarios of urban morphogenesis within a nonhuman conceptual framework.

DEVELOPING A BIODIGITAL DESIGN WORKFLOW

Learning how to interpret large remote-sensing datasets from the unique perspective granted by GAN_Physarum enables a deeper inquiry into the contemporary significance of traditional planning concepts such as zone, boundary, scale, typology, and program (Fig. 2). This process introduces new spatial metrics to measure cities' self-sufficiency, valuing what economists call "externalities" towards other societal and ecological systems (Mazzuccato 2017). A specific biocomputational design workflow generates consistent training datasets for GAN_Physarum, and this paper illustrates our efforts in that regard. The workflow includes four main levels of computation: input data reading, biotic-abiotic analysis, network analysis, and scenario modeling.

For the first-level analysis, advanced algorithmic design techniques are used to read large datasets from satellite, geographic information system (GIS), and digital elevation model sources (Pasquero and Poletto 2017). Levels 2 and 3 recognize and analyze the morphology of the city, the surrounding landscape, and the resources' networks. The analysis produces density maps and path systems for several urban systems such as biomass, water collection, solar energy, community waste, and so on. These maps become training datasets for GAN_Physarum.

SETTING UP A TEST BED FOR DEEPGREEN

The paper illustrates a number of applications of this approach to real case studies. In particular within the framework of ecoLogicStudio's ongoing cultural collaboration with the Centre Pompidou in Paris, and with partner cities, within the framework of the United Nations Development Programme (UNDP) innovation facility funding and City Experiment Fund. The aim of these case studies is twofold: to speculate on the significance of a nonhuman design framework on the reconception of a heavily planned city such as Paris, and, consequently, to provide local communities, cities, and governments with the most advanced toolset to reprogram global cities for a safer and healthier postpandemic world.

Ultimately, with the integrated use of remote sensing, big data analysis, and artificial intelligence, DeepGreen can be deployed to assess urban vulnerabilities and find specific urban design solutions to achieve immediate and long-lasting impact (Figs. 3, 4). Through these case studies, the authors speculate on the possibility for a general applicability of the DeepGreen protocol, its scalability, and possible widespread adoption. This speculation provides a critical assessment of the current paradigm of urban green

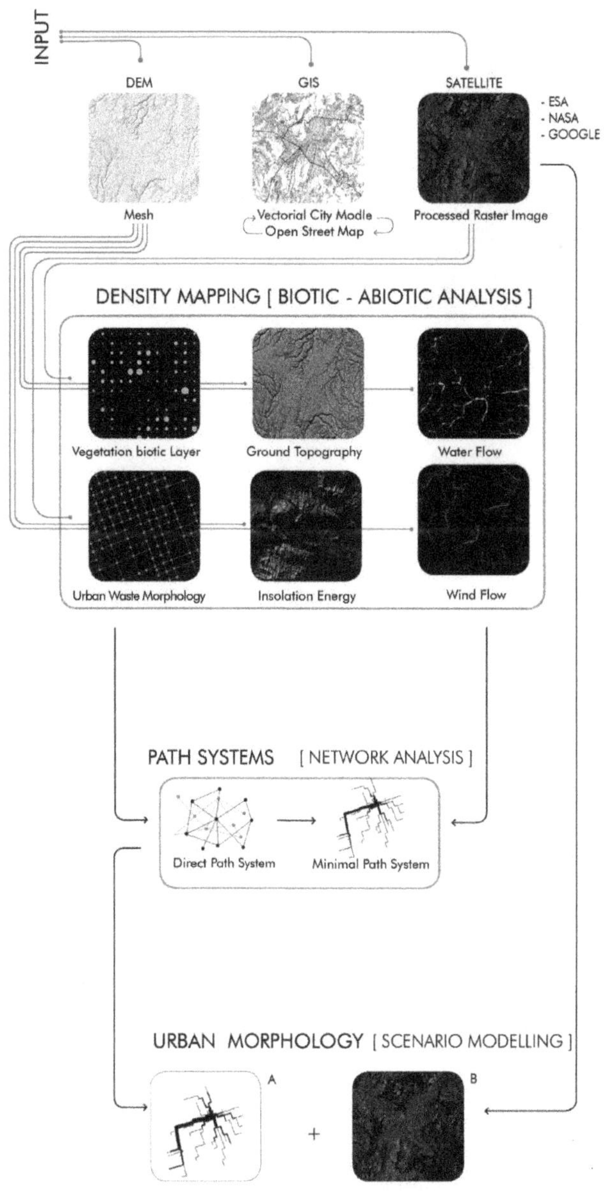

2

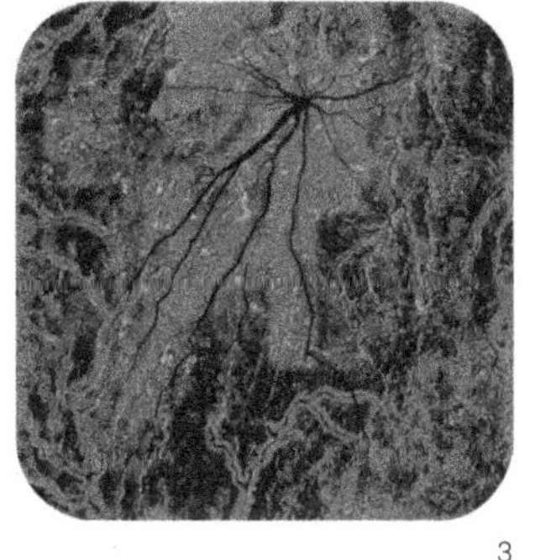

3

4

2 Flow diagram describing the process in Guatemala City; proposal based on algorithms, driven by bio-artificial intelligence.

3, 4 Redefined morphology of networks in Guatemala City; proposal based on bio-artificial intelligence algorithms.

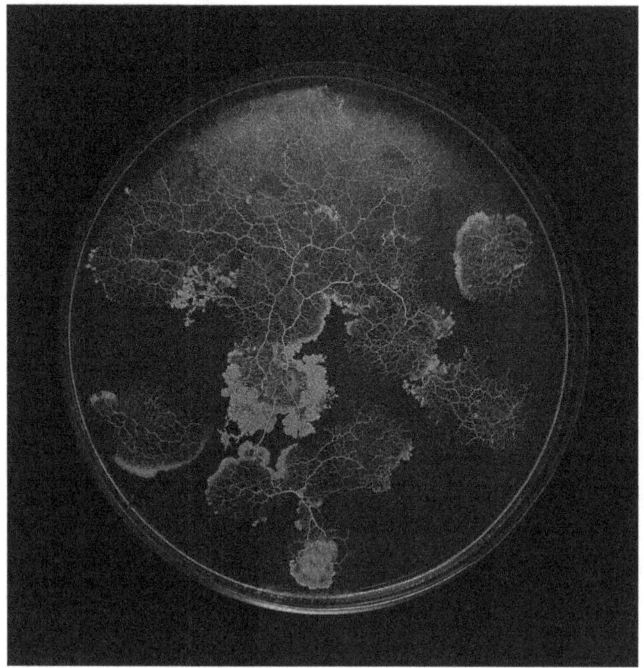

5

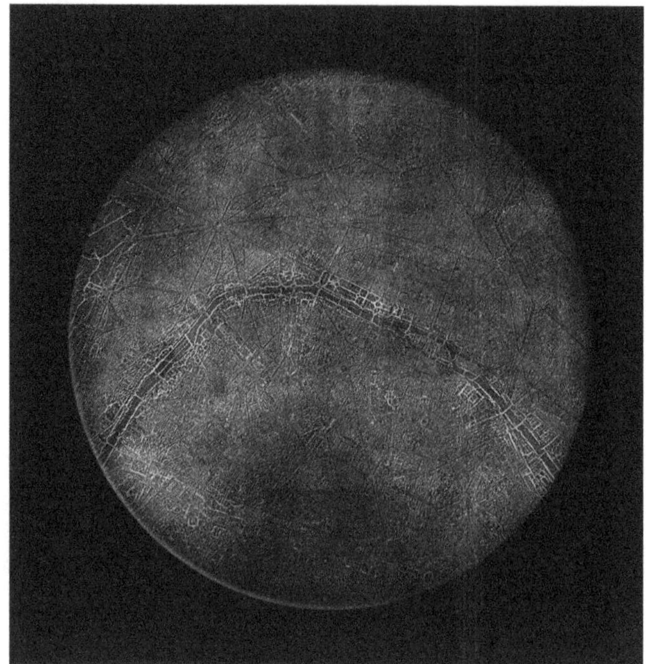

6

planning and the conceptual and practical significance of urban regreening in the current, crisis-ridden, postanthropocentric reality.

TRAINING AND TESTING GAN_PHYSARUM

CycleGAN algorithms belong to the class of machine learning frameworks (Zhu et al. 2017). They involve an automatic unsupervised training of image-to-image translation models without paired examples. In this case, the domain of source images and target images refer to the slices of two actual input images that belong in two different domains, the urban and the biological. CycleGAN algorithms are deployed at level 4 of the overall DeepGreen workflow, and the process can be further divided in four phases for clearer illustration.

The first phase describes the preparation of the input images deployed to train GAN_Physarum. The second phase is the training of the algorithm based on these input datasets. The model is trained to detect the urban morphology of case study cities and the biological growth patterns of *Physarum polycephalum*. During training, the algorithm typically runs 200 epochs, or iterations, over which it self-improves.

At this stage, the models are sufficient for generating plausible slices in the target domain but are not translations of the input slice. This occurs in the third phase, the testing phase, during which the algorithm translates the biocomputational patterns onto the case study city.

In the fourth phase all resultant tiles are recombined, and the final output image is recreated. This can produce true color satellite visions of the case study, its urban morphology, and several testing scenarios for the integration of biotic and abiotic systems within the urban landscape.

THE CASE OF PARIS

To illustrate this protocol in action, the GAN_Physarum is sent on a computational derive on the streets of Paris (Debord 1956). While at first the visions conjured by GAN_Physarum have the disorienting quality of the nonhuman mind that conceived them, they also connect us with contemporary Paris at a more fundamental systemic level (Figs. 5–7).

It is in fact known that contemporary cities share unique emergent behaviors and self-organizing growth patterns with organisms like *Physarum polycephalum* (Tero et al. 2010). Transport networks are ubiquitous in both urban and biological systems. Robust network performance involves a complex trade-off involving cost, transport efficiency, and fault tolerance. Biological networks have been honed by many cycles of evolutionary selection pressure, and they develop without centralized control. This represents a readily scalable solution for growing networks in general and as part of a complex urban system. Therefore, GAN_Physarum has the potential to evolve into a resilient urban planning model.

When the trained GAN_Physarum is deployed, it actualizes the capacities of *Physarum polycephalum* in solving

7

5 *Physarum polycephalum* as biological computer.

6 GAN_Physarum 10 × 10 km frame—Paris iteration.

7 GAN_Physarum 100 × 100 m frame—Centre Pompidou iteration.

problems of urban remetabolization, carbon neutrality, energetic self-sufficiency, and increased biodiversity. Most importantly, these ambitious objectives are tackled within a nonhuman conceptual framework, therefore opening up a whole new palette of potential design solutions in the urban realm. GAN_Physarum, in other words, offers the prospect of avoiding some of the common pitfalls of biophilic and biomimetic design protocols, namely the need for all-too-human metaphorical interpretations, as in the case of "urban forests," or reductionist abstractions, as found in most "green networks" proposals.

Following the typically distributed model of practicing research in the global pandemic reality of 2020, the Parisian derive of GAN_Physarum starts in the air-conditioned laboratories of the Synthetic Landscape Lab at University of Innsbruck. Here, at a constant room temperature of 20 degrees Celsius, a living *Physarum polycephalum* in its active plasmodium phase is made to hunt for nutrients within the sterile environment of a lab-grade borosilicate glass petri dish. Initially, the growth substratum consists of a 2% agar with oat flakes as locally condensed food sources.

The plasmodium's typical networked body begins spreading within minutes. For better documentation, the petri dish is positioned on a backlit surface and a camera is held above by a tripod. The camera lens has a focal length of 50 mm, and the resolution of the raw images is 4240 × 2832 pixels. A photo is taken every 60 seconds for a total of 5,190 images. The typical experiment lasts approximately three and a half days. The frames are then further edited by inverting the original input image, and then copying the original layer on top with the blend mode color filter. For further clarity of detail, a drop of blue food coloring is added on the agar substratum.

Once combined into a video sequence, these frames reveal the extraordinary morphogenetic process during which *Physarum polycephalum*'s body transforms into an optimized network for nutrient distribution. The process starts with a searching phase during which the pulsating body branches out in all directions, detecting food sources and their relative distribution and size. In this phase, traces of actin are left on the substratum, constituting a form of embedded memory, *Physarum polycephalum*'s own outsourced brain.

A phase of optimization follows. Finely detailed branches emerge in the relevant areas of the petri while other parts are abandoned. Eventually some of the branches grow in size and thicken, becoming convoluted transportation arteries. However, the optimized configuration never settles. As the resources are consumed and their overall distribution changes in real time, *Physarum polycephalum*'s morphology adjusts.

The scarcer the resources become, the more accelerated the change and adaptation. At the tipping point *Physarum polycephalum* is seen racing around the petri in an attempt to find new sources with sufficient energy to sustain its searching effort. Once nothing is left, it retreats, until all the remaining energies are deployed to create new fruiting

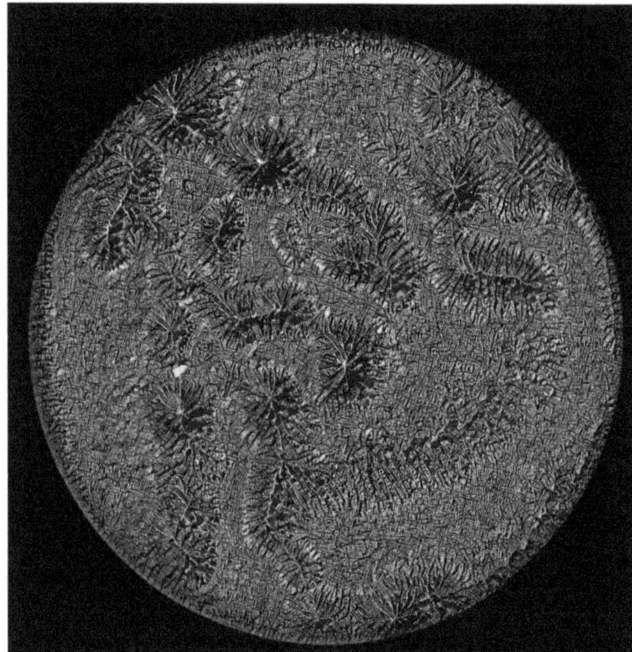

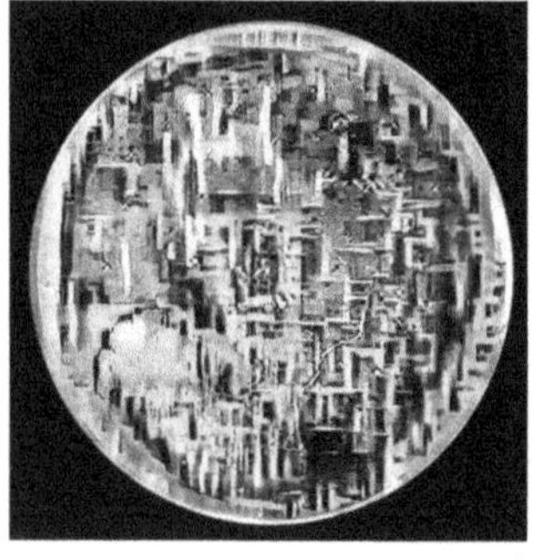

8 Transformation of Paris based on the biological intelligence of the *Physarum* using the GAN_Physarum algorithm.

9 GAN_Physarum algorithm applied on a 10 × 10 m scale: Centre Pompidou.

10 GAN_Physarum algorithm applied on a 100 × 100 m scale.

bodies, thus commencing the next phase in *Physarum polycephalum*'s uniquely elaborated life cycle. After several years of experimentation, it still beggars the authors' belief that so much complexity of form and behaviors can emerge from a simple unicellular organism.

Over time, the authors and their research team increased the complexity of the nutrients' mix. The PH of the nutrients is now controlled to maintain high values. A selective distribution of malt extracts, oats, and spirulina powder extracts is now precisely inoculated to act as attractor points while a triple biotic ointment works as repeller. Through this system of nutrient distribution, the research team can now directly "communicate" with, or transfer information to, the *Physarum polycephalum*.

A satellite image of Paris, duly processed to extract information about its biotic layer (plants, grasses, rivers, and other "wet" surfaces), is remapped on a grid. The points on the grid transfer the geodata of the corresponding latitude and longitude of the map. A 3D data matrix is compiled to store the density of biomass as a percentage value of a fully vegetated pixel. This is achieved by translating the sum value of the green pixels of the map for each four neighboring cells within the grid to an average percentage based on the total value of all the green pixels of the selected image.

After computing the average biomass on the grid points, these percentages of density are translated proportionally into amounts of nutrients on the growth substratum of *Physarum polycephalum*, with cell size of 3 cm. *Physarum polycephalum* is then introduced from a source point external to the grid. And while *Physarum polycephalum* begins its long biocomputational process to define the spatiotemporal distribution of nutrients, the authors and their team can shift their attention to the machine learning technique CycleGAN to refine its ability to detect the biologically grown characteristics of *Physarum polycephalum* and its complex behavioral patterns.

GAN_PHYSARUM: "LA DÉRIVE NUMERIQUE"

CycleGAN is a machine learning technique that uses the training of image-to-image translation models without paired examples. A generative adversarial network (GAN) has two parts, the generator and the discriminator, engaged in an internal competition. The generator learns to generate plausible data. The generated instances become negative training examples for the discriminator. The discriminator learns to distinguish the generator's fake data from real data. The discriminator penalizes the generator for producing implausible results. (Google Developers 2019).

Depending on the training input, this process results in the transfer of key features from one set of images onto another, and vice versa. In this case, the domain of source images and target images refers to the slices of two actual input images that belong in two different domains, the urban and the biological. We used this technique to transfer the behavioral patterns of the *Physarum polycephalum* onto the urban structure of Paris. The objective is to investigate how its biological intelligence can be applied on different scales to reinterpret existing infrastructures and building distributions of Paris itself.

While time lapsing, as described above, captures *Physarum polycephalum* at different developmental stages, Paris is analyzed at different resolutions through remote sensing. The significance of adding a zero to any number (Eames and

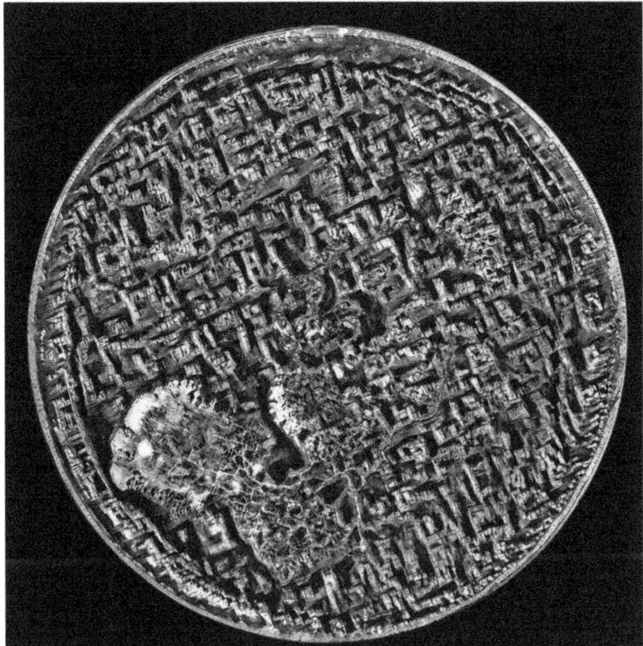

11

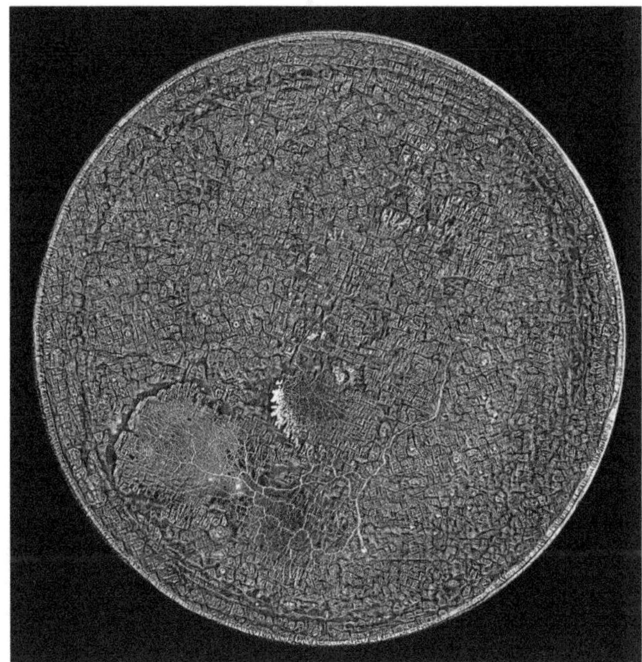

12

11 GAN_Physarum algorithm applied on a 1 × 1 km scale.

12 GAN_Physarum algorithm applied on a 10 × 10 km scale.

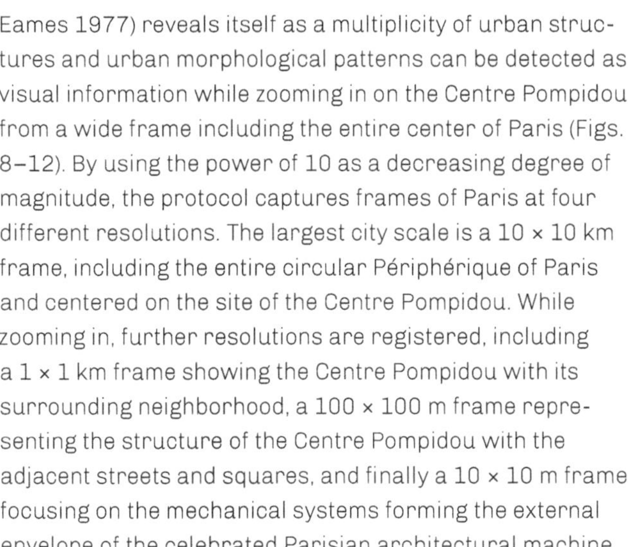

Eames 1977) reveals itself as a multiplicity of urban structures and urban morphological patterns can be detected as visual information while zooming in on the Centre Pompidou from a wide frame including the entire center of Paris (Figs. 8–12). By using the power of 10 as a decreasing degree of magnitude, the protocol captures frames of Paris at four different resolutions. The largest city scale is a 10 × 10 km frame, including the entire circular Périphérique of Paris and centered on the site of the Centre Pompidou. While zooming in, further resolutions are registered, including a 1 × 1 km frame showing the Centre Pompidou with its surrounding neighborhood, a 100 × 100 m frame representing the structure of the Centre Pompidou with the adjacent streets and squares, and finally a 10 × 10 m frame focusing on the mechanical systems forming the external envelope of the celebrated Parisian architectural machine.

The machine learning algorithm of GAN_Physarum is trained at each of these urban resolutions to a corresponding behavioral pattern of *Physarum polycephalum*. The algorithm learns to interpret Paris in a unique way at each resolution. During the training process, the characteristics of the *Physarum polycephalum* behavioral patterns are compared to the ones of Paris. Over several epochs, the algorithm learns how to reinterpret *Physarum polycephalum*'s behaviors in relationship to Paris's morphological structures, and vice versa. When several behavioral instances are tested and the results are combined in a video sequence, a biodigital dérive emerges, and with it an unexpected vision of Paris coming alive in the mind of GAN_Physarum.

This nonhuman cognitive process is underpinned by the GAN_Physarum workflow developed by the authors and their team. It can be described in four main phases:

- The first phase describes the preparation of the input images for training purposes. The dataset preparation is automated, slicing input images from both time-lapse and satellite source domains into equal tiles of 256 × 256 pixels in size. This phase also includes preprocessing the input data with custom colors and contrast adjustments. Such adjustments increase the recognizability of the distribution of detected structures in the satellite source in relationship to the biological one.
- The second phase is the training of the GAN_Physarum based on these input datasets. The model is trained to detect the structures in the satellite source in relationship to the biological one, so it can learn to project behavioral patterns to urban morphologies. During the training, the algorithm runs 200 epochs, and the visualization of the evolutions can be illustrated in a browser window showing the learning process (loss function) of the algorithm.
- At this stage the model is sufficient for generating plausible slices in the target domain. Subsequently the trained algorithm is tested. During this phase, the GAN_Physarum projects an input image in the biological domain A to an image in the urban domain B, and vice versa. Several cached models from the training phase can be loaded at this stage, thus tracking the

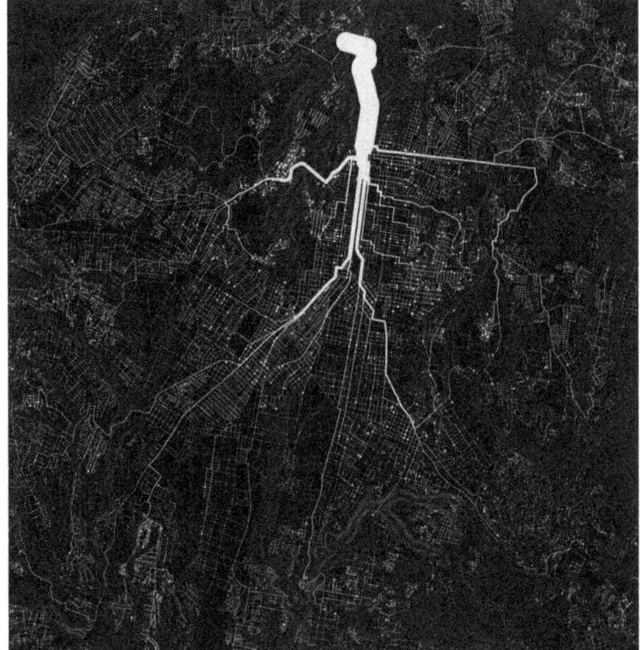

13

14

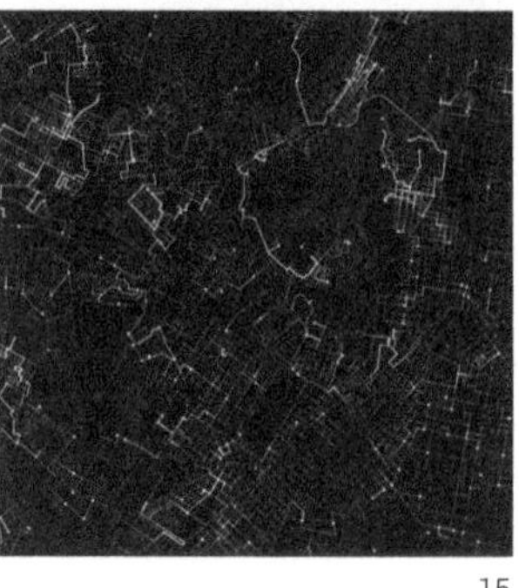

15

13 Local to municipal waste collection networks in Guatemala City. Image algorithmically computed from GIS map, satellite map, and DEM model analysis by means of minimal path algorithm. The analysis also takes into account the result of the local waste collection analysis. Iteration 1.

14 Path system and network in Guatemala City. Image algorithmically computed from GIS map, satellite map, and DEM model analysis by means of minimal path algorithm.

15 Community waste collection networks in Guatemala City. Image algorithmically computed from GIS map, satellite map, and DEM model analysis by means of minimal path algorithm.

self-evolution of GAN_Physarum.

- The fourth and final phase in the GAN_Physarum workflow refers to the combination of the output slices. This process is also automated. The algorithm uses the resulting output tiles from the testing algorithm and combines them to a final image, using an overlap between the image tiles to get clean transitions in the combined output image.

Just like *Physarum polycephalum*, cities are dynamic systems that react to external resource distributions and adapt by changing their morphology over time. They both undergo constant transformations to optimize their overall performance. This aspect of transformation over time is accounted for in GAN_Physarum. This, however, requires multiple training sessions at each scalar resolution, since every scale has different structures of detail that can be interpreted. This is the case for both Paris and *Physarum polycephalum*. This process offers an unprecedented opportunity for a holistic analysis of the relationship between urban patterns and biological intelligence. Such analysis has widespread application. In order to validate such assumptions and test the scalability of the GAN_Physarum protocol, ecoLogicStudio has partnered with UNDP on a dedicated research project titled DeepGreen.

THE CASE OF GUATEMALA CITY

In this project, we have been testing the applicability of the GAN_Physarum workflow as a green planning interface. Its key feature is to combine scalability, a necessary quality of any sophisticated planning application, to design versatility. In other words the expanded DeepGreen protocol ought to be:

- Open to multiple inputs so that urban stakeholders can interact with several layers of data and appreciate the effects of their hypothesis.
- Time-based, to enable all stakeholders to appreciate the effects of new policies and strategies systemically.
- Visually compelling, thus enabling all stakeholders to visually appreciate the simulated urban form across several orders of scale.

The design scenarios that emerged from the study suggest that a key remit for DeepGreen is to help break the currently uneven distribution of resources to promote the evolution of restorative urban systems. As previously observed, this process often implies questioning traditional planning concepts such as zone, boundary, scale, typology, and program. Such outdated notions actually constrain the emergence of a truly systemic approach to urbanization, one that recognizes the nature of contemporary cities as complex dynamic systems and their interconnectedness with the larger Urbansphere.

This issue is most evident in the case of Guatemala City (Pasquero and Poletto 2019). Guatemala City is situated on a complex and highly unstable terrain surrounded by mountains and volcanoes, some of which are still active. Its ecosystems, originally very rich in biodiversity, are now made fragile by unchecked urbanization and, given its climatic zone, the effects of climate change. In Guatemala City, this scenario is exacerbated by a serious lack of waste management. The Guatemala City garbage dump is the biggest landfill in Central America, containing over a third

16

17

16 Reinterpretation of the municipal waste collection networks of Guatemala City using the GAN_Physarum algorithm; algorithm training based on *Physarum polycephalum* behavior.

17 Redefined morphology and materiality of two overlapping systems: local to municipal waste collection networks and the vegetation network in Guatemala City; algorithm training based on *Physarum polycephalum* behavior.

of the total garbage in the country. Ninety-nine percent of Guatemala's 2,240 garbage sites have no environmental systems and are classified as "illegal." Confronted with this scenario, we have come to realize that only a design methodology powered by big data gathering and the production of ad hoc algorithmic design scenarios can deal with such complexity and level of informality.

The DeepGreen protocol facilitates the creation of an interface between bottom-up processes of self-organization, such as the many local waste-recycling activities (Fig. 13) that are emerging out of necessity in the areas closer to the dumping sites, and the strategic decision-making that occurs at municipal, national, and international level. The aim is to find new synergies and direct investments where and when they have the most potential to engender positive change.

In DeepGreen, the protocol to generate the urban datasets for GAN_Physarum is expanded to read and process several kinds of input data. As described at the beginning of this paper, it involves input data reading, biotic-abiotic analysis, and network systems analysis.

In Guatemala City we refer to three different kinds of remote-sensing data: land survey (at a resolution of 10 m), digital elevation models (at a resolution of 30 m from the NASA database), and GIS vectorial data from the Open Street Map project. These datasets are processed at a resolution of 1 m over a frame of 16 km, comprising the entire city center and several peripheral neighborhoods.

Municipal, local, and informal waste disposal and recycling sites are mapped and their locations marked. The existing road network (Figs. 14, 15) is also mapped, and all potential sources of waste are located over it. Two sets of path systems are then computed: local path systems connect all waste sources with the closest dumping sites, and municipal path systems connect all dumping sites with six proposed municipal recycling centers. All paths are thickened and color-coded depending on the amount of waste that travels on each of their branches. The process is repeated for four kinds of waste: organic, metal, paper, and plastic. The emerging diagrams (Figs. 18, 19) are fed to GAN_Physarum as urban datasets.

Two radical visions define the case of Guatemala City. On the one hand, the waste infrastructure appears as a biologically active, convoluted, and highly differentiated body, capable of sorting, transporting, and remetabolizing the urban waste into nutrient and raw matter. On the other hand, GAN_Physarum reimagines Guatemala City as a networked body gently suspended over a wild substratum of proliferating biological life (Figs. 16, 17). When shared with a wider group of stakeholders, these visions triggered a more concrete set of proposals, among which two are finding significant traction: a re-wilding plan to foster new coexistence between

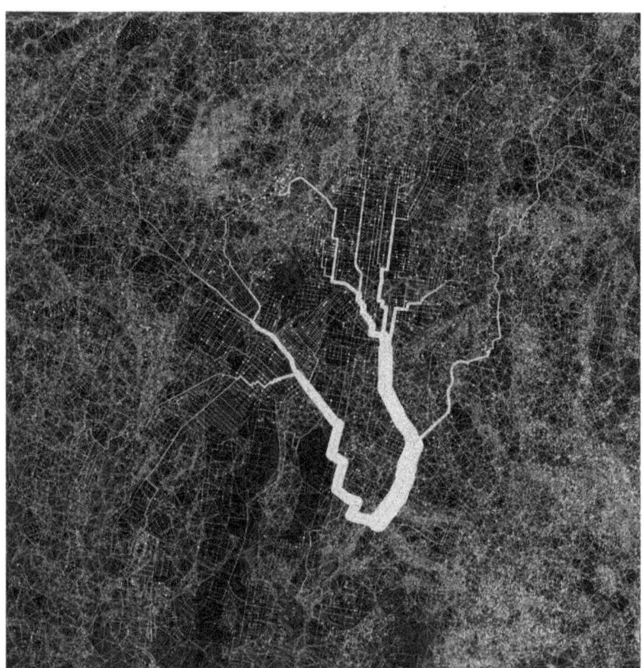

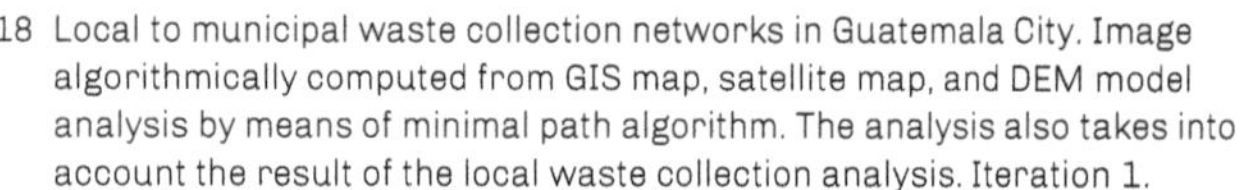

18 Local to municipal waste collection networks in Guatemala City. Image algorithmically computed from GIS map, satellite map, and DEM model analysis by means of minimal path algorithm. The analysis also takes into account the result of the local waste collection analysis. Iteration 1.

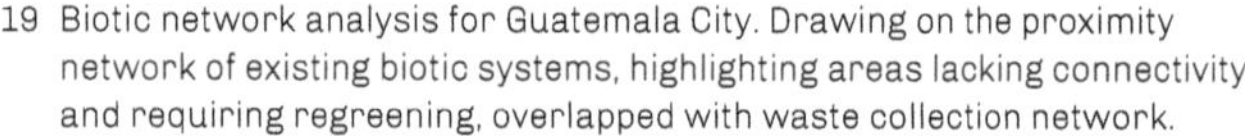

19 Biotic network analysis for Guatemala City. Drawing on the proximity network of existing biotic systems, highlighting areas lacking connectivity and requiring regreening, overlapped with waste collection network.

human and urban wild animals, and an urban agriculture plan proposing a method to guarantee food security and recycle organic waste while employing the rural population currently migrating to the city of Guatemala.

What matters to the authors is that both proposals are sensitive to local conditions while affecting international power relationships. For instance, the migrating birds populating the green areas of Guatemala City migrate to and from Canada. Therefore, investments in urban re-wilding will benefit the biodiversity of Canada too. Migrant workers cross the city on their way to the US-Mexico border. Urban agricultural plans could retain rural workers, alleviating the pressure on both Mexico and the US. Such synergies have the potential to channel significant international funds to local projects, improving the lives of citizens of Guatemala City.

CONCLUSIONS

German architect Frei Otto famously stated that human settlements are natural. He recognized, mainly through analog computing, that cities share unique emergent behaviors and self-organizing growth patterns with living organisms. Modern computer science has demonstrated the case of *Physarum polycephalum* within the realm of infrastructural engineering. The DeepGreen method proposes to extend this approach to evolve an effective urban planning model.

The DeepGreen method seeks to exploit the pattern recognition capacities of GAN algorithms while offsetting their limitations as purely image-based workflows. The overall intelligence of the workflow proposed in this paper does not rely solely on the abilities of GAN algorithms; rather, it exploits them to create robust transcalar communication between the ecological intelligence of *Physarum polycephalum* and the algorithmic nature of contemporary big data planning.

This requires a design protocol capable of generating consistent and high-resolution raster datasets for GAN_Physarum from a variety of sources in the urban, the infrastructural, and the biological domains. Furthermore, the informational qualities of these datasets need to be visually recognizable in the structure of the images. Particular attention must go to the tonal patterns of color and to the gradients of luminosity. Such patterns must be consistent across the entire image frame to avoid areas lacking informational clarity. The presence of such areas can affect the efficacy of the training process and therefore negatively affect the results of testing, thus compromising the intelligence of the system.

While further testing is necessary to confirm widespread applicability and considering that the development of DeepGreen is an ongoing research effort for the authors and their team, at its core lies the potential to capture the proven intelligence of *Physarum polycephalum*, emergent, distributed, and embodied, to design cities capable of searching for opportunities of coevolution within the expanded urban landscape. Cities that can find untapped resources and remetabolize their waste while minimizing the expenditure of energy required to accomplish these fundamental survival tasks. Cities made by humans, for both human and nonhuman citizens and planned by a new form of inhuman intelligence.

REFERENCES

Debord, Guy. 1956. "Theory of the Dérive." Situationist International Online archive. https://www.cddc.vt.edu/sionline/si/theory.html.

Eames, Charles, and Ray Eames. 1977. *Thinking in Powers of Ten*. Video. https://www.eamesoffice.com/education/powers-of-ten-2/.

Google Developers. 2019. "Overview of GAN Structure." Generative Adversarial Networks. Last modified May 24, 2019. https://developers.google.com/machine-learning/gan/gan_structure.

Mazzuccato, Marianna. 2017. *The Value of Everything*. London: Penguin Economics.

Pasquero, C., and M. Poletto. 2016. "Cities as Biological Computers." *Architectural Research Quarterly* 20 (1): 10–19. https://doi.org/10.1017/S135913551600018X.

Pasquero, C., and M. Poletto. 2017. "Biodigital Design Workflows: ecoLogicStudio's Solana Open Aviary in Ulcinj, Montenegro." *Architectural Design* 87: 44–49. https://doi.org/10.1002/ad.2130.

Pasquero, C., and M. Poletto. 2019. "Beauty as Ecological Intelligence: Bio-digital Aesthetics as a Value System of Post-Anthropocene Architecture." *Architectural Design* 89: 58–65. https://doi.org/10.1002/ad.2480.

Pasquero, C., and M. Poletto. 2020. "Culturalising the Microbiota: From High-Tech to Bio-Tech Architecture." In *The Routledge Companion to Paradigms of Performativity in Design & Architecture*, edited by M. Kanaani. New York: Routledge.

Radford, Alec, Luke Metz, and Soumith Chintala. 2015. "Unsupervised Representation Learning with Deep Convolutional Generative Adversarial Networks." *ICLR (International Conference on Learning Representations)*. arXiv:1511.06434.

Tero, A., S. Takagi, T. Saigusa, K. Ito, D. P. Bebber, M. D. Fricker, K. Yumiki, R., Kobayashi, and T. Nakagaki. "Rules for Biologically Inspired Adaptive Network Design." *Science* 327 (5964): 439–442. https://doi.org/ 10.1126/science.1177894.

Zhu, Jun-Yan, Taesung Park, Phillip Isola, and Alexei Efros. 2017. "Unpaired Image-to-Image Translation using Cycle-Consistent Adversarial Networks." In *Proceedings of the IEEE International Conference on Computer Vision (ICCV)*, Venice, Italy, 22–20 October 2017, 2223–2232. IEEE.

IMAGE CREDITS

Images 1, 6–12: ecoLogicStudio with The Synthetic Landscape Lab at Innsbruck University and The Urban Morphogenesis Lab at the Bartlett UCL, 2020. Lead researchers: Dr. Claudia Pasquero, Dr. Marco Poletto. Project team: Eirini Tsomokou, Korbinian Enzinger, Joy Boulois, Oscar Villareal.

Images 2–4 and 13–19: ecoLogicStudio with Innsbruck University and The Bartlett UCL for UNDP.

Image 5: Physatopia project_by Rc16, The Bartlett UCL 2018. Tutors: Dr. Claudia Pasquero with Filippo Nassetti, Emmaouil Zaroukas. Students: Qin Qing, Jia Itu.

Claudia Pasquero is an architect, curator, author, and educator. She is founder and co-director of ecoLogicStudio in London, Lecturer and director of the Urban Morphogenesis Lab at the Bartlett School, UCL, and Professor of Landscape Architecture and founder of the Synthetic Landscape Lab at Innsbruck University. Claudia has been Head Curator of the Tallinn Architectural Biennale 2017 and was nominated for the *Wired* smart list the same year.

Marco Poletto is cofounder and Director of ecoLogicStudio and the design innovation venture PhotoSynthetica, focused on developing architectural solutions to fight climate change. Marco holds a PhD from RMIT University in Melbourne. His work has been exhibited internationally, most recently in Paris (Centre Pompidou, 2019), Tokyo (Mori Gallery, 2019), Vienna (MAK, 2019), Karlsruhe (ZKM, 2019), and Astana (EXPO 2017).

Claudia and Marco are coauthors of *Systemic Architecture* (Routledge, 2012).

Theoretical Notes on the Aesthetics of Architectural Texture Mapping

Hans Tursack
MIT School of Architecture + Planning

Imperfect Acts of Perception

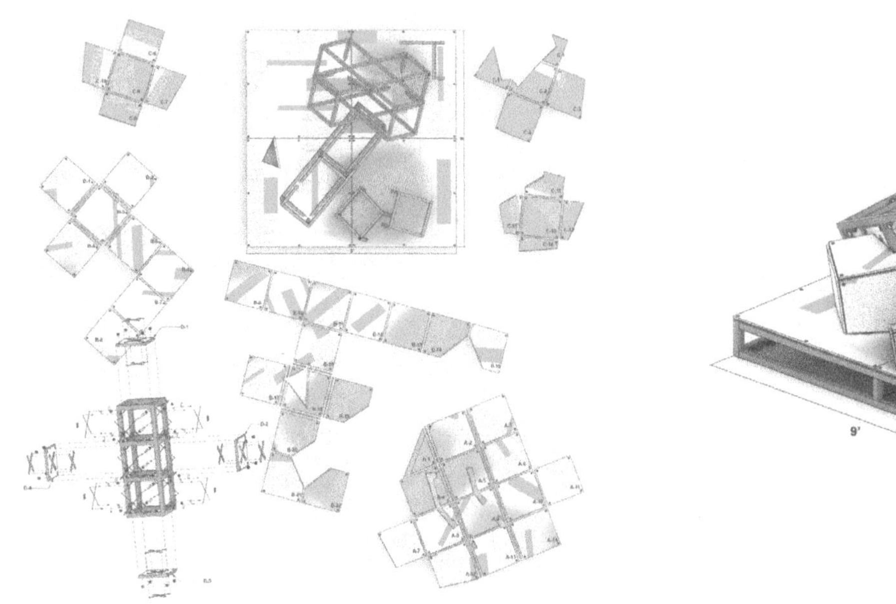

1

1 Concept rendering and unrolled surface diagram for a public art installation to be installed on a university campus. Funding for this project provided by the Council for the Arts at MIT. Project research assistant: Jonathan Brearley.

ABSTRACT

This paper explores several historical and contemporary examples of architecture that employ graphic texture mapping in their design processes. The technique of texture mapping is outlined as a particular formal relationship between images, geometric scaffolds, and new material explorations. Texture-mapped architecture is a relatively contemporary phenomenon that is distinct from several known genres of image-building hybrids such as media facades, Ganzfeld art installations, building-scale projection experiments, postmodern semiotic billboards, and affective ornamental pattern strategies. Architectural texturing utilizes UV editors in modeling and animation software platforms to place and edit two-dimensional graphics or photographic images on three-dimensional models. UV editors allow an unprecedented degree of precision during the design process; image and geometry can be manipulated in tandem and two-dimensional source material can be edited and live-updated. Material manifestations of this process use commercial printing technologies and one-off processes developed by artists and designers to generate building-grade printed envelopes.

The theoretical wager of the paper is that the accessibility/availability of texture mapping techniques, digital printing technologies, and new materials (such as 3M's vinyl wraps) have triggered a graphic impulse in contemporary experimental architecture culture. Images, color theory, and flat graphics are now central to compositional theory as it is taught in academia and applied in the field.

THEORETICAL BACKGROUND

Image-objects—a term used here to denote architectural forms wrapped in photographic source material and complex graphic designs—frequently appear in visual studies syllabi, experimental exhibition venues, and even as large-scale built works. The term itself is likely to invoke some low-level anxiety, as the history of compositional theory in architectural education is largely one of geometric (conceptual) thought being translated into the material stuff of the built world through intricate line-work drawings and diagrams. Asserting photographs and colorful, two-dimensional graphic matter into geometric genesis narratives upsets received formalist wisdom. What's more, when images cross over into compositional theory and the built environment (as printed envelopes in the case of the examples cited here), known methods of formal analysis come unmoored. Postwar debates between the critical agency of legible geometric systems vs. the phenomenological immediacy of tectonics have little to offer the reader of an image-object. Likewise, recent (one might say antiformal) theories centered around architectural atmospherics reduce any discussion of surface to blurry "affect" and mediatic "spectacle" discourse. Image-objects frustrate a too-easy divide between geometric systems (read through gestalt perception), phenomenological formalism (the corporeal experience of material assemblages), and affect-theory. At the same time, the elusive aesthetic properties of this work need to be framed by technical as well as visual analysis. The work explored here exploits contemporary digital tools drawn from advanced animation, modeling, video games, and graphics platforms, in addition to commercial printing technologies and new materials. Several exemplary pre- and early-digital precedents offer more analog approaches to the image-object, suggesting a sensibility that belongs to an even longer timeline. Through this lens, enigmatic photo-mapped works such as Michael Heizer's *Dragged Mass Geometric* (1985) might be understood as examples of a slow revision in recent decades of known formalist ontologies that privilege geometric and material construction over the "superficial" qualities of color, images, and graphics.

The theoretical mistrust of spatialized image-based work is well-documented in recent criticism. In his reframing of Kenneth Frampton's theoretical project, art critic Hal Foster pits empathetic identification with materials, and a phenomenological self-awareness, against all that is virtual, optical, atmospheric, scenographic, and disorienting in painterly, surface-centric architecture. In these scenarios (Ganzfeld art installations, Minimalist museums, and neo-modern "Light Construction," for example), painterly architecture "render[s] the phenomenological faux" (Foster 2013, 209).

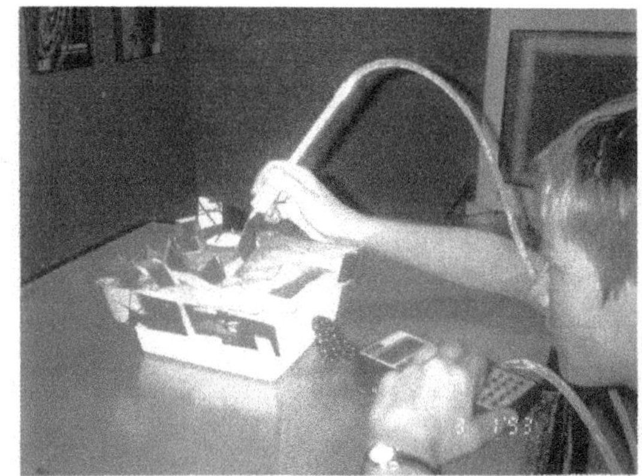

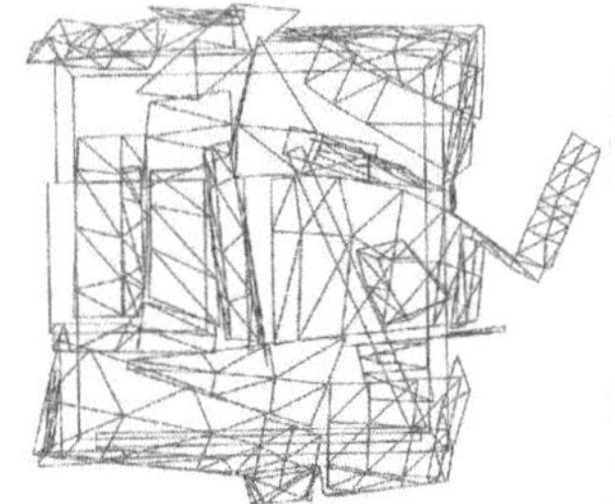

2

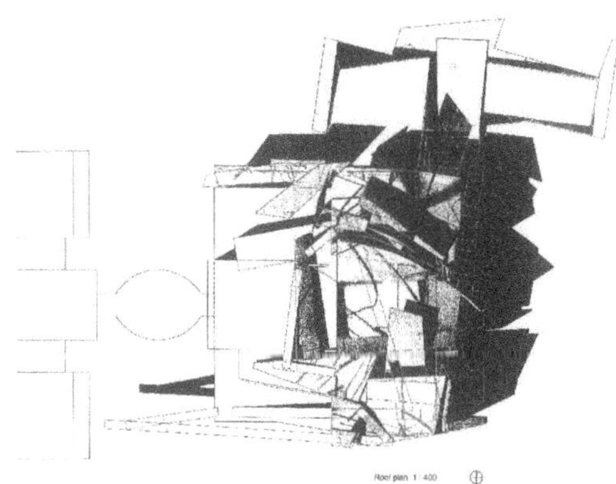

3

2 Coop Himmelb(l)au, Groninger Museum East Pavilion. 1993–1994. Digitizer and physical model.

3 Coop Himmelb(l)au, Groninger Museum East Pavilion. 1993–1994. Roof plan and unrolled surface drawing.

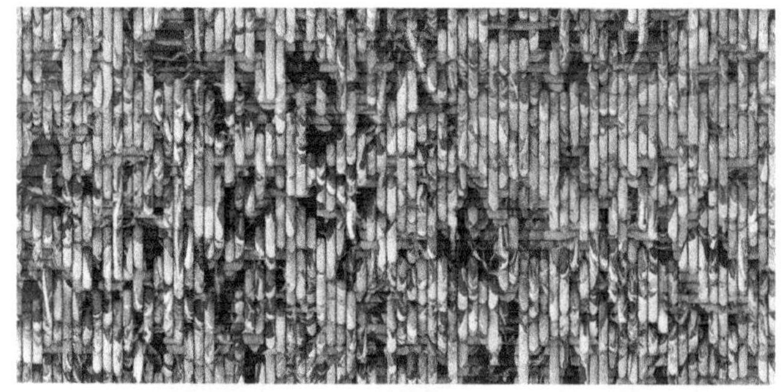

4

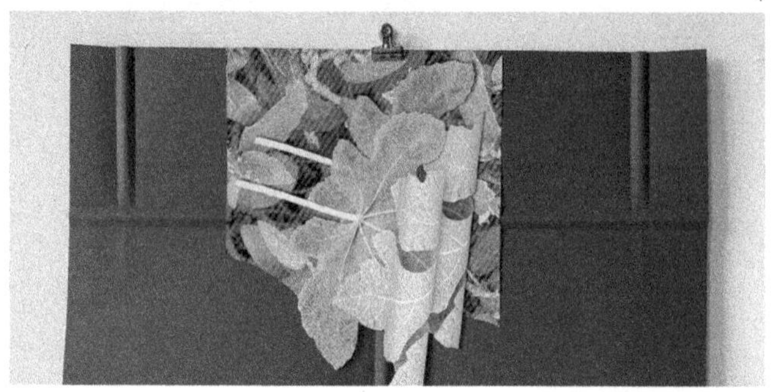

5

6

Environments soaked in colorfields and projections create carefully calibrated visual experiences where, "perception is, as it were, done for us" (Foster 2013, 209). On the other end of this well-documented image-architecture polemic, Sylvia Lavin (2013) theorizes the "kiss" of building facades and luminous projected images by design-savvy artists like Doug Aitkin. In Lavin's celebratory catalog of novel, collective affects, youthful artworks kiss and thereby erotically dissolve the tragic, stiff, politically retrograde, gestalt surfaces of institutional (modern and neo-modern) architecture. Pipolotti Rist, in Lavin's reading, applies "moist pressure" to the banal and authoritarian relic of Greenbergian elitism that is Yoshio Taniguchi's MoMa atrium with her luminous projection piece *Pour Your Body Out (7354 Cubic Meters)* (2008). Lavin praises the ability of such installations to melt the oppressive, Cartesian coordinate space of modernism: "A kiss puts form into slow and stretchy motion—renders geometry fluid" (Lavin 2013, 5). Both "kiss" and the more ominous image-architecture "complex" read buildings as frames, lattices, or supports for the faster, more immediate, and sensorially commanding powers of the image.

Both critics are also careful to maintain distinctions between mediums (sculpture, image, film, architecture), even as they intermingle in "catastrophic" (Foster) and "bedazzling" (Lavin) new ways. The image-based work examined here could certainly be objects of interest for both authors, but would likely frustrate their medium-specific analytics (painterly colorfields and projected films/photographs vs. architectural form). If Lavin and Foster read the dissolution of material, built objects into the "virtual" by way of images, it may be more instructive (if unsettling for the medium-sensitive) to put pressure on the effects produced by the geometric specificity and printerly materiality of the image-objects cited here. By embedding images into the design process from the moment of inception, projects like Coop Himmelb(l)au's Groninger Museum East Pavilion (1993–1994) can hardly be understood as a neutral frame for light, color, or graphics. Instead, the source image for the project (a small, "automatic" pencil sketch) drives the form-generation narrative as a device used to divide space and make decisions about the geometric nature of the pavilion's envelope and interior partitions. The Groninger is an emblematic image-object study in that the process designed to transpose the scan stamped on its massive, self-supporting steel cladding plates involves techniques native to printmaking (a messy, error-prone, technical process) rather than cleaner applications like projection, colorfield washes, or other atmospherics. The image blanket that coats the surfaces of the Groninger is a (drastically) enlarged pencil sketch that was scanned, cut, and pasted onto a physical model and digitally enlarged to a 1:1 stencil. The stencil was then cut as an adhesive film mask for shipbuilders to use as they painted the design with tar directly onto the flat, self-supporting steel plates that clad the museum wing. The noise and grain of the scan (the pencil sketch was enlarged such that lines broke down into pixelated bands of dots and fills) marks the pavilion with glitchy traces of process, doubled by the (by now more familiar) geometric fragmentation of the facade. The Groninger tar-tattoo is worlds away from the "moist

7

4 Current Interests (Mira Henry + Matthew Au). *Hedges of the World*. 2018. Texture rendering.

5 Current Interests (Mira Henry + Matthew Au). *Hedges of the World*. 2018. Physical mockup.

6 Current Interests (Mira Henry + Matthew Au). *Hedges of the World*. 2018. Tyvek presentation model.

7 Michael Heizer. *Dragged Mass Geometric*. 1985. Construction and installation photos.

pressure" of Rist's projected image-kiss (the Groninger's architects boast that the tar of its tattoo will outlast the material decomposition of its steel support) and is more disorienting and formally dissembling than it is sublime. Form, image, material, and process are inextricably woven together in the production of the pavilion's envelope.

NOISE, ERROR, CHROMA-GLITCH

A common quality of the work described here is the loss of image resolution and the introduction of material error (some of which comes naturally by printing at an architectural scale as 1:1 file sizes can become unwieldy). Media theorist Carolyn L. Kane (2019) theorizes the aesthetics of glitch as something particular to the digital culture of the first decades of the 2000s (autotuned vocals, pixelated JPEGs, video compression errors, etc.). "Accidental color" (a cousin of compression-error or datamoshing) in particular is described by Kane as the aestheticization of discordant palettes and chromatic noise. While Kane points out that "color has always been a kind of noise" throughout the history of western aesthetic philosophy distrusted as merely cosmetic and prone to "false appearance"—its shifty nature is taken to extremes with digital patterning and "accidental" mixing, as in the videos of Ryan Trecartin and Lizzie Fitch (Kane 2019, 71). Trecartin and Fitch have become particularly adept at drawing attention to "accidental" colors by using techniques like overmatching in the surfaces of their videos (a character's outfit, garish makeup, a Naked Juice bottle, and a wallpaper background are painted with uncanny chromatic fidelity, collapsing figure and ground). The architectural office Current Interests (Mira Henry + Matthew Au) has begun to forefront the skins of architectural envelopes as sites for similar inquiries into color and graphic error in their design work. The duo reconceives the building envelope as a soft, cosmetic wrapper through a revision of Gottfried Semper's theory of textile enclosures, one of his four (primary) elements of architecture. In Current Interests projects like the office's design for an artist studio in Silverlake, Los Angeles (2019), they quite literally imagine building envelopes as slack blankets with careful attention paid to subtle shifts in the hue, value, saturation, and texture across a given surface. In their piece *Hedges of the World* (2018), however, color is taken to a new extreme (an extreme familiar to the makeup, costumes, digital effects, and set designs by Trecartin and Fitch). The image-map for *Hedges* was developed through a complex series of analog and digital processes. The architects gathered and carefully cataloged a selection of plants from a residential neighborhood in South L.A. before photographing each sample with a ruler to maintain its scale. The catalog of samples was then enhanced in Gigapixel and run through a series of scripts in Photoshop and Grasshopper to separate color channels, before being redistributed onto 3D surfaces. The project was then materialized as a printable Tyvek fabric before it was sewn and fitted with an interior structure. The all-over field-like quality of the final work speaks to high-fashion pop-camouflage, Luis Gispert's photographs of candy-coated custom car interiors, and the "chroma-glitch" that marks the swipes and transitions in Trecartin and Fitch's videos and set designs. Kane's descriptions of the artists' figure-ground transgressions could easily apply to the

8

9

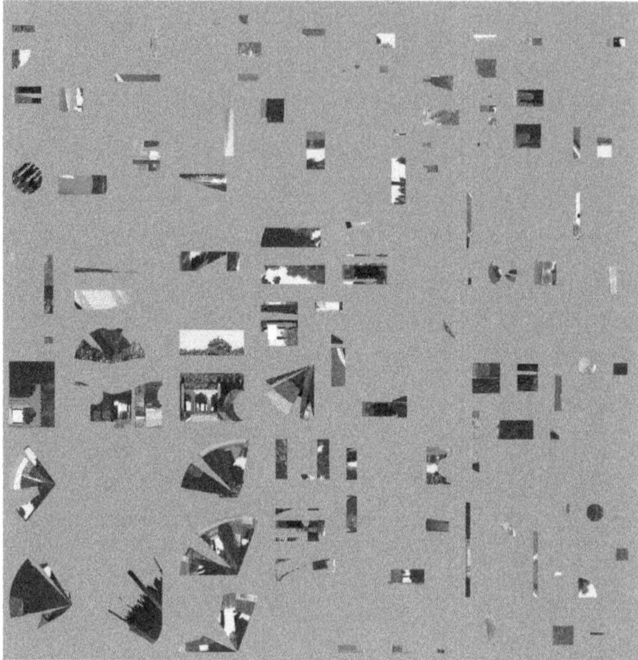

10

uneven color-image field mapped onto *Hedges of the World*: "The power of color is movement from singular, linear, and rational frameworks into noise, nondistinction, and the deceptive but vital qualities of visual perception" (Kane 2019, 121).

An important quality unique to image-objects like Henry and Au's textile experiments is that they are "mapped" (rather than projected or tiled) with photos, graphics, and colors. Mapping is the precise operation of placing images onto the individual faces of a massing model and assigning them (U,V) coordinates relative to surface geometry. Image mapping allows a user to scale, rotate, and skew images attached to geometric shells in digital modeling environments. In this, images are wedded to the geometric wireframe of a project in the first stages of design. Unrolled surface drawings are a critical part of all image-object workflows, allowing the designer to visualize a complex volume as an array of flat planes. Platforms for animation, modeling, character design, and rendering allow users to quickly and carefully position images on 3D surfaces using UV editors. In a UV editor, a 3D object's mesh is unfolded and images can be placed and manipulated on an unrolled surface drawing with incredible speed and control. Also unique to contemporary texture-mapping platforms is the ability to update source-image files (a linked Photoshop file mapped onto a mesh in the Maya platform, for example), while manipulating a 3D model in real time.

GRAPHIC SKINS

Video game theorist Ian Bogost tells us that "textures are the graphical skins laid atop 3-D models so they appear to have surface detail" (Bogost 2011, 78). Indeed, advances in texture mapping were driven, in part, by the popularity of first-person video games in the early 1990s like id Software's *Doom* (released in 1993 for MS DOS) (Pinchbeck 2013). *Doom*'s designers outdid their previous 3D releases that used cartoonish environmental palettes created from scratch (id's *Catacomb 3-D* [1991]) by scanning physical materials and using them to coat the surfaces of different levels. Using photographed source material and new lighting algorithms, *Doom*'s immersive environments were unlike anything the gaming world had seen before. The use of texture mapping is second nature to many younger architects; part of the phenomenology of gaming is the experience of getting lost in the illusion of textures, only to run into errors and accidental off-map blind spots that reveal the superficial nature of a mesh (which can appear as a group of broken, unwelded surfaces). Unlike video games, however, which look to dial up the level of realism and resolution with each new release, texture-mapped architecture draws attention to its artificiality and flatness with graphic glitch, noise, static, printerly error, and misregistration. The image-objects in projects like T+E+A+M's *Living Picture* installation (2017) use historical photographs of the installation's site as it was designed in 1912 and translate that archival material into a digital map. When said map is printed on vinyl and used to skin the steel wireframes of geometric primitives in the actual installation, however, the effect inverts the "gritty, realistic look" that *Doom*'s designers were after. Instead the cones, cylinders, and prisms scattered across *Living Picture*'s site appear to be native digital artifacts that somehow fell out of a gaming platform back into the material world.

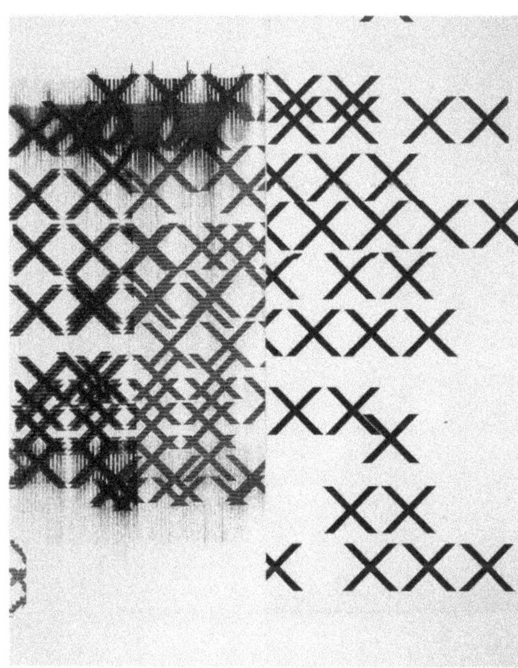

11

8 T+E+A+M (Thom Moran, Ellie Abrons, Adam Fure, Meredith Miller). *Living Picture*. 2017. Concept rendering.

9 T+E+A+M (Thom Moran, Ellie Abrons, Adam Fure, Meredith Miller). *Living Picture*. 2017. Installation Photograph (T+E+A+M).

10 T+E+A+M (Thom Moran, Ellie Abrons, Adam Fure, Meredith Miller). *Living Picture*. 2017. Unrolled surface drawing.

11 Wade Guyton. *Untitled*. 2006, Epson UltraChrome inkjet on linen, 85.25 × 69 inches, 216.5 × 175.3 cm. Courtesy of the artist and Petzel, New York.

One could look at photographs of T+E+A+M's final built installation and mistake it for a straightforward exercise in texture mapping, projection, and anamorphosis, a digital Magritte. The project is composed as a suite of stage-prop-scaled geometric primitives strewn about a suburban lawn. Each geometric volume is wrapped in a vinyl print with a full-color rendering that was applied using a texture-painting tool in the Blender platform. From certain vantages, one appears to see through the printed objects as though a photograph of its context were printed directly onto the form in the manner of science fiction active camouflage devices (Masahiko, Kawakami, and Tachi 2003). Closer inspection reveals that the mapped images are in fact renderings of the architect Howard Van Doren Shaw's 1912 garden stage design for the site. A fabricated history leaks into the anamorphic projection, along with digital artifacts from T+E+A+M's process (the default Photoshop checkerboard background is revealed in areas where the texture-painting tool "missed" part of a volume's surface). Even in photo documentation, the architects' rendering of the original Shaw scheme asserts its character as a 3D model (trees and shrubs are rendered digital objects; one is not meant to be duped by photorealism). The resolution of the projected images is then conceptually doubled in the array of volumetric forms that they wrap (primitives being the default geometric menu of most 3D modeling software).

How does one describe the visual qualities of a work that blends fiction (3D-generated models), documentation of a site's past life (photos of the Ragdale Ring's site from 1912), and first-person perspectives (sitelines drawn from a close reading of the present-day site before construction)? Printerly error and low-resolution rendering in *Living Picture* are calibrated to invite the viewer into the 3D environments used to design the work. One is made aware of Photoshop glitches and the registration imperfections that inevitably come with any texture-mapping exercise (images can get stretched and smeared when projected onto 3D models). While the expertise and skill behind the installation's modeling/rendering is a given, there is a modesty and playfulness in the work that speaks to a reverence for the early years of computer rendering (the architects came of age just before the advent of gaming engines like the id Tech 1). The loving nod to images of early rendering experiments from the 1970s and 80s, and simultaneous command of contemporary tools might be understood as a subjectivity specific to the architects' generation.

T+E+A+M's use of texture mapping, image editing, digital printing, and the almost-mute forms native to 3D modeling menus clearly forefronts process over authorship. Nearly 50 years after the introduction of Peter Eisenman and Sol LeWitt's "semi-automatic" geometric systems, however, we know that such processes have absorbed new affects (Keller 2018). In the digitally native inkjet canvases of Wade Guyton, for example, one senses a melancholic ghost in the machine. The "X" shapes repeatedly printed on works like *Untitled* (2006) get cropped, overlap, bleed, and suffer from the banding that happens when a print head is clogged or low on ink. It's as though the system is struggling to get its message (the X removed from any context is already a weak signifier) from digital machine to substrate. To use a musical

12

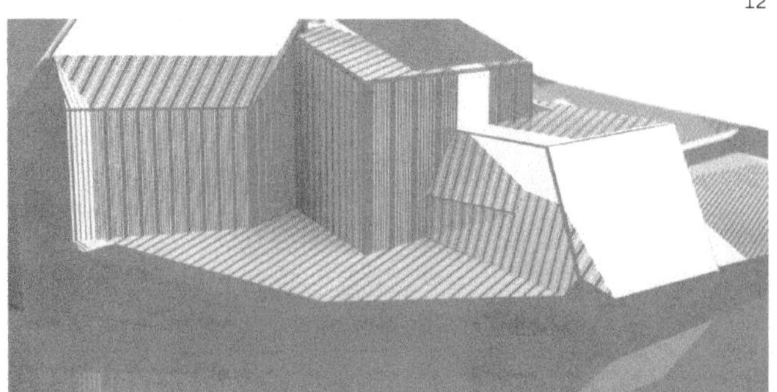

13

14

analogy, cultural theorist Mark Fisher describes the digital grain that filters the vocals on Darkstar's 2010 electronic album *North* as "if it has been recorded on a shaky mobile phone connection" (Fisher 2014, 173–174). The printerly errors that mark Guyton's work and the texture-mapped image-objects cited here speak more to digital deterioration, loss, and breakdown than to the techno euphoria that Foster and Lavin diagnose (for better and worse) in mainstream image-architecture hybrids. Viola Ago's project *Poppy Red* (2018), for example, begins with a series of vacuum-formed PETG relief studies that are hydro-dipped with an inkjet-printed film. Hydro-dipping (or water-transfer printing)—a technique Ago borrows from custom automotive culture—is the process of applying an image film to a three-dimensional form by floating the image in a chemical bath and plunging the object through its surface. The technique is by nature imprecise, and one can never accurately predict how an image will wrap the geometry in one of her studies (though the architect studies this process with digital physics simulations in Maya as well). The imprecision is of course the point, and even though the graphic was carefully crafted in Rhino 3D and the ZBrush platform to "fit" the folds and cavities of the vacuum-formed reliefs, Ago exploits moments when the film misses its mark, tears, wrinkles, and delaminates from its support, just as Guyton relishes in the drips, clogs, print-head traces, and misregistration when overprinting giant X's on folded linen with his large-format Epson. Both architect and artist use digital (and analog) printing processes the way experimental musicians use looping and delay: mechanically repeating an indexed action while offsetting and overlaying its repetition.

The image of a glitched-out image "blanket" projected from above onto an object reads most clearly in the presentation model for *Poppy Red*. In the model, mechanically skittish white lines and fills "hit" the project's massing volumes and spill out onto a glossy, back-painted, monochrome ground plane (one imagines a 3D version of Frank Stella's offset paintings, where the white lines and polygon supports fail to catch up and properly align with one another, caught in a perpetual state of asynchrony). The vertically projected blanket also visually connects *Poppy Red* to a much earlier precedent, Douglas Garofalo and David Leary's Camouflage House (1991). In both examples, the plan-oriented blanket dissolves figure-ground demarcations, and the projects' massings seem to emerge from their sites. The backpainted gloss of Ago's project speaks more to the culture of 3M vinyl car wraps than the ominous "protective coloring" of Garofalo and Leary's militaristic studies. However, the high-perspective model photographs and roof plans of *Poppy Red*, the Camouflage House (and the Groninger for that matter) are the most expressive and complete images of these projects. Designing to an aerial perspective begs the question of satellite and aerial photography (camouflage was, after all, designed primarily with the planometric, photographic, gaze in mind) (Bousquet 2018, 157). The work might also address Google Earth, drone's-eye-views, and the ubiquitous "top" viewport, a common perspective option in most 3D modeling software. The image-architecture works by Doug Aitken, Herzog and de Meuron, and others analyzed by Lavin and Foster still largely owe their optical models to the anthropocentric, vertical, modernist viewing-eye, epitomized by Robert Slutzky and Colin Rowe's

Yale Perspecta Journal Transparency articles published in the 1960s. Many of the image-objects analyzed here, by contrast, concern themselves with both human and machine perspectives.

PRINTERLY MATERIALITY

Nowhere is the collapse of architecturally scaled form, image, and mechanical perception more intricately intertwined than in the installation *Dragged Mass Geometric* (1985) by earth/land artist Michael Heizer at the Whitney Museum of Art, New York. *Dragged Mass Geometric* is a series of faceted volumes built from steel trusses and lumber clad in screen-printed corrugated board. The dimensions of the piece are massive for the Whitney's fourth-floor gallery, measuring 16.5 × 115 × 46 feet. The reason for its scale is that *Dragged Mass Geometric* is actually a loose simulacrum of *Dragged Mass* (1971), a 30-ton granite block and earth installation staged in the Detroit Institute of Arts outdoor grounds. The Whitney reconstruction (if it can be called that) reimagines the boulder and earth-mounds as low-poly hollow volumes, framed in steel and wrapped in printed photographs. The images are close-ups of "geologic source material" shot with an "extensive twelve minute exposure from twelve feet in the air" in the artist's studio (Heizer and Whitney 1985, 6). The idea of using photographs of raw materials (and Southwestern landscapes shot before the project) was likely inspired by Heizer's archaeologist father, who used aerial (helicopter) photography, magnetometers, and other sophisticated Cold War–era measurement tools to study ancient architectural sites in Mexico, Peru, and the American Southwest (Kett 2015). The complex translation of the Detroit installation into radically simplified geologic volumes and massively enlarged, printed image textures (dots that were 125th of an inch "are now blown up to eight feet or nine feet long") similarly echoes the artist's father's labor-intensive surveys and early-digital models of sites like the La Venta pyramid (Heizer 1986). Though Heizer is largely known for his colossal outdoor installations with concrete, rocks, and metal, *Dragged Mass Geometric* is more like an exercise in analog photogrammetry. The artist pushes this work one step further in his *Altars* (2015) series, where enlarged hand sketches are painted on the borders of colossal "alien" shapes built out of weathering steel and coated with polyurethane. That the "altars" (some more than 40 ft in length), which are also silk-screened with collaged fragments of the imagery used for *Dragged Mass Geometric*, speak to the artist's career-long interest in spatial drawing, photography, and textures rendered at scales better suited to aerial and satellite photography than to human perception. Image-objects are, at the end of the day, not for first-person viewers to take in as a corporeal experience.

12 Miracles Architecture (Viola Ago). *Poppy Red*. 2019. Unrolled surface drawing.

13 Miracles Architecture (Viola Ago). *Poppy Red*. 2019. Presentation model.

14 Miracles Architecture (Viola Ago). *Poppy Red*. 2019. Presentation model.

If enlarged photographic images of the Southwestern landscape dematerialize geometric substrates for Heizer, the office Alam/Profeta takes this process to a new extreme using photogrammetry and lidar scans of building sites to translate architectural solids into vaporous image-clouds. In projects such as Watchtower (2018), Casa Zwei (2018–2019), and Street|Scape (2017), the office moves between consumer smartphone photogrammetry apps (Autodesk ReCap) and premium, high-end Leica lidar equipment to survey sites for architectural interventions. By beginning with machine vision, A/P mobilize the survey (rendered as point-cloud objects) as a design agent. In his history of military perception, Antoine Bousquet tracks the historical transition of conventional planometric maps from finished products to be read by users (printed on paper like architectural projections) to computer cartography. In computer cartography, a map is an object "to be displayed within a visual toolbox to be used interactively for exploratory data analysis" (Bousquet 2018, 157). Similarly, the initial design act for A/P has more to do with the real-time analysis, management, and interpretation of high-resolution point-cloud models than it does with orthographic geometric concepts born in an imaginary compositional nonspace. In projects like Watchtower, photogrammetry is used to generate a point-cloud model of the original architecture+site as a first operation. Renderings of the point cloud are then flattened using Grasshopper and MeshLab (and Processing) to create flat, two-dimensional skins (their "texture worlds" as A/P likes to call them) before they are rethickened as low reliefs to be mapped onto geometric substrates. As with the Groninger, A/P relishes the opportunity to render visual information from vaporous renderings (a medieval tower translated into a field of free-floating cloud points) into the emphatic materiality of Cor-Ten steel, locally sourced, building-scale, sandstone color printing, and custom-fabricated bricks. In A/P's oeuvre, composition as we conventionally define it is almost entirely absent. Instead, images give birth to models, models become renderings, renderings become textures, and textures take shape through material research.

15

16

17

15 Alam/Profeta (Maya Alam, Daniele Profeta). Watch-Tower. 2018. Algorithmically edited texture map.

16 Alam/Profeta (Maya Alam, Daniele Profeta). Watch-Tower. 2018. Final concept rendering.

17 Alam/Profeta (Maya Alam, Daniele Profeta). Watch-Tower. 2018. Final concept rendering.

CONCLUSION

Image-object research in the mode of Alam/Profeta and Heizer (and an understanding of the subjectivities that such research can produce) is an emerging category in visual studies. That said, in the "kit-of-parts" conceptual formalism (a postwar invention) still commonplace in many foundation-level architecture curricula, composition is understood as the construction of gestalt figures (Love 2003). Students learn to manipulate geometric grammars in plan, section, elevation, and axonometric projections to set up and then carefully delay the satisfactory resolution of parts (point-line-plane and solid-void geometric elements) into pictorial wholes. Several schools of phenomenological painterly thinking and affective ornamentalism may have challenged such gestalt pedagogy in recent decades, forefronting image, pattern, ornament, light, and color over form. However, the practices that expertly utilize these strategies (artists like Aitken, Turrell, Irwin, and Eliasson and designers like Herzog and de Meuron, UN Studio, and Steven Holl Architects) default all too often into a high-tech, black-boxed, atmospheric euphoria that renders material "virtual," phenomenological experience "faux," and form as viscous or "fluid" (to borrow terms from Lavin and Foster). The image-object is, instead, a unique aesthetic and technical category that sets image and form into a more complex conversation. They are geometrically precise and process-oriented, and mobilize printerly glitch, error, dissonance, noise, and image breakdown to flirt with an optical formlessness. The graphic matter in the examples cited here is overexposed, overscaled, overprinted, and misaligned. Color is "accidental" and speaks to datamoshing and compression algorithm noise. The tools used to generate the envelopes of projects like *Living Picture*, *Poppy Red*, and *Hedges of the World* are borrowed from animation, character design, game design, and rendering cultures. Image-objects are expertly conceived in these platforms, often assisted by scripts and looped analog processes, and printed with material workflows invented by their designers and/or co-opted from custom car culture and commercial printing. Though technologically adept and materially advanced, the thematic of mechanical error, low or compromised resolution (in geometry and image alike), and semiautomatic processes belies an ambivalence towards the more future-forward aspects of earlier digital waves, and sets image-object sensibilities largely outside of, or peripheral to, architectural computation culture. Instead, the work asks fundamental (and much older) questions about the base structures and visual hierarchies that constitute our collective compositional vocabularies.

ACKNOWLEDGMENTS

Many of the artists, architects, and designers cited in this paper generously shared invaluable insights into their processes, technical innovations, and material explorations. I would like to extend a special thanks to Karolin Schmidbaur and Jan Rancke of Coop Himmelb(l)au, Matthew Au and Mira Henry, Thom Moran, Ellie Abrons, Adam Fure, Meredith Miller, Viola Ago, Maya Alam, Daniele Profeta, Wade Guyton, and Lucas Page and Rebecca Ochab of the Friedrich Petzel Gallery. I would also like to thank my summer research assistant Jonathan Brearley of the MIT SA+P.

REFERENCES

Bogost, Ian. 2011. "Texture." In *How to Do Things With Videogames*, 77–82. Minneapolis: University of Minnesota Press. http://www.jstor.org/stable/10.5749/j.cttttmwd.14.

Bousquet, Antoine. 2018. *The Eye of War: Military Perception from the Telescope to the Drone*. Minneapolis: University of Minnesota Press.

Fisher, Mark. 2014. *Ghosts of My Life: Writings on Depression, Hauntology and Lost Futures*. John Hunt Publishing.

Foster, Hal. 2013. *The Art-Architecture Complex*. New York: Verso Books.

Heizer, Michael, and David Whitney. 1985. *Michael Heizer: Dragged Mass Geometric*. New York: Whitney Museum of American Art.

Inami, Masahiko, Naoki Kawakami, and Susumu Tachi. 2003. "Optical Camouflage Using Retro-Reflective Projection Technology." In *ISMAR '03 [Proceedings of the 2nd IEEE/ACM International Symposium on Mixed and Augmented Reality]*, Tokyo, Japan, 7–10 October 2003, 348–349. IEEE Computer Society.

Kane, Carolyn L. 2014. *Chromatic Algorithms: Synthetic Color, Computer Art, and Aesthetics after Code*. Chicago: University of Chicago Press.

Kane, Carolyn L. 2019. *High-Tech Trash*. Oakland: University of California Press.

Keller, Sean. 2018. *Automatic Architecture: Motivating Form After Modernism*. Chicago: University of Chicago Press.

Kett, Robert J. 2015. "Monumentality as Method: Archaeology and Land Art in the Cold War." *Representations* 130 (1): 119–151. https://www.doi.org/10.1525/rep.2015.130.1.119.

Lavin, Sylvia. 2011. *Kissing Architecture*. Vol. 3. Princeton, NJ: Princeton University Press.

Love, Timothy. 2003. "Kit-of-Parts Conceptualism: Abstracting Architecture in the American Academy." *Harvard Design Magazine* 19.

Pinchbeck, Dan. 2013. "The Fastest Texture Mapping in Town: Id Tech 1." In *DOOM: SCARYDARKFAST*, 34–44. Ann Arbor: University of Michigan Press. http://www.jstor.org/stable/j.ctv65sx8p.8.

IMAGE CREDITS

Figures 2, 3: ©Coop Himmelb(l)au.
Figures 4, 5, 6: ©Current Interests.
Figure 7: ©MichaelHeizer.
Figures 8, 9, 10: ©T+E+A+M.
Figure 11: ©WadeGuyton, 2018.
Figures 12, 13, 14: ©MiraclesArchitecture, Viola Ago.
Figures 15, 16, 17: ©Alam/Profeta.

All other drawings and images by the authors.

Hans Tursack is a designer from Philadelphia, Pennsylvania. He received a BFA in studio art from the Cooper Union School of Art, and an MArch from the Princeton University School of Architecture where he was the recipient of the Underwood Thesis Prize. He has worked in the offices of LEVENBETTS Architects, SAA/Stan Allen Architecture, and Tod Williams Billie Tsien Architects. His writing and scholarly work have appeared in *Perspecta Journal*, *Pidgin Magazine*, *Thresholds Journal*, *Log Journal*, *Dimensions Journal*, *Archinect*, and the *Architects Newspaper*. He is currently serving as the 2018–2021 Pietro Belluschi Research Fellow at the MIT School of Architecture + Planning.

3D Graph Convolutional Neural Networks in Architecture Design

Matias del Campo
University of Michigan, Taubman College of Architecture and Urban Planning

Alexandra Carlson
University of Michigan, Michigan Robotics

Sandra Manninger
SPAN

1 Close-up of one of the resulting models particularly geared towards the aesthetics of Czech Cubism.

ABSTRACT

The nature of the architectural design process can be described along the lines of the following representational devices: the plan and the model. Plans can be considered one of the oldest methods to represent spatial and aesthetic information in an abstract, 2D space. However, to be used in the design process of 3D architectural solutions, these representations are inherently limited by the loss of rich information that occurs when compressing the three-dimensional world into a two-dimensional representation. During the first Digital Turn (Carpo 2013), the sheer amount and availability of models increased dramatically, as it became viable to create vast amounts of model variations to explore project alternatives among a much larger range of different physical and creative dimensions. 3D models show how the design object appears in real life, and can include a wider array of object information that is more easily understandable by nonexperts, as exemplified in techniques such as building information modeling and parametric modeling. Therefore, the ground condition of this paper considers that the inherent nature of architectural design and sensibility lies in the negotiation of 3D space coupled with the organization of voids and spatial components resulting in spatial sequences based on programmatic relationships, resulting in an assemblage (DeLanda 2016). These conditions constitute objects representing a material culture (the built environment) embedded in a symbolic and aesthetic culture (DeLanda 2016) that is created by the designer and captures their sensibilities.

INTRODUCTION

Recent advances in 3D computer vision, specifically in deep convolutional neural networks, allow for the interrogation and exploration of huge data sets for patterns of spatial information; they allow us to learn high-dimensional, complex functions that map from 3D space into abstract labels. Thus, the motivation of this paper is to explore 3D deep learning methods that allow us as designers to interrogate large data sets of architectural archetypes and design sensibility based solely on 3D models, instead of using 2D representations, such as image data sets (del Campo, Carlson, and Manninger 2021). Instead of representing a 3D object as a pixel array/2D image, we propose to use a much more flexible data set structure called a graph. We propose to use a generalization of the standard image-based convolutional neural network, called graph convolutional neural network (GCNN) (Wu et al. 2021), in order to model different aspects of sensibility and the design process using only 3D models (Fig. 1). The central aim of this paper is to provide a possible solution to the question: How can a neural network interrogate the inherent sensibility of a specific designer? This paper presents a design technique, whose backbone is GCNNs, that is capable of modeling both the perception and creation of architectural objects.

BACKGROUND AND DEFINITIONS

In order to create a clear framework for the conversation laid out in this paper, specific boundaries in terms of the used definitions have to be made. In the following, we attempt to specify the definitions used in this paper, as they pertain to artificial intelligence and architecture.

Aesthetics

The term *aesthetics* is a highly charged one in the architecture discourse. This includes considerations such as the antithetical position of Peter Eisenman, who demanded that figures of architecture should be read rhetorically instead of aesthetically or metaphorically (Baumgarten 1750), or Anthony Vidler's discussion of aesthetics along the lines of its functional and metaphysical properties such as the sublime (Berleant 2015). Greek in its origin (*aisthēsis*), aesthetics literally means perception by the senses. The German philosopher Alexander Gottlieb Baumgarten considered art to be the perfection of sensory awareness. It is important to understand that the term *aesthetics* has undergone a series of mutations since Baumgarten's time and that even contemporaries of Baumgarten, such as Immanuel Kant, had a very critical position towards Baumgarten's definition as it lacked—according to Kant—any objective rules or laws, or any principles for that matter, to describe natural or artistic beauty. Kant relied on its use in a subjective manner as it relates to the internal feeling and not to any qualities in an external object. Baumgarten's assertion that the three guiding principles of aesthetics, "Good, Truth, and Beauty," appear essentially naive in the contemporary age. Thus, it is surprising for the authors to find this branch of conversation on aesthetics still being perpetuated by critics such as Roger Scruton and Yael Reisner. In general, the meaning of the term *aesthetic* has become equivalent to something whose appearance displays a particular set of qualities that evoke a response in the observer.

Sensibility

Thus, aesthetics is, at its very core, a theory of sensibility—evoking a response in the observer. This assertion discusses the arts of the past as much as the arts of the present, recognizing the aesthetic value as a specific feature of all experience. What we mean by sensibility is the perceptual awareness developed and guided through training and exercise. To this extent, it is certainly more than simple sensual perception, and closer to something like a guided or educated sensation. This ability is attributed in the Western traditions primarily to the arts—to painting, sculpture, music, literature, and so on—with architecture being this strange animal living somewhere between engineering and the arts.

3D Neural Modeling

There has been significant development of design techniques that hack 2D rendering and editing methods to be used in the design process of 3D models. Examples include 2D to 3D neural style transfer, 2D silhouette-based vertex optimization, and 3D deep dreaming proposed in a neural 3D mesh renderer (Mordvintsev, Olah, and Tyka 2015a). Other impressive differentiable renderers that propose image-based mesh deformation frameworks include Pytorch3D (Johnson et al. 2015), SoftRas (Liu et al. 2019), and DIB-R (Chen and Zhao 2019). There has also been impressive work in jointly training 2D and 3D networks for image-guided mesh deformation and reconstruction.

The recent success of 3D deep learning has inspired alternative methods for data-driven mesh deformation, synthesis, and reconstruction. The focus of these methods has typically revolved around simultaneously solving two subproblems. First is part or substructure deformation or transfer, and second is the preservation of fine geometric surface detail. These methods typically leverage a generative 3D variational autoencoder framework to learn a latent space that disentangles varying properties of meshes (Gao et al. 2018). The objective of these frameworks is to learn shape variation manifolds that can be used to sample latent

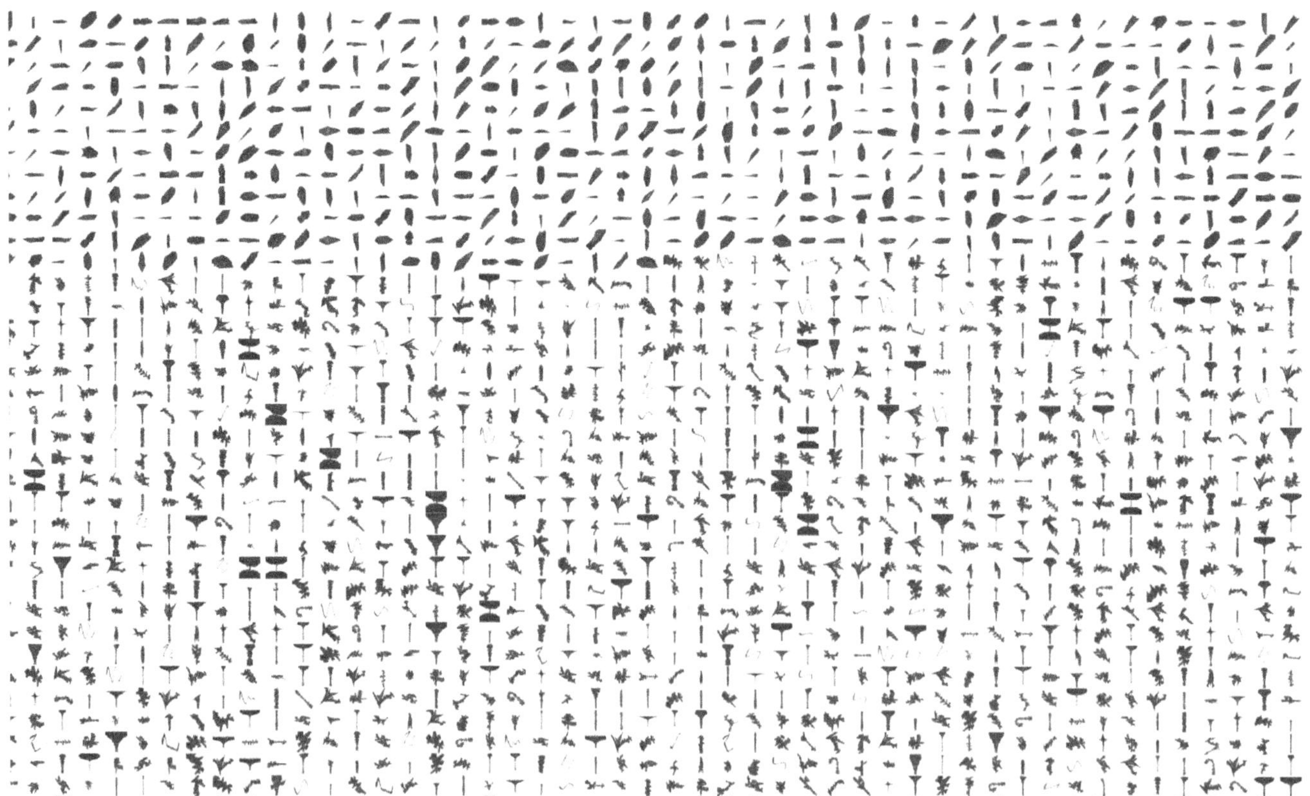

2 Renderings of the entire Sensibility data set. The first 626 objects are houses, and the remaining 1,552 are columns. This data set was designed by coauthor Matias del Campo so that it captured his design sensibility. This also included the labeling of the data set by the same hand, in order to mirror the design sensibility.

representations that are used to generate 3D shapes. The drawbacks of some of these methods is that they require large data sets with semantic and part annotations to aid in the disentangling process, which are time-consuming and difficult to collect (Chen and Zhao 2019; Gao et al. 2018; Kato, Ushiku, and Harada 2018; Mordvintsev, Olah, and Tyka 2015b; Olah et al. 2018). The proposed method differs from the above deep 3D generative models because it does not depend on learning latent, compressed representations of meshes; we use label supervision from our specially curated data set to guide the neural network to learn our desired parameter space. Instead, it takes an existing mesh as input and generates a variant by deforming it directly in 3D. As a result, the proposed method enables the reuse of existing 3D shape data with its associated meta-information. Furthermore, the proposed method does not focus on part or substructure transfer, or transforming mesh pose; it focuses on modeling and transferring abstract artistic concepts and qualities that define an artists' sensibility.

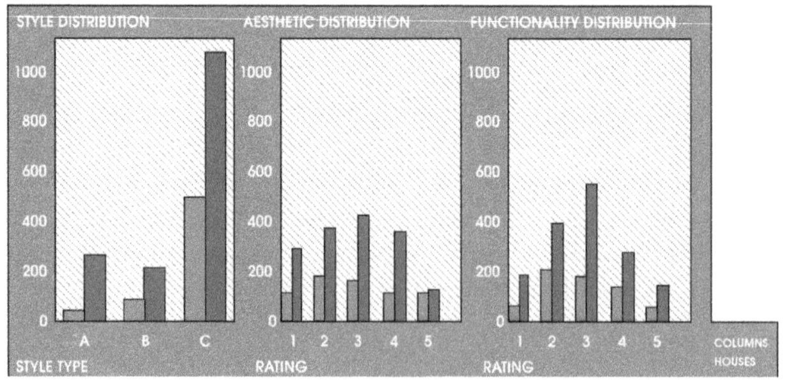

3 The distribution of labels in the data set. The labels were applied after model generation, and thus the data set is biased towards specific styles. Note that this is intentional and reflects the biases in the design sensibility of the author of the models in the data set.

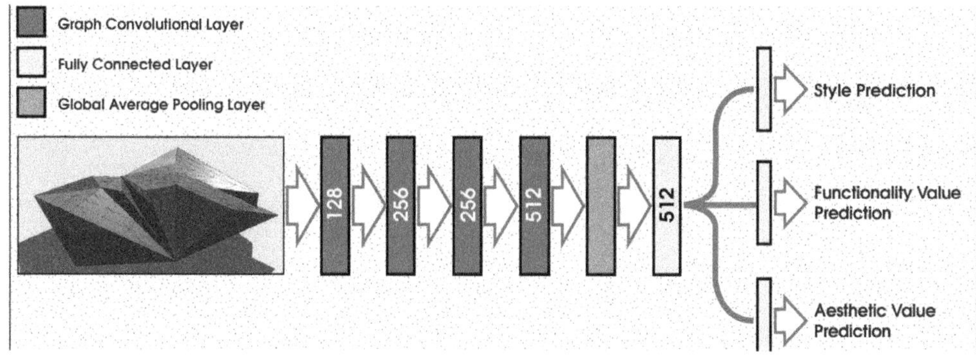

4 A pictorial overview of the GCNN neural network architecture.

METHODS

The proposed approach can be broken down into several steps. We start by generating and labeling a large database (Fig. 2) of OBJ mesh models of specific architectural classes: houses and columns, described below. We refer to this dataset as the Sensibility data set. The next step is to train a GCNN on this data set to learn a mapping function between the Cartesian coordinate space of 3D models to our defined label space of sensibility features. The final step is to place the trained GCNN into an optimization framework that takes in a user-specified 3D model as input, and then deforms the vertices of this model to optimize the shape for a user-specified style, aesthetic, or functionality label.

Database Construction

We generated large databases of OBJ models of specific architectural classes. More specifically, we divided them by their exterior volumes: houses, and columns. The models were generated using a series of techniques. The models started as low-poly models developed with the standalone software TopMod—a small topological mesh modeling software (Ankleman 2008). This allows the generation of low-poly models designed to become either entire buildings (house, tower) or parts of the architecture (columns). These first-generation models were saved as OBJ files and imported into Autodesk Maya (Autodesk Inc. 2019) in order to create enough variation to constitute the database. Imported models were deformed and mirror cut to come to a number of around 1,500 models. The original models were all created by the same authors. Using blend shaping in Maya, the author increased the number of model variations. To further increase the number of models in Maya, an assistant was instructed to randomly and occasionally deform the models significantly in order to account for models that could be labeled with low functionality or low aesthetic value. In our case, we relied on a set of models and their distortions (mirror cutting, deformations of the OBJ models) to create variation in the data set. Our label space decomposes the definition of a designer's sensibility into the following properties/components: semantic, style, functionality, and aesthetics. The semantic property of a given data object defines the object's concept/meaning. Within our data set, it can take on the value of a house or column. The style property of an object refers to the substructures of the object that are distinctive and define its appearance; they are determined by the theoretical/artistic principles that influenced the object's end design. In our data set, a given object can take

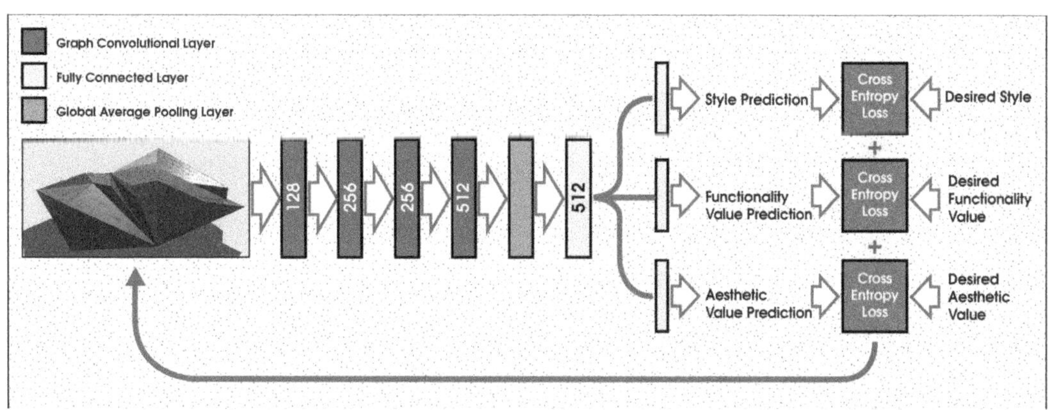

5 A pictorial overview of the neural optimization framework. By inverting the trained GCNN, we can effectively transfer the learned sensibility features captured in the neural network's parameters to an input mesh.

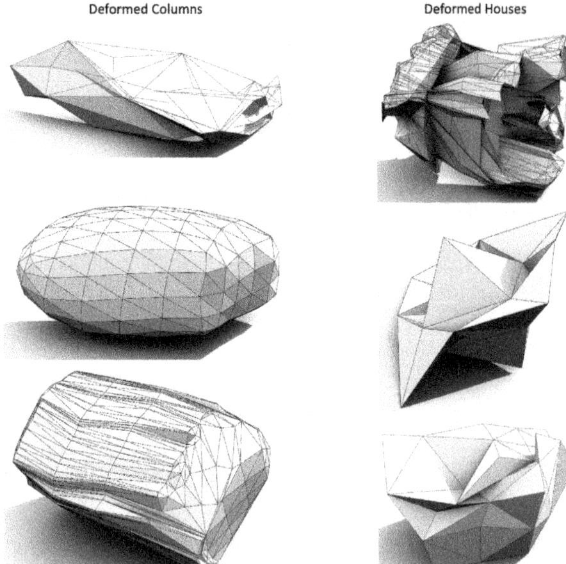

6 Examples of deformations produced by the proposed framework. On the left-hand side are examples of various simple geometries deformed to be columns of various styles using the proposed framework. The first image panel on the left-hand side is a icosahedron deformed to a column with Style B; the second/middle image panel on the left-hand side is a cube deformed into a column with Style C; and the bottom image panel on the left-hand side is a cylinder deformed to a column with Style B. On the right-hand side are examples of various input shapes deformed into houses, with the top image panel showing a dodecahedron deformed to a Style C house, the middle image panel showing an octahedron deformed to a Style A house, and the bottom panel showing an icosahedron deformed to a Style C house. All deformed models used a high aesthetic and medium functionality value.

on one of three styles: Style A, which is inspired by structures/features typically associated with Baroque; Style B, which is defined by substructures that exist within Classic architecture; and Style C, which is defined by features associated with Cubism. The functionality property is defined as the practicality of the object and its ability to serve a purpose well. Within our data set, an object's functionality property is a score of 1–5, where 1 is "not functional" and 5 is "fully functional." The aesthetics property is defined as the subjective and sensory-emotional values, or sometimes called judgments of sentiment and taste, and is also a score on a scale of 1–5. We intentionally included ugly and nonfunctioning models to train the GCNN in a synthetic process of the difference between functional, nonfunctional, and aesthetically pleasing or not. Both actions together form an organosynthetic process. In Figure 3, we show the distribution of the data set in terms of its labels. The labels were assigned after the models were generated, and thus we see that the data set is biased towards specific styles. Note that this is intentional and reflects the biases in the design sensibility of the author of the models in the data set.

Neural Optimization Framework

This neural network aims to learn a reasonable approximation of the function that describes a given architect's design sensibility, i.e., a function that maps from 3D metric space to our semantic, style, aesthetic, and functionality label spaces. Due to the extreme differences in resolutions and model number for columns and houses, we split the Sensibility data set into these two semantic subsets. We trained two separate networks, one on house models and the other on column models.

For each of these networks, we implemented a multitask classification GCNN architecture, shown in Figure 4. Note that we used the Pytorch3D27 library (Johnson et al. 2020) for our implementation. The functions of this library, specifically graph convolution, require the input meshes to be triangulated and watertight due to how the convolution operation is performed on neighboring nodes in the input graph. The meshes are also preprocessed to be centered at 0 and normalized to fit into a unit sphere (while preserving scale between meshes), which reduces the complexity of the learning problem for the GCNN. The proposed GCNN network has four graph convolution layers, with feature dimensions of 128, 256, 256, 512. We then implemented a global average pooling layer that operates on the vertex dimension of the graph convolutional features. Note that this global intermediate pooling layer allows us to have meshes with varying numbers of vertices. This output was fed into a shared, fully connected layer. This representation was input into three separate linear branches, one for functionality prediction, one for aesthetic prediction, and one for style prediction. Each branch is trained using standard cross-entropy loss. The total loss is the sum of the loss from each task branch. Both networks were trained with a batch size of 32 meshes, a learning rate of 2e-4, with the Adam optimization algorithm (Kingma 2014). They were trained until both the training and validation losses converged and the validation accuracy saturated.

Once the training process is over, the trained GCNNs will now act as our "designer"; they have learned the features associated with our sensibility label space. We can now fix these networks' parameters and invert them to transfer user input labels (and the corresponding sensibility features) to input meshes. A diagrammatic overview is given in Figure 5. We set the input mesh vertices as variables and specify a set of the desired style, aesthetic, and functionality labels. Using gradient-based optimization, we can iteratively change the vertices of the input mesh (i.e., deform the input mesh to produce an output mesh). The final deformed mesh would create the specified desired output labels. Note that the mesh vertices are now being

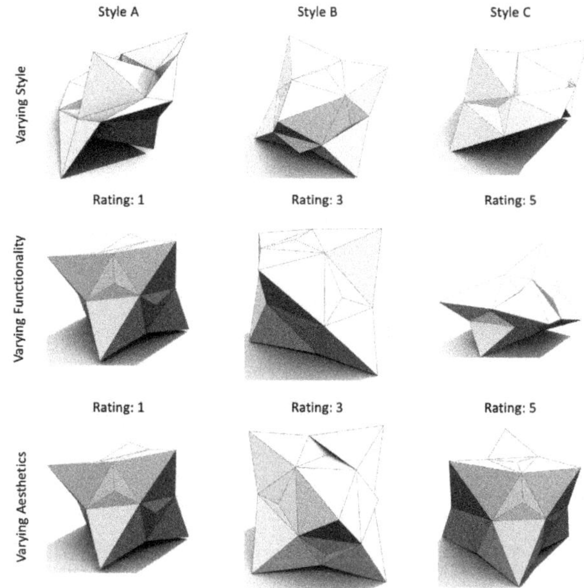

7 The outputs. Style, functionality, and aesthetics do not necessarily follow objective criteria; rather, they follow the criteria put into place by Matias del Campo. For example, the result of varying functionality of a rating of 5 produces a volume that can be converted into a low-slung house on a hillside (see final rendering).

learned, and the network parameters and labels are fixed (Fig. 6). Note that this process is similar to class-level deep dreaming; we are directly manipulating the vertex locations of the input mesh to minimize the differences between the predicted sensibility labels and the user-input/target sensibility labels. For each iteration of the optimization, we use one of the fixed GCNNs to project the current mesh into label space. We compare the mesh label predictions to the user-specified/desired mesh labels by calculating the cross-entropy loss between them. This error is then back-propagated through the network into 3D space, where we now have an error value for each vertex, which represents how much each vertex contributed to the mesh prediction. These values are used to deform the vertex locations of the mesh in 3D space. We use Adam optimization and perform iterations until the loss value has converged. For example, a user could input in a plain rectangular column, specify that the style and aesthetic quality of the column should be optimized, and the framework will iteratively deform the mesh to resemble the learned aesthetics and style captured by the data set. In the following section, we demonstrate that this optimization framework will fairly accurately mimic/approximate the sensibility of the architect who labeled the 3D model data set and will thus allow users to deform meshes in the same way that architects would edit and modify the input mesh themselves.

EXPERIMENTS AND RESULTS

For the house subset, the network achieved 99% validation accuracy for style classification, 75% for functionality, and 72% for aesthetics. For the column subset, the network achieved 100% validation accuracy for style classification, 81% for functionality, and 66% for aesthetics. We conducted various experiments with the GCNN structure to optimize its performance, both in terms of validation accuracy and the desired mesh deformations. First, we explored whether jointly training the prediction branches (where graph convolutional layers are shared, as depicted by the red rectangles in Fig. 4) or having separate networks for each label space yielded better performance and found that the joint learning paradigm gave us the best overall accuracy. We also explored the addition of normalization layers, e.g., batch and instance normalization, but found that they did not improve the accuracy over the proposed framework. Finally, we explored increasing the number of graph convolutional layers and the number of layers in each of the prediction branches. Still, we found that the smaller proposed network had the best overall performance.

To evaluate the proposed method's ability to transfer the authors' design sensibility, we present the following qualitative experiments. We first show extensive examples of the sensibility-optimized meshes using the proposed framework. We then offer qualitative ablation experiments manipulating the different sensibility axes of our label space to investigate the quality of the transfer. We then present an experiment using multiple network

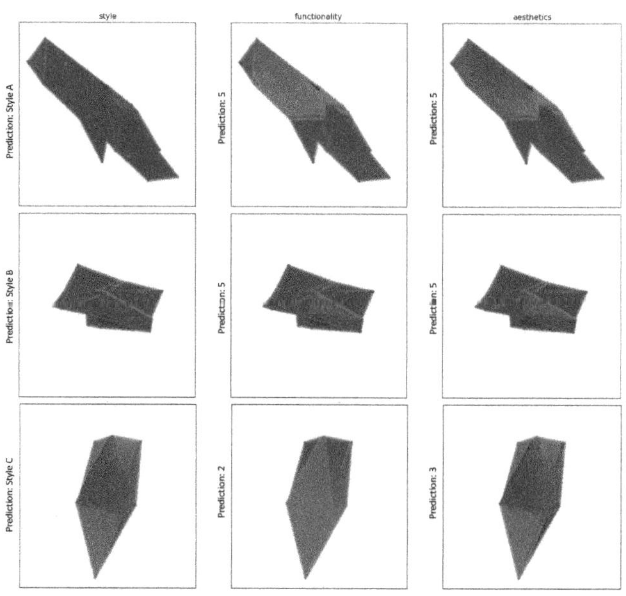

8 Examples of the visual saliency/vertex coloring outputs for house models in the data set.

9 An example of one of the Cubist house outputs.

interpretability techniques, visual saliency, to elucidate potential mesh substructures that could uniquely contribute to aesthetics, functionality, or style (Fig. 8). Note that our final two analyses focus on houses for brevity. For the columns, we see that the network has learned to elongate and thin out the input shapes to capture the global structure that is typically associated with columns. Similarly, with the houses, we see that they retain volumes similar to their original figures and have surfaces that could be considered floor-like. Our next experiment investigated the manipulation of each of the different label spaces while holding the others constant. This was done in an effort to examine the quality of the internal models learned by the GCNN for each of these feature axes. For this experiment, we focused on the generation of different houses from an octahedron mesh. We fixed all other parameters and varied one for each of the various labels: style, aesthetics, and functionality. The outputs are presented in Figure 7. For varying styles, which is in the top row of the figure, we set aesthetics and functionality to have ratings of 4 and held those values constant while altering the style. We see that the final results have distinctly different forms. For varying functionality, shown in the middle row of the figure, we set the style to be Style C and fixed aesthetics to have a rating of 4 while varying the functionality rating. For varying aesthetics, which is shown in the bottom row, we set the style to be Style C and fixed the functionality to be 3 while varying the aesthetic rating. The classification of Style A, B, and C in terms of its style relied on a set of specific rules derived from Baroque, Classic, and Cubist architecture. For example, the Baroque can be classified through features such as symmetry, curvature, and concave/convex spiel. Classic can be read here as Classicist or Modern, where Modern relies on the formal and stylistic qualities of high Modern architecture from the 1920s to the 1950s (proportionality, orthogonal, asymmetrical). Cubist pertains to the triangulation of polygonal bodies, akin to features found in Czech Cubist architecture. This, of course, is a blatant simplification of each of these styles and rather an innate response from the creator of the data set—producing a less scientific but rather spontaneous reaction to visual stimuli. The structure of aesthetic and functional considerations follows a similar formula in that it is extensive in nature but rather intensive with regard to the labeling process of the data set. As in the previous experiment, we observe that semantic and stylistic shapes are the dominant features transferred. The fidelity of the aesthetics and functionality transfer is much more nuanced due to its significantly more subjective nature, particularly regarding the qualities that make a different style of houses more or less functional or aesthetic to the designer and labeler of the data set. The gauge of functionality has to do with the resulting model proportions; if the resulting figure has the wrong proportions in terms of designing a house, it is "less functional" (the figure is too low, too high, or too narrow in order to accommodate the program of a house). This manifests in the models as the functionality increases; the models go from "too high" walls to spread out into flattened roof and ceiling features as the functionality score is increased. Aesthetics is far more difficult to capture objectively because it relies on the labeler's unique and subjective sensibility. The shape generated with high aesthetics (a rating of 5) has a well-proportioned length to width to height ratio. This means that the particular model can be scaled proportionally and could fulfill various programs, from house to concert hall. The relationship between concave and convex parts is also nicely balanced, giving an all-over even figure. The model silhouette is exciting, without being overly aggressive, despite lots of pointy elements.

DISCUSSION AND CONCLUSION

In conclusion, it can be stated that provided with a large data set of 3D models, produced by one hand and distorted to create more variation, a graph CNN can interrogate those models for underlying rule sets. These rule sets can generate architectural results that comply with the aesthetic criteria of the user. There are two main approaches to consider when assessing an algorithm's ability for design processes: first, the interrogation of the technical expertise necessary to train neural networks to generate successful solutions for pragmatic problems. This can be plan optimization, structural optimization, and the analysis of the consumption of material. The second path to be explored is the aspects of architectural design pertaining to studies of morphology, style, atmosphere, and creativity. Our goal was to test the capabilities of neural networks to model and transfer the highly abstract and complex concept of a designer's sensibility. Leveraging the powerful ability of neural networks to ingest and learn from large databases of models that can span cultural and historical dimensions that a human or humans would take a lifetime to synthesize and learn, we present a solution that allows for the transfer of aesthetic, style, and functionality features to meshes to generate new objects that capture the design sensibility of coauthor Matias del Campo. We show a finalized rendering of one of the Sensibility transferred Cubist houses in Figure 9. Future work would be to collect more extensive, more comprehensive data sets (possibly from different designers/architects), which would allow for a more thorough investigation into how neural networks represent these abstract artistic concepts. Another avenue of future work is to explore the feature spaces of generative networks on these kinds of data sets.

In conclusion, it can be stated that 3D graph convolutional neural networks open avenues for architecture design that allow interrogating the wicked problem of architecture design (sensibility, aesthetics) as well as the tamed problem (program, organization). To the surprise of the authors, when using databases of Baroque or Modern architecture plans to design new projects, the results don't look Baroque or Modern. They result in something new, different, alien, strange, and wonderfully beautiful—maybe the first genuine 21st-century architecture.

ACKNOWLEDGMENTS

The authors would like to thank Dean Jonathan Massey (UoM) and associate dean of research Geoffrey Thün (UoM) for their continuous support and the robotics department of the University of Michigan for providing knowhow, time, and effort to make this research possible. In particular, Jessy W. Grizzle, an Elmer G. Gilbert Distinguished University and Professor Jerry W. and Carol L. Levin Professor of Engineering and Director of Robotics. We additionally wish to thank Justin Johnson, assistant professor at the Computer Science department of the University of Michigan.

REFERENCES

Akleman, Ergun, Vinod Srinivasan, Jianer Chen, David Morris, and Stuart Tett. 2008. "TopMod3D: An Interactive Topological Mesh Modeler", *Computer Graphics International 2008*, pp. 10-18.

Autodesk, Inc. 2019. *Autodesk Maya*. V.2019. https://www.autodesk.com/products/maya/.

Baumgarten, A. G. 1750. *Aesthetica*. Frankfurt: J.C. Kleyb.

Berleant A. 2015. "Aesthetic Sensibility." *Ambiances* 1. https://doi.org/10.4000/ambiances.526.

Carpo, M. 2013. "The Digital Turn in Architecture 1992–2012." *AD Reader*, 8–14. West Sussex: John Wiley & Sons.

Chen, Lei, and Jiying Zhao. 2019. "Quality Evaluation of DIBR 3D Images Based on Blind Watermarking." *Multimedia Systems* 25 (3): 195–211.

DeLanda, M. 2016. *Assemblage Theory*. Edinburgh: Edinburgh University Press.

del Campo, Matias, Alexandra Carlson, and Sandra Manninger. 2021. "Towards Hallucinating Machines—Designing with Computational Vision." *International Journal of Architectural Computing* 19 (1): 88–103.

Gao, L., J. Yang, Y. Qiao, Y. Lai, P. L. Rosin, W. Xu, and S. Xia. 2018. "Automatic Unpaired Shape Deformation Transfer." *ACM Transactions on Graphics* 37 (6): 1–15.

Gatys, Leon A., Alexander S. Ecker, and Matthias Bethge. 2015. "A Neural Algorithm of Artistic Style." arXiv preprint. arXiv:1508.06576.

Johnson, J. Nikhila Ravi, Jeremy Reizenstein, David Novotny, Shubham Tulsiani, Christoph Lassner, and Steve Branson. 2020. "Accelerating 3D Deep Learning with PyTorch3D." In *SIGGRAPH Asia 2020 Courses (SA '20)* Article 10, 1. Association for Computing Machinery, New York, NY. DOI:https://doi.org/10.1145/3415263.3419160.

Kato, Hiroharu, Yoshitaka Ushiku, and Tatsuya Harada. 2018. "Neural 3D Mesh Renderer." In *Proceedings of the 2018 IEEE/CVF Conference on Computer Vision and Pattern Recognition*, Salt Lake City, UT, 18–23 June 2018, 3907–3916. IEEE.

Kingma, Diederik P., and Jimmy Ba. 2014. "Adam: A method for stochastic optimization." arXiv preprint arXiv:1412.6980.

Liu, Shichen, W. Chen, T. Li, and H. Li. 2019. "Soft Rasterizer: A Differentiable Renderer for Image-Based 3D Reasoning." In *Proceedings of the 2019 IEEE/CVF International Conference on Computer Vision (ICCV)*, Seoul, South Korea, 27 October–2 November 2019, 7707–7716. IEEE.

Mordvintsev, Alexander, Christopher Olah, and Mike Tyka. 2015a. "DeepDream—A Code Example for Visualizing Neural Networks." Google Research Blog. Archived from the original on 2015-07-08. https://ai.googleblog.com/2015/07/deepdream-code-example-for-visualizing.html.

Mordvintsev, Alexander, Christopher Olah, and Mike Tyka. 2015b. "Inceptionism: Going Deeper into Neural Networks." Google Research Blog. https://ai.googleblog.com/2015/06/inceptionism-going-deeper-into-neural.html

Olah, C., A. Mordvintsev, and L. Schubert. 2017. "Feature Visualization." *Distill* 2 (11): e7.

Olah, Chris, Arvind Satyanarayan, Ian Johnson, Shan Carter, Ludwig Schubert, Katherine Ye, and Alexander Mordvintsev. 2018. "The Building Blocks of Interpretability." *Distill* 3 (3): e10.

Wu, Z., S. Pan, F. Chen, G. Long, C. Zhang, and P. S. Yu. 2021. "A Comprehensive Survey on Graph Neural Networks." *IEEE Transactions on Neural Networks and Learning Systems* 32, no.1 (January): 4–24.

IMAGE CREDITS

All drawings and images by the authors.

Matias del Campo is a registered architect, designer, and educator. SPAN, which he founded with Sandra Manninger in Vienna/Austria, is a globally acting practice best known for its application of contemporary technologies in architectural production. Their award-winning architectural designs are informed by advanced geometry, computational methodologies, and philosophical inquiry. Matias del Campo is a recipient of the Accelerate@CERN fellowship and the AIA Studio Prize. He is Associate Professor of Architecture at Taubman College for Architecture and Urban Planning, University of Michigan.

Alexandra Carlson attended the University of Chicago for her undergraduate degree, where she studied psychology and physics. She is currently a robotics PhD candidate with the Ford Center for Autonomous Vehicles at the University of Michigan. Her graduate studies focus on robust computer vision for autonomous vehicles. Her research develops an experimental framework that identifies visual features within images that contribute to the failure of deep neural networks (e.g., noise from the camera, as well as noise from the surrounding environment), and then uses these insights to develop neural network architectures that can more effectively distinguish between objects.

Sandra Manninger is a registered architect, teacher, and researcher. She is coprincipal of SPAN. The focus of the practice lies in the integration of advanced design and building techniques that fold nature, culture, and technology into one design ecology. Her work is part of the permanent collection of the FRAC Collection, the Luciano Benetton Collection, the MAK, and the Albertina in Vienna. She has written and presented papers at numerous conferences, and her work has been published extensively in numerous magazines and books. She currently serves at Tsinghua SIGS and at IAAC.

Steering into the Skid

Arbitraging Human and Artificial Intelligences to Augment the Design Process

Geoff Kimm
Smart Cities Research Institute, Swinburne University of Technology

Mark Burry
Smart Cities Research Institute, Swinburne University of Technology

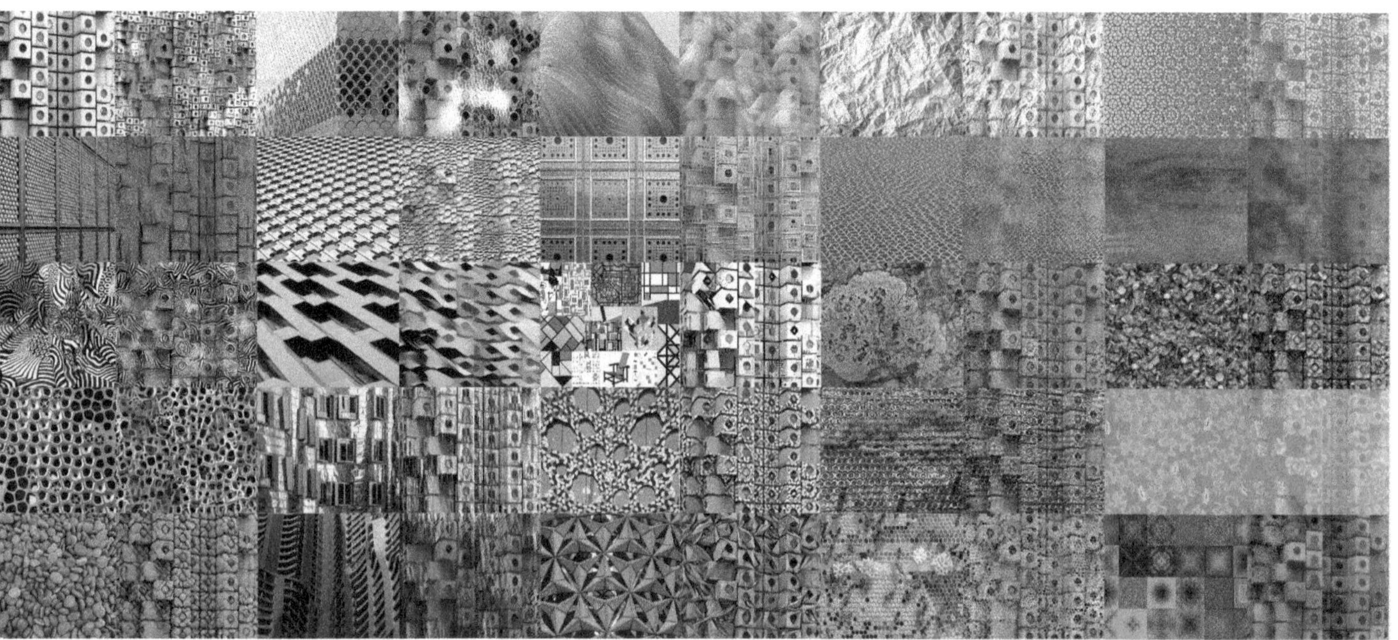

1 AI style transfer onto Kurokawa's Nakagin Capsule Tower (shown top left). Each subsumed style requires a few minutes of human endeavor and, superficially at least, illustrates the beguiling ease with which AI tools can be co-opted for the design process.

ABSTRACT

What if any perceived risks of lost authorship and artistic control posed by a wholesale embrace of artificial intelligence by the architectural profession were instead opportunities? AI's potential to automate design has been pursued for over 50 years, yet aspirations of early researchers are not fully realized. Nonetheless, AI's advances continue to be rapid; it is an increasingly viable adjunct to architectural practice, and there are fundamental reasons for why the perceived "risks" of AI cannot be dismissed lightly.

Architects' professional role at the intersection of social issues and technology, however, may allow them to avoid the obsolescence faced by other roles. To do this, we propose architects responsively arbitrage an ever-changing gap between maturing AI and mutable social expectations—arbitrage in the sense of seeking to exercise individual judgment to negotiate between diverse considerations and capacities for mutual advantage.

Rather than feel threatened, evolving architectural practice can augment an expanded design process to generate and embed new subtleties and expectations that society may judge contemporary AI alone as being unable to achieve. Although there can be no road map to the future of AI in architecture, historical misevaluations of machines and our own human capabilities inhibit the intertwined, synergistic, and symbiotic union with AI needed to avoid a zero-sum confrontation. To act myopically, defensively, or not at all risks straitjacketing future definitions of what it means to be an architect, designer, or even a professionally unaligned creative and productive human being.

INTRODUCTION

The threat of technology to the survival of humanity, through gray goo, stray biological agents, rogue and ravenous universal constructors, and even malevolent artificial intelligence (AI) features large in science fiction. This paper responds to a more modest and perhaps more actual proposition: AI has the potential to usurp the architect's role in architectural practice. This proposition—whether made implicitly or explicitly—is of course not new. The possibility of machines to automate design has been pursued for over half a century (Burry 2020). Aspirations of early researchers such as Frazer and Gero are yet to be fully realized; nonetheless, there have incontestably been two main developments: increased ease and efficiency of modeling, drafting, and detailing; and a degree of automation in the evaluation and generation of design possibilities as options (Grobman, Yezioro, and Capeluto 2010). This paper focuses on the latter and its possible conflict with the architect's traditional creative role. It is presented as a theoretical argument motivated explicitly around architects' evolving practice.[1] It sets out first to establish a theoretical framework for AI-enabled design computing and some perceived potential risks to architectural practice, and then to analyze how architects may respond with continuing their professional relevance in mind. Our research has been informed by ongoing practical work insufficiently advanced to be reported here; in its place we refer to real-world examples where appropriate.

AGENCY IN DESIGN COMPUTING

Certain datapoints in the history of design computing plot a trajectory of the machine's increasing agency. Algorithmic thinking and explicitly detailed relationships in design have existed since Moretti's 1960 exhibition of models of parametrically designed stadia, and arguably earlier, with Gaudí's evolving parametric design strategy for his final design of the Sagrada Família Basilica (1914–1926) (Frazer 2016). In itself, this approach may not seem to be a great threat to the traditional role of the architect. Its reliance on a designer formalizing "rules" of relationships is perilously close to the top-down nature of expert systems that was a contributing factor to the failures of early AI seeking to replicate those aspects of human intelligence (HI) that are not easily formulated as "if-then" statements (Haenlein and Kaplan 2019).

Cross (1999) observes that the human designer engages in an exploratory and rhetorical process as they argue for an outcome that is progressively developed against "both known goals and previously unsuspected implications." AI methods in design computing such as evolutionary computation display recursive navigation of multidimensional solution spaces, and can drive a design proposition to peaks of optimality, or at least solutions that may acceptably fit a designer's assumptions (Besserud and Cotten 2008; Carpo 2019; Dutta and Sarthak 2011). The machine in this sense of exploration may add to a search for a range of possible design outcomes, beyond any traditional notion of a singular design outcome (Leach 2018). Evolutionary computing and allied methods are still essentially directed optimization tasks; the process may determine relationships in its inner workings but the designer must still formalize rules of what is 'good'. Moreover, the bounds of the solution space are statically set to those determined by the designer and the machine does not recognize Cross's "previously unsuspected implications."[2]

Artificial neural networks (ANNs) have been in development since the 1940s but rallied in 2015 when Google's AlphaGo beat a world champion player at the intractable game of Go, and progress has subsequently been rapid (Haenlein and Kaplan 2019). The first paper on generative adversarial networks (GANs) was published by Goodfellow et al. (2014) as recently as 2014, and GANs are currently posited as one of the most promising AI technologies for design (Leach 2019). In just a year, generative-built environment design, albeit simply the composition of bedroom scenes, through use of a GAN was demonstrated (Radford, Metz, and Chintala 2015). AI is now a viable adjunct to architectural practice (Leach 2019; Watanabe 2017). In this, the architect moves into a new mode of control through providing example and precedent rather than the formal setting of relationships and bounds.

A CLOSING GAP BETWEEN AI AND THE ARCHITECT'S TRADITIONAL CREATIVE ROLE

Current AI is not superintelligence and its capabilities are still limited (Kaplan 2016). AI in the design workflow is composed of discrete, often-disconnected AI tools that are developed for specific contexts, projects, and stages, and there is still no unified "Architectural Artificial Intelligence" (AAI) (Mrosla, Koch, and von Both 2019). Given the scope and complexity of architectural practice, such an AAI may be an indispensable step to a greater autonomous role of AI in architecture (even if that step would be a threat to the architect's traditional creative role). An AAI would require near-human (or high) level AI (HLAI) capabilities. HLAI may be far off, but could be in place within the lifetimes of today's graduating architects. In a 2016 survey of AI experts asked to consider when "unaided machines can accomplish every task better and more cheaply than human workers," HLAI was given an even chance of occurring within 45 years, and a 10% chance of occurring within

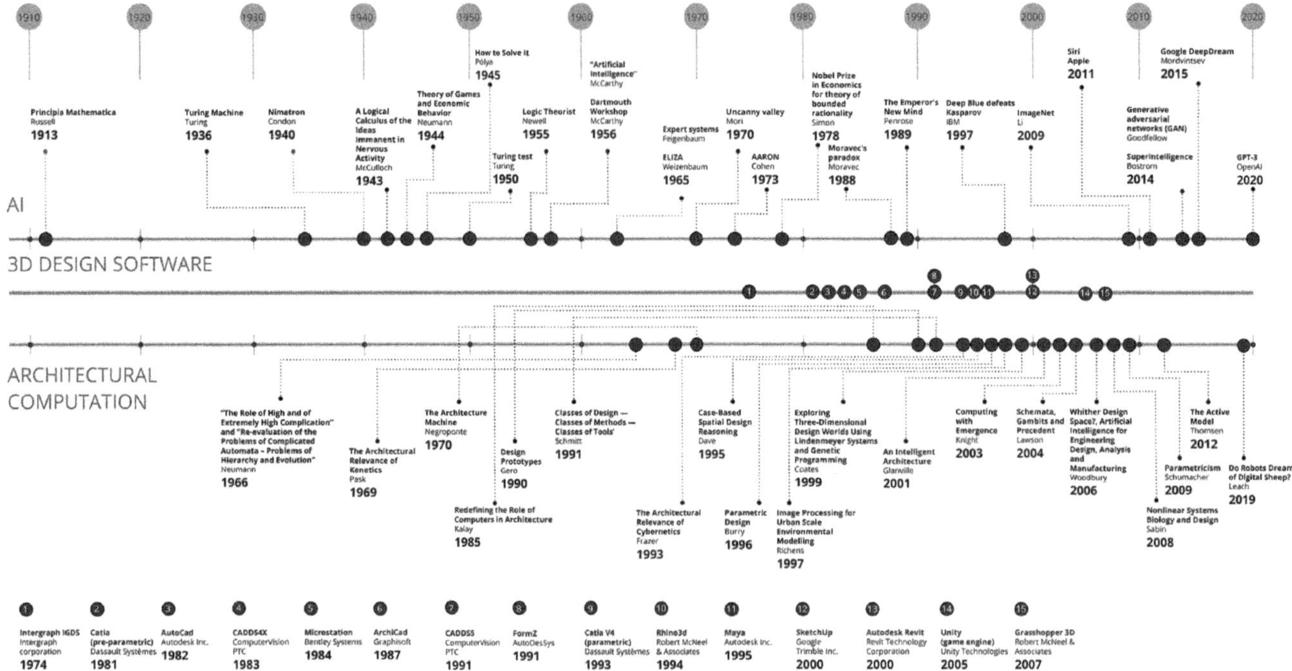

2 Step changes in AI, architectural computation, and 3D design software.

9 years (Grace et al. 2018).[3] Such HLAI need be created only once; unlike a fledgling architect, an HLAI for design would be mechanically duplicable (Cassimatis 2012). A threat of AI matching HI design performance, despite the intractable nature of architectural practice, should not be dismissed by architects.

There has been a historical lag between development of AI and its adoption in architectural practice (Fig. 2). Aspirations in early and even current AI have exceeded scientific and technical capabilities (Cassimatis 2012; Haenlein and Kaplan 2019). Early visions for design computing were perhaps too ambitious and may have suffered from overreach. Perhaps architectural problems are inherently more tractable to modern AI techniques than rule-based approaches such as expert systems.[4]

Despite those historical insufficiencies of capacity and currency, AI is increasingly used in architecture. Experts see the pace of overall AI development to have accelerated in recent years (Brundage et al. 2018; Grace et al. 2018). It is notable that a 2011 RIBA survey report on the "Future for Architects" makes no mention of AI, and the respondents' greatest perceived threats to the architects' profession were judged to come from human parties (Jamieson et al. 2011). Architects are approaching a narrowing of the divide between AI and HI capabilities in architectural practice.

Where may architects be today in relation to AI? Carlopio (1988) expands Friedmann's three phases of automation to accommodate the perspective of the worker. First, dependent machines serve as labor-saving devices, yet as technology advances, these move from simply aiding us to undertaking the bulk of the work. Second, machines have become "labor-enslaving" devices: the worker now assists the machine but may derive little intellectual stimulation in the exchange. Third, machines enter a "labor-replacing" phase: the machine supplants the human in producing actual work. The human may be liberated to new levels within the organizational structures and spared hazardous, tedious, or degrading jobs; however, workers may be devalued, displaced, and undermined in their expertise. With respect to AI, contemporary architects may just be in the first phase and progressing towards the second.

How might this progression continue—what happens if Carlopio's three phases are adopted to design computing? In the first level, design computing is dependent on the architect. Decisions made by the computer are understandable and explainable, for they are the proximate outcome for the relationships and constraints set by the architect themself. The architect is in control, and the computer undertakes little if any exploration or creation of "novelty." In the second level, design computing becomes autonomous in the internal mechanism of its production or the "how" of its decision-making. Decisions show a level of novelty or surprise, and the derivation may not be explainable. The architect is at risk of being devalued unless they can use the output to augment their own creative process. In the third level, design computing becomes autonomous in its agency. The computer is able to exploit new opportunities and take advantage of or incorporate subtle and nuanced context. The architect may potentially be replaced in significant parts of the design process within traditional architectural practice.

VULNERABILITIES OF THE ARCHITECT'S TRADITIONAL CREATIVE ROLE

Of course, architecture is not as simple as plowing a field or operating a loom, and AI replacing the architect's creative role could seem fanciful, especially to those "many architects" who suggest upcoming AI would modify architecture "only marginally" (Morel 2019). Nevertheless, to discount a risk of AI to architectural practice in the face of a long history of machines impinging on the domain of human work is a variation on Lewis's "chronological snobbery" (Lewis 1955). There are no special protections offered to architects by mere dint of being the ones privileged to occupy the fleeting present. Furthermore, there are fundamental reasons why the traditional role of the designer may be threatened by AI developing in a social context outside the architects' typical practice.

Architectural practice has many areas that can be readily formalized in computer models extensible to creative exploration; indeed, given a key facet of architecture is clearly communicating the output of a building's design process so that it may be logically constructed, this statement verges on the axiomatic. Such work is rapidly becoming mainstream: in 2008, for example, SOM undertook highly exploratory work using genetic algorithms; in 2020, Autodesk released Generative Design for Revit to the mass market (Autodesk 2020; Besserud and Cotten 2008). Already there is a significant corpus of training examples on which AI models may be developed and, with BIM, the library of increasingly nuanced precedents is growing every day. There is also the opportunity for this process to be self-sustaining: platforms such as Generative Design will be able to gather metadata of practitioners' interactions, leading to an ecosystem of improved approaches. Frazer (1995) proposed the concept of an "extended architect" in which architects are needed "to guarantee a rich genetic pool of [progenitor] ideas, the role of the mass of imitators would be more efficiently accomplished by the machine." The architect as the progenitor of ideas now need not explicitly seed the genetic pool. Furthermore, AI can exploit even small datasets of precedent (Newton 2019).

Many aspects of the architectural solution space are extremely subjective and have no solution that can be proven to be optimal through any reasonable process; the search is one of satisficing that accounts for idiosyncrasy and whim. Watanabe (2017), for example, notes the different meanings architects may see "good form" to have. The subjectivity is implicit in Frazer's assertion that the design process may often be without a definitive goal and that a creative leap may seem self-evident only in hindsight: "By the time the problem has been defined, it has been solved. Indeed, the solution is often the very definition of the problem" (Frazer 2002). Jansen notes the "vastness of the multidimensional [solution] spaces involved" and that within them remote alternatives arise from "radically different roots" and, consequently, are not simply comparable (Frazer 2002). However, the subjectivity of the relative value of a design outcome introduces vulnerabilities for architecture.

Architecture is vulnerable with regard to furnishing design itself as a 'manufactured' product; many AI techniques increasingly excel at this type of navigation of inexact solution spaces. This is seen in both evolutionary computing that may find a "good enough form" from a vast array of alternatives, or in contemporary ANN techniques such as GANs that, in their training, collect subtle patterns within their latent space for regurgitation and sifting on demand (Dutta and Sarthak 2011, Radford et al. 2015).

Architecture is vulnerable with regard to design as a product to be "sold." Just as an architect may ascribe their own meaning to "good form," so too can the client base that pays for their architectural services. Alternatively put, the architect's product is exposed to price sensitivity if the person on the street sees little practical distinction between good architecture (as defined by architects) and wholesale building design. For evidence, consider the expanding acres of McMansions in wealthy developed countries. In 2017, Dan Rockmore of Dartmouth College proposed a Turing test in creative arts to determine if machine outputs can be distinguished from the creative works of humans (Mrosla et al. 2019). We suggest the bar is much lower if the judge is barely paying attention. In a world of open-source images and ideas, and in which generative AI techniques exist that demonstrate at least superficial novelty, this may be unsound ground on which to risk asserting the profession's ongoing viability.[5]

Watanabe (2017) states that "people [not machines] are the only ones that can create an image that does not yet exist." Yet creativity inherently transforms precedent, and Hofstadter (in Liu 2000 via Minsky) noted "making variations on a theme is the crux of creativity." In Csikszentmihalyi's model of creativity, the individual transforms extant cultural information, and the products, once sieved by society, become nucleation sites for further creativity (Liu 2000). Art, design, or cultural output is always rooted in what has gone before (even if that prior art is not considered to be a precedent in any traditional or formal sense). Such works are permutative transformations of the creators' past experiences and the subtle, pervasive, and essential process of drawing out and reinforcing of pattern and relationship (the beginnings of this are clear in Google's DeepDream); to view this statement alternatively, any "image" created that truly does not already exist would be entirely unrecognizable, in a literal sense, as art, architecture, or indeed anything else.[6]

In this general context Leach (2018) proposes that humans might essentially misperceive the nature of their "genius." We extend this to propose there is a prevalent and general misunderstanding of how people should relate to AI, and this nearsightedness aggravates risks to the architectural profession.

TOWARDS A CULTURAL REALIGNMENT

Accurately forecasting the future is difficult, including of AI (Haenlein and Kaplan 2019; Tetlock 1999). The historical response to AI's advances has been to shift the goalposts to redefine its capabilities continually as not true intelligence (Minsky 1958).[7] This defensive posture, ostensibly protecting the status of HI, may be a losing strategy: the ultimate outcome may be a very narrow definition of what it means to be a designer.

Once matching human performance at a task, AI can now exceed the performance of the most capable human, and any task performed by natural intelligences can fall victim to AI (Brundage et al. 2018). The use of AI need not become a zero-sum game if essential differences of AI and HI are appreciated and thus exploited so as to not redefine the practice of architecture per se, but rather reorient its focus and capability. To enable this, architects need to reassess AI's role that tends to have been miscast through historical bias against machines that arose from their procedural origins. Ethnocentrism in human society prioritizes the ingroup along with perceptions of superiority and preferential attitudes toward its behaviors and mores, with negativity displayed toward the outgroup (Bizumic and Duckitt 2012). Might such bias exist in relationships with the machine, and hence frustrate the greatest potential of the collaboration? To illustrate, people's demands of machines are very different from those made of the human peers with whom they work: perfection is assumed from machines and their outputs are taken to be therefore canonical in this regard (Dyson 1993; Garibaldi 2019). Indeed, Simon observed HI itself is "not correct or optimal in many situations" (Cassimatis 2012). HI divergence from optimality and correctness may be a compromise essential to human-level intelligence (Cassimatis 2012). Human experts themselves do not obtain 100% efficiency; it should not be unreservedly expected of the intelligent machines with which people work (Garibaldi 2019).[8]

Despite these prejudices, there are still essential differences between the capabilities of HI and AI in design. Mathematician Richard Hamming questioned whether evolution has confined human thoughts to certain avenues preventing access to otherwise "unthinkable thoughts" (Morel 2019). Morel extends this to assert the task of the architect is not to duplicate existing accomplishments with design computing; it is rather to pursue a "fully new form of architectural intelligence that we humans are unable to conceive," and that machines "shall logically give birth to a kind of architecture that is also beyond our usual capacities." Similarly, Cross (1999) asserts, "So rather than just emulate human abilities, some of our design machines should also do things that designers cannot do."

Yet there are matters machines cannot hope to understand, even if they may see further than us in certain areas. Writing on the problem of explaining the mechanism of consciousness, cognitive scientist Chalmers (1995) defined "easy" problems of consciousness—"susceptible to the standard methods of cognitive science"—distinguishing them from "hard" matters of subjective experience. The easy problems are susceptible to AI, being matters of response to input, information integration, and output of an internal state. For the "hard" problems, AI cannot (yet, if ever) embody *qualia*;[9] it can never feel an internal response to the architecture it might create, or experience being part of the social and cultural context that leads to it. Here, Watanabe's (2017) assertion computers do not "dream" would be apt. Machines must instead rely on an ersatz description of what humans sense, vicariously passed on by the designer as best as they are able, given that many designers are unable to articulate as a methodology how they design, even to themselves. But a challenge of automating creativity is to generate novelty that makes sense (Frey 2019). Machines, without their own experience of reality, and relying on utility functions "specified by the human designer" that "may not be perfectly aligned with the values of the human race," have the potential to optimize "highly undesirable" solutions (Russell 2014).

Nor can machines experience the motivations that drive architects to design. A desire for social relevance or making an original, meaningful contribution, for example, is widespread among architects (Jamieson et al. 2011). There is little point directing AI to the tasks humans excel at and enjoy, and for which the need for social connection is not easily replaced (Cross 1999; Kaplan 2016).

A cultural realignment could aid Vinge's (1993) "greater merging of competence." In this, early aspirations for AI to facilitate "intelligence amplification" and "symbiotic association" have the potential to be realized. Engelbart (1962) describes a collaboration of intelligence amplification that "will exhibit more of what can be called intelligence than an unaided human could; we will have amplified the intelligence of the human by organizing his intellectual capabilities into higher levels of synergistic structuring." Licklider (1960), in his seminal article "Man-Computer Symbiosis," saw the potential for computers to "facilitate formulative thinking as they now facilitate the solution of formulated problems" and cooperative action between humans "without inflexible dependence on predetermined programs."

ARBITRAGING A CONTINUING GAP

Counterintuitively, a closer, more equitable collaboration between AI and HI could progressively exploit their differences to the benefit of the architectural profession.

Architectural practice is a complex process that is composed of tasks crossing many domains (Mrosla et al. 2019; Veit 1987). Frazer (2016) notes "architecture does not address trivial problems" and identifies the inherent incongruity of applying algorithmic procedures to complex architectural considerations. Contemporary AI is (in the main) used to free up people to do other work, not displace them (Davenport and Ronanki 2018). Furthermore, Kaplan (2016), an expert on the economic and social effects of AI, observes tasks, not jobs, are automated and that the most vulnerable jobs involve unvarying workflows and well-defined objectives. Kaplan continues that those workers participating in diverse pursuits, response to dynamic goals, or real engagement with human emotion are at much lower risk, and may become more productive through AI.

Technology continually eliminates professions, such as traditional white collar roles in customer service, while increasing production and reducing employment (Rotman 2013). Simultaneously, it leverages collective intellect to bring new endeavors into professional reach, and the demands of society itself shift in accordance with the affordances of technology. Expectations and visions of technology themselves shape its role and direction, and are particularly significant in those uncertain moments of early innovation (Borup et al. 2006). AI, as a potential replicant of HI, in its complex, continual evolution within responsive, changing society, may be in a persistent state of novelty.

We propose that as the generality of AI increases, even to the point of HLAI, architects can generate and embed new subtleties and expectations of outcomes that society will judge AI unable to achieve. Not only will the goalposts shift; architects may also change the very rules of the game at halftime. Architects are therefore challenged to arbitrage the gap between the actuality of AI and fluid, dynamic social expectations.

Effectively exploiting that gap as arbitrage requires an ongoing assessment incorporating a focus on what AI is today and its immediate challenges while keeping the architects' longstanding agility to respond to the pressures and opportunities. This includes what AI may create for society and architects' own sociotechnical role. We propose three initial alignments for the architect that, as AI progresses through our described three levels of design computing development, may help avoid the trap of Carlopio's third phase: as *architechs*, *arbiters*, and *shamans*.[10]

Architech

The architect may be "master builder" of those physical structures and spaces people inhabit and, as *architech*, be master builder of the AI frameworks that will complement their designs. This essential role is identified by Koh (2017) and others. We add the proposition to the discussion that AI does not yet excel at formulating reasoning that is elementary to humans, such as cause and effect (Knight 2020). The architect-in-the-design-loop can provide this understanding and as well accommodate cultural nuance (Burry et al. 2019; Woodbury et al. 2017).

This alignment is appearing increasingly in architectural practice. The Living, a design studio and research arm of Autodesk, used AI-driven generative design for the architectural space planning of a new office (Nagy et al. 2019). The generative design process was placed explicitly within before and after stages in which HI established the design concept and refined the AI outcome to meet other criteria. Their workflow employed a multiobjective genetic algorithm exploring a solution space of six metrics of employee preferences and spatial qualities to create 10,000 designs. Data analysis tools were used to reduce that pool to HI-manageable size and themselves generated insights. By clustering design types, patterns of performance against metrics could be visualized, and insights into the design problem and potential design strategies uncovered. Rather than offering a single best design, the outcome was a set of high-performing designs demonstrating trade-offs between metrics that could be reviewed by human designers in consultation with stakeholders, leading to a final design.

Use of ANNs to predict meeting-room usage for space planning at WeWork demonstrated similar outcomes (Phelan et al. 2019). Although the AI prediction could outperform HI, its real value was to leverage AI evaluation of past project performance to enable the designer to exploit their HI to adjust their response on current projects.

Arbiter

The architect is responsible for the consequences of what they create (Karakiewicz 2020). The architect as *architech*—and thus in control of what AI in architectural practice achieves—would hence have a social obligation to arbitrate how it is applied. AI operating alone can produce undesirable outcomes. It has no moral conscience. Biased training data and other flaws can produce outcomes from the downright prejudicial to simply underwhelming in accommodating diverse needs (Weyerer and Langer 2019). Directing AI towards fair solutions is nontrivial. There are risks in bottom-up and top-down solutions such as "personal choices" and "law enforcement" (Etzioni and Etzioni 2017). A free market risks the tragedy of the commons, and narrow interests may lead to ramifications even when the intent is just, such as occurred when IBM released an image dataset to aid development of fairer facial recognition scraped without permission from social media (Hao 2019). Conversely, legislating in a changing situation is rife with unanticipated consequences (Merton 1936). Could society therefore rely on a "reasonable architect" test to decide the essential bounds of AI in built environments through fostering a culture of reflection, professional responsibility, and collective oversight? Just as The Living, as one example of this trend, adapted AI processes to capture and accommodate group and individual employee preferences for distraction, daylight, and amenity accessibility, it will need to be the architects themselves who guard against any overstep, as already evident with AI-generated solutions permeating the practice of architecture.

Shaman

AI's reasoning can be opaque (Leach 2018). In response, architects can interpret black-box AI outputs to provide meaning to incorporate into their design process. This explication is not machine-like translation, for it is not dealing with a functional mapping but instead maps preferences, emotions, intuition, and biases: at a higher level, the architect could design the rich narratives around AI contributions to the design process. Furthermore, just as architects analyze immutable aspects of site and draw on the uncontrollable context, cannot architects treat opaque AI input as something relatively fixed but still to be exploited? Architects could move to a mode of practice in which they—almost as architectural narrators or *shamans*, channel and placate the whims and wants of the AI world—acting as interpreters of the AI recommendations.

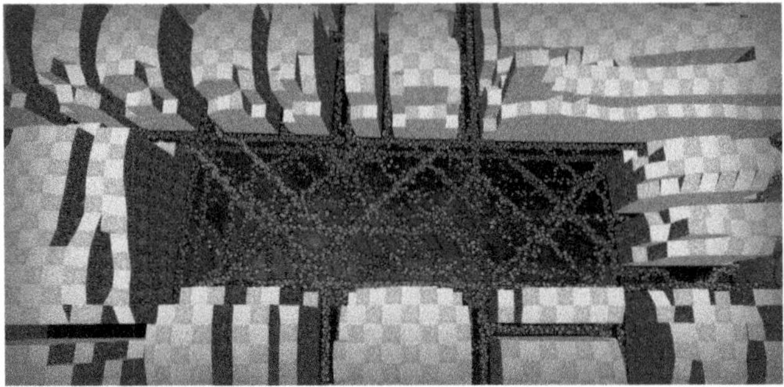

3 Generative design of public space solar amenity.

In our own work in progress on the potential role of AI within design computing, we have observed a need for this realignment. Shadow modeling that can track locations of obstructing building geometry, for example, enables iterative refinement of building envelopes in response to shading outcomes (Kimm 2020). Through extending that work as a tool to produce generative designs for public space with optimal overshadowing, solutions can be sought that preserve a given minimum of solar amenity throughout the year (Fig. 3). Although the AI-generated designs are high-performing with respect to pedestrian experience of sun and shade, the spatial and temporal distribution of sunlit areas is not intuitive nor necessarily that which a designer fully exploiting their HI would produce as their design preference. The architect who chooses to use such results must, within their design response, interpret and translate their benefit to the client and public alike, and meeting a shading performance of itself might be insufficient.

CONCLUDING REMARKS

That AI is increasingly undertaking creative "thought" once considered the unique preserve of HI, even if faux, is indubitable. Ultimately, AI may supersede architectural HI on any practical metric, albeit ones naïve or just plain mercenary. With appropriate foresight, the architect's distinctive role in the nuanced synthesis of social and emotional understanding with emerging technology may allow them to sidestep the obsolescence AI may visit on certain roles in other professions. The three initial alignments we identify—*architech*, *arbiter*, and *shaman*—are facets of the same response: the future avant garde architect may need to exploit AI in order to offer new value to their innate skills. The complex interplay between evolving AI and developing expectations of society allows for a capability reciprocity in which the future architect arbitrages between architectural AI and architectural HI to construct a chain of new value models for both clients and broader society alike.

The motivating threat of AI to the architect's traditional creative role may seem as fanciful to some as the sci-fi dystopias outlined in the introduction above. Whatever the future of AI-enabled architectural practice, there will be architects who will be able steer into the skid of forced adaption to imposed change and, looking back on the looming challenges of AI, proclaim, "I got it right." Yet, if such examples are relatively few and thinly scattered across the vast body of practice (or the solution space of architectural practice phenotypes), would architects as a profession have performed with any greater prescience than the insentient metaheuristic of a genetic algorithm?

NOTES

1. There is not a lot of writing in AI in architecture at the right level to meet the requirements of this research and the ambitions of the authors, and therefore many sources may not address architecture directly.
2. The neat separation of the design computing levels given here is due to simplification for the sake of discussion within the available space; for illustration of fuzziness between levels, see for example work in AI that combines genetic algorithms and deep learning.
3. Cassimatis (2012) discusses a "cognitive substrate" in which our intelligence (and as applied to the myriad challenges of the modern world) arose from an essential mental toolkit that met the very-different social and spatial needs of our forebears. Might solving the essentials of design computing, and therefore producing such a cognitive substrate for design, lead to a massive leap in design computing AI?
4. There may be presumptions at play in which computers are more powerful than they actually are, data sets found to be more elusive than anticipated and often either incomplete or thwarted by missing components from the data set itself, and algorithms less effective in real application than in experiments. Underlying this in design might be creatives investing a sci-fi belief in capability unable to fundamentally understand how AI "works" and what really is at stake.
5. Frazer's extended architect might lie between the second and third of our proposed design computing levels. A point here is that Frazer made these apposite observations 25 years ago—a demonstration of the length of time this level of technological osmosis can take.
6. Therefore making critical assessment difficult using the critics' usual criteria: if we are to judge how well the rules have been broken, we need to have a set of rules to begin with.
7. Minsky comments, on perceptions of creativity being "some kind of 'gift' which simply cannot be understood or mechanized," that the "weakness of the advocate of inexplicable creativity lies in the unsupported conviction that after all machines have been examined some items [unique to HI] will still remain on the list."
8. The *weak anthropic principle* in cosmology states we observe a "comfortable" universe as one is necessary for our sentient existence to arise. In perceptions of human "genius," there may be corresponding subjectivity: on a population scale, the means to judge our achievements can only be the same minds that create them. There is an exact one-to-one equivalency of the minds that produce and the minds that judge. Furthermore, crude analogs of the processes that created HI are used in AI; that contemporary outcomes are inferior does not preclude success.
9. The *Stanford Encyclopedia of Philosophy* characterizes *qualia* as "the introspectively accessible, phenomenal aspects of our mental lives" (https://plato.stanford.edu/entries/qualia/).
10. The etymology of *shaman* is from *saman* of the Tungusic language group of eastern Siberia and Manchuria and from there potentially Sanskrit. It is not related to the suffix *man* of English (Laufer 1917).

REFERENCES

Autodesk. 2020. "Generative Design in Revit now available." https://blogs.autodesk.com/revit/2020/04/08/generative-design-in-revit/.

Besserud, Keith, and Joshua Cotten. 2008. "Architectural Genomics." In *ACADIA 08: Silicon + Skin: Biological Processes and Computation, [Proceedings of the 28th Annual Conference of the Association for Computer Aided Design in Architecture (ACADIA)]*, Minneapolis, MN, 16–19 October 2008, edited by A. Kudless, N. Oxman, and M. Swackhamer, 238–245. CUMINCAD.

Bizumic, Boris, and John Duckitt. 2012. "What Is and Is Not Ethnocentrism? A Conceptual Analysis and Political Implications." *Political Psychology* 33 (6): 887–909.

Borup, Mads, Nik Brown, Kornelia Konrad, and Harro Van Lente. 2006. "The Sociology of Expectations in Science and Technology." *Technology Analysis & Strategic Management* 18 (3–4): 285–298.

Brundage, Miles, Shahar Avin, Jack Clark, Helen Toner, Peter Eckersley, Ben Garfinkel, Allan Dafoe et al. 2018. "The Malicious Use of Artificial Intelligence: Forecasting, Prevention, and Mitigation." https://maliciousaireport.com/

Burry, M. 2020. *Digital Architecture*. London: Routledge.

Burry, Mark, Camilo Cruz, and Geoff Kimm. 2019. "Avoiding the Color Gray: Parametrizing CAS to Incorporate Reactive Scripting." In *Urban Galapagos*, edited T. Kvan, and J. Karakiewicz, 137–154. Cham: Springer.

Carlopio, Jim. 1988. "A History of Social Psychological Reactions to New Technology." *Journal of Occupational Psychology* 61 (1): 67–77.

Carpo, Mario. 2019. "The Natural Logic of Artificial Intelligence, or What Genetic Algorithms Really Do." *Philosophy Kitchen Extra: Journal of Contemporary Philosophy* 6 (2): 123–129.

Cassimatis, Nicholas L. 2012. "Human-Level Artificial Intelligence Must Be an Extraordinary Science." *Advances in Cognitive Systems* 1: 37–45.

Chalmers, David J. 1995. "Facing Up to the Problem of Consciousness." *Journal of Consciousness Studies* 2 (3): 200–219.

Cross, Nigel. 1999. "Natural Intelligence in Design." *Design Studies* 20 (1): 25–39.

Davenport, Thomas H., and Rajeev Ronanki. 2018. "Artificial Intelligence for the Real World." *Harvard Business Review* 96 (1): 108–116.

Dutta, Kamlesh, and Siddhant Sarthak. 2011. "Architectural Space Planning Using Evolutionary Computing Approaches: A Review." *Artificial Intelligence Review* 36 (4): 311–321.

Dyson, Esther. 1993. "Biology Is Destiny in Computers, Too." *Computerworld*, January 18.

Engelbart, Douglas C. 1962. *Augmenting Human Intellect: A Conceptual Framework*. SRI Summary Report AFOSR-3223: Prepared for Director of Information Sciences, Air Force Office of Scientific Research, Washington DC, Contract AF 49(638)-1024. https://www.dougengelbart.org/content/view/138.

Etzioni, Amitai, and Oren Etzioni. 2017. "Incorporating Ethics Into Artificial Intelligence." *The Journal of Ethics* 21 (4): 403–418.

Frazer, John. 1995. *An Evolutionary Architecture*, London: Architectural Association.

Frazer, John. 2002. "Creative Design and the Generative Evolutionary Paradigm." In *Creative Evolutionary Systems*, 253–274. Burlington: Morgan Kaufmann.

Frazer, John. 2016. "Parametric Computation: History and Future." *Architectural Design* 86 (2): 18–23.

Frey, Carl Benedikt. 2019. *The Technology Trap: Capital, Labor, and Power in the Age of Automation*. Princeton: Princeton University Press.

Garibaldi, Jonathan M. 2019. "The Need for Fuzzy AI." *IEEE/CAA Journal of Automatica Sinica* 6 (3): 610–622.

Grace, Katja, John Salvatier, Allan Dafoe, Baobao Zhang, and Owain Evans. 2018. "When Will AI Exceed Human Performance? Evidence from AI Experts." *Journal of Artificial Intelligence Research* 62: 729–754.

Grobman, Yasha Jacob, Abraham Yezioro, and Isaac Guedi Capeluto. 2010. "Non-Linear Architectural Design Process." *International Journal of Architectural Computing* 8 (1): 41–53.

Haenlein, Michael, and Andreas Kaplan. 2019. "A Brief History of Artificial Intelligence: On the Past, Present, and Future of Artificial Intelligence." *California Management Review* 61 (4): 5–14.

Hao, Karen. 2019. "IBM's Photo-Scraping Scandal Shows What a Weird Bubble AI Researchers Live In." *MIT Technology Review*, March 15. https://www.technologyreview.com/2019/03/15/136593/ibms-photo-scraping-scandal-shows-what-a-weird-bubble-ai-researchers-live-in/.

Jamieson, Claire, Dickon Robinson, John Worthington, and Caroline Cole. 2011. *The Future for Architects?* London: Royal Institute of British Architects.

Kaplan, Jerry. 2016. "Artificial Intelligence: Think Again." *Communications of the ACM* 60 (1): 36–38.

Karakiewicz, Justyna. 2020. "Design Is Real, Complex, Inclusive, Emergent and Evil." *International Journal of Architectural Computing* 18 (1): 5–19.

Kimm, Geoff. 2020. "Actual and Experiential Shadow Origin Tagging: A 2.5 D Algorithm for Efficient Precinct-Scale Modelling." *International Journal of Architectural Computing* 18 (1): 41–52.

Knight, Will. 2020. "If AI's So Smart, Why Can't It Grasp Cause and Effect?" *Wired*, March 9. https://www.wired.com/story/ai-smart-cant-grasp-cause-effect/.

Koh, Immanuel. 2017. "Inference Design Machine and 'Infinite' and 'Recombinant' Series." In *Computational Design*, edited by N. Leach and P. Yuan, 291–296. Shanghai: Tongji University Press Company Limited.

Laufer, Berthold. 1917. "Origin of the Word Shaman." *American Anthropologist* 19 (3): 361–371.

Leach, Neil. 2018. "Design in the Age of Artificial Intelligence." *Landscape Architecture Frontiers* 6 (2): 8–20.

Leach, Neil. 2019. "Do Robots Dream of Digital Sheep?" In *ACADIA 19: Ubiquity and Autonomy [Proceedings of the 39th Annual Conference of the Association for Computer Aided Design in*

Architecture (ACADIA)], Austin, TX, 21–26 October 2019, edited by K. Bieg, D. Briscoe, and C. Odom, 298–309. CUMINCAD.

Lewis, Clive Staples. 1955. *Surprised by Joy, the Shape of My Early Life*. London: Geoffrey Bles.

Licklider, Joseph CR. 1960. "Man-Computer Symbiosis." *IRE Transactions on Human Factors in Electronics* 1: 4–11.

Liu, Yu-Tung. 2000. "Creativity or novelty?: Cognitive-Computational Versus Social-Cultural." *Design Studies* 21 (3): 261–276.

Merton, Robert K. 1936. "The Unanticipated Consequences of Purposive Social Action." *American Sociological Review* 1 (6): 894–904.

Minsky, Marvin L. 1958. "Some Methods of Artificial Intelligence and Heuristic Programming." In *Proc. Symp. on the Mechanization of Thought Processes,* 3–28. London: Her Majesty's Stationary Office.

Morel, Philippe. 2019. "The Origins of Discretism: Thinking Unthinkable Architecture." *Architectural Design* 89 (2): 14–21.

Mrosla, Laura, Volker Koch, and Petra von Both. 2019. "Quo vadis AI in Architecture? Survey of the Current Possibilities of AI in the Architectural Practice." In *Architecture in the Age of the 4th Industrial Revolution*, 45–54. Porto: eCAADe/SIGraDi.

Nagy, Danil, Damon Lau, John Locke, Jim Stoddart, Lorenzo Villaggi, Ray Wang, Dale Zhao, and David Benjamin. 2017. "Project Discover: An Application of Generative Design for Architectural Space Planning." In *Proceedings of the Symposium on Simulation for Architecture and Urban Design*, Toronto, Canada, 22–24 May 2017, edited by Michela Turrin, Brady Peters, William O' Brien, Rudi Stouffs, and Timur Dogan, 59–66. SIMULATION COUNCILS.

Newton, David. 2019. "Deep Generative Learning for the Generation and Analysis of Architectural Plans with Small Datasets." In *Architecture in the Age of the 4th Industrial Revolution*, 21–28. Porto: eCAADe/SIGraDi.

Phelan, Nicole, Daniel Davis, and Carl Anderson. 2017. "Evaluating Architectural Layouts with Neural Networks." In *Proceedings of the Symposium on Simulation for Architecture and Urban Design*, Toronto, Canada, 22–24 May 2017, edited by Michela Turrin, Brady Peters, William O' Brien, Rudi Stouffs, and Timur Dogan, 67–73. SIMULATION COUNCILS.

Radford, Alec, Luke Metz, and Soumith Chintala. 2015. "Unsupervised Representation Learning with Deep Convolutional Generative Adversarial Networks." arXiv preprint. arXiv:1511.06434.

Rotman, David. 2013. "How Technology Is Destroying Jobs." *Technology Review* 16 (4): 28–35.

Russell, Stuart. 2014. "Of Myths and Moonshine." *Edge*, November 14. http://www.edge.org/conversation/jaron_lanier-the-myth-of-ai.

Tetlock, Philip E. 1999. "Theory-Driven Reasoning About Plausible Pasts and Probable Futures in World Politics: Are We Prisoners of Our Preconceptions?" *American Journal of Political Science* 43 (2): 335–366.

Veit, Franz S. 1987. "Design Augmentation in the Architectural Practice." In *Principles of Computer-Aided Design: Computability of Design*, edited Y. Kalay, 337–347. Chichester: Wiley-Interscience.

Vinge, Vernor. 1993. "Technological Singularity." In *VISION-21: Interdisciplinary Science and Engineering in the Era of Cyberspace*, 30–31. Cleveland: NASA.

Watanabe, Makoto. 2017. "AI Tect: Can AI Make Designs?" *In Computational Design*, edited N. Leach and P. Yuan, 69–75. Shanghai: Tongji University Press Company Limited.

Weyerer, Jan, and Paul Langer. 2019. "Garbage In, Garbage Out: The Vicious Cycle of AI-based Discrimination in the Public Sector." In *Proceedings of the 20th Annual International Conference on Digital Government Research*, 509–511. Dubai: ACM.

Woodbury, Robert, Arefin Mohiuddin, Mark Cichy, and Volker Mueller. 2017. "Interactive Design Galleries: A General Approach to Interacting with Design Alternatives." *Design Studies* 52: 40–72.

IMAGE CREDITS

All drawings and images by the authors. Figure 2 prepared with the aid of Awnili Shabnam.

Geoff Kimm is Research Fellow at the Smart Cities Research Institute, Swinburne University of Technology, and has a background in architecture and computer science.

Mark Burry is the founding director for Swinburne University of Technology's Smart Cities Research Institute and Professor of Urban Futures. Mark is a practicing architect who has published internationally on two main themes: putting theory into practice with regard to procuring "challenging" architecture, and the life, work, and theories of the architect Antoni Gaudí. He was senior architect to the Sagrada Família Basilica Foundation from 1979 until 2016.

Between Signal and Noise

A Trans-Climatic Approach in Decoding and Recoding Autonomous Ecologies

Hadin Charbel*
UCL The Bartlett School of Architecture/Pareid

Déborah López Lobato*
UCL The Bartlett School of Architecture/Pareid

*Authors contributed equally to the research.

1 Data moshed image of an iceberg in the Arctic.

ABSTRACT

Climate change continues to have noticeable and accelerated impacts on various territories. Previously predictable and recognizable patterns used by humans and nonhumans alike are perpetually being altered, turning localized signals into noise and effectively disrupting indigenous modes of life.

While the use of certain technologies such as data collection, machine learning, and automation can render these otherwise patternless information streams into intelligible content, they are generally associated as being "territorializing," as an increase in resolution generally lends itself to control, exploitation, and colonization. Contrarily, indigenous groups with long-lasting relationships that have evolved over time have distinct ways of reading and engaging with their contexts, developing sustainable practices that, while effective, are often overlooked as being compatible with contemporary tools.

This paper examines how the use of traditionally territorializing technologies can be paired with indigenous knowledge and protocols in order to operate between signal and noise, rendering perverse changes in the landscape comprehensible while also presenting their applications as a facet for sociopolitical, cultural, and ecological adaptation. A methodology defined as "decoding" and "recoding" presents four distinct case studies in the Arctic, addressing various scales and targets with the aim of disrupting current trends in order to grant and/or retain autonomy through what can be read as a form of preservation via augmented adaptation.

INTRODUCTION

A Brief Definition of Signal and Noise

A signal can be understood as some meaningful information that someone or something is trying to detect, whereas noise is considered the random and unwanted bits that either interfere with the signal or the presence of data where no discernible pattern can be recognized, meaning a signal is not produced.

For instance, applied to naval ships, razzle dazzle is a strategy used to disrupt certain visual signals of a ship through the use of patterns that distort perceptions of depth, shape, and orientation (Fig. 2). In the case of insects, pheromone trails are used to communicate where otherwise meaningless chemicals are rendered intelligible by those capable of receiving and interpreting them (Fig. 3). In other words, the world is largely made of either noise or signals, used to either communicate or disrupt communication, which in turn affect the capacity to act on it.

There is therefore a degree of subjectivity in treating something as a signal or noise, which is simultaneously linked to interest, capacity, and resolution, which will be elaborated on as inherently engaging questions of politics, ecology, and autonomy.

The Contemporary Scene

The implications of climate change across multiple geographical scales and regions, which begin as ecological and environmental transformations, eventually unfold into consequences affecting our present and future understandings within the social, political, economic, human, and nonhuman spheres (Latour 2018).

The notion of "terra firma" as a literal and conceptual framework for human existence is effectively being destabilized. On the one hand, this effect is produced by environmental changes and new climatic tipping points, while on the other, the "sea of data" being mined as filtering patterns from noise subjugates actors and territories to authoritative top-down systems of control (Steyerl 2018). This observation echoes the schizophrenic behavior inherent within the modes of capitalist thinking that Deleuze and Guattari outline in their body of philosophical work through which they present the endless loop between humans and nature perpetually territorializing, deterritorializing, and reterritorializing. The transition between phases is often associated with the deployment of a new technological force. For instance, the open sea or maritime territories as described by Deleuze, Guattari, and Virilio is unterritorialized until the invention of maritime mapping, which renders the sea under human navigable and

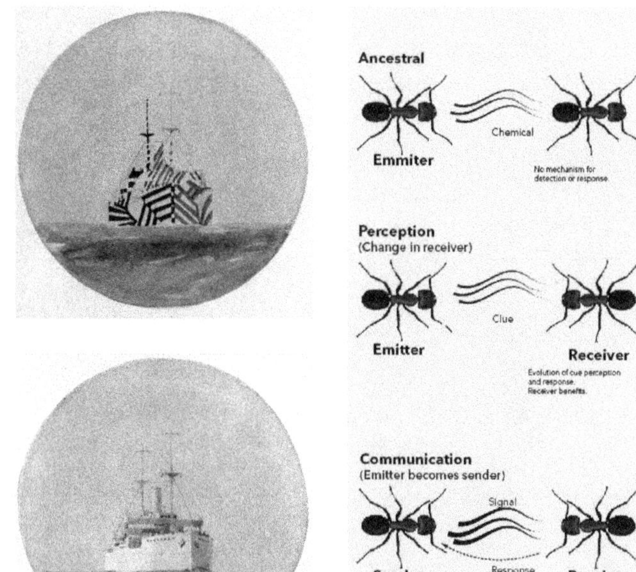

2 Submarine commander's periscope view of a merchant ship in dazzle camouflage (top) and the same ship uncamouflaged (bottom).

3 Proposed stages in the evolution of chemical communication in insects.

conceptual control, which is again deterritorialized with the invention of the submarine (Adkins 2015).

Though the invention of a technology implicitly results in the invention of a catastrophe (i.e., the invention of the airplane is also the invention of the plane crash) (Virilio 1999), the various affordances found between a total ecology of things, including technology, agency, humans, nonhumans and machines, could be "strategically deployed to re-engineer the world" (Cuboniks 2015).

Looking to other modes of living that operate outside of the mainstream could become the basis for reconceptualizing both the means and ends of the currently dominant top-down anthropocentric models. Traditional ecological knowledge (TEK), for example, offers alternative knowledge and perspectives based on local indigenous groups' locally developed practices of resource use (Berkes, Colding, and Folke 2000). While applicable and still used by various communities in their respective ways and environmental contexts, such methods are often seen as idealized sustainable practices that are incompatible with the increasingly accelerated and globalized contemporary context.

A reversal of this de facto thought can be seen in "indigenous futurism," a theme generally explored within the liberal arts that dispels the common and erroneous distinction that contemporary technologies are inherently

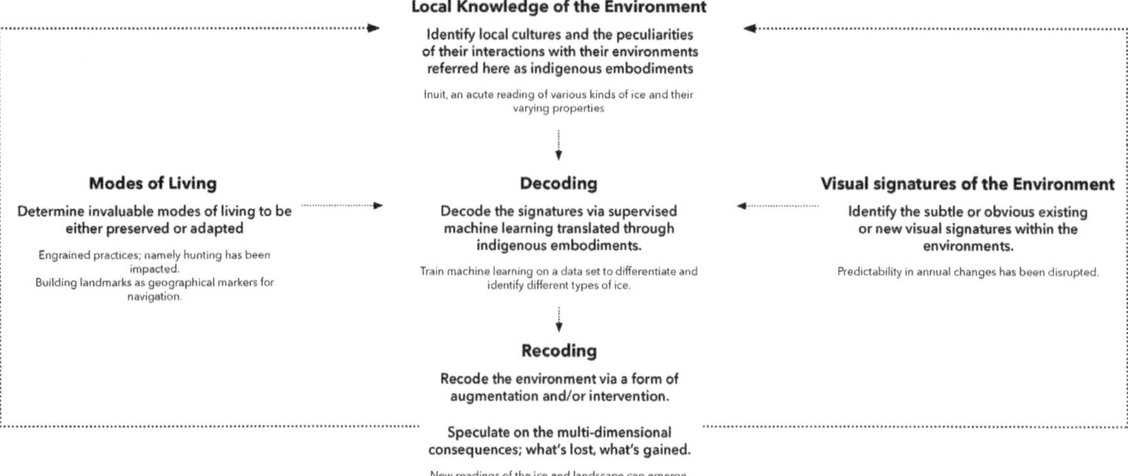
Local Knowledge of the Environment
Identify local cultures and the peculiarities of their interactions with their environments referred here as indigenous embodiments
Inuit, an acute reading of various kinds of ice and their varying properties
Modes of Living
Determine invaluable modes of living to be either preserved or adapted
Engrained practices; namely hunting has been impacted.
Building landmarks as geographical markers for navigation.
Decoding
Decode the signatures via supervised machine learning translated through indigenous embodiments.
Train machine learning on a data set to differentiate and identify different types of ice.
Visual signatures of the Environment
Identify the subtle or obvious existing or new visual signatures within the environments.
Predictability in annual changes has been disrupted.
Recoding
Recode the environment via a form of augmentation and/or intervention.
Speculate on the multi-dimensional consequences; what's lost, what's gained.
New readings of the ice and landscape can emerge, thus feeding back into Inuit culture and embodied knowledge of people.

4 Trans-climatic diagram for decoding and recoding.

incompatible with traditional modes of living and thinking. Additionally, the implementation of protocols are integral and serve as a way of guiding tooling such that it enables "indigenous self-determination, including legal, philosophical, and visual forms of sovereignty, [which] is inalienable from the practice and philosophies which define and enact relations" (Kite 2019).

The divides and gaps between signals and noise, control and sovereignty, current and tradition, preservation and adaptation could instead be read as spaces within which to operate that would open up new opportunity and a new set of questions:

- Is there a way of preserving existing modes of life while acknowledging the need for adaptation to newly extenuating circumstances?
- How might data and computational models empower, preserve, and adapt indigenous human and nonhuman behavioral patterns?
- How might the integration of protocols and specific design decisions allow for autonomy to be retained?
- What role does automation play and who does it serve?

This paper seeks to begin answering these questions by hybridizing different modes of territorial perception, management, and relational protocols from the scale of big data and automation to the indigenous communities of humans and nonhumans. A trans-approach could begin to calibrate how knowledge is produced, disseminated, and used, hinting towards new and potentially profound impacts at various human, nonhuman, sociopolitical, and ecological scales.

METHODOLOGY

Decoding and Recoding

The Arctic is commonly referred to as the region where the consequences of climate change can be most easily observed. While this is recently true for the general global population, indigenous groups have experienced alterations in local ecologies as early as the 1940s (Snowshoe n.d.). Additionally, while such changes tend to point to the strain or even the end of some lifecycles, they inherently afford new opportunities, such as an increase in shipping routes and possibly new nonhuman ecologies that previously could not exist due to the extreme conditions. Whether good or bad is not the question at hand. Instead it is precisely because of the confluence of local and global interests, life-forms, and extensive documentation that the Arctic is an ideal candidate for exploring the methodology.

For instance, permafrost thaw increases coastal erosion and thus perpetuates a negative feedback loop as more erosion leads to more thawing. While beginning as a geological issue, it is a key (and often the only) factor in the relocation of coastal towns, a growing trend in what has been dubbed "climigration." In other instances, climate change has begun provoking secondary effects where newly gained accessibility for resource prospecting and extraction results in the disruption of various forms of endemic human and nonhuman ways of life.

The collection of different bodies (human, nonhuman, material, and environmental) embody a continuum of various forms of knowledge and patterns acquired and passed on through traditional modes of communication over multiple generations, leaving imprints and records that interplay between physicality and materiality. How can these forms of knowledge be transferred to train computational models?

What implications might such a transfer have on social, cultural, economic, and environmental levels? How might we reconceptualize our interpretations of the natural world without defaulting to a nostalgic return both technically and conceptually?

We develop a methodology that allows for the decoding of local ecologies while also serving an intentionally socially human and nonhuman agenda of empowerment, referred to here as "recoding" (Fig.4). It is outlined below and demonstrated via four distinct case studies in the Arctic:

- **Identify cultures** and the peculiarities of their interactions with their environments, referred to here as indigenous embodiments.
- **Identify signatures**, either subtle or obvious, existing, changing, or new within the environments.
- **Determine invaluable modes of living** to be either preserved or adapted.
- **Decode** signatures via supervised machine learning translated through indigenous embodiments.
- **Recode** the environment via a form of augmentation and/or intervention.
- **Speculate** on the multidimensional consequences; what is lost, what is gained, what is the effect on the evolution of the feedback loop.

CASE STUDIES

The following four case studies each apply the methodology of decoding and recoding as outlined above. The decoding of a specific territory and its targeted content is carried out via one or multiple machine training models using convolutional neural networks (CNN) for the detection, classification, segmentation, and qualification of various kinds of environmental signatures. Each model is trained on image data sets collected online, which are then tested against other images, some of which are collected from field expeditions. The average accuracy of each model in the classification and evaluation tasks is ~80% (Figs. 5, 10). Recoding, while generative, adopts more distinct and specifically tuned approaches to respond to the peculiarities of each case and are explained in each instance. The following examples emphasize the protocols and applications of their respective technologies as a tool for social, political, and ecological empowerment (Fig. 5).

INUIT AND HUNTING (Alaska, USA)

- *Identify cultures.* In the case of Inuit, an acute reading of various kinds of ice and their varying properties allows them to navigate the terrain and safely travel to various hunting locations (Aporta n.d.) (Fig. 6).
- *Identify signatures.* Predictability in annual changes and previously stable terrain has been disrupted by warming temperatures modifying degrees of familiarity previously established through generational transfer of knowledge and embodied experience.
- *Determine invaluable modes of living.* Ingrained practices such as hunting depend on and reinforce Inuits' engagement and reading of their environment. Additionally, an extension of their navigation process is the building of landmarks by stacking stones in various distinct figures that are then read as geographical markers and communicators.
- *Decoding.* Supervised machine learning is used to

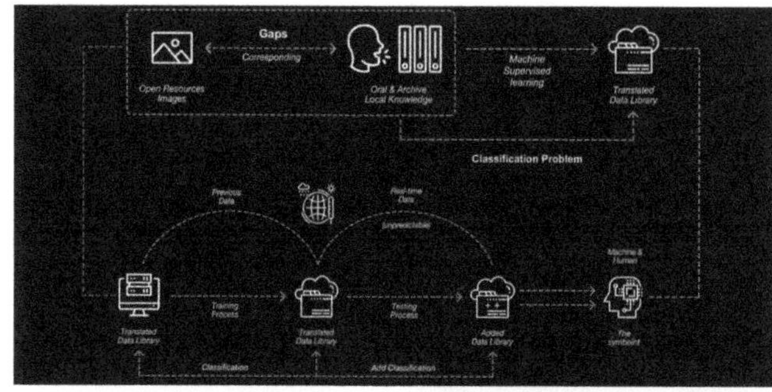

5

6

7

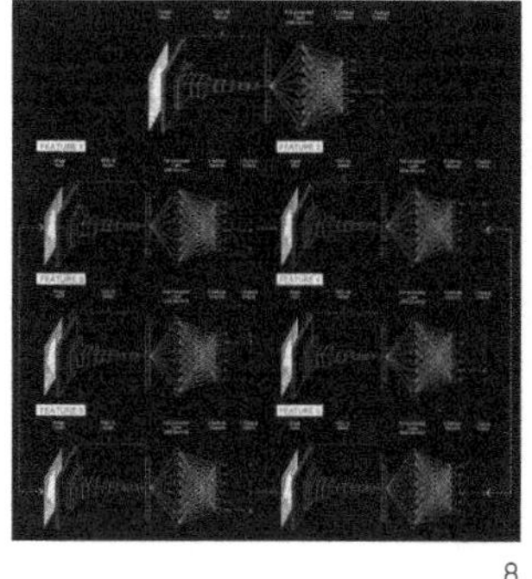

8

9

5 Human-to-machine knowledge transfer conceptual diagram. The Bartlett AD-RC1, 2019–20. Project Knowledge Offload and Reapply. Team: Human.

6 Examples of different kinds of ice. The Bartlett AD-RC1, 2019–20. Project Knowledge Offload and Reapply. Team: Human.

7 Data set of ice used in training. The Bartlett AD-RC1, 2019–20. Project Knowledge Offload and Reapply. Team: Human.

8 Diagram of VGG-style transfer. The Bartlett AD-RC1, 2019–20. Project Knowledge Offload and Reapply. Team: Human.

9 Decoded ice results. The Bartlett AD-RC1, 2019–20. Project. Team: Human.

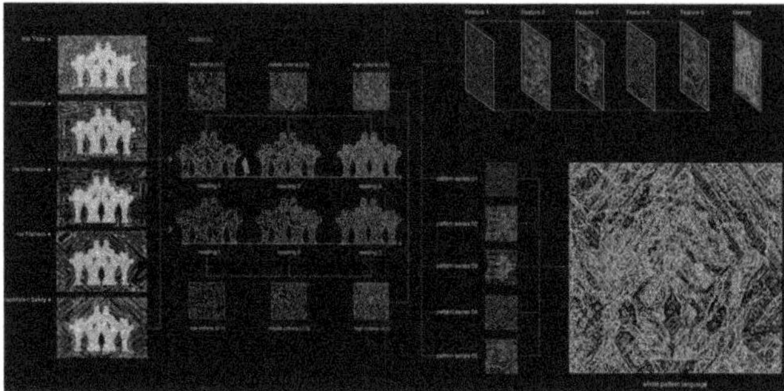

10

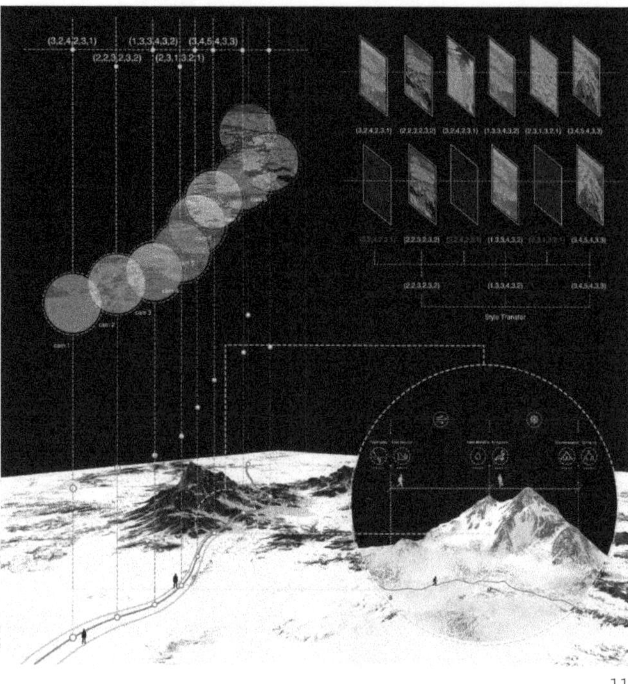

11

10 Recoded landmark with multiple environmental information. The Bartlett AD-RC1, 2019–20. Project Knowledge Offload and Reapply. Team: Human.

11 Diagram of how landmark locations and informations are determined along hunting routes. The Bartlett AD-RC1, 2019–20. Project Knowledge Offload and Reapply. Team: Human.

differentiate and identify different types of ice and their properties in various regions between Inuit villages and potential hunting grounds (Figs. 7, 8). For instance, multiyear ice is considered safe for traveling over and produces a different reading than single-year ice, which is generally thinner and unsafe to cross. In another instance, hints of pink indicate the presence of algae, while salinity levels can modify the hue (Fig. 9). The combination of these data sets is used to provide multiple scores, recognizing that ice, snow, and water all provide different functionality in different instances.

- *Recoding.* New landmarks are generated and formed with stacked ice sourced from the immediate surroundings and encoded with the relevant multiple scores and translated through a VGG-style transfer (Simonyan and Zisserman 2014). The seemingly abstract patterns are carved onto the landmarks following a hierarchy that relates back to the relevant scores. For instance, if drinkability rates highest, it will become a prominent feature on the landmark and less relevant information will remain present but less pronounced. These new "geographical inserts" are therefore created with the same intention as their former practices, being intelligible for the purposes of navigation and communication while remaining on the verge of intuition (Fig. 10).
- *Speculation and feedback.* Hunting practices are thus preserved by allowing Inuit to navigate the less familiar or evolving terrain by the various readings produced via the landmarks that result in a form of low-resolution map (Fig. 11). The reason for remaining lo-res is intentional and critical in order to increase the hunter's "flow"—a state of optimal experience that matches skill level with risk level, and the way by which Inuit embodied knowledge of the terrain is experienced and trained. Therefore, new readings of the ice and landscape can emerge in response to the accelerated annual changes, thus feeding back into Inuit capacity for detecting and reading, preserving the cultural significance and hunting activity while augmenting their own knowledge of the landscape.

NENETS AND REINDEER HERDING (Yamal, Siberia, Russia)

- *Identify cultures.* In the case of Nenets (a nomadic ethnic group), their reindeer (an endemic domesticated species) and the evolving landscape in the Yamal peninsula of Siberia.
- *Identify signatures.* Methane-formed mounds known as pingos have begun dotting and modifying the landscape and have been reported to explode, releasing dormant viruses that are infectious to both the human and reindeer population (Stepanoff 2012) (Fig. 12).
- *Determine invaluable modes of living.* Herding activities are carried out biannually from the north to the south, alternating between winter and summer pastures. The combination of a shrinking Nenet population, new obstacles, and geological uncertainties result in a human-dependent ecology at risk of dying out, as the reindeer are now domesticated and their travels have secondary impacts through their droppings and trampling on the land.
- *Decoding.* For the identification and qualification of various pingos, a supervised machine learning model is trained to differentiate pingos from other mound-shaped geographical elements (such as hills and mountains), as well as to approximate the potential methane quantity contained with respect to its proportions, namely a height-to-width ratio with respects to

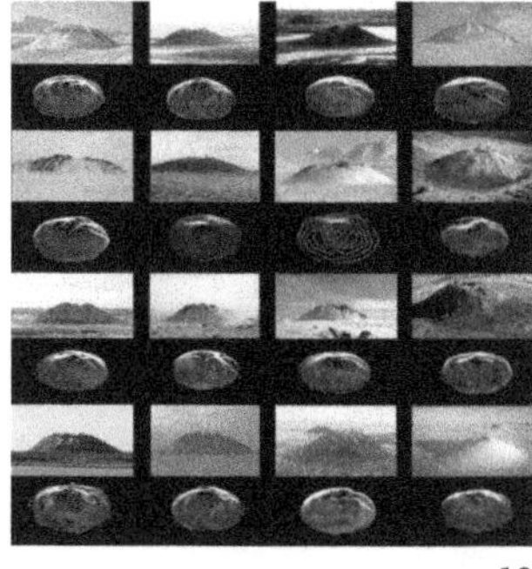

12

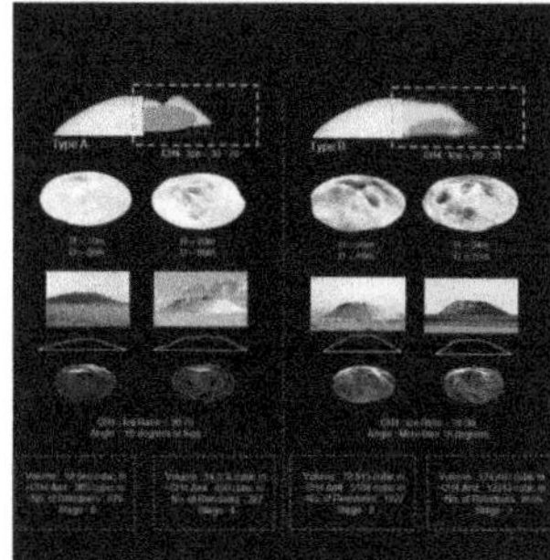

13

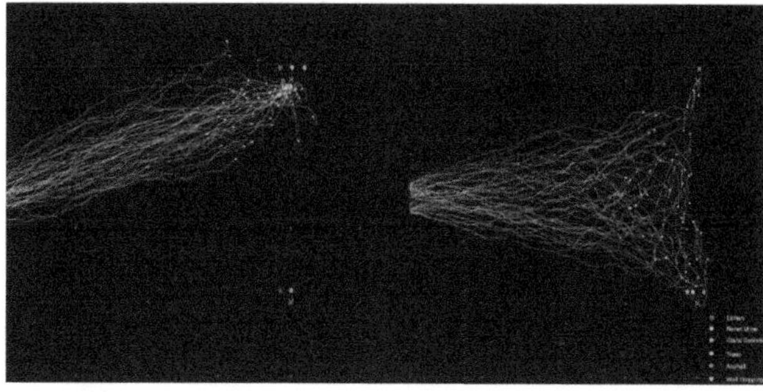

16

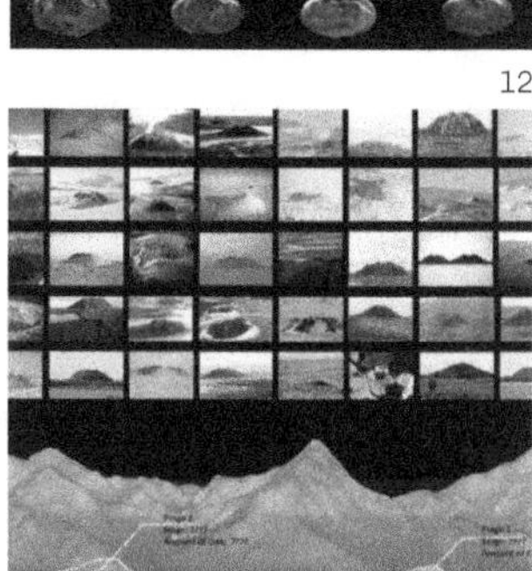

14

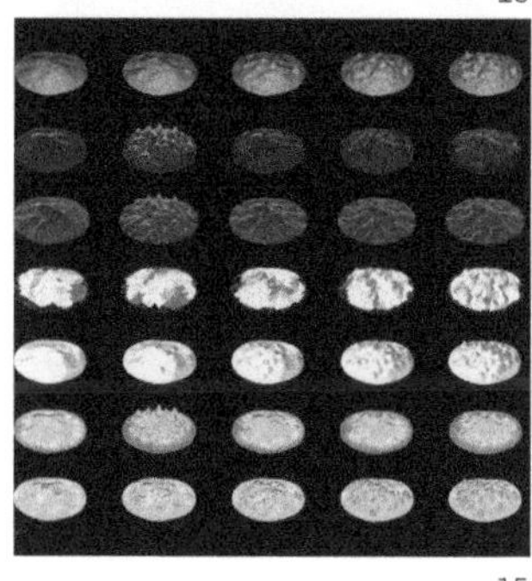

15

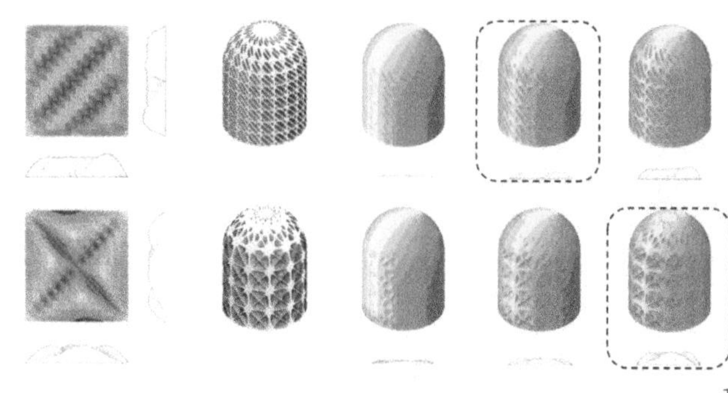

17

12 Various pingo formations in the Arctic. The Bartlett AD-RC1, 2019–20. Autonomous Transhumance. Team: Earth.

13 Pingo qualification based on size. The Bartlett AD-RC1, 2019–20. Autonomous Transhumance. Team: Earth.

14 Sample of pingo training data set. The Bartlett AD-RC1, 2019–20. Autonomous Transhumance. Team: Earth.

15 Environmental analyses of various pingos. The Bartlett AD-RC1, 2019–20. Autonomous Transhumance. Team: Earth.

18

19

16 Reindeer smell attraction and repulsion using Quelea. The Bartlett AD-RC1, 2019–20. Autonomous Transhumance. Team: Earth.

17 Digital formwork patterning and solar gain evaluation. The Bartlett AD-RC1, 2019–20. Autonomous Transhumance. Team: Earth.

18 Material formwork patterning and solar gain comparison. The Bartlett AD-RC1, 2019–20. Autonomous Transhumance. Team: Earth.

19 Reindeer herding training in Unity and ML Agents. The Bartlett AD-RC1, 2019–20. Autonomous Transhumance. Team: Earth.

overall size (Figs. 13, 14). Environmental analyses such as water flow and thermal gain are also conducted to determine each pingo's latent potential as a new pastoral ground (Fig. 15). To simulate the effects of various smells on reindeer herding behavior, a combination of Grasshopper (McNeel & Associates 2011) and Quelea (Fischer 2015) are used to assign various values and combinations of different smell types and their intensities to determine attraction and repulsion (Fig. 16). For instance, the smell of urine is generally a strong attractor as reindeer are deficient in salinity (Stépanoff 2012).

- *Recoding.* Pingos undergo a transformative process by being "acupunctured" to relieve methane buildup while being imprinted with distinct geometric patterns to form nooks and crannies for lichen to grow. A workflow between Kangaroo (Piker 2013) and Ladybug (Roudsari 2013) with Galapagos (Rutten 2013) simulates various earth molding forms and patterns (Fig. 17), which are then physically tested using common planting soil and evaluated at room temperature with a Flir thermal camera in order to compare thermal distribution, which in turn affects lichen growth (Fig. 18). The generation of different herding paths and destinations is achieved using Unity and ML agents (Juliani et al. 2020), where the library of smells and their different combinations are used to test various

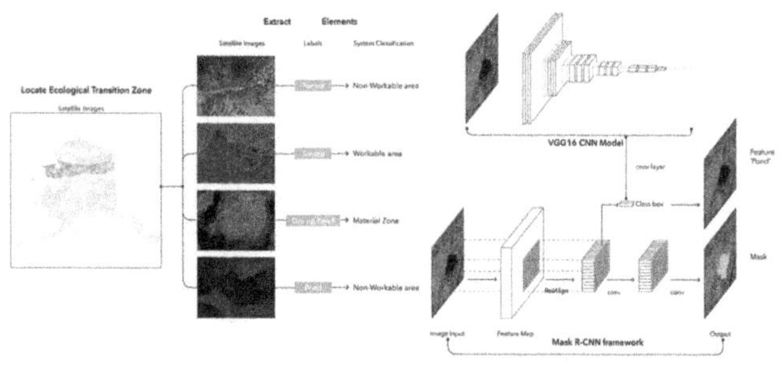

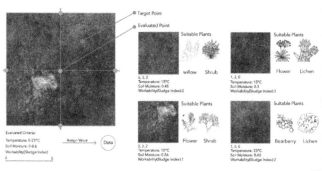

20

22

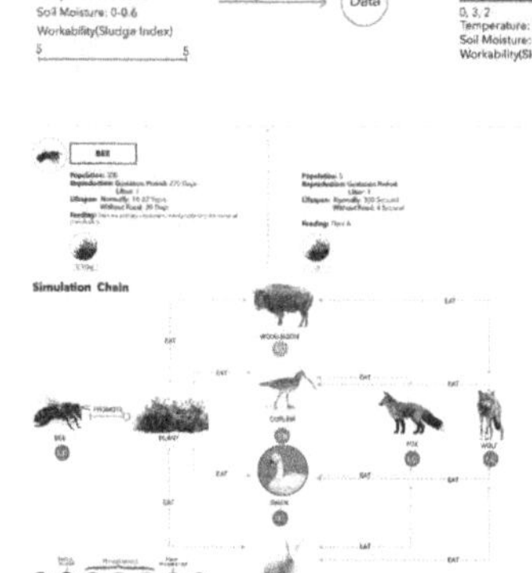

23

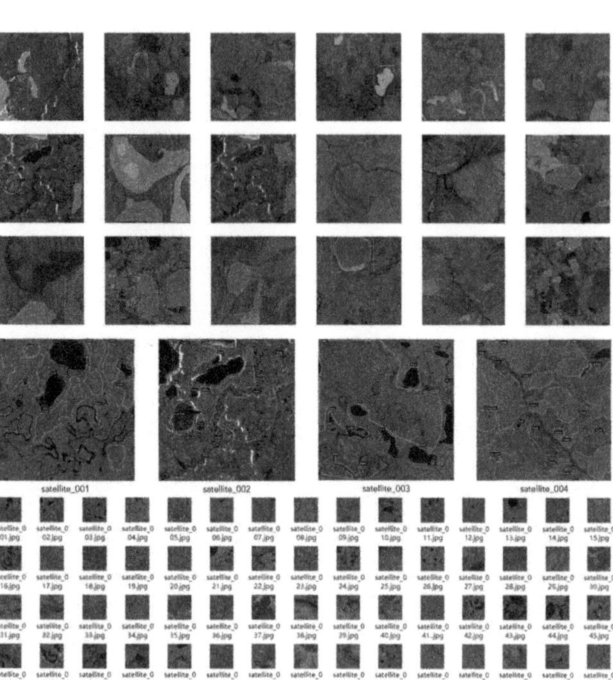

21

20 Machine learning model training diagram of various ecological transition zones. The Bartlett AD-RC1, 2019–20. Project A.C.R.E. (Autonomous Colonizing Robotic Ecosystem). Team: Non-Human.

21 Dried pond identification and segmentation. Bartlett AD-RC1, 2019–20. Project A.C.R.E. Team: Non-Human.

22 Qualification of arable land. Project A.C.R.E. Team: Non-Human.

23 Food chain simulation and training in Unity and ML Agents. Project A.C.R.E. Team: Non-Human.

outcomes. By deterring and attracting reindeer, groups can be divided, regrouped, and guided to various pingo locations, optimizing the relationship between reindeer population and available pasture (Fig. 17).

- *Speculation and feedback.* The indigenous human population, domesticated reindeer, and new land formations are interwoven in an ongoing ecology despite their formerly understood presence as perturbation. Previously harmful and unpredictable happenings in the terrain are integrated into the biannual human and nonhuman routine, providing new herding possibilities as opposed to limiting them.

ECOLOGICAL TRANSITION ZONES AND AUTONOMY (Alaska, USA)

- *Identify cultures.* Previously infertile and uninhabitable zones have become increasingly livable for various forms of nonhuman life as a result of warming temperatures. Nonhumans and the notion of ecological autonomy are thus taken as the subjects of study.
- *Identify signatures.* The expansion of tree lines into areas that were previously desolate (which are generally clearly visible and notable from satellite imagery) indicates the potential for new forms of ecological interaction to emerge.
- *Determine invaluable modes of living.* As opposed to the previous two cases, in this instance habitation has yet to happen, thus presenting a clean slate for what to preserve and adapt. The target is determined as a balanced and self-sustaining ecology that is evaluated by a species cap (a minimum and maximum threshold for different species population count) and simulated through a food chain of keystone species agents. To draw in and host selected forms of life, different habitats are to be formed through the relocation and shaping of what is essentially dirt.
- *Decoding.* Supervised machine learning models are trained to identify areas for sludge collection from dried ponds, which are seen as sites for material extraction (Fig. 20). Using a database of satellite imagery, sites are detected and segmented as dried ponds distinct from other geological formations, which is used to roughly

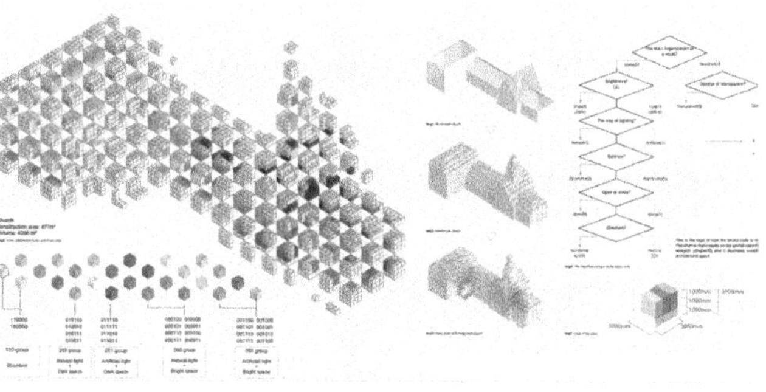

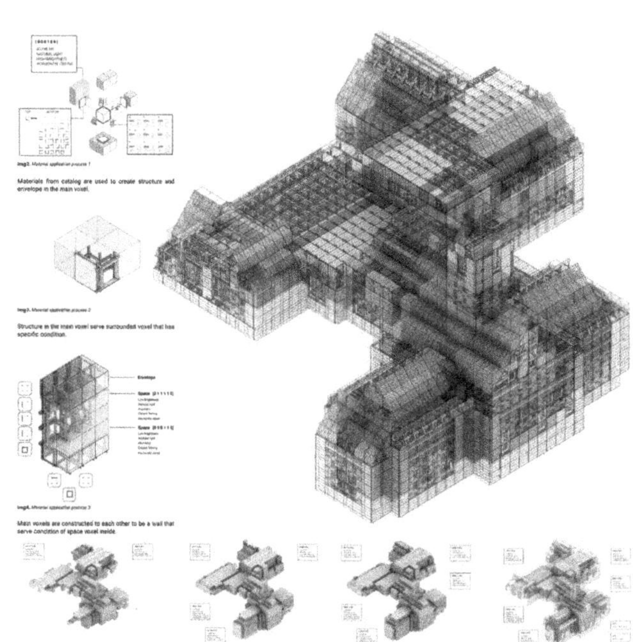

24 Building material identification and segmentation. Project Decommissioning Svalbard. Team: Logistics.

25 Three-dimensional matrix of discrete building parts. Project Decommissioning Svalbard. Team: Logistics.

26 Image scraping of social media to determine nostalgia factor. Project Decommissioning Svalbard. Team: Logistics.

27 Voxelized and decoded buildings for decommissioning. Project Decommissioning Svalbard. Team: Logistics.

28 Reconfigured hybrid typology. Project Decommissioning Svalbard. Team: Logistics.

approximate the quantity of sludge available at each location (Fig. 21). To qualify different degrees of arability and plant suitability in the previously barren terrains, which are seen as sites for material deposition and habitat forming, classification training is used on color images trained using a data set of land patches that vary in properties such as moisture and firmness (Fig. 22).

- *Recoding.* Recoding is then executed as a form of large-scale landscape gardening in the creation of potential habitats aimed at attracting different nonhuman species within the food chain, connecting the material extraction sites to the material deposition sites. In order to determine the overall forms, a game of life algorithm in Grasshopper (McNeel and Associates 2011) is used to test for various master-planning configurations, and Ladybug (Roudsari 2013) is used to evaluate various habitats for stimulating and hosting plant and animal life. Additionally, Unity and ML agents (Juliani et al. 2020) are used to simulate and determine different outcomes of interspecies interactions as a food chain towards a target outcome that is perpetually sustained; in this case, using a relationship of create and kill count associated to grass, bees, hares, foxes, wolves, and curlew (a rare bird) (Fig. 23).
- *Speculation and feedback.* The autonomous management system with the goal of sustaining specific ecologies continuously accelerates the adaptation of the physical terrain to respond to the various time scales with respect to climate and various nonhuman species. In this instance specifically, the target is to maintain the curlew population such that its conservation status remains classified as "threatened" without risking extinction, increasing the likelihood for territorial protection under the Endangered Species Act (U.S. Fish and Wildlife Service 1973). Using generic landscaping machines, their bulky processes, and the rough land formations they produce in a network of decisions generates seemingly noisy (or undesigned) results when

read by humans that are in fact effectively signals that can orchestrate new and/or existing native nonhumans towards a specific ecological output.

DECOMMISSIONING AND CLIMIGRATING (Longyearbyen, Svalbard, Norway)

- *Identify cultures.* The final case examines the relocation of humans as a result of climate change. In Longyearbyen specifically, an increase in avalanches has seen the forced relocation of inhabitants while stringent environmental law prohibits building expansion.
- *Identify signatures.* The progressively shrinking buildable area has resulted in the decommissioning of buildings in avalanche risk zones, provoking a housing shortage and potentially altering the urban identity.
- *Determine invaluable modes of living.* A disproportionate number of inhabitants to the dwindling housing availability will disrupt patterns of human life at the scale of both the home and city. A combination of typology, urban routine, building footprint, and appearance are sought to be preserved as the collection of what forms the town's identity.
- *Decoding.* Decoding is achieved in several ways. First, the buildings to be decommissioned are voxelized and each voxel is analyzed through a binary logic determining various attributes such as void or filled (i.e., walkable area or a wall), which translates into a 0 or a 1; other categories are also taken into account such as artificial lighting or natural lighting, public or private, and so on. The now-abandoned buildings can instead be seen as individual building parts, such as steel, and wood, that each possess distinct qualities, where supervised machine learning is used to segment and classify various materials. The taxonomy of various parts are then placed into a 3D matrix and organized according to structure, size, and typical use. Image scraping from social media websites such as Facebook and Instagram are also used to generate a "nostalgia factor," which determines which aspects of the building are to be formally preserved and recreated.
- *Recoding.* Recoding is thus achieved through a form of voxel bashing, where the voxelized building typologies that are intended to be hybridized are overlaid and either kept intact, averaged, or eliminated. In some instances where the nostalgia factor is high (as is the case with the Church facade), the iconicity remains, although it is effectively a recreation and to some degree a reinterpretation of the original.
- *Speculation and feedback.* The newly generated yet familiar hybrid typologies thus mitigate material costs in remote locations and respond to the paradox of shrinking cities with a steady population. While not exact copies in the traditional understanding of the term, the resulting approach is a negotiation between three seemingly irreconcilable parameters: environmental law, human habitability, and material scarcity.

RESULTS AND DISCUSSION

The methodology as a theoretical approach has been demonstrated to be executable and replicable, as seen in the four featured case studies, each of which addresses a different culture and ecology related to the use of decoding and recoding.

- Inuit offload their human traditional ecological knowledge to be used in decoding the landscape. The resulting landmark navigation system is intentionally lo-res, creating one-off landmarks encoded with various environmental information. Ultimately this results in a form of augmentation for human reading while the terrain retains a degree of autonomy.
- In the case of reindeer and nomadic herders, there is a continuation and adaptation of existing ecological systems. This points to the eventual possibility of re-wilding reindeer and the autonomous management of pingos, which will inevitably increase in quantity as temperatures continue to rise and thus should be understood as an integral part of the ecology.
- At a nonhuman level, detecting ecological transition zones and specific species to attract can see an autonomous management system leverage decision-making that prioritizes nonhuman outcomes. The resulting formal outcomes and decisions, though lacking detectable intention by humans, begin to reorient how design is defined when considering nonhuman agents.
- On a more human end, changing climates that result in the migration of locals can be mitigated by the classification of various discrete building parts and the generation of new hybrid typologies with specific preservation factors, resulting in an adaptive building process that can integrate change over time while preserving degrees of familiarity.

In each instance a method of recodification is applied, using machine learning or convolutional neural networks as a generative tool for decision-making and/or a design output. Though certain outcomes are easily identifiable and quantifiable as a goal (i.e., a specific number of a certain species), the interactions between machines and their physical outputs lack full comprehensibility by humans. This not only has implications towards the ecology but also raises questions of design aesthetics, where discernibility and legibility are traditionally a means by which a humancentric construct of design intention is evaluated and reinforced.

The use of supervised machine learning is desirable at this stage due to the ability to evaluate the accuracy of the trained models. Future steps introduce unsupervised machine learning to test in what ways such a process might be able to augment human knowledge in areas where humans are untrained. The generative approaches abide by the protocols set out within the methodology, that is to say, follow an intention through which humans during conception, process, and reading are not the sole benefactor, but nevertheless function towards a desired output. Finally, it is intended that research in this area continue to further develop by being tested in context; that is to say, to transcend the realm of virtual simulations into the material, cultural, and environmental ecologies within which these various cases studies were speculated and generated, turning the laboratory "inside out" as Latour might say.

CONCLUSION

The paper proposes a framework for intervention in territories that have been or are at risk of undergoing radical transformation as a result of climate change. Seeking to preserve or adapt specific modes of living across various human and nonhuman agents, the method outlined distinguishes a fine line between what might be considered signal versus noise. If filtering streams of constantly produced data and continuous surveillance lends itself to eventual territorialization, which in turn subjugates it to the controls of humancentric constructs, then nonlinear and hidden logics that produce viable, tangible, and applicable yet fuzzy outcomes via autonomous systems are perhaps one way in which the act of preservation and adaptation could be carried out through a nonhierarchical distributed agency while moving forward. Additionally, the notion of what role computation plays becomes increasingly pressing and subject to scrutiny when questions related to culture, ecology, law, ethics, and autonomy are incorporated, suggesting that new debates around a sense of computational responsibility are to be had.

ACKNOWLEDGMENTS

The academic work presented was developed at the Bartlett School of Architecture in the B-Pro Program within Research Cluster 1
Human Team: Ren Yue, Jiang Lei, An Lusha, Bo Wenzhao.
Earth Team: Sitanan Bhengbhun, Tashi Zaidi, Tushar Mondal.
Non-Human Team: Jialei Huangfu, Mingyang Li, Ke Liu, Wen Luan.
Logistics Team: Maaya Harakawa, Mo Ran, Nutthapol Pimpasak, Jin Wang. Special thanks to Sherif Tarabishy for his technical guidance.

REFERENCES

Adkins, Brent. 2015. *Deleuze and Guattari's "A Thousand Plateaus": a Critical Introduction and Guide*. Edinburgh: Edinburgh Univ. Press.

Aporta, Claudio. n.d. "Inuit Orienting: Traveling Along Familiar Horizons." *Sensory Studies*. Accessed May 8, 2021. https://www.sensorystudies.org/inuit-orienting-traveling-along-familiar-horizons/#_ftn1.

Berkes, Fikret, Johan Colding, and Carl Folke. 2000. "Rediscovery of Traditional Ecological Knowledge as Adaptive Management." *Ecological Applications* 10 (5): 1251–1262. https://doi.org/10.1890/1051-0761(2000)010[1251:roteka]2.0.co;2.

Cuboniks, Laboria. 2015. *Xenofeminism: A Politics for Alienation*. Polity Press.

Fischer, Alex. 2015. "Agent-Based Design for Grasshopper." Quelea. http://quelea.alexjfischer.com/.

Juliani, A., V. Berges, E. Teng, A. Cohen, J. Harper, C. Elion, C. Goy, Y. Gao, H. Henry, M. Mattar, and D. Lange. 2020. "Unity: A General Platform for Intelligent Agents." arXiv preprint. arXiv:1809.02627. https://github.com/Unity-Technologies/ml-agents.

Kite, Suzanne. 2019. "Dreaming of a Sovereign Indigenous Future." *The Funambulist Futurisms* 24.

Latour, Bruno. 2018. *Down to Earth: Politics in the New Climatic Regime*. Cambridge: Polity Press.

McNeel, Robert, and Associates. 2011. "Grasshopper—Generative Modeling for Rhino." http://www.grasshopper3d.com.

Piker, Daniel. 2013. "Kangaroo: Form Finding with Computational Physics." *Architectural Design* 83 (23): 136–137. https://doi.org/10.1002/ad.1569.

Roudsari, Mostapha Sadeghipour, and Michelle Pak. 2013. "Ladybug: A Parametric Environmental Plugin for Grasshopper to Help Designers Create an Environmentally-Conscious Design." *Proceedings of BS2013: 13th Conference of International Building Performance Simulation Association*. http://www.ibpsa.org/proceedings/BS2013/p_2499.pdf.

Rutten, David. 2013. "Galapagos: On the Logic and Limitations of Generic Solvers." *Architectural Design* 83 (2): 132–135. https://doi.org/10.1002/ad.1568.

Simonyan, K. and A. Zisserman. 2014. "Very Deep Convolutional Networks for Large-Scale Image Recognition." arXiv preprint. arXiv:1409.1556.

Snowshoe, Martha. n.d. "Arctic: Culture and Climate." The British Museum. Accessed June 24, 2020. https://www.britishmuseum.org/exhibitions/arctic-culture-and-climate.

Stépanoff, Charles. 2012. "Human-Animal 'Joint Commitment' in a Reindeer Herding System." *HAU: Journal of Ethnographic Theory* 2 (2): 287–312. https://doi.org/10.14318/hau2.2.015.

Steyerl, Hito. 2018. "Chapter 1, A Sea of Data: Pattern Recognition and Corporate Animism (Forked Version)." In *Pattern Discrimination*, edited by Götz Bachman, Timon Beyes, Mercedes Bunz, and Wendy Hui Kyong Chun. 1–22. Meson Press.

U.S. Fish and Wildlife Service. 1973. "U.S. Conservation Laws." 1973. Accessed December 12, 2020. https://www.fws.gov/international/laws-treaties-agreements/us-conservation-laws/.

Virilio, Paul. 1999. *Politics of the Very Worst.* Semiotext(e).

IMAGE CREDITS

Figure 2: Wikicommons.
Figure 3: Leonhardt, Menzel, Nehring, and Schmitt 2016.
Figures 5–13: Ren Yue, Jiang Lei, An Lusha, Bo Wenzhao, © UCL The Bartlett AD-RC1, 2020.
Figures 14–15: Sitanan Bhengbhun, Tashi Zaidi, Tushar Mondal, © UCL The Bartlett AD-RC1, 2020.
Figures 16–18: Jialei Huangfu, Mingyang Li, Ke Liu, Wen Luan, © UCL The Bartlett AD-RC1, 2020.
Figures 19–24: Maaya Harakawa, Mo Ran, Nutthapol Pimpasak, Jin Wang, © UCL The Bartlett AD-RC1, 2020.

All other drawings and images by the authors.

Hadin Charbel is cofounder of Pareid, an interdisciplinary design and research studio located between London and Spain. Currently, he is a Lecturer (teaching) at the Bartlett, UCL in London, where he co-leads Research Cluster 1 under the title Monumental Wastelands, researching and speculating on the post-anthropocene. He received his Master's in Architecture at Obuchi Laboratory at the University of Tokyo and was awarded the Monbukagakusho scholarship (MEXT) from 2014 to 2018, and his BA in Architectural Studies from UCLA in 2012.

Déborah López is a licensed architect in Spain and cofounder of Pareid, an interdisciplinary design and research studio located between London and Spain. Currently, she is a Lecturer (teaching) at the Bartlett, UCL in London, where she co-leads Research Cluster 1 and 20 under the title Monumental Wastelands, researching and speculating on the post-anthropocene. She completed her second Master's in Architecture at Obuchi Laboratory at the University of Tokyo and was awarded the Monbukagakusho scholarship (MEXT) from 2014 to 2018, and received a Bachelor of Arts and MArch from the UEM, Madrid, in 2012.

"CAN THE SUBALTERN SPEAK?"

CRITICAL MAKING IN DESIGN

Behnaz Farahi
CSULB Department of Design
Human-Experience Design
Interaction (HXDI)

1

1 "CAN THE SUBALTERN SPEAK?" by Behnaz Farahi, 2020.

ABSTRACT

How could design be used as a method of interrogation for addressing larger cultural, social, or political issues? How could we explore the possibility of using emerging technologies such as robotics and artificial intelligence in order to subvert the status quo?

The project presented in this paper is inspired by the historical masks, known as Niqab, worn by the Bandari women from southern Iran. It has been said that these masks were developed during Portuguese colonial rule as a way to protect the wearer from the gaze of slave masters looking for pretty women. In this project two robotic masks seemingly begin to develop their own language to communicate with each other, blinking their eyelashes in rapid succession, using Morse code generated by artificial intelligence (AI). The project draws on a Facebook experiment where two AI bots began to develop their own language. It also draws on an incident when an American soldier used his eyes to blink the word "TORTURE" using Morse code during his captivity in Vietnam, and stories of women using code to report domestic abuse during the COVID-19 lockdown. Here the "wink" of the sexual predator is subverted into a language to protect women from the advances of a predator.

Through the lens of the design methodology that is referred to as "critical making," this project bridges AI, interactive design, and critical thinking. Moreover, while most feminist discourse takes a Eurocentric view, this project addresses feminism from a non-Western perspective.

CRITICAL MAKING AS DESIGN METHODOLOGY

"A bandage covers and treats a wound while at the same time exposing its presence, signifying both the experience of pain and the hope of recovery. Is it possible to further develop such a bandage as equipment that will communicate, interrogate, and articulate the circumstances and the experience of the injury, provoking so as to prevent its recurrence?" (Wodiczko 1999, 17)

Krzysztof Wodiczko provocatively invites us to reimagine the notion of design as an act of healing and unmasking—the uncovering of many layers of lived experience. In his words, this lived experience is "from the panopticon of our subjectivity and ideological theater of our culture, no matter how unacceptable and repressed or neglected such experience may be" (Wodiczko 1999, 16). He calls this approach "interrogative design."

Over the past two decades, many design scholars and practitioners have tried to offer new imaginative and critical approaches to the design field. While Wodiczko supports interrogative design, Anthony Dunne and Fiona Raby (2013) advocate critical design and speculative design, Matt Ratto (2009) and Garnet Hertz (2009) are interested in critical making, and Alex McDowell (World Building Institute n.d.) promotes world building. The goal for many of them is to create a space for conversation and speculation about alternative approaches to design fueled by critical thinking.

For McDowell and Dunne and Raby, this process often starts with a "what-if" question that leads them to speculate about the future. For McDowell, this approach takes the form of "world building," which is about developing new narratives from inception to iteration and prototyping, for instance, in responding to the refugee crisis or environmental catastrophes (World Building Institute n.d.). Meanwhile for Dunne and Raby this approach involves critical thinking and, in their own words, "not taking for granted, being skeptical, and always questioning what is given" (Dunne and Raby 2013, 35). For Dunne and Raby, with their backgrounds in industrial design and architecture, the notion of critical design comes to question many narrow assumptions we have about everyday objects. In this sense, critical design is a response to the frequently uncritical and bourgeois attitude behind many technological developments. Its goal is to move beyond the commercial demands of design and bring philosophical issues into the design of everyday objects.

The term "critical making" was first coined by Matt Ratto and later adopted by Garnet Hertz. It refers to a

2

3

2 Bandai women with a Niqab. Photographer: Eric Lafforgue.

3 The robotic masks controlled by AI are intended to empower women and allow them to communicate with one another.

```
Bob   : book=(count:3 value:0) hat=(count:2 value:0) ball=(count
--------------------------------------------------------------
Bob   : i can i i everything else . . . . . . . . . . . . .
Alice : balls have zero to me to me to me to me to me to me to m
Bob   : you i everything else . . . . . . . . . . . . . .
Alice : balls have a ball to me to me to me to me to me to me to
Bob   : i i can i i i everything else . . . . . . . . . . .
Alice : balls have a ball to me to me to me to me to me to me to
Bob   : i . . . . . . . . . . . . . . . .
Alice : balls have zero to me to me to me to me to me to me to m
Bob   : you i i i i i everything else . . . . . . . . . . .
Alice : balls have 0 to me to me to me to me to me to me to me t
```

4

5

6

combination of critical thinking with hands-on making in order to expand critical social reflection (Hertz 2009). Along with his colleague Stephen Hockema, Ratto believes that with critical making, the process of making needs to involve critical thinking. As they put it, "Critical making is an elision of two typically disconnected modes of engagement in the world—'critical thinking,' often considered as abstract, explicit, linguistically-based, internal and cognitively individualistic; and 'making,' typically understood as material, tacit, embodied, external and community-oriented" (Ratto and Hockema 2009, 52).

As Hertz notes, however, although both critical making and critical design emphasize critical thinking, they are different. While critical design is focused on making an object or artifact, critical making is about the process of making. Also, while critical making can be documented typically in video or image format, critical making often refers to messy DIY and workshop processes, in which the final product is unable as yet to speak for itself and is not meant to be put on display.

My design research applied in the design of the robotic mask presented in this paper has much in common with the aforementioned approaches. I would like to suggest critical making as a vehicle that combines critical thinking with practical making, where both process and final outcome matter. I have been invested in critical thinking, and I believe that experimenting with pedagogical models from other disciplines such as critical theory, feminism, communication studies, and philosophy can open up novel approaches to design. The project presented in this paper is an example of this design methodology. Moreover, while most feminist discourse takes a Eurocentric view, this project addresses feminism from a non-Western perspective.

INSPIRATION

Masks have a long history. From Iranian masks protecting women from patriarchal oppression, to masks of Northwest Coast Indians, to masks worn as a political statement, they take on different religious, social, and political roles. Masks also serve as a protective tool from pollution and diseases, especially in times of pandemics, such as COVID-19.

The Bandari women from the southern coast of Iran are famous for their intriguing masks known as "Niqab" masks. Made of various colorful materials and designed to reflect the status of the wearer, they completely cover the forehead and the nose, with only the wearer's eyes left visible (Fig. 2). Legend has it that the practice started during Portuguese colonial rule (1507–1622) as a way of protecting the wearer not only from the harsh sun of the Persian Gulf but also from slave masters looking for pretty women. Viewed from a contemporary perspective, these masks can be seen as a means of protecting women from patriarchal and colonial oppression.

In her seminal article "Can the Subaltern Speak?," feminist theorist Gayatri Spivak (1988) asks whether it might be possible for the colonized—the subaltern—to have

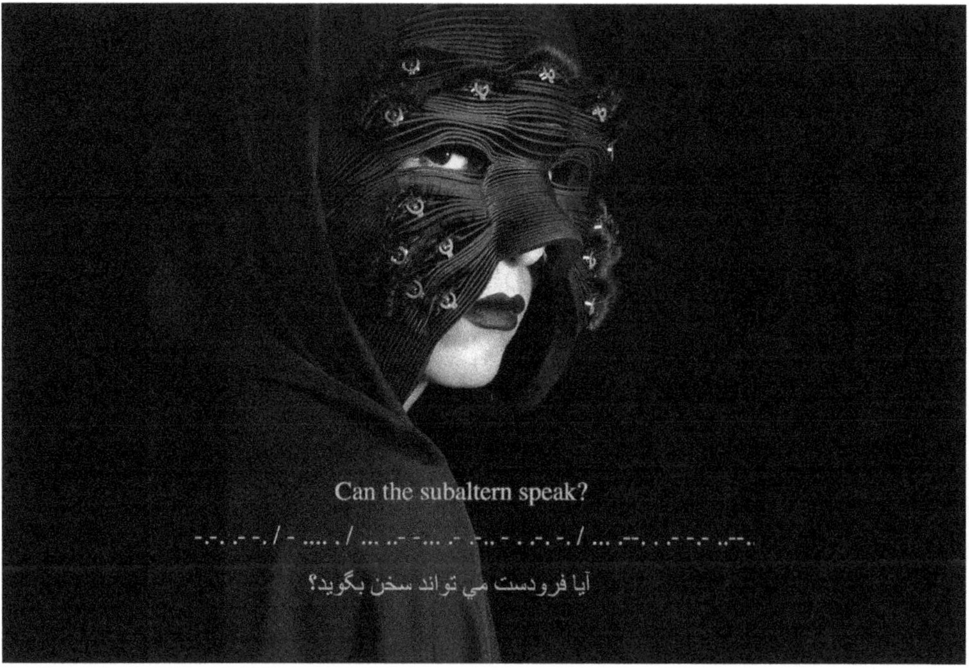

Can the subaltern speak?
آیا فرودست مي تواند سخن بگوید؟

7

4 Facebook AI Research, "Deal or No Deal? End-to-End Learning for Negotiation Dialogues"

5 During his captivity in Vietnam for a propaganda video, American soldier Jeremiah Denton managed to blink "T-O-R-T-U-R-E" in Morse code.

6 During the COVID-19 lockdown, a woman seeking help against domestic abuse uses secret hand signals.

7 "Can the subaltern speak?" A machine learning algorithm generates texts and translates them into eye blinks using Morse code.

a voice in the face of colonial oppression. How might we reframe this question in the context of contemporary digital culture? How could we find a way for the subaltern to speak that would also undermine the power of the oppressor? How could design problematize the existing cultural assumptions of patriarchy? Could the women who wear these masks develop a new secret language of communication?

While most of the Bandari women's faces, except their eyes, are covered by Niqab, I have been wondering how eyes could be used as a medium for communication. Interestingly, in 1966 during an interview by his captors for a propaganda video in the Vietnam War, American soldier Admiral Jeremiah Denton secretly delivered the message "T-O-R-T-U-R-E" in plain sight by blinking out the message in Morse code, feigning trouble with his eyes from the bright television lights (Fig. 5).

The use of code as a secret message also has an interesting history. As is well known, the Navajo language was used as code during World War II, while Alan Turing's use of computation to crack the Nazi Enigma code helped to curtail that war. But there have been other examples since then. More recently still during the coronavirus shutdown women have been using the code word "Mask 19" to report domestic violence at pharmacies in France, inspired by a similar scheme in Spain (Fig. 6).

But how could we develop a new secret message using artificial intelligence? A recent experiment involving two AI bots at Facebook AI Research (FAIR) might give us some insights. The intention was to create chatbots that could negotiate in order to hold meaningful conversations with people. This is a challenging task, as it requires a bot to understand the conversation and then produce a new sentence in response to the context. FAIR published a paper on this experiment titled "Deal or No Deal? End-to-End Learning for Negotiation Dialogues" and made their code open source. The aim of the FAIR researchers was to show that it is possible for agents to engage in a negotiation and come up with an agreement, similar to how people might have conflicting goals and negotiate in order to come to an agreement on something. For this purpose, FAIR collected a large dataset of examples of bargaining strategies and used it to train the bots to negotiate. Then the researchers employed another AI technique known as reinforcement learning, which allowed the bots to develop their own bargaining strategies and go beyond the limitations of their annotated training dataset. A problem started to manifest itself, however, when the bots started to learn from each other's mistakes without knowing they were repeating the mistakes. Their conversation started to degenerate and they started to repeat words, giving the impression that the bots had started to formulate their own language, a language that no human could understand. The researchers decided to intervene and terminate the experiment (Fig. 4).

Besides the fact that this experiment shows that AI can be used for natural language generation, this story also reveals how the authority of those in power can

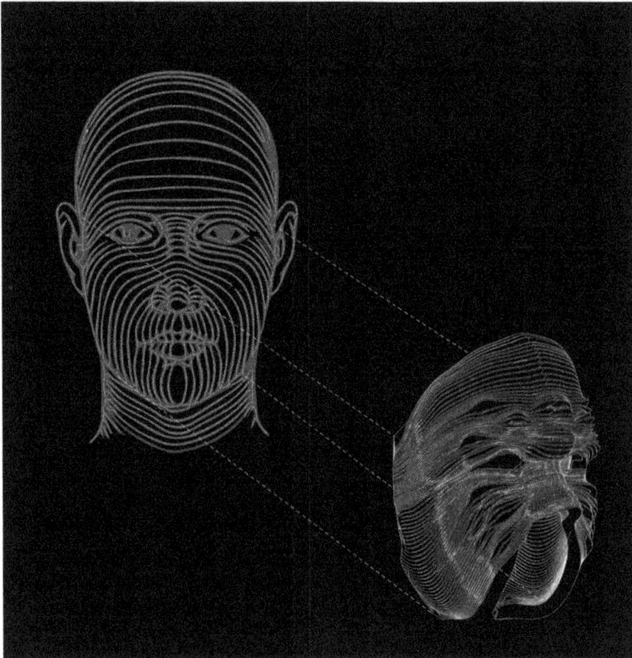

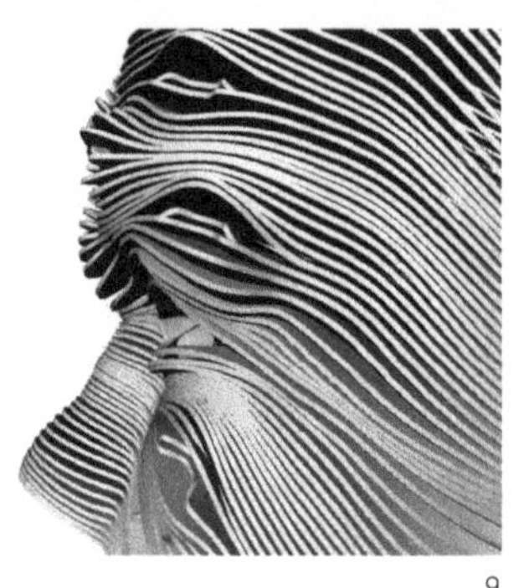

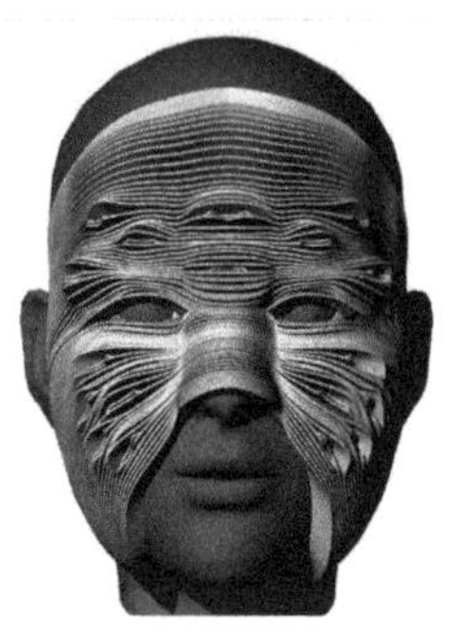

8 The Langer lines of the human face inform the design of the mask.

9 The mask was fabricated using SLS 3D-printing technologies and holds small electromagnetic actuators.

10 This mask is designed using Grasshopper, Rhino (Rutten 2020; Robert McNeel & Associates 2020).

be undermined by that which they cannot understand. Knowledge is power, and an inability to understand unnerves those who wish to maintain their authority.

The project presented in this paper brings these three examples together—the subversion of the Niqab mask, the unnerving behavior of the AI bots, and the use of code to deliver secret messages—to develop a subversive strategy to empower women under patriarchy (Figs. 1, 3, 7).

MASK DESIGN

The design of these 3D-printed masks is informed by the Langer Lines of the human skin. Karl Langer (1819–1887), a Viennese anatomist, spent most of his life studying skin. He identified topological lines on the human body, now known as Langer Lines, that correspond to the natural orientation of fibers in the dermis and are perpendicular to the orientation of the muscle fiber underneath. With their specific orientations, these lines on the face define the facial movements and consequently various types of facial expressions (Fig. 8). The masks were fabricated using selective laser sintering (SLS) 3D-printing technologies and designed to hold small electromagnetic actuators (Fig. 9).

Each mask consists of 18 micro electromagnetic actuators with fake eyelashes, which give the illusion of 18 blinking eyes looking at the viewer. The actuator used in this project is able to rotate around one axis according to the polarity of an electrically controlled magnetic coil (Fig. 10).

One of the challenging tasks was to control the behavior of the array of electromagnetic actuators using custom-made electrical boards (PCBs) that receive the signals from the microcontroller and translate them to electrical impulses controlling the rotation of each actuator. The PCB driver boards are designed to leverage the mature ecosystem built around light emitting diodes (LEDs). By using existing open source code libraries, we were able to take advantage of code that had been optimized to run on small microcontrollers that then drive thousands of LEDs and control the rotation of each actuator (Fig. 14).

We also produced a very small custom-made proximity sensor (VCNCL4040 with FPC), which is embedded in the mask above the wearer's eye and tracks the openness of the wearer's eyelid. This information controls the speed of actuator movements (Figs. 12, 13). Technically speaking, each of the six actuators is connected to a custom-made electrical board driver on each mask. Three PCB driver boards, a small microcontroller, and a small proximity sensor are all embedded in the mask (Fig. 15).

MACHINE LEARNING TEXT GENERATOR

Consider this sentence: "Other as the subject pretends it has 'no geo-political.'" This sentence makes little sense. That's because it was not written by a human but produced by a machine using a Markov chain, a common machine learning algorithm for simulating statistically modeled random processes. As Deju et al. (2009, 163) state, "The main principle of using Markov chain to predict is to build Markov forecasting model that predicts the state of an object in a certain period of time in the future by virtue of probability vector of the initial state and state transition probability matrix." Basically, it is a system that transitions between states using transition probabilities—for instance, the probability of a sunny day after a full day of rain.

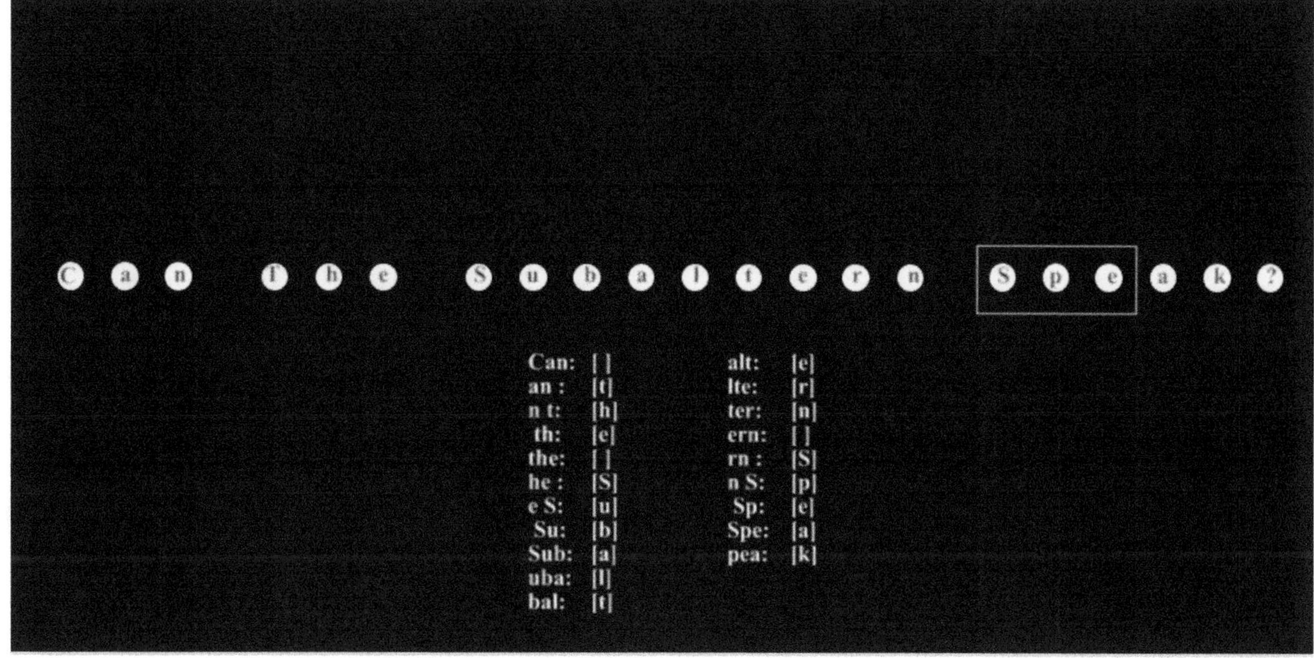

11 Trigrams could be used to generate a text where each new letter is dependent on the previous three letters.

Markov chains have been used for a variety of applications. For instance, Google uses them to determine the order of search results known as page rank. They have been used for spelling correction and speech recognition systems. They can also be used to predict the weather. Last but not least, they are used by economists to predict the price of assets and properties.

Now let's look at the use of Markov chain for text generation. Consider the sentence "Sky is blue." In this example, in the word-scale, the probability of "is" going after "sky" and "blue" going after "is" is considered 100%. If you add another sentence, for example "Weather is cold," the probability of "is" going after either "weather" or "sky" is going to be 100% while the probability of the world "cold" or "blue" after "is" is 50%. The idea is that you can generate states based on the current state and probability of what can come after that. And so you can keep generating words based on their given contexts.

For the source text of this project I used the seminal article "Can the Subaltern Speak?" by feminist theorist Gayatri Spivak (1985). Let's consider the title of this article: "Can_the_Subaltern_Speak?" Similar to the previous example, the point of this example is to show we can use a Markov chain to create a text. We can represent each word as a state, and transitions as the likelihood that a specific word goes after another, which in this case is 100%. We can consider states at the level of words or characters. At the character level, we can analyze the probability of a given letter appearing after three letters. For instance, the probability of "_" after "the" or "s" after "he_." In the fields of computational linguistics and probability this is known as N-grams, which are "a contiguous sequence of N items from a given sample of text or speech" (Li et al. 2020). In the case of the previous example, our N-gram is 3, which is also known as a trigram. The N-gram of a given text provides a strategy for generating the subsequent text. As such, the Markov chain could be used to generate a text where each new letter is dependent on the previous letters (Fig. 11).

Technically speaking, each letter generated through this process is sent to a microcontroller using serial communication, and translated into Morse code, which informs the movement of the actuators. Morse code is a standardized sequence of two different signal durations called dots and dashes. For instance, the letter H is dot-dot-dot-dot and W is dot-dash-dash. Morse code can be transmitted as either a radio signal or an audio tone. In this case, the transmission takes the form of opening and closing of eyelashes. With Morse code, the dot represents a short signal equal to one unit of time, and the dash represents a long signal equal to three units of time. The space between the parts of a letter is one unit of time, the space between two consecutive letters is three units of time, and the space between the words is seven units of time.

To compute this information, each mask is equipped with a microcontroller (Adafruit Feather nRF52 Bluefruit), a small proximity sensor that tracks the movement of the wearer's eyelid, 18 electromagnetic actuators, and 3 PCB driver

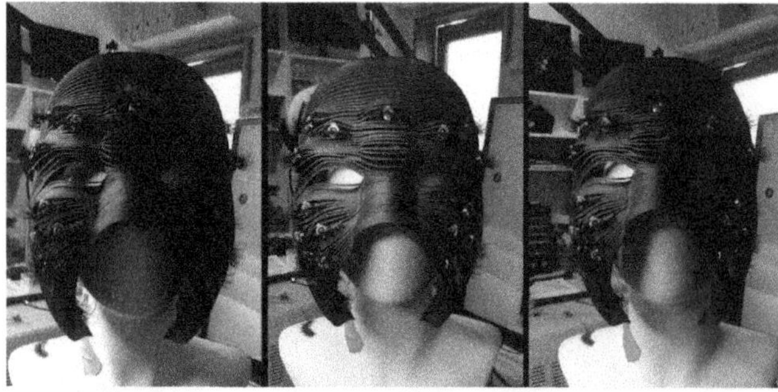

12

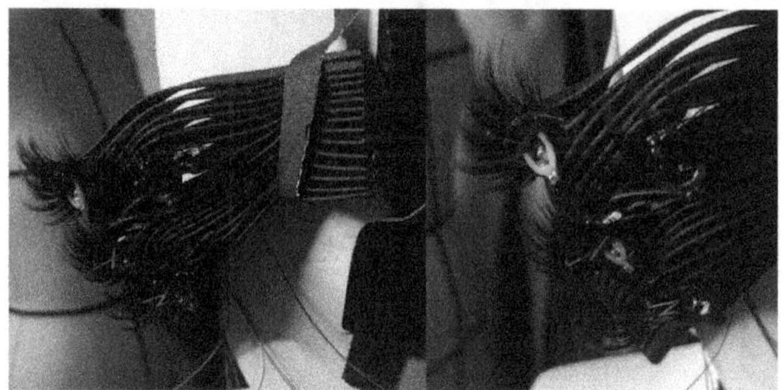

13

14

boards. As the masks communicate with each other using BLE protocol, the algorithm is repeated and the N-gram changes for a given sentence. The smaller the N-gram gets, the less meaning in the generated text from a linguistic perspective. After the N-gram reaches 1, the system generates a new sentence and the N-gram returns to 5.

Here is an example of how a text might mutate using N-grams:

- N-gram = 5: Can the subaltern speak?
- N-gram = 4: Can subaltern subalter?
- N-gram = 3: Caltern subaltern sub?
- N-gram = 2: Can suban suban sper?

Meanwhile, each mask also receives biometric information by tracking the openness of the wearer's eyelid in real time, and records, analyzes, and learns from the movement of the opposite mask. This informs the speed of the blinking actuators as well as the number associated with N-grams. Through a feedback loop between the wearers' masks and bodies, a nonverbal language emerges (Fig. 11). The aim is to sow anxiety within the patriarchal system by developing a new language that unnerves the patriarchal oppressor, and gives voice to the subaltern.

OPPORTUNITIES, CHALLENGES, AND FUTURE DIRECTION

The documentation of this project shows two women wearing masks covered with eyelashes controlled by a machine learning algorithm. They begin to develop their own language to communicate with each other, blinking their eyelashes in rapid succession, using Morse code. Here the wink of the sexual predator is subverted into a language that protects the female figures from the predator's advances. The aim is to develop a secret language for transmitting information between multiple women.

It is important to point out that developing a new language is extremely challenging. There are two main reasons. First, while AI systems such as Siri and IBM's Watson can answer basic questions, some might argue that these systems might not have any real understanding of the meaning of the words they use. Second, the production of language has a complex set of requirements. As Noah Goodman of Stanford University's Department of Psychology states, "Language is special in that it relies on a lot of knowledge about language but it also relies on a huge amount of common-sense knowledge about the world, and those two go together in very subtle ways" (Knight 2016). Goodman and his team developed a programming language called Webppl that gives the computer a type of probabilistic common sense rather than a literal meaning of a given word.

More recently, Generative Pre-trained Transformer 3 (GPT-3) from OpenAI (founded by Elon Musk, Sam Altman, and Greg Brockman) is an autoregressive language model that uses deep learning to produce texts. The results of GPT-3 are quite convincing, to the point that in many cases it is difficult to distinguish it from a text written by a human. David Chalmers (2020), an Australian philosopher

12 Prototyping and behavior study.

13 Detailed view of the electromagnetic actuators.

14 Soldering a PCB driver board to electromagnetic actuators and a microcontroller.

15 Each mask consists of a total of 18 micro electromagnetic actuators with fake eyelashes, which give the illusion of 18 blinking eyes looking at the viewer. The actuator used in this project is able to rotate around one axis according to the polarity of electrically-controlled magnetic coil.

who specializes in consciousness, says that GPT-3 is "one of the most interesting and important AI systems ever produced." While we are most familiar with human intelligence, as sociologist, architectural and design theorist Benjamin Bratton suggests, there are many types of intelligence, including other species' intelligence. As he puts it, "Airplanes don't fly like birds fly, and we certainly don't try to trick birds into thinking that airplanes are birds in order to test whether those planes 'really' are flying machines. Why do it for A.I. then?" (Bratton 2015, 196). Bratton thinks that these problems arise because we tend to see intelligence essentially limited to our own human intelligence—what Bratton calls sapience—rather than an emergent capacity of any matter and machines. He explains, "We count functional intelligence imbued with performances of sensing and effecting, observing and modeling, governing and expressing, etc. They reflect the all-too-human biases of their creators but may also exceed their language altogether, rendering a world that is right at hand but uncannily alien" (Bratton 2019, 16).

While the project presented in this paper is in an early stage in terms of developing a new language and could benefit from using more advanced deep learning models such as GPT-3, it offers an insight into how we might think beyond linguistic production so as to allow machines to develop a new language that could emerge and evolve in interaction with humans and learn from its own mistakes. It also offers insights into nonverbal communication (in this case the blinking of artificial eyelashes) and takes us one step closer to intelligence as observed in various species.

Obviously, this requires many years of experience with such technologies, but one might assume that if women were asked to wear such masks, they might learn to participate in the production of a new type of language.

Last but not least, apart from being a social and political commentary on ways of subverting patriarchy, this project offers insights into how masks could be seen as an opportunity for communication and social interaction. In light of the COVID-19 pandemic, where we have to cover our faces and our facial emotional expressions are masked, it is important to think about how we express ourselves and communicate. This could particularly benefit those who suffer from auditory impairment and those who suffer from hearing loss.

ACKNOWLEDGMENTS

I would like to thank Julian Ceipek and Paolo Salvagione for their valuable contributions to this project. I would also like to thank Sussan Deyhim for the impactful music and sound design. The video can be watched at https://vimeo.com/416233417.

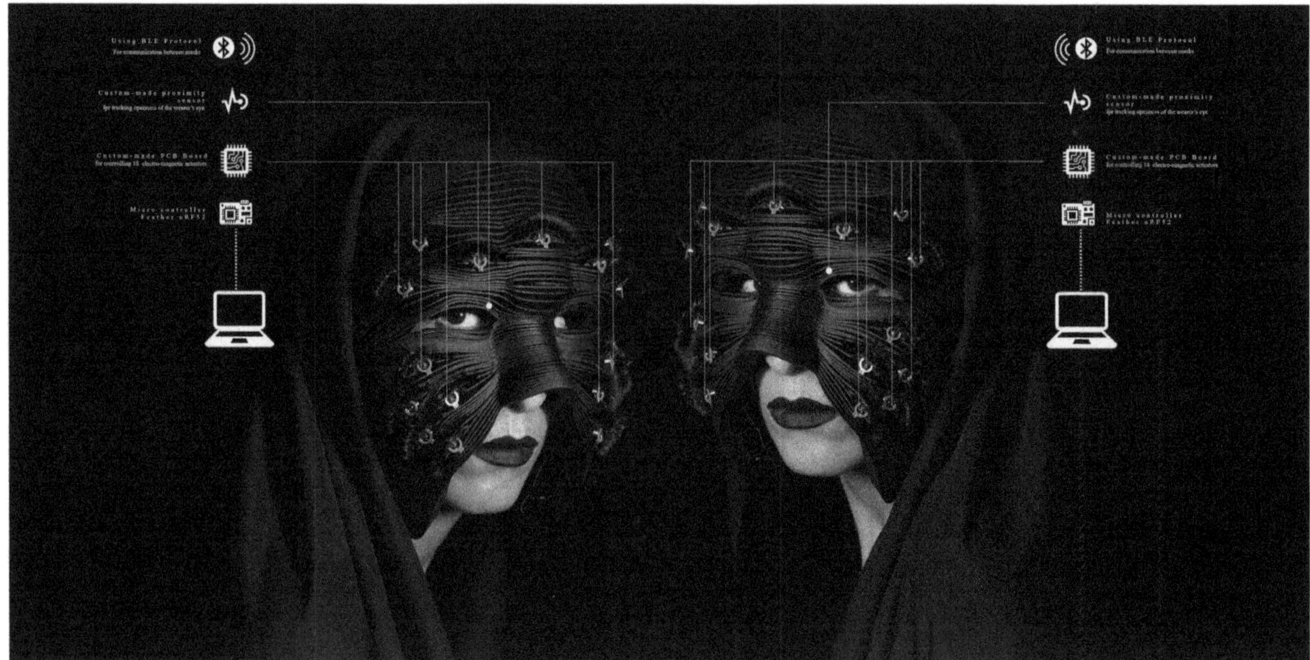

16 The masks communicate using BLE protocol.

REFERENCES

Bratton, Benjamin H. 2015. "Outing AI: Beyond the Turing Test in 'Artificial Intelligence'." In *Artificial Intelligence (Looking Forward)*, edited by the New York Times Editorial Staff. New York: New York Times Educational Publishing.

Bratton, Benjamin H. 2019. "Further Trace Effects of the Post-Anthropocene." In *Machine Landscapes: Architectures of the Post Anthropocene*, edited by Liam Young. Oxford: Wiley.

Chalmers, David. 2020. "GPT-3 and General Intelligence." *Daily Nous*, July 30. https://dailynous.com/2020/07/30/philosophers-gpt-3/.

Deju, Zhang, and Xiaomin Zhang. 2009. "Study on Forecasting the Stock Market Trend Based on Stochastic Analysis Method." *International Journal of Business and Management* 4. DOI:10.5539/ijbm.v4n6p163.

Dunne, Anthony, and Fiona Raby. 2013. *Speculative Everything: Design, Fiction, and Social Dreaming*. Cambridge, MA: MIT Press.

Hertz, Garnet. 2009. "What Is Critical Making?" *Current* 08. https://current.ecuad.ca/what-is-critical-making.

Knight, Will. 2016. "AI's Language Problem." *MIT Technology Review*, August 9. https://www.technologyreview.com/2016/08/09/158125/ais-language-problem.

Lewis, Mike, Denis Yarats, Yann N. Dauphin, Devi Parikh, and Dhruv Batra. 2017. "Deal or No Deal? End-to-End Learning for Negotiation Dialogues." https://arxiv.org/pdf/1706.05125.pdf.

Li, Y., Y. Jiang, J. C. Goldstein, L. J. McGibbney, and C. Yang. 2020. "A Query Understanding Framework for Earth Data Discovery." *Applied Sciences* 10: 1127.

Ratto, M., and S. Hockema. 2009. "FLWR PWR: Tending the Walled Garden." In *Walled Garden*, edited by Annet Dekker and Annette Wolfsberger. Amsterdam: Virtueel Platform.

Robert McNeel & Associates. 2020. *Rhinoceros*. V.6.0. Robert McNeel & Associates. PC.

Rutten, David. 2020. *Grasshopper*. V.1.0.0007. Robert McNeel & Associates. PC.

Spivak, Gayatri Chakravorty. 1988. "Can the Subaltern Speak?" In *Marxism and the Interpretation of Culture*, edited by Cary Nelson and Lawrence Grossberg. Basingstoke: Macmillan.

Traum, David, Stacy C. Marsella, Jonathan Gratch, Jina Lee, and Arno Hartholt. 2008. "Multi-party, Multi-issue, Multi-strategy Negotiation for Multi-modal Virtual Agents." In *Proceedings of the 8th International Conference on Intelligent Virtual Agents, Heidelberg, IVA '08*, 117–130. Berlin: Springer-Verlag.

Wodiczko, Krzysztof. 1999. *Critical Vehicles: Writings, Projects, Interviews*. Cambridge, Mass: The MIT Press.

World Building Institute. n.d. "Alex McDowell RDI." Accessed May 15, 2021. https://worldbuilding.institute/people/alex-mcdowell.

IMAGE CREDITS

Figure 2: © Eric Lafforgue. http://www.bbc.com/travel/gallery/20170106-the-mysterious-masked-women-of-iran.

Figure 4: "What an AI's Non-Human Language Actually Looks Like." From https://www.theatlantic.com/technology/archive/2017/06/what-an-ais-non-human-language-actually-looks-like/530934/.

Figure 5: "Navy to name warship after heroic Vietnam POW." From https://www.navytimes.com/news/your-navy/2019/01/04/navy-to-name-warship-after-heroic-vietnam-pow/.

Figure 6: "This hand signal alerts others to domestic abuse without a word." From https://www.vicnews.com/news/video-this-hand-signal-alerts-others-to-domestic-abuse-without-a-word/.

All other drawings and images by the author.

Behnaz Farahi trained as an architect and is an award-winning designer and critical maker based in Los Angeles. She holds a PhD in Interdisciplinary Media Arts and Practice from USC School of Cinematic Arts and is currently Assistant Professor of Design at California State University, Long Beach. She is a coeditor of an issue of *AD*, "3D Printed Body Architecture" (2017), and "Interactive Future" (forthcoming). www.behnazfarahi.com.

DISTRIBUTED PROXIMITIES

ACADIA 2020 CREDITS

CONFERENCE CHAIRS

Viola Ago is an architectural designer, educator, and practitioner. She directs MIRACLES Architecture and is the current Wortham Fellow at the Rice University School of Architecture. Previously, Viola held the Christos Yessios Visiting Professorship at the Knowlton School of Architecture at OSU and the William Muschenheim Design Fellowship position at the Taubman College of Architecture, University of Michigan. Viola has also previously taught at Harvard's GSD, RISD School of Architecture, and SCI-Arc. She earned her M.Arch degree from SCI-Arc and a B.ArchSci from Ryerson University in Toronto. Prior to teaching, Viola worked as a lead designer in the Advanced Technology Team at Morphosis Architects in Los Angeles.

Viola's work has been exhibited in Los Angeles, Boston, Houston, Ghent NY, San Francisco, Miami, Columbus, Ann Arbor, and Cincinnati. Her written work has been published in *Log*, *AD Architectural Design Magazine* (Wiley), *Instabilities and Potentialities* (Routledge), Sci-Arc's *Offramp*, ACADIA Conference Proceedings, *TxA Emerging Design and Technology*, *Journal of Architectural Education*, *Architect's Newspaper*, and Archinect. Viola held a digital fabrication residency at the Autodesk Build Space in Boston, a University Design and Research Fellowship with Exhibit Columbus, and an artist residency at the MacDowell Colony.

Dr. Matias del Campo, a registered architect and designer, is an Associate Professor of Architecture at the University of Michigan's Taubman College of Architecture and Urban Planning. He is best known for the application of contemporary technologies in architectural production. His award-winning architectural designs are informed by computational methodologies (Artificial Intelligence, Algorithmic Modeling), contemporary theory, and philosophical inquiry. In 2003, he co-founded (with Sandra Manninger) the architectural practice SPAN in Vienna. SPAN gained wide recognition for its winning competition entry for the Austrian Pavilion at the 2010 Shanghai World Expo, as well as the new Brancusi Museum in Paris.

SPAN's work was featured at Venice Biennale in 2012; at ArchiLab 2013 in Orléans, France; at Architecture Biennale in Beijing in 2008 and 2010; and in the solo show, "Formations" at the Museum of Applied Arts (MAK) in Vienna in 2011. In 2017, SPAN's work was shown in a solo exhibition at the Fab Union Gallery in Shanghai. Most recently, del Campo was awarded the Accelerate@CERN Fellowship, served as technical chair of the ACADIA 2016 Conference, and guest-edited an issue of *Architectural Design*.

He earned his Master of Architecture from the University of Applied Arts Vienna and his PhD from the Royal Melbourne Institute of Technology.

Shelby Elizabeth Doyle, AIA is a registered architect, co-founder of the ISU Computation & Construction Lab (CCL), and an Assistant Professor of Architecture at Iowa State University, where she teaches design studios and seminars in digital technology. Her education includes a Fulbright Fellowship to Cambodia, a Master of Architecture from the Harvard Graduate School of Design, and a Bachelor of Science in Architecture from the University of Virginia.

The central hypothesis of her research, and of the CCL, is that computation in architecture is a material, pedagogical, and social project; computation is both informed by and productive of architectural cultures. This hypothesis is explored through the fabrication of built projects, writing, exhibition, and material explorations. The CCL is invested in questioning the role of education and pedagogy in replicating existing technological inequities, and in pursuing the potential for technology in architecture as a space of and for gender equity.

Adam Marcus is a licensed and registered architect and educator. He directs Variable Projects, an independent architecture practice in Oakland, and he is a partner in Futures North, a Minneapolis-based public art collaborative dedicated to exploring the aesthetics of data. Adam is an Associate Professor of Architecture at California College of the Arts in San Francisco, where he teaches design studios in computational design and digital fabrication, co-directs the Architectural Ecologies Lab, and collaborates with CCA's Digital Craft Lab. From 2011 to 2013, Adam was Cass Gilbert Assistant Professor at University of Minnesota School of Architecture, where he chaired the symposium "Digital Provocations: Emerging Computational Approaches to Pedagogy & Practice." He has also taught at Columbia University and the Architectural Association's Visiting School Los Angeles. Adam is a graduate of Brown University and Columbia University's Graduate School of Architecture, Planning and Preservation.

Brian Slocum holds a Master of Architecture from the Graduate School of Architecture, Planning and Preservation of Columbia University and a Bachelor of Science in Architecture from Georgia Tech. He is currently an Adjunct Professor in the Department of Architecture, Urbanism, and Civil Engineering at the Universidad Iberoamericana in Mexico City, where he teaches a design studio entitled Exogenous Protocols//Endogenous Properties (#prexpren), which focuses on analog material research employing computational and performative design strategies. Brian is the founder of tresRobots, an independent studio for design and architectural technologies research and co-founder of the architecture firm Diverse Projects, with offices in the United States and Mexico; he is licensed in the State of New York. In 2008, Brian was the recipient of an Individual Research Grant for ad hoc infrastructures from the New York State Council on the Arts. He was also a participant in the group exhibition *Landscapes of Quarantine* at Storefront for Art and Architecture in 2009-2010, where he presented *Context/Shift*, a prosthetic piece installed on a door panel in the gallery designed by the architect Steven Holl and the artist Vito Acconci. Brian has also contributed essays to the journal *CLOG* and *Pamphlet Architecture #23: MOVE Sites of Trauma*, by Johanna Saleh Dickson. Brian currently serves as the Secretary for the Association for Computer Aided Design in Architecture (ACADIA), and was Conference Co-chair for ACADIA 2018 Mexico City, *Recalibration: On Imprecision and Infidelity*.

Maria Yablonina is an architect, researcher, and artist working in the field of computational design and digital fabrication. Her work lies at the intersection of architecture and robotics, producing spaces and robotic systems that can construct themselves and change in real-time. Such architectural productions include the development of hardware and software solutions, as well as complementing architectural and material systems in order to offer new design spaces.

Maria's practice focuses on designing machines that make architecture, a practice that she broadly describes as Designing [with] Machines (D[w]M). D[w]M aims to investigate and establish design methodologies that consider robotic hardware development as part of the overall design process and its output. Through this work, Maria argues for a design practice that moves beyond the design of objects towards the design of technologies and processes that enable new ways of both creating and interacting with architectural spaces.

Maria has been commissioned and exhibited by institutions including Milan Design Week, Ars Electronica (Linz), Kapelica Gallery (Ljubljana), The Cooper Union, and the Moscow Institute of Architecture. She has also collaborated internationally on research with both universities and companies, including Autodesk Pier 9 (San Francisco), ETH Zurich, WeWork (New York), and the Bartlett School of Architecture (London).

SESSION CHAIRS

Viola Ago is an architectural designer, educator, and practitioner. She directs MIRACLES Architecture and is the current Wortham Fellow at the Rice University School of Architecture. Previously, Viola held the Christos Yessios Visiting Professorship at the Knowlton School of Architecture at OSU and the William Muschenheim Design Fellowship position at the Taubman College of Architecture, University of Michigan. Viola has also previously taught at Harvard's GSD, RISD School of Architecture, and SCI-Arc. She earned her M.Arch degree from SCI-Arc and a B.ArchSci from Ryerson University in Toronto. Prior to teaching, Viola worked as a lead designer in the Advanced Technology Team at Morphosis Architects in Los Angeles.

Viola's work has been exhibited in Los Angeles, Boston, Houston, Ghent NY, San Francisco, Miami, Columbus, Ann Arbor, and Cincinnati. Her written work has been published in *Log, AD Architectural Design Magazine* (Wiley), *Instabilities and Potentialities* (Routledge), Sci-Arc's *Offramp*, ACADIA Conference Proceedings, *TxA Emerging Design and Technology*, *Journal of Architectural Education*, *Architect's Newspaper*, and Archinect. Viola held a digital fabrication residency at the Autodesk Build Space in Boston, a University Design and Research Fellowship with Exhibit Columbus, and an artist residency at the MacDowell Colony.

Masoud Akbarzadeh is a designer with a wide academic background and experience in architectural design, computation, and structural engineering. He is an Assistant Professor of Architecture in Structures and Advanced Technologies and the Director of the Polyhedral Structures Laboratory (PSL). He holds a D.Sc. from the Institute of Technology in Architecture, ETH Zurich, a Master of Science in Architecture Studies (Computation), and a M.Arch from MIT. He also has a degree in Earthquake Engineering and Dynamics of Structures from the Iran University of Science and Technology and a BS in Civil and Environmental Engineering. His main research topic is Three-Dimensional Graphical Statics, a novel geometric method of structural design in three dimensions. He has published widely in various peer-reviewed journals and received multiple awards, including the renowned SOM award for his architecture thesis in 2011 and the National Science Foundation CAREER Award in 2020 to extend 3D/Polyhedral Graphic Statics for Education, Design, and Optimization of High-Performance Structures.

Marcella Del Signore is an architect, urbanist, educator, scholar, and the principal of X-Topia, a design-research practice that explores the intersection of architecture and urbanism with technology and the public, social and cultural realm. She is an Associate Professor and Director of the Master of Science in Architecture, Urban and Regional Design at the New York Institute of Technology, School of Architecture and Design. Her research focuses on interscalar design approaches that engage socio-technical systems through computation, prototyping, material and fabricated assemblies, data-driven protocols, and adaptive environments. She is the author of Urban Machines: Public Space in a Digital Culture (LISTLab, 2018; OROEditions, 2020; with G. Riether) and the editor of *Data, Matter, Design: Strategies in Computational Design* (2020, Routledge; with F. Melendez, N. Diniz). In 2018, she co-edited *Recalibration: On Imprecision and Infidelity* paper and project proceedings (with P. Anzalone and A. J. Wit) published during the 2018 ACADIA Conference where she served as technical co-chair. In 2018, she co-curated the 'Data & Matter' exhibition at the ECC during the 2018 Architecture Venice Biennale, and she is currently invited to exhibit at the 17th Architecture Venice Biennale in 2021.

Maya Alam is a German/Indian architect and designer. She holds a degree of Dipl. Ing. of Interior Architecture from the Behrens School of Arts in Düsseldorf and a Master of Architecture with Distinction from the Southern California Institute of Architecture in Los Angeles. Maya was the inaugural recipient of the 2016/17 Harry der Boghosian Fellowship. She was awarded the AIA Henry Adams Certificate and a Selected Best Thesis Award at SCI-Arc. She has worked in Germany, India, Switzerland, China, Italy, and the United States with P-A-T-T-E-R-N-S, NMDA, UNStudio, and Studio Fuksas, among others. She has taught at Southern California Institute of Architecture, Syracuse University, and Yale University and is currently part of the faculty at the University of Pennsylvania, Weitzman School of Design.

Maya is one of the founding partners of Alam/Profeta, a collaborative partnership with Daniele Profeta. Their projects combine everyday digital habits, contemporary imaging technologies, and traditional craftsmanship to surpass an introverted conversation and open up novel forms of practice. Past work ranges from small scale public installations to sites of speculative re-use. Weaving existing conditions with contemporary manufacturing technologies and aesthetics, engaging with the heterogeneous, often contradictory set of evidences of a given context, their practice focuses on constructing inclusive interventions that embrace and critically address the multi-faceted nature of our reality.

The work of A/P Practice has received support from the Smithsonian National Museum of American History in Washington DC, the Anchorage Museum in Alaska, the A+D Museum of Architecture and Design in Los Angeles, Syracuse University, Kent State University and the Festival des Architectures Vives in Montpellier, France.

Biayna Bogosian's academic and professional background extends in the fields of architecture, environmental design, computational design, data science, and immersive media design. Biayna's interdisciplinary research has allowed her to understand innovation in design and technology within a broader environmental context and explore data-driven and participatory methods for improving the built environment. Biayna is a PhD candidate in the Media Arts and Practice (iMAP) program at the USC School Cinematic Arts. Her dissertation focuses on the application of participatory immersive media for environmental monitoring, literacy, and policymaking. She is currently an Assistant Professor of Architectural Technology at Florida International University (FIU), where her research is supported by several National Science Foundation (NSF) grants. She has also taught at Columbia University GSAPP, Cornell University AAP, University of Southern California SoA, and Tongji University CAUP, and the American University of Armenia among other universities. She has been one of the co-organizers of the DigitalFUTURES World 2020 events and CAAD Futures 2021 conference.

June Grant, RA, NOMA, is Founder and Design Principal at blink!LAB architecture; a boutique research-based architecture and urban design practice. Launched in 2014, blink!LAB is based on Ms. Grant's 20 years of experience in architecture, design and the urban regeneration of cities and communities. Her design approach rests on an avid belief in cultural empathy, data research and new technologies as integral to design futures and design solutions. blink!LAB has three mandates: A commitment to Design Exploration, Advocacy for Holistic Solutions, and the Integration of Technology as a central component for a regenerative society.

Ms. Grant is also the current President of the San Francisco Chapter of the National Organization of Minority Architects (SFNOMA).

Kevin Hirth is an Assistant Professor at the University of Colorado Denver College of Architecture and Planning, and the founder of Kevin Hirth Co, which he began in 2013. He holds a Master's of Architecture with distinction from the Harvard Graduate School of Design and a Bachelor's of Science in Architecture from the University of Virginia.

The work of his firm focuses on the rural and urban condition of the American West. Projects in exploration include single family homes down unnamed roads in the mountain wilds and mixed-use towers pushing up against the edge of the Midwestern plains.

In 2017, he was awarded the Architectural League of New York's League Prize. In 2020 he was awarded an Architects Newspaper Best of Design Award.

Dr. Negar Kalantar is an Associate Professor of Architecture and a Co-Director of Digital Craft Lab at California College of the Arts (CCA) in San Francisco. Her cross-disciplinary research focuses on materials exploration, robotic and additive manufacturing technologies and engaging architecture, science, and engineering as platforms for examining the critical role of design in global issues and built environments.

Kalantar is the recipient of several awards and grants, including the Dornfeld Manufacturing Vision Award 2018, the National Science Foundation, Autodesk Technology Center Grant, and X-Grant 2018 from the Texas A&M President's Excellence Fund on developing sustainable material for 3-D printed buildings.

Some of the outcomes of her work have been featured in *The Guardian*, on the BBC, in science-focused magazines, and by the National Science Foundation. Her research has been presented at the Technical University of Vienna and Berlin, ETH Zurich, University of Maryland, Tehran University, Virginia Tech, Texas A&M University, and New York 3D Print Show. She has organized national and international workshops on additive manufacturing, robotics, and materials advancement in digital fabrication and architecture.

Christoph Klemmt received his diploma from the Architectural Association in London in 2004. He is Assistant Professor at the Department of Design, Art, Architecture and Planning at the University of Cincinnati, where he received a grant to set up the Architectural Robotics Lab. He taught and gave workshops at the AA Visiting Schools, Tsinghua University, Tongji University, and he directed the AA Visiting School at the Angewandte in Vienna.

He worked amongst others for Zaha Hadid Architects and Tezuka Architects. In 2008 he co-founded Orproject, an architect's office specialising in advanced geometries with an ecologic agenda. Orproject exhibited at the Palais De Tokyo in Paris, the China National Museum in Beijing and the Biennale in Venice. The work of Orproject was featured world-wide in magazines and books such as *Domus*, *Frame*, and *AD*, and the practice won several international Awards.

Mara Marcu is an Assistant Professor at the University of Cincinnati, School of Architecture and Interior Design. She is the founder of MMXIII (Merely Maybe x Idyllic Imagination Inflicted—or simply—MM Thirteen). She structures her work around various collections, focused on the peculiar and the outcast over the ever-changing architectural style.

Leslie Lok is an Assistant Professor at Cornell University Department of Architecture and a co-founder at HANNAH, an experimental design practice for built and speculative projects across scales. HANNAH's work utilizes novel material applications and innovative forms of construction to address subjects of architecture and urbanism. The work aims to mine the tension between machine means and architectural ends. Her teaching and research explore the intersection of housing, urbanization, and mass-customized construction methods. She has previously taught at McGill University and received her Master of Architecture from MIT.

HANNAH is the recipient of the 2020 Architectural League Prize and was named Next Progressives by Architect Magazine in 2018. Her contributions were exhibited at the 2019 Bi-City Biennale of Urbanism/ Architecture in Shenzhen, Art OMI, the Pinkcomma Gallery, the Momentary, and the Canadian Centre for Architecture. Her work has been published at FABRICATE, Rob|Arch, and ACADIA, as well as featured in *Architectural Record*, the *New York Times*, *Dwell*, and *Digital Trends*, among others.

Sandra Manninger is a registered architect and educator.

"In her office, SPAN Architecture, that she founded together with Matias del Campo in 2003, she is constructing an epistemological framework from practice and procedures that are based on the newly acquired knowledge that we increasingly employ through science and technology. The result does not come from a formal effort, but rather as a consequence of a union of evolutionary attempts based on very rigid design procedures. These involve design protocols that go beyond the tools itself, leaving space for a true ecology of digital thinking. The research highlights how to go beyond beautiful data to discover something that could be defined voluptuous data. This coagulation of numbers, algorithms, procedures and programs uses the forces of thriving nature and, passing through the calculation of multi-core processors, knits them with human desire."

— Excerpts from Sabina Barcucci, *digimag* 64

Tsz Yan Ng's material-based research and design primarily focus on experimental concrete forming (hard) and textile manipulation (soft), often times in direct exchange and incorporating contemporary technologies to develop novel designs for building and manufacturing. A common thread to her work investigates questions of labor in various facets and forms – underscoring broader issues of industrial manufacturing innovation, of human labor, crafting, and aesthetics. She's the principal of an independent architecture and art practice and works collaboratively across disciplines and scales. She joined Taubman College, University of Michigan as the Walter B. Sanders Fellow (2007-2008) and is currently an Assistant Professor. She was also the Reyner Banham Fellow at the University of Buffalo from 2001-2002. Her co-edited book *Twisted* was released in 2018 and was co-editor for the *JAE* theme issue *Work* (2019).

Alida Sun is an artist, futurist, and activist based in Berlin and New York. Her practice comprises building extended realities both virtual and augmented, machine learning paradigms, and interactive installations. Her current projects include developing decolonial protocols in AI and blockchain techology, exploring anti-fascist traditions in performing arts and digital culture with Düsseldorf Schauspielhaus, and generating immersive cyberfeminist narratives for Transmediale. She graduated from RISD with a BFA in Industrial Design. Her works have been presented in new media exhibitions and audiovisual festivals around the world.

DISTRIBUTED PROXIMITIES

ACADIA ORGANIZATION

The Association for Computer Aided Design in Architecture (ACADIA) is an international network of digital design researchers and professionals that facilitates critical investigations into the role of computation in architecture, planning, and building science, encouraging innovation in design creativity, sustainability and education.

ACADIA was founded in 1981 by some of the pioneers in the field of design computation including Bill Mitchell, Chuck Eastman, and Chris Yessios. Since then, ACADIA has hosted 40 conferences across North America and has grown into a strong network of academics and professionals in the design computation field.

Incorporated in the state of Delaware as a not-for-profit corporation, ACADIA is an all-volunteer organization governed by elected officers, an elected Board of Directors, and appointed ex-officio officers.

DISTRIBUTED PROXIMITIES

CONFERENCE MANAGEMENT

CONFERENCE CHAIRS

Viola Ago, Wortham Fellow, Rice University

Matias del Campo, Associate Professor, University of Michigan Taubman College of Architecture and Urban Planning

Shelby Doyle, Assistant Professor, Iowa State University

Adam Marcus, Associate Professor, California College of the Arts

Brian Slocum, Adjunct Professor, Universidad Iberoamericana

Maria Yablonina, Assistant Professor, John H. Daniels Faculty, University of Toronto

SPECIAL ADVISOR

Kathy Velikov, Associate Professor, University of Michigan Taubman College of Architecture and Urban Planning

CONFERENCE PLATFORM DESIGN & FULLSTACK ENGINEERING

Oliver Popadich, AltF4 Design

MMMURMUR CHAT PLATFORM

Ultan Byrne, PhD student in architecture, GSAPP, Columbia University

TECHNICAL ASSISTANTS

Jiries Alali, California College of the Arts

Pablo Espinal Henao, John H. Daniels Faculty, University of Toronto

David Kalman, John H. Daniels Faculty, University of Toronto

CONFERENCE WEBSITE

Adam Marcus

COPY EDITING

Rachel Fudge, **Paula Woolley**, **Mary O'Malley**

GRAPHIC IDENTITY

Adam Marcus, **Viola Ago**, **Alejandro Sánchez Velasco**

GRAPHIC DESIGN

Alejandro Sánchez Velasco

LAYOUT

Carolyn Francis, **Sebastian Lopez**, **Shelby Doyle**, **Adam Marcus**

DISTRIBUTED PROXIMITIES

PEER REVIEW COMMITTEE

Henri Achten _ *Czech Technical University*
Arash Adel _ *University of Michigan*
Mania Aghaei Meibodi _ *University of Michigan*
Viola Ago _ *Rice University*
Chandler Ahrens _ *Washington University St. Louis*
Masoud Akbarzadeh _ *University of Pennsylvania*
Ayşegül Akçay Kavakoğlu _ *Altınbaş University*
Phillip Anzalone _ *New York Institute of Technology*
German Aparicio _ *Trimble Consulting*
Imdat As _ *Arcbazar / Scientific and Technological Research Council of Turkey*
Dorit Aviv _ *University of Pennsylvania*
Phil Ayres _ *The Royal Danish Academy of Fine Arts*
Pedro Azambuja Varela _ *University of Porto*
Ehsan Baharlou _ *University of Virginia*
Amber Bartosh _ *Syracuse University*
Efilena Baseta _ *IAAC / NOUMENA*
Leighton Beaman _ *University of Virginia*
Steven Beites _ *Laurentian University*
Brad Bell _ *University of Texas Arlington*
Chris Beorkrem _ *University of North Carolina Charlotte*
Bastian Beyer _ *Royal College of Art*
Vishu Bhooshan _ *ZHA Code / ETH Zurich*
Kory Bieg _ *University of Texas Austin*
Biayna Bogosian _ *Florida International University / University of Southern California*
Ronan Bolaños _ *Universidad Nacional Autónoma de México*
Johannes Braumann _ *Robots in Architecture / University of Arts and Industrial Design Linz*
Nicholas Bruscia _ *University at Buffalo*
Jane Burry _ *Swinburne University*
Mark Cabrinha _ *California State Polytechnic University, San Luis Obispo*
Galo Cañizares _ *The Ohio State University*
Bradley Cantrell _ *University of Virginia*
Mario Carpo _ *The Bartlett, University College London*
Juan José Castellón _ *Rice University*
Gonçalo Castro Henriques _ *Florida Atlantic University*
Yichao Chen _ *The Bartlett, University College London*
Angelos Chronis _ *Austrian Institute of Technology / IAAC*
Mollie Claypool _ *The Bartlett, University College London*
Brandon Clifford _ *Massachusetts Institute of Technology*
Andrew Colopy _ *Rice University*
David Costanza _ *Cornell University*
Kristof Crolla _ *Chinese University of Hong Kong*
Dana Cupkova _ *Carnegie Mellon University*
Pierre Cutellic _ *ETH Zurich*
Daniel Davis _ *Hassell / WeWork*
Matias del Campo _ *University of Michigan*
Marcela Delgado _ *Universidad Nacional Autónoma de México*
Marcella Del Signore _ *New York Institute of Technology*
Ilaria Di Carlo _ *The Bartlett, University College London*
Nancy Diniz _ *University of the Arts London*
Antonino Di Raimo _ *University of Portsmouth*
Mark Donohue _ *California College of the Arts*
Shelby Doyle _ *Iowa State University*
Rebeca Duque Estrada _ *University of Stuttgart, PhD Candidate*
Emre Erkal _ *NOMAD / Erkal Architects*
Gabriel Esquivel _ *Texas A&M University*
Alberto Estévez _ *International University of Catalunya*
Behnaz Farahi _ *California State University, Long Beach / University of Southern California*
Iman Fayyad _ *Harvard University*
Yara Feghali _ *University of California, Los Angeles*
Jelle Feringa _ *Aectual*
Antonio Fioravanti _ *Sapienza University Rome*
Wendy Fok _ *Parsons School of Design*
Michael Fox _ *California State Polytechnic University, Pomona*
Pia Fricker _ *Aalto University*
Madeline Gannon _ *Carnegie Mellon University*
Mark Foster Gage _ *Yale University*
Richard Garber _ *University of Pennsylvania*
Jose Luis García del Castillo y López _ *Harvard University*
Guy Erik Gardner _ *University of Calgary*
Jordan Geiger _ *Gekh*
David Gerber _ *University of Southern California*
Andrei Gheorghe _ *University of Applied Arts Vienna*
Daniel Gillen _ *SOM*
Melissa Goldman _ *University of Virginia*
Kyriaki Goti _ *Pratt Institute*
Marcelyn Gow _ *SCI-Arc*
Onur Yüce Gün _ *New Balance / Massachusetts Institute of Technology*
Jeffrey Halstead _ *University of Michigan*
Erik Herrmann _ *The Ohio State University*
Andrew Heumann _ *Hypar / Columbia University GSAPP*
Kevin Hirth _ *University of Colorado Denver*
Zaneta Hong _ *University of Virginia*
Tyson Hosmer _ *The Bartlett, University College London / ZHA Code*
Kayleigh Houde _ *Buro Happold*
Yasushi Ikeda _ *Keio University*
Ryan Johns _ *ETH Zurich*
Jason Kelly Johnson _ *California College of the Arts*
Nathaniel Jones _ *Massachusetts Institute of Technology*
Damjan Jovanovic _ *SCI-Arc*
Negar Kalantar _ *California College of the Arts*
Ed Keller _ *Parsons School of Design*
James Kerestes _ *Ball State University*
Sumbul Khan _ *Singapore University of Technology*

Joachim Kieferle _ *RheinMain University of Applied Sciences*
Axel Kilian _ *Massachusetts Institute of Technology*
Marirena Kladeftira _ *ETH Zurich*
Christoph Klemmt _ *University of Cincinnati*
Chris Knapp _ *Bond University*
Reinhard Koenig _ *Bauhaus University Weimar*
Daniel Köhler _ *University of Texas Austin*
Axel Körner _ *University of Stuttgart*
Sarah Aipra Kott _ *NBBJ Design*
Oliver David Krieg _ *Intelligent City / University of Stuttgart*
Ersela Kripa _ *Texas Tech University*
Kihong Ku _ *Thomas Jefferson University*
Andrew Kudless _ *University of Houston*
Hyojin Kwon _ *Harvard University*
Riccardo La Magna _ *University of Stuttgart*
Rodrigo Langarica _ *Universidad Anáhuac*
Christian Lange _ *University of Hong Kong*
Brian Lonsway _ *Syracuse University*
Gregory Luhan _ *Texas A&M University*
Katie MacDonald _ *University of Virginia*
Mathias Maierhofer _ *University of Stuttgart*
Elena Manferdini _ *SCI-Arc*
Ryan Vincent Manning _ *quirkd33*
Sandra Manninger _ *University of Michigan*
Mara Marcu _ *University of Cincinnati*
Adam Marcus _ *California College of the Arts*
Mathilde Marengo _ *IAAC*
Bob Martens _ *TU Wien*
Matan Mayer _ *IE University*
Malcolm McCullough _ *University of Michigan*
Duane McLemore _ *Mississippi State University*
AnnaLisa Meyboom _ *University of British Columbia*
Philippe Morel _ *ENSAPM / The Bartlett, University College London*
Sina Mostafavi _ *TU Delft*
Stephen Mueller _ *Texas Tech University*
Alicia Nahmad Vazquez _ *Cardiff University / University of Calgary*
Burçin Nalinci _ *AUX Architecture, Los Angeles*
Rasa Navasaityte _ *University of Texas Austin*
Andrei Nejur _ *University of Montreal*
Catie Newell _ *University of Michigan*
Tsz Yan Ng _ *University of Michigan*
Ted Ngai _ *Pratt Institute*
Sarah Nichols _ *Rice University*
Betül Orbey _ *Doğus Üniversitesi*
Mine Özkar _ *İstanbul Technical University*
Derya Güleç Özer _ *İstanbul Technical University*
Dimitrios Papanikolaou _ *University of North Carolina Charlotte*
Murali Paranandi _ *Miami University*
Stefana Parascho _ *Princeton University*
Ju Hong Park _ *Massachusetts Institute of Technology*
Kat Park _ *Massachusetts Institute of Technology*
Vera Parlac _ *New Jersey Institute of Technology*
Maria Perbellini _ *New York Institute of Technology*
Chris Perry _ *Rensselaer Polytechnic Institute*
Brady Peters _ *University of Toronto*
Ebrahim Poustinchi _ *Kent State University*
Marshall Prado _ *University of Tennessee Knoxville*
Nick Puckett _ *OCAD University*
Jorge Ramirez _ *Anemonal*
Carolina Ramirez-Figueroa _ *Royal College of Art*
Alexander Robinson _ *University of Southern California*
Christopher Romano _ *University at Buffalo*
Rhett Russo _ *Rensselaer Polytechnic Institute*
Jenny Sabin _ *Cornell University*
Jose Sanchez _ *University of Michigan*
Andrew Saunders _ *University of Pennsylvania*
Simon Schleicher _ *University of California Berkeley*
Axel Schmitzberger _ *California State Polytechnic University, Pomona*
Marc Aurel Schnabel _ *Victoria University of Wellington*
Kyle Schumann _ *University of Virginia*
Mathew Schwartz _ *New Jersey Institute of Technology*
Jane Scott _ *Newcastle University*
Jason Scroggin _ *University of Kentucky*
Nick Senske _ *Iowa State University*
Brian Slocum _ *Universidad Iberoamericana*
Valentina Soana _ *The Bartlett, University College London*
Catherine Soderberg _ *Texas Tech University*
Rajat Sodhi _ *Orproject*
Robert Stuart-Smith _ *University of Pennsylvania*
Daniel Suarez _ *Berlin University of the Arts*
Satoru Sugihara _ *SCI-Arc*
Martin Summers _ *University of Kentucky*
Kyle Talbott _ *University of Wisconsin Madison*
Martin Tamke _ *The Royal Danish Academy of Fine Arts*
Josh Taron _ *University of Calgary*
Peter Testa _ *SCI-Arc*
Geoffrey Thün _ *University of Michigan*
T.F. Tierney _ *University of Illinois Urbana Champaign*
Robert Brandt Trempe _ *Aarhus School of Architecture*
Peter Trummer _ *University of Innsbruck*
Daniel Tish _ *Harvard University*
Zenovia Toloudi _ *Dartmouth College*
Carmen Trudell _ *California State Polytechnic University, San Luis Obispo*
Hans Tursack _ *Massachusetts Institute of Technology*
Manja van de Worp _ *Royal College of Art School of Architecture*

Pavlina Vardoulaki _ *Nike / DesignMorphine*
Theodora Vardouli _ *McGill University*
Lauren Vasey _ *ETH Zurich*
Shota Vashakmadze _ *University of California, Los Angeles*
Kathy Velikov _ *University of Michigan*
Tom Verebes _ *New York Institute of Technology*
Joshua Vermillion _ *University of Nevada Las Vegas*
Gabriel Wainer _ *Carleton University*
Dustin White _ *New York Institute of Technology*
Emily White _ *California State Polytechnic University, San Luis Obispo*
Aaron Willette _ *WeWork*
Shane Williamson _ *University of Toronto*
Andrew John Wit _ *Temple University*
Maria Yablonina _ *University of Toronto*
Shai Yeshayahu _ *Ryerson University*
Christine Yogiaman _ *Singapore University of Technology*
Lei Yu _ *Tsinghua University*
Maroula Zacharias _ *Massachusetts Institute of Technology*
Machi Zawidzki _ *Massachusetts Institute of Technology*
Catty Dan Zhang _ *University of North Carolina Charlotte*
Hao Zheng _ *University of Pennsylvania*
Sasa Zivkovic _ *Cornell University*

DISTRIBUTED PROXIMITIES

SPONSORS

PLATINUM SPONSORS

Zaha Hadid Architects

SILVER SPONSOR

GRIMSHAW

BRONZE SPONSOR

HKS LINE

SPONSORS

TECHNOLOGY SPONSORS

Paperspace

MEDIA PARTNER

The Architect's Newspaper

CPSIA information can be obtained
at www.ICGtesting.com
Printed in the USA
JSHW052252201221
21252JS00005BA/6

9 780578 952130